OVERLAND TEA CARAVAN ROUTE

THE INEVITABLE RUSSIAN SAMOVAR

CHINA

BLACK AND GREEN TEAS

FIRST TEA BOOK

THE BIRTHPLACE OF TEA

DARUMA

JAPAN: GREEN TEA

CHA-NO-YU

INDIA BLACK TEA

FORMOSA: OOLONG

CEYLON: BLACK TEA

SUMATRA: BLACK TEA

JAVA: BLACK TEA

AREAS

WALTZING MATILDA

HEAVY TEA DRINKERS HERE

THE GREAT TEA RACE 1866

"ALL ABOUT TEA" COPYRIGHT 1935 BY W.H. UKERS, N.Y.

ALL ABOUT TEA

Mary E Eaton

©W.H.U.

TEA LEAVES, FLOWERS, AND SEEDS, PAINTED FROM NATURE

Branch starting at lower left is fully matured. Branch starting at lower right has young shoot
ready for plucking. At extreme left, seeds, pistil, and seed pods. The specimen shown is *Thea
sinensis* (L) Sims, variety *assamica*.

ALL ABOUT TEA

BY
WILLIAM H. UKERS, M.A.

Vol. I

NEW YORK
THE TEA AND COFFEE TRADE JOURNAL COMPANY
1935

PRINTED IN THE UNITED STATES OF AMERICA
BY KINGSPORT PRESS, INC.

To
HELEN DE GRAFF UKERS
and
ALONZO H. DE GRAFF

PREFACE

TWENTY-FIVE years ago the author made his first visit to the tea countries of the Orient and began to collect material for a work on tea. After the initial surveys, researching started in the principal European and American libraries and museums; this phase of the work continued up to the return of the final proofs to the printer in 1935.

The sorting and classification of the material was begun twelve years ago. Subsequently, the author spent a year in travel among the tea countries, to revise and bring up to date the data already in hand. The actual writing of the manuscript has extended over ten years.

The originally-contemplated single-volume companion to *All About Coffee* had to be abandoned as it was found impossible to do justice to the subject in one volume. The two volumes of *All About Tea* contain fifty-four chapters, 1152 pages and approximately 600,000 words. Among the unique features of the work are: a Complete Reference Table of the principal kinds of tea grown in the world; a Tea Thesaurus; a Tea Chronology containing 500 dates of historical importance; a Tea Bibliography containing 2000 authors and titles; a Tea Dictionary of 425 definitions, and an Index of 10,000 references.

Since Lu Yu wrote the *Ch'a Ching*, or "Tea Scripture," in A.D. 780, scores of books on tea have been published. These have dealt mostly with specific phases of the subject, and have not always been free from propaganda. There has been no serious work of a general character in English in forty years. This is the first independent work fully covering all phases, and it is intended to appeal to the general reader as well as to those directly associated with tea.

All historical references have been checked by researches among the original sources. The trade and technical chapters have been passed upon by competent authorities. No effort has been spared to make the work exhaustive and authoritative.

In addition to the more formal acknowledgments elsewhere, the author wishes to thank all those who have lent a hand in the preparation of *All About Tea*. The work has been made possible by the fine, unselfish coöperation of many in and out of the trade and industry who have assisted in the researches as a scientific contribution to our knowledge of tea.

ACKNOWLEDGMENTS

GRATEFUL thanks are returned by the author to all individuals, associations, institutions, and firms who have assisted him in the preparation of this work.

For literary aid, research courtesies, permissions to quote, reproduce paintings, photographs, etc.:

British Museum, Guildhall Library, Royal Botanic Gardens, and Victoria and Albert Museum, London; British Library of Information, New York Historical Society, Metropolitan Museum of Art, and New York Public Library, New York; Bibliothèque Nationale, Paris; Bibliothèque Centrale, Moscow; Commercial Research Museum, Kiangwan, China; Colonial Secretary's Office, Hong Kong; Boston Public Library and the Museum of Fine Arts, Boston; Congressional Library and the Library of the Smithsonian Institution, Washington; Charleston (S. C.) Museum; and Addison Gallery of American Art, Andover, Mass.

The *Connoisseur*, London; *The Blue Peter*, London; The Japan Society of London, *Transactions and Proceedings*; Royal Society of Arts, *Journal*, London; Duffield & Co., New York, publishers, *The Book of Tea*, by Okakura Kakuzo, and Peter Davies, Ltd., London, owners of the English rights; Little, Brown & Co., *Some Chinese Ghosts*, Boston; Mr. H. J. Moppett, *Tea Manufacture*, Colombo; Messrs. E. C. Elliott and F. J. Whitehead, *Tea Planting in Ceylon*, Colombo; Mr. Richard McKay, *Some Famous Sailing Ships*, G. P. Putnam's Sons, New York; Mr. Arthur H. Clark, *The Clipper Ship Era*, G. P. Putnam's Sons, New York; Captain Andrew Shewan, *The Great Days of Sail*, Heath Cranton, Ltd., London; Mr. Basil Lubbock, *Sail*, The Blue Peter Company, Limited, London; Hosea Ballou Morse, *The East India Company Trading to China*, Harvard University Press, Cambridge, Mass.; Mr. Arthur D. Howden Smith, *John Jacob Astor*, J. B. Lippincott Company, Philadelphia; Dr. Richard Dillard, *The Historic Tea Party of Edenton*, Edenton, N. C.; State Street Trust Co., *Some Merchants and Captains of Old Boston*, Boston; Mr. Merle Crowell and *The American Magazine*, "John A. Hartford"; Mr. John Masefield, *Poems*, The Macmillan Company, New York; Cicely Fox Smith, poem: "By the Old Pagoda Anchorage," *Full Sail*, Houghton, Mifflin & Co., New York; Harold Willard Gleason, poem, "At Tea Time," *New York Times*; Dr. George M. Sheahan (owner) and Mr. Anton Otto Fischer (artist), painting of the clipper "Staghound"; Mr. Thomas U. Todd, Hatton, Ceylon, photographs; Mr. A. L. McWilliam, Coimbatore, British India, photographs; Mr. J. Surrey, Calcutta, photographs; Mr. Carl von Gimborn, Emmerich-am-Rhein, photographs; Messrs. T. H. Parker, London, photographs; Sir J. C. Poole, General Manager Great Western Railway, London, photographs; The Gorham Company, silversmiths, New York, photographs; Mr. Charles De Cordova, Hall & Loudon, and Blank & Stoller, Inc., New York, photographs; and City of Baltimore, photographs.

For scientific, technical, and historical data, or for critical revision of trade and technical chapters:

LONDON.—Ceylon Association, Indian Tea Association, and South Indian Association; Sir Edward Denison Ross, Miss Octavia Murray Browne, and Mr. Z. L. Yih of the School of Oriental Studies (London Institution); Dr. Alfred Barton Rendle, Keeper of the Department of Botany, British Museum; W. T. Ottewill, Supt. Records, India Office; Anglo-Ceylon & General Estates Co., Ltd.; The Assam Co., Ltd.; Asiatic Trading Corporation, Ltd.; De Zoete & Gorton; Eastern Produce & Estates Co., Ltd.; Harrisons & Crosfield, Ltd.; Frederick Mathieson & Sons; W. J. & H. Thompson; Hon. Samuel J. Best; and Messrs. E. A. Andrews, T. Dunkerley, John Harpur, P. F. Howlett, James Insch, A. W. Matthewson, A. S. Moore, Carl Reid, W. J. Rettie, T. P. Simpson, L. G. Stephens, and T. L. Trueman.

UNITED KINGDOM.—Mr. A. H. Abbott, Oxford; Mr. Harry Barnard, Stoke-on-Trent; Mr. T. C. Crawford, Glasgow; Davidson Engineering Works, Belfast; Mr. A. J. Denison, Godalming; Dr. Harold Hart Mann, Aspley Guise, Bedfordshire; Marshall's Tea Machinery Co., Ltd., Gainsborough; Mr. H. K. Rutherford, Banstead, Surrey; and Sir George Watt, Chinsura, Lockerbie, Dumfriesshire.

NEW YORK.—British Empire Chamber of Commerce; Tea Association of the United States of America; Dr. C. Stuart Gager, Director, Brooklyn Botanic Gardens; Messrs. L. Beling, Charles De Cordova, George E. Hall, Robert L. Hecht, C. J. Hensley, C. F. Hutchinson, W. D. Loudon, Oliver Carter Macy, R. A. Mason, George F. Mitchell, Ernest A. Nathan, E. W. Payne, J. H. Swenarton, H. P. Thomson, and I. Yamashita.

UNITED STATES.—Bureau of Food and Industry, Department of Agriculture, Washington; Foodstuffs Division, Department of Commerce, Washington; Dr. B. L. Robinson, Curator, Gray Herbarium, Harvard College, Cambridge; Mr. Younghill Kang, New York; Mr. L. G. Fenton, Seattle; Mr. Sydney Greenbie, Amherst, Mass.;

Mr. A. V. Lally, Boston; and Mr. C. S. Toohey, San Francisco.

AMSTERDAM.—Bureau van Statistiek en Propaganda; Pakhuismeesteren van de Thee; Vereeniging van Thee Importeurs; Vereeniging voor de Thee Cultuur; Messrs. A. and C. Biereas de Haan, F. H. de Kock van Leeuwen, D. Lageman, F. N. Neumann, and A. J. Reynst.

BRITISH INDIA.—Indian Tea Association, Calcutta; Indian Tea Cess Committee, Calcutta; United Planters' Association of Southern India, Madras; Tea Districts Labour Association, Calcutta; Mr. P. H. Carpenter, Chief Scientific Officer, and Messrs. H. R. Cooper, S. F. Benton, and A. C. Tunstall, Tocklai Tea Experimental Station, Cinnamara, Assam; Mr. C. R. Harler, Munnar; Dr. W. S. Shaw, Scientific Officer, U. P. A. S. I. Tea Experimental Station, Devarshola, Nilgiris; and Messrs. G. S. Horton, N. J. Sherville, and J. Thomas & Co., Calcutta; and Mr. A. L. McWilliam, Coimbatore.

CEYLON.—Ceylon Chamber of Commerce, Colombo; Ceylon Estates Proprietary Association, Colombo; Planters' Association of Ceylon, Kandy; Colombo Commercial Co., Ltd.; Mr. T. Petch, former Director, and Dr. R. V. Norrs, Director, of the Tea Research Institute of Ceylon, Telawakelle; Forbes & Walker, Major J. W. Oldfield and Messrs. G. H. P. Maddocks and C. F. Whitaker, Colombo; and Mr. H. A. Webb, Peradeniya.

JAVA.—Algemeen Landbouw Syndicaat, Batavia; Batavia Tea Buyers' Association; Dr. Ch. Bernard, former Director, Dr. C. P. Cohen Stuart, former botanist-selectionist, Dr. J. J. B. Deuss, former Director, and Dr. A. Steinmann, former Mycologist, of the Proefstation West Java, Buitenzorg; Mr. H. J. O. Braund, former Tea Expert, and Mr. T. W. Jones, Tea Expert, of the Thee Expert Bureau, Batavia; and Messrs. Geo. Wehry & Co., Batavia.

SUMATRA.—Dr. A. W. de Jong, Algemeen Proefstation, and Mr. James Morton, Medan.

CHINA.—Dr. Fong F. Sec, Editor-in-Chief, *Commercial Press*, and Messrs. W. S. King, F. L. Lachlan, Chun Uck Chao, Baen E. Lee, L. A. Lyall, R. G. Macdonald, and James Y. Tong, Shanghai; Mr. B. D. F. Beith, Hong Kong; and Mr. Boris Torgasheff, Harbin, Manchuria.

JAPAN.—Japan Central Tea Association, Tokyo; Joint Tea Association of Shizuoka Prefecture (The Shizuoka Tea Guild); Tea Refirers' Guild of Shizuoka Prefecture; Tea Experimental Station of the Agricultural and Forestry Department, Makinohara; Tea Experimental Station of Shizuoka Prefecture, Makinohara; Mr. Yuzo Hori, Kakegawa; Mr. Seiichi Ishii, Shizuoka.

FORMOSA.—British Consulate, Tamsui; Government General of Taiwan; Mitsui Bussan Kaisha; North Formosa Foreign Board of Trade, and Messrs. G. S. Beebe, F. C. Hogg, S. Nakase, Robert Boyd Orr, A. L. Pink, and E. Thomas, Taihoku.

ELSEWHERE.—The Department of Agriculture, Rangoon, Burma; The Director General of Agriculture, Rio de Janeiro, Brazil; Mr. Earl S. Haskell, Director General of Agriculture, Teheran, Iran; Levuka Chamber of Commerce and Captain David Robbie, Levuka, Fiji; Mlanje Planters' Association and Mr. R. S. Hynde, Mlanje, Nyasaland; and Dr. Serrao d'Azevedo, Lisbon, Portugal.

SCHEME OF CONTENTS

Volume I

TEA AT DARJEELING, INDIA, BEFORE THE GLORY OF THE SNOWS

The tea gardens, factories, and planters' bungalows in the foreground are at an elevation of about 4000 to 5000 feet. Mt. Kinchinjunga, the Himalayan peak in the background, is 28,000 feet.

THE SUBJECT IN BRIEF

TEA is a treasure of the world. Originally the tea plant was an exclusive Chinese possession that resisted all attempts to transplant it in other soils. Tea drinking also was exclusively Chinese and had to be changed to suit local conditions in the countries of its later adoption. It proved peculiarly suited to the English scene, and even America may never know afternoon tea as England knows it. Like Henley, it is unique.

Civilization has produced but three important non-alcoholic beverages—the extract of the tea leaf, the extract of the coffee bean, and the extract of the cacao bean. Leaves and beans are the sources of the world's favorite temperance beverages. The tea leaves lead in the total amount of beverage consumed; the coffee beans are second, and the cacao beans third. For a quick "explosion" men still have recourse to alcoholic drinks, pseudo stimulants, which often are narcotics and depressants. Tea, coffee, and cocoa are true stimulants to the heart, nervous system, and kidneys; coffee is more stimulating to the brain, cocoa to the kidneys, while tea occupies a happy position between the two, being mildly stimulating to most of our bodily functions. The "boon of the Orient" thus becomes the most gracious of the temperance drinks; a pure, safe, and helpful stimulant compounded in Nature's own laboratory, and one of the chief joys of life.

In telling the story of tea, the author has divided the subject into six parts: Historical, Technical, Scientific, Commercial, Social, and Artistic.

HISTORICAL ASPECTS.—The first chapter tells of the legendary origin of tea, about 2737 B.C., and of an alleged Confucian reference in 550 B.C., but the earliest credible mention is A.D. 350. Mother Nature's original tea garden was in a portion of Southeastern Asia which includes bordering provinces of Southwestern China, Northeastern India, Burma, Siam, and Indo-China.

Tea cultivation and the use of the beverage spread throughout China and Japan under the patronage of Buddhist priests, who sought a means of combating intemperance. Tea had its first handbook in the Ch'a Ching, written about A.D. 780. The first English translation digest of this important work appears in Chapter II. The earliest notice of tea in Japanese literature dates from A.D. 593, and its cultivation, from A.D. 805.

The first account of tea reached the Arabs A.D. 850; the Venetians in 1559; the English in 1598; the Portuguese in 1600. The Dutch brought the first tea to Europe about 1610; it reached Russia in 1618; Paris, 1648; and England and America about 1650. All this in Chapter III.

Later historical aspects are entwined with the stories of Garway and his famous London coffee house in Chapter IV; the nation that fought a war on account of an unjust tea tax, in Chapter V; the world's greatest tea monopoly, in Chapter VI; the tea clippers, in Chapter VII; and the amazing development of tea in Java-Sumatra under the Dutch, and in India and Ceylon under the British, in Chapters VIII, IX, and X. The history of tea propagation in other lands is told in Chapter XI.

TECHNICAL ASPECTS.—Chapter XII describes the commercial teas of the world. Chapter XIII discusses their trade values, leaf characteristics, and cup merits, and contains a complete reference table. The succeeding eight chapters are devoted to the cultivation and manufacture of tea as practiced in China, Japan, Formosa, Java, Sumatra, India, Ceylon, and other countries. The concluding chapter of this book traces the evolution of tea machinery from the earliest Chinese hand manipulation to the latest tea-factory appliances.

SCIENTIFIC ASPECTS.—In Chapter XXIII, on the etymology of tea, we learn that the Cantonese pronunciation of the Chinese word for tea is "chah," but that it is pronounced "*tay*" in the local dialect of Amoy, and in the latter form it reached most European countries. Other countries of Europe and Asia adopted *cha*.

The botany chapter tells how the first classification of the plant by Linnæus, in 1753, as *Thea sinensis*, though later changed to *Camellia*, now is commonly accepted by botanists.

The chemistry and pharmacology of tea are exhaustively treated by Mr. C. R. Harler, former chemist of the Indian Tea Association at Tocklai, in Chapters XXV and XXVI. The constituents of the leaf, the chemical changes occuring during manufacture, and the effects of caffeine and tannin are stated in a forthright manner.

Chapter XXVII, on the healthfulness of tea, presents a digest of scientific, medical, and popular opinions in convenient form for tea connoisseurs, merchants, and advertisers.

COMMERCIAL ASPECTS.—Chapters I to IV in Volume II describe the channels through which teas pass in the producing and consuming countries; how they are bought and sold from the time they reach the primary markets until they are delivered by the retailer to the consumer. Ten chapters which follow deal with the history of the tea trade in China, the Dutch trade, the British at home and overseas, tea trade associations, tea shares and tea share trading, Japan and Formosa tea trade, and the trade in other lands. The history of the American tea trade is told in Chapter XV.

Chapter XVI presents a history of tea advertising from A.D. 780 down to the latest tea propagandas and coöperative campaigns, with some conclusions as to tea-advertising efficiency. Chapter XVII discusses the world's tea production and consumption.

SOCIAL ASPECTS.—Tea has been called "the handmaiden of fashion and refinement." Its social history begins in Chapter XVIII, which concerns itself with the period of tea's early adoption in China, Japan, Holland, England, and America. Before continuing, there is a detour, in Chapter XX, for some droll tales from the tea gardens. Chapter XXI tells of the unsophisticated pleasures of the London tea-gardens of the eighteenth century, where tea was brought into the open and publicly drunk by both sexes for the first time in England. Chapter XXII, dealing with early tea manners and customs, starts with the aboriginal Shan tribesmen, who used wild-tea leaves for food and the preparation of a beverage; describes churned-tea soup and the manner of drinking it in Tibet; and traces the origin of the graceful rite without which no English day is complete—afternoon tea.

The next chapter deals with present-day tea manners and customs around the world. Here we learn why afternoon tea is one of the "shining moments of the day" in England, and why, before America can fully appreciate its virtues, she first must learn the art of leisure. Chapter XXIV has to do with the evolution of tea-making appliances, from the primitive kettle to the American tea bag, which some believe will cause the disappearance of most of the teapots. What price efficiency?

In the succeeding "Preparation of the Beverage" chapter, Mr. Harler discusses scientific tea-brewing, and this is followed by advice to tea lovers on how to buy tea, and how to make it in perfection.

ARTISTIC ASPECTS.—Chapter XXVI, "Tea and the Fine Arts," shows how tea has been celebrated in painting, drawing, engraving, sculpture, and music; with some noteworthy exhibits of tea pottery and tea silver. The final chapter, XXVII, is concerned with "Tea in Literature," and includes quotations on the subject of tea in the writings of poets, historians, medical and philosophical writers, scientists, dramatists, and authors of fiction.

APPENDIX.—The back matter at the end of Volume II includes (1) a chronology of tea, containing dates and events of historical interest; (2) a tea dictionary, which lists and defines difficult, technical, or dialectal terms employed in the tea-producing countries and the tea trade; (3) an alphabetically-arranged tea bibliography of authors and titles of historical writings, notable books, and important periodical references; and (4) an alphabetically arranged index for ready reference.

BOOK I
HISTORICAL ASPECTS

WILD TEA GROWING IN THE PRIMEVAL TEA-FOREST COUNTRY OF BRITISH INDIA

"The Himalaya from Rangagurrah Muttack in The Jungle of Upper Assam." After a sketch made on the spot by William Griffith, 1847.

CHAPTER I

TEA IN THE BEGINNING

LEGENDARY ORIGIN, 2737 B.C.—ALLEGED CONFUCIAN REFERENCE, 550 B.C.—GAN LU LEGEND—POSSIBLE REFERENCES IN THIRD CENTURY A.D.—EARLIEST CREDIBLE MENTION, A.D. 350—BECOMES ARTICLE OF TRADE—FIRST USE AS SOCIAL BEVERAGE—FIRST BOOK OF TEA AND FIRST TEA TAX—WHIPPED TEA—MOOT QUESTION OF PLANT ORIGIN—MOTHER NATURE'S ORIGINAL TEA GARDEN—INTRODUCTION INTO JAPAN—BODHIDHARMA LEGEND—TEA CULTURE SPREAD BY BUDDHIST PRIESTS

TEA had its genesis in China untold centuries ago but its early history is lost in the obscurity of China's venerable antiquity and for the most part is traditional. Everything known of its beginning is so inextricably intertwined with things patently mythical and fabulous, that we can only vaguely surmise which is fact and which is fancy. Probably it will never be known when tea was first used as a beverage nor how it was discovered that tea leaves could be treated and used to make a palatable drink. It is equally doubtful whether we will ever know with anything like reasonable accuracy when and how the cultivation of the plant began. Just as coffee has been known and used as food and drink in Ethiopia since time out of mind, so, too, the Chinese have known the tea plant and have used its leaves for food and beverage purposes from time immemorial.

The legendary origin of tea as taken from Chinese sources dates back approximately to 2737 B.C. The earliest reliable reference is contained in a Chinese dictionary dated about A.D. 350. In the years between, a few possibly authentic and many supposed references to tea are to be found. The word "supposed" is used for good reason since the present appellation ch'a 茶 was not given to tea until the seventh century of our era. Prior to this time the Chinese used the names of several other shrubs in their mention of tea. Of the borrowed names, t'u 荼 was the one most frequently used until the time of the T'ang dynasty, A.D. 620–907, when t'u reverted to its original meaning of "sow

thistle" and ch'a came into being. Then again, so great is the similarity between the characters ch'a 茶 and t'u 荼 that it suggests a close etymological relationship and inspires some with the idea of a direct derivation of ch'a from t'u. Consequently it will be readily understood that any attempt to trace the early story of tea through ancient records has been extremely difficult, a primary difficulty being the impossibility of determining when many of the early writers meant tea instead of some other shrub.

Legendary Origin in 2737 B.C.

The Chinese have dramatized the vague and obscure advent of tea by ascribing it to the reign of a legendary emperor, Shen Nung, called the "Divine Healer," who lived about 2737 B.C. "This," says Samuel Ball with a sympathetic understanding of the Eastern habits of thought, "is not so much from the vanity of assigning it to a high antiquity, as to a kind of courtesy sanctioned by ancient usage and oral tradition, which ascribes the discovery of numerous medicinal plants, and of tea among the rest, to Shen Nung."[1]

In Shen Nung's Pen ts'ao, or Medical Book, a reference reads: "Bitter t'u is called ch'a, hsuan, and yu. It grows in winter in the valleys by the streams, and on the hills of Ichow [in the province of Szechwan], and does not perish in severe winter. It is gathered on the third day of the third month [in April] and then dried."

[1] Samuel Ball, *Cultivation and Manufacture of Tea in China*, London, 1848, p. 1.

1

Another reference mentions the tea leaf as "good for tumors or abscesses that come about the head, or for ailments of the bladder. It dissipates heat caused by the phlegms, or inflammation of the chest. It quenches thirst. It lessens the desire for sleep. It gladdens and cheers the heart." The *Pen ts'ao* of Shen Nung has been offered time and time again as a proof of the great antiquity of tea. To the popular mind this seems a prima facie case, for here, it may be argued, is a quotation from an author who flourished as far back as 2700 B.C. What a great pity to destroy such an enchanting myth, even though historical accuracy compels its destruction! Shen Nung's book was not actually written in its earliest form until the Neo-Han dynasty, A.D. 25–221, the tea reference being added after the seventh century when the word *ch'a* came into use. This was thirty-four hundred years after the time of the fabled emperor to whom the authorship of the book is ascribed.

Alleged Confucian Tea Reference

This is but one of the great errors which has crept into the literature of tea. A still greater one—greater because it is more persistent and has received a wide circulation on account of the fame and popularity of its supposed author—attributes a tea reference to the *Shih Ching*, or Book of Odes, edited by Confucius about 550 B.C. The supposed allusion occurs in Ode Ten, "The Lament of a Discarded Wife," in Part Three of the Odes of Pei, and reads: "Who says that *t'u* is bitter? It is sweet as the *tsi*." Many orientalists are agreed that no reference to tea or to the tea plant was intended in this quotation, nor elsewhere in the entire work. James Legge, 1815–97, an English missionary, whose translation of the *Shih Ching* ranks high in scholarship, translates the character *t'u* as "sow thistle," a vegetable, and *tsi* as "shepherd's purse," making the passage read,

Who says the sow thistle is bitter?
It is sweet as the shepherd's purse.[2]

In the *Ch'a Ching*, ca. A.D. 780, the first book on tea, Lu Yu, its author, has the reference read, "Who says that *t'u* is bitter?" Another passage in Lu Yu's work

reads, "*Chin* and *t'u* are as sweet as treacle." Lu Yu states that the character *t'u* in the Confucian quotation indicates a vegetable was meant, pointing out that the "grass," not the "tree" radical was used, and that tea was and is regarded as a tree. A corrupt form of the Confucian quotation has occasionally appeared, reading, "Who was it asserted that *ch'a* is bitter?" Obviously, since *ch'a* was not in use before A.D. 725, interpreting this quotation in this manner is not justifiable. There is one more possible reference of 500 B.C. even after this questionable Confucian reference has been dismissed as unworthy. It is quoted by Bretschneider, who Dr. Cohen Stuart, the eminent Dutch botanist, characterizes as an amateur Sinologue. The quotation is in the *Yen Tsu Ch'un Ch'iu* and mentions *ming ts'ai*, or "ming [tea] vegetable," as an article of food in the time of Yen Ying, a contemporary of Confucius, but whether the tea plant was meant is problematical.[3]

Over four centuries later, about 50 B.C., Wang Piu, in his *Contract with a Servant*, speaks of buying *t'u* from Wutu and of boiling it. It is barely possible this may be a dependable reference to tea. Wutu is a mountain situated in Szechwan, a province which was to become celebrated as the birthplace of the tea industry. Moreover, tea is said to have been first cultivated in the Szechwan district and several oriental scholars consider the *t'u* mentioned in Wang Piu's work to be a direct reference to tea. The inference that tea was grown there in the days of Wang Piu is not therefore unreasonable.

The Gan Lu Legend

What is sometimes considered as evidence of the early cultivation of tea in the Szechwan district is to be found in the legend of Gan Lu. The legend, which curiously is not in any of the principal Chinese works on tea, is that Gan Lu, whose family name was Wu-Li-chien, returned from Buddhistic studies in India during the Later Han dynasty, A.D. 25–221, bringing with him seven tea plants which he planted on Meng Mountain, in Szechwan. Whatever foundation the legend may possess in fact, it has the support of an allegory on tea in the *Ch'a P'u*, published long after-

[2] James Legge, *Chinese Classics*, Hong Kong, 1871, Vol. IV, Part 1.

[3] E. Bretschneider, "Botanicon Sinecum II" in *Journal of the China Bch. Royal Asiatic Society*, Shanghai, 1893. Vol. XXV, p. 130.

ward, to the effect that tea was first brought to imperial attention during the After-Han dynasty, A.D. 221–263. This might conceivably refer to Gan Lu's seven tea plants. Samuel Ball, on the other hand, dismisses the *Ch'a P'u* as designedly too full of poetic anachronisms to have any authoritative value.

Possible Third-Century Notices

After the third century of the Christian Era the mention of tea becomes more frequent and seemingly more reliable. Although the *Pen ts'ao* of Shen Nung, of which mention has already been made, was written in the Neo-Han dynasty, A.D. 25–221, the earliest forms of this work did not mention tea. The tea references were added, as previously stated, some three centuries later. However, *Shin Lun* by Hua T'o, a celebrated physician and surgeon who died A.D. 220, contains a possible reference. It reads, "To drink *k'u t'u* [bitter *t'u*] constantly makes one think better." Another reference is in Chen Shou's *History of the Three Kingdoms*. Sun Hao, A.D. 242–283, the ruler of Wu, according to this work, secretly gave *ch'uan*, or tea, to Wei Yao, one of his generals whose capacity for wine was only two shengs.[4]

Earliest Credible Mention

In the fourth century, we find Liu Kun, d. A.D. 317, a general of the Chin dynasty, writing to his nephew Liu Yen, the governor of Yenchow in the province of Shantung, that he felt aged and depressed and wanted some real *t'u*. Further notice of the tea drink, when it must have been drunk much after the fashion of the bone-set tea of our grandfathers, is to be found in the *Shi Shuo*, written in the fourth century. "Wang Mang, father-in-law of the Emperor Hui Ti," says the *Shi Shuo*, "was much given to drinking *t'u*. He would set the beverage before his friends, but they, finding it too bitter, generally declined, feigning some indisposition."

The *Erh Ya*, an ancient Chinese dictionary annotated by Kuo P'o, celebrated Chinese scholar, about A.D. 350, gives the first recognizable definition of tea under the name of *kia*, 檟, or *k'u t'u*, 苦荼, adding,

"A beverage is made from the leaves by boiling." The same work states the earliest gathering of the leaves was called *t'u*, 荼, and the latest, *ming*, 茗. This reference in the *Erh Ya* is accepted by many authorities on tea history as the earliest credible record of tea cultivation. As revised by Kuo P'o it forms the basis for the oft-published statement that the tea plant was first cultivated about A.D. 350. The tea drink of Kuo P'o's time was a medicinal decoction—and probably a bitter one—of unprepared green tea leaves, but its aroma attracted favorable attention, for Pau Ling-hui, a Chinese authoress, wrote of it under the title *Fragrant Ming*. Mention of the tea drink is also found in the *Chin Shu*, a history of the Chin dynasty, where the statement is made that the governor of Yangchow, Huan Wen, A.D. 312–373, was frugal; he only put down seven receptacles for tea and fruit when he dined.

Some light on the manufacturing process of the period, and on the medicinal drink made from tea, is to be found in an extract from the *Kuang Ya*, a dictionary by Chang I, of the Later Wei dynasty, A.D. 386–535, which states that the leaves were plucked and made into cakes in the district between the provinces of Hupeh and Szechwan; the cakes were roasted until reddish in color, pounded into tiny pieces, and placed in a chinaware pot. Boiling water was then poured over them, after which onion, ginger, and orange were added.

Tea Becomes an Article of Trade

By the fifth century tea had become an article of trade. In *The Family History of Chiang*, of the Northern Sung dynasty, A.D. 420–479, we read that Chiang Tung called attention to the fact that the sale of vinegar, noodles, cabbage, and tea in the west garden was a reflection upon the dignity of the government.[5] In his will, the Emperor Wu Ti, A.D. 483–493, indicated his fondness for tea, and stipulated that he did not want posthumous offerings of cattle; only cakes, fruit, tea, dried rice, wine, and dried meat. Wang Su, A.D. 464–501, held a contrary opinion of the tea drink. In *Hou Wei Lu*, the record of the Later

---

[4] *Sheng*, a Chinese pint; 10 shengs = 1 *tou* = 2.315 gallons.

[5] In this and the references which follow, the word is given as *ch'a*, or tea, by a later commentator, Lu Yu, who wrote after the word *ch'a* came into use; *i.e.*, after A.D. 725. The word for tea most commonly used before that time was *t'u*.

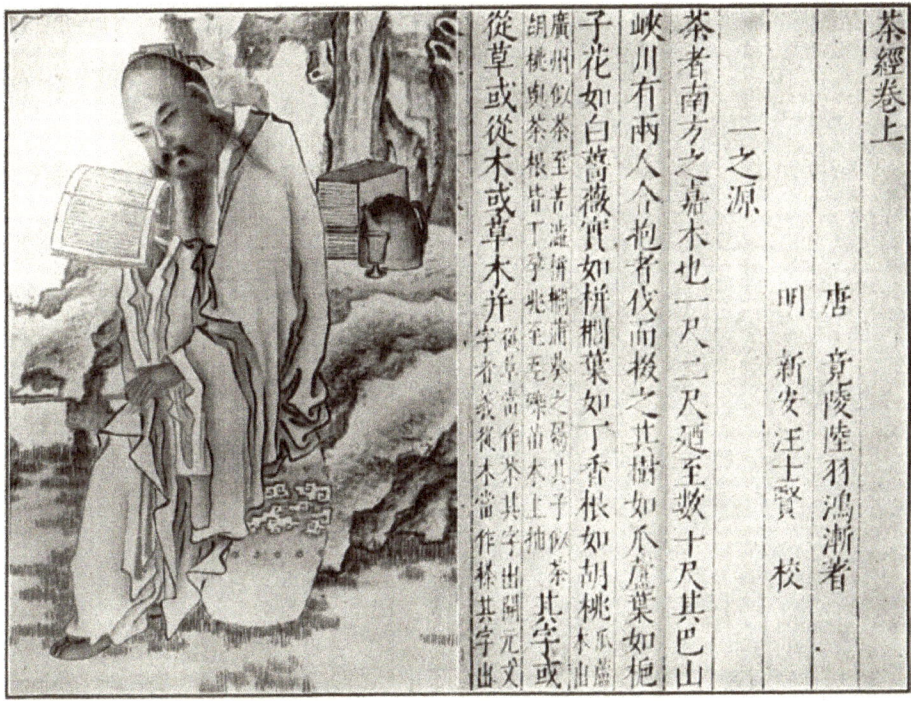

Lu Yu and a Page of the *Ch'a Ching*, the First Tea Book, a.d. 780

Wei dynasty, it is recorded that he pronounced tea much inferior to kumiss.

The custom of reserving special teas for imperial use began about this time, for we find the *Wu Hsing chi*, by Shan Ch'ien-Chih, of the Northern Sung dynasty, A.D. 420–479, stating, "Twenty lis [a li is 705 yards] west from the city of Wucheng, in the province of Chekiang, there is the Wen mountain, on which grows the tea reserved to the emperor as tribute tea."

Tea Used for Beverage Purposes

Late in the sixth century, the Chinese generally began to regard tea as something more than a medicinal drink. Its use as a refreshing beverage was epitomized by the poet Chang Meng-yan, of the Chin dynasty, A.D. 557–589, in his poem *On the Chengtu Terrace* [in Szechwan]. "Fragrant *t'u*," he wrote, "superimposes the six passions: the taste for it spreads over the nine districts."[6] The transition of the tea

drink at this time from medicinal to beverage uses is confirmed by the author of the *Kuen Fang P'u*. Tea, according to this account, was first used as a beverage in the reign of Wen Ti, of the Sui dynasty, A.D. 589–620, and was acknowledged to be good, though not much esteemed. Tea continued in high repute as a remedy, however, for the "noxious gases of the body, and as a cure for lethargy."

First Tea Book and First Tea Tax

While tea propagation became more general in the sixth century, it was not until A.D. 780 that the horticultural and other aspects of tea growing were first published in an exclusive work on tea. In this year, Lu Yu, a noted Chinese author and tea expert, wrote the *Ch'a Ching*, or Tea Classic, at the request of the tea merchants. It treats, among other things, of the qualities and effects of the beverage. In an allegory, the book quotes one of the emperors of the Han dynasty as saying: "The use of tea grows upon me surpris-

---

[6] The six passions are: content and anger, sorrow and joy, like and dislike. The nine districts included the entire kingdom.

ingly: I know not how it is, but my fancy is awakened and my spirits exhilarated as if with wine." This makes it evident that the tea drink had progressed in Lu Yu's time from the earlier rank decoction of unprepared green tea leaves into a more inviting infusion. With suggested methods to improve the manufactured leaf came better beverage quality in the drink, making the use of certain ingredients, such as spices, no longer necessary for improving its flavor. The art of tea making also showed progressive improvement, for Lu Yu stresses the choice of water and the degree to which it should be boiled. So widespread, in fact, had the use of tea become at this period that the Government made it the subject of an impost in the first year of Tih Tsung, A.D. 780. This was the earliest tax on tea. It probably met with opposition, for it was soon abolished, but in the fourteenth year of the same reign, A.D. 793, we find the duty reimposed.

The introduction of tea into general use may be said to have taken place in the two centuries between the reign of the Emperor Wen Ti, of the Sui dynasty, A.D. 589–620, to whose reign the author of the *Ch'a P'u* ascribes the first use of the beverage, and the reign of Tih Tsung in the T'ang dynasty, when the first tea duty was levied. One account of the manner of preparing it in this period is supplied by two Arabian travelers who visited China about A.D. 850. The travelers speak of tea as the common beverage of China and tell how the Chinese boil water and pour it scalding hot upon the leaf, adding, "The infusion preserves them from all distempers."[7] It is evident the Chinese of the ninth century infused the leaf much the same as to-day, and that they continued to regard it as possessing medicinal properties.

Whipped Tea Makes Its Appearance

By the time of the Sung dynasty, A.D. 960–1280, tea, according to the *Kuen Fang P'u*, was used throughout all the provinces and whipped tea had made its appearance as the fashionable mode among tea exquisites. The dried leaf was ground to a fine powder and whipped in hot water with a light bamboo whisk. Salt definitely disappeared as a flavoring agent, and the

beverage was, for the first time, enjoyed for its own delicate flavor and aroma. The enthusiasm of tea epicures now became lyrical and was reflected in the social and intellectual intercourse of the period. New varieties were eagerly sought, and tournaments were held to decide their merits. The Emperor Hwei Tsung, A.D. 1101–26, who was extremely artistic in temperament, counted no cost too great for the attainment of new and rare varieties. A dissertation on the twenty kinds of tea by this royal connoisseur specifies the "white tea" as of the rarest and most delicate flavor. Elaborate tea houses appeared in all of the cities, and in the temples Buddhist priests of the southern Zen sect, founded in India by Bodhidharma,[8] and brought by him to China in A.D. 519, gathered before the image of Bodhidharma and drank tea in solemn ceremonial from a single bowl. One or two centuries later, in the Ming dynasty, A.D. 1368–1644, the second book on tea appeared, the *Ch'a P'u*, by Ku Yuan-ch'ing, a Chinese scholar. This work has been judged of slight historical value.

Moot Question of Tea's Origin

To repeat the opening sentence of this chapter, tea had its genesis in China. There is ample corroboration of this view as far as the creation of the industry and the adoption of tea as a beverage are concerned. Speaking from a botanical point of view, however, the subject presents other aspects, and for many years controversies raged among scientific men and scholars as to whether the tea plant originated in China or in India. Plants of the China variety had been painstakingly carried to India for a long time after the native *assamica* was found there in 1823, and there are ancient stories of how tea came to China from India. Indeed, there are to-day those who believe the Chinese must have obtained the plant for cultivation from a source outside of China. Samuel Baildon, who wrote extensively on the tea industry of India in the 'seventies, was an active proponent of the idea that tea was indigenous only to India; his theory being that the plant was introduced into China and Japan from India some twelve hundred years ago. He argued there was

---

[7] Eusebius Renaudot, *Accounts of India and China by Two Mohammedan Travelers Who Went to Those Parts in the Ninth Century*, London, 1733.

[8] Bodhidharma is sometimes called Dharma or Daruma.

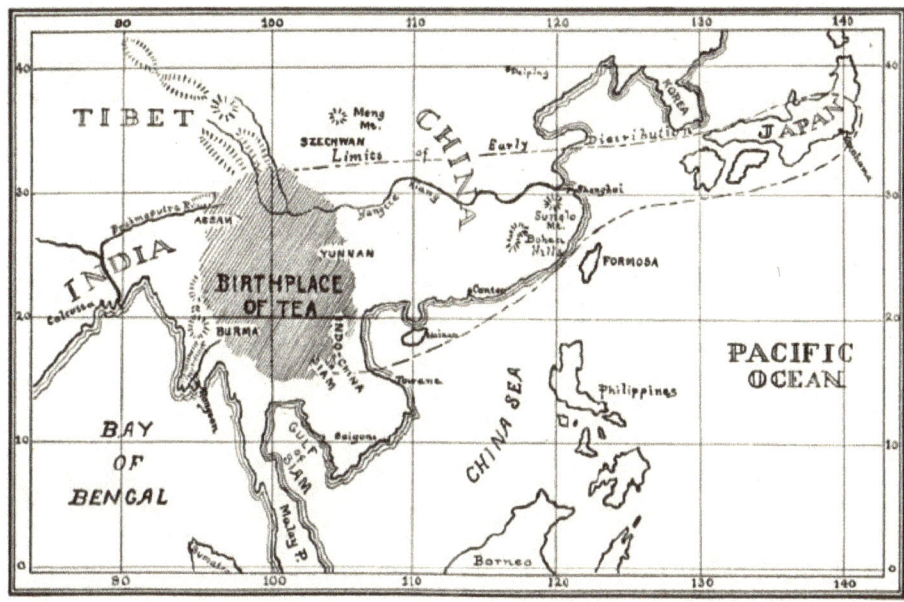

MOTHER NATURE'S TEA GARDEN IN THE MONSOON DISTRICT OF SOUTHEASTERN ASIA

but one species of tea—the Indian—and that the inferior growth and smaller leaves of the China tea were the result of the transportation of the plant far from home into an uncongenial climate and into unfavorable conditions of soil and treatment.[9]

Dr. C. P. Cohen Stuart, former botanist of the Thee Proefstation of Buitenzorg, Java, in his scholarly essay on the origin of tea, makes an exhaustive examination into the literature dealing with the wild tea plant found on the borderlands of China— the mysterious Tibetan mountain walls and the scarcely explored jungles of southern Yunnan and Upper Indo-China. In this region, according to Dr. Cohen Stuart, we must expect the solution, if one is obtainable, of the primary problem in tea history —the origin of the tea plant. The French colonies in Further India also furnish evidence of supplying important clues as to the origin of tea. Dr. Cohen Stuart declares that it is not anticipating too much to suspect that here, close to the heart of Mother Nature's first tea garden, lies hidden the answer to this age-old enigma.[10]

[9] Samuel Baildon, *Tea in Assam*, Calcutta, 1877.
[10] C. P. Cohen Stuart, "A Basis for Tea Selection" in *Bulletin du Jardin Botanique*, Buitenzorg, 1918, Vol. I, Part 4.

Mother Nature's Tea Garden

Mother Nature's original tea garden was located in the monsoon district of southeastern Asia. Many other plants now grow there, but specimens of the original jungle, or wild, tea plant are still to be found in the forests of the Shan States of northern Siam, eastern Burma, Yunnan, Upper Indo-China, and British India. Consequently, the tea plant may be said to be indigenous to that portion of southeast Asia which includes China and India. The political boundaries of the various countries where wild tea has been found are purely imaginary lines which men have traced to mark the states of India, Burma, Siam, Yunnan, and Indo-China. Before any thought was given to dividing this land into separate states, it consisted of one primeval tea garden where the conditions of soil, climate, and rainfall were happily combined to promote the natural propagation of tea.

Contemporary Chinese records establish that tea cultivation began in the interior province of Szechwan about A.D. 350, gradually extending down the Yangtze valley to the seaboard provinces. The author of the *Ch'a P'u*, however, writing at a much later date, A.D. 1368–1628, assigns the first discovery of tea to the Bohea Hills, partly in deference to prevailing popular opinion and partly, perhaps, to give greater éclat to his story by connecting it with one of the most celebrated and widely known tea districts in China. During the T'ang dynasty, A.D. 620–907, tea cultivation spread through the present provinces of Szechwan, Hupeh, Hunan, Honan, Chekiang, Kiangsu, Kiangsi, Fukien, Kwangtung, Anhwei, Shensi, and Kweichow. Hupeh and Hunan tea plants became famous for quality, and tea from these plants was reserved for the emperor.

Early legends, thought to be inspired by Buddhist priests, relate that monkeys were used to gather the tea leaves from inaccessible places. Sometimes they were trained for the work; or, when seen amongst the rocks where the tea bushes grew, the Chinamen would throw stones at them. The monkeys, becoming angry, would break off branches of the tea bushes and throw them down at their tormentors.

After the cultivation of tea had spread through the provinces, it came to the attention of travelers from other shores, and China became the fountainhead whence tea culture spread to other countries. The first of these was Japan.

"Monkeys Gathering Tea in China"

Fanciful picture illustrating an early legend. After Marquis, 1820.

Introduction of Tea into Japan

Destined to assume an even more important social position in Japan than in China, knowledge of tea was probably introduced into the Island Empire along with Chinese civilization, the fine arts, and Buddhism, about A.D. 593, in the reign of Prince Shotoku. Actual tea cultivation was introduced at a later time by Japanese priests of the Buddhist religion. These priests, many of them famous in Japanese tea history, became acquainted with the cultivation of the tea plant while pursuing religious studies in China. Upon their return to Japan they carried with them some of the seeds, and from these Chinese seeds are descended the cultivated teas of Japan.

The Bodhidharma Legend

Stream of Nine Windings, Bohea Hills
The gigantic hands were caused by water erosion. After Fortune, 1852.

Japanese mythology credits the origin of tea in China to Bodhidharma. It is related that this Buddhist saint, when overcome with sleep during his meditations, cut off his eyelids and threw them on the ground, where they took root and grew up as tea plants. As a matter of fact, tea is now so inherently a part of the social and cultural life of Japan that it is difficult for Japanese historians to conceive of a time when there may have been no tea in the temple gardens; therefore they are accustomed to speak of tea as always having been part of their civilization. According to the *Koji Kongen* and *Ogisho*, authoritative historical records, the Japanese Emperor Shomu bestowed some *hiki-cha*, or powdered tea, upon one hundred priests whom he summoned for a four days' reading of the Buddhist scriptures at the imperial palace, in the first year of the Tempei Era, A.D. 729. The introduction of this rare and costly beverage to these ritualists apparently aroused in them a desire to grow their own plants, as the records show the monk Gyoki, A.D. 658–749, crowned his life work by building forty-nine temples and planting tea shrubs in the temple gardens. This is the first recorded cultivation of tea in Japan.

The Buddhist monks were not alone in their desire to possess the divine herb of China's envied bowers, however. In the thirteenth year of the Yenryaku Era, A.D. 794, the Emperor Kammu erected an imperial palace at Hei-an-kyo, the Capital-of-Peace, adopting Chinese architecture and inclosing a tea garden. For the administration of the tea garden a governmental post was created under the medical bureau, indicating that the tea plant was then regarded as a medicinal shrub.

Buddhist Priests Spread Culture

Subsequently, in the twenty-fourth year of the Yenryaku Era, A.D. 805, the Buddhist saint Saicho, better known by his posthumous name, Dengyo Daishi, returned from studies in China, bringing tea seeds which he planted at the foot of Mount Hiyei in the village of Sakamoto, province of Omi. The present-day tea garden of Ikegami is said to be located on the site of Dengyo Daishi's original planting. The following year, the first of the Daido Era, A.D. 806, Kobo Daishi, another Buddhist monk, returned from studies in China. Like his illustrious predecessor, Dengyo Daishi, he was so impressed with this friendly plant and with the advance of civilization marking its progress in palaces and temples in the neighboring Chinese empire, that he aspired to see it take an equal or greater place in his own country. He, too, brought

a quantity of tea seeds and planted them at various places. He is said to have brought home and imparted as well a knowledge of the process of manufacturing.

Evidently the attempt of the priests to grow tea in the temple gardens was a success. The ancient Japanese histories *Nihon-Koki* and *Ruishu Kokushi* record that in the sixth year of Konin, A.D. 815, the Emperor Saga paid a visit of state to Bonshaku Temple at Karasaki, Shiga, in the province of Omi, where the abbot Yeichu regaled him with tea. It is further recorded that the temple beverage so pleased the emperor that he decreed the cultivation of the plant in the five home provinces near the capital, stipulating an annual tribute of the leaf for the use of the imperial household. Tea cultivation was successful also at the Genko Temple of Yamato, for, according to the same histories, the retired Emperor Uda, while visiting there, in the first year of Shotai, A.D. 898, was served with scented tea by the abbot Seiju Hos-shi.

First Japanese Book on Tea

At this time, when the tea drink was well on the way to become a popular social beverage of the capital at Hei-an-kyo, although still used extensively for medicinal purposes by those in high circles, it had a dramatic setback. Civil wars broke out in Japan and tea was practically forgotten for nearly two hundred years. The tea drinking custom was neglected, and no attention was paid to tea cultivation during this period. With the return of peace, tea drinking was again revived in the second year of the Kempo Era, A.D. 1191, by one of the brightest figures in Japanese tea history, the Buddhist abbot Yeisai, chief of the Zen sect, whose posthumous name is Senko-Soshi. He reintroduced the tea plant to Japan, bringing new seeds from China and planting them on the slope of the Seburi Mountain, southwest of the Castle of Fukuoka, in the province of Chikuzen. Others he planted in the temple grounds of Shokukuji at Hakata.

Yeisai not only planted and raised tea, but visioned the plant as the source of a sacred remedy, writing a book—the first Japanese work on tea—called *Kitcha-Yojoki*, literally, the Book of Tea Sanitation. In his book Yeisai acclaimed tea a

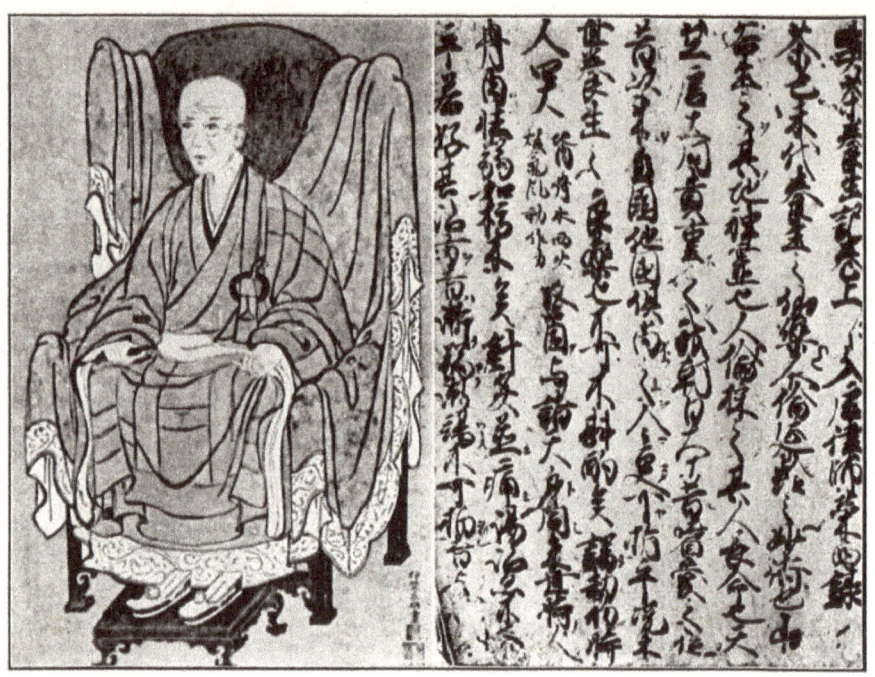

YEISAI AND A PAGE OF THE *Kitcha Yojoki*, THE FIRST JAPANESE TEA BOOK, CA A.D. 1200

"divine remedy and a supreme gift of heaven" for preserving human life. After this, the use of tea, previously restricted to a few priests and members of the nobility, began to extend to the people at large. The popularity of tea was no doubt considerably helped by a spectacular incident which focused attention upon it as a miraculous elixir. The mighty Minamoto Shogun Sanetomo, A.D. 1203-19, became desperately ill from over-feasting and summoned Yeisai to offer prayers for his recovery. Never doubting the efficacy of his petitions, the good abbot supplemented his prayers with his favorite beverage, sending in all haste to his temple for some of the tea grown there. He administered to the sufferer a drink prepared by his own hands, and lo! the great general's life was spared. Naturally enough Sanetomo wanted to know more about tea; so Yeisai presented him with a copy of his book and subsequently the shogun became a tea devotee. The fame of the new remedy spread far and wide, nobles and commoners alike seeking its healing virtues.

Its appeal as a social agent was enhanced by the appearance of a tea service provided by a skilled potter, Toshiro, who imported a special glaze from China, then under the Sung dynasty, A.D. 960-1280. Applying this to tea sets helped to bring the tea drink into fashionable vogue. It was about this time too, that to the abbot Myo-e, chief of the Mantra sect, at Togano-o, near Kyoto, Yeisai presented some tea seeds with instructions for cultivation and manufacture. Myo-e carefully observed the directions, and the tea produced from this garden was used in his temple and elsewhere.

As the use of tea as a beverage became more general, tea cultivation gradually spread to such districts as Nin-na-ji, Daigo, Uji, Hamuro, and Han-nya-ji. Later it spread to Hatori of Iga, Kawai and Kami-o-ji of Ise, Muro-o of Yamato, Kiyomi of Suruga, and Kawagoe of Musashi. This was done in order to keep pace with the constantly growing demand.

The invention of the green tea manufacturing process by Soichiro Nagatani, better known as San-no-jo, in the third year of Genbun, A.D. 1738, gave the final impetus to tea propagation in all parts of the Japanese Empire.

WATERING PLANTS IN A HILLSIDE GARDEN

PRIMITIVE PICKING AND TRANSPORT METHODS

WITHERING AND SUN DRYING

PANNING AND FIRING OPERATION

EARLY TEA CULTURE AND MANUFACTURE IN CHINA

Reproductions from a series of colored sketches made in the 18th century by a Chinese artist.

10

CHAPTER II

CHINA AND THE *CH'A CHING*

THE BEGINNING OF TEA CULTIVATION AND MANUFACTURE—ITS SPREAD THROUGH CHINA —GROWING NEED FOR A HANDBOOK OF INFORMATION RESULTS IN THE PUBLICATION OF THE FIRST WORK ON TEA—LU YU, CHINA'S ROMANTIC COMEDIAN, AUTHOR OF THE *Ch'a Ching*, OR TEA SCRIPTURE—TRANSLATION DIGEST OF THIS FAMOUS WORK—THE ORIGIN OF TEA—NECESSARY UTENSILS—MANIPULATION OF THE LEAF—PREPARATION OF THE DRINK—HISTORICAL RECORD—GENERAL SUMMARY

AS SOON as a medicinal value began to be attributed to tea by the inhabitants of Southwestern China, a demand sprang up for supplies of the raw leaf, a demand which the Chinese met by cutting down the wild trees, sometimes thirty feet in height, in order to strip the leaves from the branches. In time this destructive method threatened to completely denude the forests of tea trees, so to offset the results of such a practice, and to develop a more conveniently available source of supply, a primitive form of tea cultivation was begun, based upon the lessons learned from other agricultural efforts. For instance, the tea plant was observed by those early husbandmen to be very like the walnut tree in that "its roots spread downward until they encountered gravel, and then the tender plants grew up." From this they concluded that tea plants would best thrive in a soil composed of disintegrated stone, with gravelly soil second best, and clay quite unsuitable. Consequently, the first seeds were sown and the plants cultivated in selected ground found in the hill districts of Szechwan.

This was about A.D. 350. By the time of the T'ang dynasty, A.D. 620–907, tea drinking had become so general throughout the kingdom that a rapidly increasing demand had induced farmers in most of the provinces to plant small patches of tea in odd corners and on the hillsides. In this way the cultivation spread from the Szechwan districts down the Yangtze valley and thence along the seaboard. By the time of the Sung dynasty, A.D. 960–1127, it had reached the Singlo hill district in the present province of Anhwei, China's finest green tea area, and to the equally celebrated black tea district of the Bohea Hills, between the provinces of Fukien and Kiangsi.

The First Book on Tea

During the greater part of the time while the cultivation was thus spreading through China, such meager knowledge as existed regarding tea culture and manufacture was disseminated almost entirely by word of mouth. While it is true that some slight mention of tea had been made in contemporary writings, most of these tea references were fragmentary, and could furnish to the agriculturist little or no practical guidance. It remained for Lu Yu, a Chinese scholar, to compile, about A.D. 780, the *Ch'a Ching*, the first book to be devoted in its entirety to tea. To Lu Yu the early Chinese agriculturists were heavily indebted. And if their debt was heavy, how much more so is the debt which all the world owes. But for the knowledge imparted by the *Ch'a Ching* concerning the cultivation and manufacture of tea, the world might have remained in ignorance of the joys of tea drinking until long after the time of Jacobson, Gordon, Ball, Fortune, and others who learned much from this work at a time when tight-lipped Chinamen found it convenient to be mute. For it must be remembered that tea, then as precious as the gold of Ophir, was not a subject to be lightly discussed with foreigners, nor were the secrets of its growth and preparation to be disclosed. Yet dis-

11

Lu Yu, China's Romantic Comedian

LU YU IN HIS TEA GARDEN

By an anonymous, present day artist after an original of the T'ang period, when the tutelary God of the China tea merchants was a friend of the Emperor Taisung. From a copy on silk in the author's library. The Chinese legend recites: "Done in the peach-blossoming month at Chin Sin Kiang (Shanghai) by the man of Po Yo San (white sun mountain)."

The tea merchants, in casting about for someone to gather together all the fragmentary knowledge of their industry, happily hit upon Lu Yu, a colorful personality of high ability and wide versatility. From fugitive references here and there in Chinese literature it is easy to piece together the story of Lu Yu's adventurous life. According to the fanciful story of his origin—a story savoring of the Biblical account of Moses in the bulrushes—he was a foundling. A native of Fu-Chow, in Hupeh, he is thought to have been found by a Buddhist priest and to have been adopted by him. Later, when Lu Yu refused to join the priesthood, he was set at menial tasks in the hope that the discipline would tame his proud spirit, teach him true humility, and fit him for the practicalities of a staid and proper eighth-century conventionalism. Irked by such servile duties, Lu Yu, always an extreme individualist, heard the call of the open road, and fled. He became a clown, a long-cherished ambition. Wherever he went delighted crowds acclaimed him for his antics, but he was far from being happy. His is the old, old story of the saddened heart hidden beneath the motley jacket. In Lu Yu's case, however, the discontent came from a frustrated ambition for learning. He was a pantaloon, if you will, with a deep yearning for knowledge. One of his many admirers, an official, became a patron who supplied him with books to educate himself. China's world of books, that vast storehouse of ancient wisdom, was opened to him. He absorbed it greedily. Lu Yu then became fired with further ambition; he wanted to add to the national store of knowledge—he even yearned to create. The tea merchants offered the very opportunity he sought. They needed someone who could put together the disconnected knowledge of their growing industry; they needed his genius to emancipate tea from its crude commercialism and lead it to its final idealization. Lu Yu saw in the tea service the same harmony and order that rules in all things. He became the first apostle of tea. In the *Ch'a Ching* he gave his patrons the "Tea Memoir," or, as it is sometimes called, "Tea Scripture," or "Tea Classic." He was the first to formulate a Code of Tea, out of which, later on, the Japanese developed the Tea Ceremony.

closed they were, for the *Ch'a Ching* opened the closely guarded mystery to the prying foreigners. Undoubtedly these people from other lands would have learned all the essential facts in time, but the *Ch'a Ching* simplified their quest and hastened the day of universal knowledge. Logically, the situation was incongruous. This is apparent when we consider that the very merchants who were most jealous in guarding the secrets of tea from the foreigners were the ones responsible for the written record which disseminated the vital facts among them.

Lu-Yu found himself famous, and—what is, indeed, rare—in his own country. It was futile for him to insist his feet were of clay; his admirers knew better. They literally canonized him, and he has been worshiped ever since as the patron saint of the Chinese tea merchants. If, as Ruskin said, "to see a thing and tell it in plain words is the greatest thing a soul can do," then no one will deny Lu Yu his place among the immortals.

The last years of his life were sweet, or should have been. Lu Yu was befriended by the emperor, and none there were too rich or too poor to pay him reverence. But disillusionment stalked his footsteps. Life was a comedy, yes, but too much of a comedy not to be taken seriously. Was that, after all, its hidden meaning? He must think it out. Were the sages right? Only in meditation could he find the way. He would seek the truth in the belief it would make him whole. He would withdraw into the solitudes and again seek the solution of life's mystery. And so he arrived back at his starting point; his life had come full circle. Had not the great Confucius taught that "they who know the truth are not equal to those who love it, and they who love it are not equal to those who find pleasure in it"?

So in 775 he became a hermit. Five years later the *Ch'a Ching* was published, and in 804 Lu Yu died.

Translation Digest of Ch'a Ching

The copy of the *Ch'a Ching* from which this digest was made is in the library of the University of London. Its title page states that it was written by Lu Yu, alias Hung-Chang, of the T'ang dynasty, A.D. 620–907; that he was born in the district of Chin Ling; and that the book was edited and the proofs read by Wang Shih Hsien of the Ming dynasty, A.D. 1368–1644.

In the preparation of this digest, an acknowledgment is due the late Sir Edward Denison Ross, Ph.D., C.I.E., M.R.A.S., F.A.S.B., Director, School of Oriental Studies, London Institution, University of London. An equal debt is acknowledged to Mr. Z. L. Yih, part-time lecturer, also of the School of Oriental Studies, London Institution, for the excellent translation of the original which has been closely followed. The explanatory matter inclosed in brackets is the translator's or the author's.

[The *Ch'a Ching* consists of three volumes with ten parts in all. In the first part Lu Yu treats of the nature of the tea plant, in the second of the utensils for gathering the leaves, and in the third of the manipulation of the leaves. The fourth part is devoted to enumerating and describing the twenty-four implements of tea equipage. In this part may be noticed Lu Yu's predilection for Taoist symbolism and the influence of tea upon Chinese ceramics. In the fifth part Lu Yu describes the infusion method. The remaining chapters treat of the ordinary methods of tea drinking, an historical summary, famous tea plantations, and illustrations of tea utensils.]

LU YU WITH HIS TEA EQUIPAGE

His travel kit contained a tea pot, cups, water bottle, and fire fan. By Yamamoto Baiitsu (1784–1857). From the Bijutsu Shuyei published by The Shimbi Shoin Ltd., Tokyo. By permission.

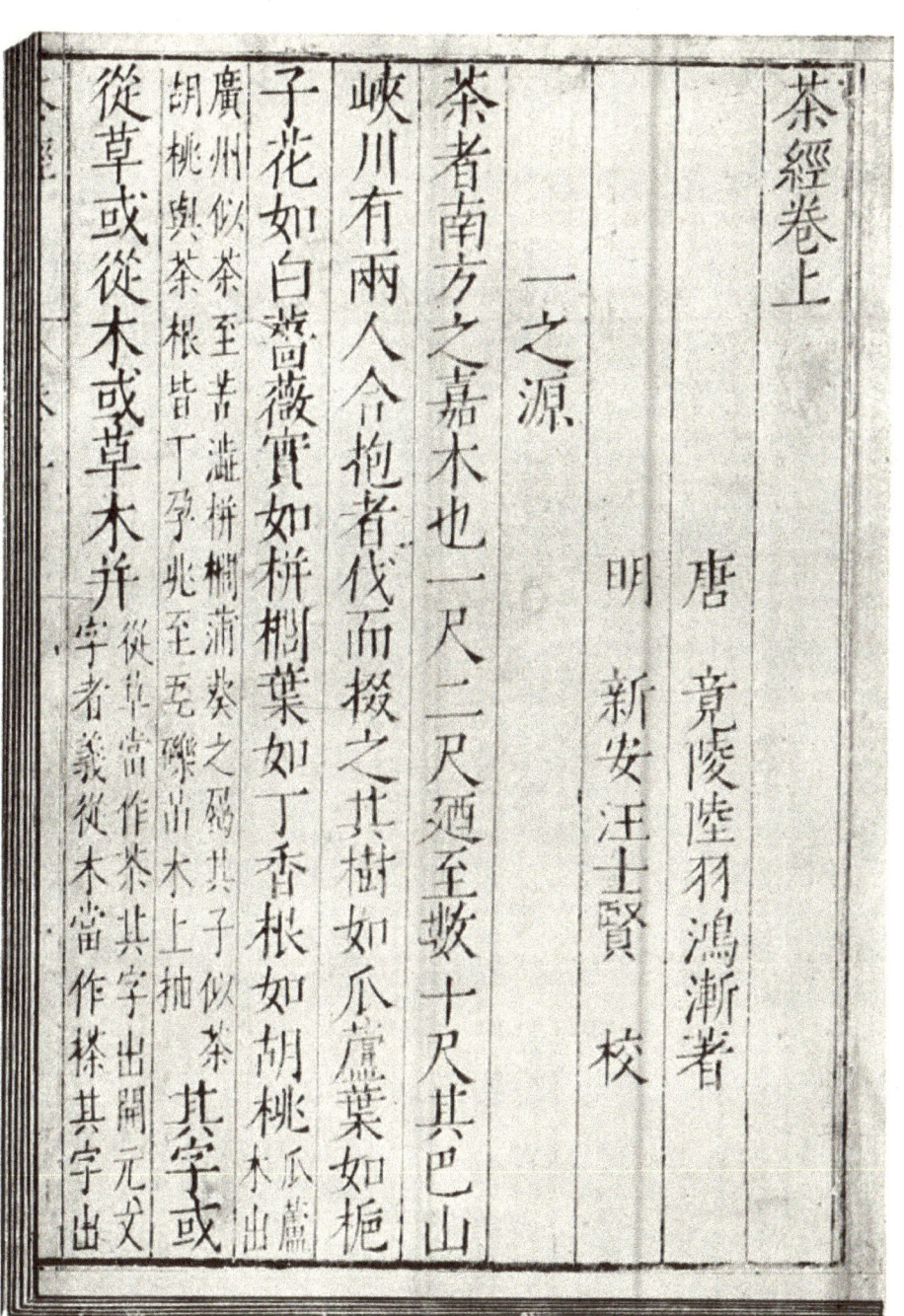

茶經卷上

茶之源

唐　竟陵陸羽鴻漸著

明　新安汪士賢　校

茶者南方之嘉木也一尺二尺迺至數十尺其巴山峽川有兩人合抱者伐而掇之其樹如瓜蘆葉如梔子花如白薔薇實如栟櫚葉如丁香根如胡桃　瓜蘆木出廣州似茶至苦澀栟櫚蒲葵之屬其子似茶胡桃與茶根皆下孕兆至瓦礫苗木上抽　從草當作茶其字出開元文字從木當作搽其字出

從草或從木或草木并　本字者義從木當作搽其字出

THE CH'A CHING, OR "TEA CLASSIC," THE FIRST BOOK ON TEA

From a Ming Dynasty copy in the University of London. Reading downwards the characters in the right-hand column say (1) Tea, (2) Classic, (3) Chapter, (4) First.

THE CH'A CHING

Part I.—the Origin of Tea

Tea is a fine tree of the South. Its height is from one to two feet to several tens of feet. The tea plants which grow on the hills and by the streams of Pa Shan [in the province of Szechwan] are sometimes so big that it takes two men to encircle them with their arms. They are cut down and then their leaves are plucked. A tea plant is like *kua lu*, a tree growing in Canton, the leaves of which are bitter and acrid in taste; its leaves are like those of the gardenia; its flowers are like the white cinnamon roses; its seeds are like those of the palm and coconut palm; its stalks are like those of the clove, and its roots are like those of a walnut tree. The roots of the two plants spread downwards until they reach gravel and broken tiles, and the tender plants shoot up.

In regard to the Chinese character *ch'a*, it has "grass," 艹, as its radical part; sometimes it has "tree," 木, as its radical part; and sometimes it has both "grass" and "tree" as its radical parts. The character with "grass" as its radical part is the *ch'a*, 茶, which is found in *K'ai Yuan Wen Tzu Yin I* [a dictionary]. That with "tree" as its radical part is the *t'u*, 梌, which is found in *Pen Ts'ao* [Shen Nung's *materia medica*].[1] The character having both "grass" and "tree" as its radical parts is the *ch'a* which is found in *Erh Ya* [the ancient Chinese dictionary, begun, as some claim, by the Duke of Chou, d. ca. 1105 B.C., and annotated about A.D. 350 by the learned commentator Kuo P'o, who added a definition of tea under the name of *kia*, 檟; *k'u t'u*, 苦荼]. In regard to the names given to tea, it is called *ch'a, kia, she, ming,* and *ch'uan.* Chou Kung said that *kia* was bitter *t'u*. Yang Hsiung [53 B.C.–A.D. 18, a brilliant scholar] said that the people in the southwestern part of Szechwan referred to *ch'a* as *she*. Kuo P'o said that what was plucked early was *ch'a*, and what was plucked later was *ming*, which was otherwise known as *ch'uan*.

The most favorable ground [for growing tea] is where there is to be found the soil of disintegrated stones. The next best is

IN A GREEN TEA DISTRICT

Scene in Kiang-nan, Anhwei, as drawn for Fortune's *Visit to the Tea Districts of China and India*, 1852.

where gravel is present in the soil; the least favorable ground is yellow clay. The method [of cultivating a tea plant] is just like that of growing the melon. The leaves can be plucked after three years.

The wild tea plants found growing in the open are of superior quality; those found growing in confined spaces are of secondary quality. Of those to be found growing on cliffs exposed to the sun or in a shady forest, the dark brown leaves are best, the green leaves are of the next quality, the new shoots are better than the buds, and the curled leaves [tips] are better than the uncurled ones. The leaves of the plants grown on the shady sides of hill slopes and valleys should not be plucked.

The effect of tea is cooling.[2] As a drink, it suits very well persons of self-restraint and good conduct. When feeling hot, thirsty, depressed, suffering from headache, eye-ache, fatigue of the four limbs, or pains in the joints, one should drink tea only, four or five times. The beverage is like dark red wine and sweet dew. If the

---

[1] The *Pen Ts'ao* is popularly attributed to Shen Nung, a legendary emperor, said to have flourished ca. 2737 B.C., but was not written in its earliest form until the time of the Eastern-Han dynasty, A.D. 25–221.

[2] The Chinese consider a medicine either of a cold or a hot nature. For example, cinnamon is of a hot, and rhubarb of a cold, nature. Tea was long regarded a medicine in China.

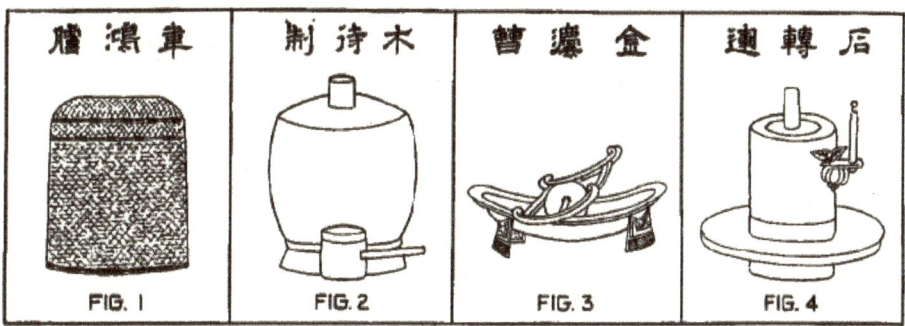

FIG. 1   FIG. 2   FIG. 3   FIG. 4

UTENSILS USED IN THE PREPARATION OF TEA IN THE TIME OF LU YU

Fig. 1 is a bamboo basket for firing tea. Fig. 2 is an anvil made of wood and an iron mallet to mould the tea into cakes. Fig. 3 is an iron grinding boat. Fig. 4 is a stone grinding mill.

tea leaves are not plucked at the proper season, are not properly prepared, and are mixed with herbs, they cause disease if consumed. The danger of tea is just like that of ginseng [the root of a plant valued by the Chinese as a strengthening medicine]. The best kind of ginseng grows in Shang T'ang [in the province of Shansi], the medium kind grows in Pai Chi and Hsin Lo [both in the south of Korea], and the inferior kind grows in Korea. Those which grow in Tse Chou [in the province of Shansi] I Chou, Yu Chou, and T'an Chou [all in the province of Chih-li] have no value as medicine. Those which are not ginseng are worse still. To know the danger of ginseng is [by analogy] to know that of tea.

Part II.—The Utensils

A square or round basket with the capacity of five *shengs*, one *tou*, two *tous*, or three *tous* is made of bamboo.[3] The tea gatherer carries it on his or her back while plucking tea. A furnace in which the pan has to be deeply sunk should not be used. A pan with broad brim should be used. There is a wooden or an earthenware steamer to which is attached a sort of mat made of bamboo. [There were seven holes at the bottom of the steamer, so a bamboo mat or a piece of cloth was necessary.] A pestle and mortar which have been in constant use are to be preferred. A round or square mold, sometimes with flowery designs, is made of iron. An anvil is made of stone, ash, or mulberry tree, half of

which is buried in the ground in order to render it immovable. A piece of cloth made of oiled silk or old cloth is put between the mold and anvil while tea is being manufactured [molded].

A network with square holes made of bamboo splints two feet five inches by two feet,[4] having a handle five inches long is an implement on which the [cake] tea is placed. An awl with the handle made of hardwood is used for boring holes in order to string the cake tea together. A bamboo implement is used for separating [the cakes of] tea.

A baking [drying or firing] ditch is constructed ten feet long, two feet five inches wide, and two feet deep, around which is built a wall two feet high.

Bamboo splints two feet five inches long are used for stringing tea for baking.

A wooden shed of two stories is built above the baking ditch. The half-dried tea is put on the lower story and the thoroughly dried tea is put on the upper story.

In some parts, as in Kiangsu and Anhwei, the tea package is made of bamboo matting. In Szechwan, it is made up with the bark of a tree. In Kiangsu and Anhwei, a large package contains one catty, a medium one contains half a catty, and a small one contains four or five ounces. In Szechwan a large package contains one hundred and twenty catties, a medium one contains eighty catties, and a small one contains fifty catties.[5] A basket with a wooden

---

[3] *Sheng*, a Chinese pint; 10 *shengs*=1 *tou*=2.115 gallons.

[4] Chinese feet and inches are meant throughout this translation. One foot, or 10 Chinese inches, equals approximately 14 English inches.

[5] Catty, 16 Chinese ounces, approximately 1⅓ pounds avoirdupois.

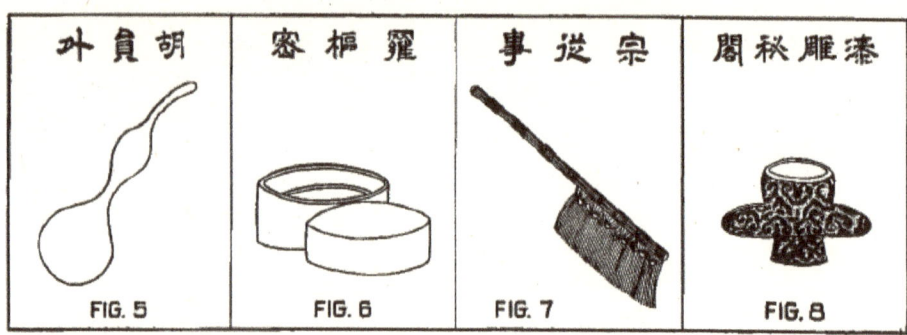

ADDITIONAL UTENSILS CALLED FOR AND DESCRIBED BY LU YU IN THE CH'A CHING

Fig. 5 is a gourd or ladle for measuring water. Fig. 6 is a sieve to separate coarse from fine tea. Fig. 7 is a brush for the removal of dust. Fig. 8 is a lacquer cup holder to avoid burning the hands.

frame is made of bamboo splints. It is divided by a partition. There is a cover on the upper part; a door opens from one side of the lower part, in which there is a receptacle containing a very gentle fire. It is an hourglass-shaped basket for refiring.

Part III.—Manipulation of Leaf

Tea is generally plucked during March, April, or May. On rich soil, the tea shoots [the flush], four or five inches long like the green stalks of the bracken and thorn ferns, are plucked. The best of the three, four, or five tea shoots growing on the thick branches is plucked. It is not plucked on a rainy or cloudy day. It is plucked only when the weather is fine. It is steamed, pounded, patted, baked, packed, and repacked. [First it was packed in a paper bag to retain the flavor and next wrapped in grass-bamboo matting or tree bark.]

There are a thousand different appearances of tea leaves. Generally speaking, some look like the Tartar's boots [wrinkled], some look like the buffalo's breast [regularly shaped], some look like the floating clouds [curled] arising from the mountains, some look like the ripples on water caused by a breeze [slightly wrinkled], some look dull brown, and some look like a piece of newly cultivated land covered with puddles [uneven] after violent rain. These are good tea. Others are like the first leaves of the bamboo shoots; they are hard and stiff, and it is difficult to steam and pound them; again, there are others which look like the lotus under frost—both the stalk and leaves wither. These are old and bad tea. [Another trans-

lation of the above passage renders it: "The best quality leaves must have creases like the leathern boot of Tartar horsemen, curl like the dewlap of a mighty bullock, unfold like a mist rising out of a ravine, gleam like a lake touched by a zephyr, and be wet and soft like fine earth newly swept by rain."]

From plucking to final packing, there are seven processes. From the appearance of the Tartar's boots to that of the lotus under frost, there are eight grades. Those who attribute smoothness, darkness, and flatness to good tea are connoisseurs of an inferior order; those who attribute wrinkles, yellowness, and uneven surface to good tea are the ordinary connoisseurs; those who hold the opinion that these qualities may or may not belong to good tea are the superior connoisseurs. Because whether tea is good or otherwise depends upon its flavor. The tea leaves which contain the juice are smooth, and when it is squeezed out the wrinkles appear. The tea which is manufactured by a slow process [consuming more than a day] is dark. If it is manufactured in a day it is yellow. The tea which is steamed and pressed becomes flat, and if it is not pressed, then its surface is uneven.

Part IV.—Implements for Preparation

[This part is addressed to the consumer, and, taken in connection with the parts which follow, presents Lu Yu's Tea Code.]

1.—A stove made of brass, iron, or mud in the shape of an ancient tripod.

2.—A basket one foot two inches in height and seven inches in diameter is

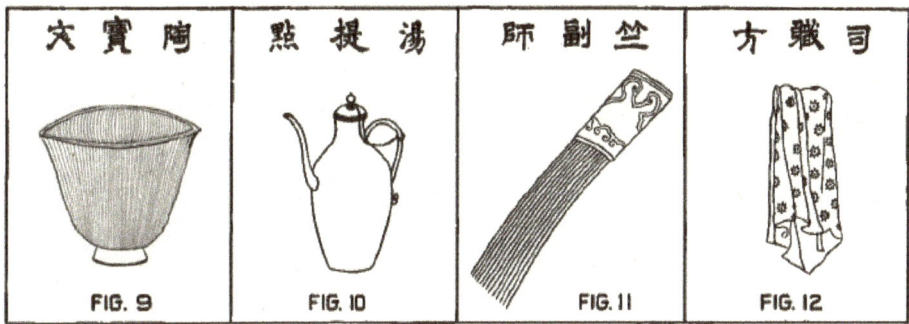

FIG. 9   FIG. 10   FIG. 11   FIG. 12

THESE ILLUSTRATIONS OF TEA UTENSILS ARE ALSO FROM LU YU'S CH'A CHING

Fig. 9 is a China cup. Fig. 10 is a China tea pot. Fig. 11 is a bamboo hand brush for washing pots. Fig. 12 is a towel for cleaning cups. All figures in this series re-drawn from the originals in the Ch'a Ching.

made of bamboo. Sometimes a container is made of rattans in the shape of a circular basket with hexagonal holes.

3.—A six-cornered poker one foot long, made of iron.

4.—A pair of tongs one foot three inches long, made of iron or brass.

5.—A boiler made of pig iron or wrought iron; its inner surface is smooth but the outer surface is rough. It is of earthenware in some places, and is made of stone in others; both are elegant utensils, but do not last long. The best is the silver boiler which is very clean and will wear well.

6.—A stand for the boiler to rest on.

7.—A small green bamboo about one foot two inches long is split just beneath its knob [joint] for baking tea; the flavor and fragrance of the latter will be improved through the bamboo juice. Where bamboo cannot be obtained, the implement is made of wrought iron or brass for its durable quality. [Sometimes, in order to improve the flavor of the tea with the juice of the fresh green bamboo, it was toasted in split bamboo tongs.]

8.—A paper bag made of thick white paper, used for keeping the baked tea so that it may not lose its fragrant flavor.

9.—An apparatus to grind tea, made of wood. The space inside is circular so as to permit the free movement of the wheel which crushes the tea as it is forced to move along. As it is square, it stands firmly and does not fall over easily. There is a tiny brush made of a bird's feather.

10.—A sieve made of bamboo and covered with a piece of gauze is put in the lid of a case in which there is a measure. The case, two inches in height and four inches

in diameter, is made of bamboo or lacquered wood, and its lid is one inch high.

11.—A measure made of a seashell, bamboo, brass, or iron. Generally speaking, a cubic inch of tea is used in one *sheng* [Chinese pint] of water. The quantity can be reduced or increased according to whether one desires to have weaker or stronger tea.

12.—A water tank with the capacity of one *tou* [about 2⅓ gallons], made of wood the cracks of which are filled with lacquer.

13.—The frame of a water-straining bag is made of unmanufactured copper, as manufactured copper is deemed to collect moss and dirt, and iron is deemed to emit offensive odors and to render the water acrid to the taste. In the mountainous regions, sometimes a bamboo or wooden frame is used, but for durability it must be made of unmanufactured copper. The straining bag is made of green [raw] silk with ornaments, and is covered with an outer bag of green oilcloth; the diameter of the latter bag is five inches, and its handle is an inch and a half long.

14.—A ladle made of a gourd or wood.

15.—A pair of sticks one foot long made of wood, the two ends inlaid with silver.

16.—A china salt-cellar four inches in diameter in the shape of a case. Sometimes it is a bottle or cup. The salt spoon is made of bamboo four inches long by one inch wide.

17.—A jar for boiled water with the capacity of two *shengs* is made of china or sand [porcelain or earthenware].

18.—The china cups from Yueh Chou [Shao Hsing, a district in Chekiang] are the best. Those from Ting Chou [Ch'ang

Te, a district in Hunan], Wu Chou [Chin Hua, a district in Chekiang], Yo Chou [Yo Yang, a district in Hunan], Shou Chou [the district of Shou in Anhwei], and Hung Chou [Nan Ch'ang, a district in Kiangsi] are not so good. [Lu Yu considered the blue glaze of the North the ideal color for the teacup, because it lent additional greenness to the beverage; whereas, the white made it look pinkish and distasteful. It must be remembered he used cake tea. Later on, when the Sung tea masters took to powdered tea, they prepared heavy bowls of blue, black, and dark brown. The Mings, with their steeped tea, rejoiced in light ware of white porcelain.]

19.—A basket made of rushes [which] can hold ten cups.

20.—A brush made of the coir [coconut] palm tied together with string between two pieces of wood or inserted in a short piece of bamboo in the shape of a large writing brush.

21.—A slop basin similar to the water tank made of wood having a capacity of eight *shengs*.

22.—A dust bin similar to the slop basin having a capacity of five *shengs*.

23.—Two cloth towels two feet long to be used for cleaning the implements.

24.—A sideboard [cabinet] six inches high, three feet long, and two feet wide is a sort of bed or stand with doors which can be shut or opened as desired. It is varnished yellow or black and is used for keeping the implements.

The all-in-one bamboo basket, one foot five inches high, two feet four inches long, and two feet wide, is for keeping all the implements. [Here may be noticed Lu Yu's predilection for Taoist symbolism.]

Part V.—Infusion

Tea should not be baked before a wind which will render the fire unsteady and which will cause uneven baking. It should be turned over often, and taken away about five inches from the fire when its surface becomes uneven as the back of a toad. As soon as it recovers its original form, it should be baked again until its flavor indicates it is baked sufficiently, or until it is as soft as if baked under the sun. At the beginning, if the tea is very tender, it should be pounded while hot immediately after being steamed; the leaves will be pulpy, but the shoots remain as they are.

After baking [as described in the first paragraph] it should be put in a paper bag so that it will not lose its fragrant flavor. It should be ground when it is cold. The fuel should be charcoal, and the next best is hard wood, such as mulberry or plane tree. The charcoal fire on which meat has been cooked, and which has been tainted with an offensive odor, should be avoided; while fragrant woods, such as juniper and pine trees, and old and rotten woods, should not be used as fuels.

In regard to water, the spring in a mountainous region is the best; the slowly flowing water is preferred, and the rapid or torrent, which, if drunk often would cause trouble at the neck, should be avoided. The water of a river is the next best, and that of a well is the last for quality. When the water first boils, there appears something like the eyes of fishes on the surface, and a little noise can be heard. Then appears something like a spring rushing forth and a string of pearls at the side; this is the second boiling. Then the waves and breakers come along; this is the third boiling. After that the water will be overboiled and should not be drunk. When the water first boils, put in a pinch of salt. The quantity should vary according to that of the water. During the second boiling, take out a ladleful and stir the water in the middle part with a pair of small bamboo sticks; as soon as the waves and breakers come along, they should be stopped by pouring in again the water just taken out; this is done to improve the quality of the liquid.

For drinking, make tea in a cup and let there be froths, which are the essence of beverages. One *sheng* of water is for five cups. The first and second cups are the best and the third one is the next best. One should not drink the fourth and fifth cups unless one is very thirsty. Drink tea while hot, as then the heavy and impure stuffs are at the bottom and the best part, which will vanish as soon as it evaporates, is floating on the top. Moreover, cold tea would cause indigestion.

Part VI.—Drinking

The birds, animals, and human beings all have to drink and eat to live. In regard to drinks, boiled water is to quench thirst, wine to drown sorrow, and tea is to avoid sleepiness.

Tea as a beverage was discovered by the [legendary] Emperor Shen Nung, and was known to the Duke of Chou [author of the *Erh Ya*, d. 1105 B.C.]; [6] Yen Ying [d. 493 B.C.], Yang Hsiung [53 B.C.-A.D. 18], Wei Yao [of the third century A.D.], Liu Kun [d. A.D. 317], and other notable personages all drank tea.

Drinking tea was very popular in the T'ang dynasty, A.D. 620–907. In some parts of Honan, Shensi, Hunan, and Szechwan the drink was universal. There is ordinary tea and ground tea. What is called cake tea is put in a jar or bottle after being pounded, and the boiling water is poured over it. Sometimes onion, ginger, jujube, orange peel, and peppermint are used, and it is permitted to boil for some time before skimming off the froth. Alas! This is the slop water of a ditch.

There are nine steps in connection with tea: (1) manufacturing; (2) distinguishing good from bad tea; (3) implements; (4) fire; (5) water; (6) baking; (7) grinding; (8) infusion; and (9) drinking. To pluck tea on a cloudy day and to bake it at night is not the proper way of manufacturing. To smell it and taste it by chewing is not the proper way to distinguish good from bad tea. A rank-smelling pot or jar is not the proper utensil. Fragrant wood and charcoal used in the kitchen are not the proper fuels for the fire. Neither rapid nor stagnant water is suitable for making tea. Being well baked outside but raw inside is not the proper way of baking. Ground tea with dust is the result of improper grinding. To make tea not with ease, and to stir suddenly, is not the proper way of infusing. To drink tea in summer, and to abandon it in winter, is not the proper way of consumption. The best are the first three cups, which are full of fragrant flavor.

Part VII.—Historical Record

[This part is a compilation of historical references to tea, which had been published by earlier authors.]

Extract from *Fang Yen* [a comparative vocabulary of words and phrases used in different parts of the empire], by Yang Hsiung [53 B.C.-A.D. 18, a brilliant scholar]:

"The people in the southwestern part of Szechwan called *ch'a* as *she*."

Extract from *Shih Ching* [Food Classic] by Shen Nung: [7] "To drink *ch'a* and *ming* constantly makes one strong and is exhilarating."

Extract from *Erh Ya*, by Chou Kung [Duke of Chou]: "*Kia* means bitter *t'u*."

Extract from *Kuang Ya* [a dictionary by Chang I, of the Later Wei dynasty, A.D. 386–535]:

In the district between the provinces of Hupeh and Szechwan the leaves are plucked and made into cakes; those made of old leaves are mixed with rice. To make tea as a drink, bake the cake until reddish in color, pound it into tiny pieces, put them in a chinaware pot, pour boiling water over them and add onion, ginger, and orange. The drink renders one sober from intoxication and keeps one awake.

Extract from *Yen Tsu Ch'un Ch'iu* [the sayings of Yen Ying, d. 493 B.C.]: "When Yen Ying was the chief official of the Duke of Ch'i, he ate unpolished rice, three roasted birds, five eggs, and took *ming* and goosefoot."

Extract from "The Biography of Wei Yao" [third century A.D.], in *The History of the State of Wu:*

Whenever Sun Hao [A.D. 242–283], the ruler of Wu, gave a dinner, he always used seven *shengs* of wine as the limit. Though he did not drink all, he used the whole quantity by pouring some on the ground. Wei Yao's capacity of drinking wine was not more than two *shengs*. Sun Hao treated him at first with special favor and secretly gave him *ch'a* and *ch'uan* instead of wine.

In the latter part of the Chin dynasty [A.D. 265–420], when Lu Na was the chief official of the district of Wu Hsing [in the province of Chekiang], the famous General Hsieh An [A.D. 320–385] often desired to pay him a visit. Lu Shu, a nephew of Lu Na, was surprised at the fact that his uncle made no preparations, and yet dared not to ask him about it; so he secretly hoarded a quantity of food sufficient for scores of persons. When Hsieh An arrived, only tea and fruit were given. Then Lu Shu gave out the chief dishes. After the distinguished visitor had taken his departure, the host gave his nephew forty strokes with a stick and said: "You have not been able to raise the social status of your uncle

6 Lu Yu was mistaken in assuming that tea was known to the Duke of Chou. The definition of tea in *Erh Ya* was added by Kuo P'o about A.D. 350.

7 The *Shih Ching*, Food Classic, of Shen Nung, is not to be confused with the *Shih Ching*, Book of Odes, edited by Confucius, for they are entirely different books.

[by becoming a high official or a brilliant scholar], so why do you seek to sully his simple mode of living by giving many dishes to the guest?"

Extract from *Chin Shu* [the history of the Chin dynasty]: "When Huan Wen [A.D. 312–373] was the governor of Yang Chou [in the province of Kiangsu], he was frugal. When he took food and drink, he only put down seven receptacles for tea and fruit."

Liu Kun, a famous general of the Chin dynasty [d. A.D. 317], wrote to his nephew, Liu Yen, the governor of Yen Chou [in the province of Shantung] and said:

A catty of dried ginger of An Chou [in the province of Chihli], a catty of the yellow-colored medicinal root and a catty of cinnamon, which I have received, are the necessary things to me. Now I feel aged and depressed and want some real tea. Send them on.

Extract from *Erh Ya Chu* [the commentary of Erh Ya, by Kuo P'o, *ca*. A.D. 350]:

The plant [tea] is as small as the gardenia, and in winter has leaves which can be made into a drink. What is plucked early is called *ch'a*[8] and what is plucked later is called *ming*, otherwise known as *ch'uan*, which is called bitter tea by the people of Szechwan.

During the rebellion of the four princes of the Chin dynasty, the Emperor Hui Ti [A.D. 259–306] left the capital. When he returned he was offered an earthenware bowl of tea by a eunuch.

The Emperor Wu Ti [who reigned A.D. 483–493], of the South Ch'i dynasty, left a will in which he said: "Do not offer me any cattle as a sacrifice, give me only cakes, fruit, tea, dried rice, wine, and dried meat."

Extract from *Hou Wei Lu* [The Record of the Later Wei dynasty]:

While Wang Su [A.D. 464–501] was an official of the Southern dynasty, he was fond of tea and a vegetable stew. When he returned to the North, he loved mutton and kumiss. He was asked as to which was the better of the two. His answer was, "Tea is not fit to be the slave of kumiss."

Extracts from *Tung Chun Lu* [a treatise on medicine]:

The people of Hsi Yang [in the province of Honan], Wu Ch'ang [in the province of Hupeh], Lu Chiang [in the province of Anhwei], and Chin Ling [in the province of Kiangsu] are fond

of tea. Some people make pure *ming*; to drink *ming* which is frothy will do one good. All beverages are mostly made from leaves; but in regard to *Asparagus lucidus*, its roots are used. The drinks are all good for human health.

In Pa Tung [a district in the province of Hupeh], there are real *ming* and *ch'a*, which if made into a drink make one sleepless. According to the custom, the leaves of sandalwood and *ta tsao li* [a kind of plum tree] are used as tea. They are taken cold.

In the South there is the *kua lu* tree resembling *ming*. The leaves, bitter and acrid to the taste, can be made into a drink as tea, and also keep one sleepless the whole night. The people who boil sea-water to get salt only consume this drink; they like to make friends. When a visitor calls, he is first of all offered this tea with some fragrant herbs.

Extract from *K'un Yuan Lu:*

Three hundred and fifty *lis* [140 miles] northwest from the city of Hsu P'u in Ch'en Chou [in the province of Hunan], there is the Wu She Mountain, which is full of tea plants. According to the barbarous custom there, people assemble to sing and dance on the top of the mountain whenever a happy event occurs.

Extract from *I Ling T'u Ching* ["The Topography of I Ling," a district in the province of Hupeh]: "*Ch'a* and *ming* are produced on the Huang Niu, Ching Men, Nu Kuan, and Wang Chou mountains."

Extract from *Ch'a Ling T'u Ching* [The Topography of Ch'a Ling, a district in the province of Hunan]:

Ch'a [tea] Ling [mound or hill] is so called because *ch'a* and *ming* grow in the valleys and on the hills. According to the section on trees of *Pen Ts'ao* [Shen Nung's work on *materia medica*], *ming* is bitter *ch'a*; its taste is sweetish-bitter; its nature is slightly cold and it is not poisonous; it cures running sores and ulcers, stimulates the activity of the kidneys, stops phlegm, quenches thirst, has a cooling effect, and makes one less desirous of sleep; if it is plucked in the autumn, it is bitter, cures the breathing trouble and improves digestion. A commentator said that it should be plucked in spring.

Extract from *Pen Ts'ao Chu* [the commentary on *Pen Ts'ao*]:

"In *The Book of Odes* [a work edited by Confucius] it says: '*T'u* is an all bitter vegetable. Bitter tea, *ming*, belongs to the family of trees, and does not belong to that of vegetables. *Ming* is plucked in spring and is called bitter *ch'a* 梏 .'" [The character used is *ch'a*, tea, with *mu*, tree, on the left.]

Extract from *Jou Tzu Fang* [prescriptions for children]: "Bitter *ch'a* made with the rootlets of onions can cure children who are frightened and tumble without apparent causes."

---

[8] Kuo P'o used the character *t'u*, not *ch'a*. *Ch'a*, tea, did not come into use until some four centuries after Kuo P'o.

Part VIII.—Producing Districts

[This part enumerates the famous tea districts of China where the best teas were obtained.]

To the South of Chung Nan and T'ai Hua mountains, Hsia Chou [Ichang in Hupeh]; to the south of the Huai River, Kuang Chou [Huang Ch'uan in Honan]; to the west of Chekiang, Hu Chou [Wu Hsing in Chekiang]; in Chien Nan [one of the ten political divisions during the T'ang dynasty]; P'eng Chou [P'eng Hsien in Szechwan]; to the east of Chekiang, Yueh Chou [Shao Hsing in Chekiang]; and from En Chou [Yang Chiang in Kwangtung]; Po Chou [Tsun I in Kweichow]; Fei Chou [Fei Hsien in Shantung]; I Chou [Chi Mo in Shantung]; Ao Chou [Wu Ch'ang in Hupeh]; Yuan Chou [I Ch'un in Kiangsi]; Chi Chou [Chi Hsien in Shansi]; Fu Chou [Min Hou in Fukien]; Chien Chou [Chien Ou in Fukien]; Shao Chou [Chu Chiang in Kwangtung]; and Hsiang Chou [Hsiang Hsien in Kwangsi].

Part IX.—General Summary

In the spring, when fire is prohibited [a festival during which cold meals are eaten], if in an enclosure on a mountainous region or around a ruined temple tea is plucked, steamed, pounded, and baked, then the implements such as the awl, bamboo splints, and wooden shed for baking can be omitted. If tea is prepared under pine trees and on a rock, then the sideboard is not needed; if dry wood for fuel and a tripod are used, then the stove, tongs, etc., are not needed; if a stream is near by, then the water tank, slop basin, and water-straining bag are not needed; if there are less than five persons, fine tea can be used, and so the sieve is not needed; if tea is baked in a cave, pounded, and kept in a paper bag, then the apparatus to grind and a tiny brush are not needed; as the ladle, cups, small bamboo sticks, brush, jar for boiled water, and salt-cellar can be put in a basket, the all-in-one basket is not needed. If, however, one of the twenty-four implements is missing in an aristocratic family inside the city, then tea cannot be prepared.

Part X.—Memo Regarding Plates

[This part of the work is addressed to the tea merchants.]

The *Ch'a Ching* should be copied out and illustrated on four or six scrolls of silk hung by the seat in one's studio, and then the origin, utensils for gathering and manufacturing tea, implements for the preparation, infusion, drinking, historical record, producing districts, and general summary can be perused at any time. Thus, the Tea Classic is complete from the beginning to the end.

CHAPTER III

INTRODUCTION OF TEA INTO EUROPE

THE FIRST MENTION OF TEA IN EUROPEAN LITERATURE IN 1559—PORTUGUESE AS PIO-
NEERS IN ORIENTAL TRADE—EARLY MENTION OF TEA BY PRIESTS AND TRAVELERS—THE
DUTCH ARRIVE IN THE ORIENT—THE ENGLISH REACH THE FAR EAST—ADOPTION OF
TEA BY FIVE EUROPEAN COUNTRIES, RUSSIA, HOLLAND, GERMANY, FRANCE, AND SCANDI-
NAVIA—EARLY CONTINENTAL CONTROVERSIES ABOUT TEA—SOME CURIOUS LATER NOTICES
IN FRENCH AND SCANDINAVIAN LITERATURE

TEA drinking is one of the great temperance customs that the East shares most generously with the West; yet it was many centuries after tea was commonly used in the Orient that Europeans learned of it. Of the world's three great temperance beverages—cocoa, tea, and coffee—cocoa was the first to be introduced into Europe, in 1528, by the Spanish. It was almost a century later, in 1610, that the Dutch brought tea to Europe. Venetian traders introduced coffee into Europe just a few years later, in 1615.

The earliest mention of tea in the literature of Europe was in 1559. It appears as *Chai Catai*, "Tea of China," in *Navigatione et Viaggi*, or "Voyages and Travels," by Giambattista Ramusio, 1485–1557, a noted Venetian author who published a valuable collection of narratives of voyages and discoveries in ancient and modern times. Ramusio, as secretary to the Venetian Council of Ten, collected some rare commercial information and met many famous travelers, among whom was Hajji Mahommed, or Chaggi Memet, the Persian merchant credited with having brought the first knowledge of tea to Europe. The story appears as "The Tale of Hajji Mahommed" in Ramusio's "Espositione," a preface to the second volume of *Navigatione et Viaggi*, a work which includes the travels of Marco Polo. The paragraph containing the tea reference reads:

The name of the narrator was Hajji Mahommed, or Chaggi Memet, a native of Chilan [Persia] on the shores of the Caspian Sea, and he himself had been to Succuir [Sakkar, India],

coming afterwards, at the time I speak of, to Venice. . . . He told me that all over Cathay they made use of another plant or rather of its leaves. This is called by those people *Chai Catai*, and grows in the district of Cathay which is called Cacian-fu [Szechwan]. This is commonly used and much esteemed over all those countries. They take of that herb, whether dry or fresh, and boil it well in water. One or two cups of this decoction taken on an empty stomach removes fever, headache, stomach ache, pain in the side or in the joints, and it should be taken as hot as you can bear it. He said, besides, that it was good for no end of other ailments which he could not remember, but gout was one of them. And if it happens that one feels incommoded in the stomach for having eaten too much, one has but to take a little of this decoction, and in a short time all will be digested. And it is so highly valued and esteemed that every one going on a journey takes it with him, and those people would gladly give a sack of rhubarb for one ounce of *Chai Catai*. And those people of Cathay do say if in our parts of the world, in Persia, and the country of the Franks, people only knew of it, there is no doubt that the merchants would cease altogether to buy rhubarb.[1]

In the time of Ramusio, Venice was the center of great commercial activity due to its geographical position between East and West. Its merchants and scholars were keenly alert for any knowledge which would add to its commercial prestige or increase the wealth of its merchant princes. Notable traders or travelers who came to Venice from the veiled East were fêted, entertained, and encouraged to tell of

---

[1] Giambattista Ramusio, *Navigatione et Viaggi*, Vol. II, Venice, 1559. This work consisted of three volumes published in the following order: Vol. I, 1550; Vol. III, 1556; Vol. II, 1559. There has been considerable difference of statement as to the year Ramusio published the first notice of tea in Europe, but this notice is included in Vol. II, which was published last.

23

ve nè tanta copia,che l'abbrucciano côtinuamente fecco incābio di legne : altri, come hanno i
lor caualli malati,glie ne danno di cōtinuo à mangiare, tanto è poco ftimata ĝlla radice in ĝlle
parti del Cataio . ma bñ aprezano molto piu vn'altra piccola radice,laquale nafce nelle monta-
gne di Succuir doue nafce il Rheubarbaro,& la chiamano Mambroni cini,et è carifsima:e lado
perano ordinariamēte nelle lor malattie,& mafsime in ĝlla de gl'occhi:perche,fe trita fopra vna
pietra con acqua rofa,vnghano gl'occhi,fentono vn mirabile giouamento,ne crede che di ĝlla
radice ne fia portata in ĝfte parti,ne meno difse di faperla defcriuere:& di piu , vedēdo il piacer
grāde,ch'io fopra gl'altri pigliauo di ĝfti ragionamēti,mi difse che per tutto il paefe del Cataio,
fi adopera ancho vn'altra herba,cioe le foglie,la quale da que' popoli fi chiama **Chiaī Catai**:&
nafce nella terra del Cataio,ch'è detta Cacianfu : la quale è cōmune & aprezzata per tutti que'
paefi,fanno detta herba cofi fecca come frefca bollire affai nell'acqua,& pigliando di ĝlla decot-
tiõe vno o duoi bichieri à digiuno leua la febre,il dolor di tefta,di ftomaco , delle cofte,& delle
giūture,pigliādola pero tanto calda quāte fi pofsi foftrire,& di piu difse efser buona ad infinite
altre malattie delle quali egli p a l'hora nō fi ricordaua : ma fra l'altre,alle gotte.Et che fe alcuno
per forte fi fente lo ftomaco graue p troppo cibo , pfa vn poco di ĝfta decottione in breue tēpo
hara digerito.& per ciò è tāto cara & aprezzata,che ogn'uno che và in viaggio ne vuol porta-
re feco , & coftoro volontieri darebbono per quello ch'egli diceua fempre vn facco di rheubarbaro per vn'oncia di **Chiaī Catai**: Et che quelli popoli Cataini dicono che fe nelle noftre
parti & nel paefe della Perfia & Franchia la fi conofcefse , i mercanti fenza dubio non vorreb-
bono piu comperare Rauend Cini,che cofi chiamano loro il Rheubarbaro . Quiui fatto vn
poco di paufa,& fattoli domandare s'egli mi voleua dire altro del Rheubarbaro , & rifpoftomi
                    non

British Museum

THE EARLIEST PRINTED MENTION OF TEA IN EUROPE BY RAMUSIO, VENICE, 1559

strange peoples and products. Such information had been eagerly sought ever since
the memorable return of Marco Polo. At
the time of Hajji Mahommed's visit, Ramusio was engaged in editing an account
of Polo's travels. It was while entertaining the Persian merchant that Ramusio
first heard of the tea plant and drink.

Parenthetically, Marco Polo's account
fails to mention tea, although the drink was
in great favor among the Chinese at that
time, 1275–92. The reason is simple. Polo
spent most of his time among the hosts of
Kublai Khan, the Tartar invader, and was
not interested in the customs of the subject people.

Portuguese as Pioneers in Orient

Following Vasco da Gama's discovery
of an all-sea route to the Indies by way of
the Cape of Good Hope, in 1497, the
Portuguese pushed on to other discoveries
and founded a settlement at Malacca on
the Malay Peninsula. From Malacca, in
1516, their first ship reached China, where
they found favorable opportunities for
trade. These Portuguese were the first
Europeans to arrive in the Orient by sea.
A fleet of several ships followed the next
year, and an ambassador was sent to
Peiping. By 1540 they reached Japan.

The Chinese, looking with suspicion upon
the Portuguese, held out no welcome, but
the Portuguese ambassador finally convinced the Chinese emperor that the newcomers had come to barter and exchange
and not to invade. The Chinese then permitted them to settle at Macao, a narrow
peninsula projecting from the island of
Hiang Shang on the western side of the
estuary of the Canton River.

Mention by Priests and Travelers

During the early years of European commerce with China and Japan there is no
record of tea having been transported, but
the Jesuit missionaries, who early penetrated both countries, became acquainted
with the tea drink and sent accounts of it
to Europe. Of these missionaries, Father
Gasper da Cruz, a Portuguese, is said to
have been the first to preach the Catholic
doctrines in China, having reached there
in 1556. Returning to Portugal about
1560, he published the first notice of tea in
Portuguese. It reads:

Whatsoever person or persons come to any
man's house of quality, hee hath a custome to of-

fer him . . . a kind of drinke called *ch'a*, which is somewhat bitter, red, and medicinall, which they are wont to make with a certayne concoction of herbes.

Further news of tea reached Italy in 1565 in a letter from Father Louis Almeida, a missionary to Japan. Father Almeida wrote: "The Japanese are very fond of an herb agreeable to the taste, which they call *chia*."

Two years later, in 1567, the first account of tea reached Russia. The news was carried there by Ivan Petroff and Boornash Yalysheff upon their return from travels in China. Their reference to tea was a casual one. They described the tea plant as a wonder of China, but they brought back neither specimens of the bush nor samples of tea.

Although an account of tea had been published at Venice in 1559, it was not until 1588 that it was again noted in an Italian work. This was when Giovanni Maffei, an eminent Italian author, printed at Florence Father Almeida's 1565 letter in an extensive collection of papers, titled *Four Books of Selected Letters from India*. In Maffei's frequently quoted *Historica Indica*, published at Rome the same year, are two other references to tea:

The beverage of the Japanese is a juice extracted from an herb called *chia*, which they boil to drink, and which is extremely wholesome. It protects them from pituitary troubles, heaviness in the head, and ailments of the eyes; it makes them live long years almost without languor.

The Japanese have as yet no use for grapes, but they make a kind of wine from rice. But that which before all they delight to drink is water *almost* boiling, mingled with the powdered *chia*. They are particular about having it well made. The most eminent sometimes make it with their own hands, taking the trouble to regulate the portions and to make the mixture for their friends. They even have certain rooms in their homes reserved for that alone. There is always at hand a kind of covered chafing-dish from which they offer their friends a drink on arriving or taking leave.[2]

Next in point of time was Giovanni Botero, a Venetian ecclesiast and author, who, in 1589, in his work *On the Causes of Greatness in Cities*, states: "The Chinese have an herb from which they press a delicate juice which serves them instead of wine. It also preserves the health and frees them from all those evils that the immoderate use of wine doth breed in us." At this time tea had been a medicinal and social beverage in China for approximately

eight hundred years, so it is fairly certain that this author is referring to tea.

Writing thirteen years after Botero, in 1602, on the etiquette of China, Father Diego de Pantoia, another Portuguese missionary, makes this reference to tea: "When they have ended their salutations, they straightway cause a drink to be brought, which they call *ch'a*, which is water boyled with a certaine herbe, which they much esteeme . . . and they must drink of it twice or thrice."

The next tea reference to appear is perhaps the most important of all early accounts, for it gives not only the details as to the price of tea, but briefly contrasts the Chinese and Japanese methods of making the drink. It was found among the letters of an Italian missionary, Padre Matteo Ricci, 1552–1610, a scientific adviser to the Chinese court at Peiping from 1601 until his death. The letters were published in 1610 by Padre Nicolas Trigault, d. 1628, a French Jesuit. The account reads:

I cannot pass by some rarities, as their shrub whence they make their *Cia* [tea—obs. Ital.]. They gather the leaves in the shadow, and keep it for daily decoction, using it at meals, and as often as any guest comes to their house; yea, twice or thrice if he make any tarrying. This beverage is always drunk or rather sipped hot, and on account of a peculiar mild bitterness is not disagreeable to the taste; but on the contrary is positively wholesome for many ailments if used often. And there is not alone a single quality of excellence in the leaf, for one surpasses the other, and thus you will often buy some at one gold escu [five francs], or even two or three escus a pound, if it is rated as the best. The most excellent is sold at ten and more, often at twelve gold escus a pound in Japan, where its use is also somewhat different from that of China; for the Japanese mix the leaves reduced to a powder, in a cup of boiling water to the amount of two or three tablespoonfuls and swallow this potion mixed in this manner; but the Chinese throw a few leaves into a pot of boiling water, then when it is tinctured with the strength and virtue of the same, they drink it quite hot and leave the leaves.[3]

The same year, 1610, in which Padre Ricci's account appeared in Italy, a Portuguese traveler and scholar published *An Account of the Kings of Persia and Ormuz* which contained a notice of tea, reading: "*Cha* is a small leaf of a herb, from a certain plant brought from Tartary which was shown me while I was at Malacca."

2 Giovanni Maffei, *Historica Indica*, Rome, 1588.

3 Padre Matteo Ricci, *Annua della Cina del 1606 e 1607 del Padre M. Ricci*, collected and published by Padre Nicolas Trigault, Rome, 1610.

our clokes when we meane to goe abroad into the towne or countrie, they put them off when they goe forth, putting on great wyde breeches, and coming home they put them off again, and cast their clokes vpon their shoulders: and as among other nations it is a good sight to see men with white and yealow hayre and white teeth, with them it is esteemed the filthiest thing in the world, and seeke by all meanes they may to make their hayre and teeth blacke, for that the white causeth their grief, and the blacke maketh them glad. The like custome is among the women, for as they goe abroad they haue their daughters & maydes before them, and their men seruants come behind, which in Spaigne is cleane contrarie, and when they are great with childe, they tye their girdles so hard about them, that men would thinke they should burst, and when they are not with Childe, they weare their girdles so slacke, that you would thinke they would fall from their bodies, saying that by experience they do finde, if they should not doe so, they should haue euill lucke with their fruit, and presently as soone as they are deliuered of their children, in stead of cherishing both the mother and the child with some comfortable meat, they presently wash the childe in cold water, and for a time giue the mother very little to eate, and that of no great substance. Their manner of eating and drinking is: Euerie man hath a table alone, without table-clothes or napkins, and eateth with two peeces of wood, like the men of China: they drinke wine of Rice, wherewith they drinke themselues drunke, and after their meat they vse a certaine drinke, which is a pot with hote water, which they drinke as hote as euer they may indure, whether it be Winter or Summer.

Annotat, D. Pad.

The Turkes holde almost the same maner of drinking of their Chaona, which they make of certaine fruit, which is like vnto the Bakelaer, and by the Egyptians called Bon or Ban: they take of this fruite one pound and a half, and roast them a little in the fire, and then sieth them in twentie poundes of water, till the half be consumed away: this drinke they take euerie morning fasting in their chambers, out of an earthen pot, being verie hote, as we doe here drinke aquacomposita in the morning: and they say that it strengtheneth and maketh them warme, breaketh wind, and openeth any stopping.

The manner of dressing their meat is altogether contrarie vnto other nations: the aforesaid warme water is made with the powder of a certaine hearbe called Chaa, which is much esteemed, and is well accounted of. The 1. Booke.

among them, and al such as are of any countenance or habilitie haue the said water kept for them in a secret place, and the gentlemen make it themselues, and when they will entertaine any of their friends, they giue him some of that warme water to drinke: for the pots wherein they sieth it, and wherein the hearbe is kept, with the earthen cups which they drinke it in, they esteeme as much of them as we doe of Diamants, Rubies and other pretious stones, and they are not esteemed for their newnes, but for their olones, and for that they were made by a good workman: and to know and keepe such by themselues, they take great and speciall care, as also of such as are the valewers of them, and are skilfull in them, as with vs the goldsmith prizeth and valueth siluer and gold, and the Iewellers all kindes of pretious stones: so if their pots & cuppes be of an old & excellet workmans making, they are worth 4 or 5 thousad ducats or more the peece. The King of Bungo did giue for such a pot, hauing three feet, 14 thousand ducats, and a Iapan being a Christian in the town of Sacay, gaue for such a pot 1400 ducats, and yet it had 3 peeces vpon it. They doe likewise esteeme much of any picture or table, wherein is painted a blacke tree, or a blacke bird, and when they knowe it is made of wood, and by an ancient & cunning maister, they giue whatsoeuer you will aske for it. It happeneth some times that such a picture is sold for; 3 or 4 thousand ducats and more. They also esteeme much of a good rapier, made by an old and cunning maister such a one many times costeth 3 or 4 thousand Crownes the peece. These things doe they keepe and esteeme so; their Iewels, as we esteeme our Iewels & pretious stones. And when we aske them why they esteeme them so much, they aske vs againe, why we esteeme so well of our pretious stones & iewels, whereby there is not any profite to be had and serue to no other vse, then only for a shewe, & that their things serue to some end.

Their Iustice and gouernment is as followeth: Their kings are called Iacatay, and are absolutely Lords of the land, notwithstanding they keepe for themselues as much as is necessary for them and their estate, and the rest of their land they deuyde among others, which are called Cunixus, which are like our Earles and Dukes: these are appointed by the king, and he causeth them to gouerne & rule the land as it pleaseth him: they are bound to serue the king as well in peace, as in warres, at their owne cost & charges, according to their estate, and the auntient lawes of Iapan. These Cunixus haue others vnder them called Tons, which are like our Lords

FIRST PRINTED REFERENCE TO TEA IN ENGLISH, 1598

It appears as "Chaa" in the first column, two lines from the bottom.

Over thirty years elapsed before the next tea reference appeared. It was mentioned by Father Alvaro Semedo, 1585–1658, a Portuguese Jesuit, in *The History of the Great and Renowned Monarchy of China*, a work first published in Italian at Rome in 1643, and later in English at London in 1655.

The next three accounts of tea were all by French missionaries. The first was Father Alexander de Rhodes, 1591–1660, who gave tea a notice in his *Voyages et Missions Apostoliques*, published at Paris in 1653, reading: "One of the things contributing to the great health of these peoples [the Chinese], who frequently reach extreme old age, is tay, which is commonly used throughout the Orient." The second of the French missionaries was Jacques de Bourges, who stated in his *Relation of the Voyage of the Bishop of Beryte to Cochinchina*, published in Paris in 1666: "During our abode at Siam, after our dinner . . . we drank some *tea* . . . we found it very wholesome, and comparing the effects of this tea with those of wine . . . it is doubtful which of these two may obtain the preëminence if not this leaf."

The last of the three was an account by the Jesuit missionary Father Louis Lecompte, 1655–1728, in his *Memoirs and Observations Made in a Late Journey Through China*, published at Paris in 1696. It reads: "In China they are subject to neither gout, sciatica, nor stone; and many imagine that *thee* preserves them against all these distempers."

Arrival of Dutch in Orient

The Portuguese had the sea trade of the Orient to themselves up to 1596, carrying silks and other rich produce on their return voyages to Lisbon, where Dutch ships became the principal carriers to the ports of France, the Netherlands, and the Baltic.

In 1595–96 Jan Hugo van Linschooten, 1563–1633, a Dutch navigator who had sailed to India with the Portuguese, published an account of his travels, a work which fired the Dutch merchants and ship captains with a desire for a share of the rich oriental trade. His account is notable because it contains the first notice of tea [as *chaa*] in the Dutch language, and throws an informing light on early Japa-

JAN HUGO VAN LINSCHOOTEN, 1563–1633

nese manners and customs. In his English translation, printed in London in 1598, Linschooten says, in part:

Their manner of eating and drinking is: Everie man hath a table alone, without tablecloths or napkins, and eateth with two pieces of wood like the men of *China*: they drinke wine of Rice, wherewith they drink themselves drunke, and after their meat use a certaine drinke, which is a pot with hote water, which they drinke as hote as ever they may indure, whether it be Winter or Summer . . . the aforesaid warme water is made with the powder of a certaine hearbe called *Chaa*, which is much esteemed, and is well accounted of among them, and al such as of any ccuntenance or habilitie have the said water kept far them in a secret place, and the gentlemen make it themselves; and when they will entertaine any of their friends, they give him some of that warme water to drinke: for the pots wherein they sieth it, and wherein the hearbe is kept, with the earthen cups which they drinke it in, they esteeme as much of them as we doe of Diamants, Rubies and other precious stones, and they are not esteemed for their newnes, but far their oldnes, and for that they were made by a good workman: and to know and keepe such by themselves, they take great and speciall care, as also of such as are the valewers of them, and are skillfull in them, as with us the goldsmith priseth and valueth silver and gold, and the Jewellers all kindes of precious stones: so if their pots & cuppes be of an old & excellet workmas making, they are worth 4 or 5 thousad ducats or more the piece. The King of Bungo [one of the ancient kingdoms of Japan] did give for such a pot, having three feet, 14 thousand ducats, and a *Iapan* being a Chieftian in the

SHIPS OF THE DUTCH EAST INDIA COMPANY BEFORE CANTON, 1655

This illustration shows the type of East India merchantmen that brought the first tea from Java to Europe in 1610. These ships carried the ambassadors of the Dutch East India Company to China in 1655. From Nieuhoff's *Embassy*, London, 1668.

town of Sacay, gave for such a pot 1400 ducats, and yet it had 3 pieces upon it. . . . These things doe they keepe and esteeme for their Jewels as we esteeme our Jewels and precious stones.[4]

Continuing now with the history of the Dutch trade, we come to 1595, the year in which the Portuguese closed their harbors to Dutch shipping. Thereupon the Dutch sent four ships to the Indies under the command of Cornelius Houtman. In June of the following year the fleet reached Bantam, in Java, where they established a depot for collecting and loading homeward-bound cargoes of oriental products. The Dutch found the natives everywhere ready to trade with them and returned home with such rich cargoes that direct trading with the Indies was given a tremendous impetus. Before the first fleet had returned to the roads of Texel,[5] a second fleet of eight ships set out, and by 1602 more than sixty-five Dutch ships had completed voy-

ages to the Indies. A ruinous competition among themselves resulted, so the Dutch East India Company was chartered that year to unite the rival enterprises and compose their conflicting interests. Also in the same year the first Dutch ship from Java reached Japan, and in 1607 some tea was transported from Macao to the depot in Java. This, incidentally, is the earliest recorded transportation of tea by any of the Europeans stationed in the East.[6]

By 1609, the first ships of the Dutch East India Company reached the island of Hirado off the coast of Japan. It was from this island that the Dutch began to take tea in 1610 to Bantam, in Java, where it was transshipped to Europe. This date, while somewhat conjectural, has been generally accepted as correct. Gaspard Bauhin, 1560–1624, a celebrated Swiss anatomist and naturalist, writing in 1623, more or less corroborates the 1610 date by asserting that "the Dutch were the first to take tea from Japan and China to Europe at the beginning of the 17th century."[7]

[4] Jan Hugo van Linschooten, *Discours of Voyages*, London, 1598, p. 46. Translated into English, by the author, from the original Dutch edition published in 1595–96.

[5] An island of the Frisian group in the North Sea belonging to the Netherlands, used as a point of arrival and departure by early Dutch Indiamen.

[6] Francis Valentijn [or Valentyn], *Ancient and Modern East Indies*, Dordrecht and Amsterdam, 1724 and 1726, Vol. V, p. 190.

[7] Gaspard Bauhin, *Theatri Botanici*, Basel 1623.

That the first teas to reach Europe were green teas is indicated by Thomas Short, 1690?–1772, a Scottish physician and medical writer, who states that "the Europeans contracted their first acquaintance with the green tea: then Bohea took its place." [8]

In the next year, 1611, the Dutch company obtained from the Japanese emperor the privilege of trading and established a trading factory on the island of Hirado. By confining their activities to trading, the Dutch found favor with the Japanese, while the earlier arrivals, the Portuguese priests, so embittered the natives by their usurpation of temporal powers that several armed conflicts resulted. The emperor, alarmed at this, decreed that all Europeans be expelled. The Portuguese and their converts took refuge in a walled settlement on a high rock overlooking the harbor. The soldiers of the emperor could not dislodge them from this stronghold. The Dutch joined forces with the Japanese and with their ships' guns leveled the Portuguese compound. For their assistance the Dutch were permitted to remain, but under humiliating conditions. They were removed from Hirado to Deshima, an island in the harbor at Nagasaki, and there were virtually made prisoners within stone walls. Under such conditions the Dutch tea trade with Japan dwindled, and they obtained their supplies from China instead.

The English Reach the Far East

At the turn of the seventeenth century the Dutch had almost complete mastery of the rich spice trade with the Indies. By 1619 they had founded the city of Batavia in Java as a new base for reaching their great eastern objective—the Spice, or Molucca, Islands. In the meantime, the English East India Company [9] was creeping out to the East. In their early voyages the English had pushed as far as Japan, and had established friendly relations at the Chinese court. By 1610–11 they had founded factories in India at Masulipatam and Pettapoli, and had settled on the island of Amboyna, in the Spice group, where the Dutch were already established. The territorial right of the English in the Indian Archipelago was disputed by the Dutch traders, who considered they had prior rights. The contention that developed culminated in 1623 in the "massacre of Amboyna," the immediate effect of which was to force the English company to admit the Dutch claim to a monopoly of the Far Eastern trade, followed by their retirement to the mainland of India and the adjoining countries. [10] This is the reason the first teas used in England in 1657 and thereafter came from Dutch sources, though they arrived, in compliance with the Navigation Act of 1651, in ships of English registry.

If we disregard two small gifts of tea for the English king in 1664 and 1666, the first importation of tea by the English East India Company was in 1669, when that company brought 143½ pounds from Bantam, in Java. So began an importation into England which in time was to build fortunes and dot the seas with tea ships. Later, Charles II rechartered the English company, granting it powers usually enjoyed only by governments. The company then proceeded to build up an oriental trade which soon far outstripped its rivals —the Dutch and the Portuguese.

Adoption by Other Countries

While tea was being carried into Western Europe over water routes, overland caravans by way of the Levant were carrying it into other parts of Europe. The first tea to so arrive was a gift of several chests brought by a Chinese embassy to the Russian court at Moscow in 1618. Eighteen arduous months were required for the journey, and if the Chinese hoped by this present to create a demand for their product the journey was in vain, for the tea failed to win Russian friends at that time. For nearly a score of years after the arrival at Moscow of the imperial tea gift, nothing of historical importance appears in connection with the early use of the tea drink in Europe.

During this period the many early ecclesiastical panegyrics on tea as a wonderful cure-all were not passing unchallenged. The first of the opponents, Dr. Simon Pauli, 1603–80, a German physician, published in 1635 a medical tract full of terrifying alarms and claiming furthermore

---

[8] Thomas Short, *Discourses on Tea, Sugar, Milk, Made Wines, Spirits, Punch, Tobacco, etc., with Plain Rules for Gouty People,* London, 1750.

[9] Chartered by Queen Elizabeth, on December 31, 1600, as "The Governor and Merchants of London Trading into the East Indies."

[10] *Encyclopædia Britannica,* 11th ed., Vol. VIII, p. 834.

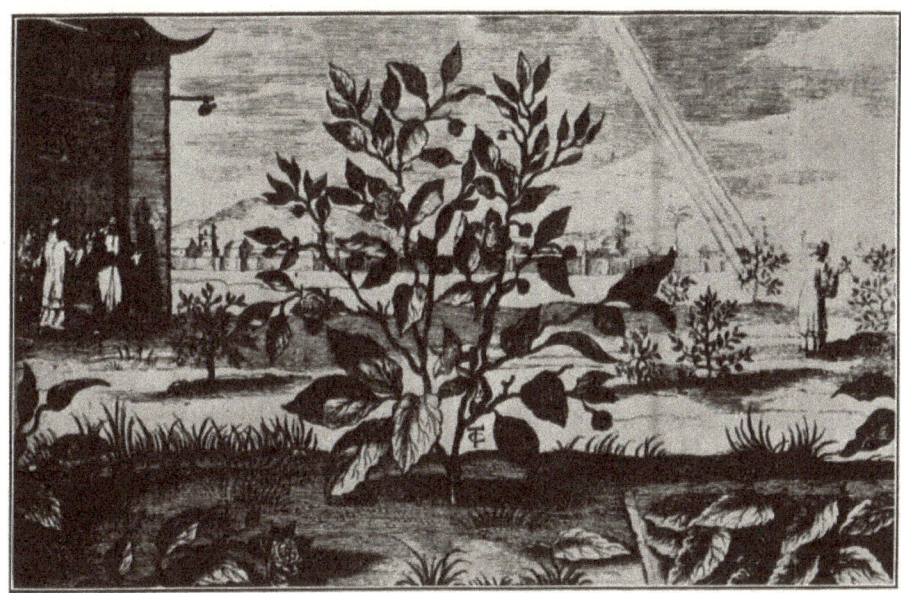

ONE OF THE EARLIEST ENGRAVINGS USED TO ILLUSTRATE THE STORY OF TEA IN EUROPE

From *China, monumentis qua sacris qua profanis, illustrata* by the Dutch Jesuit priest Athanasius Kircherus, 1668.

that tea was nothing but myrtle of the kind common throughout the world. He wrote:

As to the virtues they attribute to it, it may be admitted that it does possess them in the Orient, but it loses them in our climates, where it becomes, on the contrary, very dangerous to use. It hastens the death of those that drink it, especially if they have passed the age of forty years.[11]

The next account praises tea as much as Dr. Pauli condemned it. It is from the journal of Johann Albrecht von Mandelslo, a young German traveler who, in 1633–40, accompanied an embassy from the Duke of Holstein-Gottorp to the Grand Duke of Muscovy and the king of Persia. "At our ordinary meetings every day," he writes, "we took only *the*, which is commonly used all over the Indies, not only by those of the Country but also among the Dutch and English, who take it as a drug. The Persians instead of *the*, drink *kahwa* [coffee]."

While at the Persian court, in 1637, Mandelslo, finding his health impaired, obtained leave for a sea trip to India. Of the voyage and of the benefit of tea drinking he wrote:

We went from Gamron to Surrat [India] in nineteen days, during which the captain treated

me very magnificently. . . . He was well furnished with Fowl, Mutton, and other fresh Meat, but above all things, with excellent Sack, English Beer, French Wines, Arak, and other refreshments, which proved so well for me that . . . I found my health perfectly recovered, though I must also acknowledge, as much contributing thereto, my using *The*, to which I had so accustomed myself that I ordinarily took of it twice or thrice a day.[12]

The earliest reference to the use of tea in Holland appears in a letter dated January 2, 1637, from the "Lords XVII," the name by which the seventeen directors of the Dutch East India Company were popularly known, to the governor-general of Netherlands East India, at Batavia. It reads: "As tea begins to come into use by some of the people, we expect some jars of Chinese as well as Japanese tea with each ship." [13]

That the tea drink was indeed growing in favor in Europe about this time, 1637–38, is confirmed by Mandelslo in describing the whipped tea of the Japanese which he calls *tsia:*

As for *Tsia*, it is a kind of *The*, or Tea; but

[11] Dr. Simon Pauli, *Commentarius de Abusu Tabaci et Herbae Thee*, Rostock, Germany, 1635.

[12] Johann Albrecht von Mandelslo, *Travels into the East Indies*, English translation by Davies, London, 1669.

[13] *Uitgaend Brievenboek* [Outgoing Letter Book] of the *Oostindische Vereenigde Maatschappij*, 1637.

the plant is much more delicate, and more highly esteemed than that of *The*. Persons of Quality keep it very carefully in Earthenware pots well stopp'd and luted, that it may not take wind; but the Japonnesses prepare it quite otherwise than is done in Europe.

Writing in 1638, Adam Olearius, or Oelschlager, secretary of the embassy from the Duke of Holstein-Gottorp to the king of Persia, states that the excellent qualities of tea are well known among the Persians, who "boil it till the water hath a bitterish taste, and a blackish color, and add thereto fennel, aniseed, or cloves and sugar."[14]

In the year 1638, Vassily Starkoff, the Russian ambassador at the court of the Mogul Khan Altyn, partook of an infusion of tea, but declined a present of a quantity of it for his master the Czar Michael Romanoff, founder of the Romanoff dynasty, as something for which the czar would have no use.[15] However, if Russia and Eastern Europe were still insensible to the advantages of the tea drink, high society at The Hague was beginning, about

the year 1640, to adopt it as a fashionable, although an expensive, beverage.[16]

The first tea was introduced into Germany by way of Holland about 1650. By 1657 it had become a staple article of commerce, quoted at fifteen gulden a handful in the price lists of chemists in Nordhausen. Its use spread slowly except in districts near the sea, such as Ost Friesland, where its consumption is greater than in any other part of Germany.

Responding to a newly aroused interest in the subject, William Ten Rhyne, a Dutch naturalist, wrote of the tea plant in 1640, and in 1641 Dr. Nikolas Dirx, 1593–1674, a celebrated Dutch physician, writing under the nom de plume of "Nikolas Tulp," was one of the first Europeans of his profession to sound the praises of tea. The eulogy of tea in his *Observationes Medicae* attracted wide attention. It reads:

Nothing is comparable to this plant. Those who use it are for that reason, alone, exempt from all maladies and reach an extreme old age. Not only does it procure great vigor for their bodies, but it preserves them from gravel and gallstones, headaches, colds, ophthalmia, catarrh, asthma, sluggishness of the stomach and intestinal troubles. It has the additional merit of

---

[14] Adam Olearius [Oelschlager], *Travels of the Ambassadors*, English translation by Davies, London, 1662; first written in German, Schleswig, 1647.

[15] John Coakley Lettsom, *Natural History of the Tea-Tree*, London, 1799, p. 20.

[16] Pakhuismeesteren van de Thee, *Kolonial Memorieboek*, Amsterdam, 1918.

A Seventeenth Century Dutch Illustration of a Tea Garden and Early Picking Methods

From Nieuhof's *Beschryving van t' Gesandschap der Nederlandsche Oost-Indische Compagnie aan der Grooten Tartarischen Cham*, 1665.

preventing sleep and facilitating vigils, which makes it a great help to persons desiring to spend their nights writing or meditating. Also, all of the utensils meant for the preparation of tea are objects of great luxury, and the Chinese prize them as highly as we do diamonds, precious stones and pearls; nor do they have, as to price, an inferior place to diamonds, jewels and pearl ornaments among us.[17]

Dr. Jacob Bontius, a physician and naturalist of Batavia, in Java, still further illumines the subject in one of the quaint dialogues with which he enlivens the *Historiae Naturalis et Medicae Indiae Orientalis,* first published in 1642. This is also included in the collection of Gulielmus Piso, *De Indiae Utriusque re Naturali et Medicae.* To quote:

ANDREAS DUREAS. You have mentioned the drink of the Chinese called *Thee:* what is your opinion thereof?
JACOBUS BONTIUS. The Chinese regard this drink almost as something sacred . . . and they are not thought to have fulfilled the duties of hospitality until they have served you with it, just like the Mahommedans with their *caveeh* [coffee]. It is of a drying quality, and banishes sleep. . . . It is beneficial to asthmatic and wheezing patients.

Other famous Dutch physicians of the period, among them Blankaert, Bontekoe, Sylvius, Van Duverden, Bidloo, and Pechlin, followed with equally laudatory opinions, as did Father Athanasius Kircher, a learned chemist; Jacob Breynius, a botanist; and Johannes Baptista van Helmont, 1577–1644, a famous chemist, physiologist, and visionary. The pupils of the latter were taught that tea had the same effect on the system as bloodletting or laxatives, and should be used instead.

Of the Dutch physicians who wrote in praise of tea at this time, Dr. Cornelis Decker, 1648–86, of Alkmaar, otherwise known as "Dr. Bontekoe," was easily its most distinguished advocate. He is generally credited with having done more to promote its ensuing general adoption in Europe than any other tea protagonist. "Bontekoe advised the use of eight to ten cups of tea daily, but found no reason to object to 50, 100, or 200 cups, as he frequently consumed that quantity himself.[18] History whispers that Dr. Bontekoe may have been retained by the Dutch East India Company to write in praise of tea. At all

events, it is recorded that the company made him a handsome honorarium for the impetus given their tea sales.

The earliest mention of milk used as an ingredient for tea is recorded by the Dutch traveler and author Jean Nieuhoff, 1630–72, who accompanied an embassy of the Dutch East India Company to the Chinese emperor in 1655. Describing a royal feast given the "barbarian" ambassadors outside the city gate at Canton, he writes:

At the beginning of the Dinner, there were served several bottles of *The* or *Tea,* served to the Table, whereof they drank to the Embassadors, biding them welcom: This drink is made of the Herb *The* or *Cha,* after this manner: they infuse half a handful of the Herb *The* or *Cha* in fair water, which afterwards they boil till a third part be consumed, to which they adde warm milk about a fourth part, with a little salt, and then drink it as hot as they can well endure.[19]

Apothecaries were among the first dealers in tea. In Holland they sold it by the ounce, along with sugar, ginger, and spices, but gradually tea found its way into colonial produce shops, which subsequently developed into grocery shops. Between 1660 and 1680 its use in the Netherlands became general, first in the homes of the gentry, and later in the houses of the bourgeoisie and the poor. In homes of families with social aspirations, one of the principal rooms was specially furnished for tea drinking; while the poor utilized a small room for the same purpose, or drank it in their meeting halls. As was the case with coffee, history records no official intolerance of tea in Holland.

In Germany, a Dr. Feltman early prescribed tea as a remedy against pestilence, and Dr. Weber expressed the opinion that its use strengthened the stomach, lengthened life, and dissipated unnecessary sleep. Professor Waldschmidt of Marburg wrote: "The high and mighty gentlemen who bring upon themselves a hundred thousand pounds of care concerning the confused situation in Europe, would do well to drink hot tea-water for the maintenance of their health."

Russia began regularly to import tea from China by way of the picturesque overland caravan route through Manchuria and Mongolia after the signing of the Nerchinsk treaty with China in 1689. The

---

[17] Dr. Nicolas Tulpius, *Observationes Medicae,* Amsterdam, 1641.
[18] Doctor Cornelis Bontekoe, *Tractat van het Excellente Cruyt Thee,* The Hague, 1679.

[19] Jean Nieuhoff, *The Embassy of the Oriental Company of the United Provinces to the Emperor of China,* Amsterdam, 1665.

CORNELIS BONTEKOE, EARLY DUTCH TEA
PROTAGONIST, 1648–86

Russian trade with China was confined by this treaty to the town of Kiakhta on the northern frontier of China, which thus became the sole entrepôt for the exchange of the products of both countries.

It is likely that the Scandinavian countries first became acquainted with tea through the commercial activities of the Dutch and later through the Danes, who began to take part in the India trade in 1616.

Continental Tea Controversies

There were strenuous adversaries of tea in Germany, however, prominent among whom was the Jesuit Martino Martini, who claimed that tea was the cause of the dried-up appearance of the Chinese. He exclaimed: "Down with tea! Send it back to the Garaments and Sauromates!" There were others who clamored to have the German physicians forbidden to prescribe foreign medicaments, insisting that tea should be prohibited by public decree. There were many physicians in Holland, as well, who were of the same opinion, for, though tea found notable panegyrists, there were others who met it with taunts and gibes, calling the drink "groats and dishwater, a tasteless and disgusting liquid."

It was after ecclesiastical notices and Dutch medical comment had made the new China drink a leading topic of discussion throughout the capitals of Europe, that tea found its way to France. It is said to have appeared first in Paris in 1635,[20] but Commissioner Delamarre, in his *Traité de Police,* or Treatise on the Police (Tome III, p. 797), claims it began to be used in Paris in 1636. Alfred Franklin, however, casts doubt on both dates by declaring the earliest mention of tea in Paris to be contained in a letter of March 22, 1648, from Dr. Gui Patin, 1601–72, the celebrated French physician and writer. In this letter Patin refers to tea as "the impertinent novelty of the century," and states:

> One of our doctors, named Morisset, who is much more of a braggart than a skilful man . . . caused a thesis on *the* to be published here. Everybody disapproved of it; there were some of our doctors who burned it, and protests were made to the dean for having approved the thesis. You will see it and laugh at it![21]

While Patin was the declared enemy of all innovations, especially in medicine, he was by no means alone in opposing the introduction of tea as a medicine into France. Morisset's dissertation entitled "Does Tea Increase Mentality?" in which he hailed the drink as a "panacea," caused such an uproar in the French medical world that no other physician of the Collège de France dared to speak in its favor.[22]

According to the previously quoted work of Father Alexander de Rhodes, the Parisians, a few years later, 1653, were paying high prices for their tea. He states:

> The Dutch bring tea from China to Paris and sell it at thirty francs a pound, though they have paid but eight and ten sous in that country, and it is old and spoiled into the bargain. People must regard it as a precious medicament; it not only does positively cure nervous headache, but it is a sovereign remedy for gravel and gout.[23]

De Rhodes's testimonial to the efficacy of tea as a remedy may have inspired Cardinal Mazarin, the distinguished courtier and prime minister of France, to use it for his gout. We learn of this through another letter of the eminent Dr. Patin, dated April

[20] Myers' *Konversation Lexikon.*
[21] Alfred Franklin, "Le Café, le Thé, et le Chocolat," *La Vie Privée d'Autrefois,* Paris, 1893.
[22] Dr. Philibert Morisset, *Ergo Thea Chinensium Menti Confert,* Paris, 1648.
[23] Father Alexander de Rhodes, *Voyages et Missions Apostoliques,* Paris, 1653.

TITLE PAGE, FRONTISPIECE AND FIRST TEXT PAGE OF DUFOUR'S WORK, 1685

1, 1657, heaping ridicule on the remedy selected by the illustrious prelate. "Mazarin," sneers the doctor, "takes *the* as a preventative of gout. Isn't this a powerful remedy for the gout of a favorite!"

Other illustrious personages in France had used tea as a medicine before de Rhodes wrote, for he thus concludes his tea encomium:

I have dilated somewhat in my discourse on the subject of tea, because, since I have been in France, I have had the honor to see some people of great quality and of excellent merit whose life and health are extremely necessary to France, who make beneficial use of it and who have been kind enough to want me to tell them what my experience of thirty years had taught me concerning this great remedy.

One of the persons of quality to whom the learned author made reference was undoubtedly Chancellor Sequier, who was very fond of the new beverage and contributed more than anyone else to extending its use in the *haut monde*.

In 1657, the Chancellor accepted with enthusiasm the dedication of a thesis written by the son of the celebrated surgeon Pierre Cressy, extolling his favorite drink. This disgusted Patin, the implacable foe of tea, who wrote a politely sarcastic letter, saying: "Thursday next, we have a thesis on the subject of tea, dedicated to M. le Chancellor, who has promised to be pres-

ent. The portrait of the above mentioned gentleman will be there." The inference was that the Chancellor himself would hardly appear in person.

Dr. Patin had a surprise in store for him, however, for the younger Cressy had made a study of the effect of tea as a treatment for gout, which he advocated so eloquently for four hours that the faculty of the college not only gave up its former hostility to tea, but even smoked it like tobacco.[24] The worthy Dr. Patin yielded handsomely, and, in a letter dated December 4, 1657, acknowledged that the Chancellor was present, together with a most distinguished company, including the very precious gouty personages of the privy council. "The doctor," says Patin, "did marvelously well in discussing before such a fine company, and the chancellor did not stir on account of the discussion until high noon." Nothing less than the presence and interest of the Chancellor was needed to impress the young doctor's arguments on the minds of the faculty, and from this time the position of tea in France was assured. So assured, in fact, that in 1659 Dr. Denis Jonquet appears to have voiced the general sentiment of the medical profession in Paris by his reference to tea as

[24] Pakhuismeesteren van de Thee, *Kolonial Memorieboek*, Amsterdam, 1918.

a divine drink, while Paul Scarron, the dramatist, had already become its devotee.

French and Scandinavian Notices

A weird recipe for making tea, was brought to Europe by the returned China missionary, Père Couplet, in 1667. It was as follows:

To a pint of tea, add the yolks of two fresh eggs; then beat them up with as much fine sugar as is sufficient to sweeten the tea, and stir well together. The water must remain no longer upon the tea than while you can chant the Miserere psalm in leisurely fashion.

In 1671, Phillipe Sylvestre Dufour published at Lyons his admirable treatise *Concerning the Use of Coffee, Tea, and Chocolate*, and, in 1680, Mme de Sévigné, the famous letter writer to whom we are indebted for preserving many incidents of historic interest, records that Mme de la Sablière conceived the idea of mixing milk with her tea. This is the earliest record of the use of milk in tea in Europe. In 1684, the same illustrious letter writer states: "The Princess of Tarente took twelve cups of tea daily, and M. le Landgrave forty.

He was dying, and this resuscitated him visibly."

By 1685, we find tea in high favor in literary circles, with Pierre Daniel Huet, the noted Bishop of Avranches, celebrating his favorite beverage in a Latin poem of fifty-eight stanzas, under the title "Thea, elegia," and Pierre Petit, another learned French writer, producing a poem of five hundred and sixty stanzas entitled "Thea Sinensis" [Chinese tea]. Pomet, the Parisian apothecary, emerges out of the smoke of this literary bombardment to tell us that he was selling Chinese tea at 70 francs a pound, and Japanese tea from 150 to 200 francs in 1694. He remarks that its vogue as a drink of the middle and upper classes had suffered considerably because of the introduction of coffee and chocolate. In this connection we are told that Racine, the French dramatic poet, who died in 1699, was very fond of tea during the latter years of his life, drinking it in the morning.

The first mention of tea in Scandinavian literature occurs in a comedy, *The Lying-in Woman*, written by Baron Ludvig Holberg, 1684–1754, in 1723.

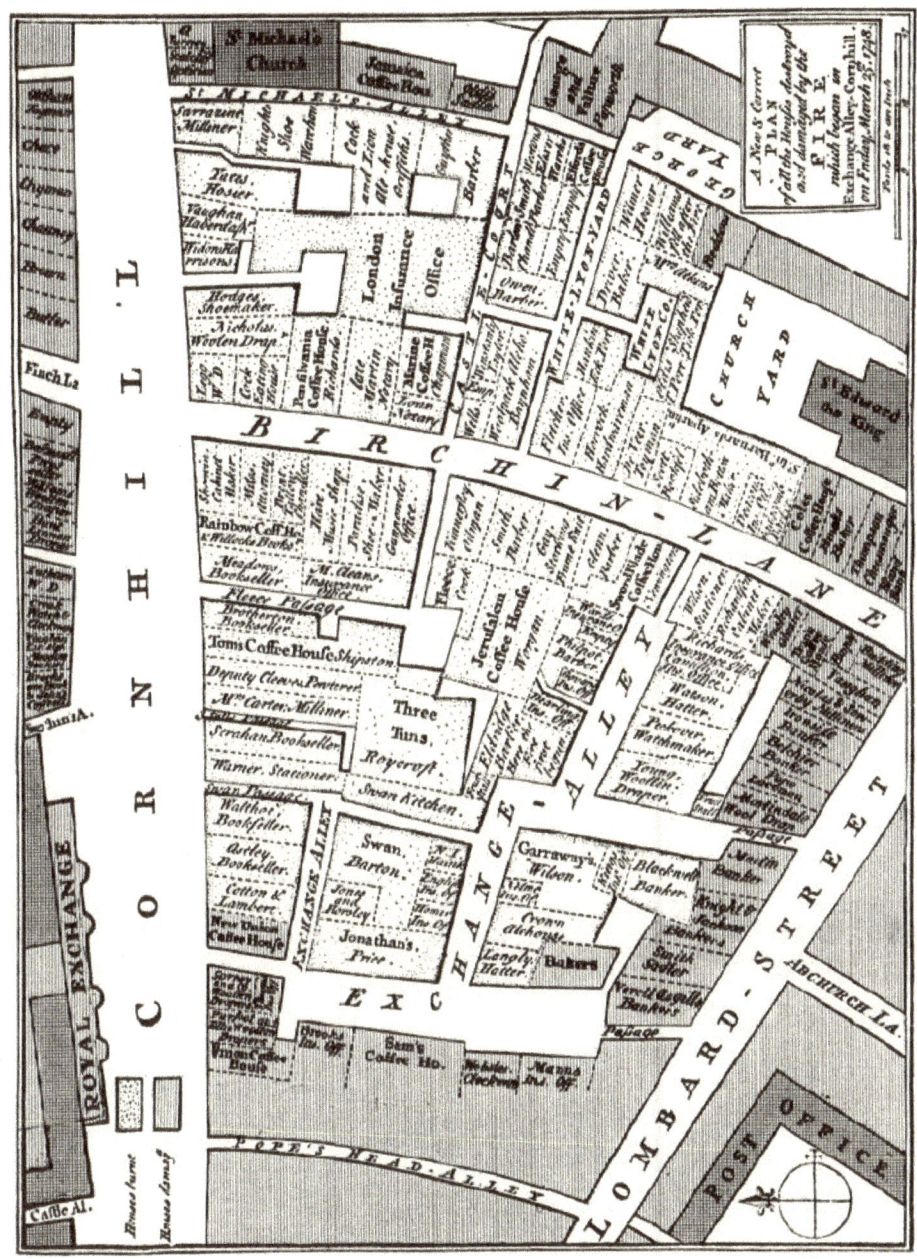

MAP OF LONDON IN THE TIME OF THE COFFEE HOUSE

This plan of all the houses destroyed and damaged by the Fire of 1748 shows the location of many of the famous places where tea was first drunk in the 17th Century, including Garraway's in Exchange Alley, Cornhill, where the fire started. The drawing originally appeared in the *London Magazine* for March, 1748.

36

CHAPTER IV

INTRODUCTION OF TEA INTO ENGLAND

FIRST REFERENCE TO TEA BY AN ENGLISHMAN—GARWAY BEGINS TO SELL TEA AT HIS LONDON COFFEE HOUSE—THE FIRST TEA BROADSIDE—THE ARCHBISHOP OF CANTERBURY MAKES INQUIRY—MR. PEPYS DISCOVERS TEA—FIRST NEWSPAPER ADVERTISEMENT—ENGLISH LADIES BEGIN TO DRINK TEA—ATTEMPTED SUPPRESSION OF THE COFFEE HOUSES—THEIR ULTIMATE DECLINE—GROCERS ADD TEA TO THEIR STOCKS—THE FIRST TEA SHOP —EARLY DAYS OF TEA IN SCOTLAND—SOME TEA CONTROVERSIES

THE introduction of tea as a drink into England forms a chapter teeming with high adventure, strange peoples, and intriguing events.

The first printed reference to tea in English, calling it *chaa*, appeared in 1598 in *Linschooten's Travels*, an English translation of a work originally published in Holland in 1595–96.

An inventory of the plate and household furnishings in Peel Castle, Isle of Man, dated November 3, 1651, has been quoted as mentioning a "Tea Cupp Gilt." This has been taken by some as indicating that tea was drunk in the Isle of Man previous to the year 1651.[1] However, antiquarian authorities in the office of the Deputy Keeper of the Records, Public Record Office, London, agree that the first letter of the item of the inventory under discussion cannot be "T" and probably is "S," the whole word being a contraction for "Silver." One "Silver Cupp Gilt," they hold, would make sense, but one "Tea Cupp Gilt" would not.

Dr. Thomas Short, 1690–1772, a Scottish physician and medical writer, is of the opinion that tea may have been known in England as far back as the reign of James I, because the first East India fleet sailed in 1601.[2] But had the use of the leaf been known, it would seem that because of its novelty, it hardly would have escaped notice by the early English dramatists, whose works mirror the prevalent tastes and humors of their time.

It seems extraordinary that the English East India Company should not have discovered and developed the possibilities of tea as early as did their commercial competitors the Dutch East India Company, who were bringing Chinese, as well as Japanese, tea with every ship in 1637. Yet it certainly was not known in England as early as 1641, for in a rare *Treatise on Warm Beer*, published in that year, the author undertakes to chronicle the advantages of the known hot drinks as opposed to cold, and mentions tea only by quoting the Italian Jesuit Father Maffei that, "they of China do for the most part drink the strained liquor of an herb called *Chia* hot." [3]

First Reference by an Englishman

The earliest known reference to tea by an Englishman is found in a letter preserved in the archives of the East India Company—now at the India office, London, S. W. Mr. R. Wickham, the agent for the company at "Firando" (Hirado), Japan, wrote to Mr. Eaton, another agent of the company, at Macao, China, on June 27, 1615, requesting him to forward to the writer "a pot of the best sort of chaw." This reference leads us to the conclusion that some Englishmen knew about tea as early as 1615.

---

[1] W. Ralph Hall Caine, *The Origin and Significance of the Name Isle of Man*.
[2] Dr. Thomas Short, *A Dissertation upon Tea*, London, 1750.
[3] Giovanni Pietro Maffei, *Historica Indica*, Rome, 1588.

GARRAWAY'S COFFEE HOUSE IN 'CHANGE ALLEY
Garway, or Garraway, claimed to have been the first to sell tea in England, in 1657.

As yet there was no word for tea in the English language, so early British authors were wont to employ some approximation of its Chinese name, *ch'a*. Tea appears as *chia* in *Purchas His Pilgrimes*, in 1625. To quote from this early English collector of travels: "They use much the powder of a certaine herbe called *chia* of which they put as much as a Walnut shell may containe, into a dish of Porcelane, and drink it with hot water." In a footnote Purchas observes that *chia* is used "in all entertainments in Iapon and China."[4]

In 1637, the English first appeared in the Orient, when a fleet of four ships entered the mouth of the Canton River, and, with characteristic aggressiveness, forced their way past the Portuguese, who opposed them at Macao. Upon reaching Canton, they established direct contact with Chinese merchants. There is no record to show that any tea was transported at this time, however, nor upon the occasion of a second visit of the English at Macao, which occurred twenty-seven years later.

Shortly after 1644, English traders established themselves at the port of Amoy, which was their principal Chinese base for nearly a century. Here they picked up from the Fukien dialect the word *t'e* ("tay") for the drink used by the Chinese, and they spelled it *t-e-a*, writing *ea* as a diphthong, *æ*, having the sound of long *a*.

First Public Sale at Garway's

There is no record of the earliest importation of tea into England. Probably this occurred more or less contemporaneously with its appearance in Holland, France, and Germany, sometime about the middle of the seventeenth century. From a broadside by a London coffee house keeper, one Thomas Garway, or Garraway, we learn that previous to the year 1657 the leaf and drink had been used only "as a regalia in high treatments and entertainments, and presents made thereof to princes and grandees." For such use purchasers were compelled to pay £6 to £10 ($30 to $50) per pound, and to get their supplies abroad, as tea was not as yet sold in Britain.[5]

The same broadside tells us that in 1657 the tea leaf and beverage were first publicly sold in England by Thomas Garway, tobacconist and coffee house keeper at his place in Exchange Alley. This famous coffee house, known to succeeding generations as "Garraway's," was a center for great mercantile transactions. Here men prominent in the commercial life of the metropolis were wont to refresh themselves with ale, punch, brandy, arrack, etc., in addition to tea and coffee.

The tea sold by Garway was reputed to possess remarkable preventive and curative qualities, but there was little general knowledge of it in London; so Garway sought directions for making the beverage from the best-informed merchants and travelers from the East, preparing it accordingly. For the benefit of customers who desired to make the drink in their homes or elsewhere, he offered to sell all comers the prepared leaf at 16s. ($4) to 60s. ($15) a pound, thus effecting a saving of from 104s. ($26) to 140s. ($35) per pound. Having established a fair price, he proceeded to

4 Samuel Purchas, *Purchas His Pilgrimes*, London, 1625. Vol. III. p. 326.

5 Thomas Garway's broadsheet, broadside, or shop-bill, entitled "An Exact Description of the Growth, Quality and Vertues of the Leaf TEA," *ca.* 1660, preserved in the British Museum.

herald the quality and virtues of tea in the broadside which has assumed historical importance as one of the earliest and most effective advertisements for tea.

The First Tea Broadside

Garway observes in the quaint advertising copy of the period:

The Leaf is of such known vertues, that those very Nations famous for Antiquity, Knowledge, and Wisdom, do frequently sell it among themselves for twice its weight in silver, and the high estimation of the Drink made therewith hath occasioned an inquiry into the nature thereof amongst the most intelligent persons of all Nations that have travelled in those parts, who after exact Tryal and Experience by all ways imaginable, have commended it to the use of their several Countries, for its Vertues and Operations, particularly as followeth, viz: The Quality is moderately hot, proper for Winter or Summer. The Drink is declared to be most wholesome, preserving in perfect health untill extreme Old Age.

Garway enumerates "the particular Vertues" as follows:

It maketh the body active and lusty.
It helpeth the Headache, giddiness and heaviness thereof.
It removeth the obstructions of the Spleen.
It is very good against the Stone and Gravel,

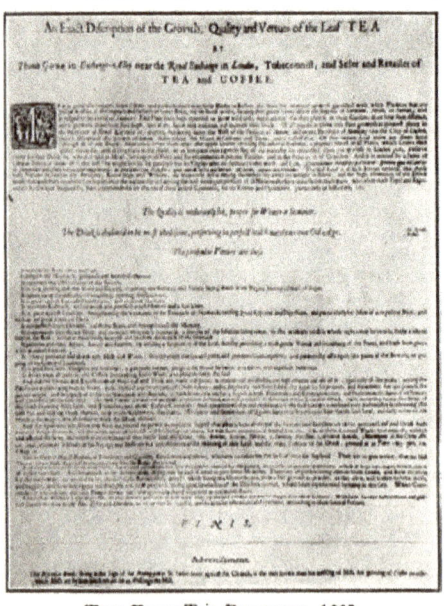

THE FIRST TEA BROADSIDE, 1660

Thomas Garway's famous advertisement of Tea as published from his Coffee House in Exchange Alley. From the original in the British Museum.

cleaning the Kidneys and Uriters, being drank with Virgins Honey instead of Sugar.
It taketh away the difficulty of breathing, opening Obstructions.
It is good against Lipitude Distillations and cleareth the Sight.
It removeth Lassitude, and cleanseth and purifyeth adult Humors and hot Liver.
It is good against Crudities, strengthening the weakness of the Ventricle or Stomack, causing good Appetite and Digestion, and particularly for Men of a corpulent Body, and such as are great eaters of Flesh.
It vanquisheth heavy dreams, easeth the Brain, and strengtheneth the Memory.
It overcometh superfluous Sleep, and prevents Sleepiness in general, a draght of the Infusion being taken, so that without trouble whole nights may be spent in study without hurt to the Body, in that it moderately heateth and bindeth the mouth of the Stomack.
It prevents and cures agues, Surfets and Feavers, by infusing a fit quantity of the Leaf, thereby provoking a most gentle Vomit and breathing of the Pores, and hath been given with wonderful success.
It (being prepared with Milk and Water) strengtheneth the inward parts, and prevents Consumptions, and powerfully assuageth the pains of the Bowels, or griping of the Guts and Looseness.
It is good for Colds, Dropsies and Scurveys, if properly infused, purging the Blood by sweat and Urine, and expelleth infection.
It drives away all pains in the Collick proceeding from Wind, and purgeth safely the Gall.
And that the Vertues and excellencies of this Leaf and Drink are many and great is evident and manifest by the high esteem and use of it (especially of late years) among the Physitians and knowing men in France, Italy, Holland and other parts of Christendom.

Who of Garway's patrons, having a corpulent body, a weak "stomack," ailing "uriters," or whatnot, but would daily seek the protection of this panacea from out the purple East, after reading the claims that were made for it in this remarkable broadside? Much editorial credit, indeed, is due Garway for the diligence by which he contrived to boil down into the limits of a single sheet practically all the claims, fantastic or otherwise, that had been made for tea as a medicine in the writings of the Chinese, or of the early Jesuit missionaries in the Far East.

The Povey Manuscript, 1686

Just what claims for tea were coming to England from the East is made clear by a manuscript now in the British Museum, which was elegantly transcribed in 1686 from a paper of T. Povey, M.P. and Civil Servant, being a translation of a Chinese encomium. It reads:

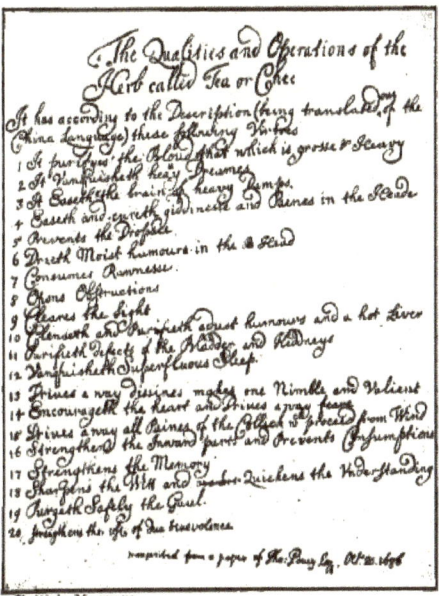

The Qualities and Operations of the Herb called Tea or Chee

It has accoding to the Description (being translated of the China Language) these following Virtues

1 It purifyes the Bloud that which is grosse & Heavy
2 It Vanguisheth heavy Dreames.
3 It Easeth the brain of heavy Damps.
4 Easeth and cureth giddinesse and Paines in the Heade
5 Prevents the Dropsie
6 Drieth Moist humours in the Head
7 Consumes Rawnesse.
8 Opens Obstructions
9 Cleares the Sight
10 Clenseth and Purifieth adust humours and a hot Liver
11 Purifieth Defects of the Bladder and Kidneys
12 Vanguisheth Superfluous Sleep
13 Drives away dissines makes one Nimble and Valiant
14 Encourageth the heart and Drives away feare
15 Drives away all Paines of the Collick which proceed from Wind
16 Strengtheth the Inward parts and Prevents Consumptions
17 Strengthens the Memory
18 Sharpens the Will and quickens the Understanding
19 Purgeth Safely the Gaul.
20 Strengthens the use of due benevolence.

transcribed from a paper of Tho: Povey Esq. Oct.20 1686

British Museum

A FAMOUS TEA MANUSCRIPT OF 1686

In which Thomas Povey, a "nice contriver of elegancies," produced a flowery testimonial from the Chinese.

It has, according to the Description (being translated out of the China Language), these following Virtues:

1. It purifyes the Bloud of that which is grosse and Heavy.
2. It Vanquisheth heavy Dreames.
3. It Easeth the brain of heavy Damps.
4. Easeth and cureth giddinesse and Paines in the Heade.
5. Prevents the Dropsie.
6. Drieth Moist humours in the Head.
7. Consumes Rawnesse.
8. Opens Obstructions.
9. Cleares the Sight.
10. Clenseth and Purifieth adust humours and a hot Liver.
11. Purifieth defects of the Bladder and Kiddneys.
12. Vanquisheth Superfluous Sleep.
13. Drives away dissines, makes one Nimble and Valient.
14. Encourageth the heart and Drives away feare.
15. Drives away all Paines of the Collick which proceed from Wind.
16. Strengthens the Inward parts and Prevents Consumptions.
17. Strengthens the Memory.
18. Sharpens the Will and Quickens the Understanding.
19. Purgeth Safely the Gaul.
20. Strengthens the use of due benevolence.

Transcribed from a paper of Tho. Povey, Esq., Oct. 20, 1686.

Prominent men in the social and religious life of Britain were much intrigued by the new China drink. A letter from Daniel Sheldon, factor for the English East India Company at Balsore, written in 1659 to another factor for the company at Bandel, urgently requested a sample of tea to send home to his uncle, the illustrious Dr. Gilbert Sheldon, Archbishop of Canterbury. He wrote:

I must desire you to procure the chaw, if possible. I care not what it cost. 'Tis for a good uncle of mine, Dr. Sheldon, whome some body hath perswaded to studdy the divinity of that herbe, leafe, or what else it is; and I am soe obliged to satisfy his curiosity that I could willingly undertake a viage to Japan or China to doe it.

There seems to have been some difficulty in securing the tea at Bandel, for Sheldon wrote again: "For God's sake, good or badd, buy the chaw if it is to be sold. Pray favor me likewise with advise what 'tis good for, and how to be used." The final outcome is not revealed by the correspondence, but, whatever this may have been, it is not likely that the Archbishop's curiosity long went unsatisfied, as tea had then been on sale in London for several years.

Mr. Pepys Discovers Tea

Samuel Pepys, 1633–1703, the gossipy English diarist and Secretary to the Admiralty, to whom we are indebted for so many intimate glimpses of the daily life and customs of his time, writes, under date of September 25, 1660: "I did send for a cup of tee (a China drink) of which I never had drank before." [6]

The directors of the East India Company apparently found tea valuable for the use of "the Court of Committees," for their books show entries covering several small purchases of from six to eight pounds thus charged and bought from the coffee house keepers.

Tea in the London Coffee Houses

Seventeenth-century records agree in showing that the real introduction of the tea drink into England began in the London coffee houses, where it was served in

---

[6] Pepys wrote his *Diary* in phonetic shorthand. The original, comprising six volumes, is preserved in the Pepysian Library at Magdalene College, Cambridge.

SAMUEL PEPYS, 1633–1703

One of the earliest incidents recorded in the famous Diary is his first cup of tea in 1660.

common with coffee, chocolate, and sherbet. Whereas its previous use in England, as Garway so well points out, was limited to rare "treatments," and the occasional entertainment of some grandee, it was now to be enjoyed by the great and the near-great in the coffee house. It soon became the talk of the town.

Other London coffee houses hastened to adopt the new beverage, and it may not be out of place to state that these unique gathering places, each with its own more or less distinct clientele, whether of business men, professional men, or literati, came to be called "coffee houses" instead of "tea houses" because the public sale of the coffee beverage, in England, antedated the public sale of tea by a few years.

The coffee houses, forerunners of London's clubhouses of to-day, were so congenial to the English character that they quickly made a place for themselves that promised to be perpetual. Here every political subject of the day was discussed; and, as not only the higher but also the middle classes frequented these new places of entertainment, a knowledge of public affairs was widely diffused.

In 1650, the first English coffee house had been opened by a certain Jew from Lebanon, Jacob by name, at the Sign of the Angel in the Parish of St. Peter in the East, Oxford. "And there," says Anthony Wood, 1632–95, an English antiquarian writer, "coffee was by some who delighted in noveltie drank." [7]

This same Anthony Wood has been erroneously quoted as having stated that Jacob "also sold chocolate and thee" in 1650. However, there is no such passage in Wood's *Life;* but there is ample evidence that the English delighted in novelty drinks, as suggested by Wood, for coffee houses soon appeared in various parts of the metropolis, as well as throughout the country, and presently they were all of them serving tea, with the other temperance beverages.

The First Tea Advertisement

The Sultaness Head Coffee House was one of the earliest to adopt the tea beverage as a part of its entertainment, and on September 30, 1658, its proprietor inserted the first newspaper advertisement of tea, in *Mercurius Politicus.* This advertisement announced: "That Excellent and by all Physitians approved *China* drink, called by the Chineans *Tcha*, by other Nations *Tay*, alias *Tee*, is sold at the Sultaness Head Cophee House in Sweetings Rents, by the Royal Exchange, London."

About this time tea was everywhere offered and accepted as a wonderful health drink. Quite possibly there may have been a bit of favorable psychology in this, for men have ever been fond of attributing remedial values to their drinks, and tea was soon to be acclaimed "the sovereign drink of pleasure and of health."

The world's three great temperance drinks gained a quick popularity in the London coffee houses, for we read in Thomas Rugge's *Mercurius Politicus Redivivus* of November 14, 1659: "Theire ware also att this time a Turkish drink to bee sould, almost in evry street, called Coffee, and a nother kind of drink called Tee, and also a drink called Chacolate, which was a very harty drink."

Tea was sold also at Jonathan's, another coffee house in Exchange Alley. In the play *A Bold Strike for a Wife*, Mrs. Centlivre laid one of its scenes at Jonathan's;

[7] *The Life of Anthony Wood*, written by himself, Oxford, 1848, p. 48.

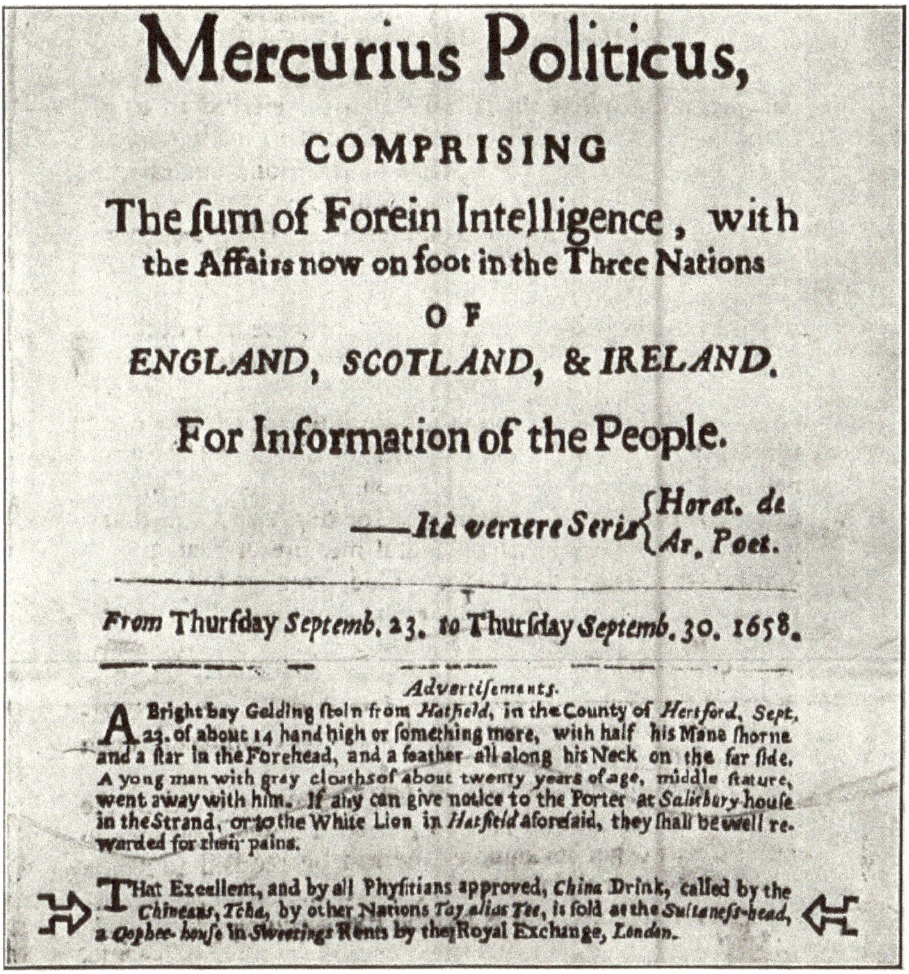

Mercurius Politicus,

COMPRISING

The ſum of Forein Intelligence, with
the Affairs now on foot in the Three Nations

O F

ENGLAND, SCOTLAND, & IRELAND.

For Information of the People.

————— Itá vertere Seriæ { Horat. de
{ Ar. Poet.

From Thurſday Septemb. 23. to Thurſday Septemb. 30. 1658.

Advertiſements.

A Bright bay Gelding ſtoln from *Hatfield,* in the County of *Hertford,* Sept.
23. of about 14 hand high or ſomething more, with half his Mane ſhorne
and a ſtar in the Forehead, and a feather all along his Neck on the far ſide.
A yong man with gray cloaths of about twenty years of age, middle ſtature,
went away with him. If any can give notice to the Porter at *Saliſbury* houſe
in the Strand, or to the White Lion in *Hatfield* aforeſaid, they ſhall be well rewarded for their pains.

T Hat Excellent, and by all Phyſitians approved, *China* Drink, called by the
Chineas, Tcha, by other Nations *Tay aliaſ Tee,* is ſold at the *Sultaneſs-head,*
a *Cophee-houſe* in *Sweetings* Rents by the Royal Exchange, *London.*

THE FIRST NEWSPAPER ADVERTISEMENT OF TEA, 1658

and while the business of the place is being enacted, she makes the serving lads cry, "Fresh coffee, gentlemen! Fresh coffee! Bohea tea, Gentlemen!"[8]

Proportionately as the coffee houses gained vogue and prospered, the taverns became deserted, and the Government, faced with a considerable diminution of revenues from wines, found it necessary to make up the deficit by imposing a tax on the liquors dispensed in coffee houses. Furthermore, such places were placed under the same kind of license as that imposed upon taverns and ale houses.

England Taxes Tea

Tea first appeared upon the English statutes in Act XXI, Charles II, c. 23 and 24, in which an excise duty of eight-pence was placed on every gallon of tea, chocolate, and sherbet sold. The Act required keepers of coffee houses to take out a license at the Quarter Sessions and pro-

[8] Bohea (bo-hē, but first pronounced bo-hay by the English), from *Vu-e* pronounced *bu-e* by some Chinese. The name of a famous range of hills where the original Bohea tea was grown. The use of the word was later expanded to include all black teas. Now obsolete except in Java, where it applies to a low grade grown and used by native villagers

vide security for the due payment of the excise duty. Neglect to do this entailed a penalty of £5 a month.

Excise officers visited the coffee houses at stated intervals to gauge and take account of the number of gallons of each liquid that was made. The plan had many disadvantages and was difficult of execution, as it was necessary for the excise officer to see and measure the taxable drinkables before they could be sold. It was customary to infuse an ample supply of tea to outlast the period between inspections and to store it in kegs to be drawn off and heated as required.

In 1669, imports from Holland were prohibited by English law, thus creating a monopoly for the English East India Company.

Tea and Coffee Tokens

On account of the scarcity of small change, coffee house keepers and other tradesmen of the seventeenth century put out large numbers of tokens, or trade coins. They were of copper, brass, pewter, and even of leather, gilded. They bore the name, address, and calling of the issuer, the nominal value of the piece, and some reference to his trade. They were readily redeemed at their face value; were passable in the immediate neighborhood, and seldom circulated farther than the next street. Concerning them, G. C. Williamson has written: "Tokens are essentially democratic; they would never have been issued but for the indifference of the Government to a public need." We must remember, however, that these were the troublous days of the Civil War and the Commonwealth in which we have a remarkable instance of a people forcing a legislature to comply with demands at once reasonable and imperative. Taken as a whole series, the tokens were homely and quaint, somewhat wanting in beauty, but not without a curious domestic art of their own.

E. F. Robinson, who traced the origin of the English coffee house system, finds an exception to the general simplicity in the tokens issued by one of the Exchange Alley houses. The dies of these tokens are such as to suggest the skilled workmanship of John Roettier. The most ornate has the head of a Turkish sultan and is the only one of the coffee house keepers'

tokens now preserved on which the word tea occurs. Its inscription runs:

MORAT Y GREAT MEN DID MEE CALL
WHERE EARE I CAME I CONQUERD ALL.
Coffee. Tobacco. Sherbet. Tea.
Chocolat. Retail in Exchange Alee.[9]

A number of the most interesting coffee house tokens have been preserved in the

"The Sultaness Head" In Sweetings Rents By the Royal Exchange, Cornhill.

"Morat ye Great" or "Turk's Head" in Exchange Alley, Cornhill.

TEA AND COFFEE TOKENS, LONDON c 1658

These were used in lieu of small change. The "Turk's Head" alone mentioned tea, although the beverage was sold at all coffee houses.

Beaufoy collection at the Guildhall Museum in London.

English Ladies Begin to Drink Tea

Tea became a fashionable drink for the ladies of England with the coming of Princess Catherine of Braganza, the Portuguese princess and tea devotee whom Charles II wedded in 1662. She was England's first tea drinking queen, and it is to her credit that she was able to substitute her favorite temperance drink as the fashionable beverage of the court in place of the ales, wines, and spirits with which the English ladies, as well as gentlemen, "habitually heated or stupefied their brains morning, noon, and night." [10]

With a population that grew from 3,000,-000 at the beginning of the seventeenth

[9] E. F. Robinson. The Early History of Coffee Houses in England, London, 1893, p. 147.
[10] Agnes Strickland, Lives of the Queens of England, London, 1882, Vol. V, p. 521.

century to 5,000,000 at its close, the England of Queen Catherine's time was, throughout its greater part, "open and un-tamed," while enjoying the culture handed down from the Elizabethans. The English poet Edmund Waller, 1606–87, wrote the first eulogy of tea in English verse to honor the birthday of Queen Catherine in the year of her marriage, 1662. The poem begins:

Venus her myrtle, Phœbus has his bays;
Tea both excels, which she vouchsafes to praise.

The queen's taste for tea may account for its selection by the directors of the East India Company as a rare and costly gift to the king in 1664. In their records for that year the following entries appear: "1664—July 1.—Ordered, that the master attendant do go on board the ships now arrived [from Bantam, Java], and enquire what rarities of birds, beasts, or other curiousities there are on board, fit to present to His Majesty." On the 22nd of August the Governor, having acquainted the Court of Directors that the factors had in every instance failed the company of "such things as they writ for," he was of the opinion, if the court thought fit, that a silver case of oil of cinnamon and some good *thea* be selected, which he hoped would be acceptable. This, we are told, the court "approved very well," and on September 30 there is an entry on the general books:

Sundry accounts oweth to John Stannion, Sec'y.
Presents—For a case containing six
   China bottles headed with
   silver £13.0.0
   More for 2 lbs. 2 oz. of *thea*
   for His Majesty............... 4.5.0

Further impetus was given to tea drinking as a fashionable entertainment at the court of Charles II when Henry Bennet, Lord Arlington, Secretary of State, and Thomas Butler, Earl of Ossory, returned to London from The Hague in 1666, bringing in their baggage a quantity of tea which their ladies proceeded to serve after the newest and most aristocratic vogue of the Continent. At this time the Netherlands represented the pinnacle of elegance in tea serving, and every home of any consequence had its exclusive tea room.

The effect of the importation by Lord Arlington and Lord Ossory was so pronounced, thanks to the teas given by their

CATHERINE OF BRAGANZA, 1638–1705
She was England's first tea drinking Queen and Waller eulogized both in a famous poem.

ladies, that Jonas Hanway, 1712–86, a benevolent English merchant and author of a famous attack on tea,[11] made the statement, somewhat widely copied, that they were the first to introduce tea into England from Holland; a statement controverted by Dr. Samuel Johnson, 1709–84, in his famous reply to Hanway, when he called attention to the well-established fact that tea had been taxed since the year 1660, and had been publicly sold in London for several years before that.

At the time that Lord Arlington and Lord Ossory returned, Abbé Raynal, 1713–96, a French historian, informs us: "Tea sold in London for near seventy livres (£2.18.4) a pound, though it cost but three or four (from 2s. 6d. to 3s. 4d.) at Batavia."[12] The price was kept up with little variation, regardless of the fact that the high cost prevented its general use. However, its vogue at court gave it added interest to the ladies; and the apothecaries of London hastened to add it to their phar-

[11] Jonas Hanway, *An Essay on Tea*, London, 1756.
[12] Abbé Guillaume Thomas François Raynal, *Philosophical and Political History of the Settlement and Trade of the Europeans in the East and West Indies*, Edinburgh, 1804; first published in Amsterdam in 1770.

macies. In 1667, Pepys records in his diary: "Home and found my wife making of tea; a drink which Mr. Pelling, the potticary, tells her is good for her cold and defluxions."

Suppression of the Coffee Houses

The influence of the coffee houses having grown to a point where they were looked upon by the Government with the utmost aversion, Charles II on December 23, 1675, issued a proclamation closing all of them—including, of course, those selling tea—as places of sedition.

Stripped of its excess verbiage, the order announced:

BY THE KING: A PROCLAMATION FOR THE SUPPRESSION OF COFFEE HOUSES
Charles R.

WHEREAS it is most apparent that the multitude of coffee houses of late years set up and kept within this kingdom, the dominion of Wales, and town of Berwick-upon-Tweed, and the great resort of idle and disaffected persons to them, have produced very evil and dangerous effects; as well for that many tradesmen and other, do herein mispend much of their time, which and probably would be employed in and about their Lawful Calling and Affairs; but also, for that in such houses . . . divers false, malitious and scandalous reports are devised and spread abroad to the Defamation of his Majesty's Government, and to the Disturbance of the Peace and Quiet of the Realm; his Majesty hath thought fit and necessary, that the said coffee Houses be (for the future) Put down, and suppressed, and doth . . . strictly charge and command all manner of persons, That they or any of them do not presume from and after the Tenth Day of January next ensuing, to keep any Public Coffee House, or to utter or sell by retail, in his, her or their house or houses (to be spent or consumed within the same) any Coffee, Chocolate, Sherbett or Tea, as they will answer the contrary at their utmost perils . . . (all licenses to be revoked).

Given at our Court at Whitehall, this third-and-twentieth day of Dec., 1675, in the seven-and-twentieth year of our Reign.

GOD SAVE THE KING.

And then a remarkable thing happened. It is not usual for a royal proclamation issued on the 29th of one month to be recalled on the 8th day of the next; but this is the record established by Charles II. The proclamation was made on December 23, 1675, and issued December 29, 1675. It forbade the coffee houses to operate after January 10, 1676. But so intense was the feeling aroused, that eleven days was sufficient time to convince the king that a blunder had been made. Men of all parties cried out against being deprived of their accustomed haunts. The dealers in tea, coffee, and chocolate protested that the proclamation would greatly lessen His Majesty's revenues. Convulsion and discontent loomed large. The King heeded the warning, and on January 8, 1676, another proclamation was issued by which the first was recalled.

In order to save the King's face, it was solemnly recited that "His Gracious Majesty," out of his "princely consideration and royal compassion" would allow the retailers of tea and its allied liquors to keep open until the 24th of the following June. But this was clearly a royal subterfuge, as there was no further attempt at molestation, and it is extremely doubtful if any was contemplated.

"Than both which proclamations nothing could argue greater guilt nor greater weakness," says Anderson.[13] Robinson remarks: "A battle for freedom of speech was fought and won over this question at the time when Parliaments were infrequent and when the liberty of the press did not exist."

All through the years remaining in the seventeenth century, and through most of the eighteenth century, the London coffee houses prospered and the sales of tea increased. They were sometimes called "penny universities," because they were great schools of conversation, and the entrance fee was only a penny. Twopence was the price of a dish of tea or coffee, this charge also covering newspapers and lights. "Regular customers," we are told, "had particular seats and special attention from the fair lady at the bar and the tea and coffee boys."

Thomas B. Macaulay, 1800–1859, in explanation of the popularity of the coffee house in England, asserts: "The convenience of being able to make appointments in any part of the town, and of being able to pass evenings socially at a very small charge, was so great that the fashion spread fast."

Evolution of the Club

Every profession, trade, class, and party had its favorite coffee house. Coffee and tea brought together all sorts and conditions of men; and out of their mixed association there developed groups of patrons

[13] Adam Anderson, *Historical and Chronological Deduction of the Origin of Commerce*, London, 1787.

favoring particular houses and giving them character. It is easy to trace the transition of the group into a clique that later became a club, continuing for a time to meet at the coffee house, but eventually demanding a house of its own.

Decline of the Coffee Houses

Starting as a forum for the commoner, the coffee house soon became the plaything of the leisure class; and when the club evolved, the coffee house began to retrograde to the level of the tavern. So the eighteenth century, which saw the coffee house at the height of its power and popularity, witnessed also its decline. It is said that there were as many clubs at the end of the century as there were coffee houses at the beginning. A few houses survived until the early years of the nineteenth century, but the social side of their life disappeared long before that time. As tea and coffee entered the home, and the exclusive clubhouse succeeded the democratic coffee forum, the coffee houses became taverns or chophouses, or, convinced that they had outlived their usefulness, just ceased to be.

Grocers Begin to Sell Tea

By the close of the seventeenth century tea had been adopted into the better-class homes, and certain London grocers began to sell it. They were called tea grocers, to distinguish them from those who did not handle it. However, tea was as yet too expensive a luxury for England's masses, and it was almost, although not quite, unknown in the sister kingdoms of Scotland and Ireland.

The First Tea Shop

An event significant of the progress tea was making in London occurred in the year 1717, when Thomas Twining transformed "Tom's Coffee House" into the "Golden Lyon," the first tea shop in England. Unlike the coffee houses, which had been patronized only by men, the Golden Lyon was frequented alike by both sexes. Edward Walford writes: "Great ladies flocked to Twining's house in Devereaux Court in order to sip the enlivening beverage in small cups for which they paid their shillings."

Tea Comes into Common Use

Notwithstanding the high price, the taste for the tea drink gained ground. It was not brought into common use, however, until about the year 1715, when the lower-priced green tea began to be used. "Till then," according to Raynal, "no sort was known but the Bohea. The fondness for this Asiatic plant," continues Raynal, "has since become universal. Perhaps the frenzy is not without its inconveniences; but it cannot be denied that it has contributed more to the sobriety of the nation than the severest laws, the most eloquent harangues of Christian orators, or the best treatises of morality."

Humphrey Broadbent, "the domestick coffee man," summed up the case in favor of tea in 1722 as follows: "It is accounted one of the best, pleasantest and safest herbs that was ever introduced into food or medicine." [14]

In 1728, Mary Delany, 1700–1788, English memoirist and daughter of Lord Granville, wrote: "The man at the Poultry [a London street still existing] has tea of all prices,—bohea from twenty to thirty shillings, and green tea from twelve to thirty."

Early Days of Tea in Scotland

In 1680, tea was first served in Scotland at Holyrood Palace, Edinburgh, by the Duchess of York, Mary of Modena, who, as the wife of James II, was later queen of Great Britain and Ireland. The duke and duchess were virtual exiles, first at The Hague, where they picked up tea drinking as a social art, and later at Holyrood, where they introduced the novel refreshment to the wonderment of their friends and devoted adherents among the Scottish nobility.

In 1705, George Smith, a goldsmith of Luckenbooths, Edinburgh, advertised green tea at 16s. and Bohea tea at 30s. a pound. There may have been some association of ideas as to values in offering tea for sale with jewelry, but how much tea was sold to the canny Scots at such prices is not recorded. However, by 1724 all classes were drinking the beverage.

Some there were who regarded the drink as a highly improper article of diet, expensive, wasteful of time, and likely to

[14] Humphrey Broadbent, *The Domestick Coffee Man*, London, 1722.

The London Gazette.

Published by Authority.

From Monday December 13. to Thursday December 16. 1680.

Lisbon, Nov. 11.

THe Court is gone to *Alcantara*, and will remain there all this month; the Queen and the Infanta being very much delighted with the place. We are expecting here the Marquis de *Dronero*, who comes in the quality of Ambassador Extraordinary from the Duke of *Savoy*, to demand the

Advertisements.

THese are to give notice to Persons of quality, That a small parcel of most excellent TEA, is by accident fallen into the hands of a private Person to be sold: But that none may be disappointed, the lowest price is 30 s. a pound, and not any to be sold under a pound weight; for which they are desired to bring a convenient Box. Inquire at Mr. Tho Eagles at the Kings Head in St. James's Market.

A NEWSPAPER ADVERTISEMENT OF 1680 OFFERING TEA AT THIRTY SHILLINGS A POUND

render the population weakly and effeminate. Such was Lord President Forbes's conviction in 1744, and it was about this time that an energetic movement was begun all over Scotland to stamp out the "tea menace." Towns, parishes, and counties passed resolutions condemnatory of the Chinese leaf and pointing strongly to the manlier attraction of beer. The tenants of William Fullarton of Fullarton, Ayrshire, in a bond which they entered into thus delivered themselves:

We being all farmers by profession, think it needless to restrain ourselves formally from indulging in that foreign and consumptive luxury called *tea;* for when we consider the slender constitutions of many of higher rank, among whom it is used, we conclude that it would be but improper diet to qualify us for the more robust and manly parts of our business: therefore we shall only give our testimony against it and leave the enjoyment of it altogether to those who can afford to be weak, indolent and useless.[15]

Early Tea Controversies

Initiating the first of several attacks on tea in England, in 1678, Mr. Henry Sayville wrote to his uncle, Mr. Secretary Coventry of His Majesty's Government, in sharp reproof of certain of his friends "who call for tea, instead of pipes and a bottle after dinner." This he characterized as "a base Indian practice."

In 1730, Dr. Thomas Short, a Scottish

[15] Robert Chambers, LL.D., *Domestic Annals of Scotland*, 1885.

physician, published *A Dissertation upon Tea*, in which he stated that he refused to take the imaginary good qualities of the beverage on trust. He believed that it threw "some Persons into Vapours" and many other disastrous-sounding ailments.

One of England's several tea controversies flared up about 1745, and we catch its echo in an old copy of the *Female Spectator*, which denounces tea in no uncertain terms as "the bane of housewifery." Again Arthur Young, 1741–1820, the most influential political economist of the period, described the effects of tea drinking upon the entire national economy as being altogether evil. He was greatly disturbed because of the growing custom "of men making tea an article of their food, almost as much as women, labourers losing their time to come and go to the tea-table, farmers' servants even demanding tea for their breakfast!" He went so far as to prophesy that if they continued to waste time and to injure their health by so bad a beverage, "the poor in general will find themselves far more distressed than ever."

However, both tea and English prosperity sufficiently survived to permit a new attack, in 1748, by no less a figure than John Wesley, 1703–91, the great preacher, who urged his followers to discontinue its use for both medical and moral reasons. Wesley inveighed against tea drinking as hurtful to both body and soul. Unlike the Buddhist priests of China and Japan who early seized on this non-intoxicating

JOHN WESLEY'S HALF-GALLON TEA POT

It was used at his Sunday morning tea parties.

beverage as a weapon to attack the alcoholic stimulants previously in use, he denounced tea in much the same terms he employed against strong drink, calling on his adherents to abstain from its use and apply the money they would thus save to charitable works.

It was because of his recovery from a paralytic disorder which, he said, disappeared as the result of leaving off tea that Wesley took this attitude. According to his philippic, he then reflected concerning tea drinkers:

> What an Advantage it would be to these poor enfeebled People if they would leave off what so manifestly impairs the Health, and thereby hurts their Business also. If one only would save all that he could in this single instance, he might surely feed or clothe one of this brethren and perhaps save one life. . . . Some objected, tea is not unwholesome to all. . . . To these I reply, you should not be so sure of this. . . . Many eminent Physicians have declared their judgment that it is prejudicial in several respects.[16]

We find that during the latter part of his life, however, Wesley became a regular tea drinker again, and it is claimed that he even gave tea parties. Rev. George H. McNeal, Minister, Wesley's Chapel, London, states that when Wesley was at home, all of the Methodist preachers in London gathered at his house for breakfast on Sunday morning before they went to their various appointments, and that at these breakfasts a teapot which held about half a gallon, and had been especially made for him by the famous potter Josiah Wedg-

wood, was regularly used. It now forms one of the exhibits in the room of the City Road house where Wesley died.

The tea drinking habit progressed steadily in the eighteenth century in spite of attempts to check it, spreading to the pleasure gardens and the rural districts of England, and by 1753 country people regularly kept tea on hand among their supplies.

One of the most famous attacks on tea was made in 1756 by Jonas Hanway, 1712–86, an apparently amiable and well-disposed London merchant and author. In his *Journal of an Eight Days Journey*, Hanway branded tea as "pernicious to health, obstructing industry, and impoverishing the nation."

The Hanway journal came in the way of Dr. Samuel Johnson, 1709–84, famous English lexicographer, who answered it with a degree of alacrity proportioned to his avowed fondness for the beverage of his choice.

Dr. Johnson was "a lover of tea to an excess hardly credible," writes Sir John Hawkins, one of his biographers. "Whenever it appeared, he was almost raving, and called for the ingredients which he employed to make the liquor palatable. This in a man whose appearance of bodily strength has been compared to Polyphemus."[17]

Knowing this foible of Johnson's, the reader will more readily appreciate the delight with which the redoubtable doctor sprang to the defense of his favorite beverage. In articles published in the *Literary Magazine* he overwhelmed Hanway with good-humored ridicule, proclaiming himself "a hardened and shameless tea drinker, who has for many years diluted his meals with only the infusion of this fascinating plant; whose kettle has scarcely time to cool; who with tea amuses the evening, with tea solaces the midnights, and with tea welcomes the morning."[18]

Other celebrated authors, among them Addison, Pope, Coleridge, and the poet Cowper, eulogized tea; and a little later Rev. Sydney Smith wrote: "Thank God for tea! What would the world do without tea? I am glad I was not born before tea."

16 John Wesley, M.A., Fellow of Lincoln College, Oxford. *A Letter to a Friend Concerning Tea,* Bristol, 1749.

17 Sir John Hawkins, *The Life of Samuel Johnson, LL.D.,* London, 1787.
18 The Literary Magazine, Number VII, Oct. 15, to Nov. 15, 1656, and Number XIII, Apr. 15, to May 15, 1657, according to Sir John Hawkins.

CHAPTER V

INTRODUCTION OF TEA INTO AMERICA

THE use of tea as a beverage was unknown to the American colonists who, early in the seventeenth century, settled along the Atlantic seaboard. Indeed, it was almost unknown in the mother countries, but, by the year 1640, the aristocracy of the Netherlands had begun to drink tea, and by the years 1660–80 its use had become general in that country. So, although there are no specific records of its earliest use in America, it is more than probable that the custom was brought from Holland, and that Dutch New Amsterdam was the first American colony to drink the beverage, about the middle of the seventeenth century.

We are not left in the least doubt as to the use of tea by the burghers of New Amsterdam, or at least by those who could afford to buy it, for some of their inventories that have been preserved show that tea drinking became as much a social custom in the colony as it did in Holland, and at about the same time. The tea board, tea table, teapots, sugar bowl, silver spoons, and strainer were the pride of the Dutch household in the New World.

The socially correct grand dame of New Amsterdam not only served tea, but she brewed several kinds in different pots so as to accommodate the tastes of her guests. She never offered milk or cream with tea, for this was a later innovation that came to America from France; but she did offer sugar, and sometimes saffron or peach leaves for flavoring.[1]

Tea was known and probably used to a limited extent in the Massachusetts colony as early as 1670. It was first sold at Boston in 1690 by two dealers, Benjamin Harris and Daniel Vernon, who took out licenses to sell tea "in publique" in accordance with the English law requiring every purveyor of tea to have a license for its sale. Apparently its use in Boston was not uncommon subsequent to that time, for we find Chief Justice Sewall jotting in his "Diary" that he drank it at Mrs. Winthrop's residence in 1709, and he makes no comment to indicate that there was anything unusual in the occurrence.

Bohea, or black tea, then popular in England, was the kind commonly used, but in 1712 Zabdiel Boylston, a Boston apothecary advertised "Green and Ordinary" teas at retail.

Small copper tea kettles were in use in Plymouth as early as 1702. The first cast-iron tea kettles were made in Plympton [now Carver], Massachusetts, between 1760 and 1765. When ladies went to parties, each carried her teacup, saucer, and spoon. The cups were of the best china, very small, containing about as much as a common wineglass.[2]

Certain contretemps arising from lack of knowledge as to how to prepare tea are recorded of the period of the early adoption of tea in New England, as in the mother country. In Salem the leaves were boiled for a long time, until an extremely bitter decoction was produced, which was

---

[1] Esther Singleton, *Dutch New York*, N. Y., 1909.

[2] Francis S. Drake, *Tea Leaves*, Boston, 1884.

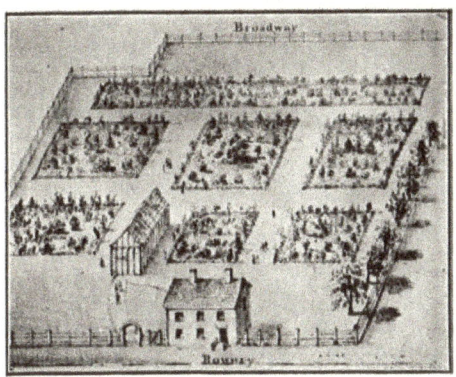

NEW YORK'S THIRD VAUXHALL GARDEN, 1803
The Astor Library was built on its site.

drunk without milk or sugar; then the leaves were salted and eaten with butter. In more than one town the liquid tea was thrown out and the boiled leaves were eaten.[3]

Tea in Old New York

New Amsterdam having passed into English hands in 1674, it was rechristened "New York" and proceeded to acquire English manners. Copying the idea of the London pleasure gardens of the first half of the eighteenth century, tea gardens were added to the coffee houses and taverns. Then, on the outskirts of the city were opened the Ranelagh and Vauxhall gardens, named after their famous London prototypes. The first Vauxhall garden—there were three of this name—was on Greenwich Street between Warren and Chambers streets. It fronted on the North River, affording a beautiful view up the Hudson. Starting as the Bowling Green Garden, it changed to Vauxhall in 1750.

The Ranelagh, which lasted for twenty years, was on Broadway between Duane and Worth streets, on the site where, later, the New York Hospital was erected. From advertisements of the period 1765–69 we learn that there were fireworks and band concerts twice a week at Ranelagh and Vauxhall. The gardens were "for breakfasting as well as the evening entertainment of ladies and gentlemen." Tea, coffee, and hot rolls could be had in the pleasure gardens at any hour of the day.

We are told, too, that there was a commodious hall in the garden for dancing. The second Vauxhall, opened in 1798, was near the intersection of the present Mulberry and Grand streets; the third opened in 1803, was on the Bowery Road near Astor Place. The Astor Library was built upon its site in 1853.

William Niblo, previously proprietor of the Bank Coffee House in Pine Street, opened, in 1828, a pleasure garden which he named Sans Souci. It occupied the site of a former circus building called the Stadium. Later, he built a more pretentious theater that fronted on Broadway. The interior of the garden was "spacious and adorned with shrubbery and walks, lighted with festoons of lamps." The place was generally known as Niblo's Garden.

Among other well-known pleasure gardens of old New York where tea was served were Contoit's, later the New York Garden, Cherry Gardens, and the Tea Water Pump Garden. The latter was a famous "out-of-town" garden located at a spring near the junction of Chatham (now Park Row) and Roosevelt streets. This spring and its surroundings were made into an extremely fashionable resort for drinking tea and other beverages. The spring itself was first mentioned in the diary of a traveler to New York in 1748. He wrote: "There is no good water in the town itself; but at a little distance there is a large spring of good water which the inhabitants take for their tea."

In order to make it possible to obtain good water for drinking and for preparing

NIBLO'S GARDEN, BROADWAY AND PRINCE STREET, 1828

[3] Alice Morse Earle, *Customs and Fashions in Old New England*, New York, 1909.

CHATHAM STREET TEA-WATER PUMP, 1748

tea, the Corporation of New York erected a tea-water pump over the spring at Chatham and Roosevelt streets. This water was considered much more desirable than that from the other town pumps, and was peddled about the streets by carters whose cries of "Tea water! Tea water! Come out and get your tea water!" were characteristic of the day. By 1757 this business had grown to such an extent that the Common Council was constrained to enact "a law for the Regulating of the Tea Water Men in the City of New York."

Tea water was also pumped from several other springs. There was Knapp's famous spring, located near the present Tenth Avenue and Fourteenth Street; another spring that was well patronized was near Christopher Street and Sixth Avenue. These two tea-water pumps—Knapp's and the one in Christopher Street—having made a name for themselves, enjoyed a large patronage from those who could afford to pay for the water, but the one oftenest referred to as the "tea-water pump" is the old pump on Chatham Street, which fashionable New York first visited with its approval.

Tea in Old Philadelphia

William Penn is generally credited with the introduction of tea into the Quaker colony which he founded on the Delaware in 1682. He also brought to the "City of Brotherly Love" that other great drink of human brotherhood, coffee. At first, 1700, "like tea, coffee was only a drink for the well-to-do, except in sips."[4] As was the case in the other English colonies, too,

[4] Ellis Paxson Oberholtzer, *Philadelphia; a History of the City and Its People,* Philadelphia, 1912, Vol. I, p. 106.

coffee languished for a time while tea rose in favor, more especially in the home. Following the Stamp Act of 1765, succeeded two years later by the Trade and Revenue Act of 1767, the Pennsylvania colony joined hands with the others in a general tea boycott, and coffee here received the same impetus as elsewhere in the colonies.

Tea Taxes That Divided an Empire

The close of the Seven Years' War, in 1763, left England supreme upon the seas and in America, and the task of readjusting fiscal relations with the colonies fell to the British Government under George III, who held that the war had been fought for the benefit of the colonies, and believed that they should be taxed for at least a part of the cost of the troops necessary for their defense. Under the ministry of George Grenville, 1712–70, the unfortunate Stamp Act of 1765 was passed, imposing a tax on tea and many other articles used by the colonists. A storm of protest arose at once, not only in America, but at home among the opponents of the Grenville ministry. William Pitt, 1708–78, was prominent in the Opposition, taking the ground that the British Parliament had no right to tax the American colonies without the consent of their assemblies.

The Government chose a middle course by repealing the Stamp Act in 1766, though asserting by the Declaratory Act its supreme right to tax the colonies and make laws for them.

Later, in 1767, Charles Townshend's Act of Trade and Revenue was passed by Parliament; duties being laid on paints, oils, lead, glass, and tea. So were lighted the

KNAPP'S TEA-WATER PUMP, 1750

CAP. XLIV.

An act to allow a drawback of the duties of customs on the exportation of tea to any of his Majesty's colonies or plantations in America; to increase the deposit on bohea tea to be sold at the India Company's sales; and to impower the commissioners of the treasury to grant licences to the East India Company to export tea duty-free.

Preamble.

WHEREAS *by an act, made in the twelfth year of his present Majesty's reign, (intituled, An act for granting a drawback of part of the customs upon the exportation of tea to Ireland, and the British dominions in America; for altering the drawback upon foreign sugars exported from Great Britain to Ireland; for continuing the bounty on the exportation of British-made cordage; for allowing the importation of rice from the British plantations into the ports of Bristol, Liverpool, Lancaster, and Whitehaven, for immediate exportation to foreign parts; and to impower the chief magistrate of any corporation to administer the oath, and grant the certificate required by law, upon the removal of certain goods to London, which have been sent into the country for sale;) it is amongst other things, enacted, That for and during the space of five years, to be computed from and after the fifth day of July, one thousand seven hundred and seventy-two, there shall be drawn back and allowed for all teas which shall be sold after the said fifth day of July, one thousand seven hundred and seventy-two, at the publick sale of the united company of merchants of England trading to the East Indies, or which after that time shall be imported, by licence, in pursuance of the said therein and herein-after mentioned act, made in the eighteenth year of the reign of his late majesty King George the Second, and which shall be exported from this kingdom, as merchandise, to Ireland, or any of the British colonies or plantations in America, three fifth parts of the several duties of customs which were paid upon the importation of such teas; which drawback or allowance, with respect to such teas as shall be exported to Ireland, shall be made to the exporter, in such manner, and under such rules, regulations, securities, penalties and forfeitures, as any drawback or allowance was then payable, out of the duty of customs upon the exportation of foreign goods to Ireland; and with respect to such teas as shall be exported to the British colonies and plantations in America, the said drawback or allowance shall be made in such manner, and under such rules, regulations, penalties, and forfeitures, as any drawback or allowance payable out of the duty of customs upon foreign goods exported to foreign parts, was, could, or might be made, before the passing of the said act of the twelfth year of his present Majesty's reign, (except in such cases as are otherwise therein provided for:) and whereas it may tend to the benefit and advantage of the trade of the said united company of merchants of England trading to the East Indies, if the allowance of the drawback of the duties of customs upon all teas sold at the publick sales of the said united company, after the tenth day of May, one thousand seven hun-*

dred and seventy-three, and which shall be exported from this kingdom, as merchandise, to any of the British colonies or plantations in America, were to extend to the whole of the said duties of customs payable upon the importation of such teas; may it therefore please your Majesty that it may be enacted; and be it enacted by the King's most excellent majesty, by and with the advice and consent of the lords spiritual and temporal, and commons, in this present parliament assembled, and by the authority of the same,

That there shall be drawn back and allowed for all teas, which, from and after the tenth day of May, one thousand seven hundred and seventy-three, shall be sold at the publick sales of the said united company, or which shall be imported by licence, in pursuance of the said act made in the eighteenth year of the reign of his late majesty King George the Second, and which shall, at any time hereafter, be exported from this kingdom, as merchandise, to any of the British colonies or plantations in America, the whole of the duties of customs payable upon the importation of such teas; which drawback or allowance shall be made to the exporter in such manner, and under such rules, regulations, and securities, and subject to the like penalties and forfeitures, as the former drawback or allowance granted by the said recited act of the twelfth year of his present Majesty's reign, upon tea exported to the said British colonies and plantations in America was, might, or could be made, and was subject to by the said recited act, or any other act of parliament now in force, in as full and ample manner, to all intents and purposes, as if the several clauses relative thereto were again repeated and re-enacted in this present act.

After May 10, 1773, on all teas sold at publick sale, if imported and afterwards exported as merchandise, to any of the British colonies in America, the whole duties of customs to be drawn back.

II. *And whereas by one other act made in the eighteenth year of the reign of his late majesty King George the Second, (intituled, An act for repealing the present inland duty of four shillings per pound weight upon all tea sold in Great Britain; and for granting to his Majesty certain other inland duties in lieu thereof; and for better securing the duty upon tea, and other duties of excise; and for pursuing offenders out of one county into another,) it is, amongst other things, enacted, That every person who shall, at any publick sale of tea made by the united company of merchants of England trading to the East Indies, be declared to be the best bidder for any lot or lots of tea, shall, within three days after being so declared the best bidder or bidders for the same, deposit with the said united company, or such clerk or officer as the said company shall appoint to receive the same, forty shillings for every tub and for every chest of tea; and in case any such person or persons shall refuse or neglect to make such deposit within the time before limited, he, &c. or they, shall forfeit and lose for times the value of such deposit directed to be made as aforesaid, to be recovered by action of debt, bill, plaint, or information, in any of his Majesty's courts of record at Westminster, in which no essoin, protection, or wager of law, or more than one imparlance, shall be allowed; and moiety of which forfeiture shall go to his Majesty, his heirs and successors, and the other moiety to such person so shall sue or prosecute for the same; and the sale*

Act 12 Geo. 3.

Act 18 Geo. 2. recited.

THE TEA ACT OF 1773 CAUSED THE BOSTON TEA PARTY

---

smoldering fires afresh, and the colonists refused to import any goods from England. In order to satisfy the English merchants, Parliament repealed every tax except the duty of threepence per pound on tea, which the colonists refused to pay, preferring to get their tea elsewhere than to sacrifice their principles by buying it from England. A brisk business in smuggled tea from Holland was started, and the American tea trade was transferred very largely to that country.

The Tea Act of 1773

In panic at the loss of the colonial markets, and faced by a huge surplus of tea on hand, the East India Company appealed to Parliament for aid. This was obtained through the active support of the prime minister, Lord North, 1733–92, in the shape of permission for the company to export

tea, a privilege it had never enjoyed before. Up to this time English jobbers had been accustomed to purchase tea from the East India Company and then resell and ship it to the colonial merchants. The passage of the Tea Act, 1773, however, authorized the company to import its teas into the colonies, cutting out the English middlemen's profit, as well as that of the American importers. It provided, further, that the company should be permitted to draw back the full amount of the 100 per cent English duty when the teas were shipped out of England, leaving only a threepenny tax to be collected by the colonial customs. It was thought that this would underprice the Dutch, at the same time giving the colonists lower-priced teas than were obtainable in England. It seems not to have occurred to those most concerned that the American colonists would refuse a bargain in tea on account of a matter of principle

76   Anno decimo tertio GEORGII III. c. 44.   [1773.

of all teas, for which such deposit shall be neglected to be made as aforesaid, is thereby declared to be null and void, and such teas shall be again put up by the said united company to publick sale, within fourteen days after the end of the sale of teas at which such teas were sold; and all and every buyer or buyers, who shall have neglected to make such deposit as aforesaid, shall be, and is and are thereby rendered incapable of bidding for or buying any teas at any future publick sale of the said united company: and whereas it is found to be expedient and necessary to increase the deposit to be made by any bidder or bidders for any lot or lots of bohea teas, as the publick sales of teas is to be made by the said united company; be it enacted by the authority aforesaid, That every person who shall, after the tenth day of May, one thousand seven hundred and seventy-three, at any publick sale of tea to be made by the said united company of merchants of England trading to the East Indies, be declared to be the best bidder or bidders for any lot or lots of bohea tea, shall, within three days after being so declared the best bidder or bidders for the same, deposit with the said united company, or such clerk or officer as the said united company shall appoint to receive the same, four pounds of lawful money of Great Britain for every tub and for every chest of bohea tea, under the same terms and conditions, and subject to the same forfeitures, penalties, and regulations, as are mentioned and contained in the said recited act of the eighteenth year of the reign of his said late Majesty.

III. And be it further enacted by the authority aforesaid, That it shall and may be lawful for the commissioners of his Majesty's treasury, or any three or more of them, or for the high treasurer for the time being, upon application made to them by the said united company of merchants of England trading to the East Indies for that purpose, to grant a licence or licences to the said united company, to take out of their warehouses, without the same having been put up to sale, and to export to any of the British plantations in America, or to any parts beyond the seas, such quantity or quantities of tea as the said commissioners of his Majesty's treasury, or any three or more of them, or the high treasurer for the time being, shall think proper and expedient, without incurring any penalty or forfeiture for so doing; any thing in the said in part recited act, or any other law, to the contrary notwithstanding.

IV. And whereas by an act made in the ninth and tenth years of the reign of King William the Third, (intituled, An act for raising a sum not exceeding two millions, upon a fund, for payment of annuities, after the rate of eight pounds per centum per annum; and for settling the trade to the East Indies;) and by several other acts of parliament which are now in force, the said united company of merchants of England trading to the East Indies are obliged to give security, under their common seal, for payment of the duties of customs upon all unrated goods imported by them, so soon as the same shall be sold; and for exposing such goods to sale, openly and fairly, by way of auction, or by inch of candle, within the space of three years from the

(margin notes, left:) Every person, after May 10, 1773, who shall be declared the highest bidder at any publick sale, shall deposit with the company 4l. for every tub or chest of bohea tea.

Commissioners of the treasury may grant licence to the East India Company to export to America any quantity of tea they shall think proper, without penalty.

An Will. 3. recited.

1773.]   Anno decimo tertio GEORGII III. c. 44.   77

importation thereof: and whereas it is expedient that some provision should be made to permit the said united company, in certain cases, to export tea, on their own account, to the British plantations in America, or to foreign parts, without exposing such tea to sale here, or being charged with the payment of any duty for the same; be it therefore enacted by the authority aforesaid, That from and after the passing of this act, it shall and may be lawful for the commissioners of his Majesty's treasury, or any three or more of them, or the high treasurer for the time being, to grant a licence or licences to the said united company, to take out of their warehouses such quantity or quantities of tea as the said commissioners of the treasury, or any three or more of them, or the high treasurer for the time being, shall think proper, without the same having been exposed to sale in this kingdom; and to export such tea to any of the British colonies or plantations in America, or to foreign parts, discharged from the payment of any customs or duties whatsoever; any thing in the said recited act, or any other act to the contrary notwithstanding.

V. Provided always, and it is hereby further enacted by the authority aforesaid, That a due entry shall be made at the custom-house, of all such tea so exported by licence, as aforesaid, expressing the quantities thereof, at what time imported, and by what ship; and such tea shall be shipped for exportation by the proper officer for that purpose, and shall, in all other respects, not altered by this act, be liable to the same rules, regulations, restrictions, securities, penalties, and forfeitures, as tea exported to the like places was liable to before the passing of this act; and upon the proper officer's duty, certifying the shipping of such tea to the collector and comptroller of his Majesty's customs for the port of London, upon the back of the licence, and the exportation thereof, verified by the oath of the husband or agent for the said united company, to be wrote at the bottom of such certificate, and sworn before the said collector and comptroller of the customs, (which oath they are hereby impowered to administer,) it shall and may be lawful for such collector and comptroller to write off and discharge the quantity of tea so exported from the warrant of the respective ship in which such tea was imported.

VI. Provided nevertheless, That no such licence shall be granted, unless it shall first be made to appear to the satisfaction of the commissioners of his Majesty's treasury, or any three or more of them, or the high treasurer for the time being, that at the time of taking out such teas, for the exportation of which a like licence or licences shall be granted, there will be left remaining in the warehouses of the said united company, a quantity of tea not less than ten millions of pounds weight; any thing herein, or in any other act of parliament, contained to the contrary thereof notwithstanding.

(margin notes, right:) Treasure may grant licence to the company for any quantity of tea to be exported to America, discharged of the customs.

Entry to be made of all tea exported by licence, and shipped by the proper officer, and such tea to be liable to the same rules, penalties, &c. as before passing this act. Officer's and collector's duty on exportation.

No licence to be granted, unless ten millions wt. of tea be left in warehouses.

THE TEA ACT OF 1773 BROUGHT ABOUT THE AMERICAN REVOLUTION

involving a little tax of threepence per pound.

With these adjustments made, the East India Company proceeded toward the execution of its plans by appointing special agents to receive the tea on consignment in Boston, New York, Philadelphia, and Charleston upon payment of the small American duty. Among the agents selected by the company were the sons and nephew of the unpopular English governor, Hutchinson, of Massachusetts, and others noted for their fidelity to the interests of the royal government and for their strong financial standing. Nor does there seem to have been much apprehension of serious trouble on the part of the eminent Britons who were financially and patriotically interested in the East India Company when the history-making chests were finally sent on their way. On the contrary, they seemed to be optimistically looking forward to recovering for England the lost tea trade of America.

Colonial Resentment Aroused

Across the water in America resentment against the Tea Act, and the various other measures which preceded it, was taking definite form. The assemblies of several of the colonies adopted resolutions of protest, and these, with a number of petitions, were sent to England, where they either went unheeded or were rejected outright. In the American seaports there were meetings and demonstrations of various sorts by organizations calling themselves the "Sons of Liberty," and many groups of colonial dames throughout the colonies were inspired to pledge themselves to drink no tea. Five hundred Boston ladies thus pledged themselves, and it is on record that the ladies of Hartford and many other American towns and villages took similar action. In a general way these agreements were in support of a non-importation movement directed against British goods, but in particular against tea after the passage of the Tea Act. In some parts of the Massachusetts colony it was impossible to purchase tea, even for medicinal purposes, without a permit. One of these permits, now preserved in the Library of the Connecticut Historical Society at Hartford, is dated at Wethersfield, Mass., and reads as follows:

To Mr. Leonard Chester
Sr:
Mrs. Baxter has applied to me for Liberty to buy a Quarter of a pound of Bohea Tea. I think by her Account of her Age & bodily Infirmities it will not be acting contrary to the Design of our Association to let her have it, & you have my full Consent thereto.
I am Yrs & c.
Elisha Williams.

For ordinary purposes various substitutes were used in place of the best-liked beverage. Liberty tea was one of these, and was manufactured by pulling up the four-leaved loosestrife, stripping off the leaves and boiling the stalks. The leaves were then placed in an iron pot and drenched with the liquor from the stalks, after which they were put in an oven and dried. The prepared leaf sold at sixpence the pound, and no quilting party, spinning bee, or other gathering of dames was considered a success without this or some substitute for the rigidly abjured tea. Strawberry and currant leaves were used to make a pseudo-tea, and ribwort, sage, and numerous medicinal herbs. Also Hyperion tea is often mentioned. It was made from the leaves of raspberry bushes.

While the patriotic women of the colonies were thus training themselves, and incidentally their posterity, against the use of tea, the men were intent on the newest aggression of the home government, by which it was proposed to take the existing colonial tea trade and turn it over as a monopoly to the East India Company. Up to this time, 1773, there had existed radical and conservative elements among the opponents to the recent measures of the royal government, and the merchants, who largely comprised the conservative group, had become indifferent to what they regarded as the vaporings of the radicals. But when they saw their tea business thus rudely taken out of their hands and gratuitously handed over to the East India Company by act of Parliament, they were filled with alarm for the future and quickly made common cause with the radicals. A circular letter issued by the Massachusetts Committee of Correspondence, under date of October 21, 1773, stated: "It is easy to see how aptly this scheme will serve both to destroy the trade of the colonies and increase the revenue. How necessary, then, it is that each colony should take effectual methods to prevent this measure from having its designed effects." [5]

In a letter dated October 18, 1773, one of the Boston consignees wrote to London: "What difficulties may arise from the disaffection of the merchants and importers of tea to this measure of the East India Company, I am not yet able to say. . . . My friends seem to think it will subside; others are of a contrary opinion."

Abram Lott, one of the New York consignees, wrote: "There will be no such thing as selling it, as the people would rather buy so much poison."

On October 25, 1773, the New York merchants met and passed a resolution of thanks to the captains of certain London ships trading to New York who had refused to take as freight from the East India Company tea which would have been subject to the hateful duty. Probably they hoped no ships would be found to bring the tea, but in this they were disappointed, for very shortly they heard that the tea had been shipped.

Decision to Prevent Landing

Discussion in the press became more heated than ever. Explaining the manner in which the tea duty was collectible, it was stated: "On a certificate of its being landed here, the tribute is, by agreement, to be paid to London. The landing is, therefore, the point in view." The merchants, backed by various patriotic groups, prominent among which were the Sons of Liberty, decided that the tea should not be landed—that it "should not pass." A British officer in New York wrote to a friend in London:

All America is aflame on account of the tea exportation. The New Yorkers, as well as the Bostonians and Philadelphians, it seems, are de-

[5] Francis S. Drake, *Tea Leaves*, Boston, 1884.

A TEA PROTEST MEETING WAS HELD AT THE NEW YORK CITY HALL, DEC. 17, 1773

General John Lamb, member of the Sons of Liberty and Special Committee of Correspondence, is addressing the indignant citizens. Mayor Whitehead Hicks and Recorder (afterwards Chancellor) Robert R. Livingston are standing by. Outside it is raining.

termined that no tea shall be landed. . . . They have on this occasion raised a company of artillery and every day, almost, are practicing at a target. Their independent companies are out and exercise every day. . . . They swear they will burn every tea ship that comes in; but I believe that our six- and twelve-pounders, with the Royal Welsh Fusileers, will prevent anything of the kind.

Opposition in Philadelphia

Philadelphia, the big boy of the colonial family, took the lead in resisting the plans of the parental government. A printed handbill was distributed throughout the city, headed, "By uniting we stand; by dividing we fall." It exhorted the inhabitants to oppose by every possible means the invasion of their rights, and characterized the consignees, appointed by the East India Company, as "political bombardiers to demolish the fair structure of liberty." The consignees were warned that all eyes were upon them and they were advised not to act. The handbill was signed "Scaevola." [6]

A mass meeting was held at the State

House on October 18, 1773, at which resolutions were unanimously adopted declaring that the tea tax was an unwarrantable duty imposed on the colonists without their consent; that the East India Company was attempting to enforce the tax; and that any person who should attempt to unload or vend the tea would be an enemy to the country.

Disaffection Spreads to New York

On October 26, 1773, a similar mass meeting was held at the City Hall in New York, and the attempted monopoly of the colonial tea trade by the East India Company was denounced as a "public robbery." A paper called the *Alarm* was appearing in New York about this time, and one of its warnings read:

If you touch one grain of the accursed tea you are undone. America is threatened with worse than Egyptian slavery. . . . The language of the Revenue Act is, that you have no property you can call your own; that you are the vassals, the live stock, of Great Britain.

After three weeks of such bombardment the New York consignees withdrew, whereupon it was announced that the customs officials would take charge of the tea upon

---

[6] Scaevola was a Roman soldier who held his hand over a lamp and burned it off to show the Etruscan king he would not shrink from torture.

THE GREEN DRAGON TAVERN, BOSTON

Known as "the headquarters of the Revolution." Opposition to the hateful tea tax crystallized here.

its arrival. There was prompt resentment of the announcement, and immediately the Sons of Liberty made it their business to warn all storekeepers against harboring the tea, declaring, as had the Philadelphians, that all who bought or sold it would be considered enemies of the country.

The Sons of Liberty

Nearly every colony had its Sons of Liberty association. Starting in Boston as the "Union Club," it took its later name from a phrase used by Col. Isaac Barré in a speech before the British Parliament. The membership included most of the early patriots, and their organization was secret, with passwords as protection against Tory spies. On the occasion of any public demonstration, the Boston members wore about their necks medals having, on one side, an arm grasping a staff surmounted by a liberty cap, and surrounded by the words "Sons of Liberty." The reverse bore a design of the Liberty Tree.[7]

The organization served its own warrants and made arrests. In secret caucus it arranged slates for elections, and laid the plans for all public celebrations. In short, under the popular leaders of the day, it controlled public conduct throughout the events leading up to, and including, the tea revolt.

In Boston the so-called North End Caucus met frequently to discuss what should be done, and on October 23 voted

that they would oppose with lives and fortunes, if need be, any attempt to land and sell the East India tea. This body, composed largely of artisans, was organized by Dr. Joseph Warren, and usually met at the home of William Campbell near the North Battery, though some of its sessions were held at the Green Dragon Tavern. The North End Caucus and another similar organization, the Long-Room Club, were local branches of the Sons of Liberty, and as such preserved the traditions of that society. Paul Revere, the famous Boston engraver and patriot, said: "We were so careful that our meetings should be kept secret, that every time we met, every person swore upon the Bible not to discover any of our transactions but to Hancock, Warren, or Church, and one or two more leaders."

Public Meetings at Boston

On November 2, the Boston consignees were summoned by the Sons of Liberty to appear at the Liberty Tree on the following Wednesday, and there publicly to resign their commissions. Flags were flown and bells rung as a crowd of five hundred or more gathered on the appointed day; but the consignees, not having presented themselves, the assemblage, among whom were John Hancock, Samuel Adams, and William Phillips, sent a committee to wait on them at Clarke's warehouse. The upshot of the matter was that the consignees refused to resign their commissions, or to promise not to attempt to land the tea when it should arrive. The committee reported this to the meeting at the Liberty Tree, and later a call was issued for a town meeting at Faneuil Hall. This gath-

PAUL REVERE'S ANTI-TEA CARTOON

In it the versatile patriot shows Lord North forcing the tea down the throat of America.

[7] The Liberty Tree at the present corner of Essex and Washington streets, Boston, where patriotic outdoor meetings were held in 1773-74.

ering, on November 5, presided over by John Hancock, settled any doubt there may have been about popular opinion as represented by the selectmen of the town and by every patriot leader, for they were all present. After careful consideration, the resolutions of the Philadelphia meetings were adopted declaring the tea tax tyrannous and arbitrary, and opposition to the policy of the ministry to be the duty of every freeman in the country.

Refusal of Consignees to Resign

A committee consisting of the town selectmen and two others was sent to communicate the resolutions to the consignees—Thomas and Elisha Hutchinson, Richard Clarke & Sons, Benjamin Faneuil, Jr., and Joshua Winslow. Highly unsatisfactory replies were reported to the meeting, which included four hundred local tradesmen, who voted the replies "daringly affrontive" to the town, and then adjourned. The Governor attempted to obtain evidence of treasonable utterances at the meeting, but could find no one willing to give it. On November 17, after a tense fortnight, word came from London that three ships, having as a part of their cargoes tea from the East India Company, had sailed for Boston, while other ships had cleared for New York, Philadelphia, and Charleston. The three ships headed for Boston were the "Dartmouth," the "Beaver," and the "Bedford," all of Nantucket. They had carried whale oil to England, and for their return trip had accepted some of the East India Company's tea.

On November 19, the Boston consignees, evidently realizing that they had to deal with a popular uprising against the tea project, petitioned Governor Hutchinson and council to be allowed to turn their persons and the properties committed to their care over to the government for protection. They also asked that provision be made for safely landing and caring for the teas until sold by the petitioners. The Governor did what he could to help the petition along, but the council decided that it was no part of their duties to act as guardians and storekeepers for the East India Company. The selectmen of Boston followed this up by telling the consignees plainly to send the tea back to London, but, in spite of the fact that some of their Tory friends advised them similarly, they still held out,

hoping, with the backing of the Governor, to carry their point.

The Boston Tea Party

The first of the tea ships to arrive at its destination was the "Dartmouth," Captain Hall, owned by the Quaker Captain Rotch, which sailed into the harbor on Sunday, November 28, with 80 whole and 34 half-chests of tea aboard. The "Beaver" and the "Bedford," commanded by Captain Bruce and Captain Coffin, arrived later. By order of Samuel Adams, the Massachusetts patriot, heading a committee from the town, the "Dartmouth" was brought to Griffin's [now Liverpool] Wharf to discharge its other cargo, but was ordered upon no account to attempt to unload any tea. A watch was maintained day and night to see that this order was obeyed. After unloading everything except the tea, the owner, Rotch, was perfectly agreeable to load outbound cargo and take the tea back to London rather than suffer highly unprofitable delay, but was unable to obtain clearance from the customs because the inbound cargo had not been wholly discharged. His application to the Governor for a pass to take the tea back to London was also refused, and the ship was compelled to lie inactive at the wharf. According to the English law the cargo would be subject to seizure and sale by the customs for the unpaid duty at the end of twenty days after entering port. The revenue officers had the right then to take possession, and since they were backed by the naval forces from two sloops of war that were guarding the mouth of the harbor against any attempt of the "Dartmouth" to sail without clearance papers, the Governor had every reason to expect the tea would be landed. The consignees had taken refuge at the Castle and were confidently awaiting this outcome. The last day of grace, before the seizure and landing of the tea would take place, was December 16, 1773. It witnessed the greatest gathering that had ever been known at Old South Church, for all business was suspended, and hundreds of people flocked in from surrounding towns. Indeed, the whole community felt the gravity of the occasion and the immediate need for action. Adams' committee reported to the meeting the failure of negotiations for a clearance, and Rotch was instructed to proceed at once to file a protest with the customs, after which he was directed to renew his application to the Governor for permission to sail the same day with the "Dartmouth" for London.

While Rotch was thus engaged, delegations from other towns reported that their communities had agreed to use no tea. The reports were received with shouts of approval, and a resolution was adopted stating that the use of tea was "improper and pernicious," and that all towns should appoint committees to prevent "this accursed tea" from reaching their communities. Samuel Adams, Thomas Young, and Josiah Quincy made ringing speeches, and at half-past four it was unanimously voted that the tea should not be landed. As the plans for events that were to follow could best be kept from Tory ears by being handled in executive session of the leaders, it was thought inadvisable to adjourn the larger gathering, so the meeting was held open until the outcome of Rotch's application to the Governor should be known. Rotch returned at six o'clock with the news that the Governor had repeated his refusal of a pass, on the entirely justifiable ground that his duty as representative of the royal government made this impossible. The meeting adjourned, and darkness fell upon the throngs of patriots who milled about the streets and the vicinity of Griffin's Wharf. "Who knows," cryptically remarked John Rowe, a prominent merchant and selectman of Boston, as the meeting broke up, "how tea will mix with salt water?" And whether or not the remark was a preconcerted signal, it was answered by war whoops from a party of men in the garb of Mohawk Indians, who appeared from the direction of the Green Dragon, and proceeded with businesslike directness to Griffin's Wharf. Their number has been variously estimated from twenty to ninety, all armed with hatchets or axes.

Swiftly they boarded the ship, and warning the revenue officers and crew to keep out of the way, brought the tea on deck, and there broke open each chest and emptied it into the harbor. A contemporaneous account of this stirring tea episode in the *Massachusetts Gazette*, December 23, 1773, concludes as follows:

Having cleared this ship, they proceeded to Captain Bruce's, and then to Captain Coffin's brig. They applied themselves so dexterously to the destruction of this commodity, that in the space of three hours they broke up three hundred and forty-two chests, which was the whole number in these vessels, and discharged their contents into the dock. When the tide rose it floated the broken chests and the tea insomuch that the surface of the water was filled therewith a considerable way from the south part of the town to Dorchester Neck, and lodged on the shores.

The wharf where the tea was destroyed is now marked by a commemorative tablet, reading:

HERE FORMERLY STOOD
GRIFFIN'S WHARF
at which lay moored on Dec. 16, 1773, three British ships with cargoes of tea. To defeat King George's trivial but tyrannical tax of three-pence a pound about ninety citizens of Boston partly disguised as Indians, boarded the ships, threw the cargoes, three hundred and forty-two chests in all, into the sea, and made the world ring with the patriotic exploit of the

BOSTON TEA PARTY

No! ne'er was mingled such a draught
In palace, hall, or arbor,
As freemen brewed and tyrants quaffed
That night in Boston Harbor![8]

In England there were some who sympathized with their kinsmen across the sea, and some protested against their "dastardly impertinence." Coercive measures were at once brought forward in Parliament, and the passage of bills closing the port of Boston and changing the charter of the Massachusetts colony to make the council appointive by the Governor, instead of elective by the people, was soon followed by the war which ended in the establishment of the American republic.

Meanwhile, accounts of the events at Boston were carried to New York, Philadelphia, and the colonies to the south, where the news was received with ringing of bells and great enthusiasm. The younger men, especially, were alive to the controversy at issue, and were ready for any action that would prevent tea bearing the hated tax from coming among them. The opportunity soon came most unexpectedly to Greenwich, a small community on a tributary of the Delaware River, in Cumberland County of southern New Jersey.

The Greenwich Tea Party

At this time Greenwich was the largest and most prosperous town in New Jersey.

---

[8] The quotation in verse is from Oliver Wendell Holmes' "Ballad of the Boston Tea Party."

THE BOSTON TEA PARTY OF DECEMBER 16, 1773

This conception of the historic event, by a modern artist, for Chase and Sanborn, Boston, was made from an old print by W. L. Greene in the Boston Public Library. By permission.

Located on the Cohansey River, it enjoyed water communication with Boston, New York, and Philadelphia, while ships from more distant ports were often seen at its dock loading the products of field and forest. Thither most unexpectedly, on December 12, 1773, came the brig "Greyhound," Captain J. Allen, bearing some of the tea. It had been destined originally for Philadelphia, but it is likely that the captain was warned by the Delaware pilots against attempting to land his cargo in Philadelphia. At all events, he slipped up the Cohansey and unloaded the tea with the utmost secrecy at Greenwich, where it was stored in the cellar of a house on Market Square, the home of Dan Bowers, a loyal subject of King George. The whole transaction was carried out very quietly, but it was soon discovered, and it required only the confirmatory news that came in a few days from the patriot leaders at Philadelphia to inspire the Greenwich Tea Party.

A general meeting of the inhabitants of Cumberland County was held at Bridgetown, but the report of the committee was too conservative to meet the approval of the younger men, who took matters into their own hands. That night horseback riders were dashing about the countryside and a group of young patriots, burning with zeal and intent on the speedy destruction of the tea, was soon mobilized. These young men were from Fairfield, Bridgetown, and Greenwich, and proceeded with a speed suggesting prearrangement to a rendezvous where they disguised themselves as Indians. Citizens of the quiet Jersey village hurried to their doors on that night, December 22, 1773, as shrill war whoops sounded and a lurid glow lit the low-lying clouds. The hated tea, together with the chests that contained it, was burning in the middle of Market Square, and none there were who dared to stay the weird figures in paint and feathers who burned it.

Suit in trespass was begun by the owners against some of the "Indians," whose make-up was not proof against identification, but various adjournments finally brought the cases to the end of royal authority in New Jersey. Efforts to have a Continental grand jury find true bills, later on, were equally unsuccessful, as successive grand juries refused to indict.[9]

_____

[9] Frank D. Andrews, *The Tea Burners of Cumberland County*, Vineland, N.J., 1908, pp. 12–13.

A monument erected on the spot commemorates the stirring event and lists as proudly remembered patriots those ancestors of present-day Cumberland County families whose acts found full justification in the ultimate success of the colonial cause.

The Charleston Tea Party

In South Carolina the colonists were not less active in resisting the tea tax. When the ship "London" arrived at Charleston early in December, having on board a consignment of the East India Company's tea, two meetings of the inhabitants were called and it was determined, "that tea ought not to be landed, received, or vended in this colony; that no teas ought to be imported by any person whatever while the act imposing the unconstitutional duty remains unrepealed." The consignees, upon learning the temper of the community, agreed that they would not accept the consignment nor pay the duty on the tea.

Anonymous letters were sent to the captain of the "London" containing threats that the ship would be burned if any attempt was made to land the tea, and these letters so alarmed him that he laid them before the lieutenant governor. The collector of customs also petitioned for protection, as, under the law, he would be obliged to seize the teas for unpaid duty at the end of twenty days. The council convened on December 31, 1773, and directed that the sheriff and peace officers take such steps as might be necessary to preserve the peace when the collector should seize the tea. At the expiration of the period, no one having come forward to pay the duty, the consignment was duly seized, and, whether by design or otherwise, was stored in damp vaults under the Exchange, where it quickly spoiled.[10] Some teas arriving later were similarly seized and stored, but on the 3d of November, 1774, seven more chests having arrived on the ship "Britannia Ball," the inhabitants of Charleston decided it was their turn to hold a "tea party." A great crowd, carrying effigies of Lord North and the king, gathered on shore. The owners, fearful lest the ship and her entire cargo might be burned, hurried aboard with the consignees, and having

chopped the chests open with hatchets, quickly dumped their contents overboard.

A somewhat similar demonstration took place soon afterwards at Georgetown, S.C. In neither the Charleston nor the Georgetown "parties" was there any disguise, or need for any, as the principals themselves joined in the destruction of the tea.

The Philadelphia Tea Party

Philadelphia, the principal American seaport in 1773, as well as the leader in population and political activity, was prompt to pick up the gauntlet flung down by the directors of the East India Company when they undertook to "cram British tea down the throats of the American colonists."

As already told, on the 18th of October, 1773, a huge public meeting was held on the State House grounds at which it was determined to resist to the utmost any attempt to land such teas. This was followed on December 1 by printed notices in the Philadelphia papers stating that the ship with tea intended for Philadelphia had sailed from London on September 27. As it was then hourly expected, the papers exhorted their readers to "be wise—be virtuous." Even before these notices appeared, however, a self-constituted "Committee for Tarring and Feathering" had issued handbills to the Delaware pilots, which read: "*Do your duty* if perchance you should meet with the [tea] ship 'Polly,' Captain Ayres."

On November 27 there were others reading: "Much is expected from those Lads who meet the tea ship—There is some talk of a HANDSOME REWARD FOR THE PILOT WHO GIVES THE FIRST GOOD ACCOUNT OF HER—How that may be, we cannot, for certain, determine: But all agree that TAR and FEATHERS will be his portion who pilots her into this Harbour." This second handbill also bore a warning, addressed to Captain Ayres, which stated in no uncertain terms that unless he stopped short in his dangerous errand and returned to the place whence he came, he would be publicly tarred and feathered and his ship burned.

At the same time demands were made upon the consignees to refuse the shipment. The Messrs. Wharton complied promptly, but the firm of James & Drinkwater took a little more time about it, although this

10 Edward M'Crady, *The History of South Carolina under the Royal Government*, New York, 1899.

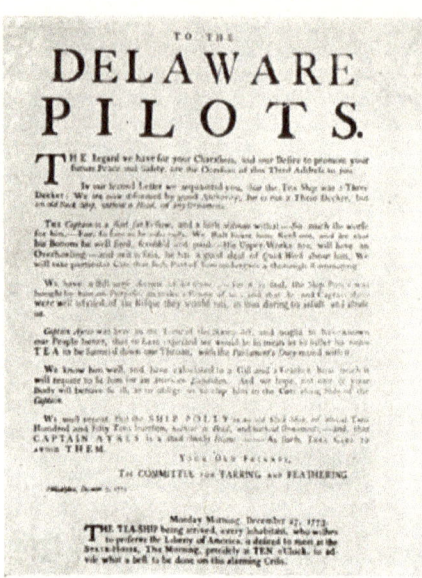

PHILADELPHIA TEA PARTY HANDBILL, 1773

This was the call to Philadelphia's Tea Party by the "Committee for Tarring and Feathering."

was probably due to no lack of patriotism, as they had united with their fellow citizens in protesting against the Stamp Act and had signed the non-importation agreement. A reply not being forthcoming from the latter firm, the following notice was sent them on December 2:

The public present their Compliments to Messieurs James and Drinkwater. We are informed that you have this day received your commission to enslave your native Country: And, as your frivolous Plea of having received no Advice, relative to the scandalous Part you were to act in the Tea Scheme, can no longer serve your purpose, nor divert our Attention, we expect and desire you will immediately inform the Public, by a Line or two to be left at the COFFEE HOUSE, whether you will, or will not, renounce all Pretentions to execute that Commission?—THAT WE MAY GOVERN OURSELVES ACCORDINGLY.

To the crowd accompanying the messenger who bore this communication Abel James, head of the firm of James & Drinkwater, gave the guaranty of his word and property that the tea should not be landed, but should go back in the ship that brought it.

On Christmas day, word reached Philadelphia that the long-expected tea ship had entered the bay and was proceeding toward the city. A committee intercepted her at Gloucester Point on December 26, and, after acquainting Captain Ayres with the resolution passed at the general meeting, requested that he anchor his ship where she lay, and accompany the committee to learn for himself the temper of the people. The captain accompanied the committee to the city, arriving there in the evening, and saw, among other things, the prominently displayed posters for his tarring and feathering.

The greatest crowd ever collected in the town up to that time besieged the doors of the State House on the following morning, and because of the impossibility of getting all the people inside, the meeting was adjourned to the Square outside. Then, with a directness and singleness of purpose that must have made a deep impression on the captain of the "Polly," the following resolutions were adopted:

Resolved that the tea on board the ship "Polly," Captain Ayres, shall not be landed.

2. That Captain Ayres shall neither enter, nor report his vessel at the Custom House.

3. That Captain Ayres shall carry back the tea immediately.

4. That Captain Ayres shall immediately send a pilot on board his vessel with orders to take charge of her, and to proceed to Reedy Island next high water.

5. That the Captain shall be allowed to stay in town till tomorrow, to provide necessaries for his voyage.

6. That he shall then be obliged to leave town and proceed to his vessel, and make the best of his way out of our river and bay.

7. That a committee of gentlemen be appointed to see these resolutions carried into execution.

Speakers then informed the crowd of the spirited action of their fellow colonists at Boston, and resolutions were adopted returning hearty thanks to the people of that city "for the determination they had exhibited in destroying the tea rather than suffer it to be landed."

Captain Ayres, who was present, pledged his word that the public wishes should be carried out in every respect, and on the next day returned to his ship and headed about for the long voyage back to London with the tea.[11]

The New York Tea Party

The ship "Nancy," Captain Lockyear, started from London with a cargo of tea

[11] F. M. Etting, *The Philadelphia Tea Party of 1773*, Philadelphia, 1873.

To the Public.

THE long expected TEA SHIP arrived last night at Sandy-Hook, but the pilot would not bring up the Captain till the sense of the city was known. The committee were immediately informed of her arrival, and that the Captain solicits for liberty to come up to provide necessaries for his return. The ship to remain at Sandy-Hook. The committee conceiving it to be the sense of the city that he should have such liberty, signified it to the Gentleman who is to supply him with provisions, and other necessaries. Advice of this was immediately dispatched to the Captain; and whenever he comes up, care will be taken that he does not enter at the custom-house, and that no time be lost in dispatching him.

New-York, April 19. 1774.

NEW YORK HANDBILL OF 1774

Announcing the first ship to arrive at Sandy Hook with contraband tea; signalizing New York's Tea Party.

bound for New York on September 27, 1773, at the same time the other tea ships sailed for Boston, Philadelphia, and Charleston, but stress of weather drove her far off her course to the island of Antigua, in the British West Indies. She finally appeared off Sandy Hook on April 18, 1774. This was the first opportunity given New York to second the action of her sister colonies.

Announcement that the tea ships had arrived in Boston had reached New York on December 15, and a meeting of the Sons of Liberty was held on the evening of December 16, at the same time the patriots at Boston were breaking open the tea chests and dumping their contents into the harbor. It was resolved not to permit the New York tea ship to enter port, and a Vigilance Committee was appointed to enforce the resolution.

Upon arrival of the "Nancy" off the port of New York, the pilots refused to take her further than the Hook. There she was taken in charge by a selected detail of fifteen husky Sons of Liberty and her small boats chained and padlocked to avoid desertions of the crew, who were needed to take her back to London. After Captain Lockyear had been told very plainly that he would not be allowed to land his teas,

nor even to take his ship into the harbor, he requested to be allowed to visit the city to obtain supplies for his ship and to consult the consignee, who, as he was informed, had resigned. The request was granted, and he proceeded under guard to the wharf, where he was met by a large number of citizens.

In charge of his custodians Captain Lockyear visited the consignee, Mr. Henry White, who refused the cargo and advised its return to London. Quartered at the Coffee House, the Captain was given every assistance in procuring the supplies needed for the return voyage, but he was not permitted to go near the custom house, nor to communicate with its officials. He was soon convinced that he had brought his tea to the wrong market, and went actively about the business of preparing for departure. On the 21st of April the tea ship committee caused a handbill to be distributed throughout the city. It read:

TO THE PUBLIC

The sense of the city, relative to the landing of the East India Company's tea, being signified to Captain Lockyear by the committee, nevertheless, it is the desire of a number of citizens, that at his departure from hence, he shall see with his own eyes, their detestation of the measures pursued by the Ministry and the India Company to enslave this country. This will be declared by the convention of the people at his departure from this city, which will be on next Saturday morning at 9 o'clock; when, no doubt, every friend to this country will attend. The bells will give notice about an hour before he embarks from Murray's Wharf.

BY ORDER OF THE COMMITTEE

FRAUNCE'S TAVERN, NEW YORK, 1854

THE TONTINE COFFEE HOUSE, NEW YORK, ABOUT 1772

Reproduction from a painting by Francis Guy, 1796, in the possession of the New York Historical Society. The Tontine Coffee House is at the extreme left; the Merchants Coffee House at the extreme right.

On April 22, 1774, while Captain Lockyear was still in the city, the ship "London," Captain Chambers, arrived off the Hook, and word having reached the Vigilance Committee that she had tea concealed in a general cargo, the pilots, acting under instructions from the committee, refused to take her into the harbor. Captain Chambers protested, denying to the pilots and the "Sons" who visited the ship that he had tea aboard. In support of his denials he produced his manifest and cockets which showed no tea. Accordingly, the ship was allowed to proceed to her wharf, but about four in the afternoon the entire body of the Vigilance Committee, being still unconvinced, went aboard with the announced intention of yanking out the entire cargo and opening every package, if necessary, to find the tea that they believed to be concealed there. Captain Chambers, seeing that further concealment was useless, acknowledged he had eighteen chests of tea aboard belonging to himself, and gave up the cocket for it. Thereupon, the committee, the captain, and the owners retired to Fraunce's Tavern for deliberation, leaving a great crowd of people at the wharf. While the conferees were still considering the best disposal of the business the crowd on the dock took matters into their own hands, breaking out the tea chests and throwing the contents overboard. There was much popular indignation against Captain Chambers for his attempted duplicity, with some talk of violence against his person, but he was not to be found, having slipped off to the "Nancy" under cover of darkness.

At eight the next morning, Saturday, April 23, 1774, all the bells in New York and its vicinity were rung, and by nine the greatest throng ever gathered together in the town up to that time was milling about the Tontine Coffee House. Then, with the band playing and the crowd cheering, the doors of the Coffee House opened, and Captain Lockyear, bowing his acknowledgment, came out on the balcony attended by a deputation from the Sons of Liberty. He thanked the citizens and the Sons of Liberty for the consideration shown him throughout the unfortunate circumstances in which he had found himself involved, and was escorted to Murray's Wharf at the foot of Wall Street, where cannon were fired and the band played the English national air in a final burst of the mutual

BURNING OF THE "PEGGY STEWART," 1774

Fired by the hand of its owner, this scene marked the culmination of the Annapolis Tea Party.

good feeling which marked the departure of Captain Lockyear from the city.

He sailed for England the next day, taking with him Captain Chambers, of the "London," as well as the entire consignment of tea with which he had started out some seven months before.

The Annapolis Tea Party

It was on October 14, 1774, that the brig "Peggy Stewart," owned by Mr. Anthony Stewart, a Scottish merchant of Annapolis, approached that city, having on board 2000 pounds of the anathematized British tea. Citizens of the entire countryside immediately assembled and listened to popular leaders in heated denunciation of the tea tax. Finally, amidst much cheering, it was resolved that the tea should not be permitted to land, the meeting adjourning till the 19th, when the ultimate fate of the cargo was to be determined.

At the meeting on October 19, the assemblage was greatly incensed upon learning that the owner, Mr. Anthony Stewart, had already defeated their principal pur-

pose by paying the duty on the tea. The feeling was so intense that preparations for lynching Stewart were being made, when that gentleman, accompanied by the consignees, appeared in alarm before the assemblage to present most abject apologies, and offering, if desired, to bring the tea ashore and publicly burn it. The crowd was not in a forgiving mood, however, and when Dr. Charles Warfield of Anne Arundel County came marching up the street at the head of the patriotic Whig Club they fell in line with his suggestions to punish the offender. They erected a gallows immediately in front of Stewart's house by way of intimidation, and gave him his choice either to swing by the halter or go with them on board and put fire to his own vessel. He chose the latter, and in a few moments the whole cargo with the ship's tackle appeared in flames. Shortly after this Mr. Stewart left the country.

A commemorative tablet now marks the building which stands on the spot where, on that eventful October day in 1774, the "Peggy Stewart" was burned by her owner. A mural painting on the west wall of the corridor of the Criminal Court in the Court House at Baltimore graphically depicts the event.

The Edenton Tea Party

Less militant, but not less patriotic, was the action of the women of Edenton, an important town in North Carolina at that time. On October 25, 1774, just six days after the burning of the "Peggy Stewart," fifty-one women drew up a paper commending the resolutions passed a short time before by colonial deputies at New Bern in condemnation of the unjust tax on tea, and then, boldly signing their names to the document, sent it to a London paper for publication. The correspondence as it appeared in *The Morning Chronicle & London Advertiser* of January 16, 1775, created a sensation in England, where many of the signers had social and family connections. It read:

Extract of a letter from North Carolina, Oct. 27.

The provincial deputies of North Carolina, having resolved not to drink any more tea, nor wear any more British cloth, &c. many ladies of this province have determined to give a memorable proof of their patriotism, and have accordingly entered into the following honourable and spirited association. I send it to you to shew your fair countrywomen, how zealously and faithfully American ladies follow the laudable example of their husbands, and what opposition your matchless ministers may expect to receive from a people, thus firmly united against them.

"Edenton, North Carolina, Oct. 25.

"As we cannot be indifferent on any occasion that appears nearly to affect the peace and happiness of our country, and as it has been thought necessary, for the public good, to enter into several resolves by a meeting of members deputed from the whole Province, it is a duty which we owe, not only to our near and dear connections, who have concurred in them, but to ourselves, who are essentially interested in their welfare, to do everything as far as lies on our power, to testify our sincere adherence to the same; and we do therefore accordingly subscribe this paper, as a witness of our fixed intention and solemn determination to do so."

Then followed the names of the fifty-one signers.

Dr. Richard Dillard, formerly a member of the North Carolina Historical Commission, has written an excellent account of the Edenton tea episode. His interesting brochure relates in part that:

The society of Edenton at this period was charming in its refinement and culture. . . . Its galaxy of distinguished patriots, both men and women, would shine resplendent in any country and any age. The tea-party then, as now, was one of the most fashionable modes of entertaining. The English were essentially a tea-drinking

THE PATRIOTIC LADIES OF EDENTON, 1774

Signing the declaration which pledged them to substitute raspberry leaves for Bohea and boycott British stuffs

nation, and consequently tea became the most universal drink of the colonies. . . . The feeling of ease and comfort inspired by an elegant cup of tea, as well as the exhilaration of the mental faculties which it produces, made it a necessary assistant to break the stiffness of those old-fashioned parties.

The incidents connected with this particular tea-party are especially interesting, as they come to us through the blue mist of a century. We can easily imagine how they sat around in their low-necked, short-waisted gowns, and after they had gossiped sufficiently, it was resolved that those who could spin, ought to be employed that way, and those who could not should reel. When the time arrived for drinking tea, Bohea and Hyperion were provided, and every one of the ladies judiciously rejected the poisonous Bohea, and unanimously and to their very great honor, preferred the balsamic Hyperion, which was nothing more than the dried leaves of the raspberry vine, a drink, in the writer's opinion, more vile even than the much vaunted Yupon.[12]

An old mezzotint printed upon glass shows the declaration spread on the table before the ladies. It states that they would drink no tea, nor wear any stuffs of British manufacture. The printer's name is said to be the same as the one who printed the celebrated letters of Junius in the reign of George III. The origin of the picture is not known.

In the rotunda of the State Capitol at Raleigh, the North Carolina Daughters of the American Revolution have placed a bronze tablet commemorating the passage of the resolutions by the women of Edenton, and on the site of the house where their tea party was held there has been placed a Revolutionary cannon surmounted by an heroic bronze teapot bearing the inscription: "On this spot stood the residence of Mrs. Elizabeth King, in which the ladies of Edenton met Oct. 25, 1774, to protest against the tax on tea."

A Non-Tea-Drinking Nation Is Born

While the American colonists were registering, through their tea parties, their determination to resist enforcement of the tea tax, the home government was taking an equally determined stand that its measures against America must be enforced.

Thus was the issue joined, and presently, amid the boom of cannon and the roar of musketry, a great republic was born—one that was soon to become the wealthiest consumer-nation in the world, but with a prenatal disinclination for tea.

[12] Richard Dillard, A.M., M.D., The Historic Tea-Party of Edenton, 6th ed., Edenton, 1925.

A VIEW OF THE EAST INDIA HOUSE, LEADENHALL STREET, LONDON, ABOUT 1826

From a drawing by T. H. Shepherd.

CHAPTER VI

THE WORLD'S GREATEST TEA MONOPOLY

WHILE it is often said that the English East India Company owed its birth to pepper, its amazing development was due to tea. Its early adventures in the Far East brought it to China whose tea was destined later to furnish the means of governing India.

During the hey-day of its prosperity John Company, otherwise the "Honourable East India Company," maintained a monopoly of the tea trade with China, controlled the supply, limited the quantity imported into England, and thus fixed the price. It constituted not only the world's greatest tea monopoly but also the source of inspiration for the first English propaganda in behalf of a beverage. It was so powerful that it precipitated a dietetic revolution in England, changing the British people from a nation of potential coffee drinkers to a nation of tea drinkers, and all within the space of a few years. It was a formidable rival of states and empires, with power to acquire territory, coin money, command fortresses and troops, form alliances, make war or peace, and exercise both civil and criminal jurisdiction.

The English East India Company was chartered in the closing days of the year

Old Dutch Print of India House, 1648.

1600. In 1601, Captain James Lancaster made his famous voyage in the company's behalf and established a factory at Bantam in Java. The Dutch had preceded the English in the Indies by four years, although the Dutch East India Company was not chartered until 1602.

There were sixteen rival East India companies of Dutch, French, Danish, Austrian, Swedish, Spanish, and Prussian origin, operating at various times from the continent of Europe, but none of them reached the position of commanding importance occupied by the English East India Company.

During the sixteenth century Portugal was the only European country that carried on a regular trade with the East Indies. It was a Crown monopoly. In 1602, the Dutch, having driven the Portuguese out of the principal Indian settlements, organized their trade under the banner of the Dutch East India Co. The French had six companies operating in the Indies at various periods between 1604 and 1790, while two Danish companies sought to get some of the wealth for Denmark—one in 1612 and the other in 1670. Two Scottish East India Companies were formed; one in 1617, the other in 1695.

The Ostend Company, Austrian, made

up of factors from the Dutch and English East India companies, began operations in 1723, but became inactive for seven years beginning in 1727, and was forced into bankruptcy in 1784. In 1731, during the inactivity of the Ostend Company, Henry Koning of Stockholm gathered a number of its servants into a Swedish East India Company that subsisted mainly by smuggling tea into England. In 1784, however, Parliament made a sweeping reduction in the tax on tea, and the company promptly expired.

A Spanish Royal Company of the Philippine Islands operated in defiance of the Treaty of Munster [1648] from 1733 to 1808 with varying fortunes. There were Prussian, Asiatic, and Bengal companies in 1750–1804 and 1755–56, respectively. An Austrian East Indian company, known as the Imperial Company of Trieste for the Commerce of Asia, was founded by William Botts, "a discontented servant" of the English East India Company in 1775–1781, but the Botts speculative genius proved its undoing in 1785.[1]

Beginnings of John Company

At the start, the trade with the East was in the hands of the Levant Company, which made huge profits out of the trade with India by way of the overland route through Asia Minor, and when the sea route to the East by way of the Cape of Good Hope had been opened certain members of the Levant Company were first to see its advantages.

Accordingly, in 1599 a number of members of the Company met and discussed the possibilities of developing the sea route to the East, for the Portuguese and Dutch were by then obtaining such a firm foothold that unless something was done immediately it was felt that the opportunity would never return. A petition to Queen Elizabeth was presented, but it was not approved until the last day of 1600, when these gentlemen were given a monopoly of the Indian trade for fifteen years. This in itself was valuable, but still more valuable was an exemption from export duties for the first four voyages, and permission to take out coin of the realm, which ordinarily was prohibited. The Company started with a practical monopoly of all the wealth

[1] Sir Geo. C. M. Birdwood, *Reports on the Old Records of the India Office,* London, 1891, pp. 31, 32.

to be found by trade or discovery between Cape Horn in the Western Hemisphere and the Cape of Good Hope in the Eastern Hemisphere. Its charter conferred the sole right of trading with the East Indies. Unauthorized interlopers were liable to forfeiture of ships and cargoes.

The Early Fleets

The first East India fleet to sail left England in the early summer of 1601, the flagship being the Earl of Cumberland's "Red Dragon," originally the "Mare Scourge," and specially designed for privateering work against Spain. The other ships of the fleet were the "Hector," "Ascension," and "Susan," with a victualer named the "Guest." James Lancaster was admiral of the expedition, but the individual captains had a good deal of authority in their own hands. The enterprise does not appear to have had any other object than the importation of spices and for this reason did not make for the mainland of India, but went to the Netherlands Indies, where they were received in very friendly fashion in spite of an embargo the Dutch authorities had laid on the traders of any flag other than their own. Not only did the English fleet collect cargo in Sumatra, but they captured more from the Portuguese, and, after coming near to losing the whole of the venture by perils of the sea, the promoters pocketed some 90 per cent profit on their capital and expenses.

Toward the end of the seventeenth century, in order to raise money for the Crown, a new East India Company was established. For a time the two companies threatened to ruin each other; but eventually they composed their differences and amalgamated.

The first East Indiaman penetrated as far as Canton in the spring of 1637, but tea does not appear to have appealed to these pioneers in the least, and, although Englishmen in China and Japan were drinking it as early as 1615, none was brought home. The East Indiamen of this day were slightly but not greatly superior to the average merchant ship of the time. In the matter of size they were not very imposing, the great majority being of 499 tons burden. The reason for this was the law that ships of 500 tons or over must carry a chaplain. The Court of Directors, while willing to pay their servants gen-

British Museum

THE FOREIGN FACTORIES AT CANTON, 1760, BY A CHINESE ARTIST

erously and to find rich jobs for themselves and their relatives, saw no reason to let any more money go out of the family than was absolutely necessary.

The first direct consignment of tea was rather less than a hundredweight, but it soon became popular and huge quantities were carried by the East Indiamen. These ships carried only the better quality of tea; although, when one reads the conditions of their voyages and compares them with the care taken nowadays, it leaves some doubt as to just what "best quality" meant. The Dutch and Ostenders were importing large quantities of the cheaper kinds, and a goodly proportion of their imports was immediately smuggled across to England and sold at very much less than the East India Company's prices. At the same time, the officers and men of the ships were very prone to smuggling, and at a rather later date it was a standing order of the revenue service that as soon as an East Indiaman dropped her anchor in the Downs every available cutter or boat was to be told off to watch her and prevent her officers and men landing the tea that they had bought as a private venture in the East.

China Added to the Monopoly

Although the East India Company had traded with China since the early days of the eighteenth century, the charter was completely revised in 1773 and it was given the monopoly of the British trade with China as well as with India. This extension of the regular run was of considerable indirect advantage, for the Company had not the docking facilities in the East that it had at Bombay, and the longer run forced it to build bigger and better ships. Both the building and the running were, however, exceedingly wasteful, and it has been estimated that it made only about two-thirds the profits it might easily have done with a little careful management.

Voyages to India were long enough, but to China they were needlessly protracted. Not only was no effort made to drive the ships as they might have been, but they were kept in Chinese waters for a long time waiting for cargoes. So long was the delay that it was customary to unrig the ships completely and refit them when they were due to sail again.

All this time the East India Company had been nothing more than a corporation of individual merchants, just as it was when founded by Queen Elizabeth. Every merchant had his own ax to grind and his own profits to make, with the Court of Directors maintaining a certain discipline. The company never owned its own ships, but for many years they were supplied by individual directors, who were known as ships' husbands. The company took them up for so many voyages, generally six, at an agreed freight, and then made them conform to its regulations.

Gradually this privilege of chartering ships for the company got out of the hands of the directors themselves, but every effort was made to keep it a close corporation, and it was very difficult indeed for an unknown man to get his ships accepted.

The Captain's Profits

Very often the ship's husband, after having his tender accepted, would sell the privilege to his captain; sometimes for as

Macpherson Collection

TYPICAL EAST INDIAMEN OF THE EIGHTEENTH CENTURY

much as £10,000. With the freight money, the generous pay and allowances, and the permission of the East India Company to trade in certain commodities privately and to carry fifty tons outward and twenty tons homeward, that officer was able to make a large sum every voyage. Also the captain frequently let his quarters to passengers, with the result that £10,000 profit to himself on a single voyage was not an unknown return. When this custom had gone on for some time, the command of Indiamen became almost hereditary, and, until the court of directors stepped in and demanded a certain amount of sea time and experience, men who had never been to sea before and were scarcely out of their teens took the command of ships.

The fare to India varied, principally according to the rank of the passenger in the company's service; for there were few travelers who did not wear its uniform. A high official would pay anything up to £250, while a young subaltern just gazetted would find that his voyage out cost him barely £100. Food and wine were liberally supplied, but, curiously enough, the company refused to fit out the cabins, and the first thing to be done after booking a passage was to purchase the necessary furniture from the riverside firms that specialized in its construction; the ship's captain or his officers generally buying this furniture for a song at the end of the voyage and selling at a big profit to homecoming travelers.

Tea Smuggling

So troublesome was the smuggling of tea in the seventeenth century that acts were passed to prohibit its being imported into England from any other part of Europe; later these had to be modified by the provision of licenses whenever the East India Company's supply fell short of the demand, an occurrence that was constantly happening. In spite of this, however, the Company carried more tea away from China than anybody else, the figures in 1766 being 6,000,000 pounds carried by it, 4,500,000 by the Dutch, and no other company nearer than 3,000,000.

The Company began to get into low water in the middle of the eighteenth century, and in 1772 had to beg the Government to remit the contributions it owed, and at the same time lend it £1,000,000. These boons were granted, but at the same time the authorities passed the India Acts, by which more economical management was enforced. Soon afterward the East India Company was granted the privilege of placing its tea in bond and paying the duty when it was taken out. This made a considerable difference to the trade, for it allowed the sales to be distributed much more evenly throughout the year; though at this time it was estimated that only one-third of the tea drunk in Great Britain paid duty, all the rest being smuggled.

End of the Indian Monopoly

In 1813, the British Parliament passed an act which gave the Government a hand in the company's commercial as well as administrative activities, and at the same time put an end to its monopoly to India. The monopoly to China, however, which consisted principally of the tea trade, was allowed to continue for another twenty years, being finally abolished in 1833, when the ships of the company's fleet were rapidly dispersed.

One or two of the ships' husbands under the East India Company soon established themselves as independent shipowners trading to India and the East. By far the best-known and most successful of these were George Green, Money Wigram, Henry Loftus Wigram, and Joseph Somes. All the ships owned by these firms, however, were the lineal descendants of the old East Indiamen, heavy frigate-built ships with no great pretensions to speed, but of solid comfort and of very fair carrying capacity. It was the Americans who made all the difference in the trade. The advent of the American clipper was in 1832. The British followed in 1846.[2]

Tea Notes From the Company's Records

The first reference to tea—as "chaw"—in the East India Company's records is the famous Wickham letter of 1615, to which reference is sometimes made as "the earliest mention of tea by an Englishman."

It is to be found in a set of old records entitled *Japan Miscellanies,* consisting of copies of letters from Richard Wickham, the company's factor at Firando (Hirado). Birdwood tells us that Wickham went out first to the Indies as a factor in the "Union" on the fourth voyage, 1608. At Zanzibar he was captured by the natives and handed over to the Portuguese who carried him to Goa where he met the traveler Françoise Pyard. In 1610, Wickham, with other European captives, was sent to Portugal, whence he made his way back to England in time to offer his services for the eighth voyage. Captain John Saris

[2] Frank C. Bowen, "John Co. and the Clippers," *Tea & Coffee Trade Journal,* New York, 1926, vol. 51, no. 4, p. 483 ff.

THE SALOON OF AN EAST INDIAMAN, AFTER A CARICATURE BY CRUIKSHANK

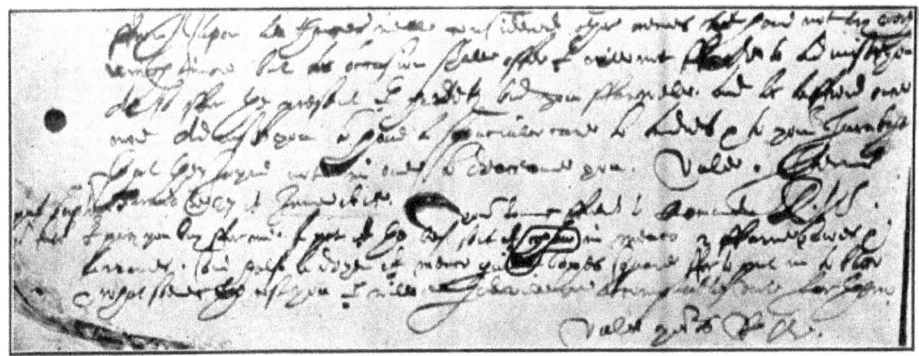

FIRST REFERENCE TO TEA BY AN ENGLISHMAN—R. WICKHAM, 1615

The reference appears as "chaw" (ringed) in the postscript and was probably the earliest pidgin-English for the Chinese "ch'a." The complete text of the now obsolete English employed by the writer appears on this page.

left him with Richard Cocks at the Firando factory. His letter book during a portion of his service there, 1614–16, is still preserved among the India Office records. Wickham left Japan in 1618 for Bantam, later going to Jacatra where he died.[3]

In his letter of June 27, 1615, to Mr. Eaton, the company's agent at Macao, Wickham wrote:

Mr. Eaton I pray you buy for me a pot of the best sort of chaw in Meaco, 2 Fairebowes and Arrowes, some half a dozen of Meaco guilt boxes square for to put in to bark (barque) and whatsoever they cost you I will be alsoe willinge accumptable unto for them.

Vale, Yors R. W.

The Old East India Company

The title of the first East India Company was, "The Governor and Company of Merchants of London trading into the East Indies." The corporation was empowered to make by-laws, to export all kinds of goods free of duty, to export foreign coin or bullion, to inflict punishments, impose fines, with many other privileges of great pecuniary benefit.

In the beginning, tea could only be procured from China. It was a very precious thing; a "treasure of the world" which appeared occasionally among the lists of gifts to sovereigns, to princes, and the nobility. The English appear to have been slow to appreciate its commercial aspects. While the Dutch were busy promoting its introduction and sale on the Continent, and were selling it to London coffee-house keep-

ers who retailed it at sixteen to fifty shillings [$4.00 to $10.00] a pound, the agents of the English East India Company were singularly neglectful of their opportunities to provide direct importations. There were, of course, good reasons for their tardiness as explained elsewhere; the principal one being Dutch supremacy in the Far East. And so it is in 1664, nearly fifty years after Mr. Wickham's famous personal request for a pot of "chaw," before we find any reference to tea in the Company's records and then it is only to note the purchase of some 2 lbs. 2 oz. of "good thea" by the Court of Directors from Thomas Winter for presentation to His Majesty in order that he might "not find himself wholly neglected by the Company." Several authorities aver that Charles II promptly transferred the gift to his Queen Consort, Catherine of Braganza, who was an ardent devotee of tea.

In 1666, among several "raretyes" provided by the secretary for His Majesty, 22¾ lbs. of thea were purchased at 50s. a pound and "for the two cheefe persons that attended His Majesty, thea @ £6.15s." There are other entries about this period which show purchases of tea from London coffee-house keepers for the use of the Court of Committees.

Meanwhile, it appears that the Company's servants occasionally reported to their masters upon the custom of the Chinese in partaking of an infusion of an aromatic plant called "tay," but these masters, being more obsessed with the idea of trading the orientals English cloth in exchange for sleeve and sewing silks, failed

[3] Sir Geo. C. M. Birdwood and Sir William Foster, The First Letter Book of the East India Company, 1600–1619, London, 1893, p. 399.

utterly to envision a future when tea would dominate all other trading on the Royal Exchange. It was 1668 before the Company's first order for importing tea reached the agent at Bantam. It instructed him "to send home 100 lb. waight of the best tey that you can get."

The first importation followed in 1669, when two canisters weighing 143 lbs. 8 oz. arrived from Bantam. This was followed in 1670 by four pots weighing 79 lbs. 6 oz. Of these two shipments 132 lbs. were found to be damaged and sold at the company's sales for 3s. 2d. per pound. The Court of Committees consumed the remainder.

Thereafter tea was imported year by year—with the exception of the years 1673-77—from Bantam, from Surat, from Ganjam, and from Madras, until 1689, in which year there is the first record of an importation from Amoy. One of the importations, 266 lbs. from Bantam, is recorded as having been "part of the present from Tywan [Formosa]," but in general the Company's factors bought at Bantam from Chinese junks trading there, and at Surat from the Portuguese ships trading from Macao to Goa and Daman. Nearer than this they could not get in reaching out for the China trade.[4]

The British presidency at Bantam sent a ship to establish a factory at Amoy in 1676. In 1678, the company imported 4717 lbs. of tea from Bantam which effectively glutted the market for several years, but in 1681 we find the directors instructing their agent at Bantam "to send home annually Tea to the value of 1000 Dollars." Three years later the English were driven out of Java. It was then that the directors placed a standing order with their agent at Madras for "five or six canisters yearly of the best and freshest tea." Thus it took nearly fifty years for the English East India Company to follow the example set by the directors of the Dutch East India Company in 1637 in ordering regular tea importations. During the decade ending in 1686 tea appears to have been selling in the London market from 11s. 6d. to 12s. 4d. per lb.

In 1686, the Company's Directors instructed its agent at Surat that teas in the future should form a part of the company's imports and not be articles of private trade. In 1687, the Court desired "that very good thea might be putt up in tintinague potts,[5] and well and closely packed in chests or boxes, as it will always turn to accompt here, now it is made the Company's commodity; whereas, before there were so many sellers of that commodity, that it would hardly yield half its cost, and some trash thea from Bantam was forct to be thrown away or sold for 4d. or 6d. per lb."

When the Company's ship "Princess" reached London from Amoy in 1689 the Court complained because tea was a drug on the market "except it be superfine, and comes in potts, tubs, or chests." That same year, there were imported from Amoy and Madras some 25,300 lbs. Again, the 1690 records show that various individuals and the Company imported 41,471 lbs. of tea from Surat, while because of the heavy duty laid upon tea the Company prohibited any but the finest kinds to be sent for their account.

Four years later, "the London dame who affected a passion for tea," says Beckles Willson, "was forced to patronize, albeit indirectly, the Dutch merchants"; but in 1699 we find the Company ordering "300 tubs of fine green teas and 80 tubs of Bohea, having both become in great request at the home sales." The orders for packing were most particular, to prevent the leaf from acquiring odor from the tutenague pots in which it was enclosed. Again, in 1701, the Company's instructions to its supercargoes were most explicit as to packing and stowage. By 1702, the demand had increased to such an extent that the Company's instructions were to send a ship's cargo of tea, to be two-thirds Singlo, one-sixth Imperial, and one-sixth Bohea.

A Frankenstein of Commerce

The close of the seventeenth century witnessed a number of subsidiary companies all in a mad scramble for a share in the lucrative trade of the Far East. Having created in the East India Company a Frankenstein of commerce, the Government found itself hard put to devise ways

---

[4] Hosea Ballou Morse, *The Chronicles of the East India Company Trading to China 1635–1834*, Cambridge and Oxford, 1926, p. 9. By permission.

[5] Tutenague (tintinague), a white alloy resembling German silver.

and means to make the monster give an accounting of its stewardship. The first hundred years had been marked by a series of duties cunningly devised to replenish the royal coffers by exacting adequate customs returns for the extraordinary privileges accorded the gentlemen adventurers trading with the Orient. These duties, representing part of the price which the Occident was to pay for its tea, continued to annoy and irritate English traders and English tea drinkers for over two and a half centuries before they were abolished in 1929, only to be reimposed three years later.

At the start, semi-private adventurers frequently realized larger profits than the parent corporation. The outcome was several

Trade Mark East India		*of the First Company*
	c 1600	

companies or corporations operating under special privileges, these in turn being harassed by private adventurers. In 1698, the interlopers set up a new East India Company which was approved by Parliament. An ultimate settlement was brought about by a consolidation, in 1708, of the different interests in "The United Company of Merchants of England trading to the East Indies."

Before this event the old company, in addition to its troubles at home, found itself beset with many vexations in its dealings with "the subtile Chinese," as Mr. Robert Douglas, chief supercargo of the "Macclesfield," so feelingly referred to them from Canton in 1700. Then there were costly clashes with Malay pirates, envious Dutch, French, and Portuguese rivals operating in the Indies, to say nothing of what the company had to suffer from the cupidity of its own servants who were ever keen to feather their own nests, which, indeed, they were privileged to do, until the privilege became abused. Consequently it required the first hundred years to consolidate the company's monopoly in trading to the Indies. It appears from the records that, in spite of the smugglers, adulterations, and internecine strife, the Government collected over £77,000,000 on tea alone between the years 1711 and 1810; a sum which exceeded the

national debt of England in 1756. The duties ranged from 12½ to 200 per cent.

During the reign of Charles II the company grew greatly in stature; successive new charters investing it with far-reaching powers. Besides other privileges it had the right to acquire territory, coin money, command fortresses and troops, form alliances, make war, conclude peace, and exercise criminal and civil jurisdiction. With the establishment, in the closing years of the seventeenth century, of the presidencies of Bengal, Madras, and Bombay in India the East India Company became a ruling as well as a trading power.

Modifications were afterwards made in the Company's constitution, designed to place it under more immediate Government control, but its great powers continued. Even as late as 1814, when privileges were granted to private traders, these were compelled to send their goods to India in vessels belonging to the Company and the same system was compulsory on the Indian merchant shipping goods to England. Its tea monopoly was most effective. Richard Bannister, Deputy Principal of the Inland Revenue Laboratory, in a lecture before the Society of Arts, London, May 12, 1890, declared that, in the later years of the Company's monopoly the British consumer had to pay nearly £2,000,000 sterling a year more on the quantity cleared for consumption than if the same quantity and qualities of tea had been bought in the open markets of the Continent.

The effect of the monopoly was observable on distributor and consumer. The Government restrictions imposed on the Company tended to increase prices, and the absence of competition enabled the Company to extort at its sales such high prices that tea could only reach the consumer at a cost, which, except to the well-to-do, was almost prohibitive. Again, because of the Government's regulations, the tea sold by the Company could not reach the consumer until it had been packed over twelve months. Indeed, at one time it is said tea was being kept on an average of seventeen months before it was put into consumption. This was not so hard on the China teas as on the teas of India, which, in the beginning, were not so well fired as the China teas. Furthermore, since the Company's monopoly enabled it to control the supply of tea, it was always to its interest to put a short supply on the market to obtain better prices at the sales. Bannister says:

Private enterprise, if allowed, would soon have remedied such a state of things, and healthy competition would have killed the monopoly. But this was not allowed, and, consequently prices were charged which had not only to cover the large profit put on the tea, but also to make amends for reckless expenditure in China and at home through the absence of commercial rivalry. Such a corporation had to work through servants; individuality was to a great extent lost ... by the red tape system of a corporation mostly governed by men of small commercial experience of any kind, and of quite as little knowledge of the requirements of their Company; men apt to resent any overture of a novel kind, however good, desiring only to pursue the high and dry methods of business which had been in vogue for centuries, but which were already quite out of date when applied to modern commerce.

Extravagance in administration, and consequent high prices of goods sold under this monopoly, led to an examination of the business of the Company, with a view of seeing whether the extravagance of working did not eat up the profits on the sales, or rather what was charged over and above the continental importers' prices. This inquiry brought out the following curious result:

	£
Profits realized by the Company in three years ending 1828	2,542,569
Average [per year]	847,523
Excess of price received for the Company's teas over the price of such teas sold at New York and Hamburg [per year]	1,500,000

There was, therefore, an absolute loss, through the monopoly, of £652,477 a year, in addition to the odium attached to a system which diminished trade, choked competition, and increased the cost of the necessaries of life. When the time came for the renewal of the charter these facts were not forgotten, and Acts 3 and 4, William IV., c. 85, abolished the monopoly, made it lawful for all persons to import tea, and thus gave power to those who wished to open up a trade with China.[6]

China Trade of Three Centuries

The British made several attempts to reach China after 1596, when Queen Elizabeth wrote a letter to the Chinese Emperor which was not delivered. British trade in the Orient was commenced by the East India Company with the opening of agencies at Taiwan [Formosa] in 1625, and at Amoy toward the close of the Ming Dynasty in 1644. An attempted opening of trade with Canton, by way of Macao,

in 1627, was frustrated by the Portuguese.

In 1635, the East India Company negotiated a treaty with the Portuguese Governor of Goa, and the "London," Captain Weddell, was admitted to the harbor of Macao. Owing to misrepresentations by the Portuguese, the English ships were fired on at the Bogue Forts which were silenced by the "London," and the Viceroy of Canton granted permission to trade, in July, 1635. The oldest record of trade in the East India Company's archives at Canton is dated April 6, 1637. Trade languished owing to the Portuguese influence until the treaty of Oliver Cromwell with King John IV of Portugal, in 1654, gave ships of both countries free access to any port in the East Indies.

In 1664, the Company secured a house in Macao and, from 1678, began direct and regular trade to China. In 1684, a site on the river side at Canton was obtained with permission to erect a factory, provided all their traders and trading operations were strictly confined within its area. This grant was probably the commencement of the European factories at Canton. The following year, in 1685, the agency at Amoy was reopened and, in 1702, a trading post was established on the island of Chusan; but it was not until 1715 that ships reached Whampoa, the Canton anchorage, for trade.

In 1760, the East India Company sent a special mission to the Viceroy of Canton protesting against the co-hong system of trade and asking for the release of their agent, Mr. Flint, who had been captured at Amoy in 1759. The mission failed to have any effect, for the agent was kept in confinement until 1762, but, with bribes, the trade continued, and in 1771 the Company succeeded in purchasing permission to reside at Canton during the business season. After the season the business agents of the various companies established in separate factories allotted to the several nationalities were annually compelled to return to Macao, or to go home. The ships arrived towards the end of the southwest monsoon—from April to September—and left during the northeast monsoon—from October to March. In 1771, the co-hong system was abolished, and replaced, in 1782, by the hong merchants who were given the monopoly of foreign trade, and were made responsible for the safe conduct of all foreigners.

[6] Richard Bannister, "Cantor Lecture on Tea" *Journal of the Society of Arts*, London, 1890, vol. xxxviii, no. 1980, p. 1023.

THE EAST INDIA COMPANY'S OWN SHIP "WATERLOO" AT THE WHAMPOA ANCHORAGE, 1817

The view is from Dane's Island looking towards Canton. The "Waterloo" is flying the Company's ensign. From a print lent by the Parker Gallery, Berkeley Square, London. Painted by W. J. Huggins; engraved by E. Duncan.

The East India Company protected its monopoly for nearly two centuries; no British subject was allowed to land at Canton without its permission, nor any British ships to trade, except under license. But private traders of other nationalities defied the Company; Portuguese from Macao, Spaniards from Manila, and Dutch from Formosa had preceded the Company, and could not be dislodged. Danish and Swedish merchants, 1732, French, 1736, Americans, 1784, and others forced their way in, and Chinese policy protected them against interference. Also, some British merchants frustrated the Company by taking out foreign naturalization papers.

The earliest pioneer of British free trade was the founder of Jardine, Matheson & Co., Mr. William Jardine, who lived in China between 1820 and 1839. Next in influence came Mr. W. S. Davidson, from 1807 to 1822; Mr. R. Inglis of Dent & Co., 1823 to 1829; the brothers Matheson, from 1826 to 1850. The Mathesons started the *Canton Register* in 1827 to disseminate the principles of free trade and to oppose a prolongation of the Company's monopoly, and, during the three or four years before the expiration of the charter, on April 22, 1834, the Company's officers had relaxed their rules and free trade had practically begun.

In 1831, Chinese authorities imposed on the foreign merchants at Canton such severe restrictions that the East India Company threatened to suspend all commercial intercourse. They finally weakened, though, and actually handed the keys of the British factory to an official in token of submission. An indignation meeting was held in Canton on May 30, to remonstrate against the policy of the company. It was attended by the little band of free traders, the Jardines, Mathesons, Dents, Gibbs, Turners, Hollidays, Braines, etc.

Although the influence of the Company was waning, the foreign community refused to submit to the caprices of the Chinese authorities. The free traders went actively about the establishment of a China trade of their own, which included large-scale importation of opium from India into China. Restriction placed on opium ships was evaded by establishing hulks outside the Bogue Forts at Lintin for the storage of opium and goods. The closing of the monopoly of the Company was fixed for the year 1834, and the Chinese Government, believing war to be imminent, issued an Imperial Edict, in 1832, ordering all maritime provinces to build forts and prepare ships of war to scour the seas and drive off any European vessels of war that might make their appearance on the coast. An order also was issued forbidding foreign ships to remain at Lintin.[7]

Among the principal articles of export in British trade from Canton during the year 1834, tea was first with 32,000,000 lbs. Evidence given by witnesses before the Committee of the House of Commons, appointed in 1847 to enquire into the commercial relations with China, contains much information with regard to the British tea trade. The recommendation of the committee was, that the duty of 2s. 2¼d. per pound, being 164 per cent on the average cost of 1s. 4d. per pound, should be reduced; most witnesses suggested that the duty should be 1s. per pound. Mr. R. M. Martin in his report on tea, July, 1845, printed in the Committee's proceedings, says: "It is more than probable that tea has now reached the limit of consumption in England and that any reduction in tax-

[7] James Orange, *The Chater Collection*, London, 1924, p. 38 ff.

ation . . . would not augment the use of this innutritious leaf." The import into England in 1846 was about 56,500,000 lbs.; in 1929 it was 560,720,000 lbs., or ten times the 1846 total.

Tea and America

The East India Company ordered its tea put "in chests and not in tubs as usual," in its instructions to the "Loyal Blisse," loading at Canton for the season of 1713. Sixty years later the Boston Indians were to find chests much easier to handle than tubs or pots.

By 1718, tea had begun to displace silk as the main staple of the China trade and in 1721, Fate began to set the stage for the drama in the West. Under the ministry of Sir Robert Walpole the import duty on tea was removed and an excise tax on withdrawals from bond replaced it.

This change of policy was followed by orders prohibiting the importation of tea from all parts of Europe, thus making the East India Company's monopoly complete; so by 1725 we find that tea had become such a sacrosanct thing in England under the aegis of the East India

Chater Collection

THE CANTON FACTORIES, 1833, BY A CHINESE ARTIST

Company's benevolent assimilation, that its adulteration was made punishable by seizure and a fine of £100. Still further punishment was added in 1730–31; owners of tea sophistications were fined £10 per pound and in 1766 the penalty was increased to include imprisonment.

In 1739, tea led in value all other cargo items brought by the ships of the Dutch East India Company to Holland. Smuggling to England and America was on the increase, for the English East India Company's monopoly was inviting the inevitable interference from outsiders. Ten years later, London was made a free port for tea in transit to Ireland and America.

By the middle of the eighteenth century, the American colonies had begun to suffer from growing pains. Most of the dispassionate twentieth century historians agree that the Revolutionary War might just as well be charged up to Big Business, represented on the one hand by the East India Company's tea monopoly and on the other by British and Colonial tea merchants. It might have been free molasses or free rum that started it, but, as a matter of fact, it was tea.

Two years before the passage of the Stamp Act, Boston merchants had already united in a club to oppose any attempts to make the tax on molasses effective. As John Adams said later, "molasses was an essential ingredient in American independence." Tea was another.

In 1765, the Stamp Act, the first measure of the oncoming madness, was passed by Parliament, causing an immediate outburst of protest and resistance from the American colonists led by Patrick Henry of Virginia. They were, then, just Englishmen making the usual fuss about being taxed. James Otis said they shouldn't be taxed without the consent of their own assemblies.

In the trade of Canton, tea had by this time assumed a position of prime importance. Incidentally, the tea shipments of the rival continental East India companies far exceeded those of the English company. The reason was obvious; most of these shipments were being smuggled into England and America; the high duties offering every incentive to "free trade."

Here it is interesting to note that the American colonists in the eighteenth century were as great consumers of tea as were the Australians in the succeeding centuries; however, they were beginning to prefer the cheaper smuggled tea to that which reached them, duty paid, from the London tea sales.

The obnoxious Stamp Act was repealed in 1766, too late for any moral effect in America, where the Dutch were scooping in all the trade in sight. There followed in 1767 the ill-fated Townshend duties and their repeal in 1770—all except the 3d. per pound on tea—and then the stage was completely set for the act of supreme folly.

In dire financial straits and with a surplus of 17,000,000 lbs. of tea on its hands, the East India Company, in 1773, complained to Parliament that the colonial tea business was being absorbed by the Dutch because the colonists would no longer buy the duty-paid English article. They suggested the time had come for England to throw overboard the rights of British export merchants and colonial importers in order that the great East India Company might be saved. Their solution was that they be allowed to export tea on their own account to America, free of the duty which other British export merchants had to pay, and then to sell it through their own agents in America upon payment of the small American duty, which the colonial merchant was refusing to pay as a matter of principle. By this ingenious method two middlemen's services and profits would be abolished, the Dutch interlopers would be confounded, the smuggling of tea would stop, and the colonist would obtain his tea more cheaply than the home consumer in England.

Parliament sanctioned the scheme and the die was cast. There was probably as much indignation among the British export merchants as among the colonial importers. In the case of the latter, however, this act of favoritism was the one thing needed to turn the scales in favor of the colonial politicians who had lately found the merchant class rather cold to their revolutionary appeals. The most promising business of the new world was being attacked. The colonial merchant was a free thinking and free trading individual to whom anything smacking of monopoly was anathema. His livelihood was being taken from him by a most unholy alliance between the government he had always trusted and the world's greatest monopoly. To arms, to arms!

The Boston Tea Party and the War of American Independence followed. The "people" of England had little to do with it. The original cause, as wittily diagnosed by the late Dean Alvord, University of Michigan, was *flapperitis exuberans*.[8] The immediate cause was the attempt to perpetuate a tea monopoly distasteful alike to British and American merchants. Thus England lost an empire to oblige the East India Company.

The Goliath's Fall

As was to have been expected, the East India Company survived the War of American Independence, muddled through its financial difficulties, and, by means of much helpful legislation from the State designed to kill off adulterations and defeat smuggling, emerged from its second century more powerful than ever.

The Commutation Act of 1784 repealed the existing duties, amounting to about 119 per cent and substituted therefor a duty of 12½ per cent computed on the sale prices obtained at the East India Company's quarterly tea sales. These were hedged around with certain restrictions, "that the company might take no advantage of the real monopoly of tea which this act would throw into their hands," but, notwithstanding this supposed protection, a general revolt against the high-handed methods of the Company by the thirty thousand wholesale and retail tea dealers of London followed. Their spokesman before the Company's directors was Richard Twining.

Pamphlets and meetings of general protest were the means employed to rouse public opinion against the company toward the close of the century. Again it was the British people warring against special privilege. The agitation was designed to force the Government to serve upon the Company the three year's notice required by law in the event of a proposed termination of its monopoly. Although it failed of its purpose at this time, the way was prepared for another attack in 1812. The directors relied upon "the wisdom of Parliament and the good sense of the nation in general," to resist these "rash and violent innovations upon the

EAST INDIA CO.'s TEA CATALOGUE OF 1786

system of the Company." They further contended that open "competition would be ruinous to the public interest; the cost of teas would be enhanced."

The American tea merchants of 1773 had established a dangerous precedent for dealing with monopolies, however, for the War of American Independence had been fought and won by rallying public opinion around a free trade ideal. Now another war with this young country was about to break. The English tea merchants were only too ready to aid and abet the Americans in bringing fresh disaster to the East India Company. They viewed the war of 1812 as a blessing. John Company stood at bay. When the Earl of Buckinghamshire gave them an evasive answer they protested against a "tide of prejudice and popular clamor being permitted to determine public counsels," but their truculent attitude could not avert the blow. In 1813, as noted earlier in this chapter, the Company's monopoly to India was ended, though the China monopoly was permitted to go on for another twenty years.

Following the Company's refusal to consider seriously the cultivation of tea in India, because it was fearful of the effect upon its only remaining monopoly, the China trade, came the discovery of indigenous tea in Assam in 1823. Ten years

---

[8] Clarence Walworth Alvord, "Lord Shelburne and the American Revolution," *The Landmark*, New York, 1927. vol. ix, p. 79 ff.

later, the Company again faced the same jealous outcry against a continuance of its special privilege, and in 1834 it was forced to yield to the agitation for the complete abolition of its trading monopoly. Indeed, the tea of China had furnished the means of governing India; or perhaps it would be fairer to say the export of tea and the import of opium, for the East India Company originally organized and financed the cultivation, shipment, and distribution of opium to China. As is recognized, it was largely the opium traffic that caused the wars between China and Great Britain in 1840 and 1855.

The profits which had accrued to "a handful of adventurers from an island in the Atlantic" as Macaulay described the Company in the House, had made possible "the subjugation of a vast country divided from the place of their birth by half the globe." Wherefore, they were permitted to continue its administrative functions in India until the India mutiny caused the transfer of the Indian administration to the Crown, August 2, 1858.

Thus ended, after 258 years of glorious adventures, the greatest of all monopolies. However, there are those who believe that this great capitalist trading organization is being repeated in the Russian Soviet government of to-day.

Undoubtedly, the attitude of the Company toward the American colonist was, in large measure, responsible for its ultimate undoing. After all, the colonists were Englishmen and the great mass of their fellow countrymen at home sympathized with their aspirations. Certainly, while they might have been more or less indifferent to the Company's dream of empire, they were very much concerned when they were asked to pay for it in the form of taxes.

John Company at Home

"At Mr. Thomas Smythe's house in Philpot Lane"—such was the first address of John Company. Here, at the city mansion of its first governor, Sir Thomas Smythe, in several modest rooms, was started the business that was to shape the destinies of empires. After twenty-one years it removed to Crosby House in Bishopsgate Street. From here, seventeen years later, in 1638, it moved to Sir Christopher Clitherow's house in Leadenhall

COAT OF ARMS OF THE OLD COMPANY

Street. A third and final move into Lord Craven's house next door was made in 1648. This property was purchased in 1710, and the company made extensions of the premises, later acquiring several adjoining houses.

After surviving the plague, the Great Fire, and the Weavers' Riots, the Company met its first real opposition in 1698 with the incorporation of a rival, the "English Company Trading to the East Indies" with which it merged in 1708 as the "United Company of Merchants of England Trading to the East Indies." The picturesque coat-of-arms of the old Company showing the Tudor roses, the Royal arms, three ships sailing an azure sea, supported by blue sea lions, the crest being a terrestrial globe with the punning motto *Deus indicat*, was succeeded by the United Company's arms, the crest of which was irreverently nicknamed the "cat and cheese." This coat of arms continued to be used until 1858.

Three views of Craven House, at different periods, have come down to us. One, known as the Dutch view because of the Dutch caption, is preserved in the Grace Collection at the British Museum. It is an etching "from a painting in the possession of Mr. Pulham of India House, twelve inches by eight." James Brook Pulham, friend and fellow clerk of

Charles Lamb, was an amateur etcher of some ability.

Another drawing of the Craven House by George Vertue is preserved in the London Museum. A third representation, the Overley view, as printed in the *Gentleman's Magazine* of December, 1784, is from a representation on the shop bill of William Overley, a joiner who is shown in the small shop in the front of the house. It furnished the description by Macaulay: "An edifice of timber and plaster, rich with the quaint carving and lattice work of the Elizabethan age. Above the windows was a painting which represented a fleet of merchantmen tossing on the waves. The whole was surmounted by a colossal wooden seaman, who from between two dolphins looked down on the crowds of Leadenhall Street."

Other views show the premises after their reconstruction, from plans by Theodore Jacobsen, Esq., in 1726–29, and in 1796–99 from plans by Richard Jupp, the company's surveyor. This third and last building became one of the show places of London. Foster thus describes it:

The new façade was about 200 feet in length and 60 feet high. Its style was classical, with an Ionic portico of six fluted columns. The tym-

India Office

THE OVERLEY VIEW OF INDIA HOUSE

panum of the pediment was filled with a group of figures designed by John Bacon, representing George III, in Roman costume, defending the commerce of the East. The composition of this excited some criticism, and not without reason; for the King was represented as holding his sword in his left hand in a decidedly unwarlike manner, while the appearance in the background of the City barge was scarcely appropriate. On the apex of the pediment Britannia sat in state upon a lion, bearing in her left hand a spear surmounted by a cap of liberty; while above the two corners of the pediment were figures of Europe on a horse and Asia on a camel. The rest of the façade was severely plain, with a double row of windows and a projecting cornice crowned by a parapet. On the iron railings in front were fixed half a dozen standards for lamps.

Previous to the rebuilding, the sales had been held in the General Court Room, and of the scene on such occasions the accompanying illustration, which is reproduced from Ackermann's *Microcosm of London*, 1808, gives an excellent idea. The view is taken from the top of the amphitheatre which filled the eastern end of the apartment. This is occupied by bidders and spectators, while on the other side of the barrier which crosses the floor are seated the presiding Director, two officials in little wooden pulpits noting the bids, and a number of clerks who are entering up bargains or writing out contract notes. Among the latter, by the way, the artist may have noticed a swarthy, Jewish-looking little man who

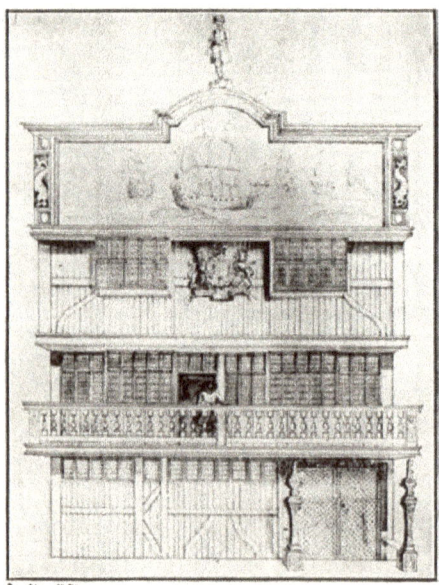

India Office

VIEW OF INDIA HOUSE BY GEORGE VERTUE

AN AUCTION IN THE SALE ROOM AT THE EAST INDIA HOUSE IN 1808

From an aquatint by Stadler, engraved by Rowlandson & Pugin.

answered to the name of Lamb, and who found the duty of attending sales a tiresome one.[9]

A new sale room was provided in the remodeled Jupp building and the old one became the assembly room of the Court of Proprietors, or General Court, which elected the Court of Directors.

For a colorful description of the scene at one of the Company's periodical sales we turn to Charles Knight's *London*. He says:

Those of Tea were the most extensive, and they are yet remembered with a sort of dread by all who had anything to do with them. They were held only four times a year—in March, June, September, and December; and the quantity disposed of at each sale was in consequence very large, amounting on many recent occasions to 8½ millions of pounds, and sometimes much higher: they lasted several days, and it is within our recollection that 1,200,000 lbs. have been sold in one day. The only buyers were the tea brokers, composed of about thirty firms: each broker was attended by the tea dealers who engaged his services, and who communicated their wishes by nods and winks. In order to facilitate the sale of such large quantities, it was the practice to put up all the teas of one quality before proceeding to those of another, and to permit each bidder to proceed without much interruption so long as he confined his biddings to the variation of a farthing, for what was technically called the upper and under lot; but as soon as he began to waver, or that it appeared safe to advance another farthing, the uproar became quite frightful to one unaccustomed to it. It often amounted to a howling and yelling which might have put to shame an O.P. row, and, although thick walls intervened, it frequently was heard by the frequenters of Leadenhall Market. All this uproar, which would induce a stranger to anticipate a dreadful onslaught, was usually quelled by the finger of the chairman pointing to the next buyer, whose biddings would be allowed to go on with comparative quietness, but was sure to be succeeded by a repetition of the same noise as at first.[10]

Richard Jupp died before the building, reconstructed from his plans, was completed. Henry Holland succeeded him and when he died his successor was Samuel Pepys Cockerell, a collateral descendant of the famous diarist. Cockerell resigned in 1824, and William Wilkins became surveyor. Several additions were made by these in the same style as Jupp's façade. The finished aspect as of 1826 is shown in the T. H. Shepherd drawing.

One of its later attractions to visitors

India Office

AN EAST INDIA COMPANY OFFICER SALUTING

This was the uniform of the R. E. I. Volunteers.

was a library and museum known as the Oriental Repository, begun in 1801, which developed into a notable collection of orientalia subsequently removed to the India Office and from thence to the Victoria and Albert Museum.

In 1858, the East India House became the India Office. When new quarters were found for this department of the Government at Westminster, in 1861, the old East India House was demolished. An office building now occupies the site.

From *Old and New London* we learn that in "the old times" John Company employed nearly four thousand men in its warehouses, and, before the trade with India closed, kept more than four hundred clerks to transact the business of this greatest tea company that the world has ever seen. The military department superintended the recruiting and storing of the Indian army. There was a shipping department, a master-attendant's office, an auditor's office, an examiner's office, an accountant's office, a transfer office, and a treasury. The buying office governed the fourteen warehouses, and so worked the home market, having often in store some fifty million pounds weight of tea; 1,200,000 lbs. being sometimes sold in one

---

[9] Sir William Foster, *The East India House*, London, 1924, p. 139-41. By permission.
[10] Charles Knight, *London*, 1843, vol. v, p. 59.

THE EAST INDIA COMPANY'S HOUSE AFTER ITS RECONSTRUCTION IN 1726–29

Showing the Company's second building, which replaced the original Elizabethan structure. After plans by Theodore Jacobsen, Esq.

THE THIRD AND LAST BUILDING, RECONSTRUCTED AFTER PLANS OF RICHARD JUPP IN 1796–99

TRANSFORMATION OF JOHN COMPANY'S HOME IN LEADENHALL STREET

day, at the annual tea sales. "The tea and indigo sales were bear-garden scenes." Foster says:

An interesting example of the conservatism of the Company is the fact that, from the very beginning right down to 1858, the Directors' letters were subscribed 'Your loving friends.' Sir George Birdwood once quoted this as a proof of the excellent relations that subsisted between the Company and its servants; but I fear that, when it closed, as it often did, a letter of stinging rebuke, it was regarded by the recipients as nothing more than a conventional formula.

Distinguished Servants of the Company

Like the leaders of many successful commercial enterprises, the success achieved by the directors of the East India Company was due to their ability to surround themselves with people cleverer than themselves.

Many of those whose names are written high on the rolls of England's great were numbered among the servants of John Company. Aside from the generals and the captains who served the Company in Java, India, China, and other stations overseas, the Company drew to itself at home many brilliant minds from the intelligentsia of the age. To mention only a few of these, there were: John Hoole, 1727-1803, the dramatist and translator, accountant and auditor for the East India Company; James Cobb, 1756-1813, also a dramatist and contemporary of Hoole; Charles Lamb, 1775-1834, poet, essayist, humorist, and critic, author of the *Essays of Elia*, who was for the greater part of his life a clerk in the office of the East India Company; James Mill, 1773-1836, the journalist, metaphysician, historian, and political economist, of the Company's examiners department; his son, John Stuart Mill, 1806-1873, the philosopher and author of *Political Economy*; Thomas Love Peacock, 1785-1866, satirical poet and novelist; and a score of lesser known but still distinguished men of letters and clerics.

For those who would dip deeper into the lore of the East India Company, recourse should be had to the works of Sir William Foster, historiographer to the India Office for over fifty years; to the *Chronicles* of Dr. H. B. Morse; and to Beckles Willson's, *Ledger and Sword*.

In its valedictory of 1858, written by John Stuart Mill, the East India Company solemnly reminded the nation that the foundations of the British Empire in the East "were laid by your petitioners at that time neither aided nor controlled by Parliament, at the same period at which a succession of administrations under the control of Parliament were losing to the Crown of Great Britain another great empire on the opposite side of the Atlantic."

This was eloquent and forceful but none the less futile. There was pathos in it, too, for it seemed to be calling upon posterity to witness that John Company must not be blamed for the loss of that Western Empire, and even if it were, not to forget that Britain's magnificent Empire of the East had been acquired for her by John Company at its own expense and that for a century of time the Indian possessions had been governed and defended from the resources of those possessions without the smallest cost to the British Exchequer.

John Company was "a corporation of men with long heads and deep purposes." Macaulay told Parliament in 1833 that it was a mistake to suppose that the Company was merely a commercial body till the middle of the eighteenth century. Commerce was its object, but, like its Dutch and French rivals, it was invested with political functions as well. It was at first a great trader and a petty prince, then it became a great Nabob, sovereign of all India.

John Company's honor roll included the names of many merchants having the sentiments and abilities of great statesmen. "The East India Company has left its mark on the world," said Sir Alfred Lyall in 1890. "It accomplished a work such as in the whole history of the human race no other trading company ever attempted and such as none surely is likely to attempt in the years to come," said the *Times* in 1873.

THE MEN OF JOHN COMPANY

Men who prepared ambrosial Sangaree,
And double Sangaree or Sangarorum:
Now took a fleet, now sold a pound of tea,
Weighed soap, stormed forts, held princes in terrorem,
Drank, fought, smoked, lied, went home and, good papas,
Gave diamonds to their little boys for taws.
    THEODORE DOUGLAS DUNN in *Poets of John Company*.

THE FAMOUS TEA RACE BETWEEN THE CLIPPER SHIPS "ARIEL" AND "TAEPING" IN 1866

From the painting by J. Spurling. By permission of the publisher and owner of the copyright, the Blue Peter Publishing Co, Ltd, London.

CHAPTER VII

GOLDEN AGE OF THE CLIPPER SHIPS

AS THE tea trade grew in importance, after the abolition of the monopoly of the East India Company, merchants began to demand more rapid transit for each new season's teas. The slow and stately East Indiamen were becoming obsolete. These frigate-built ships were jocularly known as "tea waggons."

In America a type of schooner had evolved from the swift privateers produced in Baltimore for the War of 1812, and these became known as Baltimore clippers. Sometimes they were rigged as hermaphrodite brigs, but they never carried more than two masts; whereas the sailing vessel which introduced the age of the clipper ships was three-masted.

In 1816, the famous Black Ball Line of square-rigged packet ships appeared on the New York-Liverpool run, carrying passengers, mails, and cargo. Competition increased and with the opening of the Erie Canal in 1825, New York and New England shipbuilders were besieged with orders for fast ships to sail the seven seas.

"Ann McKim," the First Sizable Clipper

In 1832, Isaac McKim, a Baltimore merchant, conceived the idea of building for the China trade a three-masted, full-rigged vessel along the lines of the fast Baltimore clippers. She was built by Kennard and Williamson of Fells Point and named the "Ann McKim," after the own-

er's wife. Being a kind of hobby with him, she was fitted with the most expensive Spanish mahogany hatches and brass fittings, including twelve brass guns. She was 493 tons register, 143 feet long and 31 feet wide. Although she proved to be one of the finest and fastest ships on the China run her carrying capacity was comparatively small for her length and crew requirements, so she failed to make any great impression upon the conservatism of other merchants of the period.

This was not true of two young enterprising marine architects employed in New York shipyards, near the yard where the "Ann McKim" was at one time undergoing repairs. They were John Willis Griffiths and Donald McKay. These lads got from her the inspiration, which was later translated into the extreme clipper ship, that was to bring both of them fame and honor.

Upon the death of Isaac McKim in 1837, the "Ann McKim," forerunner of the real clipper ship, was purchased by Howland and Aspinwall, the pioneer New York tea merchants, who afterwards introduced the "Rainbow," the first of the extreme American clippers. Later, the "Ann McKim" was sold to the Chilean government. She caused a sensation when she was first put into the China trade, despite the complacency and skepticism of maritime circles in the early 'thirties. It was beginning to be realized that tea was a cargo that was best handled quickly, while business travelers were also realiz-

THE "ANN McKIM," THE FIRST SIZABLE AMERICAN CLIPPER, 1832

From a lithograph in the possession of the Maryland Historical Society and reproduced here by permission.

ing that time was money. Accordingly there was every incentive for improving upon the little "Ann McKim" by building the famous "Rainbow," which in turn was followed by a host of other American clippers. The reign of the clipper ship furnishes the most romantic chapter in the history of America's merchant marine.

Evolution of the Extreme Clipper

With the dawning of the new era in naval architecture the blunt, full-bodied ship gave way to a radical departure in design. The "cod's head and mackerel tail" of old tradition evolved into a thing of beauty, grace, and speed. The stem was carried forward in a curve, lengthening the bow above water; the water line was concave before it became convex both at the bow and stern, while the masts shot further skyward, carrying tier upon tier of sail.

In 1841, John Willis Griffiths, 1809–1882, "a grey-eyed, dreamy-browed fellow," was employed as a draughtsman by the shipbuilding firm of Smith & Dimon. It was his genius that revolutionized the science of marine and naval architecture by the introduction of the first extreme clipper ship model. In telling the story in *Some Famous Sailing Ships and Their Builder, Donald McKay,* Richard C. McKay, the author, generously acclaims Griffiths as the designer of the type of clipper

ship which Donald McKay was later to make famous. Says Mr. McKay:

Griffiths created no small sensation in New York shipbuilding circles when he attacked the generally-held theory that it did not matter how roughly a vessel entered the water so long as she left it smoothly behind her—the theory exemplified in the Baltimore clipper's full round bows, practically flat forward floor, and narrow stern. This daring innovator proposed a model of a knife-like concave entrance, melting into an easy run to the midship section, where, instead of forward, he located the extreme breadth of beam. Thence this fullness of breadth melted again into the after end in lines almost as fine as those forward. In place of the codfish underbody he gave his innovation a dead rise amidships.[1]

"Rainbow's" Sensational Performance

Griffiths proposed the clipper ship in 1841 and designed the "Rainbow" in 1843. She was of 750 tons registry and was launched from the Smith & Dimon yards, New York, in 1845. One observer declared her bow had been turned outside in and that "her whole form was contrary to the laws of nature." Opinion was divided as to whether she would float or sink.

However, she exceeded all expectations. Her maiden voyage to China started in February and she was back in New York in September having paid her cost, $45,000,

---

[1] Richard C. McKay, *Some Famous Sailing Ships and Their Builder, Donald McKay,* New York, 1928, G. P. Putnam's Sons. By permission.

A MODEL OF THE "ANN McKIM"

From the original in the Addison Gallery of American Art, Phillips Andover Academy, Andover, Mass.

and her owners, Howland and Aspinwall, an equal sum in profit. On her second voyage she was so fast that she herself brought back to New York the news of her arrival in Canton. She had made the round trip faster than any other ship could sail one way; ninety-two days out and back in eighty-eight. Her commander, Captain John Ladd, called her the fastest ship in the world, and certainly she was one of the smartest. Although she was lost on her fifth voyage her performance had proved the superiority of the clipper type. There was a second "Rainbow" after the Civil War.

Griffiths' second clipper, the "Sea Witch," 890 tons, built for Howland and Aspinwall in 1846, was for three years considered the fastest ship that sailed the seas. She made Hong Kong in 104 days and returned to New York from Canton in eighty-one days. Later, she bettered the Canton-New York run by four days, making 358 miles in one day's run. There was a later ship called the "Sea Witch."

Other Early Clippers

Almost as soon as they had begun to send their ships overseas, Americans had appreciated the value of the China trade, and several New England merchants had made fortunes in it. Their competition was not regarded very seriously by the British, who had such a huge preponderance in numbers, and were backed by a monopoly that appeared to assure them a comfortable profit for all time. After the first China War had been fought, however, and the trade to China greatly increased, American merchants brought out a regular

fleet of clippers and captured such a large proportion of the trade that the British were forced to follow their lines.

Meanwhile, in 1844, A. A. Low & Brother, the New York tea merchants, had contracted with Brown & Bell to build the "Houqua," named in honor of a Cantonese hong merchant.

In 1846, Alexander Hall & Co., of Aberdeen built the clipper schooner "Torrington" for Jardine, Matheson & Co., to compete with the American opium clippers in the Chinese coasting trade. Frank C. Bowen considers the "Torrington" to be the first British clipper schooner, but Arthur H. Clark says the first was the "Scottish Maid," 150 tons, built by Hall & Co., in 1839.[2]

The "Torrington," which was rigged as a two-masted schooner, and differed from the American clipper in many points of construction, succeeded so well that she was soon followed by others in this particular line, and the system of construction spread to the ships that carried tea home to England. The repeal of the Navigation Laws, which limited trade between Great Britain and her colonies to British ships, permitted American ships to carry cargoes of China tea straight to England, and the competition between the two flags became keener than ever.

In 1847, A. A. Low & Brother brought out the "Samuel Russell," 940 tons, built by Brown & Bell. Among other clip-

[2] Frank C. Bowen, "John Co. and the Clippers," Tea & Coffee Trade Journal, New York, 1926, vol. 51, no. 4, p. 489, and Arthur H. Clark, The Clipper Ship Era, New York, 1910, G. P. Putnam's Sons, p. 58.

AMERICAN CLIPPER "RAINBOW," 1845

From a painting by Worden Wood in the possession of the Submarine Signal Co., Boston. By permission.

FIRST BRITISH CLIPPER, "STORNOWAY," 1850

pers built in the United States about this time, mention should be made of the "Architect," 520 tons, built for Nye, Parkin & Co. of China in 1847; and the "Memnon," 1068 tons, built in 1848 for Warren Delano of Boston.

To keep pace with American competition in the China trade, Jardine, Matheson & Co., in 1850, launched the "Stornoway," 506 tons. This, the first extreme clipper-rigged ship in Great Britain, was built by Alexander Hall & Co. of Aberdeen, who also built the clipper schooner "Torrington." Other early British tea clipper ships were the "Chrysolite," built in 1851 by Alexander Hall & Co. for Taylor & Potter of Liverpool; the "Abergeldie," 600 tons, built by Walter Hood & Co., Aberdeen, in 1851; the "Challenger" built by Richard Green of London in 1852; the "Cairngorm," 1250 tons, another Jardine, Matheson ship, built by Hall & Co. in 1853; the "Crest of the Wave," "Norma," "Flying Dragon," "Formosa," "Spirit of the Age," and "Lord of the Isles." The last named was the only tea clipper built of iron at that time. She made a remarkable run of eighty-seven days from Shanghai to London during the northeast monsoon in 1855. Other British cracks of the late 'fifties were the "Lammermuir," "Robin Hood," "Friar Tuck," "Fiery Cross," "Assyrian," "Wynaud," "Chieftain," "Morning Star," and "Warrior Queen."

It is related of the "Challenger," which was owned by W. S. Lindsay of London, that she was built to beat William H. Webb's "Challenge," owned by N. L. & G. Griswold of New York. The two never came to grips, however, although both participated in one of the early tea races, in 1852. The "Challenger" sailed from Shanghai and made the run to Deal in 113 days; while the "Challenge" sailed from Canton, reaching Deal in 105 days. There was another "Challenger," an American-built, California clipper ship of 1853.

The British "Challenger," in 1863, was the first vessel of any nationality to load tea at Hankow. Captain Thomas Macey paid the American tug "Firecracker" £1000 to tow his ship up the Yangtze to Hankow. Although considered a dangerous experiment Captain Macey's enterprise paid, and his example was soon followed by other China captains. Though the chief difficulty was the navigation of the Yangtze, the traders had to keep their armory in readiness for any eventuality. Basil Lubbock declares that two of the missionaries taken up river by the "Challenger" were actually eaten by Chinese cannibals. Captain Macey loaded 1000 tons of tea in June, 1863, at £9 per ton and made the run home in 128 days. [3]

Clipper Fleet of A. A. Low & Brother

A. A. Low & Brother's fleet of American clipper ships, beginning with the "Houqua" in 1844, was remarkable in many ways. It included some sixteen ships, several of which became famous. The "Houqua" made her first voyage to Hong Kong in eighty-four days. She made New York from Hong Kong in ninety days, and in 1850 she did the Shanghai-New York voyage in eighty-eight days. She foundered in a typhoon off the coast of China in 1865.

The "Samuel Russell" was named after the founder of Russell & Co. in China, in which firm Mr. A. A. Low formerly had been a partner. James Banks Taylor, one of Low & Brother's agents in China had

3 Basil Lubbock, *Sail: the Romance of The Clipper Ships*, London, 1927, The Blue Peter Publishing Co., Ltd., p. 89. By permission.

THE TEA CLIPPER, "HOUQUA," 1844
From the original painting in the possession of William Gilman Low, Jr. By permission.

such confidence in her speed that when new crops of tea came on the market he could afford to let others pay the highest price for them, and, three weeks later buy them more cheaply, put them on the "Samuel Russell," and still get them to New York first.

The "N. B. Palmer" was known in China as the "Yacht." Named in honor of the celebrated clipper ship captain, who commanded the "Paul Jones," "Houqua," "Samuel Russell," and "Oriental," she was beaten by the "Flying Cloud" in the San Francisco race of 1852, on top of which the two ships sailed for China and the "N. B. Palmer" won the contest by two weeks. She made the run from Canton to New York in eighty-four days. The "Surprise" was a famous and fast ship, launched in 1851, that made the voyage to San Francisco in ninety-six days, while the "Contest," a fast and beautiful ship, did it in ninety-seven days. She was later captured and burned by the "Alabama" in the Java sea. The "Jacob Bell" also was captured and burned by one of the Confederacy's cruisers, the "Florida."

The "Great Republic," the largest of the Low fleet, was not built for them; but was purchased by the firm and cut down one deck after she had burned at her pier. She was capacious and fast. She was chartered by the French Government as a transport in the Crimean War and, later, by the United States in the Civil War. She made the San Francisco run in ninety-two days.

The "Yokohama" was a barque. A story told concerning her relates that, once when she was loading in Japan, a Scottish vessel named "Caller Ou," loading at the same time, got away two days ahead of Captain Berry. Fearing he'd have hard work overhauling the Scot, beating down the China Sea against the southwest monsoon then blowing, he decided to try the longer way home around Cape Horn. He was favored by fair winds, reached New York, unloaded, took on an outward cargo and set sail. On passing out at Sandy Hook he met the "Caller Ou" coming in, to the profound astonishment of the Scottish Captain.

The "Golden State," built in 1852 by Jacob A. Westervelt, was slightly less in tonnage than the "N. B. Palmer." Her record was ninety days from China. The "David Brown," a handsome ship, built

by Roosevelt & Joyce in 1853, made the San Francisco voyage in ninety-eight days. The "Romance of the Seas" sailed from Boston two days later, but caught up with the "David Brown" off the Brazilian coast. They kept close company, finally passing through the Golden Gate side by side. After discharging their cargoes, they again put out to sea together, this time bound for Hong Kong. While they did not see each other during the forty-five-day trip they anchored in Hong Kong on the same day and less than six minutes apart. The log of the "Romance of the Seas" records that skysails and stunsails were not taken in until Hong Kong was reached.

The "Benefactor," built by Roosevelt & Joyce, was the barque, 100 tons less than the "Houqua," which brought the first cargo of tea from Japan to the United States. The "Maury," a 600-ton clipper barkentine, was named for Lieut. Maury, U.S.N., but renamed the "Benefactress" when Maury showed Southern leanings at the outbreak of the Civil War. In 1856, sailing against the iron-built "Lord of the Isles" from Foochow to London, both carrying new teas with a premium of £1 per ton on the first ship home, the "Maury" reached the Downs the same morning as her rival, which had left Foochow four days ahead of her. They passed Gravesend within ten minutes of each other, but the "Lord of the Isles," having the fastest tug, made her dock first and won the prize. Other ships in the fleet of A. A. Low & Brother were the "Penguin," "Osaca," and "Sunda."[4]

Other New York Clippers

Several other New York firms engaged in the China trade owned their own ships and, sometimes, the cargoes as well. Among these firms should be mentioned Grinnell, Minturn & Co., whose most celebrated ships were the "Flying Cloud," "North Wind," "Sea Serpent," "Sweepstakes," and "Sovereign of the Seas"; Goodhue & Co., who owned the "Mandarin"; Howland and Aspinwall, greatest of the merchant houses, who owned the "Ann McKim," "Natchez," "Rainbow," and "Sea Witch"; N. L. & G. Griswold, who owned the "George Griswold,"

4 William Gilman Low, *A. A. Low & Brother's Fleet of Clipper Ships*, 1922.

THE "ORIENTAL," FIRST AMERICAN SHIP TO CARRY A CARGO OF TEA TO LONDON, IN 1850

From the original painting by Frederic S. Cozzens in the General Office of the Great Northern Railway Co. and reproduced here by permission.

"Helena", "Ariel," "Panama," "Tarolinta," and "Challenge."

The "Challenge," 2006 tons, built in 1851, was the second largest clipper ship; "Trade Wind," built by Jacob Bell, New York, for W. Platt & Son, Philadelphia, exceeding her by 24 tons. The "Challenge" was at first commanded by "Bully" Waterman, whose exploits have furnished much colorful copy for nautical writers and abundant small talk for retired skippers. Known as "the finest and most costly merchant ship in the world," she was lost off the coast of Brazil after many years in the service of N. L. & G. Griswold, of New York.

The "Oriental" Carries Tea to London

The first American ship to carry a cargo of tea from China to London after the repeal of the Navigation Laws was the clipper "Oriental," 1003 tons, built for A. A. Low & Brother of New York by Jacob Bell in 1849. She was 185 feet long, and 36 feet in breadth. Her maiden trip to Hong Kong by the eastern passages consumed 109 days. She returned to New York with a cargo of tea in eighty-one days. On her second voyage she made Hong Kong in eighty-one days. Then she was chartered by Russell & Co. to carry tea to London at £6 per ton of 40 cubic

feet with British ships begging for London cargoes at £3.10s., per ton of 50 cubic feet

The "Oriental" delivered her 1600 tons of tea in London in 1850, being ninety-seven days out of Hong Kong, a feat of speed never before equaled. Her first cost was $70,000; her freight on this one ship-

"STAG HOUND," FIRST EXTREME CLIPPER, 1850

Original painting by Otto Fischer. By permission of the owner, Dr. Geo. M. Sheahan, Quincy, Mass.

ment was $48,000. On her voyage of 367 days from New York through Far Eastern seas to London she had sailed 67,000 miles, logging about 183 miles a day. In *The Clipper Ship Era*, Arthur H. Clark describes the "Oriental":

Every line of her long, black hull indicated power and speed; her tall raking masts and sky-sail yards towered above the spars of the shipping in the docks; her white cotton sails were neatly furled under bunt, quarter, and yardarm gaskets; while her topmast, topgallant, and royal studding-sail booms and long, heavy, lower studding-sail booms, swung in along her rails, gave an idea of the enormous spread of canvas held in reserve for light and moderate leading winds; her blocks, standing and running rigging were neatly fitted to stand great stress and strain, but with no unnecessary top-hamper or weight aloft. On deck everything was for use; the spare spars, scraped bright, and varnished, were neatly lashed along the waterways; the inner side of the bulwarks, the rails, and deckhouses were painted pure white; the hatch combings, sky-lights, pinrails, and companions were of Spanish mahogany; the narrow planks of her clear pine deck, with the gratings and ladders, were scrubbed and holystoned to the whiteness of cream; the brass capstan heads, bells, belaying pins, gang-way stanchions, and brass work about the wheel, binnacle and skylights were of glittering bright-ness. Throughout she was a triumph of the shipwright's and seaman's toil and skill. The ship owners of London were constrained to ad-mit that they had nothing to compare with her in speed, beauty of model, rig, or construction. It is not too much to say that the arrival of this vessel in London with her cargo of tea in this crisis in 1850, aroused almost as much appre-hension and excitement in Great Britain as was created by the memorable Tea Party held in Boston harbor in 1773. The Admiralty obtained permission to take off her lines in dry dock; the *Illustrated London News* published her portrait, and the London *Times* honored her arrival by a leader.[5]

Other California clipper ships that followed in the wake of the "Oriental" to London, causing the English ship owners to lose out almost entirely on the London tea trade in favor of American ships, were the "Surprise," "White Squall," "Sea Serpent," "Nightingale," "Argonaut," and "Challenge." The American clippers were able to command twice the price per ton asked by British ships.

The Famous China Clippers

The competition which followed the repeal of England's navigation laws produced those famous China clippers, which will always live in the romance of the sea. The discovery of gold in California turned

5 Arthur H. Clark, *The Clipper Ship Era*, G. P. Putnam's Sons, 1910, pp. 97-98. By permission.

DONALD McKAY, 1810-1880

"He made the clipper ship famous."

the attention of Americans very largely to their own coasts, only a few of their ships going across the Pacific to China for a tea cargo home, but the British shipping companies built against one another in competition that was just as keen as it had been against the Americans.

The type continued to improve, and the annual race home with the first of the new season's tea, for a prize of a heavy bonus and, as a rule, a very big stake, became an annual event. All through the 'fifties and the 'sixties these ships improved and they became the aristocrats of the ocean, just as the East Indiamen had been in their day. The golden age of the tea clippers spanned a generation, beginning in 1843 and ending with the opening of the Suez Canal in 1869.

The California clipper period reached from 1850 to 1860. Prominent among the first ships turned out for the San Francisco run were the "Celestial," "Mandarin," "Surprise," "Witchcraft," "White Squall," "Stag Hound," and "Flying Cloud." There was a contest of clippers around the Horn in 1850 between the "Houqua," "Sea Witch," "Samuel Russell," "Memnon," all old China clippers, and the newer California clippers "Celes-

AMERICAN TEA CLIPPER, "FLYING CLOUD," 1851, UNDER SKYSAILS AND STUNSAILS

From the painting by J. Spurling. By permission of the publisher and owner of the copyright, The Blue Peter Publishing Co., Ltd., London.

tial," "Mandarin," and "Race Horse." It was won by the "Sea Witch" in a run of ninety-seven days.

Other California clippers were: "Shooting Star," a California clipper ship of 903 tons, built in 1851 by J. O. Curtis, Medford, Massachusetts, for S. G. Reed & Co., Boston; and "Antelope," 1187 tons, built in 1852 by J. Williams & Son, Williamsburg, New York, for Harbeck & Co., New York.

Donald McKay's Ships

The appearance of the "Stag Hound," in 1850, caused a sensation and served to focus attention on Donald McKay, 1810–1880, her designer. "While Donald McKay did not originate the clipper ship," says Richard C. McKay, "he was the man who made it famous. His advance production of a vessel of the extreme clipper class proved a notable contribution to America's prestige as a maritime nation." Shipping men hailed the "Stag Hound" as being pretty near perfection of the clipper ship type. She was 1534 tons, at that time the largest merchant ship ever built. She made the run from Canton to New York in eighty-five days. She was lost by fire off Pernambuco in 1861.

In 1851, Donald McKay's second extreme clipper was launched. This was the "Flying Cloud," 1782 tons. Though built for Enoch Train & Co., Boston, she was sold while yet on the stocks to Grinnell, Minturn & Co., of New York. She accomplished the run around the Horn to San Francisco in eighty-nine days, twenty-one hours. Three years later she excelled her own record by thirteen hours. These sailing records have never been equaled. The launching of the "Flying Cloud" is said to have inspired Longfellow's poem, "Building of the Ship," with its oft quoted line, "Sail on, O union strong and great!" She was named by George Francis Train, 1829–1904, the American financier and author, junior partner in the firm of Enoch Train & Co.

Like many of the early California clippers the "Flying Cloud" had to cross the Pacific to China to get a cargo home. She made Honolulu in twelve days. One day, under skysails and stunsails, she covered 374 miles. She loaded tea at Macao and returned to New York in ninety-six days, being beaten by the "N. B. Palmer" by ten days, although the latter was three days later in starting. Later, she had her revenge, for, as previously told, she beat the "N. B. Palmer" in the San Francisco race of 1852. There were other exciting races with the "Hornet" and the "Archer," after which, in 1859, she was sold to enter the London-China run. She carried her first load of tea from Foochow to London in one hundred and twenty-three days. In 1863, she was bought by James Baines, of Liverpool, who put her into the Australian emigrant trade. She was again sold into the North Atlantic timber trade, went ashore on the New Brunswick coast and later burned at her dock in St. John in 1874.

Donald McKay also produced the "Staffordshire" and the "Flying Fish" in 1851. Both were California clippers of the extreme type; the former was wrecked off Cape Sable in 1854, the latter was wrecked in 1858 while coming out of Foochow with a cargo of tea.

In 1852, the "Sovereign of the Seas" was launched by Mr. McKay for Grinnell, Minturn & Co. of New York, owners of the Swallow Tail Line. She was 2421 tons, the largest clipper up to that time, and too big for the China tea trade. When she won the clipper ship race to San Francisco November 15, 1852, the sailors sang this version of "Oh, Susanna":

> Oh, Susanna, darling take your case,
> For we have beat the clipper fleet,
> The Sovereign of the Seas.

Mr. McKay's subsequent contributions to the California clipper service in 1852–53 included "Westward Ho," "Chariot of Fame," "Empress of the Sea," "Romance of the Seas," culminating with the "Great

"LIGHTNING," FASTEST CLIPPER, 1854

From the painting by Charles Dixon; courtesy Bank of America, New York.

Republic," 4555 tons, the largest extreme clipper ship ever built, which, as previously mentioned, was burned at her dock before she could make her first voyage, and was subsequently sold to A. A. Low & Brother, who rebuilt her on a smaller scale, 3357 tons—still the largest merchant ship of her time. Hearing the actress, Mrs. Fanny Kemble, recite Longfellow's poem, "The Building of the Ship," is thought to have been responsible for Donald McKay's naming his supreme achievement "Great Republic."

Following this, James Baines, founder of the Liverpool Black Ball Line of Australian packets, engaged McKay to build that famous clipper ship quartette: "Lightning," "James Baines," "Champion of the Seas," and "Donald McKay," launched in 1854–55. The "Lightning" specially distinguished herself by doing 436 sea miles in twenty-four hours, an average of more than eighteen miles an hour, the record for a sailing vessel for all time and a speed exceeded by only a few steamships even in our day.

The British Tea Clippers

The British began building tea clippers in earnest with the "Falcon," a 937-ton wooden ship produced in 1859 by Robert Steele & Co., Greenock, for Shaw, Maxton & Co. During the next ten years no less than twenty-six wood and composite clippers were turned out by British shipyards. Six of them became famous. They were the "Taeping," "Ariel," "Sir Lancelot," "Thermopylae," "Cutty Sark," and "Black-

"GREAT REPUBLIC," LARGEST EXTREME CLIPPER, 1853

From the painting by Charles R. Patterson; courtesy of Mr. W. R. Laidlaw.

British Clipper "Taeping," Famous Tea Racer, 1863

From the painting by J. Spurling. By permission of the publisher and owner of the copyright, the Blue Peter Publishing Co., Ltd., London.

adder," all composite ships except the last named, which was iron.

Following the "Falcon," in 1859, came the "Isle of the South," 821 tons, built by Laing & Co., Sunderland. In 1860, the "Fiery Cross," 888 tons, a champion tea racer [second ship of that name], was built by Chaloner & Co. of Liverpool; also the "Chaa-sze," 600 tons, was launched at Hall & Co's. Aberdeen yards for Turner & Co. of Canton. The "Min," 629 tons, built by Robert Steele & Co., Greenock, and "Kelso," built by Pile & Co., Sunderland, were launched in 1861. In 1863, there appeared the "Belted Will" by Feel & Co., Workington; "Serica" and "Taeping," both champion tea racers, built by Robert Steele & Co., Greenock; the "Eliza Shaw" by Alexander Stephen, Glasgow, and the "Yang-tze" and "Black Prince" by Alexander Hall & Co., Aberdeen.

Among the tea ships launched in 1864 the following stand out: "Ariel," 853 tons, and "Sir Lancelot," 886 tons, by Robert Steele & Co., Greenock; "Ada," 686 tons, by Alexander Hall & Co.; and "Taitsing," 815 tons, by Connell & Co., Glasgow. The year 1866 produced the "Titania," 879 tons, by Robert Steele & Co., Greenock;

1867, the "Spindrift," 899 tons, by Connell & Co., Glasgow; "Forward Ho," 943 tons, by Alexander Stephen, Glasgow; "Leander," 883 tons, by Lawrie & Co., Glasgow; and "Lahloo," 779 tons, by Robert Steele & Co., Glasgow; all of them noted tea fliers.

In 1868, there were more famous tea racers. Among them were: "Thermopylae," 947 tons, by Walter Hood, Aberdeen; "Windhover," 847 tons, by Connell & Co., Glasgow; and the "Cutty Sark," 921 tons, by Scott & Co., of Greenock. The year 1869 witnessed the launching of the "Caliph," 914 tons, by Alexander Hall & Co., Aberdeen; the "Wylo," 799 tons, and "Kaisow," 795 tons, by Robert Steele & Co., Greenock; the "Lothair," 794 tons, by Walker & Son, London; and the "Norman Court," a beautiful tea clipper, first commanded by Captain Andrew Shewan, Sr. The "Blackadder" was launched in 1870.

The "Fiery Cross" was owned by J. Campbell. Her commander, Captain Robinson, was considered "a hard man to beat in the tricky China seas." She won four of the exciting tea races of the 'sixties. When her racing days were over she was sold to the Norwegians. Subsequently, she caught fire and sank in one of the creeks of the Medway at Sheerness.

The "Taeping" was designed to beat the "Fiery Cross," which had won the 10 shillings per ton premium awarded to the first arrival in the 1861–62 seasons. The wood "Serica" and the composite "Taeping" had several tussles. "Serica" had been in the tea trade since 1851 and had the great good luck to win by five days her first tea race with the "Fiery Cross" from Foochow. However, the "Taeping" did not really distinguish herself until the Great Tea Race of 1866, which she won, and again in 1867 and 1868. The "Taeping" was finally wrecked on Ladds Reef on her way from Amoy to New York; her mate's boat with six men being picked up three days after.

The "Ariel" was commanded by Captain John Keay, who had previously sailed the "Ellen Rodgers" and the "Falcon" with great success. She was "the ideal tea clipper, the fastest thing the wind ever drove through the water," in the opinion of Captain Andrew Shewan, late master of the "Norman Court." Lubbock said of her that:

Like all the fairy-like Steele clippers she was a ticklish jade to handle, and it took a master to

get the best of her. If overpressed she had a habit of settling down aft and had to be quickly relieved of her mizzen canvas or she would drown her helmsman. This fault was due to a want of bearing aft, which was practically the only flaw in Robert Steele's tea ship designs.

Hawthorne Daniel, in *The Clipper Ship*, agrees that:

"Ariel" was too fine astern to make her safe in a following sea. She was sharp at the bow, as well, and in heavy weather fairly drowned her crew. But that was a failing of many British-built ships as well as of more than a few Americans. Speed was considered as being so important in the construction of these ships that seaworthiness was sometimes scamped to obtain it.[6]

In the Great Tea Race of 1866, "Ariel" was the winner at the Downs, but, for want of tidal water, had to wait in the Thames, docking twenty minutes later than her rival, "Taeping." In 1872, "Ariel" left London for Sydney and was never heard of again. She was always a ticklish ship to handle in the "roaring forties," "and it is generally supposed," says Lubbock, "that she broached to and foundered when running her easting down." There were four "Ariels" and the one here

[6] Hawthorne Daniel, *The Clipper Ship*, New York, 1928, Dodd, Mead & Co., p. 244. By permission.

BRITISH TEA CLIPPER, "SIR LANCELOT," 1864

From the painting by J. Spurling. By permission of the publisher and owner of the copyright, the Blue Peter Publishing Co., Ltd., London.

BRITISH TEA CLIPPER "THERMOPYLAE," 1868

From the painting by J. Spurling. By permission of the publisher and owner of the copyright, the Blue Peter Publishing Co., Ltd., London.

mentioned, built in England—1865—was the only one important in tea history.

The famous tea clipper "Sir Lancelot" was a sister ship of the beautiful "Ariel." Her figurehead was a knight in mail armor, his visor open and his right hand drawing a sword. She loaded just under 1500 tons of tea, and was the first ship to load tea at Hankow after the famous "Challenger," being chartered by Jardine, Matheson & Co. at £7 per ton. This was in 1866. "Sir Lancelot" was third in the tea race of 1868, making the run from Foochow to London in ninety-eight days. She was the winner of the 1869 tea race from Foochow to London in eighty-nine days, with an added day's record run of 354 miles. "Sir Lancelot" was subsequently on the Australian-Shanghai-New York run. Later, she was sold to an Indian' merchant, and foundered in a cyclone in the Bay of Bengal, 1895.

The "Thermopylae" marked a distinct advance in British tea clippers. She came out of Aberdeen, and was designed by Bernard Weymouth, whose early tea clipper, "Leander," was fast, but wet. The "Thermopylae" was built to give a good account of herself in a blow as well as in light airs. "The best all-around ship of the tea clipper fleet," Captain Shewan calls her. She was the first British clipper to bear pressing in rough weather. Twice she made the run from London to Melbourne in sixty-three days. In the 1869 tea race from Foochow she lost to "Sir Lancelot" by three days. Her biggest tea cargo was 1,429,000 lbs. She was later sold into the trans-Pacific trade and after that to the Portuguese Government which subsequently sank her off Lisbon in 1907.

"Thermopylae's" great rival was the "Cutty Sark," probably the best advertised of all British tea clippers. The "Cutty Sark" was a composite ship designed by Hercules Linton to beat "Thermopylae," and built on the Clyde to the order of Captain John Willis, the London ship-owner known as "old Whitehat." From 1870 to 1877 she made a number of tea passages, none of then sensational. After that she went on a series of wandering voyages, stopping anywhere a cargo offered. She was beset with all kinds of tragic happenings and romantic adventures until she came under the command of Captain Woodget, when she settled down to a dignified middle age in the Australian wool trade. She, too, went under the Portuguese flag and again started in quest of strange adventures, which ended in 1922 when she was restored to the British nation to be used as a stationary training ship at Falmouth.

Unfortunately, "Thermopylae" and "Cutty Sark" never had a chance of testing their powers properly, for on the only occasion on which a race could be arranged the "Cutty Sark" lost her rudder and then the jury rudder that was rigged. However, she was only a few days behind her rival, so that there was little doubt that she would have won had things gone well with her.

The "Blackadder," an iron clipper ship, sister to the "Hallowe'en," and designed for the China trade, had a disastrous maiden voyage in 1870, due to defects in construction. She did not meet with favor at the hands of the tea shippers. She was followed by a most persistent hoodoo through the 'seventies and 'eighties but later gave a better account of herself. Both these ships, however, were after their time, for the Suez Canal was practically completed and Alfred Holt, the Liverpool shipowner, had led the movement that transferred the carriage of tea from sail to steam. The later clipper ships saw the greater part of their service in the Australian trade.

The "Serica" and "Spindrift" were wrecked in 1869. The "Taitsing" was wrecked off the coast of Zanzibar in 1883.

Windjammers Give Way to Steamers

The eclipse of the sailing ship was rapid

BRITISH TEA CLIPPER "CUTTY SARK," 1868
From the painting by J. Spurling. By permission of the publisher and owner of the copyright, the Blue Peter Publishing Co., Ltd., London.

and dramatic. The opening of the Suez Canal in 1869 gave the steamships an advantage over the old windjammers that they had never possessed when forced to watch every pound of coal. Alfred Holt, who had started operations to the West Coast of Africa with a single second-hand steamer, saw his opportunity and immediately built with the idea of high speed and economy. Within a few years his Blue Funnel liners had captured the cream of the tea trade.

Other companies followed, some successful and some not, and, although the sailing ships struggled on for some years more, the best gradually drifted into the Australian trade, where gold-seekers and wool cargoes gave them their opportunity. The days of racing home with the new season's tea were over. The steamship owner weighed comparative cost carefully, and with his bigger cargo capacity and a regular schedule was able to maintain a profitable business without running undue risks. In the early 'eighties an attempt was made to revive the craze for speed in a famous steamer known as the "Stirling Castle," a 5000-ton ship with a speed of 19 knots, which reduced the time between China and London to thirty days, or about one-third the clipper ship time. The "Glenogle" did it in forty days. It was soon found, however, that the expenses ran away with the profits, and the trade reverted to the regular cargo steamers.

Clipper-Ship Days in Mincing Lane

The interest and excitement among landsmen during the clipper-ship days has been rivaled only by the Derby. The tea trade was then the highest class of mercantile pursuit, and during the tea season the cynosure of all eyes was the dashing "tea-clipper." Speeding under her enormous spread of snow-white canvas from far-away Cathay to her British or American home-port, she was freighted with the choicest of the new season's pickings, a cargo meaning a handsome profit to the consignees of the first arrival. The best sailing masters, the finest seamen, and swiftest vessels afloat were represented in the tea fleet. The racing of the tea ships was at that time the all-absorbing topic of the hour on 'Change, at the club, or by the fireside. The winner gained something more substantial than mere fame—not infrequently a fortune was the prize.

In Mincing Lane the telegrams recording the hours at which the tea ships passed certain points were read with as much avidity as present-day stock-ticker tapes; and when the news came from Start Point that the clippers were beating up the English Channel the excitement became intense. Before the days of the telegraph, when news traveled slowly, the arrival of the tea clippers had in it even more of mystery and of thrill.

Sometimes the crew of the winning ship received £500 from the owners of the cargo, for the first tea put on the market realized from 3d. to 6d. a pound more than teas on the slower ships. Swarms of sampling clerks would descend upon the docks to draw samples for brokers and wholesalers as soon as the news came that the racers had passed Gravesend. Some spent the night at near-by hotels; others slept at the docks. By 9 A.M., the samples were being tasted in Mincing Lane. Then the bids were made by the large dealers; duty was paid on the gross weight, and by the following morning the new season's Congous would be on sale in Liverpool and Manchester.

An interesting reminder of clipper ship days is still to be seen in the office of W. J. & H. Thompson, the Mincing Lane tea brokers. It is a wind-clock which hangs on the wall of the sales room where it was

WIND CLOCK, RELIC OF CLIPPER SHIP DAYS IN
MINCING LANE, LONDON

installed to keep the office informed as to the wind direction; for, in the days of sail, adverse winds could compel the tea clippers to lie out in the Downs a week or more. The arrow hand of this clock was connected with a weather vane on the roof of the building. A southwesterly wind was the kind of a "blow" calculated to bring the clippers flying up the Channel, but a northeasterly wind meant exasperating delay. While a northeaster was not so unwelcome to overworked clerks, for whom it spelled respite from their labors, the keener spirits were all for the winds that brought the sampling of the new season's teas more quickly to hand. With a move of the windclock's hand from northeast to southwest men on horseback would ride from the city to Tooting or Balham—then outlying villages of London and eight miles away—to inform merchants living there of the probable arrival of the tea ships.

The important tea races of the 'fifties and 'sixties and their winners were as follows: In 1859, the American tea clipper "Sea Serpent" won the Foochow to London race in 130 days from the "Ziba," which made it in 134 days; "Ellen Rodgers," in 136 days; "Fiery Cross" [the first], in 139 days; and "Crest of the Wave," in 147 days. The 1860 race from Foochow was won by "Falcon" in 110 days, the other contestants being "Ellen Rodgers," 119 days; "Robin Hood," 124 days; "Chrysolite," 125 days; and "Ziba," 126 days. The 1861 race was won by the new "Fiery Cross" in 101 days, her rivals being "Falcon," 120 days; "Ellen Rodgers," 121 days; "Robin Hood," 125 days; and "Flying Spur," 124 days. In 1862, "Fiery Cross" arrived first after 122 days, although the "Ellen Rodgers" made the best passage, in 116 days. In 1863, "Fiery Cross" was again the winner, in 104 days; the others being "Ziba," 106 days to Liverpool, and "Falcon," "Robin Hood," "Flying Spur," "Min," and "Ellen Rodgers" arriving at London in the order named. In 1864, out of a field of nine tea clippers that carried the season's teas from Foochow, the real contest was between the new "Serica" which won in 109 days, with "Fiery Cross" second, and "Flying Spur" third. In 1865, after doing most of the 16,000 miles from Foochow together in a perfectly matched race, "Fiery Cross" got the first tug in the Channel and won from "Serica" by one tide at the London docks.

"Taeping" and "Ariel" Passing the Lizard in the China Tea Race, 1866
"Taeping," winner at the London Dock, is to the left; "Ariel," winner at the Downs, is to the right.
From a colored lithograph lent by The Parker Gallery, Berkeley Square, London.

The 1867 race was won by "Sir Lancelot" in a run of ninety-nine days out from Shanghai, but "Ariel" was first from Foochow, with "Maitland" second. In 1868, seven cracks were enlisted, among them three new ones, "Spindrift," "Lahloo," and "Undine." "Spindrift" won from "Ariel" [both ninety-seven days out from Foochow] by six hours. In 1869, as already told, "Sir Lancelot" won in eighty-nine days from five contestants. In 1870, "Lahloo" won in ninety-seven days from four rivals. In 1871, "Titania," by a ninety-seven days' run, captured the blue ribbon from a field of four, sailing from Foochow and Shanghai. That year marked the end of the tea races.

The Great Tea Race of 1866

The story of the Great Tea Race of 1866, still a favorite topic of discussion in Mincing Lane, has been told best by Mr. Basil Lubbock in his *China Clippers*, in the *Blue Peter*, and again in *Sail*. This most exciting of all the tea races started on May 28, 1866, from the Pagoda anchorage in the Min River, below Foochow, and ended ninety-nine days later, in the London docks. Says Mr. Lubbock:

The struggle, however, began long before the ships hove up their anchors in the Min River. It began in the offices of the ships' agents and in the hongs of the Chinese merchants, fortunes in money being dependent on the winning ship. Thus the favorites for the race got the first chests, and were therefore the first to finish loading. The tea came down the Min River from Foochow to the anchorage in large sampans, and was slung aboard the ships, and stowed into every nook and cranny, even to the captain's cabin, by clever Chinese stevedores, who worked in shifts day and night.

While the tea chests were being stowed, the crews were getting the clippers ready for the fray. The most elaborate chafing gear was sent aloft. Every rope and wire were carefully examined and replaced by new if they showed the least sign of wear. The stunsail gear was overhauled, and the stunsail booms sent aloft. As each ship began to fill up, the excitement became greater and greater, and the ships resounded with a variety of noises, the pidgin English of the Chinese stevedores contrasting weirdly with the stronger seafaring English of the mates and bos'ns.

In May, 1866, there were loading at the Pagoda anchorage the following first-class tea clippers:
Ariel, 852 tons, Capt. Keay, tea cargo, 1,230,900 lbs.
Fiery Cross, 695 tons, Capt. Robinson, tea cargo, 854,236 lbs.
Serica, 708 tons, Capt. Innes, tea cargo, 954,236 lbs.
Taeping, 767 tons, Capt. McKinnon, tea cargo, 1,108,709 lbs.
Taitsing, 815 tons, Capt. Nutsford, tea cargo, 1,093,130 lbs.
Ziba, 497 tons, Capt. Tomlinson.
Black Prince, 750 tons, Capt. Inglis.
Chinaman, 668 tons, Capt. Downie.
Flying Spur, 735 tons, Capt. Ryrie.
Ada, 687 tons, Capt. Jones.
Falcon, 794 tons, Capt. Gunn.
I have put down the ships in the order in which they sailed from the anchorage. "Ariel" and "Taitsing" were new ships, and of the two

"Ariel" was made the favorite in the betting on the race. "Taeping" had made the fastest passage in 1865, and the first ships in that year were "Serica" and "Fiery Cross," the latter having the luck to fall in with a tugboat off Beachy Head, when "Serica" was leading her by two miles. But, as regards speed, there was only a slight difference between the first and last, and the race depended quite as much upon the skill and nerve of their captains as upon the ships themselves.

The "Ariel" was the first ship to finish loading but she made an unfortunate start, and had to anchor before the tide had fallen. "Fiery Cross" passed her, and put out to sea ahead, getting a day's lead. "Taeping" and "Serica" crossed the bar of the Min River together. The other ships left the anchorage on the following dates: May 31, "Taitsing"; June 2, "Ziba" [for Liverpool]; June 3, "Black Prince"; June 5, "Chinaman" and "Flying Spur"; June 6, "Ada"; June 7, "Falcon."

In a race of 100 days across three-quarters of the globe, one would imagine that a few days' start would have made little or no difference in the result, but, as a matter of fact, these racing tea ships were as closely matched as a one-design class of racing yachts, and every hour was of value. It so happened in this race that the ships were not together for any length of time. Each of the tea ships carried a picked crew ["Ariel's" numbered 32 all told, all A.Bs., no boys or O.Ss.], but there was no doubling of crews as has often been stated in print; when racing, the skipper signed on only two extra hands. "Ariel's" normal complement was 30 men.

On June 2 "Taeping" and "Ariel" were in sight of each other. A week later they were again in company in 7° N. 110° E., and "Taeping" signaled that she had passed the "Fiery Cross" the day before. Both captains congratulated themselves on the supposition that they were ahead of Capt. Robinson, but he was a hard man to beat in the tricky China seas, and very soon regained his lead.

The times at Anjer were as follows:

Fiery Cross ....at noon on June 18	21 days out
Ariel ....at 7 a.m. on June 20	21 days out
Taeping ....at 1 p.m. on June 20	21 days out
Serica ....at 6 p.m. on June 22	23 days out
Taitsing ....at 10 p.m. on June 26	26 days out

The trades in the Indian Ocean often piped up good and strong, and broken stunsail yards and booms were common. In 1866, "Ariel" carried away two topmasts, one topgallant, and one royal stunsail yard; but her daily runs, from June 22, when she passed Keeling Island, to June 30, were as follows: 215, 290, 280, 317, 330, 270, 230, 255, and 270 miles and each ship was doing as well. "Fiery Cross," still a day ahead at Mauritius, ran 328 miles on June 24, "Taeping" made 319 on the 25th, and "Taitsing" 318 on July 2.

By the time the Cape was reached, "Ariel" had nearly wiped off her lost 24 hours, being only two or three hours behind "Fiery Cross" on July 15, when both ships rounded. "Taeping" was 12 hours astern, while "Serica" and "Taitsing" still lagged behind. In the passage up the Atlantic all five ships got closer and closer to one another without knowing it. At St. Helena two and a half days covered the first four ships, the order being "Taeping," "Fiery Cross," "Serica," "Ariel," Taitsing." "Taeping," "Fiery Cross," and "Ariel" all crossed the Line on the same

day, Aug. 4. "Serica" had dropped a couple of days, and "Taitsing" was still over a week astern.

From Aug. 9 to 17 [12° 29′ N. to 27° 53′ N.] "Taeping" and "Fiery Cross" were within sight of each other in doldrum weather; "Ariel" farther to the westward having better winds and running into the lead. On Aug. 17 "Fiery Cross" saw "Taeping" pick up the breeze and run out of sight ahead in a few hours, the Liverpool crack being left becalmed for 24 hours. This, Robinson always declared, cost him the race. Nevertheless, he was up in the van again at the Western Isles. Here the times were truly remarkable, the order at Flores being:

1. Ariel ....passed on Aug. 29	91 days out
2. Fiery Cross ....passed on Aug. 29	92 days out
3. Taeping ....passed on Aug. 29	91 days out
4. Serica ....passed on Aug. 29	91 days out
5. Taitsing ....passed on Sept. 1	93 days out

With fresh westerly winds all five ships made the run to soundings in six days. At 1:30 a.m., Sept. 5, "Ariel," the leading ship, picked up the Bishop and St. Agnes Lights. At 5:30 a.m., with the sky clearing and wind fresh at about W.S.W., Capt. Keay proceeded with all possible sail.

In the skipper's private log there is this entry: "A ship, since daylight, has been in company on starboard quarter—'Taeping,' probably."

"Ariel's" times past the various lights were as follows:

Sept. 5

2.50 a.m.	St. Agnes north distant about 10 miles.
8.25 a.m.	Lizard Lights about W. N. W. 11 miles.
12.30 p.m.	Start Point Lighthouse north 3 miles.
4.15 p.m.	Portland Lights north about 6 miles.
7.25 p.m.	St. Catherine's north 1 mile.
9.45 p.m.	Owers Light north 4 miles.
12.30 a.m.	Beachy Head Light north 5 miles.
3 a.m.	Dungeness Light N. E. 8 miles.
4 a.m.	Hove to abreast of Dungeness Light, distant 1½ miles.

All this time the two ships had been tearing up Channel, with "Ariel" slightly in the lead. Captain Keay remarks in his log, "Going 14 knots royal stunsails and flying kites set, wind strong from W.S.W." At 6 p.m. "Ariel" got her anchors over, and was compelled to take in her jib-topsail and Jamie Green so as to have all clear forward. Then, when off St. Catherine's, all small sails had to come in, except the fore topmast stunsail. Off Beachy Head, "Ariel" had about an hour's lead of "Taeping," and as she neared Dungeness she began to burn blue lights and send up rockets for a pilot.

One may imagine the excitement, both aboard the two ships and ashore, where the news that two tea ships were racing up Channel spread like wildfire. From each headland the report of their positions was rushed to the nearest postoffice, and, though they had not our facilities in those days, the owners of both ships and their agents in London soon learned that the two vessels were neck and neck.

It was aboard the ships, however, that the excitement was greatest, and also the anxiety, for the prize money ran into hundreds of pounds.

Behind Captain Keay's words in his log at this point, one can feel the thrill, the tension, and the suppressed agitation, which must have almost kept his heart from beating. Captain Keay was an experienced hand in the China trade, and up to every move in the game, a calm, confident, level-headed skipper, yet that night must have tried his nerves. He missed nothing, however, and the time of every move in the contest was jotted down in his log:

"Sept. 6, 5 a.m. Saw the 'Taeping' running and also signaling; bore up lest they should run eastward of us and get pilot first; seeing us keep away, they hove to, we again hove to.

"5:30. Saw two cutters coming out of Dungeness Roads.

"5:40. Kept away so as to get between 'Taeping' and the cutters.

"5:55. Rounded to close to the pilot cutter and got first pilot. Were saluted as first ship from China this season. I replied, 'Yes, and what is that to the westward? We have not room to boast yet. Thank God we are first up Channel and hove to for a pilot an hour before him.'

"6 a.m. Kept away for South Foreland; set all plain sail; were immediately followed by the 'Taeping.' They set also topmast, topgallant, and lower stunsails one side—wind slightly quartering. We kept ahead without the stunsails or would also have set them. 'Taeping' neared us a mile or two, but was a mile astern when he had to take stunsails in [had shifted them to port side when hauling up through the Downs].

"Hoisted our number abreast of Deal we were then fully a mile ahead of 'Taeping,' and kept so until obliged to take in all sail and take steamer ahead."

The times of the five ships in the Downs were as follows:

Ariel, at 8 a.m., Sept 6 . . . .   99 days out
Taeping, at 8.10 a.m., Sept. 6 . . . . . .   99 days out
Serica, at noon, Sept. 6 . . . .   99 days out
Fiery Cross, during the night, Sept. 7 101 days out
Taitsing, at forenoon, Sept. 9 . . . . . .   101 days out

None of the other ships made a race of it with these five. The "Serica" had come up Channel on the French side. "Fiery Cross" was off St. Catherine's at 10 a.m. on Sept. 7, but she was compelled to bring up in the Downs owing to a severe W.S.W. gale.

The race was not finished until the sample boxes of tea were hurled ashore in the London Docks; but, so scared were the owners of "Ariel" and "Taeping" of losing the 10s. extra per ton on a quibble as to which ship really won that they agreed privately to divide the premium, the first ship in dock claiming. The captains knew nothing of this arrangement, and the excitement aboard both ships was still at fever heat, as shown in Captain Keay's log:

"'Taeping's' tug proved much better than ours, and soon towed past us. I thought of taking another boat, but found there would be no need as far as docking was concerned, as we could reach Gravesend two or three hours before it would be possible to go on, till tide made, therefore saved the £10 or £12 asked by the boats.

"'Taeping' reached Gravesend 55 minutes before us. We avoided anchoring by getting a tug alongside to keep us astern. Proceeded with first tug ahead, as the flowing tide gave us sufficient water to float, thus reached Blackwall and East India Dock entrance at 9 p.m. Could not open the gates till tide rose higher. 10.23 p.m., hove the ship inside dock gates. 'Taeping' had pre-ceded us up the river, but, having farther to go, did not reach the entrance of London Docks till 10 p.m.; and, drawing less water than we, also dock having two gates, they got her inside outer gate, shut it, and allowed the lock to fill from the dock, then opened the inner gate, so she docked some 20 minutes before us—the papers have it half an hour, for the sake of precision."

One can hardly imagine a more harrowing, grueling finish to a race, with the tension kept at boiling point. Since 8 p.m. a strong westerly gale had been blowing, and it is easy to imagine the language flying between the tug men and the officers of the two clippers. The air must have been blue all round "Ariel" when it was realized that her tug could not keep her ahead of "Taeping." "Ariel's" first officer, Duncan, considered the smartest racing mate in the whole fleet, had a flow of language justly celebrated for its richness and variety of expression, but the things he said to that tug skipper beat all records.

The yarn goes also that half a dozen great burly seamen, headed by the "Ariel's" bos'n, offered to board the tug, by way of the tow rope, in order to supplement the stokers and sit on the safety valve.

"However, there was no help for it, although a more extraordinary and yet more unsatisfactory finish could hardly be imagined. After such a magnificent exhibition of racing seamanship, it was no consolation to divide the stakes, and all shipping people agreed that the race should have finished when the leading ship took her pilot.

"Serica" managed to haul inside the West India Dock at 11:30 p.m., just as the gates were being closed; thus "Ariel," "Taeping," and "Serica," after crossing the bar of the Min River on the same tide, all docked in the Thames on the same tide.[1]

Captain Edward T. Miles, who was a member of the crew of the "Ariel" in this memorable race, recently wrote the author from Ringwood, Victoria, Australia:

The finish of the race as published is incorrect. The ships are said to be running up Channel with a fair wind and stud sails set, whereas we had the wind down Channel and were beating up. We made the land during the night and at daylight were making a good leg up Channel standing over towards the French Coast. Several vessels were on our lee quarter, seven or eight miles away, and our Captain, with his telescope, was endeavoring to identify them. While doing so the leading vessel of those to leeward backed ship and when broad side on, the Captain said "That is the 'Taeping.'" Being nearer the English coast, though five miles to leeward of us, they had evidently seen the smoke of a tug-boat in there and immediately tacked. We also saw the smoke and tacked ship, but, alas! our chance of getting the first tow-boat had gone and we had the mortification of seeing the "Taeping" close up her sails and steam away in tow. To avoid the possibility of our getting a faster tug-boat the Captain of the "Taeping" engaged the next tug also and it was

[1] Basil Lubbock, "The Great Tea Race of 1866," The Blue Peter, London, 1926, vol. vi, no. 56. By permission.

several hours afterwards when the "Taeping" was out of sight that we got one; even then we docked on the following tide. On the merits of the race under sail all the honour is with the "Ariel" for we were fully five miles to windward of the "Taeping" when the tug-boat hove in sight and, without the assistance of steam, must have won the race.

Palmy Days of Sail

Some likes pictures of women (said Bill), an'
    some likes 'orses best,
As he fitted a pair of fancy shackles on to his
    old sea-chest;
But I likes pictures o' ships (said he), an' you
    can keep the rest.

     •   •   •

An' I don't care if it's North or South, the
    Trades or the China Sea,
Shortened down or everythin' set, close-hauled or
    runnin' free;
You paint me a ship as is *like* a ship an' that'll
    do for me.
                    CICELY FOX SMITH.[8]

Though the palmy days of sail are no more and the race horses of the sea have disappeared, they live again in the histories of Clark, Lubbock, Shewan, McKay, and Daniel, and in the sea romances of Melville, Dana, Conrad, and McFee. America's participation in the golden age of the clipper ships extended a little over a decade; then the Civil War gave Great Britain her chance and she, too, had her decade in the sun; but Suez and the era of steam ended that.

As to records Basil Lubbock has tabulated all the day's runs of 400 miles or over by sailing vessels. There are eight, to which Prof. Samuel Eliot Morison of Oxford has added two. These ten phenomenal runs were all made by five ships in the

---

8 Cicely Fox Smith, *Pictures*. By permission.

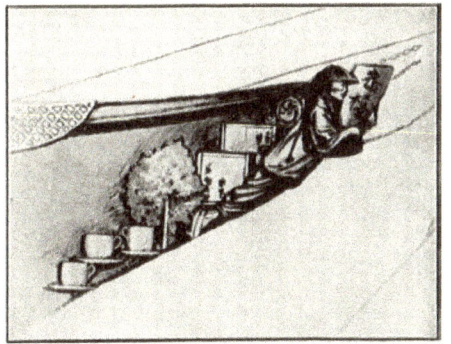

FIGURE HEAD OF THE "CHAA-SZE," BRITISH
CLIPPER, 1860

years 1853–56; four of these, the "Sovereign of the Seas," "James Baines," "Donald McKay," and "Lightning" were designed and built by Donald McKay in Boston and the fifth, "Red Jacket," was designed by Samuel A. Pook of Boston and built in Rockland, Maine. Most of these runs were made under the British flag in the Australian trade.

The tea clippers were beautiful ships, splendidly designed and substantially built, with small deck houses and ample deck space for fast working. Invariably they looked like model sailing yachts, with their black or green hulls, golden scroll work, all brass work polished, decks holystoned, and gear well found. One curious feature was their loose ballast. They carried from 200 to 300 tons of shingle [coarse, round, sea shore stones], which was adjusted to the keelson and evenly placed along the bottom of the ship, serving as a bed for the tea chests. They generally carried a crew of thirty and their skippers were men of extreme ability, not afraid to "let her rip," never troubling to snug down at night, always keen to make the fastest possible voyage between ports.

These ships were what shipping men called very "tender." They could not be shifted about easily, once they were unloaded. They stood up tall, carried a great deal of mast and rigging; were in fact fullrigged ships, i. e., they were provided with three masts, each mounting square sails. The early tea clippers were built of wood. The ships built at the close of the 'fifties and in the early 'sixties were nearly all composite, i. e., iron frames, wooden sides, copper sheathed. At the end of the 'sixties the clipper ship was built of iron right through; still later ship builders advanced to steel. "The introduction of iron," says Lubbock, "contributed more than anything else to the supremacy of the British merchant marine. It killed off the competition of our American cousins."

The sight of a clipper ship being towed into her berth at New York is a treasured memory of few present-day New Yorkers, but Mr. W. G. Low says he recalls seeing the "N. B. Palmer" being docked at the Pierrepont Stores on the Brooklyn side:

Spic and span, her newly-painted black hull decorated with a narrow gold stripe running its full length, yards squared with snowy sails neatly furled and having black crossbands to hold them in place—she was indeed a never-to-be-forgotten

THE OLD PAGODA ANCHORAGE IN THE MIN RIVER, BELOW FOOCHOW, CHINA

The name is derived from the Pagoda seen on the hill. Pagoda Island is 26 miles from the open sea. Foochow City is nine miles up the river on the left of this picture.

picture. At the top of her mainmast floated her red, yellow, and white house flag, while a brand new U. S. ensign provided a brilliant flash of color for her mizzen gaff. In the glow of the setting sun she was not only a thing of beauty, but so tall, so stately, so handsome as to make her surroundings seem a little shabby.

In the days of the clipper ships South Street, New York; India Wharf, Boston; and the water fronts of Salem, Philadelphia, and Baltimore were veritable forests of masts. The late Captain Andrew Shewan in *The Great Days of Sail* brought together the best set of reminiscences of all the tea clipper captains. Captain Shewan describes the building and launching of the "Chaa-sze" [tea taster], whose figurehead consisted of two reclining celestials supporting a shield on which was depicted the name in Chinese characters; trailing along the cutwater were representations of tea chests, tea pots, cups, and saucers, including a weird-looking object like "a birch broom in a fit," which was intended to represent a tea shrub.

Launchings of tea clippers in Aberdeen were not unlike those in America, where the public schools usually declared a holiday, and there were brass bands and several kinds of colonial "whoopee." Launching day in the fittie [footdee] district of Aberdeen was quite in the nature of a gala.

Loading tea at the Pagoda anchorage, Foochow, as described by Captain Shewan, was a picturesque scene. The opening of the market was peculiar to the Foochow tea trade. In the city of Foochow, after early May, when the first crop pickings arrived, the Chinese merchants were slow to make up their minds to sell at prices acceptable to the foreign buyers. Weeks

were spent in haggling, and finally, when the price had been lowered sufficiently, and one of the more important foreign firms was tempted to close, the market was open and the rush began. Speed was the order of the day. Forty-eight hours were required to weigh and label the tea chests. Then each hong hurried its chops by lighter to the Pagoda Anchorage, twelve miles below the city, where three or four clippers with good records were chosen as "going ships." As a rule each clipper in the running had already shipped a "ground chop," i. e., a sufficient number of chests of tea of inferior quality, carried at a slightly lower rate of freight than the new teas, to cover the shingle ballast and so provide added protection to the new crop chops.

After weeks of idling while waiting for the market to open, suddenly and as likely as not in the night, a blowing of conch shells, and much hullabaloo would announce the coming of the first tea chops. The method followed was for the men on the lighters to chant in a long drawn out wail the Chinese name of the hong that owned the tea. Thus Jardine Matheson's employees would wail out unendingly in mournful cadence: "Ee-wo! Ee-wo!"; those of Turner and Company would snap back a discordant "Wha-kee! Wha-kee!" and others in like manner through a whole gamut of barks and whines. Captain Shewan says:

Who it was that replied to them and directed them to their destinations I cannot say; certainly it was not members of the clippers' companies. I believe when they were expected Chinese rivermen were stationed in anchored boats in readiness to direct them. When day dawned, hopes and fears would be set at rest. Round each of the two or three favourite ships some half-dozen or so lighters would be gathered. The rest of the fleet were out of luck and had to exercise patience. Yet they had not long to wait. In about forty-eight hours the "Blue Peter" would be flying from the trucks of one or more of the fortunate ones, and the "tea-chops" would transfer their attentions to the ship next in turn.

The finest display of clippers that I ever remember seeing waiting for the market to open was in 1869. In that year no less than fifteen of these beauties, more like yachts than merchantmen, lay moored off the Pagoda, with holds ready, ballast levelled, ground chop stowed, waiting for the new teas. I do not suppose that in any other port in the world one could have seen such a fleet of beautiful craft as were assembled in the River Min on that occasion. Among them were the "Thermopylae," "Leander," "Windhover," and "Kaisow," all on their first trip; the "Spindrift" and "Lahloo" on their second; the proved and noted flyers "Sir Lancelot," "Ariel," "Taeping," and "Serica"; as well as the somewhat older but still handsome vessels, "Black Prince," "Falcon," "Min," "Flying Spur," and the little "Ziba."

There they lay, their hulls actually radiant, as smooth and glossy as though they had been lacquered, with scarcely a seam visible. Their copper sheathing had been burnished by hand and carefully oiled, till it glittered brilliantly in the sunlight. Aloft everything was "a-taunto"—yards freshly painted and squared to a hair's-breadth by lifts and braces; topmasts and top-gallant masts bright and oiled; standing rigging freshly blackened, and all superfluous running gear unrove; and with snow-white awnings with scalloped edges neatly stretched fore and aft of each ship. There was no great display of bunting except on gala days. The agent's house-flag was flown at the main as a guide to the "tea-chops"; while at the mizzen captains flew a pennant when they were aboard their ships, which was hauled down man-o'-war fashion as soon as "his highness" was over the gangway. Everywhere the British Ensign waved supreme. It was sometimes worn at the peak, but more often on a flagstaff over the taffrail.

It was not every shipmaster who cared to have the handling of an up-to-date tea clipper of the 'sixties. Captain Shewan tells us:

The commander of one of those tender beauties had to be continually on his guard against squalls and sudden changes of weather. Not for him the take-it-easy attitude of other shipmasters through spells of fine weather or in the region of the steady trades. Not even when the ship had been snugged down under low sail, and the more fortunate man felt he deserved and could legitimately take rest, was the tea-clipper man free from the obsession that he must crowd sail on his ship whenever the wind showed the least sign of abating. He had a China clipper under his charge, and she must never be allowed to lag. Her white wings were intended to be spread to the breeze, and anxieties were meant to be undertaken and overcome.

There was an old forecastle song, a great fa-vourite of the shellbacks of my boyhood days, which illustrates this. After describing the operation of carrying on till the last moment, and the subsequent reefing of topsails, on board a New York packet-ship, whose officers had no other object than to make a speedy passage, the singer portrays the anxiety of the skipper to keep his ship going:

> "In the very next watch
> There being a lull,
> Old Davey comes forward
> And roars like a bull:
> 'Come shake out those reefs, boys,
> More sail we must show,
> She's a flash Yankee packet—
> Oh, Lord, let her go!'"

The poetry of the clipper ship has been beautifully expressed by Margaret E. Sangster, in the following lines, which are framed on the wall of India House, New York:

THE CLIPPER SHIP

(Suggested by the design on a little coffee pot from India House)

A silhouette of silver sails against a shining sky,
A clipper ship, a ghostly shape, that stealthily
   slips by;
A crew that croons a merry song,—a phantom
   song, sung low—
"To India, to India, to India we go!"

To India.—The very name comes with the scent
   of flowers,
It speaks of gold, and precious stones, and vivid
   drifting hours,
Of wealth, adventure, dreams come true; of
   power and of fame—
The wonder of a weary world is in that glowing
   name!

The challenge of the seven seas, of cities famed
   afar,
Bombay, Calcutta,—romance towns, where living
   stories are;
The clipper ship once forged the chains that
   bound them to our side.
That drew them closer, link by link, across the
   troubled tide.

And that is why, set quietly upon a certain
   street,
An old house stands with doors flung wide, where
   kindred spirits meet,
To talk of trade and other things—to hope, and
   build and plan
The climax of the mighty work the clipper ship
   began.

And as they talk, perhaps they know that, bright
   against the sky,
Far out upon the gleaming bay, a ghostly ship
   sweeps by;
A phantom with a singing crew that carols, sweet
   and low,
"To India, to India, to India we go!"

Cicely Fox Smith thus muses on the glory that was once Foochow's:

THE "WESTWARD HO" IN THE CHINA SEA

From the original painting by Charles Robert Patterson in the possession of George W. Rogers and reproduced by permission.

By the old Pagoda Anchorage the clippers lie
    no more,
There is silence on the river, there is quiet on
    the shore,
And the silted channels seem
Still to murmur as in dream
Of the tea ships in their glory, lifting seaward
    on the tide,
All the strong and fair and fleet,
By those shores that used to meet,
And the valiant master mariners that walked
    their decks in pride,
By the old Pagoda Anchorage when clippers
    sailed the sea,
Logging fourteen on a bowline, ay, and seven-
    teen running free,
Racing home for London River—
Crack her on for London River—
Carry on for London River with her chests of
    China tea![9]

For a very good description of a tea clipper scudding before a gale Captain Shewan quotes from the diary of Mr. Frank Logan, a passenger in the "Norman Court" to Sydney in 1879, the ship being at the time south of Cape Leeuwin:

May 25th, 1879.—A very stormy day, a heavy gale blowing; ship under reefed topsails, rolling and labouring in a mountainous sea . . . Mr. Doughty and I were watching the sea over the stern-rail for some time. It was a grand sight: the high seas rolling along, following the ship. Their crests would break with a roar just as they got near us. We would be on the point of

<hr />

[9] Cicely Fox Smith, *Full Sail*, Houghton Mifflin Co., Boston and New York, 1926. By permission.

making a bolt from our vantage place, imagining that nothing could stop them tumbling on board and engulfing the poor little "Norman Court." [She was about equal tonnage with the "Ariel."] But lo and behold! her stern would rise in the air and she would be carried along on the top of the wave, with her bow pointing down into the valley, whilst another huge mountain would again be towering above her. "By Jove"! we would say to one another, "this one is a terror and will be aboard us for a certainty," but our brave little ship rode out the gale like a cork.

Captain Shewan gives his version of an amusing and oft quoted tea race incident of 1885. The Jardine flyer, "Cairngorm," Captain Ryrie, and the "Lammermuir," with Captain Andrew Shewan, Sr., in command, were racing to London for a £200 prize and found themselves together in the Java sea, in the region of the northwest monsoon, south of the line, sailing close-hauled on the starboard tack, neither making more than two or three knots.

This was the "Lammermuir's" strong point of sailing [says Captain Shewan], and the Aberdeen clipper's weak one. Like many extremely sharp ships with slightly hollow lines, she became a trifle sluggish in light winds. Thus the rather full-bowed "Lammermuir" gradually gained on her, coming up on the lee quarter. The two captains being good friends, Ryrie hung out a white table-cloth, signifying "Come on board to dinner," and Shewan, nothing loath, lowered his gig and was pulled over to the "Cairngorm."

The mate of the "Lammermuir" at the time was one Francis Moore, a native of Schleswig-Holstein, who had served John Willis almost from boyhood. He had been with my father since 1853, first as second, afterwards as chief mate. He was a first-class seaman and remained in the Willis's employ until about 1878, becoming master of the "Merse" in 1860 and successively commanding the "Whiteadder," "Blackadder," and "Cutty Sark." Moore was very proud of the "Lammermuir," and saw a chance to execute a manoeuvre that would redound to her credit for all time. This was "to go through the lee," as the phrase went, of the crack tea clipper of the day and sail round her; than which nothing could be more irritating to a proud rival.

Thus while the two captains were below at dinner the "Lammermuir" had so far fore-reached on the "Cairngorm" that Moore was able to put his helm down, come about on the port tack and stand across the bows of the other. Then, on the weather beam of the "Cairn-gorm," he tacked once more and resumed his course. The report of the officer of the watch to Captain Ryrie at the dinner table that the "Lammermuir" was crossing the bows brought the two captains on deck. After the first gasp of surprise, Ryrie was furious. "Well, I'm jiggered!" he gasped, "look at the perishing Dutchman! By the powers! I'll dress him down when I get him ashore."

I do not know whether he had his wish, but at least it was certain he was never. able to obliterate the memory of the fact that the "Lammermuir" once sailed round the redoubtable "Cairngorm."[10]

SEA FEVER

Oh, I am tired of brick and stone, the heart of me is sick,
For windy, green, unquiet sea, the realm of Moby Dick;
And I'll be going, going, from the roaring of the wheels,
For a wind's in the heart of me, a fire's in my heels.

.   .   .   .

I must down to the seas again, to the lonely sea and the sky,
And all I ask is a tall ship and a star to steer her by.

.   .   .   .

And all I ask is a merry yarn from a laughing fellow rover,
And a quiet sleep and a sweet dream when the long trick's over.

JOHN MASEFIELD.[11]

[10] Andrew Shewan, *The Great Days of Sail*, London, 1926, Heath Cranton, Ltd. By permission.
[11] John Masefield, *Poems*, New York. Macmillan Company. By permission.

CHAPTER VIII

TEA'S CONQUEST OF JAVA AND SUMATRA

FOR many years it was thought tea could not be grown and manufactured successfully except in China and Japan, so it was a long time after the Portuguese navigators had shown the way to the Indies and the Far East that the Dutch and the English were inspired to try it in their Indian possessions.

The German naturalist and doctor of medicine, Andreas Cleyer, first thought of growing tea in Java. He had become rich in the smuggling trade and it occurred to him that tea bushes would add an ornamental touch to the gardens surrounding his palatial home on the Tiger canal at Batavia. In 1684, he brought tea seeds from Japan, from which he successfully grew several tea bushes; and, although nothing ever came of his tea planting experiment, this gesture entitles him to the honor of being the first to grow tea in Java. Cleyer's garden steward, Georg Meister, subsequently transported tea plants to the Cape of Good Hope and to Holland.

F. Valentyn, the parson historian, records that in 1694 he saw "young tea shrubs from China, the size of currant bushes," growing in the garden of the country house of Governor General J. Camphuijs, near Batavia, but it is quite possible he was mistaken regarding their origin. The Governor General had been in Japan, and retained a great affection for that country; he was Cleyer's patron and a near neighbor, too, so it seems more likely that the two exchanged seeds and plants; anyway this explains how the Dutch discovered the possibilities of a new colonial industry, and Java became the first country after China and Japan to successfully grow tea. The conquest of Java by the tea plant was started with tea from Japan, followed by plants from China; but it was not until Assam tea seed was brought from British India, in 1878, that the victory was complete. Indeed, it took over two hundred years for tea to complete the subjugation of Java, for some forty years elapsed after Cleyer's importation of Japanese tea seed before the Dutch East India Company decided to grow its own tea with tea seed brought from China. They were undoubtedly actuated by jealousy of the competition from Austrian Netherlands merchants in the China-Japan trade, and were looking for a means to thwart it.

The "Seventeen Lords," the Board of Directors of the Dutch East India Company, in certain representations made to the Government of Netherlands India, in 1728, argued that China tea seed should be sown not only in Java, but also at the Cape of Good Hope, in Ceylon, at Jaffanapatnam, and elsewhere. They proposed to import Chinese labor and prepare the leaf in the Chinese manner, reasoning that the product's inferiority to China tea was immaterial since it would improve with time, and Europe was, meanwhile, ready to buy anything that was called tea. They pointed out that Java coffee, the cultivation of which was once thought impractical, was supplanting Mocha in the European markets.

The Dutch East Indian Government viewed the project coldly, promising faint encouragement. It doubted if tea could be grown in Java; however, it would make the experiment by offering a bonus to the first one who would produce a pound of the finished native product, as suggested by the "Honorable and Noble Lords." Apparently, the Dutch East India Company did not pursue the matter, for a few years later the Company had regained its monopoly of the tea trade of Europe and had ceased worrying about the growing of tea, satisfied to be sole distributor of the product on the continent.

They did not revive the subject of tea growing in Java until 1823, the year the English were discovering the indigenous tea plant in India. The President of the Royal Company of Agriculture and Herbiage at Ghent, then still a part of Holland, was the moving spirit this time. He wrote to the Minister of Public Education, National Industry, and the Colonies, asking to have certain Japanese plants sent to the Netherlands, but making no mention of tea. When this request reached the Governor General at Batavia, Dr. C. L. Blume, Director of the State Botanical Gardens, suggested that the commission be given to his friend the German physician, Surgeon-Major Philipp Franz von Siebold, 1796–1866, then attached to the Dutch East India Company's agency and settlement on Deshima, an island in the harbor of Nagasaki, Japan.

So it came about, that the first official document in the nineteenth century in which mention is made of the import of tea seed is the Netherlands India Government Resolution of June 10, 1824, No. 6, instructing the head functionary in Japan to charge Surgeon-Major P. F. von Siebold with the execution of the request of Dr. C. L. Blume. By its terms, Dr. von Siebold was ordered to "ship to Batavia, annually, plants and seeds which distinguish themselves by a useful or peculiar quality." Apparently there was no thought of starting the cultivation of tea in Java, even then. The island was selected merely as a station stop for plants on the way to enrich the botanical gardens of the Netherlands. However, these men builded better than they knew. "Of tea there was then no question," says Dr. van der Chijs, the Dutch historiographer, "but the import of new cultures was, so to say, in the air and

SURGEON-MAJOR PH. F. VON SIEBOLD
He shipped the first tea seed from Japan.

the idea of introducing tea culture into Java could not be much longer deferred."[1]

Although tea was not mentioned, and the first shipment was a failure, tea seeds were included in the second shipment, received in 1826. They were successfully sown in the Buitenzorg Botanical Gardens that year, and in an experimental garden near Garoet in 1827.

In 1820, the French naturalist, Pierre Diard, had arrived in Java, fresh from a tour of British India and Sumatra. In 1825, he was appointed inspector of all cultures, "particularly for the poppy, kapok, and all others that might be considered desirable." He played an important rôle in scientific investigation in Netherlands India.

About this time, matters had reached such a pass in the struggle between the conservative colonial politicians who were bent upon maintaining the monopoly system of the Dutch East India Company on behalf of the Government, and the liberal group who wished to open the colonies to private enterprise, that there was a shake-up which resulted in an extraordinary gov-

[1] Jacobus Anne van der Chijs, *Geschiedenis van de gouvernements thee-cultuur op Java*, Batavia and the Hague, 1903.

ernmental authority being sent out from Holland with extensive powers for radical reform. The appointee was the Commissioner General L. P. J. Viscount du Bus de Gisignies, late governor of South Brabant. His instructions from the King were to promote existing cultures and initiate new ones likely to revive the languishing colonial exchequer. Being a man of vision as well as of action, he promptly organized a Chief Commission of Agriculture, the forerunner of the agricultural experiment stations, with himself as chairman. The result was that government support was extended to private enterprise and tea became an object of the Commissioner General's particular solicitude. Agricultural stations for experiments on a larger scale were opened at Krawang and in the exile quarter at Banjoe-Wangie. This set the stage for the entrance of the real founder and father of tea culture in Java, Jacobus Isidorus Lodewijk Levien Jacobson, or, as he is more familiarly known, J. I. L. L. Jacobson.

The Story of J. I. L. L. Jacobson

Jacobson was an expert tea taster en route from Holland to Canton to sample tea for the Netherlands Trading Company. When he arrived the tea plants were doing well in the moist climate around Buitenzorg and Garoet, but search among the Chinese population of Java had failed to discover anyone who knew how the leaf should be prepared for market. Commissioner General du Bus de Gisignies gave Jacobson his great opportunity by assigning him the task of collecting and forwarding information, implements, and workmen from China, with a view to promoting the tea industry of Netherlands India. Jacobson traveled back and forth between China and Java for six years, and after that labored at his task in Java for upwards of fifteen years, during which time he wrote his name highest on the scroll of tea achievements in Netherlands India.

J. I. L. L. Jacobson was born at Rotterdam, March 13, 1799. He was the son of I. L. Jacobson, a coffee and tea broker whose business was established in Rotterdam, and it was from his father that young Jacobson learned all there was to know of the art of tea tasting at that time. The Netherlands Trading Company appointed him their tea expert for Java and China, and on September 2, 1827, he arrived at

J. I. L. L. JACOBSON, 1799–1848

From the original painting owned by Dr. C. J. K. van Aalst, Amsterdam.

Batavia. Invited by Commissioner General du Bus de Gisignies to undertake the mission of collecting information and forwarding tea seed from China for the government's tea experiments, he proceeded to Canton. There he ingratiated himself with the leading tea merchants and, during the following six years, made annual return journeys to Java; each time bringing with him valuable information and quantities of seeds or tea plants for the tea enterprise.

From various accounts of Jacobson's activities we gather that, although he was still in the twenties when he began this work, he was possessed of amazing assurance. He was a positive type who knew how to get things done, although his accomplishments stirred up much jealousy and made many enemies. From the most authoritative biographical sketch of him that has come down to us we learn that he not only gained access to the tea-making establishments in Honan, but that he even penetrated to the interior where he visited the tea gardens.[2]

Dr. C. P. Cohen Stuart, in his valuable

[2] *Winkler Prins' Geïllustreerde encyclopaedie*, Amsterdam, 1912.

monograph on "The Commencement of Tea Culture in Java,"[3] is inclined to be sceptical of the latter claim, pointing out that foreigners were forbidden to travel inland. Jacobson in his own account of his journeys[4] talks about going "a long way into Honan." But the Honan he visited may have been only a small island in the river opposite Canton. Cohen Stuart concludes that Jacobson didn't get much further than the seaport manufacturing sheds at Honan, where the semi-manufactured tea was re-fired for export.

Jacobson tells of Chinese "promises to take him to the tea gardens" and avers that he actually went there. He refers to Ting-soe-a [Tingsua], thirty miles in the interior, where he found "many tea establishments, while six miles further on were to be found "thousands of tea gardens with atmospheric conditions similar to Buitenzorg."

Some of Jacobson's critics would have us look upon him as a kind of Baron Munchausen, but the main facts of his career stand out clearly, and his contributions to the founding of Java's tea industry were many and salutary in spite of necessary allowances for youthful enthusiasm. He was what is sometimes described in America as a "go-getter." Dr. Ch. Bernard says in his monograph, "The History of Tea Culture in the Dutch East Indies": "Jacobson must be rightly considered the actual founder of this culture."[5] Dr. Cohen Stuart, while acknowledging Java's debt to other pioneers, particularly to De Serière, hails Jacobson's arrival in Java, in 1827, as "a factor of great moment in the success of the tea experiments."

Jacobson gained considerable information on his first trip to China, in 1827-28, although "he was essentially a tea taster and trader, not a tea culturist," as Cohen Stuart says, "so such information as he acquired about the culture and manufacture of tea could not have been of much importance." Another of his latter-day critics says: "It was certainly a mistake

SHIP OF CHINA AND JAVA WITH MAT SAILS

Type used for carrying first tea to Java.

to look upon Jacobson as a specialist, the right man for culture and manufacture, when as yet he could only be gauged by his value as a tea taster." However, this same critic acknowledges the man's "admirable perseverance," and agrees that his manual for planters, published in later years, was "of value for a long while."

At Canton it was Jacobson's duty, in his service to the Netherlands Trading Company, working with a fellow countryman, Thure, to assist as tea taster the super-cargo, A. H. Buchler, in buying the return cargoes. For one so young—he was only 28—he was being paid a handsome salary—$4000 a year—and he was full of ambition as well as romantic ideas. At the same time, he knew tea on the buying end, and no one else knew much about its cultivation and manufacture. He was young, too, to have thrust upon him the high honor conferred by his government, although it does not appear that he flinched from the service, fraught though it was with much danger. In those days it was an exceedingly hazardous undertaking to invade an unfriendly country and attempt to carry off men and produce, yet Jacobson did both. On returning from his second journey, in 1828-29, Jacobson brought back eleven Chinese tea shrubs, from Fukien. His third journey, 1829-30, yielded no results for tea culture. From his fourth journey, in 1830-31, he brought back 243 tea plants and 150 seeds. On his fifth journey, in 1831-32, he returned with 300,000 seeds and twelve Chinese workmen. "This was a success of some significance," says Cohen Stuart. When the workmen were subsequently murdered in a coolie row, Jacobson went on a sixth journey to China, 1832-33,

[3] Dr. C. P. Cohen Stuart, botanist at the Theaproefstation, Buitenzorg, "Het begin der theacultuur op Java," *Gedenkboek der Nederlandsch Indische theecultuur*, Weltevreden, 1924.

[4] Jacobus Isodorus Lodewijk Levien Jacobson, *Handboek voor de kultuur en fabrikatie van thee*. Batavia, 1843.

[5] Dr. Ch. Bernard, "De geschiedenis van de theecultuur in Nederlandsch-Indie," *Gedenkboek der Nederlandsch Indische theecultuur*, Weltevreden, 1924.

and brought back no less than 7,000,000 seeds, fifteen workmen—tea planters, tea makers, and box makers—and a mass of materials and implements, which he had collected. It was during this last expedition that he nearly lost his life; for the Chinese government had put a price on his head, and the mandarins attempted to capture his vessel with his tea seed and the Chinese workmen. They did get his interpreter, Acheong, who made the voyage in another ship and was mistaken for Jacobson. Acheong was later ransomed by M. J. Senn van Basel, the Dutch consul at Canton, for 502 piasters. Jacobson got away with his precious cargo.[6]

When given him originally, these assignments were recognized by the government as most difficult, and all who knew Canton with its myriad spies were doubtful of the outcome. From a cabinet letter of Governor General van den Bosch it is apparent that much importance was attached to the 1832–33 charge. "What a triumph was Jacobson's return journey for him!" exclaims Cohen Stuart. On the arrival of his ship off Anjer, cannon were fired, a swarm of prauws put off to enable him to discharge his cargo, and post horses were put at his disposal to take him to Batavia. He was the Lindbergh of his day!

Thus, in 1833, seven years after the first parcel of Japanese tea seed was safely in the ground, Jacobson began in good earnest his labors for the tea industry in Java. Up to 1833, much of the pioneer work had been carried on by others, but Jacobson brought valuable contributions of seeds, plants, men, materials and technical advice on tea making.

Among others of importance in this period Cohen Stuart gives first place to De Serière—a man gifted with the same zeal and self assurance as Jacobson, and interesting because of his diversified talents. De Serière was originally minister to Belgium, accompanying Du Bus de Gisignies to Netherlands India as his protégé. Upon his arrival in Java, he first engaged as editor of the official *Batavia*, afterwards *Java Courant*, and he became simultaneously secretary of the chief commission of agriculture; next, assistant resident of Kra-

wang, and resident of various provinces; finally governor of the Molucca Islands and Chamber Deputy. As Du Bus de Gisignies' faithful Boswell, he claimed for himself and for his patron the honor of first promoting tea cultivation in Java. With circumstantial detail he tells how the Commissioner General, in 1826, acting upon the advice of Pierre Diard, Inspector of Cultures, sent an order for tea seeds to von Siebold in Japan. The latter is said to have filled the order with a small case of tea seeds by the returning ships. There are no official papers to confirm this story, but Cohen Stuart thinks it possible that the thing could have happened, although he is careful to point out it is equally probable that this seed belonged to the annual shipment of Japanese plants with which von Siebold was charged in 1824.

However this may be, De Serière contributed much to the ultimate success of the tea growing enterprise by the care he bestowed upon the seed shipments of Von Siebold and Jacobson, and by his subsequent management of the first large-scale tea garden and factories in the Krawang region. His share in the pioneer work for tea in Java was suitably recognized at the World's Exposition in Paris, 1867, by the award of a gold medal.

It should be noted in passing that M. Diard, in 1839, laid claim to recommending

A DUTCH EAST INDIA MERCHANTMAN OF THE 17TH CENTURY

[6] "We get similar tales from the English tea seed collectors of that time. Vide, G. J. Gordon, *Journal of the Asiatic Society,* Bengal, IV, p. 95, and Robert Fortune's divers writings." *Dr. C. P. Cohen Stuart.*

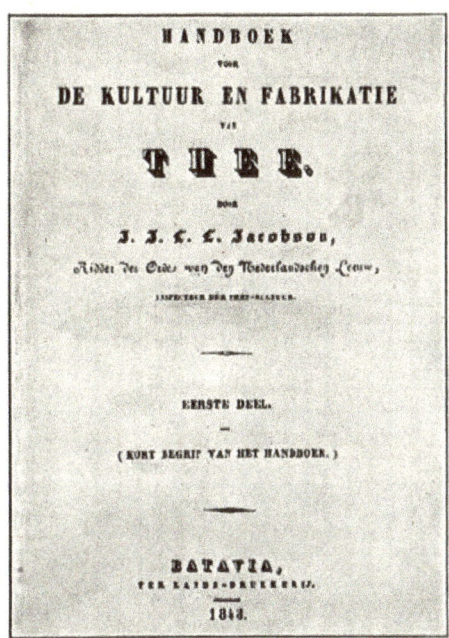

HANDBOEK
voor
DE KULTUUR EN FABRIKATIE
van
THEE.
door
J. I. L. L. Jacobson,
Ridder der Orde van den Nederlandschen Leeuw,
Inspecteur der thee-kultuur.

EERSTE DEEL.
-
(KORT BEGRIP VAN HET HANDBOEK.)

BATAVIA,
TER LANDS-DRUKKERIJ.
1843.

JACOBSON'S FIRST HANDBOOK OF TEA CULTURE AND
MANUFACTURE, PUBLISHED AT BATAVIA IN 1843

the cultivation of tea in Java as early as 1821; also that in 1822, 1823, and 1824 he had imported tea seed from China, which, however, arrived in spoiled condition. Unfortunately, official confirmation of these shipments is lacking.

The "parson-journalist," De Serière, is similarly responsible for a notation in the *Bataviasche Courant*, in 1827, that Lord Amherst or Lord Minto had imported tea plants from China and set them out in the Botanical Gardens at Buitenzorg previous to 1823. It is a fact that Dr. Blume's first garden catalogue, 1823, lists "Thea bohea."

From the reports of the chief commission we learn that in April, 1827, the tea plants at Buitenzorg from the 1826 importation of tea seed had grown so big that some of them were sent to Garoet. Here too "were sown the seed from trees whose leaves, because of their peculiar fragrant property, were mixed with the tea." This reference is to *Thea sasanqua* (THUNB.) NOIS, later identified at Parakan Salak as mandarin tea. The leaves of this species, because of their clove oil content, were formerly used in China and Japan for scenting tea.

In 1827, there were 1000 tea plants at

Buitenzorg and 500 at Garoet, but by 1828 only 750 remained of the 1000 at Buitenzorg; the "tjang kriek," Java's first insect pest, had destroyed the rest. From the survivors, which had already blossomed and borne fruit, the first sample of Java tea was manufactured by order of the Commissioner General, in April, 1828. The work was done by several local Chinamen, who volunteered their services, and Du Bus was much impressed with the result. He wrote: "That which is still lacking in the perfection of this product must be solely ascribed to the want of a sufficient supply of good implements required for the preparation of the same." The Chief Commission of Agriculture was ordered to apply itself with diligence to the extension of tea culture.

The Netherlands Trading Company, on the other hand, was not impressed. It reported on the Buitenzorg sample that it was irregularly gathered, improperly prepared, unsuitable for local consumption or export to Europe, and advised the Commissioner General to have an expert tea maker brought over from Canton. Here we find initiated the principle which later on was to emerge in the Tea Expert Bureau. That tea eventually triumphed in Java is due largely to the willingness of the Dutch always to seek expert advice.

Meanwhile, the chief commission had ordered a large quantity of seeds and plants from Japan, so as not to be hampered in their experiments. A big shipment arrived in 1828, and was distributed among the several Provincial Sub-Commissions of Agriculture in order to try the cultures in various soils and temperatures. G. E. Teisseire, an ex-high-bailiff of the Batavian outer possessions and a member of the Provincial Sub-Commission, distinguished himself by successfully raising several thousand plants. That same year, Fisscher, the inspector of coffee culture in the district of Malambong [Soemadang], reported the discovery of a number of Chinese tea shrubs imported by a Chinaman from his native country. Tea seeds were being brought over from China frequently by the Chinese about this time, but most of them failed to germinate because, in the language of the Chief Commission, "not being packed in soil they spoil."

It is interesting also to note that in this same period Chinamen were cultivating small home garden patches of tea around

WANAJASA TEA PLANTATION AND FACTORY ABOUT 1836; AFTER A SKETCH BY JACOBSON

Benkoelen and Port Marlborough in Sumatra, where the English East India Company was firmly established; so the last province in Netherlands India where tea cultivation has been established was one of the first to grow the tea plant.

For fifteen years following 1833, the indefatigable Jacobson devoted himself to the development of tea cultivation in Java, directing the planting and manufacturing in fourteen provinces. The Dutch Government rewarded his perseverance by appointing him inspector of tea cultivation with some two hundred hands to help him, and later gave him the Cross of the Dutch Lion. In 1843, he published at Batavia his *Handboek voor de cultuur en fabrikatie van thee* [Handbook for the Cultivation and Manufacture of Tea], and in 1845 his *Over het sorteeren en afpakken van de thee* [About Sorting and Packing of Tea], the pioneer technical books on tea.

The cultivation of tea introduced under his direction throughout the whole of west and middle Java increased rapidly, but he was not destined to see its ultimate triumph. He returned to his native country to work out further plans for the development of the industry, only to meet his death on December 27, 1848. In that same

year, Robert Fortune sailed for China to bring back tea plants and Chinese workmen to British India, and the first attempt was made to grow tea in the United States. China tea was still ruling the thought of tea men in all countries, for it was not until 1878, thirty years later, that Assam tea seed was introduced into Java, marking the turning point in the successful development of the industry.

First Phase—Government Failures

In December, 1828, previous to De Serière's acceptance of the appointment as secretary of the Chief Commission of Agriculture, another important event took place. This was the foundation under Diard of agricultural experiment work in Wanajasa. Tea was planted on the slopes of the Boerangrang toward the close of 1829. De Serière tells us in his 1829 report that Jacobson was well pleased with the Chinese tea-makers at Buitenzorg; that he, himself, after his second trip to China, had "made samples of green and black tea, nay, even of Souchon and Pecco," which met with the approval of the Netherlands Trading Company; and that he had been awarded a silver medal for his tea at the

Gov. General J. van den Bosch, Father of the Culture System

Com. General du Bus de Gisignies. Favored Private Ownership

first exposition ever held in Batavia, June 27 to July 10, 1829. In the catalogue of the exposition there is mentioned:

A small case with five samples of tea grown and manufactured in the State Botanical Gardens at Buitenzorg; a sample of tea produced and prepared at Lebak, in the Bantam region; three samples cultivated and prepared at Garoet, in the Preanger Regencies; four samples of tea from the State Botanical Gardens at Buitenzorg . . . ; two samples from Japan.

Within the next few years rapid progress was made, beginning with a plantation of 2783 trees which was laid out at Wanajasa in 1829. Five thousand more trees were planted in 1830 and, in 1831, there were added 119,000 trees. In 1832, the first big import from China by Jacobson and also from Japan, 425,000 trees, arrived. In 1833, there was a further shipment from Japan of 415,000 trees, making a total of 964,000 trees at the end of 1833. Supposing that all these shrubs were actually there and planted 5 x 5 feet, as Jacobson advised, then, says Dr. Cohen Stuart:

This would represent over 200 hectares [494 acres] under cultivation at an epoch, when in British India plans were just being considered for making a trial of tea culture. Moreover, in 1830, there was a small factory, with four furnaces, in operation at Wanajasa; the first in Java, and fully equipped for the packing of tea. The game had begun.

At first, tea was made now and then. There was a package for the Governor General, then the samples for the Batavia Exposition; again, in 1831, a small chest was sent to the King. However, when Jacobson arrived in 1832, with his really important shipment, and his Chinese tea makers, the infant tea industry assumed a serious aspect. Indeed, it even developed bloodshed, for dissatisfaction arose among the Chinese workmen at Tjilankap. The new Governor General, van den Bosch, favored the Chinese, because he had a very poor opinion of Javanese labor in general, and the turbulent Singkehs rose in mutiny, making it necessary to call out the military forces. The disaffection spread, and although the Chinese tea workers at Wanajasa were peaceably inclined, and had no part in the trouble at Tjilankap, the agitation led to an attack upon them, resulting in the killing of all but two.

In spite of this serious setback, De Serière pursued his experiments, but, in March, 1835, it was decided to close down the station at Tjilankap. The garden at Wanajasa remained under the management of Jacobson.

Dr. H. Burger, Von Siebold's co-worker in Japan, made an inspection of Wanajasa in 1833, and was favorably impressed by the Javanese labor employed there. He comments on their adaptability—working in the tea sheds as if they had always been accustomed to that kind of labor. "There were days, when, with four furnaces and ten Javanese boedjangs [workmen], I saw 20 catties [about 27 pounds] of tea prepared, both green and the choicer sorts."

The Governor General, afterwards Count, J. van den Bosch, in 1832, purchased at public auction, the lands of Pondok Gedeh, Tjiawie and Tjiderock, previously united under the name of the Pondok Gedeh lands, for fl. 203,000. This

THE FORMER GOVERNMENT TEA PLANTATION AT WANAJASA AS IT APPEARS TODAY.

private landed property remained in the possession of the Counts van den Bosch until 1887, when the Cultuur Company Pondok Gedeh was established. With the exception of the Herwijnen and Legok-Ngenong plots they were not planted with tea until 1890. Governor General van den Bosch was the father of the culture system, or *cultuur stelsel*, although a monopolist of the old school and diametrically opposed to the ideas of Du Bus, who encouraged private enterprise.

The Cultuur Stelsel

That the tea-growing industry remained insignificant in Java until 1860, in spite of the comparatively good start it had, is to be attributed to the agrarian fiscal policy adopted by the Dutch East Indian Government in 1830. At that time, the Commissioner General, Du Bus de Gisignies, who was an ardent believer in private initiative and liberty of action for European colonial agriculture and industry, was replaced by Governor General van den Bosch, who introduced the culture system. In the days when Java was under English rule, Lieutenant Governor Raffles, in consequence of the usurpation of power by native princes in the districts governed by them, had laid down the principle that the Government was owner of all the land, cultivated or not. The natives who settled on the land with the right to make use of it by inheritance had to pay rent for that right; the rent being equal to about one-fifth of what they could get out of the soil.

Van den Bosch ruled that the native villages should pay their land rent by giving up one-fifth of their fields to the cultivation of those crops which were needed for the European market, the Government paying the laborers who worked this portion. The land rent could also be satisfied by the provision of labor for export cultivation on hitherto unbroken ground. In this way the Government found itself able to control quantities of coffee, sugar cane, indigo, and newly introduced crops, such as tea, at slight cost, but employing much compulsion. The system failed, however, in the case of tea, for tea-growing and manufacture both demand expert care. In the period from 1835 to 1842 only a small amount of tea was grown by the Government on a few plantations, under contract with private persons. The making of the

Site of One of the Oldest Government Tea Gardens near Tjisoeroepan

China tea planted by Jacobson, 1829.

tea also was contracted for by private persons who received advances and were paid according to the quantity turned out, with the natural result that these contractors paid more attention to quantity than to quality. It proved impossible, moreover, to carry out an efficient inspection by the Government.

After 1870, the ideas of Du Bus again triumphed. The system of Government culture, bound up with feudal tenure and contracts with European planters, was found wanting as far as tea was concerned, although these same Government tea-gardens provided a foundation on which private enterprise builded real successes in later years. In 1849, the Government tea-gardens in the Krawang Residency were abandoned "without extirpation of the shrubs," and in 1851, the factories and warehouses at Wanajasa were publicly sold. Accepting a loss of six million guilders [$2,412,000] the Government monopoly of tea in Java was finally abandoned in 1860.

Meanwhile, in 1835, the first invoice of Java tea was received by the Pakhuismeesteren van de Thee at Amsterdam, and by 1841, there were eight establishments in

TEA CHEST LABEL OF 1835

From the first invoice of Java tea shipped to Amsterdam.

the Preanger. The tea, however, did not come up to the market requirements, so it was decided to have it refined at a central factory erected for the purpose at Meester-Cornelis, a suburb of Batavia. This did not help matters much, since garden labor was high and transport quite expensive. In 1859, the production costs were amounting to fl. 1.17 per pound while at Amsterdam sales the tea brought only fl. 0.81, net. Small wonder then that the Government thought to recoup its losses by transferring some of its holdings to private firms under contract, assisting them with loans. It was provided that the country-fired teas should be delivered to the central refiring establishment at Meester-Cornelis at a fixed price. The Government had closed all its holdings except those under lease in the residencies of Batavia, Preanger, Cheribon and Bagelen by 1842 and, although the product improved, the cost price continued to exceed the selling price. The Meester-Cornelis enterprise was abandoned in 1894, and the contract leases were amended so as to have the tea fully manufactured at the local factories and delivered to the Government in a finished condition.

From 1849 to 1853, the Government paid the contractors an average of 65½ Dutch cents per half kilogram, the price agreed upon being the Amsterdam market quotations. The Government's losses continued

to mount, but as long as Jacobson tested the teas at Meester-Cornelis there was continued improvement. When he returned to Holland, however, and the testing had to be done in the contractors' factories by Government officers who knew little or nothing about tea, matters grew steadily worse. It is related that unscrupulous contractors were not above tampering with lines of tea after they had been passed. The Chinese contractor at Sinagar, for example, never permitted the Government inspector to test his tea until "he had treated him as host in a royal manner."

The outcome was inevitable. All the Government undertakings were set free and offered for private enterprise at fl. 25 to fl. 50 per hectare. Some of the more notable transfers follow:

In 1862, Parakan Salak was hired to A. W. Holle; in 1863, Sinagar and Tjirohani to A. Holle and van Motman; in 1863-65, Tjioemboeleuit, Tjikembang, Tjarennang, Djatinangor and Tjikadjang, to Mr. W. A. Baron Baud; and in 1865, Bagelen, known as the Ledok Tea Gardens, was hired in part to D. van der Sluijs, who acquired 153 hectares on Tandjoengsari, and in part to W. de Jong, who acquired 137 hectares on Tambi and 218 hectares on Bedakah. These were subsequently purchased by Dr. N. P. van den Berg, and Messrs. K. F. Holle and Ed. Jacobson, under the style of the Bagelen Tea and Cinchona Company.

The Second Phase—Private Ownership

The second phase of tea's conquest of Java—the era of private enterprise—began in the years 1862 to 1865. Rid of its losing tea venture the Government turned with relief to the flourishing coffee industry, which was bringing handsome returns to the State, while the infant tea industry had caused a loss of over six million florins. Competition between the tea

Mr. W. A. Baron Baud

and coffee interests continued to be keen, and the men engaged in tea were looked upon askance when they petitioned for land having coffee possibilities. In this way tea was held in check for fear of the bad influence it might have upon the extension of

OLDEST JAPANESE-CHINESE TEA, GROWING ON TJIKADJANG, DATING FROM 1863

its rival, coffee, and because it called for much more labor than coffee required.

The private tea planting enterprise was handicapped in many directions. From the beginning the contracts held by tea planters were continually getting them into all kinds of trouble, even lawsuits, with the Government. Then, poorly selected soils brought unfavorable crops, and plant diseases multiplied. Again, only a few of the higher elevation teas like Tjikadjang and Bagelen, traveling under fancy names, were found to be serviceable in choice blends; the teas of the lower gardens were known in the trade chiefly for their sharp disagreeable "Java taste," and could not compete with the China growths. Probably the greatest of all the difficulties with which the tea planters had to contend was the transport problem. The roads were poor and the tea was usually transported by the slow moving Indian buffalo oxen, picul packhorses, or coolies. There is a specimen tea invoice in existence representing a shipment that was dispatched from Waspada in December, 1875, but which did not get to Batavia until ten months afterwards.

In 1870, there were only about fifteen plantations under cultivation. They ranged from 150 to 200 hectares. The area of the Government gardens, which in 1846 had increased to over 4500 hectares, comprising 20,000,000 plants, had dwindled in 1864 to less than 900 hectares with 6,000,000 shrubs. Likewise, production, which nearly reached 2,000,000 lbs. in 1860, had shrunk to less than 800,000 lbs.

It was not until the proclamation of the Agrarian Act of Minister de Waal in 1870, whereby lands could be leased for seventy-five years with free extensions not subject to the approval of officers having coffee culture interests, that tea prospects began to brighten. At the same time the hire contracts of existing concerns were converted into lease-hold rights. Generally speaking, however, conditions continued unsatisfactory because of low prices, and the competition of China teas, and the constantly increasing supplies from Ceylon and British India. "It was," says Dr. Bernard, "one long groping about in the dark."

At last a few tea manufacturers, quite at their wits' end, hit upon the idea of sending their tea to London and, in 1877, the first Parakan Salak invoice reached Mincing Lane. The English tea brokers were friendly but brutally frank. The tea was not only badly made, as compared with

Mr. John Peet   Mr. A. Holle   Mr. L. A. F. H. Baron van Heeckeren   Mr. E. J. Kerkhoven

IMPORTANT FACTORS IN THE INTRODUCTION OF INDIA TEA SEED INTO JAVA

that of British India, but India grew better kinds. With the difficulty thus definitely defined there were but two courses open to Java tea manufacturers; either to retire from the market or to produce better and more useful teas. Fortunately the way already had been paved for the latter course. Assam tea seed, destined to revolutionize the tea industry of Java, was first imported from British India in 1872. Bosch, the chief inspector of cultures, ordered a few maunds through Dennyson and Company, and tried it out in an experimental way on his Tjiboengoer plantation by Patjet. In 1876, the estate passed into other hands and the experiment died through neglect.

John Peet Introduces Assam Seed

In 1878, another tea pioneer, whose name will always be held in high regard by the Java tea planting industry, appeared in the person of John Peet, founder of the firm of John Peet & Co., which continues under the same name. He knew the requirements of the English market and was familiar with manufacturing methods in Ceylon and India. Acting on his advice the Java planters began the regular importation of tea seed from Assam and changed over their manufacturing methods. Mr. Peet's first Assam tea seed was sown on the Sinagar-Tjirohani [Moendjoel] property at Tjibadak by A. Holle, with Mr. Peet as a partner in the enterprise. A seed garden was laid out at Moendjoel, and in 1879 a pluck garden was made with a second parcel received by Mr. van Heeckeren at Sinagar. Seed from the Moendjoel garden was sold to many gardens over Java. Mr. R. E. Kerkhoven, Director-Administrator of Gamboeng, had sown some Assam tea seed received from Ceylon in 1877 and the years following, but with unsatisfactory results. In 1882, however, when Mr. Kerkhoven saw what a success had been achieved by his uncle, E. J. Kerkhoven, on Sinagar, he ordered some Jaipur seed from British India. That same year Mr. John Peet ordered for Messrs. Albert Holle, B. B. J. Crone, E. J. Kerkhoven, G. C. F. W. Mundt, and F. C. Philippeau, 10 maunds of seed from Calcutta. The best seeds were sent to Moendjoel and to Tendjoajoe. The former afterwards sold large quantities. The original gardens are still in existence.

Gradually, the old China plants were superseded by the sturdier Assam jats, modern machinery took the place of the old rolling methods, and mechanical driers drove out the charcoal furnaces. Thus was ushered in the third period of tea's conquest of Java; a period that was marked by great prosperity when the coffee lands became *koffie moe* [coffee tired]. The tea garden areas were extended, quality improved, and Java tea became as well known in the tea markets of the world as Java coffee had been in the old days.

The Third Phase—The Golden Age

Modern withering, one of the most important, if not the most important, phase of tea manufacture, in the opinion of Dr. Bernard, was harder to install in Java than any of the other processes. The report of H. J. Th. Netscher and A. A. Holle on their study trip to British India, in 1902, tells of their astonishment at seeing for the first time the withering "chungs" so characteristic of the country. Up to that time

Mr. R. A. Kerkhoven   Mr. K. F. Holle   Mr. A. W. Holle   Mr. G. L. J. van der Hucht

PIONEERS OF THE CULTIVATION OF TEA IN JAVA

tea in Java had been withered on *tampirs* —flat bamboo trays—in the sun, or on the factory floors. A series of withering experiments followed; the results being published in the *Cultuur Gids* [Culture Guide] of 1904.

Mention should be made of the names of some of those who strongly influenced the development of tea culture in Java at this period. First place is usually given the names of Holle and Kerkhoven. The rôle which the Holle-Kerkhoven family played and, indeed, is still playing in Java tea, is so important that the two are inseparably bound together. From 1850 to 1860 the names constantly recur—the Holles of Sinagar, Parakan Salak, Tjikadjang and Waspada; the Kerkhovens of Sinagar, Ardjasari, and Gamboeng. Mr. A. R. W. Kerkhoven, the present chairman of the Sockaboemi property and administrator of Panoembang, is a son of the founder of the house.

Dr. Bernard recalls that the period from 1875 to 1890 represents the golden age of sociability and good fellowship in the Java tea industry; the good old times when an almost royal hospitality was dispensed in the mansions of the tea barons, who lived like feudal lords and were looked up to as Great White Fathers by their thousands of estate laborers. Those were the times when journeys took days to accomplish and were full of adventures; when palanquins, "balloon" carts, and buffalo oxen provided more picturesque, if less speedy, means of transportation than the modern motor cars; the days of thrilling snipe hunts, of the races, rides to hunt, soirées, dinner parties, and gorgeous oriental festas. Not that the spirit of Dutch hospitality has changed; only that we live in a swifter age, one wherein railways, aeroplanes, motor cars, radio, telephones, superb roads, all conspire to rob life of something of the peace and serenity which characterized the "old days," and which will always linger in the memories of those of us who knew them without the modern hysteria or, as Dr. Bernard so feelingly calls it, "our present *perpetuum mobile*." And a curious part of it is the ease with which we adapt ourselves to the changing conditions. The author admits he found Dutch hospitality in Java quite as pleasant in 1924, when he covered ten times as much ground and saw and learned much more, as in 1906, when he visited only two or three estates and spent most of his time on the island as a guest of that princely host, Mr. L. A. F. H. Baron van Heeckeren tot Waliën, on Sinagar, one of the show places of the "Garden of the East."

MONUMENT TO MR. K. F. HOLLE, GAROET

Mr. R. E. Kerkhoven   Mr. A. R. W. Kerkhoven

TWO NOTABLE KERKHOVENS

The first meteorological observations on tea estates were made in 1858–59 by K. F. Holle at Tjikadjang, and from 1864 to 1869 at Tjioemboeleuit by Meijboom. In an address at the 1924 Tea Congress, Dr. Bernard pointed out that as early as 1834 there was a difference of opinion between Resident de Serière and Inspector Jacobson with regard to plant propagation; that in 1845, plantation samples of tea soil were sent to Holland for analysis; in 1847 it was recorded by Jacobson that *Helopeltis* wrought havoc on badly tilled ground.

Java Tea Associations

On December 20, 1881, eleven of the leading planters met and organized the Soekaboemi Agricultural Association. These were E. J. Kerkhoven of Sinagar, A. Holle of Moendjoel, G. C. F. W. Mundt of Parakan Salak, W. R. de Greve of Sindangsari, P. Zeper of Aardenburg, B. B. J. Crone of Tendjoajoe, G. A. Ort of Boengameloer, F. C. Philippeau of Tjisalak, G. W. Eekhout of Pasir Telegawarna, Ch. J. Hausmann of Tjikembang, and D. Burger of Malinggoet.

This was the pioneer tea association of Java. Its first chairman was Albert Holle, the first secretary G. C. F. W. Mundt.

In 1885, Mr. Mundt was sent to Ceylon to study conditions there. His observations were published in a brochure entitled "Ceylon and Java."

In 1924, there was a merger with the rubber planters' association, and since 1927 the Soekaboemi organization has been subordinated to the *Algemeen Landbouw Syndicaat*, or General Agricultural Syndicate, Batavia, and attends only to local matters, while the Syndicate looks after general agricultural affairs.

G. C. F. W. MUNDT, Knight of the Order of Orange Nassau, Officer of the Order of Cambodia, was born at Hamburg, February 8, 1845.

At the age of nineteen he went to Hong Kong, where he stayed for nearly a year, going from there to Singapore, and afterwards, in 1865, to Batavia, where for three years he was with the firm of P. Landberg & Sons. Following that connection he was in the service of the Netherland Indies Steamship Company for three years. He married Catharina Suzanna van Motmann in 1871 and became manager of the coffee estate Mandalasari, Nanggoeng. Later, he was manager at Parakan Salak, and at Tjiboengoer and Mandaling, where he died on November 19, 1904. Mr. Mundt at one time was superintendent of the Sindangsari and other estates.

The *Vereeniging voor de Thee Cultuur in Nederlandsche Indië*, Batavia, is a new organization of estate owners resident in the Netherlands Indies, similar to one of the same name at Amsterdam composed of estate owners resident in Holland.

The Tea Experimental Station

As early as 1886, the tea planters realized the need for an inquiry service and scientific observations. After a preliminary discussion between the director of the State Botanical Gardens, Dr. Melchior M. Treub, the vice-chairman of the Soekaboemi Agricultural Association, and Mr. E. J. Kerkhoven, an arrangement was perfected, in 1893, whereby several firms pledged a sum of money for the salary of an assistant who was to study tea culture

Dr. Melchior M. Treub   Mr. G. C. F. W. Mundt
Director of the State   First Secretary of
Botanical Gardens   Soekaboemi Ag. Assn.

PROTAGONISTS OF SCIENTIFIC TEA CULTURE

MANAGER'S BUNGALOW ON PARAKAN SALAK, RESIDENCE OF THE LATE MR. G. C. F. W. MUNDT

questions in the agricultural analyst laboratories of the Botanical Gardens. Dr. C. E. J. Lohmann was appointed to the post and labored at it for five years under the direction of, and in coöperation with, Dr. P. van Romburgh. The first report of van Romburgh's tea investigations appeared June 14, 1894. The funds were in the hands of a commission appointed by the Soekaboemi Agricultural Association E. J. Kerkhoven of Sinagar was the first chairman of this commission.

In 1898, Dr. A. W. Nanninga succeeded Dr. Lohmann, and in 1902, acting upon the initiative of Mr. T. G. E. G. de Dieu Stierling, the temporary institution at Buitenzorg became the *Proefstation voor Thee*, or Tea Experimental Station. Dr. Treub continued to direct the new institution, and Dr. Nanninga remained as manager.

Among others who have been active in their support of the Experimental Station, mention should be made of Mr. O. van Vloten, who for ten years was an active chairman, first of the Commission of Inspection, afterwards of the Association; and the late Mr. K. A. R. Bosscha, chairman, 1917–1929.

In 1916, the station was organized independent of the Soekaboemi Agricultural Association, having its own board of directors, chosen from the participating planter members, now representing one hundred seventy estates. It still coöperated with the Soekaboemi Association, however, and remained attached to the Department of Agriculture, Industry and Trade until July, 1925, when all scientific research work conducted by the experimental stations of the tea, rubber, coffee, and cinchona industries passed to the control of the *Algemeen Landbouw Syndicaat*, or General Agricultural Syndicate, which is

Mr. T. G. E. G. de Dieu   Mr. J. E. van Polanen
Stierling   Petel

TWO JAVA TEA PIONEERS

Dr. Ch. Bernard
1907-28

Dr. J. J. B. Deuss
1928-33

FORMER DIRECTORS OF THE PROEFSTATION

the head organization of the Netherlands Indian Mountain estates.

MR. W. J. DE JONGE, the present Chairman of the Algemeen Landbouw Syndicaat,

Mr. W. J. de Jonge

was born in Holland, September 8, 1898, and after completing his education at the Gymnasium in Nijmegen and the University in Leiden, started his business career as counsel and attorney at The Hague, later continuing in the same profession at Semarang. He was Secretary of the Syndicaat for a number of years prior to his election, February, 1933, to the chairmanship, succeeding Dr. G. H. C. Hart.

From 1907 to 1928 the scientific staff of the Experimental Station was directed by Dr. Ch. Bernard, a Swiss botanist.

DR. CH. BERNARD was born in Geneva, December 5, 1876, obtaining his degree of D. Sc. at the university at Geneva in 1902. Dr. Melchior Treub invited him to become Director of the Botanic Laboratories at Buitenzorg in 1905, and when Dr. Nanninga retired as Director of the Tea Experimental Station, in 1907, Dr. Bernard succeeded him. In 1928 he became Director of Agriculture, Industry, and Commerce, and retired in 1933.

DR. J. J. B. DEUSS was born in Limburg, Holland, in 1883, obtaining his degree in chemistry at the University of Liege in 1908. In 1912, he went to Buitenzorg as assistant to Dr. Bernard, whom he succeeded as Director of the Proefstation in 1928.

DR. IR. TH. G. E. HOEDT, the present Director of the Proefstation, was born in Java and educated in Holland. He succeeded Dr. Deuss as Director in 1933.

The Director of the Station is an adviser for native tea cultivation for which the Station is allowed a yearly Government grant of $2000. In 1907, a botanist and a chemist were engaged to conduct various experiments connected with the manufacture and chemistry of tea, diseases, manuring, etc.

Gradually the staff was increased, and in 1932 the *Proefstation voor Thee* was combined with the *Proefstation voor Rubber* under the style of the *"Proefstation West Java."*

On September 24, 1927, the new and strictly modern office building now occupied by the Tea Experimental Station at Buitenzorg was formally opened.

The Tea Expert Bureau

In 1905, on the initiative of Mr. F. D. Cochius of the brokerage firm of Dunlop & Kolff, of Batavia, there was organized the Tea Expert Bureau, first located at Bandoeng and afterwards at Batavia. This Bureau, to which planters can send samples of their teas for testing, has contributed much towards the improvement of the quality of Java tea by pointing out defects before shipment, thus safeguarding its good name in the tea markets abroad. In addition, it has made a study of marketing teas in foreign countries, as well as advertising in Australia and the United States.

Before the establishment of the Tea Expert Bureau, the planters had to await reports of valuation and tests of quality until the arrival of shipments in London or Amsterdam. As a rule these reached them eight or ten weeks after the dis-

Mr. C. E. J.
Lohmann

Dr. P. van
Romburgh

Dr. A. W.
Nanninga

GROUP OF EARLY SCIENTIFIC OBSERVERS

Mr. J. Th. Hamaker
First President

Mr. H. Lambe
First Expert

EARLY PROMOTERS OF THE TEA EXPERT BUREAU

patch of the shipment. The tea tester in the Tea Expert Bureau eliminated this delay, and gave them an opportunity to rectify any mistakes in manufacture before they shipped the tea. Thirty-three gardens were represented in the Bureau by the end of 1905, and Mr. H. Lambe was the first expert employed, remaining with the organization until 1910.

Mr. Lambe had been engaged for a number of years previously with Walker Lambe & Co., in London, and later had represented the same company under his own name at Calcutta. Then he came to Batavia to take the post of manager of the former Tea Export Corporation.

At its inception Mr. J. Th. Hamaker was chosen as the first president of the Committee re Tea Expert, and Mr. S. W. Zeverijn as secretary. A committee of three members, consisting of Messrs. H. van Son, S. W. Zeverijn, and F. D. Cochius, was appointed to act with two members from the Soekaboemi Planters' Association in charge of contributions and supervision of the office of the expert.

In 1907, Bandoeng was selected as headquarters for the tea expert, who, in addition to his duties as tester, had financial duties connected with the collection of contributions. In 1910, the Committee re Tea Expert was incorporated under the name *Vereeniging Thee Expert Bureau*, or Tea Expert Bureau Association, and the headquarters of the expert were transferred to Batavia to bring the tea expert in closer contact with the Board which at that time consisted of: Mr. S. W. Zeverijn, President; Geo. Wehry & Co., Secretary and Treasurer; Messrs. E. H. Evans, Odo van Vloten, and K. A. R. Bosscha.

The Bureau costs 60,000 to 70,000

guilders [£5,000 to £5,833] a year, this sum being raised partly by a contribution of 10 cents [2d.] for 100 kilos [220 lbs.] of tea made; of a charge of 25 cents [5d.] a sample tasted; and of an annual charge of 50 guilders [£4.3.4] for circulars on prices, reviews, etc. From the sum raised £1,000 is set aside for propaganda, which was used largely for advertising in America up to 1932, when propaganda in consuming countries was abandoned in favor of promotional work among the native population of Java.

Tea Scales The Pengalengan Plateau

The number of tea gardens increased gradually from 1880 to 1890. During this period tea completed its conquest of Java by scaling the Pengalengan Plateau, that magnificent table-land which appeared to offer all the advantages of a near-Darjeeling elevation, combined with the forcing climate of the equatorial zone. Tea cultivation on this broad elevated tract of rich tropical soil was stimulated largely by the activities of the planter-philanthropist, K. A. R. Bosscha, 1855–1928, sometimes referred to as the "agricultural king of the Praanger" and as the "tea king of Java." For over thirty years he was associated with Malabar Estate, a name which, like Goalpara, is almost synonymous with Java tea. Mr. Bosscha was the first manager of Malabar, which he opened in 1896, when it was little more than a tropical jungle. The estate now comprises 3000 acres under tea and 65 acres of cinchona.

K. A. R. BOSSCHA.—Mr. Bosscha left Holland for the East Indies in December, 1887, when only a young man, joining his uncle, Mr. Kerkhoven, on the Sinagar Estate, near Soekaboemi. He soon moved to Borneo, however, to explore for gold mines;

Mr. F. D. Cochius
Proposer

Mr. S. W. Zeverijn
First Secretary

THEY HELPED ORGANIZE THE TEA EXPERT BUREAU

one of the first Europeans to engage in a private enterprise in western Borneo. He returned to Java in 1892, making headquarters with his uncle, and founding the Preanger Telephone Company, of which he was superintendent and technical adviser till the system was taken over by the Government. He had a directing part in every phase of the Malabar development, including the invention of the Bosscha withering machines, the establishment of laboratories so that all tea is under the constant supervision of chemists, the erection of a 3000 h.p. station to supply the estate with electric power, and the building of water works, including a tunnel 4000 feet long. He was also one of the main factors in numerous other agricultural and industrial enterprises, among them the Bandoeng Electric Company, the caoutchouc factory at Bandoeng, and the Romaniet plant for the manufacture of explosives, near Batavia.

Mr. K. A. R. Bosscha

He was noted for his public and private benefactions, which included 100,000 guilders to Bandoeng University, of which he was chairman, besides innumerable gifts to hospitals, scientific societies, and other educational institutions. It was he also who took the initiative in the erection of a large meteorological observatory near Lembang, which frequently figures in the astronomical news of the world. Mr. Bosscha was chairman of the committee of the Java Tea Congress and Fair, held at Bandoeng in 1924. He died in 1928.

The successful exploitation of the Pengalengan Plateau aroused the interest of the investing public, and there was started a veritable "rush into tea." As the period of prosperity since 1890 continued, new estates were constantly started, at first in the mountainous districts of Western Java, where the most favorable soil, climate, and labor conditions were found to obtain; subsequently in other parts of Java, until around 1910 the number had increased to about 200, the majority of which were located in West Java and particularly in the Preanger.

In 1927, there were two hundred sixty-nine tea estates with 210,000 acres under tea in the island of Java alone, with twenty-six, having 31,000 acres in tea, on Sumatra. If we add to this the 63,000 acres of tea gardens owned and run by the native Malay population the total is 304,-000 acres, producing over a hundred million pounds per year, so that the conquest of the island by tea may be said to be fully consummated.

Improved methods of cultivation have raised the yield per unit area tremendously as compared with the period before 1890, so much so, indeed, that nowadays productions of 1000 to 1500 kilos per hectare are by no means exceptional.

The period of prosperity, which lasted until the middle of 1914, was followed by a series of very trying years, culminating in the panicky times between 1920 and 1922. Subsequently, conditions materially improved.

In 1924, a Tea Congress was held at Bandoeng to commemorate the first centenary of the introduction of tea culture into Java. The opening address was delivered by Dr. A. L. Rutgers, Director of Agriculture, and papers discussing phases of the tea industry were presented by Dr. Ch. Bernard, Dr. J. J. B. Deuss, Dr. R. Menzel, Dr. C. P. Cohen Stuart, and Mr. A. Keuchenius of the Tea Experimental Station Staff; Mr. H. J. O. Braund of the Tea Expert Bureau, Batavia; Mr. George F. Mitchell, Supervising Tea Examiner of the United States; Messrs. A. C.

MR. BOSSCHA IN HIS OFFICE ON MALABAR

TEA CONGRESS AT BANDOENG, COMMEMORATING THE FIRST CENTENARY OF TEA CULTURE IN JAVA, JUNE 21–26, 1924

Slotemaker, C. M. Hamaker, J. H. Müller, I. Tanabé, H. W. S. van Hooff, H. van Warmelo, M. Guillaume, R. du Pasquier, Oeij Tiauw Hok, A. Groothoff, I. G. E. Kalshoven, D. C. Sparnaay, A. T. J. Bianchi, G. F. J. Bley, A. R. W. Kerkhoven, Prof. A. Lendner, Dr. C. A. Backer, Dr. M. Kerbosch, Dr. L. G. den Berger, Dr. L. Rehfous, Dr. F. C. van Heurn, and Dr. A. W. K. de Jong.

The Tea Congress was followed four years later, in 1928, by an Estate Managers' Congress held at Bandoeng, and sponsored by the Soekaboemi Agricultural Association.

Tea Restriction

Dutch East Indian tea planters joined the planters of British India and Ceylon in an agreement for a joint restriction of plucking following the market slump of 1929. The proportion of the reduction undertaken by Java and Sumatra was 9,500,000 lbs. on the 1930 crop, but no actual decrease was effected and in 1931 the plan was dropped.

Continued overproduction brought about regulation of tea exports. The initiative was taken by the tea committee of the British Chamber of Commerce for the N. E. I. in London. British India and Ceylon joined the Dutch in a five-year plan, providing for a 15 per cent reduction in tea exports in 1933, and suitable reductions for succeeding years.

A Family of Tea Patriarchs

A few historical notes may not be amiss on that great family of patriarchs, the Holle-Kerkhovens, those sturdy Dutch pioneers who were the real founders of the tea industry in Java. For these the author is indebted to Dr. C. P. Cohen Stuart of the Tea Experiment Station.

GUILLAUME LOUIS JACQUES VAN DER HUCHT.—In 1846, Mr. Guillaume Louis Jacques van der Hucht arrived in Batavia with 33 relatives. It was a red letter day for the Hucht family, for Java, and for tea. Young van der Hucht was one of a large family of little means, and when his father was killed in the Russian war he decided to relieve his mother of his support by running off to sea. He educated himself on his voyages aboard a Dutch merchantman plying back and forth to the Indies. He bought his own school books, spending his study hours in the crow's nest. He rose to first mate and when his captain died was given the command. It was a profitable run in the days when the captains always prospered, so the poor lad became a wealthy man. Yearning for other worlds to conquer, his attention was turned to Java, whither, in 1846, he made his last voyage, taking to the promised land a ready made colony of relatives, all imbued with the same enterprising spirit as himself.

Among others on board were Mr. and Mrs. Holle, *nee* Van der Hucht. Mrs. Holle was a sister of the patriarch Van der Hucht. The Holles had seven children: Karl Frederick, founder of Waspada estate; Adriaan Walraven, manager of Parakan Salak, who married Miss J. van Motman; Herman H., manager of John Pryce and Company; Albert, manager of Sinagar, who married Miss J. R. van Motman; Pauline, who married Mr. Hoogeveen, manager of Sindangsari and Tjisalak; C. F., married to N. P. van den Berg, LL. D., president of the Java Bank; and Albertine A., married to Mr. Denninghoff Stelling of the firm of Tiedeman and van Kerchem. The father of this remarkable family became manager of the Bolang Estate, but died shortly thereafter. The parents of Mr. van Heeckeren were also in the Van der Hucht family party of 1846.

Mr. G. L. J. van der Hucht, after the death of his first wife, married Miss Mary Pryce and later established the firm of John Pryce and Company.

The son of A. W. Holle, Alexander Albert Holle, was employed at Parakan Salak under G. C. F. W. Mundt and subsequently, in 1902, made the notable study trip to India with Mr. H. J. Th. Netscher.

Johannes Kerkhoven, who married a sister of Mr. van der Hucht, died in Holland in 1859. His youngest son, Edward Julius, 1834–1905, went to Java in 1861, and was employed on Parakan Salak, under his cousin, A. W. Holle. Later, he succeeded Albert Holle as managing director of Sinagar, which, meanwhile, had been purchased from B. B. Crone by Mr. van der Hucht. E. J. Kerkhoven, known among his people as *"djoeragan sepoeh,"* or the Old Master, managed Sinagar for nine years after the death of A. Holle. It was in 1872 that his cousin, L. Baron van Heeckeren tot Waliën joined him as an employee. Mr. Kerkhoven's connection with the founding of the Soekaboemi Agricultural Association has already been mentioned.

Albert Holle, as also noted previously, was co-founder and first president of the Soekaboemi Agricultural Association. It was he who, in 1878, laid out the first Assam tea seed garden at Moendjoel.

As the Tjibadak district was developed by the Holle family so the Kerkhovens developed the district south of Bandoeng. Rudolph Albert Kerkhoven, 1820–1890, came to Java in 1865, and established the Ardjasari estate, being succeeded by his son, Augustus Emilius Kerkhoven, who died in 1924. A second son of the founder, Rudolph Eduard Kerkhoven, 1848–1918, came to Java in 1871; became acting manager of Sinagar during his uncle's furlough, and was on Ardjasarie. With his father, he began the planting of coffee and tea on the site of the present Gamboeng Estate. He put out Assam tea in 1882, and explored the Pengalengan, selecting the site occupied by Malabar as ideal for tea. Many were dubious of this, fearing the Assam jat from the plains of India could hardly be expected to do well in the mile high climate of the Pengalengan Plateau; but, after experiencing considerable difficulty in securing the necessary capital, Mr. Kerkhoven finally enlisted the financial aid of Messrs. S. J. W. van Buren and John Peet & Co. His cousin, Mr. K. A. R. Bosscha was appointed manager. The rest of the story belongs to the history of Malabar and is an ample justification of the vision and faith of the Kerkhovens as represented by Rudolph Eduard. After Malabar came Taloen, where Dr. J. Bosscha was made manager, and the foundation was laid for the Negla Estate recently developed by K. F. Kerkhoven.

Of R. E. Kerkhoven's sons, the eldest, R. A., first became manager and later director of Malabar; E. H. became director of Gamboeng and K. F. director of Negla. It is interesting to note that all the members of this family, as also A. R. W. Kerkhoven, manager of Panoembang, son of E. J. Kerkhoven of Sinagar and son-in-law of Dr. Jan Bosscha of Taloen were graduated engineers before taking up agriculture.

KARL FREDERICK HOLLE.—One of the most remarkable of the Holles was Karl Frederick, who, born in 1829, came to Netherlands India at the age of fifteen, and engaged as clerk in the resident's office at Tjandjoer. For ten years he remained in administrative occupations without becoming a "bureaucrat." He became absorbed in studying the life and language of the Sundanese and Javanese people, and prosecuted many historical researches, showing extraordinary genius in deciphering old writings. In 1856, he left the gov-

Mr. W. P. Bakhoven   Mr. B. B. J. Crone
TEA PIONEERS OF CENTRAL JAVA

ernment service to study the manners and customs of the people of his adopted country, publishing much on the subject. He became manager of Tjikadjang in 1858, and acquired Waspada in 1865.

He worked hard for the revival of the Sundanese literature, established shops in the Preanger for the sale of cheap textiles, and imported weaving looms. Finally, in 1866, he secured the establishment of a training college for native teachers at Bandoeng, whereupon the Home Government rewarded his activities with the Knight's Cross of the Netherlands Lion, offered him the residency of the Preanger and, in 1871, appointed him honorary adviser for native problems. He chose, however, to remain manager of Waspada. He wore a fez, and adhered closely to the Sundanese customs, although, at the same time, a costly ring could always be seen on his little finger reminding the natives that he was still the *djoeragan* or great master. He was at once a great agriculturist, an efficient estate owner, and a student of folk-lore. He expressed one of his convictions when he said, "The people on the estate must be treated as well as the plants, if the estate is to flourish." Many improvements which have greatly benefited the Sundanese people were introduced by him, such as the importation of merino sheep and the promotion of silk culture. Much of his sage advice is contained in booklets for the people and in a series of agricultural pamphlets published under the name *Mitra noe tani*—"the friend of the farmer."

The Government always sought his advice on all matters pertaining to Islam, popular education, agriculture, and labor. He went to Buitenzorg to live, in 1886, and died there in 1896; rounding out a life of service in which there was no seeking of fame, honor, or money for himself. On a monument erected to his memory at Garoet is inscribed, "The friend of the farmer."

Other Java Pioneers

MR. W. P. BAKHOVEN, late head administrator of the Bengelen Estates, was one of the outstanding figures in the development of the tea industry of central Java. He started tea cultivation contemporaneously with such men as Messrs. J. E. van Polanen Petel and B. B. J. Crone during the period 1870–75. He joined the Bengelen Estates in October, 1877, and continued with them for more than forty years, taking an active part in developing tea quality for the London and Amsterdam markets. Mr. Bakhoven died in 1927.

Among other pioneers of the tea industry in Java mention should be made of Mr. J. C. van Son who opened the Tjiboengoer Estate; Mr. H. van Son, the founder of Tjisaroeni, Pangerango, and Melattie Estates; Mr. H. W. S. van Hooff, lately retired as manager of Tjiboengoer Estate and one of the best-known present-day tea planters.

E. J. Hammond, Pioneer Industrialist

Among the later pioneers of the industrial development of western Java a position of high honor must be accorded to the late Ernest John Hammond, 1877–1926, managing director of the Anglo-Dutch Plantations of Java, Ltd. He was unique among the foreigners in Java. Coming to the country at a period when, apparently, it was "full up," he contrived to make a place for himself by the application of intensive cultivation methods, transforming tens of thousands of acres of jungle land into great sheets of tea, coffee, kapok, rubber, and other products. This not only made money for the owners of the property but brought undreamed prosperity to the overflow native element, which quickly moved into the new territory from the congested districts of this densely populated island. It can be said truly that he made the deserted country blossom like the rose.

Mr. Hammond was born in England in 1877, starting his commercial career in the tea-buying department of Peek Bros. & Winch, Ltd., Peek House, Eastcheap, London. It early appeared that he was particularly adept in the tasting of tea, and he quickly established a reputation as one of the best tea tasters of the London market. When Peek Brothers & Winch, Ltd., opened an office at Batavia as Francis Peek & Co., Ltd., Mr. Hammond was put in charge. Almost his first achievement was to organize the Anglo-Dutch Plantations of Java, Ltd., which company in 1909

Mr. E. J. Hammond

bought the Pamanoekan and Tjiasem lands. He became managing director in 1913.

Under Mr. Hammond's direction some 3500 acres of tea, rubber, and coffee, taken over from the Netherlands Indian Agricultural Corporation, were enlarged to almost 50,000 acres, consisting of tea, rubber, kina, coffee, sisal, tapioca, and kapok. Also during his management sixteen additional tea and coffee undertakings were bought in different parts of Java, representing a total area of 24,000 acres. The company's total land holdings are 510,000 acres.

The prosperity of the native population on and in the neighborhood of the enterprises of the company always had Mr. Hammond's personal interest. He had hundreds of native houses built, most of them equipped with electric lights, and greatly improved the water supply and living conditions generally. The Pamanoekan and Tjiasem Fund for social purposes, founded by him, provides medical service for the native population and seeks to improve the drinking water. It also provides pensions and keeps up kampong roads.

Among other things, this English captain of industry ceded to the Dutch Government the site of the army aerodrome at Kalidjatti for the sum of one guilder. He regretted he couldn't make an outright gift of it, due to a rule of his company. Both press and public opinion were profoundly moved by this gracious act, and the Queen appointed him an officer of the Order of Orange Nassau.

Java Tea Reaches Out

Tea manufacturing methods were greatly improved after 1890, as a result of which

Java tea became well established on both the Amsterdam and London markets, particularly because of its "strength" and color, which made it singularly suitable for blending with the aromatic Ceylon and British Indian teas. In some countries Java tea, as such, has attained such favor as to be consumed without blending.

By 1910, the conditions and prospects had become so flourishing as to cause a kind of "boom," resulting in the opening of more land for new plantations. All available land in Java having been practically taken up for tea or other cultures, the adjoining island of Sumatra was invaded. Owing to its greater size and scant population Sumatra offered plenty of land and splendid opportunities for expansion of the tea industry.

Tea's Conquest of Sumatra

A few native plots had been opened in the Pasemah and Semendo districts of Palembang, encouraged by zealous administration officials who furnished the seed; but the first serious attempt to introduce tea culture into Sumatra on a large scale was promoted by several prominent tea planters from the Preanger, among them Mr. O. van Vloten. This experienced tea promotor, in company with Dr. Ch. Bernard of the Tea Experiment Station, made several trips to the east and west coasts of Sumatra, and brought back samples of soils. They were found well suited to tea culture and, benefiting by the experience gained through long years of success and failure in Java, the tea industry of Sumatra has been rapidly extended.

In the early 'nineties, there had existed at Deli an Assam tea estate owned by the British Deli and Langkat Company and managed by Mr. John Inch who came from Ceylon to the Rimboen Estate to open Tandjong Goenoeng. From Rimboen in 1894 the first Sumatra tea was sent to London, where it brought 2d. per pound. Shortly thereafter, the enterprise was abandoned on account of the excessive cost of maintaining a labor force, which was principally Chinese. The importation of a satisfactory supply of Javanese coolie labor had not been possible at that time.

Tea planting was demonstrated to be a remunerative proposition in the East Coast of Sumatra as early as 1906 through the initiative, enterprise, and energy of the late Mr. C. A. [Arthur] Lampard, director of Harrisons & Crosfield, Ltd. Harrisons & Crosfield, Ltd., acquired their first estate interests in Sumatra in 1906, and as the result of Mr. Lampard's visits to the island, he became convinced that tea planting in Sumatra could be followed successfully. Accordingly, arrangements were made in 1909 for a considerable experi-

Mr. C. A. Lampard   Mr. J. H. Marinus
Two Founders of Sumatra's Tea Industry

mental planting of tea on the firm's Tebing Tinggi Estate, then under the management of Mr. F. Hess. In order to provide the requisite expert knowledge of tea cultivation, Mr. Lampard arranged for an experienced South Indian tea planter, Mr. H. S. Holder, to join the firm's Sumatra estates' staff. Consequently, Mr. Holder has been with the tea industry in Sumatra from its infancy, and still is one of the leading authorities on tea in that country.

The results of the Tebing Tinggi experiment proved encouraging, and led to the opening up in the Siantar district of Naga Hoeta and the other large tea estates of the Rubber Plantations Investment Trust, Limited. Approximately fifty rubber, tea, copra, and other tropical properties are under the local management of Harrisons & Crosfield, Ltd., and included in them are about half of the 30,000 acres of tea in the East Coast of Sumatra.

Great difficulties had to be overcome in pioneering in a new district without railway or other satisfactory means of communication. The firm was fortunate in their local representatives, however, and under the guidance of their chief planting expert in Sumatra, Mr. Victor Ris, founder and first president of the now powerful A. V. R. O. S., local planters' association, development proceeded rapidly. A Suma-

tra planter of ripe experience in tobacco, coffee, and rubber, with the energetic pioneering spirit highly developed, Mr. Ris, was assisted later by the general manager of the Trust's Siantar estates, Mr. C. G. Slotemaker, who found the task of rapid large-scale development in a new country one after his own heart. So well did tea on Naga Hoeta estate develop, that other interests—Dutch, German, and British—were speedily induced to acquire land in the district and take a hand in tea cultivation there, thus leading to the establishment of the important industry it has become.

The tobacco planters were first to push on to the *lalang*, or tall, wild grass fields, of Pematang Siantar, because tea prospectors believed that only forest soils were suitable for tea. It was soon found, however, that tea grew just as well—if not better—on grass land as on forest grounds. Simeloengoen became a tea center about 1912.

In 1912, the Nederlandsch Indisch Land Syndicaat opened the Bah-Biroeng Oeloe estate in tea, the Marihat Sumatra Plantagen Gesellschaft m.b.H. began with Bah Kasinder, and the Handelsvereeniging "Amsterdam" opened Balimbingan, Bah Kisat, Si Marimboean, and Sidamanik.

In 1926, important new developments were undertaken by the Handelsvereeniging "Amsterdam" in the Korintji district of Sumatra, where that company purchased blocks of land aggregating some 10,000 hectares. Their first estate was named Kajoe Aro, and their plans comprehended opening 25,000 acres in tea. Their tea factory at Balimbingan is the largest in the world.

The first sample of tea from Tebing Tinggi did not turn out well, but the second was sent to London, where it received a favorable report in October, 1911. The first tea from Naga Hoeta estate No. 1, was sold to London in April, 1914. Extensions of existing cultivations followed favorable reports from London, and new areas were opened on the East Coast. More recently estates have been opened on the West Coast, in Southern Sumatra, and in Atjeh in Northern Sumatra. On the East and West Coast there are thousands of hectares suitable for tea at elevations from 1800 to 4000 feet, particularly in Palembang, Benkoelen, Korintji, Moeara-Laboeh, Ophirlands, and Dairie-lands.

Conspicuous success has crowned the efforts of such pioneers as Ris, Slotemaker, von Guerard, Holder, and Marinus, so that at present there are on the island some twenty-eight estates with thoroughly modern factories; ten on the West Coast and in Tapanoeli, Benkoelen, and Palembang, and eighteen in Sumatra's East Coast. The acreage of the latter in 1926 was 14,178 hectares and their production amounted to 8435 metric tons. In 1926, the total planted tea area had increased from 3237 hectares, 1915, to 14,178 hectares with 11,063 hectares producing 8435 tons.

Planters' Associations

The various planting industries are well served with two associations; one for the tobacco interests, and the other, known as AVROS [Algemeene Vereeniging van Rubberplanters ter Oostkust van Sumatra], which represents the tea, rubber, and tropical produce other than tobacco. AVROS was established in 1910. Its headquarters are in Medan, where it also conducts an experimental station.

J. H. Marinus, Sumatra Tea Pioneer

A notable figure in Sumatra's tea industry was the late Mr. J. H. Marinus, who in 1910 founded the Nederlandsch Indisch Land Syndicaat and subsequently opened twelve big estates. Mr. Marinus played an important rôle in the development of Sumatra's East Coast.

At the age of 21, Johannes Hermanus Marinus, 1865–1930, sailed from Amsterdam for Netherlands India, where he started his planting career on the St. Cyr

tobacco estate in Deli. He was in tobacco until 1906, when he returned to Holland. His first appearance as a pioneer of tea in Sumatra, was the launching in Amsterdam, in 1910, of the Nederlandsch Indisch Land Syndicaat, and to this company he devoted much of his time and energies. The company now owns five large estates in Sumatra's East Coast, and six estates in South Sumatra [Palembang and Benkoelen]. The estates produce tea, coffee, cinchona, and oil palms.

The company has large and thoroughly up-to-date factories; Tiga Blata, with its twenty white and gold rollers, is one of the largest in the world, with a yearly capacity in excess of 5,000,000 pounds of manufactured tea. Eventually, the company expects to produce 10,000,000 to 12,000,000 pounds a year.

Mr. Marinus subsequently figured in the opening of lands in the districts of Palembang and Benkoelen. During his thirty-eight years of planting life he was responsible for the opening of twenty-five large estates in Sumatra, all of which are flourishing. Mr. Marinus retired to Hilversum in Holland in 1927, but even in his retirement took an active interest in tea and tea trading. He died in 1930.

There is room for a great many more tea plantations on the island of Sumatra. It is estimated that if all the available land were utilized the island could easily produce upwards of 100,000,000 pounds of tea per year, which would considerably exceed present production of Java. With the conquest of Java completed, it is safe to conclude that tea is now in a fair way to repeat the achievement in Sumatra on a much more imposing scale.

CHAPTER IX

THE FAR-FLUNG KINGDOM OF INDIA TEA

How India Came to Dominate the Tea Markets of the World—The Discovery of the Native Jat—Lord William Charles Cavendish Bentinck and the First Indian Tea Committee—The Bruces and Other Tea Pioneers—Rise of the Assam Company—Tea Mania and Panic—The Old Days in Assam—William Jackson and Sir S. C. Davidson—Some Planting and Agency Pioneers—The India Tea Associations—Scientific Departments.

THE dramatic and romantic story of the domination of the world's tea markets by India tea falls naturally into two main parts; the first records the vicissitudes of the tea industry preceding its establishment as a permanency in India, and the second tells the story of how British enterprise promoted the sale and consumption of the product throughout the world.

Indeed the far flung Kingdom of India Tea extends to all the countries of the earth where tea is grown or is used as a beverage; to Ceylon and Java, where her Indian jats supplanted the China varieties; to Europe, where India tea took possession of markets held inviolate by China tea for 200 years; to North America, where first China, and then Japan, were forced to give tea-drinking hostages; to the Latin countries, which for centuries have acknowledged cocoa as queen; to Brazil, where coffee is king; to Paraguay, where maté rules; to Africa, Australia, and New Zealand, where her devotees are legion; and even to China and Japan, who produce their own, but where many foreigners, and not a few natives, do India tea homage, morning, noon, and night. Verily, the sun never sets upon India tea's dominions.

The introduction of tea culture into India is in itself quite a stirring tale, for, in the first place, tea was indigenous to India, although only the aborigines knew it. Patriotic Englishmen proposed to import China tea plants and set up an industry of their own in India. Apologetic statesmen of the compromising kind, and all those more or less directly interested in preserving the English East India Company's monopoly of the eastern trade, promptly objected.

For ten years indigenous India tea begged for recognition, only to be met with cynical indifference; and when recognition came, how halting, how half-hearted it was! There was still the glamour, which for centuries had clung to China tea, and when the bewildered merchants were relieved at last of the East India monopoly incubus, they found themselves incapable of thinking in other terms save those of China tea. They continued to send thousands of miles to China for tea seeds, plants, and workmen; solemnly and laboriously trying to grow China tea in a country that was already possessed of a native jat much better suited to its requirements. This was recognized only by a few soldiers of fortune, statesmen, and scientists. These courageous souls won the day for India's indigenous tea, eventually, and then private enterprise stepped in where governmental paternalism had failed. Within the span of three generations British enterprise carved out of the jungles of India an industry that covered over two million acres, representing a capital investment of £36,000,000, with 788,842 acres under tea producing 432,997,916 lbs. annually, giving employment to one and a quarter million people; at the same time creating one of the most lucrative sources of private wealth and government tax returns in the British Empire.

The native Indian population of British

India seem to have known about tea from time immemorial. They knew of it first as a vegetable food in the form of *miang, letpet,* or pickled tea. Later, they made an infusion of it, a kind of soup, very like the butter tea of Tibet. Foreigners in India must have had early knowledge of the China drink, for the English East India Company's factors in Japan and Java undoubtedly conveyed news of it to their fellow agents in India.

The Genesis of Tea in India

In 1662, Mandelslo discussed tea drinking in India, which he visited about 1640, remarking, "at our ordinary meetings, every day, we took only *The,* which is commonly used all over the Indies, not only among those of the country, but also among the Dutch and the English, who take it as a drug. The Persians instead of *The* drink their *Kahwa* (coffee).[1] A similar statement occurs in Ovington's *Voyage to Suratt.*[2]

Cohen Stuart suggests that an ancient tea specimen in the Sloane Herbarium of the British Museum, said to have been collected on the Malabar coast between 1698 and 1702 by Samuel Browne and Edward Bulkley, might have been a China plant brought to Malabar during the period of the Dutch East India Company's ownership.[3] It was not until 1780, however, that there was a definite move made by Europeans to cultivate the tea plant in British India, and then it was only for ornamental purposes, as in the case of the first plants raised in Java.

It was in 1780 that a few Chinese tea seeds were brought from Canton to Calcutta by captains of the English East India Company.[4] Some of these were sent by Governor-General Warren Hastings to Mr. George Bogle in Bhutan, Northeastern India; others were planted by Lieutenant Colonel Robert Kyd, of the Bengal infantry, in his private botanical garden at Sibpur, Calcutta.[5] They grew well, notwith-

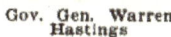

Gov. Gen. Warren Hastings   Col. Robert Kyd

PRIME MOVERS OF TEA CULTIVATION IN INDIA

standing lack of information as to their proper care, and were the first cultivated tea plants grown in India, which was then governed by the East India Company.

The earliest practical step toward the introduction of tea cultivation was taken in 1788 by Sir Joseph Banks, 1743–1820, the great English naturalist, whose hobby was the diffusion of commercial plants. At the request of the Court of Directors of the English East India Company, Sir Joseph prepared a series of memoirs on the methods to be adopted in the cultivation of new crops in India, particularly tea. He recommended Bihar, Rangpur, and Cooch Bihar as the localities in which tea cultivation was most likely to be successful. The memoirs were strongly endorsed by Colonel Kyd, but political and commercial objections connected with the company's highly profitable tea trade with China conspired to prevent the carrying out of his suggestions at the time. In 1793, however, scientists accompanying Lord Macartney's embassy to China secured seeds of Chinese cultivated tea plants and dispatched them to Calcutta, where they were planted in the Botanical Gardens according to directions furnished by Sir Joseph. It has been said of him that his fame rested on what his liberality enabled other workers to do.

In 1815, Dr. Govan, who subsequently became the first superintendent of the Government Botanical Gardens at Saharanpur, supplemented the suggestions of Colonel Kyd and Sir Joseph Banks by recommending that tea planting be introduced into

[1] Johan Albrecht von Mandelslo, "Travels into the East Indies" in Olearius' *Description of Journeys in Muskovy and Persia,* Eng. Transl., London, 1662.

[2] John Ovington, *Voyage to Suratt,* London, 1689.

[3] Dr. C. P. Cohen Stuart, "A Basis for Tea Selection," *Bulletin du Jardin Botanique,* Troiseme Serie, vol. 1, fasc. 4, Buitenzorg, 1919, p. 257.

[4] M. Kelway Bamber, *Chemistry and Agriculture of Tea,* Calcutta, 1893, p. 6.

[5] This garden formed the nucleus of the present Government Botanical Gardens, founded in 1787 at the suggestion of Col. Kyd, who was appointed the first superintendent.

northwestern Bengal, but again nothing was done.

What appears to be the earliest mention of indigenous India tea is to be found in a report made in 1815 by Colonel Latter, of the British forces in India, in which he told how the Singpho hill tribes of Assam gathered a species of wild tea, ate it with oil and garlic, after the Burmese manner, and also made a drink from it.

In 1816, the Hon. Edward Gardner, resident at the native court of Nepal, found a shrub which he thought was a tea bush, growing in the palace garden at Khatmandu. He sent specimens of the leaves to Dr. Nathaniel Wallich, 1787–1854, superintendent of the Royal Botanical Gardens at Calcutta, who decided they were *Camellia kissa*, now known as *Camellia drupifera*, and not true tea.

The Discovery of Indian Tea

In the year 1823, Major Robert Bruce, who had a flair for botanical research, went on a trading expedition beyond the eastern frontier of British India into the province then known as Burmese Assam. He visited the capital at Rangpur, now Sibsagar, with a large assortment of goods, and traded with a local Singpho chief, the Beesa Gaum. During the time of his stay Bruce made several botanical forays into the adjacent country, and found native tea trees growing on the nearby hills. Before his departure he made a written agreement with the chief for a supply of tea plants and tea seeds to be ready for him upon the occasion of his next visit.

In 1824, the Beesa Gaum delivered the plants and seeds to Mr. C. A. Bruce, a brother of Major Robert Bruce. Mr. C. A. Bruce had been ordered to the vicinity of Rangpur when war broke out with Burma, and he sent some of the plants to the Commissioner of Assam, Captain David Scott, who had them planted in his garden at Gauhati. The remainder were planted in Mr. Bruce's own garden at Sadiya in 1825. Major Bruce died that same year.

In 1825, Captain Scott sent to Mr. G. Swinton, then chief secretary to the Indian Government, and to Dr. Wallich at the Botanical Gardens in Calcutta some leaves and seed from tea trees which he discovered growing wild in the state of Manipur. Captain Scott insisted they were true tea, but the doctor pronounced them to be

SIR JOSEPH BANKS

The great naturalist, whose Tea Memoir of 1788 so strongly recommended the cultivation of tea.

Camellia. Some authorities have since thought the specimens sent by Captain Scott from Manipur may have been a common camellia, or some plant other than the genuine *Assamica* variety found by Mr. Bruce; but, be that as it may, there seems to have been a long-maintained reluctance at Calcutta to admit the identity of the Assam tea plant.

In 1827, Dr. F. Corbyn, a journalist, found some tea plants in Sandoway. He sent specimens to the Governor General, Lord Amherst, with a report, a copy of which was subsequently forwarded to the Court of Directors of the East India Company.

Meanwhile, there had been brewing in London a strong sentiment favorable to starting a tea industry in India, despite the unfriendly attitude of the East India Company. In 1825, we find the English Society of Arts offering a gold medal or 50 guineas "to the person who shall grow and prepare the greatest quantity of tea of good quality, not being less than 20 pounds in weight, in the East or West Indies, or any other British colony." Further scientific support for the theory that tea could be successfully raised in British India was

S. Faulkner Benton

SIVA'S TANK AND THE DOE TEMPLE AT SIBSAGAR (FORMERLY RANGPUR), MIDDLE ASSAM, INDIA

Indigenous tea was first found growing near Rangpur by Major Robert Bruce and his brother, Mr. C. A. Bruce, in 1823–24. Sibsagar means "Sea of Siva," or "Siva's Tank." The Doe is dedicated to the god Siva. This tank is two miles round and the water level is some twenty feet above the surrounding country. It is entirely dependent on the rainfall for its water, and leakage apparently is checked by the thorough "puddling" carried out on the bottom of the tank during construction.

supplied in 1827 by the well known botanist, Dr. J. Forbes Royle, 1799–1858, in charge of the government botanical gardens at Saharanpur, Kumaon. He urged the introduction of the China tea plant into the northwest district of the Himalaya range and was so firmly convinced of the suitability of the Himalayas for tea cultivation that he renewed his recommendations in 1831, '32, '33 and '34. At this time Assam, Cachar, Sylhet, part of the Northwest Province, and the Punjab were under native rule and not included in the British Empire.

In 1831, Lieutenant [later Captain] Andrew Charlton reported that he had been informed of tea trees growing wild near Beesa, in Assam, whence he obtained three or four young plants, and gave them to Dr. John Tytler to be planted in the Government Botanical Garden, Calcutta. However, these arrived in a sickly state, were thought to be camellias, and soon died. The following year, Dr. Christie, a surgeon of the Madras Establishment, was placed on special duty to conduct meteorological and geological inquiries in Southern India. In a short time he applied for a grant of land in the Nilgiri hills, where he started an experimental tea, coffee, and mulberry nursery. Unfortunately, he died soon after, and the work, barely begun, was discontinued. Dr. Christie's tea plants, of the China jat, were distributed to various parts of the hills for trial. Three were given to Colonel Crewe, the commandant at Ootacamund, who planted them in his garden at Crewe Hall.

The First Indian Tea Committee

In the various transplantations of the cultivated tea plant from China to European colonies, the introduction was usually due to the energy of individuals, but in the case of British India it was the result of an urgent national need. Closing its eyes to the facts in the case, the East India Company for years refused to permit any interference with its monopoly of the China tea trade, and thus did all it could to discourage tea cultivation in India. In the year 1833, however, the treaty with China expired and the Chinese government refused to renew it. There was even a possibility that, like Japan, China might soon close her ports entirely. In the face of this serious state of affairs Governor-General Lord William Charles Cavendish Bentinck, 1774–1839, in 1834, appointed a committee to inquire into the possibility of introducing China tea plants into India.

Lord William Charles Cavendish Bentinck

England owes a debt of gratitude to Lord William Bentinck. In the light of subsequent events, the most important act of his administration as governor-general of India was the introduction of tea growing. Due to his vision and insistence the question as to the suitability of the Indian soil and climate, and the kind of tea to be planted, was settled in such thorough fashion as never to call for re-opening. His method was first to get the facts, next to put them in their right order, and so arrive at his conclusions. Unfortunately he died before all the tea facts were assembled, otherwise some of the early tea mistakes might have been avoided.

Lord William Bentinck was born in 1774, the second surviving son of William Henry, third Duke of Portland. Having served in many campaigns, he became governor of Madras in 1803, but was recalled about 1805. He was commander of the troops sent to aid Ferdinand, King of Sicily, in 1810, and held at the same time the office of plenipotentiary. In 1812, he gave a liberal constitution to Sicily, and in 1814, led a successful expedition against the French in Italy, taking possession of Genoa. He was appointed governor-general of India by the Premier, Mr. Canning, in 1827. He showed himself a humane and enlightened governor, among other acts, abolishing suttee—the Hindu custom which required that widows be burned on the funeral pyre of their husbands—and suppressing the Thugs.

Lord William Bentinck had given thoughtful attention to all the various tea reports laid before him in the early years of his incumbency, but he was moved to heroic action by a Mr. Walker, in London, who announced, in 1834, that he considered it of national importance "that some better guarantee should be provided for the supply of tea than that already furnished by the toleration of the Chinese Government." He proposed that the East India Company should "resolutely undertake the cultivation of the tea plant on the Nepal hills and other districts, where the *Camellia* and other plants similar to the tea plants are indigenous."

It was on January 24, 1834, that Lord William Bentinck appointed the history-making Tea Committee. This committee, consisting in the first instance of Mr. James Pattle, Mr. George James Gordon, and Dr. Lumqua, a Chinese physician long a resident of Calcutta, was later enlarged so that it was composed of eleven English and two Indian gentlemen.[6] The members of the committee shared the general skepticism as to the ultimate success of any attempt to cultivate tea in India,[7] but the Governor-General insisted that the proposition be given a trial. The committee was charged by Lord William Bentinck with the duty of submitting to the government "a plan for the accomplishment of the introduction of tea culture into India and for the superintendence of its execution."

Accordingly the Tea Committee issued a circular on March 3, 1834, describing the climate, soil, and topographical conditions favorable to tea growing, and requesting information where these might be found. It also dispatched its secretary, Mr. George James Gordon, of the firm of Mackintosh & Co., to China, for the purpose of studying cultivation and manufacturing methods, and to secure seeds, plants, and Chinese workmen. Mr. Gordon's salary was Rs. 1000 per month.

These two acts of the committee produced lasting results, the tea circular bringing out the somewhat grudging, but none the less definite decision by the authorities that the tea plant grew in Assam; the second act bringing about the introduction of the first lot of China tea seed, which Dr. Mann calls "the curse of the India tea industry."[8]

Because of the insistence of the Governor-General the committee proceeded with the general survey work in hand, until the tremendously important discovery was made that genuine tea trees were, at that very time, growing wild in the hills of

LORD WILLIAM CHARLES CAVENDISH BENTINCK
He introduced tea growing into India and appointed the famous Tea Committee of 1834.

Assam, thus proving conclusively that tea could be grown in India.[9]

This vindication of Governor-General Lord William Bentinck's position in the matter changed apathy into enthusiam, and an ultimate transference of the British tea trade from China to India was envisioned by many of the discerning ones. The Chinese plant was more or less successfully introduced into Assam, the Himalayas, and the Nilgiri hills, together with a later unqualifiedly successful cultivation of India's splendid native teas.

It took many years for India tea to reach the impregnable position it now occupies in the world of commerce, but the credit for that success, while shared by many, is due in the first instance to the perspicacity and courage of Governor-General Lord William Bentinck. He resigned from the governorship on account of ill health in 1835, dying at Paris four years later.

It was in June, 1834, that Mr. Gordon sailed from Calcutta in the "Water Witch," accompanying the missionary Rev. Charles Gutzlaff, with whom he finally reached

[6] Messrs. James Pattle [Chairman], J. W. Grant, R. D. Mangles, J. R. Colvin, Charles E. [Later Sir] Trevelyan, C. K. Robison, Robert Wilkinson, Sir R. D. Colquhoun, Bart., Dr. N. Wallich, C. Macsween, G. J. Gordon, Radakant Deb, and Ram Comul Sen.

[7] "Everywhere," said a writer in the *Calcutta Courier*, February 7, 1834, "it [the tea plant] thrives, as far as mere vegetation is concerned, but nowhere, except in China, has any successful effort yet been made to render it a profitable product of industry."

[8] H. H. Mann, *Early History of the Tea Industry of Northeast India*, Calcutta, 1918.

[9] It was not until twenty years later that the superiority of the native *jat* was recognized.

China, after an adventurous passage during which they were attacked by pirates. Together they visited the Ankoy tea hills, and made an unsuccessful attempt to reach the famous green tea districts of the interior, where no European was permitted to go. However, Mr. Gordon secured ample supplies of Bohea tea seeds, and these reached Calcutta in 1835. Meanwhile, the committee's circular, asking about favorable spots for China tea nurseries, reached the hands of Captain [afterwards General] Francis Jenkins, who had succeeded to the post of agent for Assam, formerly held by Captain David Scott. Captain Jenkins was keenly interested in developing the natural resources of the Assam Valley. Since he was a resident of Gauhati, in the heart of the valley, he knew that tea grew wild all over the hills to the northeast. Also, he was reminded of the efforts previously made for its recognition by Mr. C. A. Bruce, in 1826; by Lieutenant Charlton in 1831; and resumed by himself, in 1832, when Mr. C. A. Bruce persuaded him to re-examine the matter.

Astonishing Results of the Tea Circular

Feeling that the time was most auspicious for renewing the agitation, Captain Jenkins answered the circular with a report to the Government at Calcutta, dated May 7, 1834, in which he told about the coarse variety of tea indigenous to the Singpho district of Beesa, and recommended Assam for the cultivation of the tea plant. At the same time he dispatched Lieutenant Charlton into the hills near Sadiya for specimens. This officer secured a complete exhibit, which included tea leaves, fruit, blossoms, and the prepared leaf used by the hill tribes for making their primitive tea drink, thus discovering the native tea plant a second time. "The prepared leaf," said Lieutenant Charlton, "is the best test that the tree is not a *Camellia* as Dr. Wallich imagines." The exhibit was sent to the Calcutta Botanical Gardens, where it arrived on the 8th of November, 1834, this time enabling Dr. Wallich to identify it as tea, identical with that of China.

In apprising the Government of this important event the committee wrote, on the 24th of December, 1834:

It is with feelings of the highest satisfaction that we are enabled to announce to his Lordship in Council that the tea shrub is beyond all doubt indigenous in Upper Assam, being found there through an extent of country of one month's march within the Honourable Company's territories from Sadiya and Beesa to the Chinese frontier province of Yunnan, where the shrub is cultivated for the sake of its leaf.

We have no hesitation in declaring this discovery . . . to be by far the most important and valuable that has ever been made in matters connected with the agricultural or commercial resources of this empire.

We are perfectly confident that the tea plant which has been brought to light will be found capable under proper management, of being cultivated with complete success for commercial purposes, and that consequently the object of our labours may be before long fully realized.

Among the local administrators, botanists and scientific men aroused by the Tea Committee's inquiry in 1834 were Mr. George William Traill, Commissioner of Kumaon, and Dr. Hugh Falconer, civil assistant surgeon then in charge of the Government's Botanical Garden at Saharanpur, where he later succeeded Dr. J. Forbes Royle, Kumaon's early tea protagonist. Commissioner Traill was quick to appreciate the economic importance of the tea question and to put into effect any suggestions from the Tea Committee. He had an able coadjutor in Mr. Robert Blinkworth, who was plant collector for Dr. Wallich at Almorah.

Because he was in sympathy with Dr. Wallich's belief that China tea was best suited for cultivation in the Indian highlands, Dr. Falconer was deputed to examine and report on possible nursery sites in the districts between the heads of the Jumna and the Ganges. In this way Dr. Falconer became the founder of the tea industry in Kumaon and Garhwal. Later, in 1843, he was succeeded by Dr. William Jameson, "the great central name which will always most justly be associated with the . . . progress of tea culture in the mountain districts of India." [10]

Still Harping on the China Jat

The Indian Government was impressed with the discovery of the indigenous plant and concurred with the views of the Tea Committee. As the first result of the announcement, Mr. Gordon was recalled from China, February 3, 1835, on the ground that his mission was now unnecessary. The

[10] J. H. Batten, "Notes and Recollections on Tea Cultivation in Kumaon and Gurhwal," *Tea Cyclopedia*, Calcutta, 1881, p. 245.

letter did not reach him, however, until he had obtained and dispatched three shipments of seeds. The first parcel contained seeds from the Bohea hills, shipped by Mr. Gordon personally, and presumed to have been collected only from plants bearing leaf suitable for preparing the superior kinds of black tea; the second and third shipments were sent from Canton during Mr. Gordon's absence from the city, and were not even inspected by him. Judging from the channels through which they were procured, they were probably the seeds of inferior varieties of tea. The last parcel arrived out of season, and was not in condition for germination.

The second result of the committee's report to the Government was the appointment, in 1835, of a scientific commission consisting of Dr. Nathaniel Wallich and Dr. William Griffith, botanists, and Dr. John McClelland, geologist, authorized to inquire into, and report on, the Indian indigenous tea, and to advise as to the most favorable locations for starting experimental tea gardens. They left Calcutta August 29, 1835, and journeyed to Assam; the trip to Sadiya, the farthest outpost of civilization, requiring about four and a half months.

At Sadiya they were joined by Mr. C. A. Bruce, who acted as guide. Between January 15 and March 9, 1836, five localities were visited where the indigenous tea was found growing wild and in great profusion. The commission dispersed on March 21, 1836. Dr. Griffith reported that the plants were remarkably vigorous and flourishing; they were of all ages, from seedlings to mature shrubs twelve to twenty feet in height, their stems were mostly under one inch in diameter, and none were more than two inches. When seen in February, 1836, most of the full grown shrubs were covered with seed buds, and some still bore blossoms. The older leaves were large, and of a fine, dark green color.[11]

The commission as a whole, however, was unable to agree on recommendations as to the most favorable localities for experimental gardens. Dr. Wallich favored the Himalayas, while Dr. Griffith and Dr. McClelland were of the opinion that the Himalayas were not as well adapted for tea

DR. WILLIAM GRIFFITH

Member of the first scientific commission to investigate the indigenous tea of Assam.

cultivation as Upper Assam. They stated further that the Assam plant beyond any doubt sprang from the same stock as the China variety, although it had degenerated on account of having grown wild over a long period. Dr. Wallich, who made no report, argued that since the native plants were actually tea, there was no need to import, as "there is no ground for supposing the various sorts of tea seeds brought from China will produce anything but the shrub in its natural [Indian] state." Dr. Griffith, on the other hand favored importing the China seed, because "a wild plant is not likely to give as good produce as one that has been cultivated for centuries."

It was finally decided that "the China plant and not the degraded Assam plant" should be used for the Government's experiments, so Mr. Gordon was again dispatched to China in 1836, and for many years China tea seed was imported regularly into India, the principal attention being given to the cultivation of the China shrub. This was the Tea Commission's first blunder.

About this time India's scientific men

11 William Griffith, *Journals of Travels*, Calcutta, 1847.

divided on the tea question as follows: Wallich, Royle, and Falconer were for the Himalayas and the China plant. Griffith and McClelland were for Assam and the indigenous plant. From the seeds sent by Mr. Gordon on his first trip 42,000 shrubs were raised at the Calcutta Botanical Gardens, and in 1835–36 these were forwarded to Upper Assam, Kumaon, Dehra Dun, and the Nilgiri hills.

The Tea Commission made a second blunder by selecting for the locality of their first experimental tea garden about the only plot of land throughout the length and breadth of Assam where it was impossible for tea to thrive. This was at Koondilmukh, where they chose a ten-acre patch of ground on a chur, at the confluence of the Koondil river and the Brahmaputra, near Sadiya. The churs are shifting sandbanks with alluvial deposits several inches deep. As soon as the tap roots of the seedlings reached the sand the plants withered and died. "In a short time," says David Crole, "the kindly Brahmaputra flowed over the site of this, the first tea garden in Assam, and buried in its waters a lamentable failure." [12]

After the Koondilmukh failure some of the shrubs were removed to Jaipur in one corner of the Lakhimpur division, at that time one of the army headquarters. Here the tea was preserved until 1840, when the area was sold to the Assam Company. Several acres are still kept as a matter of historical interest.

The next attempt was in 1837, at Chabua, now Chabwa or Chubwa, 18 miles from Dibrugarh in the center of Lakhimpur's indigenous tea district. The original name, Chabua, according to one Indian authority means "tea planted." Here, as in Jaipur, the tea plants flourished, but J. Berry White says, "it is a matter of profound regret that this experiment did not share the fate of its Sadiya predecessor, for it proved the chief means of disseminating the pest of Assam—the miserable China variety—all over the province"; [13] and vast quantities of hybrids, as he might have added. It is a curious fact that whenever an attempt has been made to transplant the China jat the result has been

C. R. Harler

ORIGINAL CHINA TEA AT CHUBWA

disastrous. It was so in Java; it followed in India, and in Ceylon. It seems as if that mysterious, hidden force, which Couperus talks about in his stories of the East, was at work to accomplish the undoing of anyone who sought to carry away the seeds of China's most venerated plant. It has been charged that the Chinese frequently boiled the tea seed before selling it to foreigners, to prevent its germination, and it is known that all kinds of strange tricks were resorted to in order to defeat the propagation of the China tea plant outside of China. Seeds and plants shipped in good condition often arrived improperly packed, mouldy, diseased, dead, or in a dying condition; and when good seed or healthy plants were taken through successfully, the tea manufactured from them was never the same as in China. Indeed, only China's soil and climate seem able to produce year after year, the distinctive China tea which the celestial accepts as a gift of the gods, designed for him alone. White men for centuries begged it from the Chinamen because they liked it, too; but, just as soon as the white man tried to produce it outside of its native China, "it bit him like a serpent" or "stung him like an adder."

[12] David Crole, *Tea; Its Cultivation and Manufacture*, London, 1897.
[13] J. Berry White, "The Indian Tea Industry: Its Rise, Progress During 50 Years, and Prospects Considered from a Commercial Point of View," *Journal Society of Arts*, London, 1887, xxxv.

A conspicuous exception seems to have been the case of Robert Fortune, who, in 1850–51 secured a huge quantity of China plants and seed, and brought them through with flying colors to Calcutta, where it was found the germinated seeds had produced about 12,000 new plants, which were added to the Himalaya gardens. This moves Dr. Cohen Stuart to remark that in the Himalayas, at least, the advice of the Tea Commission [Wallich, Royle, Falconer and Jameson] was fully confirmed, adding: "The superiority of the Assam indigenous is not universally accepted. And, as a matter of fact, the Himalaya districts furnish a conclusive proof that, under certain conditions, China tea may be the better variety."

However, the facts in the case are that the Indian teas made from the China jat or China-Assam hybrids are commercially unimportant to-day; and the indigenous Assam jats are the most eagerly sought for by tea planters in all the tea producing countries outside of China and Japan. Only a fractional acreage of China plants remain where once Fortune thought he had outwitted the China tea jinx.

In all, there were some 20,000 China tea plants in the 1835–36 shipment that was sent from Calcutta to Mr. C. A. Bruce, who had succeeded Captain Charlton as superintendent of tea culture of Assam in April, 1836. On the instructions of Dr. Wallich, Dr. Griffith, and Dr. McClelland,

ONE-HUNDRED-YEAR-OLD TREES AT JAIPUR,
CHINA JAT

the plants that survived the journey were placed in a nursery at Saikhwa, near Sadiya. When they arrived only 8000 were found to be living, and Dr. Griffith reported that many of these died after they were planted. Two years later, Mr. Bruce reported 1600 China shrubs transferred to Deenjoy, adjoining Chubwa in Muttuck [Matak], where they began yielding crop —32 pounds—in 1839.

Another 20,000 of the China shrubs were sent to Kumaon and Dehra Dun in the Himalayas, where the 2000 that survived succeeded a little better. Upon the recommendation of Dr. Hugh Falconer, Mr. George William Traill, Commissioner of Kumaon, selected two sites for experimental tea gardens; one at Bhurtpur [Bhartpur], near Bhemtal [Bhimtal], and the other at Lutchmesir [Latchmeswar], near Almora. These nurseries were planted in the latter part of 1835. Dr. Falconer later established experimental gardens for growing China tea plants in Kumaon, Garhwal, and Sirmore at elevations from 2000 to 6400 feet. They succeeded well, and plants were raised at Saharanpur from seeds obtained from one of these nurseries.

The remaining 2000 plants, shipped to the Madras Presidency of Southern India, were all reported dead within two years. These were transported in twenty packing cases, each containing 100 plants, and, upon arrival at Madras, six cases were distributed to Mysore; six to Coorg; two to the Agricultural and Horticultural Society at Madras; and six to Colonel Crewe at the Government experimental farm at Kaity, in the Nilgiri hills.

Shortly after this, Colonel Crewe died and the plants that survived from his original allotment were neglected. In August, 1836, M. Perrottet, a botanist for the French Government, found that only nine of these plants were still living. A few of the seedlings sent to the Nilgiris had been given by Colonel Crewe to Captain Minchin, stationed at Mannantoddy in Wynaad, in the Western Ghauts. These made a good start, according to a report made in June, 1836, but appear to have ultimately shared the common fate of the first extensive experiment at cultivating the China tea plant in Southern India. In 1839, however, Major Bevan wrote: "Since I left Wynaad, the cultivation of the tea plant has been introduced, and with very rea-

CHINA TEA PLANTED BY CHINESE WORKMEN AT CHUBWA IN 1835
Now abandoned, owing to being pure China jat.

sonable prospect of success. However, the discovery of the tea growing wild in Assam renders its culture in Wynaad less important than it otherwise would have been."

In the report of General Cullen, Resident of Travancore, written in October, 1859, we read:

The tree thrives well in Travancore territory, both at the level of the sea and altitudes of 1800 and 3200 feet. I first met with it in the coffee plantation of Mr. Huxam in the year 1841, on the route from Quilon to Courtalam, at a factory called Caldoorty, about forty miles inland and six or seven hundred feet above the sea. There are some ten or fifteen trees from twenty to twenty-five feet high; they were, I believe, introduced during the Government of Mr. Lushington, who, I believe, also introduced those formerly at Kaity in the Nilgiris. I procured plants from Mr. Huxam and put them down in an experimental spice garden which I established some twelve years ago at 1800 feet on a hill in the south of Travancore near Oodagherry. They are now trees of twenty to thirty feet high, growing vigorously; and I have four hundred plants procured from their seed growing on another hill near the Tinnevelly frontier, at an elevation of 3200 feet. There can be no doubt, therefore, of the facility of its introduction, although from the moderate altitude and great atmospheric moisture of the localities hitherto selected, they may possibly be considered to grow more luxuriantly than is desirable; but which, if a defect at all, can probably be easily

remedied by selecting ground more to the eastward, at greater altitudes, and with less humid climate.

Mr. H. Waddington, Madras, in 1929 wrote the author that General Cullen must have been mistaken as Lushington retired before the tea seed was distributed in 1832. He thinks it more likely that the trees at Caldoorty were from seed imported in 1834. According to Mr. Waddington:

Tea planting on a commercial scale was commenced on the Nilgiris in 1853. Thirty years ago the area under tea did not probably exceed 3000 acres on the Nilgiris, one estate of some 250 acres in the Wynaad, 315 acres on the Kanan Devans, perhaps, 5000 acres in the rest of Travancore. Of the 116,000 acres in Southern India at least 105,000 have been planted since 1893.[14]

In addition to the 42,000 China seedlings sent by the Calcutta Botanical Gardens to the various Government tea nurseries, in 1835–36, there were 9000 more sent out to 170 individual planters in various parts of India. The Hon. S. J. Best, in an address before the Rotary Club of Calcutta, recalled how the Tea Committee regarded the

[14] H. Waddington, "Historical Notes on the Early Days of the Planting Industry in Southern India," *Planting Directory of Southern India*, Madras, 1928.

ACTUAL TEA PLANTED "SEED-AT-STAKE" ON CHUBWA UNDER CHINESE SUPERVISION IN 1887

This tea is still in cultivation, being a fair hybrid of China and Assam jat.

country around Mussoorie and Dehra Dun as most favorable for tea, and that an individual planting was made at that time on Kasauni, a garden formerly managed by his firm. This garden still exists, the tea being more than ninety years old.

Besides these experimental plantings of the Chinese jat, Mr. C. A. Bruce started a nursery devoted solely to the indigenous variety at Sadiya, in 1836. This was really an extension of Mr. Bruce's original planting, begun in 1825, although kept entirely distinct. Mr. Bruce continued searching for new tracts of the wild tea. In 1837, he found several new ones in the Matak country, near Sadiya, and by 1839 he had located one hundred and twenty; the most extensive was in the Naga hills, but there were large numbers in the Tippoom and Gubru hills. "The wild tea," he said, "may be traced from tract to tract, thus forming a chain of tea tracts from the Irrawaddy to the borders of China, east of Assam."

In 1849, the Government sold the Chubwa garden to a Chinaman for Rs. 952/14/8. Being unable to make it pay, the Chinaman disposed of it two years later for Rs. 475 to the late Mr. James Warren, one of the pioneers of India tea culture,

whose descendant of the same name became chairman of the Chubwa Tea Co., Ltd., the present owner of this property. The pure China jat was gradually abandoned. In 1871, the garden area under tea was 713 acres with an outturn of 85,775 lbs. To-day, with 1548 acres in tea the outturn is 1,120,000 lbs. A fair hybrid of China and Assam, planted in 1887, is still in cultivation, as also tea planted in 1910 from Assam village seed.

In 1838–39, three more China tea gardens were planted near Tinsukia; one at Deenjoy, one in Chota Tingri, and the third in Hukanpukri.

First Fruits of Assam Tea Manufacture

The next step toward cultivation of the native tea plant was an order to the native chiefs to clear the jungle where the tea was first discovered. In the meantime the Indian Government's scientific commission had visited and defined such districts as embracing: Kuju [Cuju] and Ningrew in the Singpho country; Nadowar, or Noadwar [Nudwa] and Tingri, in the Muttuck or Bengmara country, and Gabroo Purbut in the territory of Rajah Burunder Singh.

Upon the arrival at Calcutta of the Chinese workers procured by Mr. Gordon, they were sent at once to Mr. Bruce in Assam. He had them make up a small sample of manufactured tea early in 1836, and he forwarded this to Calcutta. The tea was made from young shoots of native tea plants in the Muttuck country. Later in the same year he sent a second sample, consisting of five boxes. These samples met with approval at Calcutta, and the Viceroy, Lord Auckland, pronounced the beverage of good quality.

Speaking generally, however, the early conception of the usefulness of the indigenous tea was, as previously stated, that its presence indicated the districts in which imported China tea plants might be grown with best prospect of success. Attention centered on the speediest possible establishment of the imported cultivated plant as a basis for a quality of tea production to compete with that of China and Japan; expediency pointed to the probability that years of reclamation and selection would be required to make the native plant available.

The Discovery Medal Controversy

Quite a controversy subsequently developed regarding the discoverer of tea in Assam. Dr. Wallich first presented Lieutenant Charlton's claim, which was modified later; the claim being transferred to Mr. C. A. Bruce and his brother, Major Robert Bruce of Jorhat. Since Major Bruce had died, Mr. C. A. Bruce was awarded a medal from the English Society of Arts, presented through the Agricultural and Horticultural Society of Bengal. Both Lieutenant Charlton and Major Jenkins protested, and much acrimonious correspondence ensued. Their claims were finally established, however, and on January 3, 1842, the president of the Agricultural and Horticultural Society of Bengal presented a gold medal to Captain Charlton for being the first to establish the fact that the tea tree was indigenous to Assam, and another to Major Jenkins for his activities in bringing the inquiry to a successful termination. So it was that the only one who did not receive a medal was the original discoverer, Major Robert Bruce, who never sought it. Incidentally, Samuel Baildon, author of *Tea in Assam*, says a native named Moneram Dewan is credited

with having been the discoverer. Perhaps, after all, it was Moneram Dewan who told Major Bruce about it, or may he not have first led the Major to where the tree was growing?

The Pioneer Work of C. A. Bruce

India tea owes much to the real founder of tea cultivation in Assam, its first superintendent of tea culture, Mr. Charles Alexander Bruce. He was not a scientific man, as subsequent events proved; he was not even a good business man. He did not possess a knowledge of botany or horticulture, but he did know how to pioneer a jungle, and make it give up its hidden treasures. He was essentially an explorer, peculiarly equipped by long residence in Assam to understand the climate and the people, and possessed of an amazing store of good health and fine animal spirits, combined with tact and resourcefulness. He soon discovered that the tea plant, instead of being confined to a few isolated spots, was to be found growing in jungle colonies over a wide extent of country.

His researches through hundreds of miles of pathless jungle were first viewed with jealous suspicion by the native chiefs. He not only succeeded in removing all their prejudices, but actually persuaded them to aid him in his labors. Dr. Mann hails him as an admirable pioneer, who found out the habits of the tea plant, got over many of the initial difficulties, and made the first drinkable tea. To him, almost alone, is due the bringing of the cultivation and manufacture to such a point that a commercial company was willing to take it up. The tea under his charge consisted for the

MEDAL PRESENTED TO CAPT. CHARLTON

most part of colonies of the indigenous
Assam trees reclaimed from the jungle, and
cut back so as to form leaf bearing bushes.

Two years after the first tea was sent
to Calcutta, Mr. Bruce made his famous
shipment to England. In this same year,
1838, he published an excellent *Account of
the manufacture of the black tea as now
practiced at Suddeya, in Upper Assam, by
the Chinamen sent thither for that purpose, with some observations on the culture
of the plant in China, and its growth in
Assam.* In it he tells of finding a tea tree
43 feet high and 3 feet round, though "very
few attain that size."

Bruce found it better to plant under
shade. He even grew cuttings in the shade.
His Chinamen plucked the whole of the
young shoots as soon as they had four
leaves on them, doing the same with the
second flush, and even taking a third help-
ing if the bush grew after such drastic
treatment. He withered the leaf in the
sun, rolled it by hand, and dried it over
charcoal fires.

Mr. C. A. Bruce was a picturesque character. Before going into tea in India, his
career was most exciting. Born January
10, 1793, his life of adventure began when
he was sixteen. He tells the story in a
letter written December 20, 1836, to Captain Jenkins at Gauhati. It reads:

I left England in 1809 as midshipman on board
the H. C. ship Windham, Captain Stewart, and
was twice captured by the French on my way
out, after two hard fought actions; was marched
across the Isle of France at the end of the bayo-
net, and kept prisoner on board of a ship, until
that island was taken by the British; thus I suffered much, and twice lost all I possessed, and
was never remunerated in any way. I afterwards went as an officer of a troop ship against
Java, and was at the taking of that place. At

GRAVE OF CHARLES ALEXANDER BRUCE AT TEZPUR
First Superintendent of Tea Culture in Assam.

the breaking out of the Burmah war, I offered
my services to Mr. Scott, then Agent to the
Governor General, and was appointed to command gunboats. . . . It was my good fortune
last year to go against the Duffa Gaum and his
followers, who threatened to overrun our Frontier, and it was my good fortune to expel him
twice with my gunboat from two strong positions.

Mr. C. A. Bruce lies buried in the church
yard at Tezpur. In the church there is a
tablet to his memory. Some members of
the Bruce family are still living on tea
gardens at Tezpur.

The First Shipments of British Tea

During 1837, only "samples" of manufactured tea were produced, but in 1838,
the history-making shipment was ready for
London. It consisted of eight chests, and
Captain Jenkins, Commissioner of the
Assam Valley, proudly announced their
dispatch on May 6. They reached England, where the greatest interest had been
aroused by the event, during the latter part
of the year. They were brought to auction
on January 10, 1839, each chest being sold
separately. The *Asiatic Journal* furnishes
the following contemporary account of the
sale:

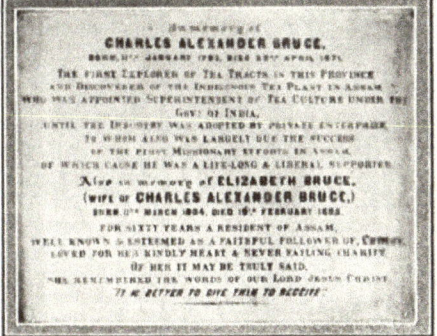

BRUCE MEMORIAL TABLET AT TEZPUR

The first importation of tea from the British territories in Assam, consisting of eight chests, containing about 350 pounds, was put up by the East India Company to public sale in the commercial sale rooms, Mincing Lane, on the 10th January, 1839, and excited much curiosity. The lots were eight, three of Assam souchong, and five of Assam pekoe. On offering the first lot (souchong) Mr. Thompson, the sale-broker, announced that each lot would be sold, without the least reservation, to the highest bidder. The first bid was 5s. per pound, a second bid was made of 10s. per pound. After much competition it was knocked down for 21s. per pound, the purchaser being Captain Pidding. The second lot of souchong was bought for the same person for 20s. per pound. The third and last lot of souchong sold for 16s. per pound, Captain Pidding being the buyer. The first lot of Assam pekoe sold after much competition for 24s. per pound, every broker appearing to bid for it: it was bought for Captain Pidding. The second, third, and fourth lots of Assam pekoe fetched the respective prices of 25s., 27s. 6d., and 28s. 6d., per pound and were also purchased for Captain Pidding. For the last lot (pekoe) a most exciting competition took place,—there were nearly 60 bids made for it. It was at last knocked down at the extraordinary price of 34s. per pound, Captain Pidding was also the purchaser of this lot, and has therefore become the sole proprietor of the first importation of Assam tea. This gentleman, we understand, has been induced to give this enormous price for an article that may be produced at 1s. per pound by the public-spirited motive of securing a fair trial to this valuable product of British Assam.

Captain Pidding was the proprietor of "Howqua mixture." He afterwards distributed small samples of the shipment at 2s. 6d. each. The gesture proved a splendid advertisement for British grown tea, even if the quality left much to be desired. However, a second lot, this time 95 chests, arrived late in 1839, and showed considerable improvement. It, too, was put up for sale by the East India Company, on March 17, 1840, after the Honourable Court of Directors had reserved 10 chests for private distribution. Several tea brokers and tea merchants valued it at from 2s. 11d. to 3s. 3d. per pound. Among them were such well known firms as W. J. & H. Thompson, Joseph Travers & Sons, William & James Bland, Richard Gibbs, Mr. Stevenson and the Messrs. Twining. Patriotic buyers pushed prices up to between 8s. and 11s. per pound, except in the case of a lot called "Toychong," which brought 4s. to 5s. per pound.

Messrs. Twining & Co. expressed the general opinion of the second shipment by saying:

Upon the whole we think that the recent specimens are very favourable to the hope and ex-

pectation that Assam is capable of producing an article well suited to this market, and although at present the indications are chiefly in reference to teas adapted by their strong and useful flavour to general purposes, there seems no reason to doubt but that increased experience in the culture and manufacture of tea in Assam may eventually approximate a portion of its produce to the finer descriptions which China has hitherto furnished.

What a fine bit of quiet reserve prophecy that was! Within six years from the time Lord William Bentinck had appointed his tea committee, the Government had demonstrated that British grown tea could be produced in marketable quantities; but twelve years more were to elapse before tea culture in India could be pronounced a commercial success. Quite as significant was this date, 1840, because it marked the beginning of the end of China tea in England.

A record of the first shipment of Assam tea into the Calcutta market is preserved in the India office. It is a handbill of a commercial sale of tea made by Government, signed by Mr. Thomas Watkins, superintendent of the Government plantations and endorsed by N. Wallich, M. D., superintendent H. C. Botanic Gardens. It is dated Jaipur, Upper Assam, March 5, 1841, and headed: "Novel and Interesting Sale of Assam Teas—The First Importation for the Calcutta Market." The tea circular announces two parcels of tea offered for sale, namely, 35 chests manufactured by the Singpho chief, Ningroola, and 95, the produce of the Government tea plantations. All of which moves Sir George Watt to the following comment: "It may thus be noted that the Singphos were actually manufacturing tea in Assam at the very time apparently that Wallich challenged the production of tea as the evidence necessary to convince him that the Assam indigenous plant was the true tea-yielding species." [15]

Rise of the Assam Company

While the various experiments previously detailed were being conducted, Upper Assam, natural home of the tea plant, was still foreign territory under a native ruler, Parundur Singh, the British maintaining a few troops and a political agent there. In 1839, in consequence of failure to fulfill his

15 Sir George Watt, *Commercial Products of India*, New York, 1908.

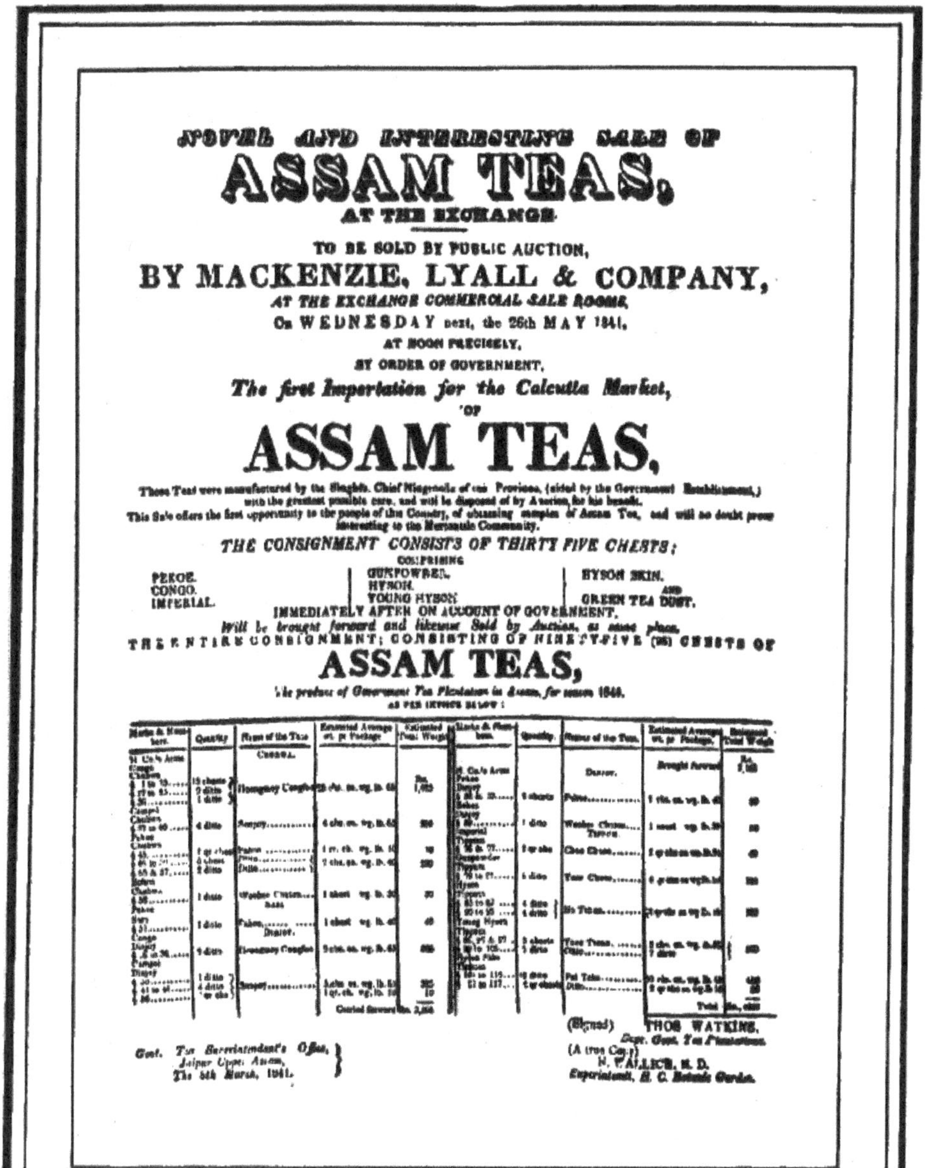

NOVEL AND INTERESTING SALE OF

ASSAM TEAS,

AT THE EXCHANGE

TO BE SOLD BY PUBLIC AUCTION,

BY MACKENZIE, LYALL & COMPANY,

AT THE EXCHANGE COMMERCIAL SALE ROOMS,

On WEDNESDAY next, the 26th MAY 1841,

AT NOON PRECISELY,

BY ORDER OF GOVERNMENT,

The first Importation for the Calcutta Market,

OF

ASSAM TEAS,

These Teas were manufactured by the Singhfo, Chief Ningroolu of the Province, (aided by the Government Establishment,) with the greatest possible care, and will be disposed of by Auction for his benefit. This Sale offers the first opportunity to the people of this Country, of obtaining samples of Assam Tea, and will no doubt prove interesting to the Mercantile Community.

THE CONSIGNMENT CONSISTS OF THIRTY FIVE CHESTS:

COMPRISING

PEKOE.	GUNPOWDER.	HYSON SKIN.
CONGO.	HYSON.	AND
IMPERIAL.	YOUNG HYSON.	GREEN TEA DUST.

IMMEDIATELY AFTER ON ACCOUNT OF GOVERNMENT.

Will be brought forward and likewise Sold by Auction, as same place,

THE ENTIRE CONSIGNMENT; CONSISTING OF NINETY FIVE (95) CHESTS OF

ASSAM TEAS,

the produce of Government Tea Plantations in Assam, for season 1840.

AS PER INVOICE BELOW :

Govt. Tea Superintendent's Office,
Jaipur Upper Assam,
The 5th March, 1841.

(Signed) THOS WATKINS,
Dept. Govt. Tea Plantations.
(A true Copy)
N. WALLICH, M.D.
Superintendt., H. C. Botanic Garden.

HANDBILL OF THE FIRST SALE OF INDIAN TEA IN THE CALCUTTA MARKET

treaty engagements, the native ruler was deposed by Col. White, British agent, who took over the administration of Sibsagar and Lakhimpur in the name of the British crown.

This annexation made private enterprise

possible and safe. The Government, feeling satisfied that it had done all that could be expected of it in an experimental way for British grown tea, rested on its oars and, in effect, said to the merchants of the empire, "observe these successful tea gardens at Dibrugarh, along the Tingri and around the Naga hills; gentlemen, the next move is yours."

The merchants were not slow to act, Calcutta taking the initiative. Some capitalists of that city, with Government approval, formed the Bengal Tea Association. In February, 1839, a joint stock company was formed at London, "for the purpose of cultivating the newly discovered tea plant in Assam." It soon became obvious that the two groups should combine, and on May 30, 1839, the Bengal Tea Association moved to form a junction with the London Company, on condition that "the local management be conducted by a committee of directors to be elected exclusively in Calcutta." In this way was evolved the peculiar constitution of India's pioneer tea company, whereby its destinies were entrusted to a double board of directors, one in London and one in Calcutta.

The Assam Company in London was approved by the heads of the East India Company, despite some opposition led by Sir Charles Forbes, who insisted that no exclusive monopoly be granted to it in Assam lest it "turn out to be a humbug." The Government turned over to the Assam Company, in March, 1840, two-thirds of its experimental gardens in Assam free for the first ten years. This included practically all of its holdings, except Chubwa.

In March, 1840, Mr. C. A. Bruce joined the company as superintendent of the northern division with headquarters at Jaipur, and Mr. J. Masters, a gentleman identified in Calcutta with agricultural and botanical pursuits, became superintendent of the southern division at Nazira, which is still the Assam Company's headquarters for India.

The Company was beset by labor troubles at once. Civil war and the Burmese invasion had almost depopulated Assam, so local labor was scarce although Masters reported he found the natives willing and promising while Mr. Bruce's Chinese laborers were few and none too willing. An attempt was made to import several hundred Chinese coolies from Calcutta and Singapore, but they were a poorly selected, quarrelsome lot. Many of them were shoemakers or carpenters from the bazaars, and knew nothing about tea making, so it was not strange that there was a clash with the natives—at Pabna—resulting in 57 of the Chinamen landing in jail. The remainder refused to go on, causing the cancellation of their agreements, and they returned to Calcutta, where they caused the authorities endless trouble. "A turbulent, obstinate, rapacious gang," is the description the company's London report gave of them. After committing many excesses, they were finally rounded up by the Calcutta police, and deported to the Isle of France, ending the first and last attempt to introduce Chinese labor into the Indian tea gardens.

A body of 652 "Dhangar Coles" was recruited next, but cholera attacked them on their way up to Assam and those who survived took to their heels and were never seen again. The mortality among Europeans as well as among the native laborers was something appalling. Even the Company's doctors died in their tracks. On every hand nature seemed to resent the intrusion of this white man's enterprise, continually nagging him in its development.

In spite of labor troubles and plague ravages, however, some 2638 acres had been snatched from the jungle and were reported under tea cultivation at the Company's annual meeting in Calcutta on August 11, 1841. During the preceding year, 10,212 pounds of manufactured tea were produced. But at what a cost! Over £65,000 had been poured into the venture by London investors. The management did not lose heart, however, and even began to whistle to keep up its courage. As an evidence of this, we read that the Calcutta board was so sanguine of the future that it estimated production in 1841 at 40,000 pounds; rising by 1845 to 320,000 pounds.

Neither the Chinese tea makers nor the European assistants gave much satisfaction. The former, according to Mr. Masters, were given to assuming the airs of fine gentlemen on their three rupees a month income, and were grossly insulted by being asked to work. "If they continue saucy," Masters wrote to the directors on February 12, 1842, "we may take a convenient opportunity of making a strike for two or three months, and when they lose their pay, they will probably become sensible that they are dependent on the Assam Company for their livelihood." "Mr. Masters hardly gives one the idea of a tactful manager," is Dr. Mann's comment.

Regarding his European assistants, Masters complained that "a passionate European, entirely ignorant of the language and of every part of his duty, can be worse than useless" in such an unhealthy climate. The main trouble with them was that they sickened and died, however, and then Masters had the same difficulties and inconveniences all over again.

By 1842, the Company's report showed that in Mr. Masters' division there were 44 poorahs [one poorah = 1.21 acres] in the Gabroo Purbut Gardens; 213 poorahs on Hatheoah; 23 on Cherideo; 20 on Deopani, and 350 newly planted on Rokanhabbi. In Bruce's division there were 31 poorahs at Kahung; 34½ poorahs on Hoholea [including Ballyjan and Tipling]; 31¼ on Hoogrijan; 10 on Tingri; 32 on Khootoon Goorie; 30 on Hookham, and 15 on Tippum. The Bazaloni seed garden was on Hoogrijan.

In spite of the optimistic forecasts of the year previous, production in 1841 was only 29,267 lbs., while the net cost of the enterprise stood at £160,000. There were ugly rumors in the air, storm clouds were gathering, and the newspapers were indulging in sarcastic comments. Said the *Friend of India*, apropos of the maiden voyage of a new river steamer: "The Assam Tea Company after having sent their new steamer on one trip up the Berhampooter, have, on her return, offered her for sale. The cause is not made known—probably her inability to steam the current of the Berhampooter."

By 1843, the Calcutta directors decided there must be something wrong and sent Mr. J. M. Mackie and Mr. Hodges into Assam to investigate. As a result both Mr. Bruce and Mr. Masters were summarily dismissed, and the London directors confessing they had been deceived, promised drastic reforms.

Then followed several lean years in which expenses were reduced and the yield increased. The directors were so pleased they declared a dividend of ten shillings a share in January, 1846, though no profit had been made. Meanwhile, there had been a full incorporation of the Company under limited liability, by special act of Parliament in 1845, and this, together with the general economies inaugurated, convinced the East India Company it was time to get out from under. This is how they phrased it:

> The sales of tea, both in Calcutta and London, judging from the statement of the cost per pound —14 annas c.i.f.—confirms the opinion expressed that the article may under proper management be cultivated at a real remunerative price, and we accede to your [the Government of Bengal] proposal that the Government should withdraw from any further connection with the cultivation or manufacture of tea in Assam.

All of these proceedings were calculated to make the general public believe the industry was an established success, but, as Dr. Mann points out, the true facts of the case did not justify any such conclusion. The estimates of yield had been falsified, hopeless mismanagement continued, and worse than everything, it was becoming increasingly evident "that nobody knew how to grow tea so as to maintain the yield of the bushes, let alone increase the amount of tea which could be made from them." In other words "the concern had reached the stage when the method of planting and plucking tea, which had been learned from the Chinese who had taught the pioneers, had definitely broken down, and it was evident, unless new methods could be found which would yield more tea and maintain the yield of the bushes better, the industry must close."

The London directors saw the handwriting on the wall. In the name of further retrenchment they closed down the Tingri and Jaipur garden groups in 1846, and in 1847 confessed there were "too small hopes of success and too limited an amount of profit to be anticipated to render it advisable to continue our operations." They even tried to unload the property on the Calcutta board at a price, but Calcutta was silent. The £20 shares were being hawked about the market at half a crown apiece. And this only two years after the East India Government had told the world that the tea industry in India was an established success.

Finally, it was decided to carry on for another year, and it was with heavy hearts and light purses that the directors faced 1848. The Company was teetering on the brink of ruin and there was no use trying to disguise it. Those were dark days for tea in Assam, and a winter of discontent for the shareholders of the Assam Company.

Twenty-one lakhs of rupees had been expended upon buildings and cultivation, which, subsequent investigation disclosed, should not have cost one-tenth of that sum. The credit and resources of the company were exhausted; they were £7000 in debt in London, Rs. 40,000 in Calcutta, and the absolutely necessary outlay required in Assam to save the wrecks of buildings and neglected plantings was staggering.

In this crisis there were some who deserted the fast sinking enterprise, but there were those, too, who had enough discernment to perceive the possibilities of the property under better management. "With a spirit, firmness, and confidence that does them infinite credit," says the *Friend of India*, "they raised funds on their own individual credit and responsibility to make one more effort to retrieve the affairs of the company."

Who among them dreamed it was the proverbial dark hour that precedes the dawn? Yet so it was, for, as often happens in time of crisis, real men were ready to be raised up to meet the emergency. In this case they were three: Mr. Henry Burkinyoung in Calcutta, Mr. Stephen Mornay and, later, Mr. George Williamson in Assam. The year was 1847.

Mr. Burkinyoung became deputy chairman of the Calcutta Board of Directors, and Mr. Stephen Mornay took charge in Assam. Inside of five years these men made over a bankrupt concern into one which was paying its own way. The improved methods and technical skill introduced into Assam by Mr. Mornay and carried out by Mr. Williamson, changed a colossal failure into a profitable industry. Says Dr. Mann: "One cannot exaggerate the debt which the tea industry owes to them. Their successors improved their results—but they it was who made a tea industry appear possible in Northeast India."

So dramatic was the transition that the Company's report for 1848 showed a profit of £3000. Out of £7000 debt, £2000 were paid off, and with the inspiration that comes from restored confidence there was a call of £1 per share [£10,000] to extend the cultivated areas. And this success in the face of continued exploitation of the "cursed China jat"!

Indeed, it is interesting to note how far careful management and intelligent direction carried the company on its upward turn despite the stock selection, for it was a long time before the native India jat succeeded to its birthright.

Calcutta was delighted and eager to push ahead, but London, often burnt, was conservatively shy. In 1849, Tingri and Jaipur were re-opened, greatly to the "fear and displeasure" of the London Board. However, profits continued, though the area was extended, and the entire indebtedness was wiped out in two years. In 1852, the first earned dividend of 2½ per cent was paid, and there was no longer any doubt that the company was on the highroad to success. It was followed by a three per cent dividend in 1853, and in that year Messrs. Mornay and Burkinyoung retired.

The new manager in Assam was Mr. George Williamson, who has been hailed as "the greatest figure in the development of the Assam tea industry." After his retirement from Assam, in 1859, he established, in the early 'sixties, the London firm of Messrs. George Williamson & Co., which was the forerunner of the Calcutta firm of Williamson, Magor & Co. The managing director in Calcutta was Mr. W. Roberts, of Begg, Dunlop & Co., afterwards with the Jorehaut Tea Company.

Mr. Williamson soon came to regard the China tea plants as an evil, for he early refers to one garden, Kachari Pookri, as possessing an advantage "in having no China plant, the inferior yielding of which in respect to quantity is now a well established fact." He condemned injudicious and ignorant plucking, and refused to be stampeded by the directors when they grew alarmed because no tea was forthcoming in March and April. "Everything will be alright," said he, and it was. He found a production over the whole of the gardens of only 235 pounds per poorah and set himself energetically to bring about the change that gradually displaced the imported China tea plants with the native tea of Assam; one of the most epochal happenings in the history of India tea. He brought to the business careful study of the tea bush, a fund of technical skill and good management, with the result of increased yield and larger dividends. The Company paid nine per cent in 1856.

This was 22 years after Governor Lord William Bentinck appointed the first tea committee, and so his faith was vindicated and his vision became reality. Already other companies were forming to enter the field, and the province was alive with prospectors. The next ten years saw such an amazing development that, because it was so well grounded, the industry rode triumphant through the succeeding speculative debacle into an era of scientific cultivation which has continued to the present day.

First Plantings in Other Districts

The introduction of tea into Chittagong dates from 1840, when some China plants from the Botanical Gardens at Calcutta and some seeds from Assam were planted in the pioneer garden near the location of the present club. This district is not favored with a suitable climate and has not developed to any great extent. The cultivation of tea in Dehra Dun started in 1842. In 1843, Dr. Falconer was succeeded by Dr. William Jameson as superintendent of tea culture for Kumaon.

Because it had done so well in the northwest provinces, the China tea plant was still foremost in the plans of the Tea Committee in the year 1848, when Robert Fortune, 1813–1880, a British traveler and horticulturist, disguised himself as a Chinaman, and, at the instigation of the English

East India Company, penetrated into the interior of China for the choicest tea seeds, plants, and workmen. His quest was in every way successful. His first shipment arrived in good order at Calcutta, in the summer of 1850. He returned to Calcutta, in 1851, with eight workmen, a quantity of seed, and more than 20,000 plants, collected in the green and black tea districts of China. There followed a tour of inspection of the tea districts in Kumaon and Garhwal, and afterward he published the results of his observations in his *Visit to the Tea Districts of China and India*, 1852. Fortune paid a third visit to China, in 1858.

In 1851, the first privately owned tea garden was opened in Assam by Lieutenant-Colonel F. S. Hannay, initiating the era of private ownership. It was stocked with China tea plants. Some of Colonel Hannay's descendants are to-day connected with important India tea companies.

In 1854, the Lieutenant Governor of the Northwestern Provinces authorized Dr. William Jameson to establish a principal tea nursery at Ayer Toli, near Byznath, which, subsequently, developed into the

AN OLD-TIME TEA FACTORY IN CACHAR—LATE 80's

On the Dwarbund tea estate, in 1889. The plantains over the fermenting room were designed to promote coolness.

AN HISTORIC HOUSE WARMING PARTY AT BALLACHERA, CACHAR, IN 1868

Standing, left to right—C. Williams, Dulcherra; T. B. Barry, Rampore; W. Aitchison, Doloo; S. C. Davidson, Barkhola; J. Harvey, Massampore; R. B. Donke, Doodputloe; Tooshe; G. Shaw, Khoreel. Sitting—H. Hawes, Rampore; Ritherden, Kurkoorie; W. Nicholl, Arcuttipore; C. Oldfield, Kalline; H. Gregg, Ballacherra; A. A. Shaw, Massampore; Reid, Doloo.

best and richest cultural district in Kumaon. Dr. Jameson's report from the Botanic Garden, Northwestern Provinces, 1855, stated:

The cultivation of the tea plant is destined ultimately to change the features of the hill provinces, and render them as valuable to the state, as those of the plains. Tea is now thriving from Kangra to Kumaon. The finer kinds of tea plants, introduced by the government through Mr. Fortune, from the northern districts of China, viz., Woo-e-san, Hwuy-Chow, Moo-yuen, Tien-tung, Silver Island, etc., have been distributed throughout the whole of the districts, and have yielded a large supply of seeds for the ensuing season.

The Assam indigenous tea was found in the Chandkhani hills in Sylhet and in Cachar, in 1855. One account credits the discovery of the tea plant in Sylhet to a native, Muhamed Warish. Later, tea was found growing wild along the Khasia and Jaintia hills, and for some time the presence of indigenous tea was taken as a sign that the area was suitable for tea growth. Tea cultivation in Sylhet was begun under the direction of Mr. Sweetland of Telaghur. Malnicherra, the first garden, was opened in 1857. The first tea in Cachar was put out in Mauza Barsanjan, in 1856, on the

hill tops which stretch from the Barail range to the Barak. The *teelas* [hillocks] were next planted, and, in 1875, the first *bheels* [swamps] were drained and planted.

Darjeeling embarked on the tea venture in 1856–59 under the fostering care of the chief Government official, Dr. A. Campbell. By the close of 1856, tea was being cultivated at Tukvar, at the Canning and Hopetown gardens in Darjeeling, and on the Kurseong flats, and between Kurseong and Pankhabari. After the industry was established as a commercial enterprise in the Darjeeling district, attention was directed to the Terai, where Champta was put out in 1862. The land east of the Teesta, known as the Dooars, was soon after explored, and Gajaldhoba was planted in 1874, followed later by Phulbari [Leesh River] and Bagrakote. As the tea area spread eastward till it ultimately reached the Sankos, the boundary of Assam, good jat indigenous tea was planted in place of the China bush with which the Western Dooars and the Terai were planted.

In 1861, tea cultivation was re-commenced in the Nilgiri hills of Southern

India by Captain Mann with China tea seed. Chittagong and Chota Nagpur started tea cultivation on a commercial scale about 1867.

Reviewing the early history of tea in Kumaon and Garhwal, J. H. Batten, formerly commissioner of Kumaon, summarizes it as falling into seven periods: *first*, ignorance and indifference; *second*, guessing and conjecture; *third*, the first actual official experiment; *fourth*, that of regular Government exploitation; *fifth*, beginning of private enterprise; *sixth*, the abandonment of official experiment; and last, the commercially successful period. All of which is fairly applicable to India as a whole.

Tea Mania and Panic

Capital began to be seriously interested in tea in India about 1851. The success of the Assam Company, and after it the Jorehaut Company, in 1858, together with the opening of new gardens in other districts focussed public attention on the new development, and there were over 50 private tea enterprises in existence by 1859. Not only in Assam, but in Darjeeling, Cachar, Sylhet, Kumaon, and Hazaribagh prospects seemed bright and alluring to investors. There was a normal, healthy development going on when, about 1860, the industry turned an unlucky corner and plunged into a speculative orgy that all but ruined it. The "tea mania" is the phrase most historians use in referring to it, and the title fits it perfectly.

In the early days of tea, Government was anxious to foster its cultivation, so it was ready to grant suitable tracts of land on easy terms. As the industry developed and land applications became more plentiful, more stringent laws were adopted, culminating in the Assam Rules of 1854. These provided for 99-year leases under heavy clearance conditions, and were most unpopular with the tea planters and investors. The dissatisfaction became so general that, in 1861, the Assam Rules were supplemented by Lord Canning's Rules which, among other reasonable concessions, permitted the redemption of the land in fee simple.

Symptoms of the tea mania had developed before the Canning Rules were published; shortly after that it broke out in all its virulence. Speculators and get-rich-quick artists were not slow to take advantage of the situation. From the good results achieved by a few of the new gardens, fancy pictures were painted of the huge profits to be made by working with big capital, and new gardens were opened with reckless abandon; old gardens were extended out of all proportion to their intrinsic value, caution and forethought were tossed aside, and the mad scramble was on. Companies were hurriedly formed, and there was a great rush for shares in the new concerns.

New companies were starting daily in Calcutta, and tea shares were sent skyrocketing by the sudden avarice of those who hoped to become rich over night. All sorts and conditions of men became obsessed with the frenzy; many of them throwing up lucrative posts to devote their time to speculation or to plunge madly into tea. "Those were greedy days," says A. F. Dowling, "and it would have been well for the tea industry had the new Rules been framed with a view to check instead of to foster speculation." [16]

Unfortunate modification of the Canning Rules by a Secretary of State at home, too far away to judge what was best, caused tea lands to be sold at the most absurd prices. Instead of a charge of Rs. 2-8 per acre to the applicant, the illiberal and unjust method of putting the land up at auction with an upset price of Rs. 2-8 was adopted. In this way the finder and applicant usually lost out to anyone who cared to bid half an anna more than he did. Rs. 10 and upward per acre were paid for wild jungle tracts.

From *Papers Regarding the Tea Industry in Bengal*, published in 1874, we get the following pen picture of conditions in the planting districts:

> The chief object of speculators during the tea mania was to get possession of one or more lots of waste land, and the suspension of the clauses in the Waste Land Rules providing for demarcation and survey previous to sale, made it very easy of attainment. The next step taken by the more honest among them was to try and bring portions of their lots under some sort of resemblance to tea cultivation in as short a time as practicable. Local labor was hired at any rate which the laborers chose to ask. Tea seed was purchased at extravagant prices. The earth was scratched up and the seed being laid down, the speculator considered himself free to form a company, which was started by selling the lands he had scarcely finished clearing and sow-

16 A. F. Dowling, *Tea Notes*, Calcutta, 1886.

ing, as accomplished tea gardens, and what still remained of undesirable waste at a cost out of all proportion to the amount he had contracted to pay for it to the state, and to what it was worth. But in time even such a pretense of cultivation was thought too slow, and more enterprising traders found their account in persuading shareholders to invest in tea gardens that were actually not in existence at all. A remarkable instance of this occurred in the Nowgong district, where the Indian manager of a promoter of companies in London was advised by his employer to clear and plant a certain area of waste land for delivery to a company to whom he had just sold it as a tea garden.

These evils were more or less common to Assam, Cachar, Darjeeling, and Chittagong at this time. In the last named district many tracts on steep hills and used-up paddy land, wholly unsuitable for tea cultivation, were sold and sold again at enormous profits. As to the effect of all this upon the public mind, Mr. J. Berry White says:

The fact was, that during the mania of 1862-63, all who held grants of waste land in Assam, and had planted a few maunds of tea seed on it, honestly believed that they possessed a veritable El Dorado, and in most cases proved their bona fides by declining to receive any cash payment, but stipulated for the entire consideration being made to them in shares. Although tea has the reputation of furnishing a beverage that cheers but does not inebriate, yet its cultivation in new districts exercises the most strangely intoxicating influences on those engaged in it, equalled only by the sanguine dreams of gold explorers. On the opening out of each new district in India, the most extravagant expectations have been formed by men who ought to have been capable of forming a reliable and dispassionate estimate.[17]

Money says it was madness to expect aught but ruin under the conditions which obtained in the tea-fever days. "Any one was taken. Tea planters were a strange medley of retired or cashiered army and navy officers, medical men, engineers, veterinary surgeons, steamer captains, chemists, shopkeepers, stable men, used-up policemen, clerks, and goodness knows who besides. Is it strange the enterprise failed in their hands?"

In the first wild rush every man thought that to own a few tea bushes was to realize wealth, and not only were existing gardens bought for eight and ten times their value, but many found to their sorrow that nominal areas of 500 acres, after being bought

EARLY TYPE OF MANAGER'S BUNGALOW
Erected in 1903 on the Urrunabund Tea Estate, Cachar, and "still going strong."

and paid for, on subsequent measurement, proved to be under 100 acres; new gardens were started on impossible sites by managers "who did not know a tea plant from a cabbage." There were highly paid boards of directors in Calcutta and London, and still more highly paid secretaries; all of whom did nothing but add to the expense. Extravagance and mismanagement were rampant in every department.[18]

The tea saturnalia reached its climax in 1865, and the inevitable reaction set in. It is not strange that the thing collapsed; the wonder is it did not do so earlier. The mushroom companies sickened and died, and once the bubble was pricked, a panic followed. In place of the rush to buy tea properties at any cost, there developed a frantic dash to sell. Tea gardens that had cost lakhs of rupees but a short time before were sold for as many hundred. Some gardens were abandoned because they couldn't get a bid of a shilling an acre, and the panic became a rout. All the holders wanted was to get their names off the registers before the bottom fell out of the market, and tea shares that had been bulled to absurd premiums were offered for next to nothing. The rout became a shambles, and there were many tragedies. Men became bankrupts because of tea; found they had borrowed money which they could not repay on account of tea; that they had ruined friends and relatives through tea; until the very word became a stench in the

[17] J. Berry White, "The Indian Tea Industry: Its Rise, Progress During 50 years, and Prospects Considered from a Commercial Point of View," *Journal Society of Arts*, London, 1887, vol. XXXV.

[18] Edward Money, *The Cultivation and Manufacture of Tea*, London, 1878.

nostrils of the investing public. Indeed, during this period, tea acquired much unenviable notoriety from being classed with the South Sea and other bubbles.

So serious was the crisis that the Government stepped in and, early in 1868, appointed a commission to inquire into the state of the industry. This commission confirmed the conviction that every thoughtful student and prudent investor had all the time, that the industry was basically sound, only needing to go ahead and get rid of its unwise inflation and stock-jobbing companions. The commission's report was confined to Assam, Cachar, and Sylhet, and disclosed that such old gardens as had escaped the speculative blight were in a flourishing state.

Confidence began to return about 1870. Several new companies were started, and the scrip of the older companies that paid dividends moved to higher levels. It was a staggering body-blow that India tea received in the collapse of the boom in lands and shares of 1866–67, with its widespread financial disasters, but the comeback was such a splendid exhibition of gameness on the part of the real builders of the industry, that it soon entered upon its new heritage, the succeeding era of scientific cultivation and of goodly profits.

Those who may wish to delve further into the early history of tea in India will find much material and many references in *Tea Cultivation, Cotton and Other Agricultural Experiments in India*, 1863, by Dr. W. Nassau Lees; *A Text Book on the Chemistry and Agriculture of Tea*, 1893, by M. Kelway Bamber, M. R. A. C., M. R. A. S. Eng., F. C. S., member of the Society of Arts, London, and late chemist to the Indian Tea Association; *Commercial Products of India*, 1908, by Sir George Watt, C. I. E., M. B., C. M., LL. D., F. L. S., formerly Professor of Botany, Calcutta University, superintendent of the Industrial Section, Indian Museum, and Reporter on Economic Products to the Government of India; *The Early History of the Tea Industry in North East India*, 1918, by Harold H. Mann, D. Sc., F. I. C., F. L. S., formerly scientific officer of the Indian Tea Association and, later, Director of Agriculture, Bombay Presidency; *A Basis for Tea Selection*, 1919, by Dr. C. P. Cohen Stuart, botanist, Proefstation voor Thee, Buitenzorg, Java.

The Old Days in Assam

The early days of tea in Assam may have been the "good old days" to those courageous souls who loved the adventure, and did not count the cost, but the tea planter's life hardly commended itself to one at all mindful of creature comforts.

Generally speaking, the country was an almost impenetrable jungle of *khagra* grass from ten to fifteen feet high, with occasional *pathar* oases, which marked abandoned rice fields, and an equal amount of heavy forest. When British enterprise started to reclaim this jungle for India tea, the wild beasts were in the ascendancy and the native Assamese were on the decline. Indeed, the terrified inhabitants were continually abandoning their villages and treking to more salubrious parts of India.

As a rule the forest jungle was preferred to the grass jungle for tea planting. Nearly all the tea in the Jorhat, Dibrugarh, and Doom-Dooma districts was put out in land recovered from dense forest.

Linde, 1879, pictures the tea planter as living like the pristine man in a grand primeval forest, the limits of which retreat further and further from his little settlement.

The woods bow beneath the sturdy strokes of his dependants, who, secluded from the rest of the world like him, regard their master in a patriarchal light, looking upon him as father, defender, and judge. Here the pioneer, whose position is exalted indeed, lives a solitary life, having not his equal, and months may pass, before the sight of a white face and the sound of the Queen's English gladdens his soul. Here, removed from all his friends, stripped of every luxury, he breathes a miasmatic air, is exhausted by a perpetual vapor bath, but bears it all, and prefers sickness, nay even death, to non-success in his undertaking.

A tea planter's bungalow in those days was a rather pathetic sight. There was a stove, a platform bed of split bamboos, a table, a box which did duty as a chair, and a medicine shelf. This last was really the principal article in the furnishings, as it provided the essentials without which no tea planter could be expected to survive; for in order to survive, the planter's health code demanded "quinine every morning, castor oil twice a week, and calomel at the change of the moon." An old Assam tea planter growing reminiscent in Calcutta not so long ago, remarked:

Sheep could not stand the climate. The Hindu

WILLIAM JACKSON, 1850–1915

He was the inventor of Jackson's tea roller, tea driers, and other epoch making machines.

population debarred beef. Religious prejudice forbade milking the cows. So the planters had to live on the skinny fowls of the country, and such ducks and geese as they could raise and save from the ocelots and the ounces. They also fattened goats for meat, and occasionally persuaded the half-wild she-goat to part with a little milk. A litter of wild piglings might sometimes be brought in by a shikari, each enveloped in a basket, with its little legs sticking out. These, no bigger than kittens, charged in all directions and bit like demons when released. For cereals there was nothing but rice, of many kinds, but all coarse. This was boiled or crushed for porridge, or rough ground to make a kind of *chapati*. To the horses and elephants it was given in husk [paddy], but no horses could thrive on this, or indeed stand the climate at all, except the shaggy little Bhutea ponies.

The planter's daily routine was to go out only after the day was well aired. After the morning quinine, he drank his coffee and ate what he could. Then with a pipe under his nose to counteract the miasma, he sallied forth to oversee his clearing, and all the countless jobs, which brought round the midday meal. Followed the afternoon siesta, or bout of ague as the case might be, and then the evening inspection. And so *da capo* from week to week, till it was time for the trip home to recruit, or else for rest in the grave.

William Jackson and His Tea Machines

One day, early in the 'seventies, a sidewheeler chunking lazily down the Brahma-

putra, went aground on one of the shifting sand bars for which the river is notorious, and due to this seeming trifle, the currents of two men's lives were turned awry and a revolution was started in tea making machinery.

The men were the brothers John and William Jackson, who were on their way home to England from a tea estate in Upper Assam. It was found that because of needed repairs, the boat would be hung up on the sand bank for a considerable period, so the passengers spent the waiting time exploring the surrounding country. In the course of their rambles, the Jacksons came across a Marshall portable steam engine, which had been doing yeoman's service in India for ten years. William Jackson became so enamored of it that he made a note of the address of the maker, and, when, later on, he found it impossible to make satisfactory arrangements in Scotland for the manufacture of the tea machines with which his head was buzzing, he went to Gainsborough, England, and formed the association with the Britannia Iron Works, which was to mean so much for the tea industry, and out of which the extensive tea machinery business of Messrs. Marshall Sons & Co., Ltd., has since developed. The association lasted until Mr. Jackson's death in 1915.

The two Jacksons pooled their ideas at the beginning, but, subsequently, John came to the United States, while William continued his work in India and at Gainsborough. Nearly all the Jacksons' patents were taken out in William's name.

William Jackson did most of his experimental work at the Nigriting garden of the Brahmaputra Tea Co., and at Jorhat, where he set up his first tea roller on the Heeleakah garden of the Scottish Assam Tea Company in 1872. He freely acknowledged the inspiration which he had received from the inventions of Kinmond and others, but it was soon apparent that he had done a new and revolutionary thing. The Jackson roller was not unlike Kinmond's and yet it was so different that, as time wore on, it was apparent that Jackson was blazing a new trail. Even Lieutenant-Colonel Edward Money, the India tea planting expert, was not won over to the idea of any machine superseding hand rolling for tea until he saw Jackson's roller. Indeed, where others groped in the dark, Jackson burst through into the light.

Jackson did not confine himself to rollers only, but let his genius play upon the firing of tea, breaking, sorting, and packing problems. As a result, he has to his credit many noteworthy inventions and improvements on machines for every department of modern tea making. The original Jackson "Cross Action," "Excelsior," and "Hand Power" rollers, were complicated machines with heavy castings and parts. In 1887, he invented his improved "Rapid" roller, which, for twenty years dominated the market. Over 250 of these machines were sold in 1889. The single- and double-action "Metallic" rollers followed in 1907 and 1909, respectively.

Jackson produced his first mechanical hot air driers in 1884. The names are as familiar to tea men as his own. Who has not heard of the good old "Victoria," "Venetian," and "Paragon" machines? The principle employed was that of a suction fan to assist nature in drawing the hot air upwards through the leaf trays. These, too, held their own for over twenty years.

That Jackson had the courage of his convictions is shown by the fact that in 1887, after he had spent fifteen years working in the general direction of the vertical crank, with bevel gears, for rolling machines, he swept the net results into the discard, and began all over again, possessed of the idea that a simple rotary movement of the crank was superior. In that same year, he also brought out his first roll breaker; in 1888, he produced a tea sorter; and in 1898, a tea packer.

Jackson's fertile brain continued to evolve new ideas on rolling, drying, and sifting machines, and many of these were patented. Messrs. Marshall Sons & Co., Ltd., produced the improved machines as fast as Jackson evolved them, and found a ready market for them, in practically every tea country. The mechanical genius of members of the Marshall family played an important part in finding solutions of the engineering problems presented in the working out of many of Mr. Jackson's ideas.

In 1910, Jackson produced a notable change in his drying machine by the application of the up-draft on the pressure principle. Until that time, all his tea driers had been employing the suction principle. The big "Empire" machine stands as a monument to his genius in this field. In this drier, the fan draws the air through the well known Jackson multitubular stove and then forces it through the leaf in the drying chamber.

In 1872, when Jackson began inventing, the cost of tea production in India was 11d. a pound. By 1913, improved machinery had cut the cost to 2½ and 3d. a pound. Eight thousand rolling machines took care of the tea which previously would have called for the hand work of a million and a half coolies. Formerly, eight pounds of good wood converted into charcoal were required to dry one pound of tea, but the Jackson machines produced the same results with any wood, grass, or refuse. Where coal was used, the amount was reduced to a quarter of a pound of Assam coal per pound of finished dry tea.

Jackson was one of the first to emphasize the idea that better results were to be gained by stopping fermentation as soon as the leaf entered the drying chamber; also, that the tea should be cooled down as soon as possible after drying. He argued that the essential oil could not escape when the leaf was cold.

In the beginning, the leaf was rolled by hand, dried over charcoal fires, and trampled into the chests by the coolies' feet, in India as in China. Jackson and his contemporaries changed all that. They ushered in the new era of scientific preparation of the leaf in the most sanitary surroundings, and, with the most meticulous attention to hygienic requirements.

William Jackson died at Thorngrove, Aberdeen, Scotland, June 15, 1915, at the age of sixty-five. His brother John, who, in 1880, accepted the invitation of United States Commissioner of Agriculture William G. le Duc to conduct tea experiments in South Carolina, died about 1890, in St. Paul, Minn., where he was engaged in cleaning tea for the trade.

Mr. William Jackson left half of his estate, about £20,000, to such charities as the Indian Tea Association might select. The Tea Planters' Benevolent Institution was formed in 1921, and in addition to receiving funds from other sources, they were granted money from the William Jackson Trust of which Sir Charles McLeod, Bart., is chairman.

Sir S. C. Davidson and His Machines

The name of Sir Samuel C. Davidson will always be held in grateful remem-

SIR SAMUEL C. DAVIDSON 1846–1921

Inventor of the famous "Sirocco" tea drier and other revolutionizing tea machines.

brance by the tea planting industry, because it is synonymous with the "Sirocco" tea drier, and other tea machines, which he invented and made famous.

Samuel Cleland Davidson [afterwards Sir] was an Irishman by birth, but of Scotch descent. He was born in 1846, in County Down, and received his early education at the Royal Academical Institution, Belfast. He left school, at the age of fifteen, to enter the office of Mr. William Hastings, a Belfast civil engineer, where he remained until 1864.

About this time, Mr. Davidson's father purchased a share in the Burkhola Tea Estate in Cachar, whither young Davidson was dispatched to learn the tea business. It was in the autumn of 1864 that he set out on this, his first great adventure. Arriving at Calcutta, he had a three weeks' journey by river boat ahead of him. Now, this trip may be made in two days by steamer and railway.

At the estate, he began his planting career as assistant manager, and after two years, when he was twenty years old, he became manager.

He bought out his father's co-partner and became sole proprietor after his father's death, in 1869. Subsequently he sold the estate, joining Messrs. Chambers, Drake, and Ferguson in the Subong garden, of which he became sole owner later.

Young Davidson was keenly observant and it did not take him long to realize the inadequacy of the primitive Chinese methods then employed for tea manufacture in India. He applied himself with diligence to evolving something better, noting the efforts of such early machinery pioneers as Kinmond, Nelson, McMeekin, Gibbs, and Barry, who fired his imagination. A machine to take the place of the ancient wicker basket for firing interested him especially, and his experimental work convinced him that better tea could be made by machinery; also that there was a greater commercial success offering in the manufacture of tea machinery than in making tea. Consequently, he sold his Subong property in 1874, returned to Belfast, and for several years thereafter, superintended the manufacture of his patented machinery by Messrs. Combe, Barbour & Combe. In 1881, he founded the Sirocco Engineering Works, where he acted as his own draughtsman and manager.

Davidson's first "Sirocco" air heater, for the tea driers, appeared in 1877, followed by his No. 1 up-draft "Sirocco" tea drier, in 1879. Afterwards, he took out many patents covering all phases of tea manufacture.

From a modest beginning with one small workshop, in 1881, when he employed only seven hands, the Davidson enterprise has grown into a private limited liability company, employing over a thousand workmen, and having branches in many countries. The Sirocco Engineering Works of Messrs. Davidson & Co., Ltd., manufacture only Davidson's inventions. These include, besides tea machines, the "Sirocco" centrifugal and propeller fan, which not only disproved and upset many of the previously accepted theories of aero-dynamics and fan design, but also did much to revolutionize factory and mining conditions and life afloat; also, a new process raw rubber machine. However, it is because of his tea machinery that Mr. Davidson will be longest remembered by tea planters. From time to time, he brought out improvements on his driers, secured patents on tea rollers, roll breakers, cutters and sorters, and packing machines. Eventually, the

Davidson line included both up- and down-draft "Siroccos."

Mr. Davidson's versatility was remarkable. It is apparent in the fact that during his career he found time to invent new types of tennis poles, belt rivets, steam engines, and even for the production of non-alcoholic beverages from tea, coffee, and cocoa. In his early days out East, he was a keen sportsman, and held several records. In later life he carried out many scientific experiments in horticulture and arboriculture on his country estate at Seacourt, Bangor, County Down. To this many-sided man must also be given the credit of being one of the first to establish agencies for the sale of India teas in America and on the continent of Europe.

During the World War, the Sirocco Engineering Works played an important part in the manufacture of munitions, and Mr. Davidson brought out several war-time inventions which were adopted by the authorities. The firm was also one of the first to pay allowances to dependents of employees who volunteered for active service. Mr. Davidson's only surviving son, Captain J. S. Davidson, was fatally wounded on the Western front in 1916.

On June 22, 1921, Mr. Davidson was made a Knight of the British Empire. As Sir Samuel Davidson, K. B. E., he lived only two months, his death occurring August 18, 1921.

Tea Planting Pioneers

A book could be written about the many who went out to India and achieved distinction as tea planters. Not all of them rose to positions of eminence in the agency business or in association activities, but distinction of some kind came to most of them; either as experts in tea cultivation, tea manufacture, or because of their successful handling of the labor problem and long years of service—twenty-five to fifty in many cases. And this in a country whose climate, generally speaking, is most inhospitable to white men.

At the risk of being charged with serious omissions, the author wishes to refer here to the following tea planters, who are entitled to honorable mention, although they may not have figured prominently as members of firms in the tea trade nor in association affairs.

MR. WILLIAM ROBERTS, one of the early planters in Assam, was chiefly interested in the Jorehaut Tea Co., of which his son, Mr. F. A. Roberts, is now managing director. He was one of those present at the first meeting of the Indian Tea Association in London.

MR. W. H. VERNER, one time chairman, Dooars Tea Co., Ltd., the Empire of India and Ceylon Tea Co., Ltd., and the Singlo Tea Co., Ltd., was identified with the tea industry in the Dooars district, and rendered valuable service to the Indian Tea Association in London, of which he was at one time vice-chairman. He died in 1902.

MR. JAMES RIDDELL was one of the pioneers of Assam. He came out to India to the Jorehaut Tea Co. in 1861, and was subsequently associated with the Darjeeling Tea Co. and Badulipar Tea Estates. He died in 1903. Shortly before his death he was asked to preside at the dinner given to Sir [then Mr.] James Buckingham; a gesture which showed the esteem in which he was held by the planting fraternity.

COLONEL DOUGALD MACTAVISH LUMSDEN, C.B., was another of the pioneers of tea planting in Assam, and was quite prominent in his planting days. He was chairman of the Dhendai Tea Co. During the Boer War, he raised a volunteer battalion, known as Lumsden's Horse, which he took out to South Africa. He died in 1915.

MR. H. LUCKMAN JOHNSON was closely connected with the tea industry in Assam for over forty years, though not as a tea planter. He was a government official in Sylhet before going to Assam, and his official position, as well as his association with the labor question, enabled him to obtain a complete knowledge of the tea industry. Mr. Johnson died in 1913.

MR. ROBERT HART, one time chairman of the Baraoora (Sylhet) Tea Co. and a prominent member of the Indian Tea Association, (London), was a planter in India before coming to London. He died in 1914.

LIEUTENANT COLONEL W. MAGILL KENNEDY, C.I.E., at one time acted as Tea Commissioner in India for the Food Controller. He had a distinguished career in Assam. His name was a household word among tea planters, because of his activities as first chairman of the Assam Labour Board, 1915–20, and as a representative of the Tea Districts Labour Association. He was murdered during a train journey in September, 1923, and, though strong efforts

Mr. Claud Bald   Mr. H. R. A. Irwin   Mr. E. Scarth   Mr. W. H. Verner

INDIA TEA PLANTING PIONEERS OF THE 1870's

were made to apprehend the murderer, he was never found.

MR. J. BERRY WHITE, was for many years in medical charge of one of the most important districts in Assam. Here he acquired an accurate knowledge of tea which he was later to place at the service of the London tea trade.

MR. CLAUD BALD, author of the best-known technical work on India tea, came out from Glasgow, where he was born in 1853. He began planting on the Lohargur Estate in the Terai in 1877, and was also on Adulpore in the Terai before he joined the Lebong Company in the Darjeeling district, where he achieved fame and honor. For twenty-six years he served the Lebong Company as manager successively at Barnesberg, Badamtam, and Tukvar. He became manager of the Tukvar Company's estates in 1907, holding the position until his retirement in 1918. Four editions of his *India Tea* have been published. He also wrote two smaller books for tea and rubber planters and general agriculturists. Mr. Bald was president of the Darjeeling Planters' Association for several years. He retired to West Worthing, Sussex, in 1919, and died there in 1924.

MAJOR SIR GEORGE A. DOLBY, a pioneer Assam tea planter, retired, was prominent during his stay in India in the Assam Valley Light Horse.

MR. EDWARD SCARTH, a Darjeeling planter who retired in 1928 after fifty years in tea planting, came out to Assam in 1877. Mr. Scarth was born in Upper Holloway, Islington, England, July 11, 1850, and came out to India as an assistant on the Brahmapootra Tea Company's garden at Nigriting, Assam, in 1877. In those

days it was a seventeen and one-half days river journey from Goalundo to Nigriting, whereas, to-day it takes three days. He was manager of the Moabund Tea Co., 1882–95; superintendent, Attareekhat Tea Co., Ltd., 1895–1900; manager, Gingia Tea Co., Ltd., all in Assam. From 1904 to 1920 he was manager of the Seeyok Tea Co., and from 1920 to 1927 manager, Chamong Tea Co. in the Darjeeling District. He was a member of the Sibsagar Mounted Rifles, afterward the Assam Valley Light Horse and the Northern Bengal Mounted Rifles. In 1928, he retired to Dersingham Vicarage, Kings Lynn, Norfolk after 50 years of planting in India.

MR. HENRY RAIKES ALEXANDER IRWIN, C. I. E., who retired in 1920 after forty-five years of tea planting in India, started his own tea estate in the Darjeeling Terai when he was seventeen. Fifty-five years later, in 1930, he paid a visit to India, still hale and hearty at seventy-one. When Mr. Irwin came out to India, in 1875, he could go only as far as Sahebgunge by rail. The remaining 200 miles to Darjeeling had to be covered by bullock cart and tonga. He was in Darjeeling from 1890 until he retired. When the author first visited India, in 1906, he learned a lot about tea from Mr. Irwin, who was then on Moondakotee and Dhajea. Mr. Irwin served four years as chairman of the Darjeeling branch of the I.T.A.; ten years as president of the Darjeeling Planters' Association; and four years as representative of the Dooars and Darjeeling tea districts on the Bengal Legislative Council. While in India, he took four cricket teams from Darjeeling to Calcutta, and in the cold weather of 1884–85 he brought a planters' polo team to the capital. He also helped form the Terai Sports Club at Siliguri. He is now living in retirement in England.

MR. A. H. R. GOWDELL, pioneer planter in the Dooars, who first introduced humidifiers on the Sam Sing garden of the Chulsa Tea Co., Ltd., retired in 1926, and is now the proprietor of the Moor Park Hotel, Chagford, Devon.

Col. Alexander J. MacLaughlin, M.B., C.I.E., V.D., India tea pioneer planter of *bheel* lands, who started in medical practice in Cachar, Sylhet, and the Dooars in 1876, going into tea in 1885, was born in Drum-rhu, Waterford County, Ireland, in 1854. After his retirement to England, he served as a director in ten India tea planting companies and was a member of the Indian Tea Association (London) for thirty years. He died at Woking in 1932.

Mr. A. W. C. Chaplin, who started his planting career in 1888, did much for the industry as chairman of the Dooars Planters' Association and as a Member of the Bengal Legislative Council. He served the Chulsa Tea Company as assistant manager, superintendent and, finally, as chairman of the company until his death at Lynwood, Ascot, in 1934. He also was a member of the boards of several other well-known tea companies.

Calcutta Agency Pioneers

Toward the close of the nineteenth century many new gardens were opened. They were more or less family concerns. The later development has been in the direction of limited liability companies, and the tea industry is to-day a highly organized one.

The length of the journey from England to India made tea agency houses a necessity in the early days, and even to-day, with improved methods of communication and the shortened journey, the agency system is still in force, for it combines the benefits of a steady policy in garden management and coöperation among sellers in shipping and marketing their crops. Most agency houses have holdings in the concerns they manage. Here we may digress to note a few of the firms that were prominently identified with pioneer tea growing in India.

The oldest of the tea agency firms in Calcutta is the firm of Gillanders, Arbuthnot & Co., which was founded in 1819 by Mr. F. M. Gillanders, who was sent to India for this purpose by Sir John Gladstone, father of the famous prime minister. The firm's first connection with tea, however, dates from 1866, when they became agents for the Golaghat Tea Estate [F. M. Paul] and the Teelwaree Tea Co. It was in 1865 that the name of Mr. Thomas Kingsley appeared as a tea planter. From then until his death, in 1899, he was an intimate and loyal friend of the house of Gillanders. In 1873, he started the Singlo Tea Garden with Messrs. J. A. Gibbons and W. Freeman. This subsequently became the Singlo Tea Co., absorbing the Jaboka Tea Co., and the Kisna Tea Co.

The agency firm of Jardine, Skinner & Co., was established in 1843. Some of their present-day gardens are among the oldest in existence, viz., Burnie Braes, Serispore Division of the Central Cachar Tea Co., and Makaibari of the Kurseong & Darjeeling Tea Co., Ltd. These gardens were formerly administered by the late Mr. C. A. Stewart.

Although the business of Williamson, Magor & Co., 4 Mangoe Lane, Calcutta, was not established until the 'sixties, Mr. George Williamson, one of its founders, with his brother, Mr. J. H. Williamson, was identified with the tea industry as early as 1853. His important pioneer contribution has already been told in the story of the rise of the Assam Co. The firm's interests are chiefly in the Assam Valley.

The firm of Begg, Dunlop & Co., was founded in Calcutta by Dr. David Begg, May 1, 1856. They first became interested in tea in 1859, when the Jorehaut Tea Co. was floated. Mr. A. B. Inglis, one of the early partners, was a pioneer of tea in the Dooars and did valuable work in developing the tea industry of Northern India.

Founded on January 1, 1859, under the style of Playfair, Duncan & Co., the present firm of Duncan Bros. & Co., Ltd., Calcutta, was later re-constituted as Duncan Brothers & Co., and converted into a limited liability company on January 1, 1924. From its early days this house has had important interests in the tea industry, at first mainly in Cachar. It took a prominent part in the development of the industry in the Dooars during the 'eighties and 'nineties.

The firm of Balmer, Lawrie & Co., Ltd., was established in 1867, being at that time interested in various small gardens. In

CLIVE STREET, CALCUTTA, WHICH CONTAINS MANY OFFICES OF PIONEER TEA FIRMS

1872, the partners of the firm and their friends formed the first of several companies for working estates in Assam.

Coincident with the expansion of producing areas, Balmer, Lawrie & Co., built up an organization for distributing tea to various parts of the world. This branch of the business, with its expert tasters, is entirely separate from the management of the estates. To-day, Balmer, Lawrie & Co., Ltd., have under their charge the cultivation of 28,000 acres of tea, the production of 20,000,000 lbs., and the distribution of 10,000,000 lbs.

The firm of Octavius Steel & Co., Ltd., was originally established at Calcutta in 1870, under the name of Steel, McIntosh & Co.

The Calcutta branch of James Finlay & Co. was established as Finlay, Muir & Co. in 1870.

A Calcutta agency house, which has been closely connected with the India tea industry for over fifty years, is the firm of Macneill & Co., established in 1872. At the present time this firm represents as

agents forty-four tea gardens situated in Assam, Cachar, Sylhet, and the Dooars, with an area of 112,223 acres, of which 30,422 acres are under tea cultivation; they have an annual outturn of approximately 16,000,000 lbs. of manufactured tea.

The founder of Barry & Co., another historically important Calcutta agency house, was Dr. John Boyle Barry, an adventurous Irishman, who, after studying medicine in the United Kingdom, decided to seek his fortune further afield. In the 'forties of last century, he enlisted as a private in a regiment bound for India. On the same transport was a certain Dr. R. Scott Thompson. In the course of the voyage, Dr. Thompson had numerous opportunities for studying Private Barry, and, discovering that his medical attainments were worthy of a better cause, bought him out from military service, and engaged him as medical attendant for R. Scott Thompson & Co. In the course of time, Dr. Barry acquired a controlling interest in this business, and in the 'sixties, when the directors of the East India Company were at a loss to find medical men, Dr. Barry was engaged as civil surgeon for Tezpur. At this period, the tea industry was passing through a severe crisis, and properties were being sold for whatever they would bring. Dr. Barry, in company with a certain Dr. Ferris, Mr. James Young, and others, purchased gardens for very little, paving the way for the establishment of an agency business in Calcutta.

The firm of Barry & Co., was actually founded in 1876 at No. 5, Lyons Range, Calcutta, although it is believed that Mr. Tom Barry, a brother of Dr. Barry, had an office at No. 5, Lyons Range, dating back to 1839, and it is certain that Dr. Barry carried on his activities in Calcutta long before the actual firm of Barry & Co. was founded. In 1876, Dr. Barry's partner was Mr. A. P. Sandeman, a Lloyds surveyor from Liverpool, who was first a Hooghly River pilot and then a tea planter. Mr. J. H. Barry, son of the founder, was a mechanical engineer and collaborated with a Mr. Gibbs of London in the invention of the Gibbs and Barry drier, one of the earliest machines to be used in the manufacture of tea. The experimental work on this drier was done in the compound of Martin & Co., in Mission Row.

Another pioneer Calcutta tea estate agency is the firm of McLeod & Co., founded in 1887. They are interested in sixteen tea companies, comprising forty tea estates, and representing an area under tea of 34,313 acres.

The firm of Shaw, Wallace & Co. is still another firm that has left its mark on the Indian tea industry, dating from the 'eighties. Two members of the firm are ex-Indian tea planters, Mr. H. S. Ashton and Mr. Gerald Kingsley, who was eleven years in Assam. Shaw, Wallace & Co. control 26,540 acres in Assam, the Dooars, and Sylhet.

India Tea Associations

As early as 1876, an attempt was made to organize the Northern India tea estate owners into an association, but it was not until 1879 that the agitation bore fruit. In that year the Indian Tea Districts Association was formed in London. To-day the Indian Tea Association represents a merger of the London and Calcutta groups.

The Indian Tea Association, Calcutta, was formed at a meeting held at the Bengal Chamber of Commerce, May 18, 1881. The following were present: Messrs. P. Playfair, W. L. Thomas, J. H. Edwards, A. Wilson, J. H. Barry, D. F. Mackenzie, C. J. Sharpe, H. J. C. Turner, R. B. McPhun, D. Cruickshank, Leslie Worke, R. B. Magor, W. Walker, T. Carritt, and A. B. Inglis.

Mr. A. B. Inglis, who had been asked to take the chair, told of the attempt made five years before to bring about a combination of the kind proposed. In the tea districts this necessity had prompted the formation of several local combinations. Furthermore the formation of the Indian Tea Districts Association in London, 1879, had made it all the more necessary that there should be a corresponding body in India. The want of united action among tea proprietors had been a great drawback up to that time, and with this remedied, the representations of such a body as the Indian Tea Association would have far more weight with the government.

Mr. A. B. Inglis   Mr. D. Cruickshank   Mr. W. L. Thomas   Sir Patrick Playfair

SOME OF THE FOUNDERS OF THE INDIAN TEA ASSOCIATION, CALCUTTA

THE ROYAL EXCHANGE, CALCUTTA, HEADQUARTERS OF THE INDIAN TEA ASSOCIATION

The feeling of the meeting was strongly in favor of the proposal for the formation of an association, and the following resolutions were adopted:

That those present at this meeting form themselves into an association, to be called, provisionally, the Indian Tea Association.

That the Rules for the incorporation of the association as submitted to the meeting, be generally approved of, and that representatives from each of the following firms be appointed as a provisional committee for the purpose of revising the rules and drawing up a scheme for the working of the association, and to report to another meeting to be held within a fortnight.

Names of firms: Messrs. Jardine, Skinner & Co., Williamson, Magor & Co., Macneill & Co., Schoene, Kilburn & Co., Begg, Dunlop & Co., Octavius Steel & Co., Barry & Co., Shaw, Finlayson & Co., Finlay, Muir & Co., Gillanders, Arbuthnot & Co., and Grindlay & Co.

The association started with a membership of companies and estate owners representing a planted area of some 103,000 acres, which had increased to 530,000 acres by the end of 1928. This area represents approximately 84 per cent of the area under tea in Northeast India. The headquarters

of the association is in the Royal Exchange Buildings, 2, Clive Street, Calcutta, but there is a branch of the association in each district, which deals with local problems. The Assam branch has its headquarters at Dibrugarh, and the Surma Valley branch is at Binnakandi, in Cachar.

The objects and duty of the association is to promote the common interests of all persons concerned in the cultivation of tea in India. Proprietors and managers of, and agents for, tea estates are eligible for election as members by the General Committee. The business and funds of the Association are controlled by a General Committee consisting of nine firms who are elected annually and who nominate gentlemen to represent them. The committee elect their own chairman and vice-chairmen. The secretary and assistant secretary of the Bengal Chamber of Commerce are ex-officio secretary and assistant secretary of the association. The 1934–35 officers are: Chairman, K. B. Miller; Vice Chairman, H. F. Bateman; Secretary, D. K. Cunnison; Assistant Secretary, A. C. Daniel; Chief Scientific Officer, P. H. Carpenter, F.I.C., F.C.S., Tocklai. The annual meeting is held in March.

Labor Supply Association

The tea industry in Northeast India also has an association for managing its labor affairs and for recruiting labor. As early as 1859, it was realized that the importation of foreign labor was essential, and a tea planters' association was formed, one purpose of which was the organization of a system of coolie emigration from Lower Bengal. The sudden expansion of the industry had created a class of contractors who supplied labor to the tea gardens, relieving the planters of all responsibilities excepting paying for the coolie. The results were so disastrous, because labor was rushed up without proper precautions, often causing serious mortality on account of competition between contractors, that in 1861 the Government appointed a committee to inquire into the system under which the emigration of labor was conducted.

As a result of this and other inquiries, various emigration acts were passed, and finally, in 1915, recruiting by contractors was abolished. Following this the only legal recruiting was that done by garden sirdars working under a licensed local agent. A garden sirdar may be described as an individual employed on an estate as a native head man, who is granted a certificate authorizing him to recruit labor for his employer in his home district, preferably in and around his own village. It was the duty of the local agent to look after the interests of the garden sirdar. The certificate was countersigned by a magistrate in the native district who investigated the bona fides of the sirdar.

In 1892, a meeting was called by the Bengal Chamber of Commerce to discuss the formation of an association to deal with the question of labor supply to gardens. The outcome was the formation of the Tea Districts Labor Supply Association, which took over the smaller associations already in existence, with the exception of the Assam Labor Association. The first recognition of these two major associations was the granting of certain concessions by the Government in connection with their operations. For instance, the power of local agents to act without the necessity of taking recruits before a magistrate, was given.

In 1915, the Assam Labor Board was created to supervise the work of the local agents on behalf of the Government. The board was given the power to make recommendations regarding the licensing of local agents. Meanwhile, the Assam Labor Association became amalgamated with the Tea Districts Labor Supply Association, and, in 1919, its denomination was altered to the Tea Districts Labor Association.

Sirdar recruiting is ideal when labor is inclined to move freely, but the average recruiting success in normal periods has been one recruit per sirdar only, making the average cost for an Assam garden to import one laborer about Rs. 150/—.

In the year 1918, India was visited by severe famine owing to the early failure of the monsoon. This synchronized with the wide-spread influenza epidemic, when more deaths occurred in India from this cause than occurred in Europe during the four years of the World War.

In 1932, a new Act was passed, removing the restriction on recruiting methods and the personnel employed, but controlling the forwarding of emigrants and paying greater attention to their welfare on tea estates. It gave every emigrant at the end of his first three years in Assam the right of repatriation at the expense of his employer. A "Controller of Emigrant Labor" was stationed in Assam. The Act applies only to Assam, and not to Dooars and Terai estates, which recruit by sirdar methods, mainly through the Association.

The Tea Districts Labor Association is managed by a committee composed of members representing London and Calcutta interests, and of planters from various tea districts. It is estimated that the Association controls recruiting for ninety-five per cent of the estates in Northern India.

The Tea Cess

This brief historical sketch of the Indian Tea Association would be incomplete without a reference to the Tea Cess Act. The Indian Tea Cess was created by Act IX, 1903, Government of India, effective April 1st of that year. It assessed an initial duty of $\frac{1}{4}$ pie [1 pie = $\frac{1}{12}d$. Eng. or $\frac{1}{8}\cancel{c}$ U. S.] on every pound of tea exported and ran for five years. The cess was renewed in 1908, 1913, 1918, 1923, 1928, and 1933. The present cess expires March 31, 1938.

From 1903 to 1921 the cess was collected at the rate of ¼ pie per pound. Act No. 21 of 1921 amended the 1903 Act so that the Government is empowered to increase the levy up to a maximum of eight annas per hundred pounds of tea exported, at the request of the tea industry. The levy was six annas until 1933 when it was increased to eight annas. The cess is collected by the customs authorities and paid into the cess fund.

The Tea Cess Committee is a body of twenty members appointed by the Government of India, under the provisions of the Indian Tea Cess Act of 1903, to take such measures as may be deemed necessary to promote the sale and increase the consumption of tea in India and other countries. Its members are selected as follows:

3 on the recommendation of the Bengal Chamber of Commerce.
1 on the recommendation of the Madras Chamber of Commerce.
7 on the recommendation of the Indian Tea Association, Calcutta.
2 on the recommendation of the Assam Branch, Indian Tea Association.
2 on the recommendation of the Surma Valley Branch, Indian Tea Association.
1 on the recommendation of the Darjeeling Planters' Association & Terai Planters' Association, jointly.
2 on the recommendation of the Dooars Planters' Association.
1 on the recommendation of the Indian Tea Planters' Association, Jalpaiguri.
1 on the recommendation of the United Planters' Association of Southern India.

The fund created by the cess is devoted exclusively to the expansion of home and foreign markets for India tea. This is done by sending special commissioners to various countries, by magazine and newspaper advertising, and by exhibits at expositions, fairs, and bazaars.

The annual meeting of the Cess Committee is held in March, and the semi-annual in July. The committee meets frequently to decide questions which may have no direct bearing on advertising.

The Scientific Department

The Indian Tea Association has a well-staffed, well-equipped scientific department for investigating the various problems connected with tea culture and manufacture. The department was first started in a small way in 1900, following a resolution passed at the Annual General Meeting of the Association in 1899. Immediately after that meeting, the opinions of the branches of the association were sought regarding the appointment of a scientist. The preponderance of opinion favored the appointment of an agricultural chemist, and Mr. Harold H. Mann, B.Sc., [now D.Sc.], F.I.C., F.L.S., was selected in London, and engaged on a three years' agreement. The initial estimated expenditure of this appointment was reckoned at Rs. 1500 monthly, which had to be met from the surplus funds of the association, augmented by grants from the government of Bengal and the administration of Assam, and from additional contributions from the different branches of the association. The initial sanction for laboratory equipment was £200. The laboratory work was inaugurated in conjunction with the laboratory accommodation in the Economic Court of the Indian Museum, Calcutta, where laboratory investigations were continued up to the year 1932. Later on, a small station was opened at Heeleakah in Assam, which in 1911 was moved to Tocklai, near Jorhat.

From these small beginnings the Scientific Department has developed into an institution employing a qualified staff of Europeans recruited from England, consisting of a chief scientific officer, two chemists, an entomologist, a mycologist, and a bacteriologist, together with Indian qualified assistants and others. The present staff includes: Chief Scientific Officer, P. H. Carpenter, F.I.C., F.C.S.; Mycologist, A. C. Tunstall, B.Sc.; Chemists, H. R. Cooper, B.Sc., F.C.S., and C. J. Harrison, B.Sc., A.I.C.; Bacteriologist, S. F. Benton, B.Sc.; Botanist, W. Wight, Ph.D., B.Sc.; Assistant Chemists, P. B. Sen Gupta, B.A., and S. N. Sarma, B.Sc.; Insectery Assistant, M. Sinha; Assistant Bacteriologist, J. N. Borthakur; Assistant Botanist, P. K. Barua, B.Sc.

In 1930, the expenditure of the department was Rs. 327,538, which was supplied by the funds collected in subscriptions at the rate of six annas per acre from all tea companies in the membership of the association. This was apart from small contributions from the Governments of Assam and Bengal and the United Planters' Association of Southern India.

DR. HAROLD HART MANN, who was the first chief scientific officer of the Indian Tea Association was born October 16, 1872.

Dr. H. H. Mann
Chief Scientific Officer
1900–07

Dr. G. D. Hope
Chief Scientific Officer
1908–11

Mr. P. H. Carpenter
Chief Scientific Officer
since 1919

Mr. C. R. Harler
Chemist and Meteorologist
1919–1932

NOTED MEMBERS OF THE I.T.A. SCIENTIFIC STAFF

He attended the Elmfield School at York; after that, the Yorkshire College, Leeds, and Pasteur Institute, Paris. He was Chemical Assistant for Research to the Royal Agricultural Society, 1895–98; Resident Chemist, Woburn Experimental Farm of the Royal Agricultural Society, 1898–1900; Scientific Officer to Indian Tea Association, Calcutta, 1900–07; Principal, Agricultural College, Poona, and Agricultural Chemist to the Government of Bombay, 1907–18; Director of Agriculture, Bombay Presidency, 1918–20 and 1921–28; Member Bombay Legislative Council, 1925; Kaiser-i-Hind Medal of the First Class, 1917. His publications are many, especially on matters relating to tea culture and manufacture, and other Indian social and economic questions. With Sir George Watt he wrote *The Pests and Blights of the Tea Plant.* He retired from the government service in 1927, but subsequently returned to India in the capacity of agricultural adviser to H.E.H., the Nizam's Government. In 1929, he returned to the Woburn Experimental Station of the Lawes Agricultural Trust at Aspley Guise, Bletchley.

MR. CLAUDE MACKENZIE HUTCHINSON, C.I.E., 1920, succeeded Dr. Mann as chief scientific officer in 1907. He was born April 29, 1869, educated at Trinity College, Glenalmond and St. John's College, Cambridge. He has written numerous memoirs and papers on bacteriology of the soil, plant pathology, green manuring, fertilizers, etc. In 1904, he went with the Indian Tea Association, leaving in 1908 to accept appointment as Imperial Agricultural Bacteriologist to the Government of India.

DR. G. D. HOPE succeeded Mr. Hutchinson as chief scientific officer in 1908, and during his term in office, marked progress was made. Dr. Hope visited Java, Sumatra, and Persia, and wrote two monographs entitled *The Tea Industry of Java and Sumatra* and *The Cultivation of Tea in the Caspian Provinces of Persia.* He was born at Thurstaston, near Chester, England, November 23, 1880. After attending a preparatory school in Rock Ferry, he took his degree of Bachelor of Science at Liverpool University, completing his education in Halle, Germany, where he received the degree of Bachelor of Philosophy. He became assistant scientific officer in 1907, and chief scientific officer in 1908, retiring in 1911. He lives at Riverside, West Kirby, Cheshire.

MR. P. H. CARPENTER, F.I.C., F.C.S., the present chief scientific officer, who succeeded Dr. Hope, was born in London, February 19, 1879, and educated at an English public school. He took his scientific training at the City and Guilds College, London. After that, he went as assistant to Mr. A. C. Chapman, F.I.C., F.R.S., F.C.S., for seven years. Then he went to India to do sugar work for Begg, Sutherland & Co., at Cawnpore. In 1909, he joined the Indian Tea Association as assistant scientific officer under Dr. G. D. Hope.

In 1915, Mr. Carpenter joined the Indian cavalry and went to Mesopotamia, returning to the Experimental Station at Tocklai in 1919, when he assumed charge; Dr. Hope having been invalided home. Since 1919, he has continued to occupy the position of chief scientific officer to the Indian Tea Association. Mr. Carpenter is

Mr. J. F. MacNair
Chairman, 1887-89

Mr. H. C. Begg
Chairman, 1900 and 1903

Mr. R. L. Williamson
Chairman, 1908

Sir A. Pickford
Chairman, 1915 and 1918

PROMINENT FIGURES IN THE INDIAN TEA ASSOCIATION, CALCUTTA, 1887-1918

a Fellow of the Institute of Chemistry and of the Chemical Society of London.

Prominent Association Figures

The first chairman of the Indian Tea Association, Calcutta, was Mr. A. B. Inglis of Begg, Dunlop & Co., who presided at the organization meeting. In 1882, he was succeeded by Mr. J. J. Keswick, of Jardine, Skinner & Co. Mr. D. Cruickshank, of Begg, Dunlop & Co., was the first secretary.

Mr. A. Wilson of Jardine, Skinner & Co., was chairman from 1882 to 1886. During this period and also for the year following, when Mr. D. Cruickshank was chairman, Mr. G. M. Barton was secretary. Mr. J. F. MacNair of Begg, Dunlop & Co., was chairman from 1887 to 1889. In 1887, Mr. S. E. J. Clarke became secretary, holding the post for 10 years.

From 1889 to 1895, with the exception of one year, Mr. J. N. Stuart of Balmer, Lawrie & Co., was chairman, and during his incumbency much of the pioneer work of developing trading in India teas with America was done. Mr. A. G. Watson of Williamson, Magor & Co., a tea planter, was chairman, 1892-93.

Mr. H. S. Ashton of Shaw, Wallace & Co., was chairman, 1895-96, and again from 1901 to 1902. He was also chairman of the Cess Committee. From 1896 to 1898, Mr. G. A. Ormiston, of Balmer, Lawrie & Co., was chairman. In 1898, Mr. W. Parsons became secretary, continuing to hold office until 1907.

Mr. G. G. Anderson, of Williamson, Magor & Co., and previously a Ceylon tea planter, became chairman in 1898, with Mr. H. S. Ashton as vice-chairman. Mr. H. C. Begg, of Begg, Dunlop & Co., was chairman, 1900-01. As noted above, Mr. Ashton became chairman for the second time in 1901. In 1902, Mr. Lockhart Smith, of Williamson, Magor & Co., a recognized authority on tea in Bengal, was chosen chairman, and, except for the 1903-04 period, he continued to occupy the office until 1907. He died in 1909. Mr. Smith was also chairman of the Calcutta Tea Traders' Association for many years.

Mr. Begg was again chairman, 1903-04, when Mr. T. McMorran was vice-chairman. From 1904 to 1906, Mr. D. A. Campbell was vice-chairman.

Mr. Gerald Kingsley became chairman in 1907. He served for one year, being returned to office again in 1912. Mr. Kingsley was a partner in Shaw, Wallace & Co., with an enviable record as a tea planter behind him. He was born in 1867, at Bowden, Cheshire. At sixteen he went to sea, and at twenty, he became interested in tea in Assam, where he achieved success both as planter and sportsman. During his first term as chairman, Mr. G. Pickford served as vice-chairman, and Mr. H. M. Haywood became secretary, a post which he held until 1926.

Mr. R. Lyell Williamson, of Messrs. Williamson, Magor & Co., was chairman, 1908-09. He was born in Calcutta, trained in the tea business with the London tea brokerage firm of W. J. & H. Thompson, became assistant to the Attareekhat Tea Co., Assam, in 1894. He was invalided home for a period after being mauled by a bear in 1896, but returned in 1898 as as-

Mr. A. D. Gordon
Nine times chairman

Hon. Samuel J. Best
Chairman, 1925

Mr. T. C. Crawford
Eight times chairman

Mr. K. B. Miller
Chairman, 1934–35

A GROUP OF LATTER-DAY CHAIRMEN OF I.T.A. CALCUTTA

sistant in Williamson, Magor & Co., working his way up to a partnership in 1904. He died in 1927. Mr. C. D. Inglis was vice-chairman during the time Mr. Williamson acted as chairman.

Mr. T. McMorran of Duncan Bros. & Co., became chairman in 1909, and served for two years. Mr. G. Pickford served as vice-chairman, 1909–10, and Mr. W. Warrington, 1910–11. The latter was a partner in James Finlay & Co., and became chairman in 1911, with Mr. H. C. Begg as vice-chairman. As already noted, Mr. Kingsley succeeded to the chairmanship a second time in 1912, with Mr. A. D. Gordon, vice-chairman. Mr. Gordon was a partner in Williamson, Magor & Co. He was chosen chairman in 1913 and was returned to the office four times thereafter.

Mr. [later Sir] R. Graham, of James Finlay & Co., was chairman, 1914–15, and Mr. [later Sir] A. D. Pickford, of Begg, Dunlop & Co., 1915–16, when Mr. Gordon resumed office for two years. Mr. R. Graham was vice-chairman with Mr. Gordon and with Mr. A. D. Pickford, who became chairman again in 1918–19. Mr. [later Sir] H. W. Carr, of Balmer, Lawrie & Co., was chairman, 1919–20, with Mr. W. A. Duncan acting as vice-chairman. Mr. Gordon was chairman again in 1920, with Hon. Samuel J. Best vice-chairman.

In 1921, Mr. T. C. Crawford, of James Finlay & Co., was elected chairman and served for three years, with Mr. J. A. C. Munro, Hon. Samuel J. Best, and Mr. A. D. Gordon as vice-chairmen, after which Mr. A. D. Gordon became chairman for the fifth time. This was 1924–25 when Mr. F. G. Clarke was vice-chairman.

The Hon. Samuel J. Best of Octavius

Steel & Co., Ltd., became chairman in 1925, with Mr. T. C. Crawford, vice-chairman. The following year, Mr. Crawford was returned to the chairmanship, and again in 1927 and 1930; the latter date marking the sixth time he held the office. Mr. A. D. Gordon became chairman for the sixth time in 1928. He was followed in 1929 by Mr. James Insch, of Messrs. Duncan Bros. & Co., Ltd. In 1926, 1927, and 1928 Mr. J. A. MacBean, of Shaw, Wallace & Co., was vice-chairman, and Mr. T. C. Crawford, in 1929. In 1927, Mr. D. K. Cunnison became secretary.

Mr. A. S. Macalister, of Macneill & Co., was elected chairman in 1931, and was succeeded in 1932 by Mr. T. C. Crawford.

Mr. Keith B. Miller, chairman of the I.T.A., Calcutta, 1934–35, was born at Calcutta, October 30, 1888. He is a partner of Williamson, Magor & Co.

Southern India Planters' Association

The United Planters' Association of Southern India was founded as a result of a conference between different planters' associations held at Bangalore in 1893 and the first general meeting was held at the same place in 1894. The chief object of this organization is to promote and protect, in all parts of the world, the interests of the various planting industries in Southern India.

Planters affiliated with the Association elect a member of the legislative council at Madras, and the association activities include a labor department with five divisional offices under European superintendents, and Indian agencies throughout Southern India. The Scientific Department at present employs three experts and maintains experimental stations for tea, rubber, and coffee respectively at Devarshola, Mundakayam, and Sidapur. The Benevolent Fund assists and relieves distress among members of the planting community. By coöperation the Buying Agency obtains special terms in return for prompt payment. In 1906, the Association started a paper at Madras called *The Planters' Chronicle*, now issued fortnightly.

The affairs of the Association are managed by a general committee, consisting of two representatives of each district planters' association, and an executive committee made up of the chairman, the planting member, a labor member, and three representatives of district associations; one each to represent the interests of tea, rubber, and coffee respectively. Four other members-in-waiting are elected at the same time to replace any casual vacancy that may occur.

The association is represented in London by the South Indian Association in London and is affiliated with the Madras Chamber of Commerce and the Employers' Federation of Southern India, Madras. It cooperates with the Indian Tea Association, Calcutta, and the Travancore Combined Planters' Association of Quilon, and is also a member of the Indian Tea Cess Committee, Calcutta. The 1933–34 officers were: Chairman, Mr. Rohan Fowke; executive committee: for tea, Mr. J. S. B. Wallace; for coffee, Mr. J. S. H. Morgan; for rubber, Mr. Eric Hall. The Secretary is Lt. Col. C. H. Brock. The tea specialist of the Scientific Department is Dr. W. S. Shaw, Ph.D., M.Sc., A.I.C., who was trained for the work at Tocklai. The

association offices are at Glenview, Coonoor P. O., Nilgiris. The annual meeting is in August.

South India Scientific Department

The establishment of a Scientific Department of the United Planters' Association of Southern India, first was proposed in 1904. Five years later, in 1909, the Government of Madras appointed Mr. R. D. Anstead as Scientific Adviser to the Association, with headquarters and laboratory, at Bangalore. Mr. Anstead devoted his entire time and services to the problems connected with tea, rubber, and coffee; part of the cost being borne by the U.P.A.S.I., and part by the Government. In 1912, two European assistants were added to the staff and paid by the Association to work in Mysore and Coorg, but resigned their posts at the outbreak of the World War, in 1914.

In the re-alignment that ensued, it was arranged that Mr. Anstead should join the Madras Agricultural Department as the Deputy Director of Agriculture, and the intention was to extend the work of the Scientific Department, but the War prevented. In 1919, efforts were made to set in motion the schemes that had been proposed, and four small experimental stations were started. One of them was located at Peermade, in Central Travancore, for work on tea. This station was supervised by an Indian official, under the direction of Mr. Anstead. In 1923, Mr. Anstead became the Director of Agriculture at Madras, and was succeeded by Mr. D. G. Munro, with headquarters at the Agriculture College, Coimbatore. After

Mr. C. E. Abbott
Chairman, 1907–8;
1911–13

Mr. C. R. T. Congreve
Chairman, 1920–21;
1930–32

Mr. H. L. Pinches
Chairman, 1921–24

Mr. Walter A. J. Milner
Chairman, 1929–30

TEA PIONEERS WHO BECAME OFFICERS OF THE U.P.A.S.I.

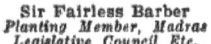

Sir Fairless Barber
*Planting Member, Madras
Legislative Council Etc.*

Mr. R. R. H. Fowke
*Chairman, U.P.A.S.I.
1925–27; 1933–34*

PIONEER TEA PLANTERS OF SOUTHERN INDIA

a period of ten years, from 1914 to 1924, the U.P.A.S.I. again took over the control of the Scientific Department; at the same time, the Government of Madras agreed to make a fixed contribution of Rs. 28,000 per annum for five years, and in 1929 renewed the contribution for another five years.

The scheme of having a single European officer responsible for work on the three products, was ultimately found inadequate, and, as early as 1921, it was suggested that each be given individual attention. In that year, a mycologist was engaged for work on rubber and, in 1924, arrangements were made for a scientific officer for work in tea. Negotiations were begun for a suitable site for a tea experimental station; the Peermade Station being considered unsuitable. In 1925, Dr. W. S. Shaw, Ph.D., M.Sc., A.I.C., was appointed Tea Scientific Officer of the present Experimental Station, consisting of twenty-seven acres of land near the Village of Devarshola, Nilgiris. In 1926, the Peermade Station was discontinued, Mr. Munro reverted to the Government Agricultural Department, and the present Scientific Department became a separate unit.

Jalpaiguri Association

The Indian Tea Planters' Association, Jalpaiguri, was organized in 1918 "to keep up a spirit of fellow feeling and of united action among the Indian planting community of Bengal, Assam, and elsewhere in British India and the native states; to take up all matters of common interest, to keep in touch with the Government and to protect the interests of the planting com-

munity in general." All tea companies under Indian management or ownership are eligible. Mr. Tarini Prosad Roy, B.L., the first chairman still holds the office.

Tea Restriction

As a result of overproduction and demoralized markets, the Indian Tea Association recommended that its members restrict the 1920 crop to not more than 90 per cent of the average crops of the years 1915 to 1919 or, as an alternative, that they cease plucking November 15, 1920. This recommendation was generally observed. A recommendation by the association for an 80 per cent reduction in the following year, based on the same five-year period from 1915 to 1919, failed of sufficient support to make an agreement possible, although a majority of the large producers followed the policy recommended.

In 1929, an overproduction of teas resulted in an agreement between British Indian, Ceylon, and Dutch Indian tea growers for a restriction of plucking the 1930 crop. Based on prices and grades during the years 1926 to 1928, India's share of the restriction was 15 per cent on teas that sold at 1s 5d per pound, 10 per cent on teas that sold at 1s 5d to 1s 7d, and 5 per cent on teas that sold at 1s 7d to 1s 9d and 3 per cent on teas that sold above 1s 9d. India and Ceylon exceeded their allotted reductions, but there was no decrease in the Netherlands Indies, so in 1931, restriction was abandoned. However, there was substituted for it in 1933 a five-year plan for regulation of tea exports from the Netherlands Indies, Ceylon, and India by which exports were reduced 15 per cent in 1933, with suitable reductions in following years.

Cooperative Tea Propaganda

A belief among tea men that restriction of output offered only a temporary remedy for overproduction and that the end of the five-year plan, in 1938, might bring them again face to face with mounting stocks and demoralized prices in the principal markets prompted British Indian planters to join with those of Ceylon and the Netherlands Indies in a joint publicity drive, which began in 1934, to increase the use of tea in countries having a low per-capita consumption.

CHAPTER X

TEA'S TRIUMPH IN CEYLON

The Dramatic Replacement of Coffee by Tea—Early Attempts at Tea Cultivation—Coffee in the Old Days—The Transition to Tea—The Worms Brothers, Tea Pioneers—Loolecondera, the Oldest Garden—The Rush into Tea—History of the Planters' Association of Ceylon and Sketches of the Men Who Made it—Tea Research Institute—The Labor Problem—Other Men of Achievement—The Ceylon Estates Proprietary Association—Some Pioneer Tea Companies

TEA'S triumph over coffee on the plantations of Ceylon is one of the most dramatic stories in the history of the industry. Coffee had been successfully cultivated on the island for nearly fifty years when the dreaded blight, *Hemileia vastatrix*, made its appearance, and within a few years destroyed an industry that had represented at its peak a capital value of £16,500,000 [$80,000,000], and had exported as much as 110,000,000 lbs. in a single year.

Tea cultivation had been tried in an experimental way only, up to that time, and when the great blight came its acreage was practically negligible—between 200 and 300—compared to coffee, which covered 275,000 acres. To-day, there are upwards of 467,000 acres devoted to tea, and the coffee acreage has dwindled to almost nothing. Tea production reached the record of 251,500,000 lbs. in 1929. The area now under tea exceeds the vanished area under coffee by some 192,000 acres.

When the British finally settled down to develop to the *n*th degree the vast resources of the "brave island, so fruitful and fair," that they had inherited from the Dutch, one of the first things they did was to carve for themselves an astounding coffee enterprise out of the virgin forests of the Kandyan country.

Coffee had been known in Ceylon at that time, 1796, for nearly a hundred years, and the natives were so predisposed in its favor that they looked upon its scientific cultivation under the English with a degree of friendliness which they never showed to tea when it succeeded to the abandoned coffee estates. Small coffee gardens were common among the peasantry. Something like five millions sterling were invested in Ceylon's coffee estates between 1830 and 1845, the period of the "coffee mania." Though the Sinhalese villagers were not disposed to help with the cultivation beyond the initial jungle clearing stage, they did not oppose the importation of Tamil labor from Southern India, which was more willing to work. To this labor element is due much of tea's subsequent success.

Early Attempts at Tea Cultivation

Wolf, writing in 1782, reports "Tea, and some other sorts of elegant aromatics are not to be found here [Ceylon]. Some trials have been made to rear them, but without success."[1] He was referring to repeated attempts by the Dutch to grow China tea in the island. Tennent also refers to these unsuccessful attempts by the Dutch.[2]

The London Observer of July 25, 1802, noted: "A late attempt has been made by a naturalist of eminence to cultivate the tea plant in the island of Ceylon, but, notwithstanding, almost all the trees, plants, and flowers of this part of the globe seem collected there the experiment has totally failed."

Cordiner, in 1805, says the tea plant was growing wild near Trincomalee and

[1] Johann Christian Wolf, *Life and Adventures*, London, 1807.
[2] Sir James Emerson Tennent, *Ceylon, an Account of the Island, Physical, Historical, and Topographical*, London, 1860, (2 vols.).

A CEYLON COFFEE ESTATE OF THE 'SEVENTIES SUBSEQUENTLY TURNED INTO TEA
This is a view of Bogahawatte, Dimbula, 4300 feet elevation, as it appeared about the transition period.

that the soldiers dried the leaves, boiled them and preferred the decoction to coffee.[3] This was not wild tea but a species of cassia, which Captain Percival also confused with genuine tea.[4] Bertolacci contradicts a report current in his day, 1813, that the tea plant grew wild in the forests of Ceylon,[5] and yet Bennett, thirty years later, in his *Ceylon and Its Capabilities* gravely publishes a colored plate of a species of indigenous tea plant. This he did on the authority of Assistant Staff

[3] James Cordiner, *A Description of Ceylon*, London, 1807.
[4] Captain Robert Percival, *An Account of the Island of Ceylon*, London, 1803.
[5] Anthony Bertolacci, *A View of the Agricultural, Commercial, and Financial Interests of Ceylon*, London, 1817.

Surgeon Crawford who sent him the specimen from Batticaloa in 1826; however, Bennett could never find the species again in the Mahagam pattu.[6]

Tennent on better authority states that the leaves of the "Rannawara" [*Cassia auriculata*] are infused in the South of Ceylon as a substitute for tea, the plant being called "the matara tea tree." The Century Dictionary under "tea-tree" lists the Ceylon tea-tree, *Eloeodendron glaucum*. Dr. Trimen describes it in his *Flora*.[7] It is a small tree common from the coast to Dimbula with leaves often strongly serrate. It was sent by General Hay MacDowall to the Royal Botanic Garden, Calcutta, as "Ceylon tea tree" which name Roxburgh adopted.

Coffee in the Old Days

Governor Sir Edward Barnes established the first European coffee estate at Gangaruwa about 1824, although it is recorded that Mr. Conradi shipped coffee, probably native, to England, in 1802. Governor Barnes was not only a pioneer in coffee, but he also built the road between Colom-

ASSISTANT SUPERINTENDENT'S BUNGALOW, 1878

[6] John Whitchurch Bennett, *Ceylon and Its Capabilities*, London, 1843.
[7] Dr. Henry Trimen, *A Handbook of the Flora of Ceylon*, London, 1893.

bo and Kandy, and made Nuwara Eliya a sanatorium, thus preparing the way for the development of both the coffee and tea industries which were to center about Kandy and Nuwara Eliya. Mr. George Bird followed Governor Barnes' lead in coffee, by opening up Sinnapittiya, Gampola, in 1824.

During the time that coffee was king, about 1864, and huge tracts of jungle in the Dimbula, Dikoya, and Maskeliya districts were being transformed into cultivated forests of young coffee trees, Mr. [later Sir] Graeme Hepburn Dalrymple-Horn Elphinstone, came out to Ceylon and began his planting career on the Dalrymple estates in Kotmalie. In 1875, he was the largest coffee estate proprietor in Ceylon. Then came the coffee leaf disease, which, while it destroyed all his great properties, was at the same time responsible for initiating a movement to turn the coffee collapse into a tea triumph. Inspired by an ex-Assam planter named William Cameron [really "Campbell"], Elphinstone became interested in tea and probably would have figured largely in its further development had not his financial difficulties presently overwhelmed him, and brought his life to an untimely end in 1900. In 1882, Cameron so improved the local system of pruning and plucking tea as to show a remarkable increase in crop returns.

SUPERINTENDENT'S BUNGALOW, DIMBULA, 1878

After the first coffee slump of 1845, due to the hysterical speculative "rush into coffee," many European-owned properties were abandoned, but the village coffee industry still flourished. This suffered with the rest when the coffee blight came in the 'seventies. The apex of Ceylon's prosperity, resulting from the coffee industry, was reached in 1877. Ten years later the government was facing a deficit, and the island seemed derelict, with the coffee smash at its worst. Like rats deserting a sinking ship, large numbers of Jaffna Tamils and frightened burghers joined the crowd of ruined planters who were leaving the island in despair, many going to the Malay States, as the coffee slump was coincident with the opening of that country.

Tea was being tried in an experimental

MID-VICTORIAN DECORATIONS IN A TEA PLANTER'S BUNGALOW ON EPPLEWATTE, DOLOSBAGE, 1878

IN THE PUSSELLAWA DISTRICT, WHERE TEA WAS FIRST PLANTED IN CEYLON IN 1841

way when the coffee blight struck Ceylon, but the financial outlook for a new industry in this direction was dour indeed. With the one highly organized agricultural industry, on which Ceylon was dependent, in ruins and the coffee trees rotting, there seemed little chance of raising money to promote tea cultivation. Only a few years before had the strange orange-red blots appeared on the under side of the coffee leaves. One lone scientist, Dr. George Henry Kendrick Thwaites, then director of the Royal Botanic Gardens at Peradeniya, raised his voice in solemn warning, but it was like the voice of one who cries in the wilderness. No one heeded him until it was too late. Like a thief in the night, the plague had descended upon the all too confident, smiling planters.

There was left only a small band of planters who made a pathetic picture standing together amid the ruins of their fortunes, but stubbornly refusing to accept defeat. To these men who faced seemingly insurmountable obstacles at the blackest period of Ceylon's history, the tea trade of the world is indebted for the raising of a magnificent industry from the ashes of the coffee estates—an industry conceived in penury and nurtured in economy, yet producing to-day the finest quality teas that reach the world's markets.

How complete was the ruin of coffee may be gathered from the fact that dead coffee trees, stripped and with branches cut level, were exported to England to serve as legs for tea tables.

The Transition to Tea

At this time, some of the coffee planters were so poor that they were unable to buy seed. Not a few were struggling along on as little as 30 to 40 rupees a month, so the recovery from the coffee slump was one of the most remarkable and striking achievements in colonial history. Families ruined by coffee returned to Ceylon, took off their coats, and started with a grim determination, which has been an example to British colonists ever since. First, cinchona was tried, with good results until —as is always the case with drugs—the price dropped out of sight. They secured cinchona seed and planted it through the coffee, and this helped to stave off the

Mr. Maurice B. Worms Mr. Gabriel B. Worms
CHINA TEA PIONEERS IN CEYLON

evil days. Quinine at that time was about 11½ rupees an ounce, but overproduction soon reduced it to 75 cents an ounce, and ultimately the bark from which the quinine was extracted was not worth taking off the trees. Then they bought tea seeds and planted them in the coffee rows. The resource, grit, self-denial, and sheer hard work shown by the Ceylon planters in a trying climate during those critical days commands unlimited admiration.

The tea experiments were well under way before coffee received its death warrant, although it was cinchona that helped bridge not a few estates over from coffee to tea.

The Beginnings of a Great Industry

In the closing days of 1839, the first tea seeds from the newly discovered Assam indigenous plants, grown by Dr. Wallich in the Botanic Gardens at Calcutta were received at the Botanic Gardens in Peraceniya. Early in 1840, 205 plants followed. In 1840-42 some of these were planted on the land of Sir Anthony Oliphant, Chief Justice, in the neighborhood of Queens Cottage, Nuwara Eliya, and some near Essex Cottage, now the Naseby tea estate.

In the meantime, Mr. Maurice B. Worms, returning from a voyage to China, in 1841, brought with him some cuttings of the China tea plant, and these were planted on the Rothschild coffee estate in the Pussellawa district. Later, the brothers Gabriel B. and Maurice B. Worms, Germans, and cousins of the London Rothschilds, planted tea on Sogamma and their other estates, and in this way a field was planted with China tea seed on Condegalla, now a part of the Labookelle group in the Ramboda district. Some tea, which is reputed to have cost a guinea a pound to produce, was manufactured by the aid of a Chinaman on the Rothschild estate. Subsequently, the Ceylon Company, Ltd.,—now the Eastern Produce and Estates Company, Ltd.,—imported skilled labor from Bengal, and, under the direction of a retired Dibrugarh [Assam] planter, a Mr. Jenkins, made tea by hand in a temporary factory at Condegalla and at Hope.

The Worms Brothers, Tea Pioneers

The Worms brothers belonged to a remarkable family. The eldest, Solomon, was the first Baron de Worms, son of Benedict Worms of Frankfort-on-Main, and his wife, who was the eldest sister of the Baron de Rothschild. The brothers were born traders and adventurers. Maurice went to England in 1827; Gabriel in 1832, and both became members of the London Stock Exchange. Maurice sailed east in 1841, and in 1842 Gabriel joined him in Colombo, where they established a shipping and banking business under the name of G. & M. B. Worms. Gabriel remained in Colombo, and Maurice looked after the planting end in the up-country. Their 2000 acre Rothschild estate in Pussellawa was famed for its completeness and efficiency, and was held up as a model by William Sabonadiere in his coffee planter's text book. Their mark was a standard for quality in Mincing Lane for over twenty-five years. They soon reached out and opened the Keenakelle estate in Badulla, Meddecombra in Dimbula, Thotulagalla in Haputale, Condegalla and Labookelle in Ramboda, and Norwood in Dikoya, making, with their Pussellawa holdings a total of 7318 acres. They held these properties for twenty-four years and sold them to the Ceylon Company, Ltd., in 1865, for £157,000—a record transfer of European-owned estates. They then retired to England. As one of the brothers expressed it, they "led useful, contented lives." Maurice died in 1865; Gabriel in 1881.

Among other famous coffee properties that afterwards went over to tea, mention should be made of the Rev. James Moncriff Sutherland Glenie's Delta estate, which adjoined the Rothschild holdings, and Captain Henry Bird's Black Forest, where Mr. F. R. Sabonadiere, founder of Sabonadiere & Co., Colombo, started.

About the same time that the Worms brothers imported and planted their China plants, a Mr. Llewellyn, of Calcutta, introduced a selection of Assam indigenous shrubs which were planted on Penylan estate, Dolosbage. It is not now known which was the earlier arrival.

Loolecondera, the Oldest Garden

Quite as early in the field, however, and more successful in a quiet way, were the proprietors of Loolecondera estate, Hewaheta, then Messrs. G. D. B. Harrison and W. M. Leake; now the Anglo-Ceylon & General Estates Co., Ltd., whose produce in the early 'eighties, under Mr. James Taylor's careful management, acquired a high reputation among Ceylon teas. Loolecondera was also a coffee estate originally. It was purchased from the crown by Mr. James Joseph Mackenzie, in 1841. As far back as 1865, Mr. Taylor, sometimes

Two Close-up Views of the Original Assam Tea Garden on Loolecondera

MANAGER'S BUNGALOW AT HINDUGALLA, OLDEST IN CEYLON, BUILT IN 1851

called the father of tea planting in Ceylon, began collecting tea seed from Peradeniya on Mr. Harrison's order. He planted it in hedge rows, along the roadsides, in 1866. In that year Mr. William Martin Leake, being secretary of the Planters' Association, moved that body to get Sir Hercules Robinson's government to send Mr. Arthur Morice, an experienced Ceylon coffee planter, on a mission to inspect and report on the Assam tea districts. The result was a valuable report published by the Government, and subsequently reproduced in the *Tropical Agriculturist* for 1865–66. That report induced Mr. Leake in 1866 to order for his firm, Keir, Dundas & Co., a consignment of Assam hybrid tea seed; the first, probably, of this kind ever imported, and this seed was handed over to the care of Mr. Taylor on Loolecondera. Mr. Taylor's first clearing, of twenty acres, was felled towards the end of 1867, a year before the Ceylon Company had felled any forest for tea. This is generally considered to be the oldest field of tea under continuous cultivation in Ceylon; many of the earlier plantings having been allowed to go out of cultivation, either permanently or temporarily, before Mr. Taylor began planting tea on Loolecondera. The Ceylon Company imported Assam seed and began planting the hybrid kind in 1869.

Mr. JAMES TAYLOR was born at Mosspark, Monboddo, March 29, 1835 and was educated in the lovely village of Auchen-

blae. He went out to Ceylon when he was seventeen, having engaged to make himself generally useful to Mr. George Pride of Kandy for three years, at £100 per annum. He went directly to Loolecondera and remained on that estate until the day of his death forty years after. In 1891, the Planters' Association presented him a silver tea and coffee service in recognition of his having laid the foundation of the tea industry in Ceylon. He lies buried in the cemetery at Mahaiyawa, Kandy, and on the memorial stone above his grave is the inscription: "In pious memory of James Taylor, of Loolecondera Estate Ceylon, the pioneer of the tea and cinchona enterprise, who died May 2, 1892, aged 57 years."

The Rush Into Tea

The devastating attacks of *Hemileia vastatrix* on the coffee plants began in 1869, and reached their culmination in 1877–78, but it was in 1875 that the first thousand acres of old coffee land was planted in tea. The subsequent "rush into tea," as it has been called, is shown by the following figures:

1875 total planted acreage			1,080 acres
1895 " " "			305,000 "
1915 " " "			402,000 "
1925 " " "			418,000 "
1930 " " "			467,000 "

In 1866–67, the director of the Botanic Gardens reported that a sample of Ceylon tea prepared from China [Bohea] jat had been favorably reported on in London, and for several years Dr. Thwaites continued directing the attention of the Government and the public to the advantages of cultivating this hardy plant. In 1868, there were 270 plants of Assam jat, two feet high and prospering well at the Hakgala gardens, and two years after the distribution of seed commenced. It was the general opinion then that the Assam variety would succeed best at an altitude above the limit of coffee. In 1872, Dr. Thwaites saw no reason why the sides of the higher mountain ranges should not be covered with flourishing tea plantations, and by 1875 the cultivation of tea in Ceylon was an established commercial success.

Mr. Taylor sold the first of the Loolecondera [Assam hybrid] tea at Kandy in 1871–72. In the following year 23 pounds, valued at Rs. 58 [£4.7s; $19] were sent to London. In 1873 and 1874, plants of both the Assam hybrid and the China variety were distributed from Peradeniya and Hakgala gardens. Later on, the chief means of supply was by the importation of large quantities of Assam seed from Calcutta. This is now prohibited by law,

Mr. James Taylor
The Father of Tea
Planting in Ceylon

Dr. G. H. K. Thwaites
Early Advocate of Tea
in Ceylon

CEYLON TEA PIONEERS

in order to prevent the introduction of blister blight, *Exobasidium vexans*, and all the seed used is from local seed gardens on the island.

The Planters' Association of Ceylon

The planters early felt the need of an organization to look after their interests, and so on February 17, 1854, the Planters' Association of Ceylon was founded at Kandy, with Captain John Keith Jolly, a partner in the firm of George Wall & Co., Kandy and Colombo, as the first chairman. The first constitution and rules were adopted in 1862. They provided that land ownership should constitute the chief basis of membership; that non-owners who so desired might be admitted upon payment of the usual subscription, but might not vote on questions involving taxes.

In 1867, the Association had 75 estates represented in its membership, but this had increased to a total of 2394 estates and private members in 1921. Some twenty-seven district associations were formed from time to time, but consolidations reduced the number to eighteen by 1931. Representatives from each district association serve on the general committee of the Planters' Association. The area under tea represented by the Association at the end of 1932 was 406,727 acres. In 1933 the membership totaled 1121.

The last thirty years have brought a marked change in the scope of the Association's activities, due to the transference of great numbers of Ceylon estates from private ownership to limited liability companies whose financial affairs are handled through managing agents. The

VICTORIA COMMEMORATION BUILDINGS, KANDY

Ferguson Hall, upper story, is in memory of A. M. Ferguson; the tower in memory of Geo. Wall; the clock in memory of Alex. Wardrop; the main entrance gates in memory of Alexander Philip.

A View of the Mariawatte Estate Near Gampola, in the Kaduganawa District, Opened by Mr. H. K. Rutherford in 1886

greater number of the association members are no longer owners of estates, and their acts have become, therefore, largely advisory. However, any recommendation from a general meeting of the association, or from its committee, always receives careful consideration by the Government and by others interested in the planting industries.

The Association was incorporated in 1916, and its constitution was revised in 1920. The revision represented an attempt to meet changed conditions at a time when a movement was started to form another association, which it was feared would result in the disintegration of the Planters' Association. Many of the members felt that a re-shaping of the constitution might still make it possible for all interests to work together under a single organization. The new constitution provided for two sub-committees of the Association, one devoted to the interests of the proprietors, and the other to deal with all matters and questions that concern superintendents and assistant superintendents of estates. The outcome was that the proprietary planters would not accept the plan, and only the superintendents' and assistant superin-

tendents' committee was formed. In the meantime the proprietary planters decided, for various reasons, to join the new association, which was promoted by the estate agents, and has been known since 1921 as the Ceylon Estates Proprietary Association, Colombo.

CAPTAIN JOHN KEITH JOLLY, 1807–1865, the first chairman of the Planters' Association of Ceylon, was the son of a Justice of the Peace and Deputy-Lieutenant of Stirling and Dumbartonshire. He saw maritime service with the Honourable East India Company until 1843, when he and his wife settled down on the Fairieland Estate. He died at Mount Lavinia.

MR. ROBERT BOYD TYTLER, 1819–1882, of the Pallakellie coffee estate in Dumbara, became the second chairman, in 1856. After serving several months he went home on furlough. Upon his return to the island he again occupied the Planters' Association chair in 1858, 1859, and part of 1860. He was born in Aberdeenshire, and spent three years in Jamaica before going to Ceylon, in 1837, at the age of eighteen. He was accounted one of the giants of the planting industry.

One of the first acts of the Planters'

Capt. John Keith Jolly | Mr. Robert Boyd Tytler | Mr. George Wall | Mr. Alexander Brown
First Chairman, 1854 | *Second Chairman, 1856* | *Third Chairman, 1856* | *First Secretary, 1854*

FOUNDERS OF THE PLANTERS' ASSOCIATION OF CEYLON

Association was to urge upon the Government "the unspeakable advantage of a railway," but it was not until 1858 that the agitation was destined to bear fruit. Robert Boyd Tytler was diligent in its behalf. He became a member of the Legislative Council. He introduced the scientific cultivation of cocoa and tobacco into Dumbara, about 1850. One of Mr. Tytler's great achievements was to develop a scheme for raising the waters of the Mahaweli-ganga 500 feet, to irrigate the Rajawella coffee estate. The engineering enterprise was a failure, but it was responsible for bringing out to Ceylon Mr. John Brown, who later became a pioneer in Uva. His name survived in his two sons, one of whom died in 1934.

MR. GEORGE WALL, F.L.S., F.R.A.S., the third chairman of the Association, was a pioneer planter, merchant, politician, and journalist. In his planting activities he enjoyed three distinctions: he drafted the circular proposing the formation of the Association, he was the first Englishman to occupy the chair, and he held the office more frequently than anyone else. Originally elected in 1856, he was re-elected nine times at four divided periods, extending to 1884. In the 'fifties and 'sixties he sat in the Legislative Council, and twice he was chairman of the Chamber of Commerce. Born in Lancashire in 1820, he went to Ceylon in 1846 to manage the Ceylon Plantations Company at Kandy. Wall's hobbies were astronomy, botany, and flute playing. He wrote two books, *The Natural History of Thought* and *Good and Evil*. He remained active until his 75th year, when, because of ill health, he left Ceylon, never to return.

MR. ALEXANDER BROWN, 1820–1876, nicknamed "Sandy," the Association's first secretary and treasurer, became chairman in 1861, succeeding Captain Gallwey who occupied the chair for a short time after Mr. Tytler's departure in 1860. He was a picturesque pioneer type. Twelve years after his arrival in Ceylon in 1845, he was proprietor or lessee of twenty-one estates. Being an accountant, he was a popular choice for the association's first secretary and treasurer, which post he held from 1854 to 1855, and from 1858 to 1861. He wrote a model planting report, and was a splendid debater. He was the author of *The Coffee Planters' Manual*. He served the Association again as its secretary for a few months before his death.

MR. C. PITTS, secretary of the Association, was senior in the Kandy firm of Pitts & Gavin, which started when the firm of Ackland, Boyd & Co. came to grief in 1848. Mr. Pitts died in 1858 after filling the position of secretary for three years.

CAPTAIN H. C. BIRD [afterwards Lieut. Col. Henry C. Byrde] was the first member of the Planters' Association to be nominated to the Legislative Council. He was elected in 1857. Captain Bird was the nephew of George Bird, who, aided by the first Colonel Bird, opened up Sinnapitiya, the first regular coffee plantation in the island, in 1824, and Weyangawatte, afterwards the famous Mariawatte Tea Estate. "Captain H. C. Bird" [he did not change his name until after he had retired to Wales in the 'sixties, after nearly thirty years in Ceylon] was again elected Member of the Legislative Council in 1860.

Captain Bird was followed in the Legislative Council by Messrs. Andrew Nicol,

Capt. H. Byrde
Chairman, 1862–68

Mr. Andrew Nicol
Rep. in Leg. Council, 1861

Mr. John Gavin
Chairman, 1862

Mr. L. H. Daniel
Secretary, 1863

PROMINENT IN THE EARLY WORK OF THE PLANTERS' ASSOCIATION

R. J. Corbet, and William Thompson.

MR. ANDREW NICOL, 1819–1889, was known as the "poor but industrious planter." He was born in Banff, and went to Ceylon from Bombay in the early 'forties, opening up coffee in Rangala and coconuts at Batticaloa. He was the representative in the Legislative Council in 1861. He went home in 1862, retiring in 1863. Twenty-two years later, in 1885, he again went out to Ceylon, to view the transformation which had taken place in Dimbula from coffee to cinchona and tea. Though no longer young, he became active in the rehabilitation of his properties. He "stuck it" for four years and then returned to Elgin, Scotland, where he died.

CAPTAIN H. BYRDE was chairman of the Planters' Association of Ceylon for part of 1862 and again from 1863 to 1868.

MR. JOHN GAVIN, 1819–1876, succeeded Captain H. Byrde as chairman in 1862. John Gavin, known as "Honest John," went to Ceylon in 1843, when he was 24, and joined the firm of Ackland, Boyd & Co. He left them, in 1848, to join the establishment of the Kandy agency firm of Pitts & Gavin. On that firm's ceasing to function, in 1858, Mr. Gavin became managing partner and subsequently head of the largest agency house of his time, Keir, Dundas & Co. Being handicapped by deafness Mr. Gavin was chairman of the Planters' Association for only a few months in 1862. After handing over a flourishing business to Messrs. G. D. B. Harrison and W. Martin Leake in 1863, he went home, returning in 1864–65 for a visit in connection with a coffee estate suit. He retired again to England, where he died.

During the incumbency of Captain Byrde and Mr. Gavin, in 1862, Mr. T. C. Hutton was secretary. When Captain Byrde again became chairman, in 1863, Mr. L. H. Daniel was secretary, to be succeeded in April by Mr. W. Martin Leake.

MR. G. D. B. HARRISON succeeded Mr. William Thompson as representative in the Legislative Council in 1864. He was reappointed in 1865.

MR. WILLIAM MARTIN LEAKE, engineer, planter, and merchant, is a name that will always be associated with the activities of the Planters' Association of Ceylon and of the Ceylon Association in London. His record with the former, in an official capacity, began in the latter part of 1863, when he was appointed secretary and treasurer; an appointment which he retained until the early part of 1868. In 1872 and in the early part of 1873, he was chairman, and he was the Association's representative on the Legislative Council during 1872 and 1873. With the Ceylon Association in London he was secretary from the date of its inception, in 1888, to the time of his retirement in 1915. He died in 1916.

Mr. Leake was born in London, April 23, 1831; educated at Rugby and St. John's College, Cambridge; and trained as an engineer. He sailed for Ceylon, in 1859, to join Mr. G. D. B. Harrison, then carrying out irrigation works in the Southern Province. He first visited Kandy in 1860, on the occasion of the ceremonial opening of the Kattugastota Bridge. Shortly thereafter Mr. John Gavin, of Keir, Dundas & Co., announced that he was seeking partners to replace Messrs. Simon Keir and G. H. Dundas, who had gone home to Scotland. Thus June, 1861, saw Mr. Leake commencing his close association with the planters and planting.

When Mr. Leake left Ceylon in September, 1861, for a visit home, everything there was peaceful; but when he returned in June, 1862, he found the countryside aflame with indignation at the do-nothing policy of the Government. In that year, the Planters' Association was remodelled.

Mr. Leake became acting secretary of the Planters' Association of Ceylon, April 18, 1863, upon the return to England of the incumbent, Mr. L. H. Daniel. He was elected to the office May 24, 1863. Mr. Leake afterwards told of the isolation of the planters at this time. The only means of communication between the Central Province and the coast consisted of two daily coaches, carrying ten passengers each way; the fare for the single journey being Rs. 25, and the time occupied, twelve hours. The voyage home to England, except by sailing vessel around the Cape, cost £100. He adds: A trip to Colombo was, therefore, a matter of rare occurrence with the average planter, and a trip home possible for the very few. I was myself for over two years in Kandy without visiting Colombo. For the same reasons, visitors from the outer world were conspicuous by their absence. The mail steamers called only at Galle, from which port access to Colombo was as difficult as it was from Kandy, and very few steamer passengers were ever seen even in Colombo. In a community so situated, cut off from the outside world, grievances were apt to rankle and complaints to find vent in unmeasured terms.[8]

It is to be noted in passing that from 1863 to 1866 the Association concerned itself chiefly with military expenditure and labor questions. It was Mr. Leake's duty to present the viewpoint of the planters to the Government and this he did with a forcefulness that he admits was excusable only because of the isolation of those associated with planting enterprises. The correspondence was frequently acerbitous, but he got results, and these without detracting from what was later to be acclaimed "a career of a man of culture and high professional training, who nevertheless, entered on the ordinary and sometimes rough work of the pioneer."

8 William Martin Leake, "Events of Eleven Years: 1863–1873," in *Jubilee of the Planters' Association of Ceylon, 1854–1904*, Colombo, 1904.

Mr. G. D. B. Harrison   Mr. William Martin Leake

EARLY PROTAGONISTS OF THE ASSAM JAT

The activities of the Association in matters political and legislative at this period eventually produced many benefits in which the general community shared.

In 1866, tea growing was brought up at the meeting of the Association for the first time as a subject of discussion. Mr. Leake had an interest in the Loolecondera Estate in Hewaheta, and the manager, James Taylor, was experimenting in the manufacture of tea from the leaves of some China bushes he had planted along the roadsides, with quite hopeful results. Arthur Morice of Mooloya also took an interest in it, and it was suggested that if Mr. Morice could be sent to India as commissioner to report on tea cultivation, it might be helpful. The Association voted £100 for the purpose on condition that the Government do likewise, which it did. After Mr. Morice's report, which appeared in 1867, the proprietors of Loolecondera at once ordered from Weinholt Bros., of Calcutta, a consignment of Assam hybrid tea seed to plant their first field of tea. This epoch-making event was mentioned by Mr. Leake in the P. A. Committee report that year as follows: "Among subjects of less importance, the Committee have to notice the publication in the course of the year of the report on the Tea districts of India by the Commissioner of the Association, Mr. Arthur Morice." Commenting on this in 1904, Mr. Leake wrote:

The Committee seems to have approved of the Report, for "as a mark of their sense of the value" of it they made Mr. Morice an Honorary Member of the Association. The coffee crop of 1866–67 was a very large one, indeed the largest in proportion to the acreage in bearing in my time. Who could have conceived that within twenty years coffee would have become a "subject of less importance" than tea?

At the end of 1867, Mr. Leake found the Association in a parlous state; in fact it had begun to be said that the Association was Keir, Dundas & Co., which, though untrue, contained a spice of truth. At the annual meeting of 1867–68 a much wider interest was created. To further his Ceylon League and its reform scheme Mr. George Wall was again seeking the chairmanship of the Planters' Association. Mr. Leake and Captain Byrde staged an election contest which gave Mr. Wall the chairmanship, but at the same time replenished the Association's depleted coffers. It was first announced that no one would be entitled to vote unless the subscription for the year had been paid before the annual meeting. The subscriptions and members came in, and the receipts that year reached £484. Instead of showing a balance of three figures on the wrong side, it exhibited a favorable balance of £205. Mr. Leake was re-elected to the post of secretary but retired shortly thereafter in favor of Captain Byrde.

In 1870, some Russian agents visited Ceylon, prospecting for cargo for a line of steamers from the Black Sea through the newly opened Suez Canal. They thought the market for Ceylon produce might be best supplied directly by this route as soon as the railway from Moscow to Odessa was opened. Mr. Leake, who was in London on holiday, thereupon paid a visit to Russia, but found that coffee consumption in that country was small and that tea was the more popular beverage. This was a disappointment in view of the fact that coffee was then the principle product of Ceylon.

On his return to Ceylon, in 1871, Mr. Leake found the island discussing the questions of manure and of *Hemileia vastatrix*. For the next ten years vast sums were spent on fighting the pest, in the hope of staying the plague, but it was hopeless. In the year 1872, the system of keeping accounts was changed; beginning January 1, accounts previously kept in sterling were re-opened in rupees and cents. In that same year, Mr. Leake was elected chairman of the Planters' Association in place of Mr. J. A. Bell. He also served on the Legislative Council that year and in 1873, when he was re-elected chairman of the

Planters' Association. It was in 1872 that Mr. Leake made the first shipment [23 lbs.] of Ceylon tea from Loolecondera to London. However, he only continued to serve the Association as chairman and planting member until September, 1873, when he left Ceylon, ending his connection with the Planters' Association. His career with the Ceylon Association in London was less romantic in a way but twenty-seven years as secretary of the London body served to add to the regard in which his abilities were held by all those with whom he came in contact.

MR. CHRISTOPHER B. SMITH was the Planters' Association representative in the Legislative Council from 1865 to 1868, when Mr. G. D. B. Harrison was again appointed to that office.

MR. G. D. B. HARRISON, head of the firm of Keir, Dundas & Co., known as "the King of Kandy," who had served the Planters' Association in the Legislative Council in 1864–66 and in 1868–69, succeeded Mr. Wall as its chairman in 1870. He continued to act as planting member of the Legislative Council until 1871 when Mr. M. H. Thomas replaced him.

MR. M. H. THOMAS who represented the Planters' Association in the Legislative Council 1871–72 went out to Ceylon in 1856, and later became a partner in the firm of Alston, Scott & Co.

MR. J. A. BELL was chairman in 1871, being succeeded by Mr. Leake in 1872.

MR. GEORGE WALL succeeded Mr. Leake as chairman of the Association in 1873, and continued to occupy the chair until 1876. During this period Mr. W. D. Gibbon was secretary and treasurer in 1874, and Mr. T. C. Anderson in 1875. Wm. Bowden Smith was the representative in the Legislative Council from 1874 to 1877.

MR. H. S. SAUNDERS, 1841–1919, chairman of the association in 1876–78, was the son of the late Hon. Frederick Saunders, who was Treasurer of Ceylon, an office later occupied by his eldest son, Sir Frederick Saunders, brother of Henry Spearman Saunders. Mr. Saunders went out to Ceylon early in life, and became interested in coffee planting. Later, he started an estate agency. It was largely due to his efforts that certain railway extensions in the mountain districts of Ceylon were brought to fruition. While he was chairman of the Association he organ-

Mr. J. A. Bell
Chairman, 1871

Mr. H. S. Saunders
Chairman, 1876–78

Mr. A. Philip
Secretary, 1876–1905

Sir W. D. Gibbon
Chairman, 1878

PLANTERS' ASSOCIATION OFFICERS OF THE 'SEVENTIES

ized a London agency which later developed into the Ceylon Association in London. He engaged in road building, organized the Colombo Club, and was a well-known sportsman.

MR. A. PHILIP, who was secretary of the Association from 1876 to 1905, had an estate agency business of his own in Kandy. As the secretarial duties were not so arduous in those days, he was able to combine both. When he died a pair of ornamental wrought-iron gates were erected to his memory at the entrance to the Victoria Commemoration Buildings, Kandy.

MR. REGINALD BEAUCHAMP DOWNALL, 1842–1888, became the planters' representative in the Legislative Council in 1877. With the exception of the years 1879, 1882, 1883, and 1884, he served until 1889. During his term of office the Uva railway extension agitation was the outstanding feature. Mr. Downall was the son of a Devonshire archdeacon. He went to Ceylon in 1863, and entered the employ of Geo. Wall & Co. Inside of a year and a half he was a full-fledged V. A. He was a great sportsman, cricketer, keeper of hounds, and patron of the turf. He stalked big game in both India and Ceylon. After becoming a Dimbula proprietor, he sold out in 1877 to purchase Dambatenne and Lemastota in Haputale. He also purchased Monarakande, which turned out to be a millstone as soon as coffee began to fail. Then it was that he had to give up Barnes Hall in Nuwara Eliya, and go to live on his estates. He clung to coffee until the last, planting tea much later than his neighbors. When attacked by cancer of the stomach he was already heavily involved financially. However, in August,

1888, he was able to get to London where he was met by his life-long friend and predecessor in the Legislative Council, Mr. W. Bowden Smith. An immediate operation served to prolong his life only a few months. He died in his 47th year, deeply mourned by all the European community.

MR. W. D. GIBBON [later Sir] was another Ceylon pioneer who rendered yeoman service to the Planters' Association. He arrived in the island at the end of 1855, and started work on the estate of his brother-in-law, R. B. Tytler. He began coffee planting at Madulkelle under Donald Stewart, later known as the "King of Coorg." Two years thereafter, Mr. Gibbon became manager of Madulkelle and Oononagalla. Still later, he became manager of Hoolankande, on the understanding that he would have the agency of Mr. Tytler's estates. The latter's farewell to the island was, however, delayed by the heavy outlay which had been incurred on the waterworks at Rejawella, and Mr. Gibbon entered the firm of J. M. Robertson & Co., first becoming manager of Oodewelle and later their chief visiting agent. He was secretary of the Planters' Association in 1874, and became chairman in 1878.

Mr. Gibbon estimated that on his travels as visiting agent, he covered by rail and carriage, on horseback and foot, nearly 50,000 miles; and that he visited or reported on every estate in Ambegamuwa, Dikoya, Dimbula, Maskeliya, Matale East, Kelebokka, Kotmale, and other districts. In 1904, he acted for six months as Member in Council during the absence of the Hon. [later Sir] Edward Rosling.

Mr. Gibbon was created a knight in 1913. He was a member of the Kandy Munic-

Mr. J. L. Loudoun-Shand
Chairman, 1879–81

Mr. J. Shipton
Chairman, 1882

Mr. T. N. Christie
Chairman, 1885–88

Mr. L. H. Kelly
Chairman, 1888–91

PLANTERS' ASSOCIATION OFFICERS OF THE 'EIGHTIES

ipal Council, and a justice of the peace part of the time he was in Ceylon. His connection with the Planters' Association extended over some sixty-eight years. He died in 1919.

MR. J. L. LOUDOUN-SHAND, who was one of Ceylon's foremost and most enthusiastic pioneers in tea, first took part in the affairs of the Planters' Association in 1866, but the best work he did for Ceylon and its planting community was when he was a member of the Legislative Council at perhaps the darkest period in Ceylon's history. Through the failure of the coffee-growing industry, the planters had become much in arrears in payments to their coolies, and many cases were instituted in the courts, aided and fomented by hangers-on. It became necessary for the Government to interfere, and a somewhat drastic labor ordinance was introduced into the council, which Mr. Loudoun-Shand had great difficulty in getting modified.

On February 17, 1879, he was elected chairman of the Planters' Association, which office he held for two years. The period was probably the worst two years Ceylon had. The Association was passing through a lean time, it had a debit balance, and many of its members had a weight of personal financial troubles. In his term, the first sod of the Nawalapitiya-Nanuoya Railway was cut by Sir James Longden.

Mr. Loudoun-Shand also took active part in bringing about the affiliation of the district associations. He recalled that, when he first went to Ceylon, there were only a few resident proprietors; most estates being in the hands of agency firms. Those powerful rivals, Keir, Dundas & Co. and George

Wall & Co., had the Planters' Association more or less in their hands. Association records of that period show how splendidly it fought the planters' battles in the face of discouragement and lack of support. However, times changed, and soon a body of residential proprietors, with important public interests to attend to in their own districts, began to rally round the Association.

Mr. Loudoun-Shand, after living in Ceylon for twenty years returned home as planting commissioner for the Colonial & Indian Exhibition in 1886, and represented Ceylon at other exhibitions in the following year; among them the Liverpool, Glasgow, Paris, and Brussels exhibitions. His work at these did much to draw attention to the tea-growing potentialities of Ceylon. He lectured also at the Royal Colonial Institute in London, the Society of Arts, and other public bodies on the fine prospects of Ceylon's tea industry.

In 1912, Mr. Loudoun-Shand was elected president of the Ceylon Association in London, and in 1913 he was again chosen for that honor. In 1925, he was made an honorary life member of the Ceylon Association in London, and Mr. W. Forsythe, in a speech, said that the good work he performed during those critical days between 1879 and 1884 would not be forgotten by any who belonged to that generation. He died at his home in Dulwich, Scotland, in 1932, aged eighty-six.

MR. G. A. TALBOT, who represented the Planters' Association on the Legislative Council in 1879, originally went out to Ceylon about 1870, when he started his career as a coffee planter under the auspices of Messrs. Lee, Hedges & Co. in

Mr. Giles F. Walker
Chairman, 1891–94

Mr. A. M. White
Chairman, 1894–96

Mr. A. W. S. Sackville
Chairman, 1896

Mr. J. N. Campbell
Chairman, 1897

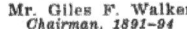

PLANTERS' ASSOCIATION OFFICERS IN THE 'NINETIES

the Dimbula district. After a short interval he was moved into the Kandy district. In 1874, he returned to the Dimbula area, where he took charge of the Great Western Estate, and became visiting agent for his firm. A few years later he bought Wallaha, a fine coffee estate, a cinchona property in Nuwara Eliya, and, in partnership with others opened land in Upper Dikoya and in Maskeliya. While resident in Dimbula, he was chairman of the Dimbula District Planters' Association. When the coffee blight came, Mr. Talbot was one of the early ones to turn to cinchona and tea.

In 1886, the Ceylon Tea Plantations Co., Ltd., was registered in London. Originally, they purchased estates belonging to the late Mr. David Reid and his partners, amongst whom was Mr. H. Kerr Rutherford. Mr. Talbot's estate, Wallaha, as well as his other interests in Nuwara Eliya and Maskeliya were absorbed into the new company. When Mr. Rutherford left for England in 1889, Mr. Talbot was appointed the company's manager in Ceylon, and made Nuwara Eliya his headquarters.

He remained there until 1896, when he retired to England, and took a seat on the board of the company, in London. Here he extended his field of operations and became chairman or director of other tea producing companies in Ceylon, Northern India, and Travancore. He was an active member of the Ceylon Association in London and of the Rubber Growers' Association. He was elected president of the Ceylon Association in London for 1904–06. He entered Parliament as member for Hemel Hempstead, being re-elected on a change of government taking place. In

the House, his long and intimate acquaintance with Ceylon proved of great benefit to the Ceylon Association. He remained a Member of the House until his death in 1920.

Mr. George Wall succeeded Mr. Loudoun-Shand as chairman in 1881, and he, in turn, was succeeded by J. Shipton in 1882. Mr. J. L. Loudoun-Shand was the Member in Council that year. In 1883–84, Mr. Wall was again chairman, with E. J. Young the Member in Council the first year; and Mr. Loudoun-Shand, in 1884.

Mr. T. North Christie was the first of three—Messrs. Christie, Kelly, and Walker —to preside over the Association for three years, and succeed each other in Council. Mr. Christie was one of the ablest planting politicians Ceylon ever had. He was a planter in Ceylon for twenty-four years. In 1878–80, he traveled in Malaya, opening land in Selangor which became the Damansara Estate. He was chairman of the Planters' Association of Ceylon in 1885–88, being their representative on the Legislative Council in 1889–91, in which years L. H. Kelly was chairman of the Association. Mr. Kelly went to the Council in 1891, 1892, and 1893; being followed by Giles F. Walker. Mr. Christie served again as member of the Legislative Council in 1896–97.

Mr. L. H. Kelly succeeded Mr. Christie as chairman in 1888, and continued in office until 1891, when Giles F. Walker came into office.

Mr. Giles F. Walker was educated at Marlborough and Tonbridge. Coming out to Ceylon in 1866, he was first an assistant on Sheen and Pundaluora under the late Alexander Fraser and Edward Hope. In

Mr. F. G. A. Lane
Chairman, 1898–1900

Sir Edward Rosling
Chairman, 1900 and 1909

Mr. A. C. Kingsford
Chairman, 1902–04

Mr. Edgar Turner
Chairman, 1904

PLANTERS' ASSOCIATION OFFICERS AT THE TURN OF THE CENTURY

1868, he took charge of St. John del Rey, Bogawantalawa, where he remained for twenty-eight years. He gave up this billet in 1896, and in 1897 became a director in the Colombo agency firm of J. M. Robertson & Co. Mr. Walker was chairman of the Planters' Association of Ceylon in 1891–94; and Representative in the Legislative Council, 1894–96.

MR. A. MELVILLE WHITE, a contemporary of Joseph Fraser and John Rettie, Ceylon tea pioneers, was chairman in 1894–96. He was able and independent. He died in 1914.

MR. A. W. S. SACKVILLE filled the chair for the year 1896.

MR. J. N. CAMPBELL became chairman in 1897. He was born in 1852 at St. Andrews, Scotland, educated at Marlborough, and went to Ceylon in 1870, sailing two years later for a five years' stay in South Africa. He returned to the island in 1880, and commenced work on Moray, Maskeliya. He took charge of Henfold in 1892, and became manager of the Anglo-Ceylon and General Estates Co.—then the O. B. Estates Co.—in 1894. In 1897–1902, Mr. Campbell was the Representative on the Legislative Council, and for sometime thereafter continued as General European member. He was the first member to be awarded the prefix "Honorable," a badge of distinction instituted by Sir West Ridgeway for ten years' service in council.

MR. F. G. A. LANE, chairman, 1898–1900, was born in India, July 4, 1852; was educated at Blackheath and St. John's College, Cambridge, and went to Ceylon in 1874. He was a proprietary planter on Blair Atholl, Dikoya; also, served the Association as chairman of the Thirty Com-

mittee and of the Labor Federation, retiring to Bloxworth, Wareham, Dorset, in 1900. He became a member of the Wareham and Purbeck Rural District Council; chairman, Board of Guardians; J.P. for Dorset; High Sheriff of Dorset, 1916; deputy president, South Dorset Conservative and Unionist Association; and chairman, General Commissioners.

MR. EDWARD ROSLING [later Sir] who became chairman of the Planters' Association in 1900, was born December 4, 1863, at South Nutfield. He was educated at Queenwood, Hampshire; went out to Ceylon in 1886; and "crept" with Mr. Causland on Templestowe. Next, he took charge of Fruit Hill as an acting appointment for seven months; went home to be married; and returned at the end of 1888 as manager of Dessford, Nanuoya. He stayed there until he moved to his own residential property, Netherleigh, Nuwara Eliya. His knighthood was created in 1913. He holds the distinction of having represented the planting interests on the Legislative Council for ten years, 1902–1913. After serving as chairman of the Planters' Association for 1900–01, he was again elected chairman for 1909–11. Returning to England in 1913, he became chairman of the Ceylon Association in London in 1914 and 1915.

MR. ARTHUR CHARLES KINGSFORD, who succeeded Mr. Rosling as chairman of the Planters' Association in 1902, was one of the youngest chairmen the Association ever had. He was a man of fine character, good breeding, and sage counsel. In company with Mr. M. Kelway Bamber, he made a tour of Java, Formosa, and Japan in 1904, the results of their joint observa-

Mr. William Forsythe
Chairman, 1905

Mr. James R. Martin
Chairman, 1906–07

Mr. H. A. Beachcroft
Chairman, 1908

Mr. G. C. Bliss
Chairman, 1911–13

OFFICERS OF THE PLANTERS' ASSOCIATION, 1905–13

tions being published in 1907. Mr. Kingsford did good work on the Kandy committees and in the Kelani valley, where his collection of statistics of traffic for the railway was acclaimed a triumph of industry. He was in charge of Rockwood, Hewaheta, in 1898. He died at Jesselton, British North Borneo, July 29, 1905.

MR. EDGAR TURNER, J.P., who was chairman of the association in 1904, secretary 1905–07, and acting chairman for six months in 1907, was born in England in 1862. He was educated at Ipswich School, and went into Mincing Lane in the 'eighties to learn tea tasting. Because of an accident suffered in the spring of 1884, he had to leave London, and three years elapsed before he could begin work again. He went out to Ceylon in 1887, and lived for a short time with N. M. Home, on Woodstock, Ambegamuwa, later joining P. E. Sewell on Rahatungoda, Upper Hewaheta. He helped to start the Maturata and Hewaheta District Planters' Association in 1896; became its honorary secretary in 1897; chairman in 1898, and again secretary in 1899. In 1903, he visited South India as one of the two labor commissioners sent over by the Planters' Association of Ceylon. He served the Association as representative in the Legislative Council from 1908 to 1911; was elected chairman of the Ceylon Estates Proprietary Association, 1921–22; for several years acted as a visiting agent before joining the firm of Geo. Steuart & Co.; retired in 1924, and since then has been living quietly at Kuruman, Walberswick, near Southwold, Suffolk.

MR. WILLIAM FORSYTHE was chairman in 1905. He was born at Scoutbush, Car-

rickfergus, Ireland, February 25, 1860; went to Ceylon in 1877 to engage in coffee planting and in 1878 planted the first tea clearing on Gallebodde, Nawalapitiya, under Mr. John Fraser. He continued in coffee until 1881, when he took charge of the Dunedin Tea Estate at Yatiyantota under Mr. P. R. Shand; became a V.A. in 1885, and held the position until he retired in 1910. He died in 1933.

MR. JAMES R. MARTIN was chairman in 1906 and a part of 1907.

MR. HENRY AWDRY BEACHCROFT, 1847–1920, held the chair in 1908. Born in London, he was a member of the bar until he went out to Ceylon in 1884. Mr. Beachcroft was succeeded by Mr. Rosling, who served until 1911, when Mr. G. C. Bliss became chairman.

MR. ALEXANDER WARDROP was the association's first full time secretary. He retired from planting to take up the post. Except for a short period in 1910, when Mr. H. North was acting, he held the office from 1907 to 1912. His genial disposition and keen sense of humor made him very popular, and his sudden death at the age of fifty-three, Kandy, 1912, came as a great shock to the planting community. A clock is installed in the Victoria Commemoration Buildings to his memory.

MR. GEORGE CECIL BLISS, J.P., F.R.C.I., chairman, 1911–13, was the third son of Dr. W. H. Bliss, D.S.C., of Magdalen College, Oxford. He was educated at Downside College, Bath, and went out to Ceylon in 1898 for the Ceylon Tea Plantations Company, Ltd. He was on Drayton, Kotagala; Atgalla, Gampola; Glenlyon, Agrapatna; and Wallaha, Lindula. At one

Mr. F. H. Layard
Chairman, 1913

Mr. Hew C. Kennedy
Chairman, 1914–16

Mr. J. Graeme Sinclair
Chairman, 1916–19

Mr. T. Y. Wright
Chairman, 1919–21

PLANTERS' ASSOCIATION OFFICERS, 1913–21

time he was chairman of the Pussellawa Planters' Association. He died at Wallaha in 1925.

MR. FRANK HENRY LAYARD, J.P., U.P.M., chairman in 1913, was born April 13, 1872. He was educated at Elizabeth College, Guernsey, and St. Anne's, Redhill; studied law at first, and in 1888 went out to Ceylon to start tea planting under the late Mr. William Gow, a founder of the firm of Gow, Wilson & Stanton. Under E. P. Willisford, on Hangranoya, Nawalapitiya, he planted Assam tea after removing the old coffee and cinchona. He was also on Blackwater, Galgoda, Penrith, Avisawella, and, finally, superintendent of Ganapalla, Yatiyantota. In 1903, he was one of the first to plant rubber over large areas in the Low Country. He was also chairman of the Thirty Committee of the Planters' Association. In 1914, he joined the Colombo agency firm of Gordon Frazer & Co., Ltd., and was presently director and inspector of estates until his retirement to Deerholme, Canford Cliffs, Bournemouth, Hants, in 1928, after forty years in Ceylon.

MR. JOHN STILL, who became secretary and treasurer of the Association in 1912, was born at Horningsham, Wiltshire, and educated at Winchester. He went to Ceylon as an archaeologist, transferred to the Land Settlement Department, and then took up planting, which he gave up when appointed secretary. At one time he was editor of the *Planting Gazette* and a director of the Peradeniya Chocolate Co., Ltd. He proceeded home for war service in 1914; was wounded and taken prisoner by the Turks; resumed his secretarial duties in 1919, and retired to "Walden," Pondtail Road, Fleet, Hampshire, in 1926. He

was secretary of the Ceylon Association in London in 1930–34. He is the author of *A Prisoner in Turkey, Poems in Captivity,* and *The Jungle Tide.* He visited the United States in 1931.

MR. HEW C. KENNEDY, planter and V.A., was chairman in 1914–16, and secretary part of this period. He was born at Castle Douglas, Scotland, October 3, 1875; went to Ceylon in 1893, and engaged in planting until the War broke out; served in France, whence he emerged as Major with a *Croix de Guerre.* He was secretary and chairman of the Maskeliya Planters' Association, 1902–14; returned to Ceylon in 1924, and was V.A. for Lipton Ltd., 1924–27; and in 1928, went to South India where he was for a time on Talliar Estate, High Range, Travancore.

MR. WILLIAM SINCLAIR was the Representative in Council during a part of Mr. Layard's administration and again during a part of Mr. Kennedy's 1915 term of office. He died in 1931.

Mr. Alex. Wardrop
1907–12

Mr. John Still
1912–14, 1919–26

SECRETARIES OF THE PLANTERS' ASSOCIATION OF CEYLON

Mr. H. D. Garrick
Chairman, 1921-23

Major J. W. Oldfield
Chairman, 1924-26

Mr. George Brown
Chairman, 1926-27

Mr. E. C. Villiers
Chairman, 1928-30

PLANTERS' ASSOCIATION OFFICERS, 1921-30

MR. R. HUYSHE ELIOT, planter and V.A., Norwood, was the Representative in Council in 1914 and in 1915-19. He died in 1920.

MR. J. GRAEME SINCLAIR, 1874-1924, chairman in 1916-19, was the son of the late Mr. James Sinclair of Balmoral Estate, Agrapatna, Dimbula, where he was born. He was educated at the Old Gymnasium in Aberdeen. Returning to Ceylon in 1892, he "crept" on Bearwell, Dimbula, with "Mattakelle" Smith, one of the finest planters of his day. His first assistant superintendent's billet was under Thomas Mackie, with whom he remained for two years. He then went to Mousa Ella, Lindula, from 1895 to 1901, and in the latter year took charge of Tillicoultry, Lindula. In 1918, he went to Bal-na-coil but returned to Tillicoultry a few weeks before his death.

Mr. Sinclair was manager in Ceylon for the Dimbula Valley (Ceylon) Tea Co., Ltd., from 1904, and for many years was a well-known V.A. He took an early interest in planting politics, and was chairman of the Dimbula Association, 1906-08. During his three years of office as chairman of the Planters' Association of Ceylon, he did much to restore the prestige of the parent body. He served as Representative in the Legislative Council in 1919, part of 1920, '21, and '22. Ill health compelled him to leave for home in 1920, but he returned to the island and his seat in the Legislative Council in 1921. That same year, he filled a temporary gap in the chairmanship of the Planters' Association, serving again in 1923. He was an officer of the European Association, of the Caledonian Society, member of the Nuwara

Eliya Board of Improvement, Justice of the Peace, and Unofficial Police Magistrate. He was also active in cricket, football, and golf.

MR. NIGEL I. LEE, solicitor, crown proctor, and secretary of the Kandy Hotels Co., Ltd., was acting secretary of the Association during the War period from 1915 to 1919, when Mr. Still returned to his secretarial duties.

MR. T. Y. WRIGHT, who became chairman in 1919 and again in 1920, was also the Representative in Council at various times during the succeeding five years. Mr. Wright was born in January, 1869, educated at the Edinburgh Academy and the College at Stratford-on-Avon, and went to Ceylon in 1889. He was in tea at Matale, at Galphele, Panwila, and manager of the Shakerley estate, Kurunegala. He was chairman of the Knuckles, Kelebokka, and Panwila Planters' Association for two years, and chairman of the Kurunegala Planters' Association for a like period. A keen volunteer, he joined the C.P.R.C. soon after his arrival in Ceylon, and served in the Boer War of 1900 with the Ceylon contingent; was officer commanding the C.P.R.C. for six years; was again put in command for a year during the World War, and is now on the Reserve with the rank of Lieutenant-Colonel. He has been an all-round sportsman, specially distinguishing himself in cricket, Rugby football, and polo.

In 1927, he joined the Colombo agency firm of Carson & Co., and in 1929, he was made a Life Member of the Planters' Association.

MR. H. D. GARRICK, chairman for a part of 1921, for the year 1922, and a part of

1923, is a planter, V.A., and manager of the Ukuwela Estates Co., Ltd. He was acting Representative in Council in 1927.

MAJOR J. W. OLDFIELD, C.M.G., O.B.E., M.C., became chairman in 1924, and was re-elected in 1925. Major Oldfield was born in Georgetown, British Guiana, October 22, 1886; went to Ceylon as a planter in 1907; was on Gallawatte, Agalawatte, and sometime chairman of the Kalutara Planters' Association. Major Oldfield had a distinguished career during the World War. He fought at the battle of Loos and the battle of the Somme, and he was gassed at Ypres. He was mentioned in despatches on six occasions and was awarded the M.C., O.B.E., Croix de Guerre, and was made a Chevalier of the Order of Leopold.

After the War he returned to Ceylon and identified himself to a greater extent with the planting, mercantile and political life of the country. In 1925, he became a director in the Colombo agency firm of Lee, Hedges & Co.; in 1926, he was vice-chairman of the Ceylon Estates Proprietary Association and was also nominated by His Majesty the King as the European unofficial member of the Governor's Executive Council. In 1932 he was elected vice-chairman of the Ceylon Chamber of Commerce and chairman of the Ceylon Tea Traders' Association. Recently he was made a Companion of the Order of St. Michael and St. George for his public services to Ceylon.

MR. CARR HAMOND, a tea planter whose Ceylon experience extends over thirty years, with intervening service in the Boer War and the World War, was acting secretary for a part of 1924.

MR. GEORGE BROWN, B.A. [Cantab.], J.P., U.P.M., planter and V.A., who was elected to succeed Mr. J. W. Oldfield as chairman in 1926, was born in Chilhampton, South Newton, Wilts, in 1876. He went to Ceylon in 1902, and "crept" under Mr. J. Rettie and Mr. H. Hoseason, two of the most prominent men in the Uva region at that time. He was secretary for two years, chairman of the Sabaragamuwa Planters' Association for two years, and had three years' service in the World War. In 1928, he was elected a member of the Legislative Council for the European Rural Electorate. In 1929, he retired to "Combe Manor," Hungerford, Berkshire.

MR. A. W. L. TURNER, planter, Old Bungalow, Mount Pleasant Estate, Pera-

Mr. B. M. Selwyn
Chairman

Mr. A. W. L. Turner
Secretary

PLANTERS' ASSOCIATION OFFICERS, 1933–34

deniya, was appointed assistant secretary to Mr. John Still in January, 1926, and succeeded him as secretary when Mr. Still retired in March of that year. Mr. Turner was born at Mansfield Woodhouse, Notts, and educated at Sedbergh, Yorkshire. He went to Ceylon in 1906 and held billets on estates in Pussellawa and Balangoda. He proceeded on war service in 1914, and was wounded at Gallipoli in 1915. Returning to Ceylon in 1919, he held planting billets in the Dimbula, Badulla, Pussellawa, and Nuwara Eliya districts. He gave up planting because of his war wounds and has been associated with the Planters' Association ever since.

MR. R. G. COOMBE, J.P., U.P.M., F.R.E.S., planter and V.A., Poonagalla Group, Bandarawela, was chairman for a part of 1927. Mr. Coombe is keenly interested in sport, especially lawn tennis, which he popularized in Ceylon. While chairman of the Tea Research Institute, Mr. Coombe ably directed the organization of a most important adjunct of the Planters' Association. He resigned in 1934.

MR. E. C. VILLIERS, J.P., U.P.M., manager, Hemingford Group, Parakaduwa, was elected chairman for 1928 and re-elected in 1929. He was born in 1880, went to Ceylon in 1909, and "crept" under the late Mr. James Duncan of Ury. He became an assistant to Mr. R. G. Coombe on Poonagalla; took charge of Keenagaha Ella, 1911–20, and became manager of the Hemingford Group in 1921. He was commissioner to the Ceylon Section of the British Empire Exhibition at Wembley in 1924.

MR. A. G. BAYNHAM, B.A., M.C., J.P.,

Mr. R. G. Coombe   Mr. R. V. Norris

THE PROPOSER AND THE DIRECTOR OF THE TEA
RESEARCH INSTITUTE OF CEYLON

U.P.M., planter of Darrawella, Dikoya, was vice-chairman in 1929, and was elected chairman of the Association in 1930, '31, and '32. He was previously both honorary secretary and chairman of the Dikoya Planters' Association. Mr. Baynham was born at Little Langford, Wilts, on May 28, 1887; educated at Charterhouse and Merton College, Oxford; went out to Derryclare, Kotagala, in 1910; and was superintendent of estates for the Anglo-Ceylon and General Estates Co., Ltd., 1912–34. In 1934 he was appointed secretary of the Ceylon Association in London.

MR. J. CARSON PARKER was elected vice-chairman in 1930, was followed in 1931 and '32 by Mr. F. H. Griffith, and in 1933–34 by Mr. Gordon Pyper.

MR. B. M. SELWYN, Udapolla, Dehiowita, who became chairman in 1933, was born February 20, 1886, in Stowmarket, Suffolk, and went out to Ceylon in 1904.

The Honorary Life Members of the Planters' Association of Ceylon are: C. G. Ryan, Esq.; Sir Edward Rosling; J. B. Coles, Esq.; Major H. Scoble Nicholson, O.B.E.; and Lt. Col. T. Y. Wright.

MAJOR H. SCOBLE NICHOLSON went to India as Ceylon Labor Commissioner in 1912. The class of labor Ceylon was getting at that time was distinctly bad, and the Government was threatening to close some of the Low Country estates. In the course of a few years recruiting improved greatly, and by 1927 as many as 170,000 Tamils came over in the twelve-month. Major Nicholson's organization was a fine piece of work, and his tact in dealing with high and low in India was a great asset. When he left, the Ceylon Labour Commission was acclaimed as one of the finest labor organizations in the world.

In addition to the Planters' Association of Ceylon, the following funds, etc., are administered from the Association office: Planters' Benevolent Fund, established 1894; Planters' Association Staff Provident Fund, 1920; Tea Research Institute of Ceylon, 1925; and Ceylon Planters' Provident Society, 1926. The Planters' Association held a Jubilee celebration in 1904.

The Tea Research Institute

In 1898, Mr. Montague Kelway Bamber, a chemist, was called upon to study the tea soils of the island, and from that time until his death, in a motor accident, at Gravesend in 1924, he worked on problems connected with the soil and the manufacture of tea. He was the author of *A Text Book on the Chemistry and Agriculture of Tea, Including the Growth and Manufacture,* and, with the late Mr. A. C. Kingsford, *A Report on the Tea Industries of Java, Formosa and Japan.* The scientific work begun by Mr. Bamber was continued in the form of cultivation and manuring experiments on tea plants by the Director of Agriculture at the Royal Botanic Gardens at Peradeniya, but this was done merely as incidental to the general experimental work in these world-famed gardens, and the Ceylon tea industry had to depend mainly on individual planter experience for its technical knowledge of tea cultivation and manufacture. This experience was slowly acquired, and its manifest deficiencies at length confronted the industry with problems that could only be solved by systematic scientific investigation.

Recognizing these facts, the plan, generally called the Ceylon Tea Research Scheme, proposed by Mr. R. G. Coombe and approved by the Planters' Association of Ceylon, was endorsed by the Ceylon Association in London in 1924. It provided for a tea experimental station under the management of a board styled the Board of the Tea Research Institute of Ceylon, and having chemist, mycologist, and entomologist technicians for factory investigations, as well as two traveling advisory officers. The plans, as originally adopted, involved the outlay of an estimated Rs. 90,000 [£6,750, Eng.; or $32,-000] annually by the tea industry, and a similar amount by the Government of Ceylon. This amounted to a tax of five Ceylon cents [$9/10$ of a penny; 1 $8/10$¢ U. S.] per 100 pounds of tea on the tea area, and an equal amount on the Government.

Originally on financial grounds, and subsequently for other reasons, the Ceylon Estates Proprietary Association was unable to give the matter its full support, so the Government finally withdrew its appropriation of Rs. 90,000 from the budget. It was then decided to abandon any idea of securing a grant from the Government in favor of having the entire expense borne by the tea industry. This involved a cess of 10 Ceylon cents per 100 pounds of tea with government coöperation for its collection. In 1930 the rate was increased to 14 cents.

Early in 1925, a referendum was taken in London and Ceylon, when it was found that representations of 378,572 acres were favorable, 8,668 acres against, and 17,000 acres indifferent; showing a percentage of 97.7 in favor of the proposal. The Tea Research Ordinance was passed by the Council on October 9, 1925, and on October 27, Ordinance No. 12 of 1925, to provide for the establishment of the Tea Research Institute and for the incorporation of its Board of Management, duly received the assent of His Excellency the Governor. The date of the imposition of the cess was announced by proclamation to commence on November 13, 1925.

The Board of twelve members is constituted as follows:

a. *Ex-officio Members*

The Director of Agriculture.

The Colonial Treasurer, or if he is unable to be present at any meeting of the Board, the Assistant Colonial Treasurer.

The Chairman of the Planters' Association of Ceylon.

The Chairman of the Ceylon Estates Proprietary Association.

b. *Nominated Members*

Three members nominated by the General Committee of the Planters' Association of Ceylon.

Three members nominated by the Ceylon Estates Proprietary Association.

One member nominated by the Low Country Products Association.

One member nominated by the Governor to represent small holders.

Nominated members hold office for three years, but may be renominated.

On March 8, 1926, Mr. T. Petch, B.A., B.Sc., the well-known botanist and mycol-

ogist, was appointed the first director of the Institute and was empowered to select his staff of assistants. He continued at the head of the Institute for three years until April 30, 1929, when he severed his connection therewith and was succeeded by R. V. Norris, D.Sc., F.I.C., previously agricultural chemist to the Government of Madras, Indian Agricultural Service, 1918–24, and professor of bio-chemistry, Indian Institute of Science, Bangalore, 1924–29.

The senior staff of the Institute in 1934 was as follows:

DIRECTOR—Roland V. Norris, D. Sc., M. Sc., F. I. C.

DEPARTMENT OF MYCOLOGY—Mycologist, C. H. Gadd, D. Sc. Assistant, C. A. Loos.

DEPARTMENT OF AGRICULTURAL CHEMISTRY—Agricultural Chemist, T. Eden, M. Sc., A. I. C. Research Assistant, C. A. de Silva, B. Sc., C. D. A. Assistant, E. N. Perera. Field Assistant, M. Piyasena.

DEPARTMENT OF BIOCHEMISTRY—Biochemist, Dr. Roland V. Norris. Tea Technologist, J. Lamb, M.Sc. Assistants, V. Mendis, E. L. Keegel, P. R. Perera.

DEPARTMENT OF ENTOMOLOGY—Entomologist, C. B. Redman King, M. A. Assistant Entomologist, G. D. Austin. Assistant, D. J. William. Field Assistants, W. T. Fonseka, K. H. M. Goonatillake.

DEPARTMENT OF PLANT PHYSIOLOGY—Plant Physiologist, F. R. Tubbs, M. Sc., D. I. C., A. R. C. S., F. L. S. Assistant, M. H. E. Koch. Field Assistants, F. H. Kehl and J. W. Reith.

SUPERINTENDENT, St. Coombs Estate, J. A. Rogers.

In the beginning, pending the acquisition of an estate on which to carry on the work of the Institute, a bungalow in Nuwara Eliya was taken over as a laboratory and office building; at the same time Director Petch visited the majority of the district planters' associations, and collected many valuable suggestions as to the relative importance of the problems awaiting investigation.

In order to avoid overlapping investigations already in progress at Peradeniya, it was decided that the Department of Agriculture should carry to completion the work it had in hand before the Institute was established, while the Institute was to undertake a wide range of new investigations connected with both the cultivation and manufacture of tea.

At the start, the work was conducted under rather trying conditions inasmuch as the Institute was in a purely temporary location, and this handicap placed a severe limitation on the scope of the investigations. However, a permanent home was secured in 1928, when the St. Coombs tea estate near Talawakelle, Dimbula district, was purchased from the Anglo and General Estates Co., Ltd., and the construction of a laboratory, bungalows, coolie lines, a model tea factory, and cart road extension was begun. The tea factory, which is electrically operated, was put in operation in October, 1929, and the final removal of the Institute from Nuwara Eliya to the St. Coombs Estate was effected late in 1930. The Estate consists of slightly over 423 acres, of which 165 are of tea in bearing, new clearings 74, and patana and swamp 184. It was purchased for Rs. 600,000. It is the idea to devote some 340 acres to commercial tea production.

It is planned to establish other experimental stations in different tea-growing districts, each of which will give attention to the problems of that district, but all cooperating to a common end—the promotion of quality Ceylon teas.

The Labor Problem

In 1904, the combined planting industries, as represented by the Planters' Association of Ceylon, established a Ceylon Labor Commissioner at Trichinopoly, in the heart of the Tamil districts of Southern India, to promote recruiting. Assistant Commissioners have been stationed in each of the surrounding districts to supervise sub-agencies. The plan has proven an unqualified success. It is now supported by approximately 75 per cent of the Ceylon estates, and forwards 95 per cent of the cooly emigration.

Formerly the *kanganies*, or native foremen, on the various estates were granted "coast advances" to finance the importation and establishment of a labor force, including the small sums necessary to pay off local debts and provide for dependents before the coolies left their native villages.

In 1921, the colony's Labor Ordinances were amended to abolish *tundus*, or discharges, covering wage advances to coolies, because the practice had been abused.

Since October, 1923, it has been required by law that the recruiter possess a license signed by the government of India and by the Ceylon Controller of Indian Immigrant Labor.

Other Men of Achievement

It would be an impossible task to tell something about all the tea men who have written their names high in Ceylon's Hall of Fame. However, there are some, in addition to those already mentioned, whose contributions to the industry have been such that it is only proper they should be referred to here, no matter how briefly. Arranged chronologically they are as follows:

1850–60.—Mr. George Shelton Anderson, the retired Dimbula planter, died 1922; Mr. Frederick Lewis, son of the coffee pioneer and author of *Sixty-four Years in Ceylon*, died at Colombo in 1930.

1860–70.—Mr. Hastings A. Clark, died 1925; Mr. Thomas Smith, known as "Tommy," died 1927, a well-known V.A., connected with Mackwood & Co.; Mr. Charles Peter Anderson, coffee and tea pioneer of the Upper Hewaheta district, died 1924; Mr. J. A. Spence, died in 1931.

Mr. JAMES SINCLAIR, planter and company promoter, who died in 1906, came out to Ceylon in 1867. After serving his apprenticeship as a coffee planter, he was one of the pioneers in the Agrapatna district in the early 'seventies. Before that he was in charge of Donside, Kotmale. He was a contemporary of Elphinstone and McLeod.

When the coffee disaster came, Mr. Sinclair had retired to Scotland but he returned at once to Ceylon and began planting cinchona. The venture was not a success, so he went to India to study tea culture. When he came back to the island in 1884, he converted the Bearwell estate, Telawakelle, into tea. Returning to London in the 'nineties he formed several successful Ceylon tea companies. In 1887, with Mr. H. Kerr Rutherford, he shared the distinction of initiating in Kandy the movement that resulted in the formation of the Ceylon Association in London. One son, the late Mr. J. Graeme Sinclair became chairman of the Planters' Association of Ceylon and another, Mr. D. Erroll Sinclair, president of the Ceylon Association in London.

Mr. A. T. RETTIE was one of a number who arrived in Ceylon in 1868 during the coffee boom, and who remained to achieve fame and fortune in tea. He retired in 1913, after forty-six years' continuous service, forty-one of which were with the

Mr. James Sinclair   Mr. A. T. Rettie   Mr. D. W. H. Skrine   Mr. H. Kerr Rutherford

CEYLON TEA PLANTING PIONEERS OF THE 'SIXTIES AND 'SEVENTIES

Spring Valley Ceylon Estates, Ltd. He not only opened several estates in tea, but converted Spring Valley from coffee to tea on its original capital. Spring Valley alone has this distinction. It was a remarkable task considering the geographical difficulties and hard times, but he was gifted with exceptional physique, character, and driving power. His son, Mr. Wilfred J. Rettie, succeeded to the management of the Spring Valley properties.

Mr. E. G. HARDING, a contemporary of the late Mr. H. S. Saunders, and now living in retirement at Hammersmith, went out to Ceylon in 1869. He began his planting career as an assistant on the Great Valley Coffee Estate in Hewaheta. He learned about tea from the great father of tea culture in Ceylon, the late Mr. James Taylor of Loolecondera. Mr. Harding delights to tell how he was wont to visit Mr. Taylor on Sundays. "The factory," says Mr. Harding, "was in the bungalow. The leaf was rolled on tables on the veranda by hand, *i. e.*, from wrists to elbow, while the firing was done in *chulas*, or clay stoves, over charcoal fires, with wire trays to hold the leaf. The result was a delicious tea which we bought up locally at R. 1/30 a pound."

Mr. L. G. PILKINGTON, another survivor of the coffee era, went to Ceylon in 1869. He opened the famous Mariawatte tea estate in Gampola which yielded 1300 lbs. of made tea per acre for eleven years in succession. Mr. Pilkington is now in retirement in Sussex.

1870-80.—Mr. James Duncan, late of the Ury Group, Badulla, died 1927; Mr. John Rettie, the Uva planter and brother of Mr. A. T. Rettie, died 1914; Mr. North Couper Davidson, died 1921;

Mr. Thomas James Jebb, died 1921; Mr. G. D. Jamieson, after 50 years in Ceylon, died at Lunugala in 1923; Mr. George Kent Deaker, planting politician, chairman Passara Planters' Association, 1896-97, died 1924; Mr. J. McCombie Murray, who was later associated with Mr. R. E. Pineo, another Ceylon planter, in the introduction of the first packet Ceylon tea in America, died 1928; Mr. Alexander Louis Kirk, three years chairman of the Haputale Planters' Association, died 1927; Mr. Gilbert F. Traill, planter, partner in the Colombo agency firm of Bosanquet & Co., and V.A., died 1927; Mr. T. G. Hayes, died 1928; Mr. Duncan W. H. Skrine, coffee and tea planter who founded the Colombo agency firm of Skrine & Co., died 1928; Mr. John Helps Starey, who transformed the coffee lands of the Worms Bros. into smiling sheets of tea, died 1928; Mr. John J. Robinson, an unrivaled *shikari*, died 1929; Mr. William Stewart Taylor, one time chairman of the Passara Planters' Association, died 1929; Mr. Robert Farquhar Spottiswood Hardie, planter and former partner in the Colombo agency firm of Leechman & Co., died 1930; Mr. William Hall, died 1930; Mr. H. G. Maddock, Dehiwala, retired; Mr. C. W. Ross Wright, died 1931. Mr. Alexander Forbes, Badulla, died 1931. Mr. A. M. Forbes, Telawakelle, died 1932.

Mr. KEITH ROLLO was another who figured in the making over of Ceylon's coffee lands into tea. He arrived in 1870, while coffee was still king, and started planting on Ingurugalla, Aranayake. He was with the Norwood Estate for a long time, and then went to Wanarajah, Dikoya, which was planted in tea later than most estates in that district. He retired

Mr. Norman W. Grieve　　　Mr. Joseph Fraser　　　Sir Theodore Charles Owen　　　Sir L. F. W. Davidson

CEYLON TEA PIONEERS OF THE 'SEVENTIES

from the latter in 1908, and settled at Oakley Cottage in Nuwara Eliya. He inherited the Rollo estates from his brother in 1905. When the author visited Ceylon in 1924, and renewed an acquaintanceship of some eighteen years, he found that, in addition to being the dean of the pioneer planters, Keith Rollo had come to be known as the "Laird of Nuwara Eliya." He died in 1926.

Mr. H. Kerr Rutherford is one of Ceylon's tea pioneers who has figured in the island's affairs at home as well as out East. Mr. Rutherford first went to Ceylon in 1871, though his association with tea did not begin until 1876. He was a civil engineer, in England and in India, previous to his railway and road building work in Ceylon. He started in tea with Weyangawatte—now Mariawatte—an abandoned coffee estate near Gampola. He later converted many old coffee areas into valuable tea properties. He was the first chairman of the Kelani Valley Planters' Association. In 1887, Mr. Rutherford published his *Ceylon Planters Note Book* which went into nine editions. It was at his suggestion that the Ceylon Association in London was formed. He returned to London in 1889, where he assumed the chairmanship of several important Ceylon tea concerns which had been developed under his direction.

At the annual meeting of the Ceylon Association in London, in 1926, when he had conferred upon him an honorary life membership, Mr. G. H. Masefield, the president, recalled that Mr. Rutherford had served the Association as vice-president or president for no less than eight years, after which he had been a member of every council and committee of the Association.

Mr. Norman William Grieve, born in 1852, went out to Ceylon in 1871, and has been closely associated since then with coffee, cinchona, tea, and rubber. He was engaged by the official liquidator of the Oriental Bank in developing numerous Ceylon estates which the bank had to take over after the stoppage of coffee. These estates having been converted into tea were eventually sold to different companies. Mr. Grieve is a past president of the Ceylon Association in London [1906–08] and was made an honorary life member in 1926.

Mr. Joseph Fraser was one of the pioneers in cinchona, tea, and rubber. He was born in 1852, and arrived in Ceylon in 1872. He learned coffee planting on Pitakanda Estate, Matale. He then went to Udahena Estate, Haputale, where he stayed for about four years, after which he returned to Pitakanda as manager, remaining there until shortly before his death at Banffshire, N.B., in August, 1914.

He was one of the first, if not the first, to experiment with artificial manures on tea; this was about the year 1895. His ideas met with a tremendous lot of opposition because planters and proprietors were afraid of the industry suffering from over-production, and at the time of the slump in 1899, 1900, and 1901 he was blamed for having caused over-production with his artificial manure. He gradually persuaded the proprietors of the tea estates, of which he was the visiting agent, to adopt his methods, however, and it can be said now that on all well cared for tea estates—and for that matter, rubber estates as well—artificial manuring is included in the year's program. Although the methods of application and the ingredients of the manures have been varied, there is no doubt that Ceylon would to-day have been much behind other tropical countries if the late Mr. Joseph Fraser had not persisted in his opinion that artificial manure was absolutely necessary. He became the leading visiting agent and authority on cultivation, and his ideas have proved to be sounder and more practical than those of many of the so-called experts.

Sir Theodore Charles Owen, whose death in 1926 robbed Ceylon tea of a man who had the best interests of the industry at heart, went out to Ceylon in 1872 to plant coffee, but the failure of the coffee industry made him turn his attention to tea. After opening several districts in tea cultivation, he wrote a book, *Tea Planting in Ceylon*. He remained in Ceylon until 1894, when he returned to London to become a partner in the firm of Rowe, White & Co. He was chairman of the Ceylon Association in London, 1920–24 inclusive, and was knighted for his services as commissioner for the Ceylon government at the Wembley Exhibition.

Mr. P. R. Shand, the veteran proprietary planter of Coolbawn, Nawalapitiya, started in 1873 as assistant to Mr. James Taylor on Loolecondera, four years after the first field of Ceylon tea was planted. He was in time to take part in the second pruning of the original tea field, now known as "Loolecondera No. 7," which is still flourishing. Mr. Shand died in 1933.

Mr. [later Sir] Leybourne Francis Watson Davidson, who knew all the vicissitudes of the transition period from coffee to tea, was born at Dean Park, Midlothian, in 1859. He was educated at George Watson's College, Edinburgh, and worked at engineering for three years before he went out to Ceylon as a planter in 1876. In 1877, he planted 130 acres of tea on the Carolina Estate. Since then he has been responsible for planting some 50,000 acres of tea in Ceylon and Southern India. He said, in 1929, that when he arrived on the island there were 300,000 acres of coffee, all doomed to perish from the leaf disease: "I well remember the Dimbula district with its 50,000 acres one sheet of white blossoms; the whole of this is now

very fine tea." He died at Worthing, Sussex, in June, 1934.

Mr. A. J. Denison has been connected with the Ceylon tea industry since 1879, when he went to Ceylon as manager of the Wangie Oya Estate in Dimbula. He, too, was a participant in the miraculous transformation from coffee to tea. During a period of twenty years in tea planting, Mr. Denison was an active worker in the Dimbula District Planters' Association, serving for a time as chairman. In 1899, he joined the firm of Cumberbatch & Co., estate agents in Colombo, where he remained until 1914, when he retired. He was president of the Ceylon Association in London in 1927.

1880–90.—Mr. B. A. Starling, died 1921; Mr. Charles Montagu Buckworth, died 1927; Mr. David Lyall, died 1928; Lieutenant-Colonel Forbes Griffith Saunder, died 1928; Captain Percy Penrose Miers, died 1929; Mr. C. C. Wilson, died 1930; Mr. T. W. B. Crowther, died 1930; Mr. S. P. Blackmore, died 1930; Mr. F. E. Waring, retired in 1934.

Mr. H. A. Webb, pioneer tea planter, is half-owner and superintendent of Hindugalla Estate near Peradeniya. For many years he has been active in the councils of the Planters' Association of Ceylon. Mr. Webb was born in England in 1858, and was educated at Winchester College. He began work with W. J. & Henry Thompson Sons, London tea brokers, and in 1880 went to Assam in the employment of the Noakacharee Tea Co., with which he remained for three years. He then moved to Ceylon, and in 1884 joined his brother as half-partner on Hindugalla. He has been a member of the Planters' Associa-

Mr. H. A. Webb   Mr. Alex. J. Ingram

Tea Pioneers of the 'Eighties and 'Nineties

tion since 1884, and has been on its general committee for many years.

1890-1900.—Mr. D. B. Williamson, died 1923; Mr. H. O. Hoseason, a contemporary of the Retties in Badulla; Mr. Edward S. Grigson, of George Steuart & Co., and Mr. Edward J. Young, J.P., U.P.M., proprietary planter, well-known V.A.'s; Mr. A. J. Ingram, the retired manager of the Pelmadulla Group, Kahawatta, identified with tea growing in Ceylon for thirty-eight years; Mr. Walter Sutherland Ross, died 1926; Mr. G. Thain Davidson, died 1927; Mr. A. E. Ogilvy, died 1928; Mr. H. M. Drummond Hay, died in 1932.

MR. G. H. MASEFIELD, who was elected president of the Ceylon Association in London for 1925 and 1926, is a former Ceylon tea planter. He went out to the island as a "creeper" under Mr. W. A. M. Denison on Kintyre Estate, Maskeliya, in February, 1897; joined Nuwara Eliya Tea Estates Co., Ltd., in December, 1897; was assistant on Portswood and Concordia, in 1898-1900; had acting charge of Park and Pedro Estates, 1901; joined Ceylon Tea Plantations Co., Ltd., 1902, as superintendent of Dewalakande; in 1910, was appointed general manager in Ceylon of the Ceylon Tea Plantations Co., Ltd., Ceylon Proprietary Tea Estates Co., Ltd., Central Tea Company of Ceylon, Ltd., and the Digalla Co. Mr. Masefield retired from Ceylon in March, 1921, having completed twenty-five years in the colony. During this time he had served for twelve years on the committee of the Planters' Association of Ceylon, 1910-21. He joined the council of the Ceylon Association in London and four years later he became chairman. He is active also in the South Indian Association in London, and has been a member of its committee for years.

1900-10.—Mr. Joseph Ambrose Magoris, formerly a planter and afterwards with the Colombo brokerage house of E. John & Co., died 1926; Mr. G. L. H. Doudney, Lipton's agent in Ceylon, who began planting in 1910.

THE FERGUSONS.—The name Ferguson has been associated with Ceylon coffee and tea for nearly a hundred years, but it is best known because of its journalistic rather than of its planting connotation. Mr. A. M. Ferguson, who died in 1892, went out to Ceylon in 1837. He planted coffee, and later tea, on Abbotsford, Dim-

bula, and in 1846 became co-editor, with Dr. Christopher Elliott, of the *Ceylon Observer*, originally the *Colombo Observer*. This publication was started in 1834 as a weekly broadsheet by the Colombo merchants under the control of one of them, Mr. E. J. Darley, of Darley, Butler & Co. Mr. A. M. Ferguson's nephew, the late John Ferguson, who died in 1913, went out in 1861 and joined him on the *Observer* in 1870. In 1881, Mr. John Ferguson started the *Tropical Agriculturist*, now published by the Department of Agriculture at Peradeniya.

THE CAPPERS.—Messrs. H. H. and Frank Capper, who had engaged in coffee planting, joined their father, Mr. John Capper, originally a Colombo merchant, in the business of publishing *The Times of Ceylon*, in the 'eighties. The elder Capper had acquired the paper in 1858. It was established in 1846 by Mr. Hugh Stuart. It is the oldest daily newspaper on the island and has actively promoted the tea industry since its inception.

Later Years of the Industry

Black tea, only, was manufactured in Ceylon at first, but in 1895, Mr. William Mackenzie, Ceylon tea commissioner to the United States, advised his principals that the Americans were, at that time, green tea drinkers; so, in 1899, the manufacture of green tea was begun under the stimulus of a 10 Ceylon-cent bonus [1¾ pence Eng.; 3½¢ U. S.] for each pound exported. The bonus was paid over a period of six years, up to and including 1904. The idea was to bring the price of green teas on a parity with black, although black tea prices went so low that it is probable that green tea would have been made without any bonus, as it has been ever since, though in constantly decreasing quantities.

About the year 1900, a heavy overproduction, coupled with poor storage facilities, put a stop to tea planting in Ceylon, and it was not recommenced until after 1906. In 1920-21, the second crisis of the present century was caused by overproduction of lower grade teas and lack of storage accommodations.

To the planters of Ceylon the credit is due of having been the first to realize that the modern consumer demand was turning largely to good tea, and they have given a

IN THE MASKELIYA DISTRICT WHICH CONTAINS MANY OF CEYLON'S PIONEER TEA ESTATES

In the distance may be seen Adam's Peak, on whose summit is the mark which legend says is the impress of a gigantic human foot, variously assigned to Gautama, Siva, and Adam.

most useful lead to the whole industry in that respect. Following the slump of 1920–21, it was decided that only fine teas of high quality would be likely to meet with a ready market. A general policy of finer plucking and most careful manufacture was then adopted. Again, in 1929, ever increasing stocks and falling prices brought about an agreement between the growers of India, Ceylon, Java, and Sumatra teas for a reduction of the 1930 crop amounting to a total of 57,000,000 lbs. In accordance with the system of grading used in the Ceylon tea gardens, the restriction amounted to 15 per cent on teas selling below an average of 1s. 5d. per pound, London, in 1926–28; 10 per cent on teas selling at 1s. 5d. to 1s. 7d. per pound; 5 per cent on teas selling at 1s. 7d. to 1s. 9d.; and 3 per cent on teas selling over 1s. 9d. The prices were based on the average for the grades. The plan was a failure and was not renewed in 1931.

Continued overproduction brought about regulation of tea exports. The initiative was taken by the tea committee of the British Chamber of Commerce for the N.E.I. in London. British India and Ceylon joined the Dutch in a five-year plan, providing for a 15 per cent reduction in tea exports in 1933, and suitable reductions for succeeding years.

The Ceylon Estates Proprietary Association

Since the close of the nineteenth century, many Ceylon tea estates have been transferred from private ownership to limited liability companies whose affairs are handled through estate agents, as in India. The proprietary interests in the Planters' Association joined with the estate agents and on August 5, 1921, formed the Ceylon Estates Proprietary Association.

The 1932 membership included 554 proprietors, representing a cultivated area of 641,925 acres, as follows: tea, 375,504; rubber, 243,100; sundry products, 23,321. Its objects are to promote the common interests of all persons concerned in the cultivation of tea, rubber, and other agri-

Sir T. L. Villiers
Chairman, 1922

Mr. G. Turnbull
Chairman, 1922–23

Mr. Clifford H. Figg
Chairman, 1923–24

Mr. C. S. Burns
Chairman, 1924

OFFICERS OF THE CEYLON ESTATES PROPRIETARY ASSOCIATION, 1922–24

cultural products in Ceylon. Proprietors of, and agents for, estates of not less than fifty acres in extent are eligible.

The first chairman of the Ceylon Estates proprietary Association was Mr. C. M. Gordon, of George Steuart & Co., who served from May to October, 1921. He was succeeded by Mr. Edgar Turner, of George Steuart & Co., who, in February, 1922, was succeeded by Mr. Thomas L. Villiers also of George Steuart & Co. Mr. Villiers was succeeded in 1922 by Mr. G. Turnbull, of James Finlay & Co., Ltd., Mr. Villiers becoming vice-chairman. Mr. Herbert Bois, of J. M. Robertson & Co., was chairman from May to August, 1923. From August, 1923, to April, 1924, Mr. C. H. Figg, of Whittall & Co., was chairman, and Mr. M. J. Cary was vice-chairman.

Mr. C. S. Burns, of Lee, Hedges & Co., Ltd., became chairman from April to December, 1924, when Mr. G. C. Slater, of Bois Bros. & Co., Ltd., was elected and served two terms until 1926. During his first term Mr. R. F. Battams of the Eastern Produce & Estates Co., Ltd., was vice-chairman and during his second term, Mr. H. F. Parfitt of Mackwoods, Ltd., held this office part of the time, succeeding Mr. Slater as chairman in April, 1926, and serving until October, 1926.

In October, 1926, Mr. W. Coombe was elected chairman and served in that capacity until April, 1930. Mr. J. W. Oldfield, of Lee, Hedges & Co., Ltd., was vice-chairman for 1926 and 1929 and Mr. Herbert Bois of J. M. Roberston & Co., was vice-chairman for the 1927 term. Mr. Coombe resigned the chairmanship on April 10, 1930, and Mr. F. F. Roe, of Gordon Frazer & Co., Ltd., was appointed

chairman to fill out the unexpired term. Major H. Scoble Nicholson became vice-chairman in 1930. Mr. Roe was elected chairman for 1930–31, and was succeeded by Mr. G. K. Stewart in 1931–33. Mr. C. E. Hawes, who was vice-chairman in 1931–33, became chairman in 1933, with Mr. L. G. Byatt as vice-chairman.

The honorary secretaries have been as follows: Mr. W. G. Beauchamp, 1921–22; Mr. H. W. Urquhart, 1922–24; Mr. C. L. Carson Parker, 1924–26; Mr. W. D. Morton, 1926–28; Mr. C. A. Meakin, 1928–30; Mr. W. D. Morton, 1930–33. Mr. E. E. Spencer became Honorary Secretary in 1933.

MR. C. M. GORDON, first chairman of the Association died in retirement at Buchromb, Dufftown, Banffshire in 1932. MR. EDGAR TURNER, the second chairman, has retired to Walberswick, Southwold, Suffolk.

SIR THOMAS L. VILLIERS, M.L.C., J.P., U.P.M., the third chairman, has been president of the European Association in Ceylon, representative of the Fort Ward in the Colombo Municipal Council, chairman of the Estate Agents Association, European urban member of the former Legislative Council of Ceylon, nominated member of the State Council, and chairman of the Ceylon Chamber of Commerce. He went to the island in 1887, and "crept" on Elbedde, Dikoya, under Mr. Alfred Tabor; later on Tillyrie, Bogawantalawa, and with the Ceylon Tea Plantations Co., Ltd., for nine years, taking charge of Scrubbs Estate, Nuwara Eliya, in 1893, and Yoxford, Dimbula, in 1895. Subsequently, he went to Brazil, where he took charge of the Dumont Coffee Company; but returned to Ceylon in 1897. He planted in Pussellawa

Mr. G. C. Slater
Chairman, 1924–26
    Mr. W. Coombe
Chairman, 1926–30
    Mr. F. F. Roe
Chairman, 1930–31
    Mr. G. K. Stewart
Chairman, 1931–33

OFFICERS OF THE CEYLON ESTATES PROPRIETARY ASSOCIATION, 1924–33

for two years and, in 1905, joined George Steuart & Co., becoming a partner the following year. He was knighted in 1933.

MR. GEORGE TURNBULL, the fourth chairman, planted in Southern India before going to Colombo to take charge of the office of James Finlay & Co., in 1917.

MR. CHARLES STEWART BURNS, seventh chairman, planted in Ceylon from 1897 to 1903. He died in 1931.

MR. WILLIAM COOMBE, J.P., U.P.M., chairman of the Association for 1926–29, inclusive, who is also a director of Carson & Co., Ltd., Colombo, has been active in Ceylon tea planting for thirty-seven years. Born at Tillingham, Essex, England, July 20, 1877, he went out to Ceylon as a "creeper" under his brother, Mr. R. G. Coombe, in December, 1896. He followed planting actively until 1911, when he became a visiting agent, and in 1919 joined Carson & Co., Ltd. In addition, he is on the boards of sixteen Ceylon tea producing companies.

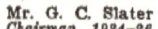

MR. C. E. HAWES has seen war service in the Transvaal, Gallipoli, France, and Belgium. He first planted tea in Ceylon in 1913, returning in 1919. In 1929–31 he was a member of the Executive and Legislative Councils. He was admitted as a partner in Whittall & Co., 1931. He was born in Chichester, Sussex, England, February 9, 1878.

Mr. C. E. Hawes

MR. FRANK FREEMAN ROE was born in London, September 23, 1888. He joined Gordon Frazer & Co., Ltd., Colombo, in 1909.

Some Pioneer Tea Companies

Among the pioneer Ceylon tea enterprises which date back from thirty to sixty-five years and which have continued under the original or new proprietorship to the present day, mention should be made of the following, the names being arranged chronologically as to dates of registry:

1865.—Spring Valley Ceylon Estates, Ltd.
1878.—Scottish Tea and Lands Co. of Ceylon, Ltd.
1880.—Lanka Plantations Co., Ltd.
1884.—Ceylon Land & Produce Co., Ltd.; Hunasgeria Tea Co., Ltd.
1885.—Ceylon Estates Investment Association, Ltd.
1886.—Anglo-Ceylon & General Estates Co., Ltd.; Ceylon Tea Plantations Co., Ltd.
1887.—Talgaswela Tea Company of Ceylon, Ltd.
1888.—Eastern Produce and Estates Co., Ltd.
1889.—Battalgala Estate Co., Ltd.; Scottish Ceylon Tea Co., Ltd.
1891.—United Planters' Co. of Ceylon, Ltd.
1892.—Carolina Tea Co. of Ceylon, Ltd.
1893.—Great Western Tea Co. of Ceylon, Ltd.
1895.—Alliance Tea Company of Ceylon, Ltd.; East India and Ceylon Tea Co., Ltd.; Nuwara Eliya Tea Estates Co., Ltd.; Vogan Tea Co. of Ceylon, Ltd.
1897.—Ceylon & Indian Planters' Association, Ltd.; Ceylon Proprietary Tea Estates Co., Ltd.; Tea Corporation (1921), Ltd.
1898.—Rajawella Produce Co., Ltd.

In addition to the above named companies, some of the pioneer tea estates which are now privately owned are: Abbotsford Estate, owned by Mrs. A. M. Ferguson; Hindugalla and Shrubs Hill Estates, owned by E. & H. A. Webb; Tamaravelly Group, incl. Tamaravelly, Wevelkelle, Eplawatte, Gonawatte, and Nartakande tea estates, owned by Mr. and Mrs. E. H. Simpson.

GENERAL VIEW OF THE FORMER IMPERIAL DOMAIN TEA ESTATE AT CHAKVA, ABOUT 1900

Since Transcaucasian Georgia became sovietized, this plantation has been the center of production and management for the people's special corporation *Chai-Gruzia*, or Tea Georgia, Ltd.

RUSSIAN PEASANTS PICKING TEA BY THE CEYLON SYSTEM UNDER CHINESE DIRECTION

This tea, planted on the hills of the former Imperial appanage at Chakva, fifteen miles from Batoum, is now under Soviet ownership and management.

RUSSIAN TEA CULTIVATION DURING THE CZARIST RÉGIME

CHAPTER XI

TEA PROPAGATION IN OTHER LANDS

Tea Growing Experiments in Sweden, England, and France—History of Propagation in the Russian Transcaucasus, Formosa, French Indo-China, Siam, Burma, British Malaya, and Persia—Cultivation in Africa, Including Natal, Nyasaland, Abyssinia, Rhodesia, Uganda, and Kenya—American Experiments in British Columbia, the United States, Mexico, Brazil, Paraguay, Argentina, and Colombia —Minor Cultivations in Australia and Various Islands, Including Borneo, Mauritius, Fiji, Puerto Rico, Cayenne, and Jamaica

IN ADDITION to the major transplantations of the tea bush from China to Japan, Java, India, Ceylon, and Sumatra it has been introduced and is cultivated on a commercial scale in Formosa, French Indo-China, Russian Transcaucasia, Natal, Nyasaland, Kenya, and Uganda. Minor cultivations exist in Siam and Burma, and the plant is grown in British Malaya, Persia, Portuguese East Africa, Rhodesia, and the Azores. Experimental cultivations in the Eastern Hemisphere have been attempted in Sweden, England, France, Italy, Bulgaria and, more recently, in the Cameroons, Abyssinia, and Tanganyika Territory.

On the continents of the Western Hemisphere, experiments have been conducted in the United States, British Columbia, Mexico, Guatemala, Colombia, Brazil, Peru, Chile, Paraguay, and Argentina. The islands where attempts have been made to grow tea include Borneo, the Philippines, Fiji, and Mauritius in the Eastern, and Jamaica, Cayenne, and Puerto Rico in the Western Hemisphere.

European Attempts

Numerous attempts have been made to grow tea in Europe, but nearly all of them were failures.

SWEDEN.—The earliest experimental success was achieved by Linnaeus—Charles or Carl von Linne—1707–1778, the distinguished Swedish botanist, who first classified tea in 1737. At the request of Linnaeus, Peter Osbeck, another Swedish naturalist, then chaplain on a vessel belonging to the French Compagnie des Indies, secured in China a magnificent specimen of the tea bush. This he hoped to carry back to Sweden, but when in sight of the Cape of Good Hope a sudden squall blew the tree overboard. The incident recalls the vicissitudes attending the transportation of the first coffee plant from France to Martinique.

Later, under the patronage of Magnus von Lagerstrom, a Swedish savant and a director of the East India Company, two China plants were safely transported to Upsal, Sweden. After being carefully tended for a year or so, it was discovered that the plants were camellias. Some time afterward, a true tea bush which had been brought as far as Goteborg, was destroyed by rats in the room of the commandant, shortly after its arrival. Linnaeus, undeterred by these failures, engaged Captain Eckburg, then in the China trade, for another attempt. The captain, before leaving China, planted seeds in an earth-filled pot to allow them to germinate during the voyage. All were well up when the ship reached Goteborg. Captain Eckburg immediately sent half of them to Upsal, but they perished in transit. The other half he carried there himself, and on October 3, 1763, delivered at Upsal the first growing tea plants in Europe.

About this time, the French Academy of Sciences concluded that the tea bush was so peculiar to China it could not be raised elsewhere, but Linnaeus, addressing them from Upsal, reported he had "in his garden a stalk of this tree, very much alive"; that he "was trying to multiply it," and concluding that "the plant did not appear any more susceptible to the cold than a great number of others that grow in our climate, like the syringa."

ENGLAND.—In 1763, the same year that Linnaeus succeeded in bringing growing plants to Sweden, English botanists successfully transported to England a number of plants which had been raised from seed aboard ship from Canton. Especial care had been taken during the voyage—fresh water and protection from the sun, wind, and salt spray having been provided. Those that survived were not put to commercial uses, but were utilized as greenhouse specimens or for ornamental purposes about lawns or gardens during the summer season. The first tea to flower in England was at Sion, the seat of the Duke of Northumberland.

FRANCE.—Some years before the Revolution of 1793, a London nurseryman, Gordon, sent to M. le Chevalier de Janssen in Paris a growing tea plant—the first in France. Shortly afterward, the Duc de Cossi acquired a tea plant. In 1838, M. Guillemin, botanical aide at the Museum National d'Histoire Naturelle, Paris, was sent by the Minister of Agriculture and Commerce to Brazil, where tea cultivation had been introduced a quarter of a century earlier, to bring back three thousand tea plants. Less than half of these survived but they received careful attention at the *Jardin des Plantes*. Experimental attempts made to acclimatize the tea tree in the environs of Saumur and Angers demonstrated the possibilities of raising it in the open air, but the yield of leaf was too light to give any promise of commercial success.

RUSSIAN TRANSCAUCASIA.—Next in order of time, but certainly first in order of importance was the introduction of the tea plant into Russian Transcaucasia. This has been the only introduction into Europe that ever reached commercial proportions. Tea was first planted experimentally in the Botanical Gardens of Sukhum, a Black Sea port, in 1847, at the instance of the Viceroy of the Caucasus, Vorontzoff. From

that date until the 'nineties, Russian agriculturists conducted further experimental cultivation on their own lands until successful tea production was demonstrated. Since 1893, when cultivation on a commercial scale was begun, it has become one of the most important sources of wealth in Transcaucasia.

A pioneer in the Russian experimental cultivation work was Colonel A. Solovtzoff, who, in 1884, planted about five and a half acres of tea with seedlings from China; but the father of tea production on a commercial scale was the late Mr. C. S. Popoff, president of the tea trading firm of C. & S. Popoff Freres. Mr. Popoff purchased three estates on the eastern shore of the Black Sea, near Batoum, and set out nurseries preparatory to opening them in tea. In 1893, he planted 385 acres with seedlings from his own nurseries and with others brought from China. Later on, he successfully planted seedlings grown from seeds brought from India and Ceylon by M. Klingen and Prof. Krasnoff. Mr. Popoff imported fifteen Chinese foremen and laborers to work the estates, and teach the natives this new industry. In 1896, he installed tea making machinery including withering racks, leaf rollers, roll-breakers, firing machines, and sorting and packing machines. The enterprise soon was established on a commercial basis to supply teas for the Russian market.

Following Mr. Popoff's lead the management of the crown lands at Chakva prepared and planted 600 acres of the crown estate in tea, and in 1900 the Ministry of Agriculture established a tea experimental station, which later supplied local landowners with seedlings free of charge.

As a result of the promotional measures of the government, great interest was aroused and many of the present cultivations were started. In 1905, the area under tea had been increased to approximately 1125 acres on forty estates, and by 1913, the prewar year, there were 2400 acres on a total of 147 estates.

In 1900, some twenty-five experimental fields of tea were planted in the Kutais area, an interior district north of Batoum. After six years' experience in these fields, many private owners in Mingrelia and Gouria made small plantings, averaging from one and a half to two acres each, and in 1913–14 many of the peasants began to cultivate patches on land leased from the

EARLY FORMOSA TEA CULTURE UNDER CHINESE DOMINATION—ABOUT 1895

villages, the average harvest amounting to 170 to 200 pounds an acre.

The World War seriously disrupted the Transcaucasian tea industry, not only because of the disturbance of communications to which all tea countries were subjected, but because the warring forces of Turks, Mensheviks, British, and finally the Soviets, surged across Batoum, making a battle ground of the tea area. During the control of the Mensheviks, 1917-1921, the cultivation dropped to 150 desiatins [405 acres], although in a brief interim of British occupation a British officer was detailed to take charge of and rehabilitate the estate and factory at Chakva, fifteen miles from Batoum. However, since Georgia became a part of the Union of Socialist Soviet Republics in 1923, the State has developed the available tea area from 1000 hectares [2470 acres] to 34,000 hectares [84,000 acres] in 1933. Tea experimental stations have been established at Chakva, Sukhum, Ozurgeti, and Zugdidi.

ITALY.—Tea has been cultivated in only two other countries of Europe—Italy and Bulgaria. In neither has it passed the experimental stage. In Italy, tea has been grown in the botanical gardens of Pavia, Florence, Pisa, and Naples. It has been grown outdoors the whole year around in the Borromean Islands of Lake Maggiore, and on the island of Sicily. In one case of experimental planting, on an estate in the commune of Bagni di San Giuliano, province of Pisa, all the plants produced flowers and seeds.

BULGARIA.—Tea plants were brought recently to Bulgaria from Russia, and planted out near Philippopolis. These have done well, and a large scale production is being projected.

Asiatic Propagation

FORMOSA.—The tea industry of Formosa —now *Taiwan*—is relatively modern as compared with China and Japan. Although tea cultivation there dates only from the early part of the nineteenth century, there is some belief that tea is indigenous to the island; a belief based upon the discovery of wild tea plants found growing at elevations of 2500 feet in the central and southern provinces of Taichu, Tainan, and Takao.

The Chinese emigrants to Formosa, who by the end of the seventeenth century had expelled the early Dutch settlers and taken possession of a large part of the island, obtained their first supplies of tea from Fukien, in nearby China. About 1810, Chinese merchants from Amoy introduced tea cultivation. They soon discovered that leaf produced on the island, especially leaf from which Oolong is made, possessed unique quality and flavor. It was not, however, until 1868 that tea propagation on a commercial scale was begun. Three principal kinds of tea are manufactured in Formosa—the well-known semi-fermented Oolong, the new three-quarters-fermented Oolong, and flower scented Pouchong. Small quantities of black and green teas also are produced.

In 1868, expert Chinese tea manufacturers were brought to the island from Amoy, and intensive Oolong production was begun. Since then, production of the different kinds has gradually increased until to-day there are approximately 112,000 acres under tea, and the total annual output is close to 24,000,000 lbs.

Pouchong tea manufacture in Formosa was started in 1881 by a Chinese tea merchant from Fukien, named Ngo Fok Ro, who found its production in China unprofitable.

Black tea was first manufactured in Formosa some thirty years ago. Mitsui & Co., Ltd., are the pioneers of its production on a scale of any importance. The Japanese Government is encouraging the manufacture of black tea for consumption in Japan where a surprising demand for India and Ceylon tea developed. Samples of Formosa black were sent to London, New York, and other markets in 1928. During 1929, about 10,000 chests were manufactured by Mitsui & Co., Ltd., and exported, principally to the London market, but also to United States, Australia, and Japan. Manufacture has been progressively increased each year since.

The process of green tea manufacture was taught to Formosa Chinese by the Byoritsu Agricultural Association about twenty years ago, and they manufactured it for local consumption. At the present time it is manufactured on a small scale only, for use in the island.

In 1923, the first factory for the manufacture of the new-type, three-quarter-fermented Formosa Oolong was erected by Mitsui & Co., Ltd., and the first samples were sent to America, where they were well received. By the end of 1928, the firm had four new and modernly equipped factories devoted to the production of this tea, with another nearing completion.

Since Japan acquired Formosa from China, at the close of the Sino-Japanese War, in 1895, tea production has made substantial gains under the watchful care of the Japanese Government. In 1902, a machine-equipped factory was established at Anpeichin. In 1910, a black tea producing company was subsidized and granted the use of the Anpeichin factory. In 1918, the Government formulated plans for aggressive encouragement of the tea industry, and started to subsidize it by granting a loan of tea-making machinery to factories organized in conformity with the plans of the Government. This was followed in 1923 by rules promulgated for the regulation of the industry and the establishment of an inspection of all teas for export.

The Joint Sales Tea Market, composed of owners of tea factories, was established in 1923 under government subsidy and control. Among various inducements offered producers to coöperate with the Joint Sales Tea Market was the creation of the Tea Forwarding Office at Heichin by the Shinchiku Provincial Government Agricultural Association. This office extends forwarding and financing facilities to producers without charge.

FRENCH INDO-CHINA.—In French Indo-China, tea has been grown by native cultivators for many centuries, so it is impossible to say even approximately when the industry was begun. Prior to two centuries ago it was an important industrial activity which lapsed into insignificance until revived by the French since 1900.

SIAM.—The aboriginal tribes of Siam, like those of Burma, and the bordering Chinese province of Yunnan, are credited by botanists with having been the first to gather and use the leaves of the *miang*, or wild tea trees, found growing on their native hills. From the wild tea leaves they continue to make small bundles of steamed and fermented tea for chewing. In earlier times they made a medicinal drink by boiling the raw, green leaf.

BURMA.—As far back as historical records go, the tea grown in Burma has been chiefly used as a vegetable relish, and by far the greater proportion of the present-day crop is consumed in this manner. In recent years there has been a movement to establish commercial leaf production in

Burma by modern methods of cultivation and manufacture. An estate was opened at Toungoo in 1919, and planting began in 1921.

BRITISH MALAYA.—In March, 1914, Mr. M. Barrowcliff, at that time Assistant Agricultural Chemist, paid a visit to Lubok Tamang, 3500 feet above sea level, and explored a portion of the Bertam Valley. He took a number of soil samples and his conclusions were that, in comparison with the best tea soils in Northeast India, the soils of Lubok Tamang were in every respect up to the standard of a good tea soil, and that there was no reason, apparently, why tea of high quality should not be grown there.

Further analysis by another chemist supported Mr. Barrowcliff's arguments, but it was not until 1925 that an effort was made to test the truth of the soil analysis. In that year a small consignment of three varieties of Assam tea was secured, and 200 seeds of each variety were taken up to Cameron's Highlands and sown in specially prepared nursery beds on low-lying land at Tanah Rata. Germination was good, and in January, 1926, 437 seedlings were raised from this stock of seed and planted out. The elevation at which they were planted was about 4650 feet above sea level, and the varieties used were the Betjan, Dhonjan, and Rajghur. After one year the plants had grown to a height of about four feet, with an average spread of over two feet. The pruning of these plants prior to plucking was undertaken in April, 1927, and plucking operations began in July. During the twelve months ending in July, 1928, the first year of cropping, the total weight of dry tea harvested amounted to 78 lbs. Taking the area of the experimental plots at one-sixth of an acre, this is equivalent to a yield of 470 lbs. of manufactured tea an acre.

More extensive experiments have been carried out in low-lying stations, one of which was the Serdang experimental station, where five acres were sown with Assam varieties of tea in 1924. Regular plucking began in 1928, but the method of manufacture employed then was somewhat primitive. A first-class modern tea factory was erected in 1933, and the planted area is being increased.

During the years 1924 and 1925, the Bigia Estate at Gurun, in the unfederated Malay State of Kedah, was opened in tea and approximately 300 acres planted. Kedah, one of the northernmost states of the Peninsula, is hilly, the climate is closely akin to that of Ceylon, and there is an abundance of cheap labor at all times. In a Chinese settlement of some 360 acres in the mining district of Sungei Besi, Chinese small-holders have planted out 140 acres with Chinese tea, which is manufactured and sold to the Chinese in the tin mines.

IRAN [PERSIA].—Tea cultivation was introduced into Persia in 1900 by a Persian prince named Kashef-es-Saltaneh, who brought seeds from India and had a Persian, who had learned the tea industry in India and China, teach the villagers to grow and manufacture it. A small amount of tea is now grown in the districts of Fumen, Lahijan, and Langrud near Resht, in the province of Gilan, on the edge of the Persian plateau, south of the Caspian sea.

Cultivation in Africa

Generally speaking, the cultivation of tea on a commercial scale has been more successful in Africa than anywhere outside of the Far East. Probably no other section of the world offers as much potential acreage for increasing the world's tea production.

NATAL.—Tea was first introduced into Natal in 1850, but was grown merely for experimental purposes in the Durban Botanical Gardens. In 1877, when a flourishing coffee industry suddenly failed, a Natal planters' association imported several species of Indian tea seeds from Calcutta, and this marked the beginning of the tea industry on a practical scale. The Assam indigenous, one of the types imported, proved to be the most suitable to the climate and soil of Natal and was soon the only kind grown. The late Sir James Liege Hulett, of Kearsney, is regarded as the Father of the African Tea Industry.

The tea seedlings were planted on estates near Stanger, Natal, and all of the tea now grown in South Africa is produced in that vicinity. The total area suitable for tea growing is 15,000 acres, although even when the industry was at its height only 4500 acres were planted.

The two principal tea growers are J. L. Hulett & Sons, Ltd., and W. R. Hindson & Co.; both having their headquarters at

Tea Growing Near Mt. Mlanje, Nyasaland's Pioneer Tea District; Elevation 2000 feet

Tea cultivation on a commercial scale was nct begun until about 1890, but Nyasaland's production already exceeds 1,000,000 pounds per year.

The Hulett Tea Estate at Kearsney, Natal's Pioneer Tea Garden; Elevation 1000 feet

Commercial tea cultivation in Natal was started i n 1877. The peak of the industry was reached about 1903. Advancing labcr costs brought a decline after 1911.

THE START OF TEA CULTIVATION ON THE EAST COAST OF AFRICA

Durban and estates near Stanger. The first-named have approximately 1250 acres under tea cultivation, and the second about 750 acres. Besides these two there are three or four small growers of tea whose production is negligible.

The first crop of tea plucked in Natal was in 1880, when the year's output amounted to eighty pounds. The highest yearly output was in 1903, when the total production was 2,681,000 lbs. The acreage remained stationary until it went into a decline after 1911, when restrictions were placed upon Indian immigration into Natal by the Government of India, causing an increased labor cost which greatly hampered the industry.

Sir James L. Hulett

The decline was due jointly to the low prices paid for Natal tea and the high cost of native African labor used in its production.

NYASALAND.—The introduction of tea into Nyasaland was first attempted in 1878 by Jonathan Duncan, a country gardner who went out to join the Mission of the Church of Scotland at Blantyre. On the long voyage out, he carried with him three coffee seedlings and a young tea plant, the gift of Professor Balfour, Curator of the Edinburgh Royal Botanical Gardens. Despite every care given to them by Duncan during the trip, however, two of the coffee seedlings and the tea plant died.

It was nine years after, in 1887, that a few other tea plants were set out in the experimental gardens of the mission at Blantyre. The average rainfall there, however, is too low for successful tea cultivation, and nothing was done with the seed produced until about 1890, when one of the pioneers, Mr. J. W. Moir, deputed the late Mr. Henry Brown, an ex-Ceylon coffee planter, to plant some of the tea seeds from the Blantyre Mission on a coffee plantation known as the Lauderdale Estate in the Mlanje district. The seeds were planted in small plots near the bungalow and the plants raised from them did well, as did the plants raised from additional seeds which Mr. Moir procured from Natal.

Mr. Henry Brown, a few years later, opened up a coffee estate for himself in the same district, and also started planting tea. By 1904, there were 250 acres under tea in the Mlanje district.

In 1898, the earliest samples of tea manufactured in Nyasaland reached England.

In 1901, on the retirement of Mr. Moir, the Lauderdale Estate passed into the hands of the Blantyre and East Africa Limited, of which Mr. Moir is one of the directors. The company, faced with the evident decline of coffee and the necessity of replacing it by some other cultivation, decided to push the planting of tea as seed became available from the established bushes, and to let the coffee gradually die out.

The only seed available was of mixed varieties, but it was later recognized that better quality tea could be had by planting pure bred Manipuri or Assam. Attempts were made to bring seed from Ceylon, but out of several importations not a single one was successful, owing to the slowness of the transport and the uncertain connections at that time. Nowadays, seed is imported yearly; chiefly from India.

Having decided upon a definite policy of growing tea on Lauderdale Estate, Blantyre and East Africa Limited extended its acreage, erected a hydro-electric plant, imported tea machinery, and placed the product on the London market. Other coffee planters in the district, seeing the success of these experiments, also engaged in tea planting, and now practically all the available land in the Mlanje area has been taken up for tea cultivation.

Blantyre and East Africa Limited, 2, Charlotte Square, Edinburgh, Scotland, present owners of Lauderdale and other Nyasaland estates, was established in 1898. They are growers of tea and other tropical products in Nyasaland Protectorate; also secretaries, and land estate agents. The head office in Africa is at Blantyre, Nyasaland. Mr. William Tait Bowie is the general manager in Africa, and Mr. Robert Edward Clegg is assistant manager. The manager of the company's tea section is Mr. William Morris Scott. The present directors are Messrs. John William Moir [chairman], Robert Ross Stark [managing director], John Liddell Officer, W. S. and John William Elder Steedman. The company was first incorporated in Edinburgh as The Scottish Central African Syndicate,

Ltd., 1898, and changed its name to Blantyre and East Africa Limited in 1901, at the same time amalgamating the properties of The Scottish Central African Syndicate, Ltd., the Buchanan Bros., Hynde and Stark, and John W. Moir situated in the Blantyre, Mlanje, Zomba, and Cholo districts. The company has succeeded in establishing and developing the largest tea growing enterprise in Nyasaland.

In 1925, the London catering firm of J. Lyons & Co., Ltd., acquired some 8000 acres at Lujeri in the Mlanje district and started operations under Mr. C. F. S. Shaw, an ex-Ceylon tea planter. They have built a tea factory with a hydroelectric power station nearby.

From Mlanje the cultivation spread to Cholo, a neighboring district, where the rainfall, although not so high as in Mlanje, is still sufficient. The average elevation of the Mlanje estates is 2000 feet, but Cholo is 3000, and consequently the quality of the tea produced there is slightly better. Mr. R. S. Hynde was the first to plant tea in Cholo, on Bandanga, then belonging to Blantyre and East Africa Limited, but now a separate estate.

The second largest tea growers in Nyasaland are the Ruo Estates, Ltd. There are also the African Lakes Corporation, Ltd., the estates of Mr. George Garden, Mr. James Millar, Mr. H. Morton, Mr. Conforzi, Mr. Scott, Mr. Harper, Mr. Wallace-Ross and others, in addition to further developments by the Cholo Land and Rubber Company's Estate and the Mandimwe property of Messrs. Maxwell. In 1932, the acreage in Nyasaland was 12,595 and the production 2,699,984 lbs.

TANGANYIKA TERRITORY.—Several attempts at tea cultivation were made by German interests before the World War in German East Africa—now Tanganyika Territory, British—and in the Cameroons. An area north of Lake Nyasa in Tanganyika, having a high rainfall and excellent soil, is suitable for tea growing; also the highlands southeast of Iringa. At present, communications are difficult but when projected railways are built, there seems little doubt that this area will be taken up largely for tea and coffee production.

RHODESIA.—In Rhodesia, tea planting started on the New Year's Gift Tea Estate at Chipinga, district of Melsetter, province of Mashonaland on the Eastern border. The original planting was made

in 1925 for seed production. From the seed thus raised, one hundred acres were planted in the spring of 1927, and a second one hundred acres, begun in November, 1929, was completed in March, 1930. The first crop, amounting to 1400 lbs. was harvested in 1930. In 1931, some 4000 lbs. were produced, and the 1932 crop was about 10,000 lbs. In addition, another tea estate is being developed by the same owners, also on the eastern border, and when this reaches full production, a total yield of 400,000 lbs. is expected, which is said to be sufficient to supply the entire colony with tea.

ABYSSINIA.—A much traveled Abyssinian, Kantibar Gebrou, first introduced the tea plant into his native land some years ago, but no trace remains of the bushes. Tea was reintroduced into Abyssinia by Mr. George Howland, one of the pioneer tea planters of Kericho, Kenya Colony. In 1928, he carried to Abyssinia eight cases of tea seed from Assam. He traveled throughout Abyssinia choosing good tea land, planting his seed in some locations and giving it away in others. In the district of Kaffa there are thousands of square miles of very good tea land. At Bonga, in this area, Mr. Howland started a successful tea nursery. Recently, plans have been made to cultivate tea on a commercial basis. Brooke, Bond & Co., are concerning themselves with the subject of developing tea plantations in Abyssinia.

UGANDA AND KENYA.—Tea was introduced into the Botanic Gardens at Entebbe, Uganda, in 1900. In 1910, seedlings were planted out on the Government plantation at Kampala, and later on the Government plantations at Kakumiro and Toro. The experimental stage proved so encouraging that Mr. F. G. Talbot, a leading planter of Mityana Township, established a tea industry there. Among the growers are Buchanan's (Uganda) Estates, with more than 500 acres under tea. The proprietor is Lord Woolavington. Another tea estate is that of Major Leslie Renton, near Mityana, with 250 acres planted. Counting plants not yet in bearing, Uganda has more than 1000 acres under tea.

In Kenya, it is said that the first settlers to plant tea were the brothers Orchardson, sons of Sir William Orchardson, the famous artist. In 1925, Brooke, Bond & Co., Ltd., and James Finlay & Co., Ltd., purchased land and began planting extensively.

Brooke, Bond & Co., Ltd., bought a 640-acre farm near Limoru and erected a factory to meet the requirements of tea production in the vicinity. Also, they organized a coöperative tea growing association, in which about fifteen planters have joined.

James Finlay & Co., Ltd., and other companies with whom they are associated, organized the African Highlands Produce Co., with £250,000 capital, to plant tea in the Kericho and Lumbwa districts, where they hold 23,000 acres of land suitable for tea cultivation. This land was inspected by an expert from Southern India before it was purchased. His report said that the soil was excellent and the rainfall sufficient and well distributed, indicating yields of tea equal to the high range of Travancore, at no greater cost.

An important step in the progress of the new industry was the formation in 1933 of the Kenya Tea Growers Association, in which all companies and individuals owning tea estates of not less than 50 acres are eligible.

In 1934, Kenya, Uganda, Tanganyika Territory, and Nyasaland agreed to limit the area of new planting of tea, and to prohibit the export of tea seed during the currency of the tea control scheme adopted by the Governments of India, etc., which expires in 1938. The total area for new planting of tea in these four territories has been fixed at 7900 acres.

Attempts in North America

On the North American continent, attempts have been made to cultivate tea in British Columbia, in several parts of the United States, and in Mexico.

BRITISH COLUMBIA.—In British Columbia, a few tea plants have been grown from six-inch seedlings brought from Japan and planted at the Experimental Station on Vancouver Island in 1915. This was not an attempt to start commercial tea growing, but rather an attempt to demonstrate the mild climate of British Columbia; and, while the plants were apparently flourishing in the open, it is unlikely that any attempt will ever be made to grow tea commercially in the Canadian province.

UNITED STATES.—The attempt to raise tea in the United States of America was a serious, sustained effort to establish it as a commercial enterprise. Plants were first brought into the country about 1795 by a French botanist, Andre Michaux, 1746–1802. Commissioned in 1785 by the French government to collect and send to France specimens of North American flora, he spent eleven years in the United States. Deterred from sending plants to France during the first two years of the Anglo-French war, he occupied his time by augmenting his botanical gardens on the Middleton Estate, fifteen miles from Charleston, S. C., with tea seeds and plants secured through American captains in the China trade. One of the supposed original tea trees, grown to a height of fifteen feet, survived as late as 1887.

The first effort to start a tea industry was made in 1848 near Greenville, S. C., by Dr. Julius Smith, who had abandoned a professional career in London. His plantation, which never passed beyond the experimental stage, "got along first rate," even surviving a snow storm of eight or nine inches, according to his report to the *American Agriculturist* in 1851. It finally stopped producing through neglect, after his death in 1852.

In 1850, another physician, Dr. Jones, planted tea at McIntosh, Georgia. This cultivation, continued by Dr. Jones for several years and subsequently by his daughter, Mrs. R. J. Screven, was finally abandoned. In 1858, the United States government became interested in the possibilities of tea growing, sending Robert Fortune, English traveler and horticulturist, to China for tea seeds, which were distributed free among the planters of the southern states. A number of bushes were raised from these seeds in North and South Carolina, Georgia, Florida, Louisiana, and Tennessee. As most of the growers prepared the leaf for their own use, no commercial production was attained, and interest in tea planting died out.

Interest was revived and cultivation experiments were conducted on a large scale when, in 1880, William G. le Duc, U. S. Commissioner of Agriculture, employed John Jackson, a tea planter of seventeen years' experience in India and a brother of William Jackson of tea roller fame, to conduct further tea experiments on 200 acres of leased land near Summerville, South Carolina. Most of the seed planted came from China, Japan, and India, but some was supplied by the few surviving plants grown from the seed previously distributed

NEGRO CHILDREN PICKING TEA IN A CHINA TEA GARDEN AT PINEHURST, S. C., 1905

by the Government. Crops of several small tea fields resulted, and Jackson manufactured sample quantities of teas, which received the commendation of competent judges in New York. Before the experiment could be fully developed, the work was abandoned because of the illness of Jackson.

Later, in 1890, Dr. Charles U. Shepard, 1843–1915, a physiological chemist and writer on chemical and agricultural subjects, began tea growing on a small scale at Summerville, South Carolina. Dr. Shepard was made Special Agent for Tea Culture, U. S. Department of Agriculture, and the enterprise became known as the Pinehurst Tea Garden. Government aid was given in 1900, and yearly appropriations, varying from one to ten thousand dollars, were made during the fifteen years following. The acreage under tea increased from 60 to 125 and the maximum annual production reached 15,000 lbs. of finished tea.

Mr. Geo. F. Mitchell, who later became United States Supervising Tea Examiner, was associated with Dr. Shepard in the Pinehurst tea enterprise for nine years, from 1903 to 1912. Tea growing at Pinehurst was abandoned in 1915.

Only one other commercial tea project was launched. In 1901, Major Roswell D. Trimble, organized the American Tea Growing Company, headed by Colonel August C. Tyler, a retired U. S. Army officer who had been Major Trimble's superior officer during the Spanish-American War. Their training camp had been situated near the Pinehurst Tea Gardens, and they became interested in Dr. Shepard's experiment. Purchasing 6500 acres of former rice fields situated between Charleston and Savanna, South Carolina, the company planned ultimately to plant one to two thousand acres in tea. During the first year, some 600,000 shrubs were grown in nurseries, and most of them were transplanted. The plantation was continued for several years, although only a comparatively small amount of tea was manufactured. In 1902, the company purchased the entire crop of Dr. Shepard's garden, selling it to the grocery trade throughout the United States, but in 1903 the venture was abandoned because of the death of Colonel Tyler and the repeal of the Spanish-American War import tax of ten cents a pound on tea.

In addition to the successive attempts made in South Carolina, a small experimental tea plantation was begun in 1904 by A. P. Borden, in coöperation with the U. S. Department of Agriculture, on the

Mackey estate, near Pierce, Texas. The results were less encouraging than at Summerville, and the experiment was dropped in 1910. In California, a few shrubs were planted in connection with the San Diego exposition in 1915. They grew successfully in the open, as have various home-grown bushes near the homes of Japanese agriculturists in the vicinity of Los Angeles, but commercial production was never again attempted.

MEXICO.—In Mexico, tea cultivation is being undertaken near Cuicatlan, Oaxaca, where, since 1929, small but commercial quantities of good quality tea have been produced.

GUATEMALA.—Guatemala is the only one of the Central American countries where tea cultivation has been attempted. In the Alta Verapaz district of that country, bushes planted by Oscar Majus at Coban grew satisfactorily, and samples of dried leaf were reported as corresponding somewhat to good India tea, but the experiment was not a commercial success.

South American Attempts

Although tea cultivation has been attempted in some five South American countries it has nowhere met with genuine success.

BRAZIL.—In Brazil, the first attempt to cultivate tea was made in 1812. After the Portuguese court had fled there in 1808, energetic steps were taken to develop this South American colony agriculturally and commercially. A botanical garden was founded at Rio de Janeiro and systematic plant introductions were made. Among the latter were tea plants brought from China in 1812. Expert native Chinese tea workers were imported to teach the colonists the proper method of cultivation and manufacture. Tea was at first planted only in the neighborhood of the capital but its culture soon spread in a small way to the states of São Paulo and Minas Geraes. Production, which reached its peak in 1852 when São Paulo produced 65,000 lbs. from thirty-nine farms, declined and was all but extinguished by the abolition of slavery in 1888.

Since 1920, the industry has been revived in Minas Geraes, where several tea estates exist in the township of Ouro Preto. Also, Japanese colonists in the states of São Paulo and Paraná are planting tea in an area where none has been grown previously. Some 22,000 tea bushes were under cultivation in 1932.

PARAGUAY.—In Paraguay, an experimental nursery to cultivate Chinese tea plants was established in 1921 in the department of Villa Rica. The experiment has been successful so far as the growth of the plants is concerned, but production has not been attempted on a commercial scale.

PERU.—The planting of tea in Peru began in 1912, although it was not until 1928 that the industry really started under the supervision of a commission brought from Ceylon by the Peruvian Government. Seventeen plantations are being cultivated, with a total of 1,349,029 plants. In 1933 the output of manufactured tea was estimated at 20,000 lbs.; and in 1934 it was expected to reach 50,000 lbs.

ARGENTINA.—In Argentina the Department of Agriculture imported some 1100 lbs. of tea seeds from China in 1924, distributing them among the farmers in the northern part of the country in the hope of developing tea growing on a commercial scale. The seeds were planted on farms in the provinces of Corrientes, Entre Rios, and Tucuman, and in the territories of Chaco, Misiones, and Formosa. The plants did well, but owing partly to difficulties involved in manufacture and marketing, and partly to the local preference for yerba maté, the popular beverage of Argentina, the industry did not assume any importance.

COLOMBIA.—In Colombia, tea is being grown on a small scale at Gachala in the department of Cundinamarca. There is only one cultivation, comprising thirty-seven acres. While most of the dried leaf produced is sold locally in Bogota, Colombia has exported small quantities to Spain.

Australia and the Oceanic Islands

Attempts have been made, with varying degrees of success, to grow tea in Australia and on several islands of the Pacific and Atlantic oceans. These have been widely separated minor cultivations, and they have occurred mostly in connection with the agricultural development in island colonies of European nations, where systematic efforts were made to establish new industries.

AUSTRALIA.—Lieutenant Charlton, a leader in the movement to secure recognition of indigenous tea in India, reported in 1834 that he had seen tea growing in Australia. No other record of this growth is preserved, but the attempt was ultimately unsuccessful. A later attempt was made about the year 1850, but the experiment failed because of the unevenly distributed rainfall during the year and also because of the violent Australian storms. The cost of labor was likewise a deterrent factor; so the attempt was abandoned. Recently, another experimental effort has been started in Queensland.

BORNEO AND THE PHILIPPINES.—Attempts at tea raising were made in Borneo and the Philippines in the years just preceding the World War, but the results in the Philippines were not such as to encourage their resumption since that time. In Borneo, however, the British North Borneo Company is experimenting. In 1926, some seed was imported from India, and plants from the India seed are still flourishing. An expert tea planter reporting on this experiment indicates the soil and climate are favorable for tea cultivation. However, the low level of the gardens, the scarcity of suitable labor and the difficult communication present great handicaps.

MAURITIUS.—On the island of Mauritius, a British colony in the Indian Ocean, small quantities of tea are grown. It was first planted by M. Jaunet in 1844 under a subsidy of the British Government, but only reached a scale of any commercial importance in recent years. The annual production at the present time is about 29,000 lbs.

FIJI.—Tea was introduced in the Fiji island group about 1870, when George Simpson, a young Englishman from Assam, opened a tea estate on the south side of Vanua Levu, the second largest of the two hundred and fifty islands of the British Fiji group. After getting the tea in growing order, sickness compelled Simpson's return to England; the plantation fell into neglect, and the tea plants disappeared. In 1880, Captain David Robbie, a British planter, acquired the Simpson estate and reopened it. The annual production at the peak of the experiment was 60,000 lbs., but this figure has since declined considerably. There are about 200 acres in the Vanua Levu tea estate and the factory is equipped with rolling and drying machines of British make. The outturn is entirely consumed in the Islands. The experiment in Fiji has demonstrated that the plant would thrive in a favorable locality, but like so many other places where tea can be grown, the labor cost is too high to make its production a commercial success.

TEA ON VANUA LEVU, FIJI

WEST INDIAN ISLANDS.—Attempts have been made on only three islands of the Western Hemisphere to cultivate tea. In Puerto Rico, where it was introduced in 1903 at the U. S. Experiment Station at Mayaguez, the plants spent their vitality in excessive flowering and produced little leafage; in Cayenne, French Guiana, where French efforts to grow the plant with imported Chinese labor failed and experiment was abandoned; and in Jamaica, the largest of the British West Indies, where there was a limited commercial production.

In 1868, an acre of tea was planted experimentally at the Government Station, Cinchona, Jamaica. Proving a success, the area was later increased. In 1900, a Mr. Cox, obtaining seeds and plants from the Government Station, planted 250 acres in tea at Ramble in St. Ann's Parish. The enterprise enjoyed for a time a measure of success. At first the tea was manufactured by hand, but later machinery was introduced to gain economy in production costs. The tea was introduced on the local market in 1903, and was found to be of good quality for blending. However, production was later curtailed and there was progressive deterioration of the plantation due to increasing labor costs. After the death of Cox in 1912, cultivation was abandoned entirely and no tea has since been grown.

BOOK II
TECHNICAL ASPECTS

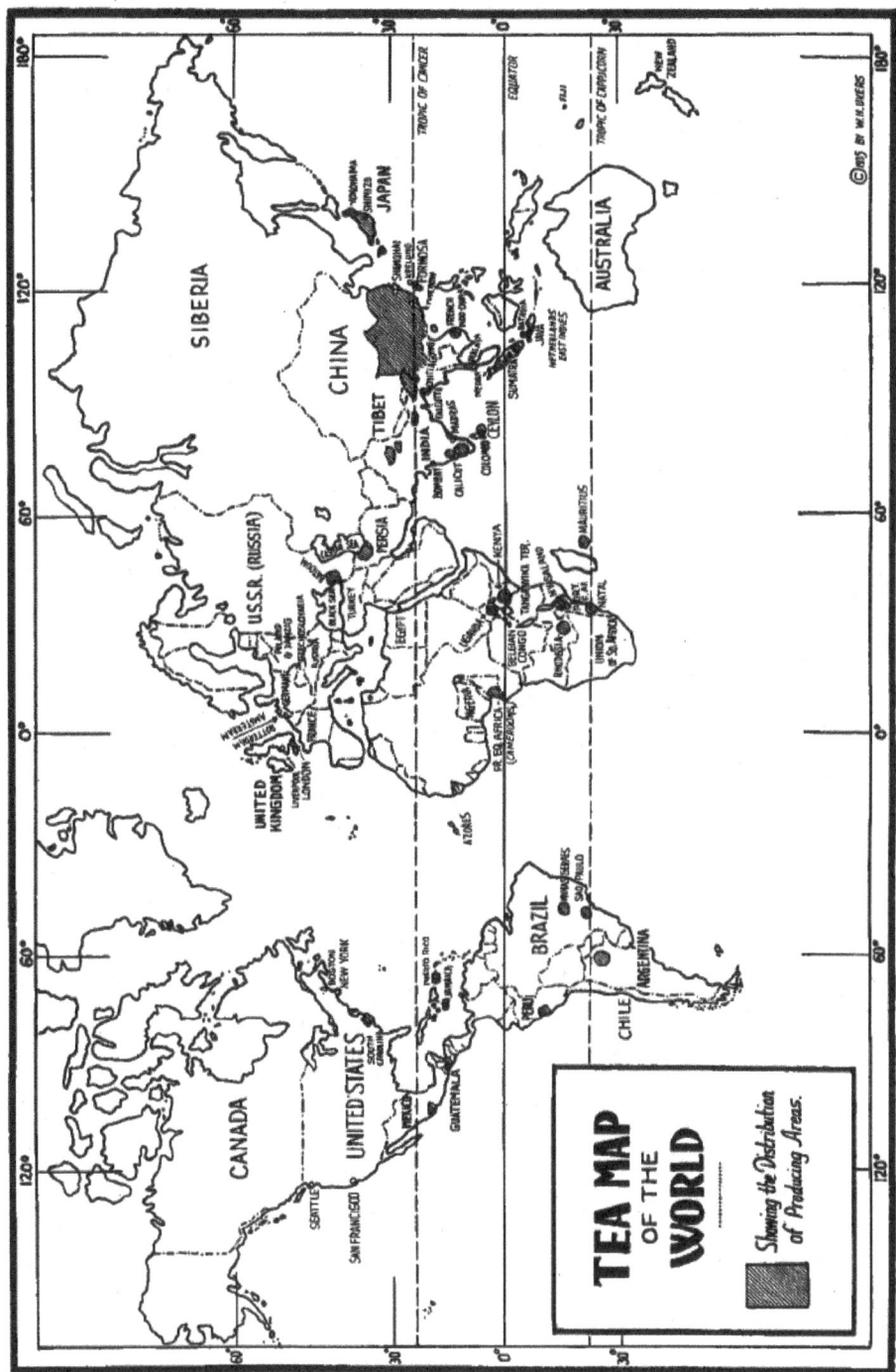

TEA MAP OF THE WORLD

Showing the Distribution of Producing Areas.

218

CHAPTER XII

COMMERCIAL TEAS OF THE WORLD

A General Survey of the Teas of Commerce—Where they come from—How they Acquire their General Classification and Their more Specific Designations—What they are Like and Where They Go—Characteristics of the Teas of Ceylon, India, China, Japan, Formosa, Java, Sumatra, French Indo-China, and Nyasaland—With a Commercial Tea Chart Showing All of the Leading Growths, Their Market Names, and General Trade Characteristics.

ALTHOUGH tea is grown successfully in some twenty-three countries throughout the world, only nine produce it in such marketable quantities as to render them commercially important. These countries are: India, Ceylon, China, Java, Sumatra, Japan, Formosa, French Indo-China, and Nyasaland.

Teas are given a general classification in accordance with their countries of origin as India teas, Ceylon teas, China teas, Java teas, etc. The different kinds and grades sold in the markets are the product of (1) different ages of the leaf and seasons of plucking; (2) different elevations at which the teas are grown and varying climatic conditions; (3) differences in soil; (4) different methods of manufacture, whereby the leaves of the tea plant become green, black, or Oolong teas; and (5) sorting by sifting and final preparation for sale either unmixed, or—as is a more general practice—in a blended mixture of various sizes and qualities of made tea.

The teas of India and Ceylon are sent mostly to England, Australia, the United States, Africa, Canada, and Russia. Java and Sumatra teas are shipped mostly to England, Holland, Australia, United States, British Indies, and Russia. China teas go mostly to Continental and Mediterranean countries, Russia, the United States, Canada, and England. Japan teas are sent almost exclusively to the United States, Canada, and Russia. Formosa teas go principally to the United States, with, how-

ever, a large amount of scented, or Pouchong tea, going to the Dutch East Indies and Siam. French Indo-China teas are consumed principally in France and her colonies. Tea from Nyasaland goes to the London market.

China produces nearly 50 per cent of the world's supply of commercial teas, although her exports are less than those of some other countries. India is second in point of production; Ceylon, third; Java and Sumatra, fourth; Japan, fifth; Formosa, sixth; Indo-China, seventh; and Nyasaland, eighth. There are certain teas which constitute the bulk of the exports from each of these countries; while others are not trade factors. For example, tea is cultivated to some extent in the Ranchi district of India, yet the quantity is too small to be commercially important; Gyokuro tea is made in Japan, but because of the high cost of production it does not appear in the world's markets. Such teas may be—in fact many are—excellent as to quality, but for one reason or another they are not known as commercial teas.

There follows a brief general description of the leading commercial teas of the world. For a more detailed description of the various growths, including a large number not mentioned here, the reader is referred to the next chapter, which deals with tea characteristics and has a complete reference table.

Ceylon produces principally black, or fermented, teas. They are divided into high, medium, and low grown. The high grown teas are produced in the hill districts in the interior of the island and are especially noted for good strength and delicate flavor. The medium grown teas have a well made leaf and a useful liquor. The low grown teas have a well made, black leaf but a plain cup, being useful, but lacking in flavor. Ceylon blacks are graded as Broken Orange Pekoe, Broken Pekoe, Orange Pekoe, Pekoe, Pekoe Souchong, Souchong, Fannings, and Dust.

INDIA is the largest tea exporting country in the world. Both black and green teas are manufactured; with black far in the lead, constituting 98 to 99 per cent of the total. The teas are known by the names of the districts in which they are grown, and also by the names of gardens or estates. The principal commercial teas of India are the Assams, Cachars, Sylhets, Dooars, Terais, and Darjeelings of North India and the Travancores and Kanan Devans of South India. In general, the dry leaf is black to brown and the cup full-bodied, rich and malty. Darjeelings, having an exquisite aroma, rank the highest in flavor and price. India teas are graded as Broken Orange Pekoe, Broken Pekoe, Orange Pekoe, etc., the same as Ceylons.

CHINA produces black, green, and Oolong teas. The North China Congous are the best known blacks. They are strong, full-bodied, and fragrant. The South China, or red leaf, Congous are light in the cup. Teas from the Ningchow and Keemun districts of North China, and the Paklin, Paklum, and Panyong districts of South China are generally favored by tea buyers.

China greens are divided into Pingsueys, Hoochows, and Country Greens. The last named includes all greens except those grown in the districts surrounding the market towns of Pingsuey and Hoochow. Greens are prepared in the following styles or makes: Young Hyson, Hyson, Gunpowder, and Imperial.

China semi-fermented teas are marketed under the name of Foochow Oolongs, and generally are inferior to Formosa Oolongs.

JAPAN produces mostly green teas. They are prepared in three styles—pan-fired, basket-fired, and natural leaf; the latter formerly known as porcelain-fired. As a whole, Japan teas have a long, straight, spider-legged leaf. The better grades possess a rich, delicate flavor peculiar to themselves. The gradings for Japan teas are: Extra Choicest, Choicest, Choice, Finest, Fine, Good Medium, Good Common, Common, Nibs, Dust, and Fannings.

FORMOSA.—Until recently Formosa manufactured two kinds of tea—the semifermented Oolongs and Pouchongs. Within the last few years, however, some black tea has been produced and three-quarters fermented Oolong, graded in Daitotei as Flowery Orange Pekoe, Orange Pekoe, and Pekoe. The Oolong is the best known in consuming markets, although some seven million pounds of Pouchong, a scented tea, are shipped annually to Siam, the Dutch East Indies, the Straits Settlements, and the islands of the Pacific. Formosa Oolongs have a greenish-brown leaf. The cup is distinguished by a natural fruity flavor. They are divided into First or Spring Crop, First Summer Crop, Second Summer Crop, Autumn Crop, and Winter Crop. The first and second summer crops are generally regarded as the best. The gradings for Formosa Oolongs, as adopted by the Formosan Government Tea Inspection Office, are: Standard, On Good, Good, Fully Good, Good Up, Good to Superior, On Superior, Superior, Fully Superior, Superior Up, Superior to Fine, On Fine, Fine, Fine Up, Fine to Finest, Finest, Finest to Choice, Choice. The trade recognizes several intermediate gradings, such as Good Leaf, Fully Standard, Standard to Good, Strictly Superior, Choicest, and Fancy.

JAVA AND SUMATRA produce black teas which are known by their garden marks. Java teas have a black and attractive leaf during the greater part of the year, but are brownish and stalky during the dry season, lasting from June to September, after which period the flavor improves. They are well made, useful blenders, soft, and of medium strength in the cup. Sumatra teas are not so readily affected by seasonal changes. The leaf is uniformly attractive. They may be said to be of the same useful cup the year round. The gradings for Javas and Sumatras are: Flowery Orange Pekoe, Orange Pekoe, Broken Orange Pekoe, Pekoe, Broken Pekoe, Pekoe Souchong, Souchong, Bohea, Fannings, and Dust.

FRENCH INDO-CHINA produces both black and green tea. The tea exported is Annam Black and Annam Green, and is

COMMERCIAL TEA CHART

The World's Leading Growths, with Market Names and General Trade Characteristics

Grand Division	Country	Principal Shipping Ports	Best Known Market Names	Trade Characteristics
Asia	Ceylon	Colombo	Ceylons High Grown Medium Grown Low Grown	Mostly black tea. Dry leaf is well made, even, black, and often tippy. Cup varies from delicate in the high grown to plain in the low grown.
	India	Calcutta Chittagong Bombay Madras Calicut	Assams Cachars Sylhets Dooars Terais Darjeelings Travancores Kanan Devans	Mostly black tea. Dry leaf is black to brown. Cup full-bodied, rich and malty.
	China	Shanghai Hankow Foochow	North China Congous South China Congous Country Greens Pingsueys Hoochows Foochow Oolongs	Black, green, Oolong, scented, and compressed tea. Wide range of appearance and cup quality. Sometimes spoken of by names of styles or makes; such as, Young Hyson, Hyson, Gunpowder, Imperial, etc.
	Japan	Shimizu	Japans	Green tea. Dry leaf long, straight, spider-legged. Better grades possess rich, delicate flavor peculiar to themselves.
	Formosa	Keelung	Formosa Oolongs	Oolong tea. Dry leaf greenish-brown. Cup distinguished by a natural fruity flavor.
	French Indo-China	Tourane Haiphong	Annams	Black, green, agglomerated, and flower tea. Dry leaf coarse. Cup strong and acrid.
Oceania	Netherlands East Indies	Batavia Medan	Javas Sumatras	Black tea. Dry leaf black and attractive. Well made, good, useful, attractive blenders.
Africa	Nyasaland	Beira Chinde	Nyasalands	Black tea, light, plain liquor, middling to good.

manufactured from inferior, coarse leaf. The tea produced by Europeans usually is well made.

NYASALAND—The British Protectorate of Nyasaland in East Central Africa produces a steadily increasing amount of black tea. It is of middling to good quality. In the cup it shows a light, plain liquor. The bushes are of British India stock.

TEA-TASTING ROOM IN A LONDON TEA PACKETING FACTORY

Here the tea tasters are to be seen at work checking the uniformity of the firm's blends. About 1500 samples are tested in this room daily.

CHAPTER XIII

TEA CHARACTERISTICS

A DISCUSSION OF THE TRADE VALUES, LEAF CHARACTERISTICS, AND CUP MERITS OF THE
LEADING TEAS OF COMMERCE, WITH A COMPLETE REFERENCE TABLE OF THE PRINCIPAL
KINDS OF TEA GROWN IN THE WORLD—JUDGING TEAS BY THE APPEARANCE, TWIST,
AND SMELL OF THE DRY LEAF; BY THE COLOR, BRIGHTNESS, AND ODOR OF THE INFUSION;
BY THE COLOR, THICKNESS, STRENGTH, PUNGENCY, AND FLAVOR OF THE LIQUOR—TEA-
TASTING AND TEA-TASTING EQUIPMENT

A STUDY of the Complete Reference Table of the Principal Kinds of Tea Grown in the World, which forms a part of this chapter, reveals that tea is grown and manufactured in Ceylon, India, China, Japan, Formosa, French Indo-China, Burma, Siam, and Iran; in the Netherlands East Indies, and the Fiji Islands of Oceania; in Natal, Nyasaland, Kenya Colony, Uganda, and Portuguese East Africa, in Africa; in Mauritius and the Azores; the Republic of Georgia, S.F.S.R., in Europe; and in Brazil, Argentina, and Peru in South America. A wide distribution, yet the bulk of the teas of the world come from only one continent—Asia. Oceania ranks next, and then comes Africa, which, while still young, is none too strong as a producer, but shows promise for the future.

Commercially, tea may be divided into three great basic classes: (1) black, or fully fermented; (2) green, or unfermented; and (3) Oolong, or semi-fermented. There are two minor classes: the native *letpet*, or pickled tea, used as a vegetable in Burma; and the miang, or chewing tea made in Siam.

All tea comes from the plant known botanically as *Thea sinensis* (L.) Sims. The different classes are a result of the treatment given the tea after plucking. If the leaves are carried at once from the tea field to a place where a certain degree of heat can be applied, they are prevented from fermenting, thus resulting in green tea. If, after physical damage by rolling, the leaves are permitted to ferment spon-

taneously for a few hours before heat is applied, the result is black tea. If the leaves are allowed to ferment for only a short time, the result is Oolong tea.

Black tea is manufactured principally in India, Ceylon, China, Java, and Sumatra. Green tea comes from Japan and China, and, to a small extent, from Ceylon and India. Oolong tea is produced in Formosa and in the province of Fukien, China.

Black, green, and Oolong tea may be further divided into leaf tea, brick and tablet tea, and soluble tea. Leaf tea is made in all countries of production. Brick tea is manufactured principally in China, and sometimes to a very small extent in India. Soluble tea is usually made in the consuming countries and is not commercially important. Both compressed [brick and tablet] and soluble tea, may be made from black, green, or Oolong tea.

Leaf tea is the tea of commerce. There are innumerable subdivisions of black, green, and Oolong leaf tea. These are caused by the age of the leaf and the time of its plucking; by differences in atmospheric influences during its growth, plucking, or manufacture; by soil characteristics; by differences in the mode of manipulation or manufacture; by assortment and separation; or by mixing the various sizes and qualities of leaf, and by many other factors.

As previously noted, tea is named after the country in which it is grown. Thus we speak of "Ceylon tea," "India tea," etc. It is further designated by the words black, green, or Oolong, and by trade

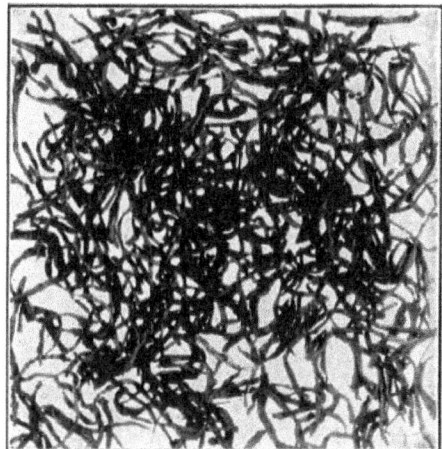

CEYLON ORANGE PEKOE
Black Tea

names, such as "China blacks," "Formosa Oolong," etc. In some cases cities, states, or districts lend their names to the tea; e.g., "Foochow Oolongs." Each tea producing country has its own individual names and gradings.

Ceylon Teas

In Ceylon, tea is produced throughout the year, but the finest pluckings are in February and March, and again in August and September, with comparatively small production during the latter period. The yield increases during April, May, and June, and again in October, November, and December, while in January the quality falls off. The principal production is of black tea.

Ceylon teas are divided into high, medium, and low grown. Of these, the first named are the best. They have no real distinction as far as style of leaf is concerned, but in the cup show good strength, combined with a delicate flavor. Some teas are successfully grown as high as 7000 feet. The mid-country teas usually have a well made leaf with useful liquor. The low grown teas have a good, black leaf which can be well rolled and well made. They have a strong, plain cup. It also can be said that teas grown below 4000 feet are useful, but comparatively plain in character; above that elevation they carry a flavor ranging from medium to fine.

For blending purposes, Ceylons lack the strength and pungency of many India teas. At the same time, their qualities render them more valuable for use unmixed, rather than for blending. It is misleading to judge either Ceylons or Indias by the Pekoe tips, as many of the coarse leaf teas possess the finest flavors.

Ceylon teas are known by their garden marks, of which there are more than 2000. These marks are stenciled on the packages. In some cases the marks are merely the initials or name of the estate owners, such as "S.V.C.E. Ld." [Spring Valley Ceylon Estates, Ltd.], or "Galaha" [Galaha Estate and Factory of the Galaha Ceylon Tea Estates and Agency Co., Ltd.]. Other marks employ geometrical figures as, for example, "Great Valley Ceylon" set in a double triangle; this being the mark of the Great Valley Estate.

With the exception of a few trade experts, chiefly brokers, no attention is paid to the district from which a tea comes; the buyers relying upon the quality of the tea, knowing from experience the estate to which to refer to find the characteristics they are seeking at the moment. Indeed, the elevation of a single district may have an altitude range of 3000 feet or more. Certain districts, such as Alagala, Kegalla, and the low country minor districts, are known to yield plain tea; others, such as Nuwara Eliya, Udapussellawa, and Dimbula, can be depended upon for very fine grades of tea.

Ceylon black tea is graded as follows: Broken Orange Pekoe, Broken Pekoe, Orange Pekoe, Pekoe, Pekoe Souchong, Souchong, Fannings, and Dust. These are separations of the same plucking and consequently possess the same character of flavor, more or less, throughout the various grades, which are physical separations, as the result of sifting through sieves of various sizes.

Through unfortunate advertising, many consumers, especially those in the United States, have come to regard the term "Orange Pekoe" as a synonym for excellence of quality. The trade distinguishes between various styles of Orange Pekoe by the addition of other terms, such as: "plain leaf," "tippy," "loose rolled," "wiry," etc. The term "Orange Pekoe," while of fanciful origin, and although originally intended to describe a certain physical appearance, has been broadened by usage to cover a more or less well twisted leaf, with

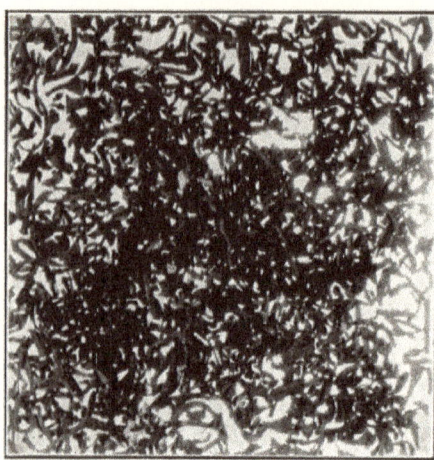

CEYLON BROKEN ORANGE PEKOE
Black Tea

or without tip, as distinguished from coarser or more broken leaf. In no sense is the term a description of quality.

In 1924, the U. S. Department of Agriculture ruled that the term "Orange Pekoe" could be applied only to fully fermented teas from India, Ceylon, Java, or Sumatra. Other teas of the O. P. leaf size could be labelled "Orange Pekoe" only with the addition of the words "leaf size" and the country of origin. A later ruling, in 1934, permits fully fermented teas of the proper leaf size from Formosa, Japan, China, and other countries to be labelled "Orange Pekoe," provided they meet the Java standard adopted by the U. S. Government from year to year. This ruling has been construed by the trade to include only "cold-fermented" East Indian type teas.

A certain amount of green tea is manufactured on a small scale in Ceylon. It does not equal the China or Japan greens because of its bitter flavor in the cup.

India Teas

India tea is a most comprehensive term and is used to include the produce of large tracts of country, which are vastly different in climate and soil, as well as latitude. Naturally, the tea produced under greatly varying conditions shows considerable variety of quality and value. The tea from Assam, for instance, is very different from the article produced in Darjeeling. The same is true of teas from Kangra,

Dehra Dun, Nilgiris, and Travancore; each produces a tea of a somewhat distinct class, but only experts can distinguish, by tasting, the sub-district from which a certain tea has come.

Both green and black tea are manufactured in India, but the black comprises the bulk of production. The small amount of green tea made is inferior to China and Japan greens. Much of it is sold over the northern border.

The two great divisions of India teas are North India and South India. The bulk of North India's teas come from Northeast India. All the North India teas are seasonal, being produced from April through November, and sold from June to the end of January. South Indias are grown throughout the year. The best Northeast India teas are the second flush and autumnals—especially in the case of Darjeelings and Dooars. The former come along during July and early August. With the approach of cold weather, the quality improves, but the appearance of the leaf begins to deteriorate; becoming brownish and containing some stalk. South India produces its finest qualities toward the end of December and during January. Quality then gradually declines until the early autumn, when the teas produced are usually the poorest of the year.

The Northeast India teas come from the provinces of Assam, Bengal, and from the native State of Hill Tippera. Teas from Dehra Dun and Kangra are known as North India teas. South India teas are produced in the native States of Mysore and Travancore, and in the Province of Madras. However, the South India growths are known by their district or subdistrict names, rather than by the name of the province.

The most important tea producing province in India is Assam. This is subdivided into the Brahmaputra Valley and the Surma Valley. Teas of the former are generally referred to as Assams, while those of the latter are known chiefly by the subdistrict names of Cachar and Sylhet. The leading Brahmaputra Valley subdivisions are: Lakhimpur, Sibsagar, Darrang, and Nowgong. In addition, there are the lesser tea producing areas of Sadiya Frontier Tract, Goalpara, and Kamrup.

Assams are full, thick, rich, heavy teas; the better grades possessing a handsome,

DARJEELING BROKEN ORANGE PEKOE
India Black Tea

tippy leaf. The medium grades have a hard, flinty, well made leaf, of a grayish black, which find a ready sale where full body and flavor are appreciated. They are the mainstay of the big British blenders. Assams draw a very full, rich-colored liquor with a great deal of strength and pungency—too much to be used individually. Therefore, they are largely used for blending with teas of a lesser strength. In the first half of June, due to slow growth, Assams are at their best as respects quality and fullness. The best Autumnal Assams are manufactured during October and November.

The Dum Duma [Doom Dooma] sub-district of Lakhimpur contains some of the finest tea areas in the world. Here quality and quantity go together.

Cachar teas have a grayish black appearance, with a leaf somewhat smaller than the teas of the neighboring district of Sylhet; and while they yield a thick, sweet liquor, they have less body than possessed by the Assams. Medium and low quality liquors are produced. Sylhets usually are attractive and well made; giving a good, medium heavy liquor with a mild smooth flavor. Both Cachars and Sylhets are useful teas.

The Province of Bengal is second in importance as a tea producer of Northeast India; its chief tea districts being Darjeeling [including the Terai], Jalpaiguri [including the Dooars], and Chittagong.

Darjeeling mountain-grown teas are cul-

tivated along the slopes of the Himalaya Mountains at elevations of from 1000 to 6500 feet. From this district come teas which bring the highest price of any that are shipped in considerable quantity. In character, Darjeelings are full-bodied, possessing rather a rich, red liquor, together with a delicious and indescribable flavor peculiarly marked as their own—a flavor sometimes referred to as "nutty." Naturally, in a district with such a wide range of elevations, some gardens produce much finer tea than others. Certain gardens produce "stand-out," i.e., outstanding teas, which bring high prices in London. While the B.O.P. and O.P. grades show handsome tippy leaf, their style is given less consideration than is the case with other teas, since it is the flavor that counts. The leaf varies from the small, very tippy, to the coarse, unsightly. However, any tea man who has examined fancy Darjeelings never will forget their distinctive flavor. They are, perhaps, the only self-drinking teas—teas which may be drunk unblended—produced in India; but are used mostly for fancy blends, being so heavy and brisk that a small proportion used with Congou [China black], Ceylon, or any other kind of tea will permeate the whole with its attractive flavor. Nowhere else in the world has the "Darjeeling flavor" been duplicated. The second flush of leaf, which is plucked in June, and the autumnal, made in October, have particularly fine character.

Teas from the Dooars have a blackish appearance and, under certain climatic conditions, stalk and reddish leaf are to be found in large quantities. They are somewhat irregular in make, and partake, to an extent, of the character of Assams; but are fuller and softer, with less pungency. In the cup they yield a soft mellow liquor, dark and full-bodied. During October and November the "rosy autumnal" teas are manufactured.

Terai teas have a black leaf, small in size, and without much style. The liquors, however, are of medium quality, usually sweet, with fair color, and at times not unlike the poorer quality Darjeelings. Terais are much used for blending. The delicate flavor of Darjeelings is apt to be killed by harder, more pungent teas. Terais, being light in liquor, are useful for blending.

Teas produced in Chittagong have a

BRITISH INDIA PEKOE
Black Tea

fairly black leaf, but of a small type. They yield colory, sweet, medium to low grade liquors. They are not, however, a great commercial factor because light and entirely lacking in character.

The province of Bihar and Orissa contains the tea producing districts of Hazaribagh and Ranchi, sometimes known as Chota Nagpur. Most of the tea is grown from China jat. It possesses some body and strength, and often has a slight brassy flavor. However, the output at present is confined to a small quantity of green tea from the district around Ranchi.

The only tea-producing district of note in the Punjab is the Kangra Valley, high up in the northwestern part of India. The climate is too cold to be perfect for tea. Mostly, green tea is made here. The tea has a peculiarly delicate flavor and brings good prices. However, much of it goes across the border into Tibet, the remainder being retained for local consumption.

The small native state of Hill Tippera, included in Bengal, contains a number of small tea estates owned by Indians. The tea manufactured is of small commercial importance, as it resembles the poorer types of Sylhets.

The tea producing districts of the United Provinces are Kumaon—subdivided into Almora and Garhwal—and Dehra-Dun. Kumaon teas have a small close leaf, and draw a light, brisk, pungent liquor; but the climate is too cool for the growth of good teas. Most of the tea grown, including a certain amount of green tea, is sold across the border to Tibet and Nepal. The teas of Dehra Dun are rather plain; lacking point and flavor.

South India teas, being geographically much nearer to the Ceylon producing districts than to those of North India, resemble Ceylons rather than Indias in general characteristics. The province of Madras includes the districts of Coimbatore, Cochin, Coorg, Madura, Malabar, Nilgiris, Nilgiri-Wynaad, and Tinnevelly.

The teas of Coimbatore usually are known by the subdistrict name of Anamalai. They possess good body and strength, and are somewhat similar to Travancores, only much stronger and preferable to them. The Cochin, Coorg, and Madura districts are commercially unimportant as tea producers. The Wynaad subdistrict of the Malabar district produces a low-grown, plain tea.

The Nilgiris, a high district with an altitude ranging from 400 to 6000 feet, yields fine flavory teas with brisk, pungent—albeit, somewhat thin—liquor. They sometimes have an attractive lemon flavor. The Nilgiri-Wynaad, half way down the slope, produces a tea on Travancore in style of leaf and fair quality of liquor. The Tinnevelly area is unimportant as a tea district.

Mysore, the native State lying immediately north and west of Madras, has so far produced but little tea; being only in the early stages of development. Tea is being planted on old coffee lands, as well as on virgin forest lands.

The native State of Travancore contains the tea producing districts of Central Travancore or Peermade, Kanan Devan, Mundakayam, and South Travancore. The teas resemble Ceylons rather than Indias. The majority are flavory in the cup, with strength, but not very stylish in the leaf.

Central Travancore, lying between the Kanan Devan and the South Travancore districts, produces a medium grade tea.

The Kanan Devan Hills, or the High Range, as its name indicates, is a mountain district where tea is grown up to an altitude of 6000 feet. A considerable quantity is of good quality.

Mundakayam teas are good, useful, plain teas. South Travancores are low grown, plain teas.

The gradings for India black teas are

KEEMUN, NORTH CHINA CONGOU
Black Tea

the same as those used in Ceylon: Broken Orange Pekoe, Broken Pekoe, Orange Pekoe, Pekoe, Pekoe Souchong, Souchong, Fannings, and Dust. The gradings for India greens generally are Fine Young Hyson, Young Hyson, Hyson No. 1, Hyson, Twankay, Soumee, Fannings, and Dust.

China Teas

China produces black, green, Oolong, scented, brick, tablet, ball, and faggot teas. The great number of distinct kinds of teas make the work of classification almost impossible. Many *hsiens*, or districts, manufacture tea which either does not appear in foreign markets at all, or is sold only in a certain country. China teas may be classified by provinces, by seasons, by trade names, etc.

The black teas fall into two great divisions—North China Congous and South China Congous. These are warm (pan) fermented teas. The former sometimes are called black leaf Congous, while the latter are known as red leaf Congous. They grow from April to October, while the most attractive quality usually is the first picking. The three pickings are April-May, June-July, and the autumn season.

North China Congous formerly were known as English Breakfast teas. They come from the provinces of Hupeh, Hunan, Kiangsi, and, to a small extent, Anhwei. North China Congous in the better grades are aromatic, full-bodied, and sweet liquor-

ing. The lower grades are mostly poor liquoring and practically "teas for price." They often are called Monings.

The three leading varieties of North China Congous are Keemuns, Ningchows and Ichangs. These have been called the Burgundies of China teas, because of their superb bouquet. Keemun tea was originally produced as green tea. In the early 'eighties it was manufactured into black. As a green tea it was quite common, but as a black it is considered one of the best China produces. Keemuns have a thick, full, liquor, combined with a rich aroma. In appearance they are not particularly attractive, but the choice grades are splendid teas. Ningchows have a handsome, hard, black leaf, with a bright and attractive infusion. They are a bit lighter in body than Keemuns or Ichangs, but are valuable teas in a blend. Ichangs have a good leaf yielding a full, rich liquor with a slightly smoky or tarry flavor.

Included among the well-known North China Congous are the Kintucks. They somewhat resemble Keemuns, having a peculiar delicate flavor, a reddish infusion, and drawing a choice quality liquor of good strength. Shantams in appearance are coarse and irregular, and the infused leaf black, hard-fibred, and unattractive. The liquor is either coarse and rank in flavor or thin and flavorless. It is a common Congou.

Kutoan, sometimes called the "Chinese Assam Pekoe," has a short, somewhat rusty leaf, and possesses strength with much point. If kept too long, it is apt to develop an herby taste.

Oonfa, sometimes spelled "Anhwa," is a favorite blending tea from the southern districts of Hunan Province. The finer grades have a bright infusion and often possess a pronounced smoky or tarry flavor.

Hohows, or Hui Hos, a name given to teas of the Makong District of Kiangsi Province, are usually classed under Kiukiangs, after the market through which they come. Kiukiang teas have fragrance and flavor, but lack body. The dry leaf is black, regular, free from dust and deteriorates quickly.

Oopacks is a general term covering the teas of Hupeh Province, the word being a derivation of the name Hupeh in the Canton dialect. Because of their similar quality and sale on the Hankow market, teas produced in the Hsiangying, Wuchang,

Hanyang, and Hwangchow Districts of Hunan also are known as Oopacks.

Other North China blacks of lesser importance include the following:

Hupeh Province [Oopacks]

Cheongshukai	Tai Sar Ping	Sienning
Tong Shan	Wun Kai	Puchi
Yanglotung	Packong	Kianghan
Yang Low Sa	Chang Yang	Kiangnan
Soon Young	Tsung Yang	Sung Yang
Hofong		Hangyang

Hunan [Oonams]

Liling	Lu Yang	Ningsiang
Taoyuan	Hsiangtang	Siang Yin
Low Young	Yun Shih	Linsiang
Wye Shan	Pingkiang	Shimen
Kou-Chao	Changsha	Siangkiang
Nipkasee		Chenyuan

Kiangsi Province

Loong Cheum	Lingtu	Siushui
Hsunyang	Wuling	Suichuen
Fulang	Shiuchang	Yuanshan

Anhwei Province

Wuhu	Liuan	Tunchia
	Chupoo	Hwei

South China blacks are variously known as South China Congous, Red Leaf Congous, Kaisows, and Foochow Congous. They grow from April to October. The most popular varieties are Paklums, Paklings, and Panyongs. The differences in soil and climate give South China blacks a character and flavor distinct from North China teas. They are the clarets of China teas.

Paklums have a small, closely twisted leaf, the better grades showing considerable white tip. They are the most stylish in appearance of all China blacks. Although bright and flavory in the cup, they lack body, character, and point.

Panyongs have rather a bold leaf. They are very serviceable teas for use in blending, the finer parcels possessing a thick, rich liquor with fine aroma and flavor. Summer crop Panyongs, sometimes known as "Thorny" Panyongs, or Assam Panyongs, are often quite distinctive, the teas being fragrant, brisk, and pungent.

Paklings have a small, even, black leaf, and are usually carefully prepared in the better grades. They have good, heavy body, with an attractive toasty flavor.

Chingwos are considered by many the best of the red leaf Congous. The leaf as a rule is evenly and tightly rolled and of a silky black complexion with some tip. The aroma is very fine and delicate, and the liquor of a bright reddish color. It imparts its flavor to any tea with which it may be blended.

Saryunes are the reddest of red leaf teas. Except for a few first crop teas, the leaf is not well made, but is open, and the second and third crops are often dusty. However, in the cup they come out strong, brisk, and ripe, with plenty of stamina.

Soomoos are good honest teas, thick and full, albeit somewhat dull. The finer varieties are distinguished by a fine, rich, Souchong flavor. They possess great body and power, and are good blenders.

Pekoe Congous are beautifully made, the leaf being black and very evenly and tightly rolled. The infused leaf is bright but the liquor, although of a dark color, lacks strength and flavor.

Padraes are highly fired teas. The dry leaf is black and crape-like, and often bold and uneven. In the cup they have brisk aroma, rich color, and great strength, with a peculiar flavor, much resembling black currants. Even the common grades, although coarse and soapy, are very strong.

Suey Kuts are evenly twisted, black, handsome teas, moderate in strength and of medium quality. The commoner grades are frequently dusty.

Ankois somewhat resemble Saryunes. The leaf, however, is a little blacker than Saryunes and the flavor ranker. They are strong, useful teas.

Singchuen is not a large nor valuable variety, except to its own special market. The leaf is rather open, and too often dust is mixed with it. It is hard liquoring.

Souchong is a generic name for the large leaf of most Congous. Specifically, the name is applied to the coarse leaf, black teas from South China. The liquor is rich and syrupy, with a slightly smoky flavor. The best known variety is Lapsang Souchong, much used to flavor high priced and delicate blends. The leaf is almost dead black, large, loose in make, and slightly curled. The second and third crops are of less strength and much softer than the first crop. There is almost no demand for these teas in America, although once much used. The term "Souchong" also is applied to certain large-leaf grades of India, Ceylon, Sumatra, and Java teas.

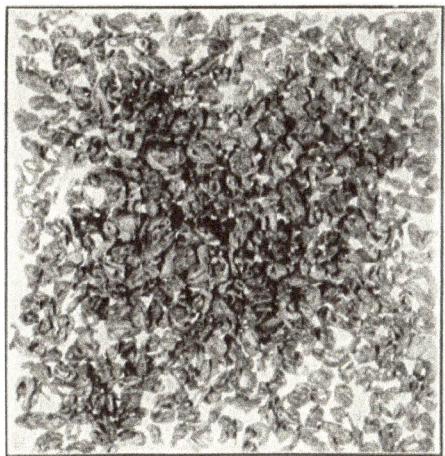

CHINA GUNPOWDER, No. 1
Green Tea

From the Province of Fukien comes a commercially unimportant tea known as Amoy Congou. It is a highly fired tea, and, when the crop is good, is brisk and strong. The dry leaf is open and bold.

Fukien also produces other small and unimportant black teas, such as Wu-I or Ai Ch'a, Pai Lian, Yang Kow, Chai Shiu, Tenyang, Shouwu, Sha Yang, Shui Ch'h, Tung Ten, Wuyuan, Tsingho and Chengho.

Formerly a class of tea known as New Makes, Province Leaf, or New District Congous, was grown, principally in the Province of Kwantung, and shipped from Canton. They are almost unknown now. The principal varieties are Hoyunes, Tarry Hoyunes, Pekoe Souchong Congous, and Honeysuckle Congous. The first two are grayish and bold, possessing great strength in the cup; the latter two are better made. There are other common New Makes which are poor and unimportant.

Hoyunes have a poor appearance. The infused leaf, however, is of a rich copper color, and the liquor has much point and quality. Tarry Hoyunes are the first pickings of Hoyunes and have a peculiar smoky taste and smell.

Pekoe Souchong [grade name] Congous have a prettily curled leaf with tip. The infusion is bright and the liquor frequently thick, rich, and powerful. Some parcels have a peculiar flavor known as "honeysuckle." These have a small reddish leaf with strong, brisk liquor.

China green teas may be roughly di-vided into Country Greens, Hoochows, and Pingsueys. Country Greens comprise all green teas, except those coming from the districts adjoining the towns of Hoochow and Pingsuey. The principal provinces for green teas are Anhwei, Chekiang, and Kiangsi, and to a smaller extent, Fukien, Kwangtung, and Hunan. The principal varieties of these districts are the Moyunes, Tienkais, and Fychows of Anhwei, the Pingsueys, Hoochows, and Wenchows of Chekiang, the Kiukiangs of Kiangsi, and the Foochows of Fukien. China greens grow from June to December. The early teas are the best.

The teas of the various districts are graded into Gunpowder, Imperial, Young Hyson, Hyson, Hyson Skin, Twankay, and Dust. These names are used only to de-scribe the style of make of the leaf after it has been manufactured. They are, there-fore, qualified in the tea trade by the name of the tea district in which the grade is made. For instance, one speaks of a Tien-kai Gunpowder, a Moyune Gunpowder, etc.

Gunpowder is made from young to me-dium leaves, rolled in balls, ranging from Pinhead to Pea Leaf. It is subdivided into Extra First Pinhead, First, Second, Third, Fourth, Fifth, Sixth, Seventh, and Com-mon Gunpowder. The three Chinese grades are *Mao Chu*, *Pao Chu*, and *Chi Chu*.

The smaller the balls, the more expen-sive the tea. Thus, an Extra First Pin-head Gunpowder is very small; a First Gunpowder is a fine, rolled, and regular leaf; a Second Gunpowder is not so closely rolled; a Third Gunpowder usually is a bit loosely rolled, etc. The Chinese name for Gunpowder is *Siaou Chu*, large leaf.

Young Hyson is made from young to medium leaves in a long, twisted style. It is thinly rolled and looks not unlike twisted thread. It is subdivided into Chun Mee, Foong Mee, Sow Mee, and siftings; and sometimes into First, Second, and Third Young Hyson. Chun Mee Young Hyson has a small, hard, twisted leaf; Foong Mee, a large long leaf of curly roll; Sow Mee, a small twisted leaf. The Chinese name for Young Hyson is *Yu Chin Ch'a*, and is graded into the following five classes: *Mi Yu*, *O Yu*, *I Yu*, *Ya Yu*, and *Si Yu*.

Imperial tea is made from older leaves, left after the Gunpowder is sorted out. It is made in Gunpowder style, but looser. It is subdivided into First, Second, and

MOYUNE, NORTH CHINA YOUNG HYSON
Green Tea

Third Imperial. First Imperial is a closely rolled, regular leaf; Second is a more loosely rolled leaf; and Third is a quite large and loosely rolled leaf. In Chinese, Imperial is known as *Ta Chu*, large leaf, and the three grades as *Tsang Chu, Tan Chu*, and *Hsi Chu*.

Hyson is made from older leaves in a coarse Young Hyson-Imperial style. It is called *Si Chuen Ch'a*, Flowery Spring Tea, in Chinese, and is graded into *Mi Si, Cheng Si*, and *Fu Si*.

Twankey is a bold, ragged, open leaf of inferior quality; Hyson Skin is even worse.

Moyunes, made in Anhwei province, are not only among the best of the Country Greens, but also of all China Greens. Their distinctive characteristic is softness of leaf, which rarely takes the shotty appearance of the Gunpowder shapes that other sorts do, because of its tender, oily quality. They also are marked by clearness and richness of cup quality. Moyunes are divided into three classes: Nankin, Packeong, and True Moyunes. The crack chops of Nankin and Packeong Moyunes are splendid drinking teas, possessing attractive flavor and full, rich, toasty body. Because of the delicate texture of the leaf, it will not stand manipulation. True Moyunes are distinguished by their pale complexion and peculiar "cowslip" scent and flavor. Ouchaines are small, granulated Moyune teas. They have great strength. Most Moyunes bear the name of the growers. For example, *Ch'a Eu*

Sung, the name of a celebrated chop, means "The Tea of Eu Sung," the proprietor's name.

There are generally three packs of each chop, the first making its appearance at Shanghai about July 1, the second about September 1, and the third about October 30. The first is the best.

Tienkais, also Country Greens, from Anhwei Province, of the crack chops, are handsomer in style, lighter in liquor and in infused leaf, and very nearly equal in flavor to Moyunes, but they lack the body and toast. The leaf is somewhat harder, permitting more manipulation than in the case of Moyunes.

Fychows, other Anhwei Province Country Greens, are good leaf teas, but are distinctly smoky in flavor. Other lesser known greens from Anhwei are Tankai, Hsihsien, Wuyuan, Suining, Chiki, Ihsein, and Taiping, all named after districts about the market center of Wuhu and, therefore, sometimes called Wuhus.

Wenchows are Country Greens grown in Chekiang Province. They are characterless, poor cup teas, with a flavor like dried apples. Soeyoans from the same province are somewhat similar to Tienkais in appearance, but have not the cup quality of the latter, and the liquor soon turns red; an indication that they will not keep.

Shanghai Packs are the products of different districts made up at Shanghai, either in regular invoices or long separate lines. They are nondescript in character.

Hoochows are light-liquoring, sweet-flavored teas of handsome appearance. They are the first China greens to make their appearance in the spring and usually are made up in invoices containing about seven or eight lines of Gunpowder, two or three of Imperial, one of Young Hyson, and one of Foong Mee Hyson. Hoochows come from Chekiang Province.

Pingsueys are similar in character to Hoochows, but are slightly metallic and usually poorer cup, with better style than Hoochows, excepting the first crop teas, which resemble Hoochows in both style and cup. They are handsome teas, being much more evenly twisted than Moyunes. Pingsueys are the product of several districts below Shaoching in Chekiang Province. Pingsuey, or Pingsui, is the name of the market town in which they are concentrated.

Both Hoochows and Pingsueys come

from Chekiang Province. Other green teas from the same province are named after the districts in which they are grown. These are the Fenghwa, Shanyin, Hweiki, and Chuchi [or Chuki] Districts of the Hweiki Circuit; the Yungka, Juian, and Pingyang Districts of the Ouhai Circuit; and the Suian and Kaihwa Districts of the Kinhwa Circuit. The green teas of the Ouhai Circuit go mostly for home consumption. A green tea known as Hangchow comes from the town of that name. Hangchow and Hoochow also export a mixture of green and Oolong teas known as Kinhwa, Yingchow, and Longchin. The Longchin grade is considered the best. Chekiang teas are sold on the Shanghai market after concentration at the local market centers of Wuhu, Hangchow, and Wenchow.

The Province of Kiangsi produces a certain amount of green tea, mostly for home consumption. The small amount for export is concentrated at the city of Kiukiang, and thence shipped to Shanghai. It is known on the export market as Kiukiang tea. The district names are Tehling, Yukan, and Wannien of the Hsunyang Circuit; Yushan, Yukiang, and Shangyao of the Yuchang Circuit; and Ji-An.

Fukien Province also produces green teas for home consumption. These teas are marketed through Santuao and Foochow. The best known are those of the Tsang An district, called Hwaisan. They are known for their sweet flavor.

Hunan Province manufactures a negligible amount of green tea for home use.

Kwangtung Province manufactures a small quantity of Hyson and Young Hyson for export through Canton.

Flowery Orange Pekoe is a green tea made in Fukien Province. In appearance it is a mass of Pekoe tips, almost white in color, and very light and fluffy. In the cup it is very light and characterless, with almost no flavor. It is mostly used for styling teas. The Chinese are consumers of all the best grades and pay high prices for them.

China Oolongs are usually divided into Foochow, Amoy, and Canton Oolongs; the first named being by far the most important. Formerly there were Kokew Oolongs also. These were loosely made, rough teas, fairly brisk and of good flavor in the better grades, but rank and nasty in the commons. Silvery Oolongs are

specially picked teas, prepared from the delicate whitish leaves of the first picking.

Foochow Oolongs were at one time of great importance, but have suffered heavily from competition with Formosa Oolongs. Foochow Oolongs have a delicate cup without much body. They are long, rough, and black in leaf. The second, or summer, crops are the best, while the autumn crop has more merit than the average thirds of other teas. There are usually four or five crops.

The famous "string" teas were Foochow Oolongs. These included the crack chops known as Tong-Lee, Tong-Mow, Tong-Shin, Cum-Wo, Choey-Wo-Loong, Wing-Wo, etc. Formerly these "string" teas were prepared with great care; the leaf being black, handsome, and very clean. In the draw they possessed a full, rich, pure, true tea flavor, which, blended with a fine Moyune Gunpowder or Young Hyson, made a satisfying high grade drink—but a costly one. At one time the demand for Foochow Oolongs was so great that Tycons, Sueykuts, and Padraes were made into Oolongs.

In the latter part of the nineteenth century, great quantities of Oolongs were exported from Amoy. For instance, in 1877, Amoy exported 90,000 piculs of Oolong tea. Then Formosa entered the market. Oolongs were made in Formosa and shipped to Amoy for re-export. In 1906, Formosa began to ship tea direct to the consuming countries. Now Amoy Oolongs are sent mostly to Singapore and Siam, and are of little commercial importance. A very small amount of Kwangtung Province Oolongs are shipped from Canton.

The main varieties of scented China teas are Foochows, which are scented teas shipped through Foochow; Cantons, which are shipped through Canton; and Macaos, which are shipped through Macao, as the names indicate. The makes are the several varieties of Scented Orange Pekoe, the Scented Capers, and Pouchong. As a whole, scented teas possess very little merit in the cup, being very light, without character or body.

Pouchong tea is a scented Oolong marketed chiefly in Foochow. Formosa Pouchong is imported into China.

Foochow Orange Pekoe and Foochow Capers may be properly considered together, as they are merely a separation, by means of sifting, of the different shaped leaves; the straight, or Young Hyson, style of leaf making the Orange Pekoe, and the round Gunpowder style producing the Caper. These teas are used mostly for blending.

Foochow scented teas are manufactured, as a rule, only under contract, and in May and June.

Foochow Scented Orange Pekoe has a small evenly curled, yellowish leaf. The infusion is small and pure. It is one of the best of the scented teas. Foochow Scented Capers are not strong enough to be used for blending. They have a peculiarly crape-like appearance.

Canton Scented Orange Pekoe has a dark green to black, long spider leaf. It is often called "Long Leaf Scented Orange Pekoe" or "Spider Leaf Pekoe." The liquor is strong, pungent, and flavory. When infused, the leaves of the Canton Scented Pekoe are much greener than those of Congou, and somewhat similar to Oolong. The quality is higher than the Scented Caper, but it rarely, if ever, possesses such grip.

There is another type known as Short Leaf Canton Scented Orange Pekoe. This is prepared to resemble the Foochow kinds. It is usually strong and rasping, but lacks flavor. The variety known as Ouchaine has a very short leaf and mixes well. It is strongly scented, and possesses much grip and pungency.

The two chief varieties of Canton Scented Capers are the glazed kind and the olive-leaf kind. They are the same tea, but the former is faced with soapstone, etc., the leaf of the other retaining its natural color. Canton Scented Capers are small and shotty, and have great pungency and grip.

Macao Scented Orange Pekoes have a fairly well made leaf, with an olive to somewhat yellowish complexion. They draw a pungent, rasping liquor. The finer grades sometimes are called "Mandarin Pekoe."

Compressed China tea may be divided into three kinds, black brick, green brick, and tablet tea. In general, brick tea represents only one-sixth of the strength of leaf tea.

Black brick tea is made in China from black leaf tea and tea dust from China, India, and Ceylon. The lowest grades of leaf and dust are used, and these are called Hwahsiangs or Huahsiangs. There are a number of different mixtures used in making black brick tea which have been developed by various private firms, who keep the formulas secret. The black brick is from eight to twelve inches long and one inch thick. The bricks are packed in bamboo baskets, averaging eighty bricks to a basket, although this may vary between 36 to 144. Each brick weighs 2¼ pounds. In some cases the Chinese adulterate the brick teas by mixing with the leaf such substances as fine tree bark, the leaves of various teas, sawdust, and even soot.

Green brick tea is made only from leaves. The bricks are packed in cases, forty-five to the case, and usually measure 7x12 inches or 8x5½ inches. The grades for both black and green brick tea are high, medium, and low.

Brick tea made at Ya-chou and Ta Chien-lu in Szechwan Province of Southwest China, is of a totally different nature. These bricks are made from exceedingly coarse leaf, even including prunings. The leaf is packed in moist hides, which on drying contract to form a strong, tight package of sixty to seventy pounds weight. These are used solely for the trade with Tibet.

Tablet tea is made in much the same way as brick tea, except that only the best Huahsiangs are used. It is composed, as a general rule, of pure dust of Chinese black teas and pure dust of Javanese and Ceylon teas. Only the finest dust is used. Tablet tea is manufactured without steam and by pressure only. It is packed in small packets of 4.788 ounces and wrapped in silver paper.

Faggot tea is made up of leaves in bundles, two inches long, tied with brilliantly colored strands of silk yarn. It is a Canton Oolong product manufactured from top shoots only. The production is negligible.

Stalk tea is composed of the stalks sometimes sifted out of the Huahsiang and sold for local consumption.

Unfired tea is exported to but a few countries, without being graded.

"Tea dust" sometimes means not only pulverized tea, but also the parts of leaves, stalk, and black powder remaining after the tea has been sifted. This is being exported in increasing amounts.

Japan Teas

Most of the Japans are green teas. They are the white wines of teas, and are as

JAPAN PAN-FIRED
Green Tea

different from Congous and Oolongs as white wines are from Burgundies and clarets. Japans grow from May to October, and are divided into first, second, and third crops. The first crop teas are the best. They draw with lighter and more flavory liquor, and the infused leaf is a brighter green than in the second and third crops. The latter two may contain many useful, stylish teas. The first crop is picked from May to about the middle of June, the second crop from the middle of July to August, and the third crop from about the middle of August to September. If the weather permits, there may be a fourth crop picked late in September.

Japan teas may be roughly divided by manufacturing methods into Pan-fired [straight], Guri [curled], Basket-fired, and Natural Leaf; the last named formerly being called Porcelain-fired. Pan-fired is made from short leaves. The color is a light green. Guri is a pan-fired tea closely resembling Young Hyson. Basket-fired is made from long leaves. Higher grades are made from young succulent leaves, which, owing to their extreme pliancy, are easily twisted into the long, dark, olive green leaf known as "Spider-Leg." Medium grades are made from older leaves, and are, therefore, less pliable and easily rolled. The lower grades are loosely rolled, and contain many large, flat, poorly made leaves. Natural leaf teas may be made in the same way as Pan-fired or Basket-fired. However, they often contain more coarse leaf.

The better grades of Japan teas possess a delicate, rich flavor, peculiar to themselves. There is no difference in the drinking qualities between Pan-fired and Basket-fired. The difference lies in their appearance.

The Japanese divide the tea according to its manufacture into Sencha, the tea of commerce; Tencha, or Hiki-cha, the ceremonial tea; Bancha, low grade tea for home consumption; and Gyokuro, a specially made tea from shaded bushes. Sencha is the principal tea exported, but an increasing amount of black tea [Ko-cha] also is being made for export.

The prefecture of Shizuoka produces most of the Japan tea intended for export. Shizuoka teas may be divided into Enshu and Suruga. Enshu, sometimes spelled Yenshu, teas have not, as a rule, much style, but excel in drinking merit. Enshu may be subdivided into Kawane, Mori, Ogasa, Kanaya, and Hamamatsu. Of these, Kawane is the best. It has a small curly leaf and a fine, full, rich liquor, rather light in color. Mori has a good leaf and good liquor. Kanaya is of medium quality, with strength, but poor color. Hamamatsu is of medium quality. Ogasa is of little commercial importance. Some Ogasa is blended with Kawane and shipped as such.

Suruga teas are the stylish teas of Japan, noted for the handsome appearance of the prepared leaf. They are principally Basket-fired. The cupping qualities are not as good as Enshu, the liquor often being neutral in flavor. There are two principal kinds of Suruga—Abe and Fuji. The former is the better, Fuji being rather thin and weak, although of good color.

From the district of Yamashiro, near Kyoto, come the best teas of Japan. They have fine liquor and flavor. Uji tea is the best subvariety. A large part of Yamashiro tea consists of special grades for domestic use, and, due to its high price, little is exported. The nearby district of Goshu [Omi] produces a good grade of tea known as Shiga. Tea from Miye Prefecture is much used for blending. Gifu Prefecture produces a curly leaf tea of fair quality.

The district extending over Irima and Tama Counties, in Saitama Prefecture, produces a tea called Sayama or Hachioji tea. It has a good leaf and good liquor, but is too high priced for export.

In the Kagoshima District of the island

JAPAN BASKET-FIRED
Green Tea

of Kyushu, a certain amount of low grade tea is manufactured. It is used principally for blending in Japan for home consumption.

Gyokuro tea is of a high grade, made by a special process from shaded bushes in the district about Uji. It is not an export tea.

Tencha, also called Hikicha, or ceremonial tea, is always powdered. Like Gyokuro, it is made from shaded bushes, but while Gyokuro is the rolled leaf, Tencha is the leaf dried in the open natural state. It is always powdered. That used for the Tea Ceremony is called Matsucha. Tencha is not an export tea.

Bancha is a low grade of tea made from the coarse leaves for home consumption. Hojicha is toasted Bancha, and is very pungent.

Nibs are the lumpy leaves which, during the process of manufacture, refuse to yield to the required twist and curl. It is obtained in varying quantities from all kinds and grades of Japan teas. The finer grades of nibs give excellent cup results, but are poorer in quality than the grade from which they are obtained.

All Japans are graded for export as follows: Extra Choicest, Choicest, Choice, Finest, Fine, Good Medium, Good Common, Nibs, Dust, and Fannings.

Formosa Teas

There are two principal kinds of tea made in Formosa; namely, Oolong, a semi-fermented tea, and Pouchong, a scented Oolong. Recently, a third kind, a three-quarters fermented tea has been developed for the American market; and a fourth, a black tea, is manufactured in small quantities for shipment to Japan. The three-quarters fermented Formosa is graded as Flowery Orange Pekoe, Orange Pekoe, and Pekoe on the Daitotei market, but in the United States it must be labeled "Orange Pekoe Leaf Size."

Pouchong tea, before the final firing, is scented with gardenia, jasmine, or yulan blossoms. Although little or no Pouchong appears in the principal consuming markets of the world, over seven million pounds are manufactured principally for the East Indian trade.

Formosa Oolongs have been called the champagnes of teas. They show a crisp, dry, greenish brown, tippy leaf, and the liquor has intense pungency and piquancy, with a most delicious and attractive natural fruity flavor. The color of the liquor runs from an amber off into brown, according to the crop and the grade. The higher the grade, the more flavor in the cup. If the color of the infused leaf is all green or nearly so, the flavor and body are not at the best; if the edges of the leaves show fermentation, the tea is much better.

The producing period for Formosa Oolongs is from April to early December. This period is divided into five crops: first or spring crop, first summer crop, second summer crop, autumn crop, and winter crop. There is much variation between these. For instance, the difference between a spring tea and a late summer tea is almost as great as between a Congou and a Ceylon, or between a Japan and a Young Hyson. In general, the spring crop is light in the cup with good style, but the first and second summer crops have the most body and flavor.

The spring teas are picked from early in April to the middle of May, and shipped out in June. They have a rough, dry leaf without much tip. The liquor is of an amber color, and very light and thin. It has an indescribable "early" flavor which is impossible to get in subsequent pickings. There is a small range of grades, usually only from Common to Fine.

The first summer teas are picked from the latter part of May to the end of June, and the second summer from the first week in July to the middle of August. Early

FORMOSA OOLONG
Semi-fermented Tea

summer teas show fair body, excellent flavor, and handsome leaf. The late summer crop teas are even more handsome in leaf and more tippy than early summer teas, and have a full, rich flavor. Some of the medium grades of this crop are so heavy in the cup that they draw like a blend of an early tea with a small proportion of Ceylon or fine Congou blended in. Summer crops have a wide range of grades, the highest grades coming out of these teas.

Autumn teas are picked from the latter part of August to the middle of October. They have good leaf and full body, but the flavor is not as good as that of summer teas. The grades rarely run above Good.

Winter teas are picked from the latter part of October to early December. They are showy in appearance and light and flashy in draw, but are so dependent on weather conditions that no general description will serve for each succeeding year. Occasionally, due to an early cold snap, a small quantity of very bright, flavory, handsome teas will be picked quite late in the fall and, strange to say, these resemble spring teas very much in cup quality. But it is only one year in perhaps eight or ten that any quantity of these are produced.

The geographical divisions of the tea area of Formosa are not important in considering quality. The two principal producing districts are Shinchiku and Taihoku.

The subdistricts of Shinchiku are Byoritsu, Chikunan, Chikuto, Chureki, Shinchiku, Taikei, and Toyen; while Taihoku includes the subdistricts of Bunzan, Kaizan, Keelung, Shichisei, Shinsho, and Tamsui. The Districts of Taichu and Tainan produce a negligible quantity. Among the foreign buyers, Oolongs are sometimes divided into North District and South District teas, depending upon whether the district producing them is north or south of Daitotei.

The old Chinese nomenclature also is used to a certain extent to chop-mark the teas. These names are as follows:

Chap Go Hoon	Mack Sai Liao	Lwan Lwan
Paichee	Am Ki	Sam Teau
Sinteam	Chim Ki	Tang Lo Kien
Chuitngka	Kimpoli	Hobe
Patchatgna	Tek Sham	Beeteng
Poon Kee Wo	Keam Chai Sang	Sakakeng
Malengki	Sim Paw	Lengsuikee
	Soy-tin-chai	

The gradings for Formosa Oolongs, as adopted by the Formosan Government Tea Inspection Office, are: Standard, On Good, Good, Fully Good, Good Up, Good to Superior, On Superior, Superior, Fully Superior, Superior Up, Superior to Fine, On Fine, Fine, Fine Up, Fine to Finest, Finest, Finest to Choice, Choice. Other intermediary gradings used in the trade are Good Leaf, Fully Standard, Standard to Good, Strict Superior, Choicest, and Fancy.

French Indo-China Teas

Tea is produced in French Indo-China in the provinces of Annam, Tonkin, and Cochin-China. In addition, wild tea grows abundantly in the mountains of Upper Laos, and some tea is made there by natives.

The principal export teas of Indo-China are Annam black, Annam green, and, to a lesser extent, *fleurs de thé*. The Annam black and Annam green, where manufactured by Europeans, are well made, and are used, principally in France, for blending. Those made by the natives are from inferior coarse leaves and have a strong, acrid liquor with little flavor. *Fleurs de thé* is, as its name indicates, made from the flowers of the tea plant. Some of it is exported to France and drunk as a novelty by Parisians.

The teas manufactured and consumed locally in Indo-China are, in addition to the above, Sun-Dried tea, Tonkin black,

JAVA BROKEN ORANGE PEKOE
Black Tea

Tonkin green, Tonkin cake, and Cochin-China green. The first three are crudely manufactured articles with little merit, the natives much preferring strength and acridness to flavor. Tonkin cake is an agglomerate tea much resembling the Ball tea of Yunnan Province in China. The best varieties are Hagiang cakes and Hanoi cakes. Cochin-China green is a coarse-leaf, astringent tea, and is not commercially important.

The Tea of Siam

Tea is made in Siam from the leaves of the *Miang* tree, a species of *Thea sinensis* (L.) Sims. There are four plucking seasons: June, August, October, and December; the latter two being considered the best. In certain parts of Siam, however, plucking goes on all the year round. The leaves are steamed and fermented. They are then flavored with salt or other ingredients and used for chewing.

The Tea of Burma

Burma tea may be divided into black and green tea, and the native *letpet*, or pickled tea. Ninety per cent of the tea grown in Burma is cultivated in the Northern Shan state of Tawnpeng Loilong. Tea is grown in the Southern Shan states, also, and, to a lesser extent, in the states of Arakan, Tenasserim, and the Northwestern border division.

Three crops of tea are gathered between March and the end of October. The second picking, coming between May and July, is considered the best and is called *Swe'pe*. The first crop is coarse, and is made into pickled tea, called by the Shans *Neng Yam*, and by the Burmese *letpet*.

The black and green tea made in Burma by Europeans is negligible in quantity and is consumed locally.

Letpet is steamed and fermented tea leaf, prepared by the natives. It is consumed locally as a salad, with oil, garlic, and sometimes with dried fish.

The second crop, or *Swe'pe*, generally is converted into dry tea called *letpet chauk*. The beverage made from this is extensively used among the Shan people. It is unpalatable to European taste.

Other Teas of Asia

Tea is grown, to a small extent, in the provinces of Gilan, Mazanderan, and Astarabad, of Iran [Persia]. It is raised from seed and plants from India and Transcaucasia. There also is one estate with some 300 acres of tea at Gurun, in the Unfederated Malay State of Kedah. As is the case in Iran, the tea is of no commercial importance.

Java and Sumatra Teas

Tea grows all the year round in Java. The teas are generally at their best during the dry season [June through September]. Quality then declines throughout the balance of the year. Only black tea is manufactured.

Java teas are known by their garden marks, to which sometimes are added the names of the districts in which they are grown, in order to give them a more precise designation. There is a great variety of flavor and distinct character of liquor in the different pluckings, as well as in the different district elevations. In general, Javas have a black and attractive leaf appearance during the greater part of the year, but are brownish and stalky during the dry season, when the flavor improves. They are well made, good, useful, attractive blenders; soft and of medium strength in the cup. It is possible to get in the higher grown teas the lighter shades of ruby tints, having the flavor and aroma of Ceylons. From other states may come

JAVA ORANGE PEKOE
Black Tea

a tea of distinct India character from Assam seed plantings. The lower grown teas lack flavor, being for the most part heavy and pointless.

The finest teas of Java come from the Pengalengan Plateau in the Bandoeng District of the Preanger Regencies. Here the dry weather teas compare favorably with the better India and Ceylon growths. The elevation is from 4000 to 6000 feet. The Preanger Regencies contain 70 per cent of Java's tea estates, the producing districts being, besides Bandoeng, Garoet, Soekaboemi, Soemedang, and Tjiandjoer.

Batavia Residency ranks second to the Preanger as a tea producer. Much fine tea comes from its highlands, the districts being Buitenzorg and Soebang.

A good quality tea is manufactured in the Loemadjang and Malang Districts of the Pasoeroean Residency. Other tea producing residencies are Besoeki, Cheribon, Kederi, Kedoe, Madioen, Pakalongan, Semarang, and Soerakarta.

Sumatra teas are not so much affected by seasonal changes as are Javas. They may be said to be of the same useful cup the year round. The leaf is uniformly attractive.

The bulk of the Sumatra crop is produced on the East Coast in the districts of Deli. The subdistricts are Asahan, Batoe Barah, Simoeloengan, and Pematang Siantar. In the last named is grown the best of the Sumatras, the elevation of the estates being from 800 to 2400 feet. There are many other districts of Sumatra which show great promise for future development. The most prominent of these is Palembang, with the subdistricts of Tebing Tinggi, Upper Palembang, Moearabliti, and Pager Alam. Some tea also is produced in the Kepahiang and Pasartjoerop Districts of Upper Benkoelen, the Korintji District of the Native Sultanate of Djambi, the Dairi District of Tapanoeli, and the Ophirlands and Moerara Laboeh Districts of the Padang Highlands of the West Coast.

Java and Sumatra teas are graded as follows: Flowery Orange Pekoe, Orange Pekoe, Broken Orange Pekoe, Pekoe, Broken Pekoes, No. 1 and No. 2, Pekoe Souchong, Souchong, Broken Tea, Dust, and Bohea.

Tea of the Fiji Islands

There is a tea plantation on Vanua Levu, the second largest of the Fiji Islands. A small amount of black tea is manufactured solely for home consumption. The low elevation mitigates against tea culture.

The Teas of Africa

NYASALAND—The most promising tea country of Africa is Nyasaland. Tea is grown in the Mlanje and the Cholo Districts. The elevation of the former is about 2000 feet, while that of the latter is 3000 feet, so that the Cholo tea is a trifle higher grade than that of Mlanje. Black tea only is manufactured. It is a middling to good tea with light, plain liquor. Nyasaland tea is becoming more important on the London market and bringing prices that compare favorably with many estate teas of similar elevation in Ceylon and India. The grades are the same as for Ceylon or India blacks.

NATAL—Tea in Natal is grown only on some six estates in the vicinity of Stanger, a hilly country, 1000 feet above sea level, just west of the Stanger coastal area and south of the Tugela River, which separates Natal from Zululand. The industry has declined and now comprises only some 2000 acres, whereas in 1909 there were 5909 acres under tea. The plucking season begins in September and lasts until June. Black tea only is produced. It is grown from Assam indigenous jat. It is graded as Golden Pekoe, Pekoe, Pekoe Souchong, and Souchong. Most of it is sold in South

Africa, although occasional small lots appear on the London market. It is a mild flavored tea of low tannin content.

KENYA—The tea of Kenya Colony is produced in the Kericho District of Nyanza Province, the Kiambu District of Kikuyu Province, and, to a lesser extent, in the Naivasha, and the Uasingishu Extra Provincial Districts. Most of this area is about 7000 feet above sea level. The tea is from various British India jats. It has a boldish leaf, thin liquor, and fair strength and quality. Although not yet commercially important, Kenya tea is developing rapidly, the total acreage under tea having increased from 382 acres in 1925 to 1689 acres in 1926.

In 1929, a representative invoice of Kenya tea was sold in the open market. A report on the samples indicated that the manufacture was conducted on similar lines to those usually followed in other countries of production.

UGANDA—A small amount of tea is grown in Uganda at an altitude of about 5000 feet. The leaf is rich in caffeine, tannin, and extractive matter; in these respects resembling India rather than China tea. It is sold in Nairobi, Kenya Colony, for local consumption.

PORTUGUESE EAST AFRICA—There are 493 acres under tea in Portuguese East Africa [Mozambique], in the territory where the Mt. Mlanje region of Nyasaland joins Mozambique. At the present time it is marketed locally and in Portugal, where it enjoys a fifty per cent preferential duty. The liquor is light and plain.

These teas are similar to those of Nyasaland, and, like them, are lacking in body and point. In style they are attractive, having the outstanding character of tip.

The Azores and Mauritius

A small amount of green and of black tea is manufactured on a few plantations on the island of St. Michael in the Portuguese owned Azores Islands. The tea is of good quality. All of it is marketed in Portugal, where it is accorded preferential duty. Tea also is grown commercially on the British island of Mauritius in the Indian Ocean. The production is approximately 30,000 pounds per annum.

Transcaucasian Tea

Considerable acreage is devoted to tea in Adzharistan, a zone under the protection of the Georgian Socialist Federated Soviet Republics in Russian Transcaucasia. The estates cover the southern slopes of the Adjar Hills near the eastern shore of the Black Sea in the vicinity of Batoum. The product is marketed in Russia. The center of production and management of cultivation is the People's Estate, "Chakva." The best quality tea is equal in some respects to many kinds of China tea, and to some of the medium and good common grades of low country India teas. The leaf has an attractive appearance, but the cup quality is rather indifferent.

Tea Tasting

It has been said that a tea taster, like a poet, is born, not made. Of course his faculties must be trained, but unless he has a delicate palate and an exquisite sense of smell to begin with, he never will be an expert judge of teas. The talent of a good taster resembles that of a maestro, who will know by the look of a score how it will sound, or that of a great chef, who will know what the taste of a dish will be by an expert knowledge of its constituents. The tea expert not only has to appraise the value of thousands of pounds worth of tea by merely tasting a sample, but he is expected to know how the various samples of different teas will blend together. It is evident, therefore, that natural talents of a high order, cultivated by years of practice and study, are requisites for a successful buyer of tea.

Tea is judged by three factors: the appearance, twist, and smell of the dry leaf, which are judged by sight and smell; the color, brightness, and odor of the infusion, also judged by sight and smell; and the color, thickness, strength, pungency, and flavor of the liquor, judged by sight and taste.

Black, well twisted leaf denotes a good wither. Brown, flaky leaf denotes a poor wither. However, leaf with a brown shade is generally the best liquoring tea; black, pretty leaf generally gives a poor liquor. Open, flat leaf infuses very quickly, and all the essence of the tea is extracted with the first water poured thereon. Leaf that is closely twisted generally gives a better second cup. For districts where the water is hard, closely twisted leaf should be chosen, while a more open leaf is the proper selection for use with soft water. In gen-

TASTING TEA IN A MINCING LANE SALESROOM, LONDON

eral, the leaf should be small, hard, well rolled and uniform. Tip is not always necessary. In the United States, where perhaps undue attention has been given to buying for style, many buyers give too much consideration to Pekoe tips as an indication of quality in black teas, whereas the best drawings of all varieties of blacks are oftentimes without any indication of tip. For example, in a fine Formosa, small, black, hard, well twisted, uniform leaf is a surer indication of quality than rough, uneven leaf with an abundance of tip, and this is also true of the choicest Darjeelings sold at the fanciest prices, the best of which are entirely black. If the tea is tippy, the tips should be golden, long, and well twisted. Some buyers test the dry leaves by taking up a quantity in the hand, gently pressing them, and noting if one sample is more springy or more flexible than another. A new tea will give under gentle compression, and return without crumbling or breaking up in the hand. An old tea will break and show dust.

Ceylon, Java, and India black tea are much alike in appearance of the dry leaf. Indeed, in instances where Java tea is grown from an Assam seed, it is well-nigh impossible to distinguish between them. China black is quite distinct from the others. Each growth, however, has a distinct aroma. It is thus possible after some practice to distinguish between them "by

the nose"; i.e., by smelling. A fair value may sometimes be placed on the teas by an expert using merely this test of the dry leaf.

The color of the infused leaf is important. In the case of black teas, a bright infusion with some greenish leaf showing in it usually goes with a brisk tea, and indicates under-fermentation. Such teas, when over brisk, are often called "raw" or "green." A dark green infusion goes with a flat leaf and often denotes under-withering, accompanied by over-fermentation. Yellow leaf with a greenish shade generally denotes pungency. Rich-golden leaf invariably denotes quality. Reddish leaf denotes rich, full liquor. Dark leaf is a sure indication of low-grade and common tea. The color should always be even. In the case of green teas, a clear, greenish-yellow or greenish-golden color, bright and lustrous to the bottom of the cup, denotes a young, early picked leaf; a dull, lifeless, dark or brownish yellow color denotes an old or low-grade leaf. The lighter the liquor of light-liquoring teas, the younger the leaf and, as a rule, the better the tea. A very high grade Japan, Moyune Gunpowder, or Young Hyson, has a remarkably light colored liquor, so much so, indeed, that it would naturally suggest a lack of body and strength. This is not the case. Extremely light colored liquor, therefore, must not be taken as evidence of a lack of other cup qualities. By smelling the infused leaf, one may distinguish variations in character of the teas and detect point and pungency, thickness, richness, and body, and burnt, or over fermented, teas. To an extent, some buyers rely on the banking qualities of the infused leaf. After the liquor has been well drained off, good banking leaf will still retain a considerable quantity, so that by pressing it like a sponge, quite a lot of liquor may be squeezed out.

However helpful the inspection of the dry leaf and the infusion, the final test of quality and flavor lies in the liquor. The ideal tea is the brisk, full, rich, flavory tea; thick or syrupy in the cup; not dark, but rich in color. The liquor of a good tea has a bright sparkling appearance immediately after it is poured out. If the tea be of the Assam variety, it will "cream down" rapidly as it cools. With the China variety there seldom is any creaming.

It is difficult to describe the different terms used in tasting tea. For instance, the tea may be brisk, full, rich, thick, insipid, grassy, fishy, smoky, flavory, harsh, metallic acrid, puckery, toasty, malty, brassy; it may have point, body, strength, pungency, bite; it may cream down. Pungency is a sensation of the gums. It is a roughness or astringency in the mouth, and not a taste. Rawness or greenness is a bitter taste. Briskness is a live, as opposed to a flat, taste; comparable to a fresh soda water against a stale one. Flavor is a sweetish taste, a honey-like smell. It also has been described as a bouquet which can be tasted. "Creaming down" means that the tea gets quite thick and looks as if a quantity of rich cream had been stirred into it; a milky film rises to the surface of the cup. It cannot be taken as an invariable test of good tea, but, when present, it may be assumed that the tea is at least strong and rich in quality. It is no indication of flavor.

Chemically speaking, tannins have a strongly astringent or pungent taste. It is this taste which gives the characteristic bite to the liquor. Tannin also is responsible for the golden, red, and brown color of the liquor, and partly responsible for the creaming down. Tannin red gives new penny color and strength; tannin brown gives old penny color; tannin itself gives pungency and briskness. Caffeine provides the stimulant; the essential oil, the aroma, and the greater part of the flavor. The total soluble solids give the thickness.

TEA-TASTING ROOM IN A NEW YORK TEA IMPORTER'S SALESROOM

In addition to the qualities mentioned above, the taster looks for "character"; *i.e.*, something distinctive. He wants a tea that can be put into blend or ordinary leaf and force its character into that blend. A tea may lack most of the desirable individual qualities, but if it has one distinctive outstanding quality or character, it will bring a good price.

Iced Tea Blends

Iced tea, drunk in tall glasses, without milk or cream, is popular as a summertime drink in America. The careful blender finds it necessary to make a thorough study of teas for this use, as some teas are somewhat cloudy in liquor; teas that cream down. Nearly all high grade, and many medium grade Assams, and high grown Ceylons, exhibit this characteristic. It has been argued that the cloudy effect, which sometimes spoils the look of an iced tea blend, is due to a too high percentage of teas that cream down. Some say it may be avoided by not allowing the tea to draw more than five minutes at the most, and by pouring it while hot into a glass filled with cracked ice. Others advocate a brew of not more than three minutes; the theory being that the longer a tea is brewed the

TESTING TEA BY THE ENGLISH METHOD

(1) Infusing pot containing the usual weight of leaf and filled with freshly boiled water. (2) After steeping 4 to 5 minutes the liquor is poured into the testing cup. (3) The infused leaf is turned into the reversed infuser lid for critical examination. (4) Liquor in the cup ready for testing under normal drinking conditions.

more likely it is to cream down. Some believe that the creaming down is caused by precipitation of the tannin and the caffeine, in the proportion of three to one. However, it is more likely caused by too great an amount of phlobaphenes [oxidized tannin products].

Of course, it is possible to make up a blend that will not develop too much precipitation. It is purely a matter of expert selection, and adaptation. Practically all low grown Ceylons, low grown Northern and Southern Indias, Formosa blacks, some of the medium grade North China growths, and all of the South China Congous, do not cream down. The component parts of an iced tea blend should be infused for six minutes and tested out with ice before being blended. Given a blend low in creaming tendency, the question of serving it successfully for iced tea purposes resolves itself largely into how soon the liquor is poured off the infused leaf. If, as indicated above, the hot tea is poured off within three to five minutes, a delightful summer beverage results.

Tasting Equipment

Light plays an important part in tea tasting. The ideal testing room has windows on the north side only. The counter or table for testing is placed where the light is steady and true, and surrounds each cup equally. If the light on each be not equal, the colors of the liquors cannot be compared. Direct sunlight or artificial light is avoided. In the Far East, a counter usually is built directly under the windows, and screens are so built outside the windows that the light is reflected down directly on the teas.

The American method and equipment for tea tasting is somewhat different from that used in England, Holland, and in the producing countries. The latter is unquestionably the more thorough and accurate; while the American takes less room and less time.

The general method of testing in all parts of the world, except in the United States, is as follows: A long counter about four feet high is used. Around part or all of the room are shelves on which rest the various samples. A kettle—preferably of copper—rests on a stove. The screens or shades on the windows are adjusted to give the proper light. The samples of dry

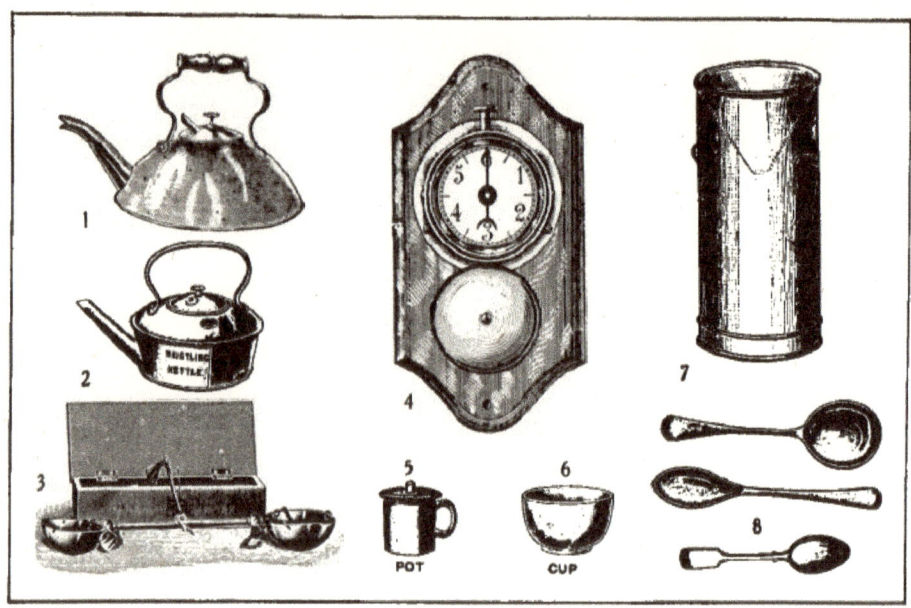

A GROUP OF ENGLISH TEA-TASTING REQUISITES

No. 1—Tea-tasting kettle; No. 2—Whistling gas kettle; No. 3—Tea-testing scales; No. 4—Tea-tasting clock; No. 5—Infusing pot; No. 6—Tasting cup; No 7—Tea-tasting spittoon; No. 8—Tea-tasting spoons.

tea to be tested are ranged in a row on the counter. Before them is placed a line of small, covered china pots or mugs. Usually they have no spouts, although in some parts of Europe pots with spouts are employed. In front of each sample and pot is a thin china cup or trier of regulation size. About one-tenth of an ounce, or forty-three grains, of tea is weighed out from each sample on a small hand-balance scale. In England the weight of a sixpenny piece is used. The tea is placed in the pots. When ten, twenty, or thirty teas have been "weighed in," the batch is ready for watering. Water, that has just reached the boiling point, always is used. It never is brought to a boiling point the second time. The water is poured over the tea and the covers placed on the pots.

The tea is then allowed to stand for a period of four, five, or six minutes. Some tasters use a sand-glass to tell the time. Others use a small wall clock with a bell attached. The clock is set for the proper period and, at the expiration of the time set, the bell rings. The pots are turned sideways in the cups, permitting the brew to drain off the leaves. After the liquor is drawn off, the infused leaf is placed on the inverted cover of the pot, which is placed on top of the pot. By this means the infusion can be examined while the liquor is tasted. A batch, as a rule, is tasted from left to right, the inferior teas receiving first attention.

In the United States, a round table with a revolving top is used. The table may be of wood, although artificial stone tops also are in use. In the center of the table is a scale resting on a base, or built on a pedestal. In the newer type of tables, a "ring-side" tray is attached to an arm extending just under the surface of the table to a point immediately outside the periphery. This tray, or "comparison shelf," remains stationary, while the table revolves. It is used to facilitate comparisons. For a space of three or four inches from its edge the top of the table is depressed a fraction from its general plane, and on this outer margin the thin, white cups are ranged, each backed by the shallow pan or tray holding the sample. The taster sits on a stool before the table. No pots are used. Tea to the weight of a silver half-dime, or its equivalent in Troy weight,

AN AMERICAN TEA-TESTING TABLE

This Burns equipment consists of a revolving artificial stone top, center-mounted scale, and Mitchell "ring-side" tea tray for holding a comparison infusion.

is placed in each cup. Boiling water is then poured thereon. The taster watches the leaves slowly unfolding at the bottom of the cup—the "agony of the leaves"— and inhales the rising steam from first one cup and then another as he turns the table. He then takes a clean spoon and moves the leaves in the bottom of each cup, noting the difference in color after this is done. A half-minute or so having passed, the leaves are cool enough to smell. A spoonful of leaves is taken up and the liquor allowed to run off them. The leaves are then brought up to the nostrils, the aroma is inhaled, and the character of the infused leaves noted. The spoon is rinsed in a bowl of clean hot water on the table, so as to prevent the transfer of the flavor from one cup to another, and the same procedure is followed with the other samples.

Next the color of the liquor is examined. Here is a sample that is "standing up"; i.e., holding its original color, better than the others. Another may be quickly darkening. The color is compared with the cup containing the tea to be matched standing on the comparison shelf, the desideratum being a dead match; i.e., a tea that shows equal qualities all round.

The tea cools rapidly and the tester comes now to the actual sipping of the liquor. He sees that the liquor is not too

hot, for to scald the mouth greatly interferes with the sense of taste. A spoonful is taken into the mouth by drawing it with a quick inward breath between the lips. The liquid is kept in continuous contact with the palate by rolling it around in the mouth, in the same manner that a wine connoisseur tastes wine. The liquor never is swallowed, for to do so would impair the sense of taste for the time being. Having fully tasted it, the taster ejects it from the mouth into a tall wide mouthed cuspidor, usually placed on the floor between his knees. These cuspidors are specially made for this purpose. In the United States they reach almost to the table top, in other countries they are sometimes much higher. They resemble an hourglass in shape. The object of tasting is, of course, to learn the true quality of the tea with a view to utilizing it either straight or in a blend.

Tea, being an infusion of leaves in water, the kind of water matters just as much as the kind of tea. Some experts have made a practice of using distilled water for testing. While such a method will invariably discover the intrinsic qualities of a tea, it will not guide a taster in the choice of a tea that will be perfectly suitable to the water of a certain district in which the tea is to be sold. In London, to counteract this condition, the big blenders have samples of the water from each district in their country. For example, if a tea is to be sold in Plymouth, the water used in tasting is South Devon water. In the United States this phase of tasting is not given much attention—more is the pity.

Certain teas, also, are more suitable for certain types of water. Young, flavory, high-grade leaf of any kind or make of

AMERICAN KETTLE OUTFITS

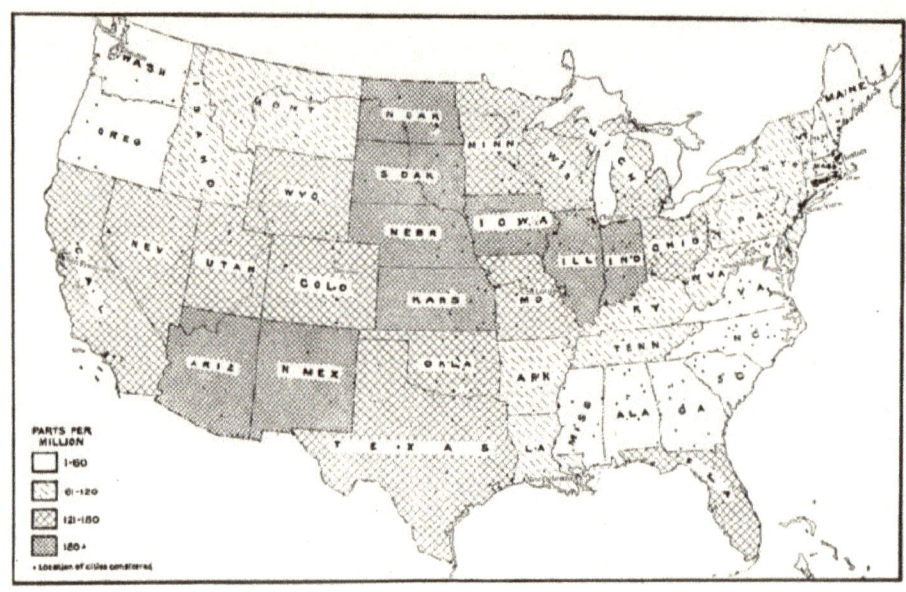

PARTS PER MILLION
1-60
61-120
121-180
180+
• Location of cities considered

WEIGHTED AVERAGES OF THE HARDNESS OF THE PUBLIC WATER SUPPLIES OF THE UNITED STATES

In a general way the shadings agree with the hardness of water furnished by the larger city supply systems. The darkness of the shadings increases with the hardness. They do not represent the actual hardness of all the water-supplies in a given state, but show the relative conditions in over 600 cities indicated by dots. From *Water Supply Paper 658*, U. S. Geological Survey.

green or black tea will yield its full fragrance, flavor, and strength when infused in pure, soft water; while the same leaf, if infused or drawn in hard water, will likely fail to exhibit the qualities required by the soft-water infusion. Highly fired teas, or teas of the rougher, harsher sorts, give better results in hard water. In countries where milk is used in tea, a final tasting is made by adding milk. Care must be taken to give an equal proportion to each cup. The usual course is to equalize the amount of liquor in each cup, and then, with a small spoon, add the same quantity of milk. Many thick-looking teas are only colorful, and, when milk is added, are tasteless and watery. The better teas will look more creamy than those of inferior quality.

Generally speaking, the London tea blender sends his strong Assam blends into Scotland; Darjeelings and Travancores into Yorkshire; Ceylons and certain of the China teas into the southwestern counties; reserving Indian and Ceylon blends for London, and the eastern counties.[1]

[1] F. W. F. Staveacre, *Tea and Tea Dealing*, London, 1929, p. 75.

There are no specific rules as to a taster's conduct while tasting. Some smoke while tasting, and some do not. Some prefer to take a bite of apple or cheese to tone up the palate between tastings, some do not. Some do all their tasting before lunch, in the belief that the palate is a bit dulled after lunch, some taste all day. Some cannot bear the sight of tea at home or out of office hours; some are very fond of it. Certain it is, however, that the old myth ascribing an early death to tea tasters is amply refuted by the number of tea tasters in the world who have lived long past their allotted three score years and ten, most of which were spent in tasting tea.

There are certain minor rules which should be strictly followed in a testing room. The cups and/or pots should be of exactly the same cubic content. The scale must be kept exactly true so that the leaves can be weighed out accurately. The kettle must be kept perfectly clean and free from odor of any kind. The tea cups and spoons should be thoroughly washed and wiped dry with a clean cloth.

COMPLETE REFERENCE TABLE

OF

THE PRINCIPAL KINDS OF TEA GROWN IN THE WORLD

With Their Trade Values and Cup Characteristics

t, indicates town or trading center; *m n*, market name;
d, district, state, county, or circuit; *s d*, subdistrict.

Grand Division	Country	Shipping Ports	State, District, or Market Name	Local Data, Definitions, Cup Qualities, Trade Characteristics, and Gradings
Asia	Ceylon	Colombo	Ceylons, *m n* [Black & Green]	*In general:* Ceylon teas are high, medium and low grown. They are known by their garden marks [of which there are more than 2000] and they are produced in 60 odd Districts in the C., S., and S. W. parts of the Island. The best pluckings are in February and March, and August and September. The dry leaf is well made, even, black, and often tippy. The high grown have indifferent leaf styles, but good strength and delicate cup quality. The medium grown usually have a well made leaf with useful liquor, but are often poor, because much village leaf is used. The low grown have a better leaf style and a strong plain cup.
			DISTRICTS	
			Alagala, *d* [Kadugannawa N.]	The elevation ranges from 700 to 2700 feet. Plain tea.
			Ambagamuwa, *d*	The wettest planting district, producing medium, to high medium grown tea at elevations ranging from 1800 to 3000 feet. Plain tea.
			Badulla, *d*	On the Uva side. Medium and high medium grown tea; elevation 1500 to 2700 feet. At times fair to good tea.
			Balangoda, *d*	Elevation 1800 to 5000 feet. Mixed quality.
			Dikoya, *d*	Formerly a flourishing coffee district. High and highest grown tea; elevation 4000 to 5000 feet. Good quality tea.
			Dikoya Lower, *d*	Medium to high grown tea; elevation 2300 to 4500 feet. Fair to medium tea.
			Dimbula, *d*	Elevation 3500 to 6000 feet. One of the best of Ceylon teas, being of very good flavor and quality generally.
			Dolosbage, *d*	Medium and high grown tea, ranging from 1300 to 4000 feet. Ordinary quality.
			Dumbara, *d*	Low grown and medium tea; 70 to 1700 feet. Ordinary quality.

Grand Division	Country	Shipping Ports	State, District, or Market Name	Local Data, Definitions, Cup Qualities, Trade Characteristics, and Gradings
Asia *Cont'd*	Ceylon *Cont'd*	Colombo *Cont'd*	Ceylons, *Cont'd* Galagedara, *d*	Elevation 800 to 2300 feet. Ordinary quality.
			Galle, *d* Ambalangoda, *s d* Elpitiya, *s d* Udugama, *s d*	Low grown tea.
			Hantane, *d*	Medium and high grown; 2000 to 3800 feet. Plain to ordinary quality.
			Haputale, *d*	Elevation 2000 to 6200 feet. Mostly fine tea.
			Haputale West, *d*	Elevation is 3100 to 7200 feet. Mostly fine tea.
			Harispattu, *d*	Elevation 1750 feet.
			Hewaheta Upper, *d*	Elevation 2400 to 6000 feet. Mixed quality.
			Hewaheta Lower, *d*	The oldest tea district. Elevation 2000 to 5300 feet. Mixed quality.
			Hunasgiriya, *d*	Elevation 2000 to 4000 feet. Medium tea.
			Kadugannawa, *d*	Elevation 800 to 3600 feet. Various qualities of tea.
			Kalutara, *d*	Low-country tea; 100 to 500 feet elevation. Plain tea.
			Kegalla, *d*	Low grown and medium tea; 400 to 1500 feet. Plain tea.
			Kelani Valley, *d* Avissawella, *s d* Yatiyantota, *s d* Ruanwella, *s d* Kitulgala, *s d*	Elevation 300 to 2000 feet. Most of Ceylon's low grown tea is in this district. Plain to ordinary quality.
			Kelebokka, *d*	Elevation 3000 to 4500 feet.
			Knuckles, *d*	Elevation 3000 to 4500 feet. Various quality teas.
			Kotmale, *d*	Elevation 2000 to 5000 feet. Mixed quality tea.
			Kurunegala, *d*	Elevation 500 to 1500 feet. Plain tea.
			Madulsima, *d* and Hewa Eliya, *d* [Badulla North]	Elevation 2000 to 5000 feet. Quality varies.
			Maskeliya, *d*	Formerly a coffee district. Elevation 3000 to 5500 feet. Fine tea.
			Matale East, *d* and Lagalla, *d*	Elevation 1200 to 4000 feet. Medium tea.
			Matale North, *d*	Elevation 1200 to 2500 feet. Ordinary quality.

Grand Division	Country	Shipping Ports	State, District, or Market Name	Local Data, Definitions, Cup Qualities, Trade Characteristics, and Gradings
Asia *Cont'd*	Ceylon *Cont'd*	Colombo *Cont'd*	Ceylons, *Cont'd* Matale South, *d*	Elevation 1000 to 1500 feet. Ordinary quality.
			Matale West, *d*	Elevation 1500 to 3000 feet. Ordinary quality.
			Maturata, *d*, including Kurunda Oya Valley	High and highest grown tea. Elevation 3500 to 6500 feet. Fine tea.
			Medamahanuwara, *d*	Elevation 2500 to 4500 feet. Quality varies.
			Monaragala, *d*	Elevation 600 to 3500 feet. Medium to ordinary tea.
			Morawak Korale, *d* or Deniyaya, *d*	Elevation 1000 to 2500 feet. Ordinary tea.
			New Galway or Wilson's Bungalow, *d*	High and highest grown tea; elevation 4000 to 6200 feet. Fine quality.
			Nilambe, *d*	Elevation 1600 to 3500 feet. Medium quality.
			Nitre Cave, *d*	Elevation 2000 to 4000 feet. Quality varies.
			Nuwara Eliya, *d*	Finest and highest estates. Elevation 6000 to 7000 feet. Very fine quality.
			Panwila and Wattegama, *d*	Elevation 1500 to 2500 feet. Ordinary quality.
			Passara, *d*	Elevation 2000 to 4500 feet. Medium quality.
			Pundaluoya, *d*	Elevation 3000 to 5000 feet. Rather fine tea.
			Pussellawa, *d*	Formerly a coffee district. Elevation 2000 to 4500 feet. Fair tea.
			Rakwana, *d*	Elevation 2000 to 3500 feet. Quality varies.
			Ramboda, *d*	One of the older tea districts; elevation 3000 to 5000 feet. Mostly fine tea.
			Rangala, *d*	Elevation 2500 to 4500 feet. Medium to good tea.
			Ratnapura, *d*, including Kuruwity and Pelmadulla	Elevation 100 to 4000 feet. Medium tea.
			Udapussellawa, *d*	Elevation 3500 to 5500 feet. Fine to very fine tea.
			Walapane Lower, *d*	Elevation 2500 to 4000 feet. Medium quality.
			Wattegama and Panwila, *d*	Elevation 1500 to 2500 feet. Ordinary quality.
			Yakdessa, *d*	Elevation 1000 to 4000 feet. Ordinary quality.

Grand Division	Country	Shipping Ports	State, District, or Market Name	Local Data, Definitions, Cup Qualities, Trade Characteristics, and Gradings
Asia Cont'd	Ceylon Cont'd	Colombo Cont'd	Ceylons, Cont'd	
			Low Country Minor Districts, including: Gampaha, Veyangoda, Matara, or Weligama Moratuwa.	Plain to ordinary tea produced throughout these sections.
			Gradings for Ceylon Blacks: Broken Orange Pekoe, Broken Pekoe, Orange Pekoe, Pekoe, Pekoe Souchong, Souchong, Fannings, and Dust.	
			Gradings for Ceylon Greens: Young Hyson, Hyson Nos. 1 and 2, Gunpowder, Twankay, Fannings, and Dust.	
	India	Calcutta Chittagong Bombay Calicut Madras Karachi Tuticorin	Indias, m n [Black & Green]	In general: The leaf characteristics of fermented (black) Indias differ with the districts in which they are produced. The manufactured leaf is usually black and assumes a browner appearance as the season progresses. In the late months stalk becomes redder and more apparent, and the so-called autumn output is generally rusty and red in color, with a marked difference in flavor from the earlier teas. In the cup, Indias are full bodied, rich, malty. India teas also are known by their garden marks of which there are more than 4000. A negligible amount of green tea is made in some districts for trading across the northern border.
			DISTRICTS NORTH INDIA	
		Calcutta Chittagong	I.—Assam, N. E. India, m n & d a—Brahmaputra Valley.	Generally referred to as "Assams." A hard, flinty, well made leaf of grayish black color, with bright golden tip in the higher grades. Rich, heavy tea, which has strength, grip, pungency, and roughness. Much used for blending. The heaviest producing districts are Sibsagar and Lakhimpur.
			Darrang, d	Ranks fourth in importance of the Assam divisions.
			Bishnath, s d	Town and steamer ghat.
			Mangaldai, s d	Market town.
			Tezpur, s d	R. R. terminus and steamer ghat.
			Goalpara, d	Market town and R. R. station. Very little tea.
			Kamrup, d	Steamer ghat is Gauhati. Very little tea.
			Nowgong, d	Market town and R. R. Station. Medium teas.
			Lakhimpur, d North Lakhimpur, s d	Some of the finest Assam teas. Pungent. Second flush very tippy. Good autumnal flavor.

Grand Division	Country	Shipping Ports	State, District, or Market Name	Local Data, Definitions, Cup Qualities, Trade Characteristics, and Gradings
Asia Cont'd	India Cont'd	Calcutta Chittagong Cont'd	North Indias, Cont'd	
			Dibrugarh, d Panitola, s d	Market town and steamer ghat. Market town and R. R. station.
			Dum-Duma, t & s d [Doom Dooma] Tingri, s d	Contains some of the finest tea areas in the world. Here quantity and quality go together.
			Sadiya Frontier, d	Little tea. Near confluence of the rivers which break from the Himalayas to form the Brahmaputra.
			Sibsagar, d Sibsagar, t & s d	Some good teas. R. R. Station.
			Golaghat, d Jorhat, d	Market town on Dhansiri River. Good medium teas; some very good.
			Balipara Frontier, d	Commercially unimportant.
			b—Surma Valley	
			Cachar, m n & d	Leaf has a grayish black appearance. Thick, sweet liquor with less body and pungency than Assams. Resembles Sylhets, but smaller in size. Thick, sweet, useful, medium and low quality liquors are produced.
			Sylhet, m n & d	Leaf attractive, well made. Liquor mild, smooth flavor. Classified as good-medium.
		Calcutta	II.—Bengal, N. E. India,	
			Darjeeling, m n & d	Appearance of the leaf varies greatly —from small, tippy to bold; grown on slopes of Himalaya Mountains, elevation 1000 to 6000 feet. The finest and most delicately flavored of India teas, possessing richness and exquisite bouquet. June and October pluckings especially good.
			Jalpaiguri, t & d	Business center for the Dooars District and for Indian-owned gardens.
			Dooars, m n & d Kalchini, s d Dalgaon, s d Binnaguri, s d Nagrakata, s d Chalsa, s d Mal, s d Oodlabari, s d	Leaf has a black appearance. Soft, mellow liquor; very colory and full-bodied. Softer than Assam. Much used for blending. Under certain climatic conditions, stalk and reddish leaf are to be found in large quantities. Autumnals especially sought after.
			Terai, m n & d	Small, black leaf. Liquor of fair to good cup quality; approaching Dooars character. Usually soft, with fair color; at times not unlike the poor quality Darjeelings.
		Chittagong	Chittagong, d	Some body and strength. A useful tea. Leaf small and black.
			Chittagong Hill Tracts, d	Small production.

Grand Division	Country	Shipping Ports	State, District, or Market Name	Local Data, Definitions, Cup Qualities, Trade Characteristics, and Gradings
Asia Cont'd	India Cont'd		North Indias, Cont'd	
		Calcutta	III.—Bihar and Orissa Hazaribagh and Ranchi, d [Chota Nagpur, m n] Purnea, d	Mostly green tea from China jat; some body and strength, slightly brassy flavor.
		Calcutta Karachi Bombay	IV.—Punjab Kangra, d	Green tea is made here; peculiarly delicate, somewhat spicy flavor.
			V.—Hill Tippera, N. E. India [Tripura, Native State]	All tea grown in native-owned gardens. Unimportant commercially.
			VI.—United Provinces	
		Calcutta Karachi Bombay	Kumaon, m n & d	Small, close leaf. Draws a light, brisk liquor. Unimportant commercially. Some green tea is manufactured in this district for trade across the border with Tibet and Nepal.
			Almora, s d Garhwal, s d	Poor grade, 5000 to 7000 feet. Poor grade, 5000 to 7000 feet.
			Dehra Dun, d	Rather plain, lacking point and flavor; poor grade of green tea sold largely to the local Amritsar market.
		Madras Calicut	SOUTH INDIA Madras	
			Coimbatore, d Anamalai, m n & d	Possesses good body and strength. Somewhat similar to Travancores, but much stronger and more preferable.
			Cochin, d	Production very small. Commercially unimportant.
			Coorg, d	Commercially unimportant.
			Madura, d	Commercially unimportant.
			Malabar, d	Low grown, poor tea.
			Wynaad, s d & m n	Average elevation 3000 feet.
			Nilgiris, d & m n	Fine flavory teas with brisk, pungent liquor.
			Nilgiri-Wynaad, d	A fair tea on Travancore style.
			Tinnevelly, d	Unimportant as a tea district.
		Calicut	Mysore [Native State]	Small production on one native estate, but now being opened up both on old coffee land and on virgin forest.
		Tuticorin	Travancore, m n [Native State]	Generally speaking, these teas resemble Ceylons more than Indias.
			Central Travancore, d [Peermade]	A medium grade tea.
			Kanan Devan, d [High Range]	A high grown, good tea.

Grand Division	Country	Shipping Ports	State, District, or Market Name	Local Data, Definitions, Cup Qualities, Trade Characteristics, and Gradings
Asia Cont'd	India Cont'd	Tuticorin Cont'd	South Indias, Cont'd	
			Mundakayam, m n & d	A good, useful tea.
			South Travancore, m n & d	Low grown, plain tea.
				Gradings for all India Blacks: Broken Orange Pekoe, Broken Pekoe, Orange Pekoe, Pekoe, Pekoe Souchong, Souchong, Fannings, and Dust.
				Gradings for India Greens: Fine Young Hyson, Young Hyson, Hyson No. 1, Hyson, Twankay, Soumee, Fannings, and Dust.
Asia	China	Shanghai Hankow Foochow Hangchow Wenchow	CHINA GREENS	In the trade China Greens are divided into Country Greens [Moyunes, Teenkais, Fychows, Soeyans, Wenchows and local packs], Hoochows, and Pingsueys. The Country Greens have rich, clear, and fragrant cup qualities. The Hoochows are flavorless and neutral. The Pingsueys are light colored and rank in the cup.
		Hangchow Wenchow Shanghai	I.—Chekiang Province	
			Hweiki	Circuit including the Districts of Fenghwa, Shanyin, Chuchi, and Hweiki.
			Ouhai, m n	Circuit including the Districts of Yungka, Juian, Pingyang.
			Kinghwa	Circuit including the Districts of Suiyan and Kaihwa.
			Pingsuey, m n	A stylish seaboard green of poorer cup than Hoochows, except first crop, which resembles Hoochow in both style and cup.
			Hangchow, m n & t	Name given to teas marketed in Hangchow.
			Hoochow, m n & t	A rather light liquoring, flavory seaboard green of good appearance; the best selections having a bright, attractive cup quality.
			Wenchow, m n & t	Poor quality Country tea.
			Kinhwa, m n & t	Mixture of green and Oolong.
			Yingchow, m n	Mixture of green and Oolong.
			Longchin, m n	Best grade mixture of green and Oolong.
			Soeyoan, m n	Name given to teas marketed in the Soeyoan District.
			Kwangtung Province	Commercially unimportant.
			Hunan Province	Commercially unimportant.

Grand Division	Country	Shipping Ports	State, District, or Market Name	Local Data, Definitions, Cup Qualities, Trade Characteristics, and Gradings
Asia Cont'd	China Cont'd		China Greens, Cont'd	
		Foochow	II.—Fukien Province Foochow, m n & t	Name given to teas marketed at Foochow.
			Santuao, t	Name given to teas marketed at Santuao.
			Wuyuan, m n & t	Teas collected in the town of Wuyuan.
			Wu-I, m n	Sweet flavored teas produced in the Chung-fu District.
			Hwaisan, m n	A number of teas of quality similar to the above, also produced in the Chung-fu District.
		Shanghai	III.—Anhwei Province	
			Wuhu, d	One of the most important green tea circuits, including the Districts of Hsihsien, Wuyuan, Siuning or Shiuling, Chiku or Jichi, Ihsien and Taiping.
			Huichow, t	Greens produced by several districts surrounding Huichow.
			Moyune, m n	Generally considered the finest of China Greens. Delicate flavor, subtle fragrance, and grayish appearance of leaf. Does not take as fine a roll as Pingsuey.
			Tienkai, m n & t	Ranking next to Moyunes. Usually the most stylish of the Country Greens, with bright cup quality.
			Fychow, m n	Great strength and pungency, but usually poor cup quality and smoky flavor.
		Shanghai Hankow	IV.—Kiangsi Province Kiukiang, m n & t	Name applied to teas marketed at Kiukiang.
			Hsunyang, m n	Circuit including the Districts of Tehling, Yukan, and Wannien.
			Yuchang, m n	Circuit including the Districts of Yushan, Shangyao, and Yuchang.
			Ji-An, m n	Popular Kiukiang green.
			Kaihwa, m n	Similar in quality to the Wuhu teas.
			Suian, m n	Similar in quality to the Wuhu teas.

Styles, Makes, and Gradings: All China Greens are prepared in the following styles or makes: Gunpowder, ranging from Pinhead to Pea Leaf, and subdivided into extra, first, second, third, fourth, fifth, sixth, seventh, and common Gunpowder, rolled round, "fine shotty" to medium; Pea Leaf [first and second], a bold round-rolled leaf; Imperial [first, second, third], large size, round-rolled; Young Hyson [long, rough, bold, and twisted leaf]; and Hyson [small, well made, curly leaf]; Waisan [brown leaf]; Sowmee [small leaf]; Hyson Skin, Twankay, and Dust.

Chinese names and grades: The Chinese name for Gunpowder is *Siaou*, large leaf, and the three Chinese grades are: *Mao Chu*, *Pao Chu*, and *Chi Chu*.

Grand Division	Country	Shipping Ports	State, District, or Market Name	Local Data, Definitions, Cup Qualities, Trade Characteristics, and Gradings
Asia Cont'd	China Cont'd	Shanghai Hankow Kiukiang Hangchow Wenchow Foochow Canton Macao Hong Kong	CHINA BLACKS [Congous, m n]	In the trade, China Blacks are divided into North China Congous, the Black Leaf Congous, or "English Breakfast" teas; which are strong, full bodied, fragrant, and sweet liquoring—the Burgundies of China teas; and the South China, or red leaf Congous, which are light in the cup with small reddish and tippy leaf—the clarets of China teas.
		Shanghai	I.—Anhwei Province:	
			Keemun, d & m n	Fine grade of North China Congou, having a thick, sappy liquor, with a rich aroma and flavor.
			Wuhu, d	Name given to teas of the Wuhu District.
			Chupoo, d	Name given to teas of the Chupoo District.
			Kintuck, m n	A flavory, full-bodied, and fine cup tea. Reddish infusion. Similar to Keemun.
			Liuan, m n	Name given to teas of the Hoshan District.
			Hwie, m n	Name given to teas from Anhwei Province, except the Keemuns.
			Hwie Chow, m n	A variety of Hwie tea.
			Tunchia, t	Teas grown around the City of Tunchia.
		Hankow	II.—Hupeh Province, or Oopack, m n	
			Ichang, n n & t	Leaf small and attractive, resembling Ningchow. Rich, full-bodied, peculiar metallic or smoky flavor.
			Yanglowtung, m n	Name given to teas of the Puchi District.
			Yanglowsu, m n	Name given to teas of the Yanglowsu District.
			Changyang, m n	Name given to the teas of the Changyang District.
			Tongshan, m n	Name given to teas of the Tongshan District.
			Tsungyang, m n	Name given to teas of the Tsungyang District.
			Sienning, m n	Name given to teas of the Sienning District.
			Puchi, m n	Name given to teas of the Puchi District.
			Kianghan, m n	Name given to teas of the Chungyan, Puchi, Hsiangnin, and Tongshan Districts.

Grand Division	Country	Shipping Ports	State, District, or Market Name	Local Data, Definitions, Cup Qualities, Trade Characteristics, and Gradings
Asia Cont'd	China Cont'd	Hankow Cont'd	China Blacks, Cont'd	
			Kiangnan, *m n*	Name given to teas from the districts surrounding Ichang.
			Sungyang, *m n*	Name given to teas of the Sungyang District.
			Cheongshukai, *m n*	Name given to teas of the Cheong-shukai District.
			Hofong, *m n*	Name given to teas of the Hofong District.
			Hangyang, *m n*	Name given to teas of the Hangyang District of Hunan, but sold under the name of Hupeh tea.
			Tai Sa Ping *m n*	Name given to teas of the Tai Sa Ping District.
		Hankow	III.—Hunan Province. "Oonams"	
			Oonfa, *m n & t* [Anhwa]	A favorite blending tea from the Southern Districts. Bright infusion; smoky flavor.
			Taoyuan, or Tangyuen, *d & m n*	Name given to teas of the Taoyuan District.
			Chang Sheo Chieh, or Chong Sow Kai, *m n*	Name given to teas of the Pingkiang District.
			Kokew, or Kou Chao, *m n*	Name given to teas of the Liuyang District.
			Liling, *d & m n*	Name given to teas of the Liling District.
			Low Yong, or Liuyang, *d & m n*	Name given to teas of the Liuyang District.
			Shantam, or Hsiangtang, *d & m n*	Name given to teas of the Hsiangtang District. Loose and spongy in make. Marked by a "mousy" taste. Quality rarely good.
			Nieyasu, or Yuin Cha Shih, *m n*	Name given to teas of the Linghu District.
			Yunshih, or Yanti, *m n*	Name given to teas of the Paling District.
			Pingkiang, or Pingkong, *d & m n*	Name given to teas of the Pingkiang District.
			Changsha, *d & m n*	Name given to teas of the Changsha District.
			Ningsiang, *d & m n*	Name given to teas of the Ningsiang District.
			Siangyin, *d & m n*	Name given to teas of the Siangyin District.
			Linsiang, *d & m n*	Name given to teas of the Linsiang District.

Grand Division	Country	Shipping Ports	State, District, or Market Name	Local Data, Definitions, Cup Qualities, Trade Characteristics, and Gradings
Asia Cont'd	China Cont'd	Hankow Cont'd	China Blacks, Cont'd	
			Shihmen, d & m n	Name given to teas of the Shihmen District.
			Siangkiang, m n	Name given to teas from the Districts of Anhwa, Siangtan, Hsiangyuin, Liuyang, Changsha, Liling, Ninghsiang, Pingkiang, and Linhsiang.
			Chenyuan, m n	Name given to teas from the Districts of Taoyuan and Shihmen, and from the circuit of Chenyuan.
			Nipkasee, d & m n	Name given to teas of the Nipkasee District.
			Wuchang, d & m n	Name given to teas of the Wuchang District.
			Hanyang, d & m n	Name given to teas of the Hangyan District.
			Hwanchow, d & m n	Name given to teas of the Hwanchow District.
		Kiukiang Shanghai	IV.—Kiangsi Province:	
			Kiukiang, m n & t	Name given to teas of the Hui Ho District in the northern part of Kiangsi. They have fragrance and flavor, but lack body.
			Hsunyang, m n	Name given to teas of the Hsunyang Circuit.
			Fowliang, m n	Name given to teas of the Fowliang Circuit. A part of these teas are known as Keemuns.
			Siushui, m n	Name given to teas of the Siushui District.
			Ningchow, m n	Valuable blending teas. A gray leaf with some tip; closely rolled, well cured, and drawing a good liquor.
			Kining, m n	Name sometimes given to Keemun and Ning Chow teas on the export market.
			Lingtu, d & m n	Name given to teas of the Lingtu District.
			Wuling, d & m n	Name given to teas of the Wuling District.
			Shiuchang, d & m n	Name given to teas of the Shiuchang District.
			Yuanshan, d & m n	Name given to teas of the Yuanshan District.
			Moning, d & m n	Name given to teas of the Moning District.
			Kutoan, m n	Sometimes fine quality. Rusty leaf with some tip. Strong for a China tea.

Grand Division	Country	Shipping Ports	State, District, or Market Name	Local Data, Definitions, Cup Qualities, Trade Characteristics, and Gradings
Asia Cont'd	China Cont'd	Kiukiang Shanghai Cont'd	China Blacks, *Cont'd*	
			Makong, *d & m n*	Name given to teas of the Makong District.
			Hohow, (Hui Ho) *m n*	Name given to teas of the Makong District.
		Hangchow Wenchow Shanghai	V.—Chekiang Province:	
			Wenchow, *m n & t*	Name given to teas marketed at Wenchow.
		Foochow	VI.—Fukien Province:	
			Panyong, *m n*	The leaf is generally black. Liquor delicate and flavory, of good body and character.
			Paklum, *m n*	Most stylish in appearance of all China blacks. Leaf is small and evenly made. Liquor pleasant but thin.
			Souchong, *m n*	Large-leaf blacks. Liquor rich and syrupy, with a slightly smoky flavor. Seldom used in America, though useful in making China blends, giving them a distinctive character.
			Pekoe-Congou, *m n*	Black leaf very evenly and tightly rolled. Infused leaf bright, but liquor lacks strength and flavor.
			Padrae, *m n*	A South China red leaf Congou; a highly fired tea. Dry leaf black and crape-like. In cup rich color; great strength; flavor resembles black currants.
			Soomoo, *m n*	A specially prepared Fukien black.
			Suey Kut, *m n*	Export name for a special grade of Fukien tea.
			Ankoi, *m n*	Resembles Saryune, but leaf is a little blacker. Strong, useful teas.
			Foochow, *m n*	Name given to any Fukien blacks concentrated for export at Foochow.
			Singchuen, *m n*	Leaf rather open; too often mixed with dust.
			Wu-I, *m n*	Otherwise known as Ai Ch'a.
			Pai Lian, *d & m n*	Name given to tea from the Minhow District.
			Yang Kow, *d & m n*	Name given to tea from the Chin Tsang District.
			Chingwo, *m n*	Tightly rolled, silky black leaf with some tip. Delicate aroma. Liquor bright reddish color, possessing considerable strength and fine flavor.

Grand Division	Country	Shipping Ports	State, District, or Market Name	Local Data, Definitions, Cup Qualities, Trade Characteristics, and Gradings
Asia Cont'd	China Cont'd	Foochow Cont'd	China Blacks, *Cont'd* Chaishiu, *d & m n*	Name given to tea from the Tsang An District.
			Tenyang, *d & m n*	Name given to tea from the Liangkian District.
			Shouwu, *d & m n*	Name given to tea from the Shouwu District.
			Sha Yang, *d & m n*	Name given to tea from the Si Hsien District.
			Shui Chih, *d & m n*	Name given to tea from the Chengking District.
			Tung Ten, *d & m n*	Name given to tea from the Shiu Ling District.
			Wuyuan, *d & m n*	Name given to tea from the Wuyuan District.
			Pakling, *m n* Pehling *m n*	Stylish appearing teas from the Foochow District. Liquor clear but thin; lacking in point and stamina.
			Saryune, *m n*	Good foundation for low priced blends. Reddish, somewhat open leaf; apt to be dusty. Rich, ripe liquor, with plenty of sap and strength.
			Lapsang, *m n*	Large leaf. Clear, bright liquor; sometimes tarry flavor.
		Canton Macao Hong Kong	VII.—Kwangtung Provnce: Hoyunes, *m n* Tarry Hoyunes, *m n* Pekoe Souchong, *m n* Honeysuckle Congou, *m n*	Teas grown here are known as New Province or New District Congous.
				Black tea gradings: (Rare) Flowery Pekoe, Orange Pekoe, Pekoe, and Souchong.
		Foochow Amoy Canton	CHINA OOLONGS	China Oolongs are semi-fermented teas and have somewhat the appearance of black teas, and a taste similar to greens. The best grades are pure straw color in the cup; the lower grades are brown and red. Oolongs are exported mostly to America and Siam.
			Foochow, *m n & t*	Name given to Fukien Oolongs marketed at Foochow. The leaf is long, rough, coarse appearing, and blackish. The cup qualities are toasty with a thin, medium flavor.
			Sueykut, *m n*	Name given to a more fermented grade of Foochow Oolong. Fairly attractive cup quality, but thin.
			Tycon, *m n*	Name given to a slightly less fermented Foochow Oolong. Cup quality thin.
			Faggot, *m n*	Canton Oolong in small, silk-tied bundles.

Grand Division	Country	Shipping Ports	State, District, or Market Name	Local Data, Definitions, Cup Qualities, Trade Characteristics, and Gradings
Asia Cont'd	China Cont'd	Foochow Amoy Canton Cont'd	China Oolongs, Cont'd Silvery, *m n*	Specially plucked Foochow Oolong, prepared from the delicate whitish leaves of the first flush.
			String Teas: Tong Mow, Tong-Lee, Tong-Shin, and Cum-Wo	Name given to a grade of Foochow Oolong less fermented than Suey-kut or Tycon, and ranging from "choicest" to "good."
			Amoy, *t & m n*	Name given to Fukien Oolongs marketed at Amoy. Commercially unimportant.
			Canton, *d & m n*	Name given to Kwangtung Oolongs marketed at Canton.
			CHINA SCENTED	Any China tea that has been scented with jasmine, or other flowers, after the final firing process.
		Foochow Canton Macao	Orange Pekoe, *m n*	A highly scented Souchong, packed at Foochow and Canton. That which comes from Foochow shows small undesirable leaf and poor cup quality. That from Canton shows long narrow leaf, and is poorer, if anything, than the Foochow variety. They are used for blending with other teas to convey to them the jasmine aroma and flavor.
			Flowery Pekoe, *m n*	A tippier grade than Scented Orange Pekoe.
			Caper, *m n*	A highly scented and inferior black tea, shaped like Gunpowder.
			Jasmine, *m n*	Any tea scented with Jasmine flowers —usually Hyson, or Hyson and black tea.
			Pouchong, *m n*	A highly scented Foochow Oolong.
			Canton, *m n*	A highly scented Kwangtung Oolong.
			Koolaw, *m n*	
		Foochow Hankow Ta-chien-lu Sungpan	CHINA COMPRESSED	Both black and green teas are compressed into various sized bricks, tablets, and balls, as a means of utilizing waste products from the manufacture of leaf teas, and reducing bulk for greater convenience in overland transport.
			Brick	Black brick tea is made chiefly from waste left over after the manufacture of black tea, including siftings, dust, and stalks. Green brick tea is made of leaves only; there is no admixture of dust, stalks, etc. Russia formerly took large quantities of China brick teas, but the consumption now is confined to Central Asia and Tibet.
		Sungpan	Baled	Tea for the Sunpan market, manufactured in the An and Shich'uan Districts, and consisting of tea plants and weeds.

Grand Division	Country	Shipping Ports	State, District, or Market Name	Local Data, Definitions, Cup Qualities, Trade Characteristics, and Gradings
Asia Cont'd	China Cont'd		China Compressed, Cont'd Cake	Known also by the name of the P'uerh Province, where it is prepared. Consumed locally.
			Tablet	Tablet tea is essentially small bricks, weighing a few ounces each, and made of fine tea dust of special quality. Consumed locally.
			Ball	A name applied to tea compressed into a ball as a means of protecting it against atmospheric changes. Consumed locally.

CLASSIFICATION OF ALL CHINA TEAS BY SEASONS	SHANGHAI MARKET CLASSIFICATION [Native Traditional Names]
Spring: First picking. *Tou Pang Ch'a*, or *Tou Chuen Ch'a*.	*Lu Ch'a*, or "Voyage Tea." All grades and all kinds coming to the Shanghai market in a finished state.
Second picking. *Er Pang Ch'a*, or *Er Chuen Ch'a*.	*Mao Ch'a*, or "Woolen Tea." Teas manufactured in Shanghai from leaf brought from the interior.
Summer: Third picking. *Sau Pang Ch'a*, or *Sau Chuen Ch'a*.	*Tu Ch'a*, or "Earth Tea." Teas manufactured at Shanghai from leaf brought from Hangchow or the vicinity of Shanghai.
Fourth picking. *Sze Pang Ch'a*, or *Sze Chuen Ch'a*.	*Yang Ch'a*, or "Graded Tea." Various teas brought to Shanghai and there blended, receiving local names on the Shanghai market. These teas are known to the export market as "Shanghai Packed."

Grand Division	Country	Shipping Ports	State, District, or Market Name	Local Data, Definitions, Cup Qualities, Trade Characteristics, and Gradings
Asia Cont'd	Japan	Shimizu Yokohama Kobe Nagasaki	JAPANS	*In General:* The export teas of Japan may be roughly divided into "pan-fired," "basket-fired," and "natural leaf"; the last named being formerly called "porcelain-fired." A small quantity of black tea is manufactured. The Japan leaf is long, straight, spider-legged. The first-crop Japan teas are the best. The better grades possess a delicate, rich flavor, peculiar to themselves. Japans are the white wines of teas.
		Shimizu	I.—Shizuoka, *d*	The Prefecture of Shizuoka produces most of the Japan tea intended for export. Various kinds and qualities come from here, such as Enshu [Kawane, Mori, Ogasa, Kanaya, Hamamatsu] and Suruga [Abe and Fuji], *q.v.*
			a.—Enshu, or Yenshu, *m n*	As a rule Enshu teas have not much style, but next to Yamashiro, are the best drinking teas of Japan. There is more Enshu tea produced than any other kind. The name sometimes is spelled "Enshi" or "Yenshu."
			Kawane, *m n*	An Enshu tea having a curly leaf and a good liquor.

Grand Division	Country	Shipping Ports	State, District, or Market Name	Local Data, Definitions, Cup Qualities, Trade Characteristics, and Gradings
Asia Cont'd	Japan Cont'd	Shizuoka Cont'd	Japans, Cont'd	
			Mori, *m n*	An Enshu tea having a good leaf and good liquor.
			Ogasa, *m n*	An Enshu tea of little commercial importance. Usually blended with Kanaya.
			Kanaya, *m n*	An Enshu tea of medium quality, with strength, but poor color.
			Hamamatsu, *m n*	An Enshu tea of medium quality.
			b.—Suruga, *m n & d*	The stylish teas of Japan, noted for their handsome and stylish appearance of the prepared leaf. The cupping qualities are not as good as Enshu, the liquor being often neutral in flavor. The principal kinds of Suruga teas are Abe and Fuji.
			Abe, *m n*	A Suruga tea of good quality.
			Fuji, *m n*	A Suruga tea, rather thin and weak, with good color.
			c.—Guri [curled]	Closely resembles Young Hyson.
			d.—Japan Black	A fully fermented tea.
		Kobe	II.—Yamashiro, *m n & d*	The best teas of Japan, having good liquor and flavor. The best known Yamashiro tea is Uji, *q.v.* Very little Yamashiro tea is exported because of its high price.
			Uji, *m n*	The best Yamashiro tea.
			III.—Goshu [Omi], *d*	
			Shiga, *m n*	A good grade tea.
		Nagasaki	IV.—Kagoshima, *d & m n*	A low grade tea from the Island of Kyushu. It is much used in Japan for blending with low price teas.
			V.—Miye, *d & m n*	A good blending tea.
		Yokohama	VI.—Saitama, *d* Sayama, *d & m n*	Often called Hachioji tea. It has a good leaf and liquor. This tea comes from the district extending over Irima and Tama Counties in Saitama Prefecture. Very little is exported because of its high price.
			VII.—Gifu, *m n*	A curly leaf tea.
			VIII.—Gyokuro, *m n*	A high grade tea made by a special process from shaded bushes in the district about Uji. It is not an export tea.
			IX.—Tencha, *m n*	Also called Hikicha or Ceremonial tea, as opposed to Sencha and Bancha, *q.v.* Tencha is always powdered and is not exported.
			X.—Sencha, *m n*	Name given to the ordinary export teas of Japan.
			XI.—Bancha, *m n*	A low grade tea made from coarse leaves. It is not exported.
			XII.—Hojicha, *m n*	Toasted Bancha—very pungent.

Grand Division	Country	Shipping Ports	State, District, or Market Name	Local Data, Definitions, Cup Qualities, Trade Characteristics, and Gradings
Asia Cont'd	Japan Cont'd		Japans, *Continued*	*Gradings:* Extra Choicest, Choicest, Choice, Finest, Fine, Good Medium, Good Common, Common, Nibs, Dust, and Fannings.
	Formosa	Keelung Tamsui	Formosas, or Formosa Oolongs, Formosa Pouchongs, Three-Quarters Fermented Formosas, and Formosa Blacks.	*In general:* Formosa teas are made into Oolongs or Pouchongs mostly. The former are sometimes referred to as the champagnes of teas.
			Oolong, *m z*	A semi-fermented, greenish brown, tippy tea. The spring crop is light in cup with good style but the summer crop has the most body and flavor. The autumn is usually of good leaf, but is thin in cup. The Formosa Oolong is distinguished by a natural, attractive, fruity flavor. The old Chinese nomenclature for the various tea producing districts is as follows: Chap Go Hoon, Tek Sham, Paichee, Keam Chai Sang, Sinteam, Sim Paw, Chuitngka, Lwan Lwan, Patchatgna, Sam Teau, Poon Kee Wo, Tang Lo Kien, Malengki, Hobe, Mack Sai Liao, Beeteng, Am Ki, Sakakeng, Chim Ki, Lengsuikee, Kimpoli, Soy-tin-chai.
				Among the foreign buyers, Oolongs are sometimes divided into North District Teas and South District Teas, depending upon whether the district in which they are produced is north or south of Daitotei.
			Pouchong, *n n*	A semi-fermented tea made by a special process and scented with gardenia, jasmine, or yulan blossoms before the final firing. Manufactured specially for the East Indian trade.
			Improved or Three-Quarters Fermented	Made from the Formosa Oolong plant, but three-quarters instead of semi-fermented. Flowery Orange Pekoe, Orange Pekoe, Pekoe.
			Formosa Blacks	A fully fermented tea made from imported Assam and indigenous plants
			DISTRICTS	
			Shinchiku	One of the two principal tea producing provinces, lying on the western side of the Island.
			Byoritsu, *d*	Town and trolley station.
			Chikunan, *d*	Town and trolley station.
			Chikuto, *d*	Town and trolley station.
			Chureki, *d*	Town and R. R. station.
			Shinchiku, *d*	Market town and R. R. station.
			Taikei, *d*	Town and trolley station.

Grand Division	Country	Shipping Ports	State, District, or Market Name	Local Data, Definitions, Cup Qualities, Trade Characteristics, and Gradings
Asia *Cont'd*	Formosa *Cont'd*	Keelung Tamsui *Cont'd*	Formosas, *Continued* Toyen, *d*	Town and R. R. station in center of tea district.
			Taichu, *s d*	A negligible amount grown in two districts.
			Taihoku, [state]	One of the two principal tea producing provinces. All "North District" teas are grown here.
			Bunzan, *d*	Town and R. R. station.
			Kaizan, *d*	Town and R. R. station.
			Keelung, *d*	Largest seaport town, N. E. Coast.
			Shichisei, *d*	Town and R. R. station.
			Shinsho, *d*	Town and R. R. station.
			Tamsui, *d*	Seaport town, Northwest Coast.
			Tainan	Small quantity produced.
				Gradings for Formosa Oolongs as adopted by the Formosan Government Tea Inspection Office are: Standard, On Good, Good, Fully Good, Good Up, Good to Superior, On Superior, Superior, Fully Superior, Superior Up, Superior to Fine, On Fine, Fine, Fine Up, Fine to Finest, Finest, Finest to Choice, Choice. The trade recognizes several intermediary gradings, such as Good Leaf, Fully Standard, Standard to Good, Strictly Superior, Choicest, and Fancy.
	Malay States (British)	Penang (Georgetown)	Kedah (State) Malay, *m n*	Commercially unimportant. Similar to Cachar tea.
			Gurun, *d*	Gives commercial promise.
			Sungei Besi, *d*	Small Chinese plots.
			Tanah Rata, *d*	Experimental plantings.
	French Indo-China.	Tourane Haiphong	Sun-Dried [Wild Tea]	A roughly manufactured tea consumed by the natives.
			Annam Black, and Annam Green, *m n*	Inferior, coarse leaf, from the Annam districts. Strong, acrid liquor with little flavor. Some Annams are exported to France and used for blending. Those made by Europeans are usually well made.
			Tonkin Black, and Tonkin Green, *m n*	Coarse, native products from the Tonkin districts, consumed locally.
			Tonkin Cake, *m n*	An agglomerate tea in three grades, consumed locally as well as in the adjoining Chinese province of Yunnan.
			Cochin-China Green, *m n*	Coarse leaf grown in the Cochin China Districts. Astringent. Consumed locally.

Grand Division	Country	Shipping Ports	State, District, or Market Name	Local Data, Definitions, Cup Qualities, Trade Characteristics, and Gradings
Asia Cont'd	French Indo-China Cont'd	Tourane Haiphong	Indo-China Teas, *Continued* Fleurs de Thé, *m n*	Tea made from tea flowers, and sometimes scented with jasmine and other blossoms. Highly esteemed by the natives, and as a novelty by Parisians.
	Burma		Native *Letpet,* or Pickled Tea, *m n*	A steamed and fermented leaf, grown and prepared by the natives, and consumed locally as a salad, with oil and garlic. The principal tea product of Burma.
			Black and Green Teas, *m n*	Cultivated and prepared by Europeans in Burma, following methods and gradings common in Ceylon. Production is consumed locally.
	Siam		Miang, or Chewing Tea, *m n*	A steamed and fermented leaf chewed with salt, and sometimes with the additions of garlic and hog fat. Consumption local.
	Iran [Persia]		Persian, *m n* Fumen, *d* Lahijan, *d* Langrud, *d*	An Indian jat, of which a small amount is grown in the province of Gilan; consumed locally; said to be of excellent quality.
Oceania	Netherlands East Indies	Batavia (Tangjong-Priok) Soerabaya Medan (Belawan-Deli) Padang Benkoelen Palembang	JAVAS AND SUMATRAS Javas	*In general:* The teas of Netherlands India are best known in the trade by their garden marks. Only fermented [black] teas are manufactured. Java teas have a black and attractive leaf appearance during the greater part of the year, but get a rather brownish appearance during the dry season [June to September], when the flavor improves. They are well made, good, useful, attractive blenders, soft and of medium strength in the cup.
	Java		RESIDENCIES	
		Batavia (Tangjong-Priok) Soerabaya	Batavia Province and Residency	Much fine tea is produced in the highlands of this District, which ranks second to the Preanger Residencies as a Java tea producer.
			Buitenzorg, *d, t & m n*	Elevation is 800 feet.
			Krawang, *d*	Town and residency.
			Soebang, *d, t & m n*	Elevation here about 1500 feet.
			Besoeki, *d*	Tea produced on only two estates.
			Cheribon, *d, ! & m n*	Relatively small quantity produced on two estates.
			Kedri, *d*	Relatively small quantity produced on three estates.
			Kedoe, *d*	Relatively small quantity produced on three estates.
			Wonosobo, *t & m n*	Elevation 3400 feet.

Grand Division	Country	Shipping Ports	State, District, or Market Name	Local Data, Definitions, Cup Qualities, Trade Characteristics, and Gradings
Oceania Cont'd	Java Cont'd	Batavia Soerabaya Cont'd	Javas, Cont'd Madioen, d	Relatively small quantity produced on one estate.
			Pasoeroean, d	A good quality tea grown on some five estates.
			Loemadjang, d, t & m n	Capital of District, and R. R. station; 50 meters above sea-level.
			Malang, t d & n n	Elevation 600 feet.
			Pekalongan, d	Relatively small quantity produced on three estates.
			Preanger Province and Residency	Make up the bulk of the Java teas. The Residency contains about 70 per cent of Java's tea estates.
			Bandoeng, d & t	Elevation 2400 feet.
			Pengalengan, d	Some of the finest teas of the Netherlands East Indies, the dry weather teas, comparing favorably with the better India and Ceylon growths. Elevation 4500 to 6000 feet.
			Garoet, d, t & m n	Elevation 2300 feet.
			Soekaboemi, t, d & m n	Elevation 2000 feet.
			Soemedang, t, d & m n	Capital of District, situated on post-road; 460 meters above sea-level.
			Tjiandjoer, t, d & m n	Capital of District, R. R. station, and 460 meters above sea-level.
			Semarang, d & t	Relatively small quantity produced on four estates.
			Salatiga, t & m n	Capital of District, R. R. station and 580 meters above sea-level.
			Soerakarta, d & t	Small amount produced on two estates.
		Medan (Belawan-Deli) Palembang Benkoelen Padang	Sumatras	Sumatra teas are not so much affected by seasonal changes as are Java teas. They may be said to be of the same useful cup the year round. The leaf is attractive.
			DISTRICTS	
	Sumatra	Benkoelen	Benkoelen, d	Small quantity produced on a few estates.
			Upper Benkoelen, s d	Capital of District of same name.
			Kepahiang, s d	Elevation 1500 feet.
			Pasartjoerop, s d	Settlement in Subdivision of Redjang.
			Korintji, d	Situated in the native sultanate of Djambi.
		Medan (Belawan-Deli)	East Coast	Makes up the bulk of the Sumatra crop.
			Deli, d	Leading East Coast District.
			Asahan, s d	Slight elevation.

Grand Division	Country	Shipping Ports	State, District, or Market Name	Local Data, Definitions, Cup Qualities, Trade Characteristics, and Gradings
Oceania Cont'd	Sumatra Cont'd	Medan Cont'd	Sumatras, Cont'd Batoe Barah, s d	In the Batoe Barah River District.
			Simoeloengan, s d	Good quality range.
			Pematang-Siantar, s d	The best of the Sumatras; elevation 800 to 2400 feet.
		Palembang	Palembang, d	Small output, but shows much promise for future development.
			Tebing Tinggi, s d	Important trading center.
			Upper Palembang, s d	On the Moesi River; R. R. station.
			Moearabliti, s d	In the Palembang Upperlands.
			Pager Alam, s d	Elevation 2400 feet.
			Tapanoeli, d	Commercially unimportant.
			Dairi, d	Elevation 3600 to 4500 feet.
		Padang	West Coast	Relatively small quantity produced.
			Padang Highlands, d	Elevation about 4000 feet.
			Loeboek Sikaping, d Ophirlands, s d	Capital of district.
			Moerara Laboeh, d	Elevation about 4000 feet.
				Gradings: for Java and Sumatra teas: Flowery Orange Pekoe, Orange Pekoe, Broken Orange Pekoe, Pekoe, Broken Pekoe, Pekoe Souchong, Souchong, Broken Tea, Dust, and "Bohea"; the latter consisting of stalks.
	Fiji Islands	Levuka	Fiji, d & m n	A small amount of black tea is grown and manufactured in Vanua Levu for local consumption.
Africa	Natal	Durban	Natal, d & m n	A black tea from Assam indigenous jat grown for local consumption.
	Nyasaland	Beira Chinde	Nyasaland, m n Mlanje, d Cholo, d	A middling to good black tea, grown from British India stock. Light, plain liquor. Becoming more important on the London market.
	Kenya Colony	Mombasa	Kenya, m n Kavirondo, N., d Kericho, d Kiambu, d Uasingishu, d	Kenya tea [grown from various British India jats] is as yet not important commercially, but is developing. It has a bold leaf, thin liquor, fair strength and quality.
	Uganda	Mombasa	Uganda, m n Mubendi, d	The leaf is rich in theine, tannin and extractive matter; in these respects resembling an Indian rather than a China tea. Consumed locally.
	Rhodesia	Beira	Mashonaland Province Melsetter, d	Commercially unimportant.
	East Central Africa	Dar es Salaam	Tanganyika Territory Southwestern Highlands, d	An experimental tea area.

Grand Division	Country	Shipping Ports	State, District, or Market Name	Local Data, Definitions, Cup Qualities, Trade Characteristics, and Gradings
Africa Cont'd	Portuguese East Africa	Mozambique	Mozambique, *m n*	Commercially unimportant. Liquor light and plain. Similar to Nyasaland teas.
	Mauritius	Port Louis	Mauritius, *m n*	Commercially unimportant.
North Atlantic Ocean	Azores	St. Michael's	Azores, *m n*	Green and black tea produced for export to Lisbon.
Europe	S. F. S. R. of Georgia (Transcaucasia)	Batoum	Georgian, *d*	Mostly of poor quality, but the best is equal to some China teas. Not a trade factor outside of Russia.
	Italy	Leghorn (Livorno)	Pisa Province	
			Bagni di San Giuliano, *d*	In experimental stage.
	Bulgaria	Burgas	Department of East Roumelia	
			Philippopolis, *d*	Experimental, with plants from Russia.
West Indies	Jamaica	Kingston	Blue Mountain, *m n*	An experimental tea.
	Puerto Rico	San Juan	Puerto Rico, *d & m n*	Purely experimental.
North America	Mexico	Veracruz	State of Oaxaca Cuicatlan, *d*	Commercially unimportant.
South America	Paraguay	Villa Rica	Department of Villa Rica	In experimental stage. Gives promise.
	Peru		Province of La Convencion	In experimental stage.
	Colombia	Buenaventura	Department of Cundinamarca Gachala, *d*	Commercially unimportant.
	Brazil	Rio de Janeiro	Minas Geraes, *d* Ouro Preto, *s d* São Paulo, *d* Paraná, *d*	Black tea from Assam seed largely for local consumption.
	Argentina	Buenos Aires	Argentina, *m n*	A tea grown from China seed. Commercially unimportant.

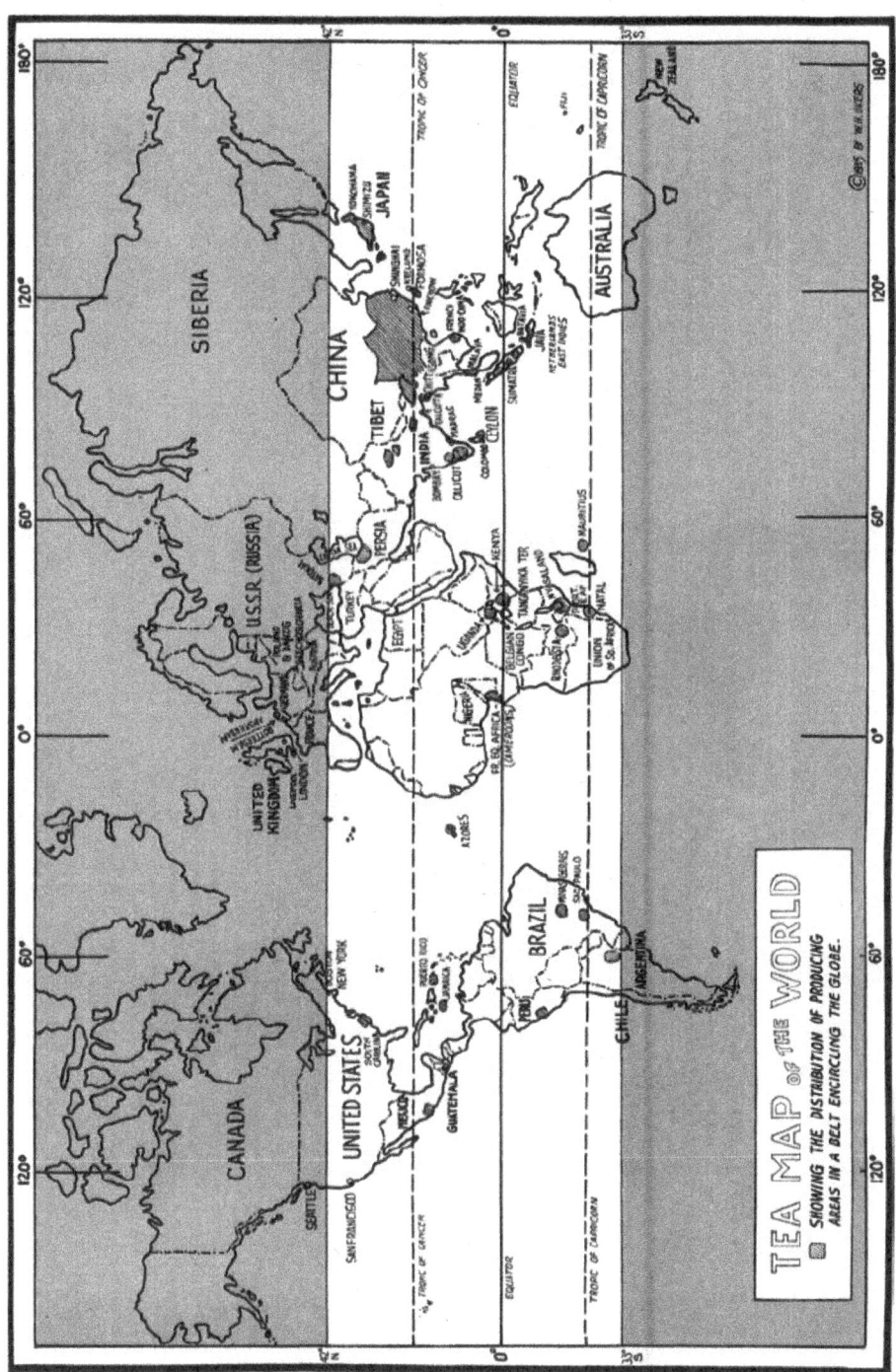

TEA MAP of the WORLD

SHOWING THE DISTRIBUTION OF PRODUCING
AREAS IN A BELT ENCIRCLING THE GLOBE.

268

CHAPTER XIV

CULTIVATION AND MANUFACTURE OF TEA

The Improvement in Methods—Soils, Climate, and Altitude—Clearing the Land—Theory and Practice of Propagation—Tillage—Shades, Windbreaks, and Cover Crops—The Use of Fertilizers—Pests and Diseases—Pruning, Plucking, and Crop Control—The Factory—Manufacturing Processes—How Black, Green, and Oolong Teas are Prepared—Brick, Tablet, Cake Teas, and Tea Fluff—Labor—Experimental Stations—Planters' Associations

THE original methods of tea cultivation and manufacture were developed in China. All of the other countries now producing tea commercially had to go to the Chinese, either directly or indirectly, to learn the secrets of its production; but these other countries have improved upon what they learned by the application of scientific agricultural methods and the use of labor-saving machinery.

In China, tea seeds are planted on steep slopes and on patches not needed for other crops. The result of indifferent treatment has been the production of bushes much smaller in size and of lower yield than those grown in India, Ceylon, and Java.

According to Chinese methods, if green tea is being made the leaf is pan-fired as soon as possible after picking; it is then rolled and dried gradually. When black tea is made the leaf is not killed by pan-firing, but is first rolled and fermented, after which it is fired.

The tea pioneers in Java and India at first imported Chinamen and Chinese plants, and the methods of China, both in the field and factory, were followed. Later, the ways of the Chinese were modified and in certain cases abandoned. The China plant was replaced by the Assam indigenous variety, the bushes were pruned and plucked in a new manner, and machinery was introduced into the factory. Present-day methods of tea management by Europeans are almost the opposite of those in China. For planting, the best available land is chosen; the seed first is put out in nurseries, the plants are selected, and then replanted. The bush is carefully pruned to give it a shape conducive to high yield, and the leaf is plucked with a view to encouraging later flushes. Such differences as exist between the methods employed in Java, Sumatra, Ceylon, and India, have come about because of climatic and topographical differences. Broadly speaking, however, the methods in the newer tea countries are quite similar.

In China, there has been little change in cultivation and preparation methods for over 500 years. The Chinese farmer still treats the tea bush as a side cultivation to his general farming, and centuries-old methods of tea-firing obtain. Sporadic efforts have been made to introduce modern processes from India and Ceylon, but there are comparatively few foreign tea-making machines in China.

Japan, on the other hand, has learned much about tea cultivation from Java and British India, and has developed a distinctive type of tea-making machinery.

Formosa, likewise, has adopted from other countries improved cultivation and manufacturing methods.

Present Day Tea Cultivation

A glance at the map will show that tea is being cultivated over a range of not less than 75 degrees of latitude—from 42° N., in Russian Transcaucasia, to 33° S., in Northern Argentina. But all the most important tea producing areas lie within a restricted range of about 43 degrees of latitude—from 8° S. in Java, to 35° N. in

Japan—and 60° of longitude—from 80° to 140° E. This area includes China, Japan, Formosa, Java, Sumatra, Ceylon, and India.

Large-scale growers of to-day bring to tea cultivation the same sort of scientific knowledge and intensive care that commercial growers bring to fruits and cereal crops. Every effort is made to assure efficiency. Experimental stations in Java, India, Japan, Sumatra, and Ceylon, are working constantly to improve methods and products, as well as to develop bush types that will resist disease, pests, and unfavorable climatic conditions.

Soil Requirements

It long was believed that tea would thrive best on poor soil, because the Chinese plant tea only on soil useless for other purposes; but early experiments in Japan, Java, India, and Ceylon soon demonstrated that a well-drained soil, which is light and friable, cannot be too rich for tea. However, tea will grow and yield well on almost any type of soil. In Assam high yields are obtained on the stiffest of clays and the lightest of sands. In Cachar, bushes growing on peat soils, or *bheels*, yield as much as 2000 lbs. of tea per acre. It may be said, though, that tea grows best, with the least attention and expense, on a light, sandy loam, well supplied in plant food, and capable of good drainage.

Since the tea crop consists of leaf, good supplies of nitrogen in the soil are essential to good yields. So far as organic matter, potash, and phosphoric acid are concerned, tea follows the same requirements as ordinary plants; but it is not a lime lover, and all good tea soils show a definite acidity. Other things being equal, the best tea is found on the more acid soils. Neutral or alkaline soils grow tea poorly or not at all.

Climate and Altitude

Tea is an evergreen and will grow in almost any climate so long as no severe drought is felt. Tea will grow in the cool, humid South of England, and it grows in Ranchi, India, where the temperature in May reaches 115° F. and the humidity falls at times to 17 per cent. Tea flourishes, however, and yields best in a tropical or subtropical climate. With a continuous hot, wet climate, like that of Ceylon or Java, tea flushes throughout the year. In Northeast India, where the monsoon ceases in October and the weather becomes cold and dry till April, the bush shuts up and gives no leaf worth gathering from December to March. The climate of China is cooler and dryer than that of India, and much smaller crops are obtained. Japan is so cold in the winter that the bushes cease flushing in spite of the rains.

Humidity is an important factor in forcing leaf. A dry atmosphere is against crop, but humidity, especially with temperatures of about 85° F., makes the bush flush.

A cool climate produces slow growth and makes for quality, as is shown in the high-grown Ceylon teas, the Darjeeling teas, the early Assams, and autumnal Dooars. Frosts, however, blacken the tea leaf on the bush.

In India, tea is cultivated in numerous, but often widely separated, hill districts at altitudes from 1000 to 7000 feet. Ceylon teas are grown from approximately sea-level up to 7000 feet; the greater part of the cultivation lying at about 3000 feet. Java tea is grown mainly at about 1000 feet, although the Pengalengan tea is planted at more than 5000 feet. In Sumatra, the elevations run from 1200 to 3500.

In China, the best black teas are produced in Anhwei Province at about 3000 feet. The most celebrated green teas are grown in the Province of Kiangsi at 4000 feet above sea-level. The finest teas of Japan are produced inland on mountain slopes along streams. Approximately half of the export teas, however, are grown much nearer sea-level in the mountainous coast prefecture of Shizuoka. In Formosa, most of the tea acreage is located on plateaus of 250 to 1000 feet elevation, but some of the most famous Oolongs are raised on broken foothill lands that range from sea-level to 300 feet.

Of prime importance for luxuriant leaf production is a copious rainfall well distributed throughout the seasons, but particularly through the cropping and pre-cropping periods. Failing this, the tea bush quickly loses vitality and becomes susceptible to pests and diseases. An annual rainfall of not less than eighty to ninety inches is usually required, with no lengthy period of drought. Many of the principal tea areas have a much greater precipita-

CHINESE RANDOM TEA PLANTING

Japan has rain all the year round and no definite dry period. September is Japan's wettest month, and January, the driest. In Kyoto Prefecture, the annual average is sixty inches, but this is supplemented by dense river fogs and heavy dews. In Shizuoka, the average is 100 inches.

Formosa has well-defined wet and dry seasons. Thunder-storms with showers occur almost daily, in the afternoon, from June until late September. Most of the rain in Formosa falls during this period.

Preparation of the Land

The first tea areas in India were put out on steep slopes in accordance with Chinese custom. Later, it was found that tea grew more luxuriantly on the flat, and the finest areas in Northeast India now are found on level ground. In Ceylon, Southern India, Darjeeling, and Java, most of the tea is planted on slopes, and in this case attention must be paid to the aspect. In Ceylon, the morning sun is preferred. On the lower slopes of Darjeeling a northern aspect is best, and this applies also to the *teelas* of Sylhet, where southern slopes often fail to grow tea, except under dense shade.

The first step in opening land, after labor has been collected and housed, is the planting of nurseries. A convenient location is selected, and the seeds are germinated and planted at intervals varying from four to ten inches. In clearing jungle land, the undergrowth first is cut and burnt, followed by the felling and burning of the big trees. It is advisable to remove all the stumps, otherwise root disease may take a heavy toll of the tea planted later. Stump removal, however, is expensive, and requires much labor, so that in many cases stumps are left to rot gradually. The clearing of grass land is simple, but such land, of course, is poorer than forest areas.

A good deal of foresight is required to lay out the road system of an estate. Many of the older properties are sadly lacking in roads, and even paths, but modern estates, when planted on the flat, are put out in small sections of ten to twenty acres duly separated by subsidiary roads capable of taking motor traffic. The more paths there are in a tea garden, the easier and better is supervision.

If slopes are being planted they usually are terraced first, and the plants put out

tion than this. There rarely is one with less, but where this occurs there are general conditions of extreme atmospheric humidity, which make up for lack of actual precipitation.

In India, the average rainfalls of the tea districts cover a wide range of variation, depending on their topographical location. Assam, in Northeastern India, is warm and moist, with rainfalls in the tea districts averaging yearly from fifty to about 150 inches. The Dooars average from 100 to 200 inches. In the Darjeeling district, the weather is cold and dry during the northeast monsoon, but extremely humid during the southwestern months,—May, June, July, and August—when rain is continuous and a precipitation of more than eighty inches for the period is common. In the tea districts of Southwestern India, the annual average is from 100 to 300 inches high up in the range.

Ceylon has a comparatively dry season from December to April, and a wet season from May to November. The annual rainfall varies from seventy-two to 271 inches.

The tea districts of Java have a well distributed rainfall ranging from 102 inches at Malabar to 168 inches at Buitenzorg. July and August are the driest months. Sumatra has a generous rainfall the year round, with the lowest precipitation during June and July. The average yearly rainfall in Siantar, the principal tea growing district, is 116 inches.

China has no clearly defined wet and dry seasons like those of Northeast India. The precipitation is distributed more or less throughout the year, but is greatest during the summer months. The approximate annual average is sixty to seventy inches.

CONTOUR PLANTING IN FORMOSA

ance being made for roads, drains, or other vacancies.

TABLE NO. 1

Bushes Per Acre by Rectangular Planting

	3 Feet	3 Feet 6 Inches	4 Feet	4 Feet 6 Inches	5 Feet	5 Feet 6 Inches	6 Feet
3 Feet.........	4840						
3 Feet 6 Inches....	4148	3555					
4 Feet.........	3630	3111	2722				
4 Feet 6 Inches...	3226	2765	2419	2150			
5 Feet.........	2904	2489	2178	1936	1742		
5 Feet 6 Inches...	2640	2263	1980	1760	1584	1440	
6 Feet.........	2420	2074	1815	1613	1452	1320	1210

TABLE NO. 2

Bushes Per Acre by Equilateral Triangular Planting

Bushes spaced 3 feet 0 inches × 3 feet 0 inches = 5590 per acre
Bushes spaced 3 feet 6 inches × 3 feet 6 inches = 4107 per acre
Bushes spaced 4 feet 0 inches × 4 feet 0 inches = 3144 per acre
Bushes spaced 4 feet 6 inches × 4 feet 6 inches = 2484 per acre
Bushes spaced 5 feet 0 inches × 5 feet 0 inches = 2012 per acre

later on the contours. Gentle slopes may or may not be contour-planted and often are supplied with *bands*, or low banks, to prevent soil-wash. The drainage system of a garden usually is put out after planting. The system of main drains, carrying water down the slope, and subsidiary drains, taking water across the slope to the mains, follows the practice of general agriculture.

After the new area has been cleared and somewhat levelled, the land is staked. With contour-planting the stakes are on the contour, and each terrace may carry one or more lines of stakes, according to the slope of the land. The greater the slope, the narrower each individual terrace.

On the flat, the whole area is staked for either square or triangular planting at distances varying from four to six feet. The number of bushes per acre varies with the planting, and, although close planting is more costly than wide, a quicker return in crop is obtained. The economic planting distance is about four feet six inches on the flat, which is reasonably cheap, and the bushes are close enough to cover the soil in about four years.

Table Number One shows the number of bushes per acre by the rectangular method of spacing, when planted on flat land, with no allowance for roads, drains, or other vacancies. In India, quite a lot of tea has been planted by equilateral-triangular spacing, the claim being made that it economizes space without over-crowding the plants. Table Number Two shows the number of bushes that can be grown per acre by this method, no allow-

Theory and Practice of Propagation

Tea is propagated from seeds which ripen on the bushes, and by vegetative propagation methods, such as cutting, layering, and grafting. Growing from seed is the rule, while vegetative methods are used where it is desirable to avoid deviation from type, as in the case of a special variety of the tea bush grown in

STRAIGHT LINE PLANTING IN SUMATRA

A Tea Seed Producer, Darjeeling, British India

Formosa to produce the delicately flavored Oolongs, or in connection with scientific work at experimental stations.

Many estates have a plot of selected tea trees that have been allowed to grow to fifteen or twenty feet in height as seed producers. Seed is picked up from the ground below the seed trees. It then is selected by sieving and floating, and carefully dried before being packed in charcoal, dried clay, or a mixture of both. The seed usually is transported in boxes.

Tea is at times "planted at stake." In India this is risky business, because drought often kills the young plants, and it is difficult or impossible to water a large area. Another drawback to planting at stake is that the plant cannot be selected, although to offset this, three seeds usually are put at each stake.

Most tea gardens are put out from nurseries placed in selected spots, either shaded by jungle or artificially shaded by thatch and leaves supported on bamboo or wooden frames. The seedbeds are about six feet wide, separated by narrow paths, and are watered in case of a dry spell.

The seed, as it arrives on the garden, has usually been selected. However, the seed is often "floated," which consists of putting it into water and discarding the light seed, which floats.

The seed is often germinated in damp sand pits. When the shell cracks, the seed is planted in the bed about one-half an inch deep, with the eye downwards. If the seed is good and guaranteed by the seller, separate germination is often left out.

Seedlings sometimes are replanted at two-months-old in Sumatra and, although they do well at this age, selection is difficult. The more common age is from six to eighteen months. In India, the plant is lifted with a clod of earth and carefully transported to the new clearing. In Ceylon and Java, where the dry season is only dry by comparison with the monsoon downpour, the plants are often transplanted "carrot" fashion; i.e., devoid of any clod.

It is not customary to manure nurseries, but when young plants are transplanted into the field, an application of cattle manure usually is given. More important, however, is shade, and for this purpose some semi-permanent green sop, like Boga medeloa, is commonly planted in the young tea. Nursery planting, while practiced to a limited extent in China, is far removed from the mass production in nurseries as developed on the vast tea estates of the British and Netherlands Indies.

Japanese and Formosan tea growers do not set out nurseries. The Japanese plant the seeds directly where they are to be grown by either bush sowing or line sowing. Line sowing is adopted where it is desirable to check soil-wash on slopes. Formosan tea growers plant their commoner, hardier tea varieties direct from seed, but they preserve the character of their best varieties by raising them from cuttings or layerings; mostly from the latter.

The operation of cutting consists in placing branches, stripped of their leaves, in moist sand, and encouraging them to put out roots.

Layering is accomplished by pegging the side branches of selected bushes into the ground with staples of bamboo. When the branch has become well rooted it is severed from the mother bush and planted out.

In Java, experiments at tea selection have been conducted over a period of sixteen years. Indo-China, China, and Japan have more recently followed this example, but neither India nor Ceylon have taken it up.

Tillage

A soil free of weeds is essential to the good growth of a tea seedling. It is common to deep-hoe the soil to a depth of about six inches at the end of the rains, and to light-hoe four or five times a year as weeds accumulate. In Southern India and Ceylon, clean weeding is practiced, and by this means the weeds are so consistently removed that few grow. In Java, the tea areas usually are under green crops, and little cultivation is necessary.

In China, the weeds are cleared away and the soil turned up around the bushes four times a year. Japanese tea gardeners practice deep-hoeing or plowing between the rows to a depth of twenty-four inches in the fall, and light-hoeing, to remove weeds and loosen the soil, three or four times from March to October. In Formosa, some, but not all, of the gardens are cleaned with a yearly hoeing or plowing, not later than the end of June. Wherever possible, tillage is by plow drawn by a buffalo, and the land is turned up to a depth of four or five inches.

On the flat areas in India, spring-tine cultivators, buffalo drawn, are often used in young tea. After three or four years, the tea is too big for this treatment and is, at the same time, producing enough foliage to control the weeds itself, to some extent. Even in young tea, however, it must be admitted that the tine cultivator is not so efficient as the hand-swung hoe. The cultivator does not clean near the trunk of the bush, as a man with a hoe is able to do.

Shades, Windbreaks, and Cover Crops

Shade trees in tea cultivation have been in use for many years, and as between shaded and unshaded areas, the former almost always produces the better tea. Trees are helpful to growing tea by supplying it with mineral food—such as potash and phosphoric acid—in a readily available form; by keeping down the deep-rooted, high-growing grasses; by opening up the soil to the action of air and water; and by protecting the tea from scorching by the sun and loss of moisture by evaporation. But trees may be disadvantageous to the tea-plants by spreading root-diseases

through the tea; by crushing the tea-bushes when, after death, it becomes necessary to fell them; by competing with the tea for moisture, plant food, and water. The mineral food supplied by trees readily can be supplied by fertilizers; the high grasses can be kept down by cultivation; and the soil kept aërated by proper drainage; and in some districts the heat of the sun normally does not scorch the tea. So it is evident that first-class tea can be grown without shade. Yet, under most conditions, the advantages of the use of trees are greater than the disadvantages; and the good effects of the trees can be more easily procured by their use than by other means.

Careful experiments on an Assam tea garden revealed that the total soluble matter in tea is increased by shading, but that the tannin is noticeably reduced.

Any one of a large number of trees can produce shade that is not too dense, but only leguminous trees have the faculty of abstracting nitrogen from the air and storing it in their branches, twigs, and leaves. Their leaf-fall and loppings constitute a valuable green manure when forked into the ground, for which reason the most commonly used shades are legumes. Among these may be mentioned *Albizzia stipulata, A. moluccanna, A. falcata, A. procera, A. lebbek, Derris microphylla, Erythrina lithosperma, Leucaena glauca,* and various *Dalbergias.*

Shade trees usually are planted eighteen or twenty-four feet square in Java and about sixty feet square in Northeast India.

Leguminous trees also are planted in

TEA GROWN UNDER DADAP SHADE, JAVA

This is *Erythrina lithosperma*, also a favorite green manure.

rows as windbreaks along the roads of tea estates, where strong winds are common. Wind is harmful to leaf production, so rows of windbreaks are frequently added to the regular shade trees. In addition to the leguminous trees, the non-leguminous silver oak [*Grevillea robusta*] is extensively planted for windbreaks in Ceylon, above about 4000 feet altitude.

Hedges of leguminous shrubs frequently are sown between alternate rows of tea when the garden is started, to supply green manure and to check soil-wash. Among those commonly used are *Crotalaria usaramoensis*, *C. anagyroides*, *Tephrosia candida*, *T. hookeriana*, *Leucaena glauca*, *Clitoria cajanifolia*, *Centrosema plumerii*, *Cajanus indicus*, *Sesbania aculeata*, *S. egyptiaca*, *Indigofera dosua*, *I. arrecta*, *Desmodium polycarpum*, *Desmodium tortuosum*, and *D. retroflexum*.

Certain herbaceous annual legumes are raised from seed sown between the tea rows and are dug into the soil when a few weeks old. Various species of the *Phaseolus*, such as the Indian *mati kalai* or *kalai dal*, the *Vigna catiang* [cowpea], the *Glycine hispida* [soya bean], *Cyamopsis psoralioides*, *Crotalaria juncea*, and the *Crotalaria striata*, are thus used.

Leguminous ground covers have replaced clean weeding in Java, and promise to do so in Ceylon, where soil-wash has extracted heavy toll. *Indigofera endecaphylla* is considered the most suitable ground cover in Ceylon, while *Vigna hosei* is the favorite in Java. Both are creeping plants, and are cut off with knives and forked into the soil when it is desired to apply green manure, after which the plants quickly grow again from the roots. The most popular ground covers in India are cowpea [*Vigna catiang*], mati kalai [*Phaseolus mungo*], sunn hemp [*Crotalaria juncea*], and dhaincha [*Sesbania aculeata*].

The Use of Fertilizers

The object of manuring, added to cultivation, is to restore to the soil the elements necessary for the growth of the tea leaf that has been lost by wash or by previous production. Experience has shown that quality does not suffer through this practice.

The question as to the exact needs of a given soil necessarily is one for a soil chemist. In order to be certain of maxi-

LEGUMINOUS GROUND COVER, JAVA

Leucaena glauca, planted as hedges along terraces in a young tea clearing to prevent wash.

mum results, it is always best for the planter who has not had this done to have an analysis made of the soils with which he has to deal, and to obtain an outline suggestion for a manuring program. India, Ceylon, Java, Japan, and Formosa have tea experimental stations with competent scientific officers, well qualified to deal with all questions of cultivation and manufacture, including the determination of soil needs.

In India, Java, and Ceylon, both inorganic and organic artificial fertilizers are used in conjunction with green manures. In India, much cattle manure is used. In Japan and China, night soil is commonly applied, and Japan is also taking up the use of artificials. Practically every available artificial manure is used in tea, although sulphate of ammonia, nitrate of soda, and calcium cyanamide—all nitrogenous manures—occur in the mixtures most commonly used. Potash salts, phosphatic manures, oil cakes, animal meals, and fish guanos are all employed if market rates are favorable.

Manures are applied annually, just before the main flushing period. In Japan, slow-acting manures are applied in the autumn and quick manures in the spring. Scientific experiment in Formosa is gradually wearing down the farmer's antipathy towards artificial manures, but in China the tea bush is generally left to shift for itself.

Pests and Diseases

The tea bush is subject to attack by a wide variety of pests and blights, but, for-

HELOPELTIS RAVAGES, SUMATRA

tunately, the greater number of them have thus far proved comparatively harmless. Probably the most serious insect menace is the *helopeltis*, the so-called "tea mosquito," whose favorite food is the sap contained in young tea leaves. This pest is serious in Java, South India, the Dooars, and Surma Valley. Various control measures have been tried, mostly resulting in failure; but superior cultivation is found to help materially.

Other industrious enemies of tea are the tea tortrix, which makes leaf-houses by enmeshing the tea leaves in its web, and the shot-hole borer, which roams over the stems and branches drilling holes that render them useless as leaf producers. The latter pest is prevalent in Ceylon. Armies of mites, presenting themselves in chromatic profusion as red spider, orange mite, pink mite, yellow mite, etc., attack the leaves during a period of drought, and, turning them yellow or black, ultimately cause them to fall off the bush. However, a good rain so stimulates growth that the bush flushes through the attack.

Another colorful pest which India shares with Japan, and probably with China, is the green fly. This insect is the only bug on record that really is welcomed by the tea planter. In India's premier hill districts of Darjeeling, where some of the world's best teas are grown, the green fly attacks the leaf, and it usually happens that from the leaf thus stunted excellent teas are made.

Not much is known about the enemies of tea in China, but in Japan the severe winters render tea, grown in that country, immune to the attacks of many trouble makers that are familiar to more southerly countries. Most of the pests that have

been mentioned have to be combated occasionally in the various tea countries and at certain elevations, but, thanks to limitations of weather and altitude, not all of them can attack the same garden.

The subject of the insect pests of tea is too extensive for more than the briefest outline in a general work, but readers desiring to study the subject in detail are referred to such comprehensive treatises as *Factors Affecting the Control of the Tea Mosquito Bug*, by E. A. Andrews, London, 1923; *Bijdrage tot het Helopeltis-vraagstuk voor thee*, by S. Leefmans, Batavia, 1916; *The Pests and Blights of the Tea Plant*, by Sir George Watt, London, 1898; and scientific monographs on tea pests, and the means of combating them, in the publications of the Indian Tea Association of Calcutta, and the Experimental Station West Java at Buitenzorg.

Various diseases of the tea bush are caused by blights, or vegetable parasites, which fasten themselves upon its leaves, stems, and roots. Leaf diseases have an especially menacing significance for growers of a leaf crop like tea, because not only do they check its growth and productiveness by attacking the plant organ responsible for future leaf and stem growth, but they reduce the immediately available crop as well. The number of blights reported to attack tea is about 150, but, with the single exception of the blister blight of Northern India, none have proven serious enough to cause alarm.

Speaking generally, it is the undernourished or otherwise weakened tea bushes that become prey to the attacks of blights; while manuring and superior cultivation methods usually cause blights to disappear. Among the leaf diseases may be mentioned: blister blight, gray, brown, and copper blight, bird's-eye spot, *Cercosporella theae*, rim blight, Japanese *Exobasidium* blight, sooty mold, *Phoma theicola*, *Phaeosphaerella theae*, scabbed leaves, etc. Each of the principal tea growing countries, except China, has recorded attacks by one or more of the foregoing, and have adopted various means of combating them, such as pruning and then burning the prunings; spraying with Bordeaux or Burgundy mixture, or lime-sulphur solution; or more intensive cultivation.

Similar treatment has been given to diseases that attack both leaf and stem, like blister blight, red rust, bacterial leaf and stem diseases, black rot, Indian parasitic thread blight, epiphytic thread blight, white stem blight, chlorosis mosaic disease, and horse hair blight. Also, such stem diseases as the two varieties of branch canker, pink diseases, three varieties of die-back, thorny stem blight, *Massaria theicola*, stump rot, velvet blight, gray fungus, collar rot of nursery plants, lichens and mosses, fasciation, galls on plucked shoots, burrs, and callous outgrowths. At present coal tar is advised for use in the prevention of infection of pruning cuts.

Root diseases usually manifest themselves to the grower by the death of the affected bushes, but seldom ascend to the stem and branches. Upon digging up a bush that has died from no apparent cause, the mycelium of a fungus is apt to be found upon its roots. Bushes, thus affected, tend to die out in patches. The commonest origin of root disease in tea is a dead stump, whose roots spread the mycelium of the .fungus in all directions. Fungoid root diseases include: *Rosellinia arcuata, Rosellinia bunodes, Rosellinia* sp., *Ustulina zonata, Sphaerostilbe repens, Diplodia*, red root, *Poria hypobrunnea, Trametes theae*, brown root, *Fomes lignosus, F. lucidus, F. applanatus, Polyporus mesotalpae, Polyporus interruptus, Irpex subvinosus*, root-splitting, "bitten-off" root, and *Sclerotium* disease.

As in the case of the insect pests of tea, the subject of the diseases of the tea bush is too voluminous for any but a specialized treatment, and this is to be found in *The*

RED RUST DAMAGE, JAVA

Diseases of the Tea Bush, London, 1923, by T. Petch, formerly botanist and mycologist to the Government of Ceylon and, later, the first director of the Ceylon Tea Research Institute.

Pruning, Plucking, and Crop Control

Generally speaking, most cultivated plants are grown under unnatural conditions. This statement is particularly applicable to the tea plant, because in its wild state it grows into a fair sized tree; while under cultivation it is reduced to the size of a bush. In most of the tea areas this is accomplished by pruning at regular intervals. Then, instead of being allowed to grow undisturbed, the bush is stripped of most of its newly formed leaves and leaf shoots as soon as they appear. This procedure is continued until the bush is no longer able to bear a profusion of leaves, due to the upset of normal balance between roots and leaves, and, when this occurs, it is the signal for re-pruning.

There are many systems of pruning in India, Ceylon, Java, and the other tea producing countries, each claiming special advantages which often are due to local conditions. All, however, have the same underlying principle and the same object —to stimulate flushing and to keep the bushes at a convenient height for plucking.

Pruning usually is done with a knife having a hooked blade four to eight inches long, according to the type of pruning to be done. Some tea planters begin, six months or a year after the shrubs have been transplanted to the field, by lightly nipping their tops with shears to induce lateral branching. Others wait as long as three years, which means that the seedling will have grown into a young tree of five to six feet in height when it is cut back with a knife about nine inches from the ground, provided there are lateral branches below this. These lateral branches are cut off at fifteen to eighteen inches from the ground, and provide a basis for the permanent framework of the bush, leaving the center open.

Later on, the bush is cut across at about eighteen inches and the subsequent cuts are made about two inches above the previous one, until the yield begins to diminish or the bush gets too high for plucking. Then it is given a heavy pruning to about fourteen inches from the ground and is subsequently pruned up two inches at a time as before.

Conditions in Assam are such as to make annual pruning the rule, although in some gardens pruning is done only once in two years. In Southern India, two to three years are commonly allowed between prunings, but in Ceylon pruning periods vary with the altitude from eighteen months to three, four, or five years. Java tea planters prune after intervals of a year and a half to two years. In Japan the tea bushes are pruned only about once in ten years, except in the case of weak bushes, which are cut down and permitted to grow up unchecked until a healthy growth is assured. Formosa planters rarely prune their tea, but those who do merely cut the bushes across about three to six inches above the ground at intervals of five to ten years.

The ordinary finger plucking, as well as the plucking by shears practiced in Japan, has the effect of a light pruning for the tea bush; it also helps to preserve a convenient plucking surface and stimulates flushing.

Flat bush tops are the rule in Ceylon and India. In Java, the earlier schools of pruning allowed the bushes to run up to high centers and deficient side growth, but the more modern practice is to keep the bushes down to three or four feet in height by cutting back the centers and diverting growth to side branches, as is done in Ceylon and India.

Well kept tea bushes in China are not allowed to attain a height above three feet, in order that pluckers of small stature may be able to work on them to good advantage. The young plants are "topped" by nipping off the center with the thumb

Pruned and Unpruned Tea, Java

nail two or three times during the first year. This causes them to spread out laterally, and the lateral branches are in turn topped, causing them to put out flush. In addition to being topped, Chinese plants in the better kept gardens are pruned when occasion requires it. This is done by seizing a handful of branches at a time and cutting them upward with a pruning knife until the height of the bush has been reduced to about two feet.

The time of the year when pruning is undertaken varies somewhat, according to local conditions. Where it is possible to so arrange it, the pruning operations are conducted in the cooler months, before the rains begin and when the plants are resting. This is the practice in India, but in Ceylon, where flushing is more or less continuous, it is customary to prune at convenient times throughout the year or until all the bushes have been gone over. Japanese tea growers, on the other hand, generally apply whatever pruning needs to be done after the first and second pluckings, at the height of the season for vegetative activity.

With the plucking operation the actual preparation of the leaf for the market is begun, and upon the delicacy and skill with which it is performed depends much of the quality in the manufactured leaf. It is nearly always done by the women and older children of the labor force, while the men are occupied with heavier tasks. Only the bud and the first and second leaves are usually taken, the larger and coarser leaves being left on the bush. This process is repeated throughout the flushing season at intervals which vary with the climatic conditions of the different tea areas. An even pluck is a most important consideration in making good teas, for with uneven leaf the finer shoots wither in less time than coarser ones, and uneven teas result. In Southern India, Ceylon, Java, and Sumatra, where no drought or cold season occurs, the bushes flush the year round and are plucked throughout the year. In Northern India, the season lasts from late March or early April until the middle of November. In China, the pluckings begin in April and are continued until autumn checks the flushes. In Japan, the season begins about May first, and there are usually not more than three or four pluckings; the latest sometimes extending into late September or early October. Formosan

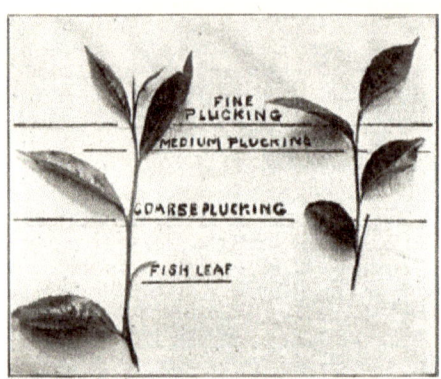

F. J. Whitehead

THE LEAVES PLUCKED FOR TEA MAKING

Showing the principal pluckings followed in India, Ceylon, and Java.

tea farmers pluck from April to the beginning of December.

An understanding of the part that leaves perform in the general economy of plant growth shows them to be the factory of the plant, where simple products are elaborated. While no harm results from plucking a certain amount of flush, some of the new leaves always have to be left if the health of the bush is to be taken into consideration. Just how much to take and how much to leave are questions which can only be answered by experience. In Ceylon, the Tamil tea plucker, using both hands, plucks about 30,000 shoots in the course of a day, and approximately 3200 shoots are needed to make a pound of manufactured tea.

When plucking the first flush, it is the general rule to allow three of its fully developed leaves to remain on the bush, exclusive of the so-called *jannum* or "fish leaf." *Jannum* is Hindustani, and means birth. When a new shoot grows from an axil, the first leaf, or *jannum*, is not serrated, and only grows to a small size. The second leaf also is sometimes undersized, and not serrated. In Ceylon and South India, the *jannum* is called the "fish leaf." The bud and two leaves are taken by nipping the stalk immediately below the second leaf. As little as possible of the stem is taken, as stems are objectionable to tea buyers. It was once the practice to take a portion of the third leaf, leaving only a small part of it on the stalk to protect the eye and axil, but this is not done to-day.

The leaf gathered for manufacture into tea is described as "fine," "medium," or "coarse," as shown in the accompanying illustration, and depends on how long the flush is allowed to grow between plucking rounds and the number of leaves taken. The illustration also shows the *jannum*, or fish leaf.

After taking the first flush, it is customary in Java and Ceylon to leave a leaf before plucking the next flush; *i.e.*, three leaves and a bud are grown, and two leaves and a bud are taken. In Assam it is common to pluck "flat" after the first flush. This type of plucking gives fine leaf, making good quality tea, but is hard on the bush.

Leaves grown from stunted buds, from which, as a rule, no further growth can be expected, are known as *banji*, Hindu for "sterile," and their treatment is the subject of much discussion among planters. Some believe prompt removal is necessary for the good of the bush, but Claud Bald holds that *banji* is a leaf that is merely resting, and should not be disturbed.[1] A more correct statement is that the *banji* leaf is still developing, but the bud in its axil is dormant. This may be for want of nourishment from the roots, heavy pruning, or drought, but after a period of necessary rest, it is not uncommon for the bud to resume activity and produce further upward growth.

Resting occasionally is resorted to as a means of restoring large areas of tea that are in poor condition. A prime requisite is to relieve such bushes of work, and to allow them to grow naturally and normally without disturbance. The work of the tea bush is the production of leaf for plucking, and to relieve it of this work rests it, and allows it to recuperate. A full season's rest is not too much for backward parts of an estate.

The resting of areas has none of the aspects of partial abandonment, for the usual cultivation is maintained, and the ground kept clear of jungle growth. At the end of the year, bushes that have been given the rest cure are pruned to two or three inches of new wood, the same as if they had been plucked. This pruning is necessary to keep the bushes from flowering and thereby needlessly reducing their

[1] Claud Bald, *Indian Tea: Its Culture and Manufacture*, Calcutta, 1922.

vitality. A modified plan of resting is to pluck during the first half of the season, and to let the bush run in the latter half.

After tea has been plucked, it frequently has to remain in the baskets for several hours while awaiting removal to the factory. If tightly packed, it becomes heated at the center, causing "red leaf" which is bad for quality in the made tea. Estimation of the tannin in red leaf taken from the center of a basket and ordinary leaf from the outside have shown that the tannin content may be reduced to half its original value by reddening.[2] It is better, therefore, to allow plenty of air to get to the leaf by loose packing, and also to transport it to the factory for withering more frequently than the usual twice daily.

The leaf is transported from the field by motor lorry, carts, light tramway, wire shoot, or on the heads of the pluckers to the factory, where it undergoes various processes which prepare it for the market.

Tea Factories

The present-day size of tea estates necessitates factories that are complete with every facility for expeditious manufacture. India, Ceylon, and Netherlands Indies are leaders in this respect. The Japanese tea factories, although well equipped, are small. China and Formosa have a few modern, machine-equipped factories, but still depend largely on hand rolling and firing in antique charcoal *chulas*.

The modern tea factory building has a light steel framework, corrugated iron roof, and brick walls, or walls of galvanized iron, lined with wood. In Assam, practically all factories are single storied, and the leaf is withered in outside leaf-houses. In the Dooars, most of the factories are two or three storied, with withering lofts above the rolling, firing, and packing rooms, which occupy the ground floor. Lofts are in general use in Ceylon, Java, and South India.

There is no standard factory, although it is the aim of every man who designs one to arrange the withering houses or lofts, the rolling room, the fermenting room, and the firing and packing rooms, in such a manner as to make organization

simple. The size of a factory, however, is based on the crop. In Assam, about three-fourths of one per cent of the annual crop is reckoned as an average big day, and one to be catered for. Thus, if the season's crop is 10,000 maunds [1 maund = 80 lbs.], machinery for a daily out-turn of seventy-five maunds is installed. In Ceylon, machinery sufficient to cope with three-fourths of the crop plucked on the busiest day is laid down. Marshall's Driers and Rollers, and Davidson's Sirocco Driers are the most common tea machinery. Certain Ceylon and Java firms also make tea machinery, and Calcutta firms recently have taken up the business.

Both the rolling and the fermenting rooms of a tea factory must be kept cool and damp. It is usual, therefore, to separate them from the firing room by a brick or stone partition, capable of insulating them from the heat of the driers. In Assam, it is customary to ferment in a separate room apart from the factory. This room is usually placed under a leaf withering house for coolness. With the installation of humidifier systems, the control of atmospheric humidity and temperature is so increased that there no longer is any need to separate the rolling and

TEA FACTORY AND WITHERING SHED, BRITISH INDIA

The upper picture shows a typical Sylhet factory; the lower, a Terai withering shed with bamboo screen against scorching winds.

2 P. H. Carpenter and H. R. Cooper, "Factors Affecting the Quality of Tea," *Quarterly Journal*, Indian Tea Association, Calcutta, 1922, part 2, pp. 11–12.

TYPICAL LOFT FACTORY COMMON TO JAVA, SUMATRA, AND CEYLON

fermenting rooms. Separation in the past was necessary because of the ease of control of atmospheric conditions in a small room. The combined rolling and fermenting room is necessarily large.

The firing room is often contiguous with the sorting and packing rooms. The sorting room normally is a dusty place, although the tendency nowadays is to install suction plants to keep the atmosphere clear.

The engine room usually is in the center of the building, but to one side. In this way, the power is transmitted to the center of the main shafting, which serves the rollers at one end, the driers in the middle, and the sorting machines at the other end.

Withering lofts are built about eight feet in height from floor to ceiling. A greater height makes it difficult to spread the leaf on the racks. Lofts of lesser height are not economical to construct. A most important consideration is the size and construction of the windows, which must be large enough to admit air if necessary, but not so large as to let in heat in case the day is hot and the window is closed.

Power in Tea Factories

The power in tea factories is obtained from steam engines stoked by wood or coal, according to locality, or by modern oil engines. In Java and Japan, where hydro-electric power is available, machinery is driven by electricity. At Malabar in Java, it also is the practice to dry tea by electrically-generated heat. The practice is, of course, only possible where electric power is cheap. Ordinarily, dry-

ing machines are heated by wood or coal, and in some cases by oil burners.

How Black Tea Is Prepared

There are four principal operations in the preparation of black tea; namely, withering, rolling, fermenting, and firing.[3] The effects of these operations may be summarized as follows:

Withering is a preliminary step to rolling, resulting in a desired loss of water, a flaccid condition of the leaf, and important changes in the constituents of the cell sap. Rolling imparts the characteristic twist, breaks the leaf-cells, and exposes the juice to the air. During fermentation, the tea tannin is partly oxidized, and the leaf reddened. The essential oil is developed in fermentation. Firing stops fermentation.

Physical Aspects of Withering

Withering methods vary somewhat in the principal black tea producing countries—British India, Ceylon, and Netherlands Indies. The atmosphere is practically always humid in Ceylon, Java, and Sumatra; whereas in British India it is only humid during the monsoon—a period of about four months. Accordingly, in Ceylon and Netherlands Indies, it is usual to wither the leaf in enclosed lofts, into which hot air, at not above 90° F., is passed at times when atmospheric condi-

[3] The following general discussions of the manufacture of black tea are recommended: P. H. Carpenter and H. R. Cooper, "Factors Affecting the Quality of Tea," *Quarterly Journal*, Indian Tea Association, Calcutta, 1922, part 2; P. H. Carpenter and C. R. Harler, "Important Points in Tea Manufacture," *Quarterly Journal* Indian Tea Association, Calcutta, 1926, parts 1 and 2.

WIRE WITHERING TATS, SUMATRA

tions make a natural wither impossible. In some parts of British India—notably in Assam—withering lofts are generally unnecessary, as the leaf withers well in the open.

For withering, the leaves are spread thinly and evenly on racks called "tats." In some districts these are made of bamboo, which may or may not be covered with Hessian cloth, while in others they are of Hessian cloth alone, or of wire mesh. It requires approximately one square yard of surface for withering each pound of fresh leaf, and the process takes from eighteen to twenty-four hours, depending on temperature and the humidity of the air. During withering, the leaves lose about one-third to one-half their weight by evaporation, become soft and flaccid, and emit an agreeable, characteristic, fruity odor.

At the same time a physical change takes place, but no definite chemical change has yet been discovered. At present, the wither is judged by the moisture content, or loss of weight, of a certain quantity of leaf. In Assam, 100 pounds of leaf are dried to about sixty-five pounds. In Ceylon, the same weight is dried to about fifty-five pounds.

The withering must be slow and even; otherwise, the leaves, being thin, shrivel and blacken before the bud and stalk have hardly dried.

Withering is governed by time, temperature, and the humidity of the atmosphere. The ideal time varies from eighteen to twenty-four hours. With an average temperature of 83° F.—that of Assam in the manufacturing season—the leaf is ready for rolling when 100 pounds have dried to about sixty-five pounds. In Ceylon, with

lower temperature, a fuller physical wither is practiced.

There is much discussion as to the best type of withering rack. Hessian or bamboo racks give an even wither, but require thin spreading, since most of the drying takes place from the upper surface of the rack. Wire racks take more leaf, because of the double drying surface, but have the disadvantage of allowing fine leaf to hang through and overdry. A drawback of Hessian racks is that they are liable to harbor harmful bacteria, and to get sour in prolonged spells of damp weather, especially in Assam, where they are open to the air at the sides.

An even wither is essential to good tea making, and, to this end, the leaf must be thinly spread. In Ceylon, a common average of rack area per pound of green leaf is ten to twelve square feet, although many factories have much greater space; some as much as thirty square feet. In India, the average is about the same as in Ceylon; but in the better tea areas, twenty-five to thirty square feet per pound of leaf is common. In Java, the spreading is considerably thicker than in India or Ceylon.

Controlled Withering

It is fully appreciated by planters that unless a suitable wither is obtained, good tea cannot be made. During prolonged wet periods it is practically impossible to obtain a good natural wither, and in many cases the leaf after standing for twenty-four hours still is as wet as when it was brought in. It follows logically, then, that attempts should be made to wither leaf artificially when natural conditions are unfavorable. The best tea is made when leaf is withered under favorable natural conditions. These include an abundant supply of fresh, moderately cool air at about 80° F., with a relative humidity of 70 to 80 per cent, flowing at the rate of fifty to 100 feet per minute. These conditions are difficult to duplicate artificially.

In Ceylon, Java, and parts of India, leaf generally is withered in lofts built above the factory. Hot air from the drying room, consisting partly of the exhaust air from the driers, is conducted into the lofts and drawn over the leaf racks by means of fans. In many lofts, the hot air enters a central bulking chamber whence it is sent with the aid of booster or pres-

HESSIAN WITHERING TATS, CEYLON

sure fans into the loft where it is needed, and is drawn through it by powerful fans into an exhaust chamber at the end of the loft. Most lofts are plentifully supplied with windows, so that in favorable weather the leaf may be withered naturally. Experience has shown that a loft should not be more than 100 feet long and forty feet wide. The 100-foot limit is necessary because the hot air, being drawn over the leaf, picks up moisture, and with a loft longer than 100 feet the air becomes saturated. A loft not wider than forty feet is best, because experience has shown that to be the maximum width which will give good results when a natural wither is possible.

It will be appreciated that the leaf nearest the bulking chamber, receiving the air at its driest and hottest, withers more quickly than the leaf at the cooler, more humid end of the loft. In order to level up the withering, a reversible arrangement of air flow has been introduced, whereby the air first flows in one direction and later in the opposite. This reversal is a simple matter, and is done by opening and shutting of doors. The temperature of the loft should not rise above 85° F. or 90° F., in order to obtain good results. It has been observed that when controlled withering is used, the leaf should be submitted to the warm, dry air as soon as it is spread; and, when a certain degree of drying has been realized, the loft should be disconnected from the air system and a wait made for the wither to proceed, as it does, without aid. Leaf withered slowly, eighteen to twenty-four hours, at a moderate temperature, around 80° F., gives the best tea.

In Upper Assam, where, on an average, some kind of physical wither can be obtained on all but about fifteen days in the year, the leaf is withered in leaf houses which are roofed, but otherwise open to the air. In spite of the fact that a full, natural wither usually can be obtained, certain factories are building controlled lofts at great expense. The success of these lofts is certain, and in a few years time most of the progressive concerns in the Assam Valley will be equipped with some kind of withering control.

In addition to loft control, many attempts have been made to dry the leaf artificially in machines constructed on the principle of tea drying machines. The leaf is run through them on an endless tray system, and submitted to an air blast of about 110° F. It is thereby reddened, but the resulting made tea usually is "harsh" and inferior to naturally withered leaf. The first drawback to artificial withering machines is the fact that high temperatures are necessary in order to get a satisfactory quantity of leaf through a convenient sized machine in a reasonable time. If the temperature is lowered to about 80° F., the machine would have to be so large, and the process so slow, as to be impracticable. It is noticeable that after rapid drying of the leaf, such as occurs in a withering machine, or as may happen on a day when a hot, dry wind blows through the withering houses, the leaf quickly becomes flabby but that after waiting for an hour or so, some of the flabbiness is lost by virtue of the redistribution of the cell moisture.

The late Mr. K. A. R. Bosscha, of Malabar Tea Estate, Java, invented an interesting withering machine. It consists of a long, octagonal cylinder with wire

BOSSCHA WITHERING MACHINES IN JAVA

sides. Leaf that has been well withered in the ordinary way is put into the cylinder, and hot, dry air at about 125° F. is blown in while the cylinder slowly revolves for about thirty minutes. The leaf loses 2 to 3 per cent of its moisture during the process, but becomes brownish and sticky, and takes on the aroma of ripe apples. In fact, it appears that the fermentation process starts, and the inventor claimed that by the use of this machine the time of fermentation is reduced from seven or eight hours to three or four hours.

Ideal Withering Conditions

Practical planters have come to the following conclusions regarding ideal withering conditions:

(a) Spread the leaf as soon as possible after plucking.
(b) Do not damage the leaf during withering.
(c) Spread evenly and thinly on clean withering space.
(d) Wither slowly and regularly in a cool atmosphere for a minimum of sixteen and a maximum of about twenty-four hours.
(e) The degree of the physical wither should depend on the temperature. At average temperatures of about 80° F., 100 lbs. of leaf should dry to about 75 lbs. At about 70° F., 100 lbs. should dry to about 55 lbs.

Chemical Aspects of Withering

As previously stated, no one has yet discovered what chemical changes occur in the tea leaf during the withering process, and analyses fail to disclose any significant chemical differences between fresh and withered leaf; but the ease with which tannin, and other soluble bodies, may be extracted by boiling water increases as the wither proceeds. Thus, if fresh leaf is placed in cold water to which a drop of ferric chloride is added, no coloration takes place for several days. When withered leaf is so treated, however, a greenish coloration is obtained in a few minutes, showing immediate diffusion of the tannin from the leaf. The tannin content and soluble extract of the tea leaf are practically unaltered by withering. The acidity of the cell-sap also is unchanged, showing a value of 4.3—4.5 in all stages of the wither.

Many theories have been formulated as to the changes in the tannin compound when the leaf withers. The earlier theories on the subject considered the tannin in fresh leaf to be in the form of a glucoside, which, on withering, was hydrolyzed. The theory that tea tannin is in some way "protected" in the fresh leaf, and hydrolyzed on withering, is a convenient one, although experimental proof still is lacking.

If fresh leaf is infused, a greenish yellow solution is obtained. As the leaf withers, the green color becomes less marked. The taste of these infusions has been reported on by tea tasters. According to these experts, fresh leaf infusion is "raw," while withered leaf infusion is "harsh." The exact significance of these terms is difficult to convey, and tasters, themselves, find great difficulty in explaining just what they mean. "Rawness," however, appears to denote bitterness, and "harshness" apparently refers to a kind of astringency.

If the leaf is at all damaged or bruised, the infusions become red. These infusions are still pronounced "raw" by tasters, but "pungency" is also detected. Pungency normally appears as soon as the leaf is rolled, and it seems that this characteristic, which is akin to astringency, and "briskness"—another tea taster's expression—results from the oxidation, i.e., fermentation, of the leaf. The "tannin red" compounds seem to be connected with pungency. This finds confirmation in the work of Peacock, who showed that the astringent principle of maté is due to the presence of phlobaphenes, or "tannin reds." [4]

The Rolling Process

The primary object of rolling is to break the leaf-cells, and liberate the juices and enzymes sealed within. A secondary object is achieved when the tea is given its peculiar and well-known twist. As soon as the leaf-cells are broken and the juices exposed to the air, fermentation begins. Oxygen is absorbed, a certain amount of heat is developed, the leaf turns from green to a copper-red color, and takes on an aroma peculiar to tea. These processes are spoken of, collectively, as "fermentation." In the earlier days of tea manufacture, the leaf was rolled by hand after withering, as is done to this day with the Congous, or black teas, of China. For many years, however, machines have been

[4] J. C. and B. L. Peacock, Jour. Am. Pharm. Assoc., Easton, 1912, vol. ix, no. 8.

A JACKSON TEA ROLLER, BRITISH INDIA
The cloth chute feeds the leaf from the withering loft above.

used to do this work in India, Ceylon, and Netherlands Indies.

A tea roller consists of a brass covered table with battens attached to its surface, upon and against which an open-bottomed leaf box is given a circular, grinding motion, while an adjustable compression arrangement makes possible the application of any desired pressure of leaf against the surface and battens of the table.

The labor-economy difference between hand-rolling and the work of a modern machine roller is remarkable. A power roller accomplishes a task that would occupy approximately seventy men, working by hand methods; it does its work evenly, and with the sanitary advantage that goes with a food product not touched by perspiring, human hands.

Although the same mechanical tea rollers are used in India, Ceylon, and Java, the system of rolling is by no means the same in the three countries. In Ceylon and Java, the rollers revolve at about forty-five revolutions a minute, and the roll may last, particularly in Ceylon, as long as three hours. In India, the rollers make up to seventy revolutions a minute,

and the normal rolling time is about one to one and a half hours.

The effect of slow and fast rolling has been studied, and, under favorable temperature conditions, no appreciable difference is noticeable in the liquors from teas made by the two methods. Slow rolling, however, involves long rolling, during which time the leaf, closed in, is liable to heat. In India, with the natural high temperatures, this heating must be avoided, and it is preferable during most of the season to get the roll finished and to thinly spread the leaf on the fermenting floor, rather than to keep it boxed up in a roller.

The slow roll in Ceylon is also connected with the full wither. It is observed that, the fuller the wither, the slower must be the roll to be effective.

So far as the appearance of the tea goes, slow rolling gives less broken tea with more "tips." Fast rolling apparently smears the "tip" with the juices from the other leaves much more than does slow rolling; the result being that much of the "tip" is indistinguishable from broken fine leaf.

In Ceylon, the leaf may be rolled as many as six times. After each roll the leaf is sifted, and fine leaf removed and taken to the fermenting room. In this manner the rolling process may take three hours, and the leaf finally left in the roller may be less than half of the original.

In India, the roll consists of two parts. First, the light roll, lasting about half an hour, by means of which the shoot is broken up and the "tip" and fine leaf detached, so that, when the green leaf is sorted, the fine stuff may be separated and taken to the fermenting room. The second roll is hard, with the pressure cap of the roller down. This roll may last for an hour.

Experience has shown that hard rolling gives strength to the tea liquors, but may expose stalk. During rolling, heat is developed, but this is mainly the heat of fermentation and not the heat of friction. A big rise in temperature is avoided by raising the pressure cap of the roller every few minutes.

As the rolling proceeds, the leaf forms into balls, which, if fermented as such, give uneven colors, for the inside of the ball is shut off from the atmosphere, and remains greenish. These balls are broken when

FERMENTING ROOM WITH OVERHEAD FACTORY-TYPE HUMIDIFIERS, BRITISH INDIA

the leaf is green-sifted, after rolling. The green-sifters are known as ball-breakers and in Ceylon the process is regarded as one of aëration and oxidation. In India, the temperature usually is so much higher than in Ceylon, that the oxidation process goes quite fast enough without additional help, and green-sifting, apart from ball-breaking, is looked upon as a means of cooling the leaf after rolling.

The rolling room must be kept cool as an aid to keeping the leaf in the rollers cool. If the leaf heats up much beyond about 85° F., the fermentation process is unduly hurried, and the best teas are not made.

The number, position, and character of the battens on the table of a rolling machine determine to a large extent the results that are obtained. Deep battens are found best for the production of broken grades, and broad, shallow battens turn off the highest percentage of well-made leaf grades. Rollers need to be carefully cleaned of all leaf at the termination of each roll; all cakes of leaf adhering inside the box, on the pressure cap, and around the battens, are carefully removed before a fresh charge is applied.

The combined roll-breaker and green-

leaf-sifting machine, to which the leaf goes from the roller, has a roll-breaking hopper provided with beaters to break up the leafy lumps, and either a sifting tray or a cylindrical sieve of generous dimensions. Two sizes of sifting screen on one tray are used in many tea factories; screens having three and four, or four and five, or four and six holes per inch, respectively, being used in varying proportions to suit local conditions. Whether more of the coarse, or more of the fine screen is used, is open to individual determination; but there seems little doubt that the combination of two sizes is preferable to a tray fitted with but a single sized screen.

A proportion of one roll-breaker to two full-sized rollers is common, but in factories where there are large numbers of rollers, the proportion is sometimes reduced to two roll-breakers to five rollers.

All machines and leaf containers require a daily scrubbing with water. The rolling room floor, where it is customary to deposit leaf, receives similar attention to assure its cleanliness.

The Fermenting Process

From the rollers and roll-breaker, the leaf, still more or less green and quite flaccid, goes to the fermenting room, where it is thinly spread on the cement, glass, or tile floor, or on glass or cement tables, to complete the process of oxidation begun and extensively developed during rolling. These fermenting spaces are washed down regularly with water, and anything in the nature of an ammoniacal smell is avoided. Although the process under discussion is given the distinctive title of "fermenting," in reality it marks the completion of that process.

During the fermentation of the tea leaf, oxidation brings about chemical changes which largely determine the flavor, strength, body, and color of its liquor; also the color of the infused leaves. The previously colorless tannin is transformed into red tannin and brown tannin, which give color to the liquor.

Fermentation proceeds best between 70° and 80° F. [cold fermentation], although in Assam it is often difficult to keep the temperature down to 80° F. in the rains. In cold areas, such as Darjeeling and the Pengalengan plateau, the leaf is sometimes spread near the driers to aid fermentation. In Ceylon, it is often spread very thinly to insure a good air supply, and, in this manner, fermentation is hastened.

The humidity in the fermenting room is maintained at a degree close to the saturation point. This is sometimes brought about through the use of Hessian curtains hung roundabout the walls of the room from perforated pipes, which sprinkle water on the curtains; also by the use of wet cloths on frames placed a few inches above the fermenting leaf. Many factories have installed humidifiers similar to those used in cotton mills.

Humidifiers of the cotton-mill type force water under high pressure through a fine nozzle, producing the desired amount of water vapor and dispensing with the use of wet curtains. Briefly, the system consists of a pump, which supplies water at a high pressure to a number of humidifying units. These units are suspended from the ceiling of the room to be humidified, in the position most favorable for complete circulation and dispersion of the humidified air, in order to obtain a uniform degree of humidity throughout the room. There are two types of these humidifiers; the open-type, and the ventilating-type. The open type is designed to supply only moisture, while the other communicates with the outside atmosphere and introduces fresh air, which is cooled and filtered before entering the room.

The objects aimed at in the humidification of rolling rooms, are: first, to reduce the working temperature in hot, dry weather; and, second, to prevent the drying of green leaf during rolling, sifting, and fermenting. If fermenting leaf dries, uneven colored infused leaf is produced.

As a general rule, the shorter the fermentation, the more pungent the liquors; and the longer the fermentation, the softer the liquors, and the deeper their colors. The chemical reason for this is that tannin in its natural state is colorless and pungent to the taste, but fermenting causes it to develop color and lose pungency.

The leaf is allowed to ferment until it arrives at the proper color, which is bright coppery-red. The time, varying from one and one-half to four and one-half hours, depends largely on the degree of the wither and the type of rolling. Locality also makes a difference; leaf from different gardens requires different types of fermentation. Only by careful experiment can the best time and character of ferment be determined.

All surfaces in the fermenting room, with which the leaf comes in contact, must be non-odorous and free from cracks and crevices that will retain juice, otherwise they cannot be kept sweet. Porous surfaces, such as wood and brick, are extremely undesirable. Iron, although nonporous, is also unsuitable, as the tannin present in tea juice acts on iron to form tannate of iron, which blackens the leaf.

Chemical Aspects of Fermentation

In order that leaf may ferment easily, it must be young and fine. Old, big leaves that are hard, and not succulent, do not easily take on the red color characteristic of fermented leaf.

Air is necessary to fermentation, and rolled leaf will not ferment in vacuo or in carbonic acid gas, but remains green. For the making of good tea, it is generally considered that the fermentation process, including the rolling time, should not last longer than about three and a half hours.

Two main factors are concerned in the rate of fermentation of leaf; namely, temperature and air supply. The course of fermentation is largely influenced by the humidity of the atmosphere.

During fermentation many reactions are going on, and, although a high temperature may merely increase the rate of these reactions and lower the time necessary for fermentation, still, experience shows that, quite apart from taints arising from bacterial action or lost flavor, the best tea is made at low temperatures. It is possible that the chemical reactions making up fermentation, proceed best at about 75° F., and that, at temperatures much removed from this, the different reactions are out of step for the production of the best tea.

The rolled leaf is spread in beds at a depth varying from one and one-half to five inches. The thicker the spread, the less chance is there of air reaching the leaf, hence longer fermentation is required. However, the thicker the spread, the more is the heat of fermentation conserved, and the hotter becomes the bed. This second factor reduces the time necessary for fermentation, but the ultimate result of a thick spread is that a longer fermentation is necessary than with a thin one.

In the hill gardens of Ceylon, where the temperatures are low, it is usual to spread very thinly—about an inch and a half—but in India, such spreading, with temperature above 80° F., would allow fermentation to go on at much too fast a rate for the production of good tea, and two and one-half inches is the average thickness of spread.

During the process of fermentation, the temperature of the bed rises steadily, after two or three hours, to a maximum at which it remains until it falls, after five or six hours. When the maximum is first attained, the aroma appears markedly, and then, for the next hour or two, seems to disappear and reappear at intervals.

Considering that fermentation consists largely in the formation of "tannin reds," which make for liquor and color of infusion, it follows that the longer the fermentation, the thicker will be the liquors at the expense of pungency, which largely is governed by the tannin, as opposed to the "tannin red" content.

Only rarely do teas show both marked pungency and strength of liquors. A tea buyer prefers one or the other of these qualities, and a tea possessing either definite pungency or strength has a better market value than one possessing both qualities, but not in a marked degree.

The question of humidity in the fermenting room may now be discussed. If leaf is fermented in a dry atmosphere, it turns the "old penny" color, to use the expression of earlier tea planters. This state is aggravated, if a dry draught blows on the leaf. When the atmosphere is humid, it is much easier to get the "new penny," or red copper, color, denoting a good fermentation. The "tannin browns" generally are held to be largely responsible for poor colors, whilst the "tannin reds," or phlobaphenes, are supposed to be responsible for good colors.

Many experiments concerning the influence of temperature, light, air, time, and humidity on fermentation have been made, and many aspects of the fermentation problem have been considered. Accounts of this work will be found in the pamphlets published by the Proefstation at Buitenzorg, Java, and by the Tocklai Experimental Station, Assam. Usually, it has been found that the best conditions arrived at empirically agree with those justified by scientific study.

In order to obtain the best results in fermentation, the following points should be observed:

(a) The fermenting floor must be kept clean and fresh.

(b) The air must be at a temperature as near 75° F. as possible and must be fresh. Draughts should be avoided.

(c) The atmosphere of the fermenting room should show a relative humidity of about 95 per cent.

(d) The leaf should be spread thinly, not more than three inches thick, and evenly, so that the temperature in the leaf never rises above about 83° Fahrenheit.

(e) The fermentation should be stopped when the aroma first appears, or when the bright copper color has developed.

The question of fermentation cannot be left without some mention of postfermentation. After tea is dried and packed, it still undergoes a slight change, and carbonic acid gas is evolved. This change is known as mellowing, and is believed to be the result of slight postfermentation.

Firing Black Teas

When tea drinking was first adopted in Europe and America, and China tea formed the only crop of any consequence commercially, *kuo* firing in shallow iron pans and basketfiring in hourglass-shaped baskets over small charcoal fires were the methods followed. Hand methods still prevail in China, Japan, and Formosa, but with the greater consumption of tea from the newer tea producing countries of India, Ceylon, and the Netherlands Indies there arose the necessity for "firing" in large quantities, and machine driers were installed.

There are various types of machine driers supplying artificial heat by different means. Some are fed automatically, the leaf falling on traveling trays that carry it from the top of the machine to the bottom, where it is discharged; others are provided with trays on which the leaf is spread and then placed in the machine, as bread is placed in a baker's oven.

The principle of drying tea consists in blowing or drawing a blast of hot, dry air up or down through an inclosed chamber through which the tea passes on trays. In the up-draft machine the hot, dry air

TEA DRIER, BRITISH INDIA
Close-up of an Imperial Venetian Firing Machine.

entering at the bottom of the chamber at a temperature of about 200° F. meets first the dry leaf, which is just leaving the machine. The air then passes through the trays bearing less dry tea. Finally, when the air leaves the machine, it is cooled to about 120° F. and is moist, having just passed the cold, wet, incoming leaf.

If tea is dried quickly in a dry atmosphere, it becomes case-hardened, and the center of the leaf remains moist. The result is that slow chemical changes take place, the tea loses quality, and sometimes even goes moldy.

Tea fermentation appears to be stopped at temperatures of about 150° F., or considerably lower in a blast of air. Thus, it has been found that if the incoming leaf meets a temperature of about 120° F. in the firing machine, the fermentation is effectively stopped. Sometimes, if the machine is overloaded, the air blast is cooled so that when it reaches the exit its temperature is below 120° F. In this case fermentation goes on for a time within the machine at an enhanced rate, and the leaf stews, producing a "flat," or over-fermented tea.

Leaf enters the firing machine with a moisture content of 50 to 65 per cent, according to the degree of the wither. In India it is usual for the leaf to contain well over 60 per cent of moisture at the time of firing, and the operation is carried out in two stages. First, the tea is fired until it contains about 30 per cent, and then, with a second firing in another machine, the moisture is reduced to about 3 per cent. It has been observed that firing to less than 30 per cent moisture—a condition known as a 12-anna fire in India —is a dangerous practice, because it always involves "stewing" the leaf and the disadvantages which go with this condition.

In Ceylon and Java, the leaf usually is more fully physically withered than in India, and is completely fired in one operation.

Regarding the high-firing, or scorching, of tea, experiments have shown that tea cannot be high-fired at 180° F. initial temperature of the air blast, although if left too long in the firing machine at this temperature after it has dried, it becomes "dry," as opposed to "sparkling," to borrow terms used in the description of wines. Teas may be fired with an initial temperature of the firing machine as high as 280° F. without being scorched, or high-fired, but if the tea, after it is dry, remains for more than a few seconds at this temperature it becomes high-fired. High-firing is a fault developed in the bottom tray, or trays, of the firing machine after the tea is dry, and just before it is discharged from the machine.

If the temperature of firing is high, the leaf may blister. Indeed, sometimes the leaf becomes covered with blisters of microscopic size, and it is believed that when such tea is rubbed, during mechanical sorting, the tops of these blisters are removed and "graying" results. A "gray" tea, as its name suggests, is one not so black as a black tea should be.

The following are the best conditions for firing:

(a) Fire at a low initial temperature; namely, 180° F, and pack the machine so that the temperature of the exit gases is at least 120° F.
(b) Fire with a full air blast.
(c) Spread the leaf thinly.
(d) See that the tea leaving the machine is dried to at least 30 per cent moisture content.

The three conditions (b), (c), (d), insure against "stewing."

When tea is fired it contains about 3

per cent of moisture. During sorting and handling it picks up moisture, so that by the time it is graded it may contain as much as 10 per cent. On this account, it is warmed in a firing machine just before it is packed, the object being to reduce the moisture content to about 6 per cent. If tea is much drier than this, it will not mellow, and, if it is much more moist, it is liable to "go off" in the box after it is packed.

In many factories, the moisture content of the tea is accurately estimated before it is packed, in order to determine whether final firing is necessary. In India, it has been observed that, during the early part of the season, when tea is packed at weekly or ten-day intervals, a final firing is necessary. In the full season, however, when tea is only kept for two or three days before packing an invoice, final firing is unnecessary.

The moisture loss throughout the manufacture of black tea may now be tabulated. It has been observed in India that the average changes in moisture content of the leaf are as shown in the accompanying table.[5]

MOISTURE LOST IN BLACK TEA
MANUFACTURE IN INDIA

Fresh leaf contains about	77% moisture
Withered leaf contains about	66% "
Fermented leaf contains about	66% "
First-fired tea contains about	30% "
Final-fired tea contains about	3% "
Packed-fired tea contains about	6% "

Sun-drying of rolled and fermented leaf is practiced in certain districts of Ceylon where long periods of favorable weather are usual. This method produces stronger, blacker, and more tippy teas than machine-firing, but a pronounced metallic taste is imparted. In order to overcome this objection, and still benefit from the advantages of the process, only a part of each day's production is sun-dried, and is mixed with the machine-fired teas in order to improve their appearance; while at the same time, the metallic taste is satisfactorily modified. The rolled and fermented leaf is spread thinly in the sunlight on a suitable surface. Often the drying is started by a brief preliminary firing in an ordinary

firing machine. This avoids, to some extent, the formation of a metallic flavor. The time necessary for sundrying is roughly from forty-five to ninety minutes, and is less when the leaf has a preliminary firing in a drying machine.

Chemical Aspects of Firing

From the chemical standpoint, the object of firing tea is to stop fermentation by destroying the enzymes and any micro-organisms which may take part in the process. This destruction is brought about by heat and the removal of moisture. In addition to this action some of the substances present in the leaf are changed by heat to give the "malty" taste and smell of freshly fired tea. This change is known as "caramelization," and is similar to the change taking place when sugar is browned in a pan. Other substances which have a cabbage flavor in fermented leaf, lose this undesirable quality when fired.

During the firing process, some valuable constituents of the tea are lost. This is, to a certain extent, unavoidable, but the loss may be minimized by careful adjustment of temperature and air blast of the firing machine. The chief loss is of those substances which give rise to flavor and aroma, and are volatile in steam. The higher the firing temperature, the greater the ease with which they evaporate along with the moisture, which is driven from the leaf. Teas fired below 170° F. are liable to "go off" on storing. In addi-

COMBINED ELECTRIC DRYING OVEN AND BALANCE, FOR ASCERTAINING THE MOISTURE CONTENT OF TEA

---

[5] C. R. Harler, "Moisture Changes During the Manufacture of Black Tea," *Quarterly Journal,* Indian Tea Association, Calcutta, 1928, part 2.

SIFTING AND GRADING MACHINE FOR BLACK TEA,
CEYLON

tion to a loss of flavoring substances, there is a loss in caffeine, but this is minimized by low-firing.

Another factor, which sometimes is responsible for loss of aroma, is the "stewing" of tea in the dryer. This follows from too thick spreading in the machine, or from a too weak air blast. It is probable that if steam is allowed to collect round the tea as it dries, there is a greater tendency for the essential oil, which is volatile in steam, to be lost, than if a full air blast is employed.

Attempts have been made to avoid these losses by drying tea in a blast of cold air, artificially dried by means of asbestos grids charged with calcium chloride. Although this process gives a very fine tea, unfortunately it gives one that will not keep unless it is partially dried by hot air. The double process of drying, both cold and hot, although it makes a good tea, is economically impracticable.

During firing, the proteins in the leaf are coagulated and rendered insoluble. These bodies, except in a degraded form, do not, therefore, enter into the tea infusion.

The red, fermented tea leaf turns black on firing, but when the leaf is infused, the red color is again observed.

At the conclusion of the firing process, the leaf is piled in heaps on the floor to cool, after which it is placed in bins, or other receptacles, ready for sorting.

Cutting, Sorting, and Packing

Big bulk in the medium grades often requires cutting, or breaking, for better ap-pearance. It is usual to put such leaf through a cutting machine before the final sifting and sorting, and this process results in a higher average of the finer grades.

It is usual to sort or pick over tea twice; once before cutting—where this is done—and once after sifting. Women are employed for this task, and their deft fingers swiftly remove all coarse red flake, stalks, and foreign matter.

Sifting follows, to separate the leaf into grades, as there is no market for unassorted teas. Sifting machines, with sieves that have meshes of many different sizes, sort the main classes into many sections; thus the Pekoe, or "top" class of black tea, is assorted into Flowery Orange Pekoe, the finest of teas, in which many "tips" are in evidence; Orange Pekoe; and Pekoe. From the coarser leaves, Pekoe Souchong, and Souchong are obtained. Also, many broken teas are sifted; the finest in quality is the Broken Orange Pekoe. Then the graders produce Broken Pekoe, and Broken tea, these being lower qualities. The very small fragments that remain after grading, are sold as "Fannings," and "Dust."

The tea is stored in bins until there is sufficient in each grade to form a sampling break. For the London market this means eighteen full, or twenty-four half-chests, or thirty-nine boxes of any one grade; but in Colombo 1000 pounds net may be cataloged and sold among the large breaks. Finally, it is bulked; i.e., the whole mass of each grade on one or more days is thoroughly mixed to secure as great uniformity of quality as is possible.

After bulking, the tea is immediately packed in chests or boxes, soldered up, labeled with the name of the estate, and dispatched to the nearest port of shipment.

Tea usually is packed by clamping one or two chests on a machine having an iron, pivoted platform, which is given a rapid vibratory motion through an eccentric connected to a power shaft. This shakes the tea down to a solid fill, and guards against undesirable rubbing or breaking-up in transit. Another type of machine combines vibration with a stamp action to press the tea down.

The requirements for tea chests are that they be light in weight, durable, and free from any strong odor. Two kinds are in use; those made of wood, lined with lead-foil, and those made entirely of metal. The wooden chests are made of shooks—small boards—or of veneer. Shooks usually are made locally, and most veneer is imported. There sometimes is an appreciable saving in the use of native wood chests where supplies of suitable timber are available, but few factories find it pays to make their own chests.

Veneer chests are made of superimposed sheets of thin wood, cut spirally in a lathe from steamed logs. After drying, three sheets are stuck together with casein glue under a hydraulic press, the two outside sheets being placed lengthwise upon both sides of the crosswise-glued sheet. Veneer chests are gradually taking the place of the old wooden chests in India.

Metal chests usually are made of steel. Their principal claims to advantage are that they hold more and weigh less. A 24x19x19-inch wooden chest, occupying five cubic feet of space, holds 90 lbs. of tea, while a metal chest of the same outside dimensions will hold 106 lbs. of tea.

Recently, chests made of wood and lined with aluminum or lead have been used. The former probably will be used extensively when its tendency to corrosion has been overcome by heating it up to a temperature of 400° C., during manufacture.

How Green Tea is Prepared

Green teas are prepared in only three principal operations; namely, steaming or panfiring, rolling, and firing. The difference between the manufacture of green tea and the manufacture of black tea is that green tea is not fermented. Leaf intended for manufacture into green tea is steamed, instead of being subjected to the slow process of natural withering, common to black tea preparation. Steaming or panfiring, not only makes the leaf pliable, but sterilizes the leaf against fermentation and blackening.

Much of the tea made in China, and most of the Japan tea, is unfermented. A small quantity of green tea is made in Northern India, and practically none in Java and Ceylon.

In China, green tea is manufactured by a similar process to black tea, except that the preliminary withering process is omitted and the leaf is immediately fired in pans at a temperature somewhat higher

STEAMING THE GREEN LEAF, JAPAN

than in the case of black tea, and for a longer period. Fermentation thus having been made impossible, the rolling and firing follows.

The leaf destined to be made into green tea is generally plucked without stalk.

In Japan, it is usual to steam the leaf immediately it is brought in and, the enzymes and micro-organisms having thus been destroyed, to roll it until dry on paper trays heated by hot, metal plates. Although the rolling process is continuous, it is divided into four periods, during which moisture is steadily lost. Many factories employ electrically driven machines, which duplicate, somewhat, the four processes used in hand rolling.

If rolling machines are employed, hot air is blown into the machine when it is box-like or the plates are warmed if it is an open machine. Tea for export is re-fired in iron pans at a central station, and dried until it contains about two per cent of moisture. The best tea is re-fired in baskets, as in China.

Two slightly differing methods are used when green teas are manufactured in India. The Assam and Ranchi tea-makers steam the leaf, and then dry it in a hydro-extractor before rolling; while in Dehra Dun and other Districts of North India, the leaf is heated in a pan before it is rolled. In both cases the rolling is done by machinery similar to that used in black tea manufacture.

Green teas are apt to emerge from firing with an uneven, dirty green appearance. The fine leaf may retain its clear green color, but the coarser leaf often turns out a blackish gray, spoiling the appearance of the tea. The Chinese and Japanese tea-makers impart a natural greenish color to their best teas by rubbing them in a warm pan for about an hour after the completion of the ordinary firing; but in the beginning this greenish tint of the "natural colored" tea failed to satisfy the demands of America, the principal market for green teas. In order to meet the desire of this market for more highly colored green tea, the Chinese and Japanese early learned to face their export teas with such substances as indigo, Prussian blue, turmeric, sulphate of lime, soapstone, and gypsum. The coloring and polishing matter was applied to the leaf at the final stage of firing, after rolling had been completed, usually in quantities too small to prove deleterious to health. Since 1911, however, all artificially colored teas have been barred from the United States. Japan at once fell in line with a law against the facing of tea, but in China no official action was taken, and faced teas still are exported to Egypt and Turkey, where there is no law against their entry.

Chemistry of Green Tea Manufacture

Much less information is available concerning the chemical changes which occur during the manufacture of green tea than is the case with black tea manufacture. The chief differences between black and green teas result from fermentation. In green tea most of the tannin is present in the original form, and the slight loss of tannin which occurs during manufacture is the result of incipient fermentation, or precipitation by proteins. Tannin red and tannin brown do not appear in a good green tea infusion, for the first step in manufacture seeks to avoid their formation.

The preliminary steaming, or heating, of the leaf kills any organisms which may give rise to the essential oil of tea, and accordingly, green tea has no such aroma and flavor as is understood when speaking of black tea.

How Oolong Tea is Prepared

Oolong tea has been described as a cross between green and black. The leaf is slightly withered before panning, and during this process, a light ferment is allowed to develop. For this purpose, the leaf is spread three or four inches deep in large bamboo baskets, and placed in the shade, where it is frequently turned over for four to five hours. The temperature of the leaf, during this time, ranges from 83° to 85° F. Finally, it changes in color and gives off a characteristic apple-like odor, which is the signal for checking any further fermentation by drying.

Oolong tea is dried by panning for ten minutes in a *kuo*, or hot pan, set in the top of a brick or clay stove. The temperature of the pan is approximately 400° F. During this time the leaf is energetically stirred by hand or by a mechanical stirrer, to prevent scorching.

The leaf is rolled on a mat immediately after panning, the operation occupying about ten minutes.

Oolong teas are fired in the type of baskets long familiar in tea manufacture. Formosa baskets are thirty inches high and twenty-seven inches in diameter, open at both ends, and slightly drawn in at the waist where the tray for the tea rests. A circular hole in the ground, about eighteen inches in diameter and twelve inches deep, contains the charcoal fire, from which all gas and flame has been burned before the tea is placed over it. The fire is covered with ashes, and the tea is dried for about three hours, during which time the baskets are occasionally removed for the purpose of stirring the leaf.

This completes the country, or local, process of preparation. Subsequently, the leaf is collected by agents for the tea hongs, who send it to tea-firing go-downs in the towns, where it is re-fired in baskets at a temperature of about 212° F. for from five to twelve hours. The best quality teas are given the longest firing. When re-firing has been completed, the tea is packed in lead-lined chests, with inner paper linings, pasted over with fancy paper, and wrapped in matting.

The Oolongs, which long have enjoyed a special market in America, are now almost exclusively produced in Formosa. They were formerly produced, to some extent, in the Foochow District of China, where teas of this character originated, but lacked the fine flavor of the Formosa product. At one time, the planters of India and Ceylon sent a scientific commission to investigate the manufacture of Formosa Oolongs, with the idea of competing in their production. The commission reached the conclusion, however, that the characteristic flavor of these teas is due to special conditions of soil and climate to be found in no other country but Formosa.

Pouchong teas have only been prepared in Formosa during the last forty years or so. They are made by mixing the Oolongs with aromatic flowers such as *Gardenia, Aglaia odorata, Jasminum sambac,* and *J. odoratissimum.* The process is the same as that employed in making black and green scented China teas. After the last firing of the tea, the flowers are added and allowed to remain for twenty-four hours, when they are picked out.

In order to obtain the most delicate perfume, it has been suggested that about one pound of strongly perfumed tea be mixed with about twenty pounds of unscented tea, and the whole hermetically sealed.[6]

Brick, Tablet, Cake Tea, and Fluff

BRICK-TEA is universally consumed in Tibet, and previous to 1917 it constituted a large part of the tea imported into the Russian dominions in Europe and Asia. All teas of this character are made in China.

The brick-teas for the Tibetan trade are manufactured by crude methods in the southwestern Chinese province of Szechwan. After removing the fine leaves for the making of high-grade teas, the tea-makers of Szechwan allow the coarse leaves, stems, and twigs to ferment in sacks for a few days. They are then sorted by hand into three grades, and steamed over a boiler. When they have become soft and flaccid, they are mixed with leaf dust that has been treated with glutinous rice water, and pressed into bricks 11x14 inches. Each brick weighs about six pounds.

Brick-tea manufacture for the Russian trade, formerly an extensive industry of Yanglowtung and Hankow in the northern tea districts of China, had its inception in an ancient Chinese industry for supplying brick-tea in form convenient for transport by camel across the plains of Mongolia. After removing the finer leaves, the coarse leaves and stalks are first sorted into three grades, and are then chopped into lengths of about an inch. From the

dusty shed where this operation takes place, the leaf goes to the factory proper. Both black and green tea is made in the usual way and, after being steamed, is squeezed, under hydraulic pressure, into heavy leaden molds. A layer of good quality tea dust is used at the top and bottom of the mold, while the middle is filled with coarse choppings. The bricks are flat slabs of various dimensions, and weigh from $2\frac{1}{4}$ to 4 pounds. Before the tea is infused, it is whittled off the edge of the brick and ground to the necessary fineness.

TABLET TEA, produced in China and Java, consists of small bricks made of special quality tea dust. A firm of English manufacturing chemists has for many years produced "Tabloid" tea in the form of small circular tablets, similar to drug tablets. They are made of a fine grade of tea from which the dust has been blown to avoid cloudiness in the cup, and are packed in small, pocket-size tin boxes. Tablet tea also was manufactured at the tea gardens subsidized by the United States Government, at Summerville, South Carolina, previous to their closing in 1915. It was compressed under 2000 lbs. pressure by an ordinary drug-tablet machine, which turned out the tablets at the rate of 115 a minute. No agglutinous substance was required for adhesion. Tablet teas are prepared for the convenience of campers, picknickers, tourists, and explorers.

CAKE TEA is made in the P'uerh District of Southern Yunnan. This tea, known as P'uerh tea in medicine shops throughout China, is highly regarded for its medicinal qualities as a digestive and nerve stimulant. The leaves have a marked bitterness. They are panned, sun-dried, and steamed; after which they are pressed into circular cakes about eight inches in diameter. Cake tea is the most ancient form of manufacture that has come down to the present time. A method of preparing cake tea was described by Lu Yu in the first book on tea, published in China about A.D. 780. It is interesting to note that the cake tea of Lu Yu was wrapped in bamboo for transport, precisely as is the P'uerh tea of to-day.

TEA FLUFF.—In tea factories, when leaf is sorted, the machines break off fine pieces of leaf and rub off leaf-hair, all of which form a fine dust. The winnowing of the tea also removes more dust, fiber, and

---

[6] C. A. Guignon, *Le Thé*, Paris, 1907.

fluff. The mass of this waste is swept up and sold for chemical purposes. The caffeine content of such material is 3.5 per cent, and this is the main source of commercial caffeine.

Tea Estate Labor

Equalling in importance the requirements of favorable climate, altitude, and soil, for the successful commercial production of tea, is an abundant supply of cheap labor. Indeed, it has happened repeatedly, in countries where minor cultivations have started, that a lack of this essential has completely nullified natural advantages.

In India, the land of "teeming millions," labor is the worst problem of the tea industry. Despite the density of the population, it is only in seasons of drought and crop failure that there is sufficient necessity to induce the indigenous population of certain districts to desert their own lands for work on the tea estates. This is true of Assam, the Dooars, and Terai. Darjeeling, on the other hand, gets plenty of labor from the hills.

The coolie labor on Ceylon tea estates is drawn from among the Tamils of Southern India. The Ceylon planters found, even before coffee planting was replaced by tea in the island, that the indigenous Sinhalese were unfitted by temperament for steady work on the estates, and early turned to Southern India for a regular supply of cheap labor. Native Tamil recruiters are sent by the Ceylon planters to engage and send over the coolies needed.

The labor forces on estates in Java consist principally of native Sundanese coolies, male and female, and are divided into *vast personeel*, or permanent labor, and *borong*, or contract labor. Although Java is sometimes called the "human ant hill," labor shortage is felt.

Sumatra tea estates recruit coolies from Java, and they are paid slightly more than they get at home, as an inducement to emigrate.

In Japan, the wages paid in tea factories have gone up rapidly during recent years. Wages on the tea plantations also have gone up, although they are less than the rates paid in the factories.

Work in the average Chinese tea garden is pretty much a family affair, the hiring of outside help being unusual. This applies also in Formosa, where tea cultivation and primary manufacture is carried on principally by Chinese.

Experimental Stations

Experimental stations for scientific investigation and analysis of all questions affecting the cultivation and manufacture of tea have been established in all the principal tea producing countries.

The Indian Tea Association established its now world-famous tea experimental station at Tocklai in 1912, with a subsidiary at Borbhetta, two and a half miles away. Reports of the work done by the Scientific Department have been published by the Indian Tea Association at Calcutta, in its *Quarterly Journal*, and continue in annual pamphlets.

The United Planters' Association of Southern India has a well-equipped tea experimental station near Devarshola, Nilgiris. The work of this station is reported in the *Planters' Chronicle*, Madras, and in Association booklets.

In Ceylon, tea experimental work is conducted by the Tea Research Institute on the St. Coombs estate, a centrally located experimental tea plantation, with a small factory for scientific investigations of manufacturing processes, near Talawakelle in the Dimbula District.

The *Algemeen Landbouw Syndicaat* controls the internationally-known *Proefstation West Java*, at Buitenzorg, which combines both tea and rubber research. The results of the experimental work are published in pamphlets that are printed from time to time. In addition to laboratory work, the estates are visited, and advice furnished as needed.

Experimental development work in China at present is but a memory. In 1915, the Minister of Agriculture and Commerce, established a tea experimental station in the Kemun District of Anhwei Province, and proposed to establish some forty subsidiary stations in neighboring districts. However, unsettled political conditions in China caused the abandonment of the work.

Japan has six principal tea experimental stations. The Kanaya National Experimental Station at Makinohara, is for both experimental and educational work. Located also at Makinohara is the Shizuoka Ken Tea Expert Training School.

From this station, or school, men are sent throughout Shizuoka Prefecture to instruct tea producers in the latest developments in tea culture and manufacture. The four others are the tea experimental stations of Kyoto-fu and of Nara, Kumamoto, and Kagoshima Prefectures.

In addition, there are numerous minor tea experimental bureaus and institutions for carrying on tea investigation and research work in the various prefectures of Honshu, Shikoku, and the Kyushu Islands. Several joint tea associations also are engaged in tea experimental work.

Formosa has a Government tea experimental station, known as the Heichin Station in Shinchiku-shu for the scientific investigation of tea cultivation and preparation. In addition, there are two tea experimental stations for the investigation of cultivation only. These are located at Bunzan-gun, in Taihoku-shu, and at Toyen, in Shinchiku-shu.

Planters' Associations

In common with many other agricultural and manufacturing industries, tea planters in every principal tea producing country, except China, have found it to their advantage to unite for mutual protection and benefit. The China tea grower is an individualist, and simply refuses to "unite."

The Indian Tea Associations of Calcutta and London are the "big brothers" of all existing tea planters' organizations. The membership is representative of all the important units in the Indian Tea Industry. The Calcutta Association keeps a watchful eye on legislation, maintains a scientific department for the assistance of tea planters, and works out plans to enlarge the world markets for Indian tea. The London Association deals with questions arising in England. There are also branches of the Indian Tea Association and numerous local district associations; notably, in Assam, the Surma Valley, Dooars, the Terai, Darjeeling, Punjab, and Madras.

The Planters' Association of Ceylon, as the oldest representative body of the planting interests of the Island, with headquarters at Kandy, concerns itself with matters affecting the practical part of the working of estates, labor, legislation, planters' benevolent fund, etc. There are some eighteen district associations, which elect representatives to serve on the General Committee of the parent body.

The Ceylon Estates Proprietary Association has 554 members, who are proprietors of, or agents for, tea, rubber, and other agricultural cultivations. Another important organization having some interest in tea is the Low Country Products Association; all proprietary members.

The Board of Directors of the Tea Research Institute of Ceylon includes representatives from all three planting organizations. It was started in 1925.

Organization of planters interested in the cultivation of tea in Java has been the rule since early in the history of tea in the island. The leading planters are members of the *Algemeen Landbouw Syndicaat*, with headquarters at Batavia. This organization, as previously stated, controls the West Java Experimental Station at Buitenzorg.

The Tea Expert Bureau of Batavia provides such planters as are members with the expert advice of a tea taster who knows the requirements of the principal world markets. Samples of all consignments are sent to the Bureau and tested before the teas are forwarded. This allows prompt correction of any mistake in preparation, and has done much for the improvement of Java teas. In addition to advising tea growers in regard to the preparation of tea, the Bureau has made a study of markets, and has directed propaganda for Java and Sumatra teas in Australia and America.

In Japan, local associations of tea growers throughout the tea-growing districts are affiliated under a parent body known as the Japan Central Tea Association. The object of this organization is the development of markets for Japan tea at home and abroad.

In Formosa, the Japanese Government of the Island is encouraging tea growers— they are mostly Chinese—to form local *kumai*, or guilds, in support of a central tea factory for each guild. This plan, initiated in 1918, has been successful wherever it has been put into effect.

CHAPTER XV

CULTIVATION AND MANUFACTURE IN CHINA

THE DISTRICTS IN WHICH THE TEA PLANT IS GROWN—THE CHINESE TEA GROWER—
CHARACTER OF THE SOIL—CLIMATE AND RAINFALL—MODERN METHODS OF PROPAGATION
AND CULTIVATION—PRUNING AND PICKING—THE MANUFACTURE OF BLACK, GREEN,
AND SEMI-FERMENTED TEAS—SCENTED TEAS—BRICK, BALED, CAKE, AND TABLET TEAS—
GRADING CHINA TEAS FOR EXPORT—CLASSIFICATIONS BY PLACE OF ORIGIN, BY MAKES,
AND BY NATIVE TERMINOLOGY—GOVERNMENTAL AID

CHINA, a Republic since 1911, is larger than all of Europe. Its area, including Mongolia, Sinkiang, and Tibet, amounts to 4,278,000 square miles, and its population, according to the latest available figures, is 438,000,000. The principal tea districts, supplying the export trade, lie between 23° and 31° north latitude, and the best districts are between 27° and 31° north latitude. Railroad transportation is practically unknown, and chests of tea are carried by coolies to the nearest river for shipment to Shanghai, Hankow, or Foochow for export.

For many centuries tea has been cultivated in sixteen of the eighteen Provinces. They are: Kwangtung, Kwangsi, Yunnan, Fukien, Kiangsi, Hunan, Kweichow, Chekiang, Anhwei, Hupeh, Szechwan, Kiangsu, Honan, Shensi, Shantung, and Kansu. Of these, the last four—Honan, Shensi, Shantung, and Kansu—are northerly provinces, producing small quantities of low grade teas, most of which are consumed locally; while the other twelve, situated in Central and Southern China, turn out more than ninety-five per cent of all the teas for local consumption and for export.[1] Black tea is produced chiefly in the provinces of Fukien, Anhwei, Kiangsi, Hupeh, and Hunan; while most of the green teas are manufactured in Anhwei and Chekiang Provinces.

The Chinese Tea Grower

Tea, in China, is grown in small patches on the hillsides, mostly by peasant proprietors, as one of several crops. Large estates, like those in India, Ceylon, Java, Sumatra, or even Japan, are unknown. The leaves are stripped from the bushes by the farmer, and are partly manufactured. In this partly manufactured state they are sold to collectors, who re-sell them to tea hongs, or factories, and these hongs in turn resell to middlemen, who supply the foreign exporter.

In the event that prices fall too low, the farmer lets his tea bushes go unpicked until the demand again makes picking an object. There is little, if any, change in the acreage from year to year, for China still would need a large part of its normal annual production of tea to supply the home demand even if the export trade vanished completely.

Character of the Soil

Investigations in the tea-growing districts by the Chinese Department of Agriculture have demonstrated that soil of loamy character, and rich in iron, which originates from porphyritic sandstone, is the most desirable for tea cultivation.

---

[1] The author has attempted, throughout the work, to follow the orthography of Chinese names favored by common usage in the tea trade. In Romanizing Chinese words, it is only possible to render them phonetically, since the Chinese have no alphabet that parallels ours; therefore, there may be, and often are, several equally correct ways of spelling them. For example: Kemun, Keemun, Kemen, Kimun, Kimen, Chimen, and Chimun. No attempt has been made to indicate the complete orthography of such words; the practice has been to adopt the form most easily recognizable by tea men.

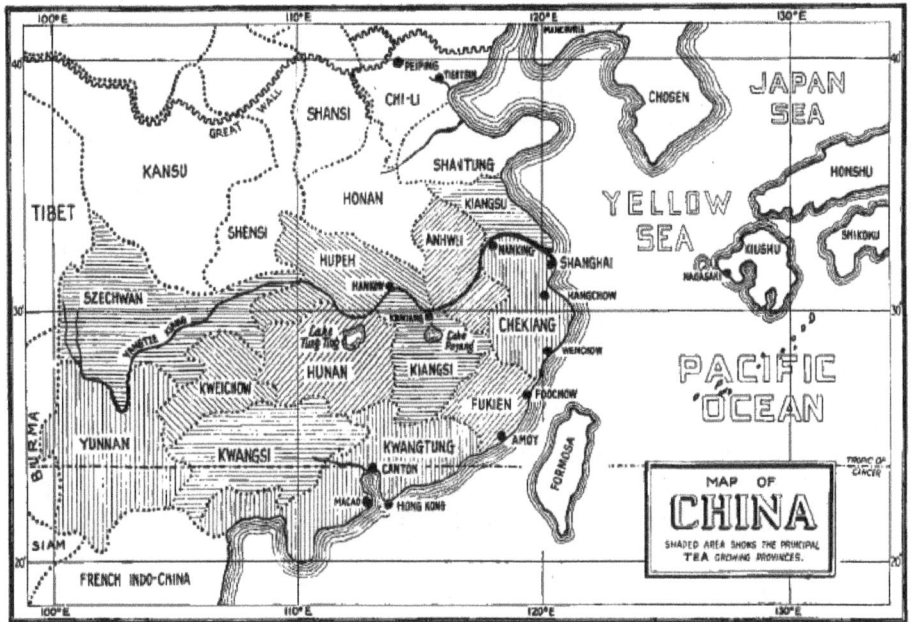

This kind of soil is abundant in southern Anhwei, where both black and green teas of superb quality are produced. China Table Number One shows a chemical analysis of typical soil of the Keemun District in the southern part of the Province of Anhwei.

CHINA TABLE NO. 1

Chemical Analysis of Keemun Soil	Per Cent
Water	2.41
Loss in ignition	6.58
Substance insol. in HCL	80.453
Silica [sol. in HCL]	1.002
Iron oxide [Fe₂O₃]	4.48
Alumina [Al₂O₃]	6.22
Lime [CaO]	0.20
Magnesia [MgO]	0.221
Potash [K₂O]	0.161
Soda [Na₂O]	0.336
Sulphuric acid [H₂SO₄]	0.117
Phosphoric acid [P₂O₅]	0.2035
Carbon	4.330
Nitrogen	0.1356
Humus matter	2.041
Total	99.9001

Speaking of Chinese tea plantations generally, it may be observed that their soils are almost exclusively moist, but well drained. Mr. G. J. Gordon, an acute observer, who reported on the cultivation of tea in China at the time tea-planting was first being attempted in India, found that the tea plant requires absolutely a free soil; not wet and not dry, but of a texture to retain moisture.

Professor Michael Faraday, 1791–1867, the eminent English chemist of the Royal Institution, made the mechanical analyses of specimen earths from China tea plantations shown in China Table Number Two.

CHINA TABLE NO. 2
Mechanical Analyses of China Tea Soils

Sample	From	Sand	Ferruginous Clay, etc.	Fragments	Total
		Per Cent	Per Cent	Per Cent	Per Cent
No. 1	A hill near Macao [the Lapa]	46.1	53.9	......	100
No. 2	Northeastern Fukien	17.7	56.53	25.77	100
No. 3	Northeastern Fukien	10.	90.	......	100
No. 4	Bohea country, 1st quality	33.08	66.92	......	100
No. 5	Bohea country, 2nd quality	44.61	55.39	......	100
No. 6	Bohea country, 3rd quality	36.15	63.85	......	100

These soils were all of similar ferruginous tints, having various shades, from

TYPICAL CHINA SCENE SHOWING RICE ON THE LOWLANDS AND TEA ON THE HILLSIDES

light yellow to reddish brown, with the exception of Number Two, which had a gray, or brownish-gray tint. All were of an adhesive-clay character, but were easily crumbled, and quickly broke down in water.

Climate and Rainfall

The climate of China is influenced to a great extent by the monsoons, or periodical winds. The northerly monsoon is attended by cold and frost, which checks vegetation, while heat and moisture accompany the southerly monsoon, stimulating vegetative growth in a high degree. There are no clearly defined wet and dry seasons, similar to those of India, as the precipitation is distributed, more or less, throughout the year, although it is much greater in summer, during the southerly monsoon.

Accurate weather statistics are available only from the larger cities, and none are obtainable from the tea districts. China Table Number Three gives average temperatures at Canton, Shanghai, and Peking, representing the southern, the central, and the northern zones of China. From these figures it is possible to form some estimate

CHINA TABLE No. 3
Average Temperatures, in Degrees Fahrenheit

City	Zone	Parallel of Latitude	Mean Annual Temperature	Mean January Temperature	Mean July Temperature	Extreme High	Extreme Low
Peking	Northern	39° N.	53	23	79	105	5 below
Shanghai	Central	31° 11′ N.	59	36.2	80.4	102	18 above
Canton	Southern	23° 15′ N.	70	54	82	100	38 above

of the temperature in the black and green tea districts of the central provinces, lying as they do, to the southward of the latitude of Shanghai, and north of that of Canton.

Methods of Propagation

In China, the tea plant is grown from seed, either planted directly in the field or started in a nursery, and later transplanted to the field. In the nursery method, when the plants are a year old, they are ready for transplanting. Tea that is grown direct from seed in the field, usually is ready for picking in three years, and somewhat later if transplanted; but the growth of the transplanted plants

TEA GROWING TOPSY FASHION IN THE YANGTZE VALLEY

It is amazing what good quality tea comes from China, considering the haphazard way in which it is grown.

TEA PICKERS IN A YANGTZE VALLEY TEA GARDEN

This is a family scene, for tea in China is mostly a family matter.

TEA IN CHINA HAS CHANGED BUT LITTLE IN A THOUSAND YEARS

is better. The usual planting distance is three or four feet apart in rows that are about four feet apart. Five or six plants are set out in each hole, but in some districts, where the soil is poor, they are planted close together in the rows, but have an irregular appearance when full grown.

Cultivation Methods

In winter the lower part of the trunk of the bushes is covered with cornstalks to protect them from being frozen and to prevent soil erosion. Where fertilizers are used by planters, they are either rapeseed cake or bean cake, both of which are rich in nitrogen. Wood ashes are used in conjunction with these nitrogenous fertilizers. Customarily, fertilizers are applied in September and February, the number of applications depending upon the nature of the soil and the age of the plant.

It is considered unnecessary to manure tea plants supplying leaf intended for black tea manufacture. They are kept clear of weeds, but are otherwise left to "make their own living." On the other hand, the plants supplying the finest green teas are manured twice a year—in spring and autumn. The weeds are cleared away and the soil is turned up about the roots four times annually. Inferior tea, called by the Chinese "hill tea," receives no attention beyond being weeded twice yearly. The weeds are left to rot about the roots of the plants.

Despite the fact that a large proportion of the tea cultivated in China is grown on hillsides, the only approach to terracing was, until recently, a mere leveling of horizontal beds, where this was easy. Of late years, however, there has been a development of modern terracing and contour planting in the Ningchow tea district in Kiangsi, distinguished as the most mountainous Province in China.

Pruning and Picking

Chinese farmers consider it undesirable to allow well-kept tea bushes to grow above three feet, on account of inconvenience in picking. When the seedlings have grown a foot high, they are "topped." That is, the crown, or head, of the young seedling is nipped off with the thumb-nail, to check growth at the center and cause the bush to spread laterally. This has to be done three or four times during the first year.

In addition to the topping of young seedlings, the producing bushes in the better kept gardens are given regular pruning. This is accomplished by taking as many branches as the left hand can hold, and then with the knife in the right hand, cutting upward; reducing the height of the bush to about two feet from the ground. Branches running along the ground are removed, and knotty, or distorted branches in the bush are cut back to within a foot of the soil. Lateral branches are cut back to within two feet of their junction with the main stem, and all short branches are reduced until only one or two eyes, or buds, are left on each.

Picking is begun when the plant is three years old, but inclines to be a hurried stripping, due to pressure of duties connected with other crops.

There are three regular pickings, and a fourth that is regarded more as a late-season clean-up than as a regular gathering. The first, called show-chun, or "first spring," begins as early as the fifteenth of April, when the delicate leaf buds appear and the foliage is covered with white down. The quantity secured in this picking is small, but the quality is superior and yields the finest teas. The next is called urh-chun, or "second spring," and usually occurs at the end of the fourth and the beginning of the fifth month, corresponding to the first part of our June, when the branches are covered with leaves and yield the greatest quantity. The third picking, called san-chun, or "third spring," takes place about a month later, when the bushes again are gone over, and the product is made into teas of the commonest sorts. The fourth gleaning, or clean-up, is called tsew-loo, "autumn dew," and yields only old, coarse leaves. No expert teas are manufactured from the third and fourth pickings; such teas being used exclusively for domestic consumption.

As is now generally known, both black and green tea may be manufactured from the leaves of the same bush, the difference being principally one of manufacture; but, it also is true that in China this is not actually done, mainly because the tea-makers of a given district are expert at either green or black tea production, but usually not at both. Also, there are dif-

A TEA FACTORY IN THE MODERN MANNER—NINGCHOW TEA GROWING CO., NINGCHOW

ferences in the manner of picking. Green tea leaves are gathered singly, without their leaf stalks, because the stalks have an injurious effect on the flavor if withered with the leaf; whereas, black tea-pickers, using both hands, nip off the leaves and their stems. The leaf stalks, or stems, improve the flavor of black tea, so they are taken with the leaf.

Each gatherer has a small basket into which the leaf is thrown as soon as it is picked. In addition to the baskets of the pickers, four larger transportation baskets are required for each section of the garden, so that two may be at hand, into which the pickers empty their small baskets, while two are sent to the firing sheds.

In the Province of Fukien, the average yearly crop is about twenty *catties* of leaf from one *mow* of tea plants, equal to a production of 160 pounds an acre. Again, speaking generally of China, it may be said that the maximum production comes from plants six or seven years old. An

FERMENTING OR WITHERING PROCESS FOR BLACK TEA

average day's picking is twenty pounds, and this work is done by women and children.

The Manufacture of Black Tea

When sufficient leaf has been gathered and sorted, it is spread out on large bamboo mats, or trays, and placed on a frame of bamboo wattles to be dried by the sun. This frame is about two feet high, and is inclined at an angle of 25 degrees toward the sun. Leaves of inferior quality, or those that have been gathered in the rain, often require a more intensive drying over a fire. Such teas are dried in flat baskets or mats placed on a bamboo framework, about six feet above the floor, in a drying room provided with charcoal fires burning in earthenware pans.

While the leaves are drying they are stirred occasionally with the hands, and tossed into the air to prevent excessive fermentation. The drying and tossing is continued until the stems are no longer brittle, and the leaves are spotted with red.

After being dried, the leaves are cooled on bamboo trays to check fermentation. They are left until they emit a faint fragrance, when they are given a light rolling for about ten minutes with the palms of the hands, after which they are again stirred and tossed for thirty minutes. Rolling and stirring are repeated three or four times, until the leaves turn dark in color and become quite soft. Firing follows immediately.

First firing occupies only about five minutes, and is done in a shallow iron pan called a *kuo*. It is circular in form and without handles, let into the top of a brick stove, and usually has its front edge depressed toward the operator. The fireplace is at the back, opposite the operator, so the ministrations of the fireman may not interfere with the firing manipulation.

The operator throws about two pounds of leaf into the *kuo* at one time, spreads it evenly over the pan, and then, with his hands, turns the leaves in every direction until they are uniformly heated. A great deal of care is necessary to prevent any of the leaves from sticking to the pan and burning, as this would injure the flavor of the tea. The pan-firing is continued until the leaves give off a pronounced fragrance, and are quite soft and flaccid. They are at once removed to circular bamboo trays for rolling, and the *kuo* is carefully swept with a splint brush to remove any remaining leaf that might burn the next firing.

In the rolling process, the workman places as much leaf on his tray as he can cover with both hands, and then rolls it to and fro until the juices are expressed onto the outside of the leaves and they take on and retain the familiar twisted form of the teas of commerce. In the rolling process, the leaves are gradually formed into a ball and exude a greenish sap, thus further reducing their moisture content. These balls are broken up and re-rolled many times, after which the leaf is returned to the *kuo* for a second firing, which is shorter in duration than the first. The processes of firing and rolling are then alternated until no more moisture can be expressed in the process of rolling. When that point is reached they are ready for final firing.

For final firing, the leaves are placed in a bamboo firing basket measuring about

HAND-ROLLING PROCESS FOR BLACK TEA

FIRING BLACK TEA IN BAMBOO BASKETS

thirty inches in diameter and three feet high, open at both ends. Halfway inside the basket is a bamboo matting partition, or sieve, on top of which the tea leaves are evenly spread. A charcoal fire is built in the ground, and the basket placed over it. During final firing, great care is taken to avoid spilling leaves into the fire, lest smoke should spoil the tea.

From the firing basket, the leaves are sifted and graded. Numerous sieves are used, the size of the meshes varying from Number One to Number Ten and even finer. The tea leaves are carefully sifted and graded for packing.

The Manufacture of Green Tea

Leaf that is to be manufactured into green tea is first picked over carefully for the removal of any remaining leaf stalks, and all dust and dirt are fanned out of it. At the earliest possible moment after plucking, the leaf is placed in a much deeper *kuo* than that used for black tea, and is given a preliminary firing that amounts to a thorough withering in steam. The green tea *kuo* is set in the top of a waist-high, brick stove, and about five inches below the level of its surface. The *kuo*, itself, is about sixteen inches in diameter and ten inches deep, making a total depth of fifteen inches from the top of the stove. For steaming the leaf, the *kuo* is made very nearly red hot with a wood fire, and into it about half a pound of leaves are thrown by the firer. These he stirs rapidly about, while they produce a crackling sound and a great quantity of steam. The operator frequently raises the leaves a little above the top of the stove,

GREEN TEA STEAMING PANS

and shakes them over the palms of his hands to separate them and allow the steam to penetrate. At length, after two or three final brisk turns about the *kuo*, the operator collects the leaf together in a heap, and, with a single deft motion, sweeps it into a basket held in readiness by another workman.

From the *kuo* the steamed leaf goes at once to a table covered with matting for rolling. The process is much the same as with black tea. After the leaves have been rolled into a ball, they are shaken apart and then twisted between the palms of the hands; the right hand passing over the left with a slight degree of pressure as the hand advances, and relaxing again as it is returned. This twists the leaves regularly and in the same direction. After rolling, the leaf is spread out in sieves and allowed to cool for a short time; then it again goes to the *kuo* for first firing. This time the fire is considerably diminished, and charcoal, instead of wood, is used for fuel, in order to avoid any smoke; but the pan is still kept so hot that the finger cannot be borne upon it for more than an instant. Close attention is given to regulating the heat; a fireman being constantly employed in this duty, while another fans the leaf throughout the entire operation.

The operator alternately stirs the leaf with his hands and twists, or rolls, it in the same manner as at the rolling table. This stirring and rolling is continued until the leaves have lost so much of their sap as to produce no more steam. After that, the leaves are merely stirred about in the pan until they are comparatively dry, turn a dark olive color, and, after being removed from the *kuo* and sifted, are once

more put back and given a third firing.

In some districts the expression of leaf-sap is hastened by placing leaf that has undergone second firing in thick cloth sacks, fifteen or twenty pounds to the sack, and having them beaten against the floor. Husky boys seize these sacks by the neck and pound them against the flooring, turning them constantly, until the leaf mass is reduced to perhaps one-third of its former volume. Then they twist and knead the bags until the contents become solid and resistant.

In the final-firing a peculiar change of coloring takes place in the leaf. It assumes a bluish tint, which is a distinguishing characteristic of this sort of tea after it has reached the correct degree of dryness. Until this color is achieved, no relaxation is allowed the workman. The three firings occupy about ten hours.

The product of these firings is called *mao ch'a*, and, when not sorted and graded on the spot, is packed in chests, and sold by the farmers and peasants to collectors, who in turn sell it to the tea hongs in the larger cities. There it passes through a succession of sifting processes, and is winnowed by being tossed about on bamboo trays or by various forms of pedal-driven fanning mills. It is then separated into commercial grades, such as Gunpowder, Imperial, Young Hyson, and Hyson.

After sifting, China greens are given a final hand sorting by women and children for the removal of foreign substances and imperfect leaves. This sorting is long and arduous, but it constitutes an important operation, designed to insure the quality of teas so delicately flavored.

It was long the custom to add artificial

FIRST-FIRING AND ROLLING GREEN TEA

BOYS BEATING GREEN TEA LEAF IN BAGS

coloring to green teas to give them style, but with the establishment of pure tea requirements by China's best customers, America and Great Britain, this has been discontinued except in the case of teas destined for Central Asia, Northern Africa, Turkey, Persia, and India.

Green tea designed for export is packed in doubly-lined, varnished chests. The liners usually are of lead, soldered to make them air-tight. The boxes are protected by an outside cover of woven bamboo grass for greater security in transit, and are marked to indicate the chop, or "sorting," and the name of the packer or grower.

Semi-fermented Teas

Semi-fermented, or Oolong teas, have some of the characteristics of both black and green teas. They are allowed to wither in the process of manufacture and partly ferment. In other respects, the processes are practically the same as for green tea. Formerly, large quantities of Oolong tea were manufactured in the province of Fukien, but better conditions for their production transferred this trade to Formosa.

Scented Teas

Chinese tea growers have an adage that "only common teas require scenting"; nevertheless, there are many scented teas, highly esteemed in China, that are far from being inferior or inexpensive. Tea that is to be scented is taken hot from the final firing and poured into a chest, so as to form a layer of two inches from the bottom. A handful, or so, of freshly plucked flowers then are strewn over the tea. In this way the tea and the flowers are spread in alternate layers, until the chest is filled. The flowers commonly used are the white jasmine, gardenia, and *yulan;* the latter being a species of magnolia. The tea and the flowers are covered and allowed to stand for twenty-four hours. The correct proportion is three catties, of one and one-third pounds each, of flowers to 100 catties of tea. On the succeeding day the tea and flowers, mixed together, are toasted in sieves, about three catties at a time, for a period of one to two hours. In some instances, the flowers are left in the tea, otherwise they are sifted out, and the tea is ready for packing.

Brick, Baled, Cake, and Tablet Teas

There are two kinds of brick tea; one made from siftings and dust, and one from leaves and stems. The former is made for the Asiatic trade and certain European Provinces of Russia and the latter for Tibet. The two kinds of bricks differ in the method of use. The Russian brick is used for ordinary infusion, but the Tibet brick tea is boiled with salt, butter, and other ingredients to form a kind of soup.

The Russian brick tea factories are located at Hankow and Kiukiang in the central tea districts; while brick tea for the Tibetan market, is extensively manufactured by the Chinese in the western province of Szechwan.

RUSSIAN BRICK TEA.—Brick tea manufacture, as practiced in the Russian factories at Hankow and Kiukiang, is simple and efficient. Heavy leaden molds, bearing elaborate designs, are placed in the

SIFTING OR SORTING GREEN TEA

FANNING OR WINNOWING MACHINE

hydraulic presses, and either black or green tea that has passed through the usual process of manufacture is steamed into pliancy and then put into the mold. First, a layer of high grade tea is used, then a thicker layer of a coarser grade, with a thin layer of high grade leaf over the top. The cover of the mold is set in place, and heavy hydraulic pressure is applied, after which the molds are taken from the press, and the bricks removed for drying. They require about three weeks to dry. The bricks weigh from about two and a half to four pounds and vary somewhat in size. For distribution, they are wrapped in paper and packed in bamboo baskets, eighty to a basket, with a net weight of 200 pounds.

Tea dusts, consisting of broken leaves, stalks, and powder, and extensively used in the manufacture of brick tea, are mostly of Chinese origin; although as much as 10,000,000 to 15,000,000 lbs. have been imported annually from India, Ceylon, and Java. These are mixed with the China leaf and fannings, and the blended bricks give a stronger liquor than those made from China tea only.

At Yanglowtung, in Hupeh Province, native tea merchants from the Northern China Province of Shansi annually establish temporary quarters, and set up their factories. Here, thousands of farmers and their families engage in the manufacture of brick tea, most of which goes to supply Russian and Asiatic markets. The second and third crop leaves are used. These are about an inch in length, have a strong taste, and are known to the Chinese as "old tea." Only wooden hand presses are used, as the temporary nature of the es-

tablishments precludes the purchase of modern equipment.

BRICK TEA FOR TIBET.—The two great market towns through which tea is supplied to Tibet are Ta-chien-lu and Sungpan, in the mountainous western part of the province of Szechwan, on the Tibetan border. Tea for the Ta-chien-lu market is grown in the District of Ya-chou and is manufactured into bricks in the towns of Ya-chou, Mingshan, Yungching, T'ienchuan, and Kiung-chou. The cultivation extends to 4000 feet elevation, and the bushes grow, smothered in weeds, to a height of three to six feet round the edges of the terraced mountainside fields. In June, July, and August, the leaves and younger stems are gathered, fired in heated pans for a few minutes, and then spread out for sun-drying. After this rudimentary preparation they are placed in large bags or loose bales and sold to agents of the brick-tea hongs in the towns where the factories are located.

Upon reaching the factory, the sacks of leaf are allowed to stand and ferment for a few days; after which the leaves and twigs are spread out and picked over into grades by women and children. There are three leaf grades and a fourth grade consisting of the oldest and toughest leaves, chopped up branches, and sweepings.

After sorting and grading, each grade is steamed in cloth over a boiler. When soft it is rammed into molds with an admixture of leaf dust treated with glutinous rice-water. It then is submitted to great pressure.

The individual bricks, thus produced,

RUSSIAN BRICK TEA

BRICK TEA TRANSPORT ON THE CHINESE FRONTIER

measure 11x4 inches, and weigh six pounds. They are set aside in racks to dry for three days, and then are wrapped in paper bearing the maker's name. Four bricks are packed together, end to end, in a bamboo wrapping, and after the coarse "packer's cakes" have been tucked in at the ends, are ready to be carried on the backs of coolies to Ta-chien-lu, to be sold to the Tibetans. The distance from Ya-chou to Ta-chien-lu is 140 miles over almost impassable roads, and the coolies, often carrying 300 or 400 pounds of tea, require twenty days to make the trip.

Bricks of the better grade, and those intended for Lhasa and the distant interior of Tibet, are taken from the bamboo at Ta-chien-lu and are repacked in parcels of twelve each in raw yak hide. The pelt is neatly sewn together, with the hair inside, and protects the tea from damage en route over the mountains.

BALED TEA FOR TIBET.—The method of manufacturing baled tea for the Sungpan market is even more primitive than that employed in the preparation of brick tea. The younger branches and leaves are picked or, more commonly, the tea plants and their overgrowth of weeds are cut together, dried in the sun, and tied into bales. Only occasionally are they panned. The bales are transported to villages where factories are located, and allowed to ferment for several days. After this, they are given a rough sorting. The sticks are chopped up with a long knife, or cutter, pivoted at one end, with a handle on the

other. The chopped branches and the leaves are steamed over a pan of boiling water and pressed into bales. After being covered with matting they are set away to dry. This tea comes from two districts. The bales from one are rectangular, measuring 2½x2½x1 feet each, and weigh 160 lbs.; while the bales from the other are oval, and weigh 90 lbs. each.

CAKE TEA.—P'uerh cake tea takes its name from P'uerh Prefecture in Southern Yunnan, where it is prepared. Packed in flat, circular cakes, eight inches in diameter, and covered with bamboo leaves, bound with strips of palm, it is a popular article in most of the medicine shops of China, as well as in the lamasaries of Tibet. The leaves are picked, panned, and sun-dried, the same as in Szechwan, after which they are steamed, and pressed into cakes. P'uerh tea is grown in the Shan States, mostly in the province of Ibang. It has a pronounced bitter flavor, and is in high repute as a medicine, being accounted a valuable digestive and nerve stimulant.[2]

TABLET TEA.—A certain amount of tablet tea is made for the European trade. The tablets are small bricks weighing but a few ounces each, and are made of very fine tea dust of special quality. The dust is placed in molds and subjected to a high pressure.

BALL TEA.—The name "Ball Tea" is applied to China tea which is compressed into a ball shape as a means of protecting it against all possible atmospheric changes.

FAGGOT TEA is a Canton Oolong made up in silk-tied bundles.

Grading China Teas for Export

After the various manufacturing processes have been completed, China teas are sifted into grades, or styles, according to the roll of the leaf—whether tight or loose —and according to the size of the leaf.

Such terms as "Pekoe," "Souchong," or "Young Hyson," refer only to style, but these names are further qualified by the names of the tea districts or place of origin. The latter form of classification is somewhat complicated from lack of uniformity. In some instances, the names employed refer to the places where the teas

[2] Henry Wilson, *A Naturalist in Western China.* New York, 1913.

are actually grown; in others, to the places where the teas are manufactured and graded. Some of the teas from certain districts are known by the names of other districts or even of other provinces, for the sole reason that the teas are similar.

There is a wide variation in methods of manufacture, whereby the same leaf, if treated in different localities, takes on different characteristics. For this reason, the place where final treatment occurs is quite important, because, even if the same methods are used, the different localities have their differences of applying them, and this inevitably influences the grade of the tea. There are various districts, for example, that are well-known producers of high, medium, or poor class teas; and the poorest grade of a favored district may be almost as good as the best grade of another. Lastly, and of great importance, is the time when the leaf is picked.

Tea exporters, confronted by the complications enumerated above, have established a classification of their own, suited to the practical demands of the trade. This classification is based partly on the source of the tea and partly on the methods of curing. It is considerably condensed, after teas have been shipped from China, by the use of new names that are usually bestowed with reference to locality or its advertising value, as "North China Congous," "Country Greens," "Oopacks," etc.

Native Chinese Classification

The native Chinese tea merchants have a classification of their own, which corresponds somewhat generally to that used by the export trade. By their classification all manufactured teas are divided into:

Hung Ch'a, or Red Tea [the black tea of the export trade].
Liu Ch'a, or Green Tea.
King Ch'a, or Yellow Tea [not exported].
RED BRICK TEA [the black brick tea of commerce].
GREEN BRICK TEA [the green brick tea of commerce].

Each of these groups is further classified as Rough, Tender, Old, or New. The twenty kinds, thus arrived at, again are divided into "well-prepared," and "ill-pre-

pared" teas, making forty classifications. In making their purchases Chinese merchants are accustomed to take into account the provinces and districts of origin to the number of 200 or more, so that the complete native classification recognizes more than 8000 grades.

The Shanghai market has a rudimentary classification based on the names by which various teas originally entered that market. It is as follows:

Lu Ch'a, or "Voyage Tea."—This includes all teas coming into the Shanghai market in a finished state.
Mao Ch'a, or "Woolen Tea."—Teas prepared in Shanghai from country leaf.
Tu Ch'a, or "Earth Tea."—Teas manufactured in Shanghai, from Hoochow, or other leaf grown near by.
Yang Ch'a, or "Graded Tea."—Teas from various sources blended on the Shanghai market and given local names. They are taken mostly from the grades of Gunpowder, Young Hyson, etc., and also are called "Shanghai Packed" teas.

Governmental Aid

In 1905, a Commission of Tea Experts was appointed by the Chinese Government and sent to Ceylon and India to study the methods of cultivation and manufacture practiced in those countries. The Commission reported that the adoption of the methods there observed would undoubtedly increase the production and lower the cost of China teas, and they recommended that small China tea growers unite in establishing centrally located factories, equipped with modern tea-making machinery. However, no steps were taken by the Government to carry out the recommendations of the Commission, and nothing more was done until 1915, when the Government subsidized what was intended for a model garden in the Keemun District; but only a few inferior samples were produced, and the cost was far in excess of that of ordinary tea. In the same year, 1915, at the urgent request of the Shanghai Tea Guild, the Government made a 20 per cent reduction in the export duty on tea and, in 1917, suspended the duty entirely; at the same time the *likin,* or inland duties, which confronted the tea all along its route to market, were reduced 50 per cent.

CHAPTER XVI

CULTIVATION AND MANUFACTURE IN JAPAN

GEOGRAPHICAL LOCATION—DISTRICTS WHERE TEAS ARE GROWN—CLIMATE AND SOILS—PROPAGATION METHODS—TOPOGRAPHY AND DRAINAGE—MANURING, TILLAGE, AND PRUNING—USE OF SHADE—HOW JAPAN TEAS ARE PICKED WITH SPECIALLY DESIGNED SHEARS, AS WELL AS BY HAND—PESTS AND BLIGHTS—KINDS OF TEA MANUFACTURED—MANUFACTURING PROCESSES—HAND AND MACHINE METHODS OF PREPARING SENCHA—GYOKURO AND TENCHA MANUFACTURE—TEA EXTRACTS—RE-FIRING, POLISHING, AND PACKING—CLASSIFICATION—TEA ASSOCIATIONS—SCIENTIFIC WORK

JAPAN proper consists of four large islands—Kyushu, Shikoku, Honshu, and Hokkaido—with a great number of small ones stretching from 30° N. to about 46° N. It embraces a population of more than fifty-nine millions and an area of 147,327 square miles. The lands suited to tea cultivation are, generally speaking, south of 40° N., and the tea plantations are located accordingly.

For the most part, the country is mountainous, with its only considerable plain located roundabout Tokyo. Tea is raised on the hillsides, or on bits of waste land, where satisfactory drainage is assured; the choicest agricultural lands being devoted to rice, and other crops. The effect of this is to relegate tea to areas often remote from the railway, and deficient in transportation.

Important Tea Districts

Although Japan heads the industrial nations of the East, her population is essentially agricultural, and 60 per cent of the people are tillers of the soil. As agriculturists, they have a wide knowledge of soil and crops, which is the heritage of thirty centuries of farming. This knowledge now is supplemented by the latest scientific discoveries, gained at the agricultural stations located in each prefecture.

The acreage devoted to tea in Japan has been steadily decreasing since 1892. In that year there were 148,714 acres under

tea. In 1931, the last year for which figures are available, there were but 93,352 acres. The number of tea factories increased from 705,928 in 1894, to a peak of 1,153,767 in 1928, while the total production advanced from 59,726,502 pounds in 1892, to 84,447,994 pounds in 1931.

The principal tea producing districts are in the Prefecture of Shizuoka, picturesquely located at the foot of Mount Fuji, also in the Prefecture of Kyoto, including the district around Uji, where the famous Gyokuro teas are produced, as well as in the neighboring Prefectures of Miye, Nara, and Shiga. Tea is grown in practically every prefecture on the islands of Honshu and Kyushu; the leaders in production. Following those already named, are: Saitama and Gifu, on the island of Honshu; and Kumamoto and Miyazaki, on Kyushu.

Nearly half of the total tea crop, and almost all of the teas, exported from Japan, are manufactured in Shizuoka Prefecture, re-fired in Shizuoka City or the surrounding towns, and shipped from the near-by port of Shimizu, or from Yokohama. But the really characteristic Japanese green tea is manufactured in the Uji District, near the city of Kyoto—the peerless Gyokuro tea, which the orthodox tea drinkers of Japan delight in drinking.

The best, and highest priced teas, come from the old province of Yamashiro, near Kyoto; a large part of its production consisting of ceremonial tea, and special grades for domestic use.

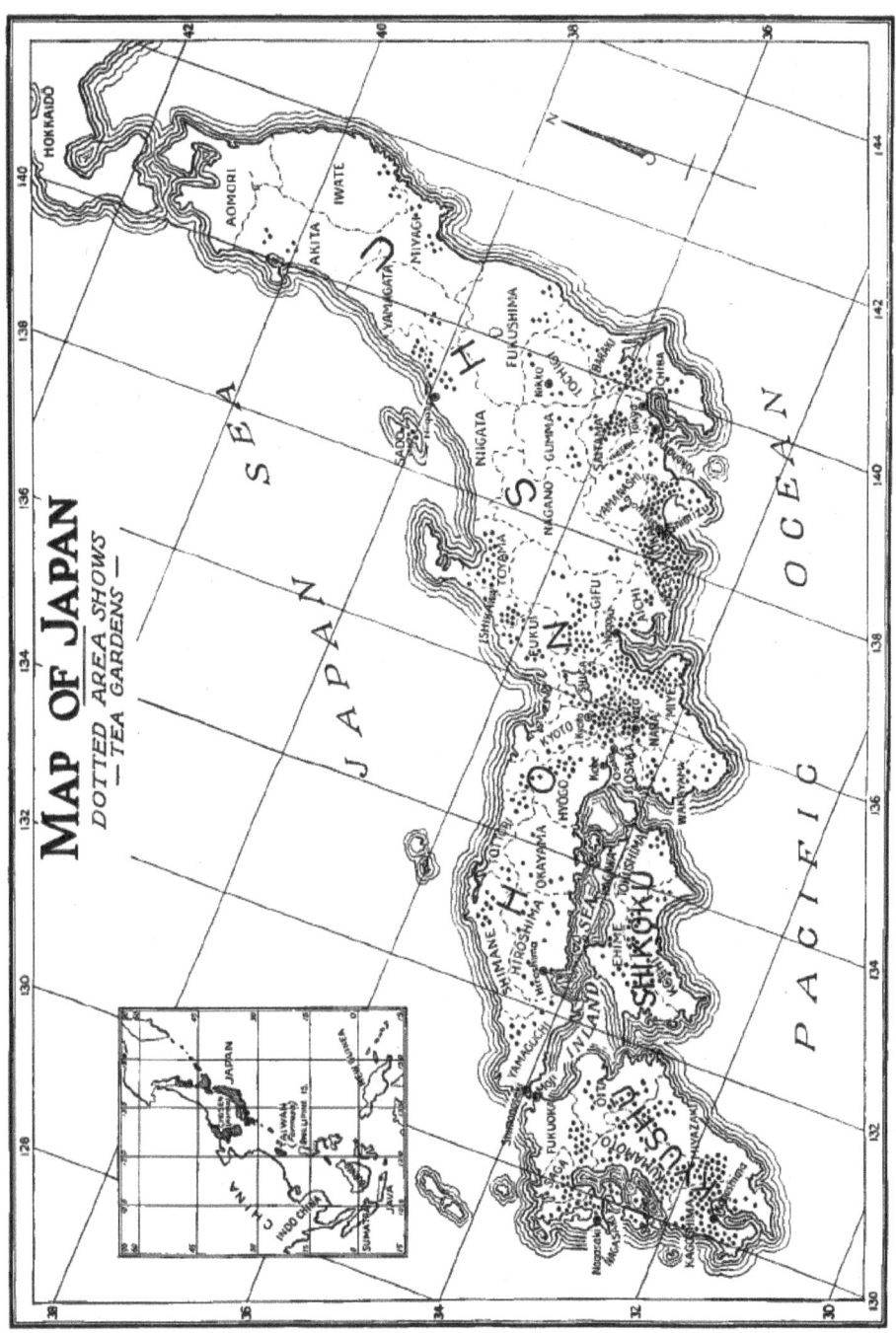

MAP OF JAPAN

DOTTED AREA SHOWS —
— TEA GARDENS —

HOKKAIDŌ

AOMORI

AKITA

IWATE

YAMAGATA

MIYAGI

FUKUSHIMA

NIIGATA

TOCHIGI

GUMMA

NAGANO

SAITAMA

CHIBA

TOYAMA

YAMANASHI

SADO

Ishikawa

FUKUI

GIFU

AICHI

KYOTO

MIE

HYŌGO

NARA

OSAKA

WAKAYAMA

HON

SHU

SHIMANE

TOTTORI

OKAYAMA

HIROSHIMA

YAMAGUCHI

KAGAWA

EHIME

TOKUSHIMA

SHIKOKU

INLAND SEA

ŌITA

FUKUOKA

SAGA

KUMAMOTO

MIYAZAKI

KAGOSHIMA

KYUSHU

Nagasaki

JAPAN SEA

PACIFIC OCEAN

CHINA

JAPAN

KOREA

INDO CHINA

SUMATRA

JAVA

The Sayama District, in Saitama Province, once famous for its production of Sayama teas, known also as Hachioji teas, which have been favored as the next best to Yamashiro tea, has, for various reasons, retrogressed as a tea district, but the name still is familiar to American buyers.

The accompanying Japan Table Number One, shows the distribution of tea areas among forty-five prefectures, wherein tea is grown; the outstanding leaders, from the standpoint of quantity produced, are Shizuoka, Kyoto, and Miye, in the order named.

The Climate

The warm climate, with frequency of precipitation, is a potential factor in Japan's tea production. There are three wet seasons: the first, *kokuu*, from the middle of April to the beginning of May; the second *nyubai*, from the middle of June to the beginning of July; and the third, *nihyaku-toka*, from early in September to early in October. June is the wettest month; January the driest.

The outstanding climatic influence is the flow of air to and from the plateau of Central Asia, commonly called the monsoon. This is caused by the Gobi Desert becoming a chimney for ascending hot air currents in summer, which causes a rush of airs from the ocean east to west across Japan, depositing their moisture on the eastern side of the islands. In winter, the desert becomes much colder than the Pacific, causing a rush of air seaward, at which time the maximum precipitation is deposited on the westerly hills of the islands. No matter in which direction the monsoon sweeps, its skirts are trailed across leagues of ocean waves, where they gather moisture to be precipitated over the tea-clad hills of these favored islands.

Favorable Local Conditions

Most of the tea gardens are on the southeastern, or warm side of Japan, and the heart of the tea districts is Makinohara in Shizuoka Prefecture. Most of the tea of Shizuoka is grown on areas exposed to the full sweep of the elements, where other crops would fail or, at best, have a struggling existence. The Nara and Kyoto tea areas, including the famous Uji gardens, are located on an average of thirty

JAPAN TABLE NO. 1
AREA OF PLANTATIONS, AND PRODUCTION OF JAPAN TEA IN 1928

Prefectures	Number of Factories	Area of Tea Plantations	Quantity of Tea Manufactured
		Chos[1]	Kans[1]
Iwate	1,432	12.5	986
Miyagi	2,572	88.9	5,901
Akita	17	2.1	73
Yamagata	79	17.4	1,377
Fukushima	7,302	84.8	7,554
Ibaraki	42,288	1,979.3	197,033
Tochigi	15,878	372.4	37,419
Gumma	5,697	118.0	8,463
Saitama	23,932	1,583.3	247,579
Chiba	23,608	645.3	73,603
Tokyo	10,995	630.0	71,901
Kanagawa	20,424	262.5	30,110
Niigata	1,013	512.1	84,027
Toyama	2,718	409.7	42,117
Ishikawa	4,889	244.0	54,174
Fukui	28,535	325.1	164,026
Yamanashi	4,078	84.1	5,480
Nagano	2,477	24.0	4,409
Gifu	47,978	863.8	218,891
Shizuoka	31,052	16,000.7	5,308,798
Aichi	25,914	231.3	70,320
Miye	26,796	1,707.0	491,242
Shiga	29,925	958.8	245,956
Kyoto	28,010	1,498.8	544,131
Osaka	4,825	201.0	88,908
Hyogo	40,561	647.6	146,024
Nara	12,118	737.0	276,180
Wakayama	26,499	365.0	94,125
Tottori	7,532	40.0	11,818
Shimane	38,537	476.8	107,315
Okayama	34,839	291.0	91,586
Hiroshima	79,575	277.4	122,342
Yamaguchi	40,741	526.1	98,605
Tokushima	18,595	435.4	89,097
Kagawa	2,080	29.4	2,430
Ehime	20,607	439.2	55,255
Kochi	37,870	1,127.6	144,968
Fukuoka	37,842	1,619.2	142,067
Saga	30,837	462.3	69,831
Nagasaki	32,721	390.7	66,487
Kumamoto	69,531	1,876.5	213,116
Oita	51,454	568.4	67,804
Miyazaki	60,550	1,059.7	211,018
Kagoshima	117,791	2,887.6	407,073
Okinawa	1,053	51.4	1,672
Total	1,153,767	43,164.6	10,423,291

[1] 1 Cho = 2.45 Acres   [1] 1 Kan = 8.28 lbs.

Report of Department of Agriculture, Ministry of Agriculture and Forestry.

miles inland, and therefore are more sheltered from storms than the Shizuoka District. Also, because they are away from the ocean, they are warmer in summer and colder in winter.

The plantations usually are located on hills along rivers, streams, or lakes, where a favorable temperature combines with dense fogs and heavy dews to produce rapid flushing. This is the condition in such famous tea producing districts as Uji, Kawane, and Sayama.

The accompanying Japan Table Number Two [shown on the next page] gives the monthly average maximum and minimum temperatures and rainfall of Kyoto and Kanaya.

JAPAN TABLE NO. 2
TEMPERATURE AND RAINFALL

Kyoto—including Uji District

Month	Maximum Degrees Fahrenheit	Minimum Degrees Fahrenheit	Rainfall in inches
Jan.	47.4	34.9	2.14
Feb.	48.7	34.2	2.62
March	52.2	33.6	4.57
April	66.8	42.1	4.38
May	74.0	50.0	3.64
June	80.9	62.4	9.45
July	89.1	70.9	5.34
Aug.	88.9	70.5	5.59
Sept.	73.1	64.6	8.91
Oct.	72.7	52.7	6.16
Nov.	61.8	41.6	3.73
Dec.	51.6	32.6	2.73
			59.26 Total inches

Kanaya in Makinohara

Month	Maximum Degrees Fahrenheit	Minimum Degrees Fahrenheit	Rainfall in inches
Jan.	47.5	33.9	2.83
Feb.	51.4	34.5	5.53
March	55.7	37.6	7.45
April	64.9	48.5	10.95
May	71.2	54.2	9.02
June	75.2	61.7	10.99
July	82.1	69.7	8.17
Aug.	84.6	70.7	12.29
Sept.	79.3	65.5	15.23
Oct.	71.0	56.1	7.80
Nov.	62.5	47.6	7.14
Dec.	52.7	35.6	3.01
			100.41 Total inches

The effect of the comparatively low temperature in Japan is apparent, in that tea picked may be stored over night before steaming, whereas, in India, in the hot, humid months of August and September, such a delay would ruin the tea.

The sunshine, which alternates brilliantly with favorable showers, is believed not only to increase the strength of the tea, but also to make it darker and more bitter in the cup. In the Shizuoka District, June and September are unfavorable for tea production, not because of the lack of sunshine, which would make for quality in green teas, but because of heavy rainfall. Leaf, that is picked wet, does not make good tea, although the scientific reason has never been determined.

Tea Soils

As previously stated, tea in Japan is not planted out on the best land, but preferably where rice and other crops cannot be grown. Except in the vicinity of Uji, tea is usually grown on steep slopes and bare wind-swept table-lands. Rows of tea bushes are grown on the banks dividing rice fields; small patches are set out in orchards, amongst mulberry bushes, and, in fact, in any odd nook where there is room. In the neighborhood of Uji alone, a considerable area of fairly low-lying ground is given over to tea cultivation.

There is apparently well-founded belief among Japanese tea growers that soil has a pronounced effect on the appearance of leaf and the quality of tea. Red clay soils are said to result in brownish yellow leaves, while humus in the soil produces dark green leaves. Sandy soils are supposed to produce light green leaves, and clay soils are thought to be specially good for producing dark colored leaf and imparting flavor to export teas. Even the shape of the leaf is said to be influenced by the soil; a red soil producing a long narrow leaf of the sort that twists well.

Shizuoka Prefecture, because of its size and topographical diversity, produces every type of soil, and each of its districts produces tea whose qualities are linked with those of its soil. Makinohara District, where red soil predominates, yields medium-quality, strong tea with poor color. The Abe District, in the neighborhood of Shizuoka City, where there is a loamy soil, produces good quality tea. The district surrounding the town of Fuji, whence the land rises to the volcanic Fuji Yama,

JAPAN TABLE NO. 3
ANALYSES OF SOILS

Kyoto District

	Uji	Kuge	Kiosawa gravelly loam
Available phosphate	0.71	0.106	
Available potash	0.010	0.010	0.02
Available lime	0.025	0.025	0.13
Humus	1.71	1.62	
Acidity [Daikuhara]	57.	48.	acid
Total nitrogen			0.44

Shizuoka District

	Shizuoka loam	Kasahara sandy loam	Makinohara humic loam
Available phosphate			
Available potash	0.008	0.010	0.006
Available lime	0.16	0.20	0.10
Humus			
Acidity [Daikuhara]	neutral	faintly	acid
Total nitrogen	0.25	0.17	0.51

HEDGE-LIKE ROWS OF TEA, DEPARTMENT OF AGRICULTURE EXPERIMENTAL STATION, MAKINOHARA

yields a thin, weak tea with good color. This greenness of color is due, not to the soil, which is black volcanic ash and humus, but to manure and shading.

The soil of mountain slopes along streams is credited with being good for tea. Kawane, a small district on the Oi River, yields the best tea in Shizuoka Prefecture.

The tea research work done thus far in Japan has been more along manufacturing lines than in the direction of soil study, so that soil analyses of many districts have never been made. In Table Number Three are given incomplete analyses of six soils of the two principal tea producing districts.

The soils of Japan appear to be rich in the elements essential to the tea bush. Their depth also is unusual, for at two feet they appear to be as rich as at the surface.

Tea Propagation

All of the cultivated teas grown in Japan are of the China type. Tentative experiments with Assam type plants at the Tea Experimental Station of Shizuoka Prefecture, Katsumada-mura, Makinohara, near Kanaya, have made little progress, owing to their apparent inability to withstand the rigors of the climate, and to resist the frosts.

Propagation as practiced in Japan is, generally speaking, field-planting from seed. Japanese farmers do not set out nurseries. Tea is occasionally, however, propagated by cutting, layering, or grafting.

Great care is taken to obtain the seeds from the best districts. They usually are gathered late in the autumn. Selection for planting generally is made by dumping the seeds in water. Those that sink are used, while those that float are discarded as poor.

There are two seasons for planting—spring and autumn. Spring sowing generally is done sometime between the middle of March and the earlier part of April, while autumn sowing takes place between the first and fifteenth of November. The quantity of seeds used for sowing is about fifty-four to seventy-two liters per *tan*, or quarter-acre.

When it is desired to reproduce the characteristics of a perfect mother plant, the propagation is done either by cutting, layering, or grafting. At Kanaya, much success has been obtained by cutting. In the month of June, a shoot, about six inches long, is cut and put into the ground after most of the leaves and buds have been taken off, in order to prevent too rapid growth. If all goes well, the shoot takes root, and is transplanted after two years. Where it is desired to employ the process known as "layering," a lateral branch of a living tea bush is scraped for an inch or so below an eye, and the branch is then pegged down so that this eye is buried. When rooted, it is cut loose from the mother bush and transplanted wherever desired. The branch may be manured with oil cake or fish manure, and is protected with rice straw.

Two methods of sowing are used: bush-sowing, and line-sowing. The bush-sowing is again subdivided into ring-sowing and group-sowing; and line-sowing is again subdivided into one-line sowing and two-line sowing. In ring-sowing, the seeds almost touching are planted in a circle about eighteen inches in diameter. The distance from the center of one circle to the center of the next is three to four feet. In group-sowing, the seeds are planted close together in a group, instead of in a circle. In either case, the tea planted grows up into a hive-shaped clump, and these clumps ultimately merge into a solid hedge-like row. The distance between rows differs according to the height at which the bushes are to be kept, but an average of five to six feet is the distance commonly allowed from the center of one ridge to the center of another.

In single line-sowing, the seeds are planted almost touching each other in a single row, and in double line-sowing the double rows are similarly planted about a foot apart. In both cases the usual space of five to six feet is allowed between the lines. This style of planting is specially suited to the preservation of slope areas.

Topography and Drainage

The best known tea districts of Japan cling to the sides of mountains along the banks of rivers. In the Uji District, tea is grown on both sides of the Uji River on gradual slopes that afford ideal drainage, and at the same time the vapors produced from the river assure a constant supply of moisture in the air.

The Oi River runs through the Kaware District of Shizuoka Prefecture, and both banks being slopes, thus provide a natural drainage. The banks of the Irima River in the Sayama District, and of the Abe River in Kiyosawa, in the Shizuoka Prefecture, have similar characteristics.

Kanaya, in the Makinohara District of Shizuoka Prefecture, is located on a bold, wind-swept plateau, between the Oi and Tenryo Rivers, overlooking on the east and south, the Pacific Ocean. Harler, describing the district, says:

> In the spring, with a stormy wind lashing the countryside with sleet, the climate seems anything but suited to tea. . . . In fine weather the scene from Kanaya is one of supreme beauty and grandeur. The promontory itself is one mass of brilliant green; green as only the tea bush can be. Away in the valley of the Oi is the beautiful patchwork of color associated with a diversity of crops, and on the farther bank of the river the land rises again, and the slopes are covered with tea, which finally gives way to pine forests.[1]

Overlooking this scene is sacred Fuji Yama, the "unique," "the only one," whose perfect snow clad cone rises in solemn grandeur from an almost level plain, 12,365 feet into the sky.

The Kyoto District is less wild than Makinohara. Uji, its most famous tea producing center, is situated on the Uji-gawa, which winds a serpentine course from Lake Biwa to the sea at Osaka. Like Makinohara, its topographical location determines its climate.

There are no drains in Japanese tea gardens, and practically no real terracing. Round about Shizuoka City, there is a certain amount of rough terracing, but, generally, wash is arrested by means of hedge planting.

Manuring

Bean cakes, dried herring guano, rape seed cakes, oil cake, dried fish, ammonium sulphate, sodium nitrate, soya cake, superphosphate of lime, potassium sulphate, artificial manures, rice bran, loam of grasses, night soil, and green manures are the principal fertilizers used on tea in Japan. Ammonium sulphate and sodium nitrate are used as quick-acting manures. In general, the only manures used are those supplying nitrogen as their chief constituent. Around Uji, as much as 230 pounds of nitrogen an acre, beside a quantity of phosphates and potash, is usual. In India, thirty pounds of nitrogen for each acre is used as a quick-acting manure.

---

[1] C. R. Harler, Ph.D., B.Sc., F.I.C., F.R. Met. Soc., "Tea in Japan," *Quarterly Journal*, Sc. Dep., Indian Tea Association, part 1, Calcutta, 1924.

For the promotion of new flushes, decomposed rape seed cakes, pulverized dried herrings, rice bran, or the quick manures, are used. This is called additional, or flush manuring. It is applied at the border line of the bushes to a shallow point in the soil, three times each year. The main manuring takes place at the time of deep ploughing, between the middle of September and the middle of October. Slow manures then are applied at a depth of three to four inches under the surface.

Although green manures are not widely used, the Japanese are employing them to some extent. Vetch, black bean, and seradella are the favorites, but red clover also is sometimes cultivated as a green crop. The green manures are spread over the surface of the soil in summer and in the fall.

Tillage

Two kinds of hoeing, or cultivating, are used in Japanese tea gardens; deep hoeing and shallow hoeing. Deep hoeing consists of ploughing between the rows of bushes to a depth of about two feet. The upper lateral roots are cut and the earth piled up around the bushes. The time for deep hoeing is not absolutely fixed, but usually is done between the middle of September and the end of October.

Shallow hoeing is done three or four times, between the middle of March and October. It is done lightly to a depth of one to two inches, just sufficient to eradicate the weeds and loosen up the soil.

Mulching with rice straw or grass bamboo is popular. The mulch is put down in the autumn, and plowed under the following year.

Pruning

For the highest quality tea—such as Oishita, Gyokuro, and Ceremonial Tea—the bush is allowed to grow as high as three feet. For medium grade tea, the bush is trimmed as low as a foot and a half. The pruning never is heavy, because this would make the bushes suffer from the cold.

The time for pruning varies, according to climatic conditions, and to the exigencies of farm work and tea manufacture. However, the pruning is generally applied immediately after the first crop, and sometimes, after the second. The primary pruning is applied when the tea bush is three to four years old, at a point 20 to 30 per cent lower than the intended height of the plants when matured. In the succeeding three or four years, the plants reach their required height, but special care has to be taken in this period to protect the weaker lateral branches. A continuous dome-shaped picking area is imparted by pruning from the crown of the bush down to the soil.

When a bush appears to be exhausted, it is cut down to its base, manured, and covered with straw for shade. After this cutting back, the leaves get bigger, and the bush improves four or five years, but then it again retrogrades. Such heavy pruning, known as *daigiri*, is resorted to only in rare cases, as a high bush is believed to give better quality tea.

In Shizuoka Prefecture, the bushes are cut back to about two feet in height once in every five or ten years, but in Kyoto, the quality gardens are only cut back once in thirty or forty years.

Shading

The use of shade trees among the tea bushes is almost unknown in Japan. On the other hand, great care is taken in shading artificially the bushes designed to furnish the finer teas; full shading being employed for Gyokuro, and partial shading for Kabuse-cha.

In general, the artificial shading is of two kinds, the shading of single bushes, and the shading of entire gardens or sections of gardens. In the former method, each bush is capped with straw, much in the manner of the caps used on haystacks. This covering, lying directly on the bush itself, retards the growth, and improves the color of the tea. Such teas are called *Kabuse-cha*, or "covered tea."

In the Gyokuro gardens, just before the picking season, the tea is completely hidden under specially constructed sun shelters. The Japanese ascribe to this practice the individual flavor and taste peculiar to Gyokuro tea. They claim it increases the sweetness of the beverage made therefrom, and imparts a dark green tint to the leaves. In April, when the buds commence to flush, a trellis about six feet high is built over the garden. When the buds open into leaves, the screens are spread open on the trellis. About ten days later,

ARTIFICIAL SHADING OF TEA AT UJI

the screens are thatched with rice straw.
After picking, the trellis is removed.

Picking

Picking begins at the end of the third
or fourth year after planting. The best
leaf is obtained between the eighth and
fifteenth years, and the ordinary life of
the bush is approximately twenty-five
years. Formerly, picking depended exclusively on hand-labor, but to-day a good
share of the work is more rapidly done
with specially designed shears. These
shears are much like those used to trim
hedges, except that they are equipped with
a baffle on the upper blade to throw the
leaf into the bag or basket, attached to
the lower one. The blades are eight
inches long. The contrivance is supported
by the right hand, while the left operates
the cutting blade. By the old hand-
picking method, a picker could bring in
from 16½ lbs. to 83 lbs. a day, the average being 45 lbs. With plucking shears,
a woman may pick from 200 to 250 lbs.
daily, and a man 300 lbs. A maximum of
432 lbs. has been picked with the shears
in one day. The ease of this method will
be appreciated when it is understood that
the Japanese tea bush resembles a box
hedge, and the flush is one continuous even
spread of leaf.

In the Uji District, the nippings of tender top buds from the shaded bushes are
made into Gyokuro tea. The coarser portions of new stems are made into Bancha.
The second flush, which is the second crop,
is made into Sencha. In Shizuoka, all
crops, from the first to fourth, are made
into Sencha.

Picking tea in Uji usually is done by
hand. The girls, in their gay costumes,
work under the straw matting, completely
hidden from view. As they pick they
sing their age-old picking songs. The
slow cadence of these songs is designed to
make for careful picking. One, which is
quite popular, may be translated into
metrical English, as follows:

The pines are in their glory;
  With branches spreading wide,
And needles fast unfolding
  Hard by the riverside.

Peace reigns within the empire,
  The fields abound with tea,
Foreshadowing for our rulers
  Days of prosperity.

Famous the bridge of Uji,
  Famous the brew prepared
From the under-flowing water
  For the ancient feudal laird.

Like lovers in their wooing,
  The fireflies at night
Illumine the thick darkness
  With softly glowing light.

No need for further singing;
  Here is the final word:
Let joy well up within us,
  And make itself be heard.

There are three or four periods for picking the tea leaves. The picking of the
first crop, or *Ichiban-cha*, begins about

PICKING WITH SHEARS, SHIZUOKA
(Insert shows shears)

May 1, and lasts until June 15. This furnishes the best of the tea, and about half the total crop. The picking of the second crop, *Niban-cha*, occupies the latter part of June and the first part of July. The picking of the third crop, *Samban-cha*, is from about August 20 to September 5. If a fourth picking, *Yoban-cha*, is made, it is a short one in late September or early October.

The pickers gather the tea into small baskets, whence it is dumped into larger ones. Two large baskets are hung on opposite ends of a pole. Coolies then carry them, with the pole over their shoulders, to the factory.

Picking Tea by Hand, Shizuoka

Pests and Blights

The severe winter climate befriends the Japanese tea gardeners by killing off many of the pests and blights common to tea in the British and Netherlands Indies. Still, Harler found most of the commoner Indian blights in Japan, including the red borer, red spider, green fly, Japan hairy caterpillar, tea looper, faggot worm, and tea tortrix. The tea mosquito, scourge of the Indies, is unknown.

Of the blights, blister blight occurs at variable times, but usually in September and November. Brown blight appears after too liberal an application of manure. Shot-hole fungus, red rust, tea canker, and root fungus [*Rosellinia* species], all are known. The latter is controlled by uprooting the diseased bushes. The Scientific Department at Makinohara issues to farmers convenient charts, which show the period at which each blight is likely to appear, and the best treatment for combating it.

Lime-sulphur and Bordeaux mixture, are freely used by Japanese farmers, who make up solutions in groups; and use them together after the picking season is finished. It has also been found advantageous to spray tea with Bordeaux mixture twenty or thirty days before picking.

Kinds of Tea Manufactured

By far, the greatest proportion of tea manufactured in Japan is green tea. More than three-fourths of the green tea is made into Sencha, or "ordinary" tea. This comprises the bulk of the exports. Next in importance is Bancha tea, a poorer grade, used largely in Japan. Then comes Gyokuro tea, and Tencha, also called Hikicha, or ceremonial tea. The latter is subdivided into Koicha [heavy tea], and Usucha [light tea]. Japan Table Number Four shows the proportionate quantities of each kind manufactured.

Black Tea Manufacture

There is a small, but increasing, production of black tea, which has trebled in the last five years. This production is encouraged, both privately and by the Government, to compete with supplies of East Indian blacks, which have gained a foothold in the domestic markets of Japan. Friends of Japan tea in America, where black tea is increasingly popular, believe that serviceable blacks can be manufactured in Japan to compete in the American

JAPAN TABLE NO. 4
Kinds of Tea Manufactured in 1928

Kinds of Tea	Pounds Manufactured
Gyokuro tea	589,528 lbs.
Sencha tea	68,588,050 lbs.
Bancha tea	16,671,838 lbs.
Black tea	45,880 lbs.
Other teas	409,553 lbs.
	86,304,849 lbs.

markets. This opinion is supported by such experts as Mr. George F. Mitchell, former Supervising Tea Examiner, Department of Agriculture, Washington, D. C., who says: "I feel sure that Japan can produce serviceable black teas."

Mr. C. R. Harler, formerly of the Tocklai Tea Experimental Station, India, who thinks there is no reason why the Japanese jat, which is the same as China, should not make good black of the China type, says:

At Shizuoka, I saw a small factory where they were making black tea in the same style as India, i.e., with a definite period during which the rolled leaf was put in a cool place to ferment before it was fired. I believe the black tea thus made was not a success; perhaps because of low temperatures. When the temperature gets below 70° F. in Darjeeling, it is found that the fermentation takes so long that the tea is not good. However, I see no reason why Japan black tea should not be as good as China black tea, if manufactured in the China way.

Manufacturing Processes

Japan tea manufacturing is divided roughly into three classes: (1) the hand method, (2) the machine method, and (3) part hand, part machine. Gyokuro and Tencha are made by hand. Nearly all Sencha teas are rolled by machine. In 1928, in Shizuoka Prefecture, 8 per cent of the tea was manufactured by hand, 71 per cent by machine, and 21 per cent by part hand and part machine.

The Hand Method

STEAMING.—The first step in the manufacture of tea by hand is steaming. The apparatus in general use is an iron water-boiling pot, with a diameter of one and one-half to two feet, and a large bottom. This pot is placed upon a brick, clay, or tile charcoal furnace, with a covered wooden steamer over it. This steamer is like a barrel, eighteen inches high, with the ends knocked out, and a perforated partition put in midway; the steam rises through the perforations. Sometimes this is varied by having a single hole bored in the partition in which is inserted an iron pipe, surmounted by a cross of two other pipes at right angles. These cross-pipes are perforated, allowing the steam to spread evenly.

Tea leaves are placed on the steamer in a steaming basket about five inches deep,

STEAMING GREEN TEA, HAND METHOD

with a wire net bottom, and covered with a lid. When steam comes from under the lid, the leaves are stirred with a pair of sticks. The length of time required for steaming varies with the volume of steam produced, but it usually takes from forty to fifty seconds at a temperature of 100° C. Under-steamed tea has a bitter taste, while over-steamed tea produces soft leaves, inferior in color and style, with a turbid liquor. After steaming, the leaves are spread on a stand for rapid cooling, which is sometimes accelerated by fanning.

DRYING is the next step. It is done in paper pans over a brick, clay, or tile charcoal furnace, three feet wide and five feet, two and one-half inches deep. The top is not level, but inclines slightly toward the front; the rear being two feet, two and one-quarter inches high, while the front is two feet high. The interior is lined with earthen walls, thicker at the bottom than at the top, making the bottom of the interior much smaller than the top.

From ten to thirteen pounds of charcoal are placed in the furnace, and lighted. This is covered with one and one-quarter to one and three-quarters pounds of rice straw. When the straw has burned, the ashes are spread over the charcoal to deaden the fire. On top of the furnace are five or six iron bars; these are covered with a mesh one foot, five inches wide, and three to three and one-half feet long. A sheet of iron or tin is placed on the mesh. This is to spread the heat evenly. On top of this is the pan, having a wooden frame and paper bottom, in which the leaves are placed. The leaves are scattered over the pan, then picked up with the fingers and rescattered. This is repeated rapidly. Care is taken to keep the leaves at a temperature only slightly above body-heat. Drying is finished when the leaves lose their glossy appearance, the stems become wrinkled, and dark spots appear on the tea.

ROLLING.—Hand-rolling in Japan is an art learned through years of practice. It is divided into six steps: (1) *Kaitenju*, (2) *Tamatoki*, (3) *Nakaage*, (4) *Naka-momi*, (5) *Denguri* rolling, and (6) *Shiage-momi*. The rolling is done on paper pans placed upon the ubiquitous furnaces.

Kaitenju, or turn-rolling, is the primary process and lasts about thirty-five minutes. The object is to dry the leaves without injuring them. If this rolling is too slow, it results in bringing a musty smell to the leaves, and injures both their color and flavor. If, on the other hand, the rotation is too vigorous, the liquor will be turbid, the taste spoiled, and the style of the leaf imperfect. Not only is it found necessary to regulate the heat according to the moisture contained in the leaves, but the speed of operation and the pressure to be applied as well. *Kaitenju* is stopped when moisture begins to appear on the surface of the leaf-mass.

Tamatoki, or roll breaking, follows turn-rolling. This is done in order to dry every leaf evenly. The process is a constant application of *momikiri* rolling, which consists in arranging the leaves in order, and rolling a handful lightly with more pressure on the ends of the bunch than the center.

Nakaage is the name given to a recess of about fourteen minutes. The leaves are allowed to cool a little, and the paper pan is wiped off.

Nakamomi, or intermediate rolling, follows. The leaves are arranged, handful by handful, and treated by the *momikiri* method, but with greater pressure. When the leaves show a dark green color, *nakamomi* is stopped. The time is about twenty-five minutes.

Denguri rolling is used to perfect the style of the leaf. Unless great care is taken, however, the cup quality may suffer. As the leaves become dried, the movement of the hands is slowed down, and the leaves are firmly pressed and rubbed against each other, so as to roll each leaf. The time is fifteen minutes.

THE MOMIKIRI METHOD OF HAND ROLLING

Shiage-momi, the finish rolling, takes about twenty minutes, and consists of rolling the mass of leaves between the hands until it is no longer sticky, but rather slippery.[2]

FINAL DRYING.—For final drying, the rolled leaf is removed to another heater, and when nearly dry it is placed in a portable drier made of wood and containing several drawers. Each drawer is three feet by three feet by three inches, and the height of the drier is determined by the requirements of the factory. Heat is furnished by a brazier of charcoal at the bottom. The drawers are interchanged at definite intervals, in order to dry the tea evenly. When the leaf becomes crisp enough to be easily pulverized between the thumb and forefinger, the drying is completed. The finished tea contains about four per cent of moisture. After the final drying, it is allowed to cool, and then is packed into air-tight containers.

The Machine Method

There has been a tremendous increase in the use of tea manufacturing machinery during the past ten years. The power used is furnished by electric motors, gasoline engines, steam engines, or water mills.

STEAMING.—In the machine method, there are two principal types of steaming apparatus—the spiral drum and the endless belt. The former, is more popular in the smaller factories. It consists of a cylindrical drum about three feet long, with an inside diameter of about one foot. The drum is built around a shaft, and revolves with it. Leaves are placed in one end, and

DRYING TEA IN PAPER PANS, HAND METHOD

[2] From data supplied by the Japan Central Tea Association.

RAW-LEAF TEA FACTORY, SHIZUOKA-KEN

travel toward the other, as the drum turns; meanwhile, they are properly steamed. This apparatus is capable of steaming 200 pounds of leaf an hour.

The endless belt machine consists of a flat box about six feet long and three feet wide. Through this travels a belt of bamboo or mesh upon which the tea is placed. The steam is introduced by means of pipes on the floor of the box. It takes from forty to sixty seconds for the leaf to pass through the box, and, as it leaves the latter, it is cooled by fans.

PRIMARY ROLLING.—The primary rolling machine does the work of leaf drying and turn-rolling. There are many varieties of primary rolling machines, but they differ only in minor details. In general, the plan of these machines comprises a cylindrical drum, fixed upon a rotating shaft. Inside the drum is a set of sweepers, and a set of fork-like "hands." The sweepers throw the leaves into the air, and the "hands" press them against the side of the cylinders. The cylinder usually is made of galvanized iron, or sheet aluminum, and the inside is lined with wood. A fan draws hot air through the machine.

Some of the best known makes of machines for this work are the Takabayashi, which is the pioneer of tea machinery in Japan; Kurita's; the Harasaki, which does the combined work of drying, primary rolling, intermediate rolling, and finish rolling; and Yagi's drying, primary rolling, and redrying machine.

INTERMEDIATE ROLLING.—The intermedi-

ate rolling machine resembles the Jackson rollers used in British India, Ceylon, and Java, except that the rolling table is not enclosed in a box. The machines are small, each roller taking from twenty to twenty-four pounds of leaf at a time. The object is to equalize the drying done by the primary machine. Coarser leaves are rolled longer than tender ones. The average time required is ten minutes. The three leading makes of intermediate rolling machines are Usui's, Mochizuki's, and Kurita's.

RE-DRYING.—The re-drier is somewhat similar to the primary rolling machine, except that it is not constructed to do any rolling. The temperature inside is kept at about 60°C., and the speed is about thirty-five revolutions a minute. The time required is fifteen minutes.

FINAL ROLLING.—The finish rolling machine is a long, rounded trough placed over a heater. A wooden roller, adjustable as to pressure and speed, moves back and forth over the leaves. The temperature is kept at about 70°C., and the tea is rolled for from forty to sixty minutes. Each machine turns out from 80 to 240 pounds every ten-hour day. The leaf taken out is finally dried as in hand rolling.

Part Hand—Part Machine Method

In manufacturing partly by machine, and partly by hand, machinery is used for the first half of the process, i.e., through the intermediate rolling, after which the tea is finished by the hand method.

Gyokuro Tea Manufacture

The first process in the manufacture of Gyokuro tea is sifting the leaves. Girls

STEAMING PROCESS, MACHINE METHOD

BLACK TEA MANUFACTURE

Upper—Withering tats.   *Lower*—Rolling machines.

then pick them over carefully, eliminating all straws, sticks, old leaves, etc. The steaming is much the same as in the manufacture of Sencha, or ordinary tea, except that more care is taken; it takes about ten seconds. The remainder of the process differs also from the manufacture of Sencha mainly in the amount of care taken.

After the final rolling, the tea is dried in a heating pan, then sifted and refined. The drying takes four hours, at a somewhat lower temperature than that used on Sencha; the whole process is done by hand.

Electric Heat in Gyokuro Manufacture

A number of the Gyokuro tea manufacturers in Kyoto have tried tea manufacturing machines that use charcoal, and other fuels, such as are common in Shizuoka Prefecture, but without success, owing to lack of uniformity in the heat supply. More recently, electric heat has been tried and found much more satisfactory. The electrically heated machines used include an evaporator for steaming the leaf, rough rolling machine, re-rolling machine, and drier.

The special advantage claimed for electric heat in tea manufacturing is that it is uniform, and can be regulated to meet any requirement. About the year 1920, the Kyoto Electric Light Company, Ltd., started experimenting, and obtaining satisfactory results by 1924, they recommended the machines to various tea factories, where they are now in operation.

Ceremonial Tea Manufacture

Ceremonial tea, known as Tencha or Hikicha, is always powdered. The first manufacturing processes are the same as those used in the making of Gyokuro. The paper pan on the tea heater, however, is larger than that used for Gyokuro or Sencha, being six feet wide, and three feet long.

The room, where the tea heater is situated, is tightly closed, a temperature of at least 50°C. being maintained inside. On each pan is spread 1¾ pounds of fresh leaves. Every five or six minutes, the leaves are stirred gently with a bamboo rake. After 60 or 70 per cent of the moisture has evaporated, they are taken out for a recess, during which the leaf is fanned. The tea then is put back into the pan, and stirred. When almost dry, the leaves are placed upon shelves for further drying.

After being thoroughly dried, the leaves are broken into small pieces, and sorted into *Koicha*, or dark colored tea, and *Usucha*, or light colored tea. These small pieces are ground up into powder by a mortar.

The standard time for drying Tencha is about thirty to forty minutes for the first drying, thirty minutes for the second, and four hours for the drying on shelves. The percentage of manufactured tea turned out is usually 17 per cent of the original leaf.

Re-firing

In 1862, expert tea makers from China brought to Japan their method of preparing tea for export by re-firing. From that time until 1911, the Chinese method was used. About five pounds of tea were placed in an iron pan over a charcoal fire. The tea was roasted for about half an hour, and then colored. In 1898, Mr. Gensaku Harasaki invented his re-firing pan, which is generally used at the present time.

Most of the tea for export is re-fired in and about the city of Shizuoka. The work done by a re-firer consists in re-firing, re-

REFIRING TEA FOR EXPORT IN HARASAKI PANS

fining, and packing. He usually has a large factory and one or more "go-downs." The factory is equipped with iron firing pans placed upon a charcoal furnace, sifting apparatus with sieves of various sized mesh, winnower, nib-cutter, polishing drum, stem-separator, and various auxiliary devices, run by an overhead shaft. For basket-fired tea, baskets are used instead of pans. The leaf used may be blended, or unblended.

There are three kinds of re-fired tea: natural leaf, basket-fired, and pan-fired. All of these come under the general classification of *Sencha*. Although natural leaf was always fired on paper pans, for some reason it became known in the early days of the Japan tea trade as "porcelain-fired." It is now, however, usually spoken of as natural leaf.

Basket-fired tea is an attractive appearing tea, made from long leaf. The highest grades are rolled some 2½ inches long, and as slender as a needle, hence the name "needle leaf" or "spider-leg" tea. It also is called *Tenkaichi*, literally, "Number One Under the Sky," a title given it many years ago by a prominent Tokyo dealer.

Pan-fired tea is made from the small leaves. Seventy per cent of the tea exported is pan-fired.

PAN-FIRED.—In making pan-fired tea, about twenty pounds of raw leaf are thrown into an iron pan. These pans usually are arranged in a row. The tea is constantly stirred in the pans by mechanical means. After twenty-five to forty minutes the tea is transferred to drums for polishing by friction.

Next, comes the refining. The tea is put into a sifting machine, which sorts it as to size, or this may be done by hand in bamboo or wire sieves. During sifting, the tea is fanned by the winnower, to blow out the fannings and broken leaf. Any leaf that is too long or broad for pan-fired tea, is sent to the cutter, where it is cut up, and refined as before. Nibs, for example, are tender portions of the leaf that, unintentionally, are made round, like Gunpowder tea, during manufacture. They have to be removed by a special cutting and sifting process. Guri tea [curled] is made after the style of Young Hyson for the purpose of export to North Africa, Russia, and Afghanistan.

BASKET-FIRED.—Long leaf tea usually is basket-fired. It is refined first, and then fired. After all of the *Bancha*, Fannings, and Siftings have been removed, there remains the finished raw leaf. About five pounds of this are put into a woven, split bamboo basket. The basket is about four feet deep, and shaped like an hourglass. At the waist is a removable bamboo tray. The basket is placed over an ash-banked charcoal fire, and fired for from thirty to forty minutes. The basket is removed from the fire several times during the process, and the leaf stirred by hand. After firing, the leaf is allowed to cool in the open air, and then is blended.

BY-PRODUCTS.—The by-products of re-fired tea are *Bancha*, Nibs, Stems, Broken Leaf, Siftings, Fannings, and Sweepings. *Bancha* is the coarse leaf removed by sorting. It goes almost entirely to the home trade. Lately, a large trade has been built up on *Hojicha*, or toasted *Bancha*. This is roasted to a coffee-color, and is very pungent.

Nibs resemble Chinese Gunpowder, in style. The quantity of Nibs in hand-rolled tea is about 3 per cent, and in ma-

BASKET-FIRING TEA FOR EXPORT

SIFTING AND POLISHING

chine-rolled, much less. The Nibs are taken out of the tea for export, but are left in for home consumption.

Stems never are exported, but are used by the Japanese to mix with *Bancha*.

Broken leaf, Siftings, and Fannings are self-explanatory, and, while some are exported, they are mostly retained for home consumption.

Sweepings are sold to chemists for the extraction of caffeine.

Polishing and Removing Stems

After pan-fired and natural leaf tea has been fired, it is thrown into a horizontal revolving drum for polishing. The time for this varies according to the nature of the leaf and the degree of polish desired. Basket-fired tea does not, as a rule, undergo this process.

The next step is picking out the stems. In the case of small-leaf teas, such as pan-fired, this is done satisfactorily by machines; but natural leaf, and basket-fired tea, must be hand picked.

Re-firing for the Home Market

Teas, for use in Japan, are re-fired by hand. The refining process is practically the same as in the case of basket-fired tea. Grades costing more than about Yen 1.60 a catty at retail are never polished by drum, as the natural green tint is much sought after. Tencha and Gyokuro teas seldom are re-fired.

Packing

After the tea has been re-fired and refined, it is removed to a "go-down," where it is blended and packed. Tea for export is packed in chests made of planed boards. The sizes vary. The boxes are papered with colored prints, lined with lead and inner paper linings, as may be required. After the tea is put in the boxes, the lead is soldered, and the box sewn into matting. This is labeled with the chop mark, numbers, and net weight. Then the package is rattaned. Sometimes, the tea is put up in small paper packages in lead-lined, or moisture-proof wooden chests, or in lead packages which are packed in unlined wooden chests. The export weights are shown in the accompanying table.

Tea for use in the home market is packed in a $14 \times 16\frac{1}{2} \times 28\frac{1}{2}$-inch box, lined with tin or zinc. Gyokuro and Tencha teas are, however, packed in smaller boxes.

Tea Extracts

As might be expected in a tea-producing and consuming country, there are a number of other kinds of manufactured tea. Among these are tea extracts; some mixed with milk, and some with lemon; some liquid, and some in powdered form. The processes used in their manufacture usually are kept secret. In general, the extract is prepared from a tea infusion in a vacuum, and centrifuged to remove the gummy matter.

Costs

The price of land for a first-class tea garden in Shizuoka Prefecture in 1928 was Yen 709 per tan; that of a medium grade garden, Yen 477 per tan; and that for a low grade garden, Yen 263 per tan. [1 tan=0.245 acres]. The annual rental of a first-class garden was Yen 31.21 per tan; of a medium, Yen 19.95; and of a low grade, Yen 11.01 per tan.

Coming to the manufacturing of tea, it is interesting to compare the production costs of machine-rolled tea as against

TABLE OF EXPORT WEIGHTS

	Half-chest	Boxes	Packages
Pan-fired.....	80 lbs.	40/50 lbs. or 5/10 lbs.	$\frac{1}{4}$, $\frac{1}{2}$, or 1 lb.
Basket-fired..	70 lbs.	40/50 lbs. or 5/10 lbs.	....
Natural leaf..	70 to 80 lbs.	40/50 lbs. or 5/10 lbs.	....

THE PRODUCTION
COST OF MACHINE ROLLED TEA

Four kammes of fresh leaf at 55 Sen...Yen		2.200
Fuel	"	.300
Labor	"	.220
Motive power	"	.040
Deterioration of equipment	"	.220
Taxes	"	.012
Miscellaneous	"	.050
Total cost of manufacturing one kamme of tea		Yen 3.042

hand-rolled tea. One factory worker, in a machine rolling plant, turns out 8 to 10 kammes of leaf a day. A laborer in a hand rolling factory turns out 1.3 kammes of tea a day. The accompanying tables give a fair idea of the difference in costs.

THE PRODUCTION
COST OF HAND-ROLLED TEA

Four kammes of fresh leaf at 55 Sen...Yen		2.200
Fuel	"	.700
Labor	"	2.300
Taxes	"	.035
Miscellaneous	"	.070
Total cost of manufacturing one kamme of tea		Yen 5.305

The re-firing charges for either pan-fired, basket-fired, or natural leaf is Yen 3 for one hundred pounds. The charges for packing in half chests, including costs of the box, lead, mattings, rattans, and labor is Yen 3 for one hundred pounds. The costs of one-pound paper packages differs according to the quality, printing, etc., but averages Yen 20 for each thousand cartons.

How Japan Teas Are Classified

With the exception of a small amount of black tea, all of the teas produced in Japan are green teas. They are classified into the following four styles, or makes:

(1) *Gyokuro*, or "Pearl Dew," reputed to be the finest tea made in Japan; grown under shade, which reduces the tannin, and increases the caffein, at the same time brightening the color of the leaf and sweetening its flavor.

(2) *Tencha*, or Ceremonial Tea, shaded in the garden, the same as *Gyokuro* tea, but made by drying the leaf without rolling, and then grinding it into powder.

(3) *Sencha*, a common tea, made of young, tender leaves and well twisted. This is the popular sort for domestic consumption and for export.

(4) *Bancha*, a coarse tea, specially made from the coarser leaves, or by separating from the raw tea of *Sencha* at the time of re-firing.

Sencha (3), the tea generally exported, is further classified as:

(*a*) Pan-fired. Re-fired in an iron pan. Its raw tea is well twisted, and somewhat curly.

(*b*) Basket-fired. Re-fired in a basket. It has a long style, and the finest is needle-like in shape. Its raw tea is well twisted, straight, and long.

(*c*) Natural Leaf. Medium in style. Used for native consumption.

(*d*) *Guri* or curled tea. The style is very curly, as the name indicates.

Tea Associations

The tea associations in Japan are under Government control; the rules and regulations are laid down by the Government. Ordinance No. 4, issued in 1891, by the Department of Agriculture and Commerce, and still in effect, gives the general plan under which every tea man, be he farmer, manufacturer, merchant, broker, or dealer, must join his local tea association. These local associations elect delegates, which form Joint Tea Associations located in different prefectures; and they, in turn, elect representatives, who make up the Japan Central Tea Association.

Each local association is composed of the tea men of a certain city, county, or prefecture. For instance, in Shizuoka Prefecture, there is the Tea Association of Shizuoka City, the Tea Association of Fuji County, and the Tea Refirers' Guild of Shizuoka Prefecture; as well as some thirteen other locals. The main object of these branches is the development of the tea industry in their respective districts by training tea men, holding tea shows, inspecting machinery, and so forth.

An idea of the activities of the joint associations may be gained from the work of the Joint Tea Association of Shizuoka Prefecture, commonly called the Shizuoka Tea Guild. This Association holds an annual meeting in March. There are delegates from sixteen locals. Beside the president, vice-president, director, and treasurer, there are employed two tea experts, with three assistants; one superintendent of tea inspection, with thirty inspectors; seven other clerks, etc. The busi-

THE TEA EXPERIMENTAL STATION OF THE AGRICULTURE AND FORESTRY DEPARTMENT, MAKINOHARA

ness of the Association comprises the regulation and inspection of tea, the improvement of production methods, market expansion, etc. The Association establishes tea inspection stations, with inspectors who visit every factory, and standard grades to prevent the manufacture and sale of inferior teas. Prizes are awarded to inventors of new tea machinery. Subsidies are given to farmers for the improvement of their gardens. Competitive tea exhibitions are held, and prizes awarded. Courses are given students on the manufacture of tea by machinery. Scientific work is carried on in the Tea Experimental Station at Makinohara. Local associations are given grants of money to assist them in their work. Correspondents are appointed abroad. Newspaper and magazine advertising and the distribution of free samples of Japan tea are carried on in foreign countries; investigators have been sent to foreign markets; tea warehouses built at the port of Shimizu; and a tea history, *Chagyo-shi*, started some years ago, was brought up to date. A magazine, *Chagyo-Kai*, is published for the members.

The by-laws of the Joint Tea Association of Shizuoka Prefecture, as revised March 1, 1924, are very strict. They are much too long to quote here, but one provision made therein is of particular interest. Section 6 provides that no one may sell any tea which has not been inspected and officially labeled. In order to be so labeled the tea must equal or exceed in quality the Tea Standards, established from the teas of the previous season, in the month of March, each year. Both the Japan Central Tea Association and the Joint Tea Association of Shizuoka Prefecture are supported by the income derived from the official labels.

As previously mentioned, the entire membership of the Japan Central Tea Association is made up of delegates from the joint tea associations of various prefectures. The work of the Central Association varies from year to year, but, in the main, it may be divided into two classes: (1) the improvement of tea production, and (2) the expansion of Japan's foreign tea markets. The first includes the holding of a competitive tea exhibition with prizes, subsidizing lecture courses, training experts, practical tea experimentation, etc. The foreign expansion work includes the sending of agents and committees to America to study the market; maintenance of pavilions and booths at fairs, and expositions in America; advertising in United States and Canadian newspapers and magazines; translation of American market reports, and their dissemination to members; subsidies given to exporters to advertise their Japan tea, etc. With the exception of tea pavilions in French and English expositions, no important work has been done in foreign countries other than Russia, Canada and the United States. However, investigations have been carried on in other countries.

Tea Experimental Stations

The scientific investigation of all questions bearing on the cultivation and manufacture of tea in Japan, and the instruction of tea-growers by lectures and demonstrations, is conducted at six principal tea experimental stations. They are:

(1) The Tea Experimental Station of the Agricultural and Forestry Department, located at the southwestern end of Kanaya Town division of Makinohara, Haibara County, Shizuoka Prefecture.

(2) The Tea Experimental Station of Shizuoka Prefecture, located at the northwestern end of Katsumada Village of Makinohara, Haibara County.

(3) The Tea Experimental Station of Kyoto City.

(4) The Tea Experimental Station of Nara Prefecture.

(5) The Tea Experimental Station of Kumamoto Prefecture.

(6) The Tea Experimental Station of Kagoshima Prefecture.

Of the foregoing, the most important from the standpoint of annual income and expenditure is the Government station (1) at Makinohara. Its work has to do with demonstration and education rather than with research. The annual appropriation, which up to 1932 averaged about Yen 16,-000 [Yen = $0.498, at par] was enlarged in that year to Yen 210,000.

The Experimental Station of Shizuoka Prefecture (2) has a staff consisting of three chemists, two agriculturists, four technologists, an engineer, and an entomologist. The station has excellent research laboratories, a first-class factory—both hand and machine—and fifteen acres of experimental tea gardens. The annual cost is approximately Yen 42,000.

In addition to the stations mentioned, there are numerous minor tea experimental bureaus and institutions which carry on research and investigation work at the Agricultural Experimental Stations of various prefectures in the islands of Honshu, Shikoku, and Kyushu. There are also several joint associations engaged in tea experiments, such as the Shizuoka Tea Guild —previously described—which has a separate building devoted to experiments in tea manufacture, like the application of electric heat to modern tea manufacturing machinery, etc. Other joint associations are conducting experiments connected with tea cultivation, the extermination of blights, etc., as well as the investigation of improved manufacturing methods.

CHAPTER XVII

CULTIVATION AND MANUFACTURE IN FORMOSA

GEOGRAPHICAL POSITION—DESCRIPTION OF TEA DISTRICTS—THEIR SOILS ANALYZED—
CLIMATE, RAINFALL, SUNSHINE, AND ALTITUDE—VARIETIES OF TEA RAISED—PRUNING—
PICKING—MANUFACTURE OF OOLONG—FIRST, OR LOCAL PROCESS—WITHERING—FER-
MENTING—PANNING—ROLLING—FIRING—SECOND, OR FACTORY PROCESS—FINAL FIRING
OR REFINING—MANUFACTURE OF POUCHONG TEA—THE "TOTTERING LILIES OF DAITOTEI"
—PACKING AND SHIPPING—PROMOTIONAL ACTIVITIES—TEA ASSOCIATIONS AND THEIR
RULES—INSPECTION REGULATIONS—GRADING

FORMOSA, or Taiwan, in the Western Pacific Ocean, consists of a main
island, elongated oval in shape, with
a group of attendant small islands, and is
situated in a semi-tropical zone, extending
over ninety-seven miles from east to west,
and 244 miles from north to south. It is
located between 21° 45′ and 25° 38′ north
latitude, and between 120° and 122° 6′
east longitude, about on a line with Cuba,
Mexico, the Sahara Desert, and Northern
Burma.

A high mountain range forms a divide,
running through the center of the Island
from north to south. The sea between the
Island and China is not more than 300 feet
deep; but deep water is found not far off
the east coast.

The Island is 752 miles in a southwesterly direction from Japan, and due east
from Amoy. It has a total area of 13,429
square miles; being a little larger than
Holland proper, but somewhat smaller than
Switzerland. The difference in standard
time between the Island and Japan, is 54
minutes.

The northern half of Formosa lies in the
temperate zone, and the southern half belongs to the semi-tropics. The Tropic of
Cancer passes through the center of the
Island near Kagi; consequently, snow seldom is experienced, except on the top of
high mountains, where it lies for short
periods in winter.

One of the best descriptions of the cultivation and manufacture of tea in Formosa is to be found in a report made to
the Indian Tea Association by Mr. James
Hutchison.[1]

The tea districts are practically confined
to the northern part of the Island, and lie
between the alluvial flat lands bordering
the sea coast and the higher mountains on
the northwest. The physical contour of
this area is of three kinds—rolling or hilly
land, table land, and broken or *teela* land.
The first averages from about 100 to 2000
feet elevation, but the greater portion of it
lies between 150 and 700 feet, and little
tea is planted anywhere at elevations
above 1000 feet.

By far the largest tea acreage is located
on the table-lands at elevations of 250 to
1000 feet, having a slight pitch, mainly toward the west. These table-lands are
completely separated from the foothills of
the main mountain range by the Tamsui
River—the largest stream in the Island—
but they are crossed by occasional water-
courses that remain dry a good share of
the year.

The *teela* land embraces the broken foothills and disintegrated rock slides to the
westward of the main range, with rice fields
between them. They range from approximately sea level to 200 or 300 feet, and it
is noteworthy that most of the localities
famous for quality of leaf are on this sort
of land.

The entire area under tea is located on

---

[1] James Hutchison, *Report on the Cultivation and
Manufacture of Formosa Oolong Tea*, Calcutta, 1904.

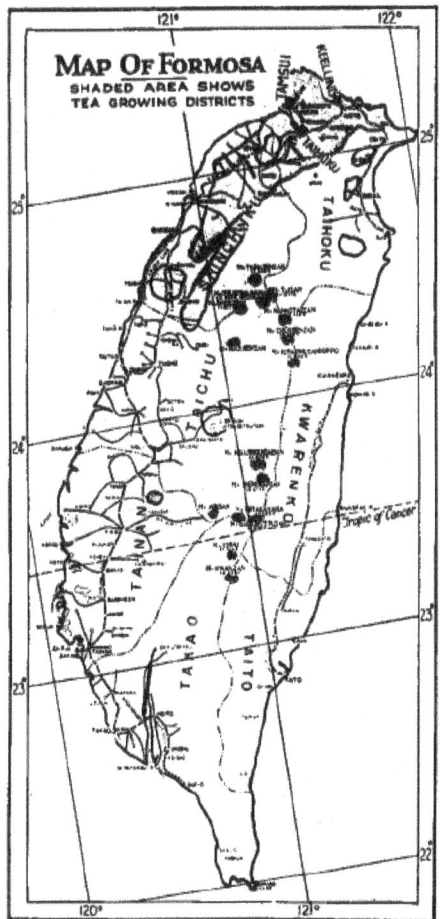

MAP OF FORMOSA
SHADED AREA SHOWS
TEA GROWING DISTRICTS

Some teas are also grown in the Province of Taichu. The average yield per *ko* is about 400 *kin* of "crude" tea, equal to 221 pounds an acre [1 *ko*=2.397 acres; 1 *kin*= 1.325 pounds].

Oolong is the most extensively cultivated tea in Formosa, amounting to about half the total production. Kokan is next in importance. Of thirty varieties grown, the following—after Oolong and Kokan—are the principal ones: Hakumoko, Tokicha, Taiyo, Taiu, Shiran, Hoshin, Fuchishu, Ukin, Chikuyu, and Byoji.

Approximately forty-five per cent of the crop is made in April and May; thirty-five per cent in summer, from June to August, inclusive; and twenty per cent in the autumn. The spring teas possess good flavor and aroma. The summer teas have good flavor and style, with much heavier body. The autumn teas have good style, but are not so heavy in the cup.

Tea growing is purely incidental to the general farming operations of the Formosan planter. He has anything from a patch to a few acres of tea, to be managed as opportunity offers with his other crops of rice, sweet potatoes, etc. On the table-lands, these general farms are larger and the areas under tea greater in proportion; but even here it is purely a family enterprise, making any attempt at cost finding impossible.

Middle-men go around and buy the tea from the makers, and they in turn sell it to the native merchants; and so it is handed about by go-betweens, until finally collected in bulk and packed. In an extreme rush time, when the gardens are beyond the capacity of the family, labor is occasionally hired, but this is not the general rule.

While the picking seasons are on, the workers are in some cases provided with refreshments in the field as often as five times a day, providing an early start has been made. Under ordinary conditions, however, the workers go home to eat.

The tea fields are given a quaint touch by the curious head-dress of the panta-looned Chinese girls, with their black scarfs pulled over their pointed bamboo hats and tied under their chins, to shield their necks from the fierce rays of the tropical sun; also by the snow white herons [aigrets] of the paddy fields, which, strangely enough, seem to have developed a coffee-spot marking on their wings, where they

lands of tertiary and quaternary formation. The acreage and average yields on the various classes of tea soils is hard to estimate accurately, on account of the extremely small and ill-defined plots on the hilly and *teela* land; but the yields will run not far from eighty to 100 pounds an acre for the *teela* country; 160 to 200 pounds for the hilly districts; and from 250 to 320 pounds for the table-lands.

The principal districts are:

TAIHOKU PROVINCE: Bunzan-gun, Kaizan-gun, Shinso-gun, Keelung-gun, Tansui-gun, and Shichisei-gun. Production about 6,000,000 *kin* annually.

SHINCHIKU PROVINCE: Toyen-gun, Taikei-gun, Chureki-gun, Schinchiku-gun, Chikuto-gun, Chikunan-gun, and Byoritsu-gun. Production about 11,000,000 *kin* annually.

A TERRACED TEA GARDEN AT SANSHIKO, SHINCHIKU PROVINCE

have forsaken their original vocation, and taken to sentinel duty among the tea bushes.

Tea Soils

Tertiary and diluvial soils of quaternary formation, in the neighborhood of the central mountain range, are the most suitable for tea growing. Such soils vary, according to location in Central and Northern Formosa, but generally are rich in organic matter, with considerable pebble content. The most fertile soil is light ochre in color.

In so far as the practical cultivation of the tea plant is concerned, there are two classes of soil on the Island: (1) a red to reddish brown loam, varying in friability in different localities according to the amount of sand it contains, and (2) a yellow clay formed from decomposing rock, with more or less grit, and pebble in it.

The red loam is characteristic of the hilly land, and on the slopes of extinct volcanoes, where it overlies boulders and water-worn gravel. But occasionally it is found over a yellow clay subsoil with an outcropping of boulders. This also is the characteristic soil of the table-lands, but here it usually is quite a bit darker than on the hilly land. On these table-lands the loam is superimposed on a stratum of coarse, round, water-worn gravel, and the depth increases from a mere covering at the lower end—say about 120 feet elevation—to six feet and more at an altitude of 450 feet. This table-land, or "low country," as the natives call it, does not produce the best quality teas.

The yellow clay soil is found almost exclusively on the broken teela country. The decomposed rocks from which it is derived are shattered and disintegrated from the ledges by the joint action of sun and rain. The finer soil washes down into the adjacent fields, forming a heavy clay land. The yellow clay district is noted for the quality of its leaf, which generally is spoken of as "high country" tea; but, as a matter of fact, the average elevation of the table-lands, or so-called "low country," is much above the most noted districts of the teela lands. There are some localities, where the red and yellow soils meet and become more or less intermingled, but these places are few, and the areas insignificant. The Chinese tea gardeners on the Island attach great importance to soil and location for the production of flavor. Their belief in this regard closely parallels that of the *vignerons* of France, who have a saying: "The poorer the vine, the better the wine." The Formosan tea grower says: "Yellow soil, small bush, good tea."

As a matter of fact, the steepness and ruggedness of the land minimizes the effect of excessive rains, and prevents waterlogging of the soil. The *teela* ground is bare in appearance, and many of the plants seem to be rooted in little else than crumbling rock. Naturally, the plants grown in such a situation are straggling, and bare in habit; but this would not account for extra quality, were it not that the soil and climate are suitable, and the roots healthy. Of course, "yield per acre" becomes entirely a secondary consideration, and "quality," as a general rule, forms the basis of all the cultivators' plans and calculations.

The tea soils of the Island were analyzed by Dr. H. H. Mann, the well-known chemist, in connection with a scientific investigation, by the Indian Tea Association, into the factors responsible for producing the flavory Oolongs of Formosa. Dr. Mann's report describes a representative soil from each of the three classes of Formosan tea lands, as follows:

No. 1 [hilly land]. This sample was taken from the center of a plot of tea fifteen years old, on the side of a "gully" up the southeast slope of a hill [which rose to an elevation of 4000 feet], at an elevation of between 600 and 700 feet. There were signs of wash, or denudation, to the extent of three or four inches. The slope was fairly steep, and stone terraced at various parts; but not where this sample was obtained. The soil was mixed with boulders. The site was about a quarter of a mile from, and 200 feet above, a sulphur mine from which fumes were constantly issuing.

. . . .

No. 4 [table-land]. This sample was taken at an elevation of 450 feet in the center of a plot of tea fifteen years old. The soil overlies a thick stratum of coarse, round gravel, and was from five to six feet deep. This district only produces second quality Oolong tea.

No. 5 [teela land]. Sample from Tzapgoanan Banzampo, one of the most renowned districts for Oolong quality in the whole Island. It was obtained from *teela* land at an elevation of between fifty and seventy-five feet.[2]

On analysis, the foregoing samples give the figures shown in Table Number One.

Dr. Mann then found that several other factors go to the making of a typical fla-

[2] H. H. Mann, *Report to the Indian Tea Association*, Calcutta, Sept. 1, 1904.

FORMOSA TABLE NO. 1
Soil Analyses

	No. 1 Hilly land	No. 4 Table-land	No. 5 "Teela" land
*Organic Matter, etc......	12.76%	6.92%	4.30%
Oxide of Iron.............	11.19	4.75	3.29
Alumina..................	24.25	10.04	6.86
Oxide of Manganese......	.01	.06	.04
Lime	.05	.02	.05
Magnesia................	.17	.35	.17
Potash..................	.28	.54	.46
Soda....................	.27	.32	.25
Phosphoric Acid.........	.20	.06	.08
Insoluble Silicates.......	50.82	76.94	84.50
	100.00%	100.00%	100.00%
*Containing Nitrogen....	.15%	.13%	.08%

vory Formosa Oolong, in addition to the soil on which it is grown. And, first in the order of importance, he is inclined to place the variety of plant from which Formosa Oolong tea is made—the so-called *che-shima*. But, at the same time, he points out that the growing of this variety involves the propagation by layering; that the yield obtained in the high quality districts is very small [eighty to 100 pounds an acre]; and, that, where the yield is greater than this, the value of the tea is correspondingly reduced. He did not mention that China had the *che-shima* plant long before it came into its own, on Formosa soil; but he may have had this in mind, when, unconsciously perhaps, he paid an Indian tea man's supreme tribute to the unique character of flavory Formosa Oolong by reporting that probably nowhere outside of its Island home could the combination of plant, climate, and soil be found to reproduce this special flavor.

Climate, Rainfall, and Altitude

Whatever may be the cause of the special quality in Formosa Oolongs, the climatic conditions are of great advantage in the production of suitable leaf, and in its subsequent manipulation. The highest temperature is 95° F., the charming verdure of the fields and mountains being enjoyed all the year round. During the hottest season, the temperature is not so high as in Kyushu, but the summer season extends over a longer period. In summer, the Island is visited by frequent showers, which are always followed by refreshing breezes, making one soon forget the oppressive heat of a few moments before.

A peculiarity of the climate is the variation in rainfall between places less than twenty miles apart, but at the same elevation. The variation is caused by the intervening hills intercepting the northeast and southwest monsoons, so that the driest month in one place, is the wettest in another. This peculiarity is intensified by the warm Japan Current, which flows up along the west coast of the Island.

Taking Taihoku as central, and comparing it with Keelung, the wettest spot on the eastern edge of the tea area, the records of the Meteorological Department show rainfall averages, over a period of five years, as shown in Table Number Two.

Deducting the rainfall for the non-producing winter months, November, December, January, February and March, we have approximately the same precipitation at both places—66.92 and 73.94 inches. These figures give a better idea of the effective rainfall over the tea districts, than the annual totals, as the cold weather rainfall in Formosa is excessive.

In the matter of sunshine, regarded as of great importance in connection with the production of quality, the records of the Meteorological Department show the percentages of possible duration of sunshine, at both of the places named, as shown in Table Number Three. This indicates an average of approximately forty per cent during the seven productive months, or about thirty-three and one-third per cent over the entire year.

There are almost daily thunderstorms, and showers in the afternoon, from early June until late September; practically accounting for all the rainfall during this

FORMOSA TABLE NO. 3

Percentages of Sunshine

Month	Taihoku	Keelung
	Percentage	Percentage
Jan............	25	18
Feb............	24	16
March.........	31	26
April..........	25	26
May...........	36	28
June..........	39	31
July..........	50	63
Aug...........	50	51
Sept..........	47	45
Oct...........	37	32
Nov..........	24	18
Dec..........	30	18
Total Mean	35	31

period, although typhoons may give two- or three-day rains, whenever one of these torrential storms visits the Island. The almost daily period of sunshine is a weather feature of the utmost importance; as it allows a large percentage of the crop to be brought in dry, and put into the sun, so as to be manufactured the same day. If it has to be held over and manufactured the next day, the quality is greatly reduced. As a rule, little or no plucking is done in wet weather.

Throughout the tea area, the temperature is comparatively equal, and the figures for the capital, Taihoku, in the center of the District, may be taken as representative of the whole. The mean temperature for the year is 71.6° F.; mean maximum, 77.7° F.; mean minimum, 65.5° F.; and mean range, 12.2° F. Taking the months of manufacture, there is a mean temperature of 78° F.; a mean maximum of 84.7° F.; a mean minimum of 71.4° F.; and a mean range of 13.3° Fahrenheit.

The elevation of Takihoku is only fifty feet, while the average elevation of the tea districts, throughout the Island, is 350 feet.

Varieties Grown

The varieties of the tea plant grown in Formosa are mostly Chinese, although the ordinary Japanese plant occasionally is seen. It is easily distinguished by its lighter green leaves of rounder shape, and peculiarly thin texture. Chinese cultivators recognize eight varieties, and these, in turn, may be divided into three groups.

FORMOSA TABLE NO. 2

Rainfall Averages over a Period of Five Years

Month	Taihoku (inches)	Keelung (inches)
Jan............	3.60	16.78
Feb............	6.38	10.43
March........	5.12	10.25
April..........	6.06	8.80
May..........	7.21	6.96
June..........	10.16	9.88
July..........	9.21	3.38
Aug..........	18.19	12.17
Sept..........	10.91	14.45
Oct...........	5.18	18.30
Nov..........	3.37	22.74
Dec..........	2.44	15.82
Total inches	87.83	149.96

The first group includes four types: *che-shima*, or "green tip"; *ang-shima*, "red," or "brown tip"; *pe-shima*, or "pale tip"; and *chekyon*, or "bamboo leaved." All of the varieties in this group give good strength; and one of them, the *che-shima*, gives a special flavor found in no other plant, when the needful conditions of soil, climate, and manufacture are met.

The second group embraces three varieties: *she-tay*, *kilam*, and *kama*. The leaves of this group are broader, and the veins branch out more nearly at right angles to the mid-rib. They are thin in texture, more fibrous, and lacking in special strength, or flavor. *She-tay* signifies "seed tea," so-called because of its seed-bearing propensity. This propensity is shared by the whole group, and differentiates it sharply from the first one; in fact, the varieties of the second group generally are propagated from seed, while those of the first group are propagated by layering.

The third group is made up of a single variety, the *pe-num-kaw*, meaning "white-haired monkey." This plant yields the fine, white, downy tea, known as *pe-kaw-chcong*, or "choice white monkey."

In addition to the foregoing, there is to be seen in the experimental gardens, a plot or two of so-called *fu-shima;* said to be a variation produced when *che-shima* is grown from seed, but it is not grouped, because of its purely incidental character and the insignificant number of such plants.

The variety, *che-shima*, is grown on approximately forty per cent of the acreage; *ang-shima* on about thirty per cent; and all other varieties thirty per cent. The reason for the large proportion of the acreage planted to inferior varieties, is said to be that during a boom in tea-planting in the 'eighties of the last century, it was impossible to get enough plants of the *che-shima* to supply the demand; so other seeds and plants were imported from China. The *ang-shima* being distinguishable only by the color of its young shoot, was the variety most liberally substituted. To-day, these two varieties are often found growing together promiscuously; especially on the table-lands, or "low country."

It is characteristic of the varieties that the *che-shima* gives only a small yield of tea as compared with *she-tay*, and the other seeded varieties of group two. *She-tay* can be picked every ten days, and *che-*

THE FINEST VARIETIES OF FORMOSA TEAS ARE REPRODUCED BY "LAYERING"

shima only once in three weeks; so extra yield is, therefore, obtained with the inferior types of plants.

The Japanese equivalents for the native [Chinese] names for the varieties of tea plants grown in Taiwan are:

NATIVE	JAPANESE
Che-shima	Seishin shu, or Seishin Oolong shu.
Ang-shima	Koshin Oolong shu
Pe-shima	Kokan-shu
Che-kyon	Chikuyo
She-tay	Jicha
Kilam	Shiran
Kama	Kokan shu
Pe-num-kaw	Hakumoko
Fu-shima	Hoshin, Ohba Oolong, Seishin Taipan, Fuchishun, Ukin, and Byoji.

Propagation

The finest varieties of Formosan teas are reproduced by layering. These include the four varieties of first-group plants previously described, namely: the *che-shima*, from which the famous Oolong is manufactured, the *ang-shima*, the *pe-shima*, and the *chekyon*. These varieties are scanty seed producers, but this is not the reason the cultivators of the Island do not plant them from seed. So jealous are they of the distinctive flavor of their best teas, that propagation from seed is never undertaken, lest the character of the leaf undergo some change.[3] Apparently, there is good reason for precaution, as *che-shima* seeds, when planted, produce the "sport," or variation from type, known to the Islanders as *fu-shima*, mentioned in a preceding paragraph.

The period for layering is during the early rains of June and July, and the plants are put out either during the cold weather or in June, when the early rains occur. The lateral branches are pegged down into the earth with bamboo staples, so they will take root; and when this occurs, they are cut loose from the original bush, and are ultimately transplanted to the spot which they are to occupy in the garden. They generally are set out, two or three together, and almost invariably more than one in a spot.

In layering a branch, the cultivators give it a sharp twist at the point where it is to be pegged into the earth. The purpose of the twist is the same as the half-cut given to such plants as carnations and verbenas—to check the full flow of sap, and thereby encourage the growth of roots at the place. The lateral branches are treated in this manner, until the parent bushes are half buried. The varieties, *she-tay* [seed tea], *kilam*, and *kama* belong to a group of copious seed bearers, and are commonly propagated from seed.

Setting Out and Cultivation

Plants are set out during the cold weather, beginning in December; or else in June, when the early rains begin.

On the *teela* lands, the traditional spacing of the plants is about 3½x3 feet, but on the table-lands the distance usually is 5x3 feet. On the *teela*, the rows are planted across the slope, but very little terracing is done.

Tillage on the table-lands, and wherever possible, is by a single buffalo-drawn plow, having a single attendant. The bushes usually are small, with a good two feet of clearance, so there is plenty of room; and the practice is to turn three furrows between the rows. The cultivation is very well done, about four or five inches in depth, and is completed so that the gardens are clean by the end of June.

Gardens on the *teelas* and steeper places are given a thorough hoeing four times during the year.

Pruning

Very little pruning is done on the *teela* land, and apparently the only time it is pruned is when a plant finally gets too stunted for even a scanty yield. Then, the practice is to cut it back, leaving only a few inches of wood.

Gardens on the table-lands receive heavy pruning, although the plants in these gardens are accorded far more considerate treatment in every way, than those on the *teela* lands. Sometimes, as much as a foot of new wood is left after a heavy pruning, but the usual practice is to leave only about three, or four inches. There is no such thing as light pruning, the picking being close enough to make that unnecessary. Heavy pruning deteriorates the quality of leaf produced; at least, the cultivators say it takes about two years to restore the quality of tea after pruning.

There is no regular time for such pruning as is done. Some plots are pruned in April, while the pruning in others is likely to run through May, and early June—after the first picking.

Picking

According to the standards of other tea-growing countries, including Japan, tea picking in the Island is even more haphazard than pruning. The underlying principle seems to be to strip all that can be gotten—including the *jannum*, or "fish leaf"—from the top to bottom of the bush, and down through the center. Later, when

CULTIVATING TEA WITH A BUFFALO-DRAWN PLOW

[3] A. C. Kingsford and M. K. Bamber, *Report on the Tea Industries of Java, Formosa, and Japan,* Colombo, 1907, part 2.

ROLLING GREEN LEAF IN A NATIVE FACTORY

the leaves are spread out for the withering process, the coarsest sometimes are picked out, and, if showing a pronounced flavor, are manufactured separately. It is surprising, though, what coarse leaf can be rolled into fair looking tea.

In Northern Formosa, picking generally takes place from April to the beginning of December. The season is divided into five crops, as follows: spring—from early April to the middle of May; summer—from the latter part of May to the end of June; second summer—from the end of June to the middle of August; autumn—from the latter part of August to the middle of October; winter—from the latter part of October to early December. Eleven to twenty pickings a year are obtained.

Toward the end of the spring flush, late in May or early in June, the leaf often becomes very coarse, and much of it is gathered in this condition. With the summer flushes, however, more care is given to the selection of leaf, and two or three leaves and the bud are taken, as often as not including the *jannum*, or "fish leaf." On the *teela* land it is not uncommon to see two leaves and a bud; or sometimes three leaves in a shoot, taken from stunted growth.

On the *teela* land ten pounds of green leaf is a good day's picking; and on the table-land, fifteen, or twenty pounds. Through much of the season, however, lesser amounts are obtained.

With such scanty yields, the picking cost would be prohibitive, were it not for the fact that almost the entire crop is handled by family labor. Extra help is hired only during a special rush of farm work and by the larger plantations.

Formosa Oolong tea first was produced in imitation of the Chinese Oolong of Fukien, to satisfy the taste of the many Fukienese who migrated thence, and settled in Formosa. The trade knows it as a semi-fermented tea; *i.e.*, one possessing some of the characteristics of black tea, with certain of the cup qualities of green tea, and resembling a blend of the two. However, the taste is quite different from the Chinese Oolong, which originated at a place half way between Foochow and Amoy, in the Province of Fukien. It gets its name from the Chinese words *Wu*, "black," and *lung*, "dragon."

The preparation of Formosa Oolong is divided into two groups of manufacturing processes, the first being performed in the tea-producing districts, and the second taking place at the tea factories.

The first preparation comprises the preliminary manufacturing operations of sunning, withering, indoor withering, panning, rolling, and firing, by which the product known as "crude tea" is produced. Since the ultimate quality of the finished product depends entirely upon the excellence of the crude tea, this first process is exceedingly important. The work is all done by hand, the result depending upon the skill of the operative, a skill acquired only by years of practice. This manipulation is a fine art, carried by experts to a perfection beyond imitation.

Sunning, or Withering

When the gathered leaves are brought in at mid-day, they are spread on a canvas mat, or placed in shallow bamboo baskets,

CHINESE GIRLS PICKING TEA AT HEICHIN

INDOOR WITHERING AND FERMENTING OF THE GREEN LEAF, UP-COUNTRY, FIRST PROCESS

each holding two pounds, and exposed to the sun to be withered. At first they are spread thinly, but as the mass becomes warmer they are doubled. The length of time varies from twenty minutes to an hour, the longer period being required on a cloudy day. Finer leaf curls slightly during this operation, but care is taken to prevent any scorching, or discoloration.

The afternoon's plucking is similarly dealt with on the same day, if possible; but if it rains and the leaf is damp, it is left in trays over night, and the process is carried out the next morning. Whenever this happens, however, inferior tea is produced.

Fermenting

After withering, the leaves are taken inside, into a room where they are spread on bamboo trays in a layer three or four inches thick, to undergo further withering and fermenting. At first they are left here for ten or twenty minutes, then mixed, and for a time are shaken up with the hands. The process of spreading out three or four inches thick, and then shaking up with the hands, are repeated at intervals of about fifteen minutes; these intervals being shortened as the processes go on.

After about two hours or two and one-half hours after it was originally placed in the sun, there is a change in the fragrance of the leaf; a tinge of brown appears on the softer leaf and on the serrations. When this discoloration has spread over the softer leaf in spots, and is noticeable along the edge of the older leaf, the leaf is supposed to be about ready for firing; but the odor, or fragrance, is the real test. The entire leaf becomes darker in color and softer, but not nearly enough so for the making of black tea. The entire operation, from the time the leaf is first put out in the sun

BASKET-FIRING ROOM, SECOND PROCESS

INTERIOR OF A MODERN FORMOSA TEA FACTORY
Showing some of the machinery that figures in the manufacture of the Improved Formosa Oolongs.

until fermenting is stopped by panning, takes about four and one-half to five hours, when the temperature is around 82° F. to 86° F. in the shade.

The more modern factories use a fermenting machine something like Bosscha's withering machine, after the preliminary sunning on cotton or bamboo.

The combined processes of withering and fermenting constitute the chief feature in the manufacture of Oolong tea, and upon the way they are done depends in large measure the ultimate quality of the tea in so far as any given leaf will produce it.

Panning

The leaves then are fired or panned over a wood fire in pans or baskets, and later they are re-fired. The panning process makes no impression on the character of the tea, except by adding to its strength, but it is designed to stop fermentation, and it makes the leaf much easier to roll.

In basket-firing, double mat baskets, open at both ends, are used. They have a screen about nine inches above the open bottom. A small quantity of tea is placed in the upper part of the basket, which is then placed over a charcoal fire. Operatives stir the tea with their hands until well softened.

For the process of pan-firing, the pan is of thin metal, usually about two feet in diameter, and seven inches deep at the center. It is set slightly sloping in a regularly made stone and mortar fireplace, or in one merely made of a bamboo framework lined with mud.

About as much leaf as can be conveniently held in the hand is placed in the pan and turned continuously toward the back, or high part, of the pan; the back leaf, in the meantime, slipping forward on the hot pan, heated to about 380° F.—although this heat is varied to suit the occasion.

Rolling

After firing, the leaves are placed upon matting, and rolled with considerable pressure, in order to break the leaf cells and liberate their juices. What with the gummy state of the stewed leaf, and the pressure exerted, the process is a short one—eight to ten minutes being the rule. Following this, the tea is shaken up and spread out to cool.

Firing

The tea is next spread thinly in bamboo trays on a circular wooden frame, about six feet high, encircling a charcoal fire. The moisture is then evaporated in three stages. A brisk fire is used for the first firing, but the leaf is kept there only about two minutes, during which time it is turned once.

After cooling, it is put on the same, or on a second fire, and spread thicker for six minutes. Then it is turned, and put aside to cool. For the last drying, a much lower fire is employed, the tea being spread to a thickness of six or eight inches, in a mat basket with a false bottom, about nine inches from its base. This is placed over the charcoal, and allowed to dry slowly. The tea is doubled in thickness for each successive stage, or firing, and then is left by the warm fireplace over night.

In the modern factories, the firing is carried out in machines.

This completes the local preparation, and the crude tea, thus produced, is packed in tea bags. At this stage of production the middle-men step in. Advances may, or may not, have been made; but traveling brokers and buyers go among the gardens and bid for the tea, either for themselves or for their principals. If one of them buys it and does not take it away with him, it is put into cotton bags holding seventy or eighty pounds, and sealed up, to be called for later. It may remain in these bags from a few hours, in the busy season, to weeks in an off season. It is transported by river boat, motor truck, and rail to the great central market at Daitotei, suburb of Taihoku, where it may pass through still other hands before final-firing and packing for shipment.

The entire-series of operations necessary for the production of crude tea requires seven or eight hours, depending upon the season. The crude tea represents a shrinkage of approximately seventy-five per cent from the weight of the green leaf.

The Second Process, Final-Firing

After the tea merchants of Daitotei buy the crude tea, they submit it to a second and final mode of preparation. Final firing is considered by some of the packers to be the most important of the tea manufacturing processes, and it receives careful attention by expert workmen.

First, the dust and foreign matter are removed, chiefly by hand, and sorting is performed by Chinese girls after fanning out the flat leaf. This work may be seen in progress any day throughout the season on the verandas of the hongs, or marts, along the streets.

After this, the tea is graded according to quality, and, when sorted, goes through the final process of refiring over a charcoal fire, and losing ten to fifteen per cent of weight.

The final firing rooms are pactically air tight. The firing stoves are in rows on a brick platform, and are about two feet in diameter and two feet in depth, with no air vents. They are filled with charcoal, and once properly lighted will burn for a couple of weeks without replenishing. A species of *accacia* wood is used for making the charcoal.

The whole room is kept warm, and the brick platform is as hot as an oven floor. The re-firing baskets of bamboo matting have openings at the ends, as have those previously described. The tea is placed in them nine inches thick around the sides, with a hollow in the middle. A tempera-

BLACK TEA MAKING IN FORMOSA
Upper view shows the drying machine; lower view shows the withering trommels.

ture of **180°** F. to **200°** F. is maintained for from eight to ten hours. The fires are never bright, but always covered with ash, and when the heat is not too great, the tea is turned only two, or three times.

This completes the second process. The tea now is ready to be packed into chests lined with tea-lead, and inner paper linings. Some of them hold twenty or thirty catties [one catty equals one and one-third pounds], others seven and one-half to fifteen catties. The larger size is called a "half chest," the smaller a "box."

After packing, the chests are covered with mats. The mats are made in China from reeds, and imported to Formosa from Canton, where they are cut to the proper size. The matting is done by especially trained men called "matting gangs." They work by hand, holding the matting down with their feet, and sewing it up with a baling needle. After the mat is on, a chest is rattaned. The rattan is wet before it is put on, in order to make it pliable, and is very rough on the hands of the matting gang. After rattaning, the chests are marked.

From Daitotei, the chests of tea are sent by train a distance of about eighteen miles to the harbor of Keelung, where they are exported.

Manufacture of Pouchong Tea

The plucking and up-country manufacture of Pouchong differs from Oolong in that the objective is to produce an unfermented infusion. The Pouchong demand does not require a small, finely rolled leaf as in the case of Oolong.

To make Pouchong, or scented tea, the Oolong leaf is mixed with quantities of jasmine and gardenia flowers, previous to final firing. The weight proportions of flowers to tea usually followed are, one of *magni* [*Jasmine sambac*], to three of tea; one of *sueng* [*Jasmine officale*], to four of tea; and equal parts of *enki* [*Gardenia*] and tea. The cultivation of these flowers forms quite an industry in the country around Daitotei.

The dried tea and the flowers are heaped upon the floor of the firing hongs for large quantities, and in circular baskets for smaller amounts, in alternate layers, the flowers being first sprinkled with water. The usual floor heap is about three feet deep. Covered with a cloth, such a heap

will generate a temperature of 104° F. overnight. Twenty-four hours is the average length of time required to soften the leaf, and fix the fragrance.

The flowers are next carefully picked or sifted out, and the tea fired as usual at a temperature of from 180° F. to 200° F. The manufacture of Pouchong tea is almost entirely in the hands of Chinese packers, and the sales of the finished product, in one or two pound packets, is practically confined to Chinese residents in the Philippines, Netherlands India, Indo-China, Siam, and Straits Settlements.

The Tottering Lilies of Daitotei

The "tottering lilies of Daitotei," is a descriptive phrase applied to the Chinese girls who work in the tea-firing, and sorting go-downs of Formosa's great central tea market. They are a gay, laughing crowd as they wend their way to work during the summer season, and altogether one of the prettiest sights of Daitotei. Terry thus describes them as they were in an earlier day, and, except for bound feet, as we hope they will always remain:

Their fresh young faces are bedaubed with white paint and rouge, their sloe-black hair combed into a shining mass to one side of the head, and adorned with a sprig of jasmine or a magnolia bloom, and, their chubby faces and snapping black eyes radiant with provocative piquancy, they step blithely along and add a quaint and interesting note to the town. The eyes are customarily the only index of emotion, and the brows are often blackened with charred sticks, or narrowed to resemble a nascent willow leaf or the moon when first seen. The following ballad pictures them well:

Eyebrows shaped like leaves of willows
Drooping over 'autumn billows';
Almond-shaped of liquid brightness
Were the eyes of Yang-Kuei-fei.

Many "tottering lilies" teeter with the throng, the tiny crippled feet encased in brilliantly embroidered shoes, and the legs in light blue or lavender silk trousers. If [says an authority] a Chinese lady ever breaks through the prohibition against displaying her person, she presents her feet as the surest darts with which a lover's heart can be assailed! Some of these tea sorters are as much addicted to maternity as the cigarette makers of Seville, and not a few carry young bead-eyed Mongolians slung in wide black bands over one hip.[4]

---

[4] T. Philip Terry, *Guide to the Japanese Empire*, Boston and New York, 1920, p. 779.

EXTERIOR VIEW OF THE MODERN TEA FACTORY AT TAIHYO

Promotional Activities

In addition to the practical work already accomplished by the Government Tea Experimental Station located at Sonampi, the Government of Formosa has done much to improve the quality of the Formosa teas, to increase production, and reduce costs. Typical of the new order, since the Japanese occupation of the Island, are the activities of the Mitsui Company, which has evolved a comprehensive plan for reviving, on an extensive scale, the declining Formosa tea industry. The principal feature of this project consists in placing the tea plantations in Taihoku, Taichu, and Shinchiku Provinces, which had been given over to tenant farmers, under the direct management of the Mitsui Company. A system of scientific fertilization, weeding, and intensive cultivation, has been adopted. It is estimated that productivity in these areas will be increased to 3200 pounds of refined tea per acre. Under Government patronage, the Company has opened many new estates, and built tea factories, equipped with modern machinery for the manufacture of three-quarters fermented, and fully-fermented teas.

Black tea production in Taiwan is increasing yearly. It is made from the Kokan variety in Taikei and Chureki, Shinchiku Province from wild tea plants, in the Hori District, and from the Assam variety, now under cultivation by Mitsui and others. When more of this becomes available for manufacture of black tea, the production may be considerable. The Taiwan Government is encouraging black tea production.

In the case of the three-quarters fermented tea, the leaf is withered rapidly in the sun, and the remainder of the process is similar to that followed in the manufactuer of black teas in other countries. The fully-fermented teas, manufactured according to the approved methods followed in India and Ceylon, have been well received in England and America.

When the author paid his last visit to Formosa, he had an opportunity of viewing at close range the initial stages of the Mitsui programme. The Company owns 84,000 acres of land suitable for tea, and an allied company, known as the Formosa Industrial Company, owns 20,000 acres.

At Taihyo, the author saw in operation a thoroughly modern tea factory. It is not uncommon to find model tea factories anywhere in Ceylon, India, or Java. One rather expects them in those countries, where railways penetrate and good roads abound; but it was not at all to be expected in wild Formosa, where the only approach was the push-car tram, and the distance interminable. However, here it was, with fermentation room, withering tats, tea rollers, firing machines, mixers, cutters, and grading machines complete, a tribute to the spirit of progress, which is typical of the Colonial Administration of Formosa, and in line with the faith which the Mitsui Company has in the future of Formosa tea.

The Government General of Formosa, since 1918, has encouraged the native Chinese tea-growers to form local associations, or kumiai, each of sufficient membership to support a central tea factory, which will perform major preparation of all teas for that unit. These plans have met with success, the number of kumiai increasing yearly.

There is a wide difference between the

primitive methods of growing and manufacture in Formosa, and the elaborate "Estate System" of such tea producing countries as India, Ceylon, and Java, under which estate owners plant, cultivate, manufacture, and export tea; thus cutting production costs, and doing away with many of the evils of production on a small scale. By the present system, there are so many middle-men between the producer and exporter, that the cost of the tea is often doubled, or trebled.

To find a solution for this difficulty the Formosan Government in 1923 appropriated funds for the improvement of the tea industry, and particularly for improvements in production. Owners of tea gardens were persuaded to organize kumiai, and machinery and equipment were loaned; while seedlings were furnished gratis, and a subsidy also was granted for the purchase of fertilizer.

The cost of organizing an "A" class association, covering an area of 600 ko [one ko equals 2.397 acres], is approximately yen 50,000 [one yen equals $0.4985]. The annual maintenance is figured to be about yen 5000, and in addition, the total sum of approximately yen 20,000 is required for the purchase of seedlings that are supplied free of charge.

One regular station for the experimental study of tea, is maintained by the Central Research Institute of the Government General of Formosa. Its official title and address are: The Heichin Tea Experiment Station, Aya Hoshin, Sonampi, Yobaisho, Chureki-gun, Schinchiku-shu, Taiwan, Japan.

Another important development is the inauguration, since 1923, of an inspection system by the Formosan Government. The object of this inspection is to prevent the exportation of inferior teas, in order to enhance the reputation of Formosan leaf in foreign markets.

As a part of the plan for improving marketing conditions, the Government General also established, in 1923, the Taiwan Joint Sales Market at Daitotei. This was done to bring the kumiai in direct touch with packers and exporters, in order, ultimately, to do away with middle-men and the profit which they now add to the cost of Formosa tea before it is shipped. However, certain middle-men will always be necessary to the effective moving of the Formosa Oolong crop.

The Joint Sales Market handles consignments of teas made by the kumiai members, as well as those from non-members. The consignments are sold through bids, the consignors usually specifying the prices at which the consignments should be sold.

In 1926, the Sales Market, as an inducement to farmers to market their tea through it, began to make loans to those who did so, of not more than fifty per cent of the cost of the tea consigned to it; the loans being redeemed with the proceeds of the tea sold through the Sales Market.

CHAPTER XVIII

CULTIVATION AND MANUFACTURE IN JAVA AND SUMATRA

GEOGRAPHICAL LOCATION—SOILS OF THE TEA DISTRICTS—CLIMATE, RAINFALL, AND ALTITUDE—CLEARING AND LAYING OUT—TILLAGE—BUILDING ROADS—DRAINAGE SYSTEMS —TERRACING—PROPAGATION FROM SEED—VEGETATIVE PROPAGATION—PLANTING—GREEN MANURING—LEGUMINOUS SHADE TREES AND WINDBREAKS—HEDGES—GROUND COVERS— FERTILIZERS—PESTS AND BLIGHTS—PRUNING—PLUCKING—FIELD TRANSPORT—MANUFACTURING PROCESSES—LABOR AND WAGES—COOLIE LINES—PLANTERS' ASSOCIATIONS— THE TEA EXPERIMENTAL STATION—TEA EXPERT BUREAU

JAVA and Sumatra are located in the Malay Archipelago, which is variously referred to as Malaysia, the East Indies, Insulinde, or Indonesia—the largest group of islands in the world. With the exception of the Philippine Islands, British Borneo, and Portugal's half of the Island of Timor, the whole group belongs to Holland, and is known as *Nederlandsch-Oost Indie*, Netherlands East India, or the Dutch East Indies. The islands are strung along the Equator between 95° and 141° longitude, east of Greenwich, and extend from 6° north latitude to 11° south.

From east to west, Netherlands India is about as wide as the United States, from New York to San Francisco. It is fifty-eight times the size of the little Holland that governs it so well, and its population of 61,000,000 is nearly seven times that of the Netherlands. The Island of Java, by far the most important in the Archipelago, is about the size of New York State, and has a population of 42,000,000, making it the most densely populated country in the world. Sumatra is almost three and a half times the size of Java, but has a population of only 7,841,000.

Java is 622 miles long, and varies in width from about fifty-five to 131 miles. The Island lies wholly between the sixth and ninth degrees of south latitude, and is one of the most fertile and productive areas in the world. Its south coast is bold and rocky, while the north coast is low and swampy. The whole interior of the Island is mountainous, and is very volcanic in structure. It is drained by fairly large rivers, few of which are navigable.

A chain of volcanic peaks, mostly extinct, forms the backbone of the Island, and between these peaks are vast plains of marvelous fertility. The tea lands are located on these plains and on the slopes of the adjacent mountains.

The Gedeh and the Salak volcanic peaks near Buitenzorg, thirty-five miles south of Batavia, form the bulwarks for a tract of country where Batavia Residency abuts on the Preangers; Gedeh rising just within the Preangers, and Salak within Batavia Residency. On the slopes of these mountains are located a number of well-known tea estates; Goalpara, on Gedeh, being one of these, and Parakan Salak, on Salak, being another.

In the Preanger Regencies to the southward of the main range is located another important mountain district, and in this district, together with the outlying districts roundabout Gedeh and Salak, are situated the greater number of tea estates. However, tea is raised on scattering estates to the eastward, almost throughout the length of the Island; the preponderant number in the western part being due to more favorable distribution of rainfall over that section.

The most important commercial centers are Batavia, Semarang, and Soerabaya, lo-

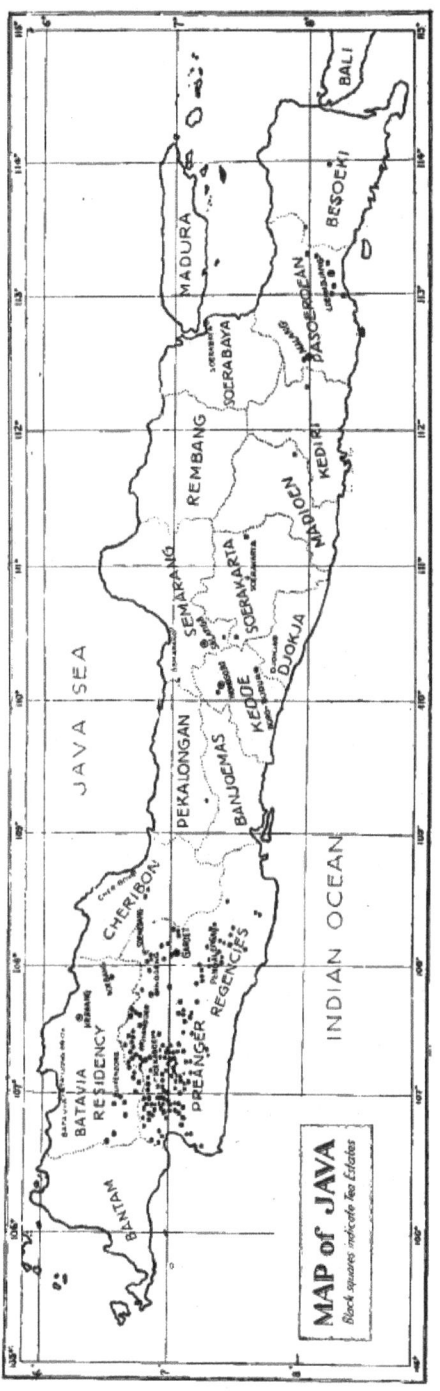

MAP of JAVA
Black squares indicate tea Estates

cated on the north side of the Island. Soerabaya and Semarang are seaports having natural harbors, while Batavia ships through its port, Tandjong-Priok, about six miles away. A railway connects Batavia, Semarang, and Soerabaya, and runs the length of the Island. Practically all of the tea that is exported is shipped from Batavia. Bantam, on the northwest coast, was the headquarters of the rich spice trade of the Dutch in the sixteenth century, but is no longer commercially important. The area of tea in production in Java at the end of 1933, the last year for which official figures are available, was 150,465 hectares, and the estates were 293 in number.

Sumatra stretches to the northwest of the western tip of Java, and is located between approximately the sixth degree of south latitude, and the sixth degree north. A chain of high mountains stretches through the length of the Island, falling away sharply to the Indian Ocean on the west, and descending into vast plains of alluvial formation on the east. Due to this configuration, the water courses to the west of the mountains are short, and few are navigable; but those on the east side are longer, and many of them are navigable for small craft.

Medan, near the northeast coast, is the principal commercial center, and is reached by rail and a good motor highway from the port of Belawan Deli. Some ninety miles south of Medan is Siantar, situated in the Sumatra East Coast Residency, 1200 feet above sea level, and the center of Sumatra's fastest growing tea district. Many of the tea estates are situated in the Siantar Highlands, but a few estates have been opened on the West Coast, in the Palembang and Benkoelen Highlands, where conditions are also favorable for tea-growing. The total area of tea in production at the end of the year 1933, the last for which official figures are available, was 33,860 hectares, and there were 41 estates. Hundreds of square miles remain of lands that are suitable for tea cultivation.

The system of land tenure for European estates in Sumatra has made it possible for European enterprises to secure property rights to large areas of land over long periods of time. While Europeans may not acquire actual ownership, the system of concessions or leaseholds, up to seventy-five years, is virtually equivalent to ownership for all practical plantation purposes and the security of capital invested. The Italian Government is operating a tea estate at Tjibitoe near Garoet, Java. Approximately fifty per cent of the capital investment in the Sumatra East Coast is non-Dutch, and, if the tobacco industry is left out of consideration, the proportion of foreign capital is considerably larger.

The rates of rental for land in Sumatra are low, ranging from Fl. 0.50 per hectare in the first year to Fl. 3.00 per hectare in the fifth and subsequent years. Florins 3.00 per hectare would seem to be a common rental rate for estates for the fifth and subsequent years after the granting of the leasehold. The rate, however, may be reduced by the Government, and would seem to depend upon conditions, such as attractiveness of the land, its situation, etc. The rate during the first years is usually calculated on a sliding scale, so that the property will not be too heavily assessed during the years of preparation, before it becomes productive. The usual practice is for one-fifth of the full rate to be charged in the first year, two-fifths in the second year, three-fifths in the third year, and so on, until the full rate comes into force in the fifth and subsequent years.

Soils of the Tea Districts

The soil, in Java and Sumatra, has been found to have less effect on the growth of the tea bush than the climate. How-

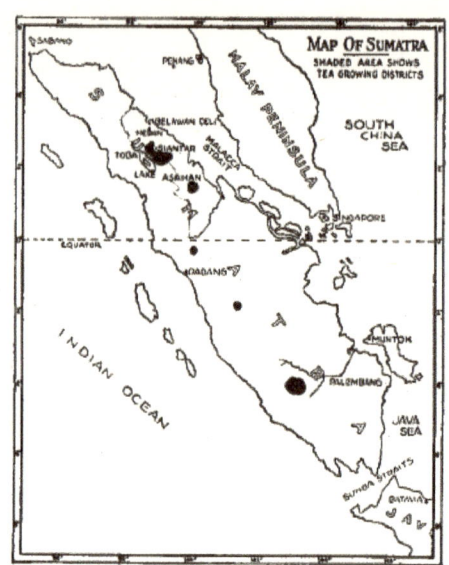

ever, the plant thrives better on loamy or sandy soils than on clay; and a light, friable soil, with sufficient humus and nitrogen, gives the best results—especially if porous and permeable.

Table Number One gives analyses of soils from a number of tea centers of Java and Sumatra.

A favorable soil proportion, consisting of one part gravel and coarse sand, two parts fine sand and silt, and one part fine sand and clay, is found in the Pengalengan soil. It is not too much decayed, but is weathered just sufficiently to be rich in mineral plant nutriments, and to be friable, and porous. The more a soil is decayed, the more clay it obtains, and the less friable it becomes. The Siantar soil of Sumatra is mostly too little decayed, and soon dries out; but the favorable climate, with its evenly divided annual rainfall, makes up for this, and is responsible for the abundant growth of the tea plant in the Island.

A good tea soil is not supposed to have less than three parts of total organic matter to two of humus. This proportion is considered important. The Siantar soils of Sumatra are apt to show a lack of organic matter and humus. Therefore, the planting of green manures on these soils has been extensively resorted to, and has brought its reward in increased tea crops.

JAVA TABLE NO. 1
Analyses of Soils

	Java Tea Districts			Sumatra
	Tjibeber	Soeka-boemi	Penga-lengan	Siantar
Mechanical Analyses				
Gravel and Stones.....	10 }33	2 }31	1 }24	18 }70
Coarse Sand..........	23	29	23	52
Fine Sand............	10 }26	23 }50	23 }54	10 }16
Silt.................	15	27	31	6
Fine Silt............	15 }42	12 }19	15 }22	7 }14
Clay................	27	7	7	7
Chemical Analyses				
Nitrogen.............	0.38	0.48	0.69	0.60
Total Potash.........	0.04	0.01	0.03	0.15
Total Phosphoric Acid.	0.03	0.10	0.11	0.05
Total Lime..........	0.08	0.05	0.74	0.03
Available Phosphoric Acid...............	0.01	0.02	0.02	0.01
Organic Matter.......	5.20	12.32	15.30	0.54
Soluble Humus...... (matiere noire)	....	2.65	5.10	0.94

GENERAL VIEW OF A TEA ESTATE ON THE PENGALENGAN PLATEAU, JAVA

Most tea soils of Java have been produced from volcanic ash. The primary rocks from which the volcanic ash of West Java is derived are mainly andesite and basalt, which decay rather easily. This decay is advanced by distribution, high temperature, and the prevailing damp; but there is a danger that, due to the rapid decay, all the mineral plant nutriments may be leached away by the heavy tropical rains, if the soil has not enough humus to absorb them. It is considered, therefore, of great importance to the wellbeing of a tea estate that the humus content of the soil be kept up. Nowadays, a great improvement is being made by the rational laying out of road and drain systems to prevent wash of top soil, which contains the most humus.

Further improvement, in the same direction, is to be noted in the planting of leguminous plants as hedges or as ground cover in the gardens. These plants not only help to prevent wash, but they also serve as green manures, and enrich the soil with organic matter, humus, and nitrogen.

In many cases, the higher a tea estate is located above sea level, the younger is the volcanic soil. The teas grown on these young volcanic soils are known for their superior quality.

The older volcanic soils are found at the foot of the mountain slopes. They are more weathered, and, therefore, contain more clay. If well kept, and regularly hoed, these soils produce large tea crops, due to the better climate conditions of the lower altitudes. Tea grown on these soils has less flavor, and is of a strong, dark color.

One reason for the predominance of tea in the western part of the Island undoubtedly is the wet climate and the volcanic origin of the soil. Reporting, in 1916, on various aspects of the tea industry in Java, Dr. G. D. Hope, then Chief Scientific Officer of the Indian Tea Association of Calcutta, wrote that "almost the whole of the big tea-growing tract in the Preanger and Batavia Residencies is of tertiary origin, and the greater part of it consists of recent volcanic ground, formed by the deposit of laval ash from volcanoes of basalt and andesite." [1]

Most of the tea estates in the Preanger

[1] Dr. G. D. Hope, *Report on Certain Aspects of the Tea Industry of Java and Sumatra*, Calcutta, 1916.

Regencies are located on the slopes of volcanoes, but a few in the south are on sedimentary ground. North of the Preangers are a number of estates, mainly in the districts of Buitenzorg and Krawang, in Batavia and in Cheribon, that also are on volcanic ground. In Central Java, tea estates are situated on the slopes of mountains in the Residencies of Pekalongan, Semarang, Kedoe, Soerakarta, Madioen, and Kediri; while in East Java, estates are to be found on mountain slopes in Passoeroean, and Besoeki.

With the exception of a few estates in the south of the Preangers, which, as previously mentioned, are on soils derived from sedimentary rocks, all of the tea estates in Java are on volcanic soils. Estates like Gedeh, Goalpara, and Perbawati, on Mount Gedeh, are on the higher slopes, and, therefore, on recent volcanic ground, while Sinagar is lower and consequently on older soil.

The sedimentary soils in the southern Preangers are volcanic in their origin, but have been covered by the sea, and sometimes overspread with a layer of coralline limestone. They now range in elevation from 2000 to 4000 feet, and are completely weathered, being of a clayish consistency.

Speaking of the Island generally, the newer soils at high elevations are gray and stony, and are, as a rule, those producing the highest priced teas; the older soils on the lower slopes are redder, have been more completely disintegrated by weathering, and contain less humus. Production on the younger volcanic soils will run about 1000 to 1500 pounds per *bouw* [about 575 to 850 pounds per acre], as against approximately 700 to 1200 pounds to a *bouw* [about 400 to 685 pounds per acre] on older soils having a smaller amount of humus. There are elevations of about 5000 feet, where the humus and nitrogen contents of the soil are high, and where some of the best tea estates in the Island are located. Their yields run as high as 2000 pounds per *bouw*, or about 1140 pounds an acre, of high quality tea. Such gardens are situated high up on the slopes of Malabar, Tiloe, Wajang, and Windoe.

The soil of Siantar, on the northeast coast of Sumatra, is volcanic in its origin, and is formed from eruptive liparitic rock. Underneath, it is clayish, and whitish-yellow in color. The surface presents a dark, friable soil, of good tilth, containing sharp fragments of quartz, which, after a heavy rainfall, cause glistening patches on the surface of the ground.

SHEETS OF TEA ON AN ESTATE IN DELI, SUMATRA'S EAST COAST

While fairly level, the ground is quite inclined to be sloping in many places, and probably the finer components of the soil are leached away by wash, accounting for a sandy character of the surface soil. This sandy soil, nevertheless, appears to be of the same nature as the under-soil, though the difference in character between the surface and the subsoils is quite pronounced. The surface soil averages about nine inches in depth, and affords the rooting area of the tea shrubs. The subsoil is more or less impervious, and water stands persistently in catch trenches after a rainfall.

Occasional patches of reddish colored soil indicate a more complete weathering, with resultant oxidation of the iron which they contain. The soils of the Siantar District have been formed by the breaking down of a very acid, liparitic, eruptive rock of a sort not found in Java. Mineral components in the sandy part of these soils are made up mainly of potash, feldspar, and quartz, with a sprinkling of mica, etc.

Tanangtaloe, a representative tea estate in the Padang Highlands of the southwest coast of Sumatra, is on flat, slightly undulating ground, with slopes steeper than those in the Siantar District. The jungle on this land is not heavy. The top layer of humus soil is fairly deep, although varying considerably, and is dark in color. It contains, in contrast to the Siantar District, a comparatively small amount of coarse sand, holds water well, and requires to be drained. Under the black humus soil there is a red-brown mixture of clay and sand. The sand is a quartz sand, occurring only in this layer, and not throughout the soil, as in Siantar. The sandy subsoil makes the ground very porous, roots penetrate it easily, and the water soon sinks through. Below this sandy soil is a layer of yellow clay, which gradually weathers upon coming in contact with the air. A still lower layer is an almost white pure clay, with no sand. This is extremely hard, impervious, and sticky. Luckily, it lies deeply in most places; but if, as sometimes happens, it immediately underlies the humus layer, it gives tea-plant roots a poor chance. The yellow clay, also, is not easily permeable, and when in direct contact with the black earth, is similarly unfortunate for tea. The tea is best where the red-brown soil underlies the black humus layer. Deep cultivation and drainage are considered as absolutely necessary in these soils.

Climate, Rainfall, and Altitude

Java and Sumatra, in common with the entire Malay Archipelago, enjoy a soft tropical climate tempered by the sea. Variations between summer and winter temperatures are small. The highest temperature on record at Batavia is 96.08° F., and the lowest 66.02°.

The southwest monsoon makes itself felt over northern Sumatra in July, the

JAVA TABLE No. 2

Rainfall in Inches

| Month | JAVA | | | | SUMATRA |
	Buitenzorg 800 feet	Kassomalang Estate 1550 feet	Goalpara Estate 3300 feet	Malabar Estate 4650 feet	Pematang-Siantar 1200 feet
January	16.93	19.11	16.73	13.85	10.14
February	15.37	15.76	15.07	12.87	7.33
March	17.33	20.16	18.84	12.95	8.81
April	15.6	17.47	19.42	10.65	8.35
May	14.04	11.65	12.64	6.63	12.62
June	10.49	7.72	8.66	4.33	6.55
July	9.67	4.21	5.7	2.54	6.05
August	9.57	1.68	5.6	2.42	9.17
September	12.75	5.3	8.39	3.82	12.35
October	16.69	7.06	14.08	7.64	15.95
November	15.89	13.88	19.81	10.92	9.48
December	13.55	16.2	20.4	13.34	9.79
Total	167.88	140.2	165.34	101.96	116.09

JAVA TABLE No. 3

Temperature—In Degrees Fahrenheit

| Month | JAVA | | | | SUMATRA |
	Buitenzorg 800 feet	Kassomalang Estate 1550 feet	Goalpara Estate 3300 feet	Malabar Estate 4650 feet	Pematang- Siantar 1200 feet
January	75.4	72.5	66.9	62.6	71.0
February	75.6	72.1	66.9	62.6	72.6
March	76.1	73.2	67.4	62.7	73.7
April	77.0	74.1	68.1	63.3	73.9
May	77.1	74.3	68.1	63.1	74.6
June	77.0	73.5	67.6	62.6	73.7
July	77.0	73.2	67.4	61.5	73.4
August	77.1	73.5	67.1	61.3	73.4
September	77.5	74.1	67.4	62.2	73.0
October	77.5	74.3	67.6	62.6	72.3
November	76.0	73.7	67.4	62.4	71.9
December	75.9	73.0	66.7	62.4	71.9
Average	76.6	73.4	67.3	62.4	72.9

same as in the southern part of the continent of Asia. At the same time, there is an area of high pressure in the neighborhood of Australia, and southeast winds affect the island of Java, and the south of Sumatra. These two prevailing influences, with minor factors, determine the wind direction in different parts of the islands in mid-year. In January, there is an air current from Asia southward, and there is a west wind all over Java that is felt more in the vicinity of the seacoast than inland; in fact, these winds are little noticed inland or at high elevations. Near the coast and near high mountains, there are the usual local air movements to be met with anywhere. The movement of wind from the east usually begins in April; and that from the west, in November. Owing to the proximity of the Equator, marked changes in air pressure are little in evidence, and cyclones are entirely unknown.

There is a distinct connection between the monsoons and the rainfall. The main characteristics to be noticed are that the west monsoon, which brings the most rain to Java, is felt in January and February, and the drier southeast monsoon in July, August, and September.

In Java and Sumatra, the tea plant thrives best in mountainous regions at elevations from 3000 to 5000 feet, where it enjoys an annual rainfall of from 100 to 160 inches, equally divided throughout the

seasons. Sunshine in the morning hours and rain in the afternoon or night are considered the most desirable weather conditions. Too much dry weather weakens the plants, making them susceptible to parasites.

The foregoing explains why tea cultivation is limited to special areas like the Preanger Regencies and the Buitenzorg District, against the Gedeh and Salak Mountains, where these weather conditions prevail. The mountains of Central Java also seem to be well adapted to tea culture, and experiments in East Java have proved successful. Java tea estates are at elevations of from 800 to 6000 feet.

In Sumatra, the ideal combination of climate and elevation has made the Siantar District, 1200 feet, near Lake Toba, the best known producing area; while the Padang Highlands of the West Coast seem also to be well adapted, and likewise, Bankoelen, 3000 to 5000 feet, on the Southwest Coast.

Tables Number Two and Three, on pages 346 and 347 respectively, give the monthly average rainfall and temperature of the chief tea districts in West Java.

It will be seen at a glance that even in the dry season, or east monsoon, lasting from April until October, the districts mentioned have no distinct dry period. The western part of Java, due to a more evenly distributed rainfall, is more suitable for tea growing than the eastern and middle parts of the Island, where a more pronounced drought occurs. Moreover, the air of West Java is more humid than that in East Java. Tea is grown to a small extent in East Java, but the prolonged drought, combined with hot dry winds, is a factor operating against the best results.

Another climate factor to be reckoned with is frost. On the Pengalengan Plateau, 5000 to 7000 feet above sea level, there are one or two estates that invariably suffer from night frosts, especially during the months of July, August, and September. During these months the sky is so clear that radiation of the heat from the ground will, under favorable conditions, cause night frosts. Usually, it is the large, flat expanses of tea on these estates that suffer, while the surrounding hills are free from frost.

Clearing and Laying Out Gardens

Java and Sumatra planters take the utmost pains to guard against loss of surface soil by wash, and terrace all steep slopes, either immediately after clearing or else soon after planting out seedlings or stumps. Terraced banks are kept up by planting leguminous plants with generous root formations, while the easier slopes are protected by contour drains, contour ridges, and catch trenches in combination with hedge systems, which also follow contour lines.

The tea is planted on terraces following around the contour. The steeper the slope, the closer together are the terraces and fewer the bushes on each contour shelf. On the steeper slopes, the terraces are so narrow that they carry only one row of tea bushes, while wider ones, on easier slopes, may carry several rows. This system is more easily carried out, because of the invariable rule of the Dutch tea planter to plant the tea-rows along the contour lines of the slopes.

On flat and very porous lands, as, for example, those occurring on the Pengalengan Plateau, precautions against wash are less urgent than on heavy clay soils mixed with *tjadas* and limestone. In all cases, however, it is found undesirable to allow too much water to be absorbed by the ground, and, therefore, the best practice provides for its overflow.

Although virgin forest land is given the preference in clearing for tea cultivation, it often occurs that only secondary forest ground is available, or plains where alang-alang grass [*Imperata arundinacea*] and underbrush grow; or else, old coffee, cinchona, or tea gardens have to be re-opened. The measures taken in each of these cases vary somewhat, but thoroughness in the preliminary work and in the steps taken to prevent wash are noticeable characteristics of the tea gardens of Java and Sumatra.

Opening the Land

In opening heavy virgin forest, a beginning is made with the cutting of roads and paths for the purpose of survey and of facilitating control. Each division of the land to be cultivated is cleared by a separate gang of workers by whom the undergrowth is cut and left to dry. Then, suitable timber trees are marked and felled, mostly at a height of from three to four feet above the ground. Stumps of large trees, over three feet in diameter, usually are very difficult and expensive to do away with, but they are uprooted so far as possible, in order to obtain a clean plantation. Where stumps are allowed to remain, they entail a risk that root disease will spread to the tea plants, especially on soils rich in humus. Branches, shrubs, and small trees are piled in small heaps and burned on prospective roads, in so far as this is possible, for the reason that there is a loss of humus where the burning is done. The large felled trees that are not sawed into timber or sold are laid in the direction of the slope, in order to prevent them from rolling and causing damage to the plantation; smaller wood is cleared by rolling it into the ravines.

The clearing of secondary forest is simpler and less expensive, but the soil is not as good.

Lands covered only with undergrowth and grasses are still easier to clear. Everything is cut, and, after drying, is burned. Following this, the roots and root stocks are carefully dug out with especial attention to grasses, in order to avoid trouble later on.

In the conversion of old coffee, cinchona, and tea gardens, all existing growths are first removed, and planting done anew. It sometimes is difficult to make the new plants take root; but in such cases reforestation has to be brought about through the use of such legumes as *Leucæna, Tephrosia,* and *Crotalaria.* By this means, and after some years, it is found possible to reopen these gardens in tea.

Beginning Tillage

After the land has been sufficiently cleared, tilling is commenced. Whether this is heavy or not depends wholly on the character of the soil. Loose sandy soils and soils that contain heavy humus, such as those of Pengalengan, are not heavily cultivated, since this may promote "dry wash." The opposite is true of clay soils, which are found responsive to heavy tilling.

In opening out, the ground generally is tilled as deeply as possible. The roots of grasses and harmful weeds are removed at the same time. Unless this is done with much care, there is risk of the growth of alang-alang or other grasses that are very difficult to root out. Close supervision is given to insure deep tilling and thorough weeding, while any weeds that appear later are promptly eradicated. In both Java and Sumatra it is considered an expensive mistake to commence tilling after the planting has been done, so the tilling is completed first.

Deep tilling is found necessary in stiff soils, in order to permit the air and water to penetrate. This causes quicker disintegration of the food reserves, and hastens growth. On loose, sandy soils the circulation of water and air is well regulated, and these soils require less intensive tilling. The same is true of humus soils, which usually are loose.

Road Building

The public roads of Java and Sumatra are excellent, and are constructed carefully and scientifically. On tea estates, after the land has been partly cleared, a systematic network of roads is laid out according to certain principles which may be briefly stated as follows:

First. Roads never are made to serve as outlet drains. On the contrary, they are protected from flowing water by special drains above the road, while any water that may collect on the road is led away as quickly as possible into the ravines or outlet drains lying below the roads. From this, it follows that the road scheme is laid out before the drainage system.

Second. On mountain land it is not found

A NEWLY OPENED TEA ESTATE IN SUMATRA

desirable to make the roads absolutely horizontal, but to give them a grade of at least one meter in forty, in order that the water may not accumulate. If the road runs along a slope, it is made highest at the ridges and sloping towards the valley, so that the drain along the road may be as short as possible.

Third. Each road having a long and regular ascent is provided with cross drains, or culverts, at intervals of not more than 150 to 300 meters, in order to free the road of any overflow of water.

Fourth. The main roads are laid in a sort of cobweb system, with the factory grounds in the center, since it may be necessary to forward the leaf to the factory several times a day. Either hard roads or light narrow-gauge rails are used for these roads. The light rails are not much more expensive than hard roads, and cost much less in upkeep. Ropeways also are used, but are generally more expensive.

In view of their possible use for light rails, the main roads are not made too steep; preferably their grade is not more than one in thirty or forty. Once planting is completed, it is very difficult to alter a road to suit the rails; so it is found advisable to pay attention to this question at the outset. When planning roads, it is taken into account that coolies always choose the shortest route, even though steep, and if a short way be found through the plantation, whatever the hindrance they will make a track.

Where the *hectarewegen,* or "hundred meters," system exists; *i.e.,* in gardens divided by the roads into squares 100 by 100 meters, the best practice is to open up the obvious short cuts to enable the pluckers to reach the receiving sheds or the factory, quickly.

Parallel roads are laid out in the same manner as the main thoroughfares, not absolutely horizontal, but sloping toward the ravines. Between the parallel roads, steeper connecting roads are made, having grades of not more than one in seven, to one in ten. For easy traffic, road junctions occur at the ridges, in so far as this is possible.

The Drainage System

The soils of Java and Sumatra are porous, and when slight showers occur, the water sinks quickly into the ground; but when heavy showers fall, these same soils are easily washed out, unless the rainwater is immediately removed.

In order to prevent the occurrence of larger streamlets by the accumulation of descending water, outlet drains straight down the slopes are necessary. This is to insure rapid removal of water at places prepared for the purpose, and though generally known, still the outlet drains often are unsuitable, not systematically laid, or else wholly omitted. Experience indicates:

First. That it is wrong to make drains any longer than they have to be, because the flow becomes too heavy at the lower end, resulting in scouring and washouts. In order to obtain relatively short drains, the highest point of the drain must straddle the hill or ridge, and the drain must slope toward the valleys on both sides of the hill at a gradient of one in twenty-five, to one in forty, or on an average, say, one in thirty, according to the nature of the land.

The relative distance of the secondary drains may be taken as fifty to 100 feet; the drains to be closer together, if:
 (a) the rainfall is heavy;
 (b) the ground is loose;
 (c) the land is steep;
 (d) the gardens are kept clean weeded.

Second. Valleys are the natural outlet drains; therefore, the main outlet drains must be laid therein with as few sharp turns as possible.

As an objection to the foregoing, it is urged that the valleys often contain the finest soil. But water travels toward the valleys, so it is found desirable to drain the latter by means of deep, main outlet-drains, because of the ground water.

The main outlet-drains, if they are steep, become deeply furrowed; but this is considered preferable to having the wash all over the land, with gradual loss of the top layer. The sides of these drains are protected by growing grass, and the rush of water is stopped to a certain extent by a series of small dams of wood or stone. The surface water is collected and carried into the main outlet-drains by means

of contour drains, having a very slight gradient. These are laid out with great care, and are flanked on their upper and lower sides by banks planted with suitable legumes. Exceptionally suitable for this purpose, is the vetiver, or *Andropogon aciculatus.* This grass grows easily, forms a thick hedge, and has an enormously wide-spreading root system that holds the ground together under the floor of the drain. The contour drains have to be cleaned out, periodically, because great damage may be caused by water breaking through them.

Catch Pits for Water

One of the most useful inventions, in use on some of the mountain tea estates, is a system of catch pits, or "water holes." In the first place, a catch pit holds a certain quantity of water during a heavy shower of rain, so that water has time to permeate the ground; and in the second place, the pit catches the soil that is washed away, and retains it until it can be restored to the ground when the pit is dug out again. In the less porous soils, the catch pits remain full of water sometimes for a day or longer; consequently, their rated capacity is not at all times available. Probably 50 per cent of capacity is a fair average. A system of water holes of 0.15 meter [6 inches] broad, 0.40 meter [16 inches] deep, and 2.70 meters [8 feet, 10 inches] long, with 0.90 meter [3 feet] between the holes, dug between alternate rows of tea bushes planted in rows of 1.20 meter [approximately 4 feet] apart, totals 1150 holes per hectare [1 hectare equals 2.471 acres], and 0.162 meter per hole. The capacity of all the holes per hectare is 186 cubic meters, which corresponds to the amount of rainfall that a shower of only nineteen millimeters deposits on the soil. Dividing this in half gives an average retention that would care for a rainfall of less than ten millimeters, which is a comparatively insignificant amount. The retention is important, however, for counteracting wash.[2]

As has been previously mentioned, it is not considered advisable to allow the soil to absorb too much water where there is a hard, impervious layer under the top

2 A. R. W. Kerkhoven, "Wash in Tea Gardens," *Handelingen van het Theecongres*, Weltevreden, 1924.

A SUMATRA TEA NURSERY

soil. In such cases catch pits have been found unsuitable. The catch pits are not made longer than, say, ten feet, since the plant-rows do not always run horizontally, and a pit that is not horizontal overflows at its lower edge, causing wash at the point of overflow.

Terracing

In the Netherlands Indies, popular opinion is fairly divided as to terracing. Much depends on the nature of the land and the rainfall; but most of the steeply sloping land is terraced, while more gradual slopes are protected by contour drains; by hedges of suitable plants; and/or by catch pits. Sometimes, both terraces and catch pits are made, but this causes the ground to absorb much more than its normal allowance of water. It is found advisable, therefore, to ascertain whether this large amount of water will be of benefit to the land in question, and whether it will not lead to lack of air in the ground.

If the ground slopes gently, and the rains are not heavy, then catch pits alone, or in combination with hedges of, say, Leguminosæ are found sufficient. If the ground is porous, and can absorb much rain, a favored system is to alternate a row of tea with long catch pits and another row with a hedge of Leguminosæ. In the narrow space at present allowed between the rows of tea plants, there is hardly room for both terraces and catch pits. A spacing of four feet or less allows the use of either terraces alone, or of pits alone. Some planters make covered terraces on steep slopes without catch pits, while on more level land they make pits without terraces. Where stones occur, they are used for facing terraces, and different plants are employed to protect the edges. On fairly broad terraces, pits are often dug at intervals along their inner edges to catch the wash when it comes from above; and when, at intervals, the pits are cleaned out, the soil that has collected in them is thrown onto the terrace above.

Propagation from Seed

In Java and Sumatra, the first work, when opening a tea estate, is to plant large nurseries of tea plants; so that after two years the young plants can be transplanted into the cleared and newly laid out gardens. However, in virgin soil and under favorable conditions, some planters prefer to plant the seed directly in the gardens at four feet spacing; the planting rows being five feet apart, and two seeds planted together. This system of planting saves much time. Where nurseries are set out, Dutch planters give them unusual care and attention. They are always made on the best soil and where water can be supplied. Such soil is tilled properly to a depth of two feet, and is cleaned of stones, weeds, and roots of trees and grasses. After this, the area is divided by main foot-paths, two feet wide, into plots twenty to sixty feet in width. On sloping ground, the main paths always follow the slope rectangularly and border the beds, which are horizontal and always follow the contour of the land. Beds are laid out within the plots with paths between, and the dirt from the paths is thrown up onto the beds until they are a foot high. Around the borders of each bed green manures are planted as hedges; Leucæna glauca, or Crotalaria usaramœnis being used for this purpose. The hedges keep the beds firm, and prevent wash, as well as being useful as shade and as ground fertilizers.

Overhead shading for nurseries is practically universal in Netherlands India, and thatch of bracken fern or a cover of alang-alang leaves is used for this purpose. Also, in order to forward germination, tea seed is often put first into germination beds, and these too are shaded with a thatch at a height of thirty inches before being planted in the nursery beds.

Germination beds are made by digging a piece of ground to a depth of six inches.

JAVA TABLE No. 4

Results of Spacing Tea Seed in Nurseries

Spacing of Seedlings Inches	Average Weight per 100 Plants Ounces	Average Height Inches	Average Circumference at Collar Inches
4	43	56	1.14
6	56	50	1.48
9	80	47	1.80
12	98	43	2.03
18	128	40	2.20

This is leveled off and covered over with fine, sifted sand, on top of which the seed is spread. The seeds are pressed half way into the sand with the eye down. They are watered abundantly every second day until the shells burst, and are then planted in the nursery beds before the young roots appear.

The usual practice is to plant seeds in the nursery beds six inches or even eight inches apart if space permits, as the plants stay in the nurseries for one and one-half to two years. Only one-and-one-half to two-year-old plants are transplanted from nurseries into the tea gardens, and this is done after their main stems have been cut to a height of six to nine inches. Table Number Four gives the result of experimental planting at various distances, as conducted at the Proefstation West Java.

With increasing distances apart, the weight and thickness of the plants increase considerably, but height decreases. Experience indicates that the best results are to be had by spacing:

    6 months old plants, 5 inches apart;
    12 months old plants, 8 inches apart;
    24 months old plants, 10 inches apart.

Triangular planting is used in seeding the nursery beds, as this style accommodates 14 per cent more plants in the same area than rectangular planting.

In an acre of nursery, good germinating results are obtained from nearly five maunds of seed planted eight inches by eight inches, triangularly. A maund of eighty pounds contains 15,000 to 22,000 tea seeds. Before the young plants appear above ground, the beds are lightly shaded by thatch five feet or more above the ground, which covers the entire nursery. This shading is commonly practiced on all estates below an elevation of 4000

feet. A common custom, also, is to cover the beds with cut grass after the young tea plants are six inches high, while shade is provided along the borders of the beds by green manure hedges; in this case, the beds are made not to exceed three feet wide.

Vegetative Propagation

Vegetative propagation, such as layering, cutting, and grafting, is not practiced in the ordinary course of commercial tea-growing in Java with the exception of tea seed gardens. The Experimental Station at Buitenzorg has published a report of the results obtained by various methods of vegetative propagation of the tea plant; this includes crown grafting, rectangular patch budding, upright stem layering, inarching, layering, and cutting. It also describes a number of methods which proved unsuccessful when applied to tea; these include veneer-grafting, shield-grafting, cleft-grafting, shield-budding, budding by veneering, splice-grafting, and crown-grafting by triangular inlaying.[3]

Planting and Planting Distances

Planting is done at the beginning of the wet season in November and December, when the regular monsoon rains have begun. It has been explained how the plant rows are laid out to follow the contour of the slopes. In the rows, the spacing of the plants is marked off by bamboo sticks, or *adjirs*, three feet high. As soon as these markers have been set, a gang of coolies under a *mandoer*, or foreman, begin digging the plant holes at the points marked by the *adjirs*. Plant holes are dug one and one-half to two feet deep, and this is done one or two months before planting, in order to give the soil time to aërate properly.

Plants a year and one-half to two years old are stumped to a height of six to nine inches above the ground, and the remaining main stem is cleaned of its branches. The stumps are then dug up for transplanting. The tap-root and the thick lateral roots are pruned, but not more than is necessary; and then the roots of these

[3] A. A. M. N. Keuchenius, "Vegetative Propagation of Tea," *Mededeelingen van het Proefstation voor Thee*, No. lxxxv, Batavia, 1923.

plants, having been freed from dirt, are examined. Thin stumps or stumps with short or crooked taproots are thrown away, as no strong tea bushes can be obtained from them. Immediately after uprooting, the stumps are packed in the leafy branches cut off from the main stem and placed in large bamboo baskets for transportation to the tea gardens.

Transplanting young plants six months old with a ball of earth, as commonly practiced in India, is hardly ever done in Java and Sumatra, because the earth is too sandy to hold together; but Sumatra planters sometimes employ the method known as *konkoak* planting, whereby young plants with a few leaves and a root about four to six inches long are planted in the gardens, two in a hole.

As previously stated, some planters prefer to plant the seed directly in the gardens and not in nurseries. At the proper distance, two or more seeds are planted together; and, when the plants have developed, the strongest are left.

The usual spacing for planting tea in Java, nowadays, is three or four feet apart in the rows, with the rows four or five feet apart; the distance varying somewhat, according to soil, climate conditions, steepness of the garden, etc. With the planting of green manures between the tea rows, spacing of five feet has been found desirable.

The great care taken in connection with tea garden operations in Java and Sumatra is notably illustrated by the use of leguminous and other trees and plants for various purposes, including green manuring, shading, windbreaks, and the protection of terraces, drains, and sloping ground against wash.

Green Manuring

As soon as the gardens are laid out and the plant holes dug, green manures—shade trees, hedges, and creepers—may be planted between the tea-rows, so that, in many instances, even before the tea is planted, the green manures are growing in the gardens.

Green manuring, as practiced in Java and Sumatra, consists in growing, pruning, and turning leguminous plants into the ground. It has been found cheaper than artificial or chemical manuring; requires less labor for a given result; is

better and more permanent in its effects, on account of its enormous supply of nitrogen and humus. Many tea estates in Java have been able to double the amount of their tea crops by cultivating green manures between the rows.

Most leguminous plants, including trees, shrubs, and creepers, have the faculty of fostering certain bacteria in a peculiar root nodule, and of absorbing free nitrogen from the surrounding atmosphere. Nitrogen fixation is known to take place through the intermediary of the nodule, which becomes richer in nitrogen than the rest of the root, and its final product is a soluble protein that is passed on to the plant.

When the leaves of a leguminous plant are fallen, or are dug into the ground, the nitrogen is speedily changed into plant food, and as soon as decay takes place, the mineral compounds—such as potassium salts, phosphates, and calcium carbonate, which the leguminous plant took from the soil—are given back to the earth in a form more available for the tea plant.

Green manuring improves the soil in organic matter, and when decaying, under favorable conditions, changes partly into humus. Cellulose forms the chief constituent of the plant residues added to the soil, and its decomposition accounts for the chief part of the humus found.

Shade and Windbreaks

The use of leguminous shade trees in tea gardens of Java and Sumatra supplies them with nitrogen and organic matter, and in addition the following benefits are claimed:

(1) The deep roots make the soil porous and friable.
(2) The shade keeps the ground cool, and damp.
(3) They break the force of a heavy rainfall, and prevent the soil from becoming compact.
(4) They bring about a healthy growth of tea, and increase the crop.

The following are the principal legumes used among tea as shade trees and windbreaks: *Albizzia stipulata, A. montana, A. moluccana,* and different species of *Acacias,* all quick-growing trees; *Derris microphylla,* a slower-growing tree, but producing stronger wood; *Erythrina lithosperma,* or dadap; and *Leucæna glauca.*

The common distance for planting these

HEDGES OF *Tephrosia candida*, A PERENNIAL GREEN MANURE, AND CATCH PITS FOR RAINWATER BE-
TWEEN ALTERNATE ROWS OF YOUNG TEA BUSHES, ON AN ESTATE IN SUMATRA

trees is eighteen or twenty-four feet apart, and as soon as they have reached a height of twenty feet, their mainstems are cut at a height of twelve feet. The trees then have an umbrella shape that produces the light shade required by the tea bush.

Leguminous trees are often planted along the garden roads on tea estates that suffer from strong winds. As is well known, wind is harmful to the tea bush, and no crop will be obtained during a windy period. Some gardens suffer so much from strong winds that, after a day or two, no leaves are left on the tea bushes. On such estates, the gardens not only have to be protected by windbreaks along the garden roads, but also by leguminous shade trees and hedges along the tea-rows. Estates that suffer from night frosts during the dry season, plant leguminous shade trees to protect the tea bush therefrom. *Acacia decurrens* is regarded as the best for this purpose. Often, shading is not enough protection against frost, but digging drains ten or fifteen feet deep at regular distances in the gardens has been found very useful.

Hedges

As a preventive of soil wash in the gardens, perennial green manures are planted between the tea-rows. When the garden is laid out, green manure seed is sown in a drill along the alternate tea-rows to form hedges. These hedges are lopped at intervals, so as to avoid hindrance to the tea bush. The loppings form a valuable mulch, irrespective of its richness in nitrogen and the store of humus added to the ground. The following are used: *Crotolaria usaramœnsis; C. anagyroides; Tephrosia candida; T. noctiflora; Leucœna glauca;* and *Clitoria cajanifolia.*

On account of the irregularity in the alignment of tea-rows, due to planting on contour lines, the control of plucking would be difficult without an easily distinguished means of marking off the unit areas. The usual method for doing this, is to divide the garden into paddocks of one-twentieth of a *bouw* [1 *bouw*=1.75 acres] by growing plants at regular intervals on the boundaries of these paddocks. *Dracœnas* are used for this purpose, since they do not interfere with the tea, and, because of their height and bright color, are easily seen. *Leucœna glauca* and several of the *Albizzias* are also used.

Ground Covers

Of late years, leguminous ground covers have been planted more and more. Their purpose is to keep the soil cool, and to prevent its being washed by heavy tropical rains. Those most used are: *Tephrosia candida, Crotolaria usaramœnsis, C. anagyroides, Indigofera endecaphylla, Calopogonium mucunoides, Vigna oligosperma,* and *Leucœna glauca.* The favorite is *Indigo endecaphylla,* which does not climb the tea bushes. In old tea gardens, where the tea is a compact growth, leguminous hedges become harmful, and it is considered better to dig them out and plant leguminous ground covers instead.

In old and already "closed gardens," the planting of ground covers is not so successful as in young gardens. It is, therefore, held advisable to plant ground covers as soon as the tea is planted. The cover plant thus has a better chance to form long trailers, and to cover the ground rapidly. When the ground has to be hoed the trailers are rolled up, and after the hoeing they are again spread over the ground.

Fertilizers

The application of artificial manure is not practiced in Java and Sumatra to the extent that it is in Japan, Ceylon, and India. This is due to Dutch foresight in terracing, protecting the gardens against wash, and the liberal use of green manures, rather than to any lack of appreciation of the value of quick working manures. For perennial cultures such as tea, where there is much rainfall, the Dutch planter prefers slowly working manures, such as oil cake, bone meal, basic slag, and wood ash. In recent years, however, sulphate of ammonia, a quickly soluble manure, has been used with success, and is generally combined with phosphate [ammophos]. Oil cake and bone meal are decayed slowly by the soil bacteria, and are not easily washed away by the rains; therefore, these manures remain for a longer period in the ground, and are preferred for their more continuous effect on the tea between prunings. In many cases, artificial manures are applied for the immediate benefit of the green manuring plants, but they come back into the soil afterwards in form more available for the tea plant, and with less liability to loss of fertilizer by wash.

Manuring usually is done shortly after pruning, as the control of the coolies, and the manuring itself, are carried out better and more easily in pruned, rather than in unpruned, gardens. The quantity of manure used is calculated on the basis of being sufficient to benefit the plant at least until the next pruning; i.e., from one to two years. The effect of dissolvable manures, such as nitrate of soda, etc., is ordinarily worked off in eight or ten months, and during a very rainy season even sooner, by leaching and wash. A suitable allowance of manure per acre is considered to be: 650 pounds of oil cake; 160 pounds of bone meal; 160 pounds of sulphate of potash, or 300 pounds of wood ash.

This supplies the three chief constituents, nitrogen, phosphoric acid, and potash—the first two in a slow-acting form. Sometimes, lime also is supplied, the quantity depending on the results of soil analyses and the acidity of the soil. When manuring with lime, the practice is to apply it a month before other manures.

It has been found that artificial manures are more economical when combined with green manures; so the latter are cultivated wherever the best results are sought. If the growth of the green manures is too slow, this is remedied by applying wood ash, lime, or quick-acting non-organic manures of potash, or phosphoric acid salts.

Nitrates, such as nitrate of soda, produce a good flush at the start; but in Java the fear that such a soluble manure may be quickly leached away is an argument against a too liberal use of it, except in small applications frequently applied.

Manuring, when properly done, returns to the soil the nutriments taken away by the yearly crop. It is not to be inferred, however, that an annual dose of a given manure will accomplish this, because the quantities of manure necessary can be definitely established only by soil analyses and manuring experiments in the gardens themselves.

Tea Pests and Blights in Java

Among all the pests in Java, the *Helopeltis*, or so-called "mosquito bug," is the most serious enemy of tea. The term mosquito is a misnomer, however, as this insect is a Capsid, and does not belong to the true mosquito family. It feeds upon the sap contained in the young leaves and in the green stalks of the young shoots of tea, and sucks the sap in the same manner that the mosquito sucks blood. Wherever the proboscis of *Helopeltis* is inserted into the leaf a liquid is introduced, which results in killing the surrounding cells. This causes a small, round patch of dead tissue, the leaf curls and blackens, and new growth is stopped.

In bad *Helopeltis* years, there is an average loss of crop amounting to 10,000,000 kilograms of fresh leaves, and sometimes more. Dr. R. Menzel, former entomologist of the Tea Experimental Station, found a parasite of this bug, a wasp of the Braconid family, *Euphorus helopeltidis*. This wasp deposits its eggs in the young larvæ of *Helopeltis*, which are thenceforth occupied by the parasitic larva. The latter leaves as soon as it has attained the nymphal stage. The host insect dies, whereas the parasitic larva makes its cocoon on the surface or in cracks of the soil, and leaves it in an adult state after sixteen or seventeen days.

The parasite has been found on various estates, but the investigations thus far conducted indicate little probability that *Euphorus* will develop into an effective check on *Helopeltis*, owing to the impossibility of developing a sufficient attacking force, for the reason that one tea mosquito will serve as host to but one parasite larva; the normal increase of the tea mosquito being, therefore, greatly in excess of that of the parasitic wasp.

Other pests are different mites; *viz.*, red spider, orange mite, pink mite, yellow mite, and purple mite. The most dangerous are the orange mite [*Brevipalpus obovatus*], which attacks gardens above 4000 feet elevations, and the purple mite [*Eriophges carinatus*], attacking gardens below 2000 feet. When a mite attack is severe, the leaves, in course of time, become reddish-yellow or black, and eventually fall off the bush. This happens mostly during drought. In the rainy season, the mites are washed off the leaf surface, and the bushes are soon flushing again.

To combat successfully all tea plant pests, it has been found necessary to keep the affected plants in good condition by manuring—especially by green manuring, and by light plucking and pruning.

Red rust [*Cephaleuros virescens*], an alga, attacks bushes weakened by *Helopeltis*, heavy pruning, or similar causes. It attacks healthy plants as thin patches on the leaves, but quickly invades weak tissues, causing the leaves to fall, and stems to crack and die.

More or less severe tea blights are the different root, branch, and leaf diseases caused by fungi which grow on all kinds of decomposing vegetable refuse, such as decaying stumps, etc., and pass from thence to the tea roots. Plants thus attacked die off and spread the disease to the neighboring bushes. There are three dangerous root fungi; *viz.*, the two species of *Rosellinia* and the red root fungus, the former being more dangerous in the high, the latter in the lower elevations.

Java also has many species of the myriad pests and blights of the lesser sort. The prevalence of the great variety of these pests and blights found on the bushes is possibly due to a practice of pruning less frequently and plucking more lightly than in India. On high gardens, lichens, moss, and insect scale attack the plant stems about the same in both countries.

Where the cultivation and general treatment of the tea gardens are good, it is noticeable that the onslaughts of pests and blights are less severe than on gardens that are neglected. Spraying and other direct methods of combatting disease are found too costly; the land everywhere being sloping and the bushes too high for this sort of thing. The best the planter can do is to be careful in selecting the strongest stocks, so that they may resist the pests, and to grow them in well drained soil using green crops. Where bushes are attacked, they are often left unplucked until they have had time to recuperate and offer resistance to attack.

The Tea Experimental Station at Buitenzorg, has treated the subject of pests and blights exhaustively in monographs, which may be read most profitably by those engaged in the scientific study of tea.

In order to ascertain whether or not dusting by aëroplanes is practicable as a means of contesting tea plant pests and diseases, a trial was made on June 16, 1928, on the Malabar Tea Estate. The experimental ground was about two hectares in extent. It was dusted within a few minutes, in four flights, with sixty kilograms of sulphur deturatum. The dusting installation worked very well, and a good and regular cloud of the dust was disseminated. At the conclusion of the experiment, the bushes were found to be covered with a thin coating of sulphuric powder. It was proved that the application of remedies for pests and blights by this modern method is quite practicable for tea culture, but only in open ground which is not too hilly, such as the Pengalengan Plateau, or in Deli, with its large sheets of tea.

Pests and Blights in Sumatra

Tea shows a vigorous growth on the East Coast of Sumatra, and few pests and blights have been seen thus far. Only fungus diseases of the roots have made their appearance extensively, and these in but a few districts, where local conditions favor the growth of fungi. In a monograph devoted to the subject of diseases and pests of tea in Sumatra, Dr. Bernard warns that it is essential to clear the land thoroughly, with particular attention to the removal of all tree-trunks, stumps, branches, and roots; this being the surest way to guard against root infection. He points out that it matters little to determine the exact species, when it is only necessary for the planter to know that numerous fungi may develop on the decomposing underground portions of the tree, from which they pass to the roots of living plants. The best method is to dig the ground over to a depth of nineteen to twenty-three inches, removing all remains of wood, and to isolate by deep ditches stumps that cannot be removed.

The principal leaf and branch parasites are brown blight [*Colletotrichum camelliae*], red rust [*Cephaleuros virescens*], and gray blight [*Pestalozzia theae*], which are found mainly on the old leaves; the younger growths being touched only on plants already weakened by other disease —a rare condition on the East Coast of Sumatra.

Little damage is reported from insect pests. *Adrama* larvæ were found on half-opened tea seed imported from Java, so it has been recommended that all such seed be sorted in rooms protected by mosquito netting, and that all infected seeds be effectually destroyed.

The *Helopeltis sumatrana* has been found on the "gambir" plant [*Uncaria gambier*], and seems to have a special predilection therefor; but experiment discloses that it may attack tea also. *Helopeltis* of another species was found on "djamboe" [*Eugenia jambolana*]; but so far has not assailed the tea plant. A species of *Pachypeltis*, which does the same sort of damage as *Helopeltis*, also is reported. The effects of *Helopeltis* attack are serious only to weakened bushes. A *Helopeltis* attack is capable of stopping a weakened bush from flushing, but a healthy bush will flush through an attack

A PRUNED TEA FIELD IN SUMATRA

with practically no loss. For this reason, it appears unlikely that *Helopeltis* will affect the plantations of Sumatra's East Coast, where the plants show great vigor.

Dr. Bernard found some traces of *Brevipalpus obvatus*, the mite which damages plantations in Java above 4000 feet elevation. The plantations of the Sumatra East Coast are not as high as this, so it is unlikely that this pest will propagate.[4] The purple mite, however, is very common in Sumatra.

There have been slight attacks of red spider, and some species of caterpillars and nettle grubs have attacked the bushes. On tea bushes growing under *Grevilleas* and *Sesbania*, certain species of *Lawana* have been found, and on the same bushes a *Reduviid* that doubtless preyed upon the *Lawana*. On the whole, however, Sumatra tea planters have been largely immune from severe attacks of pests and blights.

Pruning

Pruning was first practiced in Java on the early experimental tea gardens set out by Jacobus Jacobson, in order to learn in what period of time they were capable of producing pluck. Little was known about tea culture, and this was the only feasible means of finding out how the tea plant would behave.[5]

To-day, pruning is practiced to increase the available crop of young shoots, but not to the extent that this is done in India. Nor does it appear that this is necessary,

[4] Dr. Ch. Bernard, "Diseases and Pests of Tea on the East Coast of Sumatra," *Mededeelingen van het Proefstation voor Thee*, No. liv., Batavia, 1917.

[5] Jacobus Isodorus Lodewijk Levien Jacobson, *Handboek voor de kultuur en fabrikatie van thee*, Batavia, 1843.

for in many districts the soil is so rich and deep that single stem bushes, which never have been cut lower than eighteen inches, have, for many years in succession, borne good crops without necessity for being cut back. Indeed, Dr. Cohen Stuart points out that:

"Pruning does not imply strengthening, but loss of strength; new flush is produced at the cost of reserve food; a hard pruned bush. twice stripped of its young flush, dies from exhaustion. Hence, pruning and plucking should be effected with great care, and compensated by manuring." [6]

The object to be gained, together with its limitation, is stated by the same author as follows:

Pruning means simplifying the ramification of a plant; this necessarily diminishes the number of terminal buds and increases the size and weight of each bud; moreover, it shortens the distance between roots and foliage. It is, however, scarcely possible to obtain exact data on these effects, as in the case of a whole plant the degree of simplification and shortening cannot be determined numerically.

Two methods, or schools, of pruning are practiced in Java, and these may be roughly classified into high and low pruning; depending on the soil, and climate of the particular locality. In such districts as Pengalengan, where the soil has great fertility and the climate is ideal for tea, the planters favor high pruning. Although this system of pruning has been developed satisfactorily in these districts, it has not proven successful elsewhere, and hence the low-pruned areas.

The Malabar Garden, thirty-three miles out of Bandoeng on the Pengalengan Plateau, furnishes an example of phenomenal tea growth. The bushes are high, and the stems straight. High cutting is the rule here, and, speaking generally, it may be defined as the older, or original system of pruning in Java. M. Kelway Bamber, Scientist of the Ceylon Planters' Association, with its Chairman, Mr. A. C. Kingsford, who visited and reported on the tea industries of Java in 1904, had this to say of the older school of pruning:

The first pruning is generally very high and the work frequently indifferent, large heavy knives being employed. The style of bush grown is, in many cases, lanky and rather thin. On these estates, the wood, even on comparatively young bushes, has a gray hide-bound appearance, although when cleaned, the bark is green and healthy. In some cases, too much of the center of the bushes appeared to be cut out, especially as the new shoots are plucked very young; but this is probably done to check the tendency of the bushes to run too high. . . . The period ranges from fourteen months at low elevations to two and one-half years at 5000 feet.[7]

The newer school recognizes, as its first principle, the low pruning of bushes. As a secondary principle, it believes in pruning the centers of the bushes lower than the outsides, and recognizes that this affords a means of correcting frames that are defective from bad pruning originally. And, third, it realizes that the right place to remove a branch is at the junction with another branch. A lively interest in correct principles of cutting, combined with a careful control of their practical operation, is a noticeable feature of the newer school of pruning, and its work is on a par with the best in any of the tea countries.

Pruning is not confined to a matter of weeks or days, but is done bit by bit at any time throughout the year, preferably during the drier season to lessen the bleeding of cut branches. At almost any time of the year, some parts of the Java and Sumatra tea estates are in the process of being pruned. The general procedure is as follows:

PRUNING YOUNG PLANTS.—The plants may have been put into the ground:

(a) as seed at stake, or as seedlings not pruned when planted out from nurseries. The first cut, in this case, takes place usually when the young plant is two years old from seed, and is made at a height of from six inches to a foot from the ground. The second cut is at a height of from a foot to twenty inches. The object of leaving so much growth between the first and second cuts is to allow for a series of heavy prunings, before it is necessary to prune the first cut.

(b) as stumps or as seedlings, pruned at the time of planting out from nurseries. In this case, the usual method is to cut the seedlings at about nine inches above the ground. The next cut above this is at twelve to eighteen inches. The bush which results from this treatment is, as can be imagined, a single stem bush.

6 Dr. C. P. Cohen Stuart, "Proeven over den theesnoei," Mededeelingen van het Proefstation voor Thee, No. lxxix, Batavia, 1922.

7 M. Kelway Bamber and A. C. Kingsford, Report on the Tea Industries of Java, Formosa, and Japan, Colombo, 1907.

PRUNING MATURE BUSHES, light or heavy.—The frequency of pruning depends on the situation and elevation of the estate. Light pruning takes place at much longer intervals of time than is the case in Northeast India. One and one-half to three years is the usual interval. Heavy pruning is done about once in every five or seven prunings, and, with the fertile soil and hot climate, the growth during that time produces some very thick wood.[8]

For gardens weakened by attacks of *Helopeltis* and red rust, the Experimental Station at Buitenzorg recommends a high pruning—two to two and one-half feet—with removal of all small, dead, or sick lateral branches and twigs that may be infected by cryptogamic parasites. This method has given excellent results.

Tests made by Drs. Bernard and Deuss, of the Tea Experimental Station, to determine the best substances for covering pruning cuts with a thick, hard, and permanent protective coat, revealed:

(1) that ordinary coal tar, washed to remove the phenolic acids, is the most satisfactory of the substances tried.
(2) that its use should be confined to wood older than one year.
(3) that tarring should be done after the interval of a day after pruning.

In recent years, cement and asphalt have also been used for the larger pruning cuts.

Swedish tar was found injurious, as it burned the tissues of the branches; while the other substances tested soaked in quickly, or dripped away.

Plucking the Tea Leaf

In Java, the climate is such that the flush is plucked every eight to fourteen days throughout the year by women and children, working in gangs under a foreman, or *mandoer*.

The only breaks in the continuity of flushing are those occasioned when blocks have been pruned. An interval of sixty to ninety days is then allowed before the bushes are again gone over.

Plucking is designated "fine," when the bud at the tip of the young shoot and the two young leaves just below it are

A SUMATRA TEA PLUCKER WITH SLENDANG

plucked; "medium," when the bud and two or three leaves below are plucked; and "coarse," when the bud and three leaves below are taken. The general method of plucking in Java is what is termed "long," so that after each plucking a whole leaf is left before the next shoot is taken. The result is that the bush gets higher and higher, and just before it is pruned it may be eight or ten feet in height, in which event the pluckers have to pull down the long slender branches in order to reach the shoot.

This method of plucking has a bad influence on the growth of the shrub. It has been found better to pluck deeper at the center, than at the outside, so that the growth of "plume" will be avoided. This has the further advantage that all branches, twigs, and leaves will obtain an equal and regular supply of the circulating sap for its maintenance and development. It has been found highly important that prudence be exercised in plucking young plants in the first two to three months after pruning. The young shoots are plucked sparingly, and little crop is taken. Only as the bushes become stronger is any coarse plucking done, and that in the center of the bush.

Time studies made in a tea garden in Java shortly after the World War led to the invention of the Sperata plucking knife, which has for its object the elimination of stalks when the leaves are gathered, in order to do away with sorting for the removal of stalks after manufacture.

This knife, the invention of Mr. Carl Heinz Tillmanns, overseer of the Sperata Tea Estate, near Bandoeng, is strapped about the waist of the plucker, who gath-

---

[8] Dr. G. D. Hope, *Report on Certain Aspects of the Tea Industry of Java and Sumatra*, Indian Tea Association, Calcutta, 1916.

THE SPERATA PLUCKING KNIFE IN OPERATION

Designed to produce stalkless tea, this invention reduced labor at the sorting tables by 50 per cent.

ers the tea leaves in the usual way, but keeps the stems all pointing in one direction. When a handful has been gathered, the stems and coarse leaves are cut by pressing them into a sharp V-shaped cutter, whence they fall into a small sack attached below, while the fine leaves are thrust into the usual *slendang*, or duck bag, slung over the plucker's shoulder. The claims made for the invention that a superior product of higher value is obtained are yet to be proved. Many planters were enthusiastic at first, especially when prices were high and plucking heavy. The opinion now appears to be that, on estates at low altitudes, the stalks are so long that the cuttings constitute a high proportion; while the stalkless bulk is hardly better than before. In high gardens, where there is less coarse leaf, the knife has been more successful; however, the best practice no longer favors it.

Twice a day the coolies take their leaf to the factory, usually a large, well-equipped building, containing the most modern machinery, and operated by water, electricity, oil, or steam power. The leaf is examined and weighed, and the amount plucked by each coolie recorded; the wages depending in part upon the quantity. The payment for half a kilogram of plucked leaves varies from 0.8 to 1½ Dutch cents. One woman can pluck daily from thirty to sixty half-kilos.

Field Transport

The leaves are collected and brought to the factory at noon in a piece of cotton cloth—not usually in baskets, as in British India, and Ceylon. Ordinarily, the leaves are carried to the factory by the coolie women who pluck them, as the most economical means of transport from hillside slopes; but the field transport on such localities as the wide Pengalengan Plateau is shared by the coolie women, narrow-gauge tramways, carts drawn by horses or oxen, and the ubiquitous American motor truck, as conditions permit. On other estates, like Taloen, forty-two miles southeast of Bandoeng, aerial ropeways are used to advantage.

Ropeways, or wire-shoots as they are sometimes called, are being used more extensively each year. There are two types, one having a stationary, wire-rope cable with a suitable slope, on which a bag or basket of tea-leaf is suspended, and runs by gravity on a two-wheeled carrier; and the other, having a moving cable to which the carriers are attached.

Generally speaking, the character of field transport possible to use is governed sharply by local topographical conditions. On terraced, hillside slopes it would be manifestly out of the question to use wheeled conveyances, and here the coolie carrier is supreme, with a possible alternative of installing the more expensively maintained ropeway system of carrying. On broadly rolling plateau lands, or wherever the gradients permit the construction of suitable roadways, carts,

CLEANLINESS FIRST

Before entering any Dutch tea factory, the coolies must walk through a pool of running water.

PLUCKING TEA ON MARTOBA, ONE OF THE TRUST ESTATES ON SUMATRA'S EAST COAST

trams, or motor trucks are employed advantageously in solving the increasingly vexatious labor problem. In order to insure good ventilation, the sides of the carts or trucks are fitted with wire gauze, which keeps the leaf fresh and prevents undue heating. Some estates use trays made of wooden frames with wire gauze bottoms, which are placed one on top of the other in the cart.

On some estates the leaf is carried directly to the withering sheds or lofts; but on others it is first carried to a roomy receiving shed, where it is weighed. The plucking women are generally paid according to the quantity of leaf plucked. If the receiving shed is at ground-level and the withering done in a loft, the leaf has to be carried upstairs. This has many objections, as much of the leaf is spilled—especially when the crops are large. Some factories use a lift, others an endless carrier-belt fitted with wooden laterals or with trays, on to which the leaf is thrown.

Withering

In withering, the Java planter figures the tea leaf should lose approximately 40 per cent of its weight by the evaporation of water without undue damage to the leaf; and in order to make it soft and pliable, so that it can stand rolling without breaking, he figures that the withering should be regular and never forced.

"Natural" withering is considered the ideal way, and this is done in a *chung*, or wooden shed, with several floors, each containing racks with wooden shelves. The racks are placed back to back in pairs, and between these are passages for the coolies who carry the leaf and spread it on the shelves. Every rack consists of a certain number of wooden shelves at a distance of about eight inches above each other. They are either horizontal or have a slight slope toward the passage. The leaf is spread evenly in a thin layer on the shelves, and there it remains for sixteen to eighteen hours. The whole building is placed in such a way that the prevailing wind blows along its longitudinal axis. In the Preanger Regencies it is seldom dry enough to obtain a sufficient wither in a *chung*, and so one is never sure to have sufficiently withered leaf in the morning when the factory starts work. Therefore, *chungs* are seldom if ever, used here. Withering on *tampirs* [flat bamboo wickerwork

WITHERING LOFTS AT PASIR RANDOE, JAVA

PASIR JUNGHUHN, GOVERNMENT TEA FACTORY AT PENGALENGAN, JAVA

trays] has the same objection when fans and hot air are not available. Formerly *tampirs* were used extensively. Their size is about seven square feet, and the leaf is spread very thinly—about half a pound per *tampir*. The *tampirs* are placed one above another in such a way that good ventilation is insured; the *tampirs* of the second row being placed above the free spaces between the *tampirs* of the first row. The *tampirs* are dried as much as possible during the daytime, and they have the advantage of absorbing water, which advantage, however, planks and Hessian cloth also have; but these cannot be carried outside, like the *tampirs*, to be dried in the sun, and drying them, therefore, has to be carried out by using hot, dry air and fans, during the time that there is no leaf.

The more up-to-date withering installations are arranged in one, two, or even three lofts above the factory, or in a separate shed next to the factory. The withering lofts and separate withering sheds are arranged like the *chungs*. The racks are placed back to back in pairs, in a lateral direction with regard to the longitudinal axis of the building. A gangway usually is arranged on each side for the handling of the leaf. In this case, the racks are provided with side-walls and doors, in order to shut them off from the gangways. If the racks have wooden shelves, these are placed at a distance of eight inches, the one above the other; the highest shelf not being higher than about 8 feet 3 inches. The coolies have to use a little step-ladder when spreading the leaf on the highest shelves. Sometimes, every rack has a wooden beam running along its whole length, at an elevation of about

two feet. The coolies can stand on the two opposite beams, and so reach the highest shelves. This method also is used with other systems of withering racks. The coolies are not permitted to stand on the wooden or wire gauze shelves. With wooden shelves they can be placed either horizontally or at a slight slope. With wire gauze shelves, the planes are nearly always inclined; while Hessian cloth is always placed horizontally. When Hessian cloth is used, the ends are provided with wooden rollers, in order that the cloth may be tightened when it sags.

Various contrivances have been invented for unloading the leaf from the shelves when it has been sufficiently withered. With wooden shelves this is done very simply by brushing the leaf off with whisk brooms. If it is not done too roughly, this is a fairly useful method. Wire gauze shelves are slapped with the hands from below, and this makes the leaf "jump off,"

GREEN LEAF ARRIVING BY MONORAIL AT PASIR JUNGHUHN

but some leaves always remain hanging through the meshes, and these sometimes are damaged. Where Hessian cloth is employed, the usual system is to make one end detachable, in order to be able to shake off the leaf; and sometimes a whole rack is suspended on an eccentric axis, so that it can be turned around to allow the leaf to drop out. One simple movement empties a whole rack. Except for the gangways, the withering lofts or sheds are entirely filled with the above-mentioned racks.

Fans are placed at one or both ends of the lofts. They suck the air along the whole length of the structure. In buildings having fans at both ends, it sometimes happens that insufficient attention is given to the air supply, which comes from the factory below the loft. This air is mostly warm and moist as it comes from the driers. In the case of detached withering sheds, the hot air is supplied by a separate air-heater. It is mixed with ordinary outside air. If the mixing room is sufficiently large, regular withering can be obtained; but if the hot and cold air are sucked over the leaf without being thoroughly mixed, the withering is bound to be irregular. The fans sometimes work all night, as long as is necessary to wither; for instance, when the leaf comes in at noon the fans are set to work as soon as the leaf can be spread, and are left on until 6 o'clock in the morning. However, this is not always possible, as water power is not always available and running the fans by means of steam engines or oil motors would be too expensive in most cases. In such event, the fans are run until 11 o'clock or midnight, and then are stopped.

The Malabar Estate uses the withering machine invented by the late Mr. K. A. R. Bosscha as an aid to fermenting. After the leaf has been normally withered, it is placed in large octagonal drums fitted with wire gauze sides. The drums revolve around a horizontal axis, and hot air is blown into them through the leaf. At the end of a few minutes, the leaf is taken out and cooled, rolled, and fermented in the usual way. These machines are used on the Pengalengan Plateau, where the temperature is much lower than on the plains. The benefit claimed for their use is that they reduce the time required for fermenting by two or three hours. A light fermentation is begun in the drums, and, for this reason, Dr. J. J. B. Deuss, former head of the Proefstation, said it would be better to call these machines pre-fermenting drums. The leaf comes out of them looking fresh, having lost little moisture, but has a brownish color and a pleasant, strong smell, like that of fresh apples.

Leaf that has been well withered, and therefore does not "crack" when pressed together by the hand, has lost about 30–50 per cent of its water, and is ready to be rolled.

Rolling

Rolling, formerly done by hand, is now done by machines. These machines consist of a square or cylindrical receptacle, or "jacket," into which the leaf is thrown. This receptacle has a circular movement above the table, which affects the rolling

FERMENTING ROOM WITH MONORAIL LEAF TRAYS

of the leaf. In the "single-action" rollers the movement is confined to the receptacle, or else the latter is stationary, while the table moves. In the "double-action" rollers, both table and receptacle move in opposite directions. The "double-action" rollers are being used almost exclusively, as the result is better. Receptacle and table are nearly always brass-lined. Aluminum-lined rollers were found to be unsatisfactory, while granite-faced tables that were used at one time are now entirely obsolete.

The center of the table is fitted with brass battens in order to assist the rolling process, and with a trap-door, which allows the rolled leaf to drop out when it is desired to empty the roller. The top of the receptacle is formed by a movable cap, which can be made to slide down by turning a screw arrangement, and in this way a certain pressure can be exerted which is necessary in attaining a thorough mixing of the juices. In the case of coarse

leaf, this is quite necessary. The pressure can be regulated, and, occasionally, the cap is raised entirely in order to cool the leaf. Some rollers lack this pressure cap, and are called "open-top rollers." In these, the necessary pressure for the leaf is obtained by its own weight.

There are openings in the floors of the withering lofts into spouts, or tubes, running down to the rolling machines, through which the machines can be filled with leaf. About 330 to 440 lbs. of withered leaf are rolled at one time by each machine.

Usually the rolling is done in three stages, but sometimes in two. The fine leaf is sifted out after each rolling, and only the coarse leaf is re-rolled; for example, after filling, the leaf is rolled fifteen minutes without using pressure; then the cap is screwed down until it just touches the leaf, and the rolling is continued for five minutes, after which the pressure is taken off and the cycle repeated. After sifting, coarse leaf is rolled again, with increased pressure. The rolled leaf is dropped from the roller into a shallow, flat-bottomed trolley, which is placed under the roller, and in this the leaf is transported to the roll-breaker, which consists of a revolving, drum-shaped sieve or a flat, shaking sieve. The finest leaf is spread out for fermentation, and the rest is re-rolled.

Fermenting

The sieves do not always properly break up the "balls" of rolled leaf, and the process has often to be assisted by coolies. It is considered important that the mesh of the sieves be of the right size, otherwise too much coarse leaf is mixed with

THE CONCRETE TEA FACTORY AT PANGLEDJAR IN THE PREANGER, JAVA

A BATTERY OF TWENTY ROLLERS AT TIGA BLATA, SUMATRA'S EAST COAST

the fine leaf, thus preventing regular fermentation.

After all the leaf has been sufficiently rolled and sifted, it is fermented. During fermentation the color changes to brown, and the flavor of the tea begins to develop. Fermentation really begins during the rolling process, and sometimes, as mentioned before, during withering in the drums.

The rolled leaf is spread out to a thickness of about two inches in shallow trays consisting of a wooden frame with a bottom of bamboo wickerwork. These trays are put in rows one on top of the other, and after from one and one-half to four and one-half hours the tea is fermented.

In many of the modern factories of Java and Sumatra, the fermenting is done on a porcelain-tile floor which affords a very clean place for working; but in this case, the tea is spread in a very thin layer, as otherwise the air cannot reach the leaf sufficiently for thorough fermentation.

In order to keep the leaf sufficiently moist, wet cloths are spread over the fermenting trays. Generally, the fermenting is done in a separate room, which is a very good system, because it is easier to regulate everything properly.

Various means are employed to secure the necessary humidity in fermenting rooms, but the practice now is to install the type of compressed air humidifiers familiar in textile plants, which will saturate the air up to 100 per cent or any degree desired—usually 95 per cent—and preserve this humidity indefinitely.

The fermentation is controlled by thermometers inserted into the leaf mass. The maximum temperature occurs about the time at which the fermentation ends. When fermentation is regular, the temperature rises evenly, for the fermentation produces the heat.

Drying

After the leaf has been fermented sufficiently, it is dried at a temperature of about 90–100° C., equal to about 194° to

THE FERMENTING ROOM AT TIGA BLATA

THE IMPRESSIVE TIGA BLATA FACTORY, PERMANANGAN ESTATE, SUMATRA'S EAST COAST

212° Fahrenheit. This is done in special drying machines by means of hot air. The air is heated in an air-heater, or stove, which is fired with wood-fuel, but sometimes with crude oil. On the Malabar Estate, all of the driers are electrically heated.

Heating with crude oil is very clean, and greatly to be preferred to heating with wood. Moreover, it is easily regulated. A big drier can be heated to 212° F. in seventeen minutes, whereas it takes three quarters of an hour with firewood. At Nagahoeta Estate, about eight and one-half gallons of crude oil were used per hour, and the expense was about double that of firewood. But the expense can be reduced to the same level as firewood by transporting the oil in bulk and storing it in tanks.

The hot air is drawn across the tea leaf, which is spread on trays. This is done in different ways. In the so-called "Down-draft" Sirocco tea driers, the hot air is

sucked from the air heater to a space at the top of the drying chamber in which the leaf is spread. The air passes along the trays loaded with leaf, and is drawn off from below.

In this system, the wet leaf is in direct contact with the hot dry air; while in the "Up-draft" Sirocco's, the air enters at the bottom of the drying chamber, and rises to the top. Here the hot air comes in direct contact with the nearly-dried tea; but in case of careless working, there is some danger of burning.

In the older systems of driers, many of which are still in use, the trays consist of large, square, perforated metal plates, which are taken from the bottom of the drying-chamber by two coolies, and re-inserted at the top in order to expose the whole bulk of the leaf to the drying air. These machines have only a small capacity, but are easily controlled.

In the newer systems, the trays are continuous, and the leaf, which is mechanically spread on the upper layer of trays, drops down on the next layer, and comes out at the bottom partly or entirely dried, according to the system used—drying in one or two stages. The speed at which the trays move is regulated in such a way that the leaf comes out dried in any stage desired.

The large machines have a capacity of as much as 1400 pounds of wet leaf per hour, turning out about 500 pounds of dried tea. The drying chambers are provided with side doors, which allow easy cleaning or repairing. These are fitted with thermometers, and when the latter are not reliable, they are replaced by self-registering temperature recorders. The leaf is spread

TEA DRYING MACHINES AT BALIMBINGAN, SUMATRA'S EAST COAST

BOSSCHA ELECTRICALLY HEATED TEA DRIER

very thinly, in order to get regular drying and to prevent over-firing.

In order to cool the dried tea quickly, it is spread on *tampirs* or placed in chests with perforated ventilating tubes, which act as chimneys to carry away the hot air.

Drying tea by means of electricity has been tried and found good, as well as cheaper and more convenient. This was the conclusion reached by the late Mr. K. A. R. Bosscha, who equipped the great tea plantation, Malabar, for withering and drying tea by electricity.

Sorting

In Java, the dried, or rough tea, called "factory tea," is sorted in drum-shaped revolving sieves or, sometimes, by more complicated sorting machines with shaking sieves. Automatic sorting machines are used in practically all factories in Java and Sumatra. They consist of a tea cutter, and a series of sieves of various

SORTING TEA ON A BELT CONVEYOR, SUMATRA

mesh, operating with an oscillating motion.

Generally, the tea is re-sorted by women, who also remove the stalks, fiber, etc. This hand-sorting is very carefully done.

There are nine different market grades: Broken Orange Pekoe, Broken Pekoe, Broken Tea, Flowery Orange Pekoe, Orange Pekoe, Pekoe, Pekoe Souchong, Souchong, Dust, and the tea refuse known locally as "Bohea," which consists of the stalks and is sold usually to the native population. The sorting is regulated according to the market, and not every factory makes the same grades. The finished tea is stored in zinc or lead-lined bins, until it can be packed.

Packing

Packing is done in wooden, lead, or aluminum-lined chests, which hold about

GRADING ROOM AT KASSOMALANG, JAVA

100 pounds of tea. These chests formerly were made in the tea factory, but nowadays various "patent" chests are used. In some instances, where lead is used, it is required that the chests be provided with inner paper linings.

The filling of the chests is done by packing machines which shake the tea down by a vibratory motion. The tea is put into the machine by means of a large feed-hopper. Tea-presses also are used, in order to get more tea into a chest. Formerly, the coolies stamped down the tea with their feet.

After the chests have been closed, and the tea-lead carefully soldered, they are transported by motor truck or bullock-cart to the nearest railway station.

Many tea factories make use of water

BALIMBINGAN, THE WORLD'S LARGEST TEA FACTORY, SUMATRA'S EAST COAST
This factory has a capacity of six and a half million pounds of made tea per annum.

power, and electric lighting is used generally. The handling of the tea is done by coolies, but labor-saving transport systems are becoming more general.

Estate Management

JAVA.—The foregoing shows how tea culture, carried on by European capital, has developed in Java; especially in the mountain district of West Java called the Preanger, where, with sufficient cheap labor, good soil, and favorable climate conditions, the business has become one of the chief and most prosperous industries of Insulinde.

By far the largest proportion of tea cultivation on the estates is in the hands of resident European planters. Each estate has a manager with two to six assistants, one factory assistant, and one to five garden assistants, depending upon its size. Whereas, formerly, planters were more or less owners of their estates, to-day they are more likely to be salaried employees of large or small companies; some managed from Batavia, some from Holland.

The export and general business of the estate or company usually is in the hands of a Batavia agency, which also superintends the general conduct of the estate by means of its "visiting agent" or "superintendent," a planter of long experience, who goes over the estates at intervals, inspecting their working, estimates, accounts, etc.

SUMATRA.—The status of the estate companies in Sumatra, with reference to the marketing of their produce and management control, represents a unique development in the tea industry along the lines of modern, large-scale business. The types of estate organization are divided into three main groups, as follows:

First, large-scale companies, like the Handelsvereeniging "Amsterdam," which directly own and operate a number of estates, controlling all details of manufacture and sale by boards of directors in Europe; *Second*, estate companies originally promoted by firms that retain managerial control, and act as agents and secretaries, like the British firm of Harrisons & Crosfield, Ltd., Medan, which controls fifty estates on Sumatra's West Coast; *Third*, the small but independent estate, marketing its product locally or through direction in Europe.

Labor and Wages

The labor force of a tea estate is classified into *vast personeel*, or permanent labor, and *borong*, or contract labor. It consists of natives in West Java, generally Sundanese coolies, male and female, working in gangs under a foreman, or *mandoer*.

Normal *mandoer* wages are 10–15 guilders per month, or about 38 to 57 Dutch cents [15 to 23 cents U.S.; 7½ to 11½ d. Eng.] per day, while *boedjangs*, or coolie laborers, paid by the month, receive 8–9 guilders per month, or 31 to 34 Dutch cents [10 to 16 cents U.S.; 5 to 8 d. Eng.] per day. The financial slump which began in 1929 cut the normal wage scales from 25 to 50 per cent in both Java and Sumatra. The coolies are housed, partly on the estate, partly in their own villages, or *kampongs*, in the neighborhood, and often medically attended at the cost of the estate. On the estates also are schools for

GERMAN-BUILT TEA FACTORY IN SUMATRA

the children. The heavier labor, such as clearing forest, hoeing, and pruning, is done by the men; the lighter, such as tea plucking and weeding, by the women and children. About one hundred thousand persons are employed daily in the tea industry in Java.

In the Preanger Regencies, the teeming native population gradually develops self-confidence and a desire to work on its own account by growing the village [kampong] tea. This has furnished the tea estates an ever-growing problem that has forced them to bring the treatment of labor to a high standard.

The cost of labor is somewhat higher in the Sumatra tea gardens. Coolies are imported from Java, and normally are paid 11.20 guilders monthly, or say 43 Dutch cents [17 cents U.S. or 8½d. Eng.] per day. However, unless the coolies are engaged by legal contract for at least three years, they are not permitted to leave Java.

Native Tea Gardens

Besides the tea culture carried on by European capital, Java, since 1880, has produced many native tea gardens situated for the most part in the Preanger District. These gardens usually are small plots on steep slopes or waste ground, in or bordering on the native villages, and often planted with a mixture of crops such as bananas, tapioca, chili, etc. A few of the richer natives possess tea gardens of from two to thirty acres. The native gardens are often possessory rights, but sometimes belong to a village community. The fresh leaves usually are sold to neighboring estates and there manufactured to-

gether with the daily estate crop; but sometimes the leaves are sold to small Chinese tea factories in the Island. At the close of 1933, the last year for which official figures are available, the native area under tea in Java amounted to 46,208 hectares, or 114,133 acres.

Coolie Lines

Nowhere else in the East is the laborer so well looked after and happy as in Sumatra and Java. Insulinde always has led the other tropical countries in the matter of coolie welfare, and the native kampongs, or villages, on the tea estates of the Islands are no exception to the rule. They are complete with detached or semi-detached basket-houses of palm and bamboo, native bazaars, theatres, schools, and hospitals. In the more modern kampongs the dwellings are regularly built frame cottages, with corrugated iron roofs.

Typical of the care taken in the matter of housing on a modern Netherlands East Indies tea estate are the model coolie lines, or rows of houses, on Bah Biroeng Oeloe, one of the estates of the N. V. Nederlandsch-Indisch Land Syndicaat, near Siantar, on Sumatra's East Coast. Rows of neat cottages behind neatly trimmed hedges and fronting on well-drained streets provide comfortable as well as sanitary living quarters for the imported workers.

The shops, some of the homes, and the streets are well lighted by electricity, and happy children romp off to their own special schools, just as they would if they lived in Europe or America.

Medical care is provided by the estates,

MODEL COOLIE LINES AT BAH BIROENG OELOE, SUMATRA

according to law, and it is not uncommon to find a well-equipped hospital on a large estate. Probably the finest of the coolie hospitals is the one at Siantar, in Sumatra.

Entertainment is never lacking, as the Javan native is adept at providing amusement, and not a few musicians, dancers, and actors from the native *kampongs* have entertained audiences at various international expositions.

The coolies form their own theatrical companies, orchestras, etc., featuring native performances of the *gamelan*, an orchestra of xylophones, gongs, suspended tubes, viol, etc., and representations of the *wayang*, puppet show, and the *topeng dalang*, in which the natives from the estate frequently essay the roles of masked actors, and play in pantomime a drama recited by a *dalan*, or chorus.

Planters' Associations

JAVA.—The Soekaboemi and Rubber Planters' Association is the pioneer organization for the betterment of Java tea.

In the beginning of 1924, the former Soekaboemi Planters' Association amalgamated with the Rubber Planter's Association to look after the welfare of all the different agricultural industries; *i.e.*, rubber, tea, cinchona, coffee, oil palms, fiber plants, kapok, etc., all grown in the western part of Java. The new association became known as the Soekaboemi and Rubber Planters' Association, and has its headquarters at Bandoeng.

The *Algemeen Landbouw Syndicaat*, or General Agricultural Syndicate, with head quarters in Batavia, is the head planters' organization of the Netherlands Indian mountain estates. This body has control of the scientific research work conducted by the experimental stations of the tea, rubber, coffee, and cinchona industries. To this end, the Syndicate is divided into five groups—the Unions of the Tea, Rubber, Coffee, Cocoa, and Cinchona Estates of Netherlands India.

The *Vereeniging voor de Thee Cultuur in Nederlandsch Indie*, or Association for Tea Culture in Netherlands India, with headquarters in Batavia, is an organization of tea estate proprietors resident in the Dutch Indies.

SUMATRA.—The tea industry of Sumatra is given unity of action by an active and highly organized planters' association, which represents the plantations collectively, and serves as their mouth-piece in all matters of interest to the organization's membership. The association is known as the *Algemeene Vereeniging van Rubber Planters ter Oostkust van Sumatra*, or General Association of Rubber Planters of the East Coast of Sumatra, commonly known as the "A.V.R.O.S.," which represents not only all the rubber estates, but all estates engaged in the perennial cultures—rubber, palm oil, fiber, coffee, gambier, tea, etc.—or all cultures of Sumatra other than tobacco. The Association has its headquarters in Medan.

Aside from the administrative functions of the Planters Association in promoting the general interests and welfare of the tea and rubber industries, the Association also maintains an elaborate and highly organized experimental station for conducting

THE EXPERIMENTAL STATION OF THE A.V.R.O.S. AT KAMPONG BAROE, SUMATRA

THE TEA EXPERIMENTAL STATION AT BUITENZORG, JAVA

experimental and research work concerning all kinds of technical matters, scientific methods of cultivation, planting, seed selection, tapping, analyses of soils, preparation in the factories, methods, etc.

Buitenzorg Experimental Station

The *Proefstation West Java*, or West Java Experimental Station, at Buitenzorg, established by the Soekaboemi Planters' Association, and controlled since 1925 by the *Algemeen Landbouw Syndicaat*, undertakes all kinds of scientific investigations and experiments for the benefit of the tea and rubber planters.

Pamphlets concerning all important investigations, have been published since 1907. Besides laboratory work, estates are visited every year, reports are made thereon, and advice is given on planters' problems.

Thousands of analyses of soil from tea gardens have been made and compared with the production of the tea grown in these different soils, so that improvements can be made in enriching the soil and benefitting the crops. In the laboratory the soil is analyzed mechanically and chemically.

The mechanical analysis method is the same as that used by the Bureau of Soils in Washington, and consists in separating the soil into different grades—gravel, coarse sand, fine sand, silt, fine silt, and clay—to determine the extent of the decay of the soil. Atterberg's method is practiced to find the physical state of the soil.

The chemical soil analyses have shown that the important factors in tea growing are humus and nitrogen, besides potash, phosphoric acid, and lime.

Besides the soil analyses, many analyses of different artificial manures used on tea estates are made. Also analyses have been made of China and Assam teas to determine the percentage of caffeine, tannin, and essential oil in these teas necessary for a good quality. Experiments on tea-seed oil and tea-seed fat have been carried out.

The choice of good seed stock is very important and has so far been neglected in most countries where tea is cultivated. During the last fifteen years the Tea Experimental Station has conducted various scientific experiments in tea selection, and has studied the tea plant and its allies in a systematic manner. The aim has been to find and propagate the most productive types; also those which are superior in quality and resistance power to injurious environmental factors such as *Helopeltis*, soil, etc. It is expected that one result of this work will be to reduce the cost price.

The idea is to make graftings from the best parent trees, and to plant these graftings in isolated gardens for seed production. For this purpose extensive experiments in vegetative propagation have been carried through, with satisfactory results.

This selection program will require several decades before it is completely carried out. To meet the immediate requirements for good tea seed, official inspection service of all imported tea seed has been established, and the seed gardens supervised.

Many experiments in manuring, plucking, and pruning have been made; also, attention has been paid to soil erosion and soil deterioration by sunburn through clean weeding and dry wash.

To prevent soil erosion and soil deterioration, the Experimental Station for more than fifteen years has advised planters to plant various legumes as cover crops, horizontal hedges, and shade trees among the tea bushes. Experiments in green manuring have shown increase of tea crop everywhere throughout Java and Sumatra.

The Experimental Station has thoroughly determined the biology of *Helopeltis*, among many other pests and blights, and important results have been obtained wherever the control of the insect and careful improvement of cultural conditions are undertaken methodically and in time. Further, the Experimental Station has been able to test the insecticides on the market, and by the negative results obtained has saved planters much expense and disappointment. Natural enemies—parasites—among tea pests, and their hosts, are under investigation, and very interesting results have been obtained in combatting various caterpillars, etc. A parasite of *Helopeltis* has been discovered and observed.

The various stages of tea manufacture have been extensively studied from a theoretical as well as practical standpoint, and the Experimental Station has been able to give important advice regarding withering, fermenting, etc., by which the work in many factories has been considerably improved. In 1922, a concise guide for tea manufacture was issued, which is greatly appreciated by the planters.

The Tea Expert Bureau

The Tea Expert Bureau, of Batavia, established in 1905, is another important institute contributed to by the tea planters of Java and Sumatra. It employs the services of two tea experts, well posted on conditions in all the chief markets, (1) who are available to planters for testing samples before the tea leaves the gardens, and for pointing out any mistakes in manufacture while there is still an opportunity to correct them; (2) who make cup tests to compare with former products of the garden, and with the production of others; (3) who supply market and price

information; and, finally, (4) who give advice as to future improvement of output.

The work done by the Tea Expert Bureau has contributed heavily to the successful development of the Netherlands Indian tea trade in all of the principal consuming markets.

The fact that the quality of the tea has been notably improved, and extensive new markets successfully developed, is attributable in great part to the constructive criticisms of the tea export. Also, the organization has studied particular phases of the tea trade and directed the propaganda for Java and Sumatra teas in America and Australia. How much the work of the Bureau is appreciated is shown by its growth. In 1910, there were seventy-one members who submitted a total of 6505 samples during the year, while in 1933, there were 150 members who submitted 27,971 samples.

The Bureau has correspondents stationed in Amsterdam, London, Calcutta, and Colombo with whom it is in constant touch by cable or mail. This insures for its members reliable and prompt information on prices and conditions in the principal markets.

A Planter's Life in the N.E.I.

There has ever been a flavor of aristocracy connected with tea planting in the Netherlands Indies. The pioneers of private planting in Java were members of the first families in the Netherlands, and their descendents are well represented in the social and industrial life of the Islands. Men of great ability as industrial organizers and trained specialists in the science of tea cultivation and manufacture were later drawn into the business of tea planting, but the old flavor remains and offers the neophyte a career under auspices that are both pleasing and profitable.

JAVA.—Youthful aspirants for positions as assistants are engaged in Java or are sent out from Europe. Young men with good general knowledge are sought, although some are graduates of agricultural schools. They are given both practical and theoretical training, in the capacity of assistants, to fit those who show ability for ultimate positions as garden managers.

A junior assistant usually is paid from fl. 150 to fl. 200 a month [1 florin = 1s. 7 4/5d. Eng., or 40 2/10 cents U.S.] at the

MANAGER'S BUNGALOW AT MALABAR, JAVA

start. Later, as senior assistant, this may be increased to from fl. 200 to fl. 400 a month. The estate generally supplies unfurnished living quarters, and most of the estates pay the house tax, as well as granting free medical treatment.

Leave of absence for eight months usually is granted after five or six years of service. There is no allowance for transportation, and the arrangement for pay during leave varies. An average arrangement is full pay, with half bonus.

Managers' salaries vary from fl. 500 to a maximum of fl. 1000 a month for a first-class executive.

In addition to salaries paid, there are bonuses for the manager and his assistants based on the net earnings.

The Java tea planter's aim is, usually, to own an estate; to retire on a competence; to become an estate agent; etc. In most cases he retires to Europe on a competency after from fifteen to thirty-five years.

SUMATRA.—Young, prospective planters for Sumatra are usually imported from Europe, but some are drawn from the tea estates of Java. They start as garden or factory assistants, and learn the complete cultivation and working methods on the estate by which they are employed.

Many British assistants are employed on the British tea estates of the East Coast. Often they are young Scotchmen from the Agricultural College at Aberdeen. The Dutch estates usually import from Holland or elsewhere in Europe young men who have had agricultural training; but some of their assistants are young men who have

learned practical tea cultivation in Java.

Salaries range from 300 guilders up to 500 or 600 guilders a month [1 guilder — 1s. 7 4/5d. Eng., or 40 2/10 cents U.S.— same as florin.] The maximum salary of 500 or 600 guilders is generally reached after five or six years. In addition, there is a bonus, representing a percentage of the profits, for the manager and the assistants.

In addition to salary and bonus, the manager and his assistants are provided with unfurnished living quarters, which they fit up to suit their individual tastes. The manager's bungalow, as the official headquarters of the estate, often represents a degree of comfort bordering on luxury.

Planters' contracts vary in their details, but must comply with Government rules and regulations relating to the conditions of assistants.

The assistant gets four holidays a month, two of which must be Sundays, while the other two are, as a rule, stipulated to occur simultaneously with the two holidays a month to which the coolies are entitled. In addition, the assistant gets a fortnight's leave each year and six or eight months leave to Europe after five or six years of service. During European leave he is allowed full pay, sometimes half of his regular bonus, and free passage.

One Dutch East Coast tea company provides a pension fund for the benefit of its assistants. Otherwise, the future outlook for a Sumatra tea planter is much the same as that of his Javan contemporary. In most cases, he looks forward to acquiring a competence that will permit his ultimate retirement on the income from his capital.

THE MANAGER'S HOUSE AT TIGA BLATA, SUMATRA

HILLSIDE TEA GARDENS FACING THE HIMALAYAN SNOW RANGE AT DARJEELING, INDIA

Showing two tea estates on mountain spurs below the town, at elevations of 4000 to 5000 feet. Mount Kinchinjunga, 28,000 feet, may be seen in the background.

CHAPTER XIX

CULTIVATION AND MANUFACTURE IN INDIA

GEOGRAPHICAL EXTENT OF TEA AREAS—NUMBER AND ACREAGE OF ESTATES—RAINFALL
—TEA DISTRICTS—SOILS AND CLIMATES—PROPAGATION AND CULTIVATION METHODS—
SHADES AND GREEN MANURES—OTHER FERTILIZERS—PESTS AND BLIGHTS—PRUNING AND
PLUCKING—BLACK TEA—GREEN TEA—TRANSPORT—LABOR PROBLEMS, PAST AND PRES-
ENT—GARDEN RAILWAYS AND TRAMWAYS—INDIANS IN TEA—THE INDIAN TEA ASSOCIA-
TION—EXPERIMENTAL STATIONS—TEA CESS AND THE TEA CESS COMMITTEE—PLANTERS'
ASSOCIATIONS—TEA PLANTER'S LIFE

THE INDIAN EMPIRE, jutting southward in a great peninsula from the mainland of Asia, forms one of the brightest jewels in the British Crown. It extends from the 8th to the 37th degree of north latitude. Its length, from north to south, and its greatest breadth, from east to west, are each about 1900 miles. Including Burma, it has an area of 1,805,332 square miles, inhabited by 318,942,480 people. Of the total area, 1,094,300 square miles consists of British territory, administered directly by British officials; while the remainder, or 711,032 square miles, is divided into native states, administered by semi-independent rulers, all of whom acknowledge the suzerainty of the "Paramount Power." There are fifteen British provinces: Ajmer-Merwara, Andamans and Nicobars, Assam, Baluchistan, Bengal, Bihar and Orissa, Bombay, Burma, Central Provinces and Berar, Coorg, Delhi, Madras, Northwest Frontier Province, Punjab, and the United Provinces of Agra and Oudh. The most important native states are Hyderabad, Mysore, Baroda, Kashmir and Jammu, the Rajputana Agency, and the Central India Agency.

Nearly 77 per cent of the total area under tea lies in the Brahmaputra and Surma Valleys of Assam, and in the two contiguous districts of Darjeeling and Jalpaiguri in Northern Bengal. The elevated region over the Malabar coast in Southern India, including Travancore, Cochin, Malabar, Nilgiris, and Coimbatore, contains 18 per cent. The number of tea plantations in India and their acreage as of 1932, is shown by the accompanying Table Number One.

The average production of manufactured tea per acre plucked varies widely in the different districts, as shown by India Table Number Two on the next text page.

INDIA TABLE NO. 1
Number and Acreage of Tea Plantations in 1932

Province, or Main Division	No. of Tea Plantations	Total Acreage under Tea
Assam	998	428,100
Bengal	392	207,000
Southern India	943	153,000
Northern India	2,489	15,900
Bihar and Orissa	26	3,700
Total	4,848	807,700

The pre-war average production per acre for all India was 503 pounds. A general recourse to coarser plucking ran this up to 586 pounds in 1915, but crop restriction, manuring, and heavy pruning reduced the average to 430 pounds by 1921. In 1928, it was 572 pounds, and in 1932 it was 588 pounds.

In referring to tea in British India, it is customary to give the name of the district or subdistrict rather than the state. To mention a few examples: one speaks of

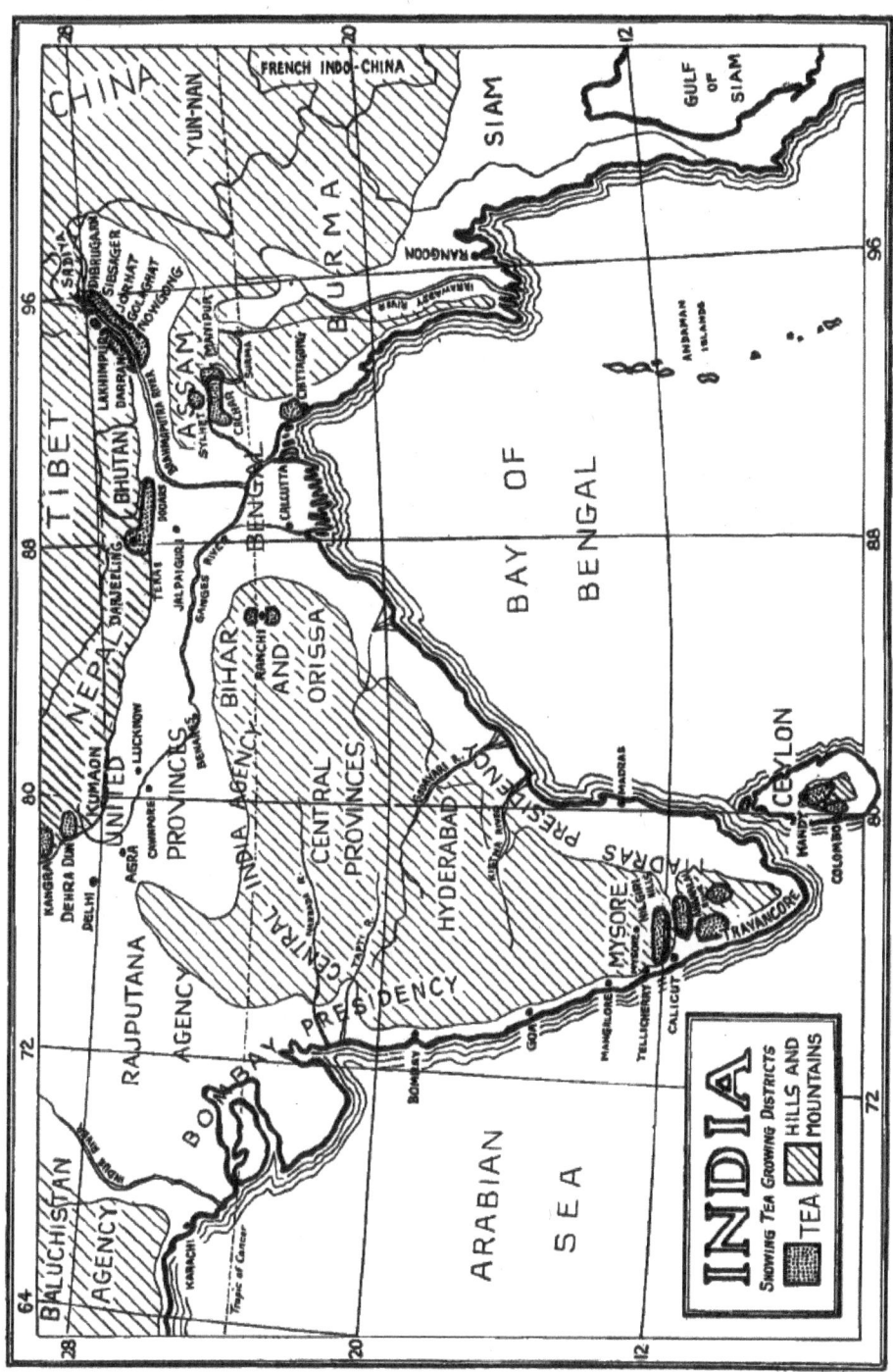

INDIA
SHOWING TEA GROWING DISTRICTS
TEA   HILLS AND MOUNTAINS

376

INDIA TABLE NO. 2

Manufactured Tea Production per
Acre Plucked in 1932

District	Per Acre	District	Per Acre
	Lbs.		Lbs.
Madura	824	Purnea	403
Lakhimpur	745	Kamrup	397
Sadiya Frontier Tract.	735	Darjeeling	376
Jalpaiguri	679	Chittagong	343
Sylhet	644	Tippera [Bengal]	288
Sibsagar	630	Cochin	286
Darrang	603	Chittagong Hill Tracts	273
Cachar	554	Mysore	259
Coimbatore	553	Dehra Dun	244
Nowgong	542	Ranchi	163
Coorg	530	Kangra	142
Malabar	520	Almora	121
Travancore	519	Tinnevelly	50
Goalpara	515	Garhwal	20
Nilgiris	423	Hazaribagh	19
		Average All-India	588

Darjeeling tea, rather than Bengal tea; Kangra, rather than Punjab; Nilgiris, rather than Madras.

Rainfall

In order to understand the climate of India, it is necessary to have some idea of the monsoon changes. Broadly speaking, there are two sets of winds blowing steadily across the earth, the trades and the anti-trades. The trade winds blow from the north and south to the Equator, but, owing to the revolution of the earth, the general direction is from the northeast and southwest. In the temperate zones, the complements of these winds, the anti-trades, blow from a southwesterly direction in the northern and a northeasterly direction in the southern hemisphere. Between these two sets of winds are two belts of calm, where are found the deserts and the Sargasso Sea.

But for the land mass of Central Asia, the peninsular portion of India would be in the course of a steady trade wind from the northeast, and Northern India would be included in the chain of deserts formed by Sahara, Arabia, Persia, and the Thar Desert. As it is, the land mass of Asia warms up in the summer months, and there follows a general flow of air from the southern latitudes to take the place of the air rising from the Asiatic plateau. Eventually, this air-flow becomes strong enough to overcome the northeast trade wind, and then the southwest monsoon begins to blow. The strength of the monsoon varies with each season, and, although the ulti-mate cause of this variation has not been decided, it depends in part, at any rate, on the oscillations of the two winds, which are pitted against each other.

West of Ceylon, the monsoon current splits into two main components, one running up the East Coast of Africa and the other round the Bay of Bengal. The current moving up the African coast sheds copious rainfall on the Abyssinian plateau, which floods the Nile and enables the Egyptian crops to flourish in a permanently cloudless sky. After meeting the Abyssinian plateau, the current makes an eastward turn, passing Cape Gardafui and the island of Socotra, and, having lost practically all its northerly component, reaches Bombay from almost due west. The rainfall at Bombay is 150 inches, but inland it decreases rapidly. Poona has an average of under thirty inches, although further from the coast there is an increase again. Arabia, Persia, and Sind thus miss the monsoon, and Karachi has a rainfall of under ten inches. The Bengal current is weaker than the African. During its movement round the Bay of Bengal, the former serves the southern part of Burma, and then comes to Bengal. Both currents are influenced by a depression, which occurs in part of Sind and Rajputana.

Towards the end of the season, the Bengal current is caught up in cyclones that whirl it across India, and the rainfall brought in this manner has a great influence on the winter crops. Before the summer is finished, the attraction towards Central Asia begins to weaken, and by the autumn the air-flow definitely begins to turn southward, and the cloud canopy is withdrawn from Northern India. The northeast trade wind, previously extinguished by the monsoon, is reinforced by cold, dry winds blowing from the desert of Tibet, which warm up as they cross the Bay of Bengal, and pick up moisture to be deposited later on the southern half of Madras.

From the foregoing brief account of the general air movements over India, it will be understood that Assam and the northeast corner are out of the track of the monsoon, yet on account of the general air drift towards the Tibetan plateau, there is a steady flow of moist air into this area. Furthermore, the Himalayan barrier and the funnel shape of the Surma and Brahmaputra Valleys insure that clouds, when they once enter the country, are

SHEETS OF TEA IN THE DOOARS GROWING UNDER ALBIZZIAS, OR SAU SHADE TREES

378

INDIA TABLE No. 3

Average Rainfall in Inches in the Tea Districts of North and Northeast India

	Brahmaputra Valley (Tocklai)	Surma Valley (Silchar)	Darjeeling	The Dooars (Sylee)	The Terai (Longview)	Bihar and Orissa (Ranchi)	Sylhet (Habiganj)	Jalpaiguri	Dehra Dun
Jan.	0.95	0.64	0.76	0.47	0.43	0.63	0.45	0.30	2.19
Feb.	1.35	2.32	1.08	0.74	0.69	1.24	1.24	0.66	2.49
March	3.59	7.99	2.01	1.12	2.34	1.10	4.53	1.36	1.46
April	7.89	13.56	4.08	3.99	4.22	0.80	9.08	3.78	0.78
May	9.66	15.72	7.83	11.09	11.35	2.33	15.42	11.07	1.57
June	12.43	20.39	24.19	33.43	30.89	9.00	19.74	23.73	8.29
July	17.04	19.98	31.74	44.56	37.01	14.46	15.82	31.28	24.33
Aug.	13.01	18.69	25.98	28.21	29.57	13.61	14.23	25.04	25.68
Sept.	10.11	13.95	18.34	28.07	23.30	8.23	11.78	19.94	9.30
Oct.	4.47	6.40	5.35	7.49	6.40	2.79	5.90	4.90	0.29
Nov.	0.92	1.31	0.24	0.98	0.50	0.37	0.83	0.20	0.92
Dec.	0.37	0.54	0.20	0.19	0.15	0.16	0.27	0.11	0.67
Total	81.79	121.49	121.80	160.34	146.85	54.72	99.29	122.32	77.97

shepherded round the hills till they are deposited as rain. Because of this, Assam is one of the permanently green provinces in a continent where conditions are, on the whole, arid. It will be seen also that the western side of Ceylon and South India are served mainly by the southwest monsoon, which a week or two later arrives by a different route in Assam. The eastern side of Ceylon and South India are served mainly by the northeast monsoon, which blows dry over Northeast India before reaching the Bay of Bengal.

India Table Number Three shows the average rainfall in the tea districts of North and Northeast India.

In South India, the extremes of rainfall are shown by Madras on the Coromandel Coast, facing the Bay of Bengal, and at Cannanore on the Malabar Coast, facing the Arabian Sea. Toward the West Coast are the tea districts. The Nilgiris District

is the one farthest from the sea, but the Anamalais and Travancore are directly exposed to its storms. The rainfall in South India is shown in Table Number Four.

Northeast and North India Districts

ASSAM.—This is by far the largest district in India in point of tea production. Upper Assam, according to Harold H. Mann, D.Sc., former Scientific Officer to the India Tea Association, possesses the ideal climate for tea.[1] In general, it is warm and moist, with no prolonged droughts. The rainfall varies over a wide range. At Cherrapunji, one of the wettest spots on earth, it averages 381 inches, with a maximum record of 905. In Silchar, it

[1] Sir George Watt, "The Cultivation of Tea," in the *Commercial Products of India*, New York, 1908.

INDIA TABLE No. 4

Average Rainfall in Inches in South India

	Madras	Cannanore	Nilgiris	Anamalais	Travancore
Jan.	1.14	0.25	2.38	0.40	0.41
Feb.	0.30	0.26	2.32	0.12	1.47
March	0.34	0.18	1.94	0.21	0.44
April	0.63	2.15	4.12	3.48	2.52
May	1.84	7.78	6.00	3.99	11.77
June	1.97	38.22	4.08	28.56	48.67
July	3.84	35.07	4.74	83.18	74.33
Aug.	4.54	18.83	4.33	23.70	40.47
Sept.	4.86	8.63	6.63	17.34	26.47
Oct.	11.15	7.95	14.35	8.17	19.69
Nov.	13.61	3.67	10.16	3.35	23.85
Dec.	5.35	0.61	4.30	0.33	0.51
Total	49.57	123.60	65.35	172.83	250.60

is 122 inches; in North Lakhimpur, more than 160 inches; and at Dibrugarh, 112 inches. In the shadows of the Mikir Hills of the Golaghat District, it drops to about 50 inches.[2]

Assam is roughly divided into two main divisions—the Brahmaputra and the Surma Valleys. Teas coming from the first named usually are known as Assams, while those of the latter are known by the subdistrict names of Cachar and Sylhet. The leading subdistricts in the Brahmaputra Valley are Dibrugarh and Dum Duma included in the Lakhimpur District; Sibsagar, Jorhat, and Golaghat, in the Sibsagar District; Bishnauth, Tezpur, and Mangaldai, in the Darrang District; and Nowgong, in the Nowgong District.

The Surma Valley has 141,542 acres of tea, producing 80,716,222 pounds [1932 figures]. The climate varies from the rest of Assam; the rainfall being heavier, but not so well distributed, and usually broken by spring droughts. During the first four months of the year, the maximum temperatures are about 7° F. higher than in the Brahmaputra Valley, and in October, November, and December they are between 4° and 8° higher. During the monsoon, they are about equal. One effect of the spring drought in the Surma Valley is that the season there starts somewhat later than in the rest of Assam, although plucking usually continues till the end of December, due to the higher autumn temperatures. The early drought seriously reduces the crop at the beginning of the season, when the shoots cease to lengthen and produce leaves. Any *banji* shoots are broken back unless they appear well below the plucking surface. In March and April, Sylhet is subject to winds known as *tufans*, or typhoons, blowing from the northwest of Assam. Hail storms may be frequent. The first tea in Cachar was planted on low hills known as *teelas*. In laying out the estates, no attempt was made to conserve the surface, which was, in consequence, washed away in a few years. Since then, tea has been planted on the flat lands, or *bheels*, lying between the hills, after careful and thorough drainage has been effected. This land is swampy, with a rich surface soil and an impervious subsoil.

Tea is grown also on the plateau lands of Cachar and Sylhet. However, on the whole, the climate is not equal to that of the Brahmaputra Valley.

The Brahmaputra Valley comprises a total of some 286,538 acres of tea, and produced 176,341,711 pounds in 1932. It is separated on the south from the Surma Valley by the Garo, Khasi and Jaintia, and Naga Hills, and by the Shillong Plateau. The Himalaya Mountains bound it on the north. The valley runs from east to west, the width varying largely. It rises about a foot per mile. The soils of the Brahmaputra Valley are mostly alluvial, differing, however, in their physical condition. Near the river they usually are sandy, becoming heavier as they approach the hills, and, in certain spots, clayey. The best results for tea have been obtained on fairly light, red, coarse sand or silt, or on the stiffer and redder alluvium found on small plateaus in certain subdistricts. Assam, to use the name generally accepted for the Brahmaputra Valley, is not in the tropics, being from 26 to 28 degrees North. It has, therefore, a definite summer and winter. The mean temperature in July is 83° and in January 60°. The main crop must be gathered between April and November. July, August, September, and November generally are the heaviest crop months.

The Lakhimpur District, the highest yielding tea area in Assam, consists of a broad plain on either side of the Brahmaputra. To the south the hills rise only a few thousand feet above sea level, but to the north they extend to a continuous chain of snowy peaks. On the south of the river the plain is fairly high, and a broad belt of country along the foot hills is clothed in dense forest. In the center of this area the country is cleared, and cultivated under tea and rice. The drainage is carried on by *jans* and small rivers, and there are few swamps, or *bheels*.

On the north bank of the Brahmaputra the country is much lower and *bheels* are common, while during the monsoon the country side is inundated. This is a country of grass and high reeds, although towards Sadiya forest abounds.

Although Lakhimpur is surrounded on three sides by hills and mountains, almost the whole area is flat, level plain. An outlying spur of the Naga Hills stretches from the Disang River, and near Jaipur, Mar-

[2] C. R. Harler, "Meteorological Observations in Assam 1924," *Quarterly Journal of the Scientific Department of the Indian Tea Association*, Calcutta, Part I, 1925.

TEA PLUCKING ON THE BORDUBI TEA ESTATE, DUM DUMA, LAKHIMPUR

gherita, and Digboi there are a few hills. Although Dibrugarh is about 1000 miles from the sea by river, its elevation is only 340 feet. Sadiya is not much higher, having an altitude of 440 feet.

Naturally, the tea areas have spread from the more to the less accessible spots; from the river inland, and, generally speaking, the gardens in the east of the district are younger than those in the west and south. The newest area, which is in process of opening out, lies to the east of Dum Duma in the Lakhimpur Frontier Tract, and almost in Khamti country. This area is spoken of as the Burhi Dihing District.

As denoted by the crop returns, the tea in Dibrugarh is very fine, and the average prices obtained are second only to those of Darjeeling in Northeast India.

DARJEELING.—The most romantic and interesting tea district in all India, Darjeeling lies wedged between Nepal, Sikkim, and Bhutan—three forbidden kingdoms. The tea gardens are practically all situated in that portion of the district west of the Teesta River, an area composed of a system of ridges and spurs, with deep valleys between. It is a mountain region, rising abruptly from the plain of the

Terai, which forms the southern boundary; the northern boundary being the valley of the Great Rangit River; the eastern, the valley of the Teesta; and the western, the hills of the Singalia Range to the north and the valley of the Mechi River, to the south.

The seasons at Darjeeling follow in general those of all India; i.e., cold weather, hot weather, and the rains. D. G. Munro, B.Sc., former Scientific Officer of the United Planters' Association of Southern India, reported on the Darjeeling seasons as follows:

The cold weather is divided into two portions. The first, at the end of the rains, is mild and pleasant, and the atmosphere tolerably clear, and generally free from dust and cloud. This is the autumn, if autumn there be at Darjeeling. Toward the beginning of December, the first touch of winter comes with hoar frost, and at the end of that month and in January the ground is sometimes frozen the whole day long. The air is cloudless, dry, and bracing. In the early morning it is very cold, but later in the day there is bright sunshine and it becomes pleasantly warm, although it remains bitterly cold in the shade. Occasionally, snow falls in January to February, but such an occurrence is comparatively rare.

In March, a brief Himalayan spring is ushered in by high blustering winds. It is very short, lasting only till the end of the month.

A DARJEELING TEA ESTATE SHOWING SLOPING GARDENS AND MANAGER'S BUNGALOW

During April and May, there is a short summer, accompanied by showers of rain, which become heavier and more frequent till the setting in of the rains in the beginning of June. For three months after this, Darjeeling is exposed to the full force of the monsoon, drenched with rain, and shrouded in mist. The alluvial plain between it and the mouth of the Ganges is almost a dead level; the foot of the hills being only 300 feet above sea-level, and consequently the vapor laden southerly winds from the Bay of Bengal reach the outer range of hills without impediment. The humidity is very great, and Darjeeling is at this period of the year one of the dampest stations in India.

The rains continue during June, July, and August; twenty-four inches average falling in June, thirty-two inches in July, and twenty-six inches in August. The rainfall varies greatly in different parts of the district. In September a decided change takes place, the continued rainfall giving way to showers, which become less and less frequent, while the sun shows itself oftener and for longer periods. About the beginning of October, the rains cease altogether. Even then, however, the weather cannot be depended upon, and Darjeeling is subject to almost constant cloud and fog, which rises from the deep valleys, and hangs for days together over the station.[3]

Most of the tea grown in Darjeeling is raised at altitudes ranging from 1000 to

3 D. G. Munro, "Report on Tour in Assam for 1924-25," *United Planters' Association of Southern India Scientific Department Bulletin,* Madras, 1925.

6000 feet and even higher. The mean temperature is but two degrees above that of London, but conditions range from subtropical at the lower elevations to temperate at the top. At an elevation of between 4000 and 4500 feet there is a distinct mist line, and above it mist might almost be said to be the rule during the monsoon. At 4000 feet, there is a distinct change in temperature and humidity. The appearance of the tea is different; growth is slow, and the stems and branches become festooned with moss and jungle.

The greater part of Darjeeling is not alluvial, but is formed in situ from the rocks of the district. It is a loamy, but highly porous soil, rich in mineral nutrients for plants. Tea from this district brings the highest price of any India tea. There were 60,424 acres of tea, producing 22,096,177 pounds in 1932. However, the yield per acre was but 376 pounds, as against 824 in the Madura District.

Dooars.—Southeast of the Darjeeling District, but still in Bengal, lie the Dooars. They are situated in what is known as the Jalpaiguri District. Some 132,000 acres in the Dooars are planted with tea. The whole area is covered with new alluvial deposits, varying from gravel to clay, in accordance with the present and past direction of the rivers; but there are large areas of much older soil, the exact origin of which is still a matter of conjecture.

The climate differs from that of the Assam Valley, the average maximum temperature being 3° to 5° higher than that of Assam, while as low as 38° has been recorded in February. In gardens close to the hills, about 180 inches of rain falls yearly, while in gardens some distance from the hills, about 125 inches is usual. Tocklai, in Assam, averages but 79.18 inches. Formerly, the health and vigor of the tea in the Dooars was thought to be due largely to the fact that the soil formed a good mulch. This was subsequently disputed and field experiments tended to confirm this view.

TERAI.—The Terai is bounded on the north by the Darjeeling foothills, on the west by the Mechi River, which forms the Nepal frontier, and on the east by the Teesta River, beyond which is the Dooars. The word "terai" comes from the Persian, and signifies damp. The term may be applied to the strip of country lying along the total length of the foothills of the Himalayas, but so far as the tea industry is concerned, it refers to the area at the immediate foot of the Darjeeling hills. The Dooars are actually in a terai area.

Sir Joseph Dalton Hooker, eminent botanist and traveler, in his *Himalayan Journals* introduces the Terai as follows:

> Siligooree stands on the verge of the Terai, that low malarious belt, which skirts the base of the Himalaya from the Sutlej to the Brahmakoond in Upper Assam. Every feature—botanical, geological, and zoölogical—is new on entering the district. The change is sudden and immediate: sea and shore are hardly more conspicuously different; nor from the edge of the Terai to the limit of perpetual snow is any botanical region more clearly marked than in this, which is the commencement of Himalayan vegetation.[4]

In the Terai, there are some 19,000 acres under tea. The soil is of good quality for tea, and varies widely over a range almost identical with that in the Dooars, but there is not as much rain during the early part of the year as the planter could wish for. The soil is generally very sandy and is usually darker than the soil of the high land.

CHITTAGONG.—The smallest of the tea districts of Bengal is Chittagong, with a total of 5400 acres planted to tea. The district lies directly northeast of the port of Chittagong on the Bay of Bengal, rising from lowlands near the coast to the hill tracts in the rear. The climate is better than Assam in that there is much less cold weather, but on the other hand there is less rain in the spring. Generally speaking, the soil resembles that of Sylhet, and that found on the hills is similar to the Assam soil. The topography of the country closely resembles that of South Sylhet. The tea is generally put out on small *teelas*, which are beautifully terraced. The southern slopes of the *teelas*—the slopes facing the sun—are much poorer than the northern.

BIHAR AND ORISSA.—The name of this district, the same as that of the province, includes the tea producing subdistricts of Hazaribagh and Ranchi, sometimes known in the trade as Chota Nagpur, the name of a plateau subdivision of Bihar and Orissa.

[4] Sir Joseph Dalton Hooker, *Himalayan Journals*, 1854.

ROAD THROUGH THE ESTATE OF THE NAMDANG TEA CO., MARGHERITA, LAKHIMPUR, ASSAM

THE VALLEY OF THE DUN AFTER THE RAIN; A VIEW FROM MUSSOORIE, FAMOUS HILL STATION

The hill on which Mussoorie is built rises from the plains in the form of a horse-shoe enclosing in the hollow a number of ridges where tea is grown. Mussoorie is 6000 to 7200 feet. In the distance may be seen the Siwaliks, or outlying hills of the Himalayas, and to the right a tributary of the Jumna. Far away are the plains of the United Provinces.

There are 26 estates containing some 3600 acres in tea near Ranchi, and one estate with thirty acres in tea near Hazaribagh. From this district come many of the coolies employed in the gardens of Northeast India. The Mundas and Oraons, for example, come from round about Ranchi. The few tea gardens are labored by recruits drawn largely from the neighboring villages.

The tea district is a plateau with few trees, and has an elevation of about 2000 feet. The climate is bad for tea, because the early drought persists right up to the break of the monsoon—June 15. As the heavily foliated tea bush thrives best on a high humidity, the climate is far from ideal. Accordingly, the tea suffers, and the yield is 163 pounds per acre in Ranchi and 19 pounds in Hazaribagh against an average of 572 pounds in Assam.

The jat in Chota Nagpur is generally China. The Assam and Burma jats do not do so well, for they are better fitted by nature to thrive in a moist atmosphere.

KUMAON.—This is a district of the United Provinces on the border of Tibet and Nepal. It is divided into the subdistricts of Almora and Garhwal. The altitude is from 5000 to 7000 feet. There are sixteen tea estates with 1200 acres under tea. Lieutenant Colonel Edward Money, who had actual experience in growing tea in this district, speaks disparagingly of it.[5] The cold climate and the distance from a seaport make tea planting a hazardous occupation, so most of the tea originally put out has been abandoned. The soil, however, is rich and productive. Orchards and tea gardens are intermixed. Kumaon has some trade with merchants from across the northern border, notably in green tea.

DEHRA DUN.—Lying northwest of Kumaon, in the same province, is the district of Dehra Dun. The outer ranges of the Himalayas are separated by narrow, longitudinal valleys or depressions called *duns*. It is from these that the district takes its name. There are twenty-one gardens in the district, with 5054 acres under tea. The hot, dry weather of the Northwest is

[5] Lieutenant Colonel Edward Money, *The Cultivation and Manufacture of Tea*, London, 1878.

not suited to the tea plant. The early drought is so severe that the bushes are completely defoliated. Flushes are few. Labor is plentiful and cheap, but transport is expensive.

KANGRA.—The only tea producing district of any note in the Punjab is the Kangra Valley, high up in the northwestern part of India, south of Kashmir and west of Tibet. Here we find 2464 gardens with 9693 acres under tea. The extraordinary number of gardens is due to the fact that most of the tea-growing companies are small ones, run by Indians or European proprietary managers. In many cases, tea is grown among fruit trees.

Although a Himalayan district, the elevation of the gardens in the Kangra Valley is not very great, running from 2000 to 6000 feet. The climate is too dry and too cold to be perfect for tea. The soil is good, and labor plentiful. The teas produced are of a peculiarly delicate flavor, and often bring good prices. As in the case of Kumaon, however, much goes over the border to Tibet and Nepal, or is retained for local consumption; so that the quantity exported is too small to have any appreciable influence on the market.

HILL TIPPERA.—Tripura, or Hill Tippera, is a small native state adjoining

SHOLAYER TEA FACTORY, COIMBATORE
Largest fully equipped factory in India.

South Sylhet and Chittagong, and similar to these districts. There are 47 gardens with 8800 acres under tea. As Europeans are not granted land in Tippera, all the gardens are owned by Indians.

South India Tea Districts

The tea industry of South India resembles that of Ceylon and differs from that of Northeast India in that tea is grown with other crops. It is usual for an estate to deal with three or more commodities. In Assam, the planter deals with no other crop than tea; in South India, three main crops—tea, coffee, and rubber—are commonly raised.

A HIGH RANGE TEA GARDEN, TRAVANCORE, SOUTHERN INDIA

MODERN TEA FACTORY ON KODANAAD, NILGIRIS, SOUTHERN INDIA
Showing the upper or withering loft floors with ventilating fans.

The acreage under tea is distributed as shown in Table Number Five.

The tea planting districts of South India are generally to be found in the hills formed by the Western Ghats. These run from the southern tip of India to a point above Bombay. They form the great sea wall for the west side of the peninsula, with only a comparatively narrow strip between them and the shore. At Palghat, there is a gap separating the Travancore part of the ghat—the Cardamom Hills—from the main range. This gap is about sixteen miles wide, and scarcely more than 1000 feet above sea level. The Madras Railway, running through it, forms the chief line of communication between the two sides of the peninsula. North of the Palghat Gap, the hills are known as the Nilgiris.

The western side of the range faces the southwest monsoon, and hence the tea is put out there. The average rainfall along the Malabar coast averages 100 inches, and increases to 300 inches high up in the mountains. The southwest monsoon comes in April, May, and June and the northeast in November and December. The estates are all on hill sides, which, while not so rugged as those of the Darjeeling District, are much steeper than the *teelas* of Cachar and Sylhet. The soils vary from light, gravelly, lateritic soils to fairly heavy clays.

In a special report on taxable lands in Southern India made by Mr. A. H. A. Todd, I.C.S., Special Settlement Officer, and published by the Government of Madras in 1927, it is stated that in the last twenty years the area under tea in Wynaad Taluk of the Malabar District increased from 4654 acres to 15,000 acres, and that in the Gudalur Taluk of the Nilgiris District, from 2496 acres to 5880 acres. The tendency is still for the acreage to expand

INDIA TABLE NO. 5
Acreage and Production [1932] in South India

	TEA AREA	TOTAL PRODUCTION	
	Acres	Black	Green
MADRAS			
Nilgiris	35,347	12,481,712	
Malabar	12,690	5,948,272	
Coimbatore	24,756	11,199,333	
Tinnevelly	602	950	
Madura	118	30,497	
TRAVANCORE	74,357	32,640,970	
MYSORE	4,239	153,842	
COCHIN	523	88,791	
Total	152,632	62,544,367	

at a striking rate. Mr. Todd found that the profits per acre on a certain estate, over a series of years, worked out as follows: £4.75, 1.56, 8.70, 5.24, 3.74, and 2.87. In the case of this estate, the Settlement Officer says, the profit does not greatly exceed the ordinary rate of interest on the money sunk, which in the case of a new estate would now be £60 to £80 per acre, etc. In respect of another large estate, he found that the cost of bringing 500 acres of tea into bearing was *Rs.* 3,50,725, excluding cost of building factory and value of land, rents, and taxes; but including some forty to fifty other items, from the manager's salary down to medical comfort for coolies. This *Rs.* 3,50,725 is spread, including a share in the factory buildings, over five years, after which time the tea is in fairly full-bearing. An area of 1000 acres produced on an average for a period of five years—some pre-war, and some during the war—541 pounds of made tea annually per acre, and the cost of production per pound was 4.78*d.*, free on boat. Mr. Todd found the annual profit per acre averaged at least £5.

NILGIRIS.—This is a high district, the altitude being from 4000 to 6000 feet. The tea produced is good, and in some cases equal to the best.

Preparation of Land

In opening new land for tea gardens in British India, brushwood and undergrowth are cut immediately after the close of the rainy season. These are burned, and then the trees are cut down, and the stumps, in so far as possible, are pulled out, since they are likely to cause root disease. In parts

ELEPHANT CLEARING JUNGLE FOR TEA ESTATE

of Assam and in Darjeeling, a ring is often dug around the tree, and the lateral roots are cut until the weight of the tree itself causes it to topple over. In this way, no stump is left. In many instances, a few trees, preferably those of the leguminous variety, are allowed to stand, in order to give shade. After grubbing out the trees and stumps, the land is hoed. Stones and roots are removed, and the soil well mixed. If the garden is on level land, drains are laid out and put in.

Seed

Many India gardens have a plot of carefully selected tea, especially cultivated to produce seeds. This plot is removed as far as possible from the rest of the garden, in order to insure it against hybridization. Formerly, this tea was not pruned and, in the case of all but the China plant, grew to its normal height of thirty to forty feet. Of late years, some planters have preferred to prune repeatedly until a shrub some twelve feet high and fifteen feet in diameter, is evolved. This makes the question of fighting blights easier than if the tree were allowed to grow to its natural height. On other India estates, seed is selected promiscuously from the healthiest plants over a large area.

Tea Nurseries

Land used as a nursery is carefully dug over, and the soil pulverized. All bits of roots, stones, etc., are removed. The nursery is laid out in rectangular beds some five feet wide, with paths between. The seeds are deposited about an inch deep, and from four to nine inches apart. The Tocklai Experimental Station advises that if plants are to be transplanted at the age of six months, the seeds should be five inches apart; for twelve months, eight inches apart; and for twenty-four months, ten inches apart.

Great care is taken in shading, watering, and manuring. The shading is done by means of raised *tatties* of grass or mats. These shades are made of thin thatch spread on bamboo frames some five feet high. All weeds are removed by hand.[6]

Broadly speaking, there are four varie-

[6] H. R. Cooper, "Tea Nurseries," *Quarterly Journal of the Scientific Department of the India Tea Association*, Calcutta, Part III, 1924.

TRANSPLANTING TEA SEEDLINGS

ties of tea bush to be seen in tea gardens in Northeast India: the China; the Assam, or light-leaved indigenous; the Burma, or dark-leaved; and the Manipuri bush. In the plains districts of Northeast India the large-leaved varieties are preferred. The dark-leaved bush is hardier than the light-leaved Assam bush, and although both yield about the same, the Assam bush invariably gives the better tea. In Darjeeling, where the climate is severe, the China type of bush is preferred. In the Dooars and the Surma Valley, where climatic conditions are often difficult, the dark-leaved variety is favored, but in the Brahmaputra Valley the light-leaved bush of the Assam variety is preferred.

The tea flower appears any time between August and October, and the fruit takes from twelve to fourteen months to ripen.

The seed is gathered as it falls, and is spread out on a cool floor over night. In the morning, it is sorted over to remove stones, refuse, empty shells, etc.

Seed is usually tested by the water method; that is, the seed is thrown in a trough filled with water, where the dried or partly empty seeds float and are skimmed off. The others are dried quickly. Sometimes the "light" seeds are kept in moist sand for a few days and again floated, when a certain percentage become "sinkers" and are planted, producing good tea plants.

The area which can be planted with one maund—eighty pounds—of seed, if the lining is rectangular, is shown in Table Number Six. With triangular planting, about 15 per cent must be deducted.[7]

7 Claud. Bald. *Indian Tea; Its Culture and Manufacture*, 4th ed., Calcutta, 1922.

Propagation by cuttings or layering has not been successful in India on a commercial scale.

Transplanting

Seedlings are left in the nursery for varying periods. Some planters prefer to set out the tea at six months, others at twelve, and still others at eighteen months. Lines are staked, and the seedlings laid out at regular intervals along these lines. Opinions differ as to the distance advisable between the plants. Much depends upon the quality of the soil and the variety of the jat. Generally speaking, the plants are put out from four to five feet apart; i.e., from four to six feet distant from the nearest plant in any direction. When the lines have been formed, and the distances decided upon, stakes are driven to mark where holes should be dug for the plants; these holes being at least a foot wide and ten inches deep. The land is then ready for the plants.

Although much tea is transplanted by hand, there are several good transplanting implements in use in Northeast India. These insure a proper clod of earth over the roots of the plant. One of the oldest is Jeben's transplanter. The plant is taken up by this device with its surrounding earth, and slipped into a tin cylinder having a movable bottom. The plants are carried from the nursery to the garden. The bottom of the cylinder is slipped out, and the cylinder set in the hole previously prepared. The surrounding space is filled in with earth, and the cylinder removed over the top of the plant. Then the earth is tamped down gently around the plant. Seedlings of eighteen months or more are too large to be transplanted in this way. Elliott's transplanter, a later and simpler device, employs a semi-circular spade, a trowel of similar shape, and about ten car-

INDIA TABLE NO. 6
Nursery Planting

Feet Apart	Plants per Acre	Acres per Maund of Seed
4x4	2722	3
4½x4	2420	3½
5x4	2178	4
5x5	1742	4½
6x6	1210	7

HOEING BETWEEN THE ROWS OF TEA

rying tins to each spade. Two men are required, one to use the spade, and the other to place the tins and release the cones from the spade.

Hoeing

In most tea districts of Northern India, hoeing is practiced. The soil around the young plants is frequently loosened to a depth of three inches for a distance of some twelve inches around. While the tea is young, and weeds are able to grow quickly on the uncovered soil, it receives both deep hoeing and light hoeing. At the beginning of the dry season, deep hoeing is undertaken. A depth of eight inches is aimed at, but seldom attained. Every six weeks, light hoeings—about three inches deep—take place. The object of the light hoeing is to keep down the weeds. During the monsoon, when the weather is forcing all plant growth, the weeds often get the upper hand. In Southern India, where the soil is more granular, less cultivation is required, and clean weeding is the rule.

In 1922, extensive cultivation experiments were started at the Tocklai Experimental Station and, although this work is still in progress, all the results point to the fact that it is the harmful effect of the weeds, rather than the beneficial effect of stirring the soil during cultivation, that influences the tea crop. Accordingly, it is becoming the custom to let the sides of the bushes grow so that they cover the soil, and tend to keep down weed growth. It has been found that such a procedure not only reduces the need for hoeing, but also keeps the soil in good tilth, approximating jungle conditions.

Motor tea-cultivators, designed to cut down the expense of hoeing, have been introduced into India, but have yet to prove their practability.

Shade Trees and Windbreaks

The shade tree most commonly used on British India tea estates is the ordinary Sau, or *Albizzia stipulata*. It gives a light, even shade, although in some districts it requires lopping. The falling leaves form a valuable manure, and act as a mulch on the surface. It is deciduous, losing its leaves from December to January, and flushing again from April to May. In many districts its life is twenty-five years.

Following the Sau closely in popularity is the Koroi, or *Albizzia procera*, which has the advantage of keeping free from canker longer than the Sau. The Bor medeloa, or *Dalbergia assamica*, also does rather well but is late coming into leaf. *Derris robusta* is sometimes used as a shade tree. It will grow almost anywhere. Dadap, or *Erythrina lithosperma*, is used generally in South India, but not in Northeast India, where it has been proved that it encourages root disease. The *Dalbergia sissu* and the *Albizzia lebbec* are also in common use.

In South India, a much used shade tree is the Ceylon Sau, or *Albizzia moluccana*, which has a large leaf and grows rapidly. In fact, it is so leafy and bushy, if left to grow naturally, that it commonly does damage to surrounding tea. It is non-deciduous, bearing its leaves through the cold weather, and hence its dense shade and consequent heavy call on the reserves of soil moisture mitigate against its use in Northeast India.

All of the trees mentioned are leguminous, but non-leguminous trees sometimes are used in South India. These include the Silver Oak, or *Grevillea robusta;* the Nahor, sometimes called Nagessar, or *Mesua ferrea;* and the *Ficus* species.

Perhaps the commonest bushes used for windbreaks in South India are the several varieties of *Dalbergia*. Their dense evergreen foliage makes them particularly effective. The silver oak, *Grevillea robusta,* also is planted extensively.

Green Manures

The use of green manures is well-nigh universal in British India, which is particularly fortunate in having a large number of *leguminosæ* indigenous to the country. Green manures may be divided roughly into trees, shrubs, and herbaceous plants.

As mentioned before, the *Albizzia stipulata*, or Sau tree, is planted as a shade tree, and at the same time acts as a green manure. Other varieties of the same tree family also are used. The *Dalbergia assamica* has been specially recommended for its suitability in certain sections of the country.

The principal shrubs in use are *Tephrosia candida*, commonly known as *Boga medeloa*, and in Darjeeling as *Bodlelara*; the *Cajanus indicus*, or *Arhar Rahar*; the *Sesbania aculeata*, or *Dhaincha*; the *Sesbania egyptiaca*, or *Jyanth*; the *Indigofera dosua*; the *Indigofera arrecta*, or Natal Java Indigo; the *Desmodium polycarpum*; the *Desmodium tortuosum*; the *Desmodium retroflexum*; the *Leucæna glauca*; and the *Clitoria cajanifolia*.

In the case of the herbaceous annuals used for green manuring, the plants are raised from seed sown between the tea and dug into the soil when a few weeks, or months old. The plants ordinarily used for this purpose are the different species of the *Phaseolus*, such as *Mati Kalai*, or *Kalai dal*; the *Vigna catiang*, or cowpea; the *Glycine hispida*, or soya bean, sometimes called *Bhot mas*; the *Cyamopsis psoralioides*, or *Guar*; the *Crotalaria jauncia*, or Sunn hemp; and the *Crotalaria striata*.

Other Manures

Except in special cases, fertilizers usually are applied to tea in India every year or every second year. This is done in the spring. The manures are spread broadcast at the time of the first light hoeing, and are hoed in. Often, if certain bushes are backward, a quick-acting nitrogenous manure is specially applied.

Practically every type of manure in the market is used on tea. These include: Sulphate of ammonia, nitrate of soda, calcium cyanamide, oilcakes, blood meal, fish manure, animal meal, steamed horn meal, skins and sinews, sardine guano, sterilized animal meal, superphosphate, bones, basic slag, Belgian flour phosphate, Algaricum flour phosphate, ground Sunghbhum phosphate, radiophosphate, saltpeter or nitrate of potash, muriate of potash, cattle dung, and lime.

Fertilizers sometimes are rotated, one of the systems being:

First year.—Phosphate and a quick-growing green manure, such as the cowpea.
Second year.—Nitrogen and potash.
Third year.—*Boga medeloa.*
Fourth year.—The prunings of *Boga medeloa,* deeply hoed in.

Formerly it was thought that, when circumstances made it necessary, an application of lime should be made the first year, after which the fertilizers were rotated, making a five-year rotation. Latterly it has been established that lime is never required on a tea soil. Any soil not definitely acid can be improved by a dressing of ground sulphur. Nitrogen is the most important factor. The cheap soluble artificials are mostly favored.

Mulching and Top Dressing

In some cases, it is inadvisable to break up the surface of the land, and mulching is resorted to. Leaves and other vegetable matter are spread upon the ground. They serve to protect the tea in the hot, dry season by conserving the soil moisture, and the material as it rots becomes good manure. However, this practice does not obtain in N. E. India.

Although a rather expensive process, top dressing has been found an effective means in India to improve the quality of poor land. If a rich bed of soil or peat exists near by, good soil is secured, and the work is done at some time when there is less work than workers. The depth of the top dressing varies, but frequently is about three inches. As much as 500 tons of earth to the acre may be applied.

Pests and Blights

As in all tea producing countries, certain insect pests and diseases are continually to be fought in British India. Most important among the pests are the "tea mosquito" bug, *Helopeltis theivora*, the red spider, the pink mite, the green fly, and the thrips.

Helopeltis appears in the Terai as early as the end of July. It is, however, at its worst in all affected districts from September until the end of the season. The usual insecticides applied against it are kerosene emulsion and soap solution, but they are by no means a cure. Experiments have been made to ascertain the effectiveness of potash manures as a preventive, but with little success. Thorough cleaning of the bushes from all fungi and poor growth at the pruning season, seems at present to be the best thing science has to offer for damage by *Helopeltis.*

The red spider, *Tetranychus bioculatus,* appears about the end of April, when the leaves of the first flush begin to mature. It disappears about the middle of June. It is more often found on China bushes. The treatment for checking the spider is to dust the bushes with sulphur when they are wet with rain or dew. Twenty pounds to an acre usually is effective; the cost being about *Rs.* 20 per acre.

The pink mite, *Phytoptus theae,* seems to prefer the jats of Assam indigenous tea. It appears in late April or early May. The introduction of heavier shade into the garden does much to mitigate this evil, as well as that wrought by the red spider. Sometimes, flowers of sulphur are used. The scarlet mite, *Brevipelpus,* and the yellow mite, *Phytoptus theae,* also do damage occasionally.

The visitation of the green fly, *Empoasca flavescens,* usually is regarded as a promise of fine, flavory tea. However, when the blight becomes severe, it has been believed that it seriously stunts the growth of the tea. Recent experiments seem to prove, however, that the green fly does not, as has been supposed, produce the stunting of the flush.

The thrips, a tiny torpedo-shaped insect, first attracted attention in Darjeeling in 1906, and its attack appears to have attained serious proportions in 1908. There are three species found in Northeast India.

The best means of prevention against thrips is to increase the vigor of the bushes; to cultivate freely; and to use soap insecticides, alone or with kerosene and sprayed on with a fine spray.

In addition to the principal pests, which have been described, there is a formidable array of others. Amongst the *Orthoptera*— crickets—*Brandrytypes postentosus* often give considerable trouble; especially in nurseries and heavily pruned tea.

Of beetle pests of tea, *Coleoptera,* the most important is the orange, or Peal's beetle, *Diapromorpha melanopus,* which, by eating partly through the succulent shoot of the flush, causes the upper portion to die off. Cockchafer grubs, *Lachnosterna* spp., attack the roots of the plant.

The list of caterpillar pests, *Lepidoptera,* is a long one. The most important are the faggot and bag worms, or *Clania* spp.; bark-eaters, or *Arbela* spp.; red slug, or *Hoterusia magnifica;* red borer, or *Zeuzera coffeae;* looper, or *Biston suppressaria;* bunch caterpillar, or *Andraca bipunctata;* sandwich caterpillar, or *Agriophora rhombata;* leaf rollers, or *Homona menciana,* and *Grecillaria theivora;* and nettle grub, or *Thosea* spp. The caterpillar of one moth, *Blastobasis spermogens,* lives inside the teaseed.

The tea aphis, *Toxoptera theaecola,* by curling and stunting the young, growing shoots, may cause a considerable check to young plants in the nursery and to bushes commencing to grow after pruning. Scale insects do considerable damage in the hill districts of Darjeeling; although, in the plains the more vigorous growth of the bushes reduces their damage. *Chionaspis manni,* in particular, does much damage by sucking the downward stream of sap from the branches. The tea mealy bug, *Dactylopius theaecola,* which attacks the roots of the plant, is a noteworthy pest in Darjeeling. The tea-seed bug, *Peecilocoria latus,* is a serious pest in the tea-seed gardens, as by puncturing the seed it permits the entrance of fungi to the interior, causing ultimate destruction of the seed.

Among the pseudo-neuroptera, termites, or white ants, are often troublesome. They swarm into the bush, primarily in search of dead pruning snags, etc., and ultimately extend their ravages to the entire frame of the bush. Of the varieties found, *Odontotermes,* which lives in the ground, is the most widespread.

Beside the insect pests, tea in India is beset by certain vegetable blights. Those most common are gray blight, brown blight, copper blight, blister blight, thread blight, black rot, stump and root diseases.

Disease Treatment

The Tocklai Experimental Station furnishes its members with ten rules for the treatment of tea blights, as follows:

In the case of stem or leaf diseases:
1. Isolate the bushes concerned by preventing coolies, cattle, etc., from touching them. All necessary cultivation, etc., should be carried

out by special coolies, using specially marked implements. At the conclusion of the operations for the day the coolies and implements should be sprayed with lime-sulphur solution on the spot, so that the disease will not be carried about. The lime-sulphur solution does not injure the skin or clothing, but should not be allowed to get into the eyes.

2. Pluck or prune off all the diseased portions and burn them on the spot. If they are too green to burn alone, a little kerosene will help matters.

3. Spray the bushes thoroughly with a fungicide, e.g., lime-sulphur.

4. Repeat the plucking, pruning, and spraying at intervals, depending on the nature of the disease.

5. Where there are numerous outbreaks occurring at the same time, treat the small ones first, isolating the larger areas until time permits treatment to be carried out on them.

In the case of root diseases:

1. The areas containing the dead or dying bushes should be isolated, and all the implements used in cultivation, etc., of such areas should be kept separate. There is no need to disinfect the coolies.

2. The edges of the large areas, and all small areas, should be dealt with first by digging out the dead and diseased bushes, taking great care to remove all the dead wood from the soil.

3. All the dead wood should be burned on the spot, if possible. If this is not feasible, it should be removed in old bags or baskets, and burned elsewhere. Care should be taken either to burn the bags or baskets, or to disinfect them thoroughly with lime-sulphur solution.

4. Watch for new outbreaks, and deal with them at once.

5. Dig out all dead stumps.

The susceptibility of the tea plant to the attacks of many of the commoner blights has been found to be associated with cultural cefects and it is often possible to control such blights without specific treatment by modifying conditions of growth. It has also been shown that much serious disease may be prevented by avoiding undue reduction in plant reserves.[8]

Pruning

Pruning in British India generally is done in the cold season, from December through February, the different varieties being pruned in the order in which they cease to flush; i.e., China first, hybrids second, and then the indigenous varieties. It is carried out on different lines in different districts, and by different planters. In Northeast India, the practice has been to prune the whole estate once a year. When tea is left unpruned at the end of the season, a larger outturn generally is

8 A. C. Tunstall, "Heavy Pruning and Stem Disease," *Quarterly Journal of the Scientific Department of the Indian Tea Association*, Calcutta, Part III, 1931.

PRUNING TEA IN THE DOOARS

secured from the unpruned area during the early part of the season, and less tea during the latter half of the year.

Different districts require different times for pruning; for example, in Sylhet, pruning is done late, because the district is subject to hail storms and drought at the period of the year when early pruned tea would have re-commenced flushing, and the young shoots might be destroyed. In Chittagong or any hill district where the temperature in spring is low, early flushes would be liable to be killed by cold. In the Dooars or Terai, also, late pruning is the most suitable; although early pruning sometimes is resorted to as a supposed means of checking blight.

Pruning is done by means of a curved knife with a blade four to eight inches long, according to the type of pruning required. Opinions differ as to the age when tea should first be pruned. Some begin as early as six months after planting; others as late as three years. More often this is regulated by the amount of growth. The first pruning frequently consists in cutting the main stem as low as six to nine inches from the ground, always provided there are side branches below this. These side branches are cut off at about fifteen or eighteen inches from the ground. The second pruning is to a height of some fifteen to eighteen inches, the plants being cut straight across. Succeeding prunings are similar, each being about two inches above the previous cut.

Heavy pruning in India means cutting near the ground to a height of nine to fifteen inches. This is done only at intervals of about ten years. It causes a reduction of crop for that year amounting to a loss of as much as half the crop for the season, and on the hill gardens, a loss of two-thirds to three-fourths.

Collar pruning is the most drastic type of pruning, which some tea scientists believe is never needed if the bushes are properly treated. It should not be necessary in any case in less than twenty years. Many planters will have nothing to do with collar pruning. Collar-pruned bushes may be cut at any place up to eight inches above the ground. Some planters have adopted a method of scraping away the earth and cutting just above the spread of the roots, but this method is less popular than it was twenty years ago.

In India, the ideal is to prune each bush on its merits, but generally the unit is a field, or section. The usual form of bush is that with a flat surface, although some planters prefer the sugar-loaf, which involves side pruning and plucking.

"Skiff" pruning, or "switching," is done by cutting off the tops of all the shoots a trifle, whether the bushes be high or low, weak or strong. One system of doing this is to furnish the coolie with a measuring rod marked at a certain place. This rod is placed against each bush and all the growth above the mark cut off, thus leaving the weaker bushes untouched.

Closely allied to pruning are such processes as cleaning-out, thinning-out, spacing-out, and the removal of centers. Hope and Carpenter define cleaning-out as a method of pruning which comprises the following five distinct operations:

(a) Removal of all thin, unproductive shoots and twigs.
(b) Removal of dead wood and snags.
(c) Reducing the number of pruned shoots of new wood at the end of the heavy-bearing

branches to one or two; the outmost one not necessarily being left.
(d) Cutting off the smaller branches arising from the heavier framework of the bush, so as to reduce the branches to a comparatively small number of strong ones.
(e) Heading back all stout shoots of new wood from low down to a height of about six inches from the point of origin.[9]

Thinning-out comprises operations (a) and (b) only, while spacing-out comprises operations (a), (b), and (c).

The prunings usually are hoed into the soil, unless they consist of wood older than one year. In the latter case, they are burned, for the reason that decaying wood in the soil spreads disease. Buried prunings add to the humus of the soil.

Plucking

In Southern India, as in Ceylon, there is no drought or cold season comparable with Northern India. Accordingly, the bush flushes all the year round and is plucked from January to December. In Northern India, when the wind turns and blows cold and dry from the Tibetan plateau, the bushes cease to flush and manufacture stops. In March, the spring flush materializes and the planter watches the bright green color creep over his garden as he prepares for another season. The second flush comes in late May or early June. Teas then made are very tippy and bring high prices. After the second flush, which is a very definite one, the others are not well marked, because the shoots growing from axils below the plucking level in time reach that level and give a continuous

[9] G. D. Hope and P. H. Carpenter, *Some Aspects of Modern Tea Pruning*, Calcutta, 1914.

TEA PLUCKERS ON A HILLSIDE GARDEN, DARJEELING

THREE TYPES OF INDIAN TEA PLUCKERS AT WORK

At the left is a plucker of the type seen on the tea gardens in Darjeeling and the Dooars. She uses both hands to pluck. In the centre is a plucker on an Assam estate, also using both hands. To the right is another Assam garden plucker, using one hand and with slendang instead of basket.

supply of the leaf. The plucking season extends from late March or early April until about the middle of December. The number of flushes run from ten to fifteen, although a garden may be plucked from thirty to thirty-five times a year if labor is available—and even weekly during the flushing season. In Southern India, plucking generally continues throughout the year, although during the height of the monsoon the bushes may close. There are two big flushing periods; the first being April–May, when about 25 per cent of the total crop is made, and the second, September to December, when 35 to 40 per cent is made. Great variations in plucking intensity is shown, however, in different districts.

In plucking, the practice in Southern India is to take two leaves and a bud, leaving three fully developed leaves on the bush exclusive of the sheath leaf, which is variously designated as the *jannum* or "fish leaf." From the second flush on till the end of July, the rule is to leave at every plucking one fully developed leaf beside the *jannum*. From the first of August, close plucking, *i.e.*, the plucking of all strong bushes to the *jannum*, may be resorted to. The intervals between pluckings are from seven to nine days. The yield of each plucking, during the height of the season may touch 120 pounds or more of leaf per acre and thus give about thirty pounds of made tea.

Plucking may be coarse or fine; close or long. Fine plucking takes off two leaves and a bud, and coarse plucking, three or four leaves. Fine plucking makes

for quality. The composition of a shoot is:

Bud	14 per cent of shoot plucked.
First leaf	21 per cent of shoot plucked.
Second leaf	38 per cent of shoot plucked.
Stalk	27 per cent of shoot plucked.
	100 per cent.

Long plucking, means plucking at a distance from the old wood of a bush. Tea which has been heavily pruned must be plucked on a long growth of new wood, otherwise the bush suffers. As the bush gets older, and the top thickens up, the plucking may be made close; *i.e.*, to within about six inches of this wood. Close plucking makes better tea than long plucking, and the best tea is made by plucking close and fine.

The general rule for plucking in Northeast India is "two and a bud." Naturally, the severity of the plucking must depend on the health of the bush; but there is more in the problem than that. To mention the word "plucking" at any planters' club is to start an argument; for example, some planters let a bush grow to a certain height, about three feet, and then pluck it level. Others take the first flush, and then raise the height of the imaginary level before plucking again.

After a certain amount of tea has been plucked, a leaf with a dormant bud is formed at the extremity of a shoot, which then grows no further. This leaf is called a *banji*. Whether or not these *banji* leaves should be plucked is a problem still unsolved, but experiments carried on at Tocklai Experimental Station indicate *banjies* must be plucked or the crop suffers.

All plucking is done by hand, usually by women. The practice of putting the plucked leaf into a cloth bag carried in front of the plucker has been frowned upon, because of the tendency of the leaf to ferment. Even in baskets, temperatures as high as 140° F. have been recorded in the center of the leaf. When leaves are thus heated, they turn red. It is impossible to make good tea from a mixture of red and fresh leaf.

To prevent premature withering, it is customary to take the leaf to the factory at least twice a day. Here it is weighed in, either in the original baskets or after being transferred to other baskets; or it may be weighed in the field, so that the pluckers can continue their work uninterruptedly and thus earn more pay.

Withering

The atmosphere in Ceylon and Southern India is practically always humid, whereas, in Northern India it is only humid during the monsoon, a period of about four months. Accordingly, in Southern India it is usual to wither the leaf in enclosed lofts. Some of the lofts are provided with warm air circulation, the same as in Ceylon; but in many cases there is no such arrangement. In Assam, withering lofts rarely are used, as the leaf withers quite well on open air racks. In the Dooars, Terai, and Darjeeling, however, where the monsoon weather is rather more humid than in Assam, lofts are in general use.

The leaf house or withering shed may be one of two types. The "chung," or frame type, consists of a series of bamboo floor racks covered with Hessian. The chungs are three feet apart; just enough to allow boys to creep in and spread the leaf. They cover the whole floor except for a center aisle. There may be as many as ten tiers of chungs in a shed. The other type consists of a series of shallow racks of wire netting, although bamboo or coarse Hessian also are used. These racks are built on a slant six to nine inches apart, reaching a height of about six feet.

The newer withering sheds are made of iron; are tin roofed, and fitted with weather board. In some cases, movable mats or blinds are used to keep off the direct rays of the sun, or to shut out the rain. The floors are made of strips of bamboo covered with hessian. This type of leaf house

Bourne & Shepherd

TRANSPORTING THE LEAF TO AN OPEN-AIR "CHUNG" IN ASSAM

This illustrates the loft type of leaf house. In this case the withered leaf is dropped through chutes to the rollers on the ground floor.

Bourne & Shepherd

ROLLING, FERMENTING, AND FIRING ROOM IN A COMPACT FACTORY

FOUR IMPORTANT STEPS IN THE MANUFACTURE OF INDIA TEA

AN OLD FERMENTING ROOM, DARJEELING

is the most expensive, but general experience shows that it is the best so far as getting a good wither is concerned.

Chung withering is more even than the wire rack method, and the better tea made more than compensates for the extra cost in construction. The leaf is spread thinly. With a wire rack, about nine square feet are allowed for one pound of green leaf; but with a chung a greater area usually is given—sometimes as much as fifteen square feet. The thickness of spreading is controlled by the quantity of leaf brought in and by the spreading space available. Therefore, on many days the spreading is by no means ideal.

When lofts are used, fans are employed. These are of two types, wall fans and centrifugal cased fans. Among the better known makes are the Sirocco cased fan, for erection on the floor; the Sirocco wall fan; the Blackman box-bladed fans, placed in the end walls, and exhausting into the open air; the Blackman stream line fan; and the Keith open-type wheel.

The time consumed in withering is from eighteen to twenty hours. Leaf which has been withered in a warm room has a current of cold air passed over it for five or ten minutes before it is swept off the racks and taken to the rolling room.

Rolling

The system of rolling in British India is divided into three parts. First comes light rolling, which continues from ten to thirty minutes. After this the balls are broken in the *kutcha* sorter, or roll breaker. The flat type of *kutcha* sorter is preferred to the rotary type. After this comes forty-five minutes of heavy rolling with about

ten minutes of pressure on, and five off; or seven on, and three off. The third rolling is not always given. It consists of a final rolling for about ten minutes after fermentation. The periods vary.

Early in the season, with only part of the machinery in use, the tables often revolve at a speed of about eighty revolutions to the minute. The usual speed, however, is seventy to seventy-five revolutions per minute. In Darjeeling, they are slightly slower—sixty-five to seventy—and in Southern India the rate is forty to forty-five revolutions per minute, with a consequent longer rolling period and a greater number of rolls.

The rolling tables usually are covered with brass plates. After the brass wears out, cement slabs are sometimes used to replace the brass. The work is done by machine, the Jackson Rollers being the most popular. A full-sized machine takes four or five maunds, or 320 to 400 pounds, of withered leaf at a charge; the equivalent of one maund, or eighty pounds, of finished tea. In Northeast India, a modern roller deals with about 1000 maunds, or 80,000 pounds, of finished tea in a season.

Fermenting

The fermenting room usually is separated from other parts of the factory, but conveniently near the rolling room. It is the coolest place in the factory, being kept under 85° Fahrenheit.

According to the most modern practice, the leaf is spread on cement floors. Plate glass and tile beds are sometimes employed but cement beds are mostly favored in the newer factories. In others, shelves, tables, or tiers of trays may be found.

The leaf is spread from one to four inches thick, according to the season and

MODERN FERMENTING ROOM, ASSAM

FIRING OR DRYING MACHINES IN A DOOARS FACTORY

In practically all tea factories in British India, firing is done by machine. The drying is a continuous process.

TURNING OUT "ORANGE PEKOES" AND OTHER LEAF GRADES

This sifting and grading machine in a Darjeeling factory illustrates the last step in the manufacture of India teas.

TEA FIRING, SIFTING, AND GRADING EQUIPMENT IN NORTHERN INDIA

SIFTING THE FINE LEAF AND BREAKING UP THE BALLS BEFORE FERMENTATION, DARJEELING

the condition of the leaf. Quite commonly, it is covered with a wet cloth, which is so spread as not to come in direct contact with the leaf. The time required for fermenting is from two to six hours, depending on climatic conditions. In some of the modern tea factories, the fermenting rooms are being fitted with humidifiers similar to those used in cotton mills. These humidifiers force water under high pressure through a fine jet, and the result is a cloud of water vapor.

Firing or Drying

In practically all tea factories in British India, firing is done by machine. The drying is a continuous process. The leaf is put in at the top of the machine and comes out at the bottom. The hot air enters at the bottom, and the exhaust is at the top; consequently, the hottest air meets the driest leaf. There is a constant falling off in temperature of the air blast, and the fresh, wet leaf at the top is met by a temperature of about 140° Fahrenheit.

The first firing must be to three-quarters dry. A second firing then is carried out, except in Southern India, where tea is often subjected to but one firing. Large automatic machines are used generally for the first firing, and smaller hand-controlled machines for finishing. The time required for firing varies, but it is commonly about 30 to 40 minutes.

A large machine does work, which, by the old charcoal drying method, would require thirty to forty men to do. In some factories, the machines are so placed that the stoking of the furnaces may be done

from the veranda. The method of drying is not the same on every estate. On some, it is the rule to only partially dry the leaf in an endless chain drier, and to finish it off in smaller driers, while on other estates the tea is completely dried in the large drier. It is interesting to note the expressions used in India for designating the various degrees of dryness. The currency of the country is employed for this purpose. There are 16 annas in a rupee; consequently the planter speaks of "12 annas" dried tea to convey the fact that it is 75 per cent dry.

Some of the best known tea driers in use in India are: the "Sirocco" line, consisting of the Sirocco Tray Up-Draft drier, the Sirocco Up-Draft drier, the Sirocco Down-Draft drier, the Sorocco Enclosed Tilting Tray Pressure drier, and the Sirocco Endless Chain Pressure drier, all made by Davidson & Co., Ltd.; also Jackson's patent machines made by Marshall's Tea Machinery Co., Ltd., in addition to the "Paragon," the "Empire," the "Venetian," "Imperial Venetian," and the "Victoria" machines.

Sifting, Sorting, and Cleaning

After firing, the tea usually is put through a cutting machine to reduce the size of the larger leaves. Then it is put through sifting and sorting machines that separate it into grades. The sifting machines in use in British India are of two general types—revolving and oscillating. In both cases, the tea is made to pass over a wire mesh, which is agitated in such a way as to cause as much of the tea as possible to pass through the mesh. The mesh employed usually is of five different sizes, to suit the commonly accepted grades.

As a rule the first sieve the tea passes over has a No. 13 or 14 mesh, and makes about twenty-five revolutions a minute. This separates the Broken Orange Pekoe. The rest then goes on a No. 12 mesh to take out the Orange Pekoe, while a No. 10 is used for the Pekoe. The balance comprises the Pekoe Souchong, which goes to a cutting machine. The dust is taken out by a No. 24 sieve.

The classes produced are Broken Orange Pekoe, Orange Pekoe, Pekoe, Broken Pekoe, Pekoe Souchong, Fannings, and Dust. Some estates make fancy teas—Golden Tips, Flowery Orange Pekoe, and Flowery Pekoe—but these are not in such general use as the recognized standard grades. There is also the "fluff," which rises from the tea as it is sifted, and settles about the room, to be swept up later. The "fluff" is sold in Calcutta for use in the manufacture of caffeine.

The sorting and cleaning of tea is a long and expensive process. In the best factories, the tea is picked over by hand several times; generally after sifting. This work is done by women and boys. Generally, stalk and other extraneous matter is removed in this way, although a stalk extractor is coming into use.

Winnowing machines are used for cleaning tea. They remove the fiber. After the tea has been graded, each grade, including fannings and dust, is winnowed. The only winnower manufactured solely for use in tea is "MacDonald's deflector." Some planters use ordinary winnowing machines, similar to those used by farmers on grain. In Dum Duma and some other districts of India, the tea is dumped from baskets through the air current from an electric fan, thus cleaning the tea and separating it from the fannings and dust.

"Gaping," or Final-Firing

The practice of giving the tea a final fire after sorting, and before packing, to drive off any moisture accumulated during storage, is referred to in different districts as "gaping," "pucca-batti-ing," and "final-firing." During the time that elapses between the second fire and packing, as much as 10 or 12 per cent of moisture may be absorbed from the atmosphere of the factory. Tea keeps best with a moisture content of under 6 per cent. If tea contains more than this percentage, it "goes off," loses briskness, and becomes flat. There also is risk of moldiness. If tea is too dry, it does not "mellow," but remains with a certain indefinable harshness peculiar to newly made tea. Thus, gaping aims at reducing the moisture content to 5 or 6 per cent, but not more. There is no point in gaping tea already at 5 per cent moisture content. The apparatus for rapid determination of the moisture content in teas is cheap, the process simple, and capable of being carried out by the average clerk. It may be obtained from any Calcutta chemical dealers, at a cost of *Rs.* 200–250, and consists essentially of an oven, a weighing-balance, a drying jar, and some small basins. A quantity of tea is weighed into a basin and heated in a steam oven for a few hours. It then is cooled in the drying jar and weighed again. The loss in weight represents the moisture driven off and, calculated on a percentage basis, is an indication whether gaping is necessary, and if so, to what degree.

Bulking and Packing

Following sorting, tea usually is kept in the factory until sufficient bulk is collected to make a "break"—that is, a marketable quantity—and in the meantime it is stored in bins. Usually, it is subjected to a final-firing at about 150° F. in order to dry it thoroughly and reduce the moisture content to 5 per cent; which is sufficient to allow for mellowing of the tea, but not enough to permit the tea to become moldy.

In bulking, baskets of tea are placed around a canvas sheet spread on the floor, and then are dumped on the sheet, one by one. The pile is turned over and mixed by means of wooden spades.

There are several kinds of packing machines, but all of them work on the same principle; i.e., the chest is shaken rapidly while the tea is being put in. In one machine, the lead- or aluminum-lined chest is placed on a platform which oscillates at 2000 revolutions a minute. Another popular packer consists of a rocking table, upon which one or two chests are clamped, and which is subjected to a rapid vibratory movement.

A break of common teas may consist of

anything from fifty to 300 chests or more. In the case of fine quality teas, not more than twenty-five to forty of one class make up a break. About two ounces extra of tea in excess of the invoice weight are put in each chest to cover loss by evaporation.

The chests used generally are three-ply; the "Imperial," the "Luralda," and the "Venesta" being popular makes. Some gardens still use board chests of "shooks," made locally; but the extra weight of the chest itself costs as much or more in freight than the saving effected by their use. Three-ply chests are manufactured at Ledo, in Upper Assam. The tea chests are lined with lead or aluminum foil. In some instances where lead is used it is required that the chests be provided with inner paper linings.

After the chest has been packed, a sheet of lead is soldered on top, and the chest is carefully nailed up. Then it is stenciled with the garden mark and the progressive number, after which it is ready for shipment.

Green Tea

Green tea has been made in British India for more than seventy-five years. At one time, it was made in all the tea districts, but the manufacture at the present time continues only in Kangra, Travancore, Sylhet, Dehra Dun, Ranchi, Cachar, Nilgiris, Chittagong, Mysore, Almora, Malabar, Garhwal, and Tinnevelly—named in the order of the quantity of green tea each district produces.

The hand process of manufacturing green tea is much the same as that used in China. The late Mr. Charles G. L. Judge, who invented several machines for making green tea, described the process as follows:

The freshly gathered leaf is thrown into iron pans, which are some thirty-six inches in diameter and twelve inches deep. These pans are kept almost at a red heat by stoves burning wood or charcoal as fuel. The leaf in the pans is rapidly turned over and over and round and round by the hand or by sticks to prevent it scorching or burning.

In about three minutes, the fresh leaf is thereby rendered quite soft and the mass reduced to about half its original bulk. The leaf is next removed to the rolling tables, and there rolled by hand; a peculiar twist being given to it, much greater than that required for black tea, as green tea requires a curly leaf.

If there is any sun, the rolled leaf is thinly spread out in the sunshine until it becomes a blackish green, and is very sticky to the touch; or, if the weather is cloudy, the roll is put in mesh trays, or *chalnies*, over charcoal fires until it comes to the same condition.

It is then put in smaller iron pans, some twenty-five inches in diameter by twelve inches deep, and placed over a slow fire. These pans are only heated to such a degree that they are too warm to touch. The pans are about half filled, and the leaf in them is kept turning over and over until it has become quite soft again, when it is again taken to the rolling table and rolled for appearance.

When the day's batch has all been rolled a second time, the small pans are filled to the brim, the heat being gradually lowered and the tea is constantly turned about as before for about four hours, until it is almost dry to the touch. If a large percentage of Gunpowder tea is required, the leaf, at this stage, is crammed into long, narrow bags of stout fabric and well beaten together until it forms a compact mass. If a predominance of Hyson is preferred, the tea is stored in bins, where it may be left for weeks awaiting the finishing process. This process is carried out in the small heated pans above described. The pans should be heated until just too hot to touch and about half filled with tea, which is worked by hand rapidly from side to side and round and round, until it takes a light greenish tint, which it will do in about an hour and a half. It is then sorted into grades, fanned, and picked. The grades, before being packed for market, are again returned to the small pans and worked in the above described manner, with or without facing or coloring matter, until it has taken all the bloom it will take. This takes about two hours, when the tea is ready to pack for market.[10]

Tea that has been faced is often called "Finished Green" or "True Green," while the unfaced is described as "Unfinished Green" or "Natural Green." The usual material for facing is soapstone, one teaspoonful being required for four pounds of tea.

Machines have been invented to eliminate much of the hand process in green tea manufacture. Early in the 'nineties, Mr. Horace Drummond Deane, a Ceylon tea planter who later moved to Travancore, obtained patents on his steam process of treating the leaf for making green tea. It was not until 1902, however, that the first steaming machines were imported into India. Shortly after, Mr. Judge invented his centrifugal machine to throw off the condensed water from the leaf; i.e., a centrifugal drier.

To improve the color, a green tea finishing and glazing machine also was invented by Mr. Judge. This consists of a hexag-

10 Charles G. L. Judge, *Green Tea*, Calcutta, 1920.

MODERN ASSAM TEA FACTORIES

The upper picture is a view of Kutchujan, Tinsukia. The lower shows the factory and railway siding at Panitola, Dibrugarh.

onal, revolving drum some four feet in diameter, having a capacity of 600 to 750 pounds. A central stationary drum of copper is in the center, while mesh windows, protected by baffles, afford proper ventilation. Other green tea finishing and glazing machines appeared on the market later.

In Dehra Dun, the leaf is sterilized by placing it in a shallow pan kept hot by a fire directly underneath. The leaf crackles and splutters, and after vigorous turning suddenly settles down. It then is ready for rolling, and must be removed from the pan immediately to prevent burning.

When green tea is made in Assam the process is as follows:

As soon as possible after plucking, the leaf is brought to the factory, where it is placed loosely in a long hexagonal box into which steam is blown for about ninety seconds. The box is revolved at about twenty-five revolutions per minute. Then the leaf is removed, cooled, and dried in a hydro-extractor making about 1000 revolutions per minute. During the process, much liquid is drawn off containing a considerable quantity of solids. About 15 per cent of the solids are lost during this process. This means that the leaf makes 15 per cent less than it would if black tea were being made. When the leaf is drained, it is taken from the extractor and opened out, as it cakes somewhat. Next, the leaf is rolled in an open-top roller for

about half an hour, after which it is partially dried in an ordinary firing machine to a degree just short of crispness. The semi-dried leaf again is rolled for half an hour. The final firing is done in an ordinary machine at about 180° Fahrenheit.

Green tea is polished by being rotated in a hexagonal box lined with sheet iron. The addition of one per cent French chalk puts on a polish.

To make the best green tea, hard or *banji* leaf is carefully avoided. The grades of green tea are Fine Young Hyson, Young Hyson, Hyson No. 1, Hyson, Soumee, Twankay, Fannings, and Dust.

Green tea made by the hot pan process is better than that made by steaming, and in addition, there is no need to centrifuge the leaf, because it never gets wet, thus obviating the centrifuge loss in liquors.

Attempts at Brick Tea Manufacture

Sample lots of brick tea were prepared at one time in Darjeeling and Kumaon for the Tibetan and Bhutan markets, but none is made at present.

As long ago as 1883, the possibilities of introducing Indian brick tea into Tibet were discussed. In 1905, James Hutchison was appointed Commissioner by the Indian Tea Association to visit China and investigate the process of making brick tea and the possibilities of the market. His report is most interesting.[11] However, the Lamas have a monopoly of the brick tea trade in Tibet, and have effectually opposed entrance of Indian brick tea into a

[11] Jas. Hutchison, *Indian Brick Tea for Tibet, Report on a Mission to Szechuen,* Calcutta, 1906.

COOLIE TEA TRANSPORT, DARJEELING

Showing the approved method of transporting tea chests from the tea estates up the steep paths to the nearest railway or level road.

market already well served from Chinese sources.

Transportation

The difficulty of getting the tea from the producing districts to the market at Calcutta has been an ever present one in India; for example, Dibrugarh is 830 miles by railway from Calcutta. In Assam and the Dooars unbridgeable rivers hamper the way.

The main traffic artery of Assam was, until the beginning of the present century, the Brahmaputra—the *Bara Naddi*, or Big River—in some places two miles or more in width. A service of paddle steamers plies between Calcutta and Dibrugarh, a distance of approximately a thousand miles, which is covered in about a fortnight. The outlet for districts on the north bank still is by steamer as far as Gauhati.

In the Surma Valley, the Barak River was the main outlet before the railway was opened, and much tea still is brought by country boats to the Brahmaputra, where it is transhipped to steamers. Besides this, the Surma Valley is in direct railway communication with Chittagong. To get to Calcutta, it is necessary to change at Chandpur and go by steamer to Goalundo, whence the broad gauge section of the Eastern Bengal Railway goes to Calcutta.

The Dooars is served by the Bengal Dooars Railway, which connects with the Eastern Bengal at Lalmanirhat, where contact is made with the line from Assam to Calcutta. This line continues to Santahar, where it joins the broad gauge road from Siliguri. Tea must be transhipped at Santahar. An alternative exit for tea is via Dhubri on the Brahmaputra, where the tea is transhipped to the river steamer and taken direct to Calcutta.

The first railways in Assam were the Jorhat Provincial Railway and the Dibru-Sadiya Railway, both built with the idea of connecting the tea districts with the Brahmaputra. Then the Assam Bengal Railway was constructed from Chittagong to Tinsukia, crossing from Cachar into the Assam Valley at Lumding. Following this, the line from Lumding to Gauhati was completed, and an alternative route to Calcutta was by railway to Gauhati, and then by river steamer to Dhubri, where connection is had with the Eastern Bengal

RIVER TRANSPORT, ASSAM

Upper—Type of country boat used for transporting tea from isolated gardens. *Lower*—Transferring tea chests from box cars to Brahmaputra River barges.

Railway. The last link in the chain of communication between Calcutta and Assam was completed when the line from Lalmanirhat to Amingaon, opposite Gauhati, opened for operation. During the last few years several important branch lines have been built in Assam.

Darjeeling suffers the inconveniences of transport that are unavoidable in a hilly district. In many cases, the main trouble is to get the tea to the Darjeeling Himalayan Railway, a two-foot gauge line, which runs from Darjeeling, at a height of about 7000 feet, down to Siliguri in the plains, where it joins the broad gauge to Calcutta.

To get the tea to the railways it sometimes is necessary to haul it by lorries [motor trucks] or bullock carts for several miles. This demands good roads. In Assam, the roads are of dirt and, accordingly, are thick either with dust or mud. Many places are isolated in the rains except for bullock cart traffic.

OLD AND NEW COOLIE LINES

Upper—Old-style lines on the Bokel Tea Estate, Dibrugarh. *Lower*—New-style lines on the same estate.

In the Surma Valley, some of the roads are better, partly because laterite from the *teelas* is available, and partly because much of the traffic is down the small rivers, thus reducing the road traffic. In the Dooars, roads are numerous and good all the year round. The trouble there is the rivers, which cut the district transversely, thus making it difficult to bridge them.

In Dehra Dun, bullock carts and lorries are used to carry tea to the railway running to Calcutta. This also is the case in Ranchi. In Kangra and Kumaon, some of the gardens are remotely located, making it necessary to have coolies carry the tea to the nearest road. In Chittagong, the roads are atrocious, so the tea is mostly shipped by sea—to Calcutta and London.

South India has a good railway system; one branch running near the Anamalais; another to Ootacamund, etc. In addition, the roads are of excellent macadam, and the tea, in many cases, is taken 100 miles by bullock carts and lorries to the railway. The drawback, however, is the heavy rainfall; sometimes amounting to forty or fifty inches in a single month. This, naturally, tends to wash out the roads, and communications are held up for a few days or a week.

Labor Problems, Past and Present

It seems strange that in India, the land of "teeming millions," the worst problem of the tea industry is labor. This is partic-

ularly true of Assam, the Dooars, and Terai. The trouble in these districts is that the indigenous population is fully occupied in the cultivation of private lands. However, satisfactory labor has been found, mainly in Chota Nagpur and the Santal Pergannas in the province of Bihar and Orissa, in the Central Provinces, and in the distant provinces of Madras and Bombay. Mundas, Oraons, and Santals are the favorite types recruited in Bihar and Orissa, and Gonds in the Central Provinces.

The Tea Districts Labor Association may be regarded as the labor recruiting branch of the Indian Tea Association, some 92 per cent of the tea interests in Assam being members, while some 70 per cent of the Dooars and Terai interests are members. The secretaries are Messrs. Begg, Dunlop & Co., Ltd., Calcutta.

Formerly, it was the practice to place laborers on contracts, which could extend to three years under the Workmen's Breach of Contract Act, or Act XIII of 1859. Laborers recruited by *sirdari*, or native foremen, were eager to place themselves under Act XIII contracts. The reason for this was the attraction of the advance necessary before such an agreement could be entered into. Such advances being at the rate of about 12 rupees per annum, if a man and his wife entered into an agreement, the advances enabled them to purchase plough cattle for their private cultivation. Several years ago, however, the period of the contract was reduced to one year, and on June 30, 1926, Act XIII was repealed. There was substituted for the Act XIII contract a purely civil form of agreement, for the breach of which redress lay only in the Civil Court.

Later, it was found that limiting recruiting to that done by *sirdari* was too great a handicap on new gardens and extensions, and in 1932 a new Act was passed which removed restrictions on recruitings, but controlled the forwarding of emigrants, paying greater attention to their welfare, and providing for their repatriation at the end of the first three years in Assam. The Act does not apply to Dooars and Terai tea estates, which recruit voluntarily by *sirdari* methods, mainly through the Tea Districts Labor Association.

Tea will thrive only on land not subject to inundation, consequently, there are, on the majority of grants, certain lands unsuitable for its growth. The proportion of such lands may rise in some areas to as much as 50 per cent of the grant. These lands are, however, just what are required for paddy, or rice, cultivation. Accordingly, on most estates, laborers who intend to settle are granted paddy lands for their personal cultivation, either rent free or at a very nominal rent. The majority of the 500,000 settled laborers in Assam hold their own land.

Paddy land is, however, not altogether an unmixed blessing to a tea estate; the coolie spends too much of his time on his own cultivation, and very largely limits his work to what under the former Workmen's Breach of Contract Act used to be the minimum task. This task takes an experienced laborer from two and one-half to three hours. The position of these laborers, therefore, is rather that of feudal tenure holders; they hold paddy lands and recognize an obligation to do a certain minimum task on twenty-four days of each month. This necessitates a labor force of at least one to one and a half coolies per acre for efficient cultivation.

Table Number Seven, prepared by the Department of Commercial Intelligence and Statistics, indicates the gradual rise in wages paid to coolies. In scrutinizing these wages, it must be borne in mind that the great majority possess about an acre of paddy land per family, which alone is sufficient to maintain them.

In addition to his wages a coolie on an estate receives the following advantages:

Housing: Cost, 300 rupees per room—a
  very low estimate—say 3 persons per
  room, 100 rupees per head capital costs,
  representing a rental of 10 rupees per
  head per annum 10.00
Loss on rice provided for their use........11.25
Medical aid 5.00
Sick relief 2.00
Feeding children 5.30
Concessions, such as gratuities at births,
  marriages, deaths, festivals, and other
  ceremonies 3.62
Blankets, one per head per annum....... 3.00

Cost per head per annum.................40.17
Cost per head per day, reckoning 26 days
  per month .... .13

In addition to the foregoing, the estate coolie enjoys free of cost to himself a pure water supply laid on close by; his temple, or a choice of several, equally convenient; free schooling for his children; good shed built by the estate for his cattle; a creche where his children can be left in safety when he and his wife are out at work; firewood to be had for the picking up; and a garden plot, where he can grow vegetables. Worked out for an estate of 500 acres, the amount spent on the labor force, over and above their wages, comes to 20,605 rupees per annum.

With a reduction of pressure on the soil in the recruiting districts, land in Assam ceases to have an attraction for the possible laborer in Chota Nagpur or Madras. Only those will emigrate who are temporarily embarrassed, and the planter who has become accustomed to the settled labor system, where his feudal tenure holders work a minimum task without much supervision, is faced with the problem of adapting conditions to newcomers who demand the opportunity of earning from 12 annas to a rupee a day, and who need constant supervision. Such people emigrate for short terms only—from six months to two years.

Assam is suffering from a clash of the two systems; the settled laborers are prone to become unsettled at the sight of high wages paid to the newcomers, while the latter obviously are jealous of the life of ease lived by the settled labor. Superadded to this is the effect of the general custom that but three hours work a day is the proper quota for a self-respecting laborer. In short, on a tea estate, class and the pride of leisure are intruding themselves into the tea garden Eden, and causing trouble as did the serpent of old.

The problem of labor in the Dooars and Terai is very similar. Here there is no

INDIA TABLE NO. 7
Average Monthly Wages of Laborers Employed in the Tea Gardens in Assam During the Years 1926–27 to 1930–31

Year	NON-ACT LABORERS								
	Men			Women			Children		
	Rs.	A.	P.	Rs.	A.	P.	Rs.	A.	P.
1926–27......	11	6	1	9	8	5	5	14	0
1927–28......	12	4	5	10	6	8	6	6	6
1928–29......	13	2	3	10	6	3	6	10	10
1929–30......	12	11	3	10	3	5	6	11	11
1930–31......	12	10	7	9	12	2	6	8	8

NOTE.—The average wages are calculated on the average daily working strength of two typical months (September and March). The figures refer to all cash earnings but exclude non-cash payments.

restrictive labor act, but, as has been indicated above, managers of tea estates
have been driven further afield in their
search for labor, and today the field is
co-extensive with that prospected by
Assam.

Recently, a Dooars Branch of the Tea
Districts Labor Association has been
formed, which is operated altogether separately, and governed by an elected
Dooars Control Committee. The interesting point about this move is that members have voluntarily assumed what in
some quarters are considered the statutory
shackles which burden the Assam planter.
For instance, members bind themselves to
restrict their operations solely to garden
sirdars, just as Assam planters are obliged
to do by law. An exception is made in a
small area of Madras, where labor is recruited by local recruiters ,and distributed
to estates under a pool system, in order
to give the estates the nuclei for sirdari
recruiting.

The system of working labor is very
similar to that obtaining in Assam, except
that an estate sirdar is employed as a
gangman and gets a small commission on
the earnings of his gang, which may number from fifteen to a hundred. He is not
a contractor, nor is he responsible for the
recruitment of members of his gang.
Herein he differs from the *kangani*, or
maistrie, of the Southern India estates,
who is, in some respects, similar to the
Italian *padrone*.

On both Assam and Dooars Estates may
be found representatives of practically
every caste and tribe in India. The problem of dealing sympathetically with their
heterogeneous labor forces can well be imagined, and calls for the exercise of no
little tact. A handbook of castes and
tribes employed on tea estates in Northeast India has been compiled by the
Tea Districts Labor Association, and
twelve language handbooks have been
issued. These consist in the main of a
complete set of phrases dealing with life
on a tea estate, and were contributed by
the planters. The following list indicates
the range of languages:

1. Mundari	7. Oraon
2. Santali	8. Nepalese
3. Telegu	9. Assamese
4. Kanarese	10. Khond
5. Gondi	11. Sadhani
6. Oriya	12. Kharia

Manuals of Hindustani and Bengali are'
not included, as suitable handbooks of
these languages are already on the market.

The races most sought after on tea estates are the Dravidian aboriginals, who
fall roughly into two groups:

(a) Dravidian Speaking [Oraon and Telegu
are types]. Thirty-one castes and tribes.
(b) *Kolarian Speaking* [Mundari and Savara
are types]. Twelve castes and tribes.

The Dravidian languages are indigenous
to India, while the Kolarian fall into the
Austric group, with links ranging to Australia. The Dravidian speakers are probably aborigines, and the Kolarian speakers
are supposed to be the earliest invaders
from what is now Australasia. Neither
language has any relationship whatever
with the Aryan languages—Bengali, Hindi,
and Assamese—nor with the Mongolian
dialects spoken on the Indian borders.

A third section, also highly regarded,
consists of the quasi-aboriginals, or Dra-
vidians, who have become more or less absorbed within the Hindu polity. These
include sixty-seven castes and tribes.

Newly arrived emigrants soon acquire
the garden *bat*, a mixture of Assamese,
Hindustani, and Bengali, so that it is seldom necessary for a manager to speak any
other dialect. However, those planters
who have interested themselves to the extent of mastering Mundari, Santali, Gondi,
or one or another of the local dialects, have
been rewarded by better contact and understanding of their help.

The planter who learns the languages of
his laborers inevitably acquires a knowledge of their psychology in so doing. He
learns, for instance, that leave is essential
on the occasion of certain festivals, and
knows their significance; also, that three
or four days off are necessary each year
for the performance of *sradh* ceremonies
for relatives who have passed into the
hereafter. He is not, therefore, moved to
laughter when a recurrent request is made
year after year, beginning with the formula "my father is dead." He knows better than to house a Dom and a Kurmi
close together, even in perfectly appointed
barracks; but instead, grants each a location where he may be with his own caste
and build his own *busti* [village]. He is
the sort of *sahib* to whom it is possible
for the coolie to turn for sympathetic understanding and, if need be, for an ad-

GREEN LEAF TRANSPORT, ASSAM

Upper—Steam locomotive and leaf wagons bringing in the leaf from out-lying gardens, Panitola Tea Estate, Dibrugarh.
Middle—Bullock transport, Muttuck Tea Estate, Dibrugarh.
Lower—Chevrolet lorry and trailer for leaf transport at the Tippuk Tea Estate, Talup, Dum Duma.

vance of money. Such a master becomes an epitome of the attractiveness of an estate where it is possible to live and work in comfort, and without peril to the soul.[12]

Garden Railways and Tramways

On large estates, wire tramways have come into use for transporting the leaf to the factory. If the slope is down hill, the endless rope system is used; the loaded basket pulling up the empty one by means of its weight. Single wire tramways, consisting of a wire rope stretched fairly tight, over which the load is hooked on grooved pulleys, are common. They work by gravity and may extend a distance of over a mile. The drawback to this type is that the empty baskets must be carried back by hand. Power ropeways also are used to transport tea over ground where it is impossible to use gravity. Top soil, fertilizers, etc., also are carried by wire tramways.

When an estate is situated far back from the main lines of shipment, light steam railways or push car tramways are

[12] Tea Districts Labor Association, *Handbook of Castes and Tribes*, Calcutta, 1924.

in use. This is particularly true of Assam, where light railways connect the gardens with the Brahmaputra River's steamer *ghats*.

Indians in Tea

According to one authority, the first Indian tea estate was started by an inhabitant of Sylhet in 1876. This man, Mr. B. C. Gupta, and his companion, Mr. D. N. Dutt, are credited with being the pioneer Indians in tea. Others have followed, among them being Raja Girischandra Roy of Sylhet, Manikohandra Barua of the Brahmaputra Valley, Rai Bahadur Bishnuram Barua of Assam, and a group of Indians in Jalpaiguri. Since 1907, more than thirty native companies have been started in Sylhet, with others in Comilla and Brahmanbaria, Jalpaiguri, Rangoon, and Calcutta. In 1920, many of these failed.

In Assam proper, very few gardens are Indian-owned, but in Kangra, Darjeeling, the Dooars, and the Terai fair areas are owned by Indian companies, and Jalpaiguri is the headquarters of the Indian Tea Planters Association. There are one or two gardens owned by Indians in Chittagong, and in Hill Tippera all the gardens are so controlled.

The Indian Tea Association

The Indian Tea Association, parent organization of the Indian tea industry, is a merger of two earlier associations—the Indian Tea Association of Calcutta and the Indian Tea Districts Association of London.

The London association dropped the name "Indian Tea Districts Association" in 1894, the date of the merger. All questions arising in England are handled by the London branch, and all questions arising in India are handled by the Calcutta branch. Each association appoints a General Committee to manage its affairs, and issue recommendations to members on various questions arising from time to time, but without authority to enforce any recommendation.

Speaking generally, the more important objects of the Indian Tea Associations of Calcutta and London are to promote the common interests of all persons concerned in the cultivation and marketing of tea in Northern India, and to expand the home and foreign markets therefor. The latter includes advertising campaigns, together with exhibits and pavilions at expositions.

The Calcutta branch is composed of tea estate owners, managers of, and agents for tea estates, including limited companies. The London branch is composed of individuals, companies, and firms in London interested in the production of India tea.

The subscription for each garden belonging to the Calcutta branch is fixed annually; an average year's rate being about nine annas per acre under tea cultivation.

The business and funds of the Calcutta branch are controlled by its General Committee consisting of nine firms elected annually by the members of the Association. Each of the nine firms elected nominates a representative to serve on the General Committee, and the Committee, in turn, elects its Chairman and Vice-Chairman.

The Secretary and Assistant Secretary of the Bengal Chamber of Commerce are ex-officio Secretary and Assistant Secretary of the Association, which has been connected with the Chamber since 1885. Also, the Association has a representative on the Bengal Legislative Council.

The headquarters of the Indian Tea Association, Calcutta, are located at the Royal Exchange, No. 2, Clive Street. There are two branches—the Assam branch, with headquarters at Dibrugarh, and the Surma Valley branch, with headquarters at Binnakandi in Cachar.

Functions of Scientific Department

The functions of the Scientific Department of the Indian Tea Association are three in number—research, correlation of results, and dissemination of the knowledge gained. The principal work consists in research, which is carried out in the laboratories, and correlated with observations made in the field. The mycological, entomological, chemical, botanical and bacteriological laboratories are staffed by Indians and directed by Europeans, each a specialist in his own branch. Much of the work done appears on the surface to be far removed from the more active aspects of the industry, but it is noticeable that purely academic work often turns out to be of prime practical importance.

In the chemical laboratory, soils are analyzed and a detailed study is made of soil acidity as it occurs in the tropics. Much work also has been done on the chemical changes which take place in the leaf during manufacture, and this work has been facilitated by the erection of a model tea factory at Tocklai.

Insect enemies of tea are studied in the entomological laboratory, for it is only through knowledge of the detailed life history of pests that they can be successfully circumvented. At present, the main problem of the entomological laboratory is mosquito blight. This is not caused by the mosquito that interests itself in human beings, but by a quite different insect, which looks something like the familiar variety. The tea mosquito gets its food by puncturing the young leaves of the bush, and sucking the sap. The young shoots are thus destroyed and millions of pounds of tea are lost annually.

In the mycological laboratory, the fungus diseases of the plant are considered. There is a large range of leaf, stem, and root diseases to be studied, and the particular predisposing causes and preventives to be ascertained. As time goes on and study is intensified, more and more pests and blights are discovered, until now the number which a planter must deal with is bewildering.

The bacteriologist studies the soil bacteria that are responsible for making food available for the plant. Here again, the history of the microörganism is as important to know as are the conditions favorable to its growth. Another problem for the bacteriological laboratory is that of the bacteria concerned with the fermentation of the tea leaf. This subject has been investigated by many scientists, but much still remains to be done.

The second function of the scientific staff is coördinating or correlating laboratory results with happenings in the field. Since conditions in agriculture are never exactly repeated, it follows that each piece of work done by the planter is in the nature of an experiment. For example, one year a certain type of pruning does well, and the next year it fails utterly. Why? Is it a question of weather, a difference in the condition of the bush, or what is it? It needs a mind scientifically trained to sort out the true facts in this or any garden problem. Under ideal conditions, a certain operation will lead to certain results, but all too often things

THE TEA EXPERIMENTAL STATION OF THE INDIAN TEA ASSOCIATION AT TOCKLAI, CINNAMARA, ASSAM

do not come out according to theory. There is an inevitable gap between theory and practice that it is the scientific observer's job to bridge and explain, and this is constantly being done by members of the staff at Tocklai.

Continually visiting gardens, as the scientific officers do, they have a unique opportunity to observe methods and results from one end of the country to the other, and the information thus collected is invaluable.

The third function of the Scientific Department is the business of disseminating the knowledge and experience gained. This has been done partly by the publication of the *Quarterly Journal*, now an annual journal, but mainly by touring the gardens. Every planter is keen to know what is going on in other districts, and to hear the experience of others.

Tocklai Experimental Station

The Tea Experimental Station of the Indian Tea Association at Tocklai, near the village and post office of Cinnamara, Assam, in Northeast India, consists of chemical, mycological, entomological, bacteriological, botanical laboratories, model tea factory, guest house, bungalows, coolie lines, etc., and covers about twelve acres. In addition, there is a much larger tract of land, belonging to the Station, at Borbhetta, two and a half miles away.

Only about five acres at Tocklai are put out under tea. The main plot, which is called the Tocklai Clearance, is devoted to jat, or variety, trials. Broadly speaking, the *jats* are divided into three main groups —China, Assam, and Burma. Here each is observed as to its hardiness, yielding ca-

pacity, suitability to the climate, etc. Smaller plots are occupied by more than fifty varieties, including Indo-China, High Burma, Low Burma, and others having slight differences to be detected only by an experienced eye.

Numerous pruning experiments are in progress, for there are many methods of turning the tea shrub into a bush low enough to be plucked by a woman. The most drastic of these is to cut the young plant close to the ground, and build up a bush gradually. This method is called collar-pruning. Another method is to cut through the bush at about eighteen inches from the ground, and then, by judicious removal of branches from year to year, build up a bush without loss of crop through the early years. The beauty of the Tocklai pruning demonstration is that the planter can come and see the results of many styles of pruning side by side, together with accurate crop records over the preceding decade.

After the pruning comes plucking, and although tea bushes have been plucked for hundreds of years, men have not yet agreed upon the ideal method. Naturally the severity of the plucking must depend on the health of the bush, but there is more to it than that. Take an imaginary flat-topped table through the bush at a height of about three feet from the ground, and the problem is whether it will pay to pluck all the shoots of two leaves and a bud which appear above that table, or whether it is better to take the first lot, and then, before plucking again, to raise the height of the imaginary table. A simple problem it seems, until one sets about its study and realizes the diversity of opinion on the subject, and the wide variation in crop returns from apparently identical experiments.

Another study at Tocklai is that of the green manures best suited to tea gardens. Also, a fairly well equipped meteorological observatory has been erected at the station in order to permit study of the correlation of tea crops with the weather. This permits conclusions as to how much of crop increase is due to improved methods, and how much of crop decrease is due to pests and blights.

At Borbhetta there are now about sixty acres of tea planted out for experimental purposes. As at Tocklai, the situation is by no means ideal either from the standpoint of rainfall or of soil; in fact, the site was chosen because of soil poverty.

The Tocklai experiments are repeated and amplified at Borbhetta, and the problem of finding how the bush grows is under constant investigation. A planter who must raise tea to turn a profit is often debarred from doing what he knows to be best in the long run. In 1921, tea sold on the Calcutta market for two annas [2d Eng., 4¢ U. S.] a pound. In 1924, it sold for about two rupees [3s Eng., 72¢ U. S.] a pound. Naturally, the method of working a garden under conditions existing in 1921 was different from that in 1924, although the tea bush was growing in the same way, and had had the same physical requirements in both years. The problems connected with plant growth present themselves year after year irrespective of market fluctuations, and on this account a station must, within reason, be run regardless of cost.

Tea is put out in nurseries at Borbhetta, and after about a year is transplanted. The best kind of shade for nurseries, the best method of sowing the seed, the best time to transplant, and a dozen other problems are studied.

And then, there is the study of manuring. The tea crop consists in the leaf, and nitrogenous manures make for leaf. How important is it, then, to know which kind of nitrogenous manure pays best, when and how is it best applied, and how much can be used with safety. The tea bush has a very hard time of it. It is pruned hard, plucked hard, and then is forced by manuring to give more than its natural outturn of leaf; but there is a limit beyond which it cannot be pushed with profit, and this limit is one of the problems under study at Borbhetta. It was held by some

that too much nitrogen made the bush susceptible to certain fungus diseases, but it was later found that the trouble was not due to excessive nitrogen but to the form [nitrate of soda] in which it was supplied and that sulphate of ammonia gave better results.

As at Tocklai, pruning experiments are being carried on, and plucking also receives further attention. Then comes the problem of cultivation, a major one because of its bearing on the vexed question of labor. Practically speaking, all tea garden cultivation is done by hand, because the bushes are too close together to permit ordinary mechanical cultivators to work without damaging the branches. Several types of light, bullock-drawn cultivators are being tried. In addition, the effects of various types of cultivation—deep-hoeing, trenching, light-hoeing, and weeding—are being watched.

One of the most interesting experiments is that of seed selection. According to Mendelian tenets, when two plants are crossed, the characteristics of the parents are, in some cases, mixed in the offspring; while they come through pure, in others. Now, in breeding from a mixed offspring some of the next generation will be mixed and some pure, or not so mixed as others. As has been previously mentioned, tea jats are divided into several groups, so, by breeding from the purest strain obtainable and then by selection from successive generations, it may be possible to obtain, eventually, a pure strain bush. It takes about three years for a seed to grow and produce more seed, and as it will take many generations of selective breeding to produce a pure strain, the results of the experiment on hand will fall to some future generation of tea planters.

The study of tea manufacture, on the whole, has made little progress in recent years. The discovery in Java of a yeast which occurs in tea leaf and flourishes in fermenting tea, and which was thought, when discovered, to be a very important factor in tea manufacture, has not been followed up thoroughly. A similar yeast has been found in India and there are indications, uncertain as yet, of its connection with the production of flavor. There is no doubt that one of the greatest services which science now can render to the tea industry is the thorough and systematic study of tea manufacture, and the combination of a special chemist and a bacteriologist now available at Tocklai, with the small experimental plant for the conduct of the various operations of tea manufacture under controlled conditions, provide an opportunity of great value.

Tocklai and Borbhetta are not places to be visited only once or twice. An annual visit is necessary in order to watch experiments develop, and to realize the changes that are taking place. Practically every aspect of tea growing can be seen, and although the business center of the Indian tea industry is at Calcutta, the front line trenches may be said to be at Tocklai and Borbhetta.

In addition to the experimental work at Tocklai and Borbhetta, in Assam, the Indian Tea Association established in 1925 a temporary substation in the Dooars, located at Sylee Tea Estate, with Mr. C. R. Harler, chemist from the staff at Tocklai, in charge. The planters in the Dooars expressed themselves as anxious to have this temporary station converted into a permanency, but owing to the increasing expenditures of the Scientific Department it had to be discontinued. It has been suggested that substations be opened in the Terai, in Darjeeling, and in the Surma Valley of Cachar and Sylhet. The research center would continue to be at Tocklai, however, while the subsidiary stations would study conditions from the local angle, and apply the results of the research at Tocklai. A permanent station, for field work only, was established at Tulsipara, Dooars, in 1930.

No account of the work of the Scientific Department would be complete without mention of the lecture courses for tea planters at Tocklai. Men come from all over the tea districts in groups of twenty, and stay for a week of lectures in the fall.

The Scientific Department receives most of its financial support from the Indian Tea Association, which in turn collects an acreage tax on the estates of members, and receives special grants and subscriptions from the Governments of Assam and Bengal, as well as various District Planters' Associations. The expenditure has been increasing gradually, as the demand increases for more and more scientific work. It now averages about seven annas [7d. Eng., 14¢ U. S.] per acre, and comprises about 80 per cent of the total funds of the Indian Tea Association.

The financial affairs of the Department are conducted in Calcutta, at the headquarters of the Indian Tea Association, and all accounts are kept there. The Chief Scientific Officer has a cash advance from which he pays the subordinate staff and laborers, as well as all petty miscellaneous expense; reporting the same in a monthly expenditure statement, which is printed and circulated to the members of the Association.

The Scientific Department subcommittee of the Indian Tea Association meets fortnightly in Calcutta, and all excesses on the votes for the Department have to receive the sanction of this body before they are incurred. The subcommittee also has power to sanction adjustments between votes. Every quarter the Chief Scientific Officer attends a meeting of this committee, and reports on the work that has been carried out during the period under consideration and at present in hand by the various scientific officers.

Tea Planters' Associations

In addition to the Indian Tea Association of Calcutta, which has an Assam Branch at Dibrugarh and a Surma Valley Branch at Binnakandi in Cachar, there is the United Planters' Association of Southern India, which serves the general planting interests of its section of the country, various district planters' associations scattered throughout the planting areas of both Northern and Southern India, and the Planters' Benevolent Institution at Calcutta.

The district organizations serve a most important purpose in unifying the efforts of planters toward the solution of the problems affecting the collective planting interests.

The Indian [native] Planters' Association has been organized recently in Travancore to promote the interests of the Indian planters of the state. There is a similar Indian Planters' Association in the Dooars, with headquarters at Jalpaiguri. It controls all the tea area under native cultivation in the Dooars and Terai.

The planters' associations afford their members opportunity for discussion and united expression on legislation, either pending or otherwise, and their recommendations always receive due consideration.

In local matters the associations take up

such urgent questions as railway and highway communication, and press for needed improvements.

Not the least of the benefits conferred by the associations on their members are the opportunities afforded at the meetings to hear practical talks by visiting scientific or practical tea men, hygienists, and others.

U.P.A.S.I. Tea Experimental Station

The Tea Experimental Station of the United Planters' Association of Southern India, Devarshola P. O., Nilgiris, consists of twenty-seven acres of land on Woodbriar Estate, leased from the owners, Messrs. G. W. and E. A. Fulcher. The buildings include the Scientific Officer's bungalow, the laboratory and office building, Assistant Scientific Officer's bungalow, Farm Manager's bungalow, Clerk's Bungalow, three sets of coolie lines, power house, and battery house. All of the buildings have been built of bricks made on the spot, and they are roofed with tiles. The bungalows of the European staff and the office and laboratory are equipped with water and electric lights.

Advisory work is an important part of the task of the Scientific Department of the U.P.A.S.I. It involves recommendations on manuring, treatment of pests and fungoid diseases, cultivation, pruning, suitability of land for the growth of tea, and all other questions connected with tea culture. Small articles, as a general rule, are published in the *Planters' Chronicle*, the recognized organ of the Association. In addition to full *Annual Reports*, the following publications have been made by the Tea Scientific Officer:

    1. *Principles and Practical Considerations Involved in Tea Manuring.*
    2. *Observations on Helopeltis for South Indian Planters.*
    3. *Suggested Treatment of Root Rot.*
    4. *Tannin in Tea.*

Touring the tea districts occupies a certain portion of the Tea Scientific Officers' time; the general plan being that each Scientific Officer shall tour respective halves of the tea districts in alternate years.

Considerable laboratory work has been done looking to exact determination of such constituents of tea as tannin, etc. Also, chemical investigations of the decomposition products of tea tannin [phlobaphenes], the synthetic compounds of tea tannin with alkaloids, and of the material responsible for "creaming down" of tea. Interesting results are expected.

The Tea Scientific Department of the U.P.A.S.I. is financed from a cess of eight annas per acre on all tea of district planters' associations belonging to the U.P.A.S.I. In addition, *Rs.* 28,000 is contributed by the Government of Madras to be divided between the three products—tea, coffee, and rubber—according to the acreage of each.

The Tea Planter's Life in India

A tea planter's job in India is no sinecure. In addition to knowing how to cultivate, prune, pluck, and manufacture tea, he must know how to grow bamboos, burn bricks, build houses, construct bridges, and make roads. He must be something of an engineer, a surveyor, and an accountant. Self-reliance and an indomitable spirit are necessities.

The planter must settle disputes among his laborers, doctor the sick, and know what is going on in the villages adjoining his grant. He must be *ma-bap*, or mother and father, to the hundreds of coolies he employs. In short, he must be able to manage labor. No matter how good he may be at his garden and office work, however keen in his observation and meticulous in

MANAGERS' BUNGALOWS, ASSAM
Upper—The assistant's bungalow at Daisajan, Talup.   *Lower*—Manager's bungalow, Woodbine Tea Estate, Dibrugarh.

BUNGALOW OF THE JOREHAUT TEA COMPANY'S SUPERINTENDENT AT CINNAMARA, ASSAM

his methods, he is only moderately successful unless able to manage his workmen.

To do this properly is a gift. The coolie must be understood. His confidence must be gained. It requires infinite patience to manage him. A man clever with labor can feel, as soon as he goes into the garden, whether the workers are happy or discontented.

The climate and living conditions of the planter are trying and in many cases unhealthy. Especially in Northern India, some estates are isolated and all are situated at immense distances from their base—Calcutta. Communications are bad, train service poor, and roads worse. Many of the supplies must come from Calcutta. Social amenities are provided for mostly in the way of clubs and visits to neighboring tea gardens.

European tea planters in India usually are recruited from England, Scotland, and Ireland. For factory work, engineers are required; but for general assistants, men with agricultural training are preferred. However, men are engaged on their merits, be they public school boys, or specially trained men. There is a good sprinkling of university men.

Hundreds of young men leave the British Isles each year, bound for remote estates in Assam, the Dooars, and other famous tea districts. It is equally a tribute to British courage under hard knocks and to the subtle allurements of a tea planter's life, that so few of them go back before they have succeeded in their occupation.

Young men usually are brought out as assistants on a three or four years' agreement. Each firm has its own scale of pay, giving an average of about Rs. 250 a month, with an extra allowance of Rs. 25 to Rs. 50 for engineers. A not uncommon scale of remuneration is Rs. 250 a month, the first year; Rs. 275, the second; Rs. 300, the third; and Rs. 325, the fourth. Assistants also receive a pony allowance of Rs. 35 to Rs. 50, and managers from Rs. 60 to Rs. 100, according to circumstances. A manager also gets a free, usually unfurnished bungalow, two or three servants, and other allowances.

The new staff member, if an engineer, may be employed entirely in the factory, but is more likely to be employed partly inside and partly outside, as occasion requires. The general practice is to give engineers opportunities of becoming conversant with field as well as factory work, in order ultimately to qualify them as estate managers.

A general assistant is employed in the supervision of field work. It requires considerable time for him to learn the work, and he also has to learn the garden *bat*, or jargon, with possibly one or more native languages. Not all his preparatory experience is gained in the field, however, as he is given factory experience, in order to train him for management. He works his way from junior assistant to senior assistant, by which time his pay ranges from Rs. 400 to Rs. 500 a month, with a small commission, which may be one-half or one per cent on the garden profits. After ten or twelve years he may become acting manager at an advance of Rs. 50 a month,

SUPERINTENDENT'S BUNGALOW, DOOM DOOMA TEA CO., DUM DUMA, ASSAM

and, if he is successful, will probably get the management of the garden.

Salaries of managers vary under different managing agencies and in various districts. They range from *Rs.* 600 to *Rs.* 1000 a month, with a commission of five and in some cases as much as ten per cent on the profits. In a good year the commission is likely to exceed the salary—sometimes very considerably. In the matter of living quarters and expenses, nearly every agency has a different arrangement; but a bungalow, often of palatial size, with servants, always is provided for the manager, as well as living accommodations for the assistants.

Planters have no definite hours. They always are on duty. They usually see that the coolies start work soon after dawn, and are present at the weighing in of the leaf in the evening; but, with the exception of certain months at the height of the season, there is ample time for the sports and amusements that are available. During the cold weather in Northern India, from November to March, the work is lighter, and there is scope for various pastimes—tennis and polo being the favorites. There are many golf courses, and the shooting and fishing rank with the best the world affords.

The majority of tea estates are within reasonable distance of a club having facilities for these sports, together with such amusements as bridge, billiards, and dancing after sunset. Most estates have their own tennis court or courts, as well. In the few instances, where estates are beyond the reach of club life, they are practically certain to be in excellent territory for shooting and fishing; although it may not be necessary to lend credence to the story of the planter who won a wager that he would bag a tiger and a snipe with a right and left from his double gun, and, after doing so, found that in his excitement he had slain the snipe with a lethal bullet from the right barrel, and the tiger with a charge of bird shot from the left.

Club activities in the tea districts are likely to be restricted to one or two days a week, except in large centers, such as Jorhat, Silchar, and Dibrugarh. These club days likewise are the occasion for parades of the local cavalry detachment of the Imperial Auxiliary Force, which employers usually expect all assistants to join. The experience is far from distasteful, however, and even if, at these gatherings, "cavalry spirit" is more in evidence than "cavalry training," the recruit learns something of martial preparedness, and combines the undoubted pleasure of numerous camps and gymkhanas; to say nothing of a horse allowance, that goes far toward the upkeep of a polo pony. Teams from the tea districts, representing the various regiments of the Auxiliary Force, become the center of no little interest when they play in the annual Calcutta Polo Meet at Christmas time.

The young planter's life in India is not all play, however; indeed, he has serious business before him from the outset. He is encouraged to devote time to recreation and club life, but whatever be his recreation, or however late he may stay at the club, he must be on the garden in time for roll call soon after dawn the next morning.

He must learn the vernacular, for, although the sirdars sometimes speak English, the only satisfactory way to deal with the personal problems in connection with labor is by direct contact.

The assistant must be up with the lark. Soon after the sun has stirred the early mists, the *chota sahib*, or assistant, is at breakfast. Half an hour later the day's labor has begun.

Finally, the assistant, having passed the initial stages, becomes a full-fledged manager—a *burra sahib*. The manager who makes good, finds himself well off. The roomy, picturesque, creeper-clad bungalow is thrown in rent free; while the flower and vegetable gardens are maintained at the expense of the estate. The salary is usually adequate; the commission on output often enables the recipient to put by rupees toward eventual retirement; and, if the *sahib* is provided with a smart assistant and good, native sirdar, his life can be a pleasant one.

The manager's day begins after an early breakfast. At this time he deals with the mail, and then goes around the garden to examine the work, and to decide which areas need plucking the following day, if it happens to be in plucking season.

Reports are received from the overseers, who first make their salaams. The *sahib* chides the lazy ones, praises those who display industry, and listens impartially to complaints. His judgment is as that of Solomon; every one cheerfully abides by it.

At midday, the manager returns to the bungalow, where a much needed, warm bath awaits him. Tiffin follows. Then comes the siesta, or "shut-eye" of the East, after which he has a cup of tea. After tea,

when the shadows begin to lengthen, the *sahib* looks in at the factory to satisfy himself that all is as it should be. Here the manufacture of the tea has the eagle-eyed manager's attention. At dusk, he receives the foremen, gets their reports for the day and issues instruction for the morrow, unless he has a European assistant to act as adjutant.

Periodically, the coolies enact a play; the manager, his assistants, the *babu* [English speaking native], the doctor, the accountant, and the overseers forming the audience. The ground facing the bungalow veranda serves as a stage, and the players, their faces rubbed with powdered chalk and cochineal, strut and posture until the show is over.

Assistants usually are granted six months' leave out of India every four or five years; managers every three or four. Managers and assistants usually get full pay during their leave, and they also receive an allowance sufficient to cover the cost of passage to and from India. The latter concession also is extended to the planter's wife as well.

The average planter's length of time in India is approximately thirty years. His ultimate aim is to retire after earning sufficient capital to insure a reasonable income. Capable men may become superintendents of groups of estates or inspectors of Calcutta agency houses; but the majority retire either to the South Coast of England, where there are entire colonies of retired planters, or to warm colonies such as Australia, New Zealand, etc., where the climate is most congenial to those who have been long in the tropics.

Many planters who have retired to England have had successful careers crowned by being placed on the boards of the companies they formerly managed. This merely entails a monthly visit or so to London for attendance at meetings.

Tea planting, as a profession, is unrivaled in the varied interests it involves; but its greatest attraction lies in the fact that it appeals to the creative instinct in man. Many a man has been set down in the middle of the jungle with a few sacks of tea seed and the order to go ahead. When the garden has grown to a thousand acres or more, several years later, it often happens that the man is reluctant to go into retirement and leave it all.

TAMIL TEA PLUCKERS AT WORK ON A HIGH-ELEVATION ESTATE IN CEYLON

CHAPTER XX

CULTIVATION AND MANUFACTURE IN CEYLON

GEOGRAPHICAL DESCRIPTION—DISTRICTS WHERE TEA IS GROWN—THEIR SOILS, CLIMATE, RAINFALL, AND ALTITUDE—CLEARING THE LAND—PROPAGATION METHODS—LAYING OUT ROADS AND DRAINS—SHADES, WIND BELTS, AND SOIL COVERS—FERTILIZERS—DISEASES AND PESTS—CULTIVATION METHODS—FIELD TRANSPORT—HOW CEYLON TEAS ARE MANUFACTURED, PACKED, AND SHIPPED—THE BUILDINGS AND MACHINERY USED—CAPITAL COST, VALUE, ETC.—COOLIE LABOR AND HOUSING—PLANTERS' ASSOCIATIONS—TEA RESEARCH INSTITUTE—PLANTERS' LIFE IN CEYLON

CEYLON is the premier Crown colony of Great Britain. It lies off the southeast tip of India, where it hangs suspended like a pearl pendant in the Indian Ocean, midway between the Arabian Sea and the Bay of Bengal, six to ten degrees north of the equator and approximately in the same latitude as Sierra Leone in Africa, or the Guianas in South America. Hakluyt, the English historian, once spoke of it as a "brave island, very fruitful and fair." The island is 272 miles long, and its greatest breadth is 137 miles. Its total area is 25,481 square miles, about the size of Holland and Belgium together, or half the size of England. The English call it "the Clapham Junction of the East," and certainly it is a most important station on the highway to the remotest ends of the earth.

Ceylon is well equipped in the matter of railways, roads, hotels, rest houses, and motoring facilities. In the hills, its climate at the right seasons is well-nigh perfect, and its delights are many and varied. Colombo, which ranks as one of the world's largest shipping ports, has a harbor that is daily crowded with shipping of all nationalities, from the stately liner to the adventurous dhow or buggalow of the native shipowner.

Tea is grown in six of the nine provinces of Ceylon. In the order of their importance they are Central, Uva, Sebaragamuwa, Southern, Western, and Northwestern. There are fifty-one districts in these provinces where the tea estates are located. The number of estates and the acreage under tea in each district are shown in Ceylon Table Number One, Page 419.

The principal tea districts are located in the mountainous Central Province at elevations up to 7000 feet, and most of them above 3000. However, there are some extensive districts in the southwestern plains, and notably in the Kelani Valley. Above 2500 feet tea forms practically the only cultivation, and the district between Kandy and Nuwara Eliya affords one of the most striking examples in the world of a country under a single crop. The tea estates of Ceylon, vary in size from five to 3000 acres. They are distributed among the fifty-one districts over an area of approximately fifty miles square, within three to twelve hours' ride from Colombo.

It is possible to visit most of the tea districts by rail. Ceylon has 740 miles of railways. The train journey from Colombo to Badulla is most interesting. For the first fifty miles, the line runs through rice lands, but as soon as it starts to rise, coconut, cacao, rubber, and cardamoms come into view. Quite some distance out of Kandy, which is 1600 feet above sea level, the tea estates appear. In the Kandy district many estates grow cacao, rubber, and cardamoms, as well as tea. From Peradeniya a branch line serves Kandy, Matale, and the surrounding tea, rubber, and cacao areas. Above Kandy the main line of the railway runs south through

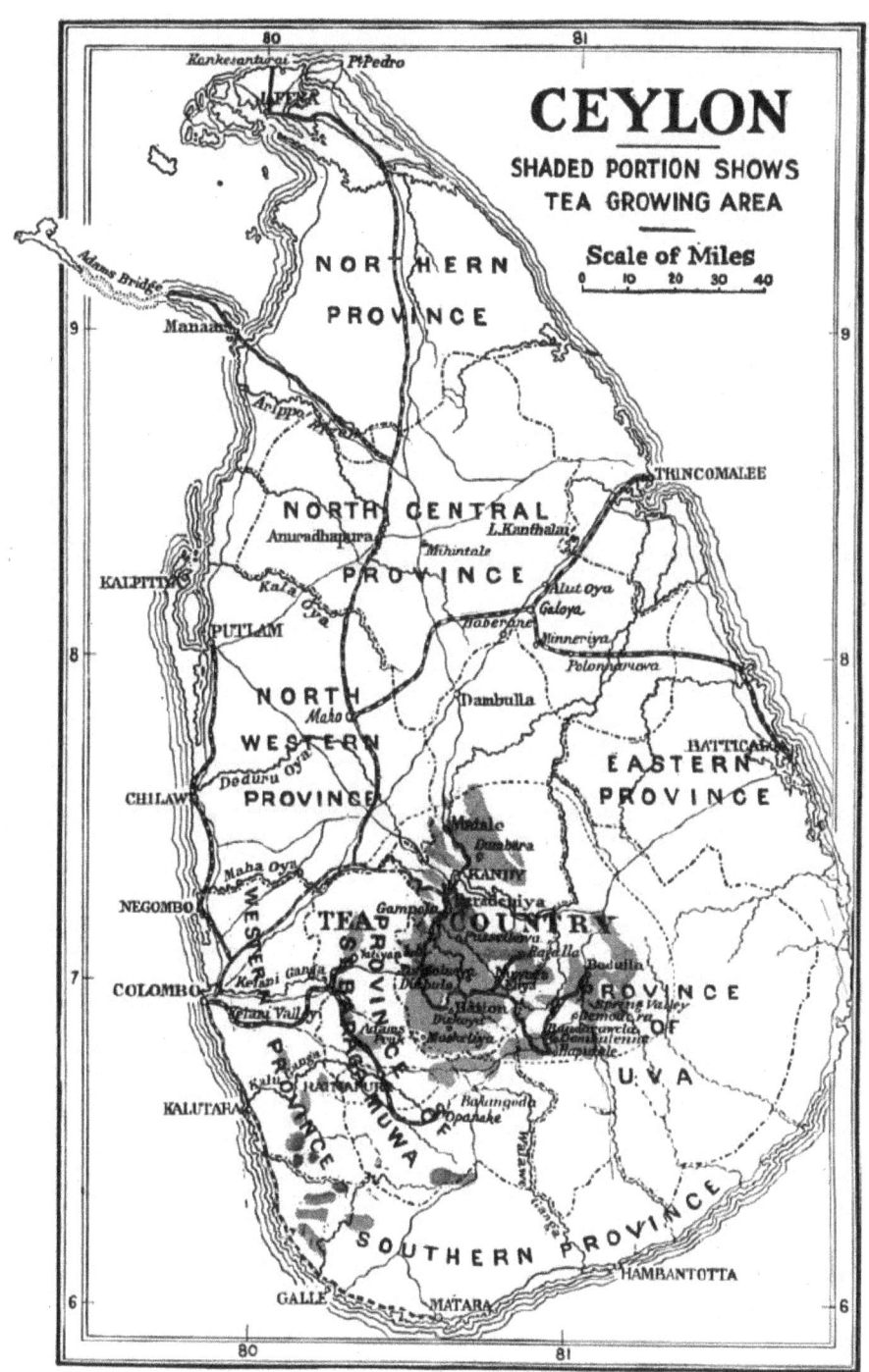

numerous valleys mostly devoted to tea. Rubber stops at Nawalapitiya. After that the tea bushes may be seen rising on each hand and crowning every rocky crest. It appears that no slope is too steep to cultivate. From Nawalapitiya the tea districts proper are entered, the line rising south and east to Hatton, Talawakele, and Nanuoya.

Badulla, at the extreme eastern end of the tea districts which center around Kandy and Hatton, is a journey of only fourteen hours from Colombo, a distance of 180 miles. Contrast this with the journey of forty-eight hours from Calcutta to Dibrugarh, the premier tea district of Assam, which is 700 miles from Calcutta and 1,000 miles from the sea; or the two weeks' journey from Shanghai to the Keemun tea-growing district of China.

Out of Hatton lies Dikoya, which was formerly a flourishing coffee district, and a few coffee factory relics are still to be seen nestling in the valleys. There are over 40,000 acres under tea in Dikoya Upper and Lower, and as the estates extend over a range of 2300 to 5000 feet, the factory is sometimes to be found in a warm, damp valley where the quality of the tea is not so good, or on an open hillside, depending upon the availability of water power.

The Dimbula district, which adjoins Dikoya, is the largest in Ceylon and one of the finest. Nearly 50,000 acres are under tea, and the observant traveler will notice that above 5000 feet the acacia has been substituted for the dadap as a shade and leguminous tree. The *Grevillea*, or silver oak, on the other hand, is grown throughout the tea districts as a shade and for fuel. From Nanuoya a narrow-gage line runs through Nuwara Eliya and the Uda Pussellawa tea districts to Ragalla. Here are to be found some of the finest and highest estates in Ceylon. A few reach an altitude of 7000 feet. Government restriction makes it no longer possible to open jungle land above 5000 feet.

The main line reaches its highest point, 6225 feet, at Pattipola, where a tunnel gives access to the *patanas*, or grassy downs, of the Uva district on the eastern side of the island. It is quite an experience to make this trip in June or July, when the southwest monsoon is beating its fiercest against the mountain range that divides the island and piling up the clouds

CEYLON TABLE NO. 1
Number of Gardens and Acreage under Tea by Districts in 1934

There is little change from year to year

District	Properties in District	Tea Alone, Acres	Tea and Rubber, Acres
Alagala	30	4150	175
Ambagamuwa	37	6050	850
Badulla	83	33300	.....
Balangoda	55	13450	400
Dikoya	69	30260	.....
Dikoya Lower	25	10200	.....
Dimbula	111	47900	.....
Dolosbage	42	12100	400
Dumbara	28	800	100
Galagedara	53	1600	700
Galle	186	9800	1800
Hantane	61	6800	600
Haputale	76	23100	300
Haputale West	13	2700	.....
Hewaheta Upper	13	6000	5
Hewaheta Lower	21	7000	15
Hunasgiriya	10	3530	.....
Kadugannawa	40	3200	1625
Kalutara	238	8500	2300
Kegalla	113	7000	600
Kelani Valley	274	11200	1700
Kelebokka	12	5300	.....
Knuckles	19	7400	.....
Kotmale	20	11500	50
Kurunegala	95	1000	50
Madulsima and Hewa Eliya	27	10000	.....
Maskeliya	48	20000	10
Matale East	70	10000	700
Matale North	44	1150	500
Matale South	27	3000	800
Matale West	32	2000	480
Maturata	15	7000	.....
Medamahanuwara	14	3250	.....
Monaragala	11	600	.....
Morawak Korale	62	9800	125
New Galway	18	3700	.....
Nilambe	21	6900	120
Nitre Cave	10	310	.....
Nuwara Eliya	20	4850	.....
Passara	17	9850	.....
Pundaluoya	16	5700	.....
Pussellawa	68	17100	1100
Rakwana	53	6600	270
Ramboda	15	6300	.....
Rangala	14	5900	.....
Ratnapura	164	24300	550
Udapussellawa	37	14700	.....
Walapane Lower	4	1000	.....
Wattegama	32	2300	190
Yakdessa	7	1050	.....
Lowcountry Minor Districts	124	2600	700
Total 51 Divisions	2694	453740	17215

in ominous masses that blot out the landscape. With a shriek the train rushes through the rain or mists, and plunges into the blackness of the tunnel, only to emerge in a few minutes into a land of sunshine and magnificent views with such dramatic suddenness as to make one catch one's breath at the wonder of it. On some tea estates, such as Warwick at Ambawella, which are set out actually on the rain divide, a walk of a mile or so may well take one in and out of the monsoon several times.

At Haputale the railway turns north to

TEA GARDEN AND FACTORY, MONARAKANDE GROUP, HAPUTALE DISTRICT, 1200 TO 4200 FEET

Bandarawela, Demodera, and to Badulla, the capital of the province of Uva. There are 40,000 acres under tea in Uva. Most of Ceylon's low-grown tea is in the Kelani Valley on the southwestern side of the island.

The possibilities of extending the cultivation of tea in Ceylon are limited by the fact that there is little, if any, more land to be had for the purpose. It is the intention of the Government to create a landed peasantry to take the place of the growing number of landless natives. The consequence is likely to be that much of the available land will be earmarked for allotment to villagers in the near future.

Comparing the average price realized, over a period of one year, from estates at equal elevations on the eastern and western sides of the Island, it was found that those on the west command a higher market average. There is not much difference in value between estates in the southwestern or northeastern sides of the Island, although judging by share values the investor considers the Dimbula and Nuwara Eliya districts worth more per acre than any other in Ceylon.

It has been stated that tea will grow in almost any soil that is well drained, but for the growing of tea as a commercial crop the soil must contain nitrogen, phosphoric acid, and potash, as has been pointed out by Bamber of Ceylon, Mann of India, and Nanninga of Java. The average Ceylon tea soil contains the essential plant foods as follows: nitrogen, 0.10 to 0.15 per cent; available phosphate 0.005 per cent; available potash 0.01 to 0.015 per cent.

Tea Soils

The rocks found in the interior of Ceylon belong to the Archaen period of geology, and are related to the gneisses and granites of Southern India. Round about the coast, where the coconut plantations are situated, the soil is sandy, but toward the interior it becomes heavier, and the proportion of laterite increases. The heaviest soils are found near Nuwara Eliya.

The tea lands are divided into forest, patana, and *chena* areas. Land that is covered with dense forest is best for opening in tea, but there is now little of this left in Ceylon. The *patanas* are grassy downs, common in Uva province. *Chena* is land that has been burnt over by the natives before cultivation. This land is like the *jhoomed* areas of Assam, and is only planted when no other land is obtainable. Present extensions are being made mostly on the *patanas*. These soils, though lacking in humus, are mechanically in good condition and respond rapidly to sound cultivation. Their tendency is to dry into a hard-pan during droughts, as is shown by the lack of trees and vegetation, but this is overcome by planting leguminous cover crops and overhead covers that provide a liberal leaf mold.

Most of the tea soils have been formed where they lie from the rocks beneath them. Mainly they are red, although light patches of soil overlie quartz. On the hillside slopes, the soil that has been retained is not true to type, due to the tremendous amount of erosion. The true-type soil is to be found only in the jungle areas.

The high percentage of iron and alumina appearing in chemical analyses of Ceylon soils may be taken as proving an extreme age for the soils. Insoluble sand and silicates are often lower than 50 per cent in Ceylon, a figure seldom equalled in India, except in the peat soils of the northeast provinces. Assam soils do not show insoluble silicates like Ceylon, even in heavy clays. With the exception of the Bogawan-

talawa district there is no soil in Ceylon that matches up to the peat soils of Cachar in India. However, a Bogawantalawa soil containing 0.799 per cent of nitrogen yielded a crop of 2235 pounds per acre, as compared to a crop of 2400 pounds in Cachar.[1]

Climate, Rainfall, and Altitude

Ceylon has a moist tropical climate with considerable variation, due to the hills. The proximity of the sea saves the low country from the extremes of temperature found in many parts of India. Colombo, the capital and principal sea port, averages 81° F., and the smallness of variations both between day and night and between one part of the year and another are noteworthy. At Nuwara Eliya, 6000 feet, the mean temperature is 59° F., the variation between day and night is considerably greater than at the coast, and frosts are not unknown.

The year can be divided into two monsoons, during which there is fairly con-

[1] C. R. Harler, "Tea in Ceylon," *Indian Tea Association Quarterly Journal*, part 4, 1924, Calcutta, 1925.

NUWARA ELIYA NARROW-GAGE RAILWAY AND ADJACENT TEA COUNTRY, UVA SIDE

tinuous wind from the southwest and northeast respectively, and two intermonsoon periods of less regular wind, but considerable rainfall. The heaviest rain occurs during the monsoons on the windward sides of the hill country, and is associated with a shielding effect on the lee side. The intermonsoon periods provide a more general rainfall throughout Ceylon. The rainfall neither reaches the maxima nor is retarded to the minima by the shielding effects of the mountains, such as operates during the monsoons. The local rains that occur during the intermonsoon period are frequently referred to as part of the monsoons that follow them, in fact many people still use the word "monsoon" as identical with "rainfall." A rough estimate of the chief periods of weather—and only a very rough one is possible—would be: southwest monsoon, May-September; intermonsoon, October-November; northeast, November-February; intermonsoon, March-April. Taking the island as a whole, February is the driest month of the year. The southwest monsoon is decidedly more regular than the northeast, as the rainfall of the latter, and of the intermonsoon period that precedes it, is in part due to the effect of depressions; hence, it fluctuates considerably according to the different paths taken by those depressions in different years.

In this setting and with such a climate, the island produces an amazing vegetation, which includes tea, rubber, rice, coconuts, cacao, spices, tobacco, and a little coffee; but the greatest of these is tea. The climate of the tea producing districts differs considerably with the elevation and geographical position; the mountains of Ceylon affording considerable protection to certain districts during the southwest or northeast monsoon. The average rainfall varies from 72 to 251 inches, while mean temperatures range from 65° to 85° F., or higher. It is generally agreed that the climate of an average tea estate is quite agreeable to those accustomed to a European climate, while the conditions at 5000 feet can be described as most pleasant; long periods of incessant rain and mist being the only drawback to an otherwise ideal climate.

The effect of climate on the flavor of tea is very marked, the colder, less tropical conditions in the hills tending to check the actual rate of growth, while promoting the fuller development of the essential flavoring constituents. During the months in which growth is more active—namely, March to May, and again, to a less extent, in October and November—quality decreases even in the highest estates, and returns again when growth is less rapid. In the Uva district, a few days of dry, windy weather will completely change the character of the crop, producing a flavor that immediately enhances the value of the tea. The same effect is produced at high elevations during January and February, when bright days and cold nights, often accompanied by slight frosts, are experienced.

The southwest monsoon period of May-September and the northeast monsoon period of November-February are distinctly marked at Colombo and Ratnapura, but Ratnapura with its background of hills has a much heavier rainfall than Colombo. Kandy, due to its central situation and not being shut off on either side by high mountains, receives an evenly distributed rainfall. Nawalapitiya is at the altitude for maximum rainfall, with an average of 251 inches annually. Nuwara Eliya escapes the extreme effects of the monsoons, but receives a liberal rainfall. Badulla, in the province of Uva, is east of the rain divide, and consequently gets most of its rainfall from the northeast monsoon.

The mean annual temperature at Ratnapura in 80° F., at Kandy [1600 feet] it is 74.4° F., at Nuwara Eliya [6188 feet] it is 59.2° F., and at Badulla [2225 feet] it is 73.7° F. There is practically no change in the mean throughout the year, but the maxima and minima vary somewhat.

March, April, and May are the heaviest flushing months in both the northeast and the southwest monsoon areas. Many of the estates obtain three-fifths of their crop during the first six months of the year. In June, July, and August the monsoon brings lots of wind and rain with poor flushing. After August the crop increases up to a second maximum in November. December, January, and February again are poor months in the southwestern districts.

Dry winds are said to impart pungency and flavor to the leaf. Generally over the island, during the heavy flushing months of April and May, as well as during the heavy monsoons in June, July, and August, the teas are poor, except in Uva, in the latter period, where the southwest mon-

DEVON FALLS, ON THE CRAIGIE LEA ESTATE, DIMBULA, 3900 FEET

soon blows dry. On the other hand, Uva teas are poor in quality during the humid months of November, December, and January when the northeast monsoon is blowing, while the Nuwara Eliya district where the northeast monsoon blows dry gives flavory teas in January.

The flavors of Ceylon teas are also influenced largely by the elevations at which they are grown; teas from estates in the low country are strong, and have practically no distinctive flavor, while choice flavor is produced by estates of medium elevation, and very fine flavor is characteristic of teas grown in certain areas and in districts 6000 feet above sea level. Low country teas compensate for their lack of quality by their greatly increased yield; high-grown teas, on the other hand, are strongly required for their good quality, and fine flavor.

The existing tea plantations of Ceylon monopolize practically all of the best land suited to tea growing in the hill regions; little or no forest remains in private hands, and all belonging to the government is strictly conserved in order to preserve the

quantity and distribution of the rainfall. There is a limited area of *patana*, or grassy land, at good elevations, that is still available for opening in tea, and in the middle and low country, jungle and *chena*, or burnt over, scrub land may be purchased from the government.

Clearing Land for Tea

A tract of land having been acquired, it is first surveyed and laid out in the best possible arrangement by a competent surveyor. A Sinhalese or Moor contractor is then engaged to fell the jungle or clear the *chena* or *patana* at an agreed fixed rate.

A great deal of later trouble and expense is eliminated by a satisfactory burn-off. Not only does a good burning mean less clearing up to be done, but a thorough baking of the surface soil destroys quantities of seeds that have lain dormant under the jungle, merely awaiting the necessary light and air to germinate and put out sprouts. After the burn off, the stumps and logs that were too large to burn with

IN THE PUSSELLAWA DISTRICT—ROTHSCHILD TEA GARDEN AND FACTORY

the brush are left to rot, for the reason that their elimination costs more than it is worth. When the jungle has been burnt off, and the *chena* undergrowth piled and burned, the next step is the reservation of sites for coolie lines and other estate buildings including the factory, and for the nurseries for tea plants.

Propagation, Tea Seed, Etc.

All of the tea grown in Ceylon is raised from seed. When a new area is to be opened on an old tea estate, it is usual to prepare nurseries where seed is sown a year and a half or two years in advance, in order to provide a supply of tea plants or stumps when required. On an entirely new estate, however, this is not always practicable, but in such cases nurseries at convenient locations are started as soon as possible, to supply the plants needed for replacements. A nursery site is preferably located in a well sheltered hollow, where there is good soil and an unfailing supply of water.

Before germination is attempted the seeds are tested by immersion in water; those that are light enough to float being either discarded entirely, as not likely to germinate, or else germinated separately. Seed is either germinated between coir mattings or in specially prepared beds. The latter comprise a thick layer of well rotted cattle manure overlaid by two inches of fine sand. The heavier tea seeds are spread closely over the sand, but not actually touching each other, and then are covered over with a thin layer of sand and straw.

The germinating beds are sometimes shaded from the sun by light framework covered with ferns or any slow withering foliage that is handy, and are thoroughly watered every alternate day. The seed germinates in about thirty days and is picked out daily. High jat seed has the thinnest shell, and therefore germinates first.

Seeds of both the light and dark leaved Assam indigenous, China, and China hybrid varieties are common. In Ceylon the usual bush is a medium hybrid that stands the climate better than the others. *Jat,* or type, of tea plays an important part in results. Good *jat*, though high in yield, is quickly affected by adverse weather conditions, and takes a long time to recover. So far as Ceylon is concerned, the best and most suitable, from the standpoint of price and quality, is a medium hybrid. The most popular seed now is a dark leaf hybrid Manipuri. In Northeast India and the Netherlands Indies, however, only pure *jats* are planted nowadays.

Germinated seed is planted out as seed at stake in the garden proper or else in nursery beds, as the case may be. Where nursery plants are wanted, it is planted in beds at a depth of one inch and three to four inches apart. After the holes have been prepared, a single germinated seed is placed in each, with the rootlet downward, and is then lightly covered with soil. The nursery beds are then shaded in the same manner as the germinating beds.

The shrubs are ready for transplanting in about eighteen months; sometimes with a clod, but generally as a stump. The young plants are cut to a height of four to eight inches, the soil is loosened, and the plant pulled up. In some localities the stump can be pulled without loosening and is sent long distances for planting. However, as a preventive measure against the shot-hole borer, government permits are necessary for transferring stumps from one district to another, and no stumps are permitted to be carried from a district where the pest is bad.

Quantities of Indian tea seed formerly were imported into Ceylon, but this is now forbidden on account of the risk of introducing blister-blight.

A few tea clearings in Ceylon have been

A CEYLON TEA NURSERY

planted with cuttings taken from tea prunings on older gardens; but although these particular plantings grew well, the practice has not been a usual one.[2]

Laying Out Roads and Drains

The excellence and number of Ceylon's roads is always a subject for remark by visitors to the island, and this is true not only of the public roads, but of roads on the estates as well. After the sites for the various buildings have been selected, a system of roads is carefully planned and built that will lead to the bungalow, coolie, and factory sites, as well as provide intercommunication between the various blocks and the main roads. Unless this is done in a way to provide the shortest routes, the coolies make their own short cuts, to the detriment of the tea bushes. The main roads are cut twelve feet wide and the bypaths four feet, with due care to slope their surfaces toward the drains so that, in wet weather, water will flow into them and not run along the roads.

The system of drains is not laid out until after the roads have been planned, as it is essential that they shall protect the roads against washouts. Drains are started from the top of each hill, and carry off the surplus water into the leading drains, with care to protect the roads from any possible overflow. Natural ravines provide most of the leading drains required, but where these are too widely separated, artificial leaders are cut. The side drains emptying into the leaders are kept as short as possible, 150 feet on either side of the main drain being the rule for the side drains, in order to avoid any great amount of water being discharged into the leader at any point. The tendency, in the dry Uva area, is to cut drains on the lock and spill method, which retains the rainfall.

Terracing in Ceylon is being adopted and is becoming more popular as the realization grows that soil erosion is a serious problem. Terraces are laid out midway between drains, so far as possible, and follow the contour in order to make them horizontal, or nearly so. All the loose stones are gathered up and used for facing the terraces, in order to protect them against wash; and where sufficient stone

[2] E. C. Elliott and F. J. Whitehead, *Tea Planting in Ceylon*, Colombo, 1926.

THE PLANTING OPERATION

is not to be found, thick hedges of *Tephrosia candida* are planted between the drains to hold the soil together, while also providing a green manure.

Planting

In Ceylon, the planting season varies with the district. In the southwest monsoon area, the season is June, July, and August, while in Uva Province, where the northeast monsoon is the wettest period, the planting season is during this monsoon—October, November, and December.

The commonest planting distance for tea in Ceylon is three feet by three-and-a-half, considerably closer than in Assam on the flat, but like that employed on the Sylhet *teelas*.

The tea plants are set out in straight parallel rows running horizontally across the hillsides, as in Java.

When planting, an *alavangoe*, or digging bar of steel or wood, is thrust deeply into the center of the hole and worked round and round until a satisfactory opening is made. The plant or stump is dropped into the hole and firmly embedded by further manipulation of the *alavangoe*, to insure the soil coming in close contact with the roots.

When seed at stake is planted, it is first placed in germinating beds and then planted out in the holes made for it, at a depth of one inch. Seed at stake is usually planted only on *patana* land, as cut-

worms and other grubs are likely to attack it if planted on jungle or *chena* land.

Shades, Wind Belts, Soil Covers

Trees of the *Leguminosae* are given the preference for shading tea. They also provide necessary wind breaks, but other trees are used as well. For protection from the sun's rays, a primary requirement is for a well distributed and light shade. The production of ample leaf-mulch and a usefulness for fire-wood are also desirable attributes. The *Grevillea robusta,* a non-leguminous tree, possesses all of these advantages, and is also an excellent wind break, but it is a slow grower. Where it is desired to form a wind belt, the procedure is to plant several rows at right angles to the direction of the wind which threatens damage to the crop. *Grevilleas* do not grow well by themselves in a clearing, but thrive under cultivation amongst the tea at the mid and lower elevations.

Albizzia moluccana, A. stipulata, Acacia decurrens, Erythrina lithosperma [the dadap], *Gliricidia maculata, Leucæna glauca,* several varieties of *Eucalyptus,* and other trees are also used for shades and wind belts. These trees have to be removed every seven to eight years, to prevent root disease in the tea. Each has its advantages and limitations, varying with the altitude, and these considerations naturally influence the selection in a given case.

The subject of leguminous cover crops for the prevention of soil erosion and the enrichment of the soil is beginning to attract considerable attention, marking a distinct departure from clean weeding, although this method is still the most popular.

A recent development in soil covers is a plan of selective weeding, by which one sort of weed is allowed to grow, while all others are removed, with the result that the ground between the tea rows is soon carpeted with this cover, protecting it against wash. Opposing this, the advocates of clean weeding point to the likelihood that the cover weeds will absorb much moisture needed by the tea plants during a dry period. *Oxalis corniculata*—in Sinhalese, *hin-embul-embiliya*—is one of the plants that are allowed to remain when weeding selectively. It is very common in Ceylon, putting out long creeping stems, which take root at intervals. The leaves are somewhat like clover, and it is often called "shamrock." It flowers and the seed pod is long and narrow. When ripe it explodes if touched.[3]

Tephrosia candida, or *Boga medeloa,* and *Vogili* are now often planted in hedges more or less horizontally across the fields of tea, in alternate rows, to obviate soil wash and supply humus.

Manuring

The yield of the tea plant is greatly improved by manuring. Between the rows of tea are grown green manure plants, and these are periodically lopped of their small twigs and branches or are cut down for incorporation into the soil. The dadap is the most popular plant for growing among tea as a green manure, but does not grow at all elevations. The acacia is being largely used at elevations above 5000 feet, while in the drier districts use is made of *Grevilleas* and *Tephrosia.* Other quick-growing, leguminous plants are planted among the tea, and are buried when mature, with the object of improving the humus content of the soil. Rotation of green crops, both overhead and creeping varieties, is receiving close attention.

Cultivation methods have greatly improved in recent years, and greater attention is given to systematic cultivation and to the application of manures.

The Tea Research Institute is making extensive experiments with all kinds of artificial manures with the idea of finding out the best time to apply them in relation to pruning and the season of the year, as well as to establish which are the most economical in use. Little definite data is yet available and the old principle of applying a pruning mixture and a general mixture or two between prunings is generally in vogue.

Some planters maintain that the pruning mixture should contain more nitrogen than either phosphoric acid or potash but others still prefer a large quantity of potash during the pruning period whilst, as a rule, the general mixtures are well balanced to contain approximately $\frac{3}{7}$ nitrogen, $\frac{2}{7}$ phosphoric acid and $\frac{2}{7}$ potash. These figures are not, of course, by any means accurate but vary in different estates under different managements. Some planters prefer to use quick acting mixtures containing possibly 75 per cent nitrogen and 25 per cent phosphoric acid, applying a few months before pruning. It is generally the custom to employ manure frequently in smaller quantities than in large quantities at less frequent intervals.

Green manuring is not practiced in Ceylon on the scale usual to Northeastern India. Cow peas [*Vigna catiang*], sunn hemp [*Crotalaria juncea*], or dhaincha [*Sesbania aculcata*], which can be grown and hoed in six weeks, are not used on most Ceylon estates owing to their steepness. Instead, some of the leguminous shade trees and wind breaks are lopped periodically and the loppings are buried. At other times, the loppings are left as mulch. Tests made at Peradeniya show that the dadap, or *Erythrina lithosperma,* yields about 10,000 pounds of loppings per acre, and the *Gliricidia maculata* about double that amount. The Ceylon sau, or *Albizzia moluccana,* can be lopped, but is not commonly used that way. The wattle, *Acacia decurrens,* is regularly lopped, but the silver oak, *Grevillea robusta,* which is non-leguminous, is not.

Deep Cultivation

Deep cultivation with various types of forks is put in at any time of the year, but generally with the manures. The deeper the forking the better. The handle of the fork is thrust outward, away from the user, thus introducing what is known as "envelope" forking, which reduces soil-wash to a minimum.

Tea Diseases and Pests

Tea has not suffered exceptionally from plant enemies in Ceylon, although most of the tea diseases and pests common in Northeast India are also to be found on the Ceylon estates. Mr. T. Petch, former Director of the Tea Research Institute, describes some sixty diseases, but points out that:

"The conditions under which tea is usually grown do not unduly favor disease. As it is kept pruned down, the bushes are not subject to a permanently high humidity, while the periodic pruning, though it may, on occasion, induce consequences which are not desirable from the point of view of plant pathology, affords an opportunity of getting rid of various diseases. The systematic manuring which is now generally practiced also assists in keep-

[3] T. Petch, "Cover Plants." *The Tropical Agriculturist,* Vol. lxiii, No. 6, Peradeniya, 1924.

ing disease in check. Nevertheless, opinions are not lacking that, as the tea bush grows older, diseases are becoming more prevalent.[4]

Leaf diseases common to Ceylon's tea estates are: gray, brown, and copper blights, whose names are due to the characteristic discolorations which they cause to the leaf; witches broom, because it forms tufts of shoots; chlorosis, in which leaves turn yellow, and a disease as yet unnamed in which branching occurs abnormally; and *Cercosporella theae* PETCH. Up to the present time none of these has had any serious effect on any of the estates in Ceylon. The methods that have been suggested for the control of leaf diseases include:

(1) Plucking and burning the diseased leaves.
(2) Manuring and general cultivation.
(3) Spraying.
(4) Removal of Acacias and other shade trees susceptible to, and propagators of, *Cercosporella theae.*

Plucking and burning never has been done on a scale to permit of a proper estimate of its actual economic returns. Manuring and general cultivation are the chief factors at present combating any increase of leaf disease. Spraying is objected to as impolitic, although probably not actually harmful to the ultimate user of tea as a drink, and as being impractical, because *Cercosporella theae* attacks only the flush.

The leaf and stem diseases found in Ceylon are mainly red rust and black rot, although there are a number that are less important. The dreaded blister blight, referred to by Dr. Watt as "one of the very worst blights on tea," has not yet been recorded in Ceylon, and it is hoped that measures taken by the Government to exclude infected seed will be effectual to keep it out of the country.

Stem diseases include various forms of branch canker, stump rot, and die-back, as well as many others less prevalent. One of the latter, known as thorny-stem blight, and confined at present, so far as known, to Ceylon, has the strange characteristic of producing black thorns on the plants attacked.

Root diseases most prevalent in Ceylon are *Ustulina zonata, Fomes lamenoensis, Poria hypolateritia, Botryo diplodia,* and *Rosellinea arcuata* PETCH. In Ceylon, as elsewhere, the usual cause of disease in the tea roots is a decaying stump.

Insect pests do their share of damage to tea in Ceylon, but thus far their attacks have been confined largely to the low and mid-country districts. The tea tortrix [*Homona coffearia*], shot hole borer [*Xyleborus fornicatus*], and the nettle grub are the ones that cause the greatest damage.

Red spider is a pest in the higher country, and is worse during dry periods. The Kalutara snail is common in the low country. White ants are plentiful in the Central Province and tea bushes attacked by them are dug out, or, if not too badly eaten, they are treated with creosote or solignum. White ants only attack dead tissue; generally that caused by termites or branch canker. Nettle grubs are yearly becoming more of a menace on the Uva side. Purple mites appear to cause little damage beyond, possibly, weakening the constitution of the tea bush. Scarlet mites may actually kill bushes. Yellow mites merely harden the younger leaves.

Helopeltis theivora, the so-called "tea mosquito," is sometimes met in the low country, though not to any great extent. Harler says it is often confused with *Cercosporella*, a leaf disease whose mark resembles that left by the mosquito, and unless the mosquito itself is seen, its presence is to be doubted. The Ceylon planter has never suffered from *Helopeltis* as have planters in other countries.

Pruning

After a year or more of continuous plucking, the tea bush loses vitality, and it is necessary to remove surplus wood and leaves by pruning. This pruning operation is regarded as the most important on the tea calendar. In many districts of Ceylon, where the rainfall is continuous, it is done all the year round. However, the frequency of the operation varies with the elevation, soil, *jat*, cultivation, and plucking, and takes place at intervals of from twelve months to three or more years.[5] As a result of the pruning, the bush is generally kept below three feet in height. The top of the bush is made as level as pos-

---

[4] T. Petch. *The Diseases of the Tea Bush.* London. 1923.

[5] H. K. Rutherford, *Ceylon Planters' Note Book,* Seventh edition. Colombo, 1925.

THE PRUNING OPERATION

sible by "tipping," which is done by breaking the tips of the primary shoots.

Pruning time varies with the climate in districts where rains are not continuous, in order to avoid the drought. It is considered a mistake to prune immediately before a period of dry weather. On the southwest side of the island pruning is done from February to March, and again from mid-June to mid-September. In the Uva district pruning is done mostly from June to September.

A young plant is unable to withstand the monsoon unless it is cut to about four inches in the nursery. This first cut is applied to the bush about eighteen months after it has been transplanted, the time varying with the altitude. It is a horizontal cut about four inches from the ground. Afterward the bush is tipped eighteen to twenty-four inches higher than this. The next pruning is a cut on two or three inches of new wood above the first four inches, and the bush is again tipped above this.

An ordinary pruning on old tea bushes is a cut made about two-and-a-half inches above the previous one, although the cut is made lower down on the straight wood when the stem becomes knotty. It has been found best to remove knots gradually—not all at one time. In some districts it is the practice to prune up three times and then to cut lower. Speaking of Ceylon generally, light pruning is now the rule. Naturally there are many variations in these methods due to climate, soil, jat, and altitude. Following the pruning operation, the bush is not touched for a period that varies with the altitude. In the low country it is tipped from six to eight weeks

after pruning, and the first flush appears about eleven weeks after pruning. In mid-country it is usual to tip about three to five months after pruning. In the high country these periods are still longer.

Collar pruning is rarely practiced in Ceylon, although it has been successful in the Matale district. It is necessary periodically to cut a bush down to a low level because the sap in its upward and downward course is impeded and deflected by snags formed in the stems and branches, and it is imperative that the obstructions be removed. Drastic down-pruning is sometimes successful on comparatively young and vigorous bushes, and especially on bushes that have been topped too high originally. However, a more gradual method of elimination is now generally favored. Lung pruning, i.e., leaving a branch for the bush to breathe through, is also being practiced. On old fields of tea, selective pruning is adopted whereby snags, knots, decaying branches, and rotting stumps are dealt with at each pruning; only the worst features being eliminated to start with. The remedial work is continued at each successive pruning until the frame of the bush has been restored. If this is found impossible, the bush is dug out and replaced.

All heavy cutting is done with saws, the lighter cuts being made with well sharpened pruning knives, which are used also for smoothing off saw cuts. Hacking thick branches with knives is forbidden, as it splits the wood, and permits the entrance of fungi. Unhealed wounds are sometimes treated with tar or other suitable material, to keep out water and avoid decay, but this treatment is not always efficacious.

Plucking

Gathering the tea leaves requires practice and careful supervision. The buds at the tip of the new shoot, and two or three leaves below them, are plucked by hand, usually by the women and older children, while the men do the heavier tasks such as pruning, forking, manuring, and cutting drains. Plucking is repeated every seven to fourteen days throughout the year according to the elevation.

The first and several subsequent plucks after pruning are specifically referred to as "tipping," and are done by a gang of expert pluckers under the supervision of a

PLUCKING TEA IN UDAPUSSELLAWA, 5000 FEET

well-trained *kangany,* or native foreman. This may be a routine leaf picking of the usual sort, or, if a drastic down-pruning has been done and time has been allowed for new growth to get well under way, it may be necessary to break back runaway shoots to the desired level. The tipping level is usually about six inches above the last horizontal pruning cut. The succulent young shoots are allowed to develop until brown wood has begun to show at the base, and then coolies are sent in to nip off the top buds, and check the sap. The lower wood then gets the benefit of the checking, and increases in size and strength. A length of two leaves above the central pruning cut usually provides ample wood on bushes of medium or good jat, and a sufficient number of buds on the primary stem to throw out a good secondary flush; but in low jat tea the leaves are often so crowded on the primaries that three or even four leaves have to be left at the first tipping, if a satisfactory length of wood is to be obtained.

After the secondary flush develops, a *jannum,* or "fish" leaf, is formed just above the junction of the parent leaf with the primary stem. It is the practice to leave one, or sometimes two, complete leaves above the *jannum* to put forth a bud and elaborate the sap to nourish it.

When the tipping period has been passed, ranging from a few months in the low country to nearly a year at high elevations, the field is turned over to the main gang

of pluckers to be picked. In the best gardens only the youngest leaves are plucked. The tip of the shoot, including two leaves and the terminal bud, is the standard fine pluck. A medium pluck includes the terminal bud, two leaves, and the soft portion of a third leaf with one or, at the most, two *banji.*[6] The pluck is said to be coarse when three or more leaves with two or more *banji* are taken.

The coolies gather the flush by plucking with the thumb and finger, and although they become very skillful, it is, of course, impossible that every single shoot should contain the exact leaf specification desired. A good average is all that is obtainable at any reasonable cost. Also, it unavoidably happens that a certain amount of hard stalk and coarse leaf is gathered by the pluckers, but it is usual to have them pick this out of their baskets, under supervision, while they are resting.

Leaf is collected in a cane or bamboo plucking basket, about twenty-four inches in depth by thirteen inches in diameter, which is furnished each cooly by the estate. Such baskets hold from fifteen to eighteen pounds of green leaf when filled loosely. If the leaf is pressed down in order to make the basket hold more, it becomes bruised, and fermentation of the juices is begun. Therefore, the practice is strictly forbidden and a number of weighing periods have been established in order

---

[6] A *banji* leaf is one with a stunted bud, from which no further growth of flush is to be expected.

CLOSE-UP OF A TAMIL TEA PLUCKER AT WORK

TAMIL GIRLS PICKING OUT STALK FROM THE MORNING'S PLUCK ON DAMBATENNE, 6000 FEET

to avoid crushing. By 4 o'clock in the afternoon, when work ceases, a good plucker will have gathered from seventy to eighty pounds of green leaf, according as the bushes flush well or otherwise. The leaf is usually weighed in the field at 9 A.M., at noon, and again at 4 P.M., daily, and is then despatched to the factory, where it is once more weighed by the teamaker.

The average yield on Ceylon estates is usually between 400 and 600 lbs. per acre, although on some estates the yields run much higher, and 700 to 900 lbs. is not unusual. On one of the high grown estates the following yields are reported:—

First year after pruning   500 lbs.
Second "   "   "   900 "
Third "   "   "   950 "
Fourth "   "   "   850 "

A bush generally announces a need for pruning by going *banji*. It is then sometimes given a light plucking, immediately before pruning. A light plucking at this time, rather than a hard one, has been found to insure a quicker recovery.

On estates where the factory is within easy reach of the field, the green leaf is carried to it on the heads of the pluckers; but where the distance to be covered is considerable, as in the case of two or more

estates sharing the same factory, considerations of economy compel the use of other means of transportation. On such estates, the leaf is emptied from the pluckers' baskets into large baskets, coir bags, or jute sacks, and then is taken to the factory by bullock cart, motor lorry, wire shoot, wire ropeway, or tramway. Each in its own way seems well adapted to the pur-

TWO LEAVES AND A BUD, AS PLUCKED

H. E. H. Sladen

A RECORD TEA BUSH ON THE BATTAWATTE GROUP ESTATES, MADULSIMA, BADULLA, 4000 FEET

What is thought to be the world's largest tea bush is pictured here as it appeared in the spring of 1934. Growing from one stem it has a diameter of 24 feet and a circumference of 67 feet. The bush is in a thriving condition and on the occasion of taking the photograph four pounds of green leaf were plucked from it.

pose, with the possible exception of wire gravity shoots, which are said to damage the leaf by the unavoidable concussion at the end of the run. Some estates try to minimize the bump given the leaf by heaping a cushion of *mana* grass in front of the bumper at the foot of the shoot; however, it quickly becomes packed under the pounding.

Withering

After it has been weighed at the factory, the leaf is spread out to wither in special withering lofts. Outside withering houses are not used in Ceylon and all the withering space is above the tea factory, so that the wither can be controlled irrespective of weather conditions.

The upper stories of the factory are filled from top to bottom with banks of withering tats made of Hessian [burlap], with or without wire edges, attached to frames or running beltwise over wide rollers, on which the tea is spread to wither. These lofts are fitted with tightly closing trap doors, while there are windows all round the building. Usually, there is a duct or a central bulking chamber from the drier on the ground floor to supply hot air when needed, and fans at the ends and

center of the middle floor, so that by opening and closing certain doors and windows a current of controlled air can be circulated in either direction through the tats for a reversible or alternating wither, or, when the outside weather permits, the windows and doors may be flung open for a natural wither. Also, a combination of the two is frequently found desirable.

It is generally held that a natural wither, made at a lower temperature, is preferable to a controlled wither obtained by the use of heated air, because the higher the temperature of the air supplied to the leaf, the more quality is lost. With this in view, all

SACK OF TEA LEAF PASSING OVER ROPEWAY STANDARD FROM FIELD TO FACTORY

T. U. Todd & H. J. Moppett

WIRE SHOOT STOP WITH MANNA GRASS BUFFER

the withering lofts are plentifully supplied with windows to be used for natural withering in fine weather; but are capable of being shut up and made airtight, for controlled withering in humid weather.

Many of the earlier Ceylon tea factories were converted coffee factories and usually were located in more or less shut-in valleys to get water power. In the modern ones the ground-floor walls are of brick or stone and the upper of corrugated iron; and are built on more open situations calculated to catch the breeze for withering purposes. Experience has demonstrated that there is a vast gain in the potentiality for natural withering in a factory on an elevation and open to every wind. In the older class of buildings good natural withers can seldom be obtained, while in the newer and better located factories natural withers predominate. However, there is unavoidable difficulty, during wet weather, in obtaining a good natural wither within eighteen to twenty-four hours, the period beyond which tea leaf appears to deteriorate rapidly if it is not then in a suitable condition to be rolled. Furthermore, if leaf is retained on the tats beyond twenty-four hours, the factory schedule is upset and manufacture cannot proceed on a daily schedule.

So far as practical experience is a guide, heated air is the only medium for applying artificial withering to tea leaf during wet periods; but temperature is not the principal factor involved. It is the relative humidity of the heated air that is most important. This is tested by a hygrometer, an instrument for measuring the degree of moisture in the air.

Formerly, it was considered sufficient to circulate heated air among the withering tats at a temperature somewhere between 90°F. and 100°F., and yet, it was frequently noticed that, even at these temperatures heated air had to be circulated for about twelve hours to secure a wither— a period injurious to the tea, in addition to being wasteful of power and heat. Then it was discovered that the tea driers, below-stairs, when filled with wet leaf, sent heated air that was heavily moisture laden up to the withering tats on the floors above, and that this heated air had a stewing effect on the leaf instead of withering it. This led to more attention being paid to the humidity of the air in the withering lofts and to the ultimate recognition that temperature is of little importance, the controlling factor being the relative humidity, or drying power of the air.[7]

In most factories the leaf is weighed after withering, and from this weight and the fresh-leaf weight, the degree of the wither is computed. If 100 lbs. of fresh leaf withers to a weight of 55 lbs., it is called a 55 per cent wither, and the leaf contains about 54 per cent of moisture. A 60 per cent wither, corresponding to about

[7] F. J. Whitehead, *Notes on the Artificial Withering of Tea Leaf*, Colombo, 1923.

ROLLER WITHERING TATS OF THE OLD-FASHIONED TYPE, GLEN ALFIN GROUP, BADULLA

WITHERING LOFT, SHOWING LEAF SPREAD ON WIRED TATS

After the leaf is withered it is dropped through the funnels, one of which is shown in the foreground of this picture, to the rollers on the ground floor.

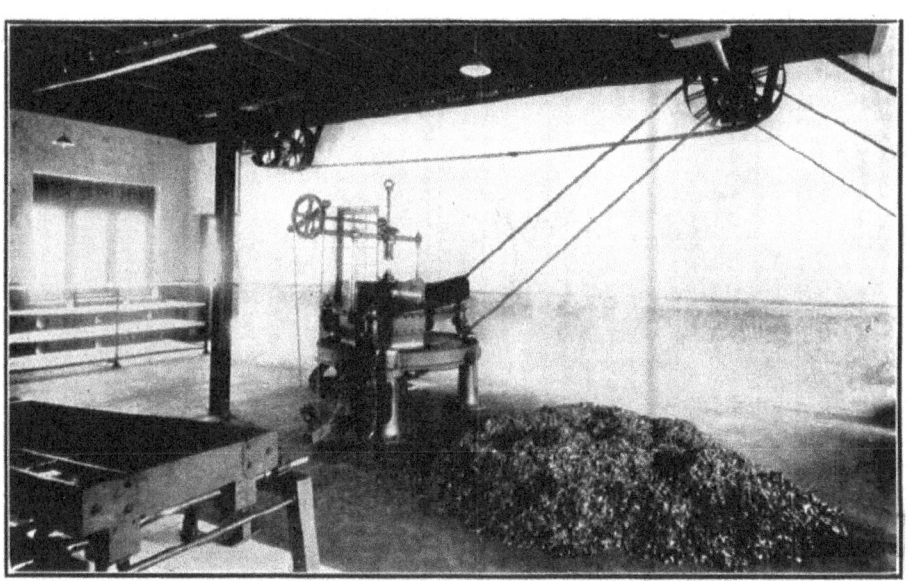

TEA-ROLLING MACHINE AND ROLL BREAKER WITH FERMENTATION TABLES IN BACKGROUND

THE WITHERING AND ROLLING PROCESSES IN A CEYLON TEA FACTORY

58 per cent of moisture, is a light wither; and a 50 per cent wither, corresponding to about 50 per cent of moisture, is a hard wither. A soft or under-wither will give soft, but thick liquor; a hard wither gives pungent teas, but thin liquor.

According to the latest ideas on closed-loft withering, the hot air is not allowed to circulate for more than one hour at a time. The windows are then opened and the foul air expelled, after which the hot air is again circulated. The rotation is continued as long as may be required. The enzymes, which withering develops, are present after about eighteen hours of withering.

When the withering is complete, the tea leaves become soft and velvety, and when twisted or rolled, retain the new shape. The correct degree of wither is determined by feel and smell—sufficiently withered leaf having the scent of fresh apples. The immediate object of withering is to obtain leaf in suitable condition for rolling, and it is very necessary to the success of the later manufacturing operations that the leaf be neither over- nor underwithered. The wither must also be even, and this is accomplished by thin spreading, since nearly all estates now have sufficient withering space to provide for this procedure. This process completed, the leaf is chuted to the rollers on the ground floor.

Rolling

The leaf is passed through the rolling machines from three to eight times. This twists the leaf and breaks the leaf-cells, releasing the properties that give color, flavor, and strength to tea in the cup. The first roll is usually without pressure, the next light, and the succeeding rolls with increased pressure. After each roll, the leaf is dropped out of the roller in lumps, and is removed to the combined roll-breaker and green leaf sifter, where it is sifted for about ten minutes. When pressure is applied, it is usually raised every five minutes for a few minutes to avoid heating. Tender young leaves become sufficiently rolled sooner than the hard older leaves, and these are sifted out. Only the leaf requiring further rolling is returned to the roller. Mr. H. J. Moppett, a former Ceylon planter, makes these suggestions with regard to rolling:

For general appearance the leaf should be just over a medium wither and should be rolled as follows:

25 minutes,	no pressure.	
25 "	" "	
30 "	15 minutes light pressure	
	15 " half "	
44 "	full pressure, 10 minutes on and five minutes off.	

A suggestion for making a large percentage of broken grades on gardens at altitudes not under 3500 feet is as follows:—

30 minutes,	no pressure	
30 "	" "	
30 "	half "	
20 "	fairly hard pressure	
20 "	pressure as hard as possible and three minutes break at half time	
20 "	same as the preceding period	

At higher altitudes the rolling may be extended, but it should be reduced at lower altitudes. In the low country the following program may be followed:—

40 minutes,	no pressure	
40 "	medium " seven minutes on and three minutes off	
40 "	same as the preceding period	

The slower the rolling, within limits, the better. 45 revolutions per minute is a rate often observed in Ceylon factories. In case of an over-wither, Moppett recommends that a bucket of water or less, according to the condition of the leaf, should be splashed gradually into the roller with the leaf.[8]

The tea rolling machines commonly used in Ceylon are of several types and makes, but all are designed to approximate the rolling of leaf between the hands by a circular movement of one palm against the other; a process that lends itself readily to mechanical treatment. A rolling machine in its simplest form may be described as a box without a bottom placed just above a table fitted throughout its surface with ribs or battens. This box is given a circular motion by cranks. When the box is in motion, the leaf placed in it is scrubbed and rolled across the battens until the leaf-cells are broken and their juices liberated to set up an even fermentation. These juices are spread stickily over the surface of the leaves and, after firing, become a dry residue that is readily soluble in boiling water.

Jackson rollers predominate in Ceylon tea factories. They are:—Jackson's 32" Square Rapid, 24" and 36" Circular Rapid, 36" Double Action Metallic, Single Action Metallic, and the 24", 28", and 32" Eco-

[8] H. J. Moppett, *Tea Manufacture: Its Theory and Practice*, Colombo, 1922.

TWO TYPES OF ROLL BREAKERS IN A MODEL TEA FACTORY

nomic. Brown's Triple Action roller and, more recently, the Colombo Commercial Company's special roller, designed to stand hard rolling, are also much used. The type of machine used is largely a matter of individual choice. Some planters prefer a roller with a square box, others favor circular boxes. Triple action is the *sine qua non* of some, while others say single action produces the best teas, and many claim that a 24" roller produces a better twist than a larger machine. Then there are also brine-cooled rollers.

The withered tea is fed into the box which is provided with adjustable screw pressure, like a wine-press, to hold the leaf against the rolling table below. The amount of pressure to be applied depends largely upon the character of the tea produced on a given estate. Heavy pressure is said to bring out strength in tea, but is likely to destroy tip, and, speaking generally, it is least employed where fine flavor exists. Extremely hard rolling gives broken grades that require little subsequent cutting.

It is considered an important item in the perfect coördination of a Ceylon tea factory to have a sufficiency of roll-breakers for the number of rollers used. A recognized standard for a small factory is one combined roll-breaker and green leaf sifter to two rolling machines, but where there are a large number of rollers, a proportion of two roll-breakers to five rolling machines is sometimes favored. The roll-breaker is a simple sifting machine with a large oscillating sieve, having a mesh of four or five to the inch, designed to sift the fine leaf from the coarse, and furnished with a hopper feed box fitted with beaters to break up the lumps formed in the roller.

Fermenting

The question of rolling room temperature and humidity is receiving closer attention than formerly. Since fermentation is known to begin during the rolling process, it is now realized that a humid and constant temperature is just as important in the rolling as in the fermenting room, and that the rolling and fermenting rooms may well be combined.

After rolling, the leaf is spread thinly on cement tables, with free access of cool air, but no direct draft, to ferment or oxidize. Oxidation of the tannin, and development of the essential oil, which is responsible for the flavor, begins as soon as the juices are released by rolling. In Ceylon, as in India, any possible drying of the fermenting leaf is feared as likely to interfere with the process, therefore the fermenting shelves are hung round about with either "dammer" or Hessian cloth, kept damp by water from perforated pipes; or, in some factories, damp cloth is spread over, but not touching the leaf. The use of dammer cloth is preferred as it is without odor.

The damp cloth, in addition to supplying moisture to the air, also tends to reduce its temperature, through evaporation; and this is important for the reason that a temperature much in excess of 82° F. during fermentation causes the formation of a dark brown oxidation product and loss of quality in the made tea. As a matter of fact, fermentation in Ceylon is conducted at much lower temperatures than this—sometimes down to 65° F., or even less; while in Assam it is not uncommon to work at temperatures above 85° F. The best temperature for fermenting is considered to be 70° F. and this must be constant. At the same time the hygrometer is supposed to show a reading not in excess of 2° between the wet and dry bulbs. No variation is best, but this is seldom attained except in modern factories with humidity systems.

The fermenting room is always on the ground floor of the factory, and arranged with numerous loopholes to get the full benefit of the prevailing winds at different times of the year. Moppett has made the suggestion that difficulty in supplying air to every part of the room may be met by installing a fan that is not so powerful as to cause drying of the spreads. The leaf is spread about one inch thick, but at the higher altitudes and cooler temperatures it is often necessary to spread more thickly in order to conserve the heat generated in the process. The finer leaf ferments in two-and-a-half hours, and the coarse in four, from the time the rolling starts.

Where flavor and pungency are sought, a light ferment is given and the leaf is taken early to the firing machine. If, on

CEMENT FERMENTING TABLES IN A CEYLON TEA FACTORY

On reaching the upper end of the Automatic Feeder and Spreader the leaf falls lightly and uniformly on to the top row of trays of the drier, which convey it into the drying chamber.

THE CUTTING, SIFTING, GRADING, AND BULKING OPERATIONS TAKE PLACE HERE

THE FIRING AND SIFTING ROOMS IN A MODERN CEYLON TEA FACTORY

the contrary, strength and body are desired, fermentation is allowed to proceed for a longer period. There is a conflict of interests in regard to the production of flavor on the one hand and a good liquor on the other, and therein lies the scope of a good tea-maker's experience. He knows when to stop fermentation for a given result, but there are no hard and fast rules for it, as allowance must be made for local conditions. As the fermentation progresses, the leaf rapidly changes color, finally developing a bright copper shade and the characteristic aroma of finished tea.

Firing or Drying

When the leaf has attained the desired stage of fermentation, it is removed to a machine with hot air passing through or over a number of trays on which the leaf is placed. The object of this operation is to stop fermentation and dry the leaf. The fermentation enzyme is destroyed as quickly as possible by the action of heat. This is accomplished by the application of a degree of heat that will absorb the greatest possible amount of moisture without loss of quality. It has been established that the capacity of a drier is determined by temperature and air-flow, but high temperature and insufficient air-flow cause loss of pungency, while low temperature causes "stewing" and produces teas that will not keep.

Some factories dry the leaf for a few minutes at a temperature of 240° F. and finish it at 180° F.; others successfully employ temperatures as low as 170° F., drying the leaf more slowly and spreading it thinly. The latter plan requires a greater investment in machines when a heavy crop is to be handled, but is considered as giving the most satisfactory results.

In Ceylon, the tea is dried in one operation, unlike Assam, where the practice is to double-fire. The rolled and fermented leaf containing from 46 to 62 per cent of moisture is dried to not more than 3 to 5 per cent. The machines commonly used are the Paragon drier, Endless Chain Pressure, the Down Draft Sirocco, Double Tilter, etc., while the Colombo drier and Brown's Desiccator, made by Colombo firms, are the favorites. The Colombo drier is a six-tray, up-draft machine with an output of 120 to 150 lbs. an hour. Brown's Desiccator has a smaller hourly capacity, 80 to 90 lbs., but is highly regarded for its excellent work. The Farbridge drier with perpendicular tubes is becoming increasingly popular.

After the withered and rolled leaf has been subjected to the operation of the drier for twenty-five minutes, more or less, it is converted into the familiar dry and brittle black tea of commerce, but is uneven in size and style. In order to correct this, it next goes to the sifting room to be sifted into the various grades.

Final firing is occasionally employed in damp weather. As previously stated, Ceylon teas are usually dried in one operation, but dried leaf readily absorbs moisture and this it may do in wet weather, while it is being sorted for packing. Finished tea does not keep well if packed with more than five to six per cent of moisture; so, although it is recognized that any unnecessary heating reduces flavor, a virtue is made of necessity in case excess moisture is found, and a final firing applied. It is not easy to tell by touch or smell whether tea contains an undue amount of moisture, but some factories use a chemical balance and small steam oven to determine the exact moisture content of each bin.

Sorting and Sifting

After the firing process, the leaf is removed for sifting into grades; but before this is begun, the various lots are carefully sorted by hand for the removal of all red flake, stalks, and foreign matter. The grades of tea usually prepared in Ceylon average approximately: Broken Orange Pekoe, 50 per cent; Broken Pekoe, 20 per cent; Orange Pekoe, and Pekoe, 20 per cent; Pekoe Souchong, Dust, and Fannings, 10 per cent.

The type of sifting machine commonly used consists of a number of sieves with different-sized mesh set one above the other on a slope, and held together by a frame. A crank arrangement off a main shaft imparts to the frame an oscillating or rotating motion. The topmost sieve has the coarsest mesh while the finest is at the bottom. With the shaft in motion the leaf passes onto the first sieve, the finer leaf falling through until it reaches a screen through which it cannot pass. Each size of leaf finally passes into a collecting box.

A cutting machine is used to reduce the larger, coarser leaves, in order that the entire day's manufacture may be reduced to uniform grades. This cutter consists principally of a roller with small holes all over its surface, operating against, but not quite touching a cutting edge. When the leaf is fed into the cutter the small leaf gets into the holes, but the coarser leaf sticks out, and is brought against the cutter. The size of the holes in the roller used determines the size to which the leaf may be reduced.

Graying of tea occurs during sorting and sifting if the surface of the leaf gets too much rubbing. In fact, any sifter or cutter that rubs the surface of the leaf very much, tends to cause grayness. This effect is greatly increased in machines run at high speed, consequently, cutting machines are run at the lowest speed that circumstances permit. Sifters that impart a hopping motion to the leaf gray it less than those that give it a sliding motion. The Moore sifter, which is now very popular, gives practically the same results as a hand sifter.

Green Tea

Only a comparatively small amount of green tea is now being manufactured in Ceylon. It consists of freshly plucked green leaf that has been made ready for rolling by an initial steaming process; the chief divergence from the process of black tea manufacture being that green tea is not allowed any process of fermentation. This is accomplished by carefully avoiding any bruising in plucking or transit to the factory, and by an immediate sterilization upon arrival there. The leaf is introduced into a hexagonal revolving drum made of wood through which runs a perforated steam pipe. The steam penetrates the leaf thoroughly as the drum turns; and at a gauge pressure of 30 to 40 lbs., the leaf is sterilized in about two minutes.

The leaf is next spread out for a brief cooling, after which it is placed in the roller box and compressed, to force out the surplus water. When the pressure is taken off, the leaf is rolled for 10 minutes. Then it is rolled for 10 minutes with light pressure, and again without pressure for five minutes. At this point the partly rolled leaf still contains an excess of water, and this is removed by passing the leaf rapidly through a firing machine, at a temperature of 200° F. Any lumps are broken up by hand during this part of the process, but not until they become pliable. Firing is continued until the leaf assumes a slight stickiness and an olive green color. It is then spread out to cool, and is rolled again for from twenty to thirty minutes. This final rolling is for the purpose of imparting the necessary twist to the leaf, and only the pressure required to do this is applied. From the rolling machine the leaf is passed through a roll-breaker and any remaining lumps are broken up by hand. Then the leaf is given a final firing at a temperature of 180° F. to 200° F., after which it is ready for sifting and grading. The grades usually prepared are Young Hyson, Hyson No. 1, Hyson No. 2, Gunpowder, and Dust.

Packing and Shipping

As quickly as possible after sifting, the finished teas are bulked or mixed in bins that are made as nearly air tight as possible, in order to keep them from accumulating moisture.

When sufficient quantity of each grade is accumulated to form a sampling break, the tea is packed and despatched for sale. The packages are commonly filled on a special vibratory machine that shakes the

VIBRATORY PACKING MACHINES

A MODERN FIVE-STORY TEA FACTORY ON BOGAWANTALAWA, DIKOYA

tea down very rapidly, without the use of compression. The machine consists of a small platform on which the package—chest, half-chest, or box—is clamped, after which an eccentric on a rapidly revolving shaft gives the platform a rapid vibration.

The tea chests hold from 80 to 130 lbs., and half-chests from 50 to 90 lbs., according to the size of the leaf. Sheet-lead or aluminum lining is placed in the packages before filling, and is afterward folded over the top and carefully soldered, in order that no moisture shall reach the leaf. In some instances, where lead is used, it is required that the chests be provided with inner paper linings. The lids are nailed on, and the packages bound with hoop iron as an added safeguard against damage in transit. The tea is then despatched to Colombo, where it may be shipped directly to the London sales, or sold at the Colombo auction.

Buildings

Bungalows are built at locations on an estate suited to the duties of the executive staff and clerks. Most of them have but a single story, although in the low country some are built with an upper floor for greater coolness. Only the superintendent's, or manager's, bungalow is planned for family acommodation; while the others are built to the probable requirements of bachelor occupancy. They usually combine comfort, and often a degree of luxury, with suitability to their environment. Some of the earlier examples of bungalow construction involved poor materials that invited dry rot and rapid deterioration, but modern bungalows on Ceylon tea estates

are built for permanency. Engineering firms can now provide good selections of plans at slight cost, and these include specifications that cover the best and most satisfactory ideas on bungalow construction.

A modern tea factory is a steel-frame building having iron roofing and galvanized iron side walls lined with wood. This rests on a stone foundation that is carried up to a height of about three-and-a-half feet above the ground floor, and, where it surrounds the rolling room, it is built up to the first floor level in order to make the rolling room as cool as possible. The arrangement always used in Ceylon tea factories places the rolling and fermenting rooms, the firing and packing room, and the sifting room on the ground floor. The withering lofts occupy the upper stories of the factory. In some of the older and smaller buildings, only two stories were provided for this purpose; but in factories with a production of 350,000 lbs. or more

T. U. Todd & H. J. Moppett

ENTRANCE TO A WELL-KEPT FACTORY

TRANSPORTING TEA CHESTS BY BULLOCK CARTS ON AN UP-COUNTRY ESTATE

of tea annually, three, or even four withering lofts are built.

Capital Cost, Value, Etc.

The capital cost of opening land for tea varies greatly, but may be put at *Rs*. 750 to *Rs*. 1200 an acre [1 rupee = 1s.6d Eng.; 36¢ U. S.], which may be spread over about four to five years, with greater cost in the first, third, and fourth. These figures include the erection of a factory, with necessary machinery, and all other works required for the running of the estate. The waiting period, before any return is received on the investment, is four to five years. In purchasing a tea estate as a going concern, the purchase period is generally taken as ten years. The value per acre of a good tea estate in full bearing varies from *Rs*. 1200 to *Rs*. 3500.

Coolie Labor

The labor on most of the tea estates in Ceylon, and on all those up country, is provided by Tamils from Southern India. Native Sinhalese are also employed where they are available. Conditions of estate life, and the wages earned, offer considerable inducement to South Indian peasants to leave their villages, where, in most cases, they are dependent on a fair season for the crops, which are often their sole means of existence. There are some 589,000 Tamils employed on tea and other estates in Ceylon.

The Tamil labor force consists of *kanganies*, or native foremen, sub-*kanganies*, and the coolie field and factory hands of both sexes and of various ages. The old method of recruiters enlisting coolies is now no longer followed but, instead, the head of the family, who is usually a sub-kanganie, is encouraged to bring over his own relations. The Ceylon Labor Commissioner at Trichinopoly and his assistants do no actual recruiting, but act as propagandists and bankers for the estates.

Under the present system, a coolie must first undergo an examination as to his suitability for estate labor. If passed in accordance to the regulations, he is sent to the Quarantine Station at Mandapam. This station is maintained by the Ceylon Government. Here he is given a medical examination, and is held six days for observation before being allowed to proceed to Ceylon. The expense of the coolie's keep in this camp is met by the Common Fund subscribed at fixed rates by all employers of Tamil emigrants. For estates having ten acres or more in tea the subscription rate to this Fund varies annually per acre according to requirements. In return, the Common Fund takes care of the transportation and subsistence costs, as well as the emigration fees, of all unskilled Indian recruits and of any recruiters accompanying them, from the time they are accepted at any of the Commission's agencies. The law prohibits recovery of any portion of this expense from the immigrants.

Eight hours is the fixed working day for field coolies. Work begins at 7 A.M. and ends at 4 P.M. There is a growing tendency to pay tea pluckers according to the amount plucked and most of the estates offer a bonus of extra pay to laborers as an inducement for them to work more than, say, twenty-one days a month, or, in certain seasons, to work more than nine hours a day.

During recent years considerable attention has been paid to the general conditions of estate labor in Ceylon. Estate schools are provided, and housing and sanitation are carried out according to Government regulations. Tea estates must have creches for the care of infants while their mothers are away in the fields. The larger properties have their own well-equipped hospitals, and there is a resident dispenser on nearly every estate qualified to treat and prescribe for minor illnesses and to carry out the instructions of the district medical officer, who is available in serious cases. Rice is usually supplied by the estates at less than cost price, and housing accommodations and medical attendance are provided free.

The rates of pay drawn by newly-arrived Tamil coolies, as revised in 1934, are as follows:

	Up-Country	Mid-Country	Low-Country
Men	49 cents	43 cents	41 cents
Women	39 "	35 "	33 "
Children	29 "	25 "	24 "

NOTE: the figures given are Ceylon cents, equal to one-fifth of a penny, or two-fifths of a cent, U.S.A.

In Ceylon the building of coolie lines is standardized by a law which also compels the modernization of all old lines to

MOTOR TRUCK TRANSPORT FROM TEA FACTORY TO RAILWAY STATION, NAWALAPITIYA, DOLOSBAGE

After its dispatch from the tea estate by bullock cart or motor lorry, the tea chests are transported by train to Colombo, where they are stored in godowns to await shipment overseas.

meet, as nearly as possible, the new regulations respecting the housing of labor.

The Government specification calls for tiled, iron, or shingle roofs having a certain pitch from the main ridge. No coolie lines may be erected until the plans have been duly approved by the principal civil medical officer, and not more than an average of 3.2 persons may occupy one room.

The best sites for coolie lines are on gentle slopes with gravelly soil. A good water supply is, of course, essential, and it pleases the Tamils to have the habitations built in colonies wherever this is possible.

Coolie lines are provided with verandas, and these the regulations require shall be protected against weather by an extension of the eaves to a point two feet beyond the edge of the veranda. Floors are required to be twelve inches above the ground level, and may be built of brick laid up with cement, or they may be laid with a mixture of stamped gravel, covered with a mixture of cow dung and mud.

An unobstructed ventilator must extend from end to end of the main ridge of all coolie lines, and the type of such ventilators is prescribed. There must be at least one window, three feet square, for each room, and the size of the doorways is also prescribed. They must be not less than six feet high by two feet, six inches wide.

A pavement impervious to water must be laid around each set of coolie lines.

The cost of building coolie lines may be roughly estimated at *Rs.* 350 per room for double lines, and *Rs.* 375 for single.

Where timber is scarce all-iron lines are erected at a cost of 20 per cent more.

Planters' Associations

The Planters' Association of Ceylon is the representative body of the chief planting interests on the Island. All proprietors, firms, and individuals who are interested in the planting industries are eligible for election. The headquarters of the Association are located in the Victoria Commemoration Buildings at Kandy, and here the general and committee meetings are held.

There are seventeen subsidiary, or district associations in various tea districts of the island that hold meetings for the discussion of local questions and matters pertaining to planting politics generally. Delegates from each branch association also serve on the General Committee of the Planters' Association of Ceylon.

The Ceylon Estates Proprietary Association membership includes 554 proprietors or companies, representing a cultivated area of 641,925 acres, as follows: tea, 375,504; rubber, 243,100; sundry products, 23,321. Its objects are to promote the common interests of all persons concerned in the cultivation of tea, rubber, and other agricultural products in Ceylon. Proprietors of and agents for estates of not less than fifty acres in extent are eligible as members.

Another organization having some interest in tea is the Low Country Products Association. It is open to owners of twenty-five acres cultivated with low

THE TEA RESEARCH INSTITUTE, ST. COOMBS ESTATE, DIMBULA
General view of the factory, equipped for commercial as well as experimental tea manufacture.

THE MANAGER'S BUNGALOW AT DAMBATENNE, HAPUTALE

country produce, principally coconut, rubber, and cinnamon, and to owners of mills or factories working any produce above mentioned. The membership is 412.

The Research Institute

During the last few years the problems of the tea industry of Ceylon, particularly those relating to the physiology of the tea plant with regard to soils and manures, have been subjected to scientific investigation in the Tea Research Institute, now on the St. Coombs Estate, Telawakelle. Important questions, to which the staff of scientists have given study recently, are: the quantity of lime needed by various soils; the effect of insecticidal and fungicidal sprays upon insect pests and the tea made from the leaf of bushes sprayed with them; and the chemical constituents of the raw tea, as well as of the best prepared tea, to determine what changes should be brought about by manufacture.

Attention has been given, also, to the breeding of a colony of a parasite of *Tortrix, Trichogramma erosicornis,* of such size that hundreds of thousands of parasites have been available when needed for distribution to infected estates. The

Diploda disease, too, is better understood since the discovery that the tea bushes which die of it after pruning are devoid of starch. This information reveals the possibility of overcoming the trouble by the application of internal food reserves. The cause of the previously unrecorded disease, *Dadaps,* has been found to be a small eelworm, *Heteroda radicicola.*

These and other results of the work carried on in the Institute are published in *The Tea Quarterly.*

Tea Planters' Life in Ceylon

The budding planters who come out to Ceylon are mostly English, Scotch, or Irish public school lads or, occasionally, univer-

GOVERNMENT STANDARD COOLIE LINES

THE SUPERINTENDENT'S BUNGALOW ON LOOLECONDERA, HEWAHETA LOWER

sity or ex-service men. Some Ceylon tea planting firms import their assistants on a straight three- or five-year agreement, while others—and this is a custom peculiar to Ceylon—accept on probation "creepers," or novices, who pay a premium for instruction, board, and lodging. After six to eight months time those who show aptitude for the work are eligible for appointments as assistants.

There is a strong divergence of opinion regarding "creeper-mongering," as it is termed by its opponents. Advertising for premium paying pupils in the United Kingdom newspapers seems to be universally condemned, but premium paying of say £100 by selected young men, consisting of relatives, friends, or acquaintances of those having tea interests in Ceylon, is upheld in some quarters; although those who hold the latter view appear to be in the minority. Most of the estate agents condemn the importation of premium-paying creepers as certain to produce in time more young men than there are billets for, with consequent unemployment, and hold that it is much better, in the interests of the planting industry, that the recruitment of European assistants be confined to actual requirements. Some even go so far as to say they would refuse to consider applications for billets from men who had paid a premium. They point out that young men go out to Sumatra and Java on agreements carrying

a salary from the start, and contend that it should be the same in Ceylon.

Opposing this view are other agents who prefer to engage a youngster who has come out as a creeper through someone they know, and who has been a good man while creeping, rather than a man sent out by the London agents. Certainly there is less creeper-mongering than twenty or twenty-five years ago, and while there is nothing good to be said of the man who attempts to make a living out of the game and advertises in the papers with this in view, as has been done, still a suitable young man who comes out with a good reference has, to date, been fairly sure of a job at the end of his creeping period.

The young European planter starts as a junior assistant to the superintendent in charge of 200 or 300 acres of tea. His salary the first year is about Rs. 250 a month, or £240 [$1200] per annum in addition to free housing, two native servants—a gardener and a house servant, free firewood, and tea as allowances. Each year his salary rises by increments of Rs. 50 or more a month until it reaches a figure of Rs. 800 to Rs. 1000 a month, or, £720 [$3500] to £950 [$4600] a year. In the meantime, he has been promoted first to senior assistant [sinna durei], occasionally acting for the superintendent [periya durei], and then to the superintendence of the estate. Later, he may be appointed manager or visiting agent.

In addition to his salary, a superintendent or a manager as a rule receives a bonus on profits ranging from £70 to £1000 per annum in good years, a furnished bungalow, four servants and, where necessary, a horse or motor car allowance.

As manager, a Ceylon planter may receive as high as £2500 on one or two of the largest groups of estates, but the average is £600 to £700 per annum. He can supplement this by visiting estates, if he is allowed to do so, bringing his salary up to, say £3000 [$14,600].

A visiting agent or inspector of estates who does nothing else can earn £3000 to £5000 a year [$14,600 to $24,000].

As a rule, there are no contracts, as these are generally regarded as standing in the way of promotion. However, some firms favor them—generally for three years, but sometimes for five, the assistant being paid from the start, including his passage to the island. At the expiration of the period the contract may be renewed, and so on.

In the matter of holidays, leave for absence in the island averages three weeks per annum, and six months home-leave on full pay is given after three to five years, according to length of service and conditions of employment. Extensions of two to four months are often obtainable at half pay. Most estates now allow a first class return passage to England for a planter and his wife, provided he returns to his employer. Otherwise he forfeits the return passage.

The average Ceylon planter's daily routine of work and play begins when he rises at 5:30 A.M., in time for muster at 6. He has early tea between 6 and 6:30. Rounds of field and factory from 7 until noon, when he has breakfast. He resumes duty at 2 P.M., and concerns himself with office work until evening muster at 4, after which he is served with tea. Field, factory, or office duties claim his time from 4:30 to 6. Usually, Saturday afternoons and all Sundays are free. At such times he is apt to turn for recreation and amusement to tennis, golf, shooting, or visiting friends, with bridge or attention to private correspondence in the evening. In the busy season, Sunday morning is occupied by visits to the fields.

The average length of a planter's active service in Ceylon is approximately twenty-eight years. If he is ambitious, his goal frequently is to become manager of a group of estates, a visiting agent, a proprietor, or a large stockholder in an estate. In the latter case, he aims to retire to England as soon as possible, retaining connections with Ceylon by going on the boards of limited companies as a director, and then paying periodic visits to the island to see that his interests are being properly looked after.

Some planters aspire to leading parts in the planters' associations, the Ceylon Association, London, or in local politics. The unambitious merely look for a livelihood, and are content to drift, looking for a favorable turn of the wheel of fortune. As a rule the Ceylon planter finds his work fascinating and hates to leave it.

A FIELD OF MATURE TEA ON THE STATE PLANTATION AT CHAKVA

FIRING MACHINES AT THE NEW CHAKVA TEA FACTORY, NEAR BATOUM, GEORGIA, U. S. S. R.

Due to the high cost of labor, mechanization has been introduced into every process of tea production in Russia. Automatic leaf spreaders here take the place of hand labor.

VIEWS OF SOVIET RUSSIA'S TEA DEVELOPMENT IN TRANSCAUCASIA

CHAPTER XXI

CULTIVATION AND MANUFACTURE
IN OTHER COUNTRIES

MISCELLANEOUS TEA CULTIVATIONS ON THE CONTINENT OF ASIA AND ELSEWHERE—THE PRIMITIVE METHOD OF PREPARING WILD TEA FOR CHEWING, IN SIAM—THE MANUFACTURE OF LETPET, A TEA SALAD, BY THE BURMESE—CULTIVATION AND PREPARATION OF COMMERCIAL TEAS IN BURMA, FRENCH INDO-CHINA, THE MALAY STATES, IRAN, NATAL, NYASALAND, PORTUGUESE EAST AFRICA, UGANDA, KENYA, TANGANYIKA TERRITORY, THE AZORES, RUSSIAN TRANSCAUCASIA, AND BRAZIL

THE ABORIGINAL tribes of Siam, Burma, and the bordering Chinese province of Yunnan are credited by scientists with having been the first to gather and use the leaves of the *miang*, or wild tea tree, found growing on their native hills. From the wild tea leaves they still make up small bundles of steamed and fermented tea for chewing. In early times, they made a medicinal drink by boiling the raw, green leaf. It was this beginning that suggested to the Chinese the cultivation of the leaf and its preparation by drying, in order that it might be available throughout the year as an addition to their materia medica; and from the Chinese, at a much later time, the countries to the south learned to preserve leaf tea for beverage use, though on a limited scale.

SIAM.—The native *miang* is the only tea produced in Siam. It is all consumed locally; none being exported. Siam is an importer of tea, most of which is consumed by foreigners and a few Siamese who have adopted European customs. In Northern Siam, the inhabitants of the mountain valleys chew steamed and fermented *miang* leaves with salt or other ingredients, such as garlic and hog fat. The *miang* has a stimulating effect, and a chew of it often enables a man to carry on at his work for a considerable time without food.

In districts where there are large *miang* gardens, the plant sometimes is grown from seed planted by natives, while others seed themselves. Wherever the wild trees are found in the forest, a clearing is made around them, and thither the villagers go to obtain the leaf. Where *miang* is sowed by hand, the seed is planted in a hole two or three inches deep, and three stout stakes are driven round each hole for protection. The seed then is left to care for itself; there is no transplanting. Planting of this sort is done among other *miang* trees.

The young trees are not picked until they reach a height of six or seven feet, and they grow to an average height of from sixteen to twenty feet. Exceptional trees grow as high as twenty-five to thirty feet. The trunks of the trees will average eight to nine inches in diameter at three feet above the ground, and just above this the branches begin.

No attention is given the trees beyond cutting the weeds and undergrowth round them twice a year. They are never pruned, nor are they freed from the epiphytes—such as mosses, ferns, and orchids—with which they become loaded. The most serious pest of *miang* is a caterpillar that destroys the young leaves and shoots.

The *miang* trees have leaves that are larger than those of the Chinese tea plants and smaller than those of native Indian tea, but all three belong to the same species—*Thea sinensis* (L.) Sims. Usually, four plucking seasons are observed—June, August, October, and December.

The October and December pickings are regarded as superior, for the reason that the June and August pickings are too sour;

although the latter are preferred by some. Each picking is continued for two to three weeks, depending on the amount to be gathered and the number of pickers.

In some localities, as in the extensive *miang* areas in the Muang Pua District, northeast of Nan, no fixed seasons are recognized; the picking going on, to a greater or lesser extent, throughout the year. These gardens belong to a race known as the Tins, whose picking methods differ somewhat from those common to the other districts, as explained later.

A common arrangement, to provide the labor for picking in the various *miang* districts, is for the owner to let out the leaf gathering on a fifty-fifty, or share alike, basis. Ordinarily, the picking is done in the morning, but sometimes continues throughout the day. In most of the districts, the pickers, either men or women, remove only about two-thirds of each of four or five terminal leaves, nipping them off with the thumb and finger of the right hand, and then transferring them to the left, where they are held until a good sized handful is obtained. They are then tied with a bamboo slip into a compact bundle, known as a *kam*. The *kams* remain intact throughout the manufacturing process, and become the unit of measurement and sale. The Tins of the Muang Pua District pick by nipping off the entire young shoot—with three or four leaves, leaf stalks, and all—and manufacture it into *miang*. About twenty to thirty *kams* is a fair yield for an average tree in any of the districts, and a good picker will gather 120 *kams* in a day.

The preparation of *miang* consists in steaming the leaves for two hours, tightly pressing the cooled *kams* into a container, such as a basket or an internode of bamboo, and allowing them to ferment for about a month; then the product is ready for use. Tea in these packs will keep for about a year. Occasionally, *miang* in bamboo joints is buried in the ground to preserve it, but this is only done when there is a supply beyond the market demands.

Miang leaves sometimes are dried and manufactured by the pan-firing and hand rolling process into leaf tea for beverage purposes. This is done, to a small extent, in the hills northwest of Chiengmai.

The demand for *miang* exists only in Siam, and, to a limited extent, in Burma; but there seems to be no reason why, with proper methods, good commercial leaf-tea should not be produced in the *miang* districts, and in almost unlimited quantities.[1]

BURMA.—The total area under tea cultivation in Burma is approximately 55,000 acres. Of this area, 50,000 acres are located in the Northern and 2000 acres in the Southern Shan States. These figures represent mere estimates of the ancient native industry as it exists at the present time. In addition, there are four districts in the states of Arakan, Tenasserim, and the Northwestern Border Division where tea is cultivated. These districts and their acreage are as follows: Akyab, in Arakan, sixty-two acres; Toungoo, in Tenasserim, 700; Katha, 503; and Upper Chindwin, 1840 acres. The total production is between twenty and twenty-five million pounds, annually; practically all of which is consumed by the Burmese and Shan people.

As to the varieties of the Burma and Shan tea plants, too little is known of them to allow of their critical separation from their near neighbor, the Manipur indigenous plant of India. The leaves are thicker, smaller, more acutely serrated, and distinctly more elliptic in shape than other teas. Possibly, what difference there is from the Manipur jat may be accounted for in some measure by the fact that the Burma plant has been grown for centuries more as a vegetable than for infusing a beverage. The Manipur variety occurs wild in considerable areas of the valleys of the Chindwin River and its tributaries in the northwestern part of Burma. It is believed to be one of the hardiest types of tea known.

Of late years, some Assam indigenous seed has been introduced into Burma. As this gives a distinctly better quality of tea than the Manipur, the Government of Burma is recommending its planting wherever the soil and climate are favorable. But where this is not the case the Manipur type is preferred, as it will flourish under conditions that would cause more delicate varieties to become the prey of pests and diseases.

Ninety per cent of the tea grown in Burma is cultivated in the Northern Shan state of Tawnpeng Loilong, which is a mass

---

[1] "Report on the Cultivation of Miang." *The Record*, issued by the Ministry of Commerce, Bankok, 1923.

of hills ranging 6000 feet above sea level. The soil is a dark brown, clayey loam of considerable depth, and covered on the surface with large quantities of decaying vegetable matter. The tea is allowed to grow with a single stem, which often is thick enough to be called a trunk. It luxuriates in the shade, and has a leaf nine inches in length when fully developed. Pruning soon kills it.

For tea cultivation, parcels of land covered with dense forest usually are selected. Blue oak, or scrub jungle is considered best. Land covered with pine forest is seldom planted. The gardens are almost invariably situated on the slopes of the hills. The ridge is left under primeval jungle, and both slopes are planted almost down to the foot. In some places they are precipitous, and on such slopes the plants usually are much smaller. There are many bare spots, caused by the dying off of trees. The gardens are not planted on any system, but are laid off at random.

Seed collected in November is sown in nurseries in February or later. The plants remain in the nursery until they are two feet high, generally in their second year, and are planted in August or September on cleared and burnt slopes. No manure is used, but the plants are freely watered during the dry season. Weeding is done only before the rains and after October, when the ground is often dug up with hoes. The trees are never pruned, either to a special shape or to regular dimensions, but are allowed to straggle freely. Vacancies among the plants are filled every year with seedlings from the nursery.

Each cultivator has his own garden, which he cultivates in the same primitive manner as has been done for hundreds of years. Until recently, no tea plantations in Burma were cultivated in a scientific manner.

The leaves are first picked in the fourth year, and the trees continue bearing for ten to twelve years. Three crops are gathered over a period from March to the end of October. These correspond to the number of flushes. The middle crop, between May and July, is considered the choicest, and is called *Swe'pe*. The picking is promiscuous, any and all kinds of leaves being gathered. The first crop is coarse, and usually is manufactured into wet, or pickled tea, called *neng yam* by the Shans and *letpet* by the Burmese.

The manufacture of *letpet* is peculiar to Burma, the Shan States, and some of the hills lying between Assam and Burma. There are two ways of preparing it. By the first, the leaves are thrown into boiling water and allowed to remain for a short time, until they become soft. They are then taken out, rolled by hand on mats, and allowed to cool. The process which follows consists in ramming the leaves down tight into an internode of a bamboo; a wooden ramrod being used for the purpose. A stopper then is made of jack or guava leaves, and the bamboos thus charged are kept in the shade for a couple of days, with the stoppered ends downward to allow any water to drain off.

The bamboos are not filled quite to the top with *letpet*, and the space thus left is packed with ashes mixed with a little water. This is done to prevent insects from getting to the tea. The bamboos then are buried in the ground until the *letpet* has matured [fermented] and is required for sale. If not buried, the tea turns black and spoils. To be good, it should be of a yellowish color. When the *letpet* is about to be sold, it is taken out of the bamboos and packed into wicker baskets lined with leaves. This method is in vogue west of the Irrawaddy River.

By the second method, used east of the Irrawaddy, the leaf is steamed, and then rolled by hand. After this process, the leaves are allowed to cool, and then are deposited in a pit lined with planks or bamboo matting. They are covered over and pressed down with heavy weights. Here they remain until a purchaser is found for the entire batch. When removed, the *letpet* is transferred into bamboo crates.

This *letpet*, or "siloed" tea, is made ready for consumption by soaking in oil, and by adding garlic and dried fish. The concoction thus formed is eaten, and considered a great luxury.

The middle season, or *Swe'pe*, crop generally is converted into dry tea. The leaves are steamed over night, and the next morning are compressed and rolled. Then they are loosened and spread out on bamboo mats to dry in the sun. While drying, they are rolled three or four times during the day. When perfectly dry they become *letpet chauk*, or dry tea, and are stored away in baskets.

The beverage made from *letpet chauk* is

TEA ON THANDAUNG ESTATE, BURMA

extensively used among the Shan people, and small quantities are exported each year into the Western China province of Yunnan. In former times this was an important trade. The infusion is not palatable to European taste. The Shans make it by boiling the prepared leaf in an earthen kettle, and then drink it with salt.

In recent years, there has been a movement to establish commercial leaf tea production in Burma by modern methods of cultivation and manufacture. Full manufacturing production was not reached for some time, due to delay in the arrival of machinery. However, samples of tea prepared by temporary process, were well received in the local market.

The report on the operations of the Department of Agriculture, Burma, for 1929 included this note:

> There is only one tea estate proper in Burma, viz., the Thandaung Tea Estate, which has 360 acres under tea, although there is a large trade in pickled tea between the Shan States and Burma. Tea of high quality has been produced, and sold at 3s.6d. per pound. . . .

Recently, the Managing Agency of the Thandaung Tea Estate has been transferred to Messrs. MacGregor & Co., Ltd., of Rangoon, and at the same time they acquired a controlling interest. This estate is at an altitude of 4500 feet on hill slopes of newly cleared virgin soil, and has an annual rainfall of 188 inches. The cultural methods are similar to those followed in Ceylon.

Plucking is carried on throughout the year, but during the periods of more vigorous flushing, the bushes are plucked every seven or eight days; while at other times there may be an interval of from one to three weeks. The *jats* introduced have

been principally good Ceylon and Assam varieties, and, of the two, the Ceylon plants do best, giving a more satisfactory yield. Tea from the Shan States also is being grown on a small scale.

The success that has thus far attended this pioneer effort to establish the tea industry in Burma lends encouragement to the belief that it may be commercially successful. If so, it will have introduced a new crop on land that is valueless for other cultivation.

FRENCH INDO-CHINA.—The natives, inheriting ancient tea manufacturing methods brought from China, have long since dropped the original Chinese processes of cultivation and manufacture, and are, with the encouragement of the Government's Experimental Station at Phu Tho, Tonkin, gradually approaching essential commercial standards.

The native population prefers strong, acrid teas to those of delicate flavor. For such teas, the older, larger leaves are required. Teas for the natives, therefore, form a valuable byproduct of the fine tea industry now being developed by Europeans.

The tea areas are located chiefly in the provinces of Annam, Tonkin, and Cochin-China, named in the order of their importance. Also, wild tea grows abundantly in the mountains of Upper Laos, and there is some native production, although most of the original cultivations in this province died out many years ago.

About 60,000 acres are cultivated in Annam, and 8000 acres in Tonkin. The ex-

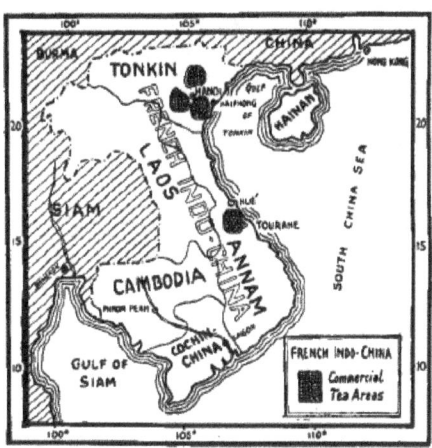

MODERN TEA CULTURE, ARBRE BROYÉ TEA ESTATE, FRENCH INDO-CHINA

ports from French Indo-China in 1930 amounted to 533,000 kilos, valued at 2,500,000 francs; in 1929, 1,012,400 kilos were shipped, valued at 10,000,000 francs.

The native cultural methods are rudimentary in the extreme, and the plantations rarely comprise more than 100 to 300 trees planted near the dwellings. Propagation is from seed planted directly in the field; nursery planting being unknown. The seeds are sown two or three together in holes twenty-three to thirty-two inches apart. When the plants come up, the strongest one is kept, and the others are pulled up. The plants are given little or no care beyond weeding, as their hardiness makes this unnecessary. Plucking begins, as a rule, when the plant is three years old, and thereafter practically all the leaves are stripped from the bush two or three times a year. The younger leaves and buds are disregarded; only the mature leaf is taken. On account of the severe plucking to which they are subjected, the bushes frequently present a ragged appearance, and fall easy prey to pests and blights.

Numerous variations of process are applied by the natives to the manufacture of the teas they produce. One process, used to some extent in all of the tea districts of

Indo-China, consists of a slow drying, corresponding to withering, followed by maceration in a rice mortar and further drying, which is substituted for the usual rolling and drying. This produces a coarse, unfermented tea.

In Cochin-China and parts of Tonkin, green tea is prepared by first steaming the whole leaf in a hot pan, and then transferring it to a second pan, where it is rolled either by hand or foot. The leaf mass is next broken up and spread out in the sun

NATIVE METHOD OF ROLLING TEA LEAVES, FRENCH INDO-CHINA

to dry for an hour; after which, rolling is resumed with a final complete drying.

A process for the production of coarse, black tea in Tonkin consists in hacking the leaves on a hardwood block immediately after plucking, and then distributing them in little piles, lightly sprinkled and covered with cloth, to ferment. After from twelve to twenty-four hours, fermentation is stopped by spreading the leaf in the sun, where it is dried for many days. The beverage made from this tea is sour, bitter, and lacking in aroma.

The process applied to the leaves of the wild varieties, *mien-luang* and *mieng-noi*, which are much affected by the natives of the province of Laos, is a trifle more elaborate than the simple method of drying in the sun. The leaves brought from the forest by the pluckers are dumped into iron basins, which have been previously heated to the desired temperature. On these hot surfaces the leaves are stirred about until dry, and toward the end of the operation are rolled by hand. A considerable part of this product, which makes a near approach to being acceptable to European tastes, is sold to the Chinese of Yunnan.

Contrasting sharply with the native production are the excellent teas now being manufactured on some six European estates in Annam organized and equipped along the lines of the British Indian, Ceylon, and Netherlands Indian tea estates. Four of them have well-equipped, modern tea factories and two more plan to build them in a short time. The areas of the estates range from 500 to 1200 acres, not all in production.

The first European tea estates were started in the low country, where the natives already had tea gardens, but this was soon recognized as being a mistake and the later estates were started higher up in the mountains.

The most serious mistake made at first was the assumption that the climatic conditions were identical with those in Java. The climate of Indo-China is not equatorial, and the winter is severe and dry, comparing more closely with the high and dry parts of the Uva district in Ceylon. Not only are the temperature, rainfall and humidity different from Java, but the whole climate is influenced by the mountains in the northeast and the dry cold winds coming from North and Middle Asia.

Speaking generally, the soil is not exceedingly rich, but is of good physical condition for tea. The gardens are planted with Assam-type bushes, which are started in nurseries and then transplanted. The original seeds were imported from Java and Sumatra, with a small part from British India, but all of the estate tea is of the regular Assam type, well developed as low bushes. Low pruning has been found to give the best results.

Annam coolies, who supply the labor force on the estates, are excellent workers, with considerable Chinese influence in this direction. Both the men and women do their work in a correct way, so plucking and other important operations are properly performed.

Plucking is fine, every seven or eight days in the rainy season—only the bud and two leaves are taken. In the dry season plucking is done every ten to twenty days.

Among recent promotions, the Société des Thés de l'Indochine has brought two plantations into a productive phase; the "Arbre Broyé," of the Société Indochinoise de Cultures Tropicales, is high in the mountains near Dalat; four other estates are on flat land near Kontum, at 2500 feet; and there are the estates of "Ia-Puch," "Ban Methuot," "Plei-Ku," "Duck-Phu," and "Dah Doa."

MALAY STATES [British].—Tea planting in British Malaya, Straits Settlements, was first demonstrated a success in the small experimental planting begun at Tanah Rata, Cameron Highlands, several years ago. There are some 2000 acres in Selangor, Pahang, and Kedah. There is an experimental factory at Serdang. Malaya tea is similar to Indian tea from the Cachar District.

The only tea area of any commercial promise is the Bigia Estate at Gurun, in the unfederated state of Kedah, where about 500 acres recently came into bearing. In the mining district of Sungei Besi, Chinese small-holders have a total of about 140 acres under tea, which they manufacture by hand, and sell locally to Chinese laborers at the tin mines.

IRAN [PERSIA]. About 570 acres of land are under tea cultivation in four districts near Resht, province of Gilan, Iran. The annual production is estimated at about 200,000 pounds.

The four districts where the tea is grown are Fumen, Lahijan, Lakan and Langrud.

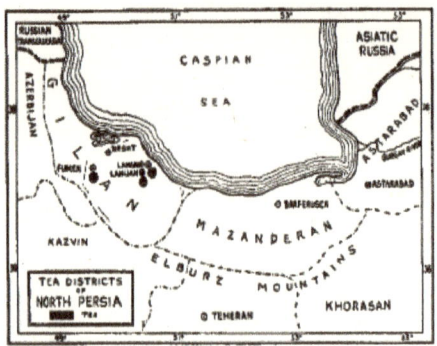

MAP OF TEA DISTRICTS IN IRAN [PERSIA]

Some tea also has been planted in the province of Mazenderan. The climate, situation, and soil are well suited to tea, according to Mr. G. D. Hope, former Chief Scientific Officer of the Indian Tea Association at Calcutta, who visited and reported on tea growing in Northern Persia.

The seed is sown from November to as late as April, and the seedlings are left in the nursery until they are two years old, when they are about a quarter of a zar high [1 zar=40.95 inches]. They are planted out in spring or autumn. The tea is not plucked until it is four years old from seed, but the ground is hoed to remove weeds. After the tea reaches the age of four years it is plucked regularly during the summer months. The leaf plucked in spring is of better quality than that plucked later in the season. If there is drought during the summer, the plants stop flushing. The pluckings are at intervals of about ten days. Pruning consists of cutting down the bushes in the autumn to a suitable height by means of clippers. Plant diseases are practically unknown, but seedlings are sometimes destroyed by excessive wet. Hoeing is carried on every ten days and at the same time as plucking. The tools used for cultivation are a bil, a kind of hoe, and a japar, a spade with a bar of iron placed so as to enable the digger to exert pressure by putting his foot on it. The latter is a typical Persian spade.

If the plant is strong and healthy, two pluckings are possible in ten days.

The tea plant in Iran is affected by no pests except an ivy, which, if permitted to grow around the plant, tends to stifle it; and by a white spider, which spins its web on the top of the plant.

On each jereeb [about 2.7 acres] of land, 10,000 plants can be put out, and if more than one zar [40.95 inches] is left between, then it is possible to plant three plants in one hole, thus facilitating the plucking.

The country most suitable for tea cultivation in Iran is thinly populated, and a deficiency of labor promises to be the great problem for the Government in connection with extension of the present acreage. The labor for plucking and curing tea costs from Rials 1.25 to Rials 2.50 a day [Rial-about $0.03].

One jereeb [i.e., 10,000 square zar, or about 2.7 acres] is worked by two laborers. In Lahijan, there are no gardens larger than five jereebs.

The methods of manufacture are primitive in the extreme. After the leaf is plucked, it is left for about fifteen hours before it is manufactured, and this permits a certain amount of withering. It then is hand rolled and dried in a wooden box resembling a small Sirocco drier and containing a set of four trays made of wood with mul-mul [muslin] bottoms. The box is heated from below by means of a charcoal fire, and the drying takes from one to one and one-half hours.[2]

Labor is the greatest problem in the way of extension of the present acreage, as even the poorest of the inhabitants are comparatively well off, and prefer to work their own land to becoming the servants of others. However, the Iran Government is reported to be studying the possibility of extending tea cultivation in the region bordering the Caspian Sea.

NATAL.—Tea production in Natal has declined somewhat, due mainly to the prohibition placed by the Indian Government on the emigration of coolies to Natal. The Assam indigenous is the only kind grown, and all of the tea growing is confined to a single hilly district, near Stanger, 1000 feet above sea level. The total area suitable for tea growing is approximately 15,000 acres, but only about 2000 are now under this cultivation.

The climate of this part of Natal is favorable for the cultivation of tea. It is equable, and with plenty of sunshine and rainfall. There is no danger from frost

[2] G. D. Hope, The Cultivation of Tea in the Caspian Provinces of Persia, Calcutta, 1914.

INDIAN COOLIES PLUCKING TEA ON THE HULETT ESTATE, KEARSNEY, NATAL

and very little from insect pests. The plucking season begins in September and usually lasts until June.

Practically all of the labor in connection with the growing and manufacturing of tea is done by coolies originally brought from India for that purpose. Their term of indenture now having expired, however, they are engaged by the planters at a much higher wage than when under indenture. The coolie women and girls are especially deft in leaf gathering. The natives [Zulus] also are used to a certain extent since the importation of Indian laborers has been abolished, but the Zulu, compared with the Indian, is neither as steady nor as capable a worker.

There are two principal tea estates in Natal where tea cultivation is being carried on. They are owned by Messrs. Sir J. L. Hulett & Sons, Ltd., and Messrs. W. R. Hindson & Co., both of Durban. In addition, tea is being grown in a small way by four other planters. On the two large estates are factories where the entire manufacturing process is carried out— withering, rolling, fermenting, firing, sorting, boxing, and shipping. The largest of these is on the Kearsney Estate of Sir J. L. Hulett & Sons, Ltd., and has a manufacturing capacity of 1,500,000 pounds of tea yearly.

Natal tea is graded as Golden Pekoe, Pekoe, Pekoe Souchong, and Souchong. If all available land were utilized, this province could readily produce every ounce of tea consumed in South Africa, and leave a considerable surplus for export.

According to the *Official Year Book* of the South African Government, capital to the amount of £350,000 is invested in the tea industry.

NYASALAND.—Tea cultivation in Nyasaland is well beyond the experimental stage, and developments are going on apace. The country, however, never will become a large tea exporter, as the area suitable for tea growing is limited by rainfall and climatic conditions. Most of the tea is grown in the Mlanje District at 2000 feet elevation, with a heavy, well distributed rainfall. A good many plantations have also commenced operations in the Cholo District, which has a lesser rainfall than Mlanje, but is nearly 1000 feet higher.

It is not likely that tea planting will succeed in the Blantyre and Zomba Districts, as the rainfall there is barely sufficient for tea, and cannot compare with the heavy precipitation at Mlanje and Upper Cholo.

The largest grower of tea in Nyasaland is the Blantyre & East Africa, Limited,

TEA PLANTER'S BUNGALOW, MLANJE PLATEAU, NYASALAND

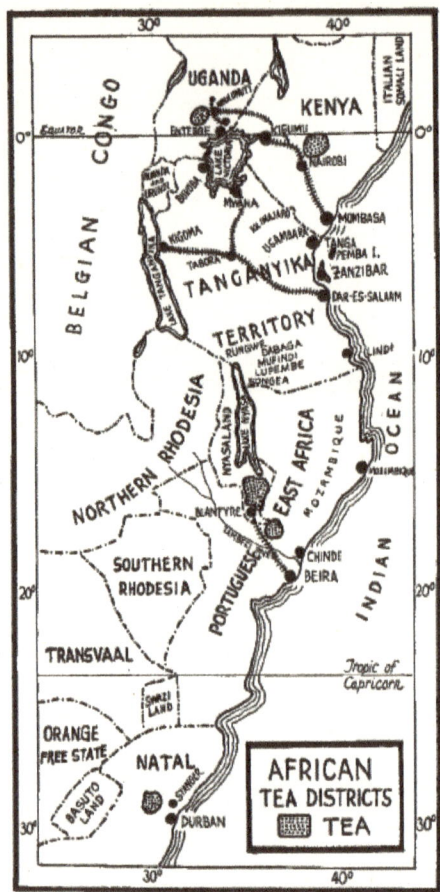

A MODERN TEA FACTORY, NYASALAND

ties, and the estates of Mr. George Garden, Mr. James Millar, Mr. H. Morton, and others.

A new development has been the advent of Messrs. Lyons & Co., Ltd., the London catering firm, which has opened a large tea property at Lujiri, Mlanje. No expense has been spared in the opening of the Lujiri Estate, and over 1200 acres have been planted in tea, in addition to the erection of a thoroughly modern and up-to-date

TEA PLUCKING SCENES, NYASALAND

Upper—Native pluckers in a Mlanje tea garden. Mt. Mlanje, 9800 feet high, in the distance. *Lower*—Tea pluckers bringing in the leaf.

owner of the Lauderdale, Glenorchy, and Limbuli Estates in the Mlanje District, and the Zoa Estate in the lower Cholo District. In 1929, the Blantyre & East Africa, Limited, had a total of 2149 acres planted with further clearings in hand.

The oldest tea estate is Lauderdale, where about 940 acres are planted in tea. The yield in 1929 amounted to 410,000 pounds, as against 324,000 in 1928. The rainfall amounted to 104 inches, compared with 72 the preceding year, and other climatic conditions were favorable.

The Ruo Estates, Ltd., probably are the second largest growers of tea in Nyasaland. They have three estates situated in the Mlanje District. Following them are the estates of the African Lakes Corporation, Ltd., the late Mr. Henry Brown's proper-

TEA ESTATE AT THE FOOT OF MOUNT MLANJE, NYASALAND, EAST AFRICA

four-storied tea factory. The soil is deep and rich, and the rainfall ample.

Recent developments in the Cholo District include the opening of tea gardens by Mr. Conforzi, Mr. Scott, Mr. Harper, Mr. Wallace-Ross, and others, in addition to further developments at the Bandanga Estate, the Zoa Estate, the Cholo Land & Rubber Company's Estate, and the Mandimwe property of Messrs. Maxwell.

Indian jat seed is imported or raised locally, and rigorous seed selection is being carried out. The acreage has increased from 260 in 1904 to 12,595 in 1932, and is gaining steadily. The latest tea machinery has been imported, and factories erected on India and Ceylon models. The export, which began with 1613 pounds in 1904, was over 3,000,000 pounds in 1933.

The methods of cultivation are modeled on those of India and Ceylon. Propagation is by seed sown in nurseries, and when the plants are about a year old they are transplanted to the fields. They go unplucked for a period of about three years, being cut back occasionally to make them branch out into small bushes. These bushes, throughout their subsequent growth, are annually pruned back to a height which varies between two and five feet.

At the end of the fourth year from seed, after the annual pruning, the terminal bud and the youngest two or three leaves are plucked by hand by native laborers. Each laborer carries a basket into which the young shoots are thrown, and two or three times a day the pluckers carry the green leaf to the factory. In about a week a second plucking is taken, and this is continued at intervals throughout the growing season. The time between the flushes varies from five to ten days, or even longer, depending on the weather. The quantity of tea produced per acre varies from 250 pounds up to 500 pounds.

The growing season is from October until May. The pruning season from May to August. Plucking, as a rule, begins heavily in December, and continues until April, when the approach of the cold, dry season slows things down.

After plucking, the leaf is weighed at the factory, where it is taken to the upper stories and spread thinly to wither on shelves made of wire netting or Hessian cloth. In this process the leaf loses about a third of its moisture. The average time for a wither is eighteen hours, but this depends entirely on the state of the atmosphere.

Both natural and artificial withering are practiced. The tea being grown in districts of high humidity, the atmosphere is often near the point of saturation, and, while a natural wither is preferred whenever possible, artificial withering is resorted to when necessary—the same as in Ceylon.

After withering, the tea is passed down chutes to the rolling room on the ground floor, where it is submitted to the rolling process in regulation English rolling machines. These machines carry charges of about 350 pounds of withered leaf. Two or more rollings may be given of not more than forty minutes each. After being passed through ball-breakers and green leaf sifters, the leaf is removed to the fermenting rooms, where it is spread on concrete, glass, or copper covered slabs and allowed to remain for a certain period, varying from half an hour to two hours or more.

When fermentation is complete, the tea is put through the regulation firing in mechanical dryers. After firing, the leaf is run through separating machines, which sort it into the usual black tea grades.

Only black teas are manufactured in Nyasaland. They are packed for export in the usual lead-lined chests, and are sold in London at prices that compare favorably with estates of similar elevation in Ceylon and India. There is a tea association at Mlanje.

As regards the future of tea growing in Nyasaland, the possible limits of cultivation soon will be reached in the Mlanje and Cholo Districts. The climate, especially the rainfall, is the limiting factor. There are, however, areas on the west shores of Lake Nyasa which have a relatively high rainfall, and which could be devoted to tea whenever communications are sufficiently developed to make the export commercially profitable. The average price of freehold land is £5 an acre.

Dr. H. H. Mann has reported that the industry should flourish and furnish one of the real foundations for the country's prosperity.[3]

PORTUGUESE EAST AFRICA [Mozambique].—On both sides of the river forming the boundary between Nyasaland and Mozambique, where the Mt. Mlange region of Nyasaland joins Portuguese East Africa, there are several small areas climatically

TEA GROWING IN UGANDA

Upper—Newly laid out garden on Kireta Estate.
Lower—Four year old Manipuri-Assam, Bajo Estate.

adapted to tea growing. One large plantation undertaking, with headquarters in Lisbon, the *Empreza Agricola do Lugella, Limitada,* has opened 500 acres under tea. A small factory has been established, and the annual production is approximately 90,000 pounds.

UGANDA AND KENYA.—Experimental tea cultivations in the British colonies of Uganda and Kenya having demonstrated that tea of good quality can be produced there, commercial cultivation has been begun, but is still in its infancy. The soil in the tea districts is a rich, red clay loam, and the land in Uganda is selling at about £4 an acre, and in Kenya for about £10. The altitude of the Uganda tea lands is about 5000 feet, and in Kenya, that of the Limuru District is 7300 feet and the Lumbwa District, 7000.

Soil analyses are available only from Uganda, where the Government plantations are located, but there is little variation in any of the soils in the farming districts of East Africa.

3 Harold H. Mann, *Tea Cultivation and Its Development in Nyasaland,* published by the Crown Agents for the Colonies, London, 1933.

GENERAL VIEW OF THE KIMUGU TEA ESTATE AND FACTORY, KENYA

A serious obstacle confronting the future of tea in Uganda and Kenya is the labor question, and upon its successful solution will depend, in a large measure, the outcome of the present experiments in tea-growing on a commercial scale.

In Kenya tea is cultivated in the Kiambu district of Kikuyu province; the Nandi, Uasin Gishu, and Trans Nzoia districts of Nzoia Province and in the Kavirondo North, Kisumu Londiani, and Kericho districts of Nyanza Province. The industry is regarded as well established in the Kericho and Limuru districts. The area under tea is about 12,000 acres and the production is approximately 3,000,000 pounds per year.

TANGANYIKA TERRITORY.—The prospects of establishing tea plantations in Tanganyika Territory, East Central Africa, were forwarded somewhat by the publication, in 1929, of an important agricultural report, *Tea Planting Prospects in the Southwestern Highlands of Tanganyika*. This established good grounds for believing that it was possible to grow tea of high quality within the heavy rainfall belt.[4]

4 Captain M. F. Bell. *Report*. Department of Agriculture, London, 1929.

In a more recent report, Dr. Harold H. Mann said that a comprehensive tea policy might develop a tea industry in the territory with an area up to a maximum of 50,000 acres in the Usambara Mountains, the Mufindi district in the Southern Highlands and the Rungwe district. Dr. Mann estimated that this combined area could produce enough tea to supply all local needs with a large excess available for export, and at the same time supporting a considerable number of planters, whether these be European, Indian, or African, and forming a means of maintenance for a large prosperous and contented labor population.

However, Dr. Mann was careful to point out that the inherent difficulties of organization could be overcome only if the development were undertaken by large firms or interests, as has been the case in many of the more newly developed tea areas of the world. In their absence it might be possible with communities of small settlers with not less than £2000 each and a central factory, developed either coöperatively by independent financial interests or in any other way, but such development would require a great deal more active interest on

FERRO-CONCRETE TEA FACTORY AT CHAKVA, RUSSIAN TRANSCAUCASIA

the part of Government than has been considered hitherto.[5]

ST. MICHAEL, AZORES ISLANDS.—There are four or five tea plantations on the island of St. Michael [São Miguel, 37° 30' N. latitude and 25° 30' W. longitude], in the Portuguese-owned Azores Islands, producing both green and black tea of good quality; the greater part of the former being exported to Portugal, where it is accorded preferential entry. The Gorreana Tea Plantation was started in 1841 with the help of four or five experienced Chinese tea-growers imported for the purpose, but their methods did not seem to be adapted to the soil, climatic conditions, and labor supply; so a local technique was ultimately developed.

RUSSIAN TRANSCAUCASIA.—Tea production is one of the most important sources of wealth in Adzharistan, a zone under the

[5] Harold H. Mann, *Report on Tea Cultivation in the Tanganyika Territory and its Development*, published by the Crown Agents for the Colonies, London, 1933.

protection of the Georgian Socialist Federated Soviet Republics in Russian Transcaucasia. Most of the tea plantations in this area are located on the southern slopes of the Adjar Hills near the eastern

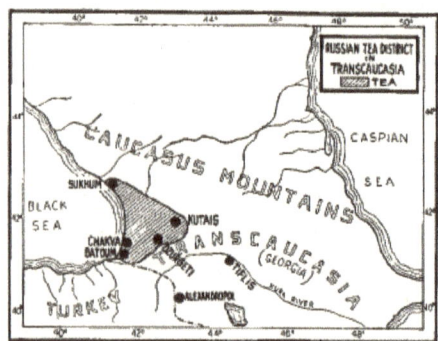

shore of the Black Sea in the vicinity of Batoum, the capital. The chief area of the tea plantations is in the hands of the Government, and the center of production and

INTERIOR VIEWS OF THE CHAKVA FACTORY—ROLL BREAKER AND ROLLING MACHINES

TEA PLUCKERS ON THE CHAKVA ESTATE NEAR BATOUM, TRANSCAUCASIA

management of cultivation is Chakva.

Until Adzharistan had become sovietized, the "Chakva" grounds belonged to the Imperial Appanage properties, but now they are under control of the People's Agricultural Committee of Georgia. In 1913 there were 1825 acres under tea in western Georgia. In 1934 this had been increased to about 80,000 acres.

The teas produced hitherto have been of an ordinary type, or, as one Mincing Lane expert put it, "They are clean, sweet liquoring teas of a nondescript neutral character." However, Dr. H. H. Mann thinks some of them compare favorably with Darjeeling growths.

The tea districts are located in 41° 30' to 42° 30' N. latitude and 42° E. longitude. This is the farthest north that tea is cultivated. The climate is subtropical, and the long slopes of land on the hills, where the tea is grown, are protected from cold blasts by the Caucasus Mountains; while moisture laden breezes from the Black Sea, make the climate of these districts correspond closely to that of other tea producing countries. The average winter temperature for Batoum is in the neighborhood of 44° F., and the average rainfall is from 100 inches near Batoum to

about 50 inches in the northern part of western Georgia. The soil is red clay.

Two-year-old seedlings were used for transplanting into these estates, with 2430 to 3240 plants to the acre; although some seeds were, and are, planted directly in the fields. Cultivation consists in digging to a depth of fifteen or twenty inches, weeding, and pruning. Plucking is begun when the plants are four to five years old, and is repeated three times annually by women and children, who collect from eighteen to twenty-two pounds of green leaf daily. The yield is 700 to 1400 lbs. of green leaves per acre, or 300 to 350 lbs. of dried leaf. Both black and green teas are manufactured. Rolling was formerly done mostly by hand, according to the Chinese method, although large growers used machines. As a result of recent developments, however, machine rolling is likely to become more general.

All the tea plantations in the country are under the direction of a special corporation, *Chai-Gruzia* [Tea Georgia, Ltd.], which was organized in 1925 with a capital of 5,000,000 rubles. The stockholders in this state corporation are the Agricultural Commissariats of Georgia, Adzharistan and Abkhasia, and the *Centrosoyus* [Central Union of Consumers' Coöperatives.]

By 1937, the end of the second Five-year plan as applied to tea, the Soviet Union expected to attain an annual production of 100,000,000 pounds from approximately 250,000 acres, the ten year goal. The annual consumption of tea in all Russia before the Revolution was 132,000,000 pounds a year, importing all but 600,000 pounds.

The development of tea culture is being promoted by the State through the granting of long-term credits to peasants in the form of money and seeds. The original seeds came from China, Japan, India and Ceylon. Today hybrid and China jats are favored. Only the poor and middle peasants are aided by money and seed credits. The organization of peasants into collective farms has shown rapid progress in the tea sections of western Georgia. Tea Georgia, Ltd., has organized two State farms, Chakva and Salibayuri.

The Tea Georgia, Ltd., has established three experimental tea stations; a central station in Ozurgeti with branches in Chakva and Zugdidi. These stations are carrying on research to determine the best types of seeds and the best methods of growing, as well as to ascertain the most favorable regions into which to extend tea culture. In addition, the agronomic personnel of Tea Georgia, Ltd., is investigating the natural conditions of the Black Sea coast. The results of this study will show to what extent, at what tempo, and in which sections tea culture may be developed.

Mechanization is the order of the day in field and factory. Large tractors and deep plowing machines with sub-soil attachments are used to prepare the soil. For

PLUCKING ON A JAPANESE TEA ESTATE NEAR REGISTRO, STATE OF SÃO PAULO, BRAZIL

inter-cultivation, a small motor cultivator made by Siemens-Schuchert of Germany is employed. The world's first tea plucking machine, constructed by Sadovsky, has recently been tested in the field and showed excellent results. It does the work of 25 pluckers. Two other designs of tea plucking machines are being tested. One of these machines is reported to pluck 3¾ acres in ten hours, as against 30 days for hand labor. New withering machines are also being tried out. Dr. Harold H. Mann, in a recent report, stated that this conception of tea manufacture as an entirely automatic process, this passion for doing things by mechanical devices, may enable the Georgian authorities to reach a degree of mechanization which has not been attained elsewhere in the world. Just the same he feels Russia can never be entirely dependent, for its tea supply, on tea produced within its own borders.[6]

BRAZIL.—Considerable progress has been made within recent years in the cultivation of tea in Brazil, particularly in the states of Minas Geraes, São Paulo, and Paraná. In the last two there are 15 estates owned and operated by Japanese immigrants. Assam seed is employed and the production is consumed locally.

SADOVSKY'S TEA-PLUCKING MACHINE

---

[6] Harold H. Mann, *The Recent Tea Developments in Georgia*, I.T.A. Quarterly Journal, Part II, Calcutta, 1932.

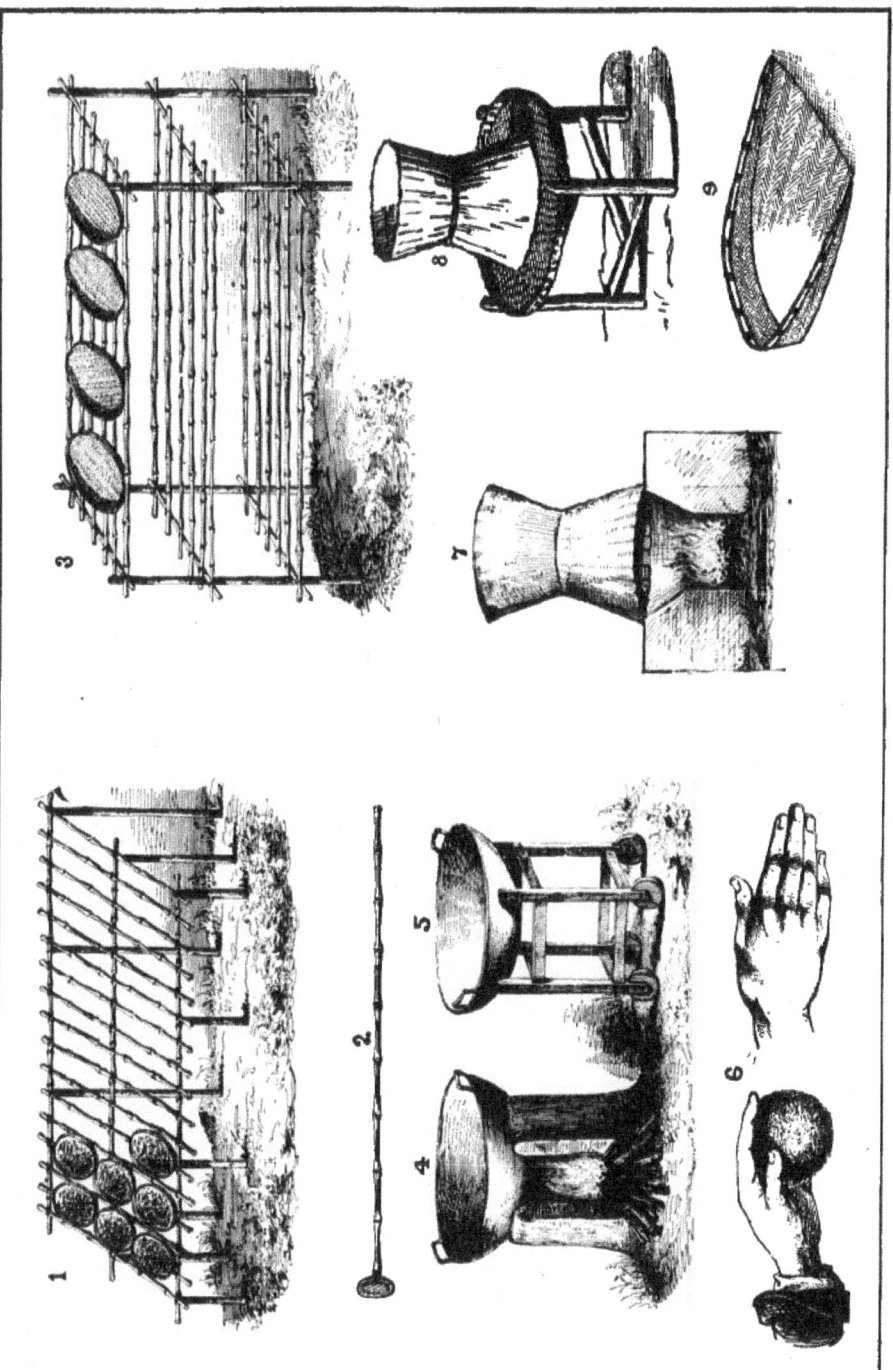

EARLY CHINESE APPARATUS FOR THE MANUFACTURE OF TEA, AND THE FIRST TO BE USED IN INDIA

No. 1—Stand and, trays for sun-drying. *No.* 2—Rod for moving trays up or down. *No.* 3—Withering stand, set in the shade. *No.* 4—Cast-iron pan for steaming or "panning" the leaf. *No.* 5—Trolley transport. *No* 6—Rolling by hand. *No.* 7—Basket-firing over charcoal fire. *No.* 8—Tray for dried or fired tea. *No.* 9—Hand-picking tray. After drawings by C. A. Bruce, 1838, and J. C. Houssaye, 1843.

464

CHAPTER XXII

EVOLUTION OF TEA MACHINERY

How the Present-Day Tea Factory Developed from the Ancient Chinese Hand
Manipulation—Pioneer Methods in Java and India—First British Patents—
Kinmond's, Nelson's, Dickinson's, McMeekin's, Money's, Gibbs', and Barry's Ma-
chines—A Study of India's Tea Machinery—Holle and Kerkhoven's Work in
Java—Jackson's and Davidson's Epoch-Making Inventions—Other Tea-Making
Apparatus Evolved During the Past Seventy-five Years

FROM the beginning of our knowledge of tea, when its manufacture was
almost entirely a process of hand
manipulation, down to the present, when
hand labor is almost completely done away
with, the trend of the industry has been
toward constantly improved machinery.

Tea manufacture was all a hand process in China, so it followed naturally,
when the cultivation and preparation of tea
spread to Java, India, Ceylon, etc., hundreds of years later, that the Chinese
manufacturing methods were the ones first
adopted. But western people differed in
temperament from the Chinese, who were
content to carry on in the age-old way, and
it is a far cry from the little Chinese farms
of the first century, where the tea was
hand rolled and fired over rude charcoal
ovens, to the modern British and Dutch
tea factories of today, with their withering
tats, rolling machines, roll breakers, cement
fermenting floors, glass fermenting tables,
mechanical driers, and machines for cutting, sorting and sifting, and packing.

Early Chinese Practice

From early Chinese literature, it would
appear that each consumer of tea not only
brewed the beverage, but manufactured the
leaves as well. An early Chinese manuscript gives the following instructions for
commercial tea manufacture:

Spread the leaves about five or six inches
thick on bamboo trays, in a proper place for
the air to blow on them. Hire a workman, or

ching fu, to watch them. Thus, the leaves continue from noon until six o'clock, when they
begin to give out a fragrant smell. They are
then poured into large bamboo trays, in which
they are tossed with the hands about three or
four hundred times: this is called to ching. It
is this operation which gives the red edges and
spots to the leaves.

They are now carried to the kuo and roasted;
and afterwards poured on flat trays to be rolled.
The rolling is performed with both hands in a
circular direction about three or four hundred
times, when the leaves are again carried to the
kuo and thus roasted and rolled three times.
If the rolling be performed by a good workman, the leaves will be close and well twisted;
if by an inferior one, loose, open, straight, and
ill-looking.

They are then conveyed to the poey long, the
fire fierce, and the leaves turned without in-
termission until they are nearly eight-tenths
dried. They are afterward spread on flat trays
to dry until five o'clock, when the old yellow
leaves and the stalks are picked out. At eight
o'clock they are "poeyed" again over a slow
fire. At noon they are turned once, and then
left in this state to dry until three o'clock,
when they are packed in chests.

It was a complicated and laborious
process, yet we find no move toward labor-
saving machinery—save for the invention
in Japan, in 1672, of an improved oven, the
"Hoiro," for re-firing, by Mihei Kamibay-
ashi—until the middle of the nineteenth
century.

Pioneer Methods in Java and India

In Java, J. I. L. L. Jacobson, in his
Handboek voor de cultuur en fabrikatie
van thee, published in 1843, gives us a
good picture of tea manufacture in that

SHOWING THE EARLIEST METHOD OF FIRING TEA IN CHINA
This is a Chinese tea factory scene reproduced from an 18th century water color.

day. The fresh leaves were first exposed to the sun on *tampirs* [bamboo trays]. The *tampirs* were placed upon tables and after twenty to twenty-five minutes were shaken. After another twenty minutes this operation was repeated, and again in fifteen minutes. After sunning, the *tampirs* were brought into the leaf shed and placed on racks. Beside the racks, in the shed, there was a horizontal octagonal cylinder revolving on an axle, for use in withering when there was no sun. This crude withering drum was run by a hand crank.

After withering came the so-called firing. This was done in *kwalies* [earthenware pans], over a brick oven burning charcoal. Jacobson cautions that "care must be taken to prevent the *kwalies* from bursting as they are only and exclusively to be obtained from the province of Canton." The leaves in the *kwalies* were constantly stirred by hand. As they commenced to dry, they were removed, placed in a *tampir*, and rolled. This was repeated four times over fires of different temperatures. Then the tea was spread on large *tampirs*, covered over, and left till the next day.

The manufactured tea went to an outside establishment for sorting and packing. One of these was located at Meester-Cornelis, near Batavia. Thither the tea was brought in large sacks, baskets, and chests. The baskets were lined with bamboo leaves, covered with thin paper. The tea for export was sorted by hand, and packed in chests of light wood, lined with lead, and highly decorated on the outside.

The successive stages in the manufacture of tea, as introduced by the Chinese instructors into Assam, may be enumerated as follows:

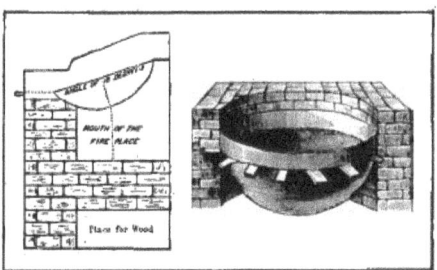

EARLY CHINESE GREEN-TEA FIRING APPARATUS
Left—Twankay stove. *Right*—Hyson stove.

1. *Drying.*—The plucked leaf was exposed in large, flat baskets to the full glare of the sun,

the baskets being arranged on a light bamboo framework.

2. *Withering.*—The baskets of dried leaf were removed from the sun, and placed upon a stand under cover in the shade until the leaves became soft and flaccid.

3. *Panning.*—The withered leaf was thrown into a cast iron pan, heated almost to a dull red over a primitive fireplace, while the leaf was vigorously stirred by hand.

4. *Rolling.*—The heated leaf was then turned out upon a table, and rolled by hand into a ball; the rolling being continued between the hands.

5. *Drying.*—The final process was a drying or firing of the manufactured leaf. The rolled leaf was dried in tall baskets, shaped like an hour-glass; the leaf being placed in the upper inverted cone, which was lined with paper, the lower cone fitting over a charcoal fire.

On some gardens the process was more complicated. Lieutenant-Colonel Edward Money, a pioneer India tea planter, in a prize essay written in 1872, lists twelve operations in making tea and recommended they be reduced to five.[1]

The time of "battying," or drying, was cut from twenty hours to four hours. An anonymous planter writing to Balmer, Lawrie & Co., Calcutta, in 1880, says: "These

[1] Lieutenant Colonel Edward Money, *The Cultivation and Manufacture of Tea,* London, 1878.

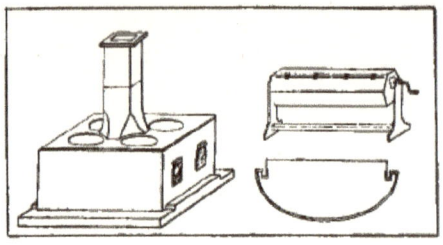

MR. JACOBSON'S BLACK-TEA FURNACE AND WITHERING MACHINE WITH TAMPIR, 1830

two things, non-panning and light battying, were brought in force about 1871, I think. Still planters used to pan if they found their packing getting in arrears, and you generally find old planters pan their own drinking teas, because it makes better drinking tea and keeps longer."

The First British Patents

It was natural that the planters of India, Ceylon, and Java, being Occidentals, should seek mechanical means to alleviate the labor of tea manufacture. Mechanically inclined men began to devise machines about 1855. Indeed, we find Charles Henry Olivier was granted a Brit-

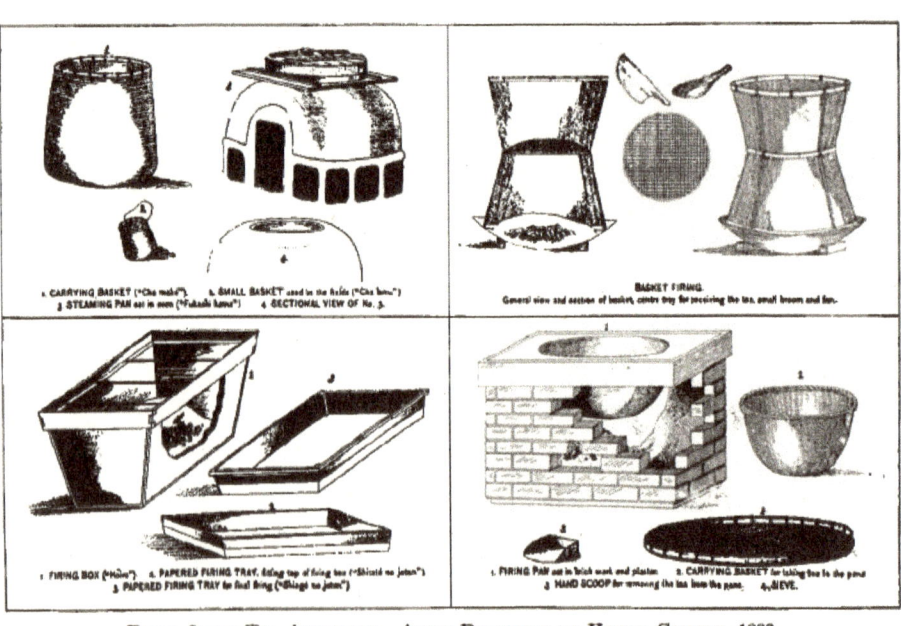

EARLY JAPAN TEA APPARATUS. AFTER DRAWINGS BY HENRY GRIBBLE, 1883

BOHEA TEA MANUFACTURE, CHINA, 18TH CENTURY

ish patent October 26, 1854, on an "improved apparatus for drying tea." In the next year, Alfred Savage of London, son of Edward Savage, who, in 1812, founded the present firm of Savage & Co., patented a "means or mechanism for treating tea, coffee, chicory, and such substances as require the processes of separation, reduction of size, and mixing or anyone or two thereof." In 1860, he obtained another patent covering improvements on his tea sifting and cutting machines.

On April 30, 1859, Edward Francis was granted a British patent on a tea sifter. On August 6, 1860, Henry de Mornay was granted a British patent on an "apparatus for sorting and preparing tea for the market." The first United States patent on tea machinery was granted on April 11, 1865, to K. Goddard, of Philadelphia. This was for a tea roller.

Kinmond's and Nelson's Machines

About the year 1867, James C. Kinmond, an English civil engineer, invented a rolling machine. This consisted of two wooden disks, the upper moving on the stationary lower one with an eccentric motion. The adjacent faces of the disks were made rough by steps in the wood, cut in lines diverging from the center to the circumference. Over these rough faces was nailed canvas. The motive power might be by animal, manual labor, or steam. The plates sometimes were of metal, but it was found that in that case the leaf would become discolored. By the use of this machine, tea could be produced ready for final firing at six annas per maund, or less than one pie per pound. A machine

with two pairs of plates would make twenty maunds of tea a day and one with four pairs, forty maunds. The four-plate size was sixteen feet long, five feet broad, and four and one-half feet high. In 1876, Mr. Kinmond was granted a British patent on improvements in this machine. A year later, he invented a machine for sifting tea and one for drying tea.

Another early pioneer was James Nelson of Cachar. He constructed a patent tea-leaf-rolling machine in which the leaf was rolled in bags, between plates.

Dickinson's Patents

Benjamin Dickinson was granted a British patent on a drier in 1865, and in 1868 he obtained another patent on improvements in his machine. J. F. W. Watson, who wrote a prize essay on tea in 1871, speaks thus of Mr. Dickinson's apparatus:

A machine invented by Mr. Dickinson professes to wither leaf as well as dry tea, and I should think from what I have seen of it that it would do so pretty well. The leaf is placed in trays in drawers and hot air is driven through them by a fan which is worked by a gin and bullock or by the hand. Whether this machine be good for the desiccation of the leaf or not, I cannot say, and it does not seem to have come into any general use, but I should think it would be well worthy of a trial for withering tea. It burns very little wood, costs little, and does not take up any great space.[2]

Dickinson also invented a roller, but it was designed only to prepare the leaf for hand-rolling. It consisted of a large box, which worked on rollers. The box was

[2] J. F. W. Watson, *Prize Essay on the Cultivation and Manufacture of Tea in India*, Calcutta, 1871.

EARLY CHINESE METHOD OF ROLLING TEA

filled with stones, and was then rolled over leaf which had been placed in gunny sacks.

McMeekin's Pioneer Inventions

Thomas McMeekin, manager of the Doodputlee Tea Estate in Cachar, was one of the earliest to realize the waste which came from the use of dhools for firing tea. Under the then prevalent custom, a single wicker sieve was inserted inside a bamboo frame called a "dhool," which was placed over a charcoal fire made in a hole in the ground. On the sieve the roll was placed, and all the heat, after passing through this one sieve, was wasted. McMeekin's idea, which he evolved in 1876, was to use the heat on many sieves. His apparatus was nothing more than a low chest of drawers, or trays, fitted in a frame one above another; the bottom of each tray being fine, iron wire, so that the heat of the charcoal coming from the masonry receptacle, over which the chest was placed, ascended through all of the trays, and thus fired, or dried, a large quantity of roll at the same time. The lowest tray was placed at the ordinary height above the fire, and the upper ones at just sufficient distance apart to admit of their easy removal. The position of the trays varied with the progress of the firing. A door, lined on the inside with tin, shut the "chest" off from the outside air. This apparatus was widely used.

Mr. McMeekin also invented a rolling table of battens. This served to sort the tea, after a fashion, because, while rolling the leaves on it, many of the small leaves fell through. The objection to it, however, was that the leaf had to be rolled lightly.

Hot Air Succeeds Charcoal Fumes

Meanwhile, discussion became rife among planters as to whether charcoal was necessary for firing tea, or whether other fuel might be used. Making charcoal was an expensive, and arduous process. Lieutenant-Colonel Edward Money, an authority on tea, as well as numerous other planters, made extensive experiments with a view to determine whether wood, coal, or any other fuel might not be used. To Colonel Money is given the credit for being the first to show by practical results that the fumes of charcoal were in no way necessary to make tea. This was in

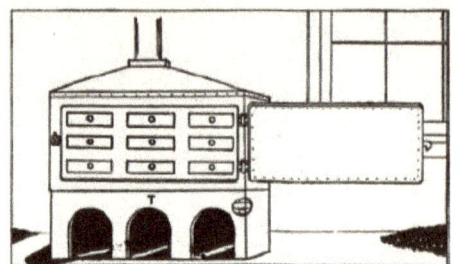

ORIGIN OF THE TEA DRIER, 1876
Mr. Thomas McMeekin's crude chest of wire-mesh trays, or drawers, for drying the leaf.

1870–73. Colonel Money invented a "furnace," which was erected at Soom, in Darjeeling, and was inspected by many planters. By means of this "furnace" the tea was fired by hot air, reducing the temperature of the tea house, ridding the air of obnoxious charcoal fumes, and lessening the labor and fuel cost.

The Gibbs and Barry Drier

William Alfred Gibbs of Essex, England, was granted a British patent August 1, 1870, on a "drying apparatus for drying agricultural, mineral and chemical and commercial products," among which, he included tea. In 1886, he was granted another British patent on a tea-withering and drying machine. These were followed by four other patents for improvements on his machine. In 1896, he collaborated with G. W. Sutton on another drier.

James Hewett Barry, son of Dr. John Boyle Barry, founder of Barry & Co., Calcutta, agents and tea merchants, was a mechanical engineer, and collaborated with Mr. Gibbs on his first drier. It was known as the Gibbs and Barry Drier.

In 1871, William Howorth received a British patent on a machine in which tea leaves were rolled in bags.

Study of India's Tea Machinery

Just here it may be helpful to the lay reader to introduce a comparative study of the development of modern tea machinery for the manufacture of black tea in British India.

Each of the three main processes of tea manufacture for which machinery is used —rolling, drying, and sifting—has its own peculiar mechanical requirements. Tea

CHINESE METHOD OF DRYING TEA IN INDIA

rollers have been invented and patented for rolling tea leaf only. There is no other manufacturing process which utilizes the peculiar rolling and twisting action required for successful tea leaf rolling. Drying machines are used in many trades and processes of manufacture. Drying tea has certain peculiarities, but the principles involved are much the same as the drying processes in other manufactures; consequently, there are innumerable patent specifications, which, although possibly dealing with machines designed for some other particular material, add, as part of their claim, that they can be used in drying "tea, coffee, or other substances." Sifting is entirely different in its mechanical requirements from rolling and drying; but is a process which is not peculiar to tea, and machines which are used for grading and sifting all sorts of substances and materials are similar in principle, and in many details, to those specially designed for tea manufacture.

ROLLING.—Hand-rolling, as practiced in Indian tea gardens before the introduction of machinery, was carried out by coolies, working on long wooden tables. The operator took a double handful of withered leaf in his two hands, and rolled it out in two directions—first, say to his left front and back again, and then to his right front and back again, using the palms of his hands and his forearms to rub and roll it on the surface of the table. This motion, in two directions, gives the necessary twist to the leaf, and may be analyzed as a movement like a figure eight. That figure is reproduced perfectly by any point between the two superimposed flat surfaces, recipro-

cating in straight lines at right angles to each other, as in the old "Cross-Action" roller [Jackson's], and, to all intents and purposes, is maintained in rollers of the "Rapid" type, where the upper and lower rolling surfaces are suspended on, and worked from, three or more doublethrow vertical cranks.

The first attempt at machine rolling produced the bag roller, and is due to the previously mentioned Mr. James Nelson, who was manager of a tea garden in Cachar. The genesis of this machine is said to have been that Nelson was watching his coolies at hand-rolling, and pondering on the possibilities of quickening the process by dealing with larger quantities of leaf than just the handful each man individually could tackle. It occurred to him that if one of the long tables on which the coolies worked was turned upside down, and put on top of another table, and then was drawn backwards and forwards with leaf between the two tables, the rolling action would be much the same as by hand, and leaf could be treated in larger quantities. However, it became clear to him at once on trying this, that the leaf had to be contained in something to hold it together. Nelson's mind jumped to the idea of a bag container, and he sent to the bungalow for a pair of his white drill trousers. He cut off the legs, filled them with leaf, tied up the ends, put the bags between the two tables, sat some coolies on the top one to add weight, and set the others to pull and shove the top, inverted table over the bottom one. The leaf in the trouser legs was rolled, and the Nelson roller was invented. It took the form of a long,

PRIMITIVE TEA ROLLER AT RANCHI, INDIA

weighted wooden box, guided longitudinally to travel backwards and forwards on top of a long wooden table; the action being obtained by a crank and connecting rod. It was the first bag roller, and others followed by Howorth and Lyle, in which the action became revolving, instead of reciprocating.

The Lyle bag roller, which was considerably used for a time, consisted of a wood covered cylinder, or drum, mounted on a horizontal shaft, inside a cylindrical squirrel cage casing, which was formed of wood rollers on iron rods, free to revolve each on its own axis. The leaf was filled into bags, like giant sausages. Part of the casing slid back, and the bags were thrown into the rollers. The drum, revolving, rolled them against the wood rollers of the casing. On opening the door in the casing, the bags were ejected; the roller being self-discharging.

EARLY INDIAN TEA-ROLLING TABLE

In the meantime James C. Kinmond had solved the problem of mechanical tea leaf rolling, and had done away with the necessity of bags by confining the leaf in a box, or jacket, and rolling it between "two super-imposed surfaces." This was improved on by William Jackson, who, after an arrangement as to patent rights with Mr. Kinmond, added the gear necessary for adjusting pressure by screwing down the upper plate, and produced in turn the "Cross-Action," "Rajah," "Excelsior," and finally the "Rapid" rollers. The "Rapid," with three double-crank suspensions for both tables, or surfaces, and equipped with pressure cap and screw adjustment, has held the field, and any improvements added since have been simply in detail.

During the developments from Kinmond's machine to the "Rapid," attempts were made with circular plates working on

JACKSON'S FIRST TEA ROLLER, 1873

a horizontal axis and inside a cylinder, as in Barber's and Thompson's machines. The plates revolved in opposite directions, and could be brought together by screw adjustment; but the distribution of the charge of leaf between vertical surfaces was unsatisfactory. Surfaces simply revolving in opposite directions do not give the "figure eight" twist, and, though conical surfaces were introduced, the work done was not to be compared to the results obtained by the Kinmond-Jackson combinations.

It is a peculiarity of the tea rolling machine that it works upon a given quantity of material for a given time and has to be filled and discharged. It is not continuous in action. Modern automatic driers are continuous; the rolled leaf is fed in and dried tea discharged continuously. Sifters also are fed continuously, and discharge themselves in a like manner. A

EVOLUTION OF JACKSON'S TEA ROLLER, 1880

UP-DRAFT "SIROCCO" TEA DRIER, 1878

good deal of thought and experiment have been expended on the idea of a continuous roller, but without any practical success. It is doubtful if the continuous roller, even if invented, would be a practical improvement. The process of fermentation, coming between rolling and drying, and requiring three to four hours for its completion, would make the use of such a machine very difficult. It would seem to necessitate the fermentation process being carried out on bands, or conveyors, and this, for a process requiring three or more

OLD-TIME CHULAS IN AN INDIAN TEA FACTORY

hours, would add too great a complication to a tea factory.

DRYING.—Tea drying machinery has developed from the old method of drying on bamboo trays over a charcoal *chula*, or stove, by means of hot fumes coming directly from the charcoal.

The first, and basic improvement, was substituting heated air for the gases and fumes of the fuel. Mr. S. C. Davidson, with his sectional Sirocco stove, solved this. In this stove the sections were alternate, one carrying the products of combustion to the chimney, the next opening to the air at one end, and communicating with the drying chamber at the other. To this he added the use of an air-duct, or casing, surrounding the chimney and communicating with the top of the drying chamber at its lower end; thus utilizing the heat of the chimney stack to induce a draft through the drying chamber. This, as in Davidson's Up-Draft Sirocco drier, was developed and made in many sizes, from the original No. 1 Sirocco, with four small trays, to eight, twelve, sixteen, and twenty-tray machines. They did good work, whether fired with wood or coal, regardless of whether they were "end slide" or "side-drawer" machines. They required a good deal of labor, as they were all hand-operated; but the process of drying was under excellent control.

William Jackson then came on the scene with driers fitted with tubular stoves, in which the draft through the

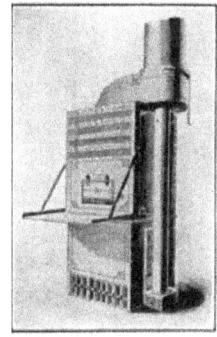

THE ORIGINAL No. 1 UP-DRAFT "SIROCCO" DRIER

stove and drying chamber was induced by a fan. First, we must consider the Venetian drier, which was, and is, a hand-operated machine. The trays are not drawn out and replaced by hand, as in the Up-Draft Sirocco, but being formed of leaves, or slats, of perforated metal, they are emptied one on to the other by turning a handle. Davidson then produced the Down-Draft Sirocco, in which he used a fan; the hot air being drawn through the stove and down from the top of the drying chamber to the

FIRST "VENETIAN" TEA DRIER, 1880

bottom. The trays, on which the leaf was spread, were inserted by hand at the bottom, and lifted, step by step, by a lever and rack-motion, to the top, where they were taken out by hand. This machine incorporates a principle which would seem to be correct; namely, that the tea leaf travels in the opposite direction to the draft of hot air, and as it dries it meets warmer and less saturated air. In later years, Davidson produced his Tilting-Tray drier; an up-draft fan machine, in many ways comparable to the Venetian.

Before proceeding to a discussion of the automatic drier, on which the bulk of tea drying is now done, we may consider two interesting machines which stand in a class by themselves. First, the Kinmond drier, a hand-operated tray machine, with a fan, and probably the first tea drier to use a fan. This machine is an example of the originality of Kinmond as an inventor. It consisted of a drying chamber fitted with small trays, or drawers, withdrawn by hand like the trays in a side-drawer Sirocco. A brick fireplace was covered with a wrought iron plate of peculiar shape, and this plate formed the major part of the heating surface of the stove. The fan was at one end, on floor level, drawing air over this plate and discharging it into the drying chamber placed above the stove. The air discharged at top of the drying chamber was partly returned to the stove and reheated. This drier undoubtedly was very efficient. The work done in proportion to the tray surface employed was noticeably high, but the furnace gave a lot of trouble; the wrought iron plate burning out, and the renewal of this, from its size

and position, was expensive, and necessitated dismantling the whole machine.

Then we have the Gibbs and Barry drier, which must be classed as the first automatic tea-drying machine. The drying chamber consisted of a large cylinder with axis slightly inclined, revolving slowly on rollers, similar in general arrangement to concrete mixers of to-day. The internal surface of the cylinder was ribbed. The tea leaf, fed in at the upper end, was continuously carried up by these ribs only to fall back again, owing to the inclination of the cylinder, gradually traveling to the lower end, where it was discharged. Drying was accomplished by blowing the products of combustion from the furnace through the cylinder with a fan, and, to obviate the necessity of using charcoal fuel, a filter of broken limestone was inserted, through which the gases passed on their way to the drying chamber. The machine, as constructed, was bulky, but did a lot of work. The continual rolling of the leaf inside the cylinder produced a very tightly curled and twisted tea, but tended to "gray" the leaf. The gases were never thoroughly filtered, and it was a very hot and unpleasant machine in a factory. In comparatively recent times, an attempt was made, but without any conspicuous success, to adapt the main design of this machine to a pressure-drier with a closed cylinder and regulated exits for hot air blown into the cylinder.

Modern automatic driers are represented

END-SLIDE TYPE, UP-DRAFT "SIROCCO" TEA DRIER

FIRST "VICTORIA" TEA DRIER, 1880

in Jackson's [Marshall's] Paragon and Empire driers, and Davidson's Endless Chain Pressure driers. These are all web, or band, machines. The drying surface consists of webs made up of perforated trays or slats carried in chains at the sides of the drying chamber. The chains are actuated by passing over sprocket wheels at the ends, and supported on angle iron attached to the sides of the drying chamber. These characteristics, with certain variations in detail, are common to all the successful automatic tea driers that have been introduced.

The first practical and successful drier of the type was Jackson's Victoria, introduced about 1885. This was a great advance in capacity and construction on any previous drier. The arrangement of the drying chamber, stove, and fan, in fact, the completeness of the whole design, bear comparison with the most modern machines; and Victoria driers installed as long ago as 1886 are still in constant use.

The most interesting point in the construction of this type of drier—the traveling web, or band, drier—is the mechanical action of the trays or slats, of which the web is composed.

Ansell of Darjeeling is credited with being the first exponent of the web machine. His name does not appear in the list of patents; probably, if patented, his ideas were only patented in India, and the writer has not been able to trace where his machine was constructed, or if it ever was more than an experimental attempt. In Ansell's web, the trays or slats passing over the sprocket wheels delivered their contents through chutes to the next web beneath, which was traveling in the reverse

direction. The trays turned completely round the sprockets, and traveled back flat on the underside of the chain; i.e., it was a closed band, utilizing only the upper side for carrying tea leaf. The trays being perforated, some of the finer portions of leaf, the *doolgoorie*, would fall through the perforation on to the returning underside of the web, and, to some extent, would be trapped there. This might tend to cause a jam, but in any case the fine leaf, held up and exposed too long to the hot draft, would get over-fired and burnt, and possibly even taint the rest of the tea in the drying chamber. Jackson avoided this difficulty in the "Victoria" drier. His trays passed over the sprocket wheels and delivered to the next band, but they returned along the bottom side of the band hanging down, and any fine tea falling through fell at once to the next band.

Thompson of Gainsborough, who had been connected with the manufacture of Jackson's machines, brought out a web drier in which he utilized both sides of the band. The trays were caused to drop the leaf they carried before reaching the sprocket wheel, and returned level, carrying leaf back on the underside of the web, or band, where it dropped again, before reaching the sprocket wheel, to the band below, and so on. He thus utilized the full surface of the bands for drying purposes, and his webs all traveled in the same direction.

Thompson's machine, called the "Power" drier, was an up-draft, induced draft machine, like the "Victoria," but provided with two fans to equalize the draft throughout the drying chamber. Jackson, in the meantime, having produced the "Britannia" drier, a variation, but hardly

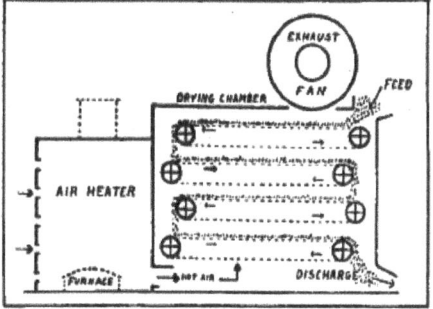

DIAGRAM SHOWING THE WORKING OF AN UP-DRAFT TEA DRIER

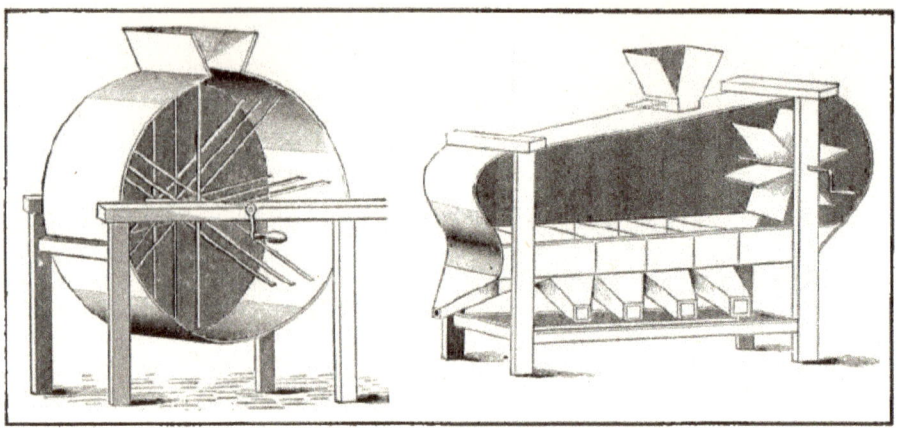

TWO EXAMPLES OF EARLY INDIAN-TEA APPARATUS
Left—Tea beating machine. *Right*—Winnowing and grading machine.

an improvement on the "Victoria," adopted Thompson's method of utilizing both sides of the band, and produced the "Paragon" drier. Thompson's tray action had included a spring-trigger gear, to ensure a sharp and positive turning down, or drop, to the individual trays. Jackson discarded this, and, with a heavier and broader tray overcame any difficulty on this point. The Paragon drier remained Jackson's leader for many years, and still is built by Marshall's Tea Machinery Co., Ltd. It was followed by Jackson's "Empire" drier, in which there are numerous improvements of detail in feed and discharge, and in stove construction. The air distribution is on the pressure system, the air being blown into the drying chamber and escaping at the top, which is not closed. The essential features of the web, or band, construction remain.

Later, Davidson entered the field with an automatic drier. Here, the web construction is the same, and based on Thompson's arrangements, but the machine—the Endless Chain Pressure drier—is a pressure, or plenum, machine. The fan is in circuit between the stove and the drying chamber, inducing a draft through the tubes of the stove into the drying chamber, which is partially open at the top. The machine is made in several sizes and various types as regards the relative positions of stove and drying chamber. These, with the Empire machines, hold the field at present as the most modern and efficient automatic tea driers.

One other interesting automatic drier, produced about 1893, may be mentioned. This was the invention of Sharpe, and manufactured by Foster & Co., of Lincoln. In this machine, the drying chamber was a vertical cylinder with a single central driving shaft. The drying surfaces consisted of rows of perforated trays, each segmental in shape, supported on their outer edges on angles bolted to the cylindrical casing, and driven by the vertical shaft. The trays turning on pivots, dropped and discharged their leaf at varying points in the circumference. It was an induced up-draft machine, and was interesting as an alternative to the band machine. But, while it was very simple, mechanically, the distribution of air and spreading of the leaf presented difficulties; and, though several machines were made and put into use, the type was not continued.

SIFTING.—Sifting, in India, originally was all done by hand on circular bamboo mesh trays handled by women. As soon as engine-power was introduced, to drive rollers, it soon was found that any sort of sieve to which a reciprocating or jogging motion could be mechanically imparted would sift tea, and factory-made sieves, driven by a small crank, were easily constructed. These were elaborated by certain inventors, like Ansell, Cooke and Jackson, into machines with several tiers of sieves of adjustable inclination. The sieves were fitted with mesh of varying size. Tea

REID'S ORIGINAL TEA CUTTER
It was patented in the late 'seventies by Mr.
George Reid, an Assam planter.

passing through the mesh was collected on
trays attached below, and delivered into
chutes; the tea passing over the end of the
mesh was directed to the sieve next below,
and so on. Thus, the finer grades were
sorted out first, and the coarser ones in succession. The cylindrical sieve also was introduced in the form of the Baillie &
Thompson sifter; a conical cylindrical sieve,
revolving on a horizontal shaft. The tea was
fed in at the smaller end, and traveled down
the inclination of the coned cylinder, which
was fitted with varying-sized meshes. Of
late years sifters such as the "Magic" sifter
and Moore's sifter have been introduced,
with moving parts carefully balanced, well
constructed and designed. These have a
very large capacity for work, and are free
from the troubles caused by shaking themselves to pieces.

A sieve rotating in a horizontal plane is
suitable for broken or small leaf, but to
extract wiry pekoes a reciprocating jigger
motion is better. This partly up-ends the
leaf; also, a rotary motion provides longer
travel which may be detrimental to
quality.

Sifting and grading necessitates the use
of breakers, or cutters, to cut the larger
dried leaves to the required size. The original machine was George Reid's breaker
[now known as a tea cutter], followed, in
more modern times, by Jackson's equalizer,
and the Savage breaker and cutter. These

machines are, in principle, modifications of
the revolving, toothed drum and the fixed
knife or edge. Improvements have been
in the direction of better regulation and
adjustment, cleaner work, and less dust.

Fanning machines, based on the winnower, also have been introduced, to assist
in cleaning and sifting teas. The final act
of tea manufacture is packing, and in this
the engineer has been most useful. The old
system of putting the tea into chests in
layers, and treading it down by foot, with
a cloth between the tea and the naked sole,
has been superseded by machinery. Davidson's packer, Jackson's packing machine,
and the Briton packing machine, are all
efficient examples of the application of mechanical means. No pressure is used. The
chest is shaken, or vibrated, continuously,
so that the tea settles itself into place,
and fills the chest completely. It does not
seem a difficult thing to arrange, but, as
a matter of fact, the packing machine must
be well made. The motion is very slight
and very rapid; the revolving parts of the
machine must rotate at high speed.

In this study, nothing has been said of
one very important process in tea manufacture—withering; but in the list of patent
specifications appear a few for withering
machines. It has seemed doubtful if a
withering machine could be produced
which would take the place of withering
in lofts; if only from the fact that fresh
leaf weighs four times as much as the tea
produced from it, and is immensely greater
in bulk. A withering machine may have
its use as an accessory to the withering
loft, to put on the final touches, so to
speak, to the process—especially in bad
weather. Tea planters have contended
that difficulties in withering are more likely
to be overcome by some system of controlled withering in lofts, such as controlling the temperature and the volume of air
passed through the loft by fans. However,
in 1927 Marshall Sons & Co., Ltd., after
several years of experimentation, introduced a tea-withering machine which has
produced practical results.

First Machinery In Java

In Java, the first attempt to apply mechanical means to the roller was made in
the early 'seventies by A. Holle at Parakan
Salak. This machine consisted of a round,
wooden table on which a second wooden

MARSHALL'S TEA LEAF WITHERING MACHINE

table rested. The upper table revolved on a vertical axle, and had an arrangement whereby it could be raised or lowered. The leaf was slipped between the two tables, and the upper turned round by oxen until the leaf worked itself out. The trouble lay in inserting the leaf. To remedy this, R. E. Kerkhoven, in charge of the administration of Sinagar, reversed the machine so that the lower table revolved. This was a distinct improvement, the leaf being easily put in through an aperture in the fixed upper table. However, the leaf always had to be rolled by hand afterwards.

Mr. Kerkhoven also devised a means of drying, whereby hot air passed under iron plates, and thence to a chimney. The hot air was obtained from the fire under the *kwalies*.

Jackson and Davidson Patents

The real development of tea manufacturing machinery has been due largely to William Jackson and Samuel Cleland Davidson. Both Jackson and Davidson held patents on machinery for withering, rolling, breaking, drying, and sifting machines.

Jackson set up his first rolling machine on the Heeleakah Garden of the Scottish Assam Tea Company, in 1872, and in the year following it rolled 64,000 pounds of tea.

Davidson first turned his attention to tea drying. The first Sirocco air heater, for the use of tea driers, was invented in 1877. This was the forerunner of many other and larger driers. In 1879, the No. 1 Up-Draft Sirocco tea drier was placed on the market.

Other Patents of the 'Seventies

Other planters and manufacturers also were working on tea plantation machinery. In 1873, Josiah Pumphrey, of Birmingham, England, was granted a British patent on "sifters or screens for sifting or screening tea." In the following year, William Stewart Lyle of Dibrugarh, Assam, was granted a British patent on a rolling apparatus. In 1876, Francis William Mackenzie, C. E., patented a machine known as "F. W. Mackenzie's Steam Tea-Dryer." Mr. Mackenzie lived on the Gelahating Tea Estate, Bisnauth, Assam. His machine was designed to burn wood, straw, grass, or seeds.

Meantime, in England, tea mixing, milling, and blending machinery was constantly being improved. In 1872, John Bartlett, an iron founder of Bristol, England, was granted a British patent on an improved tea mixing machine. This was the beginning of the Bartlett line of machinery for tea milling, sifting, and blending, and for many years the manufacture of these machines was carried on under the name of Bartlett & Son, Ltd. In 1911, an amalgamation was effected with the firm of Henry Pooley & Son, Ltd., which has since carried on the manufacture of all Bartlett tea machinery.

In 1877, J. P. Brougham was granted a British patent on a machine for winnowing and sifting tea. This was not the first apparatus for sifting. Jackson's already was on the market.

In 1876, the first Jackson roller in Java was installed by the Administrator of Tjisalak. In 1879, Jackson invented his ro-

EARLY CHINESE METHOD OF PACKING TEA

tary cylinder for rolling tea leaves. In 1880, he was granted a British patent on a tea drier. Davidson, too, continued experimenting with tea driers.

Early Packing Methods

At this time, i.e., about 1870–75, tea was being packed in India in wooden boxes made on the estate or purchased outside. The boxes were lined with sheet lead. Green teas always were packed hot, just as they came from the pans after the final coloring. They never were pressed down, but a little was put in the box at a time, and then the box was well shaken. Sometimes, black tea was packed hot, but was pressed down, usually by being trodden upon. The boxes were marked with the factory mark or brand, the description of the tea, the break number, and the chest number. On chests of the fancier teas, a fancy bordering or scroll was added.

In Java, it was still the time of glorious labeling of the cases, and the block cutters on the estates competed in flowery motives. Rattan bands were tied round the cases to protect the labeling. The bands were, however, a nuisance in stowing cargo on the ships, and when fancy labeling disappeared the bands also went.

Inventions of the 'Eighties

In 1880, the first tea rolling machine made in Ceylon was manufactured by John Walker & Co., later Walker, Sons & Co., Ltd., Colombo. In 1882, the first tea drying machine in Ceylon was erected on the Windsor Forest Estate in Dolosbage.

William Jackson, through Marshall Sons

& Co., in 1884, shipped to India the first hot air drying machine with mechanically induced draft.

In 1885, John Brown invented a tea drier. This was the beginning of the now well-known Brown's Patent Tea Desiccator, made by the Colombo Commercial Co. It was capable of firing from eighty to ninety-five pounds of tea per hour. In 1892, Brown patented his triple-action tea roller. The rolling tables of this machine were carried on sliding surfaces on a cast-iron frame, which admitted of the passage of a trolley underneath the lower table, to receive the rolled leaf as it was discharged. The lower table was circular, and covered with wooden or metal battens. It had a rotary motion, while the upper had both a rotary and a gyrating motion. This combination of motions was designed to prevent the leaf from becoming stagnant in

NOTABLE CEYLON TEA MACHINES
Upper—Brown's "Desiccator." Lower—Brown's triple-action tea roller.

TWO OF RANSOMES, SIMS & JEFFERIES MACHINES
Left—"Empire" tea roller.   *Right*—"Power" tea drier.

the upper portion of the box when heavy pressure was brought to bear upon it. The leaf receptacle, or box, was made of brass.

In 1885, H. Compton was granted a British patent on an "apparatus for drying tea," and A. Bryans one on "an apparatus for withering tea."

In 1885, Kenzo Takabayashi patented in Japan the first machines to aid in the preparation of Japan green teas. These were two rolling machines.

In 1886, Jackson turned his attention to simplifying and improving his rolling machines, and for the first time introduced the crank in a vertical position, driven by bevel gears. In 1887, he made a clean sweep of these, and introduced the simpler rotary movement of the crank, and mounted the rolling table on three of these. The first machines of this design were the "Square Rapid" rollers, which attained much popularity.

Jackson introduced his first roll breaker in 1887. It consisted of a revolving, inclined screen-cylinder with a half-inch mesh. In the center of the cylinder was a pronged beater, which rotated at high speed. The leaf was put in the open end of the cylinder. The small leaf fell through, and the balls were broken up by the beaters.

Davidson was granted a British patent, in 1887, on "employing and heating air in drying or baking vegetable substances." In the following year, he patented improvements on his apparatus for drying tea.

The year 1887 also marked the beginning of the "Sharpe" line of tea machinery, which was manufactured for some time by Richard Moreland and Sons, later More-

land, Hayne & Co., Ltd., London, who have, however, given it up.

Coming back to 1887, we find that Henry Thompson of Gainsborough, England, was granted a British patent on a drier, with additional patents in 1888 and 1890. These machines were built by Ransomes, Sims & Jefferies, Ltd., in Ipswich. All were of the automatic up-draft type. Thompson also invented a tea roller in 1888.

In 1888, John Richardson of Lincoln, England, was granted a British patent on a rolling machine which was characterized by the use of glass for the rolling surfaces.

William Jackson brought out his first tea sorter in 1888. This machine consisted

EVOLUTION OF THE TEA SORTER
Upper—Original Jackson machine.   *Lower*—Later "Eureka" development.

A GROUP OF EARLY MARSHALL MACHINES

1. Square "Rapid" tea roller. 2. Circular "Rapid" tea roller. 3. Rolled-leaf ball breaker. 4. "Paragon" tea drier. 5. Rotary tea sifter. 6. "Venetian" tea drier.

of two tables, the upper moving on the lower. The upper table was fitted with a grating having inch-and-a-half squares. The bottom table was provided with a galvanized iron wire mesh, through which the tea was forced under the action of the upper table.

Meanwhile, S. C. Davidson had been busy improving his various tea machines. In 1888, he was granted a British patent for improvements on his apparatus for drying and withering tea, followed by two similar patents in 1889. In 1890, he patented a roll-breaker and, in 1891, an apparatus for cutting and sorting tea.

Patents of the Early 'Nineties

Previous to 1891, the firm of Bartlett & Son, Ltd., Bristol, England, had been carrying on the manufacture of mixing and blending machines under the patents of John Bartlett, aforementioned. In that year, a revolutionary change in the design of blending machines was made by Charles Bartlett. This, in effect, concerned the alteration from the old method of emptying the mixer drum by the rim to that of an axial discharge, which was far more efficient and increased the working speed. This he followed with a patent on making the axial discharge through an enclosed chute, and the blades and sieve were so

designed as to prevent the separation of the different grades of fineness during the discharge.

In 1893, Charles Bartlett invented an improvement for cutting or breaking machines, consisting of an apparatus for extracting nails and other foreign substances which used to get in the rollers and damage the knives and cells. His apparatus was called the Triple Knife nail-passing gear.

In 1892, Edward Robinson of Surrey, England, was granted a British patent on a tea-drying machine, consisting of a rotating perforated cylinder enclosed in a chamber. Heated air was drawn upward

MARSHALL "PARAGON" TEA DRIER, 1894

through the cylinder. In 1897, Mr. Robinson invented a steam-heated, automatic tea-drying machine. He also devised a dry warm-air system of artificial withering, which, according to contemporaneous reports from Ceylon tea estates, proved most efficacious.

In 1892, the Waygood-Tupholme Grocers' Machinery Co. and Beeston Tupholme, both of London, were granted a British patent on "apparatus for cutting, equalizing and blending tea." The Waygood-Tupholme Grocers' Machinery Co. was the result of the amalgamation of Waygood-Tupholme, Ltd., and the Grocers' Engineering Co. Later, in 1908, the business of John Whitmee & Co., founded in 1831, was absorbed; the name then becoming The Grocers' Engineering & Whitmee, Ltd. The business now is carried on as The Whitmee Engineering Co., Ltd., London.

Meanwhile, Jackson and Davidson were working steadily to improve their machinery. In 1892, Jackson was granted two British patents on improvements in his rolling apparatus and, in 1893, another patent was given him on his drier. Davidson, in 1891, was granted a patent on "apparatus for cutting and sorting tea"; and one in 1892 and another in 1893

for improvements in his drying machine.

In 1893, William Cameron, a planter of Ythanside, Ceylon, and James Brown, of Brown & Co., Hatton, Ceylon, invented a tea breaker, one feature of which was that it cut longitudinally instead of across. In 1894, W. Gow of London was granted a British patent on a ball breaker.

Marshall Sons & Co., Ltd., brought out their "Paragon" drier, operating on the same principle as the "Victoria," but with a larger capacity. W. Jackson was granted two patents on this in 1894. The "Paragon," also had improved feeding arrangements and air heater. It was followed by a "Venetian," of larger size than that of 1884, and with improved tilting arrangements of trays. In 1895, Jackson was awarded two patents on his roller and one on his drier. In the following year, 1896, he was the patentee of further improvements on his drier, and also of a "discharging apparatus for hot air drying chambers in tea drying machines."

In 1894, Davidson, with F. G. Maguire, obtained a British patent on an apparatus for packing tea in bulk. The first machines for packing teas had been those operating by means of stamps, with a vibrating or oscillating platform. This type of machine was superseded by those work-

A GROUP OF EARLY DAVIDSON MACHINES

1. "Sirocco" tea roller. 2. Up-draft "Sirocco" drier. 3. Down-draft "Sirocco" drier. 4. Large tea sorter. 5. Tea packing machine. 6. Packing machine with hopper.

The "Sirocco" Double Down-Draft Tea Drier

ing without the stamps. The Davidson-Maguire apparatus was of the latter type.

Again in 1894, Davidson obtained a patent on improvements in his apparatus for withering tea and on his tea drier. In 1895, he obtained three patents on his drying machines, one on his packer, and one on his roller. In the following year, 1896, he was awarded two patents on his packing apparatus, two on his roller, one on his drier, and one on a tea-cutting machine.

In 1895, the late P. C. Larkin of Toronto, Canada, founder of the Salada Tea Co., invented a tea packeting machine. The packet was formed about a box, the bottom was closed, and the packet and box were inserted into a mould, where they rested on the top of a plunger. Tea was then poured into a hopper-shaped receptacle and thence into the box, where it was pressed down by a plunger. The box was removed, and the top of the packet folded and pressed.

Patents of the Late 'Nineties

C. H. Bartlett, in 1895, patented an improvement on his tea blender in the form of a central discharge, through a chute.

In 1896, a British patent was granted to J. M. Boustead of Colombo, Ceylon, on an electrically heated drying apparatus, comprising iron coils coated with porcelain or the like. The heating frame was of slate. In a machine of one pattern, the tea was placed upon sieves over or under the heating frames; and, in another, it was carried on an endless belt over or under them.

In the same year, J. S. Stevenson of Hatton, Ceylon, was awarded a British patent on another electric drier.

In Japan, in 1898, Gensaku Harasaki invented a labor-saving mechanical re-firing pan for use in preparing Japan green teas.

In 1899, B. H. Watson and H. C. Walker, trading as the Grocers' Engineering Co., London, were granted a British patent on a mixing and blending machine.

In 1901, B. H. Watson obtained another patent on improvements for his "20th Century" automatic tea mill.

During the years 1897, 1898, 1899, and 1900, S. C. Davidson was granted ten British patents, seven of them for improvements on his tea drying apparatus. The "Sirocco" Automatic Endless Web tea drier made its appearance in 1897. It worked on the same principle of continuous feeding of the leaf as the modern Endless Chain Pressure drier, but differed from the latter in that the hot air was drawn through the layers of leaf by suction, whereas, in the modern machine, the air is blown into the drying chamber.

The "Sirocco" Endless Chain Pressure drier was introduced in 1907-8, and was followed about a year later by the Tilting Tray Pressure drier.

In 1914–15, the Single Tilter was superseded by the Enclosed Type Tilter.

In 1914, the "Sirocco" Automatic Feeder and Spreader for the Endless Chain Pressure driers, also was brought out, but owing to the intervention of the World War, it was not until 1919 that it was possible to fully develop this important feature of the drier. It was fitted in large numbers to existing Endless Chain Pressure driers, and now has been embodied as a component part of the standard drier.

Returning to 1898, it was in this year that Jackson introduced his first tea packer. The special feature of the machine was the manner in which the platform was mounted on angular bracket-shaped steel springs, without any joints or links. To the platform, a very fast vibratory motion was imparted, a corresponding motion being communicated to the tea in the chest. Tea could be packed into the chests by this machine as fast as it could be filled in by one man. Also in 1898, Jackson was granted a British patent on improvements in his rolling machines; and in 1899, on improvements in his sifting apparatus, and in 1900, was awarded a patent on a machine for "dividing" tea.

Green Tea Machinery

Practically all the tea-producing countries have, at one time or another, made green tea; although India, Ceylon, and Java, have now turned their attention almost exclusively to black.

Naturally, in the Occidental countries the trend was toward the use of machinery in the manufacture of green tea as well as of black. The first apparatus was invented in Ceylon by Horace Drummond Deane, a tea planter. About 1890, he evolved a method of rendering the tea leaf pliable, for purposes of rolling and twisting, by the application of live steam. The machine consisted of a hexagonal wooden drum, nine feet long by thirty-three inches in diameter, mounted by means of cast iron flanges on bearings carried on standards. The drum was revolved by power, although smaller machines could be turned by hand. Steam inlets led into the drum at both ends. But it was ten years before there was any demand for Deane's machine. Then, about 1900, a slump in the black tea market caused a rush, on the part of the planters, into the manufacture of green tea. After some trouble in establishing his patent rights, Deane arranged with Brown & Co., Ltd., of Colombo, to manufacture the machines. Later, a Mr. Rae collaborated with Deane in the Deane & Rae patent green tea machine, now being made by Brown & Co., Ltd.

It was in 1902 that Charles G. L. Judge, inventor and journalist, turned his attention to green tea. Going into partnership with Deane, he brought some of the latter's machines into India, and an arrangement was made with Heatly & Gresham, Ltd., of Calcutta, to manufacture them. However, planters complained of the mess made in expressing the steam from the leaf, and to correct this, Judge adopted the centrifugal idea used in sugar manufacture. The centrifugal threw off all the steam water in from two to three minutes, and dealt with nearly 3000 lbs. of leaf per hour. Thus, the leaf was delivered to the rollers free of excess moisture. Judge and Deane, in 1903, received a patent on this in India.

Beside the centrifugal, the Deane-Judge process comprehended the dipping of the leaf for half a minute or so in deep cauldrons of boiling water on the out-gardens. This was to keep the leaf fresh until it reached the factory. Kelway Bamber, the well-known chemist, who was at that time Scientific Officer for the Ceylon Tea Association, improved on this by adding free carbonic acid gas to the water used to sterilize the leaf; thereby imparting a better color to the leaf, and improving the cup quality. But, although the green tea now gave a correct liquor in the cup, it had not the proper color, being too olive. This could be overcome by firing in heated pans, but the process was costly and troublesome. Therefore, in 1902, Sir William Butler in Ceylon and Charles G. L. Judge in India simultaneously invented finishing and glazing machines.

Butler's process required two machines. The first was a long, narrow, revolving-drum mixer, in which dry green tea was

DEANE & RAE'S GREEN TEA MACHINE

McDonald's "Deflector" Tea Fanner

revolved for two or three hours, either plain or with "facing" matter. Then it was removed and taken to the glazer, a smaller revolving drum with sides of fine wire mesh. After this, the tea had to be final-fired—usually in a Sutton vacuum drier—before it was packed. Judge's one machine did the work of coloring, glazing, and final-firing. In 1903, Judge brought out a "pan-firing machine."

In 1902, Whittall & Co., of Colombo, brought out the "Mitrailleuse" machine for pan-firing. In the same year, H. M. A. Alleyn of Maskeliya, a well-known planter, invented a similar machine, which, as it depended on a revolving drum, was shut out in Ceylon, by Sir William Butler's patent. The interior of the Alleyn machine was fitted with shelves to prevent the tea falling on itself, and breaking. However, it was not heated and, therefore, the tea had to be final-fired. Alleyn and J. Grieve were granted another patent in India, in 1902, on apparatus for finishing, or polishing, green or Oolong teas.

Other inventors brought out machines for glazing green tea. In 1902, Messrs. D. Reid and Dale of Baraoora, India, produced an apparatus with a large metal drum, heated from the outside. In 1904, Davidson & Co., Ltd., brought out a machine for green tea glazing.

G. W. Sutton, in 1904, put forward a steam-jacketed drum for glazing. In the same year, he invented a tea panning and rolling machine, with a steam-heated table revolving under a fixed open frame.

In Japan, many years ago, the tea-finishing firms devised and used a hand-power glazing machine. It consisted of a paddle-wheel working longitudinally in a metal

trough heated by a charcoal stove or used without heat. The tea was placed in the trough, and the wheel revolved by hand.

As for the rolling, A. H. Ayden of Whittall & Co., Colombo, in 1903, invented a machine to roll green teas in imitation of the "needle leaf" teas of Japan.

In the early part of the twentieth century, while the United States Government was experimenting in tea-growing in the State of South Carolina, the late Dr. Charles U. Shepard, who was in charge of the experiments, developed a tea-rolling machine that would roll tea similar to the basket-fired teas of Japan.

Various attempts have been made to "roast" the leaf, so as to reproduce the style of China greens, but without much success. In 1903, G. Streeting, H. Tarver, and F. E. Mackwood of Ceylon, invented a "revolving heated receptacle with scraper and fixed end door, and feeding hopper for steaming, drying, roasting, firing and finishing tea." Charles G. L. Judge was granted a patent, in 1904, on a somewhat similar apparatus heated by a central, steam-heated drum.

The Twentieth Century

By the beginning of the twentieth century, hand methods of tea manufacture in India, Ceylon, Java, and, to some extent, in Japan were becoming obsolete.

Out of the many inventions, the best were beginning to emerge. The remainder faded out. From 1900 on, we find fewer inventors, and fewer patents.

In 1900, J. N. F. Greig of Rajmai, Assam, was granted a British patent on a tea rolling machine. In 1907, he collaborated with A. F. Greig in two patents on apparatus for drying and withering tea.

Also in 1900, G. W. Sutton was granted a patent in India on tea drying or wither-

Left—Davidson Tea Packer
Right—"Sirocco" Rotary Roller

MARSHALL'S DOUBLE-ACTION "RAPID" ROLLER

ing apparatus, with concentric, revolving cylinders, air supply, and steam or electric heating. In 1904, he patented a tea cultivating machine, a motor tea cultivator, and a fermenting apparatus.

In 1900, W. F. Perman of Assam was granted a British patent on a tea roller. Perman's auto-expressor, to remove surplus moisture from the leaf charge, came later, in 1912.

In the United States, in 1900, Robert Burns secured a patent on a tea-mixer. This machine is manufactured by Jabez Burns & Sons, Inc., of New York.

Charles Bartlett, meanwhile, was constantly improving upon his cutting, mixing, and blending machinery. In 1901, he was granted a British patent on improvements in his tea-cutting machine, and in 1903, he secured another similar patent.

British patents, in 1901, also included one granted to F. E. Winsland and G. E. Moore, of North Lakhimpur, India, on machinery for packing tea in bulk.

H. M. Alleyn of Maskeliya, Ceylon, who invented some green tea machinery, was granted a British patent, in 1902, on apparatus for breaking, cutting, grading, or sifting tea. In 1905, he received a United States patent on this apparatus.

In 1902, the late Dr. Charles U. Shepard, before-mentioned, received a U. S. patent on a green tea sterilizer, consisting of a

rotating cylinder, with interior, specially arranged flanges. At one end of the cylinder was a flue, through which hot air was blown in, and a hopper. The tea was fed through the hopper and rotated through the cylinder, with a gradually diminishing temperature, to a bin on the opposite end.

William Jackson and Marshall Sons & Co., Ltd., were constantly patenting improvements. In 1902 and 1904, Jackson was granted patents on improvements on his tea rolling machines, and in 1904, 1906, and 1907, he registered improvements on his driers. S. C. Davidson also was awarded three British patents, in 1906 and 1907, on improvements in his drying apparatus.

In 1905, Job Day & Sons, Ltd., of Leeds, England, began manufacturing machinery for packeting tea.

C. P. Bartlett, of Bartlett & Son, Ltd., London, continued to improve his milling, blending, and sifting machinery. In 1906, he was granted three British patents on improvements on his tea-mixers. In 1911, he obtained a patent on an apparatus for extracting dust during blending.

A recent Bartlett invention is a tea cutting and sifting machine, which has been specially arranged for double cutting, single cutting, and straight.

In 1907, John McDonald, a Cachar tea planter, invented a machine for winnowing and sifting in a manner least liable to gray the teas. It is called McDonald's Patent "Deflector" tea fanner.

In 1908, J. Begg was granted a patent in India on a spreading device for use with withering machines. Begg was awarded a British patent on this device

MITCHELL'S TEA PRUNING MACHINE

BATEMAN'S COMBINED MILLING AND STALK-EX-
TRACTING MACHINE

in 1913. Also in 1908, a patent in India
was granted to W. G. Firman on a feeding
device for tea sifters, with adjustable hopper flaps.

In 1908, the late K. A. R. Bosscha, Malabar, Java, invented a withering drum. He
also invented an electrically heated drier.

J. Howden was granted a patent in India, in 1909, on a tea withering, fermenting, and drying process. The leaf was
withered in a revolving apparatus supplied
with air of regulated pressure and temperature. The fermenting was conducted
in a closed vessel, under pressure. The
drying was done in a revolving apparatus,
under vacuum.

In 1907, Jackson and Marshall Sons &
Co., Ltd., brought out the Single Action
"Metallic" roller, which had a much larger
capacity than the Square "Rapid" roller,
and introduced metal instead of wood,

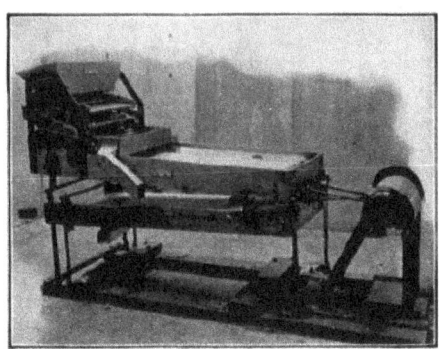

MYDDLETON'S TEA-STALK EXTRACTOR

wherever possible, to prolong the life of
the machine. Jackson was granted British patents on his rolling machines in 1908
and 1914; on his drying apparatus in 1908;
and on his machinery for sifting, or classi-
fying, the tea leaf, in 1914. About the
year 1910, a large increase in planting and
production took place and, to meet this demand, larger drying machines were found
necessary. In 1910, the first up-draft
drier on the pressure principle was made.
This principle of forcing the hot air
through the leaf, instead of drawing it, was
found to give more even drying and to
penetrate more thoroughly to all parts of
the drying chamber. The largest Jackson
machine employing this principle is known
as the "Empire."

Davidson, too, was constantly bringing
his apparatus up-to-date. He was granted

MARSHALL'S "BRITON" TEA PACKER

three patents on his rolling machines in
1909; one in 1910; another in 1911; still
another in 1912; and one in 1915.

In 1910, Gensaku Harasaki, senior managing director of the Fuji Co., Japan tea
exporters, invented a tea re-firing apparatus.

In 1911, George F. Mitchell was granted
a U. S. patent on a tea pruning machine
which, in trials on the Pinehurst Tea
Estate, Summerville, S. C., was found to
reduce pruning costs from $2 and $3 an
acre to 40 cents an acre.

Brooke Bond & Co., Ltd., and Gerald T.
Walker were granted a British patent, in
1915, on apparatus for feeding tea to cutting or crushing rollers. In 1919, the Phillips Engineering Co. and G. T. Walker obtained two British patents on a tea cutter.

In 1920, C. S. Bateman, an India tea

A GROUP OF LATE MARSHALL MACHINES

Upper left—Brine-cooled rolling machine. *Upper right*—New "Empire" drier. *Lower left*—Four-tray balanced sifter. *Lower right*—Anti-friction sifter.

planter, was granted a patent in India on apparatus for "cutting or sorting tea." Later, Marshall, Sons & Co., Ltd., placed on the market Bateman's Automatic combined tea milling and stalk extracting machine.

Myddelton's tea stalk extractor is also popular in India. It embodies two superimposed trays.

In 1924, C. H. Tillmanns, overseer on the Sperata Tea Estate in Java, invented the Sperata *theepluckmes*, or tea-plucking knife.

In 1927, Marshall, Sons & Co., Ltd., brought out the Marshall mechanical withering machine.

Marshall, Sons & Co., Ltd., also brought out, in 1927, their "Briton" tea packer. It is made to deal with either one or two chests at a time, and can be adapted for half or full chests. Recent developments in the Marshall line have been mostly refinements of mechanical efficiency, more absolute temperature control, and increased ease of operation. An open-top roller was brought out in 1930 to meet the demand for an initial rolling without pressure. Marshall's became the Marshall Tea Machinery Company, Ltd., in 1934.

THE McKERCHER "C.T.C." TEA MACHINE

AUTOMATIC TEA ROLLER CONTROL
Upper—The Gawthropp gear. *Lower*—"Sirocco" pressure-indicator attachment.

About 1926, a machine for crushing tea leaf was patented by T. A. Chalmers of Rajghurali, Assam. This was followed in 1931 by Marshall, Sons & Co., Ltd., with Sir William McKercher's C.T.C. (crushing, tearing, curling) process machine, designed

"SIROCCO" DUPLEX TILTING-TRAY PRESSURE DRIER

MOORE'S CONTINUOUS AUTOMATIC TEA-SORTING MACHINE

to produce a higher quality leaf. For some years Mr. (now Sir) William McKercher experimented with leaf crushing machines at Amgoorie, in Assam, and finally evolved the C.T.C. machine. It consists of two metal, ribbed rollers which work like a mangle. One roller makes about 700 r.p.m. and the other about 80 r.p.m. Partially rolled leaf is fed into the machine, and as it passes between the rollers it is not only crushed but distorted. The leaf is only under pressure for a fraction of a second and has no time to heat, whilst any expressed juice is reabsorbed by the leaf immediately it passes through the rollers.

In 1926, Balmer Lawrie & Co., Ltd., of Calcutta, brought out Moore's Continuous Automatic "Chota" tea-sorting machine. It is the invention of G. E. Moore, a practical planter. The action is a horizontal circular motion, having the same principle as hand sorting, with circular sieves, similar to those used in China. It is continuous in operation, it being unnecessary to start up and stop for each charge. One machine is capable of sorting ten maunds of cut tea per hour.

In 1927, Bever Dorling & Co., Bradford, England, brought out an improved "Lanka" tea roller, fitted with Sutton's patent stainless-steel corrugated rolling table.

Another popular tea sifter is the "Chalmers," manufactured by the Britannia Engineering Co., Titaghur, India. In 1928, Mr. A. L. McWilliam, of the aforementioned firm, patented a new double-action tea roller with ball-bearing crank shafts.

In 1930, Hoare & Co. (Engineers), Ltd., Colombo, introduced the Farbridge patent "Multiflu" tea drier [J. R. Farbridge pat.], with special claims to fuel economy.

In 1931, the Colombo Commercial Co. brought out its "C.C.C." single action tea

A GROUP OF LATE DAVIDSON MACHINES

Upper left—"Sirocco" O.C.B. Roller. *Lower left*—"Sirocco" Endless Chain Pressure Drier. *Upper right*—"Sirocco" Ball Breaker. *Lower right*—"Sirocco" Sorter.

roller in standard-perforated and shallow-jacket types. In 1932, they introduced their "C.C.C." multiple roll-breaker and green leaf sifter, designed to deal with a system of green leaf grading originated by Neville L. Anley, Mahatenne Estate, Elkaduwa, Ceylon.

An outstanding development of the year 1931 was the introduction by Marshall, Sons & Co., Ltd., of the brine-cooled "Marshall-Boustead" tea-leaf rolling machine [R. C. Boustead pat.], which controls the temperature of the leaf mass by circulation of calcium chloride.

The latest developments in the "Colombo" tea drier and the "Economic" tea roller, introduced by Walker & Sons Co., Colombo, in the 'eighties are their "Automatic" pressure drier and "Super-Economic" tea roller which, while incorporating important improvements, are substantially of the same design. Recently, this firm introduced a "Pentagonal" green leaf sifter, designed as an improvement

upon the hexagonal and cylindrical sorters.

In 1932, Sadovsky introduced his tea plucking machine in Russia. Others followed.

In 1932, Marshall brought out the Gawthropp gear for automatic control of pressure caps on Marshall tea rollers. This device, invented by Mr. S. C. Gawthropp,

THE CHALMERS TEA SIFTER

TEA MACHINERY OF GERMAN MANUFACTURE
Left—Krupp's tea roller. *Right*—Krupp's tea drier.

manager, Deepling Tea Estate, Assam, regulates the action of the cap so as to produce light, medium or hard pressure, making the roller practically automatic and "coolie-proof."

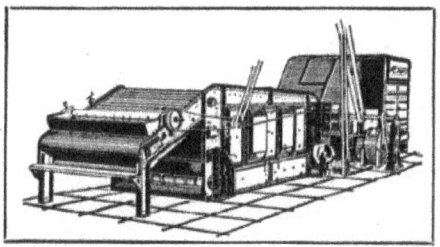

HOARE'S "MULTIFLU" (FARBRIDGE PAT.) TEA DRIER

Among the inventions or improvements that have been developed in connection with the Davidson line of "Sirocco" tea machinery since the death of Sir Samuel C. Davidson, mention should be made of the "Sirocco" Enclosed Type Single tea packer, which is similar in principle to the earlier packer, but has all the rotating parts and bearings completely enclosed.

Mention also should be made of the introduction, in 1927, of the "Sirocco O.C.B." tea roller, an improved type of roller, the special features of which are the overhead crank bearings. These ensure the smooth running and quiet operation of the machine, and greatly reduce the wear and tear. A recent addition to the Davidson line is the "Sirocco" Duplex Tilting Tray Pressure drier for final firing. It possesses the advantages of hand operation and control, and is capable of dealing with the output of a large Endless Chain Pressure drier. It is similar in design to the Enclosed-Type Single Tilter, but has a double width drying chamber divided into two sections which are operated independently of each other.

In the early part of this century German inventors became interested in tea machinery. Their most important efforts are represented in the complete line manufactured by Fried. Krupp Grusonwerk, Magdeburg.

LATE CEYLON TEA MACHINES
Upper—"C.C.C." roll breaker, 1932. *Lower*—"C.C.C." Single-Action tea roller, 1931.

BOOK III
SCIENTIFIC ASPECTS

CHAPTER XXIII

ETYMOLOGY OF TEA

THE DERIVATION OF THE WORD FOR THE LEAF, PLANT, AND BEVERAGE OF THEA SINENSIS
IN THE LANGUAGES OF THE CIVILIZED WORLD, AS OBTAINED DIRECT FROM CHINA, WHERE
TEA WAS FIRST CULTIVATED AND MANUFACTURED—THE ORIGIN OF THE TWO FORMS THE
WORD HAS TAKEN IN ITS PROGRESS AROUND THE WORLD—THE CHINESE, JAPANESE,
PERSIAN, ARABIAN, TURKISH, RUSSIAN, PORTUGUESE, DUTCH, AND ENGLISH WORDS FOR
TEA—THE WORD IN OTHER LANGUAGES

THE languages of the civilized world derive their respective words for "tea" direct from China, the home of its earliest cultivation and preparation. The native name for tea in China is 茶 , romanized as ch'a, pronounced "chah," in Cantonese; and changing to t'e, pronounced "tay," in the dialect of Amoy. From one or the other of these two sources the term has found its way with little or no alteration into practically every modern language.

The Chinese were forced to borrow the names of other shrubs for their earliest references to tea, as it did not receive its present appellation [ch'a] until about A.D. 725; consequently, there is some uncertainy when tea or something else was meant by authors who wrote before that time.

Wang Piu, about 50 B.C., in his Contract with a Servant, writes of boiling 茶 t'u that was purchased from Wutu. As Wutu is a mountain in one of the famed tea districts of Szechwan, it is possible that tea grew there when Wang Piu wrote; and some oriental scholars consider Wang's reference to t'u as a possible reference to tea.

The Chinese character t'u was one of the earlier borrowed names for tea. It had three different meanings: (1) sow-thistle, or bitter cabbage, (2) grass, or rush, and (3) tea. The context has to be relied upon to indicate which was meant in a given case.

It appears that t'u still was used to indicate tea in the fourth century after Christ. According to Dr. E. Bretschneider, 1833–1901, a distinguished German botanist, attached to the Russian legation at Peking [now Peiping], it is stated in the Shi Shuo that "Wang Mang, father-in-law of the Emperor Ai Ti [P'ing Ti], in the middle of the fourth century, was very fond of drinking t'u," tea evidently being meant.[1]

In the time of the Tsin dynasty [sixth century after Christ], the poet Chang Meng-yang made a supposed allusion to the beverage in the lines, "Fragrant t'u superimposes the six passions; the taste for it spreads over the entire kingdom."

Dr. John Dudgeon, a medical missionary to China, confirms the use of the word t'u by the following quotation from Kwang Hsi's dictionary: "Everybody says that tea is the ancient t'u; but they do not know how many sorts there are of tea. The t'u of kai k'u t'u, is the present tea. Sun says, the t'u is not a clean plant, and is not the so-called ku ts'ai [bitter vegetable]."[2]

Kia 檟 was another borrowed term for tea. It was used for a time by early Chinese writers. Its use was due to their confusion of mind as to the correct bo-

---

[1] Dr. Emil Bretschneider, "Botanicon Sinicum, Part II," Journal of the China Branch of the Royal Asiatic Society, vol. xxv, Shanghai, 1893, pp. 130–131.
[2] Dr. John Dudgeon, The Beverages of the Chinese, Tientsin, 1895, p. 4.

tanical classification of the tea shrub. Thus, in a symposium translated from Chinese authors in *The Chinese Repository*, we read: In the dictionary *Ehr Ya*[3] tea is called *kia*, meaning "bitter tea." Kuo P'o commenting on this, says—"The plant is small, like the *chi* [*Gardenia radicans*], sending forth its leaves in the winter season [that is, it is evergreen]."[4]

Kuo P'o, a Chinese author of the Tsin dynasty, A.D. ca. 265–317, who revised the ancient Chinese dictionary, *Erh Ya*, included in it the definition of tea, to which the Chinese symposium alludes, as follows: " 梹 *Kia* 苦茶 *K'u t'u* [bitter *t'u*] a small evergreen tree resembling the 梔 *chi* [*Gardenia*]. A beverage is made from the leaves by boiling. Now the earliest gathering is called *t'u*, the latest 茗 *ming*. Another name for the plant is 荈 *ch'uen*. The people of 蜀 *Shu* [Szechwan] call it *k'u t'u*."

Kuo P'o also gave two other definitions for the character *kia* in connection with trees or shrubs totally unrelated to *Thea sinensis* [L.] Sims.

茗 *Ming* was another early name for tea. It was derived from the Siamese [Hakka dialect] *miang*, becoming *ming* in the dialect of Yunnan. It was first applied to tea as an article of diet. Dr. Bretschneider informs us that the *yen tsz ch'un ch'in*, written some centuries B.C., mentioned the *ming ts'ai*, or "tea vegetable," as an article of food in the time of Yen Ying, who was a contemporary of Confucius [ca. 500 B.C.].

Reference again is made to tea under the name of *ming* in the *Account of Aliments*, popularly ascribed to the lengendary Emperor Shen Nung, ca. 2737 B.C., but actually written in the time of the Neo-Han dynasty, ca. A.D. 25–219.

In the fifth century of the Christian Era, tea was still called *ming;* for about that time, Pao Ling-hui, a Chinese authoress, wrote eulogistically of the beverage, calling it "fragrant ming."

The *Ch'a p'u*, meaning literally "tea section," compiled by *Ku Yüan Ch'ing* of the ming dynasty A.D. 1368–1628, states that in the reign of the Emperor Wen Ti, A.D. 580–800, a Buddhist priest first recommended the boiled *ming* leaves as a medicine for the emperor, who suffered from headache.

Gradually, as tea came into more general use throughout the Flowery Kingdom, the character 荼 *t'u*, of many meanings, evolved by the elimination of the upper stroke of its lower member into 茶 *ch'a*, which, henceforth, was the Chinese ideograph for tea. This character never has had any other meaning. Yen Shih Ku, a commenator of the seventh century after Christ, records that the change of the character 荼 *t'u* into 茶 *ch'a*, occurred during that period.

In the succeeding century, or approximately the year 780, Lu Yu, a noted Chinese author, wrote the first comprehensive work on tea, the *Ch'a Ching*, or "Tea Book." According to Dr. Bretschneider, the use of the character *ch'a* for tea was not general before the publication of the *Ch'a Ching*.

In the *Ch'a Ching*, Lu Yu mentions the names for tea in use at the time he wrote. He says that there were five:

茶	*Ch'a*	Tea
梹	*Kia*	"
蔎	*She*	"
茗	*Ming*	Spring Sprouts
荈	*Ch'uen*	Old Leaves

Dr. Dudgeon states that the character *ch'a* does not occur in any of the ancient records. He states further that "The character first appeared in the *Herbal* of Su Kung, an official, who revised and completed the T'ang dynasty [A.D. 620–904]

The strokes of the character *ch'a* are inscribed in the order set forth in the accompanying illustration; beginning at the top and writing downward, after the Chinese fashion.

HOW THE CHARACTER—"*Ch'a*" IS INSCRIBED

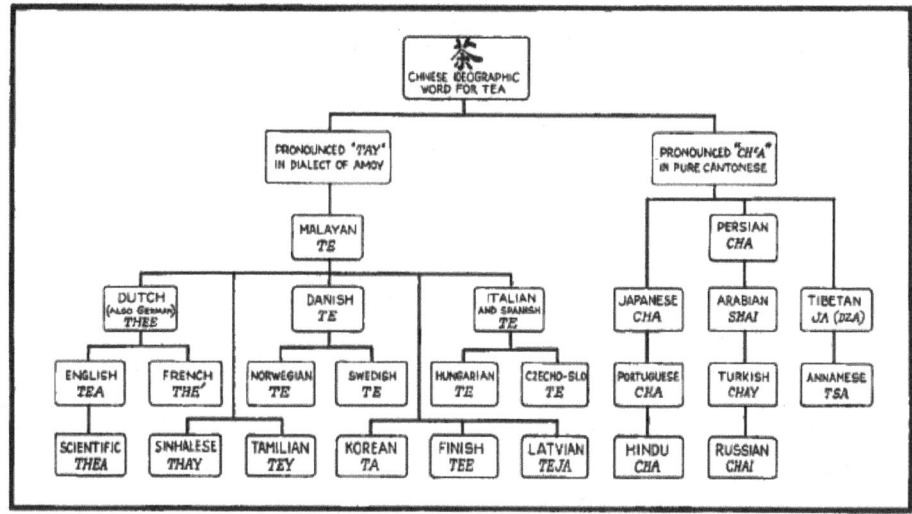

CHART SHOWING THE PROBABLE ETYMOLOGICAL DERIVATION OF THE WORD FOR "TEA" IN VARIOUS LANGUAGES OF THE WORLD

Pen t'sao, or *Materia Medica.* . . . He published a work which may be translated, *Omissions in Previous Works of Materia Medica.* It is said to have been falsely included in Shen Nung's [*ca.* 2737 B.C.] *Account of Aliments*, but in reality it was not 'falsely,' but actually added to that work by later writers. . . . Why do we know it was added afterwards? Because, before the time of Kuo P'o's commentary on the *Ehr Ya*, there was no such character as ch'a."

The translation of the Chinese word for tea into other languages undoubtedly began with the earliest sale of the commodity to a foreign people. Brinkley tells us that tea first became an article of export when Turkish caravans appeared on the nothern border of China in the last quarter of the fifth century of the Christian era.[5] Later, the Arabs obtained China tea through the Usbeck Tartars, and the first Arabian writers called it *chah*[6] or *sax*,[7] depending on the system of literation used. Both the Arabs and Turks of to-day have similar words. The Arabs call it

shai, and the Turks, *chay*, which is derived directly from the Cantonese *ch'a-ye*, meaning "tea leaf."

The Japanese imported the word *cha* as well as the Chinese manner of writing it, in the eighth century after Christ—at the time when they imported the first tea seeds from China.

The Persians, also, took the Chinese word in its pure form. In a description of an embassy in 1633 from the Duke of Holstein to the King of Persia, Adam Olearius, 1600–1671, wrote that the Persians were great drinkers of *cha*, which they obtained from the Usbeck Tartars.[8] The original word, *cha*, has remained unchanged in Persia [now Iran].

Tea became generally known in Russia in the middle of the seventeenth century, about the same time that Western Europe accepted it; but, unlike the countries of Western Europe, Russia's first teas came overland by caravan, and, therefore, it is not surprising to find that the Russian term for tea, *chai*, is derived directly from the Chinese *ch'a-ye*, tea-leaf, like the Turkish and Arabian words, *chay* and *shai*.

Portuguese was the only European

[5] Capt. F. Brinkley, *China; Its History, Arts, and Literature*, Boston and Tokyo, 1902, vol. x, p. 137.
[6] Eusebe Renaudot [translator], *Ancient Account of India and China, by Two Arabian Travelers in the Ninth Century* [*A.D.* 850] *with Notes and Illustrations*, Paris, 1713. [Eng.] London, 1733.
[7] Dr. Bernard Laufer. *Irano-Sinica*, Chicago. 1919, p. 553.

[8] Adam, Olearius [Oelschlager], *Beschreibung der Muscowitischen und Persischen Reise.* Schleswig, 1647. [Eng.] *Travels of the Ambassadors*, translated by John Davis, London, 1662.

language to adopt the Cantonese *cha;* but one can understand this, because the Portuguese were the first Europeans to established themselves commercially in China [1516], and had their dealings with merchants from Canton. The Dutch, who were the next and the greatest pioneers of oriental commerce, imported their first tea from Bantam, in Java, where it was brought by Chinese merchants from Amoy, in Fukien Province. Therefore, they followed the Amoy dialect in the use of *t'e,* "tay," for tea and romanized it as *thee.* All the other European countries, except Portugal, obtained their earliest supplies of tea from the Dutch, and their derivatives of the Chinese tea-word, likewise, followed the *t'e* of the Amoy dialect.

The English word "tea," originally pronounced "tay" and later "tee," was derived through the Dutch.

In the records of the English East India Company tea was spelled "thea" in 1664; but by 1668 it had changed to "tey." The word was an entirely new one in the language, and is not an adaptation of any former word in English or in the classic languages of Europe. It applies, properly, only to the plant, leaf, and beverage of *Thea Sinensis* [*L.*] *Sims,* and is merely a borrowed word when used for the infusions of other plants or herbs; as, Paraguay tea, *Ilex paraguayensis;* Jesuit tea, *Psoralea glandulosa;* New Jersey tea, *Ceanothus americanus;* etc.

The word is not to be found in the Bible, the works of Shakespeare, or any publication in English previous to the latter half of the seventeenth century. In the known references to tea in English, during the years 1650–1659, the word appears in its earlier form as "tee," and was pronounced "tay."

It was first spelled "tea" in 1660, but continued to be pronounced "tay" until the middle of the eighteenth century.

> "Here thou great Anna! whom three
>   realms obey,
> Dost sometimes counsel take—and
>   sometimes tea."
>   *Rape of the Lock,* Pope, 1711

The change in pronunciation must have taken place between 1720 and 1750, according to the *Hobson-Jobson* dictionary, for about the latter date we find in the verses of Thomas Moore:

> "One day in July last at tea,"
> And in the house of Mrs. P.,"
>   *The Trial of Sarah* [9]

And in Zedler's *Lexicon,* 1745, it is stated that the English write the word either *tee* or *tea,* but pronounce it "*tiy,*" which seems to indicate our modern pronounciation.

The word "*Thea*" as it applies to the tea plant, or to tea, is the botanical name for the genus of the *Theaceae* family, which includes also the familiar flowering camellia. It appears first to have been used by Dr. Engelbert Kaempfer, 1651–1716, a German naturalist, whose work, *Amoenitates Exoticarum,* was published in 1712.

"*Thea*" is the Latinized version of *Oeá,* the Greek word meaning "a goddess"— hence, perhaps, "the divine herb"—but whether or not this significance was considered by Kaempfer, its author, the word must have been derived, more or less directly, from *t'e,* the Amoy dialect form of the Chinese word for tea, the same as the French *thé,* Dutch and German *thee,* and the English "tea."

Linnaeus [Charles, or Carl von Linne, 1707–1778], the celebrated Swedish naturalist and botanist, classified tea under two names, *Camellia* and *Thea,* in 1737, having borrowed or accepted the latter from Kaempfer.

The modern terms for "tea," in various languages, derived from the Chinese character 茶 romanized as (1) *ch'a,* in Cantonese, and as (2) *t'e* in the dialect of Amoy, are:

(1) Japanese, 茶 *cha;* Russian, Чай *chai;* Arabian, *shai* [pronounced "shi"]; Turkish, *chay;* Portuguese, *cha;* Iranian, *cha;* Hindu, *cha;* Urduan, *cha;* Italian, [obsolete], *cia;* Spanish [obsolete], *cha;* English, military slang, *chah;* Tibetan, *ja* [dza]; Annamese, *tsa;* Bulgarian, *chi.*

(2) English, *tea;* Dutch, *thee;* German, *thee;* Danish, *te;* Swedish, *te;* French, *thé;* Italian, *te;* Spanish, *te;* Malayan, *te,* or *teh;* Fukienese dialect, *t'e* or *teh;* Latin [scientific], *Thea;* Sinhalese, *thay;* Tamilian, *tey;* Yiddish, טהעע , [reading from right to left] *thee;* Finnish, *tee;* Norwegian, *te;* Esperanto, *téo-a;* Latvian, *teja;* Czecho-Slovakian, *te;* Hungarian, *te;* Korean, *ta.*

THEA SINENSIS (L) SIMS, VAR. BOHEA AND VAR. MACROPHYLLA

Two varieties of the original China tea plant as painted from specimens at the New York Botanical Gardens by Mary E. Eaton. *Upper*—macrophylla; *lower left*—bohea; *lower right*—seed pod, fruit, and ovary.

CHAPTER XXIV

BOTANY AND HISTOLOGY OF TEA

COMPLETE CLASSIFICATION OF TEA BY DIVISION, CLASS, ORDER, FAMILY, GENUS, AND
SPECIES—TEA FIRST CLASSIFIED BY LINNAEUS AS *Thea Sinensis*, AND LATER AS *Camellia*—THE FIRST CLASSIFICATION NOW COMMONLY ACCEPTED—GENERAL CHARACTERISTICS OF *Thea Sinensis*—ITS MANY VARIETIES AND RACES—SUBSTITUTES FOR TEA—ADULTERANTS USED TO INCREASE THE BULK, ADD TO THE WEIGHT, OR IMPROVE THE
APPEARANCE OF TEA—MICROSCOPICAL STRUCTURE

THE plant from which tea is made belongs in the division of *Angiospermae*, or flowering plants, and to the largest and most important class of that division, the *Dicotyledones*. It is of the order *Parietales*. The name of the family is *Theaceae*, although it has been sometimes called *Camelliaceae*. All this is well established, and meets with agreement among botanists. It is only when we come down the scale of botanical nomenclature to the matter of genus and species that we encounter differences of opinion.

Carl von Linné, 1707-78, the Swedish botanist, best known as Linnaeus, was first to employ binomial names for the species of plants. This change came in 1753 when he published the *Species Plantarum*, a work considered the start of modern systematic botany.

So important is this work considered that, in 1905, when botanists from all over the world gathered at the International Congress of Vienna, and formulated what are known as the International Rules, Article 19 was worded as follows: "Botanical nomenclature begins with the *Species Plantarum* of Linnaeus, ed. 1 [1753], for all groups of vascular plants."

Linnaeus listed the tea plant as *Thea sinensis* on page 515 of Volume I of the *Species Plantarum*. On page 698 of Volume II of the same work, he listed it as *Camellia*. The question concerning tea that has caused confusion in the botanical world since then is twofold; (1) whether there are two distinct genera, *Camellia* and *Thea*, and (2) whether or not in joining *Camellia* and *Thea* the resulting genus should be *Thea*.

It seems well established that the diagnosis of the tea plant by Linnaeus was based on insufficient material, and, as later botanists became acquainted with additional related species, some of them became convinced that the separation of the genera *Thea* and *Camellia* could not be upheld. Thus, the question arose as to which name the united genus should bear.

Robert Sweet, F. L. S., 1783-1835, famous English botanist, was one of the first to unite the two under the genus *Camellia*, which he did in 1818.[1] Heinrich Frederick Link, 1767-1851, German naturalist and physician, did the same in 1822.[2] However, according to the International Rules, Article 46, when two or more groups of the same nature are united, the name of the oldest is retained. In the case of *Thea* and *Camellia*, Volume I of *Species Plantarum* was published in May, 1753; while Volume II did not appear till August of the same year. Thus, *Thea* antedates *Camellia*, and in the case of a union of the two, the genus should be *Thea*. Therefore, if one is to follow the International Rules, the genus of the tea plant undoubtedly is *Thea*. If *Camellia* and *Thea* are to be considered as separate and distinct genera, the tea plant is still of the genus *Thea*.

There are botanists who hold that *Camellia* and *Thea* cannot be considered sep-

---

[1] Robert Sweet, *Hortus suburbanus Londonensis*, London, 1818.
[2] Heinrich Frederick Link, *Enumeratio plantarum hortiregii botanici Berolinensis*, Berlin, 1822, vol. ii.

arate genera, and who reduce *Thea* to a species name. Notable among these are Sir George Watt, M.B., C.M., F.L.S., C.I.E., the well-known authority on economic plants;[3] and S. E. Chandler, D.Sc., F.L.S.,[4] both of whom designate the tea plant as *Camellia thea* Link.

However, of late years, the majority of botanists have adopted the first name that Linnaeus gave the tea plant; *i.e.*, *Thea sinensis* Linn. Of course, *Thea sinensis* hardly is geographically correct. Linnaeus, himself, in the second edition [1762] of the *Species Plantarum*, discarded the name *T. sinensis*, and identified a specimen with six petals under the name of *T. bohea*, and another with nine petals as *T. viridis*; thus, rather arbitrarily following the treatise on black and green tea by John Hill, 1716–1775, that curious English miscellaneous writer, who, styling himself "Sir" John Hill, was, in the course of his picturesque career, an actor, an author, an apothecary, a gardener, and a botanist.[5]

It is interesting to note how some modern botanists view the question. Dr. C. P. Cohen Stuart, former botanist at the Algemeen Proefstation voor Thee, Buitenzorg, and author of many botanical treatises, says:

> The latest name that has been adopted for the tea plant coincides with the first name that Linnaeus, the famous Swedish botanist, assigned to it in 1753, viz., *Thea sinensis* Linn. Since that time, the genus *Thea* has come to include the Linnaean genus *Camellia*, which is chiefly known for its greenhouse representative "Camellia," now *Thea japonica*, with its big white or red flowers. Scientists have recognized the close affinity of both genera, as more of their representatives were discovered. While, however, the scientific name *Thea sinensis* has maintained itself until now, it no longer stands for the Chinese tea plant alone, as it did in Linnaeus' days. In 1823, the Assam tea plant was discovered in jungles of the Brahmaputra Valley, and the scientific world was confronted with the puzzle whether it should be classed with the Chinese bush or be considered as a distinct variety of *Thea sinensis*, or even as a distinct species. Under the impression of the remarkable differences between both forms, the majority of botanists felt strongly inclined to adopt the latter view, and distinguished the Assam plant by the name of *Thea assamica*. Although the alternative-species, or variety, is largely a matter of taste, now that we have

learned to consider Assam and China tea as perfectly equivalent and tea-yielding plants, it would seem the time has come to pull down the ancient barrier raised by prejudice, and to restore species *Thea sinensis* of Linnaeus to its former position. It must then comprise both China and Assam tea, as well as any variety, form, or grade of tea plant that we know.[6]

The late Charles Sprague Sargent, A.B., LL.D., foreign member of the Linnaean Society of London, Director of the Arnold Arboretum and Professor of Arboriculture at Harvard, favored the name *Thea sinensis*.

Alfred Barton Rendle, F.R.S., F.L.S., Keeper of the Department of Botany of the British Museum, prefers *Thea sinensis*.

Benjamin L. Robinson, A.B., Ph.D., Curator of the Gray Herbarium, and Asa Gray, Professor of Systematic Botany at Harvard, agree with other leading present-day authorities who generally are taking *Thea sinensis* as the valid name for the species to which the tea plants belong. While the genus *Thea* is undoubtedly very close to the genus *Camellia*, and the two have often been united by those who have taken a somewhat broader view of the generic classification, this is a matter of judgment, and Dr. Robinson thinks the weight of authority is distinctly in favor of recognizing the genus *Thea* as separable from *Camellia*, and, if it is so regarded, there can be no question about the correctness of the name *Thea sinensis*.

Dr. Alfred Gunderson, of the Brooklyn Botanic Garden, Brooklyn, N. Y., says: "As the flowers of the tea plant differ from those of the ornamental *Camellias* in several characteristics, it is now usually, with related species, considered a genus separate from, though closely related to, *Camellia*. The accepted name then is *Thea sinensis*, as in the *Species Plantarum* of Linnaeus."

The Royal Botanic Gardens at Kew, London, hold: "The effective publication of the generic name *Thea* L. dates from Linnaeus' *Species Plantarum*, page 515 [May, 1753], whereas, *Camellia* L. was published in *Species Plantarum*, page 698 [August, 1753]. The tea plant should be called *Thea sinensis* L. as this was the first name given to the species."

---

[3] Sir George Watt, *Commercial Products of India*, New York, 1908.
[4] *Bulletin of the Imperial Institute*, London, 1913, vol. ii,
[5] John Hill, *Exotic Botany*, London, 1759.

[6] In a letter to the author, April, 1926.

CLOSE-UP OF AN ASSAM INDIGENOUS TEA BUSH

However, as J. Sims, in his *"Thea chinensis*, var. *B. Bohea* tea-tree" [*Curtis's Botanical Magazine*, volume xxv, 1807], was the first botanist to join *bohea* with *viridis*, *cantoniensis*, etc., under the common name of *Thea sinensis*, the complete name for the tea plant is *Thea sinensis* [L.] Sims.

To recapitulate, then, the botanical classification of the tea plant is as follows:

Division .... *Angiospermae*
Class .... *Dicotyledones*
Order .... *Parietales*
Family .... *Theaceae*
Genus .... *Thea*
Species .... *sinensis*

General Characteristics

The tea plant is a tree or shrub, sometimes reaching a height of thirty feet. The leaves are alternate and evergreen, ellipticlanceolate or obovate-lanceolate, acuminate, serrate, glabrous, sometimes pubescent beneath. In their adult stage, they are dark green, leathery, and smooth; ranging from one to twelve inches in length. The young shoots are more or less pubescent, with thin pointed buds [Pekoe].

The flower buds originate singly or in clusters from side buds springing from the leaf axils. They are globular and pendulous, as are the flowers. The latter are white and fragrant, about one inch in diameter; with five to seven leathery, permanent sepals and five to seven petals, which form one ring; with very numerous stamens; and are dropped as a whole. The anthers are two-celled. The ovary is hairy, three or four celled; the style is glabrous, with three or four long stigmas. The cells of the cotyledons of tea contain a large amount of oily and other matter, and act as reservoirs of nutriment for the use of the embryo during the process of germination.

The fruit is glabrous, brownish green, and about one inch in diameter. It is one to four lobed, depending on whether seeds have developed in one or more cells, and there are one to three seeds in each cell. The outer surface usually is smooth, but marked with furrows that show the point of union of the constituent ovaries. The seed is dark brown, one-half inch in diameter, spherical or flattened, and smooth. In the seed the two large, oily lobes are the cotyledons, and, when separated, the plumule and radicle can be easily distinguished, especially during the process of germination. The pericarp of the fruit, before the ripening of the seed, is hard in texture and green in color, but when ripe, it assumes a dark brown color.

CHINA TEA, VAR. BOHEA, DRAWN FROM NATURE

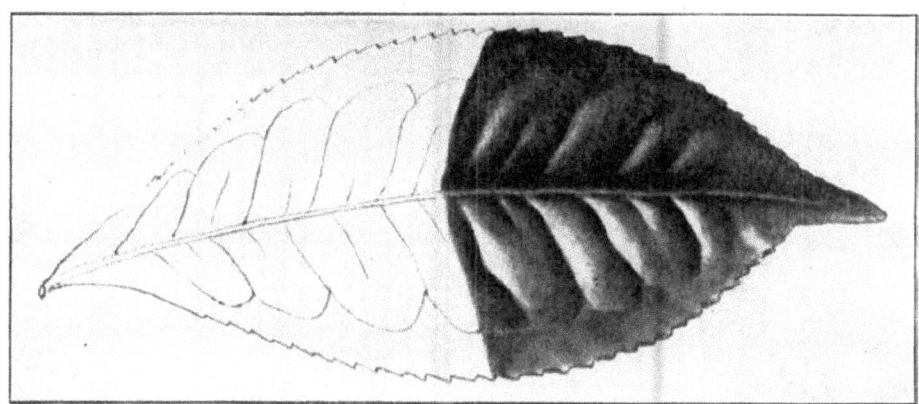

DRAWING OF AN INDIAN TEA LEAF, NATURAL SIZE

From a color sketch by Mr. Gerald Atkinson, botanic artist, Jodrell Laboratory, Royal Botanic Gardens, Kew. This is a Cossipore jat.

Varieties and Races of the Tea Plant

Differences of opinion exist as to the correct varietal division of *Thea sinensis*. The varieties are inclined to intergrade, and are separated only by minor traits, which have, in botanical classification, little diagnostic value. In the case of any widely cultivated plant, it is usual for the growers to recognize many strains differing slightly in their qualities, and, for commercial reasons, well worthy of distinction, which, however, are not capable of botanical definition; that is, they do not possess sufficiently constant characteristics to permit their separation with scientific exactness. These varieties, which are developed by selection in cultivated plants, are often given distinguishing names.

Watt names four principal varieties of the tea plant; i.e., var. *viridis*, var. *bohea*, var. *stricta*, and var. *lasiocalyx*. Under var. *viridis* he places the six races—(1) Assam indigenous, (2) Lushai, (3) Naga Hills, (4) Manipur, (5) Burma and Shan, (6) Yunnan and China. Variety *stricta* is a small bush which, according to Watt, may be seen in Indian seed gardens, flowering and fruiting freely. The leaves are thick and leathery, from $1\frac{1}{16}$ to $2\frac{1}{2}$ inches long, and vary from $\frac{1}{16}$ to $\frac{3}{4}$ of an inch in breadth. It seldom has more than eight definite nerves. Variety *lasiocalyx*, according to the same authority, is perhaps the most tropical of all the forms of *Thea* cultivated for tea. It is a Singapore or Penang plant.[7]

Cohen Stuart substitutes for the classification of Watt a system of four, or even more, groups, of which the extremes, the typical Assam bush and its China-kin, he designates by the names var. *assamica* and var. *bohea;* the latter a name used by Linnaeus, and derived from the Wu-yi, or Bohea, Mountain Range in Eastern China, which was famous for its black tea. He

[7] Sir George Watt, *Commercial Products of India*, New York, 1908.

ASSAM TEA LEAVES, FLOWER, AND SEED POD
Drawn from nature.

NORWOOD JAT CEYLON TEA, FROM A MANIPUR JAT

also adds var. *macrophylla*, found in the southern and western parts of China, and the indigenous "Shan-type," of Siam and Burma.[8]

Dr. C. R. Harler, former chemist, Tea Experimental Station, Tocklai, Assam, after a study of the recent work of Cohen Stuart, names four varieties of *sinensis*—var. *bohea;* var. *macrophylla;* var. *shan* form; var. *assamica*. Variety *bohea* [China tea], a small stunted bush, densely branched, with small [under three inches] rigid leaves, which possess ten to fourteen pairs of rather inconspicuous veins and hardly any acumen. The leaf buds often are purple. The bush flowers profusely. Variety *macrophylla* is "Chinese" in appearance, but larger in growth [about fifteen feet], and leaf size [up to six inches]. The leaves have eight or nine pairs of veins and hardly any acumen. The "Shan-type," for which a Latin name is not yet proposed, is clearly related to "Assam." The trees are fifteen to thirty feet high. The leaves have about ten pairs of veins, and are acuminate. They are smaller, thicker, more acutely serrated, and distinctly more elliptic in shape than other teas. Variety *assamica* [Assam indigenous] is a tree reaching up to thirty

[8] In a letter to the author, April, 1926.

feet in its wild state, sparsely branched, with big [six to twelve inches] accuminate leaves, having ten to sixteen pairs of lateral veins, so prominent as to form distinct hollows on the under side of the leaves. The flowers are sparse and solitary.

Other botanists recognize as important the variety *cantonensis* Lour. This, according to João de Loureiro, 1715-1796, the Portuguese botanist, is a bush four feet high, and densely branched. The leaves are lanceolate, sharply serrated, glabrous, rather thick, and very short. The flowers are solitary, and the fruit three-celled and three-lobed.[9]

Races

As before mentioned, Watt gives six races under var. *viridis*. The first of these, Assam indigenous, has been dealt with as a variety. He describes the others as follows:

RACE NO. 2. "LUSHAI."—This becomes a poplar-like, small tree of perhaps fifty to sixty feet in height. Leaves, when full-grown, average from eight to fourteen inches in length, and as much as four to six inches in breadth. It is the largest-leaved form of the tea plant as yet made known; far larger than anything recorded regarding the tea plants of China. The leaves possess from twenty-two to twenty-four prominent veins, but in texture and surface markings are identical with the Assam indigenous. This form has only to a small extent been grown in Sylhet and Chittagong, and it exists almost entirely as a local manifestation of the wild plant.

RACE NO. 3. "NAGA HILLS."—This is a small, straggling tree, with few ascending branches.

[9] *Flora Cochinchinensis*, Lisbon, 1790.

JAPAN TEA PLANT, THEA SINENSIS

INDIA TEA AND MATÉ COMPARED

1—Specimen of India tea.　2—The Paraguay tea
or maté.

It is specially plentiful near Pherima at an altitude of 2000 feet. Leaves much elongated, linear, oblong, from four to nine inches in length, and only two to three in breadth at their greatest diameter. In texture, etc., it much resembles the Assam. It has, to some extent, been cultivated in Assam, as, for example, at Amguri, and it is reported to have been specially used in crossing with the Assam indigenous.

RACE No. 4. "MANIPUR."—The wild tea plant of Manipur is never cultivated in the State of Manipur; it is there purely and simply a wild plant, found in the forests. When carried to Cachar, Sylhet, and even Assam, however, the Manipur stock has been fairly largely grown and even crossed with some of the other stocks. It is characterized by exceptionally broad leaves, almost elliptic, oblong in shape, and measuring six to eight inches in length, and two and a half to three and a half inches in breadth. In texture, the leaves are soft and leathery, are of a dark green color, and have the reticulations sparse and open. This is, in fact, one of the broadest-leaved forms of Indian indigenous races, and has probably contributed largely toward the formation of the specially dark green plants seen in many plantations, but which are regarded as being Assam indigenous tea.

RACE No. 5. "BURMA AND SHAN."—Too little is known regarding these tea plants to allow of critical separation from the other races; the present position is, therefore, only preserved to allow of more careful elaboration in the future. They constitute a series that blend into the Manipur stock on the one hand; into that of Yunnan on the other. The leaves are smaller, thicker, coarser, more acutely serrated, and much less smooth than the Manipur, but distinctly elliptic in shape. The Formosan leaf, recently brought into notice in connection with the inquiry into Oolong tea, is a little more oblong than the Burma and Shan leaf, but otherwise is very similar. I have not seen, however, more than a few separated leaves of the Oolong plant, and cannot be certain regarding its identity. So far as I can judge, it stands every chance of proving a distinct and well-marked race, fully worthy of separate recognition.

RACE No. 6. "YUNNAN AND CHINESE."—Too little is known of races of the tea plant in China to allow of a classification being furnished similar to that given for India. . . . In most herbaria the plant is fairly well represented from China, but by no means exhaustively so, until in very recent times—more especially through Dr. Henry's collections. Dr. Henry had studied the tea plant of the forests of Yunnan, and his specimens have been widely distributed in herbaria. He tells me that it is a small, sparsely-branched tree, met with under the dense shade of forests—precisely the condition of the Indian truly wild forms.[10]

Other botanists have classified these races otherwise, identifying them with different varieties. On the other hand, an almost infinite number of other varieties, races, and subraces have been "discovered."

Tea Surrogates

Besides the leaves of the tea shrub, the flowers are sometimes dried and a beverage made from them in the same way in which the leaves are brewed. Tea flowers may be said to represent a surrogate for tea.

Perhaps the most important surrogate is maté, also known as yerba maté, Paraguay tea, or Brazilian tea. It is made from the dried leaves of *Ilex paraguayensis*, a shrub belonging to the family of *Aquifoliaceae*. The leaves are from six to eight inches long, shortly stalked, with a somewhat acute tip, and finely toothed at the margin. The small, white flowers grow in forked clusters in the axils of the leaves; the sepals, petals, and stamens, are four to five in number. The berry has four seeds. *Ilex paraguayensis* grows abundantly in Paraguay and Southern Brazil. The harvesting of maté is done prin-

10 Sir George Watt, "Tea and the Tea Plant," *Journal Royal Horticultural Society*, vol. xxxii, 1907.

cipally by Indians, who climb the trees and cut off the leafy branches with knives. The branches are bundled together, and pulled through an open fire, so that the leaves are withered, but not scorched. After this treatment, the faggots are taken to the factory for the final drying, which takes from fourteen to sixteen hours. The next step is to pound the leaves into a coarse powder, after which the powder is packed into bags for market. Occasionally, the drying is done in iron pans over brick ovens, in much the same way that tea is dried in China.

In Paraguay and the Argentine, the leaves are stripped off the mid-rib before roasting. This is called *caa-miri*, or *caa-mirien*. Maté prepared from the larger, older leaves, together with sprigs and small stems, is used chiefly in Brazil; and is called *caa-guacu*, *caa-gazu*, or *yerva do polos*. A superior quality is made from the very young leaflet not yet opened out, and is of a reddish color. This is called *caa-cuy* or *caa-cuyo*.

Maté seems to have been used from time immemorial by the Indians, although the Jesuits were the first to attempt its cultivation. The word *maté* comes from the language of the Incas, and originally meant a calabash. *Caa* is the native Indian word for the plant, while the Spaniards called it *Yerba*.

Maté is made in a small silver-mounted calabash about the size of a large orange, the top being open. Sugar and a little hot water are first placed in the gourd, the maté is added, and finally the vessel is filled to the brim with boiling water or heated milk. A little burnt sugar or lemon juice sometimes is added in place of milk.

The beverage is drunk by means of a small tube, six to seven inches long, formed either of metal or of reed. It has at one end a bulb of extremely fine basket-work or of metal, perforated with minute holes. The maté is sucked up through the tube, which is called a *bombilla*. In family circles, the gourd and the bombilla are passed from hand to hand. Maté also may be brewed as tea and drunk from cups.

A beverage called "cassina" is made from the cured leaves of a caffeine-containing species of holly, *Ilex cassine*, indigenous to North America. The Bureau of Chemistry of the United States Department of Agriculture has developed a proc-

ess of curing the leaves. The product is made into green cassina, black cassina, and cassina maté; the last resembling very closely yerba maté.

The list of tea substitutes is well nigh endless. Most countries have their peculiar "teas," and the exigencies of the World War caused numerous ancient formulae to be raked up and new ones added.

One of the most important substitutes is faham, fa-am, or Bourbon tea. This consists of the dried leaves of a species of orchid, *Angraecum fragrans*. It is indigenous to Africa, but especially to Madagascar, Reunion, Bourbon, and Mauritius. It was first believed that the plant possessed a vanillic odor. This was later found by Cabley to be due to the cumarine content. The orchid has a few narrow-shaped leaves and white fragrant flowers. "Tea" is made from the dried leaves. The natives of Reunion, and Mauritius, have been drinking it since time immemorial.[11]

Kaporie, koporka, or iwan tea, consists of a mixture of leaves of the *Epilobium angustifolium*, the narrow-leaved fire weed; *Filipendula ulmaria*, the meadow-sweet, or "Queen of the Meadow"; young foliage of the *Sorbus aucuparia*, the rowan-berry; and the leaves of re-colored, used tea. The dried leaves of this mixture are allowed to swell up in hot water. Then, they are mixed with humus by rubbing, and, with a weak solution of sugar, are dried and perfumed.

South Sea tea is made from the leaves of *ilex vomitoria*, a shrub or small evergreen tree of the holly family, *Aquifoliaceae*. It is a native of the southern part of the United States.

New Jersey tea, *Ceanothus americanus*, is a shrub of the buckthorn family, *Rhamnaceae*, also known as North American tea.

Mountain tea, also known as Canada, red, and Newfoundland tea, is made from *Gaultheria procumbens*, a low, trailing evergreen of the heath family, *Ericaceae*, a native of Canada, and Northern United States. It is sometimes called the checkerberry or teaberry.

Bohemian, or Croatian, tea consists of *Lithospermum officinale*, stone-seed. This plant is cultivated under the name of *Thea sinensis*, and green, as well as black, "tea"

11 *Journal de Pharmacie et de Chimie*, 3, xviii.

is manufactured therefrom. This plant also is used as an adulterant of real tea.

Labrador tea is the common name for *Ledum palustre*, an erect small-leaved, bushy shrub of the heath family. It is a native of Northern United States, and of Canada and Labrador.

Oswego, or Pennsylvania, tea is made from *Monarda didyma*, a perennial of the mint family, *Labiatae*. It is a native of Canada and Northern United States, and is used as a tonic and a stomachic.

Bergthee, or mountain tea, from the Harz Mountains of Germany, consists of flowers of the yarrow, blackthorn, lavender, colt's-foot, and peppermint. Sassafras, root bark, and the roots of licorice, are added to it.

Winterberry tea is from *Ilex glabra*, an evergreen, smooth-leaved, bushy shrub of the holly family. It is a native of Northern United States and Canada, and is commonly called inkberry.

Benkoelen, or Malayan, tea, used in Sumatra, is from a shrub, *Leptospermum* [alaphyria] *nitida*, of the myrtle family, *Myrtaceae*. It is a native of the Malayan Islands. Several other species of the myrtle family, especially of the genera *Leptospermum*, and *Melaleuca*, are known in Australia and New Zealand as "tea shrubs."

Mexican, or Jesuit, tea, *Chenopodium ambrosioides*, is a perennial of the Chenopodiaceae family, a native of Mexico, but long naturalized in Southern Europe. It often is known as goosefoot, or pigweed.

Botany Bay tea, *Smilax glycyphylla*, sometimes called sweet, or Australian, tea, is an Australian species of the smilax family, *Smilaceae*. It is an evergreen shrubby climber.

Bush, or cape, tea is made from the leaves of *Cyclopia genistoides*, and other allied species.

Brazilian tea, *Stachytarpheta jamaicensis*, is a tall, single-stemmed biennial, with spikes of blue flowers, of the verbena family, *Verbenaceae*. It is a native of the West Indies and tropical America.

West Indian tea is made from the leaves of a shrub, *Capraria biflora*, of the figwort family, *Scrophularaceae*. It is said to be a native of North America, but has become naturalized in the West Indies. It is known also as goatweed.

Abyssinian tea, sometimes c a l l e d

Arabian tea, is made from the leaves of the *Catha edulis*, and it is used in Arabia.

Algerian tea is a species of *Paronychia*, from whose flowers a medicinal "tea" is made.

Barbary tea is the box-thorn, or Duke of Argyll's tea tree, *Lycium barbarum*.

Blue Mountain tea is made from the leaves and flowers of the *Solidago odora* of North America. It also is called golden rod tea.

Teamster's tea is a North American plant, *Ephedra antisyphilitica*, and is used as a remedy for venereal affections.

Theezan tea, *Sageretia theezans*, is a thorny rhamnaceous shrub of South China, whose leaves are said to be used by the poorer classes for tea.

Chamomile, or camomile, tea is made from an herb indigenous to England and Western Europe, *Anthemis nobilis*. The drink is made from the flowers, and has a slightly bitter taste. The plant is cultivated in England, France, and Belgium.

European tea is made from the flowerheads of the *Veronica officinalis*. It has a very aromatic, bitter taste.

French, or Greek, tea comes from the *Salvia officinalis*, a sage of Southern France. It has a strong, aromatic odor, and a pronounced taste.

There are many other substitutes for tea, of which some of the more important are:

Lemon grass, used by the natives of India; coffee leaves when roasted, used in Sumatra; *Printyia aromatica*, used at the Cape of Good Hope; a plant of the rose order, *fragaria*, used by natives in China; *Acoena sanguisorba*, used in New Holland; a form of hydrangea, used by the Japanese; *Laoten*, used by the Siamese; *Eupatorium*, used in Central Africa and Ceylon; *Catha eduus*, used in Arabia and Abyssinia; the cowslip, formerly used in England; mullein, still used in Germany and other European countries; a leguminous plant, in Chile; *Tulasi* plant, used by the natives of India; a species of heath, used to make Salvador tea; plants of the myrtle tribe, used in Australia, Tasmania, and Falkland; *Glaphyria nitida*, used in Malay; Canary tea, or *Sida canariensis*; Appalachian tea, the leaves of *Viburnum casinoides*, *Ilex vomitoria*, or *I. glabra*; Carolina tea made from *Ilex cassine*; Hottentot's tea, *Helichrysum serpyllifolium*; Kaffir tea, *Helichrysum nudifolium*; marsh tea, *Ledum palustre*; St. Helena tea, *Frankenia portulacifolia*; peppermint; lemon verbena; balm; thyme; Angelica tea; broom; clover; ivy; rue; sage; Cordova tea; silverwood; southernwood; yarrow; insomnia tea; primrose; lime; orange buds; flowers of the bass-wood tree and dried leaves; orchid-roots; sassafras; sage; mint;

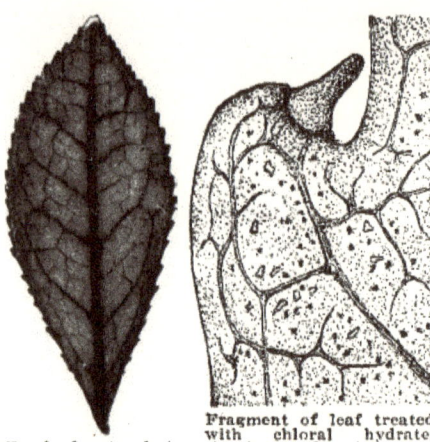

Tea leaf, natural size. (Moeller.)

Fragment of leaf treated with chloral hydrate, showing tooth, veins, crystal rosettes, and stone cells. Somewhat enlarged. (Schimper.)

catnip; Liberty tea, or leaves of the four-leaved loose-strife; Hyperion tea, or raspberry leaves; boneset tea, or thoroughwort; ribwort; strawberry leaves; black currant leaves; organ tea, or marjoram; pennyroyal; nettle tea, or mugwort; sloe-leaves; cowslip tea; senna tea; and Arabian tea, or *Catha edulis*.

Adulterants

The most common adulteration consists of the addition of leaves of other plants. Leaves which, by their nature, have an astringent taste and a toothed border are

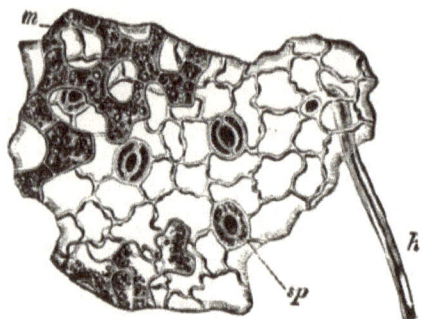

The lower epidermis showing *h* hair and *sp* stoma, and *m* spongy parenchyma of mesophyl, seen from below. X 160. (Moeller.)

most commonly used. Some of these are the leaves of the beech [*Fagus sylvatica*], hawthorn [*Crataegus oxyacantha*], Camellia sassanqua, sloe [*Prunus spinosa*], and the *Chloranthus inconspicuus*. How-

ever, trusting to the indifference of the consumer, leaves of the oak, poplar, maple, and other trees, which bear not the slightest resemblance to tea, also have been employed.

Another formerly widespread adulteration was the addition of extracted tea leaves. The leaves were collected from restaurants, hotels, etc., and dried. Then they were mixed with real tea. Sometimes, no fresh tea was added, but the spent leaves were impregnated with catechu, caramel, campeachy wood, indigo, Berlin-

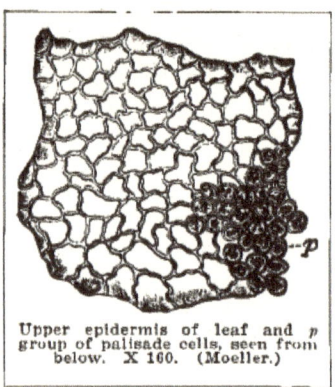

Upper epidermis of leaf and *p* group of palisade cells, seen from below. X 160. (Moeller.)

blue, curcuma, humus, graphite, etc. The so-called "Thé de caravane," "Spar-tea," and "Königs-tea," are said to have been made in this way. A so-called "Caucausian tea" is a mixture of extracted tea leaves and leaves of the *Vaccinium arctostaphylos*. This sort of adulteration defies microscopic detection, but often can be discovered by chemical means; particularly determinations of hot-water extract, tannin, and total and water-soluble ash.

Numerous adulterants have been used to "load" tea to increase its weight. Among these are clay, gypsum, iron-filings, sand, etc. Chemical analysis will quickly reveal these.

Formerly, much tea was "faced" to improve its appearance. In the case of green tea, talc, Prussian blue, ultramarine, indigo, turmeric, soapstone, and gypsum were used. Black tea frequently was coated with plumbago. Leach gives the following microchemical tests for the detection of facing:

The most delicate test for facing is to examine, under the microscope or lens, the dust obtained by sifting the leaves or the sediment obtained after shaking with water. Plumbago appears glossy black; soapstone, gray; gypsum, white; Prussian blue, ultramarine; indigo, shades of blue; and turmeric, yellow. Prussian blue is decolorized by sodium hydroxide solution. Ultramarine is not affected by alkali, but is decolorized by hydrochloric acid. Indigo is not decolorized by either reagent.[12]

In the United States, where colored teas are barred, the simple, mechanical Read test is used to disclose coloring matter. The late Miss Alberta Read, employed in the United States Bureau of Chemistry, discovered that, by simply shaking the dust from tea on white paper and mashing it with an ordinary chemist's spatula, any coloring matter, whether Prussian blue, indigo, or ultramarine blue, would be streaked on the paper; and that when the same test was applied on black paper, any facing material, such as talc or barium sulphate, could be immediately detected. This test has the advantage of being so simple that any tea importer or buyer may perform it in his own office.

Dr. J. J. B. Deuss, former Director of the Tea Experimental Station at Buitenzorg, Java, gives the following as the analytical requirements of genuine tea:

1. Tea may, when microscopically examined, not show traces of exotic leaves.
2. The percentage of water in tea should vary between 8 and 12 per cent. The figures

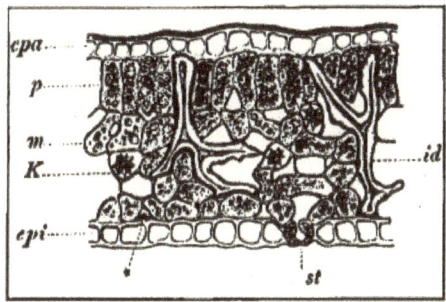

Cross-section of the tea leaf. *epa* upper, *epi* lower epidermis, *st* a slit opening, *p* palisade layer, *m* mesophyl with crystal glands K, *id* idioblast, * cross-section of an idioblast.

are, in fact, the limits for the water-percentage of pure tea in Europe.
3. Tea may contain, at the most, 8 per cent of mineral components, but not less than three

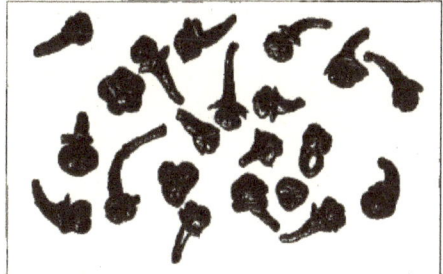

Tea fruit. Natural size. (Winton.)

per cent. Much kitchen salt or ashes may point to damage, as also lead.
4. Green tea contains at least 20 per cent of watery extract; black tea at least 24 per cent. A good tea possesses from 30 per cent to 40 per cent total watery extract. In a cup there is less; what is given above applies to the watery extract obtained after thorough extracting.
5. The percentage of caffeine must be at least 1 per cent and the percentage of tannin at least 10 per cent for green and 7.5 per cent for black teas.
6. Tea may not show traces of strange coloring matter.
7. If the tea contains lead, it should be rejected as a drink, and it may only be considered for the manufacture of caffeine.[13]

Microscopical Structure

Microscopic mounts of tea are prepared in several ways according to the part of the leaf one wishes to examine. In preparing the mounts the method most commonly used is to soak the leaves in boiling water, and then to place one of them in a solution of two parts of chloral hydrate and one part of water.

Examining the epidermis on the under surface, peculiar hairy growths are found. These are highly characteristic of tea. They are more abundant on the young leaves than the old; often forming a dense pubescence. They frequently attain a length of 500 to 700 μ. They are bent at right angles near the base, so that they lie almost flat on the surface of the leaf. They are thickly walled, and made up of one long cell. Sometimes, they are surrounded at the point of insertion by radially arranged epidermal cells.

The cells of the epidermis of the under

[12] Albert E. Leach, *Food Inspection and Analysis*, New York, 1914.

[13] Dr. J. J. B. Deuss, *Overdruk uit het Nederlandsch, Indisch Rubber en Thee Tijdschrift*, 8e jaargang, nommer 1, 15 Maart, 1923.

surface may be best examined if they are soaked in chloral hydrate, then in glycerin, and finally transferred to water. The contour of the cells is wavy, becoming more so in older leaves. Among them are numerous stomata. These are broadly oval, and are surrounded by three or four accompanying cells, which are narrow and tangentially arranged. The stomata exhibit a narrow ostiole. They, too, are

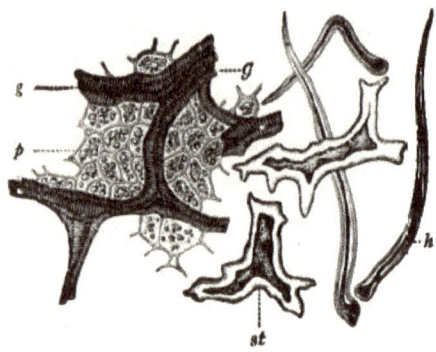

Tissues of leaf isolated by warming in alkali and squeezing with cover glass; *g*, spiral vessels of nerves; *p*, chlorophyl parenchyma; *st*, stone cells; *h*, hairs. X 160. (Moeller.)

characteristic of tea. The epidermis of the upper surface consists of small, delicate, polygonal cells, with no stomata.

The margin of the leaf is toothed. Each tooth is a conical mass of parenchymatous cells, covered with a layer of glandular cells, which, according to Cohen Stuart, produce a mucilaginous substance in the buds. When a tooth falls off, it leaves a brown scar in the old leaves. A veinlet runs up to this scar.[14]

Taking a transverse section of the leaf, below the upper epidermis are found the palisade parenchyma, sometimes consisting of the two strata. The palisade cells are circular in outline when in surface view. Below the epidermis of the under surface is the spongy parenchyma, which exhibits large air spaces. In the center of the leaf there are numerous cells containing a crystal substance [calcium oxalate].

The most characteristic feature of the tea leaf is found in the mesophyl. It is the large, colorless, peculiarly shaped sclerenchyma, or stone cells [idioblasts].

[14] C. P. Cohen Stuart, *Handelingen van het Eerste Ned. Ind. Natuurwetenschappelijk Congres,* Buitenzorg, 1919, p. 139.

They increase as the leaf matures. They are sometimes star-shaped, sometimes branched, almost always with deeply wrinkled sides. They support the upper and the lower epidermis. Albert E. Leach, S.B., and A. L. Winton, Ph.D., well-known American writers on the subject of food analysis, say: "They may be seen to best advantage in a section of the stem, or mid-rib, made parallel to the surface of the leaf. To make such a section, soak the leaf, first in water, and afterwards in alcohol."[15] Henry C. Greenish, F.I.C., F.L.S., Professor of Pharmaceutics to the Pharmaceutical Society of Great Britain, and in the University of London, finds that they can be made conspicuous by staining with phloroglucin and hydrochloric acid, as their walls are strongly lignified. The interior of the leaf is composed chiefly of ground tissue, having rounded cells full of chlorophyl grains and the fibro-vascular bundles of the veins. Greenish also gives the following diagnostic characteristics of the tea leaf:

(a) The hairs, their shape and size, together with the radiate arrangement of the cells at the base.

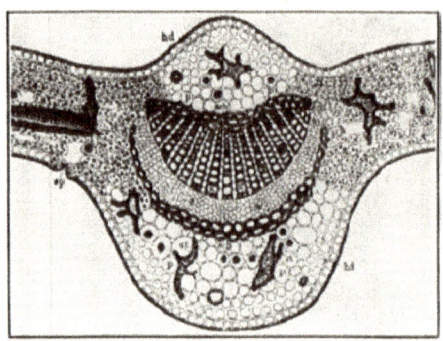

Transverse section through the midrib—*hd* hypoderma, *g* vessels in wood, *p* parenchyma, *s* sieve tissue, *sch* sclerenchymatous fibres, *sp* stoma, *st* sclerenchymatous idioblasts. X 130. (Warnecke.)

(b) The crystals of calcium oxalate; they are cluster crystals, and are often accompanied by crystal sand.

(c) The sclerenchymatous idioblasts, especially those of the petiole and mid-rib; they are never entirely absent.

(d) The stomata.

(e) The teeth at the margin, or the scars left by them.[16]

[15] Albert E. Leach, S.B., and Andrew L. Winton, Ph.D., *Food Inspection and Analysis,* 4th ed., 1920.
[16] Henry C. Greenish, F.I.C., F.L.S., *The Microscopical Examination of Foods and Drugs,* 3rd ed., 1923.

CHAPTER XXV

THE CHEMISTRY OF TEA

NATURE OF THE DISCUSSION—ANALYSIS OF FINISHED TEA—CONSTITUENTS OF THE TEA
LEAF—TEA TANNIN—VARIATION IN TANNIN CONTENT—CAFFEINE—THE ESSENTIAL OIL
OF TEA—OTHER CONSTITUENTS OF THE TEA LEAF—TEA SEED OIL—"FERMENTATION"
IN TEA MANUFACTURE—ENZYMES, BACTERIA, AND YEASTS—CHEMICAL CHANGES IN THE
LEAF DURING MANUFACTURE—THE WITHERING, ROLLING, FERMENTATION, AND FIRING
OF BLACK TEA—MOISTURE CONTENT AND POST-FERMENTATION—PREPARATION OF CHINA
BLACK, OOLONGS, AND GREEN TEAS—RESUMÉ

BY C. R. HARLER, PH. D., B.Sc., F.I.C., F.R. MET. Soc.

Former Chemist, Tocklai Experimental Station, Indian Tea Association, Assam, India

BEFORE attempting to give some account of the chemistry of tea, it is necessary to outline the nature of the subject under discussion, and to indicate the general trend of scientific research on tea problems.

The earliest work on the subject consisted of simple analyses of the finished tea of commerce. Later on these analyses were repeated on fresh leaf in tea growing countries.

About 1890, the study of the changes which take place in the tea leaf during manufacture was begun, and, during the following twenty years or so, the general chemistry outline of the process was formulated. Since that time, information has accumulated steadily, which, from time to time, has led to modifications of the earlier ideas on the subject.

The study of the enzymes, bacteria, and yeasts concerned in the manufacture of black tea was taken up scientifically at the beginning of the present century.

Our knowledge of the chemistry of tea is still most incomplete and vague. This follows from the nature of the subject, and from the present state of knowledge regarding most bio-chemical problems. In addition to this, however, chemists working on tea in Java, India, and Ceylon have suffered from the disadvantage of isolation from western scientific centers.

Accordingly, the results achieved have not been outstanding from a purely scientific viewpoint, and have usually consisted of the application to tea problems of hypotheses and methods worked out in connection with similar problems in the West. In most cases the need for results of a practical, commercial value has influenced the course of research, which has seldom been of an entirely academic nature.

In the account which follows, some attempt has been made to outline the development of our present ideas on the chemistry of tea, and, for this reason, the work and conclusions of the earlier chemists are described. After discussing the chief constituents of tea and the enzymes and micro-organisms connected with the leaf, a brief description of the chemical changes taking place during manufacture, as far as they are known, also is given.

Analysis of Finished Tea

Throughout this chapter an attempt has been made to render as much of it as possible intelligible to the reader with no special chemical knowledge. On this account many definitions and detailed descriptions are given. Most of these, however, only go to illustrate certain lines of argument or reasoning, and are not intended to satisfy the specialist.

Perhaps it would be more logical to consider first the analysis of fresh leaf, and then that of finished tea, than to consider these subjects in reverse order as we have done; however it has been thought more desirable, for historical reasons, to deal first of all with the analysis of the manufactured teas of commerce.

EARLY STUDIES.—Mulder,[1] Peligot,[2] and Rochleder[3] carried out some of the earliest chemical work on tea between 1840 and 1850. The first two workers made analyses of the product, according to the chemical standards of their time. Rochleder studied the tannin found in tea, and also isolated what he termed boheic acid, so called after *Thea bohea*, the plant designated at that time as the source of supply of China black tea. Hlasiwetz and Malin[4] in 1861 detected gallic acid in tea, and later claimed to have found quercetin in China tea. Hlasiwetz demonstrated that the so-called boheic acid was a mixture of gallic acid, oxalic acid, tannin, and quercitrin.

During 1860 and the years following, many analyses of tea were made which increased in detail as the knowledge of chemistry expanded. By 1880, fairly full analyses were available.

A paper by Blyth, published in 1879,[5] names the constituents of tea as essential oil, thein [now called caffeine], boheic acid, quercetin, tannin, quercitrinic acid, gallic acid, oxalic acid, gum, chlorophyll, resin, wax, albuminous, woody and coloring matter, and ash. Several analyses made on black teas of Russian commerce by Dragendorff are quoted, showing the percentage of water soluble substances, caffeine, nitrogen, tannin, potash, and phosphoric acid. The figures reveal a wide variation but they are typical of what present analyses show.

It is of interest to note the observations made by Blyth on the tea analyses available in 1879, and the future use of chemical analyses in evaluating teas. "We possess no complete analyses of tea; partial analyses are numerous," he writes. This statement still holds true, and although

the entire content of tea may be accounted for in a general way an analysis merely denotes a number of groups of substances.

In the same paper Blyth continues: "The time is probably not far distant when the tea trade will buy entirely by analysis, supplemented by taster's reports. An experienced palate will detect particular flavors which analysis may fail to show, but a fairly complete analysis of tea is of the highest value, whether as a guide to the purchaser or merely to show freedom from adulteration." This was written more than fifty years ago, but, in spite of the advance of chemistry, we still depend wholly on the taster's valuation of tea.

Deuss,[6] writing as recently as 1924, after making many estimations of the caffeine, tannin, and soluble substances in a tea taster's infusion, concludes by saying: "In my opinion, it is impossible to establish a relationship between the content of these substances and the quality of tea." The substances mentioned are known to be responsible for the stimulus, and, in part, at any rate, for the pungency and liquoring quality of tea.

In 1910, a series of tea analyses was conducted in the laboratory of the London *Lancet*. It was claimed at that time that the analyses tended to show that caffeine and tannin usually are present in high grade teas as the compound, caffeine tannate, whilst in common teas these substances largely are present in the uncombined form. It was suggested further that any harmful effects resulting from tea drinking were minimized if the caffeine and tannin were present in the combined form. In the main, however, these experiments were later discredited.

RECENT ANALYSES.—In 1914-15, Carpenter and Cooper[7] made numerous analyses on India teas, estimating the total caffeine, tannin, and water soluble extract. Some study of the compound of tannin and caffeine also was made. They, however, failed to correlate to a significant degree any of their estimations with the market value of, or the taster's reports on the teas.

Deuss[6] estimated the caffeine, tannin,

[1] P. Mulder, *Annalen Physik Chemie*, Leipzig, 1838, vol. xliii, p. 161.

[2] E. Peligot, *L'Institut*, Paris, 1843-45, pp. 238-239.

[3] Rochleder. *Annalen Chem. Pharm.*, Leibigs, Heidelberg, 1847, vol. lxiii, p. 202.

[4] Hlasiwetz and Malin, *Jahresberichte Fortschritte Chem.*, 1861, p. 923, and 1867, p. 732.

[5] A. W. Blyth, *Analysis and Chemical Description of Tea and its Adulterants*, London, 1879, quoted in *Tea Cyclopaedia*, Calcutta, 1881, p. 19.

[6] J. J. B. Deuss, "L'analyse chimique du thé en rapport avec sa qualité," *L'Agronomie Coloniale* Paris, 1924, no. 80.

[7] P. H. Carpenter and H. R. Cooper, *Quarterly Journal Indian Tea Association*, Calcutta 1922, part 2.

CHEMISTRY TABLE No. 1
Caffeine and Tannin Extractable by a
5-Minute Infusion

	Caffeine	Tannin	5-Minute Soluble Extract
Java black teas.....	2.7 to 4.4%	6 to 20%	16 to 26%
Japan green teas....	2.0 to 3.3%	4 to 12%	16 to 26%
China black teas....	2.0 to 3.7%	5 to 10%	16 to 22%
Formosa Oolong teas	3.1 to 3.7%	12 to 23%	23 to 25%

and solids extractable by a five-minute infusion on many samples of Java, Japan, China, and Formosa teas, and, after comparing the results with the quality of the tea, came to the conclusion quoted above. This opinion was based on the figures shown in Chemistry Table Number One.

The method employed in estimating the caffeine is described later under the section dealing with this substance.

The tannin was estimated as follows: The tea was extracted with boiling water, and the aqueous extract was treated with 40 per cent formol. Strong hydrochloric acid was added and the mixture warmed for fifteen minutes. A brown precipitate of tannoform, a compound of tannin and formol, was thus formed; one gram of tannin giving 1.24 grams of tannoform. This method is not perfect, but Deuss holds that it gives consistent results.

It should be noted here that hydrochloric acid and formaldehyde precipitate what are known, according to the old classification, as "catechol" tannins, and precipitate only in part or not at all the "pyrogallol" tannins. The method assumes that tea tannin is of the catechol type.

The consensus of opinion amongst chemists engaged in the study of tea today is that the market value of the product cannot be gauged by the figures given in chemical analyses as at present carried out.

Of recent years, however, it has been noted that some measure of the quality of Japan green tea is given by the anthocyan content of the tea infusion.[8] The anthocyans are bodies formed in the leaf under the action of bright sunlight. These substances have a bitter taste and detract from the quality of green tea; hence the best green tea is made from shaded bushes.

The anthocyan test was worked out at the Kanaya Experimental Station in Japan, and now is used with absolute confidence as an estimate of one of the qualities of Japan green tea. The test is a simple one, and is made as follows: To the tea infusion, as made by the tea taster, a few drops of dilute hydrochloric acid are added. The presence of anthocyans is thereby denoted by a red coloration, the intensity of which increases as the anthocyan content. By means of a scale of standard colors, minute quantities of anthocyans can be quickly estimated. One part of anthocyans in 10,000 parts of tea solution gives a bitter taste, and appreciably detracts from the quality of the tea. Gyokuro, the best Japan tea, contains no anthocyan bodies.

The occurrence and changes undergone by the anthocyan and the related flavone pigments which occur in small quantities in the tea leaf are receiving further study in Japan. Reference again will be made to these groups of substances.

The anthocyan test is not applicable to black tea.[9]

There undoubtedly is a close connection between the quality of the black teas of India, Ceylon and Java and the tannin and tannin products in the infusion, although the tannin estimated by the usual methods shows no such relationship. If sulphuric acid, or salt, or sulphate of ammonia be added to a black tea infusion, a precipitate is obtained and the tannin of the solution reduced. Some workers consider that by means of these precipitating agents a distinction may be made between the different bodies which go to make up "tannin" in black tea infusion. Observations on this aspect of the subject by a worker in the Lancet laboratory were published in 1911.[10] More recent work has been carried out in Assam[11] and Ceylon.[12]

The results thus far obtained are not conclusive. This aspect is discussed more fully later in this chapter under the section on tannin and also in connection with the formation of caffeine tannate in the section on caffeine.

---

8 C. R. Harler, "Tea in Japan," *Quarterly Journal Indian Tea Association*, Calcutta, 1924, part 1.

9 J. J. B. Deuss, "On the Presence of Quercitrin in the Leaf of Camellia theifera and in Made Tea," *Recueil des Travaux Chimiques des Pays-bas*, Chemical Society of Netherlands, Leyden, 1923, vol. xlii, nos. 7 and 8, p. 623.

10 "The Chemistry, Physiology and Aesthetics of a Cup of Tea," *The Lancet*, London, January 7, 1911.

11 P. H. Carpenter and C. J. Harrison, "The Manufacture of Tea in North East India," *Indian Tea Association Publication*, Calcutta, 1927, p. 40.

12 "The Tea Research Institute of Ceylon," Annual Report for the Year 1927, Kandy, Ceylon, 1928, *Bulletin* no. 2.

CHEMISTRY TABLE No. 2
Showing Chief Constituents of Black Tea and
Indicating Range of Values

Moisture	5 to 8%
Caffeine	2.5 to 5%
Nitrogen	4.75 to 5.50%
Tannin	7 to 14%
Soluble matter	38 to 45%
Ash	5 to 5.75%

Such are the indications by which some of the qualities of tea may be determined by a chemical analysis, but it is doubtful whether the chemist will ever supplant the tea taster.

Chemistry Table Number Two shows some of the chief constituents of black tea, and indicates the range of values which may be reasonably expected. It must be added that teas often give values outside this range, with no corresponding reference in the taster's report or evaluation.

Green teas show as wide a range of variation as black teas. Table Number Three sets forth the ordinary limits of analyses made on Gyokuro and on Sencha, the common green tea of Japan.[13]

The values of tea analyses show such

CHEMISTRY TABLE No. 3
Showing Analyses of Gyokuro and Sencha
Teas of Japan

Chemical Contents	Gyokuro	Sencha
Moisture	3 to 7%	4.5 to 5%
Caffeine	3 to 4%	2.5 to 3.2%
Nitrogen	6.2 to 6.8%	5.5 to 5.8%
Tannin	10 to 13%	14.5 to 18%
Soluble matter	37 to 43%	43 to 46%
Ash	6 to 6.5%	5.4 to 5.8%

CHEMISTRY TABLE No. 4
Kosai's Analysis of Dried Leaf, Green Tea, and
Black Tea

Chemical Contents	Dried Leaf	Green Tea	Black Tea
Crude protein	37.33%	37.43%	38.90%
Crude fiber	10.44%	10.06%	10.07%
Ash	4.97%	4.92%	4.93%
Caffeine	3.30%	3.20%	3.30%
Tannin	12.91%	10.64%	4.89%
Hot water extract	50.97%	53.74%	47.23%
Ether extract	6.49%	5.52%	5.82%
Total nitrogen	5.97%	5.99%	6.22%

[13] "The Chemistry of Green Tea," Tea Experimental Station Publication, Kanaya, Japan, 1923.

wide variations that an average has little significance. This applies equally to the values in Table Number Two.

Constituents of the Tea Leaf

EARLY STUDIES.—Some of the earliest chemical analyses on fresh tea leaf were made between 1880 and 1890. In 1886–87, Kellner[14] made detailed analyses on fresh leaf, and on the ash of the leaf gathered at regular intervals. A collection of analyses and notes made between 1887 and 1892 on the chemistry of tea was published by Paul and Cownley,[15] which was very useful at the time. In 1890, Kosai,[16] studying tea in Japan, took a quantity of leaf, part of which was quickly dried at 80° C., part made into green tea, and part into black tea. Analysis of the three products gave the results shown in Table Number Four.

The significant changes take place in the soluble tannin and the hot water extract. About 8 per cent soluble tannin is lost during black tea manufacture, which is about two-thirds of the total.

The first systematic work on the chemistry of tea and the changes taking place during manufacture was done by Bamber in India and Ceylon, and by van Romburgh, Lohmann, and Nanninga in Java.

Bamber first worked in Northeast India for the Indian Tea Association in 1891–92, and his book, The Chemistry and Agriculture of Tea,[17] deals largely with his experiments in Assam. In 1898, he entered into an agreement with the Ceylon Planters' Association to investigate the soils of Ceylon and the manufacture of tea in the island. His report, entitled Ceylon Tea Soils, contains much regarding the chemistry of tea.[18] Many of Bamber's later views and experiments were published in Indian Planting and Gardening.

Van Romburgh, Lohmann, and Nanninga made their reports, dating from 1892, in

[14] O. Kellner, Journal Chemical Society, London, 1887.

[15] B. H. Paul and Cownley, Pharmaceutical Journal Translations, London, 1887–88, vol. xviii, p. 417, 1891–92, vol. xxi, p. 61.

[16] Y. Kosai, "Researches on the Manufacture of Various Kinds of Tea," Bulletin no. 7, Imperial College of Agriculture, Tokio, 1890.

[17] M. Kelway Bamber, The Chemistry and Agriculture of Tea, Calcutta, 1893.

[18] M. Kelway Bamber, Ceylon Tea Soils and Their Effect on the Quality of Tea, Colombo, Ceylon, 1900.

the Dutch journals published in Java.[19] Deuss published a resumé of the results of their investigations, covering a period of fifteen years.[20]

From 1900 to 1907, Mann worked in Northeast India and did much to advance the biological side of tea chemistry, while Bernard and Welter worked along similar lines in Java.

Frequent reference is made to the work of these earlier chemists in the succeeding pages. From 1910 onwards, the increasing number of chemists studying tea problems and the ever-widening field of research robbed the work of much of its personal aspect.

The more recent workers on the subject have made a full study of the empirical side of tea manufacture.

THE GREEN LEAF.—The young tea leaf differs from the leaves of most plants in that it contains a high percentage of tannin and is rich in caffeine. The moisture content of a young tea-shoot varies from about 75 to 80 per cent. The substances which make up the ash amount to about 5.5 per cent of the dry matter in the leaf.

Tea leaf consists mainly of cellulose and crude fibre, protein matter, tannin, caffeine, gummy matters, dextrin and pectin, fats and waxes, and the ash constituents. These substances make up 95 per cent or more of the solid matter in the leaf. The remainder consists of chlorophyll and its allied pigments, together with small quantities of starch, sugars, gallic acid, oxalic acid, quercitrin, and other coloring matters.

Fresh leaf contains also some volatile constituents, which can be obtained by steam distillation of the leaf. This volatile fraction, which has a decided aroma, is acid and contains small quantities of ketone and a reducing substance.[12]

The water soluble extract of fresh leaf

CHEMISTRY TABLE No. 5

Indicating Matter Extracted by Boiling Water from Powdered Dry Leaf

Chemical Contents	Composition of Water Soluble Extract
Tannin......................	27.7%
Total nitrogen...............	2.5%
Non-protein nitrogen, chiefly caffeine	1.56%
Gummy matters, dextrin, pectin, etc.	6.0%
Ash...........................	5.03%

varies, often widely, with each sample. Table Number Five indicates the nature of the matter extracted from powdered dried leaf by boiling water.[12] The values are calculated on the dry matter in the leaf.

Brief mention of the solubility of tea leaf, and of tea in other solvents, such as chloroform, ether, ethyl acetate, and alcohol, hereinafter is made under the sub-section dealing with fermentation of black tea.

Other things being equal, the best tea, both black and green, is made from the small, soft, slightly yellowish shoot of two leaves and a bud. On analysis, such leaf is generally found to contain more tannin, caffeine, and water soluble solids than poorer leaves grown under the same conditions. Table Number Six gives typical analyses of good and poor leaf collected in Assam; the good leaf being soft and succulent and the poor leaf harder and dryer, but still young. The analyses refer to fresh leaf extracted with boiling water for an hour.

MANUFACTURED TEA.—During the manufacture of black tea, important chemical changes take place, the chief of which are the development of flavor and aroma, and the formation of certain tannin compounds. Some of the tannin compounds are soluble

19 P. van Romburgh, *Jaarverslag van 's Lands Plantentuin*, Buitenzorg, Batavia, 1892; P. van Romburgh, A. W. Nanninga, C. E. J. Lohmann. "Negen verslagen over de onderzoekingen betreffende Java gecultiveerde theeën," *'s Lands Plantentuin*, Buitenzorg, Batavia, 1893–1901; P. van Romburgh and A. W. Nanninga, *Zesde verslag idem*, Buitenzorg, Batavia, 1899; A. W. Nanninga, "Verslagen van het Proefstation v. Thee," 1902 –06, Buitenzorg, Batavia; "Onderzoekingen betreffende op Java gecultiveerde theeën," Buitenzorg, Batavia, 1900–1902; "Verslagen van het Proefstation v. Thee," Buitenzorg, Batavia, 1902–1906; *Mededeelingen uit 's Lands Plantentuin*, Buitenzorg, nos. 46, 65, 72.

20 J. J. B. Deuss, *Mededeelingen Proefstation v. Thee*, Buitenzorg, 1914, no. 31.

12 *loc. cit.*

CHEMISTRY TABLE No. 6

Typical Analyses of Good and Poor Leaf Collected in Assam

Chemical Contents	Percentage of Dry Matter	
	Good Leaf	Poor Leaf
Tannin............	25%	15%
Caffeine............	4%	2%
Soluble solids.......	47%	35%

in the tea infusion and give it characteristic color. Others are insoluble and do not enter into the infusion. Usually the aroma and flavor are qualities associated with the essential oil of tea.

During the manufacture of green tea no soluble colored tannin bodies are formed, and most of the tannin remains soluble. No essential oil forms during green tea manufacture.

A black tea infusion consists chiefly of tannin and tannin products, caffeine, carbohydrates, and small quantities of nitrogenous substances other than caffeine. A trace of essential oil is present, and small quantities of pigments. A green tea infusion consists chiefly of tannin, caffeine, gummy substances, carbohydrates, and small quantities derived from quite a number of nitrogenous bodies other than caffeine, and pigments.

The most important substance in tea, both green and black, is caffeine; because without some such stimulant it is doubtful whether tea, as a beverage, would have made such a wide appeal.

Tea tannin is regarded as the second most valuable constituent of many of the black teas of India, Ceylon, and Java; not only because it imparts the characteristic pungency or astringency to the tea liquor, but because it gives rise to the coloring bodies of the infusion. The "cream" which settles from cold tea consists in part of tannin bodies.

If flavor and aroma are present in any appreciable quantity in tea, other characteristics count for little, so highly are these qualities priced. Many of the finest Keemun and Ningchow China black teas are valued almost entirely on their flavor. The same may be said of many Darjeeling and Ceylon teas. The tannin content of these teas often is low and certainly is not, in such cases, an important factor.

In determining quality, the thickness of the liquor, or "body" of the infusion, is an important factor. This factor depends on the solids extracted by hot water; the "soluble extract," as the percentage of water soluble matter is called, is important both in green and black teas.

As previously mentioned, the quality of green tea is influenced by the anthocyan content. Quality in green tea varies directly as the nitrogen content of the leaf, which in turn influences the percentage of nitrogenous bodies in the infusion.

CHEMISTRY TABLE No. 7
Showing Extractable Solids after a 1-Hour Boiling, and a 5-Minute Infusion

Chemical Contents	1-Hour Boiling	5-Minute Infusion
Tannin	12.4%	7.3%
Caffeine	4.8%	3.6%
Soluble extract	44.5%	23.2%

However, no strict rules can be laid down regarding the amount of the major constituents in good or poor teas, whether they be green or black. The importance of the essential oil in black teas and the deleterious effect of anthocyans in Japan green teas, already have been mentioned. Both essential oil and anthocyans appear in minute qualities.

In discussing the soluble constituents of tea and their influence on the quality of the infusion, it should be noted that it takes about an hour to extract the leaf thoroughly. A taster infuses tea for six minutes, and the solution he examines contains about half the tannin, three-quarters of the caffeine, and about half the total of extractable solids. Extractions made on Assam teas gave the results shown in Table Number Seven.

Tea Tannin

THE TANNINS.—The term tannin is variously employed by different writers; at times to denote a particular substance, viz., the tannin of oak galls, and sometimes for a whole group of substances possessing certain characteristics in common. In the present discussion the term tannin will be used in its general sense.[21]

The chief properties of the tannins may be summarized as follows:

1. They are mostly uncrystallizable, colloidal substances with astringent properties.
2. They form blackish-blue or blackish-green compounds with ferric salts; these compounds having been used originally in the form of inks.
3. They have the property of combining with skins and hides, producing an effect known as "tanning," from which results the leather of commerce.
4. All tannins are precipitated by lead acetate, and catechol tannins are precipitated by an excess of bromine water.

[21] H. Neuville, *Technologie du Thé*, Paris, 1926, gives a comprehensive account of the chemistry of tea tannin and the other constituents of the tea leaf.

5. They precipitate alkaloids and substances of a basic nature.

6. In alkaline solution the tannins and many of their derivatives readily absorb oxygen; becoming dark in color.

7. In acid solution the catechol tannins produce insoluble red substances, known as phlobaphenes or tannin "reds."

8. The tannins are slightly acidic in nature.

Tannin, using the term in its generic sense, is very widely distributed in the vegetable kingdom. In the higher plants, it occurs more or less generally throughout a tissue, for example in bark, or it may be restricted in the more mature parts to special cells, which may be isolated. Tannin also is found in special structures in many plants. It especially is abundant in pathological growths, such as galls, which may contain from 25 to 75 per cent of tannin.

In the plant cell the tannin occurs in the cell sap, and, since tannin precipitates with albuminous matter, it follows that the layer of protoplasm round the tannin vesicles is impermeable to it, otherwise the protoplasm would be tanned by the production of tannin.

The more important sources of natural tannin materials may be mentioned briefly, thus indicating the wide distribution of tannins. Among the barks most widely used are those of several varieties of oak. The bark of hemlock, larch, spruce, fir, mimosa, babool, willow, and birch are used in various countries. Among the various woods, quebracho, grown in South America, is the richest in tannin. The tannin from chestnut, oak, and cutch wood also are used—the last named in India as a mordant for dyeing leather. The leaves and twigs of the gambier in India, and the sumach in Sicily, are gathered for tannin.

The pods of divi-divi, extensively grown in South America, and the dried, unripe nuts of the myrobolan tree of India also are used as tannin sources. Among the roots extracted for tannin, those of the palmetto, grown in the United States, and the canaigre, of Mexico and Australia, are, perhaps, the most common.

The chemical nature of tannin differs widely, according to its source. The extensive study of the reactions of many different tannins has furnished a basis for several schemes of classification. The tannins fall into two general classes, which have been named *pyrogallol* and *catechol*, from the fact that on dry distillation tannin materials yield one or the other of these substances. The pyrogallol tannins contain about 52 per cent carbon as against about 60 per cent in the case of the catechol tannins. Several classifications based on this grouping have been compiled.

Procter [22] classified the tannins as follows:

1. Pyrogallol tannins, including divi-divi, galls, sumach, myrobolans, oak galls and wood, and chestnut tannins, have the following characteristics:

(a) They give a dark blue color with ferric salts.

(b) They give no precipitate with bromine water.

(c) They produce on leather a "bloom" consisting of ellagic acid.

2. Catechol tannins, including all the pine, acacia, mimosa and oak barks [but not oak wood or galls], quebracho wood, cassia, canaigre, cutch and gambier, have the following characteristics:

(a) They give with iron alum a greenish-black color.

(b) They precipitate with bromine water.

(c) The addition of a drop of strong sulphuric acid to one of the tannin solution produces a dark red or crimson ring at the junction of the liquids.

(d) They deposit no "bloom," but, when boiled with acids, deposit red insoluble coloring matters, known as phlobaphenes.

Some of the tannins in this group, notably gambier and cutch, contain the phloroglucinol radical in their molecules.

A new classification of natural tannins, more discriminating than the older pyrogallol-catechol categories, was suggested in 1918 by Perkin and Everest.[23] They consider three groups as follow:

1. Depsides [old gallotannins].

2. Diphenyl methoid [old ellagitannins].

3. Phlobatannins [old catechol tannins].

This classification marks an advance in that it takes into consideration the structure of the tannin molecule.

In 1920, Freudenberg offered a still more distinctive classification than the one set forth above,[24] made possible by the great advances in tannin research during recent years. The outstanding feature of chemical investigation in this sphere was the synthesis of gallotannic acid by Emil Fischer

[22] H. R. Procter, *The Principles of Leather Manufacture*, London, 1903.

[23] A. C. Perkin and A. E. Everest, *The Natural Organic Coloring Matters*, New York, 1918.

[24] K. Freudenberg, *The Chemistry of the Natural Tannins*, Berlin, 1920.

in 1918,[25] which profoundly modified previous views on the subject of tannin chemistry. Freudenberg, formerly associated with Fischer, is carrying on that great master's work, and both he and Nierenstein have done much toward determining the constitution of catechin, which stands, with regard to the catechol tannins, somewhat as gallotannic acid does to the pyrogallol tannins.

Freudenberg divides the tannins into two main classes:

1. Hydrolyzable tannins, in which the benzene nuclei are united to larger complexes through oxygen atoms.
2. Condensed tannins, in which the nuclei are held together through carbon linkages.

Group One embraces (a) esters of phenolcarboxylic acids with each other or with oxyacids [depsides], (b) esters of phenolcarboxylic acids with polyatomic alcohols and sugars [tannin class] and (c) glucosides. The most important criterion for group number one is hydrolysis to simpler components by enzymes, particularly tannase [secreted by Aspergillus niger] or emulsin.

Tannins of Group Two are not decomposed to simple components by enzymes. Generally, but not always, they are precipitable by bromine, and when treated with oxidizing agents or strong acids condense to high molecular tannins or "reds." They are divided into two classes according to whether or not phloroglucin is present. With some exceptions, the catechins belong to the phloroglucin class; e.g., quebracho, and probably oak tannin are in this class.

A word on the physiological rôle of tannins in plants may here be written. The question regarding the reason for their formation is still under dispute. They probably are not direct products of photosynthesis, although they are elaborated in the green leaves of plants and translocated thence to the stems, roots, etc. Their close connection with the photosynthetic carbohydrates has led many investigators to seek the establishment of some significant function for tannin as a food material.

There is ample evidence that tannins are elaborated where intense metabolism is in progress, such as occurs in green leaves during the early growing season, in the rapid transformations which take place after the stings of insects producing galls, etc.

It appears to be fairly well established that tannins are intermediate products in the formation of cork tissue. They also may play a part in pigment formation.

TEA TANNIN EXTRACTION.—In the preparation of tea tannin there is always the difficulty of oxidation to be overcome, and the easy formation, even in dilute acids, of a tannin-red product. Moreover, it is extremely difficult to prepare any pure tannin.

An account of the earlier chemical work on tea tannin is given by Dekker.[26] Nanninga prepared tea tannin by first extracting dried, fresh leaf with chloroform to remove the caffeine and chlorophyll, and then followed with acetic ether, free from acetic acid, to remove the tannin. The extract then was repeatedly precipitated with chloroform. However, a pure product was not obtained.[27]

Deuss[28] prepared pure tea tannin by a modification of the process indicated by Löwe.[29] The method used follows: Fresh tea leaves were dried in warm air at 90–100° C. They were pulverized and extracted with warm benzine to remove the chlorophyll, resins, etc. The excess benzine was driven off, and the powdered leaves were treated with warm alcohol. From the extract thus obtained the alcohol was distilled off till a syrupy mass remained, to which water was added. Certain impurities were thus precipitated and the tannin dissolved. In order to facilitate the precipitation of the impurities, a little salt was added, and the solution was filtered. The filtrate was agitated with ether to remove traces of gallic acid, then with ethyl acetate which dissolves the tannin. To facilitate the latter solution, the addition of salt is advantageous. The tannin solution was dehydrated over sodium sulphate and concentrated in vacuo. Next, this last solution was poured into dry chloroform, which entirely precipitated the tannin. The precipitate was then filtered as quickly as possible and dried in vacuo.

The substance thus obtained is usually

[25] E. Fischer, Berichte deut. chem. Gesell., Berlin, 1918, vol. li, p. 1760, and 1919, vol. lii, p. 829.

[26] J. Dekker, Die Gerbstoffe, Berlin, 1913, part 2, p. 79.
[27] A. W. Nanninga, Mededeelingen 's Lands Plantentuin, Buitenzorg, no. 46, part 1, p. 23.
[28] J. J. B. Deuss, Mededeelingen Proefstation v. Thee, Buitenzorg, 1913, no. 13.
[29] Löwe, Zeit. Anal. Chem., Wiesbaden, vol. xx, p. 210.

yellow, but if it is prepared from manufactured tea, it is brown and difficult to purify. The product is purified by re-dissolving the ethyl acetate and re-precipitating with chloroform several times.

TEA TANNIN PROPERTIES.—Analysis and molecular weight determinations gave $C_{20}H_{20}O_9$ as the formula of the tea tannin obtained above, its properties being as follows: With ferric chloride it gives a black precipitate and a blue-black coloration in very dilute solutions. With lead acetate it gives a yellow-grey precipitate, and with bromine water a yellow precipitate. Potassium permanganate oxidizes it completely, while nitric acid oxidizes it to oxalic acid. It reduces Fehling solution, gives a yellow precipitate with phenylhydrazine, and reduces ammoniacal silver solution, which shows it contains a ketonic group. When boiled with 5 per cent sulphuric acid, it precipitates a red compound similar to that obtained from oak tannin. With acetic anhydride, together with dry sodium acetate it yields an acetylated tannin, $C_{36}H_{36}O_{17}$, in which it is concluded that eight hydrogen atoms of eight phenolic groups are replaced by the acetyl group. The reactions indicate that the tea tannin molecule contains at least one ketonic group, eight hydroxyl groups, and no carboxyl group.[30]

Pure tea tannin is a white powder, which easily oxidizes in air to a brown gummy mass. This change is very rapid in humid air. Tea tannin is easily soluble in water, ethyl and methyl alcohol, acetone, and acetic anhydride; it is less soluble in ethyl acetate, sulphuric and acetic acids; it is insoluble in chloroform, benzine, and dry ether.

To return to the red product obtained by the action of weak acids on tea tannin, this substance is formed in the absence of air, and Deuss considers that it is due to the splitting of water from the tannin. This "red" is insoluble in an aqueous solution of tea tannin.

If a little ammonia is added to a tea tannin solution, a brown substance is formed which may be reduced by zinc dust and weak acid back to what is probably the original tannin. Deuss considers that this brown product is formed during black tea manufacture through the action of the

oxidizing enzyme on tannin. This substance dissolves in an aqueous solution of tea tannin.

TEA TANNIN CLASSIFICATION.—The exact classification of tea tannin is still under discussion. Primarily, tannins may be considered those subjects of vegetable origin which may be found in many plants as water soluble bodies, exhibiting certain chemical behavior, possessing astringent properties and being capable of converting animal hide into leather. Although tea tannin possesses the necessary chemical properties, and precipitates gelatine and hide powder from solution, it does not convert animal hide into leather. It is therefore termed a pseudo-tannin.[31]

Referring now to the chemical classification of tea tannin, Dekker placed it in the gallic acid group, along with the gallotannins,[26] a group in his [Dekker's] own scheme of classification,[32] and included in the pyrogallol group in Proctor's classification. Deuss objected to this classification,[28] and, by its analysis, and the easy formation of red compounds in the presence of acids, classed tea tannin with the oak or catechol tannins. According to the Perkin and Everest classification, tea tannin would be designated a phlobatannin.

Freudenberg's scheme of classification placed tea tannin in the group of hydrolyzable tannins under the second class; that is, the class comprising esters of phenolcarboxylic acids with polyatomic alcohols and sugars. Deuss, however, argues that, by the fact that tea tannin is precipitated by bromine and that it forms red-brown products by the action of acids and by oxidation, it ought to be placed amongst the condensed tannins.[36] Freudenberg has indicated that condensed tannins are not converted by enzymes to simpler bodies. In the manufacture of black tea, the tannin is oxidized to an insoluble brown product, soluble in tea tannin solution. A solution of tea tannin obtained by Deuss's method, fails to react with the enzymes obtained from tea juice by precipitation with alcohol. This, Deuss considers, con-

[30] J. J. B. Deuss, *Recueil trav. chim.*, Leyden, 1923, vol. xlii, p. 496.

[31] R. W. Thatcher, *The Chemistry of Plant Life*, New York, 1921, p. 97.
[26] *loc. cit.*
[32] J. Dekker, *The Tannins*, Amsterdam, 1906.
[28] *loc. cit.*
[33] J. J. B. Deuss, *Recueil trav. chim.*, Leyden, 1923, vol. xlii, p. 1053.

firms his suggestion that tea tannin is a condensed tannin.

Deuss has not yet shown the presence or absence of the phloroglucinol radical in tea tannin, which is characteristic of many tannins of the condensed class.

Deuss distinguishes between phlobaphenes and the "red," both obtained from tea tannin. The first he considers to be the brown product obtained by the oxidation of tannin in the absence of acids and salts, whilst the "red" results from the treatment of tea tannin with dilute acids.[33]

Mention will be made of gallic acid, flavones and anthocyans, substances related to tannins, in a later section of this chapter.

Variation in Tannin Content

In accordance with the importance of the tannin content of the tea leaf, innumerable estimations of this substance have been made at all stages of growth and manufacture. Unless otherwise stated, all the tannin values quoted have been estimated by a modification of Löwenthal's method.[34] The conversion factor of 0.0416 has been established by the hide powder method. Unless a statement is made to the contrary, tannin figures refer to the amount of tannin extracted by water after one hour's boiling, and are calculated on the dry matter in the leaf.

IN THE GREEN LEAF.—Tea tannin is unevenly distributed throughout the plant, and is principally found in the leaves. The wood and the roots contain about 1 per cent tannin, and the seeds but a trace. Tea flowers have been shown to contain about 1.5 per cent tannin.[6] Table Number Eight shows the distribution of tannin throughout tea shoots which are grown in Assam.

A shoot consisting of two leaves and a bud, taken during the full growing season in India, Ceylon, or Java will contain from 19 to 22 per cent tannin, although figures wide of these may be observed. Some variation also has been recorded due to the variety of bush grown in the aforementioned countries, but the differences are small.[8] In Japan only about 15 per

CHEMISTRY TABLE No. 8

Showing Distribution of Tannin Throughout Tea Shoots in Assam

Bud	.....	27.8% tannin
First leaf	.....	27.9% "
Second leaf	.....	21.3% "
Third leaf	.....	17.8% "
Fourth leaf	.....	14.5% "
Upper stalk	.....	11.7% "
Lower stalk	[2nd and 4th leaves]	6.4% "

cent tannin is found in the leaf,[6] and in the Caucasus values somewhat above 15 per cent have been observed.[35]

It will be appreciated that *fine* plucking, consisting of two leaves and a bud, will give a shoot richer in tannin than *coarse* plucking, which includes three or more leaves. In this connection, a table showing the percentage composition by weight of the average fine shoot is presented herewith.

Even in a finely plucked shoot, the second leaf and stalk constitute more than 60 per cent of the shoot. When three leaves and a bud are taken, the extra leaf and stalk make up about half the weight of the shoot as then constituted, and the tannin content is commensurably lowered.

In Assam, a general seasonal change in the tannin content of the shoot has been observed. At the beginning of the season in that area [March and April], the tannin content is low. It rises to a maximum in August and September, and falls off somewhat towards the end of the season. Table Number Nine illustrates the variations in tannin content of Assam tea shoots.[36]

In Japan[13] and the Caucasus[35] it has been noted that the earlier pluckings of

PERCENTAGE COMPOSITION OF THE AVERAGE FINE SHOOT

Bud	14% weight of total shoot.
First leaf	21% weight of total shoot.
Second leaf	38% weight of total shoot.
Stalk	27% weight of total shoot.

[33] loc. cit.
[34] "Procter's Modification of Löwenthal's Method," Bulletin no. 13, part 7, p. 80, U. S. Dept. Agric., Div. Chem., Washington, D. C.
[6] loc. cit.
[8] loc. cit.

[8] loc. cit.
[35] J. Galy-Carles, "Review of Applied Botany, Agricultural College," Bulletin no. 86, p. 683, Paris, 1928.
[13] loc. cit.
[36] P. H. Carpenter and C. R. Harler, Quarterly Journal Indian Tea Association, Calcutta, 1922, III.

CHEMISTRY TABLE No. 9

Illustrating the Variations in Tannin Content of Assam Tea Shoots

May	Shoots contained	......	11.6% tannin
June	"	"	......20.2% "
August	"	"	......21.3% "
September	"	"	......21.7% "
October	"	"	......19.2% "
November	"	"	......18.2% "

CHEMICAL TABLE No. 10

Showing Total Soluble Extract Estimated after Precipitation in Four Different Pluckings During the Day

	First Period	Second Period	Third Period	Fourth Period
Total extract...	36.4%	42.7%	46.1%	46.9%
Precipitated by alcohol	nil	2.4%	4.0%	6.7%
Tannin........	17.7%	19.0%	20.4%	20.4%

the season contain less tannin than the later ones. In Java, where the climate is such that the bushes flush throughout the year, preliminary observations have shown that the flushes following on the biennial pruning, contain less tannin than those later on.[37] In Ceylon, also, it has been recorded that the tannin varies according to the age of the leaf from pruning. Estimations made on the leaf from an up-country estate in Ceylon showed that in five months from pruning the tannin content of the shoot was about 14.4 per cent; sixteen months from pruning it was about 18.7 per cent; and thirty-four months from the time of pruning it was about 17.3 per cent.[18]

The chemical constitution of the leaf varies throughout the day, and some of the photosynthetic products have been shown to increase in the leaf from morning to evening. As the day advances, a gummy substance is formed in the leaf, which interferes with the estimation of tannin by the formol method; and, unless it is removed, complete precipitation of the tannin is not obtained. Following up this point, it has been observed that the gummy material is precipitated by alcohol, after which process the true tannin content can be estimated.[38]

The figures in Table Number Ten show the total soluble extract, the gummy matter precipitated by alcohol, and the tannin, estimated after precipitation, in leaf plucked at four different times during the day.

It will be noticed that the increase in total extract is largely made up of gummy matter precipitated by alcohol and by tannin.

Shade has an effect on the quality of both green and black tea. Reference has been made to the influence of shade on the green teas of Japan. In Assam it has been observed that, generally speaking, shade adversely affects the quality of black tea.[39] Bamber[18] has shown that the outer leaves of the tea bush, exposed to direct sunlight, contain more tannin than the inner leaves, and that only green leaves were capable of producing tannin. Later, Hope[40] observed that by shading bushes either with grass or shade trees the tannin content was reduced.

It is customary in the Uji District of Japan to shade tea areas under grass matting supported by bamboos, about three weeks before the first flush is plucked. As previously described, the most important result of this process is considered to be the reduction of the anthocyan content of the leaf. Study of the tannin content of the shoots from shaded bushes has shown that shading may reduce it as much as 3 per cent during the period of shading.[13]

Observations in Assam have failed to show any appreciable influence of various types of manuring on the tannin content of the tea leaf.

The amount of tannin in the shoot varies with the plucking and pruning treatment the bush receives. The more naturally and freely the bush grows, the less the tannin content of the shoot. Thus, in Assam, shoots from a tea seed bush, which had never been pruned or plucked, were shown to contain less than 20 per cent tannin, while bushes producing forced, rapid growth under the stimulus of fre-

[37] J. J. B. Deuss, Archief Theeculture, Batavia, 1928, nos. 1 and 2, p. 123.

[18] loc. cit.

[38] T. Petch, The Tea Quarterly, Colombo, Ceylon, 1928, vol. i, part 4, p 114.

[39] H. R. Cooper, Quarterly Journal Indian Tea Association, Calcutta, 1926, part 2, p. 89.

[18] loc. cit.

[40] G. D. Hope, Experiments on the Quality of Tea, Indian Tea Association, Calcutta, 1910.

[13] loc. cit.

quent pruning and regular plucking, contained about 25 per cent tannin.

Leaf which is *bhanji* [Hindu for sterile], so that for the time being the bud has ceased to develop, although the leaves already formed continue to grow slowly, shows a low tannin content. *Bhanji*-ness is a natural phenomenon occurring at intervals during the growth of the branch. If, for any other reason, such as the attack of certain fungus diseases, the rate of growth of the shoot is slowed up, then the tannin content is reduced.

The length of the plucking has an effect on the amount of tannin in the shoot. The longer the plucking, the less the tannin content. *Long* plucking denotes the kind made on a long growth of new wood, and *close* plucking, that made on a short growth of new wood.[41] In one case in Assam, it was noticed that bushes pruned back to a height of nine inches, and plucked at thirty-six inches, yielded shoots showing an average tannin content throughout the season of 22.7 per cent. Similar bushes, top-pruned at thirty inches, and plucked at thirty-six, yielded shoots with an average of 24.2 per cent.

Some mention should be made of the influence of the variety of the tea bush on the tannin content of the shoot. In attempting to classify the varieties of the tea plant, botanists have considered various dimensions of the leaf, among others being the length of the leaf tip.[42] Cohen Stuart observes some slight correlation between the length of the tip and the tannin content, and concludes that only the varieties with a leaf tip over 9 mm. in length yield shoots containing more than 15 per cent tannin. This would indicate that bushes belonging to the China race should be poorer in tannin than those of other races.

DURING MANUFACTURE.—The change in the soluble tannin content of the leaf during manufacture has been the subject of considerable study. It is not proposed to discuss here the nature of the chemical changes bringing about this loss, but merely to indicate its trend and magnitude. Table Number Eleven indicates the

CHEMISTRY TABLE No. 11

Indicating the Tannin Content at Various Stages of Black and Green Tea Manufacture

Kind of Leaf	Water Soluble Tannin		
	Ceylon Tea[18]	India Tea[43]	Japan Green Tea[43]
Fresh leaf	22.3%	22.2%	15.2%
Withered leaf	22.1%	22.2%	....
Rolled leaf	20.8%	....	....
Fermented leaf	13.2%	12.9%	....
Finished tea	12.9%	12.0%	12.2%

tannin content at various stages of black and green tea manufacture.

It will be noticed that the greatest loss in soluble tannin during the manufacture of black tea, occurs in fermentation, as the oxidation process in tea manufacture is termed. Leaf, which is to be manufactured into green tea, is heated as soon as possible after plucking, which procedure renders fermentation impossible.

The loss of soluble tannin during green tea manufacture is slight, and averages as shown in Table Number Twelve.[8]

A remark on the tannin content of black teas of India, Ceylon, and China may here be made. The values shown in Table Number Thirteen were obtained by precipitating the tannin with quinine sulphate.[44]

These values may be taken as fairly indicative. The values for China tea are low, largely because the original leaf contains less tannin than that from the large leaved varieties grown in India and Ceylon. The method of manufacture in China, which entails a very full fermentation, also tends to reduce the tannin content of the made tea. Several contributary causes may be given to explain the fact that Ceylon teas generally contain less tannin than those of India. Much of the tea in Ceylon is of the hybrid variety, which usually contains less tannin than the pure Assam varieties. The high elevation of most of the Ceylon gardens, which tends to slow up the rate of growth, and

41 A discussion of the plucking problem will be found in *Mededeelingen Proefstation v. Thee*, Buitenzorg, 1919, no. 45, by C. P. Cohen Stuart, E. Hamakers, and E. L. Slahaj.

42 C. P. Cohen Stuart, *Zeit. Pflanzenzücht*, 1920, vol. vii, p. 189; R. du Pasquier, *Bull. econ. Indochine*, Hanoi, 1924, no. 169.

18 *loc. cit.*

43 C. R. Harler, "Tea in Ceylon," *Quarterly Journal Indian Tea Association*, Calcutta, 1924, part 1.

8 *loc. cit.*

44 A. C. Chapman, *Analyst*, London, 1908, vol. xxxiii, p. 95; R. R. Tatlock and R. T. Thomson, idem, 1910, vol. xxxv, p. 103.

CHEMISTRY TABLE No. 12
Showing That Loss of Soluble Tannin Is Slight
During Green Tea Manufacture

Fresh leaf	15.2% tannin
After first roll	12.8% "
After third roll	12.3% "
After final roll	12.2% "

the fact that the plucking is longer than that usually practiced in India, are both factors tending to lower the tannin content of the shoot, and, in turn, that of the made tea.

It has been stated that the tannin content of black tea infusions cannot be correlated with pungency, briskness, strength or color; qualities which are wholly or partly influenced by the tannin and soluble tannin products in the infusion. This may be due to the fact that the ordinary tannin estimation does not distinguish between the

CHEMISTRY TABLE No. 13
Showing Values Obtained by Precipitating
Tannin with Quinine Sulphate

India black teas	13.32 to 14.98% tannin
Ceylon black teas	10.31 to 13.91% "
China black teas	7.27 to 10.90% "

tannin bodies, which, although they have the common property of combining with gelatine, may have different functions in making up a tea infusion. Table Number Fourteen gives account of the attempts to distinguish between these tannin bodies.

When weak sulphuric or hydrochloric acid is added to an infusion of tea leaf or tea, the tannin value of the solution is decreased. With withered or fermented leaf a precipitate also is obtained. This loss in tannin value becomes greater as manufacture proceeds. Thus in Ceylon the changes shown in Table Number Fourteen have been recorded.

Adding Tannin to Tea

It has been suggested that the loss of tannin on the addition of acid represents a stage in the conversion of soluble into insoluble tannin, and that the precipitate obtained on acidification is closely related to the brown oxidation products of tannin, and probably determines, to some extent, the nature of the tea made.[12]

[12] loc. cit.

CHEMISTRY TABLE No. 14
Illustrating How Loss of Tannin Value Becomes
Greater as Manufacture Proceeds

Kind of Leaf	Soluble Tannin	
	Total	After Adding Acid
Withered leaf	23.6%	22.8%
Withered leaf rolled 30 minutes	23.3%	19.8%
Withered leaf after 2nd roll	19.8%	16.9%
Withered leaf after 3rd roll	17.5%	12.4%

Further reference to the precipitate obtained by the addition of acids to black tea infusions is made in connection with the compound caffeine tannate, discussed hereinafter under the sections on caffeine.

Considering that tannin is such an important factor in many teas, it might be expected that attempts would be made to improve quality by the addition of this substance. This has been done in Java[45] with reported good results at first, which, however, could not be repeated. It has been suggested that the failure may have been due to the fact that the tannin added was of the gallnut-type, and not of the oak tannin-type, to which type tea tannin belongs.[21]

Caffeine

Caffeine first was discovered in coffee in 1820. It was discovered in tea in 1827, and named theine. It was later found in maté and various other plants. Eventually it was shown that the theine of tea was identical with the caffeine of coffee, and the term theine then was dropped.

Caffeine is a powerful alkaloid, acting as a stimulant to the human system, and both tea and coffee are drunk largely because of the caffeine they contain. There is a considerable demand for caffeine for use in medical preparations, and for the manufacture of certain non-alcoholic drinks. The caffeine of commerce is commonly prepared from damaged tea and tea waste.

Pure caffeine forms long, white, silky needles, which readily form light fleecy

[45] K. A. R. Bosscha and A. D. Maurenbrecher, *Mededeelingen Proefstation v. Thee*, Buitenzorg, 1913, no. 24.
[21] loc. cit.

```
HN—CO           HN—CO               HN—CO                CH₃N—CO
 |   |           |   |                |   |    CH₃         |    |    CH₃
OC  C—NH        OC  C—NH            OC  C—N   >CH        OC   C—N   >CH
 |   ‖  >CO      |   ‖  >CH           |   ‖               |    ‖
HN—C—NH         HN—C—N             CH₃—N—C—N            CH₃—N—C—N
  Uric acid       Xanthin             Theobromine           Caffeine
```

masses. The needles are hexagonal, crystallizing from water with the retention of one molecule of that liquid. When heated to 150° C., the crystals lose their water. At 234° C. caffeine melts. It dissolves sparingly in cold water, and easily in alcohol and ether. Acids dissolve caffeine with the formation of unstable salts. On heating, caffeine forms a vapor which settles out as a solid on cool surfaces. This process, sublimation, starts at 120° C. and is complete at 178° C.

The constitution of caffeine has been established by synthesis in the course of the classic researches on the purine group by Emil Fischer.[46] The similarity between caffeine, theobromin [the chief alkaloid of cocoa], xanthin [one of the soluble constituents of meat], and uric acid, is shown by the formulæ at the top of this page.

Caffeine is tri-methyl-xanthin. The formulæ indicate the chemical relationship between these members of the purine group, but it must not be supposed that because the structure of these compounds is similar, their physiological actions will be likewise. The presence and orientation of the methyl groups [—CH₃] in the caffeine molecule is probably the controlling factor which makes its action differ from that of other members of the series.

TEA CAFFEINE EXTRACTION.—Caffeine may be quantitatively extracted from tea in various ways. By some methods, the leaf is extracted with a caffeine solvent, such as chloroform, alcohol, or benzine; sometimes in the presence of lime, magnesia or ammoniacal solution. By other methods the tea is extracted with a weak solution of lime, magnesia, or ammonia; after which this solution is extracted with chloroform.

The alkali is used with the object of dissociating the caffeine from the combinations in which it may exist in the natural state. In all methods of extraction recourse is made to secondary means of eliminating other substances, which are dissolved along with the caffeine.

Two methods will be described herein in some detail. The method of Power and Chesnut[47] is one commonly used. Dry tea is extracted with warm alcohol and the extract treated with a 10 per cent solution of magnesium oxide. It is next evaporated to dryness. The solid thus obtained is dissolved in warm water and filtered, then treated with dilute sulphuric acid and boiled for half an hour. The liquid is filtered, extracted with chloroform and, to the chloroform extract is added a small quantity of caustic potash to destroy any coloring matter present. The liquid is then evaporated to dryness and the residue dissolved in chloroform, which takes up the caffeine, leaving the impurities. Final evaporation of the chloroform leaves pure caffeine.

Deuss has employed the following method.[6] Ten grams of tea containing 20–25 per cent moisture are treated with chloroform in a Soxhlet apparatus for two hours. After the extraction, the chloroform is driven off and the residue treated with boiling water, to which is added a few drops of lead acetate solution. The solution is diluted to 125cc. and then filtered. Of the almost colorless filtrate, 100cc. is taken and treated three times with 60–70 cc. chloroform. All the caffeine thus dissolves in the chloroform, which is driven off by distillation. The caffeine is dried at 100–102° C. and weighed.

COMMERCIAL EXTRACTION.—For the commercial extraction of caffeine from tea a simple and cheap method is required, and one which permits of a fairly complete extraction. Two such processes were outlined by van Romburgh and Lohmann.[48]

In the first method, the tea waste is extracted with water and the extraction progressively treated with weak sulphuric acid, milk of lime, and lead acetate. Hav-

47 F. B. Power and V. K. Chesnut, *Journal American Chemical Society*, Easton, 1919, vol. xli, p. 1298.
6 *loc. cit.*
48 P. van Romburgh and C. E. J. Lohmann, *Verslag 's Lands Plantentuin*, Buitenzorg, 1899.

46 E. Fischer, *Berichte deut. chem. Gesell.*, Berlin, 1892, vol. xxviii, p. 3137; 1899, vol. xxxii, p. 435; 1900, vol. xxxiii, p. 3035.

ing thus precipitated much of the soluble matter other than caffeine, the liquid is evaporated and an impure caffeine obtained. The alkaloid is extracted with chloroform and purified by re-crystallization.

The same two chemists [van Romburgh and Lohmann] also considered the possibility of using the direct method of chloroform extraction industrially. They concluded that this method was applicable to tea waste containing 20–25 per cent moisture. With dryer tea waste, the extraction is less complete. The extra expense of using chloroform in this process would be balanced by the saving in plant needed, if the longer process is used.

Nowadays, caffeine commonly is extracted as follows: Tea waste is moistened with water about 25 per cent of its weight, and then extracted with benzol or toluol. The extract is then distilled with a small quantity of water, and the hydrocarbon thus passes off and the caffeine is left in solution, from which it may be crystallized. The first crystallization gives a product 95 per cent pure, and, if the process is repeated three times, the last with animal charcoal, a pure product is obtained. The yield varies from $2\frac{1}{2}$ to 3 per cent of the waste treated. This process follows along the same lines as those employed by Watson, Sheth and Sudborough,[49] who estimate caffeine in tea by extracting with benzine or toluene at 90 to 100° C. in the presence of lime water.

CAFFEINE IN THE TEA LEAF.—Little can be said of the state in which the caffeine exists in the leaf. Van Romburgh and Lohmann [50] studied this question many years ago. Fresh leaf and finished tea were extracted with alcohol and acetic ether till a colorless extract resulted. The leaf thus treated was acted on with dilute sulphuric acid, the object being to decompose the caffeine compond, if any still remained unextracted. No further appreciable quantity of caffeine was obtained by this treatment. They found also the same quantity of caffeine in fresh leaf as in made tea.

In spite of these results, the same experimenters persisted in believing that caffeine existed in combination in the leaf, and that this compound was in some way decomposed during manufacture. After searching in various liquors obtained in extraction processes, they did find a substance which appeared to be combined with caffeine. The nature of this substance and the combination still are unsolved problems.

The natural role of caffeine in the leaf has not yet been determined. Caffeine collects in the old leaves by a process of inanition, rather than of synthesis. It has been suggested that the alkaloid is used to build up the protein molecule in the process of the plant's growth. Hartwich and du Pasquier [51] concluded that caffeine was not so employed, but, on the contrary, resulted from the decomposition of proteins.

VARIATION IN CAFFEINE CONTENT.—Caffeine is irregularly distributed throughout the tea shoot. Van Romburgh and Lohmann compiled Table Number Fifteen, indicating the caffeine content of various parts of the tea plant.

In Japan it has been shown that the caffeine content of the shoot does not vary much throughout the season, although generally it is greatest in the first plucking made in the spring.[13] In Java, also, it has been shown that the caffeine content is fairly constant, and that it is greatest in the pluckings made following on the pruning.[37]

In Assam it has been demonstrated that the caffeine content cannot be appreciably altered by manuring with heavy or light doses of fertilizers.

At the United States Government Tea Experimental Station at Pinehurst, North Carolina, it was found that shading the tea increased the caffeine content as much as 50 per cent.[52] In Japan, also, it has been observed that shading increases the caffeine in the leaf.[13]

Although the caffeine content does not change appreciably during manufacture, many suggestions have been made regarding the breaking down and formation of

[49] H. E. Watson, K. M. Sheth, and Sudborough, *Journal India Institute of Science*, Calcutta, 1923, vol. v, p. 177.

[50] P. van Romburgh and C. E. J. Lohmann, *Verslag 's Lands Plantentuin*, Buitenzorg, 1895.

[51] C. Hartwich and P. A. du Pasquier, *Apoth. Zeit.*, Berlin, 1909, vol. xxiv, p. 109.

[13] *loc. cit.*

[37] *loc. cit.*

[52] Private communication from Geo. F. Mitchell, Supervising Tea Examiner, Washington, D. C.

Parts of Plant	Caffeine Content
First and second leaves	3.4%
Fifth and sixth leaves	1.5%
Stalk between fifth and sixth leaves	0.5%
Tea flowers	0.8%
Shell of green fruit	0.6%
Seed	0.0%
Hairs of young leaves	2.25%

caffeine complexes during the processes involved in tea making. Hartwich and du Pasquier[51] give a table showing the amount of "free" and "combined" caffeine at various stages of manufacture.

Much work has been done on the compound of caffeine and tannin which exists in tea infusions. Workers in the Lancet Laboratory[10] found that when weak sulphuric acid or sulphate of ammonia is added to a tea infusion, a precipitate containing caffeine and tannin in the ratio one to three by weight was obtained. This observation was used to show that most of the tannin in China tea was present in the combined form, whereas the tannin in Ceylon and India black teas was largely present in the free form.

Later work, however, has shown that no such steady ratio of caffeine to tannin can be precipitated, for the proportions vary from one to three up to one to twelve, according to the concentration of the tea solution, and the strength of the precipitant used.

Deuss has prepared caffeine tea tannate in the absence of water, and has observed that this compound is decomposed by water.[21] The compound of tea tannin and caffeine hence differs from the compound formed with other tannins.

The Essential Oil of Tea

The essential oil of tea is prepared by distilling black tea with steam, and extracting the oil in minute quantities from the water which distills over. This oil is sometimes called "theol." Bamber[17] found about three parts per 10,000 parts of tea, and described it as forming colorless highly refracting, irregular drops. Van Romburgh[53] considered only the non-water-soluble substance which distilled over in steam, and obtained six parts of oil per 100,000 parts of tea.

The quantity of essential oil being so small, its properties have been imperfectly studied. Van Romburgh noticed that the water soluble part of the steam distillate contained methyl alcohol, and a very volatile product giving aldehydic reactions. There also was a little acetone in this portion. The actual oil which collects as a drop on the water distilled from tea, has a penetrating odor of tea. It has a specific gravity of 0.866 at 26° C. and is faintly optically active. Van Romburgh, by distillation, separated the oil into two parts, one boiling at 170° C. and the other above that temperature. This oil of lower boiling point is a colorless liquid having the odor of tea. Analysis indicates for it an empirical formula of $C_6H_{12}O$. The fraction boiling above 170° C. contains a small percentage of methyl salicylate [oil of wintergreen].

Gildemeister and Hoffmann[54] state that the principal constituent of the essential oil is an alcohol of the formula $C_6H_{12}O$.

The oil, when exposed to the air, resinifies, owing to oxidation. It is found in fermented tea and has not been definitely shown to exist in fresh leaf. As soon as the leaf is rolled and left to ferment, the oil rapidly appears. Bamber[17] observed that the oil continues to increase during the first part of the firing process, after which it decreases.

The oil is not found in green tea, but Mulder[1] claimed to have found considerable quantities in unfermented teas.

Hartwich and du Pasquier[51] consider that the chief constituents of the essential oil are present in fresh leaf in glucosidal combination, and during manufacture these are liberated. Staub[55] believes this liberation to be the result of enzyme ac-

51 loc. cit.
10 loc. cit.
21 loc. cit., p. 19.
17 loc. cit

53 P. van Romburgh, Schimmel's Berichte, Leipzig, 1897, p. 40; Proc. Academy of Sciences, Amsterdam, 1920, vol. xxii, p. 758.
54 R. Gildemeister and F. Hoffmann, Les huiles essentielles, Leipzig-Paris, 1900, p. 606.
17 loc. cit.
1 loc. cit.
51 loc. cit.
55 W. Staub, Bull. Jardin Botanique, Buitenzorg, 1912, no. 5, p. 156.

tion, and not that of yeasts or bacteria. Deuss [56] is of the opinion that during manufacture a sugar is formed from some more complex body, which is capable of providing the alcohol of the essential oil.

In addition to the normal flavor of all black teas, which is attributed to the essential oil of tea, there are other flavors peculiar to certain districts and seasons. No definite chemical information regarding the substances giving these flavors has been obtained. When a tea is described as "flavory," the expression refers to flavor other than that attributed to the essential oil of tea.

Other Constituents of the Tea Leaf

Having discussed the three most important constituents of tea, it now remains to mention briefly some of the other components which are less well known, and generally are less important, so far as the quality of tea is concerned.

PIGMENTS.—Chlorophyll, the green coloring matter of plants, and its allied pigments are, of course, present in the tea leaf. Chlorophyll is essential to photosynthesis in plants. The chlorophylls a and b, and the allied pigments carotin and xanthophyll, may amount to as much as 16 per cent of the dry matter of some plants. No reliable figures are available for the content of these pigments in tea.

Although chlorophyll is insoluble in water, the greenish color of tea leaf and green tea infusions suggests that some form or product of chlorophyll enters the tea solution. It usually is supposed that part of the chlorophyll is destroyed during the fermentation of black tea.

Members of the flavone and anthocyan groups also are present in tea. The flavone and flavonol pigments are yellow bodies similarly constituted, and having similar properties. They occur in plants frequently as glucosides. Quercitrin is a flavonol found in tea. It is a glucoside which on hydrolysis yields quercetin [tetra-hydroxy-flavonol] and rhamnose—a sugar.

Deuss [57] showed the presence of quercitrin as follows: A tea extract, obtained either from fresh leaf or finished tea, was boiled under a reflux condenser in an atmosphere of carbon dioxide with ½ per cent hydrochloric acid. A brown precipitate thus was obtained, consisting largely of tannin "red." When this was dried and extracted with ether, quercetin was obtained. No quercetin was found either in fresh leaf or made tea, hence Deuss considered that the glucoside quercitrin occurs in tea.

The content of quercitrin was calculated to be about 0.1 per cent of the dry matter, both in fresh leaf and finished tea.

Nanninga [58] has described a glucoside which he separated from tea, and which possibly was quercitrin.

Shibata [59] has shown that tea grown in the sun contains a greater quantity of flavones than that grown in the shade.

The importance of the anthocyan pigments in green tea already has been treated. A close connection between the flavones and the anthocyans is known to exist, and both groups of bodies are related to catechin. Freudenberg [60] uses the term "catechins" as a collective name for the group of such substances obtained from plants.

Anthocyans usually occur in plants as glucosides, and as such are termed anthocyanidins. The anthocyans occur in minute quantities in the tea leaf, but as yet no detailed study has been made of them.

GALLIC ACID.—Small quantities of gallic acid are found in tea. This substance occurs also in gall nuts, the bark of some trees, and various plants.

Gallic acid crystallizes in silken needles. It forms brown products in alkaline solution and reduces Fehling solution, but it does not precipitate gelatine. From gallic acid is obtained digallic acid. And the relationship of the latter substance to gallotannic acid, the tannin of oak galls, was shown by Fischer in his synthesis of pentadigalloyl-glucose, which is practically identical with gallotannic acid, the best known of the pyrogallol tannins. [25]

The presence of gallic acid in tea probably influenced the earlier workers in

[56] J. J. B. Deuss, *Mededeelingen Proefstation v. Thee*, Buitenzorg, 1912, no. 18.
[57] J. J. B. Deuss, *Recueil. trav. chim.*, Leyde, 1923, vol. xlii, 4th ser. vol. iii, pp. 623–4.
[58] A. W. Nanninga, *Verslag onderzoekingen Java gecult. theeën*, Buitenzorg, 1900.
[59] K. Shibata, *Botanical Magazine*, London, 1915, vol. xxix, p. 343.
[60] K. Freudenberg, *Berichte deut. chem. Gesell.*, Berlin, 1920, vol. liii, p. 1416.
[25] loc. cit.

classing tea tannin with the pyrogallol tannins.

THEOPHYLLIN, ETC.—In 1888, Kossel [61] isolated theophyllin, $C_7H_8N_4O_2$, from tea. It occurs in minute quantities. Theophyllin is an isomer of the alkaloid theobromine, which occurs in cocoa.

The presence of minute quantities of xanthin, hypoxanthin, adenine, and theobromine in tea also has been reported. No definite study of these substances has been made in connection with tea.

PROTEIN BODIES.—The nitrogen content of tea or dry leaf is about 5.5 per cent of which about one-fifth is accountable for as caffeine nitrogen. The "crude protein" content of the leaf, calculated empirically, is thus about 26 per cent. This value includes proteins, amino and amido compounds, and other nitrogenous bodies. The "pure protein" content, which consists of nitrogenous bodies not extracted by a mixture of alcohol and 2 per cent acetic acid, is about 15 per cent, both in fresh leaf and finished tea. This value was given by Peligot in 1845,[2] and has since been confirmed.

During the manufacture of tea, the proteins are partly precipitated by the tannin, and partly coagulated by the heat during the drying process. The result is that even the water-soluble albumins, which are present in the leaf, are rendered insoluble; and, even if this were not so, the boiling water used for infusing tea would render them so. A tea infusion contains small quantities of nitrogenous bodies, other than caffeine, which may be calculated as proteins.[13]

In Japan it has been found that amino acids play an important part in the quality of green tea. Analyses of Japan green teas usually quote crude protein, pure protein and amino acids.

It has been observed in Japan that heavy nitrogenous manuring increases the nitrogen content of the leaf, and thus improves quality.[8] Heavy nitrogenous manuring also has been shown to increase the nitrogen content of the leaf in Assam, although no improvement in quality has been recorded.[62]

CARBOHYDRATES, ETC.—Cellulose occurs in considerable quantity in both fresh leaf and in tea, as the leaf structure is made up largely of cellulose. The cellulose content is about 12 per cent, but, being insoluble in water, it does not enter the tea infusion, nor does it apparently take part in the changes of manufacture.

Small quantities of sugars occur in the tea leaf. Maurenbrecher and Tollens [63] found galactose and arabinose in the leaf. Study in Japan [13] has shown that the sugars stored in the tea leaf vary somewhat, according to the conditions of growth, shading, etc. The total sugar calculated as hexose was found to be about 1.2 per cent in both shaded and unshaded bushes grown for Gyokuro tea. The shaded bushes, however, contained only a trace of reducing sugar, whilst the unshaded bushes showed quantities varying from a trace to 0.4 per cent. The quantity of cane sugar, calculated as hexose, was found to be about 0.9 per cent in shaded bushes and 0.6 per cent in unshaded. The total sugar in Gyokuro tea was found to vary from 1.2 to 1.8 per cent.

Gummy matter, dextrin, and pectin, occur in considerable quantity and may represent 6 or 7 per cent of the dry matter in the leaf. During the firing of tea some of these substances may be caramelized, and the "malty" smell of black tea as it leaves the dryer possibly is due, in part, to this change. These substances dissolve to a large extent in boiling water and influence the thickness of the tea liquors.

The amount of starch in the young tea leaf is very small, about 0.5 per cent, but it is greater in the older leaves. The woody parts of the bush contain 15 per cent or more starch, and the seeds about 30 per cent. The amount of starch in shoots taken from bushes growing naturally—from tea seed bushes—is much greater than that in bushes which are regularly pruned and plucked. Bhanji shoots show a considerable starch content. Generally speaking, leaves containing much starch contain less tannin than those containing little starch.

The starch content of the leaf slightly increases during the day. During the withering process the starch practically disappears.

[61] A. Kossel, Berichte deut. chem. Gesell., Berlin, 1888, vol. xxi, p. 2164.
[2] loc. cit.
[13] loc. cit.
[8] loc. cit.
[62] P. H. Carpenter and C. R. Harler, Quarterly Journal Indian Tea Association, Calcutta, 1922, part 4.

[63] A. D. Maurenbrecher and B. Tollens, Zeit. Rübenzüchter Indus., Berlin, 1908, p. 1044.
[13] loc. cit.

The leaf contains various mineral and organic salts. The pectinate, oxalate, and phosphate of potash were identified by Nanninga, both in the fresh leaf and in finished tea. Most of the phosphoric acid is present as the potash salt.

The ash, which constitutes about 5.5 per cent of the weight of the dry matter of the leaf, consists of about 50 per cent potash, and 15 per cent phosphoric acid. The rest is made up of lime and magnesia principally. There are small quantities of iron, manganese, soda, silica, sulphur, and chlorine. Some of the Japan teas show an ash content as high as 9 per cent.

Other products of the leaf, such as fats, waxes, crude fiber, and oxalic acid, cannot be discussed here. The fats and waxes constitute about 1.5 per cent of the leaf, and the crude fiber about 10 per cent.

Tea-Seed Oil

It might be well to mention here the subject of tea-seed oil. It must first be remarked that this oil is quite distinct from the essential oil of the fermented tea leaf.

On tea plantations managed by Europeans the tea-seed is not utilized, except when a tea-seed garden is laid out. In this case the leaf is not plucked, and the bush is allowed to grow up and produce seed. On a plucking area seed is regarded as detrimental to leaf production and it, or the flower, is cut off at pruning time.

Tea-seed oil is produced commercially in China, Indo-China, and Japan. The chief centers of production in China are East Kiangsi and South Yunnan, while the chief export cities are Hankow and Wuchow. The oil is expressed from the seeds of various varieties of *Thea*, but usually from other than those cultivated for leaf. The oil content, which depends on the variety of seed, and the region in which it is produced, ranges from about 15 to 45 per cent.

Deuss [64] found an average of 42 per cent oil in tea seeds produced in Java. The seed from China bushes he found to contain 30 to 35 per cent oil, and that from Assam bushes 43 to 45 per cent.

The oil, which ranges in color from yellow to orange, is of the non-drying class.

The crude oil has an unpleasant odor, and a more or less bitter taste, both of which can be removed by proper refining methods.

The finest quality oil is used as hair oil. The better grades of the ordinary tea oil are taken for edible purposes, chiefly in the countries where it is produced. The poorer grades are utilized in soap making, and as an illuminant.

"Fermentation" in Tea Manufacture

Having given some account of the chemistry of the constituents of the tea leaf, it now is necessary to describe the enzymes found within the leaf, and the microörganisms found on the leaf, for without some knowledge of this side of the subject the significance of the various processes of manufacture cannot be appreciated.

The enzymes and microörganisms assume most importance in black or fermented tea and Oolong or semi-fermented tea. The first process in the manufacture of these teas is withering, in which the leaf is partially dried at the normal air temperature. The leaf then is rolled and the leaf cells thereby broken, and the juice exposed to the air. This exposure is called "fermentation." Fermentation denotes the decomposition of carbohydrates by yeasts or enzymes to form alcohol and gas, or acid and gas. Although various workers have suggested that true fermentation may go on to a small extent during tea manufacture, since yeasts exist on the leaf and carbohydrates are present in the leaf juice, and an alcohol is found in the essential oil, which is produced during fermentation, by far the main process taking place during the "fermentation" of tea is the oxidation of the tea tannin.

The term "fermentation" in connection with tea manufacture, is essentially a planter's expression. Bamber in his earlier work uses the term oxidation to denote this process, and Mitchell [65] in his bulletin on tea in the United States consistently uses this term.

In the following discussion the expression "fermentation" will be employed on account of its general use by Europeans interested in tea.

The oxidation of tea tannin is brought

[64] J. J. B. Deuss, *l'Agronomie Coloniale*, Paris, June, 1913.

[65] G. F. Mitchell, *Bulletin* no. 234, U. S. Department of Agriculture, Washington, D. C., 1912.

about by the aid of enzymes. In green tea manufacture the leaf is heated before being rolled, and in this manner the activity of the enzymes is stayed and no oxidation takes place. Green teas are referred to as unfermented teas.

ENZYMES, BACTERIA, AND YEASTS.—Before giving an account of the work on the enzymes and microörganisms of the tea leaf, it is necessary to define these bodies briefly.

There is a large group of organic substances termed enzymes, many of which occur in every plant. They have a certain characteristic in common; i.e., they bring about chemical reactions in the plant without undergoing any permanent change themselves. In other words, they are organic catalysts. Many of the reactions which take place in the plant cell with considerable rapidity at ordinary temperatures, owing to the presence of enzymes, need prolonged heating at high temperatures when brought about by artificial means.

Enzymes generally can be extracted from the plant with water, if the tissues are thoroughly disintegrated. Their chemical constitution is unknown at present. They usually are destroyed at temperatures greater than 60° Centigrade.

Many processes which enzymes control in the plant can be brought about by them in vitro under suitable conditions. The majority of known plant enzymes control both hydrolysis and its converse, synthesis, by condensation with elimination of water. Under artificial conditions, however, hydrolysis most frequently occurs.

Hydrolysis and synthesis are not the only processes catalyzed by enzymes. Thus the oxidizing enzymes bring about the oxidation of substances, notably of aromatics, in the plant. There also are coagulating, fermenting, and reducing enzymes.

Enzymes aid the formation of the products of photosynthesis in the leaf. During the process of respiration, when complex bodies are broken down to simpler ones, enzymes again play a part. They also are active in rendering insoluble materials soluble, and thus capable of translocation in the plant. The full extent of the number of plant reactions catalyzed by enzymes is not yet known.

Enzymes are specific in their actions and generally are classed accordingly. The commoner plant enzymes may be classified under the following heads:

(a) Hydrolytic Enzymes. These add or eliminate water and are subclassed according to the substances on which they act. Thus, there are fat-splitting, carbohydrate-splitting, glucoside-splitting, and protein-splitting hydrolytic enzymes.

(b) Oxidizing Enzymes. Peroxidases decompose peroxides, setting free oxygen in an "active" state, probably as atomic oxygen. Catalases set free oxygen from hydrogen peroxide in an "inactive" condition. Catalases are not regarded as true oxidizing enzymes.

(c) Fermenting Enzymes, e.g., zymase of yeasts, bring about the decomposition of certain hexoses with the formation of alcohol and carbon dioxide. The butyric ferment, which occurs in certain bacteria, breaks down certain acids to butyric acid.

Since the enzyme concerned in tea fermentation is an oxidase, this class will be considered in some detail.

The presence of oxidizing enzymes in plants was long ago associated with the following phenomena: If the expressed juices, or water extracts, of the tissues of some plants are added to a solution of guaiacum gum in the presence of air, a deep blue color is obtained in a short time. On the other hand, the juices or extracts from other plants produce no such color. On the addition, however, of a few drops of hydrogen peroxide, in the latter case, the color rapidly develops. Plants are said to contain an oxidase when the extracts give a blue color with guaiacum alone, and a peroxidase when the addition of hydrogen peroxide is necessary to bring about bluing.

The oxidase-containing plants also show another phenomenon. If the tissue extracts are left exposed to the air, they become dark-colored—generally brown, or reddish brown. The same effect may be produced very rapidly by chloroform vapor. These phenomena are absent from plants giving the peroxidase reaction only.

Various hypotheses have been suggested in explanation of the reactions of oxidizing enzymes. The one often accepted is that the oxidase consists of two components—a peroxide and a peroxidase. The peroxide may be either hydrogen peroxide, or an organic peroxide. The peroxidase acts upon the peroxide, depriving it of an atom of oxygen which is transferred in an "active" condition to the substrate, which then is oxidized. Guaiacum is the substrate in the above experiments.

It is assumed, on the basis of the above hypothesis, that an organic compound capable of acting as a peroxide is present in the juice, or extract which gives the oxidase reaction. Evidence further goes to show that plants which give the oxidase reaction and turn brown on injury contain an aromatic substance with the catechol grouping. On the death of the plant cell, brought about by injury or chloroform vapor, this substance is oxidized by the peroxidase, with the formation of a brown color and an oxidation product, which then acts as an organic peroxide in the oxidase system.

Hence, it appears that the oxidase reaction of plants, as detected by guaiacum, is the outcome of post-mortem changes after the death of the cell. The actual functions of the oxidase system in the metabolism of the living plant still is a matter under discussion.

Unlike enzymes, bacteria are living bodies capable of reproduction. They are minute vegetable organisms, for the most part unicellular and devoid of chlorophyll, which multiply by simple transverse division or fission. They are the lowest forms of plant life. Under optimum conditions for each species, bacteria will multiply very rapidly.

Bacteria may be found almost anywhere, in water, foods, the soil, the stomach, and intestines of all animals, etc., but not in the blood or tissues of healthy animals or plants.

Bacteria generally thrive in feeble light. All bacteria are killed by a temperature of 150° C. if maintained for half an hour. They also are destroyed by disinfectants.

The term yeast is applied to a large order of simple unicellular fungi, many of which have the power of producing alcohol when grown in the juice of fruits, malt extract, and other solutions containing sugars.

The yeasts, like bacteria, are minute vegetable organisms, but are a rather more highly-developed form of life than the latter. Yeasts have optimum working conditions and are killed by high temperatures. The power of yeasts to break down certain sugars to alcohol and carbon dioxide, depends on the enzyme secreted within the yeast cell. This enzyme can be extracted by grinding with sand, and subjecting the cells to high pressure. The enzyme thus extracted has the power to bring about fermentation, but is incapable of growth or reproduction.

EARLY STUDIES.—The nature of tea fermentation has been discussed for many years. The *Tea Cyclopaedia*,[66] published in 1881, contains many letters from planters setting forth arguments relative to the nature of tea fermentation. Some considered the change was one comparable to the malting process undergone by barley, when the starchy material is hydrolyzed, while others considered tea fermentation to be a process of incipient decay or rotting.

The scientific study of the subject was taken up at the beginning of the century. The first point considered was, what caused the change in color of the withered leaf from green to bright copper, after it had been rolled. Bamber[17] first considered the change to be a purely chemical one, unaided by enzymes or microörganisms. Later[18] he managed to separate an enzyme from the leaf, almost simultaneously with the parallel discovery by Nanninga in Java.[58] In Japan, Aso also showed that the leaf contained an enzyme.[67] Newton studied the enzyme concerned with tea fermentation, and gave it the name *thease*.[68] Mann supplied much information on the subject,[69] and later, further details were given by Bernard, Welter,[70] and Staub.[71]

Bamber showed that the enzyme concerned in tea fermentation is an oxidase, which oxidizes some of the contents of the leaf during fermentation. Aso concluded that the black color of tea is due to the action of the oxidase on the tannin, and that green tea owes its color to the fact that the enzyme is destroyed during the first process in the preparation.

Bacteria can be separated from the leaf, and many years ago it was suggested by

66 *Tea Cyclopedia*, Calcutta, 1881, p. 208, *et seq.*
17 *loc. cit.*
18 *loc. cit.*
58 *loc. cit.*
67 K. Aso, *Bulletin Agricultural College*, Tokyo, 1901.
68 C. R. Newton, "The Fermentation of the Tea Leaf," *Indian Planting and Gardening*, Calcutta, 1901.
69 H. H. Mann, *The Ferment of the Tea Leaf*, Indian Tea Association, Calcutta, 1901, 1903, 1904, parts 1, 2, and 3.
70 C. Bernard and H. L. Welter, *Mededeelingen Proefstation v. Thee*, Buitenzorg, 1911, nos. 12 and 13.
71 W. Staub, *Mededeelingen Proefstation v. Thee*, Buitenzorg, 1912, no. 18.

Kosai,[16] and later by Wahgel,[72] that tea fermentation was a bacterial action. The earliest argument against the idea, or, in fact, against the theory of the agency in any controlling form of microörganisms, was that they would not have time to develop sufficiently during the fermentation period. Later work, consisting of the sterilization of the leaf and its subsequent fermentation, confirmed the view that the main action was due to agents other than microörganisms.

Bernard[73] isolated yeasts from fresh tea leaf and made pure cultures. In his paper on yeasts, Bernard discussed the three theories of tea fermentation in the light of the evidence then available. They were:

(a) Chemical theory—Simple oxidation.
(b) Enzyme theory—Oxidation with the aid of enzymes, found within the leaf, known as oxidases.
(c) Microörganism theory—Oxidation, not by enzymes within the leaf, but in the cells of microörganisms growing on the leaf.

The first theory was discarded, since all evidence was against it. Although the enzyme theory was the one generally accepted at the time, and believed in by Bamber, van Romburgh, Nanninga, and Mann, certain experiments seemed to suggest that the yeasts might have an important influence on fermentation. Bernard, however, recognized that the bacteria are not essential to tea fermentation, and that they often had a harmful effect on the fermentation process, so far as the quality of the tea was concerned.

Bosscha was of the belief that the yeast cells played an overwhelming rôle in tea fermentation, and his opinion gave occasion for the controversy on the subject between Nanninga and himself.[74]

Later work has brought forth no further evidence that microörganisms play an important part in tea fermentation. Evidence goes to show that the main reaction is influenced by the oxidizing enzyme, bacteria usually are harmful, and yeasts may play some minor part. There always is the possibility that the yeast may be concerned with the aroma of tea and, although the development of this quality is a minor reaction in the general course of fermentation, it is important from the point of view of the value of the tea.

LATER WORK.—Bernard and Welter,[70] and later, Welter,[75] made detailed studies of the enzyme, which they separated from the leaf by the same method used by Mann.[76] Fresh leaf is pulped with hide powder, which precipitates the tannin. The removal of the tannin is necessary because it interferes with the guaiacum reaction, used for detecting the enzyme. The mixture of pulped leaf and hide powder is squeezed through a cloth and the liquid thus obtained contains the enzyme, which is precipitated as a slimy mass by alcohol. It dries to a whitish powder.

Bernard and Welter found about the same amount of oxidase and peroxidase in all parts of the plant, and noted no appreciable change in the amount of enzyme in the leaf during manufacture. The activity of the enzyme, as measured by the guaiacum reaction, was found to be about the same, between 25 and 75° C. At 78° C. the action became slow and feeble and above this temperature there was no action. The enzyme is, however, resistant to heat, and is only permanently incapacitated if kept for some time at a temperature above 80° Centigrade.

Welter showed that phenol, or sulphuretted hydrogen, destroys the power of the enzyme, as does also an excess of hydrogen peroxide. Acids hinder its action, and one part sulphuric acid to 1,000 parts leaf, by weight, is sufficient to stop fermentation entirely. Carbonic acid slows up the reaction.

The same worker satisfactorily demonstrated that the enzyme was responsible for the coloring of the tannin during fermentation. He also showed that when the yeasts were destroyed, fermentation still took place. However, since the yeast also contains a peroxidase, there still was the possibility that this would take part in the fermentation after the yeast itself had been destroyed. In order to obviate this

[16] loc. cit.

[72] H. Wahgel, Chem. Zeitung, Göthen, 1903, vol. xxvii, p. 230.

[73] C. Bernard, Mededeelingen Proefstation v. Thee, Buitenzorg, 1907, no. 5.

[74] J. Bosscha, "The Ferment of Tea," Notulen Soekaboemischen Landbouw Verein, September, 1909. "More About Tea Fermentation," Ind. Mercuur, Batavia, 1910, no. 41, p. 814; A. W. Nanninga, "Discussion of Communication Concerning Yeasts," Ind. Mercuur, 1910, no. 34, p. 680, and no. 39, p. 775.

[70] loc. cit.

[75] H. L. Welter, Mededeelingen Proefstation v. Thee, Buitenzorg, 1912, no. 15.

[76] H. H. Mann The Fermentation of Tea, Indian Tea Association, Calcutta, 1906, 1907, parts 1 and 2.

possibility, Welter took the unopened buds of tea shoots, presumably free from yeasts, and, after treatment with chloroform, rolled them. Fermentation took place as under normal conditions with ordinary leaf.

Welter also found that finished tea, when extracted with cold water, showed the peroxidase reaction with guaiacum. From this, an explanation of the mellowing or post-fermentation of tea is obtained, as well as an idea of the great power of resistance to heat and drying possessed by the enzyme.

In 1923 Deuss [77] reviewed unpublished investigations made by Bernard and Welter on the subject of tea fermentation.

Evans, in Ceylon, has recently taken up the study of the enzyme system in tea fermentation.[12] He has observed the rate of absorption of oxygen by crushed leaf, and found it to proceed rapidly for the first three or four hours, after which it slows down. The relationship between the amount of oxygen absorbed and the time taken, can be represented by a smooth die-away curve characteristic of enzyme reactions. Oxygen up-take is characteristic of fermenting tea, and if the leaf is dried at a high temperature, or steamed for a few minutes before it is crushed, this power is lost. Further, fresh leaf can be dipped in a 1 per cent solution of mercuric chloride without detriment to its power of taking up oxygen. This characteristic, then, is not due to the presence of microorganisms.

Evans has also studied the action of the catalase in the tea leaf, and, by measuring its rate of evolution of oxygen from hydrogen peroxide, noticed that its activity increased slightly during withering and declined during fermentation. Four hours after the leaf cells had been ruptured the catalase reaction became negligible.

Referring again to the microörganisms of the tea leaf, it has been shown that fresh leaf has a considerable bacterial flora, although very little specific work has been done on the subject. In fermenting leaf, many more bacterial species are found, and Bamber [18] recognized the butyric ferment in considerable quantity in leaf which had been fermenting for more than four or five hours. The sourness of over-fermented tea he attributed to the action of the butyric ferment. It also has been suggested that other "taints" in tea may be due to bacterial action.[78]

Bosscha and Brzesowsky,[79] making a survey of the microörganisms of the fermenting tea leaf, found many types of bacteria, most of which apparently do no harm to the quality of tea. It appears that the harmful bacteria are introduced from outside sources.

Mention has been made of the possibility that yeasts may play a part in tea fermentation, and the opinion is held by some observers that yeasts may be responsible for the district and seasonal flavors of some teas. In this connection it has been recorded that, in Assam, the tea leaf is rich in yeasts in the spring and fall, when flavor is obtained in that area, and poor in the Monsoon period, when there is rarely any flavor apart from the normal tea flavor, which is attributed to the essential oil.[78]

The yeasts of the tea leaf, like the bacteria, increase in numbers during the manufacture of black tea.

It has been shown also [79] that fermenting leaf, besides containing microörganisms in the form of bacteria and yeasts, may contain certain higher organisms in the form of molds; viz., *penicillium*, *aspergillus*, *mucor*, and *dematium*.

Chemical Changes in Manufacture

The manufacture of black tea in India, Ceylon, and the Dutch Indies follows along approximately the same lines. These same methods have been adopted in other countries, where the industry is controlled by Europeans. They consist of five processes, namely, withering, rolling, fermenting, firing, sorting. Methods are sufficiently different in China to necessitate separate mention of the procedure.

The last process is wholly mechanical, and needs only enter the present discussion in so far as the moisture content of the packed tea is influenced by the manner in which the leaf is exposed during sorting. Briefly, the various processes bring about the following changes:

[77] J. J. B. Deuss, *Chem. Weekblad*, Amsterdam, 1923, vol. xx, pp. 253-4.
[12] loc. cit.
[18] loc. cit.

[78] A. C. Tunstall, *Quarterly Journal Indian Tea Association*, Calcutta, 1923, part 4.
[79] K. A. R. Bosscha and A. Brzesowsky, *Mededeelingen Proefstation v. Thee*, Buitenzorg, 1916, no. 47.

In withering, the leaf loses moisture and becomes flaccid and capable of being suitably rolled. As soon as the leaf is bruised, fermentation sets in and proceeds more rapidly when the leaf is exposed to the air in the fermenting room. During firing, the leaf is almost completely dried, and the reactions of fermentation are thus practically stopped.

Withering in Black Tea Manufacture

When the leaf is withered, the most important change taking place, so far as present knowledge goes, is loss of water. This occurs principally from the under surface of the leaf.

During withering, the cell wall becomes more permeable. This can be demonstrated by soaking fresh and withered leaf in water and noting that the former gives no coloration with ferric chloride, whereas the latter shows a coloration in a few minutes, denoting immediate diffusion of the tannin. The ease with which tannin, and other substances, may be extracted with boiling water, also increases as the wither proceeds.

After the leaf is plucked, the process of respiration continues, but at a reduced rate. It has been recorded that leaf withered till it contains about 55 per cent moisture, is actively respiring still, but at a slightly lower rate than fresh leaf. The rate of respiration of withered leaf is retarded immediately after it is crushed, whereas that of fresh leaf is not appreciably altered by this process.

During withering, not only is water lost from the leaf, but part of the solid matter also disappears as the result of respiratory changes taking place. The amount of solid matter thus lost is appreciable. There is an apparent increase in the water soluble matter of the leaf during withering, but when a correction is applied for respiratory losses, it becomes evident that there has been no real appreciable increase in the water soluble percentage.[80]

The earlier tea workers in Java registered a decrease of 1 to 2 per cent in the water soluble extract during withering. This may have been due to over-withering, or the effect of high temperatures during the withering process. An extreme case of the effect of high temperatures often is met in practice when leaf is permitted to heat up in the plucking baskets. In certain cases temperatures of 140° F. have been recorded in the middle of a basket of leaf. The water soluble tannin in such instances is reduced to about a half its original value.

The acidity of the cell sap is unchanged during withering, showing a pH value of 4.3 to 4.5 at all stages of the process. The small amount of starch present in the leaf practically disappears during withering. Withered leaf takes on a fruity odor.

If fresh or withered leaf be infused, a greenish-yellow solution is obtained. According to tea tasters, these infusions are "raw" or "harsh"—terms difficult to translate. If leaf, either fresh or withered, is damaged and kept for a few minutes, it gives a red infusion. This infusion still is pronounced "raw" by tasters, but "pungency" also is detected. Pungency develops as soon as the leaf is rolled, and it would appear that this characteristic results from fermentation, and is connected with the oxidation products of tannin. It is of interest to record that Peacock[81] considers that the astringent principle of maté is due to the presence of phlobaphenes.

Summing up the evidence concerning the changes which take place in the leaf during withering, it appears that the chief reason for withering tea leaf is to get it in a flaccid condition suitable for rolling. In practice, the degree of the wither is judged in various well-known ways, most of which consist of tests of turgidity of the leaf and stalk. At present there is no test for the state of the wither other than the physical ones.

There is evidence, however, that time is a factor in withering, and experience supports the contention that the best wither is obtained when the requisite loss of moisture is realized in about eighteen hours. The consideration of time as a factor has led to the belief that some important chemical change takes place in the wither; but numerous investigations in Java and India have failed to indicate any appreciable change. It is, however, fully realized that unless the wither is carried out with care, chemical changes may take place to the detriment of the made tea.

[80] "Report of Tea Research Institute, Ceylon," *Tropical Agriculture*, Colombo, 1918, vol. lxxi, no. 3; *The Tea Quarterly*, Colombo, 1929, vol. ii, part 1.

[81] J. C. and B. L. Peacock, *Jour. Am. Pharm. Assn.*, Easton, 1922, vol. ix, no. 8.

The effect of time on the wither has been explained on the hypothesis that the drying of the leaf causes a concentration of the cell sap, so that the degree of dispersion of the cell constituents is altered. The increase in concentration thus affects the physical condition of the colloidal material of the leaf, with consequent changes in the permeability and of the surface area, which is of so great importance for cell oxidative processes. Since coagulation is affected by time and temperature, as well as by changes in concentration, it will be realized that variations in the time taken and the temperature employed to attain the requisite loss of moisture will affect the degree of dispersion of the cell contents. The amount of surface available for oxidation will thus vary according to the manner in which the leaf has been withered.[82]

Rolling in Black Tea Manufacture

The object of rolling the leaf is to break the leaf cells and to mix the contents thereof. From the point of view of the chemical changes attending this process, rolling is intimately connected with fermentation, and the changes will be discussed hereinafter in the section dealing with fermentation.

The amount of change taking place during fermentation is governed largely by the amount of rolling, or, in other words, by the number of leaf cells ruptured.

During rolling, some heat is developed in the roller, and it is common for the temperature of the leaf to rise from 3° to 15° F. This heat is mainly that evolved by fermentation.

When leaf is insufficiently withered, or is rolled very hard, juice is expressed from the rollers. This juice reddens very quickly in the warmer tea districts, and in these it usually is thrown away. In Assam it has been observed that if the juice is put back with the leaf a "flat" [over-fermented] tea results.[83] This is partly because the juice ferments much more quickly than the leaf. Estimations show that the expressed juice contains from 1 to 1.5 per cent of solids, and from 0.25 to 0.35 per cent tannin, the composition being richer, the fuller the wither.

With well withered leaf very little juice is expressed.[84]

Fermentation in Black Tea Manufacture

During fermentation in black tea manufacture most of the chemical changes involved take place. Color, strength, pungency, and aroma are developed during fermentation. Within limits, the harder and longer the rolling, the more strength and color are developed. Hard rolling may, however, for mechanical reasons, expose stalk in the finished tea.

Old, hard leaf will not ferment satisfactorily, partly, no doubt, on account of its poverty in tannin, and partly because the cells are difficult to break in rolling.

The fermentation of tea has reached a satisfactory stage when a certain color and aroma have developed. In practice, it is customary to check the fermentation on the taster's report, and in this manner to obtain, by empirical methods the average fermentation conditions which produce the kind of tea suitable for a certain market.

Leaf will not ferment in vacuo, nor in an atmosphere of carbonic acid gas. Oxygen is essential to fermentation, and the amount of this gas absorbed by the fermenting leaf increases with the rolling. Withered leaf absorbs more oxygen when it is rolled than does fresh leaf.

Since oxygen is necessary to fermentation, it will be understood that the depth of the heap in which the fermenting leaf is spread, is important, since this regulates the air supply. Generally speaking, the thinner the leaf is spread, the quicker it ferments.

Humidity in the atmosphere aids fermentation, and, if the air is dry, the surface of the leaf dries, and the oxidation of the leaf does not proceed favorably. It is likely that tea fermentation, by nature a surface action, requires a fluid medium on the leaf for satisfactory development.

The question of the part played by microörganisms in tea fermentation still is awaiting complete solution, although the general practice in tea factories is to keep the fermenting floor clean and free of microörganisms. This does not, of course, exclude organisms brought in on the leaf

[82] D. I. Evans, *The Tea Quarterly*, Colombo, 1928, vol. i, part 4.

[83] P. H. Carpenter and H. R. Cooper, *Quarterly Journal Indian Tea Association*, Calcutta, 1922, part 2.

[84] C. R. Harler, *Quarterly Journal Indian Tea Association*, Calcutta, 1922, part 4.

itself, but merely avoids their accumulation.

It has been shown that light may hinder the action of enzymes, and, although it has not been proved that light is detrimental to tea fermentation, it is the practice to keep bright sunlight out of the fermenting room.

Nanninga studied the changes taking place during fermentation in the solubility of the leaf constituents. By extracting fresh dried leaf and finished black tea with chloroform, ether, ethyl acetate, alcohol, and water, he was able to note the following changes:

Apparently, part of the chlorophyll is destroyed during manufacture, although this point has not been definitely proved. Much of the soluble tannin disappears, and the soluble extract is reduced from about 62 per cent to 50 per cent. The substances left after the various extractions consist mainly of albuminous bodies, cellulose, and fibrous matter.

Regarding the effect of time on the extent of the chemical changes of fermentation, Nanninga showed that the soluble tannin decreased with time, and the tea became less astringent. The soluble tannin is often reduced to half its original value during fermentation. The water extract of the leaf first increases as fermentation develops, and then decreases.

Nanninga studied the effect of temperature on fermentation and found that the lower the temperature, the slower the transformations. Below 15° C. [59° F.] the progress of fermentation is negligible. Temperatures above 30° C. [86° F.], he found to be unfavorable, because aroma is lost, and the soluble matter in the leaf is decreased at such high temperatures. He discovered that the best results were obtained by fermenting at about 27° C. [80° F.], when the complex reactions constituting fermentation apparently march in best order. He did not find fermentation favorable at low temperatures because the long period of the process thus necessary tended to lose aroma. Nanninga stresses the point that hard and fast rules governing time and temperature of fermentation cannot be laid down.

Modern experience shows that an air temperature in the fermenting room of about 25° C. [77° F.], should be aimed at. The temperature of the leaf may rise during fermentation from 25° C. to about 30° C. [86° F.], according to the thickness the leaf is spread, and this rise apparently does no harm. A total fermentation time of three to four hours, including rolling, has been found to give the best results.

The exact nature of the chemical changes undergone by tea tannin during manufacture are imperfectly understood at present. A tannin oxidation product, soluble in tea infusion, is formed. Some of the tannin is rendered insoluble by the proteins in the leaf. Practically nothing is known of the formation of the essential oil during the process of fermentation.

Firing in Black Tea Manufacture

Chemically, the object of firing tea is to render inactive the enzymes and any microörganisms which may take part in the fermentation of the leaf. Heat, and the removal of moisture, practically stop fermentation.

During firing some of the products of the leaf are changed, and the "cabbage" flavor of the infusion of unfired leaf gives place to a "malty" flavor on firing. Partial caramelization of some of the leaf products may take place.

Some of the valuable constituents of the leaf, namely the substances giving rise to aroma and flavor, may be partially lost in firing. These substances, which constitute the essential oil, are volatile in steam, and high temperatures tend to accentuate their loss. When firing machines are overloaded, so that steam accumulates and the leaf is "stewed," flavor is notably lost. In order to retain the maximum of the essential oil, tea should be fired at a low temperature and spread thinly.

At one time high firing temperatures were supposed to reduce the caffeine content of the tea, and the grayish powder, which is often seen in firing machines, was assumed to be mainly caffeine. However, Keiller[85] reported this substance only contained about 3 per cent caffeine, the same as ordinary tea fluff.

Nanninga studied the effect of firing temperatures on the chemical constitution of the leaf, and, by successively extracting the made tea with moist ether, ethyl acetate, and alcohol, concluded that high firing at 110° C. [223° F.], gave tea con-

85 P. A. Keiller, *Tropical Agriculture*, Colombo, 1923, pp. 366-8.

taining less free tannin [soluble in moist ether], than did firing at a lower temperature; *viz.*, 85° C. [185° F.]. He found high firing to be detrimental to quality in tea.

Experience has shown that if tea is fired below 170° F., it will not keep well.[86] Attempts to cool dry tea with artificially dried air have produced teas rich in flavor but which will not keep. In order to stop fermentation sufficiently, temperatures not lower than about 170° F. apparently are necessary.[43]

The fermented leaf turns black on firing, but when the tea is infused the wet leaf again appears red. Successive infusions remove much of the red coloring matter, leaving it a dark greenish-brown.

During firing the proteins in the leaf are coagulated and rendered insoluble. Nitrogenous compounds, other than caffeine, enter the tea infusion, but these probably are degraded forms of proteins.

Moisture Content and Post-Fermentation

During the withering and firing processes the tea leaf loses moisture. The accompanying table of observations may be taken as typical of the course of the moisture loss in North East India.[87]

In Ceylon the leaf is withered till it contains about 55 or 60 per cent moisture, and in Java about 60 per cent. In both these countries the tea generally is fired in one operation.

Experiments both in India and Java have shown that tea is best packed containing 6 to 7 per cent moisture, for in this condition post-fermentation, or "mellowing," takes place. Tea packed with much less moisture will not mature after packing; whilst tea containing much more is liable to "go off" on keeping.

Although tea when discharged from the dryer contains about 3 per cent moisture, in the average sorting room it invariably picks up additional moisture during sorting according to the humidity of the atmosphere of the room. A series of experiments made by Deuss[88] has shown that tea handled in an atmosphere with a relative humidity of 65 per cent picks up or loses moisture, according to its original condition, till its moisture content is about 6 per cent.

Preparation of Black Tea in China

In China, it is customary to manufacture black tea on the same day the leaf is plucked. A quick wither in the sun is followed by alternate rolling and spreading in a cool spot. The firing is a process which takes place in several phases, with periods of rolling in between. The very thorough hand rolling which the leaf receives ruptures the leaf cells to a fuller extent than is realized by machine rolling. In China the careful manipulation of the leaf aims at keeping the juice as much within the leaf as possible. It is thus possible that the changes undergone by the tannin follow along somewhat different lines from those experienced in India, Ceylon, and Java, where the juice is deliberately exposed to the air.

The very thorough mixing of the cell juices entailed by China methods, combined with the frequent heating of the leaf to temperatures insufficient to stop fermentation, ensures a very full fermentation. Thus, in addition to the fact that the fresh leaf in China contains less tannin than that in India, Ceylon, or Java, the preparation in that country makes for a tea poor in tannin. It is probable that a greater proportion of the tannin is precipitated by proteins in China manufacture than by western methods. If this is so, there should be a shortage of tannin "reds" in China teas, and, in fact, the light liquors given by these teas indicate that such is the case.

Preparation of Oolong Teas

The Oolong teas are prepared in much the same manner as the China black teas, except that the fermentation is stopped

---

[86] E. C. Elliot and F. J. Whitehead, *Tea Planting in Ceylon*, Colombo, 1926, p. 170.

[43] *loc. cit.*

[87] C. R. Harler, *Quarterly Journal Indian Tea Association*, Calcutta, 1928, part 2.

[88] J. J. B. Deuss, *De Thee*, Buitenzorg, Sept., 1926, p. 97.

TABLE INDICATING COURSE OF MOISTURE LOSS IN NORTH EAST INDIA

Fresh leaf	contains about	77%	moisture
Withered leaf	" "	66%	"
Fermented leaf	" "	66%	"
First fired tea	" "	26%	"
Final fired tea	" "	3%	"
Packed tea	" "	6%	"

much sooner. With Oolong teas, as with the fine China black teas, the development of aroma is the chief aim. As might be anticipated from the mode of preparation, the Oolong teas, being less fermented, generally contain more soluble tannin than the corresponding black teas.

Preparation of Green Teas

In China, when green tea is manufactured the preliminary withering process, which is necessary to black tea preparation, is omitted, and the leaf is immediately pan-fired at a high temperature sufficient to inactivate the enzymes and microörganisms. Fermentation having been rendered impossible and the leaf made soft and pliable, alternate rolling and firing follow till the leaf is too crisp for further manipulation. The tea is finally fired in baskets or pans.

In Japan, the preliminary heating process usually is done by steam, while in the few places in India where green tea still is made, both steam and pan-firing are employed. In Japan the leaf is either hand rolled on a hot plate, as in China, or rolled mechanically in specially constructed machines, which are so warmed that rolling and drying proceed together, the latter at a steady rate. The accompanying table indicates the course of the loss of moisture, as shown by estimates made in Japan.[8]

Tea for export is fired at a central station before packing, and the moisture content reduced to about 3 per cent.

The chief difference between black and green tea results from fermentation. In green tea most of the tannin is present in the soluble form in which it occurs in the fresh leaf. The slight loss of tannin during manufacture probably is due to its precipitation by proteins in the leaf. The loss from fermentation which might take place before the preliminary heating if any leaf damage occurs is negligible, judging by the lack of red color in green tea infusions.

In Japan, the tannin content drops from about 15 to 12 per cent during manufacture,[8] while in Northeast India the tannin value has been shown to fall to 14 per cent in green tea made from leaf originally having a tannin content of about 20 per cent.[89]

A few estimations indicate that the caffeine in green tea is more easily extractable than that in black tea made from similar leaf.[89]

After the infusion of green tea, the wet leaf must assume its natural green color again, with no brown or copper admixture, this latter being the mark of fermented tea. It is assumed that during the preparation of green tea, the chlorophyll does not undergo any drastic change.

No essential oil is formed in green tea manufacture.

Résumé

To attempt to summarize the chemical changes taking place during the conversion of tea leaf into black or green tea is a task made difficult by the lack of definite knowledge on the subject.

During manufacture the leaf loses moisture. In tea preparation in China, Japan, and Formosa the loss proceeds steadily throughout manufacture; but in India, Ceylon, and Java the loss takes place only during withering and firing. Fresh leaf contains about 77 per cent, and finished tea from 3 to 8 per cent moisture.

The tannin of the leaf undergoes considerable change during black tea manufacture, and the soluble tannin is reduced to about half its original value. The loss is partly accounted for by the formation of oxidized tannin, and partly by the combination of some of the tannin with proteins to form insoluble compounds. In the manufacture of green tea the tannin loss is small, and probably due to the combination with proteins. No soluble colored tannin products are formed during green tea manufacture.

The part that caffeine plays in the changes of manufacture is still unknown, but indications suggest it is a small one.

TABLE INDICATING COURSE OF MOISTURE LOSS IN JAPAN

	Machine Rolled	Hand Rolled
Fresh leaf......	76% moisture	76% moisture
After first roll...	59% "	69% "
After second roll.	59% "	51% "
After third roll..	28% "	32% "
After final roll...	11% "	17% "

[8] loc. cit.
[89] C. J. Harrison. Quarterly Journal Indian Tea Association, Calcutta, 1927, part 2.

[89] loc. cit.

The caffeine content does not change during manufacture.

The flavor and aroma of black tea are qualities connected with the essential oil of tea which is developed during the fermentation process in tea manufacture. Since green tea is not fermented, no essential oil appears in the product.

The proteins in the leaf are coagulated during manufacture and do not enter into the tea infusion. Nitrogenous bodies other than caffeine are considered to be of importance in green tea infusions. These bodies are usually reckoned as proteins, but they probably are degraded protein bodies.

The gums, dextrins, and pectins do not undergo much change, although it is possible that the dextrins may undergo some kind of caramelization during the firing process as carried out in India, Ceylon, and Java.

The cellulose and crude fiber do not enter the tea infusion, and they probably undergo no change during manufacture. Little is known of the fats and waxes which occur in small quantities in the leaf, and are unimportant from the point of tea manufacture.

The chlorophyll is insoluble in water and may not enter the tea infusion. It is of importance, however, in that it gives the green color to infused green tea leaf. It is generally assumed that part of the chlorophyll is decomposed during black tea manufacture, but not during the manufacture of green tea. The other pigments, flavones, and anthocyans, enter the infusion and are important in green teas, but not in black.

The oxidizing enzyme of the tea leaf is responsible for most of the change taking place in black tea manufacture. Bacteria are not necessary to tea fermentation and in some cases have been shown to be harmful. The function of the yeasts, if any, in

CHEMISTRY CHART

Showing Some of the Changes Occurring during the Manufacture of Black Tea
in India, Ceylon, Java, and Sumatra

[Percentages are Approximate and Calculated on Dry Matter]

Fresh Leaf	Withered Leaf	Fermented Leaf	Fired Tea	Characteristics Imparted to Finished Tea
Tannin............22%	22%	13%	12%	pungency, strength, and color.
		Tannin oxidation products formed	?	
Caffeine............4%	no change detected		4%	stimulus
?	aroma developed in fermentation		traces of essential oil	aroma, flavor
Crude proteins.....27%	render some tannin insoluble		coagulated	
Gums, dextrins, pectins, etc...............7%	may be partially caramelized		3%	thickness of liquor
Salts............5.5%			5.5%	
Cellulose, fiber, fats and waxes.......25%	probably do not change			
Chlorophyll and pigments	chlorophyll partly destroyed in fermentation			
Oxidising enzyme........	constant in quantity	oxidizes tannin	destroyed	
Yeasts and bacteria......	increase in numbers		destroyed	
Total Soluble Matter 48–55%			38–45%	

The moisture in the fresh leaf is reduced from about 77 to 60 per cent during withering. No further appreciable moisture change takes place in fermentation. Firing reduces the moisture to about 3 per cent, and this value rises to about 6 per cent during sorting, at about which figure tea is packed. The percentages given in this chart represent the various constituents extracted by boiling water for one hour. A tea taster's infusion is made by adding 125 c. c. boiling water to 3 grams of tea and waiting for six minutes. In this time about half the total soluble matter, i.e., 19 to 22 per cent of the dry leaf weight, is extracted. This matter is made up of about 7 per cent tannin, and tannin bodies, about 3 per cent caffeine, 3 per cent mineral salts, a certain quantity of gums, dextrins, pectins, etc., small quantities of nitrogenous bodies, other than caffeine, minute quantities of leaf pigments, and traces of essential oil. The figures denoted herewith refer, as in the chart, to percentages of the dry tea.

black tea manufacture, is still unsettled. During firing, the yeasts and microörganisms are practically rendered inactive, although slight post-fermentation apparently takes place after the tea is made.

In green tea manufacture, the preliminary heating process renders the enzymes and microörganisms inactive and no fermentation takes place. The enzymes do not increase during the manufacture of black tea, but the microörganisms do.

In black tea manufacture, the water soluble matter in the leaf is reduced by about 10 per cent, largely on account of the changes brought about in the tannin. The reduction is much less in green tea.

With the limited information available, a chart has been prepared denoting some of the changes taking place in the manufacture of black tea. The figures are approximate, and refer to black tea prepared only in India, Ceylon, Java, and Sumatra and not in China.

Ultra-Violet Rays on Tea

Experiments conducted in London in 1934 to find out the effect of ultra-violet rays on dry tea are said to have resulted in an appreciable reduction in the percentage of tannin as well as an improvement in quality. It has been suggested that, with the advent of the all-electric factory, further obvious developments would be along lines of experimenting with the use of ultra-violet rays on raw leaf during the manufacturing process.[90]

[90] *Home and Colonial Mail*, London, April 27, 1934, p. 11.

CHAPTER XXVI

THE PHARMACOLOGY OF TEA

The Widespread Use of Tea and Reasons for its Popularity—The Effects of Caffeine—Caffeine in Tea—How Caffeine Affects the Heart Action, Muscular Activity, the Mental Processes, and the Entire Human System—Elimination of Caffeine from the Body—Caffeine-free Teas—Effects of Tannin—Tannin in Tea—Tannin-free Teas—Proteins, Calories, and Vitamins in Tea—Results of Vitamin Content Experiments in Japan and the United States—Content of Tea as Variously Brewed—Conclusions.

By C. R. Harler, Ph.D., B.Sc., F.I.C., F.R. Met. Soc.

Former Chemist, Tocklai Experimental Station, Indian Tea Association, Assam, India

THE effect of tea, coffee, and other beverages on human digestion and health has been the subject of long and unsettled debate. The reason is that exact experiments on problems of this nature, checked by careful controls are difficult to conduct. The problem has been further complicated by the fact that commercial interests have frequently given wide publicity to opinions based on insufficient evidence. In this chapter it is proposed to give an account only of experiments carried out on strictly scientific lines and to detail the conclusions drawn therefrom.

Arguments used against the healthfulness of tea are frequently founded on the experience of individuals or on the assumption that tea is taken in excess. Tea is the beverage of people in many parts of the world, living in every kind of climate. Although the general use of tea cannot, in itself, be used as an argument in favor of its healthfulness, nevertheless, it indicates that tea has a very general appeal and it is instructive to inquire into the nature of this appeal.

What, then, in most general terms, are the facts with regard to the widespread use of tea? In China, the four hundred million odd inhabitants are said to consume about eight hundred million pounds of tea annually. Custom may have something to do with the habit here, and it

has been suggested also that in a country like China, where the water often contains many harmful bacteria, tea is a safe drink. However, no such reasons can be given in the case of the United Kingdom, where the consumption is more than nine pounds per head per annum. It might be suggested that the English climate calls for a drink like tea. But the English climate cannot be the essential reason for its use, for in Australia, a hot, dry country, the per capita consumption is nearly as much as in the United Kingdom. In India, too, the Englishman still prefers hot tea as his drink. The Indian, himself, now is taking to tea, and although the consumption per head is still very small, India, as a whole, annually consumes about fifty million pounds.

Reasons for the Popularity of Tea

What, we must inquire, in the second place, are the reasons for this widespread popularity of tea? Without detracting, in any way, from the virtues of tea as a drink, the fact that it once was a monopoly of the East India Company, and that later, when India and Ceylon took up tea planting, tea became an Empire product, had a great influence in establishing tea as the English beverage. In the same way, the Dutch people, who now consume about

3.64 lbs. of tea per head, are, no doubt, influenced in so doing by the fact that tea is produced in the Dutch East Indies. English colonists may have retained the custom of tea-drinking, in part, in order to preserve a social bond with their mother country. And the peoples of Japan, China, India, and other Asiatic countries, may consume tea partly because they grow it and it is a notable source of national wealth.

Such reasons for the custom of tea-drinking are but partial. They do not explain the use of tea in Germany, France, Russia, and South America; nor its use to any degree in the United States, where the traditions of patriotism might be expected to lead to its complete rejection. We must look to the nature of tea itself for the essential causes, which have recommended it above all its competitors to almost all the peoples of the earth.

Tea is consumed for its lightness of touch and weight; for its easy digestibility under normal circumstances; for its warmth, yet a warmth which produces a subsequent coolness due to free perspiration, when humidity and temperature are high; for its piquant palatability and aroma; and, chiefly, for its stimulation of the nervous and muscular system, which induces a state of consciousness midway between gentle excitement and easy repose. It is not drunk on account of its food value, for it is merely an auxiliary food, as are many beverages. A cup of hot tea is said to take away, in evaporation from the skin, fifty times as much heat as it brings to us.

Green tea contains about the same percentage of tannin, caffeine, and soluble extract as black tea, and gives as great internal comfort and stimulus if taken strong and warm. However, drunk in its weak state, as is generally the custom in the Far East, its value is little more than a thirst quencher.

It is necessary now to consider the action of the various constituents of tea on the human system.

The Effects of Caffeine

When the harmful effects of tea-drinking are discussed, the two constituents, caffeine and tannin, are those invariably mentioned. Tannin is considered to have a harmful effect on digestion, and caffeine is objected to because it is a stimulant.

When caffeine is used as a drug, the *British Pharmaceutical Codex* states, it has the following action on the human system:

Caffeine exerts three important actions, (a) on the central nervous system, (b) on muscles, including cardiac, and (c) on the kidney.

The action on the central nervous system is mainly on that part of the brain, connected with physical functions. It produces a condition of wakefulness and increased mental activity. The interpretation of sensory impressions is more perfect and correct, and thought becomes clearer and quicker.

With larger doses of caffeine the action extends from the psychical areas to the motor area and to the cord, and the patient becomes at first restless and noisy, and, later, may show convulsive movements. Caffeine facilitates the performance of all kinds of physical work, and actually increases the total work which can be obtained from a muscle. In the normal man, however, it is impossible to say how much of the action in the muscle is central and how much peripheral. But, as fatigue shows itself first by an action on the centre, it is probable that the action of caffeine in diminishing fatigue, is mainly central. Caffeine accelerates the pulse and slightly raises the blood pressure. It has no action in any way resembling digitalis; by increasing the irritability of the cardiac muscle, its prolonged use rather tends to fatigue than to rest the heart.

Caffeine and its allies form a very important group of diuretics. The urine is generally of a lower specific gravity than normal, since it contains a lower proportion of salt and urea; but the total excretion of solids both as regards urea, uric acid and salts, is increased. Caffeine by exciting the medulla, produces an initial vasco-constriction of the kidneys, which tends, at first, to retard the flow of urine.

The medical dose of caffeine is 6 to 30 centigrams (1 to 5 grains).[1]

This account represents the considered opinion of British medical men, and contains only matter which is thought by them to be sufficiently established for general publication.

The average caffeine dose given by the *Pharmacopœia of the United States* is 15 centigrams [2½ grains].[2]

The Amount of Caffeine in Tea

Before describing some of the experiments made with regard to the effect of caffeine on the human system, it will be instructive to consider the quantity of the drug taken by average tea drinkers.

In Great Britain, the most important tea consuming nation from the point of view of the European-managed tea industry,

---

[1] *British Pharmaceutical Codex*, Ed. 1923, p. 228.
[2] *United States Pharmacopœia*, Ed. 1926, p. 84.

the per capita consumption of tea is about ten pounds a year. Reckoning the average caffeine content of tea at 3 per cent, the amount of the drug contained in the tea used by an average person would be 4.80 ounces per annum, or about 5¾ grains a day. This assumes that all the caffeine is extracted and drunk, which is, of course, not quite true. In a five-minute infusion, about three-quarters of the caffeine is extracted. A longer infusion, or subsequent waterings of the leaf, extract part or all of the remainder. It seems probable then, that the average daily dose of caffeine taken in Great Britain by virtue of tea drinking, is under four grains.

A cup of tea contains, on the average, less than one grain of caffeine, figuring 200 cups to the pound. The cup of tea made by the tea taster in London, Calcutta, or Colombo, however, contains about 43 grains Troy [the weight of a sixpenny piece, or a silver four anna piece] of tea, and is infused for six minutes. Tea made thus permits the brewing of 160 cups to the pound, and each contains, on the average, about one grain of caffeine.

In considering the effect which a cup of tea has upon the human body, we must remember that the caffeine which it contains is not administered as a pure drug, and is not available for assimilation at once, and that which finally is consumed in the course of drinking a whole cup becomes completely available to the system only by degrees, and sometime after it is taken. Therefore, the effect of the taking of any given amount of caffeine in tea is not nearly as great as the results recorded by the *British Pharmaceutical Codex* [quoted on page 539] would indicate, in which reference is made to the direct ingestion of the pure drug.

The amount of stimulation which a person may be expected to get from a cup of tea cannot be stated. It depends upon the condition of his nervous system, the strength of the decoction, and the nature and freshness of the leaves which he employs. When drunk in its weak state, in small quantities, tea is little more than a thirst quencher and an agent to increase perspiration. But when taken strong and continuously throughout the day, the aggregate gives a considerable stimulus to the system.

It is sometimes considered that the caffeine in coffee is in a form more available

to the human system than it is in tea, and it has been suggested that in the latter the caffeine may be, in part, inactivated by reason of its combination with tea tannin. This supposition, however, is not supported by scientific observation. A cup of coffee generally is more stimulating than a cup of tea, because it contains more caffeine. Thus a pound of tea contains about 210 grains of caffeine, of which some 170 grains are extracted in the first brew. A pound of tea makes from one hundred and sixty to two hundred cups, so that one cup of the first brew contains on the average less than one grain of caffeine. A pound of coffee contains about 140 grains of caffeine, and makes, on the average, less than forty cups, hence a cup contains about 3.5 grains of the drug, for coffee is almost exhaustively extracted. These considerations are sufficient to explain the greater stimulus given by coffee.

Caffeine and Heart Action

The evidence obtained from papers dealing with the action of caffeine is often contradictory. Much of the work has been carried out on dogs, cats, guinea pigs, birds, etc., and doses, big and small, have been given and injected with varying results.[5] The difficulty in work of this kind comes largely from the fact that a greater number of subjects than have yet become available must be studied in order that the average is not unduly influenced by exceptions.

In experimenting with the action of caffeine on lower animals, it has been found that the alkaloid increases the pulse rate, strengthens the cardiac contractions, and stimulates the vasomotor centre. When experiments have been made on human beings, the results have not always been as detailed above, partly, no doubt, because the dose administered to animals has, in proportion, been very large. Thus, Wood studied the effect of small doses on human beings. By giving a dose of 6 grains he was able to detect no marked rise in blood pressure.[6] Some workers have found that the effect of caffeine on the blood pressure

---

[5] Salant and Rieger, "The Toxicity of Caffeine," *Bureau of Chemistry Bulletin*, no. 148, United States Department of Agriculture.

[6] Wood, "The Effects of Caffeine on the Circulatory and Muscular Systems," *Ther. Gaz.*, 1912, vol. xxviii, no. 1, p. 6.

of a dog, which has a circulation similar to that of man, is greatly to increase it. Wood accounts for the difference by the fact that, in experiments on dogs, as much as 10 centigrams of caffeine per kilo weight of the dog had been administered. This is equivalent to a dose of 100 grains to a man of average weight. When a small dose is used on a dog [1 centigram per kilo], no increase is observed in pulse rate.[7]

By using therapeutic doses on men [about 3 to 6 grains] the same observer [Wood] noticed that they set up only slight increases in the cardiac contractions, causing some elevation in the general arterial pressure.

Caffeine and Muscular Activity

The influence of caffeine on the force of muscular contractions has been studied by many investigators. In 1892, De Sarlo and Bernardini used a dynamometer to show that caffeine increases this force.[8] Many other workers, mostly using the ergographic method [9] have also shown the stimulating effect of caffeine. The conclusions of other workers are, in the main, confirmed by Rivers and Webber, who also conclude that the increase in muscular work is not due to any psychical factors of interest or suggestion.[10] Wood also studied the effect of caffeine on the movement of the voluntary muscles, using only therapeutic doses. He concluded that caffeine acts as a stimulant to the reflex centers in the spinal cord, enabling the muscles to contract more vigorously, without producing a secondary depression. The sum total of work that can then be done, by a man under caffeine, is greater than can be done without it.

The peculiar state, similar in appearance to post-mortem rigor, induced in the muscles by large quantities of the drug has no bearing on its effects when used in quantities likely to be ingested by human beings under normal conditions.[7]

Caffeine and the Mental Processes

The influence of caffeine on the mental processes also has been the subject of much study. Kraepelin writes: "We know that tea and coffee increase our mental efficiency in a definite way, and we use these beverages as a means of overcoming mental fatigue. In the morning, these drinks remove the last traces of mental fatigue, and in the evening, when we have intellectual tasks to dispose of, they aid in keeping us awake." [11] Wedemeyer, however, considers that with the regular administration of caffeine, the psychic influences decrease after four or five weeks.[12]

Caffeine and the Entire Human System

In addition to the foregoing specialized investigations, a general study of the influence of caffeine upon the human system has been made by H. L. Hollingworth at Columbia University, New York. In his work, every effort was made to eliminate the errors which creep into many experiments of this nature, owing to too small a number of subjects.

The conclusions [see table, page 542] are based on an enormous number of measurements. The chief tests employed were the steadiness, tapping, coördination, typewriting, color-naming, calculations, opposites, cancellation, and discrimination tests, together with the familiar "size-weight" illusion.

The experiments were carried out in a specially equipped laboratory. For details of the experimental technique, the reader is referred to a monograph in the *Archives of Psychology* entitled "Columbia's Contribution to Philosophy and Psychology."

The caffeine was used in capsules and in syrup solutions, and control subjects received capsules and syrup solutions, minus the caffeine. No subject knew whether or not he received caffeine.

[7] Reichert, *Ther. Gas.* 1890, vol. vi, p. 294.

[8] *Revista sper di Freniatria*, vol. xviii, p. 1.

[9] Mosso, *Arch. Ital. de Biol.*, 1893, vol. xix, p. 241; Koch, *Inaug. Diss.*, Marburg, 1894; Rossi, *Revista sper di Freniatria*, 1894, vol. xx, p. 458; Sobieranski, *Cent. Physiol.*, 1896, vol. x, p. 126; Hoch and Kraepelin, *Physiol. arbeit*, 1896, vol. i, p. 378; Destree, *Jour. Med.*, Bruxelles, 1897; Benedicenti-Moleschott's *Untersuchungen*, 1899, vol. xxiv, p. 170; Schumberg, *Arch. Anat. Phys.*, supp. 1899, p. 289; Hellsten-Skand, *Arch. Physiol.*, 1894, vol. xvi, p. 197; Joyteko, *Trav. du Lab. Physiol. Inst. Solvany*, 1904, vol. vi, p. 361.

[10] *The Influence of Alcohol and Other Drugs on Fatigue.*

[7] loc. cit.

[11] Kraepelin, *Ueber die Beeinflussung einfacher psychischer Vorgänge durch einige Arzeneimittel*, p. 221.

[12] Wedemeyer, *Arch. Exp. Path. Pharm.* 1920, vol. lxxxv, p. 338.

EFFECT OF CAFFEINE ON MENTAL AND MOTOR PROCESSES

st. = stimulation; O = no effect; ret. = retardations.

Process	Tests	Small Doses	Medium Doses	Large Doses	Action Time Hours	Duration Hours
Motor Speed....	1. Tapping	st.	st.	st.	¾-1½	2-4
Coördination ...	2. Three hole	st.	O	ret.	1-1½	3-4
	3. Typewriting (a) Speed	st.	O	ret.	Results show only in total day's work.	
	(b) Errors	Fewer for all doses.				
Association.....	4. Color-naming	st.	st.	st.	2-2½	3-4
	5. Opposite	st.	st.	st.	2½-3	Next day
	6. Calculation	st.	st.	st.	2½	Next day
Choice.........	7. Discrimination, Reaction time	ret.	O	st.	2-4	Next day
	8. Cancellation	ret.	?	st.	3-5	No data
	9. S.-W. illusion	O	O	O	....	....
General.........	10. Steadiness	?	Unsteadiness		1-3	3-4
	11. Sleep quality	Individual differences				
	12. Sleep quantity	....			2?	....
	13. General health	Depending on body weight and conditions of administration.				

Briefly stated, the purposes of the investigations were as follows:

(1). To determine, both qualitatively and quantitatively, the effect of caffeine on a wide range of mental and motor processes, by studying the performance of a number of individuals for a long period—forty days in the case of the experiment—under controlled conditions.

(2). To study the way in which this influence is modified by sex, weight, age, and idiosyncrasies of the subject, and the degree to which it depends on the amount of the dose, and the time and conditions of the administration.

(3). And to investigate the influence of caffeine on the general health, on the quantity and amount of sleep, and on the food habits of the individual tested.

The results of the investigation are set forth in the accompanying chart.

The doses varied from 1 to 6 grains; above 4 grains being reckoned a large dose. No secondary reaction was observed in any test.

The general conclusions are that the effect of caffeine on motor processes is quickly realized and is transient, while that on mental processes comes more slowly, but is more persistent.

The two principal factors which seem to modify the degree of caffeine influence are body weight and presence of food in the stomach at the time of ingestion of the caffeine. In practically all of the tests the magnitude of the caffeine influence varied inversely as the body weight, and was most marked when taken on an empty stomach or without food substance. This variance in action was also true for both the quality and amount of sleep, and seemed to be accentuated when taken on successive days. The effect of caffeine does not seem to be influenced by age, sex, or previous caffeine habits. Those who during the experiment, had given up the use of beverages which contain caffeine did not report any craving for the drinks as such.

The absence of any trace of secondary depression is of importance, and, although the actual reason for the production of an increased capacity to work is not clearly demonstrated, the main fact is that the individual's standard of work is raised by caffeine. The conclusion drawn from this work is that the taking of caffeine beverages is justified.[13]

Elimination of Caffeine from the Body

Now comes the question of the elimination of caffeine from the system. Salant and Rieger studied the elimination in the case of rabbits, guinea pigs, cats, and dogs, and found that it depended partly on the manner in which it was administered. They found it was eliminated partly unchanged in the urine, into the gastrointestinal canal, and into the bile. It was concluded that in carnivora more caffeine is demethylated than in herbivora, and that the former utilize this action as a means of defense against the deleterious action of the drug, which is more toxic to carnivora than to herbivora.[14]

The structural relationship between caffeine, uric acid, and other members of the purine group is shown in the chapter on the Chemistry of Tea. It can there be seen that the demethylation [removal of –CH₃ groups] and oxidation [substitution, in this case, of oxygen for hydrogen] of caffeine may give uric acid.

Animals eliminate only small quantities of caffeine—less than 10 per cent of the amount administered—in the urine after ingestion; and Rost has shown that man eliminates only about 2 per cent in the urine.[15]

Mendel and Wardel state that the increase in the excretion of caffeine in the urine after the addition of tea, coffee, or caffeine to a purine-free diet seems to be proportional to the amount of caffeine ingested.[16] However, Clark and Lorrimer do not agree with this in a recent paper in which they describe experiments carried out on the inmates of San Quentin Penitentiary in California. Although the ingestion of caffeine increases the amount of

that substance eliminated in the urine, Mendel and Wardel do not find a definite relationship between the two amounts. By the ingestion of caffeine, more uric acid is eliminated in the urine, but they do not consider that this extra uric acid is due to the demethylation and oxidation of caffeine. They find also that caffeine ingestion increases the uric acid concentration in the blood.

The authors state also that since the drug was administered orally, there was no means of telling how much was absorbed by the system. This would depend on many things; e.g., the bulk of food residues, bacterial activity, peristaltic rate, and so on.[17]

K. Okushima has shown that on drinking tea or coffee, the excretion of caffeine in the urine increases after an interval of an hour. The caffeine excretion increases to a maximum after three or four hours, after which it persists at a reduced rate for a further four or five hours.[18]

These studies on caffeine elimination do not take into account the excretion in the sweat, and by way of the intestinal tract. The whole problem is one requiring much further study before any important conclusions can be drawn.

Caffeine-Free Teas

Before leaving the subject of caffeine, some mention must be made of the preparation of caffeine-free tea. The same attention has not been given to this subject as has been directed towards the development of a similar coffee product. This is probably due to the relatively smaller consumption of tea in Germany and America, where most of this type of work has been done. The fact that coffee may be efficaciously treated in the green state at any time prior to roasting, while the only time that tea may be treated prior to the completion of manufacture is on the plantation, also is a factor contributory to the lack of development of teas freed from caffeine.

Meyer and Wimmer, in order to obtain a tea freed from caffeine, treated the leaves with a volatile solvent, such as ether, petro-

13 H. L. Hollingworth. "The Influence of Caffeine on Mental and Motor Efficiency," Ther. Gaz., vol. xxviii, 1912, no. 1, p. 1.

14 Salant and Rieger, "The Elimination of Caffeine; An Experimental Study on Herbivora and Carnivora," Bureau of Chemistry Bulletin, no. 157, United States Department of Agriculture.

15 Rost, Arch. Expt. Path. Pharm., 1895, vol. xxxvi, p. 56; and Diss. Heidelberg, 1895.

16 Mendel and Wardel, Jour. Amer. Med. Assn., 1917, vol. lxviii, p. 1805.

17 Mendel and Wardel, Amer. Jour. Physiol., 1926, vol. lxxvii, no. 2, p. 491.

18 K. Okushima, Chem. Zeit., vol. cxxix.

leum spirit, benzene, or chloroform, to remove the aromatic substances. After the removal of this solution, the tea was treated with steam and gaseous ammonia, sulphur, sulphur dioxide, or hydrochloric acid to free the caffeine from the combination in which it is present. The liberated caffeine was thus extracted, and the tea was impregnated with the volatile solvent solution of aromatic constituents. The volatile solvent was distilled off, and the leaves dried, leaving a caffeine-free tea which was not completely devoid of aromatic qualities.[19] Seisser followed substantially the same process.[20]

But why bother about a caffeine-free tea at all? True, the physiological action of tea is, in fact, due to caffeine, but in the quantity consumed in a cup of tea it is not to be feared. In addition, the caffeine action is a protracted one in the case of tea. Caffeine in the free state creates a relatively great peak of stimulation lasting over a short time, while that produced by the alkaloid in tea is less intense, but spread over a longer period.

In certain cases, however, there are undoubtedly good reasons why caffeine should not be taken. For example, in the case of a person suffering from gout, everything must be done to lower purine ingestion and thus to lessen the load on the already overburdened kidneys. In such cases a caffeine-free beverage is advisable.

The Effects of Tannin

Tannin is, from the physiological point of view, a drug, the pharmacology of which is well known. So far as tea is concerned, tannin is generally looked upon as the main source of mischief in excessive tea-drinking. The popular idea seems to be that tea, on account of its tannin content, tends to tan the stomach.

The following extract from the British Pharmaceutical Codex is taken from the account given under the heading, "Acidum Tannicum or Tannin":

The properties of tannin depend upon its chemical interaction with protein or gelatine. . . . The free acid only is astringent and when it is neutralised by albumin or alkalies its astringent properties are lost.

When taken by the mouth it gives the characteristic property of astringency, coagulates the protein material surrounding the epithelium, and even penetrates some of the superficial cells.

In the stomach it combines with alkalies and albumin to form tannates. Albumin is digested like other coagulated protein, the tannin being liberated and rendered free to recombine. Its presence in the small intestine, by coagulating proteins and diminishing secretions, tends toward constipation. It is therefore occasionally used in diarrhoea.[21]

Tannin, in any part of the alimentary canal, the mouth, the gullet, the stomach or the intestines, may be harmful—depending upon the quantity taken, their other contents and their constitution. When milk is added to tea, the casein therein fixes the tea-tannin, and prevents its action on the mucous membrane of the mouth, and on that part of the alimentary canal leading to the stomach. If unmilked tea is drunk, the tannin combines with proteins in the stomach, provided by any undigested food there.

Whether tea-tannin be fixed by the casein in milk, or by proteins in the stomach, the tannate so formed is digested like any other coagulated protein, and the tannin again liberated when the partly digested food passes into the smaller intestine. The smaller intestine is alkaline, and the freed tannin here forms alkaline tannates. It is in this region that the harmful effect of tannin, if any, is exhibited; and to people unaccustomed to tea drinking the mildly astringent action tends to cause slight constipation. In the case of constant tea drinkers, a degree of tolerance to tea tannin is gradually established.

It is generally considered harmful to take tea at meals when meat is eaten, the idea being that the protein in the meat will be precipitated by the tea-tannin, and thus rendered indigestible. It is of interest to examine this question carefully.

First of all it should be remembered that much of the tea-tannin has been fixed with the casein in the milk, added before the tea is drunk. Secondly, it must be mentioned that four ounces of raw meat contain about 350 grains of protein matter; i.e., about one-fifth of the weight of the uncooked meat. An average cup of tea, before the addition of milk, contains not more than about 10 grains of tannin in the astringent form. From these figures it may

[19] British Patent, 18, 612, Aug. 20, 1906; United States Patent, 897, 764, Sept. 16, 1908.
[20] German Patent, 223,783, July 16, 1908.

[21] British Pharmaceutical Codex, Ed. 1923, p. 51.

be concluded that the amount of meat protein precipitated by a cup of tea is very small, even assuming that one part of tannin can precipitate completely six parts of protein. This latter proportion is given as a very safe limit and one considerably in excess of the capacity of tannin for protein precipitation.

Proteins are assimilated in the intestines where, as mentioned above, any tannin-protein complex is broken down and free tannin liberated. Hence, in face of this discussion, it may be argued that meat and tea may be taken together without any harmful effects. Indeed, the "high-tea" habit of Australia gives support to this.

In spite of all this, however, many people do not like to take tea and meat at the same meal. I do not, either.

The concensus of medical opinion is that excessive tea drinking is bad, largely because of the effect of the tannin on the digestive tract, where its astringency may constipate the bowels, and its reduction in intestinal secretions may bring about indigestion.

In order, therefore, to get the best out of tea, the brew should be a short one of five minutes. In this time as much as three-fourths of the caffeine may be extracted, and as little as one-third of the tannin. A second brew from the same leaf extracts most of the remaining caffeine, which is only about one-quarter of the original total, and less tannin than was extracted in the first brew. The second brew, being poorer in stimulant than the first, does not produce the same feeling of well-being and comfort.

There is no great difference in the therapeutic action of green and black tea. Both contain, as essentials, tannin and caffeine, and green tea often contains more tannin than black, but the difference is of no practical moment. Green tea more readily gives up its caffeine to infusion than does black. By some authorities it is regarded as an aphrodisiac.

The proper tannin dose is stated by the *British Pharmaceutical Codex* to be 3 to 6 decigrams [5 to 10 grains]. The dose suggested in the *United States Pharmacopœia* is 5 decigrams [8 grains].

The *acidum tannicum* of pharmacy is a pentadigalloyl glucose [$C_{14}H_{10}O_9$].

Tea-tannin has the formula $C_{20}H_{20}O_9$ and, in detail, differs from the tannin above described, but it has the general properties

of all tannins.[22] It combines with albumins or gelatin to form insoluble tannates and it is astringent.

The Amount of Tannin in Tea

It is of interest to calculate how much tannin is consumed by a tea drinker. The average tannin content of black tea is about 10 per cent, although with an ordinary brew, followed by one watering, not much more than half the tannin is extracted. Assuming, to be on the safe side, that three-quarters of the tannin is extracted, then a cup of tea contains about two grains, when a pound of tea makes two hundred cups.

Little work has been done on this subject, but it has been demonstrated that about 60 per cent of the tannin extracted in a five-minute infusion is pungent or astringent, while the rest, although it forms tannates, is not astringent. This pungent tannin was shown to make up color and liquor in the infusion. Taking this figure as some guide, it seems that the average cup of tea will contain less than 1½ grains of astringent tannin.

Tannin-Free Teas

Many efforts have been made to remove or reduce the tannin in tea. The principle generally employed utilizes the property tannin has of combining with albumins. Thus Christopher and Leftwich took the tea infusion and evaporated it to dryness in a vacuum pan. The dry product was finely ground, mixed with powdered gelatin, and re-dissolved. The tannin products were removed by filtration, and the remaining liquor, tannin-free, was claimed to have no injurious effect on the digestive organs.[23] Grimshaw precipitated the tannin in a similar manner, except that the gelatin substance was added before the infusion was made.[24] Sonstadt precipitated the tannin with milk, or skim milk, using about eight ounces of milk to the extract of one pound of tea. The casein in the milk forms insoluble casein tannate, which is separated as a compact mass.[25]

22 Dr. J. J. B. Deuss. *Mededeelingen Proefstation voor Thee*, no. 27, Buitenzorg, Java.
23 *British Patent* 14,877. Oct. 16, 1888.
24 *British Patent* 982. Jan. 20, 1890.
25 *British Patent* 6,596, Mar. 29, 1893.

Many other patent processes, of a similar nature to those above mentioned, have been registered.[26] Bell, although not endeavoring to reduce the tannin in tea, tried to establish a balance between the tannin and caffeine present, so that the final proportion in the tea should be one part caffeine to three of tannin. Tea containing an excess of tannin is brought to this equilibrium by spraying a solution of caffeine, or of a salt thereof, into the air currents used for drying the leaf; or by bringing the solution of caffeine into intimate contact with the tea during fermentation.[27]

In spite of the fact that tea may behave badly physiologically, the consumption of the beverage becomes more general every year, and none of the processes for making tea free from tannin have made headway. The fact is, that the removal of tannin decreases not only the astringency, but also the strength and body of the tea, and physiological effect takes second place to taste, in the tea drinker's mind.

In 1911, a paper was contributed from *The Lancet* laboratory in which it was claimed that in good teas the tannin was combined with caffeine and, in that state, it could not "tan."[28] Later chemical work has, however, shown that the conclusions drawn were not sound ones. Tea infusions, whether made from fine or poor teas, have a certain amount of pungency or astringency.

It is true that India, Ceylon, and Java teas contain more tannin than do the average black teas of China, and on this account a dyspeptic would do well to avoid the pungent liquors of the former. In Great Britain, Australia, and other countries, where people are inveterate tea drinkers, the beverage certainly is taken largely on account of the tannin it contains, and the lighter liquors given by many China black teas are by no means sought after.

The Proteins in Tea

Caffeine and tannin are by far the most important chemicals in tea, from the phar-macological standpoint; but it is instructive to consider the beverage from the point of view of food values.

The nutriment in tea is gained from the milk and sugar added, rather than from the tea infusion itself. The actual composition of a cup of tea, without milk or sugar, obviously varies with the tea and the method by which it is made. A cup of black tea made in the average English home contains from $\frac{3}{4}$ to 1 grain of caffeine, and from 5 to 10 grains of tannin and tannin products. There also are small quantities of nitrogenous bodies other than caffeine, gummy substances, and other carbohydrates, and an infinitesimal amount of the essential oil of tea.

Tea leaf contains about 30 per cent of what is conveniently termed "crude protein" by chemists. Very little work has been done on the proteins in tea, but as long ago as 1843, Peligot estimated that the fresh tea leaf contained about 15 per cent pure protein.[29] During manufacture this is, however, rendered insoluble, and infusions of finished tea contain practically no proteins, because heat coagulates the protein and renders it insoluble. However, some nitrogenous bodies are present, and in the case of Japan tea these are of importance.

Experiments on green tea show that only about one-fifth of the crude protein is extracted in a tea infusion, and that, of this, only a small percentage can be reckoned as pure protein, or degraded protein.[30]

Tea, then, cannot be reckoned to have any protein food value, although the usual addition of milk [about a tablespoonful] adds about 10 grains of protein to a cup of tea. The significance of this amount is realized when it is stated that the average man daily requires about 3 ounces [1312 grains] of proteins in his diet, although few people are as moderate in the consumption of protein foods.

Certain Asiatic people consume fresh tea leaf in various forms and, in so doing, follow a rational course, since they thus profit by the nutritive properties of the leaf. In some cases a kind of soup is made by boiling the leaf with grease and sugar, and then seasoning.

[26] Alexander-Katy, *German Patent* 91,826, Aug. 9, 1897; Martin, *British Patent* 27,460, Nov. 23, 1897; Davidson, *British Patent* 4,299, Feb. 27, 1899; Bergheim, *British Patent* 11,948, July 2, 1900; and *British Patent* 26,254, Nov. 28, 1902.
[27] *British Patent*, 10,471, May 2, 1912.
[28] *The Lancet*, London, Jan. 7, 1911.

[29] *L'Institut*, Paris, 1843–1845, pp. 238–239.
[30] *The Chemistry of Green Tea*, compiled by the Tea Experimental Station, Kenaya, Japan.

The Calories in Tea

The energy value of foods, and the energy requirements of the body, are estimated in calories. Foods rich in fats have the highest caloric value, while foods rich in protein, sugar, and starch, have greater caloric values than those containing much water.

The official "Dietetic Food List," circulated by certain restaurants in America, gives the calories in an eight ounce cup of tea, hot or iced, as ten—one calory of protein, one of fat, and eight of carbohydrates. Whether the value thus attributed to tea is accurate or not, is difficult to say, for the better known tables of food values ignore tea entirely as they do coffee.

An idea of value of calories is obtained when it is stated that an average man requires a diet giving from 2,500 to 3,000 calories a day. If to a half pint cup of tea, one tablespoonful of milk is added [ten calories], and one lump of sugar [twenty-five calories] the cup then yields a total of forty-five calories, taking the value given above for the beverage as correct. The value is not great, considering that a small roll of bread provides one hundred calories, as does also a slice of canned pineapple.

The same "Dietetic Food List" gives the calories in a cup of coffee as twelve, and in a cup of "Postum," cereal coffee-substitute, as ten.

The Vitamins in Tea

During the last few years the question of vitamins has been much to the fore, and recently the vitamin content of tea has been discussed. During the manufacture of tea from the tea leaf, the heat applied during the drying process, combined with the air blast in the drying machine, would be expected to destroy most of the vitamins. This is what largely does happen in practice, so far as the present known vitamins are concerned. Yet all of the vitamins are not destroyed, however, as various workers have found evidence of vitamins present in finished tea. Green tea, especially when hand made, is not submitted to such high temperatures, nor to an air blast, as is machine fired black tea; and it is possible that the vitamin content of green tea is greater than that of black tea.

Though not supported by experimental data, Vivia B. Appleton called attention to the vitamin content of tea a few years ago. In recording observations on diet in Labrador, along the Straits of Belle Isle, she observes:

> Every family has from twenty to forty pounds of tea a year. It is the universal beverage, and two or three cups are taken at every meal by young and old. . . . By February, people with scant supplies had little left but flour and tea . . . new summer supplies did not begin to arrive until late in June. . . . We have here a diet chiefly of cereals. There is an excess in carbohydrates and at least a partial deficiency in vitamins and suitable proteins . . . vitamins are probably provided in part by wild berries, small quantities of condensed milk, vegetables, and molasses. The importance of tea in the diet, together with the relative scarcity of deficiency-diseases following such restricted diet, leaves little doubt, that the vitamins present in tea are of considerable value.[31]

In 1922, the discovery in tea of vitamin-B was announced by Shepard.[32] Experiments were made in which both the tea leaf and the infusion were used as the vitamin source. There has been no confirmation of this work. [Vitamin-B or water-soluble-B is the anti-beri-beri vitamin.]

Masataro Miura and Michiyo Tsujimura, two Japanese chemists, in 1924, published a paper in which they claimed to have found water-soluble-C, the anti-scorbutic [relieving or preventing scurvy] vitamin. They observed that green tea has a reasonably high anti-scorbutic potency, whilst black tea almost lacks that power. The authors suggest that this loss of vitamin-C comes about in the oxidation [fermentation] process in black tea manufacture.

Guinea pigs were used as a means of showing the presence of the vitamin in tea. The usual procedure was followed in the experiment. The animals were fed on a food mixture lacking vitamin-C. To this mixture, freshly prepared tea infusion was added, and the animals were thus kept free from scurvy. Hence it was assumed that the tea infusion contained the necessary vitamin-C, which made the food mixture a complete one.

The potency of both new and old tea was examined with the results shown in the

[31] *Journal Home Economics*, May, 1921, vol. xiii, p. 199.
[32] *Duluth Herald*, Mar. 10, 1922.

accompanying table. The figures express the quantities necessary to prevent or cure scurvy in guinea pigs.

New tea................	0.4 to 0.6 grams a day
One year stored tea.......	0.75 grams a day
Two years stored tea......	1.00 grams a day
Three years stored tea....	no appreciable potency

Thus with a guinea pig weighing from 270–330 grams, the infusion obtained from ¾ gram of one-year-old green tea, as sold in ordinary stores, was shown to protect the animals from scurvy for more than sixty days, and sometimes no scorbutic sign was shown for one hundred and eight days. As the tea was stored for longer periods, its anti-scorbutic properties decreased, and, after three years, disappeared.[33]

Miura and Okabe also claim to have shown that Japanese green tea effected a prompt and complete cure of scurvy in a monkey, by daily additions to the diet of the infusion from half a gram of green tea.[34]

In 1925, a paper was read before the American Association of Anatomists at Cleveland entitled "The Anti-sterility Vitamin, Fat-soluble E." In this paper it was stated that the paucity of vitamin-E, even in its most abundant depots in animal tissue, contrasts with its concentration in certain plants, especially in seeds and green leaves. It was claimed that this vitamin is unhurt after careful desiccation of such leaves; i.e., lettuce, alfalfa [lucerne grass], pea, and tea. The paper also states that the new vitamin exists in the greatest quantities in the finest qualities of tea; namely, the finest leaf from India and Ceylon teas.[35]

Recently, J. R. Murlin, of Rochester, New York, examined the problem of the presence of vitamin-C in tea. In the absence of satisfactory chemical tests, the biological method was, of course, employed for determining the relative amounts of the anti-scorbutic vitamin. The guinea pig again was the subject used in the tests. Pan-fired and basket-fired green teas, Oolong and black tea infusions were used in the experiments. All the animals died of scurvy, except in the case of those fed on the pan-fired green tea, in which case the results indicated the presence of the vitamin-C.[36]

Mattill and Pratt at the Department of Vital Economics, University of Rochester, enlarged on Murlin's work and arrived at similar conclusions. However, their results had distinct limitations. They did not know how long after packing the tea would retain its vitamin-C, and they tried only one lot of tea. Furthermore, the use of tea as a possible source of vitamin-C was not recommended, except where food sources were out of the question.[37]

In 1928, Helen S. Mitchell, Ph.D., Director of the Nutrition Laboratory at the Battle Creek Sanitarium, Battle Creek, Michigan, decided, after experimentation, that a Japan green tea infusion contained no vitamin-C.[38] When this result was challenged, the experiments were repeated, and in 1929 the conclusion was that there is no demonstrable amount of vitamin-C in green tea.[39]

In June, 1929, Masataro Miura published certain notes on the effects of the temperature of water employed for the infusion of Japanese green tea, "in view of the recent reports of Mattill and Pratt, as well as of Mitchell."

From the notes on these experiments it appears that the guinea pigs in the Japanese experiments were forcibly fed immediately after the test infusion was made, instead of permitting the animals to consume it at their leisure during twenty-four hours, "thus risking its incomplete consumption, and at the same time its gradual loss of vitamin activity."

Miura found that if green tea were mashed with water at about 65° C. [water boils at 100° C.] for about five minutes, approximately two-thirds of the total vitamin-C is thereby extracted. The remainder is obtained by means of a second, similar mashing. About 1 gram of tea was treated

[33] Jour. Agric. Chem. Soc., Japan, Oct. 1924, vol. i, no. 1.

[34] Miura and Okabe, Publ. Assoc. Tea Merchants, Feb. 1926.

[35] Paper, "The Anti-sterility Vitamin, Fat-soluble E," read before the American Association of Anatomists, Cleveland.

[36] J. R. Murlin, "Tea as an Anti-scorbutic," Tea and Coffee Trade Journal, Nov. 1927, vol. liii, no. 5, pp. 1257–60.

[37] H. A. Mattill and A. D. Pratt, "Note on Tea as a Source of Vitamin-C," Pro. Soc. for Experimental Biology and Medicine," 1928, vol. xxvi, pp. 82–85.

[38] Helen S. Mitchell, Good Health, Sept. 1928.

[39] Helen S. Mitchell, "Vitamin-C in Green Tea," Tea and Coffee Trade Journal, May, 1929, vol. lvi, no. 5, pp. 756–60.

with 10 cc. of water each time; i.e., 20 cc. in all. By this means a tea infusion showing a strong anti-scorbutic action was obtained.

Furthermore, it was found that if tea is stewed at 70 to 75° C. for some time, about 74 per cent of the anti-scorbutic value of the infusion is lost. If green tea is extracted with boiling water, then it loses much of its anti-scorbutic property; the loss depending on the rate of cooling of the water and increasing with sustained high temperatures. With quick cooling and decantation, about 33 per cent of the original activity is retained. The activity of the infusion prepared by mashing with water at 65° C. as described above, is lost after standing for about two hours.

The above results, according to Miura, explain the failure of other experimenters to detect appreciable quantities of vitamin-C in green tea infusions.[40]

It has been suggested that because the native Japanese tea receives only a light firing, its vitamin-C content might be appreciable, whereas in the Japanese teas exported, which are re-fired at from 210° to 260° F. it might well be negligible.

In support of the above, the following may be quoted: "The only vitamin that seems to be injured by heating," says S. Josephine Baker, "is the one known as vitamin C." The same writer goes on to say that, since this vitamin occurs in lemons, oranges, and grape fruit, it can be easily introduced into the diet.[41]

Recent work suggests that the destruction of vitamin-C is to be credited rather more to oxygen than to high temperature.[42] It is believed that if the temperature employed in the drying of tea goes up to 210° C. the vitamin-C will be destroyed.

The Bureau of Home Economics of the United States Department of Agriculture, at the request of the Food, Drug, and Insecticide Administration and the Federal Trade Commission engaged in an investigation of the vitamin-C content of samples of tea in the early part of 1929. According to a *Bulletin* issued on the subject by the United States Department of Agriculture on July 28, 1929, green tea was found to be unsatisfactory as a source of vitamin-C. This *bulletin* was as follows:

Popular interest in good diet, and especially the recent emphasis on the importance of vitamins in our food, has led some dealers to make claims that can not always be substantiated by laboratory investigations. Green tea is one of the products for which distributors have claimed value as a source of vitamins— a claim which appears reasonable to many people because they know that only the young tender leaves of the tea plant are gathered for the market.

The Bureau of Home Economics has received a great many requests for information as to the reliability of these claims. A 3-month feeding experiment was therefore undertaken with guinea pigs, since other laboratory investigations seemed to present conflicting results. Tea, of course, is not consumed in the dry form, but as an infusion. The infusions fed to the guinea pigs were made according to the standard method specified by the Supervising Tea Examiner of the United States. A sample of Japan green tea was used from a package described on the label as "rich in vitamin-C."

Of the 14 guinea pigs used in the experiment, 10 were fed tea in addition to a basal diet that contained no vitamin-C, 2 as negative controls were given the basal diet only, and 2 as positive controls were given the basal diet and orange juice, which is known to be an excellent source of the vitamin.

The guinea pigs that received the tea lived from three to six days longer, on the average, than the negative controls on the basal diet only. This indicated the presence of a very small amount of vitamin-C in the tea. The symptoms of scurvy in these guinea pigs were just as severe as in the controls. The guinea pigs receiving 2 cubic centimeters of orange juice daily, lived throughout the experimental period of 90 days and made significant gains in weight. They showed no signs of scurvy. In other words, 2 cubic centimeters of orange juice furnished very nearly enough vitamin-C to meet the requirements for normal growth of the guinea pigs, while 15 cubic centimeters of the tea infusion did not furnish enough of this factor to prevent decline and death before the expiration of the 90-day period. This evidence tends to show that the claims made that this Japan tea is "rich in Vitamin-C" are not substantiated.[43]

The first series of experiments in feeding the tea infusion to guinea pigs, conducted by the Bureau in 1929, was repeated, in order to be sure that the tannin in tea in no way influenced the results on vitamins. The recent experiments not only remove any doubt as to the effect of tan-

[40] Masataro Miura, "On the Effects of the Temperature of Water Applied for the Infusion of Japanese Green Tea upon its Anti-scorbutic Potency." Abstracts from *Rikwagaku-kenkyu-jo Iho* [The Bulletin of the Institute of Physical and Chemical Research], Tokyo, June, 1929, vol. viii, no. 6.

[41] S. Josephine Baker, M.D., *Ladies' Home Journal*, Philadelphia, April, 1928.

[42] Private communication to the author.

[43] *Clip Sheet Bulletin*, no. 578, United States Department of Agriculture, July 28, 1929.

nin, but give additional proof that no one of the three samples of green tea tested contains an appreciable amount of vitamin-C.

The tests were repeated again and again, under the direction of Dr. Hazel E. Munsell, until it was certain that tea did not contain enough vitamin-C to keep a guinea pig alive, drink as much as he could.[44]

The evidence so far adduced regarding the vitamins in tea is not very definite, and though it demonstrates their presence, it does not make this fact of ultimate importance, so far as our present knowledge of the subject of vitamins goes. If there is only a small lack of a certain vitamin in a given diet, the addition of tea might supply sufficient to prevent the appearance of the characteristic deficiency disease.

Content of Tea as Variously Brewed

Having now concluded that tea is drunk, not on account of its value as a food, but primarily because of its stimulating value, and, in a lesser degree, on account of the taste of its liquor, it is necessary to determine just how to get the best out of tea. In order to settle this problem, the Tea Growers' Association of Netherlands India, in Amsterdam, put before the Trade Museum in Amsterdam the question of whether or not it would be possible to determine analytically the influence of different methods of tea brewing, and whether the taste of the tea extract could be expressed in figures. This latter, of course, is an impossible task in the light of our present knowledge, but the effect of different methods of tea brewing can be determined by ordinary analytical methods, and the values thus obtained are of use.

In brewing tea, about 75 per cent of the total caffeine is extracted in five minutes, and about 40 per cent of the tannin. If the brewing is prolonged more than five minutes what goes into solution is mostly tannin and coloring matter.

In the average estimation of tea infusions, however, attention is not paid to comparing the effects of the ordinary methods of preparing tea in daily life, and it was this aspect that the Trades Museum chemists set about to study. Three samples of Java tea were considered. The

composition of these samples was as follows:

	Caffeine	Tannin	Soluble Substances
Tea 1.........	3.21%	21.00%	44.3%
Tea 2.........	3.10%	18.60%	42.6%
Tea 3.........	3.53%	16.40%	38.1%

In all three samples the tannin content is very high.

When dry tea is covered with boiling water, and the mass allowed to stand, the quantity of substances extracted will depend on the temperature of the water and the time of standing, as it is reasonable to suppose that less will be extracted at lower temperatures than at higher. In order to quicken the process of extraction, it is necessary to prevent too great loss of heat, and for this purpose the teapot may be under a heat insulating mass [tea cozy], or set over a "waxine" light, or alcohol lamp, or samovar. In the former case, loss of heat is prevented, and in the latter case, heat is lost, but new heat is supplied by the light or lamp. If the temperature of the infusion is the same in both cases, equal quantities of soluble substances will be extracted.

Some people object to setting a tea pot over a lamp on the ground that the pot may thereby become locally overheated, so that the tea leaves lying at the bottom may be decomposed by the heat. Unless an extra large quantity of leaf be used, this contingency does not arise, and experiment has shown that the temperature in a tea pot warmed over a lamp is practically the same throughout. The real objection to a lamp under the tea pot comes from the practical certainty of loss of volatile oil in the steam which may be evolved.

However, seeing that it is the custom in some countries to keep the tea hot by means of heat supplied externally, the result of such procedure was studied.

In the experiments 18 grams [about ⅔ oz.] of air-dry tea was covered with 900 cubic centimeters [0.95 Imp. quart] of boiling water, left for five minutes and then the infusion was poured off. To the partly spent leaf, 900 cubic centimeters of boiling water was again added and a wait of twenty minutes made before the infusion was poured off. In some cases the first infusion was for thirty-three minutes.

44 Dr. Hazel E. Munsell, "Vitamin Content of Green Tea Negligible," *U. S. Daily*, Washington, D. C., March 8, 1930.

The accompanying table gives the average of the constituents extracted from the three teas above mentioned.

Method of Extraction	Caffeine	Tannin	Soluble Substances
1.—5-mins. under cozy... Second brew with boiling water 20-mins. under cozy........	82%	38%	61%
2.—33-mins. under cozy.	21% 96%	21% 64%	24% 81%

The table clearly illustrates the advantage of a quick brew, if excessive tannin is to be avoided and a stimulating drink is sought.

Experiments made at Tocklai with Assam teas show values for caffeine and soluble substances generally of the same order as the above, although the proportion of tannin extracted usually is about 60 per cent. Most Assam teas contain about 10 per cent tannin, so that a 60 per cent extraction with such a tea indicates about the same weight of tannin as that extracted from the Java teas in question.

The accompanying table shows the percentage of caffeine, tannin, and soluble substances, extracted when the tea pot is kept warm by means of an alcohol lamp.

Method of Extraction	Caffeine	Tannin	Soluble Substances
1.—5-mins. over alcohol lamp............. Second brew with boiling water, 20-mins. over alcohol lamp.............	86%	37%	63%
2.—33-mins. over alcohol lamp.............	17% 98%	23% 65%	24% 84%

The figures in the latter table run in the same way as those obtained for tea kept warm under a cozy.

Dr. Bernard, formerly of the Tea Experimental Station, Buitenzorg, has commented on the results of the above work which, he says, confirm previous knowledge gained in empirical ways. From these facts, he continues, we can immediately draw one conclusion: For obtaining a good cup of tea it is not advisable to put an excessive amount of tea into the pot and limit the "drawing" to a short time. If this is done one will indeed obtain a very flavory drink, since the etheral oils dissolve very quickly in warm water; but the taste of the tea will then be too bitter, and a part of the desirable character of brewed tea will be missed. The tannin must be present also in sufficient amount. This gives the brew a good color and a bit of sour-harsh taste that is the base of the full-mouthed quality of good, brewed tea. Tea may well be compared in this connection with wine; a red Burgundy that contained no tannin, would be rated by an expert as worthless. Similarly with tea, the "tannin" taste is expected. For this reason, tea drinkers have empirically settled down to the practice of allowing about 3 grams of tea to draw for five minutes in 100 to 125 cc. of water. Thus an infusion is obtained having a good color, and possessing the bitter-aromatic and sour-harsh properties in just the right degree.

Scientific Conclusions

The conclusions to which the foregoing scientific analysis of brewed tea would lead us, are as follows:

A cup of tea contains, on the average, a little under a grain of caffeine, and about two grains of tannin. The tea infusion is very faintly acid, its pH value being between 5 and 6, which means that it is almost neutral. The gastric juice shows a pH value between 1.0 and 2.0, which is at least 1000 times as acid as tea.

When milk is added to tea, the tannin is fixed by the casein in the milk. The sugar added to the tea merely sweetens it and adds to the value of the drink as a food.

The addition of milk to tea robs it of practically all its astringency. When the infusion is drunk, it passes first into the stomach, where the sugars are absorbed as ordinary foods, and the ingestion of caffeine begins. The comforting effect of the warmth of the drink is at once felt, but the stimulus due to the caffeine comes about a quarter of an hour later.

The compound of tannin and casein may be digested like any other coagulated protein, and the free tannin, thus liberated, passes into the smaller intestine, where it exhibits a mildly astringent action.

Although many people are opposed to tea drinking on account of the tannin content, small though it be, this constituent with its fermented products is such an essential to the beverage, that a tannin-free tea is difficult to imagine. In the same way, the stimulus from the caffeine is such an essential, that caffeine-free tea would make no appeal to tea drinkers.

CHAPTER XXVII

THE HEALTHFULNESS OF TEA

LOOKING AT THE TRUTH OR FALSITY OF ATTACKS THAT HAVE BEEN LAUNCHED AGAINST THE BEVERAGE SINCE THE EARLY DAYS—SOME QUESTIONS WITH THE BEST ANSWERS— A DIGEST OF SCIENTIFIC, MEDICAL, AND POPULAR OPINIONS BY COMPETENT AUTHORITIES COLLECTED FROM NEWSPAPERS, PERIODICALS, AND WORKS OF KNOWN STANDING AND RESPONSIBILITY—DATA DESIGNED TO BE INFORMATIVE AND USEFUL TO TEA CONNOISSEURS, MERCHANTS, ADVERTISING MEN, AND TEA PROTAGONISTS

SO many things that are not so have been published about tea, as about coffee, that it has been deemed expedient to assemble in one place many of the best answers to such intolerances as have persisted since the early days of the beverage, together with a few notable observations by authorities who ought to know whereof they speak, when tea is the subject.

What follows is a digest of scientific, medical, and popular opinions by competent authorities collected from newspapers, periodicals, and works of known standing and responsibility. References are given in each instance. No opinion has been included unless it was uttered by a person in authority, or emanated from an authoritative source. Some differences of opinion may be noted. These may be due to lack of suitable control observations; for this reason it has been deemed wise to separate these opinions from the pharmacology chapter, which is purely scientific.

The Wholesome Drink

BY DR. LOUIS LÉMERY, "Regent-Doctor of the Faculty of Physik," Paris:

Tea is very wholesome, since it produces many good effects and few bad ones. We see some who will drink ten or twelve dishes a day without any hurt at all.

It is good for disorders of the brain and nerves. It refreshes the spirit.

It agrees at all times with any age and constitution.—*A Treatise on Foods*, Paris, 1702.

Tea an Aid to the Liver

BY BARON JUSTUS VON LIEBIG, the distinguished German chemist:

We may say of these nitrogenized compounds, caffeine or theine, that they are food for the liver, since they contain the elements by the presence of which that organ is enabled to perform its functions.—*Animal Chemistry*, 1842.

The Psychological Value of Tea

BY THE LANCET, London:

It has a strange influence over mood, a strange power of changing the look of things, and changing it for the better, so that we can believe and hope and do under the influence of tea what we should otherwise give up in discouragement and despair; feelings under the influence of which tissues wear rapidly.—*The Lancet*, London, 1863.

The Drink of Sobriety

BY C. W. CHANCELLOR, M. D., Secretary of the Maryland State Board of Health:

Tea not only contributes to the sobriety of a nation, but it imparts all the charms to society which spring from the enjoyment of conversation, without the excitement which follows upon strong drink.—"Light Wines and Table-Tea,"— *Maryland State Board of Health Reports*, Jan., 1878.

The Drink of Pleasure and of Health

BY W. GORDON STABLES, M. D., C.M.:

In the forenoon, or heat of the day as some call it, a kindly cup of tea is more cooling, calming, and invigorating than wine; it is moreover more staying, it is not so soon followed by the reaction that craves repetition of the stimulant to the injury of health.—*Tea: The Drink of Pleasure and Health*, London, 1883, p. 103.

Tea Best for Prolonged Fatigue

By Thomas Inman, M. D., London:

I have been a careful reader of all those accounts which tell of endurance of prolonged fatigue, and have been touched with the almost unanimous evidence in favour of vegetable diet and tea as a beverage, that I have determined in every instance where long nursing, as of a fever patient, is required, to recommend nothing stronger than tea for the watcher.—*Tea and Tea-Drinking* by Arthur Reade, London, 1884, p. 67.

Tea Conquers Heat and Cold

By Professor Edward A. Parkes, London:

As an article of diet for soldiers, tea is most useful. The hot infusion, like that of coffee, is potent both against heat and cold; is most useful in great fatigue, especially in hot climates, and also has a great purifying effect on water. Tea is so light, is so easily carried and the infusion is so readily made, that it should form the drink *par excellence* of the soldier on service. There is also a belief that it lessens the susceptibility to malaria.—*Tea and Tea-Drinking* by Arthur Reade, London, 1884, p. 67.

Tea Lessens Tissue Waste

By Mr. Wm. B. Marshall, United States Museum:

Most of us have experienced the refreshing effects of tea when a day of unusual strain has made demands which have depleted the store of physical and mental energy. While these effects are but temporary, they for the time bolster up the flagging spirits, thus giving the physical being time to make repairs free from the retarding influences of a fretful mind. When the physical nature reports all well, the mental nature is not disposed to complain of conditions within or without. Tea has no evil after-effects. Its use on such occasions is rather a means of setting in order a disordered house. . . . The caffeine has the property of lessening the waste of tissue.—"Tea," *American Journal of Pharmacy*, Philadelphia, Feb. 1903.

Tea a Nerve Nutrient

By Sir Jonathan Hutchinson, F. R. C. S., M. D., London:

In reference to my suggestion to give children tea and coffee, I may explain that it is done advisedly. Making allowance for a few exceptions, there is probably no real objection to their use even at early ages. They rouse the dull, calm the excitable, prevent headaches, and fit the brain for work. . . . To stigmatize these invaluable articles of diet as "nerve stimulants" is to me an erroneous expression, for they have probably a right to rank as nerve nutrients.—*London Times*, Oct. 1, 1904.

The Machine-Age Tranquilizer

By George F. Shrady, M. D., New York:

The essential volatile elements [of tea] are mildly stimulating to the nerves, having a quieting or anodyne effect upon the digestive and nervous systems, which is neither permanent nor cumulative. The active principle [caffeine] is of undoubted benefit in soothing the nerves and arresting undue tissue waste. In these days of rush and ceaseless high-power endeavor tea is perhaps the best stimulant to use under the circumstances.—*New York Herald*, Nov. 28, 1905.

Tea Cures Brain-Fag

By George Lloyd Magruder, M. D., Lecturer on Therapeutics, Georgetown University, Washington, D. C.:

I cannot understand how there can be any discussion upon the effect of tea drinking and the result to the nervous system. In moderation tea helps the average person. A woman spends the day in hunting bargains, and gets home in the evening thoroughly worn out. She is in that condition known as "brain fag", and has resort to a cup of tea. Within a few minutes she feels refreshed and has a characteristic sense of well-being. That is the action of caffeine.—*New York Herald*, Dec. 1, 1905.

Moderation in All Things

By Edward Anthony Spitzka, M. D., New York:

Tea is such a universal beverage and has so many good qualities that one cannot speak disparagingly of it. Really, in discussing tea and the possible effects of overindulgence, one must consider that intemperance is not confined to this beverage. Excessive use of tobacco, whiskey or other things will have a bad effect on the system as well as the nerves.—*New York Herald*, Dec. 2, 1905.

The Mild and Harmless Stimulant

By Yorke Davies, M. D., Royal College of Physicians, London:

Tea taken in moderation is a mild and harmless stimulant. . . . Caffeine appears to have the power of appeasing hunger. Besides being a stimulant it also tends to allay the excitement from and counteract a state induced by the use of alcoholic stimulants.—*New York Herald*, Dec. 1, 1905.

Criticism of Tea, Interested Claptrap

By G. F. Lydston, M. D., Chicago:

Given a person in good health and without any individual nervous peculiarity . . . and the moderate drinking of tea, coffee, and cocoa is not harmful. Much that is said on this point is claptrap, and promulgated often for a strictly selfish commercial end.—*New York Herald*, Dec. 2, 1905.

Temperance In Tea Drinking

By THOMAS DARLINGTON, formerly President of the New York Board of Health:

Tea drinking as practiced in this country is not harmful. It is only when tea is used in excess, or when it is not properly prepared, that there is danger of injurious effects. There should be temperance in tea drinking as in all things."—*New York Herald*, Dec. 11, 1905.

Tannin Has No Ill Effect

By ISAAC OPPENHEIMER, M. D., New York:

So far as the tannin is concerned I should say that its effect was nil.—*New York Herald*, Dec. 7, 1905.

Promotes Cerebration

By WILLIAM STIRLING, M. D., Lecturer, Royal Institution, London:

Tea, coffee, and cocoa are true promoters of increased cerebration, but alcohol in whatever form, whether in the shape of the delicate and seductive champagne or vulgar pot house beer, is a paralytic from the first. Tea and its fellows promote the action of the mental faculties; alcohol, on the other hand, is a depressant."— "Food and Nutrition," *Tea and Coffee Trade Journal*, New York, July, 1906, p. 365.

Tea An Adjuvant Food

By WOODS HUTCHINSON, M. D.:

Few discoveries of the wit of man have added more to the comfort and happiness of life and less to its miseries than tea and coffee. . . . Though not foods themselves, they enable the majority of people, and especially women, to eat with a relish considerable amounts of bread, butter, crackers, meat, cake, etc., for which otherwise they would have little appetite. In other words, they are a splendid "introduction committee." Instead of diminishing the amount of food consumed, they increase it. Moreover, they are usually taken with sugar and cream or milk, and a cup of tea or coffee with plenty of these "trimmings" is the nutritive equivalent of a small saucer of breakfast food. *No disease known to the medical profession is attributable to them.—McClures Magazine*, New York, 1907.

Five or Six Cups Daily, Not Harmful

By MAJOR ROSWELL D. TRIMBLE, United States Army:

Tea is a stimulant; in fact, one of the best, for the reason that unless it is improperly used there is practically no reaction. If we are not

to use any form of stimulant there will not be much left to subsist on, as anything that arrests waste or builds up is a stimulant. Even water, by itself, under certain conditions is a stimulant. All stimulants are not intoxicating, and neither is tea. . . . Whether tea is injurious or not may be answered both yes and no. If poor tea is used, necessitating the leaving of the water on leaves over five or six minutes, if the tea is boiled, or if people try to drown themselves in it, then it is apt to hurt. Should we stop eating because a few people suffer from over-feeding. Use good tea, brew it properly, and the average person may drink five or six cups a day without harm.— "Beneficial Effects of Tea," *Tea and Coffee Trade Journal*, Sept. 1907, p. 136.

The Stuff to Feed the Troops

By CAPTAIN CARL REICHMANN, Seventh Infantry, United States Army:

In the war which I witnessed in Manchuria two nations were engaged which are known as tea drinkers. The exertions they put forth no one can appreciate who has not seen them. In the summer the heat was humid and stifling, and alternated with torrential rains, so that the roads were always muddy and marching became a painful fatigue. In the great battles the troops marched and fought day after day, night after night, were always under fire, had little sleep and little food; they were terribly fatigued, but never collapsed; they brewed a cup of tea and on they went. . . . Nothing quite so satisfied thirst on a hot day as a glass of tea. Nothing quite so well stifled a growling stomach, so quickly warmed up a frame stiffened with cold as a glass of tea; when in the saddle without food for thirty-six hours or more nothing so restored the physical balance as a glass of tea, and my first care in getting into camp was to have my canteen filled with weak tea.—*The Lancet*, London, April, 1908, pp. 299–300.

The Sustaining and Invigorating Beverage

By SURGEON GENERAL DE RENZY of the British Army:

All I can say is that on a long march, and where troops are exposed to great hardships, a cup of Assam tea is one of the most sustaining and invigorating beverages a soldier could have.—*The Lancet*, London, April, 1908, p. 301.

Tea, a Pure Stimulant

By C. W. SALEEBY, M. D., F.R.S., Edin.:

Directly we venture to lay down the law it is only to encounter some one who believes that tea keeps him awake, but coffee never—and so finds it; there being one part of nature in which beliefs determine facts, but one only. . . .

So long as alcohol is called a stimulant, and similar drugs are called stimulants, it will remain impossible for people to understand the fundamental difference which obtains between the employment of alcohol and other narcotics on the one hand, and that of tea or coffee on the other hand. Medical men are misguided by words, like the rest of mankind. When, however, we discover that caffeine is a pure stimulant with no second stage of depression, we shall begin to look at things rightly. Some of the few defenders of alcohol who really endeavor to argue have much to say in condemnation of tea and coffee. But there is probably no such thing as "theisme" or "cafeisme." The words, I admit, exist, but that is not quite the same. One offers a challenge, then. Let these controversialists, if they wish to be thought honest, inform us as to the lethal dose of caffeine, or let them show us under the microscope any results whatsoever of the long-continued action of caffeine; let them point to a single tissue change, to a single symptom complex worth mentioning, to a single crime or death. They cannot, and they know they cannot, and one wonders why one notices them at all.—*Health, Strength, and Happiness,* New York, 1908.

Milk Makes Tannin Innocuous

By A. E. DUCHESNE, A. B., Lecturing before the Indian Tea Association:

Tannin does not appreciably affect living tissue. Its action on the coats of the stomach is negligible. Milk renders tannin innocuous by precipitation in an insoluble form, probably tannate of casein. The tannin in the tea comes out in the infusion much more slowly than the caffeine. Therefore, the liquor of properly infused tea contains little tannin and sufficient caffeine.—"Tea," a Lecture before the Indian Tea Association, London, 1910.

Tea Promotes Cheerfulness

By ARNOLD LORAND, M. D., Physician to the Baths at Carlsbad, Czechoslovakia:

After taking a cup of tea there is a feeling of great comfort; we feel lighter and less fatigued, which is due, as discovered by Koch and Kraepelin, to the combined action of the essential oils and of the theine.—*Old Age Deferred,* 1911.

Caffeine, the Good Samaritan

By C. W. SALEEBY, M. D., F.R.S., Edin.:

Caffeine is a true stimulant and has no other action. It has been proved to increase the amount of combustion in the body in whatever dose it be taken; it tends to raise the temperature. Its truly stimulant action is still more conspicuous if we consider the mind—and mind is the only important matter. The larger the dose of opium or alcohol that be taken, the more certainly and rapidly will you sleep; the larger the dose of this true stimulant that be taken, the more certainly and persistently will you keep awake. About 15 grains of caffeine will entirely abolish both the desire for and the possibility of sleep for a whole night and longer, and will make it possible to do hard, intellectual work at high speed, and of the best

quality possible for the brain in question, during the hours which sleep would otherwise have certainly claimed.

The stimulant caffeine, favors the life of the body, promotes the processes of combustion on which life depends, increases vitality, and that power to work which is the expression of vitality. Everywhere men find that a cup of tea or coffee is refreshing; it produces renewed vigor; it heightens the sense of organic well-being, the consciousness of fitness and capacity. This is utterly distinct from the action of alcohol or opium in deadening the sense of ill-being. Tea antagonizes the sense of ill-being not by deadening one's consciousness of it, but by stirring the sources of vitality and by the positive substitution for it of that sense of well-being which is the index of vitality. Here is a true stimulant—something that favors life. . . .

Caffeine is a good thing in its essence because, like sunlight itself, it is a true stimulant, in that it favors the essential processes of life. Taken in reasonable quantities, such as very few people desire to exceed, it [caffeine] differs fundamentally from all the sedatives, in that it does not produce a need for a continuous increase of the dose. It relieves worry, not by a temporary and actually nutritive and fostering submergence of it, but by attacking its causes.—*Worry, the Disease of the Age,* 1911.

Tea for the Aged

By GEORGE M. NILES, M. D., Professor of Physiology, Southern College of Pharmacy:

It [tea] is mildly stimulating to the nervous system, refreshes the mental machinery, and relieves bodily fatigue. For headache arising from "run-down nerves," it often affords prompt surcease. Many elderly people find tea particularly satisfying and soothing after reaching a period of life when the functional activity of the stomach is gradually weakened. At this time, when "the shadows are lengthening" and the digestive department finds difficulty in furnishing a sufficiency of heat and energy units, generous libations of tea often cheer up the flagging stomach and intestines, enabling them to better perform their necessary tasks.—"A Dietist on Tea," *Tea and Coffee Trade Journal,* New York, July, 1912, pp. 36–37.

Tea Stimulates the Reflex Centers

By H. C. WOOD, JR., M. D., Professor of Pharmacology of the Medico-Chirurgical College, Philadelphia:

Caffeine acts as a stimulant to the reflex centers in the spinal cord; it enables the muscles to contract more vigorously without producing a secondary depression, so that the sum total of muscular work which can be done by a man under caffeine is greater than that done without it. I cannot resist pointing out how confirmatory of this conclusion is the universal experience of mankind with caffeine beverages—tea, coffee, etc.—*Tea and Coffee Trade Journal,* New York, October, 1912, p. 356.

Too Many Alarmists

By F. H. BARNES, M. D., Stamford, Conn.:

I do not believe tea and coffee are harmful if used in reasonable quantities. . . . It is my opinion that we have too many extremists and alarmists in the medical profession and among the laity as well.—*Tea and Coffee Trade Journal*, Oct., 1912, p. 357.

More Mental and Physical Work

By G. WILSE ROBINSON, M. D., Professor of Nervous and Mental Diseases, University Medical College, Kansas City:

Even in small doses, one cup of coffee or tea per day acts as a stimulant to nerve or muscle tissue. The general results of the action of caffeine upon the nervous system are to increase the reflex irritability of the cerebral cortex; mental functions primarily improve; ideas flow more rapidly; the threshold stimulus of all the senses is lowered; the sense of fatigue is lessened; wakefulness supervenes, and mental and physical inertia are dissipated.—*Tea and Coffee Trade Journal*, New York, October, 1912, p. 357.

Critics of Tea Not Sincere

By CHARLES D. LOCKWOOD, M. D., Pasadena, Cal.:

Tea and coffee are harmless to the vast majority of healthy people when used in moderation. Most of the prejudices and fear existing in people's minds with reference to tea and coffee have been created by shrewdly worded advertisements of fake substitutes.—*Tea and Coffee Trade Journal*, New York, October, 1912, p. 356.

Tea, the Savior of Civilization

By SIR JAMES CRICHTON-BROWNE, M. D., former President of the London Medical Society:

Tea has been one of the saviors of mankind. I verily believe that, but for the introduction of tea and coffee, Europe might have drunk itself to death.—*Tea and Coffee Trade Journal*, New York, April, 1915, p. 317.

Caffeine Is a Proper Stimulant

By V. C. VAUGHN, Dean of the Medical Department, University of Michigan:

I believe that caffeine used as a beverage and in moderation not only is harmless to the majority of adults, but is beneficial. Of course, there are some individuals who have an idiosyncrasy to caffeine, just as there are individuals who have a like idiosyncrasy to strawberries, buckwheat, etc. This is no proof that caffeine is harmful or is not beneficial to the majority of people. I have no use for coffee unless it contains caffeine. I have tested the caffeine-free preparations, and they are not what I want, nor do I think that they supply the body with the proper stimulants. I believe caffeine, which is trimethyl xanthin, is a physiological stimulant, one that we need to thoroughly awaken and rouse us and put us in good running condition. —"Caffeine Beverages Beneficial," *Tea and Coffee Trade Journal*, New York, May, 1913, p. 455.

Caffeine Effects not Cumulative

By SEVERAL GERMAN SCIENTISTS:

The experiments of P. Pletzer, performed in 1887 [reported in *Berliner Klin. Wochschrift*, No. 40, 1889], shows that the effect of caffeine is rapid and that it has no cumulative action. This also is borne out by Liebreich [*Encyc. der Therapie*, Vol. 1, 1896]. By experimenting, this learned author found that a cumulative action, like that of digitalis, does not belong to caffeine.

Bela Szekacs [*Pester, Med.-Chir. Presse*, No. 39, 1885; *Orvosi Hetilap*, No. 32–33, 1885], found as follows: "A great advantage of caffeine consists in its not having a cumulative action."

J. Pawinski, [*Zeitschrift f. Klin. Med.*, Vol. 23, 1893], found that caffeine does not produce a cumulative action, but is rapidly eliminated, so that there is no danger of intoxication.

O. Seifert [*Mitt. aus der Wurzburger Med. Klinik*, 1, 1885], found that caffeine-action usually is only of a brief duration, due to its rapid excretion.—Harold Hirsch, "Caffeine a Normal Stimulant," *Tea and Coffee Trade Journal*, New York, June, 1914, p. 541.

Caffeine Overcomes Extreme Cold

By A. MONTUORI AND R. POLLITZER, working at the University of Rome:

It has remained for A. Montuori and R. Pollitzer, working at the University of Rome, to discover the ideal stimulant for maintenance of body temperature under conditions of extreme cold—caffeine. The caffeine acts directly on the nerves, stimulating them, and thus overcomes the nerve depression which follows exposure to extreme cold.—F. H. Frankel, Ph.D., "Caffeine a Body Warmer," *Tea and Coffee Trade Journal*, New York, Oct., 1916, p. 355.

Tea Best for Muscular Effort

By M. A. STARR, M. D., Emeritus Professor of Neurology, Columbia University, New York:

It has been the custom of athletic trainers in many colleges to give strong tea before contests in tennis or ball or rowing. It is well-known that Swiss Alpine guides carry tea and urge its use in climbing mountains. In Russia, where tea is drunk more generally as a beverage than in any other country, those who are called upon to make muscular efforts are given tea in large quantity. During the war the English troops were freely supplied with tea and carried it instead of water in their canteens. . . . General experience, clinical and laboratory, derived from the study of cases, and personal, from the social use of tea, lead us to the conclusion that much solace and satisfaction are to be obtained from "the cup which cheers but not inebriates."—*New York Medical Record*, 1921.

Harmless Stimulants

BY WILLIAM BRADY, M. D., Brooklyn, N. Y.:

One or two cups of coffee with or without cream and sugar for breakfast every morning must be acknowledged to be harmless for most adults, and in my judgment should be deemed wholesome and beneficial for most adults. This is true also of one or two cups of tea with meals every day.—*Brooklyn Eagle*, 1922.

Tea Destroys the Typhoid Germ

BY MAJOR J. G. McNAUGHT, M. D., United States Army Surgeon:

The typhoid germ, in pure culture, becomes greatly diminished in numbers by an exposure of four hours to tea. After 20 hours it was impossible to recover it at all from the cold tea. He recommends the use of cold tea as a substitute for water in soldiers' canteens during active service.—*Tea and Coffee Trade Journal*, New York, July, 1923, p. 129.

Tea Not Cause of Nervousness

BY MARTIN EDWARDS, M. D., Boston Specialist on Dieting for Health:

I can agree that the majority of Americans are more nervous and restless than ever before, but I cannot agree that this condition can be charged to the increasing use of coffee and tea. . . . The Chinese have indulged in tea for centuries, yet it can hardly be argued consistently that they are a highly nervous or excitable people. . . . Take the mountain dwellers of Peru and Bolivia. They chew the leaves of a plant which contain a considerable amount of caffeine, and yet they seem capable of doing more laborious work than the white man in the Bolivian climate, and stand up under it longer. They are a healthy and long-lived people. . . .

With the Britisher, afternoon tea has become a daily habit, and there is an excellent reason for the custom. There are two periods of the day when the nervous tide in the human being is at ebb. One is in the early hours of the morning, and the other is in late afternoon. Those are the times for coffee and tea. . . . Five o'clock tea would do us no harm in America.—*Boston Post*, Boston, April, 1924.

Tea Increases Working Capacity

BY R. PAULI, PH.D., Professor of Psychology in the University of Munich:

The psychological action of tea shows itself in an acceleration of the phenomena of consciousness in such processes as addition, committing to memory, choosing, riming, estimating time, perception of relations, acts of attention, differentiation [E. Kraepelin]. This effect

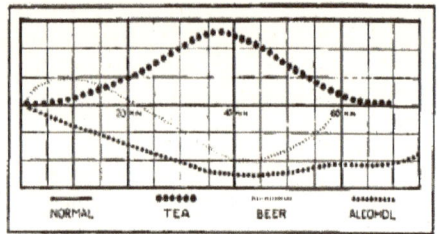

PHYSIOLOGICAL EFFECTS OF TEA AND ALCOHOL

In this chart (after Pauli) the unbroken line through the center represents the normal mental state. Note the stimulating effect of a cup of tea, extending over an hour; the stimulus from beer at first and the marked decline in the subject after indulging in strong drink.

reaches its maximum in about forty minutes, and in another thirty minutes it disappears. . . .

Recent investigations which the author carried out in the Psychological Institute of the University of Munich, in collaboration with the German Research Institute for Food Chemistry, have afforded further evidence of particular modes in which mental work is promoted by tea. . . . A half-liter of Munich beer containing 15 grams of alcohol brought about an acceleration of mental action for twenty minutes, followed by a period of noticeable depression lasting twice as long. A cup of tea, on the other hand, drove the mental capacity higher by about 10 per cent for three quarters of an hour, after which the subject of the experiment returned to normal without experiencing the ill effects that followed the alcoholic stimulant.—*Tea and Coffee Trade Journal*, New York, July, 1924, pp. 54–56.

The Idiosyncrasy Factor

BY S. C. PRESCOTT, Massachusetts Institute of Technology:

If individuals are especially sensitive to tea or coffee, its use, except in extremely limited amount, is not to be recommended. In this respect it should be treated in exactly the same manner as are many kinds of food—meat, shellfish, eggs, milk, or fruits which do not "agree" with one person or another.—*Tea and Coffee Trade Journal*, New York, Jan., 1924, p. 47.

Tea Purifies the Body

BY DANIEL R. HODGDON, M. D., formerly President of Hahnemann Medical College and Hospital, Chicago, and President of the College of Technology, Newark, N. J.:

Good tea, properly made, is one of the most delicious and economical of beverages. Taken in moderation, it has a wholesome tonic effect on the system, stimulating the body functions and relieving fatigue. . . . In the case of elderly people, who are likely to drink much tea, it aids digestion. . . . Tea is one of the cheapest drinks available. Two or three cups may be made for a cent.—*Tea and Coffee Trade Journal*, New York, December, 1924, p. 942.

Sensible Use of Tea not Harmful

By ROYAL S. COPELAND, M. D., former Health Commissioner of New York City, and United States Senator from New York:

The sensible use of tea is not harmful to an adult. It is not wise to have the tea so strong as to be like a tincture of tannic acid, but when freshly made it is a beverage which may be safely indulged in a couple of times a day. The most trying hours in life are between four o'clock and the evening meal. A cup of tea at this time adds a lot of comfort and happiness. Reasonable use at meals will assist digestion and add to the enjoyment of the table.—*Tea and Coffee Trade Journal*, New York, Dec., 1925.

Tea Preserves the Mental Equilibrium

By H. H. BUSBY, M. D., Dean of the College of Pharmacy, Columbia University, New York:

Tea and coffee are directly stimulating to cerebral activity, and stimulate all its functions. Thus, the mental equilibrium is preserved, and quantity of mental activity is increased without any sacrifice of quality.—*Tea and Coffee Trade Journal*, New York, August, 1925, p. 342.

Tea Induces Tranquility

From an interview with F. G. BANTING, M. D., Toronto, discoverer of insulin:

The famous Canadian doctor now comes out to plead for afternoon tea as a tranquillizer, an inducer of the meditative, the inventive, the creative, frame of mind. There is something vital beneath the trivial teacup chatter. Afternoon tea he regards as a valuable promoter of efficiency of the most practical, hard-headed sort. It has been tried out in factories, large offices, department stores, banks [Canadian or English, and to some slight degree in America it has gained foothold], and greater output and better quality of work results from the twenty minutes' break for refreshments. . . .

"At a tea, Dr. Banting aptly remarked, that it was one of the best and most grateful promoters of friendly understanding. This brief period of peaceful meditation before we put the finishing touches to our daily task is a habit, a ritual of priceless value, he argues. It is not merely a pleasure, it is a psychic balancer of most vital potency.

If there is one thing we Americans need, it is a few minutes off each day to take time to think, to ask ourselves why all the hurry, whither all the excitement is leading us. I like the idea of the 4 o'clock recess.—*Tea and Coffee Trade Journal*, New York, January, 1925, p. 58.

Tea in Moderation, Not Harmful

By MORRIS FISHBEIN, M. D., Editor, *Journal of American Medical Association*:

The best scientific evidence indicates that, taken in moderation, tea and coffee are not harmful. Many persons are known who have taken tea or coffee daily for fifty or sixty years without apparent ill effects.—*Tea and Coffee Trade Journal*, New York, Oct., 1927, p. 1131.

Action of Green and Black Tea

By THE EDITOR OF *Hygeia*, in answer to a reader's question:

There is no great difference in the therapeutic action of green and black tea, the essential action being that of the caffeine. Both teas do contain some tannin, but in the amount used for an ordinary cup it is doubtful if the small variation in the tannin content would be of practical moment.—*Hygeia*, Chicago, Feb., 1927.

Tea, the Great Consoler

By SIR JAMES CRICHTON-BROWNE, M. D.:

Tea is undoubtedly one of the most beneficial gifts which the West owes to the Orient. It is impossible to estimate the benefits it has bestowed upon mankind. Those who have passed through sickness and sorrow know its value. It is the great consoler, and many a poor woman has been saved from suicide by a timely cup of tea.—*Tea and Coffee Trade Journal*, New York, Oct., 1927, p. 1138.

A Necessity of Modern Life

By J. CAMPBELL, M. D., Member of the Food Committee of the New Health Society, London; Scientific Adviser to the Ministry of Food during the World War:

Tea may be regarded as almost a necessity of modern life, a stimulating and harmless beverage, giving a fillip to a jaded brain and heart at the time of the day when it is most needed. It forms a most welcome change in flavor from coffee, and no ill effects accrue, either nervine, cardiac, or dyspeptic, if properly prepared from good quality leaves and taken in moderation.—*Tea and Coffee Trade Journal*, New York, March, 1928, p. 376.

"The Best of Cocktails"

By SIR JAMES CRICHTON-BROWNE, M. D.

We see in the newspapers from time to time warnings as to the injurious effects of the excessive consumption of tea. Well, the cranks and the croakers we shall have always with us. No doubt, if you substitute tannin for tea, it is injurious. No doubt excess of anything, of cold water or ginger beer, is injurious, to say nothing of more exhilarating beverages, but I do not believe that in one case in ten thousand is the slightest harm done by what our dietetic

Pharisees would call an excessive use of tea. It is a boon and a blessing, and its effects are generally beneficial, conducive to contentment, clear thinking and sobriety. It is the best of cocktails.—From a speech delivered at the annual dinner of Bovril, Ltd., to the President, Council, and Officers of the Institute of Certified Grocers, London, Oct., 1928.

A Stimulating, Healthy Beverage

BY SIR W. ARBUTHNOT LANE, BART., M. D.:

Wisely used, good tea is a most beneficial and stimulating, healthy beverage. . . . The best tea is the cheapest and most economical in the long run.—*London Daily Mail*, Oct., 1928.

A Useful Antisoporific

BY R. J. S. McDOWALL, Professor of Physiology, University of London:

We may conclude, then, that so far as we know, the moderate consumption of properly made tea has no serious disadvantages, and that taken with meals it acts as a useful antagonist to the somewhat soporific effect of the meal itself.—"The Physiological Action of Tea as a Beverage," *The Practitioner*, London, 1928.

Tea Not Productive of Acid

BY A. L. HOLLAND, M. D., Assistant Professor of Clinical Medicine, Cornell University Medical College, New York City:

The harmful action of the caffeine in tea is probably negligible, except where tea is indulged in excessively. Theoretically, tannin taken regularly in any considerable amount should cause some impairment of the glandular activity in the stomach and upper intestinal canal, but the amount taken in properly made tea is so small that there is but little chance that it does exert any marked action on these tissues, particularly if milk or food is taken along with the tea. . . .

Several years ago, at the Cornell Medical College Clinic in New York, the writer endeavored to ascertain the effect that tea has upon the production of acid in the stomach. For this purpose the patients, whose cases were under investigation for stomach disorders, were given test meals of bread and water, and after an hour, the stomach contents were extracted and tested for acid. After establishing the average acid level for each of those patients, plain tea was substituted for the water of the test meal and the observation continued as before. After a reasonably prolonged research, carried on in this manner, it was concluded that tea under these conditions in moderate amounts, does not materially raise the acid production of the gastric glands. . . . It is not unlikely that tea is often unjustly blamed for abnormal behavior of the digestive and

other organs, where the cause may be found in constitutional deficiencies or structural irregularities.—*Tea and Coffee Trade Journal*, New York, May, 1928, p. 638.

Harmless and Refreshing Amenity

BY SIR RONALD ROSS, K.C.B., M.R.C.S., D.P.H., F.R.C.S., L.I.D., D.Sc., M. D., COL. R.A.M.C.

Like most people in this country [England] I have drunk tea twice or thrice daily all my life, and consider it to be wholly unobjectionable if so taken, and I regard its introduction as a notable addition to the amenities of civilized life—as harmless as it is refreshing.

It is worth noting that Great Britain consumes about 10 lbs. of tea per head per annum, and that as the consumption of tea has increased enormously in the last century, the consumption of alcohol has correspondingly decreased, while the longevity of the nation has increased by over twenty years in the last eighty years, according to the *Annual Report* of the Medical Officer of Health for the County of London for 1923.—From a letter written Mr. W. Shakspeare, President, the Ceylon Association in London, Oct. 25, 1929.

Beneficial to the National Health

BY SIR MALCOLM WATSON, LL.D., M.D., C.M., D.P.H.

Great excess of anything, of course, produces physical and mental disorder; and in great excess tea and coffee will disturb sleep, cause headaches, and other nervous disturbances. But so few people drink tea and coffee to this extent that in our experience, extending over thirty years of practice in both temperate and tropical climates among tea and coffee drinking people, we have not met any. There is, we believe, no proof that the drinking of tea has a deleterious affect on the national health. On the contrary, there is proof that the increasing consumption of this refreshing beverage and the facilities now provided in the great cities of Britain for its enjoyment have been most beneficial.—From a letter written Mr. W. Shakspeare, President, Ceylon Association in London, Oct. 31, 1929.

Tea Drinking Promotes Slenderness

BY HUGH A. McGUIGAN, Pharmacologist, B.S., PH.D., M.D., Chicago:

Tea and coffee drinking cause much less injury than over-eating—an important thing to consider in these days when young and old are desirous of a svelte appearance, and when over-eating is the commonest vice of each group. Indeed, these beverages lessen the sense of hunger and thus, to some extent, prevent over-eating.—*Tea and Coffee Trade Journal*, New York, April 1930.

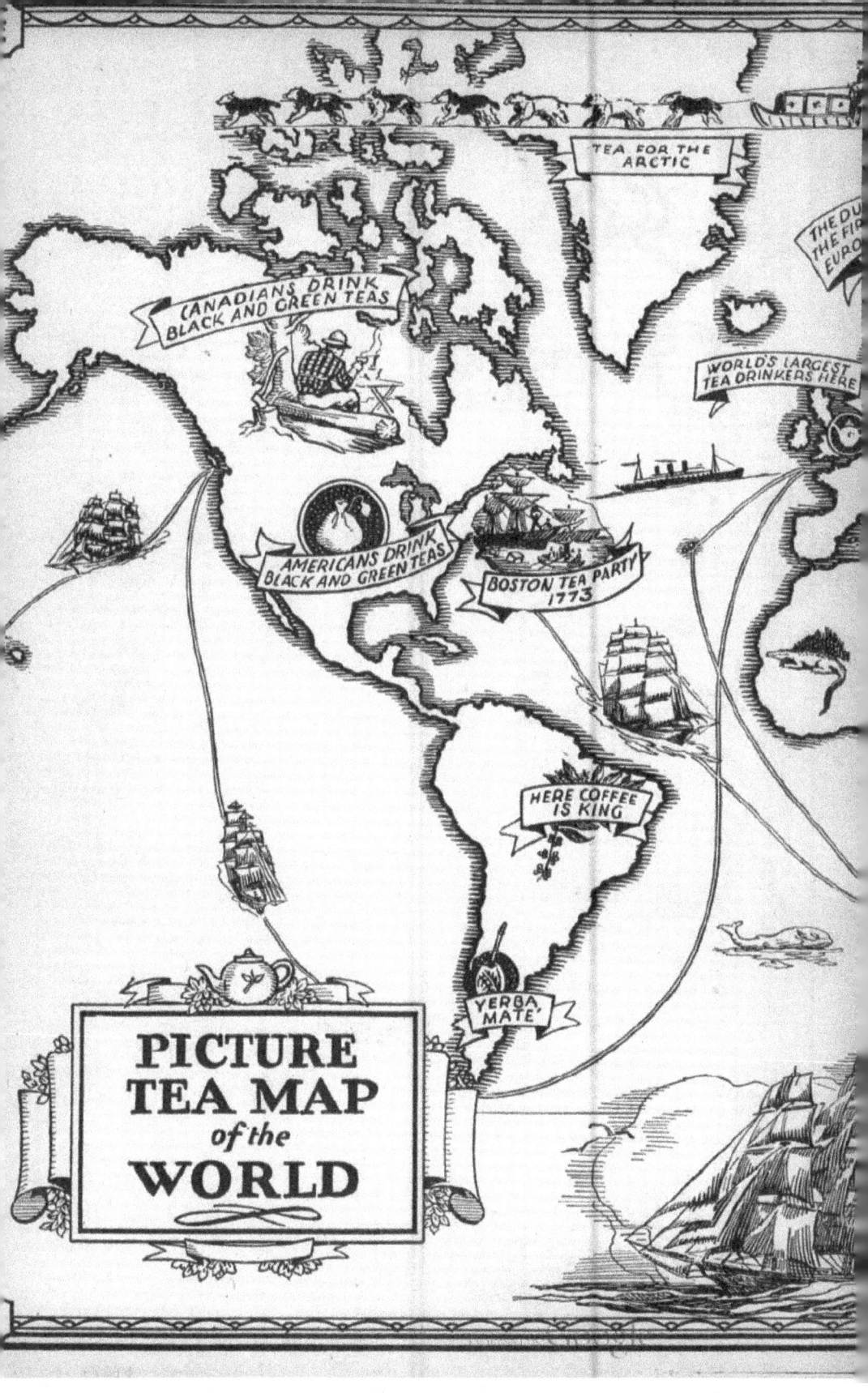

PICTURE
TEA MAP
of the
WORLD

Printed in August 2023
by Rotomail Italia S.p.A., Vignate (MI) - Italy